FODOR'S BED & BREAKFASTS AND COUNTRY INNS

America's Best Bed & Breakfasts

Over 2,000 Delightful Places to Stay in All 50 States

Portions of this book appear in Fodor's *California's Best Bed & Breakfasts, The Mid-Atlantic's Best Bed & Breakfasts, New England's Best Bed & Breakfasts, The Pacific Northwest's Best Bed & Breakfasts, The South's Best Bed & Breakfasts, The Southwest's Best Bed & Breakfasts,* and *The Upper Great Lakes' Best Bed & Breakfasts.*

Fodor's Travel Publications, Inc.
New York • Toronto • London • Sydney • Auckland
http://www.fodors.com/

America's Best Bed & Breakfasts

Editor: Anastasia Redmond Mills
Contributors: Sue Berg, Marianne Camas, Deke Castleman, Scott Duncan, Susan English, Audra Epstein, John Filiatreau, Donne Florence, Wendy Hale, Robin Hill, Deborah Lale, Jane McConnell, Diana Lambdin Meyer, Carlotta Mills, Candy Moulton, Jolie Novak, Barbara Palmer, Helayne Schiff, Linda K. Schmidt
Creative Director: Fabrizio La Rocca
Cartographer: David Lindroth
Illustrator: Alida Beck
Cover Photograph: Chris Mead
Cover Design: Guido Caroti

Special Sales

Fodor's Travel Publications are available at special discounts for bulk purchases for sales promotions or premiums. Special editions, including personalized covers, excerpts of existing guides, and corporate imprints, can be created in large quantities for special needs. For more information contact your local bookseller or write to Special Markets, Fodor's Travel Publications, 201 East 50th Street, New York, NY 10022. Inquiries from Canada should be directed to your local Canadian bookseller or sent to Random House of Canada, Ltd., Marketing Department, 1265 Aerowood Drive, Mississauga, Ontario L4W 1B9. Inquiries from the United Kingdom should be sent to Fodor's Travel Publications, 20 Vauxhall Bridge Road, London, England SW1V 2SA.

PRINTED IN THE UNITED STATES OF AMERICA

10 9 8 7 6 5 4 3 2 1

Contents

Introduction

You'll find B&Bs in big houses with turrets and little houses with decks, in mansions by the water and cabins in the forest, not to mention structures of many sizes and shapes in between. B&Bs are run by people who were once lawyers and writers, homemakers and artists, psychotherapists and architects, singers and businesspeople. Some B&Bs are just a room or two in a hospitable local's home; others are more like small inns. Every B&B stay has a quality of serendipity.

But although that's part of the pleasure of the experience, it's also an excellent reason to plan your B&B travels with a good B&B guide. The one you hold in you hands serves the purpose neatly.

To create it, we've handpicked a team of professional writers who are also confirmed B&B lovers: people who love the many manifestations of the Victorian era; who go wild over wicker and brass beds, four-posters and fireplaces; and who know a well-run operation when they see it and are only too eager to communicate their knowledge to you. We've instructed them to inspect the premises and check out every corner of the premier inns and B&Bs in the areas they cover and to report critically on only the best. They've returned from their travels with comprehensive reports on the very best B&Bs—establishments that promise a unique experience, a distinctive sense of time and place. All are destinations in themselves: not just places to put your head at night, but an integral part of a weekend escape. In our writers' evaluations you'll learn what's good, what's bad, and what could be better; what they liked and what you might not like. We also include names and addresses of B&B reservations services, just in case you're inspired to search out additional properties on your own. Reviews are organized by state, and within each state by region.

A double room is for two people, regardless of the size or type of beds it contains. Unless otherwise noted, rooms don't have phones or TVs. Regarding bathrooms: Note that even the most stunning homes, farmhouses and mansions alike, may not provide a private bathroom for each individual. What we call a restaurant serves meals other than breakfast and is usually open to the general public. Credit-card abbreviations are as follows: AE, American Express; DC, Diner's Club; D, Discover; MC, MasterCard; V, Visa. MAP stands for Modified American Plan and indicates that both breakfast and dinner daily are included in the rates; AP, American Plan, means all meals are included. Rates are listed from the lowest amount charged for a room to the highest, year-round except for those B&Bs in and around New Orleans. Hence, the lowest rate might not be available in high season and the highest rate in low season will most likely be quite a bit less than the highest rate quoted in the text. The New Orleans rates do not apply during special events: Prices skyrocket for Mardi Gras, the Sugar Bowl, Jazz Fest, and the Super Bowl; also, in addition to having three- to five-day minimums, inns sometimes request full payment in advance. On the other hand, when summertime temperatures in New Orleans soar, rates can plunge much lower than those quoted, and attractive packages are often available.

Although we abhor discrimination, we have conveyed information about innkeepers' restrictive practices so that you will be aware of the prevailing attitudes. Such discriminatory practices are most often applied to small children, traveling with their parents, who may not, in any case, feel comfortable having their offspring toddling amid breakable bric-a-brac and near precipitous stairways.

When traveling the B&B way, always call ahead. If you have mobility problems or are traveling with children or pets, if you prefer a private bath or a certain type of bed, or if you have specific dietary needs or any other concerns, discuss them with the innkeeper. If you're traveling to an inn because of a specific feature, make sure that it will be available when you get there and not closed for renovation. The same is true if you're making a special detour to take advantage of specific sights or attractions. Every care has been taken to ensure the accuracy of the information in this guide, and all prices and dates quoted here are based on information supplied to us at press time. Still, time brings changes, and we cannot accept responsibility for errors that may have occurred.

It's a sad commentary on other B&B guides today that we feel obliged to tell you that our writers did, in fact, visit every property in person, and that it is they, not the innkeepers, who wrote the reviews. No one paid a fee or promised to sell or promote the book in order to be included in it. (In fact, one of the most challenging parts of our writers' work is persuading the innkeepers and B&B owners that they need provide nothing more than a tour of the premises and the answers to a few questions!) Fodor's has no stake in anything but the truth. If a room is dark and has peeling wallpaper, we don't call it quaint or atmospheric—we call it rundown and then steer you to another section of the same property that's more appealing.

So trust us the way you'd trust a knowledgeable, well-traveled friend. Let us hear from you about your travels, whether you found that the B&Bs you visited surpassed their descriptions or the other way around. (We're at 201 East 50th Street, New York, NY 10022). And have a wonderful trip!

Karen Cure
Editorial Director

Map 1: Connecticut, Maine, Massachusetts, New Hampshire,

Connecticut
Connecticut
River Valley, **21**
Litchfield County
South and
Ridgefield, **19**
Northwest Corner, **20**
Southeastern
Coast, **22**
Southwestern
Coast, **18**

Maine
Down East, **1**
Mid-Coast, **3**
Penobscot Bay, **2**
Sebago Lake, **4**
The Southern
Coast, **5**

Massachusetts
The Berkshires, **33**
Boston, **30**
Cape Cod, **28**
Martha's
Vineyard, **26**
Nantucket, **27**
North Shore, **31**
The Pioneer
Valley, **32**
Southeastern, **29**

New Hampshire
Fitzwilliam, **9**
The Lakes Region, **7**
The Seacoast, **6**
The White
Mountains, **8**

New York, Rhode Island, Vermont

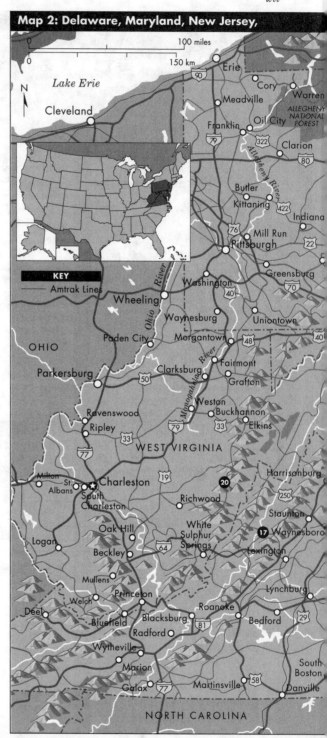

Map 2: Delaware, Maryland, New Jersey,

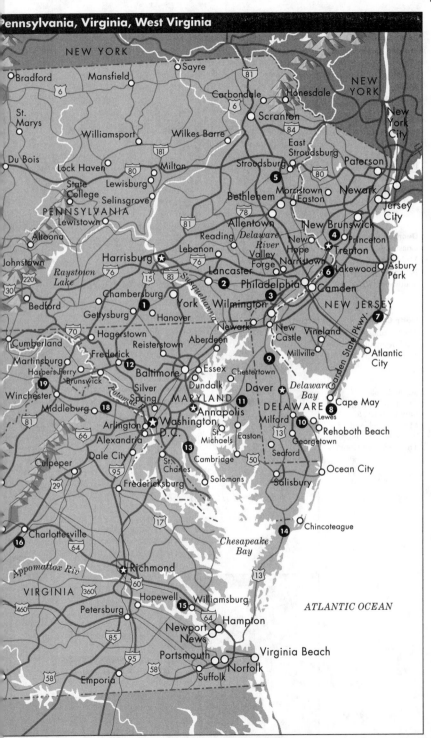

NEW YORK

NEW YORK

New York City

Bradford
Mansfield
Sayre
St. Marys
Williamsport
Wilkes Barre
Carbondale
Honesdale
Scranton
Du Bois
Lock Haven
Milton
East Stroudsburg
Stroudsburg
Paterson
State College
Lewisburg
Selinsgrove
Bethlehem
Morristown
Easton
Newark
Jersey City
PENNSYLVANIA
Lewistown
Allentown
New Brunswick
Altoona
Reading
Delaware River
New Hope
Princeton
Trenton
Johnstown
Harrisburg
Lebanon
Valley Forge
Norristown
Lakewood
Asbury Park
Raystown Lake
Chambersburg
Lancaster
Philadelphia
Camden
Bedford
York
Wilmington
NEW JERSEY
Gettysburg
Hanover
Newark
New Castle
Vineland
Cumberland
Hagerstown
Reisterstown
Aberdeen
Millville
Atlantic City
Martinsburg
Frederick
Baltimore
Essex
Chestertown
Harpers Ferry
Brunswick
Dundalk
Dover
Delaware Bay
Cape May
Winchester
Potomac
Silver Spring
MARYLAND
DELAWARE
Middleburg
Arlington
Washington D.C.
Annapolis
Milford
Lewes
Rehoboth Beach
Alexandria
St. Michaels
Easton
Georgetown
Culpeper
Dale City
Cambridge
Seaford
Ocean City
St. Charles
Fredericksburg
Solomons
Salisbury
Charlottesville
Chesapeake Bay
Chincoteague
Appomattox Riv
Richmond
VIRGINIA
Hopewell
Williamsburg
ATLANTIC OCEAN
Petersburg
Hampton
Newport News
Virginia Beach
Portsmouth
Norfolk
Emporia
Suffolk

Map 3: Alabama, Florida, Georgia, North Carolina,

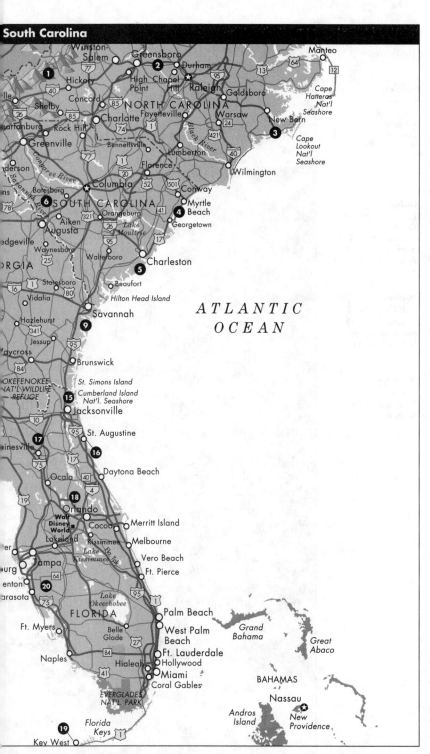

Map 4: Arkansas, Kentucky, Louisiana, Mississippi

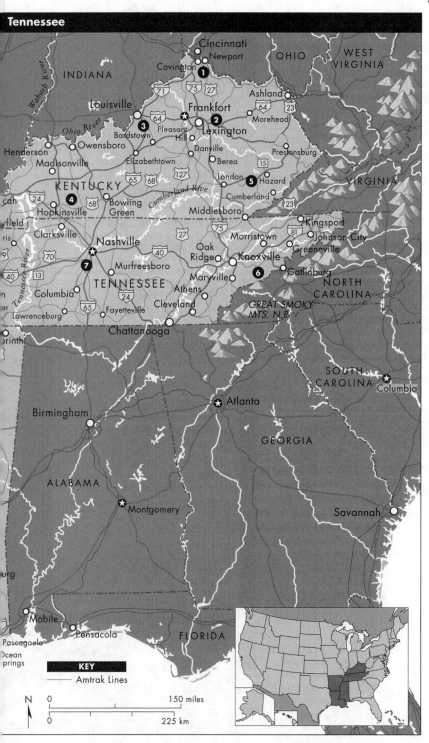

Tennessee

KEY

— Amtrak Lines

N

| 0 | 150 miles |
| 0 | 225 km |

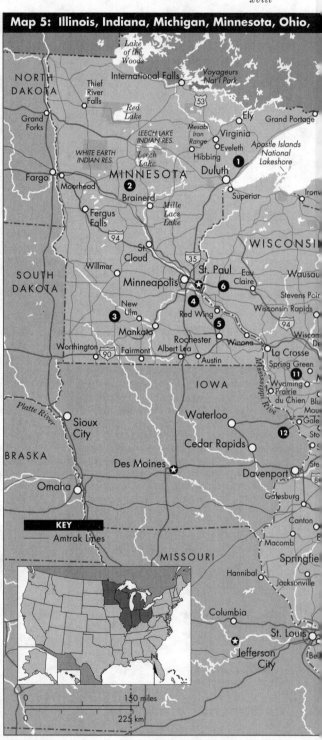

Map 5: Illinois, Indiana, Michigan, Minnesota, Ohio,

Wisconsin

CANADA

Isle Royale
Nat'l Park

Lake Superior

Keweenaw
Peninsula
Copper
Harbor
Houghton

Sudbury

Marquette
Sault
Ste. Marie

26

Mackinac
Island

MICHIGAN

Iron
Mountain

Escanaba

Beaver
Island

25

Mackinaw
City

Manitoulin
Island

*Georgian
Bay*

Marinette

Northport

Petoskey

75

Alpena

*Lake
Huron*

Green
Bay

Sturgeon
Bay

23

24

Traverse
City

MICHIGAN

23

Toronto

8

Manitowoc

Cadillac

Bay
City

25

7

Appleton

*Lake
Winnebago*

131

Saginaw

51

Oshkosh
Fond
du Lac
Sheboygan

31

75

Flint

69

Port
Huron

*Lake
Erie*

Baraboo

10

43

*Lake
Michigan*

Grand
Rapids

96

Lansing

21

94

Ashtabula

Madison

94

Waukesha
Milwaukee

22

Battle
Creek

Jackson

Ann
Arbor

Detroit

Cleveland

90

New
Glarus

9

Racine

196

Kalamazoo

94

Port
Clinton

Sandusky

20

Akron

Youngstown

Rockford
Arlington
Heights
Elmhurst

Kenosha
Waukegan

Evanston

South
Bend

69

80
90

Toledo

80
90

80

Savanna

Chicago

19

Angola

Auburn

Mansfield

Canton

Aurora

Joliet

18

Gary
La
Porte

Huntington

Ft.
Wayne

Lima

Marion

OHIO

77

Zanesville

Wheeling

La Salle

13

55

Kankakee

65

Logansport

24

69

Wapakoneta

71

70

Peoria

57

INDIANA

Muncie

Bloomington

74

Danville
Lafayette
Anderson

Dayton

70

Columbus

71

Marietta

Champaign

36

Crawfordsville
Zionsville

17

Chillicothe

Decatur

51

Indianapolis

WEST VIRGINIA

55

70

Terre
Haute

Columbus

74

50

Cincinnati

36

ILLINOIS

16

Bloomington

65

Madison

E. St.
Louis

57

Vincennes

New
Albany

15

Centralia

64

Gentryville
Corydon

Louisville

KENTUCKY

Mount
Vernon

14

Ohio R.

Evansville

Carbondale

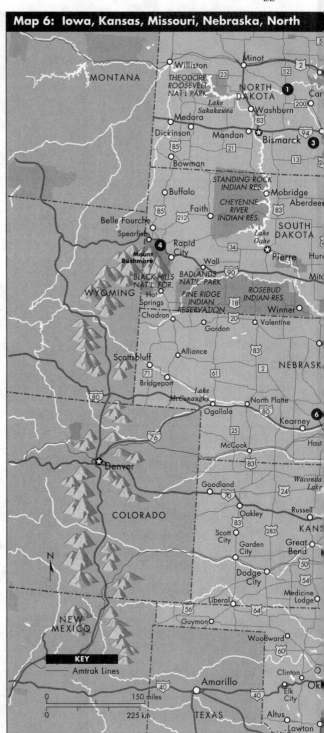

Map 6: Iowa, Kansas, Missouri, Nebraska, North

Dakota, Oklahoma, South Dakota

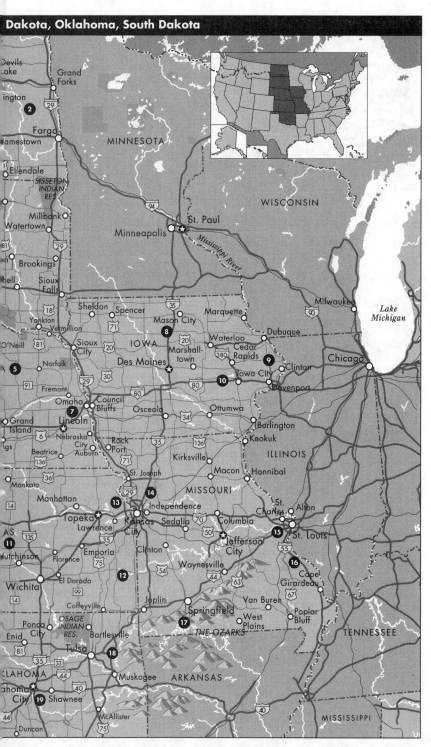

Devils Lake
Grand Forks
ington 2 29
Fargo
Jamestown
MINNESOTA
Ellendale
SISSETON INDIAN RES.
Millbank
Watertown
29
81
en
Brookings
hell
Sioux Falls
18
Sheldon
Spencer
35
Marquette
WISCONSIN
Lake Michigan
Milwaukee
90
Yankton
Vermillion
Mason City
8
20
Waterloo
Dubuque
71
O'Neill
81
Sioux City
20
IOWA
Marshall-town
Cedar Rapids
Clinton
9
Chicago
5
Norfolk
Des Moines
380
Iowa City
91
Fremont
30
80
Davenport
Omaha
Council Bluffs
Osceola
10
Grand Island
7
Lincoln
Nebraska City
34
Ottumwa
Burlington
6
Rock Port
35
136
Keokuk
gs
Beatrice
Auburn
71
ILLINOIS
136
St. Joseph
Kirksville
Macon
Hannibal
Mankato
36
14
Manhattan
29
14
MISSOURI
13
Independence
St. Charles
Alton
Topeka
Lawrence
Kansas City
Sedalia
70
Columbia
15
St. Louis
AS
135
35
50
Jefferson City
55
11
Hutchinson
Florence
Emporia
Clinton
16
Cape Girardeau
Wichita
El Dorado
75
12
54
Waynesville
44
63
67
14
99
Joplin
Van Buren
Poplar Bluff
Coffeyville
Springfield
West Plains
TENNESSEE
Ponca City
OSAGE INDIAN RES.
17
THE OZARKS
Enid
Bartlesville
81
35
33
Tulsa
18
LAHOMA
44
40
ARKANSAS
ahoma City
19
Shawnee
Muskogee
44
McAllister
75
Duncan
MISSISSIPPI
40

Mississippi River

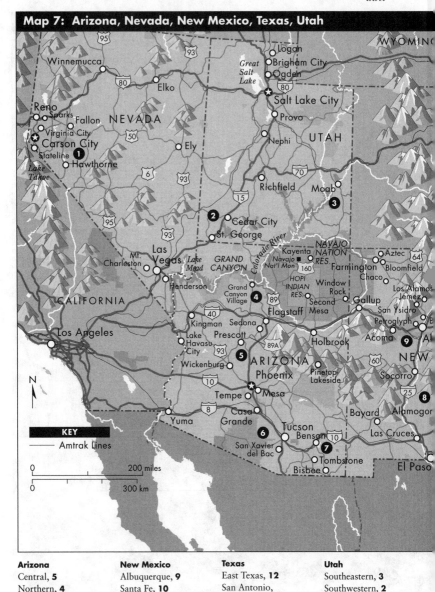

Map 7: Arizona, Nevada, New Mexico, Texas, Utah

KEY
— Amtrak Lines

0 —— 200 miles
0 —— 300 km

Arizona
Central, **5**
Northern, **4**
Southeastern, **7**
Tucson, **6**

Nevada
Carson City
and Environs, **1**

New Mexico
Albuquerque, **9**
Santa Fe, **10**
Southern
New Mexico, **8**
Taos, **11**

Texas
East Texas, **12**
San Antonio,
Austin and the
Hill Country, **13**

Utah
Southeastern, **3**
Southwestern, **2**

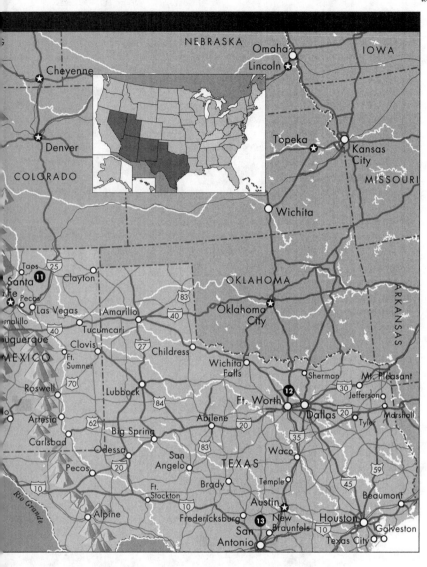

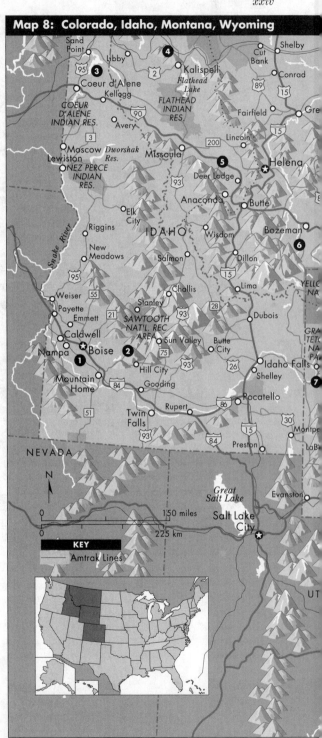

Colorado
Denver, **11**
High Rockies, **12**
North Central, **10**
South Central, **13**
Southwest, **14**

Idaho
Boise Valley, **1**
Central Rockies, **2**
Northern
Panhandle, **3**

Montana
Glacier Country, **4**
Gold West Country, **5**
Yellowstone Country, **6**

Wyoming
Jackson and
Vicinity, **7**
Northern, **8**
Southern, **9**

Map 8: Colorado, Idaho, Montana, Wyoming

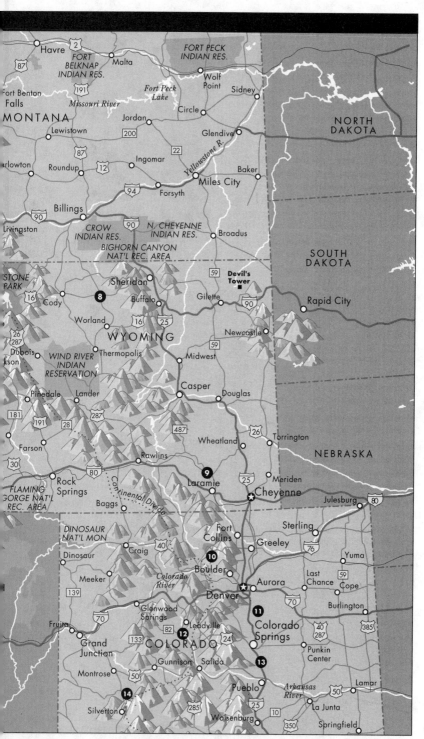

Map 9: California, Oregon, Washington

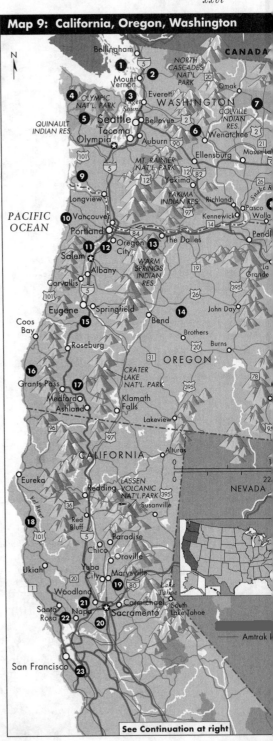

See Continuation at right

See Continuation at left

KEY
—— Amtrak Lines

NEVADA

CALIFORNIA

ARIZONA

PACIFIC
OCEAN

MEXICO

100 miles

150 km

Map 10: Alaska and Hawaii

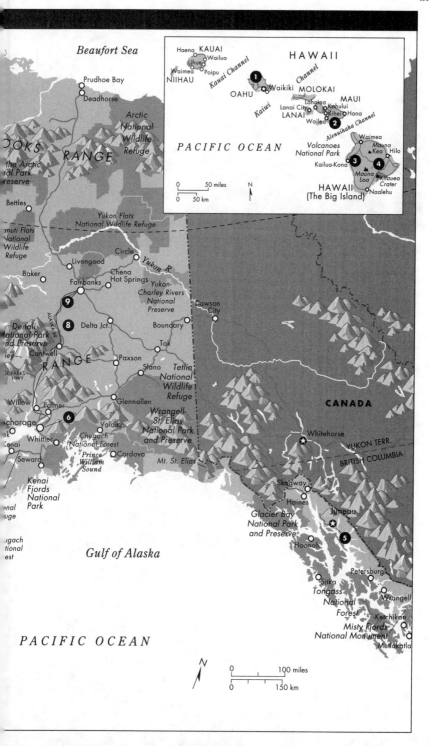

Beaufort Sea

Prudhoe Bay
Deadhorse

Arctic
National
Wildlife
Refuge

OOKS   RANGE

the Arctic
al Park
reserve

Bettles

Yukon Flats
National Wildlife Refuge

onuti Flats
National
Wildlife
Refuge

Baker

Circle
Livengood   Yukon R.
Chena
Hot Springs
Fairbanks
Yukon-
Charley Rivers
National
Preserve

9

8   Delta Jct.
Boundary

Denali   Boundary
ational Park
nd Preserve
Tok

ley
Cantwell   Paxson
RANGE   Stano   Tetlin
National
Wildlife
Refuge
Willow   Glennallen
Palmer
chorage   6   Wrangell-
St. Elias
National Park
and Preserve
Valdez
Whittier   Chygach
Kenai   National Forest
Prince   Cordova
Seward   William   Mt. St. Elias
Sound

Kenai
Fjords
National
Park

nal
uge

ugach
tional
est

Gulf of Alaska

Dawson
City

CANADA

Whitehorse

YUKON TERR.
BRITISH COLUMBIA

Skagway
Haines
Glacier Bay
National Park
and Preserve
Hoonah

Juneau

5

Petersburg
Sitka
Tongass
National
Forest   Wrangell

Ketchikan
Misty Fjords
National Monument
Metlakatla

PACIFIC OCEAN

N   0   100 miles

0   150 km

Inset map:

Beaufort Sea

Haena   KAUAI
Lihue   Wailua   **HAWAII**
Waimea   Poipu
NIIHAU   Kauai Channel   Channel

1   Waikiki
OAHU   MOLOKAI
Kaiwi   MAUI
Lahaina   Kahului
Lanai City   Kihei   Hana
LANAI   Wailea
2   Alenuihaha Channel

PACIFIC OCEAN   Waimea
Mauna
Volcanoes   Kea   Hilo
National Park
3   4
Kailua-Kona   Mauna   Kilauea
Loa   Crater
HAWAII   Naalehu
(The Big Island)

0   50 miles   N
0   50 km

Alabama

Grace Hall

North Alabama

Lodge on Gorham's Bluff

101 Gorham Dr. (Box 160), Pisgah, AL 35765, tel. 205/451–3435, fax 205/451–7403

In the early 1990s, the McGriff family began to develop their land 3 miles north of Pisgah, into a new town that will eventually have scores of homes, shops, an artists' workshop district, meetinghouse, town green, and post office. This new town, or neighborhood, is being built with a nod to tradition: Sidewalks and front porches, for instance, are common. The Lodge on Gorham's Bluff is the crown jewel of their endeavor. An amphitheater adjacent to the lodge hosts events such as a music festival in June, theater festival in August, and storytelling festival in September.

The whitewashed, 2½-story lodge has upstairs and downstairs porches across the front. It is strategically built with a view of the Tennessee River and passing barges—an unexpected treasure in a region where major cities are rare. The McGriffs, with roots in nearby Sand Mountain, where he is a CPA and she a former schoolteacher, have outfitted their lodge with thick robes, smooth cotton sheets, down-filled pillows and comforters, bath salts, and whirlpool tubs. Soft music plays throughout common areas and in bedrooms, but guests have volume controls at bedside.

Third-floor rooms, ideal for honeymooners, have whirlpool tubs for two and fireplaces that open both into the bedroom and bath. Second-floor rooms have one-person jetted tubs, and balconies with rocking chairs and abundant planters. The glass-enclosed tower with a widow's walk is a good place to savor the view.

In the first-floor living area, guests have access to a VCR, a collection of videotapes, an extensive book collection, and a small kitchen stocked with snacks and cold drinks. A 20-seat restaurant at the lodge serves Sunday lunch and candlelight dinner Thursday through Saturday evenings. Reservations are required; lodge guests have priority. In the morning the smells of the hearty southern breakfast prepared here waft upstairs to waking guests.

The Overlook Pavilion is a good place to watch the river and spot soaring eagles. This new Appalachian town is a welcome respite from the bustle of big-city living.

🏠 *6 double rooms with baths. Restaurant, air-conditioning, phone, whirlpool tub, and fireplace in rooms, VCR in common area; fishing, kite flying, hiking. $110–$150; full breakfast, snack-filled kitchen. AE, MC, V. No smoking, no pets, some age restrictions for children.*

Mentone Inn

Rte. 117 (Box 290), Mentone, AL 35984, tel. 205/634–4836 or 800/455–7470

Lookout Mountain in extreme northeastern Alabama forms the backdrop for the Mentone Inn, a building perfectly suited to its setting. Stone steps, dark wood, flagstone paths, flowers, and evergreens invite visitors to the inn's entrance. A stone foundation supports the screened-in porch, set with rocking chairs, a swing, and small tables where breakfast can be served. Rolling hills and valleys on all sides are ablaze in the fall with foliage too dramatic to seem real.

The inn is owned and operated by Frances Waller, a retired social worker who perceives her innkeeper's role as a continuing way to serve people. (She even offers reduced rates to fellow social workers and therapists.) Mrs. Waller has a way with people, pausing often to listen and to talk. She has brought her own touch to this hideaway she bought in 1995. Her grandmother's sheet music and handwritten recipes fill walls in the inn and create the feel of a favorite relative's home you visited as a child. A glance around shows family photos from the 1920s—the same era as the house—plus china hand-painted by Mrs. Waller's mother.

Near a stone fireplace, guests play dominoes or bridge in the cozy parlor, then for a change sit on the porch. In the glassed-in dining area, paneled walls oversee a long table and several smaller ones, all with views of the mountains. There's complimentary coffee—and sometimes homemade cookies—in the kitchen. Everything feels the way a relaxed country inn should.

A handsome staircase made of pale wood leads upstairs. Walls in the house are wood-paneled in natural beaded pine; some are painted, some left their natural color. Bedrooms are outfitted with period furnishings. Five of the bedrooms have two beds so that more than two guests may stay comfortably.

Several yards behind the house, backed by a grove of trees, is a wooden deck, weathered a soft gray, which holds lounge chairs, small tables and a hot tub.

🏠 *12 double rooms with baths. Air-conditioning, cable TV in living room; hot tub. $70; full breakfast, afternoon refreshments. AE, MC, V. Restricted smoking, no pets.*

Wood Avenue Inn

658 Northwood Ave., Florence, AL 35630, tel. 205/766–8441

Square and octagonal towers rise high above the garden of this three-story Queen Anne house on a tree-lined street in this college town. Built in 1889, it is pure Victorian, with 14-foot ceilings, multipane leaded windows, nooks, crannies, and bay windows.

Owners Alvern and Gene Greeley have both worked in various fields, he as a clergyman turned auto-parts salesman, she as the dean of a Bible college and then as a real estate agent. With her radiant smile and enveloping warmth, Alvern makes innkeeping an art form. Since she likes to pamper people, she is doing what comes naturally in running a bed-and-breakfast and delights in making home-cooked delicacies. Her zucchini bread is unsurpassed.

The house has an inviting porch with green wicker furniture and begonias in flower boxes. Two formal parlors open off the wide central hall, which bisects the two lower floors. One drawing room has dark-green walls with gleaming white woodwork, a red velvet sofa 150 years old, and a cabinet in a corner. Its rosewood shelves have held china for more than a century. But it's the bric-a-brac that sets the tone. Arranged among and around the furniture are enough figurines, artificial flowers, bows, wreaths, footstools, and ruffled cushions to stock a theatrical warehouse. Five minutes in that room and you know exactly how the well-to-do characters in a Dickens novel live.

Fireplaces are in every room, even the bathrooms, two of which have narrow tubs resting on claw feet. Beside the tub a table holds a bottle of sparkling cider and two silver-wrapped chocolates. After a good soak, you climb into a huge bed, its pale-rose-colored satin spread topped by matching pillows against the 19th-century-look wallpaper.

Outside the back door, wisteria climbs over an arbor, and a black carriage handmade by the Amish stands under a protective roof. Not far away a winding path leads to the bridal cottage and to other accommodations kept readied for guests who want to reserve for longer stays.

🏠 *6 double rooms and 2 singles with baths, 2 suites. Air-conditioning; catering on request, cable TV in lounge; badminton, horseshoes. $57.50–$90; full breakfast. MC, V. Restricted smoking, no pets.*

Other Choices

Madaperca. 5024 Alabama Hwy. 117 (H.C. 68, Box 20), Mentone, AL 35984, tel. and fax 205/634–4792. 2 double rooms with baths, 1 suite. Air-conditioning, phones, cable TV/VCRs; VCR library, ceiling fans, fax, copier, laundry; canoes. $70–$105, full country breakfast. D, MC, V. No smoking, no pets, 2-night minimum on weekends and during special events.

Winston Place. 353 Railroad St. (Box 165), Valley Head, AL 35989, tel. 205/635–6381 or 888/494–6786. 4 double rooms with baths, 1 suite. Air-conditioning, TV in common area. $85–$200; full breakfast. MC, V. No smoking, no pets.

Central Alabama

Grace Hall

506 Lauderdale St., Selma, AL 36701, tel. 205/875–5744, fax 205/875–9967

Among the stately homes of Selma is Grace Hall, built in 1857 and also known as the Ware-Baker-Jones House, after the three families who lived here for more than 110 years. The mansion became run-down apartments and then a grungy boardinghouse, but today, resplendent again, with many original antiques, it shines as brilliantly as ever. The owners are Coy and Joey Dillon, he a former steel executive, she a designer. Since the age of 16, when Joey bought her first antique (an oval mirror for $10), she has been interested in old buildings. She jumped at the chance to buy and restore Grace Hall. The Dillons drifted into B&B management when the mayor of Selma asked them to put up a visiting dignitary.

The house is a certified restoration of an antebellum home, an interesting alternative to the Federal-style mansions in the area. It is stunning, with double parlors, a pressed-tin ceiling in the study, red-stained glass, Romantic portraits in the hallway, heart-pine floors, and windows 10 feet tall. The dining room has its original mahogany pedestal table, seating 12, and a smaller room behind used for guests' three-course breakfast. Solid brass chandeliers light the house; on the south porch overlooking the manicured garden and its huge live oak is original wicker furniture.

The large bedrooms in the main house have marble fireplaces, where fires are lit as soon as guests arrive. Other features include antique, step-up carved rosewood beds; oak desks; Oriental rugs; and hand-painted enamel clocks. Wallpapers are copies of 19th-century designs; in one bedroom, the Brighton pattern fits perfectly with a four-poster bed flanked by brother-and-sister walnut chests. TV sets are concealed in cabinets. Leading off the back is a latticed, galleried wing, whose porches, facing the garden, provide open-air sitting space for three more smaller, but just as charming, bedrooms. Fitting the southern surroundings, an overhead fan turns lazily above a large bowl holding branches full of cotton bolls. To prevent intruding on visitors' privacy, the Dillons give tours to outsiders only when there are no guests on the premises.

🏠 *6 double rooms with baths. Air-conditioning, cable TV and phone in rooms, free home tour. $69–$99; full breakfast, evening refreshments. AE, D, MC, V. No smoking indoors, pets only if prearranged, children over age 6 only, BYOB.*

Historic Oakwood

715 E. North St., Talladega, AL 35160, tel. 205/362–0662

Historic Oakwood was commissioned in 1847 by the first mayor of Talladega. Painted white, with green shutters, tall columns, chimneys, and a freestanding balcony, it is the quintessential Federal-style southern mansion. It has a garden full of azaleas and dogwoods and faces a street lined with carefully tended houses and yards.

Historic Oakwood is done on a large scale: The rooms are 20 by 20 feet, the ceilings are 11 feet, and the windows almost as tall. The original heart-pine floors have been redone. In the wide entrance hall, a broad staircase invites you upstairs and contributes an air of welcome and elegance. Throughout the house, the wallpapers have been copied from original designs.

Home owners and innkeepers are engineer Stephen Smith and his wife, Donna, who home-schools their two children. The Smiths live upstairs and vacate their quarters when demand exceeds their two downstairs guest bedrooms. The children add a vitality not found in child-free B&Bs. The family has dogs, which may be a consideration for allergic travelers. Some guests will be pleased to learn that, unlike most other innkeepers, the Smiths are receptive to visiting pets, if arrangements are made in advance.

One bedroom has a spool bed, the others antiques. At the top of the stairs and with a charming view of life on North Street is a frilly room decorated with light, floaty curtains; old white wicker chairs and sofas; and a few baby dresses hanging here and there. The upstairs back bedroom is set off at the top of the stairs with a jag in the steps that turns left into a private hallway that can be closed off for added privacy.

Throughout the house, long sweeps of draperies are copies of fabrics of the period. Out back is a large, plain, treated-wood deck that has an arbor, a swing, and benches. It is a great place to sit, to swing, and to let the world pass you by.

🏠 *4 double rooms share 2½ baths, 1 suite with 2 baths. Air-conditioning, TV/VCR in common area, ceiling fans, laundry, soft drinks in guest refrigerator; bikes, volleyball, badminton, horseshoes, croquet. $45–$105, full breakfast. No credit cards. No smoking.*

Jemison Inn

212 Hwy. 191, Jemison, AL 35085, tel. and fax 205/688–2055

The 1930s redbrick, red-roofed Jemison Inn—with arches and a wraparound porch filled with ferns and antique wicker—was built by the small town's first physician. Rumor has it that the house was built close to the road so the doctor's spinster sister could swing while gossiping with passersby. Innkeepers Joe and Nancy Ruzicka, both retired, spent their careers dealing with people—she as a university librarian, he as a businessman. Their gracious hospitality shows much evidence of their experience.

B&B guests arrive to find a front-porch easel with a welcome message including their names. It is the first of many thoughtful touches. Completely renovated, the home has a Victorian air, although it was built in 1928–29. The parlor, a mix of furniture from 1890 to 1930, sets the rose theme that follows in public areas. Set against rose, cream, and green, the look continues with moire draperies, Oriental rugs, crushed velvet and tapestry upholstery, collections of Nippon, Roseville pottery, Victorian silver, and walnut Eastlake furnishings. There are 1930s facings on doors and windows, lots of glass, hardwood floors, crown molding, and period wallpaper.

The Duffee Room has a 1900 golden-oak high-back bed, North Wind chairs, large oak armoire, ball-and-claw tables of oak, a crocheted bedspread, floral wallpaper, hooked rug, oil paintings, beaded purses, and unusual lamps. The private bath has a claw-foot tub, pedestal sink, and oak baker's rack. Across the hall, the McNeil Room features an 1880 marble-top walnut twin beds made into a king, hand-stitched quilts, an Eastlake marble-top walnut dresser, a hall tree, needlepoint rugs, and tapestry draperies. The Johnson Room has 1900 mahogany classic furnishings with appointments in gold, blue, and white.

Across from the house, only a few miles from Interstate 65, is the Ruzickas' antiques shop, which they open for guests' private viewings.

▦ *2 double rooms with bath; 3 doubles share 1 bath. Air-conditioning, ceiling fans, fruit, flowers; fireplace in 1 room;* *cable TV in 2 common areas, laundry, fax, copier, turndown service with mints, champagne in room for honeymooners; gardens, swimming pool with poolside refreshments. $65; full breakfast, afternoon refreshments, access to snacks in kitchen. AE, D, DC, MC, V. No smoking, no pets, some restrictions on children.*

Kendall Manor

534 W. Broad St., Eufaula, AL 36027, tel. 334/687–8847, fax 334/616–0678

Kendall Manor stands majestically on a hill two blocks from the center of historic Eufaula, a town filled with the state's second most abundant collection of structures on the National Historic Register. Filled with moss-draped trees, Eufaula draws visitors to its spring Pilgrimages, fish-laden Lake Eufaula, and nearby golf courses. A treasure of architectural history, the inn, built in 1872, is a beautiful and comfortable home with southern hospitality and charm.

Transplanted northerners, Timothy and Barbara Lubsen left the corporate world to live out their dream of owning a B&B. It was an ambition they harbored more than a decade while he worked as a research director and she as a travel director and interior designer.

Ruby-etched glass panels accent 10-foot entrance doors that open to reveal spacious rooms with 16-foot ceilings and elaborate moldings. Kendall Manor's parlor has detailed carvings in rosewood and walnut, windows topped with gold-leaf cornices, antiques, and Oriental rugs. A rosewood square grand piano and a sunroom filled with assorted reading materials are available for guests' use. Those with more energy may climb on the adult-size rocking horse in the upstairs sitting area.

Rooms upstairs have wood floors, Oriental-style rugs, 10-foot windows with venetian blinds, and cloud shades. The Alabama Room, with yellow and black accents, includes a king rice bed, antique armoire and chest, love seat, chair, and ottoman. Floral wallpaper is the backdrop in the Georgia Room. Flowers in rooms and goodies such as lemon bars or brownies are standard. Wine is by request.

Verandas with intricately carved capitals atop slender columns extend around three sides of the home. A second-story sitting porch, outfitted with rocking chairs and wicker furniture, overlooks the front lawn's dogwood and magnolias and makes a good morning spot. Chippendale railings surround the rear deck, which leads to a fountain, bench, and gardens where breakfast is sometimes served.

In the rooftop belvedere, earlier visitors have left their mark: Hundreds of signatures, some dating to the home's early years, have been scrawled on the walls.

▥ *5 double rooms with baths, 1 suite. Air-conditioning, cable TV and phone in rooms, ceiling fans, fax, copier, free home tour; bikes, croquet. $85–$109; full breakfast, welcome beverage, afternoon refreshments, dinner by request. AE, D, MC, V. Smoking outside only, no pets, children over 14 only, minimum stay during special events.*

Orangevale Plantation

1400 Whiting Rd., Talladega, AL 35160, tel. 205/761–1827

Orangevale Plantation, on 150 acres 4 miles south of Talladega, once was the center of a 3,000-acre cotton plantation. Built in 1854, the main house is Greek Revival with six 25-foot-tall pillars and white exterior.

Orangevale is run by the charming Billy Bliss and her husband, Richard, a physician who served in three branches of the U.S. military. With two married sons living nearby, the Blisses maintain cattle, sheep, horses, ducks, geese, an orchard, berry farm, cornfields, fishponds, and a vineyard. Guests can enjoy the farm by strolling a nature trail lined with azaleas, dogwoods, and ferns.

The Blisses live downstairs in their antiques-filled home and leave the upstairs, which has its own living-room area, to guests. In typical antebellum fashion, the bedrooms open off a central hall, and, though these rooms have their own bathrooms, you have to tiptoe down the hall to reach them. Both bedrooms have four-poster beds with down comforters, Sheraton chests, brick fireplaces, and large windows.

There are three outbuildings. The farthest, which the innkeepers reach via golfcart, overlooks the orchard. Each of its two rooms, connected by a dogtrot, has a queen-size and single bed, a freestanding brick fireplace, a rocking chair, and walls and ceiling made of rough-hewn wood. A 1932 GE refrigerator purrs away in the kitchen (and still keeps sarsaparilla, or whatever you choose to put in it, perfectly chilled).

Behind the main house and within view of the tree-canopied brick patio are two units, both with exposed wood, kitchenettes, living areas, and baths. Cabin interiors, carrying the sweet aroma of old pine logs, appear rustic but are exceptionally comfortable.

Guests find plenty of fresh fruit and produce, and Billy's specialty—iced tea sweetened with mint sprigs that grow abundantly on the grounds. Breakfast often is served at the kitchen's lazy Susan, where the Blisses' four children once gathered when growing up here. Orangevale gives a true taste of the Old South, and the Blisses are well suited for their roles as caretakers of the past.

▥ *2 double rooms with baths, 1 cottage, 2 cabins. Air-conditioning, TV in common areas, guest kitchen, fax, copier, laundry; nature trail, 2 fishing ponds. $95, full breakfast. No credit cards. No smoking, no pets, children over 12 only.*

Other Choices

Lattice Inn. 1414 S. Hull St., Montgomery, AL 36104, tel. 334/832–9931 or 800/525–0652, fax 334/264–0075. 4 double rooms with baths, 1 cottage. Airconditioning, phones; cable TV in library, pool, outdoor hot tub. $55–$75, full breakfast. AE, D, MC, V. Restricted smoking, no pets, 1 child under 12 per adult.

Red Bluff Cottage. 551 Clay St., Montgomery, AL 36104 (Box 1026, Montgomery, AL 36101), tel. 334/264–0056, fax 334/262–1872. 4 double rooms with baths, 1 suite. Air-conditioning, TV in living room, games, laundry. $55–$65; full breakfast, prebreakfast coffee, soft drinks. AE, D, MC, V. No smoking, no pets.

Gulf Coast Delta

Bay Breeze

742 S. Mobile St. (Box 526), Fairhope, AL 36533, tel. 334/928–8976, fax 334/928–0360

Not far from downtown Fairhope, a winding white-shell driveway leads through a beautifully landscaped camellia and azalea garden to a stucco-and-wood guest house built in the early 1930s. Owners Bill and Becky Jones, who have restored and enlarged her childhood home, live in their own wing, while guests enjoy the main house and nearby cottages that offer their own privacy. The house fronts Mobile Bay, where, not far away, is the Yankee ironclad *Tecumseh,* which sank with 116 sailors. Stretching into the bay is a private 462-foot pier with a fully equipped kitchen, where Bill often cooks Saturday breakfast or a seafood supper. Fortunate guests may find themselves here for Jubilee—a natural phenomenon that takes place only two places in the world when lack of oxygen forces bottom dwellers—crab, shrimp, flounder—to shore.

A large front lawn has a stone fountain and pine benches. In the sunny living room are china and rare books in a cabinet next to a musket from the War of 1812. The Bay Room has white wicker chairs facing large French windows and the bay. A cozy sitting room hides an upright piano and brick fireplace. Breakfast is served in the open kitchen; a view of ducks and the bay enhances the meal.

The three bedrooms in the main house have wooden floors, brass double beds, old family portraits, large windows, and antique furnishings. Cottage suites are light and spacious, decorated with antiques, Oriental and hooked rugs, brick floors, and white pine paneling. In one suite, the bedroom has a large queen brass bed. Its living room contains a comfortable sofa sleeper that increases accommodations to four, and it also has a furnished minikitchen.

Becky, a retired biology instructor, loves sitting at the end of the pier and weaving tales while guests revel in this casual escape on historic Mobile Bay.

3 double rooms with baths, 2 cottages. Air-conditioning, cable TV in rooms, games, VCR in game room, ceiling fans, fax, bikes, pond. $85–$95; full breakfast, refreshments on arrival. AE, MC, V. Restricted smoking, 2 night minimum stay during special events.

Portman House Inn

1615 Government St., Mobile, AL 36604, tel. 334/471–1703 or 800/471–1701, fax 334/471–1718

Nestled in the heart of Mobile's National Historic District, Portman House Inn, built in 1922, is a charming and luxurious home turned inn. Designed by the same architect who masterminded the famed Bellingrath Gardens and Home, Portman House exemplifies the Mediterranean revival architecture of Addison Mizner found in the Palm Beach area.

Adjacent to Mobile's Central Business District, the home is surrounded by what makes Mobile wonderful—historic houses and gardens, shopping, antiques stores, fine dining, museums, art galleries, a convention center, universities, and downtown's entertainment district.

Owned by local investors, the home is overseen by Bridgett Murray-Ellis and Lex Ellis. Bridgett's innkeeping expertise is extensive and evident in the attention to detail, including turndown service with chocolates. Computer guru Lex presents breakfast in the antiques-laden dining room. If you even whimper a morning idiosyncrasy—like needing a diet cola to wake up—Lex is quick to attend to it.

Distinguishing the handsome house are heavy-cut moldings and trims, tongue-and-groove paneling, fanned windows, cut and stained-glass windows, functional fireplaces, wood floors with area rugs, traditional furnishings, and a relaxing ambience. Beautifully appointed rooms—some with sunny sitting rooms, terraces, or porches—have abundant windows. From one room, guests see the back gardens filled with azaleas, crepe myrtles, and banana trees. From a front room, the view includes ancient oak trees and bustling Government Street.

Comfortable and spacious guest rooms have individual climate controls, feather beds, complimentary toiletries, coffeemakers, fireplaces, and private baths with whirlpool tubs. Apartments have full kitchens. For large families and corporate guests, the inn can combine two suites to offer two bedrooms—one with a king bed and one with two queen beds—with two baths, two living areas, four TVs, two hot tubs, two balconies, a kitchenette, and a full kitchen.

The inn makes a wonderful honeymoon spot or, during the week, is a corporate haven, with a business center and proximity to the town's heart. A stay is enhanced by the innkeepers' savvy and willingness to share tips on local places to eat and visit.

▥ *3 double rooms with baths, 1 suite, 1 carriage house. Air-conditioning, cable TVs, phones, ceiling fans; business center, laundry. $119–$209; Continental breakfast, cocktails, and hors d'oeuvres. AE, D, DC, MC, V. No smoking in main house, no pets.*

Other Choices

Church Street Inn. 51 S. Church St. (Box 526), Fairhope, AL 36533, tel. 334/928–8976, fax 334/928–0360. 3 double rooms with baths. Air-conditioning, TVs, ceiling fans; bikes. $85; full breakfast, snacks in kitchen. AE, MC, V. Restricted smoking, minimum stay during special events.

Guest House. 63 S. Court St., Fairhope, AL 36532, tel. 334/928–6226 or 334/928–0720. 3 double rooms with baths, 1 twin room (2 twin beds) with bath, 1 carriage house. Air-conditioning, TVs; video library, guest kitchen, ceiling fans, laundry, pond. $85; full breakfast, evening wine and cheese. AE, MC, V. No smoking, no pets. Closed week after Christmas.

Alaska

Anchorage

Aurora Winds

7501 Upper O'Malley Rd., Anchorage, AK 99516, tel. 907/346-2533, fax 907/346-3192

Aurora Winds' facilities rival those of downtown hotels: four stone fireplaces, big-screen TV, hot tub, sauna, and work-out area with four-station Nautilus, stairclimber, and treadmill. For outdoor recreation, the entrance to Chugach State Park is just up the road.

This contemporary home is an eclectic mix of styles, from neoclassical to hightech, art deco to Oriental. Exposedbeam ceilings enclose 5,200 square feet of space, all of which is open to guests. The formal living room showcases a white baby grand piano and Oriental screens, while the den downstairs has a slot machine, billiard table, 52-inch projection screen TV, 150-gallon aquarium, and fireplace.

The Garden Room is the brightest of the five large suites, each of which has its own bathroom, sitting area, phone, and TV/VCR. This upper-story room has a queen-size bed, leather recliner, and a Murphy bed. Down the hall, the Mountain View room is classically deco-

rated and masculine in feel, with a wood armoire and mule bed. The Southern Comfort room is contemporary in design, with black wrought iron, ceramics, and flowing fabrics. A small kitchenette sets the Copper Room apart from the others. The grandest of the rooms is the McKinley Suite, which, in addition to the standard queen bed, also has a queen-size hide-a-bed, walk-in closet with ironing board and robes, and, behind the mirrored door, a small office, complete with computer, printer, and fax. The spacious bath has a built-in habitat environmental chamber (when it's working, lie down and experience wind, rain, steam, sun, and music), double Jacuzzi, and double vanity.

Your host in all this is James Montgomery, who sets out a Continental breakfast for those with early morning departures. But you really don't want to miss his full breakfast, which often includes French toast with Grand Marnier syrup.

▦ *2 double rooms, 2 triples, and 1 quad with baths, TV/VCRs, 4 fireplaces, 52-inch projection screen cable TV in den, exercise equipment, billiard table, slot machine, hot tub. $55–$175, full or Continental breakfast. AE, D, MC, V.*

Oscar Gill House

1344 W. 10th Ave., Anchorage, AK 99501, tel. 907/258-1717, fax 907/258-6613

Innkeepers Mark and Susan Lutz bought this historic, two-story, clapboard house in 1993 for $1, moved it to its current site across from the Denaley Park Strip downtown, and spent the next year converting it into their home and three-bedroom B&B. The Lutzes have done a wonderful job breathing new life into the home, which was built around 1913 by Oscar Gill, an Iditarod mail carrier, lighterage businessman, and speaker of Alaska's Territorial House. Historic photos hang in the entry way, including a photo of Gill himself. The house is full of interesting knickknacks yet does not feel cluttered; an old leather suitcase holds magazines, while glass cabinets upstairs display political pins. A wood stove, antique tables, and comfortable chairs with reading lamps make the small living room inviting; family photos, scattered books, and a child's rocker give it a homey feel. The dining room, also small, has a nice view of the park strip, which is approximately 12 blocks long and one block wide and has a rose garden. The dining room chairs arrived in Seward, Alaska, in 1914 as a wedding present for a now anonymous pioneer bride; much of the rest of the home's furnishings have come from secondhand stores and yard sales.

All the guest rooms are upstairs and have light-colored walls and simple, light-colored furniture. A front bedroom has a double bed, rocker, and dresser; a back room has twin beds and a writing desk. A shared bath has a claw-foot tub. The third room is larger, with a queen bed as well as a single. On a clear night you can see Mt. McKinley from the room's large window. The private bath has a whirlpool bath. Each guest room has down comforters and guest robes, and bathrooms provide Body Shop amenities.

Popular breakfast items include omelets, pancakes, fresh fruit, and old-fashioned oatmeal. The nearby coastal trail is the ideal setting for a ride, ski, or after-dinner stroll.

🏨 *2 double rooms with shared bath, 1 triple with private Jacuzzi bath. Phones, TV available, crib, complimentary bikes and skis, laundry facilities, freezer space. $55–$95, full breakfast. AE, MC, V.*

Healy

Rock Creek Country Inn

Mile 261 of the Parks Hwy., 20 miles north of Denali National Park; HC1 Box 3450, Healy, AK 99743, tel. 907/683-2676

Driving up to Wayne and Lolita Valcq's B&B is like arriving on the set of a made-for-TV movie about life on the last frontier. Manicured grounds have interesting Alaskan touches such as a collection of antlers out front, totems, and old traps and snowshoes mounted on outside walls.

Since they moved to Alaska in 1978, the Valcqs have built a spacious log home, three guest cabins with running water, a workshop with a two-bedroom suite above it, and an outdoor shower house on this site overlooking the Nenana River. There's even a two-seater outhouse complete with curtains and crocheted seat covers.

In the main house, the two rooms upstairs have twin beds; guests use a shared bath downstairs. A spacious room in the finished basement has a queen bed and two twins and a large, private bath across the hall. The cabins, which are in the woods behind the house just yards from the river, offer a variety of sleeping arrangements. The largest has a double bed, two twin beds, and a double hide-a-bed.

Lolita has decorated each clean but simple accommodation with homemade quilts, original wildlife paintings, and other Alaskan touches. The cozy sitting room and dining area in the main house contains trophy birds and mammals, many of which Lolita has stuffed. There's also a snowshoe and antler chandelier and a table lamp crafted from moose hooves.

In addition to running the B&B year-round, the Valcqs mush sled dogs and house 29 huskies in the lot next to the house. Wayne has competed twice in the Yukon Quest, a grueling race from Fairbanks, Alaska, to Whitehorse in the Yukon Territory.

🛏 *1 double and 2 singles with baths, 2 doubles share 1 bath, 1 suite, 3 cabins. Common sitting area with TV. $75–$110, full breakfast. MC, V accepted if reservations are made through Alaska Private Lodgings/Stay with a Friend, Box 200047, Anchorage, AK, 99520–0047; 907/258–1717; fax 907/258–6613. No smoking.*

Fairbanks

Forget-Me-Not Lodge/The Aurora Express

Box 80128, Fairbanks, AK 99708, tel. 907/474–0949, fax 907/474–8173

The three guest rooms in this home are spotless, the floral decor bright and cheerful, and the views of the Tanana River expansive. But it is the chance to stay in one of the refurbished Alaska Railroad sleeper cars that makes this B&B unique.

Mike and Susan Wilson have done a wonderful job turning the 1956 Pullman cars into comfortable guest quar-

ters. The sleeping compartments have themes: a richly appointed bordello, can-can room, gold mine, and chapel. These rooms, as well as a large room in a caboose, have beautifully painted, arched 10-foot ceilings; crystal chandeliers; and gilded bath fixtures in addition to queen beds and private baths with showers. The chapel compartment, modeled after Fairbanks's historic Immaculate Conception church, has a stained-glass window, altar chairs, and prayer bench.

Guests staying in the National Emblem room have the run of an entire car. Up to seven guests can stay here, each tucked into a tiny room with a single bed. There are two toilets and sinks at the front of the car, two showers at the rear, and a sitting area decorated with rich green drapes and pillows.

A full breakfast of fresh fruit, pastries, pancakes, salmon quiche, or omelets is served in the main house.

🛏 *Lodge: 2 doubles share bath, 1 suite. Train: 5 doubles with baths, plus large sleeper car with private bath and entrance that can accommodate up to seven people. $60–$325, full breakfast. MC, V. Rooms in lodge available year-round; train rooms available June 1–Sept. 1.*

Homer

Island Watch Bed & Breakfast

Box 1394 Homer, AK 99603, tel. 907/235–2265

One mile up scenic West Hill Road and five minutes from downtown Homer, this rambling, secluded B&B is perfect for relaxation. Guest rooms in the spruce log cabin and main house are casually comfortable with queen beds, modern facilities, and private baths. There are also great views of Kachemak Bay and the Kenai Mountains that set this B&B apart.

Eileen Mullen grew up along the Kenai River and for several years she fished commercially. As it became harder and harder to make a living off the sea, this gracious, soft-spoken woman moved to Homer and in 1991 opened her home to guests. The two-bedroom suite on the lower level of Eileen's home is perfect for families with small children: One bedroom has two single beds, the other a queen-size bed, and a built-in bench provides sleeping space for a fifth person. Within the suite are also a large bath with tub and shower, a sitting and dining area, and a kitchen. A spacious third-floor room sleeps three, with a private bath across the hall. Outside there's a large yard and picnic table.

The spruce cabin, which Eileen built, has two queen beds (one in a sleeping loft reached by a spiral staircase), a day bed, a small kitchen, a radio, tape player, and board games. But again, it's the view that makes this place special—a deck with a swing chair facilitates your enjoyment of the scenery.

A roomy, lower unit beneath the cabin sleeps three, has a private bath and entrance, and is accessible to people who use wheelchairs. It is above ground and looks out on Eileen's horse pasture and Kachemak Bay.

Eileen serves a large, heart-healthy breakfast from 5:30 to 8:30 AM (to accom-modate those going fishing) that often features buckwheat hotcakes with garden-fresh rhubarb-strawberry sauce.

▦ *1 cabin that sleeps up to 5 with kitchen, private bath and deck; 2-bedroom suite with 2 single beds and a queen, plus kitchen and private bath; a triple room with private bath across the hall; handicapped accessible unit with sleeping space for 3 and private bath. The latter is the only room available year-round. $30–$40, full breakfast. D, MC, V.*

Juneau

Pearson's Pond. 4541 Sawa Circle, Juneau, AK 99801–8723, tel. 907/789–3772, fax 907/789–6722. 3 bedrooms with queen beds, private baths (stocked with robes, slippers, hair dryers, and toiletries), kitchenettes, private entrances, and decks. Adjoining doors make it possible to convert the rooms into suites. Sitting room with fireplace, deck, hot tub, pond, dock. CD players, TV/VCR, phone, computers with Internet access; travel/tour services. $89–$245, Continental breakfast. AE, D, MC, V.

The attention to detail doesn't stop when you step outside. There are bikes, rowboats, and beautiful garden paths to enjoy, as well as a barbecue and a hot tub. In the winter, you can go cross-country skiing and ice skating.

Arizona

El Tovar Hotel

Northern Arizona, Including the Grand Canyon, Sedona, Flagstaff, and Indian Country

Birch Tree Inn

824 W. Birch Ave., Flagstaff, AZ 86001, tel. 520/774-1042 or 800/645-5811

This 1917 white clapboard house is in a residential neighborhood across the street from a grassy city park and from the Coconino National Forest. Joseph Waldhaus, Flagstaff's then mayor, lived here during the 1930s. After doing time as a fraternity house in the 1970s, the by-then well-worn property was rescued in 1988 by four friends from California, who turned it into a bright, clean bed-and-breakfast. The two couples, Donna and Rodger Pettinger and Sandy and Ed Znetko, take turns running the inn.

A wraparound porch runs the length of their spacious house. Inside, a handsome pool table and a piano fill a bay-windowed game room. Guests often lounge in the adjoining living room, which has a stained-oak floor and brick fireplace.

Upstairs are the guest rooms. The corner Wicker Room is decorated in blue and white. The Pella Room, named for a town in Iowa with many residents of Dutch descent, has a delft-blue ceiling, a hand-stitched tulip quilt, Dutch lace curtains, a brochure for an Iowa tulip festival on the bureau, and two pairs of wooden shoes on the floor.

The Southwest Suite, occupying the northeastern corner, has a king bed with stucco headboard and large bath with separate tub and shower; wall-to-wall carpeting echoes the soft pastel color scheme. Carol's Room is done in hunter green and beige, with a Shaker pine queen bed and matching bureau and end table. The Wagner-Znetko Room, decorated in beige and emerald green, is reminiscent of grandma's attic, with an 80-year-old rocking chair and an ancient sewing machine.

Guests enjoy afternoon refreshments— lemonade and crackers in summer, hot spiced cider and cookies in winter—in the parlor and a full breakfast in either the sunny dining room or on the long veranda. The hosts have 14 breakfast menus, all included in their 95-page bed-and-breakfast cookbook. Popular recipes include baked French toast stuffed with cream-cheese-and-pineapple filling and homemade praline sauce;

or spicy ranchero-style potato casserole, made with chilies, cheese, and turkey breakfast sausage.

🏠 *2 double rooms with baths, 2 doubles share bath, 1 suite. TV in living room. $50–$89; full breakfast, afternoon refreshments. AE, MC, V. No smoking, no children under 10, no pets.*

Briar Patch Inn

3190 North Highway 89A, Sedona, AZ 86336, tel. 520/282–2342, fax 520/282–2399

Shaded by a canopy of sycamore, juniper, canyon oak, pine, elm, and cottonwood trees, 16 log cabins nestle on the floor of Oak Creek Canyon, just north of Sedona. The murmur of the spring-fed creek blends with the rustle of the leaves to create a relaxing, peaceful ambience on this wooded, 9-acre property. It isn't hard to believe that the Briar Patch Inn has been called a "healing, magical oasis."

In the early 1880s, this was the site of a goat barn; there sheep and peacocks are now residents. The cabins were built during the 1940s to provide a summer getaway from the heat of urban Phoenix; at an elevation of 4,484 feet, this area is always temperate. The place became a bed-and-breakfast in 1983.

June through August, guests enjoy the quiet strains of a violinist and classical guitarist who play by the creek during breakfast. Sunday afternoons bring outdoor chamber music concerts on the lawn. The library is stocked with volumes on Native American culture and the history and geography of the Southwest. Innkeepers JoAnn and Ike Olson also like to schedule small workshops on the creative arts here: Navajo weaving, Native American arts, painting, photography, philosophy, self-healing, and more.

The cabins are rustic cozy, with log walls, beam or plank ceilings, Southwestern furnishings, and private patios

or decks. All except the three on the creek—Deck House, Creekside, and Kingfisher—have fireplaces, and a supply of aromatic, shaggy-bark cedar firewood is stacked outside the front door. The newest cabin, Eagle, has a Native American theme, featuring a lodgepole-pine bed, table, and chairs; polished clear-pine floors; and an armoire, paneling, and bath done in knotty pine. One windowed wall faces the tree-shaded creek. Blue Jay, the oldest cabin on the property, has the smallest windows.

Iced tea, coffee, and cookies are always available in the main building. In the morning, a heart-healthy buffet breakfast includes home-baked seven-grain bread or muffins, granola, yogurt, fresh eggs, hot apple sauce from local apples, and seasonal juices and fruits. Guests can take a tray to their room, dine at private tables in the main building, or eat at tree-shaded picnic tables overlooking the creek.

🏠 *12 2-person cabins, 4 4-person cabins. 12 cabins have kitchens, masseuse available. $135–$215, full buffet breakfast. MC, V. No pets.*

Canyon Villa Bed & Breakfast Inn

125 Canyon Circle Dr., Sedona, AZ 86351, tel. 520/284–1226 or 800/453–1166

Opened in 1992, Canyon Villa combines the personal comforts of a traditional inn with the amenities of a first-class resort. Innkeepers Chuck and Marion Yadon researched the business for 18 months, visiting B&Bs from New England to California, before distilling their knowledge into this two-story, state-of-the-art accommodation.

The site at the edge of the Coconino National Forest offers uninterrupted views of Sedona's main attractions: the red sandstone cliffs of Castle Rock, Bell Rock, and Courthouse Butte. This is prime property, and staying at Canyon Villa is very much like visiting the mansion of a wealthy Arizona rancher. Guests' spaces include a well-stocked library: a beam-ceiling, skylit modern living room with a glass-enclosed fireplace; and a 32-foot heated swimming pool in the garden. Snacks and beverages are set out each afternoon in the dining room.

A broad stairway covered with thick carpeting leads to the five upstairs guest rooms, all with large windows and glass French doors to capitalize on the breathtaking scenery; the less expensive room on the ground floor has less stunning views. All the rooms are named after the flowering cacti and shrubs found in the Sedona area and have private baths, balconies or patios, wall-to-wall carpeting, individual heating and cooling units, telephones, cable TV, 10-foot ceilings with fans, and eclectic Southwestern decor; the larger ones also offer double sinks and fireplaces.

Santa Fe–themed Ocotillo has a wrought-iron four-poster bed and a fireplace. The bed in Manzanita, done in blue, is also a four-poster. The corner Strawberry Cactus Room, with white wicker furniture and a gray-blue carpet, has views from two sides and a bath with a stained-glass window. The Spanish Bayonet is perfect for honeymooners, with its fireplace and a bathtub two steps from the king-size bed.

Two long tables, each with eight purple-accented place settings, fill the huge, carpeted dining room, where Marion's catering background is revealed at breakfast time. Marion, Chuck, and hired help (there is a staff of 11) serve a nutritious breakfast of fruit, just-baked bread, and an entrée such as chile tortilla strata, pumpkin pancakes, or sour cream waffles.

🏨 *11 double rooms with baths. Whirlpool tubs, robes, pool towels. $135–$215; full breakfast, afternoon snacks. MC, V. No smoking, no pets.*

El Tovar Hotel

Grand Canyon National Park Lodges, Box 699, Grand Canyon, AZ 86023, tel. 303/297–2757, fax 303/297–3175

In 1540, the Spanish conquistador Francisco Vásquez de Coronado led an expedition of 1,000 men north from Mexico seeking the legendary Seven Cities of Cibola. While the main force headed east from Arizona, a scouting party split off from the Zuni Pueblo in New Mexico and headed west. Don Pedro de Tovar reached the three Hopi mesas in northern Arizona and pioneered the route to the Grand Canyon—thus the name of this historic hotel.

The challenge to El Tovar architect Charles Whittlesey was to design a building that would fit naturally, unobtrusively, on the edge of the world, and one that could accommodate 200 people without defacing or distracting from the natural grandeur of the canyon. Nine decades later, most agree that Whittlesey met the challenge superbly.

Constructed of native boulders and Douglas fir logs brought in from Oregon by rail, the hotel is four stories high on the south end and three on the north. The north wall of the structure is only 50 feet from the canyon's edge, providing many rooms with spectacular views. This place is as popular as the canyon itself; reservations are accepted up to 23 months in advance.

The lobby, with polished maple flooring, black hand-hewn columns and beams, a huge stone fireplace, copper chandeliers, and mounted animal heads, reflects an earlier era of adventure. Adjoining is the hotel's dining room, a cavernous room modeled after a Scandinavian great hall, which for decades has enjoyed a reputation for fine food. The Southwestern menu changes seasonally but includes a daily vegetarian special along with innovatively prepared fish, poultry, and meat dishes; free-range chicken breast with smoked tomato pinenut sauce or sweet corn and lobster tamale might be among the dinner options.

There are 17 different room types, each with a tub/shower bath. The furniture reflects the period: wrought-iron beds, sleigh beds, and mahogany two-posters are paired with upholstered lodgepole-pine couches and chairs.

▥ *65 double rooms with baths, 18 suites. Phones, TVs, room service, tearoom, lounge, gift shop, concierge, kennel available (pets not permitted in rooms). $115–$300, no breakfast. AE, DC, MC, V.*

Graham B&B Inn

150 Canyon Circle Dr., Sedona, AZ 86351, tel. 520/284–1425

This luxurious lodging, designed by Bill and Marni Graham in 1985, was the first to be expressly built as a B&B in Arizona; it helped pioneer the proliferation of inns in Sedona. When Carol Redenbaugh and her husband, Roger, bought the place in 1992, they vowed to maintain the Grahams' reputation for excellence. They have.

Carol and Roger's touches include a lavish, three-room honeymoon suite. At center stage in the suite's bathroom, large enough for a game of handball, is a double whirlpool bath and a shower for two. The contemporary, two-story inn has a heated outdoor pool and spa, a walled, landscaped lawn and garden, and a broad deck for outdoor dining.

A beamed ceiling, two stories high, vaults over a spacious living/dining room carpeted in a dusty rose selected to match Sedona's red cliffs, and warmed by a double-face fireplace. In the dining area, cut-glass chandeliers hang above two round glass tables.

The warm rose carpet leads up a staircase to the guest rooms, each with a marble bath, ceiling fan, and spectacular views of the red rocks from a private balcony. The Southwest Room has a rustic Taos bed; a Sedona-red, beige, and teal color scheme; a fireplace; and a whirlpool bath. The corner Garden Room, green with white wicker furniture, has a flowered, half-canopy bed. The Country Room is out of a Norman Rockwell painting, with floral wallpaper, lace curtains, and an iron bed covered with a hand-sewn quilt. The San Francisco Room is done in soft peach and gray in a contemporary art-deco style and has the largest whirlpool bath in the inn.

The most romantic of all is the Champagne Room. A huge figure from a Sistine Chapel detail overlooks a hand-carved French king-size bed. Antiques, views, and a sitting area with wing chairs in front of a fireplace, complete the picture.

Breakfast may be savored in the dining room or outside on the deck. Popular entrées are German pancakes, maple bread pudding, and *huevos rancheros*. Fresh-baked goodies include Roger's bread or Carol's cinnamon bubble rolls or apricot/banana bread.

▥ *5 double rooms with baths, 1 suite. Robes, phones, TV/VCRs, videos, pool towels, guest refrigerator, pool, bicycles. $109–$229; full breakfast, afternoon refreshments. D, MC, V. No smoking, no pets, 2-night minimum on weekends.*

Grand Canyon Lodge

TW Recreational Services, Amfac Parks and Resorts, 14001 East Iliff Ave., Suite 600, Aurora, Colorado, 80014, tel. 303/297–2757 (reservations weekdays only), fax 303/338–2045, tel. 520/638–2611 (lodge switchboard for general information), fax 520/638–2554.

Less than 5 feet from the edge of America's greatest abyss, the Grand Canyon Lodge has one of the most stunning locations in the world. The grounds are heavily forested with pine, spruce, fir, and aspen. An easy ½-mile trail from the lodge to Bright Angel Point rewards strollers with breathtaking views of the canyon and a glimpse of Roaring Springs, while the gentle 1½-mile Transept Trail travels from the lodge to a campground and general store.

The first lodge on the site was completed in 1928. Built by a subsidiary of the Union Pacific Railroad, it was one of the last in a long line of elaborate railroad lodges in western national parks. Craftsmen were recruited from small Mormon communities nearby; their construction materials came from local quarries and logging camps. When the original lodge burned down in 1932, the railroad designed and erected a second (present) lodge, opened in 1936.

The vaulted ceilings of the main lobby and dining room are spectacularly crossbarred by thickset Ponderosa-pine beams; hand-hewn Kaibab stone unites the walls, floors, and fireplaces. Six carpeted steps lead down to the cavernous dining room, three stories tall. The menu, which changes every season, is surprisingly sophisticated for the rustic locale: Marinated pork kebabs, grilled swordfish, or linguine with cilantro and pesto might be among the entrées, which change seasonally. A Sun Room and outdoor patio with spectacular views are equipped with lounge and rocking chairs.

Grand Canyon Lodge has a variety of cabins and motel accommodations. If you reserve two years in advance, you might be able to get a Rim View cabin with a private porch overlooking the canyon. All rooms have phones and private baths, but some have only showers. Motel accommodations are generic; the rustic Pioneer and Frontier cabins with wood-beam walls have more character. Most deluxe are the Western cabins, with two double, extra-long beds, full bath, dressing room, and private porch.

🏨 *40 motel rooms with baths, 54 Western cabins (for up to 5 people), 84 Frontier cabins (up to 3 people), 23 Pioneer cabins (4 or 5 people). Dining room, cafeteria, bar, gift shop, transportation desk, National Park Service Information desk. $58–$95, no breakfast. AE, D, DC, MC, V. No pets. Closed in winter.*

Inn at Four Ten

410 N. Leroux St., Flagstaff, AZ 86001, tel. 520/774-0088, or 800/774-2008

Now a friendly bed-and-breakfast, the Inn at Four Ten was built in 1907 by Tom E. Pollock, a wealthy banker and cattle rancher, as the manor house of his grand estate; its extensive grounds included a stable and separate quarters for the grooms. After Pollock died, the property was split up. Some years later, the main building became a fraternity house. It was in serious need of repair when Carol and Mike Householder purchased it in 1989.

After completing extensive renovations, including the installation of an all-white commercial kitchen, they opened for business in 1991. Howard and Sally Krueger bought the inn in 1993 and in 1995 began upgrading the rooms. Guests step from a broad front porch into an open living room with polished-oak floors, bookcases, door frames, and ceiling beams, as well as a flagstone fireplace. South-facing windows in the adjoining dining room let in the soft morning light.

A great deal of detail went into the decoration of the guest rooms. Downstairs, Suite Nature, which can sleep four people in three beds, is distinctly woodsy, with a stained-glass window. The elegant Tea Room has a mahogany bookcase wall, a wrought-iron king bed, hunter green with pink roses on the carpeting, a whirlpool bath for two, a gas fireplace at the foot of the whirlpool bath, and a 7-foot walnut burl armoire; polished-oak doors lead directly into the dining room. Also downstairs, The Southwest is furnished in Santa Fe style, with a Saltillo-tile floor, kiva fireplace, whirlpool bath for two, and queen bleached log bed imported from New Mexico.

Upstairs, The Conservatory has turn-of-the-century decor with a music theme, a queen four-poster bed and a sitting area with fireplace. Dakota has two rooms in a rustic cowboy decor with barn wood from Sally's family farm. Sunflower Fields, a vibrant country charm in blue, yellow, and red with a sunflower motif, has a queen antique iron bed, fireplace and window seat.

Guests have breakfast in the sunny dining room or under the gazebo in the garden. They're given a choice of juices and fruits daily; granola and yogurt are always available, too. All entrées are low-fat and low-cholesterol, yet very tasty. Favorites include Paul's oat pancakes and peach bread pudding.

▦ *7 double rooms with baths, 2 suites. Kitchenettes in 4 rooms, whirlpool baths in 2, fireplaces in 2, coffeemakers, mini-refrigerators. $100–$150; full breakfast, afternoon tea, and snacks. AE, MC, V. No smoking, no pets.*

Other Choices

Bright Angel Lodge. Box 699, Grand Canyon, AZ 86023, tel. 303/297–2757 (reservations), 520/297–2757 (switchboard), fax 303/297–3175. 11 double rooms with baths, 13 doubles with half-baths, 6 dormitory-style doubles, 47 cabins. Phones, TVs, some refrigerators, coffee shop, steak house, lounge, tour desk, kennels available. $55–$275, no breakfast. AE, D, DC, MC, V. No pets in rooms.

Canyon Country Inn. 442 W. Rte. 66, Williams, AZ 86046, tel. 520/635–2349 or 800/643–1020, fax 520/635–9898. 13 double rooms with baths. Phones, TVs. $60–$95; Continental breakfast, fruit basket at check-in. AE, D, MC, V. No smoking, no pets.

Casa Sedona. 55 Hozoni Dr., Sedona, AZ 86336, tel. 520/282–2938 or 800/525–3756. 15 double rooms with baths.

Phones with free local calls, TV in living room. $120–$185, full breakfast and afternoon snack. MC, V. No smoking, no pets.

Cathedral Rock Lodge Bed & Breakfast. 61 Los Amigos La., Sedona, AZ 86336, tel. 520/282–7608, fax 520/282–4505. 2 double rooms with baths, 1 suite, 1 cabin. TV/VCR in living room, fresh fruit at check-in, nearby stable, homemade jam on departure. $70–$125, full breakfast. MC, V. No smoking, no pets.

Country Elegance Bed & Breakfast. Box 10793, Sedona, AZ 86339, tel. 520/634–4470, or 800/432–3529, fax 520/634–3227. 2 double rooms with bath, 1 suite. TV, ceiling fan, turndown service, 24-hr beverage bar, library. $85–$95, full breakfast. D, MC, V. No smoking, no pets, 2-night minimum on weekends, 3-night minimum on holidays.

Coyote Pass Hospitality. Contact Will Tsosie Jr., Box 91, Tsaile, AZ 86556, tel. 520/724–3258. Hogans (Navajo dwellings) accommodate 1–15 people. Guided tours, full meal service available. $85 first person, $10 each additional person; full breakfast. No credit cards. No smoking.

Cozy Cactus Bed & Breakfast. 80 Canyon Circle Dr., Sedona, AZ 86351, tel. 520/284–0082 or 800/788–2082. 5 double rooms with baths. Cable TV in living room. $90–$110; full breakfast, afternoon beverages. AE, D, MC, V. No smoking, no pets.

Lantern Light Inn Bed & Breakfast. 3085 W. Hwy. 89A, Sedona, AZ 86336, tel. 520/282–3419. 2 double rooms with baths, 1 triple with bath. TVs; refrigerator in 2 rooms; private, locked entries; Shiatsu massage. $80–$120, full breakfast. No credit cards. No smoking, no pets.

Lodge at Sedona. 125 Kallof Pl., Sedona, AZ 86336, tel. 520/204–1942 or 800/619–4467, fax 520/204–2128. 10 double rooms with baths, 3 suites. Whirlpool bath in 6 rooms, fireplace in 2 rooms, TV in parlor, library, spa. $110–$225; full breakfast, evening hors d'oeuvres. MC, V. No smoking, no pets.

Saddle Rock Ranch. 255 Rock Ridge Dr., Sedona, AZ 86336, tel. 520/282–7640, fax 520/282–6829. 3 double rooms with bath. Terry robes and pool towels, concierge, house phone, pool and spa. $120–$140; full breakfast, afternoon snacks and beverage. No smoking, no pets, no children under 14, 2-night minimum stay, 3-night minimum in spring and fall.

Thunderbird Lodge. Box 548, Chinle, AZ 86503, tel. 520/674–5841 or 800/679–2473. 71 rooms with baths, 1 suite. Gift shop, horse rentals nearby. $83–$88, no breakfast. AE, D, DC, MC, V. No smoking, no pets.

Reservations Services

Bed & Breakfast Inn Arizona (Box 11253, Glendale, AZ 85318, tel. 602/561–0335, fax 602/561–2300). **Mi Casa Su Casa B&B Reservation Service** (Box 950, Tempe, AZ 85280, tel. 602/990–0682, reservations 800/456–0682).

Central Arizona, Including Phoenix, Prescott, and the White Mountains

Greer Lodge

Box 244, Greer, AZ 85927, tel. 520/735–7216

An alpine lodge that could have come straight from the drafting board of a Hollywood set designer, this 1948 building in the White Mountains is made entirely of polished logs, exposed inside and out. The spacious lobby is replete with deer antlers, a black bearskin, wagon-wheel chandeliers, lodgepole-pine furniture, and plank floors. A stone fireplace crackles with juniper logs.

The backdrop—pine-studded Greer Valley, at an elevation of 8,500 feet, with deer and elk grazing in the meadows—is equally picture perfect. The Little Colorado River, stocked with trout and dammed here and there by beaver colonies, meanders through the grounds.

The rooms pick up the rustic theme, with knotty pine or polished log walls, oak or pine plank floors, and cheerful chintz curtains and bedspreads; each has a private bath and individual electric heat controls. First choice are the corner rooms, such as Nos. 2, 4, and 5, which offer views of both the valley and the wooded mountains. On the third floor, under the peaked roof, is a romantic pine-paneled room with a clear view to the south. In addition to the accommodations in the lodge, there are similarly furnished rooms in the Little Lodge, a four-bedroom log cabin with a kitchen and a deck overlooking the river; and rooms in a variety of smaller cabins, some with kitchens and fireplaces.

Breakfast, lunch, and dinner are served in the skylit solar-heated dining room, open to the public. It's surrounded by glass, and every table overlooks the creek, three ponds, an expansive lawn populated with ducks and geese, and the wooded hills beyond. Breakfast possibilities include Belgian waffles with strawberries, biscuits and gravy, and blueberry pancakes. At lunchtime, salads, burgers, and hot and cold sandwiches are available.

No license is required to fish in the Lodge's two fishing ponds, but there is a fee. If you catch something in the larger fly-fishing pond, you have to throw it back, but you can keep whatever bites in the smaller bait-fishing pond.

7 double rooms with baths, 2 suites in Lodge; 2 1-bedroom cabins; 5 2-bedroom cabins; 1 4-bedroom cabin. Restaurant, bar, cable TV in lounge, fruit basket upon arrival, fly-fishing classes *Apr.–Oct. Lodge $120, Little Lodge $35 per person, cabins $110; no breakfast. AE, MC, V. No pets, 2-night minimum on weekends, 3-night minimum on holidays.*

Lynx Creek Farm

Box 4301, Prescott, AZ 86302, tel. 520/ 778-9573

There are more than 200 fruit trees, including seven varieties of apple, at this 25-acre property on a hilltop east of Prescott overlooking Lynx Creek, Lonesome Valley, and the Blue Hills; in addition, there's a menagerie of chickens, pigs, parrots, goats, cats, and dogs. At the bottom of the hill, Lynx Creek meanders through a shady grove of tall cottonwood trees. This idyllic setting is equally suited to honeymooners and families, offering privacy as well as plenty of space and activities for restless children.

Built in the early 1980s, the farm was bought by Greg and Wendy Temple in 1985 and turned into a bed-and-breakfast. Across the driveway from the main house, where Greg and Wendy live, is a guest house with two rooms; each has a wood-burning stove and there's a shared hot tub on the viewside deck. The cozy pine-paneled Sharlot Hall Room, named for a Prescott pioneer woman, is filled with antiques, books, and memorabilia. One of the room's two king-size beds is set in a low-ceiling loft reached by ladder—an ideal space to stow the kids. The White Wicker Room next door is light, lacy, and romantic, with wicker furniture and a queen bed with a soft feather comforter.

In 1992, Greg added a handsome log cabin with four inviting rooms. All have wall-to-wall Berber carpets, wood-burning stoves, king beds, and private hot tubs on outdoor decks that afford views of the valley. The Old West–style Chaparral Room is decorated with beat-up saddles, antlers, and a hand-stitched quilt, while the more romantic Country Garden Room features lots of plants and whitewashed log-beam ceilings. A living room with kitchenette can be connected to any of the rooms to create a two-room suite; two daybed couches open up into four single beds for extra family members.

Mornings bring guests to the breakfast room of the main house, decorated with blue ribbons that the Temples were awarded for their apples, or to the wide deck overlooking the creek below. Large breakfasts usually feature organically homegrown fruits, quiches made with fresh eggs, homemade yogurt, fresh-baked muffins, breads, and coffee cakes. On request, a Continental breakfast-in-a-basket will be delivered to your door.

🛏 *4 double rooms with baths, 2 suites. Terry robes, phone and TV on request, playground, basketball, volleyball, horseshoes, hiking. $85–$140; full breakfast, evening refreshments. AE, D, MC, V. No smoking.*

Maricopa Manor Bed and Breakfast Inn

Box 7186, Phoenix, AZ 85011, tel. 602/ 274-6302

Business travelers appreciate this all-suite facility, centrally located near downtown Phoenix and just minutes from the Heard Museum, the Herberger Theatre, and the America West Arena. Innkeepers Paul and Mary Ellen Kelley raised 12 children in this 1928 residence, on a quiet, palm-shaded street, before turning it into an elegant executive retreat.

The immaculate Spanish Colonial–style home is decorated with fine art and stocked with countless books. Visitors have the run of the high-ceiling family room, living room, dining room, and outdoor patio. Stressed guests can let off steam by tickling the ivories on the restored piano in the music room, soaking in the hot tub in the gazebo, or taking a dip in the newly installed pool with a waterfall out back.

The accommodations have every amenity offered by the posh Phoenix resorts—fresh flowers, expensive toiletries—and even some they don't have: an array of paperbacks in each room, access to AT&T bilingual international operator service, and rubber duckies in the bathtub.

The Victorian Suite is in the main house. Set off the family room, it is done in satin, lace, and antiques; the private bath is across the hall. The other accommodations are arrayed outside in adjoining buildings. A private entrance leads to the Library Suite, with volumes of leather-bound books, a desk, and a canopied king-size bed.

In an adjoining guest house with its own carport and a gated driveway are two more spacious suites. Reflections Past offers a fireplace, antique mirrors, and king-size bed with a tapestry canopy. Reflections Future, done in black and white with a Chinese flavor, has a living room, a full kitchen with breakfast area, and a small study with a desk and phone.

A Franklin stove sets the tone for the traditional American decor in the Palo Verde Suite, which has two bedrooms, one with a king-size canopy bed and a smaller one with a ¾-size spool bed set off the enclosed sunporch.

Breakfast—orange juice, hot coffee, a fresh fruit plate, homemade bread or pastries, and a hot cheese mini-quiche—is delivered to your door, at the hour you specify, in a wicker picnic basket.

🛏 *4 1-bedroom suites (1 with private bath across the hall), 1 2-bedroom suite. Bathrobes, TVs, phones. $79–$159, full breakfast. AE, D, MC, V. No pets.*

Marks House

203 E. Union St., Prescott, AZ 86303, tel. 520/778–4632

The mayor of Territorial Prescott and a man with successful interests in ranching, mining, and wholesale liquor, Jake Marks spared no expense when it came to building a house for his wife, Josephine. Redwood was imported from California, the glass in the turret windows was curved to match the rounded sills, the cast copper door hinges were engraved with decorative designs, and parquet floors were laid in the formal dining room. In all, it took two years to construct this two-story Queen Anne–style mansion on Nob Hill, overlooking the central Court House Square; it was completed in 1884.

Restoration on the building, which served for a time as a boardinghouse and a rest home, began in 1980; it debuted as a bed-and-breakfast in 1987. Today it is listed on the National Register of Historic Homes and owned by Beth Maitland, the young actress who plays Traci on CBS's "The Young and the Restless." Her parents, Dotti and Harold Viehweg, manage the inn and continue to improve it.

Like the rest of the house, the bay-windowed living room is furnished with antiques from the 1870s through the 1890s and wallpapered with a reproduction Victorian print; filled to the rafters with lacy doodads and knick-knacks, it hosts a boutique for decorative items. The formal dining room, which enjoys a view out over Court House Plaza, has room for three linen-covered tables and matching oak sideboards.

The jewel in this B&B's crown is the Queen Anne Suite adjoining the circular turret; it's furnished in white wicker and has a claw-foot tub in the bath. The view north from the curved windows sweeps over the tall trees surrounding the Court House, across the city to majestic Thumb Butte in the distance. Princess Victoria, also upstairs, is done in mauve and lavender with floral patterns; an unusual, hammered copper tub in the bath was salvaged from an 1892 bathhouse in New York State.

Breakfast is served family style at whatever hour guests agree upon in advance. Popular entrées include blackberry dumplings made from an old family recipe, a deep-dish egg casserole with meat, and French toast.

🏠 *2 double rooms with baths (1 adjoining), 1 1-bedroom suite, 1 2-bedroom suite. Welcome mineral water in rooms, gift shop. $75–$135; full breakfast, afternoon hors d'oeuvres. D, MC, V. No smoking, no pets.*

Paisley Corner Bed & Breakfast

Box 458, Springerville, AZ 85938, or 287 N. Main St., Eagar, AZ 85925, tel. 520/333-4665

This imposing two-story redbrick mansion occupies a corner lot on the main street of Eagar, a small town near the Little Colorado River. Innkeepers Cheryl and Cletus Tisdell worked three years to restore the 1910 Historical Landmark to its pre–World War I grandeur, and probably surpassed it. They used the hammered-tin ceilings from the old Fox Theatre in Phoenix to create wainscoting, borders, and ceilings throughout the house.

Opened as a bed-and-breakfast at the end of 1991, the mansion boasts furnishings authentic to the period. An enameled wood-burning stove and formal walnut table dominate the dining room. The two front rooms retain their original stained-glass windows. In the "ice cream parlour," across the front hall from the living room, Cletus shows off his two jukeboxes, which play 78 rpm records; his working antique Coke machine; and his collection of American memorabilia.

The names given the guest rooms, all upstairs, were popular ones for women at the turn of the century. Each room has wall-to-wall Irish rose carpeting and a lazily rotating ceiling fan. Fanny's black-and-gold wrought-iron bed fronts a three-faced dressmaker's mirror and a maple vanity in an unusual cattail design; the spacious bathroom, with a claw-foot tub and 19th-century pull-chain commode, is next door. In Miss Lily, most aptly called a boudoir, mauve wallpaper in a rose pattern wraps around a lace-covered, white-and-brass bed that reposes regally on a step-up platform with formidable wooden banisters. The bath sports a circular, ribcage shower.

Entry to spacious Mabel Joy is through a pair of etched-glass doors with porcelain handles secured by a pink satin rope; the room has dark-green wallpaper with a hammered-tin border, as well as a massive, carved-oak canopy bed and matching beveled-glass vanity. Fontanille, a two-bedroom suite, boasts an artificial fireplace with tiger-oak columns and an ornate 1820s carvedwalnut bed with an 8-foot-high headboard. Recently added in the courtyard is a gazebo with a hot tub inside.

Cheryl's full breakfasts are prepared on a 1910 gas stove and served on rosepattern china set on a lace tablecloth. Fresh-ground coffee precedes fresh juice, fruit, potatoes, and home-baked breads or muffins. The main dish may be quiche; a rich breakfast casserole of bacon, hard-boiled eggs, and sour cream; or French toast with real maple syrup.

🏠 *3 double rooms with baths, 1 2-bedroom suite. TV in living room, welcome basket. $65–$75, full breakfast. MC, V. No smoking.*

Victorian Inn of Prescott Bed & Breakfast

246 S. Cortez St., Prescott, AZ 86303, tel. 520/778-2642

Prescott lays claim to being the only town in Arizona with an entire neighborhood of Victorian homes dating to the 19th century. Tamia Thunstedt's blue-and-white trim Queen Anne could easily be that neighborhood's center-piece. Built as a single-level square house in 1875, 11 years after Prescott was settled, it was purchased in 1883 by John C. Herndon, who imported milled lumber and handcrafted wood-work by train from back East and grad-ually remodeled it into his gingerbread dream house, adding bay windows and a second story with a conical turret.

Between 1982 and 1988, the building was restored. The small living room now looks as it must have 100 years ago, filled with formal Victorian an-tiques and lots of plush red velvet. The stained-glass windows and 17 chande-liers are all original to the house.

Four upstairs guest accommodations are also meticulously furnished in pe-riod style. The Victoriana Suite, done in rich burgundy and royal blue, has its own fireplace, two bay windows, and 1860s walnut pieces; it's the most spa-cious room and the only one with a pri-vate bath. The smallest is the Teddy Bear Room, dominated by a 19th-cen-tury mahogany four-poster bed and populated by stuffed bears of various sizes and colors.

The Rose Room, decorated in mauve with complementary linens, features a brass bed and antique lace curtains. Eve's Garden Room has white wicker furniture and a chiffon canopy bed with raspberry satin sheets. The bathroom shared by the three rooms has a thick, wall-to-wall carpet, a claw-foot tub with brass fittings, and a handheld shower nozzle.

At check-in, Tamia's tour of the house and detailed briefing on guest proce-dures, including fire safety, lasts nearly 15 minutes. That's nothing. She says her formal breakfast for eight takes 12 hours to prepare, and it's easy to believe: It's an elaborate production, with a setting—antique, floral-pattern china, fine linens, and gold-plated uten-sils—and food suitable for Queen Vic-toria. Entrées range from blueberry buttermilk Swedish pancakes or French

toast basted in orange sauce and served with Canadian bacon florets, to Swedish *strata*, layered bread pudding of eggs, sausage, and cheese, served with warm amaretto applesauce.

▦ *3 double rooms share bath, 1 suite. Prebreakfast coffee, tea, and newspa-per; gift shop. $90, Victoriana Suite $145; full breakfast. AE, D, MC, V. No smoking, no pets.*

Other Choices

Bartram's White Mountain Bed & Breakfast. Rte. 1, Box 1014, Lakeside, AZ 85929, tel. 520/367–1408 or 800/257–0211. 5 double rooms with baths, 1 suite. TV in living room. $85 ($20 for each extra person), full breakfast. No credit cards. No smoking, no pets.

Billings' Country Retreat. H.C. 66, Box 2614, 63 E. Turkey Track, Pinetop, AZ 85935, tel. 520/367–1709. 2 double rooms share bath. TV in living room, use of laundry, barbecue grill, refriger-ator. $45–$55, full breakfast. MC, V. No smoking, no pets.

Coldstream Bed & Breakfast. Box 2988, Pinetop, AZ 85935, tel. 520/369–0115. 4 double rooms with baths (1 across hall), 1 suite with whirlpool bath. Terry robes, TV/VCRs, pool table, bicycles, enclosed outdoor spa, horse boarding. $95–$135; full breakfast, afternoon tea. MC, V. No smoking, no pets, no children under 10.

Cottages at Prescott Country Inn. 503 S. Montezuma St., Prescott, AZ 86303, tel. 520/445–7991. 2 1-room units, 7 2-room units, 2 3-room units, 1 4-room unit. TVs, phones, clock radios, whirl-pool bath, off-street parking, outdoor barbecue. $95–$149; Continental break-fast, complimentary lunch and dinner at a choice of 5 Prescott restaurants. D, MC, V.

Hassayampa Inn. 122 E. Gurley St., Prescott, AZ 86301, tel. 520/778–9434 or 800/322–1927. 58 rooms with baths, 10 suites. Restaurant, bar, lounge, TVs, phones. $89–$175 rooms, $135–$175 suites; full breakfast, afternoon cocktails. AE, D, DC, MC, V. No pets.

Juniper Well Ranch. Box 11083, Prescott, AZ 86304, tel. 520/442–3415. 2 cabins, 1 2-bedroom ranch house. Hot tub, barbecue pits, kitchens. Cabins: $105, full breakfast. Ranch house: $100 for 4 people, $10 per additional person; no breakfast. AE, D, MC, V. No smoking.

The Meadows. Box 1110, Pinetop, AZ 85935, tel. 520/367–8200. 6 double rooms with baths, 1 suite. Restaurant, wine bar, room service. $70–$155, full breakfast. Smoking in designated area only, no pets, 2-night minimum weekends, 3-night minimum on holidays.

Mt. Vernon Inn. 204 North Mt. Vernon Ave., Prescott, AZ 86301, tel. 520/778–0886. 4 double rooms with baths, 3 cottages. Phones, TVs and kitchens in cottages. $90, full breakfast. Cottages $100–$120, no breakfast. D, MC, V. No smoking, no pets.

Noftsger Hill Inn. 425 North St., Globe, AZ 85501, tel. 520/425–2260. 3 triple rooms and 1 double with bath. Wheelchair ramp. $45–$75, full breakfast. MC, V. No smoking, no pets.

Pleasant Street Inn Bed & Breakfast. 142 S. Pleasant St., Prescott, AZ 86303, tel. 520/445–4774. 2 double rooms with baths, 2 suites. TV in living room, fresh flowers in rooms. $85–$125; full breakfast, afternoon hors d'oeuvres. D, MC, V. No smoking, no pets.

White Mountain Lodge. Box 143, Greer, AZ 85927, tel. 520/735–7568, fax 520/735–7498. 6 double rooms, 1 twin, all with baths; 3 cabins. TV/VCR in living room, guest fax and refrigerator. $50–$95, full breakfast. No credit cards. 2-night minimum weekends, 3-night minimum on holidays.

Reservations Services

Arizona Association of Bed & Breakfast Inns (3101 North Central Ave., Suite 560, Phoenix, AZ 85012, tel. 602/ 277–0775). **Bed & Breakfast Inn Arizona-Arizona Accommodations Reservations** (8900 E. Via Linda, Suite 101, Scottsdale, AZ 85258, tel. 602/ 860–9338 or 800/266–7829, fax 520/ 860–9338). **Mi Casa Su Casa B&B Reservation Service** (Box 950, Tempe, AZ 85280, tel. 602/990–0682; reservations only 800/456–0682).

Tucson and Environs, Including Pima and Santa Cruz Counties

El Presidio Bed & Breakfast Inn

297 N. Main Ave., Tucson, AZ 85701, tel. 520/623–6151 or 800/349–6151

"It's a loyal restoration," says Patti Toci of her Victorian adobe home. "We wanted it just as it was when people lived here in the 1880s." She and her husband, Jerry, labored for 12 years toward that goal and admirably achieved it by 1987, when they opened their bed-and-breakfast.

Listed on the National Register of Historic Places, the Territorial-style home has 21-inch-thick walls made of adobe brick and a 17-foot ceiling with hand-hewn beams in the *zaguan* (center hallway). Polished-oak flooring added during the 1920s and numerous antiques, including a pair of early 18th-century cherrywood corner cases and a stolid grandfather clock, all museum-quality pieces, create a more formal, Victorian atmosphere. The Veranda Room, once the mansion's back porch, is now the dining room. Broad windows look onto a cobblestone courtyard banked with geraniums, snapdragons, and rosebushes, and are shaded by mature trees— among them Aleppo pine, fig, desert ash, and grapefruit—that attract hummingbirds and cactus wrens. The birds also like to frolic in the three-tiered fountain that Jerry found in Magdalena, Mexico.

Each of the three suites has a different theme. The Victorian Suite, in the main house, has a parlor decorated with white wicker furniture, a kiva fireplace, and a braided rug. French doors line two sides of the room: One pair leads into the zaguan living room, and the other faces a lovely, tree-shaded garden. The Gate House Suite, with a huge blue wicker bed and a private entrance, has the feel of a French country manor. The brick veranda of the Carriage House Suite is topped by a Mexican-tile roof. Inside is a kitchenette with a stocked refrigerator, a living room, a rose-themed bedroom with a pine two-poster bed, and a bath with a countertop made of imported Spanish tile.

Guests enjoy an elaborate breakfast, which varies daily, at a handsome walnut dining table that can expand to seat 10. Among the delightful possibilities are chorizo and eggs on corn tortillas, gingerbread pancakes with fresh strawberry sauce and shirred eggs, or sweet potato waffles with sautéed apples and yogurt with sunflower seeds. Patti's lemon muffins, topped with lemon streusel, are made with lemons picked from the tree outside the window.

🎫 *3 suites. TVs, phones, bathrobes, kitchen in 2 suites stocked with beverages and fruit, TV in sitting room, privileges at nearby health club. $95– $115, full breakfast. No credit cards. No smoking, no pets. Some years closed July.*

Mine Manager's House Inn

1 Greenway Dr., Ajo, AZ 85321, tel. 520/387–6505, fax 520/387–6508

When the Phelps Dodge copper mine closed in 1985, and all the miners packed up and left, everyone assumed Ajo would become a ghost town. Not Martin Jeffries. He and his wife, Faith,

began buying up the vacant properties being sold off by the company. Their prize purchase was the empty 1919 mine superintendent's house and its 3 acres of neglected, terraced gardens.

The imposing, 5,000-square foot mansion overlooks the entire town from its site atop the highest hill in Ajo. The Jeffries completely refurbished the solid masonry structure, installed all new wiring, and furnished the rooms with period furniture and art. And on New Year's Day 1988, they opened a bed-and-breakfast.

The public areas include a library/sunroom, a spacious living room, and a formal dining room with a view out over the town. A hot tub in the back is wonderful for soaking tired muscles after a day of desert travel.

Each of the five individually decorated rooms has high ceilings and ceiling fans. The Greenway Suite, also called the "honeymoon suite," is the largest one and boasts a marble bathtub and vanity, an upholstered headboard with flowers and cupids, and pretty floral drapes. The Nautical Room has two queen-size brass beds and a 180° view out over the town; parts of an old schooner, including the steering wheel, are worked into the decor.

In 1990 the Jeffries sold the Mine Manager's House to a French Canadian couple from California, Micheline and Jean Fournier, who built on the B&B's early success and maintained the Jeffries' tradition of comfort and service. Each evening, for example, guests are offered a dish of gourmet English toffee ice cream or peach frozen yogurt.

Breakfasts are served on linens and fine china in the superintendent's light-filled formal dining room. The meal may feature eggs Benedict or Belgian waffles with a raspberry sauce, in addition to coffee, fresh juices, and seasonal fruits.

🎫 *2 double rooms with baths, 3 suites. TV/VCR in living room, library, guest* coin laundry, outdoor hot tub, barbecue grill, off-street parking, off-site pet boarding. $69–$105, full breakfast. MC, V. No smoking.

Peppertrees Bed and Breakfast Inn

724 E. University Blvd., Tucson, AZ 85719, tel. 520/622–7167 or 800/348–5763, fax 520/622–7167

Early settlers who came to the Arizona Territory at the turn of the century tried to create pockets of civilization in what was then a dusty desert outpost. Some 80 years later, perhaps in a similar spirit, Marjorie Martin brought antiques from her family home in the English Cotswolds to furnish her 1905 redbrick Victorian. After a careful restoration, she opened the Peppertrees in 1988. The classic residence is two blocks from the main gate of the University of Arizona and near the Fourth Avenue shopping district.

To check into the inn, guests enter the main house. Rooms with 12-foot-high ceilings and pine floors covered with Oriental carpets highlight Marjorie's furnishings, most of which date back to the last century. The mahogany-and-glass bookcase in the living room contains the family's Royal Doulton china.

Penelope's Room has windows on three sides; the one to the south looks out on a mature pomegranate tree and landscaped patio. It's decorated in Victorian style, with a white wrought-iron bed, a frilly rose-patterned comforter, and a 150-year-old mirrored mahogany dresser.

Adjacent to the main house is a 1917 bungalow-style home with a large, comfortable living room and two bedrooms decorated with mahogany furniture, frilly, patterned comforters, and lace curtains. Behind the main house, across a cozy garden with a splashing Mexican-tile fountain, are two fully equipped guest houses. Each duplex

unit, furnished in contemporary style, has two bedrooms upstairs with a shared bath. Downstairs are a half-bath, living room, dining area, full kitchen, and private patio.

A gourmet cook, Marjorie published her *Recipes from Peppertrees Bed and Breakfast Inn*. Breakfast is served buffet-style in the dining room or, on those perfect southern Arizona mornings, outdoors on the patio. There is always fresh fruit and home-baked breads or scones and a main dish such as blue-corn pancakes or savory French toast filled with cream cheese and orange. Special diets can be accommodated with advance notice.

🏨 *3 double rooms with baths, 2 2-bedroom duplex guest houses. Guest houses have phones, TVs, washer/dryers. $78–$165, full breakfast. D, MC, V. No smoking, no pets.*

Tanque Verde Ranch

14301 E. Speedway Blvd., Tucson, AZ 85748, tel. 520/296–6275 or 800/234–3833, fax 520/721–9426

"We want to get the guests involved in the desert," says Bob Cote, owner of the Tanque Verde Ranch. "Then they can see the delicate balance of nature here, the fragility of this specialized ecosystem." Viewing the flora and fauna of the Sonoran Desert is just one of the many ways in which guests at this historic lodging, built as a frontier cattle ranch in the 19th century, will find themselves immersed in the experience of the Old West. Many European visitors who'd previously seen cowboys only in the movies come back year after year for the real thing.

The first adobe building erected in Tucson, on land granted by the Spanish government, the ranch dates back to 1868. In this century, it became one of the early guest ranches in Tucson and was devoted exclusively to that purpose for many years. Recently, the 640-acre property once again became a working cattle ranch, with 300 cows and 21 bulls at last count.

More than 100 years of additions to the original small ranch house have resulted in a complex with 60 units, extensive dining areas, and a wide range of recreational facilities. There are some 130 horses to ride and many opportunities to ride them, from the daily morning trot out to a campfire breakfast cookout, to all-day pack trips into the nearby Rincon Mountains. Don't worry if you're a tenderfoot: Riding lessons are included in the room rates. Ranch activities also include daily nature walks with the ranch naturalist and evening lectures.

Less nature-oriented activities can be pursued at the ranch's five tennis courts; health club with sauna and whirlpool; shuffleboard, volleyball, and basketball courts; and heated indoor and outdoor swimming pools. Although the rooms are decorated in southwestern style, with exposed beam ceilings and, in many cases, kiva fireplaces, they're hardly rustic: All have private baths, individually controlled cooling and heating units, and telephones. Nor are meals in the franks 'n' beans mode: The chef since 1971 has built an international reputation for his fine Continental and American cuisine.

🏨 *14 double rooms, 34 deluxe (up to 3 people) rooms, all with baths, 12 suites. Private patios for many rooms, extensive indoor and outdoor recreational facilities and programs. $225–$360, including 3 meals and all recreational activities. AE, D, DC, MC, V. No pets.*

Other Choices

Casa Alegre Bed and Breakfast Inn. 316 E. Speedway Blvd., Tucson, AZ 85705, tel. 520/628–1800 or 800/628–5654. 3 double rooms with baths, 1 2-bedroom suite with kitchen. TV/VCR in Arizona Room, pool and hot tub, fireplaces. $80–$95, full breakfast. D, MC, V. No smoking, no pets.

Casa Tierra Adobe Bed & Breakfast. 11155 W. Calle Pima, Tucson, AZ 85743, tel. 520/578–3058, fax 520/578–3058. 3 double rooms with baths. Microwaves, mini-refrigerators; outdoor hot tub, access to barbecue and coffeemaker. $85–$95, full breakfast. No credit cards. No smoking, no pets. Closed June–mid-Sept.

Duquesne House Bed and Breakfast. 357 Duquesne St., Box 772, Patagonia, AZ 85624, tel. 520/394–2732. 3 suites. Radios, wood-burning stove in 2 rooms, ceiling fans. $70, full breakfast. No credit cards. No smoking, no pets.

Elysian Grove Market. 400 W. Simpson, Tucson, AZ 85701, tel. 520/628–1522. 2 2-bedroom suites, 1 with full kitchen. Fireplace, refrigerator, microwave, phone, radio, and tapes. $75, Continental Mexican-style breakfast. No credit cards. No pets, no smoking, no children.

Guest House Inn. 3 Guesthouse Rd., Ajo, AZ 85321, tel. 520/387–6133. 4 double rooms with baths. Individual heating/cooling controls in rooms, fireplace and TV in common room, patio. $79, full breakfast. DC, MC, V. No smoking, no pets.

La Posada del Valle. 1640 N. Campbell Ave., Tucson, AZ 85719, tel. 520/795–3840. 4 double rooms with baths, 1 cottage. Each room has private entrance, 2 have phones, TV in living room and cottage, Tucson Racquet Club privileges available. $90–$125, full breakfast. MC, V. No smoking, no pets.

Ramsey Canyon Inn. 31 Ramsey Canyon Rd., Hereford, AZ 85615, tel. 520/378–3010. 6 double rooms with baths, 2 housekeeping cottages. Fireplace in living room, gift shop. $90–$105; full breakfast, evening dessert. No credit cards. Smoking on patio only, no pets.

Rimrock West Hacienda. 3450 N. Drake Pl., Tucson, AZ 85749, tel. 520/749–8774. 2 double rooms with baths, 1 cottage with kitchen. Ceiling fans, TV, air-conditioning, pool. $95–$140, full breakfast. No credit cards. No smoking, no pets, no children under 16.

Triangle L Ranch Bed & Breakfast. Box 900, Oracle, AZ 85623, tel. 520/896–2804. 4 cottages. Kitchens in 2 cottages, fireplace in 1 cottage. $90–$110, full breakfast. D, MC, V. No smoking, no pets. Closed June–Aug.

Reservations Services

Arizona Association of Bed & Breakfast Inns (3101 North Central Ave., Suite 560, Phoenix, AZ 85012, tel. 602/277–0775). **Bed & Breakfast Inn Arizona–Arizona Accommodations Reservations** (8900 E. Via Linda, Suite 101, Scottsdale, AZ 85258, tel. 602/860–9338 or 800/266–7829, fax 602/860–9338). **Mi Casa Su Casa B&B Reservation Service** (Box 950, Tempe, AZ 85280, tel. 602/990–0682; reservations only 800/456–0682). **Old Pueblo Homestays B&B Reservation Service** (Box 13603, Tucson, AZ 85732, tel. 520/790–0030 or 800/333–9776, fax 520/790–2399). **Premiere Bed & Breakfast Inns of Tucson** (3661 N. Campbell Ave., Box 237, Tucson, AZ 85719, tel. 520/628–1800).

Southeastern Arizona: Cochise and Graham Counties

Clawson House

116 Clawson Ave., Box 454, Bisbee, AZ 85603, tel. 520/432–5237 or 800/467–5237

The Clawson House sits regally atop Castle Rock, the craggy buttress of Tombstone Canyon, and surveys Old Bisbee. Once the home of S. W. Clawson, the superintendent of the Copper Queen Mine, it was built in 1895 on the only flat acre in town, an executive fortress overlooking its fiefdom.

In 1988, Californians Wally Kuehl and Jim Grosskopf purchased the proud old redwood structure and spent two years restoring and furnishing it with the art and antiques they had collected during the previous 30 years. Many of the fittings are original to the house, including the etched Italian crystal windows, glass French doors, creaky oak floors, and crystal chandeliers. The Oriental carpets in the living room, the fireplace in the grand parlor, and the white-paneled china cabinet in the formal dining room all reflect the fussy glory of the period, as do the stuffed animal heads, mounted horns, ceramics, and other assorted collectibles that fill practically every inch of surface. Nor are the walls left bare: Both public areas and guest rooms are lined with Currier & Ives prints, framed battle scenes, landscapes, and portraits of long-lost Victorians.

But if you tire of Victorian clutter, all you need do is step out to the sunporch for the world to open up. To the south you can look out over the once wild and bawdy Brewery Gulch, past the raw, gaping, Lavender Pit Mine to the silhouette of the San José Mountains in northern Mexico on the distant horizon. To the north, the eye follows Tombstone Canyon, lined with 19th-century homes and the occasional giant cottonwood trees, to the crest of the Mule Mountains.

Upstairs, two spacious, well-lighted rooms share a bath that still has the original floor tiles and claw-foot tub. The downstairs bedroom has a 6-foot mahogany bedstead with mirrored mahogany vanity to match, a ruby-domed gas chandelier converted to electricity, and a standing lamp with a tasseled, red velvet shade.

Jim's elaborate breakfasts are served in what was originally the water tower, now a cozy dining nook attached to the modern kitchen. A fresh fruit compote with lemon yogurt might be followed by home-baked zucchini/pineapple bread and Swiss cheese and chili quiche, still hot from the oven.

▥ *1 double room with bath, 2 doubles share bath. Cable TV, use of house phone, off-street parking. $65–$75, full breakfast. AE, D, MC, V. No pets.*

Olney House Bed & Breakfast

1104 Central Ave., Safford, AZ 85546, tel. 520/428–5118 or 800/814–5118

George Olney was a sheriff of Graham County in the Wild West days of the 1870s. Unable to budget a salary, the county fathers agreed to pay him $2.50 for every arrest. Within two years he had amassed $30,000. Much of these earnings were spent on this classic, two-story example of Western Colonial Revival, completed in 1890. From the bay windows on the second floor, with a 180° view of Safford and the verdant Gila River Valley, Sheriff Olney could look for local desperados.

In 1988 the National Park Service announced that 20 Safford buildings had qualified for listing in the National Register of Historic Places: the 1920 Arizona Bank, the 1920 Southern Pacific Railroad Depot, a 1915 schoolhouse, a 1920 hotel, and 16 private residences. The oldest of these was the Olney House.

Innkeepers Patrick and Carole Mahoney, from San Francisco, spent four years renovating the redbrick, 14-room mansion. In 1992 they opened it as Graham County's first B&B. The home boasts 12-foot ceilings (now with circulating fans); five fireplaces with unusual, ceramic-tile detailing; polished oak and maple floors; and lots of elegant wood paneling. The bright corner dining room fills with morning light from three wide, 7-foot windows. Many of the furnishings are treasures brought back by the Mahoneys from travels in Southeast Asia. Upstairs there are three corner bedrooms.

A huge pecan tree shades two cottages in the back. Other trees on the landscaped corner lot include willows, cottonwood, Italian and Arizona cyprus, native pine, ash, and paloverdes. Each year the Mahoneys harvest fresh fruit from their apple, plum, and peach trees to make jams.

The breakfast coffee beans, ground fresh daily, are from Graffeo in San Francisco. The dill and cilantro in the omelettes and potatoes are picked from the garden. Guests have a choice of muesli with yogurt, honey, and fruit; oatmeal with pecans, wheat germ, honey, and fruit; or a cheese omelette spiced with roasted New Mexico chilies (mild, medium, or hot).

▥ *3 double rooms share bath, 2 cottages. Cable TVs, fireplace in living room, spa. $80, full breakfast. MC, V. No smoking, no pets.*

School House Inn Bed & Breakfast

Box 32, 818 Tombstone Canyon, Bisbee, AZ 85603, tel. 520/432–2996 or 800/ 537–4333

The two-story brick Garfield School, in the Tombstone Canyon neighborhood on Bisbee's west side, was built in 1918 to educate children in grades 1 through 4. The original four large classrooms, one for each grade, were divided into apartments in the 1930s and used as a nursing home in the 1970s. Abandoned by 1981, the building was refurbished and converted to a B&B in 1989.

Like most schools of the era, this one has solid masonry walls, maple floors, and high ceilings. The large dining room downstairs is carpeted; one corner is a family room with a couch and easy chairs positioned around a television set.

Current proprietors Marc and Shirl Negus took the built-in-schoolhouse theme and ran with it. Depending on how you feel about your school days, the guest rooms, all on the second floor, may strike horror into your heart or fill you with fond memories. Here's your chance to sleep, with impunity, in the Principal's Office, the Library, the Music Room, or the History Room, among others; just pick the subject you found the most soporific. Oh yes, and a cast-iron desk hangs over the stairwell.

The spacious accommodations are country comfortable, with flowery quilted comforters, dark-wood furniture, lace curtains, and stenciled wall borders; some have writing desks, wall-to-wall carpeting, or area rugs on the maplewood floors. Those at the front of the building provide views of upper Tombstone Canyon and the Mule Mountains. All rooms offer comfortable seating areas for reading and relaxing. In the Arithmetic Suite, old math books and flashcards are available to test your skill with numbers.

When the weather is fine, guests can enjoy breakfast—pancakes, say, or a crustless green chili quiche served with walnut bran muffins—on the outdoor patio, shaded by a magnificent oak tree; birds of all kinds like to splash in the patio's gurgling fountain, and hummingbirds dart to several overhead feeders. Just below the inn, there's a large public park with volleyball and basketball courts.

▥ *6 double rooms with baths, 3 2-bedroom suites. Library, off-street parking. $50–$70, full breakfast. AE, D, DC, MC, V. No smoking, no children under 14, no pets.*

Other Choices

Bisbee Grand Hotel. 6 double rooms with baths, 1 double room with detached bath, 1 room with twin beds and detached bath, 3 suites. Ceiling fans, sinks (in all but 1 room), claw-foot tubs in suites, off-street parking. $69–$110, full breakfast. AE, D, MC, V. No smoking, no pets.

Buford House B&B. 113 E. Safford St., Box 98, Tombstone, AZ 85638, tel. 520/457–3969 or 800/263–6762. 1 double room with bath, 1 twin with bath, 3 doubles share bath. Sinks, barbecue. $65–$95, full breakfast. AE. No smoking, no children under 4, no pets.

Copper Queen Hotel. 11 Howell Ave., Drawer CQ, Bisbee, AZ 85603, tel. 520/432–2216 or 800/247–5829. 45 double rooms with baths. Restaurant, bar, phones, TVs, radios, pool, gift shop. $72–$100, no breakfast. AE, D, MC, V.

Grapevine Canyon Ranch. Box 302, Pearce, AZ 85625, tel. 520/826–3185, fax 520/826–3636. 3 2-person cabins, 2 casitas for up to 3 people, 4 casitas for up to 5 people, 3-bedroom lodge for up to 9 people. Pool, hot tub, games room, TV/video room, gift shop, unscheduled live entertainment. $150–$170 per person, 3 meals included. AE, D, MC, V. No pets, no children under 12.

Judge Ross House. 605 Shattuck St., Bisbee, AZ 85603, tel. 520/432–4120 or 520/432–5597. 2 double rooms with baths. Garden. $60–$65, full breakfast. MC, V. No smoking, no pets.

Kelly's Whistlestop Bed and Breakfast. Box 236, Dragoon, AZ 85609, tel. 520/586–7515. 2 double rooms share bath. Refrigerator, coffeemaker, electric skillet, and sink in shared sitting room; sundeck, barbecue grill, horse corral. $55–$60, full breakfast. No credit cards. No smoking.

Main Street Inn. 26 Main St., Box 454, Bisbee, AZ 85603, tel. 520/432–5237 or 800/467–5237. 3 double rooms share 2 baths, 4 doubles share 2 baths, 1 2-bedroom suite. House phone, off-street parking. $45–$65, Continental breakfast. AE, D, MC, V. No pets.

OK Street Jailhouse. 9 OK St., Box 1152, Bisbee, AZ 85603, tel. 520/432–7435, 800/821–0678 (message phone), fax 520/432–7434. 1 duplex suite. Phones, TVs. $100 ($75 each additional night), no breakfast. MC, V.

Priscilla's Bed & Breakfast. 101 N. Third St., Tombstone, AZ 85638, tel. 520/457–3844. 3 double rooms share bath. $55, full breakfast. AE, MC, V.

Tombstone Boarding House. 108 N. Fourth St., Box 906, Tombstone, AZ 85638, tel. 520/457–3716. 7 double rooms with baths, 1 1880s miner's cabin. Piano and TV in living room. $60–$80; full breakfast, evening wine. No credit cards. No smoking.

Reservations Services

Arizona Association of Bed and Breakfast Inns (3101 N. Central Ave., Suite 560, Phoenix, AZ 85012, tel. 602/277–0775). **Bed & Breakfast Inn Arizona–Arizona Accommodations Reservations** (8900 E. Via Linda, Suite 101, Scottsdale, AZ 85258, tel. 602/860–9338 or 800/266–7829, fax 602/860–9338). **Mi Casa Su Casa B&B Reservation Service** (Box 950, Tempe, AZ 85280, tel. 602/990–0682; reservations 800/456–0682).

Arkansas

Empress of Little Rock

The Ozarks

Arkansas House Bed and Breakfast

Box 325, Jasper, AR 72641, tel. 800/274-6873

People still stop in the middle of the road just to chat in the quaint historic town of Jasper, nestled among the Ozark Mountains along the Buffalo National River. While the town seems sleepy, the area does offer many attractions. Guided hiking trips and floating along the Buffalo are very popular, with spectacular scenery like majestic 500-foot bluffs and 200-foot waterfalls.

Built during the 1940s, this unique rambling structure has a bottom floor that is made from individual stone casings and that once served as the Newton County Jail. Complimentary refreshments are available in the spacious common area, which has a stone fireplace, working antique pump organ, piano, and for more modern tastes, a satellite big-screen TV.

One of the most notable attractions at Arkansas House is the resident pet, Coco, a 5-year-old 600-pound black bear who arm wrestles, gives kisses, and eats 40 to 50 pounds of food each day. Coco, of course, stays outside in his air-conditioned den, but guests are welcome to visit him.

The Visnoskys moved here from Texas in 1994 and bought the restaurant adjacent to what is now Arkansas House. A short time later they purchased the rest of the property, remodeled it, and opened the Arkansas House in 1996. Larry Visnosky is retired from the military and his wife Karen taught English and drama. She now lends her dramatic touches to each guest room, filling them with old books, antiques, and memorabilia. Though each room is individually decorated, Old English style predominates, with four-poster beds and antiques in every room.

Breakfast begins in the Cedar Room with Karen's specialty, Slovakian povatica bread, fresh fruit, coffee, tea, and juice. Guests are then invited next door to the family's diner for a complimentary breakfast of their choice.

🏨 *3 double rooms with baths, 1 suite, 1 housekeeping suite. Air-conditioning, cable TV/VCRs, whirlpool tubs, phones, ceiling fans, coffeemakers, washer/dryer off common area. $65–$85, full breakfast. MC, V.*

Bridgeford House

263 Spring St., Eureka Springs, AR 72632, tel. 501/253-7853

This humble 1884 Victorian, a former residence of a Civil War captain, is centrally located for exploring downtown Eureka Springs. A fashionable spa at the turn of the century, this Ozark town attracted everyone from Carry Nation to Diamond Lil. Today, it's a thriving arts-and-crafts colony, with residents from around the globe lending a cosmopolitan air.

Owners Denise and Michael McDonald came to Eureka Springs on vacation in 1990 and were bewitched by extravagant Victorians alternating with rough-hewn limestone buildings; crooked staircases and terraced gardens careening down steep hills; and hiking trails vanishing into thick foliage.

There are strict laws in Eureka Springs ensuring that the Bridgeford House (on the National Register of Historic Places), and every building downtown (a National Historic District), conforms to its original look. This B&B's sole embellishments are a gable roof, a lone bay window, and a cotton-candy paint job—predominantly peach and apricot with accents of maroon and blue. But its simplicity is deceptive: Like many buildings in this hilly, "crazy quilt" town, it has entrances on several levels. Denise added such welcome luxuries as cable TVs, coffeemakers and mini-refrigerators, as well as lace curtains, down comforters, and such traditional country English antiques as brass and walnut beds and cherry armoires.

With a background in restaurant management, Denise loves catering to special occasions—two to three weddings a month are held here. Low rock walls, old trees, and a large stone fountain in the flower garden provide a romantic atmosphere.

Denise lays a meticulous table in the small but sunny breakfast room. Her bountiful meals often include fresh fruit, cheese soufflés, German apple pancakes, and homemade muffins. Conversations are always lively, since the McDonalds are outgoing and keep the ball rolling without being intrusive.

▦ *3 double rooms with baths, 1 housekeeping suite. Air-conditioning, cable TV, coffeemakers, mini-refrigerators in 1 room and suite. $85–$105, full breakfast. MC, V.*

Heartstone Inn

35 Kingshighway, Eureka Springs, AR 72632, tel. 501/253-8916 or 800/323-8534

A white picket fence and an inviting pink-and-cobalt patio spilling over with Boston ferns and potted geraniums greet visitors to this sprawling 1903 late Victorian inn on Eureka Springs's historic loop. This gabled two-story home might have been used as the set of *It's a Wonderful Life*; innkeepers Iris and Bill Simantel complete the picture of small-town warmth and hospitality.

Iris hails from London, and her tasteful touch is evident throughout. Most notable is her superlative collection of antique English pottery: Handsome royal blue–glazed Torquay pots and humorous Toby mugs adorn both the parlor (which doubles as an informal gallery) and the cheerful breakfast room, where Iris serves chocolate-chip muffins made from scratch, crêpes, frittatas, German apple pancakes, and all the not-so-trim trimmings like bacon and sausages. Often, classical musicians play softly on the deck, or in the gazebo on weekend mornings in the summer.

All rooms have English country antiques, including brass or four-poster beds; many also have rocking chairs and intricate tracery. Each is individually decorated, Laura Ashley–style, according to a floral theme. The Devon Wildflower room—its large bay window overlooking the garden—has delicate hues of teal, pink, and ecru, and displays framed pressed flowers; the Rose Arbor room is fittingly garnished with a profusion of roses and lace. The English Garden suite suggests a conservatory, with an ivy-covered white trellis, neoclassical garden statues, floral wallpaper, and plush, forest-green carpeting. Tucked away in the garden, the cozy Country Cottage is ideal for honeymooners, with floral decor, a private deck (including a porch swing and a barbecue), and modern conveniences like cable TV and a full kitchen. The 1882 Victoria House is crammed with antiques and has polished oak and pine floors under lofty 10-foot ceilings, a working fireplace in the master bedroom, and its own terraced garden.

▦ *8 double rooms with baths, 2 suites, 1 1-bedroom housekeeping cottage, 1 2-bedroom housekeeping cottage. Air-conditioning, cable TV, ceiling fans, radios, refrigerators and coffeemakers in both suites, wet bar and double whirlpool tub in 1 suite, fireplace in 1 cottage, small gift shop, off-street parking, massage therapy available. $65–$120, full breakfast. AE, D, MC, V. Closed mid-Dec.–mid-Feb.*

Wildflower Bed and Breakfast

Courthouse Sq., Box 72, Mountain View, AR 72560, tel. 501/269–4383 or 800/591–4879

The Wildflower Inn sits on the northeast corner of Courthouse Square in the sleepy town of Mountain View. Its Ozark Folk Center is dedicated to preserving local culture, offering daily craft demonstrations, storytelling hours, cooking classes, and musicales. Local musicians still congregate in the square each warm Saturday evening for "pickin' and grinnin'," the sweet zing of their fiddles and dulcimers filling the air.

You don't come to the Wildflower for the rooms per se, though they're certainly comfortable enough. You come for the almost vanished tradition of hospitality that is pure old-time Ozark; for the music and the pride in heritage; for the gentle scenery of rolling hills, thickly wooded hollows, lakes, and streams. The inn is a simple two-story affair—teal with burgundy trim and gray shingles—whose most notable feature is its wraparound portico. It opened in 1907 as the Commercial Hotel; Todd and Andrea Budy saved it from demolition in 1982. The Budys moved to Mountain View from Colorado, heading to the state where Todd's grandfather had been a chef in the ultragrand Arlington Hotel in Hot Springs. A recognized poet, Andrea became entranced by the quiet mystical beauty of the Ozark region. She is currently artist-in-residence at Arkansas College.

The rooms are furnished plainly in old-fashioned Ozark style, with most of the original handcrafted dressers and iron bedsteads, along with hand-sewn curtains and dust ruffles, and more modern solid-color quilts. Some feature an "Ozark closet," walls with embellished 2½-foot wrought-iron rods forged by local blacksmiths. Each room is named for a local wildflower, with colors to match. Dogwood, for example, is a delicate whitish pink; an artist's painting of the blossoms hangs on the wall. Columbine's hue is a soothing rust. The Jonquil, in bright yellow, is ideal for families, with its kitchenette and bunk nook for kids.

There's no TV on the premises, but no one seems to mind as there's always live entertainment. People rock on the porch, listening to crickets and to the musicians that stop by nearly every afternoon and evening. Kids play games on the courthouse lawn or swim à la Huck Finn and Tom Sawyer in one of the many nearby streams.

Guests gather for a large breakfast buffet, supplied by the on-site bakery (under different ownership), featuring delectable pastries, muffins, breads, fresh fruit, and homemade jams.

▦ *3 double rooms with baths, 2 doubles share 1 bath, 3 suites, 1 housekeeping suite. Air-conditioning, bakery, book shop. $50–$85, Continental breakfast. D, MC, V. Closed Jan.–Feb.*

Other Choices

Arsenic & Old Lace. 60 Hillside Ave., Eureka Springs, AR 72632, tel. 501/253–5454 or 800/243–5223. 5 double rooms with baths. Double whirlpool tub and fireplaces in most rooms, TV/VCRs, book and video library. $90–$150, full breakfast and mid-afternoon snacks. AE, D, MC, V.

Brambly Hedge Cottage Bed & Breakfast. H.C.R. 31, Box 39, Jasper, AR 72641, tel. 501/446–5849 or 800/272–6259. 3 double rooms with baths. TVs, CD/tape player in 1 room and tape player in 2 rooms, massage therapy available. $55–$75; full breakfast, evening dessert. No credit cards.

Brownstone Inn. 75 Hillside St., Eureka Springs, AR 72632, tel. 501/253–7505. 2 double rooms with baths, 2 suites. Air-conditioning, cable TV. $85–$95, full breakfast. MC, V.

Crescent Cottage Inn. 211 Spring St., Eureka Springs, AR 72632, tel. 501/253–6022 or 800/223–3246. 4 double rooms with baths. Double whirlpool tub in 2 rooms, fireplace in 1 room, cable TV/VCRs. $75–$125, full breakfast. D, MC, V.

Inn at Mountain View. W. Washington St., Box 812, Mountain View, AR 72560, tel. 501/269–4200 or 800/535–1301. 10 double rooms with baths. Air-conditioning, TV and piano in common rooms. $59–$95, 7-course breakfast. D, MC, V.

Olde Stonehouse Inn. 511 Main St., Hardy, AR 72542, tel. 501/856–2983, fax 501/856–4036. 6 double rooms with baths. Ceiling fans, radios. $55–$85, full breakfast. AE, D, MC, V.

Piedmont House. 165 Spring St., Eureka Springs, AR 72632, tel. 501/253–9258 or 800/253–9258. 8 doubles with baths. Air-conditioning, off-street parking. $69–$129, full breakfast. AE, D, MC, V.

Ridgeway House. 28 Ridgeway St., Eureka Springs, AR 72632, tel. 501/253–6618. 1 double with bath, 2 doubles with shared bath, 2 housekeeping suites. Air-conditioning, cable TV in suites, whirlpool tub in 1 suite. $79–$139, full breakfast. D, MC, V.

Reservations Services

Arkansas Ozarks Bed & Breakfast Reservation Services (H.C. 79, Box 330A, Calico Rock, AR 72519, tel. 501/297–4197 or 800/233–2777). **Bed and Breakfast Association of Eureka Springs** (7 Kingshighway, Eureka Springs, AR 73632, tel. 800/401–4667). **Eureka Springs Chamber of Commerce** (Box 551, Eureka Springs, AR 72632, tel. 501/253–8737 or 800/638–7352).

Central Arkansas: From Hot Springs to Helena

The Empress of Little Rock

2120 Louisiana, Little Rock, AR 72206, tel. 501/374–7966

The music of *Gone With the Wind* dips and swells as Rhett and Scarlett greet you upon entering this magnificent Gothic Queen Anne mansion in Little Rock's Quapaw Quarter Historic District. It is your imagination, but if the ambience alone doesn't remind you of the mansion Rhett built for Scarlett in *Gone With the Wind*, then its history will.

James Hornibrook moved from Canada to Little Rock where he opened a saloon and became very wealthy during the Civil War occupation, as did many "carpetbaggers." Although he quickly became one of the wealthiest men in

Little Rock and the state of Arkansas, he was shunned by the town's upper crust. He got his revenge by building the grandest, most elaborate house in town, Hornibrook Mansion, for his wife, Margaret, at a then-exorbitant cost of $20,000.

Perhaps the most stunning features of the mansion are the double walnut-and-chestnut staircase and 64-square-foot stained-glass skylight. Many of the rooms are octagonal, including the corner tower room where legend says Hornibrook carried on illegal high-stakes poker games while paying young boys to act as lookouts from the tower windows. The five guest rooms are beautifully decorated in the Victorian style with many authentic antiques and large floral Aubusson rugs. Three of the rooms have baths with showers and two have claw-foot soaking tubs.

Sharon Welch-Blair, a financial services consultant for New York Life, and her husband, Bob, who is in upper level management at Southwestern Bell, bought the Hornibrook mansion in 1993, restored and renamed it, and opened its doors in late 1995. When asked about the house, Sharon's eyes take on a sparkle, making her love for the mansion and its history obvious. She is in her element, sometimes even wearing period costumes when she leads tours through the Empress.

Sharon serves a full candlelit gourmet breakfast on china in the graceful dining room. A few of her favorite dishes are ham and asparagus roll-ups with hollandaise sauce, croissants à l'orange, and Russian raspberry soup. She feels an elegant breakfast is part of the whole experience at the Empress. "You can go anywhere for just bacon and eggs," says Sharon.

▥ *5 double rooms with baths. Air-conditioning, cable TV available in each room, phones, radios, fax and copier available. $85–$125, full breakfast. AE, MC, V.*

Stitt House Bed & Breakfast Inn

824 Park Ave., Hot Springs, AR 71901, tel. 501/623–2704

Everyone from Hernando de Soto (in 1541) to Al Capone took the cure at Hot Springs, Arkansas. At the turn of the last century, it was one of the country's leading spas; in the Roaring Twenties, the city was a hotbed for bathtub gin, gambling, and flappers. The elegant buildings and fragrant magnolias of Hot Springs, boyhood home of President Bill Clinton, have withstood the years gracefully, and its waters still draw people from all over the country. Today the springs are administered as part of the Hot Springs National Park; the spectacular Spanish Renaissance Revival–style Fordyce Bathhouse serves as the park's visitor center.

The Stitt House, an 1875 pre-Victorian restored mansion and the oldest dwelling still standing in Hot Springs, specializes in service. Gourmet breakfasts, which may include eggs Benedict, baked berry French toast, quiche, and fresh fruit, is served in bed, in the formal dining room, or on the open front veranda. Complimentary fruit and refreshments are provided for weary sightseers and a heated outdoor swimming pool is open April through September.

Horst and Linda Fischer purchased the Stitt House in 1983, and Linda applied her expertise in gourmet food to open the Stitt House Restaurant in the mansion. She later moved her business, naming it Grady's Grill Restaurant, to the Majestic Hotel at one end of Hot Springs' historic Bathhouse Row. Horst is general manager of the Arlington and Majestic hotels. In February 1995 the Fischers opened the 6,000-square-foot Stitt House as a bed-and-breakfast inn, providing many of the amenities one expects at a luxury hotel.

The hand-carved oak staircase in the entry hall is breathtaking, while the four guest rooms are accented by antiques and interesting European artifacts.

The extensive grounds viewed from the front veranda are meticulously landscaped and include exotic trees and foliage. In response to a comment on the beauty of the grounds, a good friend of the Fischers, and native of Hot Springs, Mary Jo Rogers, exclaimed, "Oh yes, it's a wonderful yard. We'd all come here to play as kids. In fact, Bill Clinton lived right up the street, too, and we we would all gather in this front yard for hide-and-seek and tag."

🌐 *3 double rooms with baths, 1 suite with whirlpool tub. Air-conditioning, TVs, robes, turndown service, heated outdoor swimming pool, off-street parking. $95–$110, full breakfast. AE, MC, V.*

Other Choices

Carriage House. 1700 Louisiana St., Little Rock, AR 72206, tel. 501/374-7032. 2 double rooms with baths. Air-conditioning, clock radios, TV in sitting room. $89, full breakfast and afternoon tea or evening dessert. No credit cards.

Edwardian Inn. 317 S. Biscoe St., Helena, AR 72342, tel. 501/338-9155. 7 double rooms with baths, 5 suites. Air-conditioning, cable TV, phones, radios. $59–$69, full breakfast. AE, DC, MC, V.

Gables Inn. 318 Quapaw Ave., Hot Springs, AR 71901, tel. 501/623-7576. 4 double rooms. Air-conditioning, ceiling fans, clock radios, TV and refrigerator in common room. $50–$85, full breakfast. AE, MC, V.

Hotze House. 1619 Louisiana St., Little Rock, AR 72206, tel. 501/376-6563. 5 double rooms with baths. Desks, phones with dataports, gas fireplaces, cable TV, party/meeting facilities. $80–$100; full breakfast, complimentary snack bar. AE, MC, V.

Pinnacle Vista Lodge. 7510 Ark. 300, Little Rock, AR 72212, tel. 501/868-8905. 2 double rooms with baths, 1 suite. Cable TVs, pool table, pinball, jukebox in common area, 23 acres, hiking, fishing, horseback riding. $89–$115, full breakfast. MC, V.

Stillmeadow Farm. 111 Stillmeadow La., Hot Springs, AR 71913, tel. 501/525-9994. 2 doubles with baths, 2 doubles with shared bath, 1 cottage. Air-conditioning, 70 wooded acres, hiking trails, riding stable next door. $60–$85, full breakfast. MC, V.

Wildwood 1884 Bed & Breakfast. 808 Park Ave., Hot Springs National Park, AR 71901, tel. 501/624-4267. 5 double rooms with baths. 3 rooms with private porches, 6 blocks from Bathhouse Row, wedding/party packages available. $85–$95, full breakfast. D, MC, V.

Reservations Services

Dr. Witt's House State Bed and Breakfast Referral Service (tel. 501/376-6873, referrals over phone only). **Hot Springs Convention and Visitors Bureau** (134 Convention Blvd., Box K, Hot Springs, AR 71902, tel. 800/772-2489; listings only—call for brochure). **Phillips County Chamber of Commerce** (Box 447, Helena, AR 72342, tel. 501/338-8327; listings in Helena only).

California

Archbishops Mansion

San Diego County, Including North Country and the Temecula Wine Country

Brookside Farm

1373 Marron Valley Rd., Dulzura, CA 91917, tel. 619/468-3043

Edd and Sally Guishard have created a mountain retreat out of an old dairy farm in the tiny hamlet of Dulzura, a 30-minute drive from downtown San Diego. Set on 4 tree-shaded acres bisected by the seasonal brook for which the inn is named, the farm is surrounded by colorful gardens planted with geraniums, poppies, roses, and sweet peas.

Rooms, scattered throughout the property—in the main house, built in 1928, in the old stone dairy barn, and in two cottages—have farm motifs. The Delft-blue Room With a View actually has two views: a treetop scene from the deck outside and a crackling fire in a see-through fireplace visible from the bathtub or the bed. Pink Jennie's Room has a separate step-up sitting area behind a white fence and Sally's childhood doll collection. The bright-green

Sun Porch room in the main house has wooden car-siding walls, wraparound windows, and a small garden patio; you can hear doves cooing and a fountain gurgling nearby. One of two very private cottages, the Hunter's Cabin, hangs right over the brook. Originally the pump house, it is decorated in an Old West style and has a wood-burning stove standing in front of an iron bed and a screened-porch entry.

While no longer a commercial farm, Brookside still has animals—chickens and geese, a pair of Nubian goats, and a pig—and gardens planted with corn, tomatoes, berries, lettuce, zucchini, and herbs. These ingredients are used in the excellent four-course dinners prepared by Edd, a professional chef, on weekends. Featured entrées might be chicken Mirabella, chicken Louis in tarragon sauce, or grilled chicken with rosemary. Accompanied by soup, salad and dessert, meals are a bargain at $15 per person.

While Edd enjoys cooking, Sally likes to party. You're likely to find yourself part of a celebration: tacky-crafts party, honeymoon in June, tricycle-race weekend. Guests tend to return time and again. "We have a sort of extended family here," Edd says. "Brookside Farm is everybody's second home."

🏨 *8 double rooms with baths, 2 suites. Air-conditioning, fireplace in 6 rooms, refrigerator in 4 rooms, library, guest refrigerator and phone, outdoor hot tub, badminton, horseshoes, croquet. $65–$115; full breakfast, dinner ($15) Fri.–Sat. AE, MC, V. No smoking, no pets, 2-night minimum on weekends.*

Heritage Park Bed & Breakfast Inn

2470 Heritage Park Row, San Diego, CA 92110, tel. 619/299–6832 or 800/995–2470, fax 619/299–9465

This turreted Victorian in a historic park is the ideal headquarters for touring San Diego's Old Town, a shopping-restaurant complex across the street. It's also convenient for exploring San Diego's other attractions via the Old Town Trolley, which stops at the zoo, Seaport Village, Coronado, and Balboa Park.

The inn consists of two adjacent historic buildings. The main one is a beautiful 1889 Queen Anne. It has a wraparound veranda decorated with spindle work, a variety of chimneys, stained-glass windows, and very ornate millwork on its banisters and wainscoting. Furnishings include an unusual double Eastlake panel bed with carved sunflowers, four-poster canopy beds, an antique fainting couch, and antique quilts. The second, smaller building, has an expansive suite and function space.

Rooms range from smallish to ample; most are bright and cheery. Those upstairs have views of the park and Mission Bay beyond. One of the most popular rooms is the Turret, which has a sitting room in the inn's two-story tower that offers city and park views. From Queen Anne, a spacious room on the second floor, you can gaze out to the water through a squared bay window. Downstairs, the Garden Room, which looks out on the sunny Victorian garden, is another guest favorite.

When they purchased the inn in early 1992, longtime San Diegans Charles and Nancy Helsper brought a new vitality to the Heritage Park and developed a number of packages to entertain guests. Five-course, catered candlelight dinners are now served in the dining room. The Helspers will also make arrangements for picnics at the waterfront Sunday pops concerts, balloon excursions, and Sunday-morning breakfasts at Tiffany's, with a ride in the antique Bentley that Queen Elizabeth II rode to her coronation.

Breakfast is served in a formal dining room with burgundy flowered wallpaper. Nancy, formerly director of catering at a San Diego resort hotel, puts out her best antique Spode china and stemware and offers a varied menu that includes entrées such as banana walnut pancakes and eggs Benedict.

🏨 *9 double rooms with baths, 1 suite in adjacent house. Fireplace in 3 rooms, robes, whirlpool bath in suite, old-time movies shown at night. $90–$225; full breakfast, afternoon refreshments. MC, V. No smoking, no pets, 2-night minimum on weekends in July and Aug.*

Inn at Rancho Santa Fe

5951 Linia del Cielo, Box 869, Rancho Santa Fe, CA 92067, tel. 619/756–1131 or 800/654–2928, fax 619/759–1604

One of California's most elegant hideaways, this family-operated inn dates from 1924, when architect Lillian Rice designed what was known as the Inn at La Morada. Originally used by the Santa Fe Railroad to house prospective purchasers of land the company was developing northeast of San Diego, the inn became a gathering place in the 1930s for movie stars such as Errol Flynn, Bette Davis, and Jimmy Stewart. A celebrity staying here today would enjoy the same pampering and tranquillity that attracted earlier stars.

Steve Royce, a former pitcher with the New York Giants, purchased the inn in 1958; the family has operated it ever since. Duncan Royce Hadden, a grandson, is the current innkeeper. Despite its size this is a surprisingly homey place. Family memorabilia decorates much of the inn. Team photos of Steve Royce taken in 1914 line corridors; embroidery and needlepoint canvases done by Duncan's grandmother adorn guest-room walls; and Chinese paintings collected by family members hang in the living room.

Accommodations are in the original structure and in a series of red-tile-roof cottages scattered around 20 acres of manicured, eucalyptus-shaded grounds. Those in the main building tend to be smallish, while newer rooms in the cottages are more spacious, some with large living rooms and private flower-decked patios. Decor is traditional, but colors tend to be bright: reds, greens, blues.

Over the years the inn's dining rooms have become popular gathering places for Rancho Santa Fe's wealthy residents, who enjoy Sunday brunch in the Garden Room or the book-filled Library. The fare is as traditional as the inn itself: scrambled eggs, eggs Benedict, and French toast.

Just a few miles away at the beach at Del Mar, the inn maintains a cottage for guest use. The inn also owns box seats at the famed Del Mar racetrack and makes seats available to guests during the summer thoroughbred season. Guests at the inn also have privileges at the exclusive Rancho Santa Fe Golf Club.

🏨 *76 double rooms with baths, 12 cottage suites. Air-conditioning, TVs, phones, fireplace in 45 rooms, wet bar in 30 rooms, whirlpool bath in 6 suites, restaurant, room service during meal hours; pool, fitness facilities, 3 tennis courts, croquet. $95–$510, breakfast not included. AE, DC, MC, V. 2-night minimum on selected holiday weekends.*

Loma Vista Bed and Breakfast

33350 La Serena Way, Temecula, CA 92591, tel. 909/676–7047

The first bed-and-breakfast accommodations in California were the 21 missions built during the 18th century by the Spanish padres, providing lodging and food along El Camino Real. The missions are also the inspiration for the design—and the hospitality—of the Loma Vista Bed and Breakfast.

The inn, which sits like a terra-cotta crown atop a hill in the Temecula wine country, about an hour's drive north of San Diego, is the creation of Betty Ryan, who designed it from the ground up. The look is more like a hacienda than a mission. Carefully tended rose gardens border red-tiled patios. Hummingbirds poke their long beaks into the hearts of fragrant flowers.

Inside, the inn is cool and inviting, with ceiling beams and other oak details. Objects collected from years of world travel, from African brass work to Thai silk-screen hangings, are displayed throughout the house. Large picture windows in the common rooms reveal gardens and vineyard-covered hillsides. The views from the bedrooms upstairs are more dramatic, unfolding in a broad panorama of citrus groves, distant mountains, and even the Mt. Palomar observatory.

The guest rooms are named for varietal wines, but the connection ceases there. Zinfandel is swathed in green and peach, with Colonial reproductions that include a handsome Chippendale-style secretary bookcase with bonnet top. Chardonnay is furnished in oak and has a Laura Ashley look. Art deco describes Champagne, with a black lacquer bed, tubular steel chairs, and photographs of Marilyn Monroe and Fred Astaire on the walls. Each room is stocked with fresh fruit and sherry. Weeping wisteria frames the edges of balconies of four rooms.

Whichever room you select, the setting is lovely. Don't miss the chance to spend some time sitting on the veranda sipping local wine, enjoying the fresh, cooling breezes, colorful gardens, or setting sun.

Champagne at breakfast, served family-style in the inn's large dining room, makes this a festive meal. Specialties include a variety of southwestern favorites, such as *huevos rancheros*. And you can count on tasting some tangy grapefruit juice freshly squeezed from the trees just beyond the front door.

⚏ *6 double rooms with baths. Air-conditioning, outdoor hot tub, fire pit. $95–$125; full breakfast, afternoon refreshments. D, MC, V. No smoking, no pets, 2-night minimum on weekends.*

Orchard Hill Country Inn

Washington St., Box 425, Julian, CA 92036, tel. 760/765–1700, fax 760/765–0290

Orchard Hill Country Inn offers a level of luxury and service not usually expected in rustic, Gold Rush–era Julian. Owners Darrell and Pat Straube reconstructed four Craftsman cottages from the foundation up and added a massive Craftsman-style lodge, complete with soaring two-story high windows, open beam ceilings, a great stone fireplace, and patios tucked under soaring overhangs.

Guest rooms are in both the lodge and the cottages that are spotted on a hillside overlooking town. Each cottage contains three beautifully appointed guest rooms surrounded by a broad veranda furnished with big green wicker chairs. Cottage rooms have private entrances, whirlpool tubs, see-through fireplaces visible from both bedroom and bathroom, wet bars, and window seats. One of the nicest accommodations is the large McIntosh. It's

decorated with green plaid wallpaper and contains a bathroom accessible to guests with disabilities. The Black Gilflower is also a charmer, with pillow-ticking-style wallpaper and an oversized Jacuzzi in the bathroom.

Rooms in the lodge are smaller and less luxurious, but with an attractive "Grandma's attic" feel to them. They feature skylights over the bathtubs, small desks, overstuffed chairs, hand-made quilts, fluffy down comforters, and the best views of the town and surrounding mountains.

Orchard Hill sits on 4 hillside acres, which are planted with a profusion of native plants including deep-blue ceanothus, golden poppies, and fragrant white locust trees. In spring, guests can explore paths that meander through fields of yellow and purple iris, sit in a secluded corner and admire the roses and peonies, or doze in a hammock strung between trees.

The food at Orchard Hill surpasses that found at other Julian lodgings. A full breakfast served in the bright dining room might include Gruyeure Egg Puff, blintzes, seasonal fresh fruit, baked goods, and cereal. A prix fixe four-course dinner, served to guests several nights a week, features seafood, pasta, or steak, depending on the season.

⚏ *22 double rooms with baths. Air-conditioning, TV/VCR, refrigerators, fireplaces in 11 rooms, wet bar in 12 rooms, coffee service in 12 rooms, whirlpool bath in 8 rooms, 2 rooms with private patios, robes, video library, meeting facilities. $140–$170; full breakfast, afternoon refreshments. AE, MC, V. No smoking, no pets, 2-night minimum on weekends.*

Rancho Valencia Resort

5921 Valencia Circle, Box 9126, Rancho Santa Fe, CA 92067, tel. 619/756–1123 or 800/548–3664, fax 619/756–0165

Secluded hideaways are especially rare in sprawling southern California, and this partially accounts for the popularity of Rancho Valencia, a striking collection of Mediterranean-style casitas.

The tennis resort, surrounded by horse ranches and millionaires' homes—including one owned by former Clinton administration Secretary of the Treasury Lloyd Bentsen—attracts well-heeled patrons who demand luxury and top-notch service.

There are 20 pink-stucco, red-roof casitas scattered among the gardens, each containing two uncommonly large and private guest accommodations. All the suites are bright and airy with windows all around, and include sunken sitting-dining areas or separate bedrooms, terra-cotta-tile floors, sand-colored walls, hand-painted decorator tiles, adobe fireplaces, and open-beam ceilings. Spacious bathrooms have tiled countertops, walk-in closets, and separate dressing areas. Outside each suite is a private flower-filled patio with dining table and chairs and chaise longues.

As beautiful as the suites are, the grounds—lush gardens of crimson bougainvillea, hibiscus, palm and citrus trees—astound even more; look up at sunset and a squadron of hot-air balloons drifting over a nearby hillside completes the already-mesmerizing picture.

Rancho Valencia has 18 tennis courts, a staff of eight pros, group and individual instruction, and tennis workout programs for men and women. Golf privileges are available at four area courses. A professional conditioning program provides personal training, fitness assessment, bicycle touring, and nutritional counseling. Those interested in less strenuous activities can take advantage of the resort's walking-hiking program; complimentary conducted walks take place daily. Spa services are also available.

The Rancho Valencia Restaurant earns raves from guests and locals for its serene setting, attentive service, and innovative cuisine. The dinner menu, which changes quarterly, features contemporary cuisine, such as sautéed sea scallops with sweet-pepper coulis and duck foie gras with turnip confit. Vegetables come from nearby Chino Farms, where Alice Waters and other famed California chefs buy their vegetables.

▦ *43 suites. Air-conditioning, 2 TV/ VCRs, 2 phones, fireplace, stocked minibar, safe, coffeemaker, robes, hair dryers; newspaper, fresh-squeezed orange juice, and cut rose delivered each morning. 24-hr room service, children's programs, gift shop, guest laundry, conference facilities; 2 pools, 2 outside Jacuzzis, tennis, golf, fitness facilities, spa. $315– $825, breakfast not included. AE, DC, MC, V. Pets accepted ($75 per night), smoking suites available, 2-night minimum on weekends, 3-night minimum on holiday weekends.*

Other Choices

Bed and Breakfast Inn at La Jolla. 7753 Draper Ave., La Jolla, CA 92037, tel. 619/456–2066, fax 619/454–1510. 14 double rooms with baths, 1 double shares public bath, 1 suite. Air-conditioning, robes, hair dryer in some rooms, fireplace in 3 rooms, refrigerator in 8 rooms, TV in suite and sitting room, private deck off 1 room. $85– $225; Continental breakfast, afternoon refreshments. MC, V. No smoking, no pets, 2-night minimum on weekends.

Butterfield Bed and Breakfast. 2284 Sunset Dr., Box 1115, Julian, CA 92036, tel. 760/765–2179, 800/379–4262, fax 760/765–1229. 5 double rooms with baths. Cable TV in 3 rooms, private entrance to 4 rooms, fireplaces in 2 rooms, robes, game room with pool table, gazebo. $89–$135; full breakfast, afternoon refreshments. AE, D, MC, V. No smoking, no pets, 2-night minimum on weekends.

Cottage. 3829 Albatross St., San Diego, CA 92103, tel. 619/299–1564, fax

619/299–6213. 1 double room with bath, 1 cottage suite. Woodstove and phone in cottage, TV and refrigerator in both rooms. $55–$95, Continental breakfast. AE, MC, V. No smoking, no pets, 2-night minimum.

Lake Sutherland Lodge. 24901 Dam Oaks Dr., Ramona, CA 92065, tel. 760/789–6483, 800/789–6483, fax 760/788–9832. 3 double rooms with baths, 1 detached bath. Air-conditioning, fireplace in 1 room, balcony off 1 room, gardens, horseback riding packages, picnic baskets available. $95–$165; full breakfast, after-dinner desserts; horse boarding $20 per day. AE, D, MC, V. No smoking, no pets, 2-night minimum on weekends.

Pelican Cove Inn. 320 Walnut Ave., Carlsbad, CA 92008, tel. 619/434–5995. 8 double rooms with baths. TV and fireplace in rooms, whirlpool bath in 2 rooms, railroad-station pickup. $85–$175; full breakfast, afternoon refreshments. AE, MC, V. No pets, 2-night minimum on weekends.

Scripps Inn. 555 Coast Blvd. S, La Jolla, CA 92037, tel. 619/454–3391, fax 619/456–0389. 9 double rooms with baths, 4 suites. TVs, phones, refrigerators, safes, hair dryers; fireplace in 2 rooms, kitchenette in 5 rooms. $90–$180, Continental breakfast. AE, DC, MC, V. 2-night minimum on weekends.

Reservations Services

Bed and Breakfast Guild of San Diego (tel. 619/523–1300). **Bed and Breakfast International** (Box 282910, San Francisco, CA 94128, tel. 415/696–1690). **Eye Openers B&B Reservations** (Box 694, Altadena, CA 91003, tel. 213/684–4428 or 818/797–2055, fax 818/798–3640).

The Desert and the San Bernardino Mountains from Palm Springs to Lake Arrowhead

Apples Bed & Breakfast Inn

42430 Moonridge Rd., Box 7172, Big Bear Lake, CA 92315, tel. 909/866–0903, fax 909/866–6524

With its pink facade and ornate design, this new inn stands out among Big Bear's predominantly rustic architecture. In designing and building Apples, Jim and Barbara McLean integrated contemporary comforts and Victorian accents. Their inn, set amid an acre of pine trees, feels remote and peaceful despite its location on the busy road to the ski lifts.

Colorful floral wallpapers and linens adorn the rooms, named for historic apples. Each room has either a king-size four-poster or canopied bed; some have dressing areas separate from the bathroom. Apple-scented soaps and bath gels and down comforters are among the extra touches that make a stay here special.

The second-floor Royal Gala room is bright and appealing, with a forest view, bay windows, and sunny yellow wallpaper. Two rooms on the first floor have contrasting atmospheres. Jonathan, done in shades of hunter green and pink, has a cozy feel; it's dominated by a king-size, roll-top panel bed. The four best rooms are in the recently completed turret. Somewhat larger, they have separate sitting areas and double whirlpool baths.

Common areas include a gathering room in the center of the inn, which contains an enormous sectional sofa, a grand piano, and a large reading loft. The dining room has a table long enough to seat 24 people. French doors are everywhere, leading to the broad veranda out front, shady gardens, several decks, and a hot tub out back.

Barbara, a fine cook, ran a catering business before moving to Big Bear. A typical four-course breakfast might include cold strawberry-pineapple soup, thick and crunchy French toast, herb scrambled eggs, and apple cider syrup.

Celebrities who like to hide out in summer or ski in winter in Big Bear have discovered the pleasures to be found at Apples. Autographed pictures of Robert Wagner, Stefanie Powers, Mike Connors, and Lucinda Crosby already grace the dining room walls.

▦ *12 double rooms with baths (1 room accessible to people who use wheelchairs). Fireplaces, TV/VCRs, whirlpool bath in 4 rooms, hot tub and sports court in garden, ski and mountain bike storage. $145–$185; full breakfast, afternoon refreshments, snacks available. AE, D, MC, V. No smoking, no pets, 2-night minimum on weekends.*

Chateau Du Lac

911 Hospital Rd., Box 1098, Lake Arrowhead, CA 92352, tel. 909/337–6488 or 800/601–8722, fax 909/337–6746

Dramatic architecture and sweeping lake and mountain views are the primary draws at this contemporary inn, perched on a hillside above Lake Arrowhead. Chateau Du Lac is an exceptionally bright space with more than 100 windows, some two stories tall. The three-level house, which wraps around an atrium containing an ancient oak tree, has numerous places to relax or curl up with a good book: on the decks surrounding the house, in a hammock strung across the gazebo, in the library, or up in the secluded tower room.

As seen from the second-floor Lakeview room, which extends across the front of the house, Lake Arrowhead shimmers like a bowl of clear-blue water rimmed by green trees. The view commands attention from all points, including the whirlpool bath strategically positioned in the large master bathroom. Another spacious room on this level has quirky nooks and crannies set into gables, providing a cool, dark alternative to the brightness elsewhere in the house.

Owners Oscar and Jody Wilson moved to the mountains from the Los Angeles area, where he had a long career on the technical side of the entertainment industry and she operated a catering business. Their breakfast buffet is one of the day's highlights. In fine weather, which is most of the time, the Wilsons place several tables on the deck so their guests can enjoy the view. If it's cool, Oscar stokes up a fire to warm the dining room. Taking afternoon tea is another pleasure at Chateau Du Lac. Jody normally keeps things informal, but from time to time lucky guests get a chance to experience an English high tea.

Although the main appeal of this inn is the chance to bask in the lovely surroundings, there are nearby hiking and nature trails and good picnic sites as well. The innkeepers direct casual hikers and joggers to a pine-shaded, abandoned road in Willow Creek, about a mile from the house. Just a few yards from the inn, serious hikers can find trails to Little Bear and Hook Creek.

▦ *5 double rooms with baths. TV/VCRs, phones; fireplace in 2 rooms, whirlpool bath in suites and 1 room, private balcony off 2 rooms, library with games and TV, gazebo. $125–$240; full breakfast, afternoon tea. AE, D, MC, V. No smoking, no pets, 2-night minimum on summer weekends.*

Other Choices

Bracken Fern Manor. 815 Arrowhead Villas Rd., Box 1006, Lake Arrowhead, CA 92352, tel. 909/337–8557, fax 909/337–3323. 8 double rooms with baths, 2 double rooms share 1 bath. Guest refrigerator, TV, miniature pool table in game room, sauna, outdoor whirlpool bath. $65–$185; full breakfast, afternoon refreshments. AE, MC, V. No smoking, no pets.

Eagle's Landing. 27406 Cedarwood, Lake Arrowhead, Box 1510, Blue Jay, CA 92317, tel. 909/336–2642 or 800/835–5085. 4 double rooms with baths. Fireplace, TV/VCR, stereo, refrigerator, private deck in 1 room; robes, beach-club guest privileges. $95–$185; full breakfast, Sunday barbecue brunch, afternoon refreshments. AE, D, MC, V. No smoking, no pets, 2-night minimum on weekends, 3-night minimum on holidays.

Ingleside Inn. 200 W. Ramon Rd., Palm Springs, CA 92264, tel. 760/325–0046 or 800/772–6655, fax 760/325–0710. 28 double rooms with baths, 2 double suites. Air-conditioning, TV/VCR, phone, stocked refrigerator, whirlpool bath, and steam shower in rooms, fireplace in 13 rooms, restaurant, lounge, meeting facilities, room service, outdoor pool and whirlpool, limousine pickup at local airport. $95–$385, Continental breakfast. AE, D, MC, V. 2-night minimum on weekends Oct.–May.

Korakia Pensione. 257 S. Patencio Rd., Palm Springs, CA 92262, tel. 760/864–6411. 10 double rooms with baths, 7 suites. Air-conditioning, kitchen in 8 rooms, refrigerator in 17 rooms, balcony or patio off 5 rooms, fireplace in 5 rooms, guest kitchen, pool. $79–$169, Continental breakfast. No credit cards. No pets, 2-night minimum on weekends. Closed in August.

L'Horizon. 1050 E. Palm Canyon, Palm Springs, CA 92264. tel. 760/323–1858 or 800/377–7855. 22 double rooms with baths. Air-conditioning, TVs, phones; kitchens in 7 rooms, private patios, pool, outdoor whirlpool bath, barbecue, gardens, bicycles, library, games. $115–$140; Continental breakfast, afternoon refreshments. AE, D, DC, MC, V. No smoking, no pets, 2-night minimum on weekends. Closed July through September.

Truffles Bed and Breakfast. 43591 Bow Canyon Rd., Box 130649, Big Bear Lake, CA 92315, tel. 909/585–2772, fax 909/585–2772. 5 double rooms with baths. TV in rooms, video library, guest refrigerator, gift shop, gardens, ski storage. $115–$140; full breakfast, afternoon refreshments, desserts, beverages available all day. No smoking, no pets, 2-night minimum on holidays.

Villa Royale. 1620 Indian Trail, Palm Springs, CA 92264, tel. 760/327–2314 or 800/245–2314, fax 760/322–3794. 23 double rooms with baths, 10 housekeeping suites, 3 double housekeeping suites. Air-conditioning, TVs, phones; fireplace in 16 rooms, whirlpool bath in 8 rooms, kitchen in 10 double rooms, restaurant, cocktail lounge, massage and facials available, room service during restaurant hours, 2 pools, hot tub. $75–$225, Continental breakfast. AE, D, MC, V. No pets, 2-night minimum on weekends, 3-night minimum on holidays.

Windermere Manor. 263 S. State Hwy. 173, Box 2177, Lake Arrowhead, CA 92352, tel. 909/336–3292 or 800/429–2583, fax 909/336–4748. 5 double rooms with baths. Fireplace in 3 rooms, robes, clock radios, hair dryers, magnifying mirrors, guest refrigerator, gazebo. $105–$135; full breakfast, afternoon refreshments. AE, D, MC, V. No smoking, no pets, 2-night minimum on weekends.

Windy Point Inn. 39015 North Shore Rd., Box 375, Fawnskin, CA 92333, tel. 909/866–2746, fax 909/866–1593. 5 double rooms with baths. TV/VCR on request, fireplace in rooms, stocked refrigerators and wet bars in rooms, whirlpool bath in 2 rooms, ski storage; outdoor hot tub, private beach on lake, security entrance. $105–$225; full breakfast, afternoon refreshments. AE, D, MC, V. No smoking, no pets, 2-night minimum on weekends.

Reservations Services

Bed and Breakfast International (Box 282910, San Francisco, CA 94128–2910, tel. 415/696–1690). **Eye Openers B&B Reservations** (Box 694, Altadena, CA 91003, tel. 213/684–4428 or 818/797–2055, fax 818/798–3640).

Los Angeles with Orange County

Blue Lantern Inn

34343 St. of the Blue Lantern, Dana Point, CA 92629, tel. 714/661–1304, 800/950–1236, fax 714/496–1483

The Blue Lantern Inn has quite a following. This contemporary Cape Cod–style hotel is perched on a bluff above the Dana Point Marina in southern Orange County. One of the few small inns around, it offers sweeping marina and ocean views from almost every room. You can watch as the more than 2,000 small boats move in and out of their slips, or keep an eye on the children as they explore a replica of the tall ship *Pilgrim*, immortalized by Richard Henry Dana in his book *Two Years Before the Mast*.

The Blue Lantern is operated by the Four Sisters Inns group, which owns a number of inns and small hotels, mostly in northern California. Each guest room contains an unusually spacious bathroom; most have double sinks, showers, and whirlpool baths. The decor is contemporary; light mauve with accents in soft green and cream is a favorite color scheme. There's a tall mahogany four-poster bed in the Tower Suite; other rooms have brass, sleigh, or rattan beds. Wicker side chairs, small boudoir

chairs, and Queen Anne–style desks can be found in nearly every room, as well as armoires that conceal TV sets, and refrigerators stocked with complimentary soft drinks.

The lobby is set up with tables for two and four for the buffet-style breakfast. French doors lead to an outdoor sitting area, where many visitors take coffee and the morning paper. The library, which contains a small collection of books you might actually want to read, is where guests gather in the afternoons for wine and hors d'oeuvres.

Although visitors might be tempted to spend an entire weekend enjoying the beauty and comfort of the inn, the marina complex offers a number of activities. Bicycles are available for exploring the many trails that crisscross the surrounding hills. The innkeepers will make arrangements for sail- or powerboat charters or whale-watching excursions in season. They will also prepare a picnic basket for guests to enjoy at one of the two parks within walking distance of the inn. In addition, guests can visit the mission and the chic boutiques, art galleries, and antiques stores at San Juan Capistrano, just a 10-minute drive away.

▦ *29 double rooms with baths. Air-conditioning, robes, whirlpool baths, refrigerators, TVs, phones; fitness center, conference facilities, picnic baskets available, bicycles. $135–$350; full breakfast, afternoon refreshments. AE, MC, V. No smoking, no pets.*

Casa Tropicana

610 Avenida Victoria, San Clemente, CA 92672, tel. 714/492–1234 or 800/ 492–1245, fax 714/492–2423

Rick Anderson, a young building contractor, had a dream: to turn the somewhat seedy oceanfront of San Clemente into a showplace. The centerpiece would be his unique bed-and-breakfast inn. Casa Tropicana, the inn and restaurant he created and opened in 1990, has a young, beach-bum-casual ambience—the kind of place where guests are more likely to be parking their boogie boards than their BMWs.

The five-story, whitewashed Mediterranean-style inn sits on a narrow hillside across the street from the historic San Clemente pier. On a clear day, the view from some rooms goes all the way to Catalina Island. Right across the street is a prime surfing beach where most of the year surfers can be seen riding the breakers to shore. The Tropicana Grill occupies the ground floor, and guest rooms are on the upper floors. Each level has its own deck overlooking the ocean.

Every room offers the fulfillment of a different tropical fantasy. Out of Africa holds a step-up four-poster bed topped with faux mosquito netting; guests can soak in the double whirlpool tub while watching TV or enjoying the view through a peekaboo window. Other rooms are equally fantastic. Coral Reef has a bed with a peach rattan-clamshell headboard. Emerald Forest is cool and green with vines hanging from the ceiling. The Penthouse has a three-sided fireplace and a deck with an outdoor whirlpool spa. Only the rooms facing the ocean have a view or much outside light; if you tend to be claustrophobic, take one of these.

The laid-back atmosphere carries through to the Tropicana Grill, whose bar is tucked under a thatched roof. The reasonably priced menu offers Cabo swordfish tacos, pizzas, and Ragin' Cajun garlic ribs. Room service is available beginning at 7:30 AM. Guests can select breakfast from the restaurant menu and have it delivered to their rooms or outdoor deck.

▦ *7 double rooms with baths, 2 housekeeping suites. TVs, refrigerators, phones; double whirlpool bath in 8 rooms, fireplace in 9 rooms, restaurant, room service, evening entertainment weekends. $75–$350; full breakfast, complimentary champagne. AE, D,* MC, V. *No smoking, no pets, 2-night minimum on weekends.*

Channel Road Inn

219 Channel Rd., Santa Monica, CA 90402, tel. 310/459–1920, fax 310/454–9920

Originally the home of Thomas McCall, a pioneering Santa Monica businessman, this house was moved from a hilltop site to its current location tucked in a hillside of Santa Monica Canyon, one block from the beach. With the help of the local historical society, innkeeper Susan Zolla saved the Colonial Revival building from demolition and turned it into a gracious inn.

The house is sheathed in blue shingles, a rarity in Los Angeles and for a Colonial Revival house. The architectural details are pure Craftsman. Windows are very large and abundant, to take advantage of cool ocean breezes and bright sunlight. The honey-color woodwork in the living room is unusually elegant, with moldings and baseboards carefully milled. Other woodwork has been painted white, which Susan says is historically accurate.

The decor covers a variety of styles, with a common thread of wicker throughout, including the dining room, library, and several of the guest rooms. Beds are the focal point: four-poster beds, pencil-post canopy beds, and sleigh beds. Special attention has been paid to the needs of guests, particularly business travelers who require phones or writing surfaces. Not all rooms, however, have comfortable chairs for extended sitting.

Several rooms have access to balconies or decks with views of the flowering hillside and a glimpse of the ocean. There's an attractive garden sitting area for people who want to relax at the inn. Robes and oversize towels are provided for beachgoers or spa users.

The inn serves a generous breakfast in the bright dining room, where the atmosphere is generally convivial. Selections include healthy items such as cereal, yogurt, and fresh fruit, plus a tasty egg dish.

The broad white-sand beach is just across Pacific Coast Highway; it's bordered on one side by a 30-mile-long bicycle path that stretches north to Malibu and south to Venice Beach. The Venice portion of the path is a colorful carnival on weekends as crazily clad street musicians beat out tunes, vendors sell everything from food to art, and skaters zip by. The J. Paul Getty Museum, with its lovely gardens and superb collection specializing in ancient art, is only a five-minute drive away.

▦ *12 double rooms with baths, 2 suites. Cable TVs, phones; refrigerator in 4 rooms, fireplaces in rooms, VCR in 8 rooms, outdoor hot tub, bicycles. $95–$225; full breakfast, afternoon refreshments. AE, MC, V. No smoking, no pets.*

Christmas House

9240 Archibald Ave., Rancho Cucamonga, CA 91730, tel. 909/980–6450, fax 909/980–6450

Built by wealthy ranchers in 1904, this late Queen Anne mansion was known locally as thè Christmas House because of the many lavish holiday parties thrown here. Indeed, when Jay and Janice Ilsley opened the inn in 1985, they held to custom and had a Christmas party of their own. Holiday celebrations have been a tradition at the inn ever since.

Set amid an acre of grapefruit and tangerine trees, this inviting house has turrets, gables, stained-glass windows, sweeping verandas, seven working fireplaces, dark wood wainscoting, and a grand staircase leading to the second floor. Colors are cool deep greens and burgundies. Among the inn's fine group of antiques are a 150-year-old brass bed and a family collection of framed handkerchiefs.

Guest rooms are on the first and second floors of the main house and in a carriage house behind. Accommodations in the latter are unique: Decorated with an English floral theme, Elizabeth has a private rose-garden entry, a black iron bed and green wicker furnishings; French doors lead to a romantic tropical plant-filled grotto containing a massive outdoor shower. The adjacent Carriage Room has a more masculine feel, with its fireplace, burgundy sofa, and dark antiques, including a sleigh bed. This room has a private garden with a whirlpool tub set into a gazebo.

In the main house, one ground-floor room has a private courtyard with its own hot tub. Upstairs in the front of the mansion, the Celebration Suite, a huge double room with bedchamber and parlor divided by an enormous pocket door, is a popular choice of honeymooners. It has fireplaces in the corners of both rooms; a dining table set up in front of one fireplace, where breakfast is served; and a lace-draped antique canopy bed.

Convenient to the companies of the nearby city of Ontario and to Ontario International Airport, the Christmas House has become a favorite address of business travelers, but it continues to attract leisure visitors, too. Festivities include a monthly murder-mystery weekend and a follow-the-actors production of *A Christmas Carol* during the holidays.

▦ *3 double rooms with baths, 2 doubles share bath, 1 suite. Air-conditioning, robes, fireplace in 4 rooms, TV/VCR in 1 room, hot tub in 2 rooms, TVs available, library. $80–$180; full breakfast, afternoon refreshments. AE, D, MC, V. No smoking, no pets.*

Inn at Playa Del Rey

455 Culver Blvd., Playa Del Rey, CA 92093, tel. 310/574–1920, fax 310/574–9920

This brand-new luxury inn is close enough to Los Angeles International

Airport to serve as an overnight stop for an ongoing traveler, but remote enough to have a 350-acre bird sanctuary in its backyard, and the main channel of Marina del Rey behind that. Such is the human sanctuary created by owner Susan Zolla and her staff.

This three-story gray-and-white clapboard Cape Cod–style inn, completed in 1995, offers several levels of luxury: from glamorous suites with sweeping wetland and marina views to small, but well-equipped rooms designed for a budget traveler. The most spacious suite, filling a third-floor corner, is all done in tan and white; it has a large living room with a fireplace, two bathrooms, a whirlpool tub, and a view of the wetlands and sailboats from beyond the deck. More modest rooms have see-through fireplaces and double whirlpool baths. But even the least expensive rooms have work spaces and unexpected windows or balconies, and they are stocked with thick towels and bubble bath. The decor is contemporary, but comfortable, with many hand-painted beds and armoires, canopied beds draped with gauze curtains, and quilts and fresh flowers.

As lovely as the rooms are, guests will also want to linger in the inn's spacious living room and savor a fresh ocean breeze from the wraparound deck (no doubt while sipping a glass of icy lemonade and munching on some homemade cookies). For interested birders, the innkeepers will provide a guide to the more than 90 species that inhabit the sanctuary.

Susan, mindful of her guests' occasional need to catch early flights, puts coffee out at 5 AM, while a buffet breakfast appears in the dining room at a more civilized hour. Selections include home-baked breads, cereal, fresh fruit with yogurt, and an egg dish such as chili cheese puff or cheese soufflé.

19 rooms with baths, 2 suites. Air-conditioning, TVs, phones, robes; fireplace and whirlpool bath in 8 rooms, *private decks, voice mail, data outlets, private garden with hot tub, bicycles, parking, conference facilities. $95–$225; full breakfast, afternoon refreshments. AE, MC, V. No smoking, no pets.*

Inn on Mt. Ada

398 Wrigley Rd., Box 2560, Avalon, CA 90704, tel. 310/510–2030 or 800/608–7669, fax 310/510–2237

Chewing-gum magnate William Wrigley Jr. built this impressive Georgian Colonial mansion in 1921 as his Catalina Island summer home. Occupying a 5-acre hilltop site, it has a stunning view of Avalon Harbor, the coastline, and the mountains beyond from nearly every room.

Though the home is grand, Wrigley furnished it as a less-formal (for his times) retreat for his family and guests, who included U.S. presidents Calvin Coolidge and Herbert Hoover, and the Duke of Windsor. But you don't have to be royalty to enjoy the millionaire's mansion that Susie Griffin and Marlene McAdam transformed into an inn in 1986. From the moment they pick you up at the boat terminal you'll feel pampered here: a guided tour of Avalon on the way to the inn, an invitation to lunch even before you check into your room, instruction in use of the golf cart provided to each guest for island transportation. You'll be tempted to collapse into a chair on the expansive veranda and admire the view of jewel-like Avalon harbor. Or you may want to select a book or magazine from the inn's library, spy on the town through the telescope that's set up in the solarium window, or sample the cookies that are always out.

Furnishings are comfortable rather than elegant: overstuffed sofas and wing-back chairs in the living room, natural wicker in the downstairs den. The rooms range from spacious to small, but all offer a sea view and they come with little touches such as a ladies dressing table in Ada Wrigley's suite. Not surprisingly, the standout room is Wrigley's own suite, which occupies a second-floor corner; it has a large living room that opens onto a very private deck.

Guests staying in the east-facing rooms have a beautiful early morning view of the sun rising over the Los Angeles basin—illuminating the San Gabriel Mountains, the sprawling city, and the ocean below.

The innkeepers, longtime island residents, can provide a wealth of information on what to see and how to explore on Catalina. The backcountry, beyond Avalon, is particularly rugged and is home to a herd of buffalo that may be seen on tour.

Meals at the Inn on Mt. Ada include a full breakfast, a buffet-style lunch, a three-course dinner, evening wine and hors d'oeuvres, and beverages.

▦ *4 double rooms with baths, 2 suites. Fireplace in 4 rooms, robes, TV/VCR on request, conference facilities, golf cart for island transportation. $250– $620, all meals included. MC, V. No smoking, no pets, 2-night minimum on weekends and holidays.*

Malibu Beach Inn

22878 Pacific Coast Hwy., Malibu, CA 90265, tel. 310/456–6444 or 800/255– 1007, fax 310/456–1499

The Malibu Beach is one of the few southern California inns actually right on the waterfront. Its location, ocean views, and high level of service and amenities draw the occasional famous guest. This inn is the creation of two couples, Skip and Lee Miser along with Marty and Vicki Cooper, local developers who previously owned a restaurant and small motel on the property. When a storm in 1983 destroyed the restaurant, the partners decided they liked being innkeepers better than restaurateurs and opted to construct new lodgings instead of an eatery.

The pink-stucco, Mediterranean-style inn has what is coming to be called the "Malibu look": red-tile roof, terra-cotta floors, soft pink and blue accents on hand-painted tiles in the lobby and bathrooms. All the rooms have an ocean theme, with images of sea horses, scallop shells, and sea snails stenciled on warm, white walls. Rattan headboards and dresser modules were specially made in the Philippines for the inn. All rooms have private balconies, work spaces, sofa beds, and bathrooms with separate dressing areas. A deep tiled deck extending the length of the inn on the ocean side is an ideal spot to sit and watch the surfers work the waves at Surfriders Beach off Malibu Point, and to enjoy breakfast and the morning sun—or wine and the evening sunset.

Guests have the option of serving themselves from the huge bowls of fruit and baskets of muffins and croissants set up in the inn's lobby, or having breakfast brought to their rooms. The innkeeper has also made arrangements with Alice's Restaurant, on the Malibu Pier just a few steps away, to cater lunch and dinner for guests.

From the inn, guests can explore the historic Malibu pier or shop with the rich and famous at the Malibu Colony Plaza. Outdoor activities include hikes in the hills at nearby Malibu Creek State Park, or snorkeling, sailboarding, and jet skiing at the beach.

▦ *44 double rooms with baths, 3 suites. Air-conditioning, TV/VCR, phone, refrigerator, honor bar, wet bar, coffeemaker, hair dryer, robes, hot tub in 7 rooms, fireplace in 42 rooms, 24-hr room service, beach towels and lounge chairs, picnic baskets, gift shop. $150– $275, Continental breakfast. AE, DC, MC, V. No pets, 2-night minimum on weekends and holidays.*

Seal Beach Inn and Gardens

212 5th St., Seal Beach, CA 90740, tel. 562/493-2416 or 800/443-3292, fax 562/ 799-0483

Marjorie Bettenhausen has a romantic spirit. It's what drove her to purchase a 70-year-old hotel that had once been headquarters for rumrunners in Seal Beach—a 1920s-era seaside resort just south of Long Beach—and turn it into an antiques-filled, flower-decked bed-and-breakfast inn. Opened in 1977, it was one of the first B&Bs in southern California.

Marjorie's romantic spirit also took her to Europe, where she became enchanted with the exquisite furnishings, lush gardens, and striking colors of the inns along the Mediterranean coast of France. She brought back the antique treasures guests will find at the inn: a 2,000-pound iron fountain from Paris; a red phone booth from Britain; Mediterranean tile murals; flower-filled Napoleonic jardinieres; stately 1920s streetlights; and classic wood-inlaid beds—including one from John Barrymore's estate.

The delightful French Mediterranean-style inn includes five interconnected one- and two-story buildings adorned by ornate white iron balustrades, geranium-filled window boxes, and classic blue awnings surrounding a courtyard. Another building faces a quiet residential street.

The most lavish rooms face the courtyard. Most are suites with kitchens as well as sitting rooms; furnishings include four-poster beds, stained-glass windows, and floral wallpapers and bedspreads. The Honeysuckle Suite, with windows on four sides, a sunset view, a large private deck, and a triangular two-person whirlpool bath, is the most dramatic. There are also a few attractively decorated small rooms designed for budget-minded travelers.

The inn's gorgeous gardens are colorful all year. Boxes and planters lining walkways and courtyards display showy roses, shy impatiens, golden marigolds, and crimson bougainvillea.

In fine weather guests enjoy breakfast and afternoon refreshments around the pool. When it's cool, they can retreat to the cozy library or breakfast room, where tables are set up in front of the fireplace. A number of packages are offered to guests, including a chocolate-lovers package, and a gondola getaway cruise through the canals of nearby Naples, a quaint seaside community within Long Beach Harbor.

🛏 *9 double rooms with baths, 14 suites. Air-conditioning, TVs, phones, robes, refrigerators; fireplace in 5 rooms, whirlpool bath in 5 rooms, pool, beach towels, picnic baskets, library, gift shop. $118–$255; full breakfast, afternoon refreshments. AE, DC, MC, V. No smoking, no pets.*

Other Choices

Bissell House. 201 Orange Grove Ave., South Pasadena, CA 91030, tel. 818/441-3535, fax 818/441-3671. 3 double rooms with baths. Air-conditioning, double whirlpool bath in 1 room, robes, stocked guest refrigerator, library, fireplace in living room, gardens, pool, outdoor whirlpool. $100–$150; full breakfast weekends, Continental breakfast midweek. MC, V. No smoking, no pets, 4-night minimum on New Year's.

Inn at Laguna Beach. 211 N. Coast Hwy., Laguna Beach, CA 92651, tel. 714/497-9722 or 800/544-4479, fax 714/ 497-9972. 70 double rooms with baths. Air-conditioning, TV/VCR, phone, refrigerator, honor bar, robes, hair dryer in rooms, microwave in 30 rooms, video rentals, beach umbrellas, chairs and towels provided, pool, outdoor whirlpool, conference facilities. $99–$349, Continental breakfast. AE, MC, V. No pets, 2-night minimum weekends in July and Aug.

Inn at 657. 657 W. 23rd St., Los Angeles, CA 90007, tel. 213/741–2200 or 800/347–7512. 6 suites. Air-conditioning, TV/VCR, phone, kitchens, coffeemaker in rooms, video library, gardens with outdoor spa, USC tram stop. $95–$150, full breakfast. No credit cards. No smoking, no pets.

Mansion Inn. 327 Washington Blvd., Marina del Rey, CA 90291, tel. 310/821–2557 or 800/828–0688, fax 310/827–0289. 38 double rooms with baths, 5 suites. Air-conditioning, TVs, phones, refrigerators, hair dryers, free movies nightly. $79–$125, children under 12 free; Continental breakfast. AE, D, DC, MC, V. No pets.

Old Turner Inn. 232 Catalina Ave., Box 97, Avalon, CA 90704, tel. 310/510–2236. 3 double rooms with baths, 2 suites. Fireplace in 4 rooms. $100–$180; Continental breakfast, afternoon refreshments. D, MC, V. No smoking, no pets, 2-night minimum most weekends, 3-night minimum some holidays.

Portofino Beach Hotel. 2306 W. Oceanfront, Newport Beach, CA 92663, tel. 714/673–7030, fax 714/723–4370. 15 double rooms with baths. Air-conditioning, TVs, phones; whirlpool bath in 11 rooms, private sundeck off 3 rooms, restaurant, room service during dinner hrs, lounge. $100–$235, Continental breakfast. AE, DC, MC, V. No pets, 2-night minimum on weekends.

Venice Beach House. 15 30th Ave., Venice, CA 90291, tel. 310/823–1966, fax 310/823–1842. 3 double rooms with baths, 4 doubles share 2 baths, 2 suites. TVs, phones, fireplace in 1 suite, 2 balconies, 1 private entrance, massage available. $85–$165; full breakfast, afternoon refreshments. AE, MC, V. No smoking, no pets.

Reservations Services

Bed & Breakfast International (Box 282910, San Francisco, CA 94128–2910, tel. 415/696–1690, fax 415/696–1699). **Eye Openers** (Box 694, Altadena, CA 91003, tel. 213/684–4428 or 818/797–2055, fax 818/798–3640).

Central Coast from Santa Barbara to San Simeon

Blue Whale Inn

6736 Moonstone Beach Dr., Cambria, CA 93428, tel. 805/927–4647

Like many southern Californians, Fred Ushijima had been visiting the town of Cambria regularly for years, attracted by the laid-back beachfront atmosphere, good restaurants, and the shops and galleries of a growing artists' colony. Cambria's proximity to the Hearst Castle at San Simeon has always meant large numbers of visitors, but the village hasn't become touristy or overdeveloped.

Fred decided to sink roots in Cambria, and he found the perfect location on a triangular point of land jutting out to the sea along Moonstone Beach Drive. A visual delight, the Blue Whale consists of six guest rooms stepped back from the ocean at such an angle that each captures a bit of the view (the best views, surprisingly, are from the rooms farthest back). At the front of the inn is a spacious living room furnished with overstuffed sofas and chairs and a wood-burning stove; it adjoins the dining area, and the two together create a great room with a wall of windows revealing the ever-changing ocean vista.

A tiny Japanese-style garden, created by Fred, separates the guest rooms from the parking lot. Planted with a colorful selection of native plants—including lupine, coreopsis, and thyme—the garden is punctuated by a series of stepping-stones that lead from the parking area to the decks in front of the guest rooms. Guests often contemplate the beauty of nature while sitting on the garden's wooden bench or watching its tumbling waterfall.

In sharp contrast to the expansive views of sea and sky outside, the inn's interior is a riot of wallpapers and flowered fabrics, mostly in shades of blue; whitewashed pine is the wood of choice. Appointments are comfortable: step-up canopy beds, love seats, desks, a coffee table, and a side chair in each room. Skylights punctuate each vaulted ceiling. Bathrooms, also skylit, have adjacent dressing areas complete with a sink set into a long vanity.

Although Fred is often at the inn, gardening and sharing his dining suggestions ("a walking menu," one guest observed), Karleen and Bob Hathcock are the day-to-day innkeepers. Karleen is the breakfast chef, known for her croissant French toast with strawberry sauce.

▦ *6 double rooms with baths. Fireplace, refrigerator, cable TV, gift shop. $145–$195; full breakfast, afternoon refreshments. MC, V. No smoking, no pets, 2-night minimum on weekends and holidays.*

Cheshire Cat

36 W. Valerio St., Santa Barbara, CA 93101, tel. 805/569–1610

Two words sum up these adjacent gray-and-white Victorian-era houses linked by a brick patio: "Laura" and "Ashley." If you like the late designer's delicate floral fabrics, bedding, and wallpapers, then you'll be in heaven here. Owner Christine Dunstan, who once owned and ran a B&B in Scotland, gave her American inn a thoroughly British look, from the picket-fenced flower gardens to the formal entry and fireplace-warmed sitting area. Some masculine English antiques offset the frilly prettiness of the public rooms, most notably the huge refectory-style table and weighty sideboard in the dining room.

Dunstan has the help of a manager, Amy Taylor, and a small crew of friendly folks to cook the substantial full breakfast and tend to the guests and the property. There's a fair amount to tend to: the main house, all Victorian turrets and bays; the neighboring house, a Georgian-style box with shutters and bay windows; the Tweedledum & Tweedledee house, a simple clapboard cottage, in back; and the various garden areas, including a gazebo-covered whirlpool spa and a large brick patio where a first-rate breakfast is served. Often on the menu are quiche (sometimes made with artichoke hearts, other times with hash browns), fresh-squeezed juices, cereal, and fresh fruit in summer, cooked fruit in winter.

Larger and more upscale than most other B&Bs in town, the Cheshire Cat is popular with small groups for retreats or meetings, but most of its customers are couples seeking romance. They generally find it, particularly if they splurge on the Eberle Suite, which has a brick fireplace and a whirlpool tub for two; the White Rabbit Suite, whose private patio overlooks the gardens; or the swank Tweedledum Suite in the newer back house, complete with living room, dining room, kitchenette, fireplace, TV, king-size bed, and whirlpool tub.

The west-facing rooms in the main house can be a bit noisy, since they're the closest to busy Chapala Street. On the plus side, the inn is a short walk from the shops and restaurants of State Street.

▦ *7 double rooms with baths, 7 suites. Phones, chocolates, liqueurs; fireplace in 4 rooms, whirlpool bath in 4 rooms, TV in 2 rooms, meeting room for 8 to 12 with fireplace, mountain bicycles, spa in gazebo. $89–$249; full breakfast, afternoon wine. MC, V. No smoking, no pets, 2-night minimum on weekends.*

Just Inn

11680 Chimney Rock Rd., Paso Robles, CA 93446, tel. 805/238-6932 or 800/ 726-0049, fax 805/238-6932

Justin and Deborah Baldwin may at first glance seem like yet another high-powered couple who fled the stresses of chasing a big buck (Justin was an investment banker) for the gentle charms of the wine-making life. But this is no ordinary little winery/inn. The same passion and drive that made them successful in the big city are leading them to create a flawless French-style country inn and winery. They have spared neither expense nor talent, and the results are exceptional.

In the traditional French estate fashion, Justin grows all his own grapes and follows the Bordeaux style of wine making, producing a delicious Bordeaux-style meritage blend and a chardonnay. (Actually, a large staff does most of the work, in proper gentleman-farmer tradition, but the Baldwins live on the property and supervise everything.) As their wines grew in popularity, the Baldwins were hosting more and more distributors and wine-industry folks, so to accommodate them they built two suites in a gray-and-white, wood-sided building next to the tasting room, all set amid acres of rolling vineyard. Soon travelers heard rumor of these suites, and before long the Baldwins found themselves in the innkeeping business.

The two suites, Tuscany and Provence, live up to their names. Walls are meticulously sponge-painted in rich tones of sienna and ocher. Tapestry-covered wing chairs rest in front of stone fireplaces. Lamps sit on antique pine tables. The bedrooms are filled almost entirely with massive beds topped with featherbeds and first-rate linens. The bathrooms hold large spa tubs. Outside are gardens, vineyards, a pool and a spa. Breakfast—perhaps a frittata or trout amandine, with fresh juice and croissants—is served on bone china in the French Provençal–style tasting room. One would be justified in confusing this with the French or Italian countryside.

Dinner has not been neglected by these perfectionists. If guests want to dine in, the Baldwins summon their freelance chef, Laurent Grangien, who trained with Michel Guerard and Michel Rostang and who is planning to open his own restaurant in town. Laurent prepares a light but luxurious candlelit meal, for $100 a couple, wine excluded. On occasional weekends, notable guest chefs from around the country cook dinner for visitors.

Amusements hereabout include exploring the small town of Paso Robles, 16 miles away; sampling some of the local wines; and visiting Hearst Castle, just 5 miles away. The innkeepers will pack picnic lunches and arrange for bicycle or horseback outings, golf, massages, and whale watching on the nearby coast.

🏠 *2 suites. Air-conditioning, fireplace, whirlpool bath, TV/VCR, restaurant, pool, spa. $225, full breakfast. AE, D, MC, V. No pets, 2-night minimum on weekends and holidays.*

Los Olivos Grand Hotel

2860 Grand Ave., Los Olivos, CA 93441, tel. 805/688-7788 or 800/446-2455, fax 805/688-1942

Ronald Reagan and Michael Jackson have ranches hereabouts, as do lots of less famous but similarly moneyed folks. This explains this country inn's haute-bourgeois style and high prices. Those who value rusticity should look elsewhere; those looking for creature comforts (and who don't mind paying for them) are likely to have a memorable stay.

About 45 minutes up a lovely, sharply winding mountain road from Santa Barbara, Los Olivos is tucked into the oak-dotted ocher hills of the Santa

Ynez Valley. Vineyards and ranch land occupy most of the valley, and the town isn't much more than a dozen art galleries, a wine shop, a gas station, a saddlery, a couple of restaurants, and this inn. Entertainment in these parts is genteel: wine tasting, horseback riding, hiking, dining, gallery hopping, and taking in the night air from the confines of a steaming hot tub.

The Grand Hotel hews to the polished (as opposed to the rustic) French-country style. Classical music wafts through the lobby, with its stone fireplace, gleaming piano, French doors, and various clusters of sofas, wing chairs, and Queen Anne furniture. At one end is Remington's, a good Continental-American restaurant named for the western artist; downstairs, the Wine Cellar, a private dining room, is great for larger parties.

Each of the large suites (set in two low-lying Victorian buildings) is individually styled; vaulted, beamed ceilings, Pierre Deux–style fabrics, iron or brass beds, hand-painted tile fireplaces, and Impressionist paintings are the norm. The Monet Suite, with its bay window, restful blues, and comfy chaise, is particularly lovely, but there isn't a loser in the bunch. Luxurious touches abound, from wet bars to down comforters.

The inn was recently purchased by the Four Sisters Inns group, which also operates other inns along the California coast. The staff exudes friendly professionalism and will tend to most any request, from arranging a private tour of a winery to delivering a freshly brewed cup of tea to your room at 3 AM.

▥ *21 suites. Air-conditioning, fireplace, phone, cable TV, wet bar, refrigerator, whirlpool bath in 4 rooms; restaurant, lounge, meeting and banquet rooms, room service, pool, spa, bicycles, picnics extra. $160–$325; full buffet breakfast, afternoon wine and hors d'oeuvres. AE, D, DC, MC, V. No pets, 2-night minimum on weekends.*

Old Yacht Club Inn

431 Corona del Mar Dr., Santa Barbara, CA 93103, tel. 805/962–1277 or 800/676–1676, fax 805/962–3989

When former school administrator Nancy Donaldson and teacher Sandy Hunt opened Santa Barbara's first bed-and-breakfast in 1980, they set out to provide a homey atmosphere in which guests would feel comfortable putting their feet up—and so pampered that they'd want to return again and again. In addition, there would be the outstanding food prepared by Nancy, a member of the American Wine and Food Institute.

Initially the inn consisted of only the historic 1912 Craftsman house with its broad porches, tiny balcony across the front, white brick fireplace, and colorful gardens. Just a block from the beach, it had been built as a private home, and during the 1920s served as the headquarters for the Santa Barbara Yacht Club. In 1983 the innkeepers acquired the more spacious house next door, which they transformed into the Hitchcock House.

The Hitchcock is a monument to the families of the innkeepers, with its four rooms named and decorated to honor parents and grandparents. The Julia Metelmann is decorated with photographs of the mother of a former inn partner. The photographs depict Julia as a young pioneer in North Dakota, and furnishings include a red lacquer Chinese chest that once belonged to her.

There are five rooms in the main house: four on the second floor, and one downstairs. The upstairs rooms offer a light and airy ambience. In the two front-facing rooms French doors open onto a balcony where guests can sip wine while taking in the afternoon sun. Downstairs, the sunny Captain's Corner opens onto a private patio.

Saturday-night dinners are served in the inn's dining-living room on three

Saturdays a month. Nancy uses fresh local ingredients in her five-course gourmet dinners: fresh fish from the bay, artichokes from nearby fields, sorrel grown in the backyard. Breakfast, served daily, features the lightest of light omelets, pancakes, French toast, home-baked breads, and fresh fruit.

🏨 *9 rooms with baths. Whirlpool bath in 2 rooms, bicycles, beach towels, chairs. $90–$150; full breakfast, evening refreshments, dinner (3 Sat. nights monthly), about $25. AE, D, MC, V. No smoking in guest rooms, no pets, 2-night minimum on weekends.*

The Parsonage

1600 Olive St., Santa Barbara, CA 93101, tel. and fax 805/962–9336 or 800/ 775–0352

In 1981, Hilde Michelmore transformed a dreary school for problem children (formerly the home of the parson of nearby Trinity Episcopal Church) into an excellent bed-and-breakfast, immediately becoming a leader of Santa Barbara's just-developing B&B scene. She tried to retire in 1993 but couldn't leave her pride and joy.

Although Hilde has considerably renovated her big, boxy hillside Queen Anne Victorian (circa 1892), she hasn't tampered with the uncluttered Victorian look (if that's not an oxymoron). Most rooms are wearing new paint, wallpaper, and upholstery, and whirlpool tubs have been added to the Honeymoon Suite and Peacock Room.

On the ground floor are the large, bright living and dining rooms, which combine polished woodwork, Oriental rugs, subdued antiques, and white-lace curtains to create a formal yet unfussy look. Hilde's pride and joy is the Oriental dining room table, with its subtly beautiful painted top. Her blend of antiques and styles of several periods—from the Louis XVI dresser and mirror in the Versailles Room to the Victorian settee in the Las Flores

Room—emphasizes homeyness, not museum-style perfection.

The Honeymoon Suite may be one of the most romantic accommodations in town. A huge three-room suite that wraps around a front corner of the house, it offers stunning views of ocean, city, and mountains; it also has a glass-walled solarium. Good sea views can also be had from the bay windows of Las Flores, and the other two second-story rooms offer mountain views.

Weather permitting—which is most of the time—breakfast is served on bone china on the outdoor deck or in the stately gazebo. The breakfast fare includes coffee cakes, cinnamon rolls and substantial breakfast entrées, such as soufflés, egg creations, and creative varieties of French toast. Later in the day home-baked cookies are often set out on the dining-room table, along with pitchers of iced tea or lemonade.

🏨 *5 rooms with baths, 1 suite. Fireplace in 2 rooms, whirlpool bath in 2 rooms. $100–$185; full breakfast, afternoon refreshments. AE, MC, V. No smoking, children under 12 discouraged, no pets, 2-night minimum on weekends, 3-night minimum on holidays.*

San Ysidro Ranch

900 San Ysidro La., Montecito, CA 93108, tel. 805/969–5046 or 800/368–6788, fax 805/565–1995

The San Ysidro's luxuriousness belies its humble roots as one of the Santa Barbara Mission's working ranches. It became a guest ranch in the late 1800s after cottages were added to the 1825 adobe, which still stands, and became famous in the 1930s, when owners Ronald Colman (the actor) and Alvin Weingand (a state senator) attracted stars, writers, and royalty. Here Vivien Leigh and Laurence Olivier married, John and Jackie Kennedy honeymooned, and Winston Churchill wrote some of his memoirs.

Nestled in the hills above Montecito, one of the country's wealthiest small towns, the Ranch, as it is known to faithfuls, had become shabby by the '60s. New owners restored the cottages and added some luxurious new ones, and Hollywood was once again in residence. In 1987, Claude Rouas, owner of Napa Valley's luxe Auberge du Soleil, took over and set out to bring the atmospheric stone restaurant, the ranch's old packing house, up to France's country-inn standards, a goal he and American chef Gerard Thompson have achieved in spades.

The inn itself remains as swell as ever. Winding paths connect the various board-and-batten cottages, which house everything from smallish double rooms to huge two-bedroom suites with soaring beamed ceilings. The decor is American country gone elegant: clean-lined antiques, down comforters, Oriental rugs, and a lavish use of high-quality pine.

Some highly stressed guests (including many of the very famous) just hide out by their fireplaces and order room service. Others stroll the gardens and orchards, hike through the 540 acres, swim, play tennis, ride horses, play chess in the games room, have a drink in the cozy Plow & Angel bar, or venture into downtown Montecito or nearby Santa Barbara. Families are increasingly in evidence, thanks to the new petting zoo, play area, videos, and kids' menus. Even the family dog is welcome. Everyone gets what he or she came for: clean air, charm, comfort, pampering, romance, and enough peace and quiet to finish writing that script.

▥ *26 double rooms with baths, 18 suites and cottages. Air-conditioning, fireplace or woodstove in all rooms, cable TV, private deck, wet bar, refrigerator in all rooms, whirlpool bath in 3 rooms; outdoor private Jacuzzi in 12 rooms; restaurant, bar, room service, pool, spa, tennis, picnics extra. $295–$950, breakfast not included. AE, MC, V. 2-night minimum on weekends.*

Secret Garden Inn and Cottages

1908 Bath St., Santa Barbara, CA 93101, tel. 805/687–2300 or 800/676–1622

Slowly but surely, luxuries are creeping into this understated complex of bungalows: a hot tub here, new linens there, and, in the case of three rooms, a complete makeover. Hence the decision to change the name from the Blue Quail Inn to Secret Garden Inn and Cottages. Since buying the inn in 1994, partners Jack Greenwald, who ran a five-star restaurant in Scotland, and Christine Dunstan of the nearby Cheshire Cat, have maintained the service and style that generated so much repeat business for the Blue Quail, while adding the creature comforts that guests have requested.

The antithesis of Santa Barbara's typical grand Victorian B&B, this collection of five little shingled bungalows is low-key and quiet, with an overall decor that will appeal more to lovers of American-country style than of Victorian formality. The main cottage houses a homey, carpeted living room; a dining room with hardwood floors, tan striped wallpaper, country-pine antiques, and an inviting window seat; a tiled country kitchen, where someone friendly is often baking something cinnamony; and two of the more modest guest rooms.

On the side of the property is the inn's most private quarters, the Wood Thrush cottage. There are luxurious white-on-white French linens on the king-size bed and large, comfortable wicker armchairs in the living room. The cottage itself is a bit creaky, however, and a rehab is planned soon. Those who prefer a Ralph Lauren look should try the Cardinal Suite, with its veranda, wicker bed, botanical prints, and rich fabrics in paisleys and stripes. American-country fans will love the smaller Mockingbird, with its cheerful yellow floral fabrics and yellow, blue, and white quilt on the wall. Best of all are the three freshly renovated rooms and suites, Nightingale, Oriole, and Kingfisher, each with some luxurious touch, from a fireplace to a private deck with hot tub.

Outside, the cool gardens are thick with ferns and fragrant with jasmine; in fair weather (almost always), breakfast is served on the patio. The many good restaurants, shops, and sights of State Street are a comfortable stroll or quick bike ride away; the beach is just a short drive.

Families take note: This is one of the very few Santa Barbara B&Bs that happily welcome young children, as long as they stay in one of the more private suites.

▦ *5 double rooms with baths, 5 suites. Fireplace in 1 suite, hot tubs in 2 rooms and 2 suites, TV in main house, bicycles. $85–$165; full breakfast, afternoon and evening wine and refreshments. AE, D, DC, MC, V. No smoking, no pets, 2-night minimum on weekends.*

Simpson House Inn

121 E. Arrellaga St., Santa Barbara, CA 93101, tel. 805/963-7067 or 800/676-1280, fax 805/564-4811

Although red-tile roofs are the norm in Santa Barbara, Victoriana runs rife as well, since so many Brits settled here in the late 1800s. One such emigrant was Robert Simpson, the Scotsman who built this Eastlake-style house in 1874. Glyn and Linda Davies restored the house and made it their home in 1976; more recently, they have transformed it into one of the finest B&Bs in the Central Coast.

Set on a quiet, exquisitely landscaped acre in the heart of town, the Simpson House Inn offers something for almost everyone. Traditional B&B fans should stay in the main house, where larger-than-average rooms are paeans to Victorian style, color, and elegance. One room pays tribute to famed Victorian designer Christopher Dresser; several display custom hand-printed wallpaper, produced by Bradbury & Bradbury, famous for its period designs. Oriental rugs, English lace curtains, wicker, and claw-foot tubs add to the atmosphere.

Those put off by Victorian primness and the occasional discomforts of 100-year-old bathrooms should consider the newest additions to the property: three cottages and a restored 100-year-old barn. The cottages are among the most romantic quarters in town—each has its own private courtyard (with bubbling fountain), queen featherbed, love seat set beside a wood-burning fireplace, teak floors, in-room whirlpool, superb shower, hidden TV/VCR, and plenty of privacy. Though a bit less dreamy, the four large suites in the barn are exceptional. Oriental rugs rest on antique pine floors, French doors open to private decks, king-size beds wear high-quality linens, English pine armoires hide TVs and VCRs, showers are modern and roomy, and fireplaces burn real wood, not those ubiquitous metal logs.

Resident innkeeper Gillean Wilson oversees the substantial breakfast, which can be taken on the veranda, in the garden, or in one's suite. But it is the early evening that is most memorable, when guests toast the balmy Santa Barbara twilight with local wines and elegant hors d'oeuvres while knocking around croquet balls, stoking the fireplace, or sitting for a spell on a wicker sofa in the gardens.

▦ *6 double rooms with baths, 3 cottages, 4 suites. Air-conditioning, robes in rooms, fireplace, TV/VCR, and coffeemaker in cottages and suites, bicycles, croquet, beach chairs, towels, picnics extra. $140–$300; full breakfast, evening refreshments. AE, D, MC, V. No smoking, no pets, 2-night minimum on weekends.*

Union Hotel/ Victorian Mansion

362 Bell St., Box 616, Los Alamos, CA 93440, tel. 805/344-2744 or 800/230-2744, fax 805/344-3125

In the tiny Old West outpost of Los Alamos, some 50 miles north of Santa Barbara, these two inns present a study in fantasy fulfillment. The Union Hotel, a onetime Wells Fargo stagecoach station dating from 1880, was renovated by Dick Langdon in 1970 and turned into one of the first bed-and-breakfasts in California. The whimsical Old West atmosphere, which begins in the lobby peopled with mannequins costumed in frontier finery, is carried into the saloon with its mahogany Ping-Pong table supported by marble statues, and continues in the bedrooms with their French and patriotic wallpapers.

In the neighboring yellow three-story 1864 mansion, mere whimsy gives way to flat-out fantasy. Dick, who died in 1994, created a sort of Disneyland for adults here, the spirit of which is kept alive by his children, who now run both facilities. Take the Egyptian Room, designed to make a couple feel like Antony and Cleopatra camping out in the desert. A step-up white bed, canopied with gauze, stands in the middle of the room facing a wall-size mural of a desert. Walls are draped with Near East–motif fabrics, and there's a step-up hot tub and a marble-faced fireplace flanked by floor cushions. The bathroom door is a life-size statue of King Tut, opened by tugging his beard, and the bathroom itself resembles the inside of a pyramid. Desert robes, backgammon, computer-controlled background music, and videotapes of such film classics as *Lawrence of Arabia* and *The Wind and the Lion* round out the fantasy.

Other rooms are equally fantastic: Roman, Gypsy, Pirate, '50s Drive-In, and French—each with fitting murals, bed, theme robes, music, movies, games, and menus. Breakfast is delivered to the theme rooms through lockers concealed in the walls.

Over the years, Dick employed a community of artists and artisans who gave life to his fantasy. Among the grounds' distinguishing features are the largest hedge maze west of the Mississippi and a 67-foot yawl that once belonged to the King of Denmark.

▦ *Hotel has 3 rooms with baths, 11 rooms with sinks share 2 baths; mansion has 6 rooms with baths. Air-conditioning in mansion; TV/VCR, tapes, phones, hot tubs, fireplaces, robes, refrigerators; restaurant, saloon, shuffleboard, Ping-Pong, pool, spa in gazebo. Hotel $66–$121, mansion $198–$242; full breakfast. AE, D, MC, V. No pets. Restaurant open for dinner daily, for lunch Sat.–Mon.*

Other Choices

Ballard Inn. 2436 Baseline Ave., Ballard, CA 93463, tel. 805/688-7770 or 800/638-2466, fax 805/688-9560. 15 double rooms with baths. Air-conditioning, fireplace in 7 rooms, carriage rides. $150–$220; full breakfast, afternoon wine tasting. AE, MC, V. No smoking, no pets, 2-night minimum on weekends.

Beach House. 6360 Moonstone Beach Dr., Cambria, CA 93428, tel. 805/927-3136. 7 rooms with baths. Cable TV, fireplace in 2 rooms, mountain bikes. $125–$155; full breakfast, evening wine and cheese. MC, V. No smoking, no pets.

Bella Maggiore Inn. 67 S. California St., Ventura, CA 93001, tel. 805/652-0277 or 800/523-8479, fax 805/648-2150. 28 rooms with baths, 2 suites. Cable TV, phone, fireplace in 6 rooms. $75–$150; full breakfast, evening hors d'oeuvres. AE, D, DC, MC, V. No pets.

Crystal Rose Inn. 789 Valley Rd., Arroyo Grande, CA 93420, tel. 805/481-1854 or 800/767-3466, fax 805/481-9541. 9 double rooms with baths. TV in parlor; restaurant, exercise room, bicycles. Children welcome in carriage-house rooms. $85–$175; full breakfast, afternoon high tea, evening hors d'oeuvres. AE, MC, V. No smoking, no pets.

Fern Oaks Inn. 1025 Ojai Rd., Santa Paula, CA 93060, tel. 805/525–7747. 4 double rooms with private baths. Air-conditioning, private deck in 1 room, in-room massage available; pool. $95–$110; full breakfast, evening wine and hors d'oeuvres. No credit cards. No smoking, no pets.

Garden Street Inn. 1212 Garden St., San Luis Obispo, CA 93401, tel. 805/545–9802. 9 double rooms with baths, 4 suites. Air-conditioning, radios with tape decks; fireplace in 5 rooms, whirlpool bath in 6 rooms. $90–$160; full breakfast, afternoon refreshments. AE, MC, V. No smoking, no pets, 2-night minimum on holiday and special-event weekends.

Glenborough Inn. 1327 Bath St., Santa Barbara, CA 93101, tel. 805/966–0589 or 800/962–0589, fax 805/564–8610. 6 rooms with baths, 2 rooms share 1 bath, 3 suites. Fireplace in 4 rooms, hot tub in 2 rooms. $100–$225; full breakfast, afternoon and evening refreshments. AE, D, DC, MC, V. No smoking, no pets, 2-night minimum on weekends.

La Mer. 411 Poli St., Ventura, CA 93001, tel. 805/643–3600, fax 805/653–7329. 5 rooms with baths. Old-fashioned radio in rooms, fireplace in 1 room, beach towels, antique carriage rides. $105–$155; full breakfast, afternoon refreshments. AE, MC, V. No smoking, no pets, 2-night minimum on weekends.

Montecito Inn. 1295 Coast Village Rd., Montecito, CA 93108, tel. 805/969–7854 or 800/843–2017, fax 805/969–0623. 53 double rooms with baths, 7 suites. Air-conditioning in public rooms, cable TV, refrigerator, VCR, some no-smoking rooms, room service; pool, spa, sauna, fitness center, bicycles. $150–$695, Continental breakfast. AE, DC, MC, V. No pets, 2-night minimum on weekends and holidays.

Olallieberry Inn. 2476 Main St., Cambria, CA 93428, tel. 805/927–3222 or 888/927–3222, fax 805/927–0202. 6 double rooms with attached baths, 3 with detached baths. Fireplace in 6 rooms. $85–$165; full breakfast, evening wine and hors d'oeuvres. MC, V. No smoking, no pets.

Squibb House. 4063 Burton Dr., Cambria, CA 93428, tel. 805/927–9600. 5 double rooms with baths. Fireplaces. $95–$125; Continental breakfast, afternoon refreshments. DC, MC, V. No smoking, no pets, 2-night minimum on weekends.

Theodore Woolsey House. 1484 E. Ojai Ave., Ojai, CA 93023, tel. 805/646–9779, fax 805/646–4414. 5 double rooms with baths. Air-conditioning, fireplace in 2 rooms, phone in 3 rooms, TV in 3 rooms, pool, outdoor whirlpool bath, volleyball court, croquet, horseshoes. $85–$125; Continental breakfast, afternoon refreshments. No credit cards. No smoking, no pets, 2-night minimum on weekends.

Tiffany Inn. 1323 De la Vina St., Santa Barbara, CA 93101, tel. 805/963–2283 or 800/999–5672, fax 805/962–0994. 5 rooms with baths, 2 suites. Fireplace in 5 rooms, whirlpool bath and refrigerator in suites. $125–$200; full breakfast, evening wine and hors d'oeuvres. AE, D, MC, V. No smoking, no pets, 2-night minimum on weekends.

The Upham. 1404 De la Vina St., Santa Barbara, CA 93101, tel. 805/962–0058 or 800/727–0876, fax 805/963–2825. 46 double rooms with baths, 3 suites. Cable TV and phone, fireplace in 7 rooms and 1 suite; restaurant, conference and banquet rooms. $105–$325; Continental breakfast, evening wine and cheese. AE, D, DC, MC, V. No smoking, no pets, 2-night minimum on weekends.

Villa Rosa. 15 Chapala St., Santa Barbara, CA 93101, tel. 805/966–0851, fax 805/962–7159. 18 rooms with baths. Phone, fireplace in 4 rooms, kitchen in 3 rooms; pool and spa. $85–$210; Continental breakfast, afternoon wine and cheese, evening port and sherry. AE, MC, V. No pets, 2-night minimum on weekends.

Reservations Service

Santa Barbara Bed & Breakfast Innkeepers Guild (Box 90734, Santa Barbara 93190, tel. 800/776–9176).

Monterey Bay, Including Santa Cruz and Carmel

Babbling Brook Inn

1025 Laurel St., Santa Cruz, CA 95060, tel. 408/427–2437 or 800/866–1131, fax 408/427–2457

This inn offers a combination of romantic setting, California history, and a convenient location for business travelers. In the heart of Santa Cruz, the inn's "babbling brook," wooded grounds, and gardens help to make guests feel worlds away from the city.

The inn consists of four cedar-shingle-sided buildings set on different levels of the hillside property. Portions of the main house's stone foundation date from 1796, when the mission fathers built a gristmill for grinding corn. In 1981, when it became a bed-and-breakfast inn, three cottages were added. After a seven-decade absence, the historic waterwheel was recently returned to its original pond setting in front of the building.

The rooms are decorated in French-country style: soft colors, floral-print curtains, and iron beds covered with floral spreads. The most charming are in the main house, especially the romantic Honeymoon Suite, which offers couples seclusion (breakfast in bed is available to guests staying here) as well as a private deck overlooking a waterfall. The expansive Garden Room has a wood-burning stove and a great

garden view. The Countess Room has two queen-size beds and a fireplace. The rooms in the outbuildings get more street and parking-lot noise, but they also have decks facing the garden. The Babbling Brook's gardens are often the setting for weddings, with a wrought-iron white gazebo as the centerpiece, the brook meandering through the property, and flowers adorning every inch of hillside.

The Babbling Brook's many business travelers appreciate the attention to their needs in the form of an early breakfast, late check-in, and copies of the *Wall Street Journal*. In the afternoon, the innkeepers serve tea and freshly baked cookies; later, a congenial wine-hour takes place in front of the fire in the comfortable living room. The inn's beer and wine license allows for after-dinner drinks as well.

A buffet-style breakfast of frittatas or other egg dishes, fruits, and fresh muffins and croissants with jam is set out in the living room, although guests can go either into the adjacent dining room or outside to enjoy their meals in the shade of the redwood trees.

▦ *12 double rooms with baths. Cable TV, fireplace in 10 rooms, whirlpool bath in 4 rooms, picnic baskets available. $85–$165; full breakfast, afternoon refreshments. AE, D, MC, V. No smoking, no pets, 2-night minimum on weekends.*

Green Gables Inn

104 5th St., Pacific Grove, CA 93950, tel. 408/375–2095 or 800/722–1774, fax 408/375–5437

The Green Gables Inn, a striking landmark along the oceanfront of Pacific Grove, dates from 1888, when Los Angeles businessman (and amateur architect) William Lacy built the two-story, half-timbered and gabled Queen Anne for his lady friend.

This elegant house, in which nearly every room has a three-sided bay window, offers sweeping views of the Monterey Bay shoreline from almost every room. Framed entirely of redwood, it has solid maple floors; countless angles, slopes, and nooks; exposed ceiling beams; intricate moldings, woodwork and arches; and even stained-glass windows framing the fireplace. The windows, fixtures, and woodwork are all original.

Roger and Sally Post bought the house as a family home for their four daughters in 1970. The Posts began renting out rooms to summer visitors, and in 1983 the Green Gables became a full-time inn (and the cornerstone of the Four Sisters Inns group).

Guest rooms in the carriage house, perched on a hill out back, are larger than those in the main house and have more privacy as well as views of the ocean. They also offer more modern amenities, but the rooms in the main house, with their intricately detailed molding and woodwork, have more charm. The Lacy Suite on the main floor, doubtless a converted parlor and library, has a fireplace, built-in bookshelves, and a claw-foot tub in the bathroom. Upstairs in the Gable Room, a window seat under leaded-glass windows overlooks the ocean. The Balcony Room is like a sleeping porch, and the Chapel Room actually resembles a church, with a vaulted ceiling and a pewlike window seat stretching across the front of the room.

The food, always fresh, is served family-style. The ample buffet breakfast includes frittatas, a fruit plate, an assortment of breads and scones, and apple pancakes. Afternoon refreshments include wine and hors d'oeuvres. The young staff is gracious and can offer assistance with dinner reservations and sightseeing information.

▥ *6 double rooms with baths, 4 doubles share 2 baths, 1 suite. Fireplace in carriage-house rooms, picnic baskets*

available, bicycles. $110–$160; full breakfast, afternoon refreshments. AE, MC, V. No smoking, no pets.

Inn at Depot Hill

250 Monterey Ave., Box 1934, Capitola by the Sea, CA 95010, tel. 408/462–3376 or 800/572–2632, fax 408/462–3697

Innkeeper Suzie Lankes and her partner, Dan Floyd, have created one of the most beautiful bed-and-breakfasts in California—perhaps anywhere. And they provide guests with exquisite pampering to complement the splendid surroundings.

Once a historic railroad station in the beachside village of Capitola, the Inn at Depot Hill is now a vision of turn-of-the-century European-style luxury. Most rooms have a Continental theme: Dutch Delft, a corner suite, includes a big blue-and-white sitting room, a bedroom with a huge featherbed draped in Belgian cutwork lace and real linen, a private patio filled with tulips and irises, and a gray-marble bathroom with double shower. Romantic Paris, a study in black and white, has walls upholstered in French toile, windows curtained in lace, and a bath done in gray marble. Portofino captures a sunny Italian mood, with a vine-and-leaf-decorated bed and a private Mediterranean garden planted with orange and lemon trees. Departing from the European motif, the Railroad Baron's room honors local history. This masculine accommodation, resembling a posh railroad car, has deep red brocade upholstery, a red-and-gold sitting room, rich woods with gold leaf, a circular lit dome over the bed—and an eagle presiding over all.

Last year Suzie and Dan bought the house next door, expanding the inn to include another double room and two more suites, one with a Japanese theme (modified for Western habits) with an outdoor hot tub and glassed-in garden shower, and one with two bedrooms. A large conference room with business presentation equipment can hold 25 comfortably.

But this is first and foremost a romantic inn. Although Suzie and her staff encourage guests to mingle, most prefer to retreat to the privacy of their rooms. Others find enjoyment walking among the inn's gardens or reading in the parlor-library that has a piano tucked into one corner.

The food here is ample and well prepared. The in-house gourmet chef prepares a late-afternoon hors d'oeuvre buffet with local wines, a canapé tray and crudités and dip. A homemade dessert and port and sherry welcome guests returning from dinner. For breakfast there are breads, fruit, cereal, and an egg entrée. Service is elegant, with silver, linens, and china displaying the inn's logo. When the weather is nice, breakfast is served outside in the brick courtyard.

▦ *5 double rooms with baths, 7 suites with hot tubs. Fireplaces, fax or modem connections, robes, hair dryers; cable TV/VCR and videotape lending library, phone (on request), stereo, clothes steamer, coffeemaker, private landscaped patio, double showers and hot tub in 9 rooms; access to outdoor hot tub by appointment for 3 rooms. $165–$250; full breakfast, afternoon and evening refreshments. AE, MC, V. No smoking, no pets, 2-night minimum on weekends.*

Mangels House

570 Aptos Creek Rd., Box 302, Aptos, CA 95001, tel. 408/688–7982 or 800/ 320–7401

Once the country home of California sugar barons Claus Mangels and his brother-in-law Claus Spreckels, Mangels House is set on 4 acres of lawn and orchard. The big, white square Italianate structure with deep verandas is close to the entrance of the Forest of Nisene Marks State Park and surrounded by nearly 10,000 acres of second-growth redwoods.

The Mangels family built the house in 1886 as a retreat from San Francisco; each summer the family—with children, governess, and servants—would move to the then logged-out forest for a three-month stay. At the time of its construction, the house boasted some of the most modern conveniences, including fully plumbed marble-topped vanities, still in use in the bedrooms today. Vintage gaslight fixtures in the ceilings have more recently been converted to electricity.

English-born innkeeper Jackie Fisher is the force behind the inn's genteel ambience. She came to the business naturally, after raising children, living abroad with her radiologist husband Ron, and serving as hostess on many occasions. "I love meeting new people," she explains as she pours late-afternoon tea for guests in the inn's 40-foot-long sitting room. Usually conversation turns to shared experiences and personal adventures, such as the time the family lived in Zaire.

Indeed, the inn reflects the family's life. One African-theme bedroom displays artifacts collected in Kenya and Zaire, including a collection of carved animals, banana-leaf art, dolls, and medicine men. By contrast, Timothy's Room features a pair of beautiful, locally thrown vases and a unique carved wooden headboard that Jackie herself designed.

Guests gather each morning in the dining room for a hearty English breakfast, which Jackie serves family style. It starts with Jackie's homemade crumpets, "a vehicle for getting melted butter to your mouth." Accompaniments include fruit compote, spicy cheese-egg puff, oatmeal scones, and dessert—plenty to keep one going on a long morning hike through the forest.

Jackie's English garden, planted a few years ago, is now maturing into a pleasant scene of wildflowers and rosebushes, with a small fountain and fishpond.

⊞ *6 double rooms with baths. Fireplace in sitting room and 1 guest room, English garden, games including table tennis and darts. $105–$155; full breakfast, afternoon refreshments. AE, MC, V. Restricted smoking, no pets, 2-night minimum on weekends.*

Martine Inn

255 Ocean View Blvd., Pacific Grove, CA 93950, tel. 408/373–3388, fax 408/373–3896

Elegance and grace are the keys to the Martine Inn, a nearly 100-year-old mansion perched on a hillside above the tiny cove of the Monterey Bay that frames Pacific Grove. Originally a Queen Anne with turrets and towers, the home was owned until World War II by Laura and James Parke (of Parke Davis Pharmaceutical Company) who remodeled it in Mediterranean style, with a stucco exterior and windows framed by arches. Don Martine's family acquired the house in 1972; by 1984 he and wife Marion had opened it as an inn.

Don and Marion have assembled one of the most extensive antiques collections to be found in any California bed-and-breakfast inn, mostly American pieces dating from 1840 through 1890: an Eastlake suite used by publisher C. K. McClatchy; a mahogany suite exhibited at the 1893 Chicago World's Fair; Academy Award–winning costume designer Edith Head's bedroom suite; and an 1860 Chippendale Revival four-poster bed. There are two pianos in the main house, one a music-reproducing baby grand in the dining room that plays itself during the complimentary wine and hors d'oeuvres hours.

Guest rooms are on the ground and second floors of the main house, with stunning views of the water through arched front windows upstairs in the Parke, Victorian, and Maries rooms. Other rooms are in what was once the carriage house off the courtyard. An abundance of antique mirrors brighten the rooms by reflecting the ever-changing light of the bay. Original fixtures grace the large bathrooms, which were recently retiled.

The inn has many common areas. The parlor, which occupies the glassed-in front of the house's main floor, lures guests to savor the stunning ocean view. A small library contains a personal collection of books and magazines, and two small solarium sitting rooms adjoin guest rooms on the ground and second floor. A games room contains an 1870 oak slate pool table, a 1917 nickelodeon, and a slot machine from the 1930s. Tucked in the back stables are three antique MGs from Don's collection of more than 20 classics from the 1920s to the 1950s.

Breakfast may be the best time of the day at the Martine. In the dining room, Marion serves up a lavish spread, including eggs poached in cream sauce, cereal, muffins, and fruit. Guests eat at large lace-clad tables set with Marion's best Sheffield silver and look out at a sweeping sea vista that competes with the food and decor for their attention.

⊞ *19 double rooms with baths. Phones, refrigerators, robes; fireplace in 7 rooms, daily newspaper, conference facilities, picnic meals available, garden, whirlpool bath. $130–$235; full breakfast, afternoon refreshments. MC, V. Restricted smoking, no pets, 2-night minimum on weekends, 3-night minimum on holidays.*

Old Monterey Inn

500 Martin St., Monterey, CA 93940, tel. 408/375–8284 or 800/350–2344, fax 408/375–6730

When Gene Swett was transferred to Monterey from the Bay Area in 1968, the family needed a house that was big enough for eight. Although the house they found, an English Tudor–style home built in 1929 by Carmel Martin, then the mayor of Monterey, was run down, the Swetts purchased it, reno-vated it, and created what would become one of the loveliest inns in California.

In the Old Monterey Inn, Ann and Gene Swett have elevated the business of inn keeping to a high art, offering their guests quietly elegant accommodations in a historic home—and the type of pampering that anticipates every need.

Outside, Gene made an oasis of year-round color. Inside was Ann's domain. She searched for antiques and furnishings to suit the ever-changing themes and color schemes of the rooms. Influenced by her travels, she continues to change the rooms to reflect her latest passion: The new American Room was influenced by an Andrew Wyeth exhibition Ann recently saw in Washington, DC. The room once known as Madrigal is now Serengeti, evoking a turn-of-the-century African safari, with mosquito netting over the bed, rattan chairs, pith helmets, antique leather hatboxes, and a brass-elephant birdcage stand. In the Library Room, floor-to-ceiling book-shelves contain volumes of nostalgic children's literature. The Brighstone Room feels almost like a tree house set in the upper branches of the massive oak just outside the window.

Guests have the option of having breakfast in bed. But unless you're honeymooning, consider, instead, being served in front of the fireplace in the formal dining room, at a table set for 14 with exquisite Oriental china or, weather permitting, in the Rose Garden. Guests dine on fruit, breads, and quiche, served course by course. Gene is the consummate host, mingling and getting to know each and every guest to determine food preferences before sending everyone off to dinner. He can also recommend a half dozen romantic picnic spots and advise guests on local galleries and shops worth a visit.

▥ *8 double rooms with baths, 1 suite, 1 cottage suite. Fireplace in 8 rooms,* *whirlpool bath in 1 room, robes, picnic baskets available. $170–$240; full breakfast, afternoon and evening refreshments. MC, V. Restricted smoking, no pets, 2-night minimum on weekends, 3-night minimum on holidays. Closed Christmas Day.*

Post Ranch Inn

Hwy. 1, Box 219, Big Sur, CA 93920, tel. 408/667–2200 or 800/527–2200, fax 408/667–2824

A significant new addition to northern California's high-end getaway circuit, Post Ranch Inn is on 98 secluded acres overlooking the Big Sur coastline. It blends elements of country inn, resort spa, and nature retreat into one seamlessly innovative package. "We don't fit any particular mold," declares general manager Larry Callahan. "We just fit Big Sur."

The redwood-and-steel individual units rest on either side of a quiet ridge-top trail; six more rooms are in the three-story Butterfly House. All include the same plentiful amenities, which range from king-size beds and hand-carved walking sticks to whirlpool tubs whose sliding windows yield a strictly private nature view.

As the first such venue approved by local politicos in 20 years, Post Ranch has embraced environmentally kind precepts and then some. Ocean-side cottages are built into the slope, their earth-covered roofs blending into the landscape—deer occasionally nibble at the wildflowers that grow there. "Mountainside" dwellings are mostly "tree-houses," built on stilts so as not to disturb existing ground vegetation. Floor plans are unique to each structure with the decor handsome but not fussy. The effect is both luxurious and in harmony with the tranquil surroundings.

Complementing the panoramic coastal views is commissioned artwork, scattered throughout the property. Their uniquely Californian style is echoed in room furniture, in the wooden benches along paths, and in Dan Wood's "rust"-ic custom steel grillwork. Next to the spectacularly situated Sierra Mar restaurant, where complimentary breakfast and optional prix fixe dinners are served, are a sundeck and a trellis-obscured Jacuzzi. Down the hill, past architect Mickey Muennig's striking reception/craft-store building, you'll find a 20-by-60-foot lap pool.

Up and running just since 1992, Post Ranch is still in the process of adding some new elements, such as a fully equipped health spa. But this "work-in-progress" is already one of the most distinctively designed, romantically secluded spots to be found anywhere.

▦ *29 double rooms with baths, 1 suite. Fireplace, whirlpool bath, private deck, stereo system, massage table, coffee-maker, hair dryer, robes, walking sticks in all rooms; basking and lap pools, guided walks/stargazing, yoga/exercise classes, picnic lunches, massage, aromatherapy, facials, tarot readings, gift shop, limousine service (fee) from Monterey. $285–$545; Continental breakfast, complimentary wine tastings. AE, MC, V. No smoking, no pets, 2-night minimum on weekends, 3-night minimum on holidays.*

Stonepine

150 E. Carmel Valley Rd., Carmel Valley, CA 93924, tel. 408/659-2245, fax 408/659-5160

To enter this fabulous 330-acre Carmel Valley estate, originally the weekend home of the Crocker banking family, you'll pass through two electronically controlled gates, drive by the Equestrian Center with its adjacent paddock, survey acres of oak-covered hillsides, and eventually pull into the parking area in front of the imposing, 1920s pale pink villa, where a Phantom V Rolls-Royce waits to whisk guests to the far corners of the manicured property.

The Mediterranean-style château, built in the 1920s, was designed for lavish entertaining. The elegantly appointed public rooms have graceful stone arches, Roman columns, and gracious gardens shaded by rare Italian stone pines. Walls separate the award-winning garden areas, including the rose garden, the perennial garden, the fruit garden, and the cutting garden, from the meadows behind the main house. Antiques abound: a hand-carved limestone fireplace from Italy in the grand living room; 18th-century French tapestries in the living room, the foyer, and the spiral staircase; a carved French writing desk in the Cartier bedroom; 18th-century burnished-oak paneling in the library and dining room.

Guest rooms in the château are elegantly but simply furnished with over-stuffed chairs and canopy beds. Bathrooms are dramatic, offering sweeping garden views, sunken marble Jacuzzis, and expansive marble countertops with double sinks. Tattinger, the original master bedroom, done in black and white, offers a sitting room–office, separate his and hers bathrooms, and a hidden tower room. Four bedrooms in the Paddock House are done in casual country plaids with horsey themes.

Lessons in horseback riding, both Western and English, hunter-jumping and dressage, and sulky and two-in-hand are available at the Equestrian Center, which stables a wide variety of breeds of well-groomed horses. This property dates back to the 1930s, when it was known as the Double H Ranch, then the foremost thoroughbred breeding farm in California.

Following an evening champagne and hors d'oeuvre reception, guests are escorted to dinner in the château dining room, where tables are set with Baccarat crystal, Limoges china, and sterling silverware. A typical six-course menu, prepared by two French chefs, offers choices such as roasted

Chateaubriand and sautéed salmon with dill beurre blanc, accompanied by soup, salad, dessert, Stilton, and port. Service here, as one might expect, is attentive and discreet.

🏨 *8 rooms with baths, 4 suites, 2 2-bedroom cottages. TV/VCR, fireplace, whirlpool bath, phone, robes in all rooms; video and book library, restaurant, room service, honor bar, picnic baskets, gardens, tennis, pool, croquet, archery, health club, hiking and riding trails, equestrian center. $225–$1,250, full breakfast; dinner ($65) available. AE, MC, V. No pets, 2-night minimum on weekends and holidays.*

Other Choices

Bayview Hotel. 8041 Soquel Dr., Aptos, CA 95003, tel. 408/688–8654 or 800/422–9843, fax 408/688–5128. 10 double rooms with baths; 1 2-room suite. Fireplace in 2 rooms, TV on request; restaurant, gardens. $90–$155, full breakfast. AE, MC, V. No smoking, no pets, 2-night minimum on weekends.

Blue Spruce Inn. 2815 S. Main St., Soquel, CA 95073, tel. 408/464–1137 or 800/559–1137, fax 408/475–0608. 6 double rooms with baths. Phone and computer-modem capacity in all rooms, fireplace in 5 rooms, whirlpool bath in 2 rooms, TV/VCR in 2 rooms, robes; gardens with outdoor hot tub, picnic baskets available. $90–$150; full breakfast, afternoon refreshments. AE, MC, V. No smoking, no pets, 2-night minimum on weekends.

Carmel Garden Court Inn. Torres and 4th Sts., Box 6226, Carmel, Ca 93921, tel. 408/624–6926, fax 408/624–4935. 9 double rooms with baths, 5 garden patio minisuites, 1 2-bedroom suite with full kitchen. Fireplaces, phones with modems, cable TV/VCRs, wet bars with refrigerators; gardens. $125–$245; expanded Continental breakfast, afternoon refreshments. AE, MC, V. No smoking.

The Centrella. 612 Central Ave., Pacific Grove, CA 93950, tel. 408/372–3372 or 800/233–3372, fax 408/372–2036. 16 double rooms with baths, 2 doubles share bath, 8 suites. Phones; cable TV in 15 rooms, refrigerator in 8 rooms, wet bar in suites, fireplace in 5 suites. $90–$195; expanded Continental breakfast, afternoon refreshments. MC, V. No smoking, no pets, children under 12 in garden suites only, 2-night minimum on weekends.

Cliff Crest Bed and Breakfast Inn. 407 Cliff St., Santa Cruz, CA 95060, tel. 408/427–2609, fax 408/427–2710. 5 double rooms with baths. Phones, robes; fireplace in 2 rooms, TV on request; free fitness center passes when available. $90–$150; full breakfast, evening refreshments. AE, D, MC, V. No smoking, no pets, 2-night minimum on weekends.

Country Rose Inn. 455 Fitzgerald Ave., No. E, San Martin, CA 95046, tel. 408/842–0441, fax 408/842–6646. 4 double rooms with baths, 1 suite. Air-conditioning, fireplace, whirlpool bath in 1 room, gardens, picnic baskets available. $89–$179; full breakfast, afternoon refreshments. MC, V. No smoking, no pets.

Cypress Inn. Lincoln and 7th St., Box Y, Carmel, CA 93921, tel. 408/624–3871 or 800/443–7443, fax 408/624–8216. 34 double rooms with baths, 4 with separate entrances. Cable TVs, free decanters of sherry, fruit baskets, bottled water; daily newspaper; courtyard and gardens. $95–$245; full breakfast, afternoon refreshments. AE, MC, V. No smoking, 2-night minimum on weekends.

Gosby House. 643 Lighthouse Ave., Pacific Grove, CA 93950, tel. 408/375–1287. 20 double rooms with baths, 2 doubles share bath. Phone in all rooms, whirlpool bath in 2 rooms, fireplace in 12 rooms, picnic baskets and wine available, bicycles. $85–$150; full breakfast, afternoon refreshments. AE, MC, V. No smoking, no pets.

Los Laureles Lodge. 313 W. Carmel Valley Rd., Box 2310, Carmel Valley, CA 93924, tel. 408/659–2233 or 800/533–4404, fax 408/659–0481. Lodge: 25 rooms with baths, 6 suites; Hill House: 3 bedrooms with 2 baths. Air-conditioning, cable TVs; conference facilities; pool, spa, massage on-call, game room, bar, restaurant, equestrian facilities, garden, outdoor barbecue. $80–$450, Continental breakfast. AE, MC, V. Some no-smoking rooms, no pets, 2-night minimum on weekends.

Robles Del Rio Lodge. 200 Punta del Monte, Carmel Valley, CA 93924, tel. 408/659–3705 or 800/833–0843, fax 408/659–5157. 22 double rooms with baths, 4 suites with kitchenettes, 4 1-bedroom cottages with fireplaces and kitchenettes, 1 2-bedroom house with full kitchen, laundry, outside terraced patio and barbecue pit. Cable TVs; fireside conference room for up to 40, bar; restaurant, pool, sauna and whirlpool bath, tennis court, outside barbecue, gazebo, porch, hot tub under oak trees. $99–$275, full breakfast, AE, MC, V. No smoking, no pets, 2-night minimum on weekends, 3-night minimum on holidays.

Seven Gables Inn/Grand View Inn. Seven Gables: 555 Ocean View Blvd., Pacific Grove, CA 93950, tel. 408/372–4341. Grand View: 557 Ocean View Blvd., Pacific Grove, CA 93950, tel. 408/372–4341. Seven Gables: 14 double rooms with baths. Grand View: 10 double rooms with baths. Picnic baskets, refrigerators, gardens, parking. Seven Gables: $125–$225, Grand View: $125–$185; full breakfast, afternoon tea at both. MC, V. No smoking, 2-night minimum on weekends, 3-night minimum on holidays.

Reservations Service

Tourist Information Room Finders (tel. 408/624–1711 or 800/847–8066).

San Francisco from North Beach to the Sunset District

Archbishops Mansion

1000 Fulton St., San Francisco, CA 94117, tel. 415/563–7872 or 800/543–5820, fax 415/885–3193

The Archbishops Mansion is an elegant European manor reborn in San Francisco. The Second Empire–style residence, built in 1904 for Archbishop Patrick Riordan, faces Alamo Square and its "postcard row" of restored Victorians. Designers Jonathan Shannon and Jeffrey Ross have restored the home, now managed by Joie de Vivre Hotels, to that era of opulence. Ornate Belle Epoque furnishings and reproductions, such as the crystal chandelier that hung in Scarlett O'Hara's beloved Tara in *Gone With the Wind*, fill the rooms. Everything about the mansion—the scale, the ornamentation, the Napoléon III antiques—is extravagant.

A three-story redwood staircase rises majestically from the coffered foyer. Above, sunlight filters through a 16-foot-wide, oval leaded-glass dome, which miraculously survived the 1906 earthquake. While you sip your complimentary evening wine in the front parlor, which is dominated by a massive redwood fireplace with fluted Corinthian columns, you'll be serenaded from the hall by a 1904 ebony Bechstein piano once owned by Noel Coward.

Inspired by the Opera House several blocks away, guest rooms are unabashedly romantic. The gold-hued Don Giovanni Suite conveys a Renaissance formality and, not surprisingly, has an impressive bed. The zebrawood canopy four-poster bed found in a castle in southern France was masterfully carved during the Napoleonic period.

The Carmen Suite's outstanding feature is its bathroom: A claw-foot tub sits in front of a fireplace to enhance your soaking pleasure. A second fireplace warms the Carmen's bedroom, where the 1885 settee has its original horsehair covering. Billowing draperies, canopied beds, and ceramic-tile fireplaces are routine here.

A breakfast of bakery muffins, cakes, and tea or coffee is brought to your room on a silver tray, or you can join the other guests in the formal dining room for an expanded Continental breakfast. Complimentary wine and hors d'oeuvres are offered in the early evening in the parlor.

🏠 *10 double rooms with baths, 5 suites. Phones, cable TVs; fireplace in 11 rooms, robes in 7 rooms, whirlpool bath in 2 suites; elevator, laundry service, room service for wine, beer, and snacks, conference facilities. $129– $385; Continental breakfast, evening refreshments. AE, MC, V. Restricted smoking, no pets, 2-night minimum on weekends.*

Chateau Tivoli

1057 Steiner St., San Francisco, CA 94115, tel. 415/776–5462 or 800/228– 1647, fax 415/776–0505

A stay in this ornate fin de siècle château in the historic Alamo Square district may forever alter your decorating sensibilities. Built in 1892, this historic painted lady wears no fewer than 22 colors, from raisin brown to turquoise, with ornamentation picked out in 23-karat gold leaf.

The château's past is even more colorful than its exterior. Designed by 19th-century British architect William Armitage, the house once belonged to lumber baron Daniel Jackson and later to Mrs. Ernestine Kreling, owner of San Francisco's Tivoli Opera House. Over the past few decades, when the Alamo Square district saw some rough times, the building was everything from a halfway house to a famed ashram. Current owners Rodney Karr and Willard Gersbach purchased the château from new-age guru Jack Painter in 1985.

Rodney and Willard have carried the flamboyant appearance of the exterior inside, tightly packing every room, hallway, and wall with antique furnishings and art (some from the estates of Cornelius Vanderbilt and Charles de Gaulle), housewares, knickknacks, and a somewhat haunting taxidermy collection. Competing for attention are the cornices and carved oak paneling of the entrance hall, double parlor, and staircase.

The riotous, museumlike quality of the château's busy public areas is carried over into the guest rooms. A sultan and his elephant could both stay comfortably in the glorious Mark Twain suite; its Renaissance Revival–style parlor alone is 500 square feet. Romantics will relish the Luisa Tettrazine suite's marble bath with double showerhead, huge French Renaissance canopy bed, and frescoed ceilings. Five additional bedrooms are equally spacious. From the bowed windows and Aesthetic Movement furniture in the Joaquin Miller room to the intimate tower dining nook and French wash walls of the Jack London room, there's something at the Chateau Tivoli for anyone open to the owners' flair for dramatic decorating. The only drawback is the neighborhood, which can be a tad dicey at night and is sometimes noisy.

A Continental breakfast of muffins or croissants, cereals, juices, and fresh fruit is served at a grand dining room table that seats eight, with a more intimate table for two nearby. A champagne brunch is served on Saturdays and Sundays.

🏠 *1 double room with bath, 4 doubles share 2 baths, 1 suite, 1 double suite, 1 2-bedroom suite with cave grotto ceilings, bath, sitting area and private*

street entrance on ground level.
Phones; fireplace in 1 room and 1 suite.
$80–$200; Continental breakfast week-
days, champagne brunch weekends,
complimentary wine and beverages.
AE, MC, V. No smoking.

Inn at the Opera

333 Fulton St., San Francisco, CA
94102, tel. 415/863–8400 or 800/325–
2708, fax 415/861–0821

Half-hidden behind the Opera House
(currently undergoing a seismic up-
grade, as is nearby City Hall) and the
Veterans Building, near the Civic Center, this impeccable inn with its lavish
floral arrangements and elegant furnishings manages to be a paradigm of
superb taste without being stuffy. In
1986, owner-manager Tom Noonan
turned a neglected seven-story hotel
into a resplendent hideaway for performing artists and their fans: Mikhail
Baryshnikov, Luciano Pavarotti, Her-
bie Hancock, and Dizzy Gillespie are
among the notables who have stayed
here. Noonan is a congenial host, overseeing every detail and maintaining the
inn's reputation for fine service and
hospitality.

The plush little lobby, all pale green
with Oriental porcelain and damask
chairs, resembles the foyer of a European inn. Excellent American grill cuisine is served in the adjoining Act IV
restaurant, against the swank backdrop of wood paneling, tapestry-covered walls, leather chairs, and a green
marble fireplace; a formally dressed
pianist plays old standards on a glossy
black grand. The inn offers a package
including show, dinner, dessert and
champagne, and overnight accommodations.

The hotel's 47 rooms are discreetly
romantic, glowing with pastel colors and
Old World finesse, from the half-canopy
beds and fluffy pillows to the handsome antique armoires and gorgeously
framed color reproductions of delicately

etched flowers and birds. Subtle grace
notes abound, such as a basket of red
apples and armoire drawers lined with
sheet music. Under filmy curtains and
drawn-back drapes, window shades
gently let in the morning light through a
lacy diamond-shape cutout near the bottom. Larger suites have two bedrooms,
each linked to its own bath, and a central
sitting room with a well-stocked minibar
and microwave. Guests can have a complimentary European-style breakfast
brought to their rooms with a morning
newspaper or head for Act IV's buffet
breakfast. Those in the know prefer the
rooms in the back, as the front ones do
get street noise.

▦ *30 double rooms with baths, 17*
suites. Cable TVs; 2-line phone with
data port, minibar, robes, microwave in
suites, irons and ironing boards, hair
dryers available, fireplace in restau-
rant/bar, morning newspapers, compli-
mentary pressing on arrival, overnight
shoeshine, 24-hr room service, busi-
ness-secretarial service, laundry ser-
vice, packing service, staff physician,
complimentary limousine service to
financial district, valet parking. $125–
$260. AE, MC, V. 4 no-smoking floors.

Mansions Hotel

2220 Sacramento St., San Francisco,
CA 94115, tel. 415/929–9444 or 800/
826–9398, fax 415/567–9391

If inns were awarded prizes for show-
manship, the Mansions Hotel would
win top honors. First, there's the
decapitated head of the resident ghost,
Claudia, who reads minds. And where
else can you see the innkeeper, clad in
sequined dinner jacket, play the saw?
They're just part of the live "magic
extravaganzas" held every weekend at
the Mansions.

The inspiration behind this zaniness is
the aforementioned innkeeper, Bob Pritikin. The author of *Christ Was an*
Adman, Pritikin isn't afraid of innova-
tion in his hotel, two adjacent Queen

Anne Victorians a short walk from the chic boutiques and eateries of Pacific Heights. The cabaret, free to overnight guests, also draws diners from the highly praised hotel restaurant.

The Mansions Hotel is as visually flamboyant as its entertainment, although the west wing has a simpler, country-inn look. In the public areas no surface has been left unembellished. Objects, wall murals, curios (a selection of ugly ties, for example), and sculptures, many by Beniamino Bufano, are everywhere. The porcine theme in the room known as the International Pig Museum is tough to miss, surrounded as you are by an old wooden carousel pig and wall painting depicting a swine-filled picnic in progress.

All of the east-wing rooms have murals that depict the famous San Francisco personage for whom the room is named. The authentic and Victorian reproduction decor might include a rolltop desk, four-poster canopy bed, and Tiffany-style lamp. The west-wing rooms have Laura Ashley flower-print wallpaper and matching bedding, with a preponderance of pine furniture. Particularly lavish is the Louis IV room, where such guests as Barbra Streisand, Robert Stack, and Michael York have enjoyed the immense gold-leaf half-tester bed and wardrobe and private redwood deck.

A full breakfast of fresh fruit, cereal, eggs cooked to order, potatoes, and juice can be delivered to your room. There you'll find a traditional "Chinese crystal ball" to take home. According to legend, rub it gently and your fondest wish will come true.

▦ *13 double rooms with baths, 8 suites. Phones; fireplace in suites, whirlpool bath in 1 room, restaurant, evening entertainment, complimentary newspaper and coffee, limited room service, laundry service, billiard table. $129–$350, full breakfast. AE, D, DC, MC, V.*

Queen Anne

1590 Sutter St., San Francisco, CA 94109, tel. 415/441–2828 or 800/227–3970, fax 415/775–5212

This majestic, four-story Victorian ranks among the loveliest of San Francisco's classic painted ladies. Its rose and green gables and distinctive corner turret rise proudly above a neighborhood of vivid Victorians in lower Pacific Heights; walking tours of this colorful district can be arranged at the hotel. Japantown with its restaurants and the Fillmore shopping area are just around the corner.

The building's roots as a luxurious boarding school for girls (not to mention its later incarnations as a bordello and a private men's club), constructed by silver mogul and Senator James G. Fair in 1890, still show in its rich cedar and oak paneling and the lofty staircase winding four flights up to an antique skylight. A sprawling lobby full of Victoriana—from brocade chairs to crimson walls—encompasses most of the ground floor. Guests can curl up with coffee or sherry before a crackling fire or partake of the breakfast buffet here each morning (many prefer to take a tray back to their room). Among the offerings at breakfast are English coffee cake, raspberry and blueberry scones, a variety of fruit juices and as many as 10 different teas.

The hotel's spacious public area, which fans into adjoining conference chambers, makes it ideal for weddings and business meetings. The front-desk staff is adept at attending to guests's faxing, computing, secretarial and copying needs.

All the rooms and suites are different, blending contemporary comforts with historic accents. The plush carpeting, modern bedspreads, and hair dryers in the baths are offset by old-fashioned details such as brass-necked lamps, English antiques, and lacy curtains. Fireplaces warm many quarters; one enormous room has two brick hearths at either end. The accommodations, large for a small hotel, range from a two-bedroom, split-level town house with a private deck to a snug top-story room with slanted ceilings and a framed picture of George Washington.

🏨 *45 double rooms with baths, 3 suites, 1 town house suite. Phone and cable TV in all rooms, fireplace in 10 rooms, minifridge in suites, fireplace in parlor, irons and ironing boards available, conference and reception facilities, concierge-secretarial service, laundry service, morning newspaper, complimentary morning limousine downtown. $99–$275; Continental breakfast, afternoon tea and sherry. AE, D, DC, MC, V. No pets.*

Sherman House

2160 Green St., San Francisco, CA 94123, tel. 415/563-3600 or 800/424-5777, fax 415/563-1882

The words "crème de la crème" best describe this French-Italianate white mansion in Pacific Heights a block off Union Street. More showcase than home-sweet-home, the Sherman House exudes old money, from the silken-striped Empire chairs of the second-floor gallery-salon and the sweeping staircase to the Old World splendor of the music hall. There are, however, homey touches such as soft lighting, window seats, piped-in classical music, and finches who chirp sweetly from an enormous cage modeled on a French château.

Built in 1876 by music lover–instrument maker Leander Sherman, the house once attracted patrons and world-class musicians such as Enrico Caruso and pianist Jan Paderewski, who performed in the magnificent music hall; string quartet and piano concerts still make the chandeliers quiver today. Iranian economist Manouchehr Mobedshahi and his art historian wife, Vesta, saved this urban palace from demolition when they bought and

restored it in 1980. Designer William Gaylord added antiques and objets d'art from estates and auctions, largely in French Second Empire style. A solarium with diamond-shape windowpanes and a connecting chamber lit by a flickering fire make up the petite (and expensive) in-house restaurant, which serves superb French-inspired cuisine and is for guests only. At press time there were plans to offer rates inclusive of meals.

Great care went into the guest rooms, one more sumptuous than the next. Marble fireplaces with gas jets, bowls of heady potpourri, and featherbeds enclosed in heavy drapery are common denominators. The dark, wood-beamed, and wainscoted look of the Biedermeier and Paderewski suites contrasts sharply with the airy feel of the Leander Sherman Suite; its enormous rooftop terrace with a view of the Golden Gate Bridge could hold a party of 25. Behind the main house, half an acre of garden—a princely estate in land-pinched San Francisco—encircles a carriage house containing the hotel's largest, priciest quarters, the Garden Suite. Decorated in a rattan motif, with a house-in-the-country aura and its own gazebo and private garden, this set of rooms is popular with honeymooners.

🏨 *8 double rooms with baths, 6 suites. Phones, cable TV with stereo, robes, hair dryers, whirlpool bath or Roman-style tub in 10 rooms, fireplace in 13 rooms; restaurant, music room, concierge, personal valet service, massage service, chauffeur available, laundry service, 24-hr room service, business-secretarial services, valet parking, garden. $295–$825, breakfast extra. AE, D, MC, V. Restricted smoking, no pets.*

White Swan Inn

845 Bush St., San Francisco, CA 94108, tel. 415/775-1755 or 800/999-9570, fax 415/775-5717

Fireplaces in every room, romantic furnishings, delicious food, top-notch amenities, and a location just four blocks from Union Square make the White Swan Inn one of the premier bed-and-breakfasts in San Francisco. This circa-1908 building has the look of a London town house, and the decoration is studiously English. Walk into the library, and you'll think you've been admitted to an exclusive gentleman's club, with tufted wing chairs; rich, dark wood; sparkling brass fixtures and hardware; hunting scenes on the pillows; and a red tartan couch.

The guest rooms, predominantly green and burgundy with touches of yellow and rose, have a more informal look than the public rooms. All are similarly furnished with reproduction Edwardian pieces in cherry and other dark woods. Four-poster beds, wing-back or barrel chairs, TVs enclosed in an armoire or a cabinet, wooden shutters, and Laura Ashley–style floral wallpaper are standard in most rooms. Four rooms have bay windows. A bedside switch allows you to control the gas fireplaces.

The hotel is one of the Four Sisters Inns group, owned and operated by the Post family, and often, a family member will greet guests in the common rooms. Their trademark teddy bears cuddle in the reception area, peeking through banisters and perched on the mantel over the perpetually lit fire. A plush bear also adorns each guest room.

The Four Sisters properties are known for their food, so you're urged to find an excuse to be back at the White Swan in the afternoon. You'll be rewarded by such complimentary snacks as lemon cake, vegetables with curry dip, stuffed grape leaves, and specialty cheeses, accompanied by wine, sherry, and other drinks. Typical breakfast fare includes Mexican quiche, soda-bread toast, Swiss oatmeal, fresh fruit, granola, and doughnuts. Everything is homemade. Guests have made so many requests for the recipes that the family has released its own cookbook.

▥ *23 double rooms with baths, 3 suites. Phones, TVs, wet bars, refrigerators, hair dryers, robes; laundry service, conference and catering facilities, coffee and wine room service, complimentary newspaper and shoe-shine service, valet parking available. $145–$250; full breakfast, afternoon refreshments. AE, DC, MC, V. No smoking, no pets.*

Other Choices

Anna's Three Bears. 114 Divisadero, San Francisco, CA 94117, tel. 415/255–3167 or 800/428–8559, fax 415/552–2959. 3 suites. Cable TV, clock radios, fireplace, fax. $225–$295, Continental breakfast. AE, MC, V. Restricted smoking, no pets, 2-night minimum stay on weekends.

Auberge des Artistes. 829 Fillmore St., San Francisco, CA 94117, tel. 415/776–2530 or 415/775–7334, fax 415/441–8242. 2 double rooms with bath, 1 shared bath, 2 suites. Fireplace in 3 rooms, clock radios, parking $5 per night, full kitchen and phone on each floor, picnic baskets arranged on request. $55–$100, full breakfast. AE, D, MC, V. No smoking.

Bed and Breakfast Inn. 4 Charlton Ct., San Francisco, CA 94123, tel. 415/921–9784. 5 double rooms with baths, 4 doubles share 3 baths, 2 housekeeping suites. Phone in 7 rooms, TV in 6 rooms, complimentary coffee, sherry in rooms with baths and in parlor. $70–$275, Continental breakfast. No credit cards. Restricted smoking, no pets.

Dolores Park Inn. 3641 17th St., San Francisco, CA 94114, tel. and fax 415/621–0482 or 415/861–9335. 3 rooms (one single and two doubles) share 3 baths, 1 suite, carriage house. Air-conditioning, TVs, clock radios, fireplaces. $40–$75, expanded Continental breakfast. No credit cards. No pets, no smoking, 2-night minimum, 3-night minimum for carriage house.

Inn at Union Square. 440 Post St., San Francisco, CA 94102, tel. 415/397–3510 or 800/288–4346, fax 415/989–0529. 23 double rooms with baths, 7 suites. Phones, cable TVs; fireplace in 2 rooms, wet bar in 2 rooms, whirlpool bath, sauna, and refrigerator in 1 suite, complimentary newspaper and shoeshine service, laundry service, room service, honor bar, catered dinner in room available, valet parking. $130–$300; Continental breakfast, refreshments. AE, DC, MC, V. No smoking, no pets.

Inn San Francisco. 943 South Van Ness Ave., San Francisco, CA 94110, tel. 415/641–0188 or 800/359–0913, fax 415/641–1701. 17 double rooms with baths, 5 doubles share 2 baths. Phones, TVs, refrigerators, clock radios; hot tub on deck of 1 room, whirlpool bath in 5 rooms, fireplace in 4 rooms, hot tub in garden. $75–$195; full buffet breakfast; complimentary tea, coffee, and sherry. AE, D, DC, MC, V, personal checks. Restricted smoking.

Jackson Court. 2198 Jackson St., San Francisco, CA 94115, tel. 415/929–7670. 10 double rooms with baths. Phones, TVs; fireplace in 2 rooms, fireplace in lobby. $125–$180; Continental breakfast, afternoon tea and cookies. AE, MC, V. No smoking, no pets.

Nob Hill Inn. 1000 Pine St., San Francisco, CA 94109, tel. 415/673–6080, fax 415/673–6098. 3 single rooms with baths, 12 double rooms with baths, 6 suites. Phones, cable TVs, gas fireplaces. $89–$229; Continental breakfast, afternoon tea and sherry service. AE, MC, V. Restricted smoking, no pets.

Petite Auberge. 863 Bush St., San Francisco, CA 94108, tel. 415/928–6000 or 800/365–3004, fax 415/775–5717. 26 double rooms with baths. Phones, TVs; fireplace in 13 rooms, whirlpool bath in 1 room, laundry service, coffee and wine room service, valet parking. $110–$220; full breakfast, afternoon refreshments. AE, DC, MC, V. No smoking, no pets.

Victorian Inn on the Park. 301 Lyon St., San Francisco, CA 94117, tel. 415/931–1830 or 800/435–1967, fax 415/931–1830. 12 double rooms with baths, 1 suite, 1 double suite with 2 baths. Phones, clock radios; fireplace in 2 rooms, TV available, meeting facilities. $99–$320, Continental breakfast. AE, D, DC, MC, V. Restricted smoking, no pets, 2-night minimum on weekends, 3-night minimum on holiday weekends.

Washington Square Inn. 1660 Stockton St., San Francisco, CA 94133, tel. 415/981–4220 or 800/388–0220, fax 415/397–7242. 10 double rooms with baths, 5 doubles share 2 baths. Phones; TV on request, complimentary newspaper and shoe-shine service, laundry service, room service for beer, wine, and soft drinks, valet parking ($17). $95–$185; Continental breakfast, afternoon refreshments. AE, D, DC, MC, V. No smoking, no pets.

Reservations Services

Bed & Breakfast International (Box 282910, San Francisco, CA 94128–2910, tel. 415/696–1690 or 800/872–4500, fax 415/696–1699). **Bed & Breakfast San Francisco** (Box 420009, San Francisco, CA 94142, tel. 415/479–1913, fax 415/921–2273).

Bay Area, Including Marin, East Bay, and the Peninsula

Captain Walsh House

235 East L St., Benicia, CA 94510, tel. 707/747–5653, fax 707/747–6265

Reed and Steve Robbins didn't start out intending to be innkeepers. But once they began remodeling the 1849 Captain Walsh House, they realized the house was too much for just the two of them. The inn opened as a bed-and-breakfast in 1991; a fifth guest room was added last fall. Reed, an architectural designer, and Steve, a former IBM salesman, did all the work themselves: opening up fireplaces, enlarging closets, adding bathrooms, installing molding, painting floors and walls. The result is an unusual inn, where every square foot reflects the owners' personalities, tastes and quirks.

The house was built as a wedding gift for Epiphania, a daughter of General Mariano G. Vallejo, who lived in a matching home in Sonoma that is now run by the California State Park Department. A few years later, the home was purchased by Captain John Walsh, a retired sea captain who presided over the Customs House in Benicia, and his wife Eleanor, whose spirit is rumored to visit the house from time to time.

While no two rooms are alike, certain themes and elements repeat: gargoyles, Gothic shapes, family crest forms and quirky collections of stuffed animals (not of the teddy bear variety, but real dead animals, attractively preserved, of course). Epiphania's Room, which has a view of the Carquinez Strait, is decorated in lavish ivory fabrics that engulf the canopied four-poster bed set in the center of the room. To one side is a classic claw-foot tub—but with 24-karat gold claws! The Harvest Room is dominated by a walnut Gothic armoire and matching bed and a fireplace made of white brick. Regency furniture adorns the Salon guest room which has a marble fireplace offset by gilt-edge Gothic wall panels. The Library (another guest room) has vaulted ceilings, dark-green walls, shelves lined with books, and a private reading loft that resembles an elaborate crow's nest, inevitably evoking thoughts of old Captain Walsh.

The parlor is decorated in similar whimsy, mixing old things, such as antique chairs and mirrors, with new finds, such as elegant fabrics. Reed haunts the local antiques shops to continually add to the collections in the house, whether it's a mixed set of antique luggage, or a bountiful supply of old silver trays that come in handy when wedding receptions are booked at the inn.

Breakfast is a fancy affair, with such items as smoked-pheasant omelet, apple pancakes, and crab crepes on the menu; orange juice is fresh-squeezed from the trees on the inn's property.

▦ *5 double rooms with baths. Air-conditioning, TVs; phone in 2 rooms. $110, full breakfast. AE, D, DC, MC, V. No smoking, no pets.*

Casa Madrona Hotel

801 Bridgeway, Sausalito, CA 94965, tel. 415/332-0502 or 800/567-9524, fax 415/332-2537

Occupying an enviable hillside in the heart of Sausalito, Casa Madrona is several inns in one. There are 100-year-old rooms, cozy cottages and highly contemporary accommodations, all located at different levels above the main street, Bridgeway, which runs along the shoreline of Richardson Bay.

The Casa Madrona was a decaying 1885 Victorian mansion that was on the verge of tumbling from its steep hillside perch above the Sausalito Marina until John Mays renovated and reopened it as a hotel during the late 1970s. The New Casa, a multilevel addition, is stepped down to the street below like an Italian hill town.

The New Casa's guest rooms all share a magnificent view of the marina across the street, Belvedere and Angel islands, and the forested hills of Tiburon beyond. Many rooms have private balconies. Each room has a distinct personality. The Renoir Room, hung with prints of the artist's work, has a window seat, large deck, fireplace, and, in the bathroom, a claw-foot tub surrounded by an impressionistic mural of a flower garden. In the Artist's Loft, an easel and watercolor paints, set beneath a skylight, await your talents.

Guest rooms in the original Victorian building are decorated in period style, with high ceilings, Victorian-era American furniture, and four-poster or brass beds. Rooms facing east or south have views. There are also five cottages, each with a different decor.

Casa Madrona is more small hotel than homey bed-and-breakfast, and except for a large outdoor deck at the New Casa, the Victorian's parlor and balcony are the inn's only common areas. In the evening, wine, cheese, and fruit are served in the parlor, and guests can relax in the antique settees or in the balcony's wicker chairs while taking the night air.

A buffet-style breakfast is served in the Mikayla Restaurant, attached to an upper level of the New Casa just below the original building. Designed by local artist Laurel Burch, it opened in 1995. A 12-foot mural of a sea goddess, complete with flowing hair festooned with sea creatures and flowers, sets the sort of abstract mythic tone for which Burch's jewelry is known. Likewise, colors are vivid and on the rich, dark side of the spectrum, and there are scatterings of art pieces from unnamed foreign lands, such as urns, vases and whimsical fish fashioned from terracotta. The restaurant has a dining terrace with retractable roof and sliding glass walls, which are opened in decent weather to enhance the stupendous view of the bay and parts of San Francisco. Casa Madrona's owner knows better than to even think about dethroning Neptune as god of the kitchen. Seafood reigns supreme, though the cooking is billed as "American West Coast Cuisine with a Healthy Influence." Chef Terry Lynch oversees a menu that emphasizes ethnic accents such as ahi tuna with chili and lime and caramelized scallops with snap peas, jalapeños and bacon.

🏨 *27 double rooms with baths, 3 suites, five cottages. Phones; TV in 23 rooms, fireplace in 18 rooms, minibar in 17 rooms, room service during restaurant hours, conference facilities, business and secretarial services, outdoor hot tub, valet parking. $105–$245, Continental breakfast. AE, MC, V. No smoking in restaurant, 2-night minimum on weekends.*

Inn at Occidental

3657 Church St., Occidental, CA 95465, tel. 707/874–1047 or 800/522–6324, fax 707/874–1078

Although many country inns boast antiques and collectibles, it's unlikely you'll see anything on the order of Jack Bullard's place. The decor of each room at this hillside inn was inspired by a different collection amassed over the years by the East Coast native who remodeled this home in 1994. The Ivory Room, for example, has a grouping of dramatic antique ivory carvings used by the Japanese as toggles to hold their money and other valuables when they wore the traditional kimono. Contemporary photographs and antique English and cut-glass jars dating back to the mid-1800's (the latter placed in cabinets designed to enhance their beauty) make the Cut Glass Room distinctive. Most unusual of all is the Leaf Umbrella Room, which displays a portion of the innkeeper's collection of cranberry and blue leaf-umbrella pattern glass objects.

Other rooms in this light-filled country inn have their own allotment of treasures. In the Tiffany Room, Tiffany silver is set out near the four-poster mahogany Charleston queen bed, complete with matching canopy, dust ruffle and window treatments. The Sugar Suite (accessible for visitors with disabilities) is furnished with an antique pine king-size bed and a patio overlooking the courtyard and English country garden. It is named for the shelves laden with 19th-century pattern glass made to hold the then-coarsely ground sugar. Anyone who remembers real marbles will probably want to stay in the Marble Suite, where marbles of all materials and colors are a major accent, along with an antique pine bed and a watercolor of koi fish. Dedham Pottery is named for the early 20th-century blue-and-white crackle-glaze dishware on display here, where a view to the south and west includes Occidental's community church and steeple against a background of California redwoods.

Many of the rooms are also supplied with boldly patterned quilts in the event of cool country nights. Throughout the inn are Bullard's many black-and-white photographs, most of them nature scenes and many the work of the innkeeper himself.

Oriental rugs set out on pristine hardwood floors give the pale yellow living room a cozy but sophisticated look. The ground-floor room is also decorated with some of Bullard's many books, silver pieces and unusual antique clocks. Even with lots of fresh flowers, mostly orchids, added to this eclectic mix, the place manages not to look cluttered, only interesting.

Visitors who have dined the previous night at one of the family-style restaurants for which the town of Occidental is known may have gone to bed thinking they'd never be hungry again. But when they are seated on wicker chairs on the inn's sunporch, and served fresh fruit and East Coast specialties such as Vermont maple syrup poured over apple-thyme pancakes, they may change their minds. Although the shops and restaurants are only steps away, guests may prefer to linger on the wide veranda or in the landscaped garden.

▦ *6 double rooms with baths, 2 suites. Phones; TV in 1 suite (portable TV on request), conference room. $125–$195, full breakfast. AE, D, MC, V. No smoking, no pets.*

Mill Rose Inn

615 Mill St., Half Moon Bay, CA 94019, tel. 415/726–8750 or 800/900–7673, fax 415/726–3031

Set amid a lush flower garden, the Mill Rose Inn is one of the most indulgent, romantic hostelries in northern California. The word *pampered* takes on new meaning here—guests are provided virtually everything they need for a carefree stay. Most of the guest rooms have Eastlake and Arts and Crafts antique furnishings, brass beds, down comforters, billowing draperies, and fireplaces framed with hand-painted tiles. All come equipped with a stereo, TV with VCR, refrigerator stocked with beverages, fruit and nut basket, candies, coffeemaker with herb teas and cocoa, sherry and brandy, hair dryer, and more. Sinfully rich desserts are always available in the parlor, and you'll wake to a generous champagne breakfast.

The Mill Rose Inn is 30 miles south of San Francisco, in the ocean-side hamlet of Half Moon Bay. Innkeepers Eve and Terry Baldwin both hold degrees in horticulture and take full advantage of the gentle climate. The front garden is an explosion of color, with more than 200 varieties of roses, lilies, sweet peas, daisies, Iceland poppies, irises, delphiniums, lobelias, and foxgloves, all framed by the inn's crisp white exterior. Tourists and local residents stop by just to photograph the spectacular floral displays. In the town's historic district, the inn is five blocks from Half Moon Bay and a short drive to Pacific coast beaches.

In contrast to the building's spare exterior, virtually no corner of the guest rooms has gone undecorated. Each is done in rich, deep tones with floral-patterned wall coverings, burgundy carpeting, custom-made brass chandeliers and wall sconces, and watercolor paintings. All have private entrances opening to a balcony that faces the back courtyard, with its hanging potted flowers, brick patio, and whirlpool spa secluded in an old-fashioned gazebo.

In the breakfast room, bouquets on each table and a fire in the hearth, with its hand-painted tiles reading "Welcome All to Hearth and Hall," set the stage for evening desserts and sumptuous breakfasts. Courses might include an orange-banana frappé, fresh fruit, raspberry crème fraîche soufflé, crisp bacon, enormous croissants, local champagne, and Mexican hot chocolate made with cinnamon and almonds.

▦ *4 double rooms with baths, 2 suites. Phones, TV/VCR, stereo, clothes steamers in all rooms, fireplace in 5 rooms, conference facility. $165–$265; full breakfast, afternoon wine and snacks. AE, D, MC, V. No smoking, no pets, 2-night minimum on weekends.*

Pelican Inn

Star Rte. (Hwy. 1), Muir Beach, CA 94965, tel. 415/383–6000, fax 415/383–3424

Upon first seeing the Pelican Inn, you may think you've taken a wrong turn and somehow stumbled into the English countryside. Just off Highway 1 in Marin County, the Pelican Inn is fronted by a formal English garden and set in an expanse of lush lawn. This whitewashed Tudor with black timbers is a replica of a 16th-century British inn—the realized dream of Englishman Charles Felix, who built it in 1977.

Now run by Englishman Barry Stock, the hostelry is a favorite stopping place for San Franciscans out to celebrate a special occasion and for tourists visiting the nearby Muir Woods. Muir Beach is just a short walk from the inn.

Guests are especially drawn to the Pelican's pub. Amiable bartenders, a dart board, an assortment of beers, stouts, and ales, and an inviting selection of ports, sherries, and British dishes create a convivial setting. The aptly named Snug is a parlor set aside for registered guests only. English-coun-

try antiques, old books, prints and curiosities that Stock has brought back from his homeland, as well as a comfortable sitting area by the wood-burning fireplace, make this an ideal sanctuary.

The inn's restaurant is right out of Merry Olde England, with heavy wooden tables, and a dark, time-worn atmosphere, enhanced by foxhunt prints and an immense walk-in hearth with large cast-iron fittings. During breakfast and dinner, the room is lit only by the fireplace, the tall red tapers on each table, and cut-tin lanterns on the walls. Tasty, moderately priced meals include beef Wellington, prime rib, and chicken dishes. Breakfast, served here or in your room, is hearty fare, with eggs cooked to order, breakfast meats, and toasted breads. Lunch specialties include bangers and mash and fish-and-chips as well as pastas and salads. In the backyard beer garden, sunlight filters through a greenery-entwined trellis, and a brick fireplace keeps things cozy.

Planked doors with latches open to the guest rooms, some of which are decorated with antiques from different periods. Each room has leaded, multipane windows, Oriental scatter rugs, English prints, heavy velvet draperies, hanging tapestries, and half-tester beds. Even the bathrooms are special, with Victorian-style hardware and hand-painted tiles in the shower.

▦ *7 double rooms with baths. Restaurant and pub, garden. $145–$165, full breakfast. MC, V. No pets, closed Christmas Eve and Christmas Day.*

Other Choices

Bancroft Hotel. 2680 Bancroft Way, Berkeley, CA 94704, tel. 510/549–1000 or 800/549–1002, fax 510/549–1070. 22 double rooms with baths. Phones, cable TVs; balconies off 6 rooms, conference facilities, next-door parking ($6 per day), café adjacent. $89–$99, Continental breakfast. AE, DC, MC, V. No smoking, no pets, 2-night minimum on weekends.

Blackthorne Inn. 266 Vallejo Ave., Box 712, Inverness Park, CA 94937, tel. 415/663–8621. 3 double rooms with baths, 2 rooms share bath. Outdoor hot tub. $105–$185; full breakfast, afternoon dessert and tea. MC, V. No smoking, no pets, 2-night minimum on weekends. Closed Christmas Day.

Cypress Inn. 407 Mirada Rd., Half Moon Bay, CA 94019, tel. 415/726–6075 or 800/832–3224, fax 415/458–2490. 12 double rooms with baths. Phones, fireplace; whirlpool bath in 4 rooms, TV on request. $150–$275, full breakfast. AE, MC, V. No smoking, no pets.

East Brother Light Station. 117 Park Pl., Point Richmond, CA 94801, tel. 510/233–2385, fax 510/232–5325. 2 double rooms with baths, 2 share bath. Fireplace in 1 room. $235 single, $295 couples; full breakfast, dinner. AE, MC, V. No smoking, no pets. Closed Mon.–Wed.

Gerstle Park Inn. 34 Grove St., San Rafael, CA 94901, tel. 415/721–7611 or 800/726–7611, fax 415/721–7600. 2 double rooms with baths, 6 suites. Whirlpool or steam baths in 5 rooms. Cable TVs; conference room, dual-line phones. $119–$179, full breakfast. AE, MC, V. No smoking, no pets.

Inn Above the Tides. 30 El Portal, Sausalito, CA 94965, tel. 415/332–9535 or 800/893–8433, fax 415/332–6714. 28 double rooms with baths, 2 suites. 24 rooms with decks; 22 with fireplaces. $195–$400, Continental breakfast. AE, MC, V. No smoking, no pets.

Inn at Saratoga. 20645 4th St., Saratoga, CA 95070, tel. 408/867–5020 or 800/338–5020, fax 408/741–0981. 39 double rooms with baths, 7 suites. Whirlpool bath in 7 rooms. Honor bars; cable TV, mini-refrigerators. $150–$440, Continental breakfast. AE, DC, MC, V. No pets.

Mill Valley Inn. 165 Throckmorton Ave., Mill Valley, CA 94941, tel. 415/

389–6608 or 800/595–2100, fax 415/389–5051. 22 double rooms with baths, 2 cottages, 1 penthouse. Fireplace or woodstove in 10 rooms, kitchenette in penthouse, concierge, in-room dining service from nearby restaurant. $125–$299, Continental breakfast. AE, MC, V. No smoking, no pets.

Roundstone Farm. 9940 Sir Francis Drake Blvd., Box 217, Olema, CA 94950, tel. 415/663–1020. 5 double rooms with baths. Fireplace in 4 rooms. $135, full breakfast. AE, MC, V. No smoking, no pets, 2-night minimum on weekends. Closed first 2 weeks of Dec.

Ten Inverness Way. 10 Inverness Way, Box 63, Inverness, CA 94937, tel. 415/669–1648, fax 415/669–7403. 4 double rooms with baths, 1 suite. Hot tub in garden cottage. $125–$165; full breakfast, complimentary beverages. MC, V. No smoking, 2-night minimum on weekends, 3-night minimum on holidays.

Reservations Services

Bed & Breakfast International (Box 282910, San Francisco, CA 94128–2910, tel. 415/696–1690, fax 415/696–1699). **Bed & Breakfast San Francisco** (Box 420009, San Francisco, CA 94142, tel. 415/931–3083 or 800/452–8249). **Inns of Marin** (Box 547, Point Reyes Station, CA 94956, tel. 415/663–2000. **Inns of Point Reyes** (Box 145, Inverness, CA 94937, tel. 415/663–1420).

Wine Country, Including Napa, Sonoma, Southern Mendocino Counties

Auberge du Soleil

180 Rutherford Hill Rd., Rutherford, CA 94573, tel. 707/963–1211 or 800/348–5406, fax 707/963–8764

Partially obscured by groves of gray-green olive trees, the "inn of the sun" is nestled into a hillside on the eastern edge of the Napa Valley. Claude Rouas, the French-born restaurateur who made San Francisco's L'Etoile the virtual headquarters of the society set, opened a restaurant on this site in 1981. "The restaurant took off immediately," recalls Rouas. "But I had always dreamed of opening an inn in the style of the country inns in Provence, like La Colombe d'Or. I wanted something with that Provence feeling but also something that would be fitting in the Napa Valley."

The guest accommodations also had to suit the existing restaurant, a stunning structure with light-color walls and an extended balcony entwined with grapevines. To this end, Rouas went back to the original design team—architect Sandy Walker and designer Michael Taylor. Together they built nine *maisons* (each named for a French region) on the 33-acre site below the restaurant; two others were added in 1987. The result is a low-rise blend of southwestern French and adobe-style architecture.

Each room has its own entrance and a trellis-covered veranda facing the valley. The rooms have a fresh, streamlined look with smooth, hand-glazed terra-cotta tiles on the floors and framing the fireplaces. The walls are a soothing pale stucco, and tall double doors, covered with white wooden shutters, open onto the balcony. High ceilings and air-conditioning fight the summer heat; on winter nights, however, guests may want to pull the soft leather chairs close to the fireplace for warmth.

The Auberge du Soleil is eminently suited to honeymooners, who can remain sequestered, thanks to room service. But the inn also has ample public spaces where groups can gather. The restaurant remains one of the valley's most popular. Although Rouas is often on the premises, the day-to-day business of management is left to George A. Goeggel, another European, who came to the inn from the Rosewood Hotel Group.

🏨 *31 double rooms with baths, 19 suites. Phones, TVs, air-conditioning, refrigerators; fireplace in 48 rooms, whirlpool bath in 12 rooms, 24-hr room service, massage room, restaurant, beauty salon, conference facilities; outdoor pool and whirlpool bath, tennis courts, tennis pro. $250–$800, Continental breakfast. AE, D, MC, V. Restricted smoking, no pets, 2-night minimum.*

Camellia Inn

211 North St., Healdsburg, CA 95448, tel. 707/433–8182 or 800/727–8182, fax 707/433–8130

This Italianate Victorian is set amid a garden of camellias on one side and, on the other, a tiny tiled pond in a shaded patio. Inside, it is replete with 12-foot ceilings, Oriental rugs, and a plethora of four-poster, queen-size canopy beds best entered via upholstered step stool. The pale apricot-and-white ground-floor double parlor has twin marble fireplaces. High ceilings keep the rooms cool even during Healdsburg's warm summers, and a pool out back provides a good respite from the heat on superhot days.

Of the nine double rooms (most of them named for varieties of camellia), three are upstairs in the main house, two in the rear, two in a separate building that once housed the dining room, and two in the former water tower, which was remodeled in 1989. In contrast to the other rooms, which are ornate, Tower East and Tower West are a refreshing vision of whitewashed pine, with willow furnishings.

🏨 *8 double rooms with baths, 1 suite. Air-conditioning, fireplace and whirlpool bath in 4 rooms; pool. $70–$145, full breakfast. D, MC, V. No smoking, no pets, 2-night minimum on weekends.*

Highland Ranch

Box 150, Philo, CA 95466, tel. 707/895–3600, fax 707/895–3702

The approach to the Highland Ranch is enough to make the nearby town of Philo look like an urban metropolis, but after 4 miles of narrow twists and turns, one arrives on a knoll overlooking a broad clearing. To one side, the 100-year-old ranch house is hidden in the shade of old oaks; to the left of the road, a handful of cabins look like little more than bunkhouses. Only slowly does the newcomer notice the strategically located ponds, the tennis court and small pool, the barn and riding ring in the back, and four hammocks strung beneath ancient redwood trees.

Highland Ranch didn't look this good in 1988, when George Gaines and his family took possession of what had become a rather run-down retreat. It took a mammoth effort to bury the electrical wires and perform the other feats of illusion that have resulted in a smooth-running operation. After a globe-trotting career as an international businessman, West Virginia–born Gaines came to California so that his wife, Mary Moore, could complete her studies to become an Episcopal priest. Depending on one's inclinations toward sociability, a sojourn here may be centered in the farmhouse, where guests gather in a well-worn living room lined with books, games, and memorabilia of the family's residences abroad, or in the privacy of one of the 11 cabins. These are homespun affairs, with good reading chairs and plenty of windows through which to watch deer and jackrabbits bound across the landscape.

This is not a turndown-service, basket-of-amenities type of place, but one where travelers can get some exercise and fresh air, good food, and a sense of peace so pervasive it might unnerve a big-city dweller. After breakfast, guests may take a short or an all-day horseback ride or hike, or go clay-pigeon shooting or fishing; at the end of the day, they may enjoy the sunset on their small private decks. Given the natural beauty of the setting, few visitors care that the walls of their cabin are fir plywood, the floors are Douglas-fir plank with only sparse carpeting, or that decoration consists of family collections of china or framed paintings—or even an old nonfunctioning camel horn that Gaines used to toot whenever he closed a particularly good deal.

▦ *11 cabins with baths. Phones; fireplace, deck, cribs available; pool, tennis court (racquets and balls provided), fishing, horseback riding, hiking, clay-pigeon shooting. $175 per person, including all meals, beverages, and activities. No credit cards. No pets, 2-night minimum.*

Kenwood Inn

10400 Sonoma Hwy., Kenwood, CA 95442, tel. 707/833–1293 or 800/353–6966, fax 707/833–1247

Terry and Roseann Grimm deserve an award for transforming a ramshackle antiques shop into a romantic Italian-style retreat facing the vineyards that lie on the hillsides across Highway 12. The two-lane road, in fact, is the biggest drawback to the Kenwood Inn, although there is little traffic noise after dark. This inn is separated from the road by a large flagstone patio, a pool, and extensive grounds landscaped with dozens of rosebushes, as well as persimmon, fig, apple, and—most appropriately—olive trees.

In 1994, the inn embarked on a $1 million remodeling to add eight accommodations and a full-service spa on the premises. In addition, the pool area has been renovated to include a large stone deck shaded by trellises and grapevines. The new rooms are decorated in a bit more luxurious style, with rich fabrics in colors such as ocher and gold.

The owners have paid lavish attention to detail, from the down mattresses covered with Egyptian-cotton sheets to the aromatic sprigs of fresh-from-the-garden herbs used to garnish breakfast dishes. Although there is no regular food service beyond the morning meal, guests are welcome to make special requests, whether it's a late-afternoon platter of fruits and cheeses or a specially catered dinner for private parties. Advance notice for the latter is, of course, required.

One room in the main house, decorated in leafy green and lush burgundy, has a queen-size bed and a separate living room with paisley wallpaper and moss-color draperies. It also has a private patio and garden entrance and is separated from the other two ground-floor accommodations by a large living room furnished simply with glass-and-wrought-iron console tables along the walls, antique ebony straight-back chairs imported from Mozambique, and two overstuffed sofas, upholstered in Italian prints, flanking the fireplace. The Tuscany Suite, upstairs, claims the most privacy and the best view. A four-poster king-size bed is canopied in fabrics of mango, burgundy, and black.

▦ *10 double rooms with baths, 2 suites. Fireplace; pool, sauna, steam bath. $195–$375; full breakfast, complimentary wine. AE, MC, V. No smoking, no pets, 2-night minimum on weekends.*

Madrona Manor

1001 Westside Rd., Healdsburg, CA 95448, tel. 707/433–4231 or 800/258–4003, fax 707/433–0703

A fraction of its former size, this estate dates from 1881, when San Franciscan John Paxton commissioned a mansion to be built on 240 acres on the outskirts of Healdsburg. To the Eastlake-style architecture he added gingerbread flourishes, steeply pitched dormers, gables, a mansard roof, and a wraparound porch. He filled it with massive furniture; many pieces, including a rosewood square grand piano, are still in use.

Today the estate comprises an 8-acre wooded knoll. In 1981 it was bought by Carol and John Muir, who had been living in Saudi Arabia. After redecorating the Carpenter Gothic carriage house, they added four third-floor guest rooms in the main house for a total of nine.The bedroom suite in number 203 is American Victorian Renaissance, with circular mask crests on both the chest and the double bedstead. The only guests who might feel crowded are those in the first-floor room, where more than one visitor has reported seeing a ghost during the night.

The accommodations in the outbuildings lack the elegance of the original rooms. The Meadow Wood Complex, with its very private bedroom and deck, is headquarters for travelers with children and dogs.

The Garden Suite, set in a secluded spot beyond the garden, is decorated with rattan furniture and a marble fireplace. The carriage house, with its massive Nepalese hand-carved rosewood door, houses eight rooms, as well as the newer Suite 400, which has contemporary French furnishings and a Grecian marble bathroom. The whirlpool bath has shutters that open onto the sitting room, facing the fireplace.

Herbs and some vegetables from the inn's extensive gardens find their way to the dinner menu at Madrona Manor. Local fish, poultry, and game are often smoked on the premises, and the marmalade at breakfast is made from mandarin oranges picked from several trees on the property.

▦ *18 double rooms with baths, 3 suites. Air-conditioning, fireplaces; restaurant, pool. $140–$240, full breakfast. AE, D, MC, V. No smoking.*

Other Choices

Beltane Ranch. 11775 Sonoma Hwy., Box 395, Glen Ellen, CA 95442, tel. 707/996–6501. 2 double rooms with baths, 2 suites. Hiking trails, horseshoes, tennis court. $100–$145, full breakfast. No credit cards. No smoking.

Foothill House. 3037 Foothill Blvd., Calistoga, CA 94515, tel. 707/942–6933 or 800/942–6933. 3 double rooms with baths, 1 suite. Radio/cassette players, coffeemakers; fireplace, whirlpool bath in 5 rooms, TV. $135–$250, full breakfast. No smoking, no pets.

Harvest Inn. 1 Main St., St. Helena, CA 94574, tel. 707/963–9463 or 800/950–8466, fax 707/963–4402. 54 double rooms with baths. Wet bars; TV, radio, refrigerator; fireplace in 49 rooms, 2 pools, 2 outside hot tubs. $159–$366, Continental breakfast. AE, D, DC, MC, V. Restricted smoking, no pets.

Healdsburg Inn on the Plaza. 110 Matheson St., Healdsburg, CA 95448, tel. 707/433–6991 or 800/431–8663. 10 double rooms with baths. Phones, cable TV/VCRs; fireplace in 7 rooms, whirlpool in 1 room, balcony in 1 room, shared balcony in 3 rooms. $155–$205, full breakfast. MC, V. Restricted smoking, no pets.

Inn at South Bridge. 1020 Main St., St. Helena, CA 94574, tel. 707/967–9400 or 800/520–6800, fax 707/967–9486. 21 double rooms with baths. TVs, phones, robes; turndown service, voice mail, fax/modem ports, restaurant, conference room. $175–$255, Continental breakfast. AE, DC, MC, V. No pets.

Maison Fleurie. 6529 Yount St., Drawer M, Yountville, CA 94599, tel. 707/944–2056. 13 double rooms with baths. Air-conditioning, gas-log fireplace in 5 rooms, wine cellar, pool, hot tub, bicycles. $109–$190, full breakfast. AE, MC, V. No smoking, no pets.

Thistle Dew Inn. 171 West Spain St., Sonoma, CA 95476, tel. 707/938–2909 or 800/382–7895, fax 707/996–8413. 6 double rooms with baths. Phones; fireplace, whirlpool bath in 3 rooms, TV available, outdoor hot tub. $110–$175, full breakfast. AE, MC, V. No smoking, no pets.

Vintners Inn. 4250 Barnes Rd., Santa Rosa, CA 95403, tel. 707/575–7350 or 800/421–2584 in CA, fax 707/575–1426. 39 double rooms with baths, 5 suites. Phones, TVs, radios; fireplace in 18 rooms, refrigerator in suites, conference facilities, outside hot tub. $158–$205, buffet breakfast. AE, DC, MC, V. 2-night minimum on weekends Mar. 15–Oct. 31.

Reservations Service

Bed & Breakfast Inns of Sonoma County (Box 51, Geyserville, CA 95476, tel. 707/433–4667).

North Coast and Redwood Country, Including Mendocino and Eureka

Applewood

13555 Hwy. 116 (near Guerneville), Pocket Canyon, CA 95446, tel. 707/ 869-9093

Jay Gatsby would feel right at home at this country inn surrounded by forests of giant redwoods in the heart of the Russian River resort area. The creation of two refugees from the Bay Area, Jim Caron and Darryl Notter, Applewood occupies a designated landmark home built in 1922 by the flamboyant financier Ralph Belden. Jim and Darryl have recently completed construction on a new building in the same Mission Revival style as the original.

Jim and Darryl discovered the house while they were visiting the Russian River on vacation. "The area had long been a popular vacation spot for people from the Bay Area, including my family," Jim says. "But it had become run-down by the 1960s. One of our goals with Applewood is to restore the former elegance."

At the heart of the inn, on the main floor, are the three connecting common rooms. The former solarium, with windows on three sides and a full-width skylight, is now a dining room that seats 20. On cold afternoons a fireplace provides a crackling counterpoint to the room's garden ambience. The living room feels more subdued; with burgundy carpet, a heavy-beamed ceiling, and the back of the two-sided great stone fireplace, it evokes the feeling of a country lodge. Through a set of double doors lies a more formal dining room; from here, a pair of French doors open onto the pool area.

Guest rooms—on the main floor, a lower level, and in the adjacent addition—are decorated in bright, clear jewel tones and furnished with comfort and understated elegance. They all boast sitting areas and plenty of light and are variously furnished with overstuffed love seats, boudoir chairs, chaise longues, and small desks.

The innkeepers pride themselves on their food. Both are accomplished cooks, Jim having learned at his mother's knee and Darryl at a cooking school in Bangkok. The fare tends more toward the hearty than the nouveau—eggs Florentine in the morning, steak or leg of lamb at dinner. Space allowing, seating at evening meals is open to non-guests.

▦ *16 double rooms with baths. Phones, hair dryers, cable TVs; fireplace, private balcony or patio, whirlpool bath in 2 rooms, shower for two in 5 rooms; heated pool, outdoor hot tub. $125–$250, full breakfast; dinner available (about $30). AE, D, MC, V. No smoking, no pets, 2-night minimum on weekends.*

Elk Cove Inn

6300 S. Hwy. 1, Box 367, Elk, CA 95432, tel. 707/877–3321 or 800/275–2967, fax 707/877–1808

A night spent in one of the cottages on the bluff at Elk Cove is the closest thing around to sleeping right on the beach. No matter where you stay at this inn, which boasts an oceanfront location in a hidden cul-de-sac off the Coast Highway, you can drift off to sleep to the sounds of the surf and awaken to the songs of birds. Some visitors insist on staying in the main house—usually, says the innkeeper, East Coast guests nervous about earthquakes—while others demand one of the cottage rooms time and time again, lulled by the siren song of the sea.

Alabama-born Elaine Bryant had plenty of experience as an innkeeper when she took over Elk Cove Inn in 1994. Her first property was The Elms in Calistoga, but when she found herself returning time and again to the Mendocino coast for vacation, she finally bought this 1883 Victorian and filled it with the pottery, oak and pine antiques she'd accumulated over the years. The main house was built as an executive guest house for the L. E. White Lumber Company, back when the bustling area was known as Greenwood. It became a bed-and-breakfast in 1968.

Guest rooms on the second floor of the main house share a parlor, with French doors leading to a roof deck overlooking the ocean and nearly a mile of beach below the bluff. There are long window seats in front of 8-foot-wide dormer windows for reading, gazing at the sunset, and admiring the raised beds where Elaine grows herbs and flowers for the inn. Two sitting rooms are on the second floor; one inside, the other on a protected deck. The decor throughout is simple: old-fashioned floral wallpaper, Victorian-style light fixtures, antique furnishings (even in the bathrooms) and plenty of bare wood.

Separate from the house, four cheek-by-jowl cabins offer more privacy; two have high-beamed ceilings, woodstoves and white-paneled walls. Outside, benches and a Victorian-style gazebo are perched on the edge of the bluff, which is covered in Queen Anne's lace and other wildflowers in spring and summer. Two large boulders offshore seem strategically placed to provide the soothing sound of distant waves crashing on the rocks. One of the best features of the Elk Cove Inn is the beach, accessible by a steep wooden staircase. Be forewarned, however: if you take an early-morning walk, Boomer and Asta, Elaine's German shepherd and wirehaired fox terrier, will probably drag out their leashes and beg to be taken along.

The first floor of the house shares a corner with a pub that opened in 1995, where beer and wines from the nearby Anderson Valley are sold by the glass from behind a 19th-century oak bar. Elaine prides herself on her ability to serve guests a different breakfast for as long as two weeks, hardly ever using the same place settings, thanks to the serious collecting she's done over the years. Even the morning juices are served in art glass pitchers. Breakfast always has at least one Southern-type dish such as a creamy corn pudding or peach-pineapple bread pudding with a rum-ginger sauce.

🏨 *10 double rooms with baths. Robes, coffeemakers, beer and wine bar. $98–$168, full breakfast. AE, MC, V. No smoking, no pets.*

Gingerbread Mansion

400 Berding St., Box 40, Ferndale, CA 95536, tel. 707/786–4000, fax 707/786–4381

The Gingerbread Mansion has long been a tourist attraction in and of itself; visitors are constantly making the detour from U.S. 101 to the Victorian village of Ferndale so they can take a picture of its bright-orange-and-yellow exterior and its flower-filled English gardens. The Gingerbread, with its spindle roof ridges and icicle eaves, its bay windows and shingled turret, must be one of the most photographed buildings in California. Pity those who never

get inside to enjoy the whimsical fantasy rooms and the warm hospitality of innkeeper Ken Torbert and his staff.

The Gingerbread Mansion has served many different purposes in the years since 1899, when it was built as a doctor's residence. A 1920s expansion converted the Queen Anne–Eastlake mansion into a hospital. Over the years it turned into a rest home and later an American Legion hall; when Ken purchased it in 1981, it had become an apartment house. "Alice's experiences in Wonderland guided my renovating ideas," he says. The inn is full of surprises—pleasant ones, such as rooms with mirrors for people of all heights, and a pair of claw-foot tubs set toe to toe on a white-fenced platform. In 1995, Torbert transformed the top floor into a Roman fantasy full of fine marble, gleaming brass fixtures, a mammoth glassed-in shower, several seating areas and an antique claw-foot tub.

The bathrooms are a special delight. The Fountain Suite bath has side-by-side claw-foot tubs facing a mirrored wall in which the flames in the newly added tiled fireplaces can be seen flickering. The claw-foot tub on a platform in the Rose Suite bathroom is surrounded by floral wallpaper under a mirrored ceiling; bathing there gives one the feeling of being in a garden. The actual gardens are Ken's pride and joy. Narrow brick paths meander through sculptured boxwood and past blossoming rhododendrons, camellias, and azaleas in winter, and fancy fuchsias throughout the summer and fall.

There are thoughtful surprises, too. Rooms are straightened, and the lamps and shades are adjusted at turndown each evening. Umbrellas stay at the ready for protection when it rains. Morning coffee is prepared to order for each guest before breakfast, which is served at two large tables in the dining room. This is the time for conversation over a variety of home-baked breads, a selection of unusual local cheeses, and fruit.

⌂ *8 double rooms with baths, 2 suites. Robes in rooms, fireplace in 4 rooms, guest refrigerator, bicycles. $140–$350; full breakfast, afternoon high tea. AE, MC, V. No smoking, no pets, 2-night minimum on weekends and holidays.*

Harbor House

5600 S. Hwy. 1, Box 369, Elk, CA 95432, tel. 707/877-3203

Some of the guests who arrive at Harbor House never want to leave. Some don't: Innkeepers Helen and Dean Turner fell in love with Harbor House and purchased it in 1985.

Twelve years later, those who love the ever-changing character of the sea will find themselves mesmerized by the view from this country inn perched right on the edge of the coast. Guests who book one of the inn's four red-and-white cottages can savor the view from their own furnished deck. In most of the rooms visitors can warm themselves by a fireplace while studying the sea. Those who want to see the ocean close up need only descend the steep path to the inn's private beach; although swimming is treacherous, and not advised in the rocky surf, this is a good place for a picnic.

Harbor House's magnificent setting is just one of its attractions. The rustic-elegant lodge dates from 1916, when it was built as an executive residence for the Goodyear Redwood Lumber Company, which shipped the lumber it logged out of the cove below. The main building—an enlarged version of the Home of Redwood, designed by Louis Christian Mullgardt for the 1915 Panama-Pacific International Exposition in San Francisco—was constructed entirely of virgin redwood.

The living room is a stunning example of the carpenter's craft. The floors, walls, and vaulted ceilings are made of old-growth redwood; they were rubbed with beeswax, a natural preservative, to achieve the luster they still have today. This comfortable room beckons you to curl up on one of the overstuffed sofas flanking the enormous stone fireplace.

The guest rooms, also furnished with overstuffed chairs and sofas, are equally comfortable. The Cypress and Harbor rooms, occupying corners on the first and second floors respectively, are both large enough to hold two big beds plus two sitting areas. Both have sea views, as does the Lookout—the smallest room in the inn, although a private deck makes it appear larger. Its white cast-iron bed is spread with a wedding-ring quilt.

Breakfast and dinner are served in the dining room. Menus feature fresh local seafood and meats as well as organically grown vegetables.

⌂ *6 double rooms with baths, 4 cottages. Fireplace in 9 rooms, restaurant, private beach. $175–$265, full breakfast and dinner. No credit cards. No smoking in restaurant, no pets, 2-night minimum on weekends, 3- or 4-night minimum on some holidays.*

Joshua Grindle Inn

44800 Little Lake Rd., Box 647, Mendocino, CA 95460, tel. 707/937-4143

Like many buildings in Mendocino, the Joshua Grindle Inn looks as if it were imported directly from New England and plunked down on the California coast. And in a way it was. Joshua Grindle, like many of the area's settlers, hailed from Maine. A raftsman for the Mendocino Lumber Company, he built the two-story redwood farmhouse for his bride in 1879; it stayed in the family until 1967.

The inn displays many of Mendocino's best qualities: functional New England architecture, a respect for the land, and a casual, relaxing ambience. It stands on a 2-acre hilltop near the turnoff into town from Highway 1. The original farmhouse has five guest rooms, a parlor, and a dining room. Three bedrooms upstairs are bright and airy, with either ocean or treetop views. The guest room called the Library is particularly appealing. A small, cozy room, it has its own seating area, a four-poster queen-size bed, and floor-to-ceiling bookcases flanking a fireplace decorated with hand-painted tiles depicting Aesop's fables. In the late afternoon guests converge in the farmhouse parlor, reading or playing backgammon, sipping sherry, or fingering the antique pump organ.

There are two outbuildings. The weathered redwood Watertower has three rooms, including one on the second level with windows on four sides and, naturally, a splendid view of the ocean and town as well as the mountains to the east. The Cottage, which has two rooms, is shaded by cypress trees that Joshua Grindle planted 100 years ago. Furnishings throughout the inn are simple but comfortable American antiques: Salem rockers, wing chairs, steamer-trunk tables, painted pine beds.

Innkeepers Arlene and Jim Moorehead, purchased the inn in 198 after corporate careers in San Francisco. "It was a natural move," Jim said. "We love old houses, good food, and people." At breakfast guests gather around a long, 1830 pine harvest table. Although the table isn't big enough to accommodate everyone when the inn is full, no one seems to mind enjoying a prebreakfast cup of coffee on the veranda. After breakfast, which may include quiche, frittata, and a warm fruit compote, guests frequently take the short walk into town to shop for antiques or explore the art galleries.

🏨 *10 double rooms with baths. Fireplace in 6 rooms, guest refrigerator. $95–$175, full breakfast. MC, V. No smoking, no pets, 2-night minimum on weekends, 3-night minimum on holidays.*

Timberhill Ranch

35755 Hauser Bridge Rd. (Timber Cove Post Office), Cazadero, CA 95421, tel. 707/847–3258, fax 707/847–3342

The two couples who created Timberhill Ranch were seeking a refuge from their harried, urban, corporate lives; they found it on 80 acres of rolling hills in Sonoma County—just a stone's throw from the coast, but worlds apart. Tarran McDaid and Michael Riordan and Barbara Farrell and Frank Watson admit that they created Timberhill mainly for their own pleasure. It has the kind of features they enjoy: privacy, expansive views of rolling hills (green in winter and spring and gold the rest of the year), tennis courts, a pool, miles and miles of trails for quiet strolls in the woods, an excellent dining room, and outstanding and discreet service.

With 15 cottages tucked beneath trees on the hillside above a small pond, the focal point of the ranch is the quietly elegant lodge. The lodge contains an expansive living room with a Sonoma fieldstone fireplace and floor-to-ceiling windows with a view of the pool and the hills beyond.

The dining room is another point of pride. Candlelit and formal in the evenings, it's a marked contrast to the casual atmosphere of the rest of Timberhill. An à la carte dinner featuring California cuisine is served nightly. A typical menu features such entrées as house-smoked pork loin, duck with port sauce, pan-seared Hawaiian fish and honey-glazed rack of Sonoma county lamb.

The cottages are identical in design but differ in decor. Small log cabins built of sweet-scented cedar, they have tall windows and decks where many guests enjoy the Continental breakfasts the innkeepers deliver. The beds are dressed with handmade quilts, the walls are tastefully decorated with original oils, and the fireplaces are stocked up and ready to light. Timberhill provides terry-cloth bathrobes and huge fluffy towels.

This is a ranch, so there are animals: horses in the white-fenced paddock close by; ducks and geese cruising the pond in formation; a pair of llamas; and two dogs—Banger, an Australian shepherd, and Bridgette, a shih tzu—who trot behind the innkeepers as they make their daily rounds.

🏠 *15 double rooms with baths. Fireplace, minibar, refrigerator, coffeemaker in rooms, pool, outdoor hot tub, tennis courts, hiking trails. $335–$365; Continental breakfast and dinner, picnic lunches ($30). AE, MC, V. Restricted smoking, no pets, 2-night minimum on weekends.*

Whale Watch Inn by the Sea

35100 Hwy. 1, Gualala, CA 95445, tel. 707/884–3667 or 800/942–5342, fax 707/884–4815

There's no other inn quite like this one on the California coast. Located high on a cliff with views of the Pacific to the west and the gorgeous coastline to the south, the Whale Watch Inn is especially popular during the winter months when the Pacific gray whales are migrating between Alaska and the Sea of Cortez. Larger-than-average accommodations, attentive but reserved service, and the scent of pine and cypress wafting through sliding glass doors (not to mention the in-room hot tubs), are enough to keep guests room-bound for days on end.

Started in the mid-'70s, when original owners Irene and Enoch Stewart added a guest house to the original building to accommodate their frequent visitors, the Whale Watch has since added three more buildings, for a total of five. The luxurious modern rooms are decorated in light colors and feature high, angled, skylighted ceilings. Individualized furniture gives each room a different feeling, from Victorian to Asian. All rooms have a fireplace and a private deck, with most featuring an individual or two-person whirlpool bath. In some, large wall mirrors give one the impression of being surrounded by the ocean vistas; each has been carefully designed to preserve the sense of isolation. Four condolike suites in the Sea Bounty building, equipped with full kitchens, are designed for longer stays.

After a delicious full breakfast served in their rooms, guests may brave the steep stairway down to the beach to explore tidal pools or watch wet-suited abalone fishermen heading out to sea in rubber boats. Other paths lead visitors on short strolls along the cliffs, through cypress groves and well-tended flower gardens. The Whale Watch building contains a large, comfortable common area with a sweeping view of the ocean. The nearby town of Gualala has its share of restaurants and tourist attractions, and recreational facilities are within easy reach, but the Whale Watch seems designed less for activity than for relaxation, contemplation, and above all, privacy.

🏠 *11 double rooms with baths, 7 suites. Fireplaces; whirlpool bath and ice-maker in 12 rooms, kitchen in 5 rooms; private beach access. $170–$265, full breakfast in room. AE, MC, V. No smoking, no pets, 2-night minimum on weekends, 3-night minimum on holiday weekends.*

Other Choices

Avalon House. 561 Stewart St., Fort Bragg, CA 95437, tel. 707/964–5555 or 800/964–5556. 6 rooms with baths. Whirlpool bath in 4 rooms. Ice machines, TV in parlor. $70–$135, full breakfast. No smoking.

Carter House. 1033 3rd St., Eureka, CA 95501, tel. and fax 707/445–1390. 3 double rooms with baths, 2 suites. Phone in rooms, fireplace and whirlpool bath in 1 suite, restaurant at adjacent Hotel Carter. $155–$225; full breakfast, afternoon and evening refreshments. AE, D, DC, MC, V. Smoking in parlors only, no pets.

An Elegant Victorian Mansion. 1406 C St., Eureka, CA 95501, tel. 707/444–3144 or 707/442–5594. 3 double rooms with 3 shared baths, 1 suite. Robes; Swedish massage available, Finnish sauna, laundry service, bicycles. $95–$175; full breakfast, afternoon ice-cream sodas. MC, V. No smoking, no pets.

Greenwood Pier Inn. 5928 So. Hwy. 1, Box 336, Elk, CA 95432, tel. 707/877–9997, fax 707/877–3439. 8 double rooms with baths, 5 cottages with fireplaces and hot tubs. $110–$225, Continental breakfast. MC, V. No smoking, 2-night minimum on weekends, 3- or 4-night minimum on holidays.

Little River Inn. Drawer Box B, Little River, CA 95456, tel. 707/937–5942, fax 707/937–3944. 65 rooms with baths. Phone, TV/VCR in all rooms, whirlpool bath in 19 rooms, fireplace in 34 rooms, wood-burning stove in 6 rooms, restaurant, bar, golf course, tennis courts, hiking trails, beach access. $85–$255, full breakfast. MC, V. No pets.

MacCallum House. 45020 Albion St., Box 206, Mendocino, CA 95460, tel. 707/937–0289 or 800/609–0492. 17 rooms with baths, 1 suite. Fireplace in 6 rooms, TV and phone in 5 rooms, restaurant, bar. $90–$190, breakfast not included. MC, V. No smoking, no pets.

Rachel's Inn. Hwy. 1 (2 mi south of Mendocino at Little River), Box 134, Mendocino, CA 95460, tel. 707/937–0088. 2 triple rooms with baths, 5 double rooms with baths, 2 suites. Fireplace in 6 rooms, wet bar and refrigerator in suites, beach access. $96–$185, full breakfast. No credit cards. No pets, 2-night minimum on weekends, 3- or 4-night minimum on holidays.

Stanford Inn by the Sea. Coast Hwy. and Comptche-Ukiah Rd., Box 487,

Mendocino, CA 95460, tel. 707/937–5615 or 800/331–8884, fax 707/937–0305. 23 double rooms with baths, 10 suites. Fireplaces, refrigerators, phones, TV/VCRs, CD players; indoor pool, conference room, exercise room, canoes and bicycles available. $175–$540, Continental breakfast. AE, D, DC, MC, V. No smoking, 2-night minimum on weekends, 3-night minimum on holidays.

Stevenswood Lodge. 8211 Coast Hwy., Little River, Box 170, Mendocino, CA 95460, tel. 707/937–2810 or 800/421–2810, fax 707/937–1237. 9 suites with baths. Fireplace, TV, phone, refrigerator, honor bar. $95–$195, full breakfast. AE, D, MC, V. No smoking, no pets.

Reservations Services

Bed and Breakfast International (Box 282910, San Francisco, CA 94128, tel. 800/872–4500, 415/696–1690 outside the U.S.). **Mendocino Coast Innkeepers Association** (Box 1141, Mendocino, CA 95460, tel. 707/964–0640 or 800/382–7244).

Sacramento and the Central Valley, Including the Sierra Foothills

Amber House

1315 22nd St., Sacramento, CA 95816, tel. 916/444–8085 or 800/755–6526, fax 916/552–6529

Michael Richardson admits that running a bed-and-breakfast inn has its challenges. "I want every guest to feel special. It's like having your mother-in-law for Christmas dinner every day of the year," he says. Still, Michael and his wife, Jane Ramey, former southern California residents, have no regrets about their decision to move to Sacramento in 1986 to become proprietors of

Amber House, a meticulously restored Craftsman home from 1905.

Jane, a former merchandise manager for Marriott hotels, redecorated the original house's five guest rooms, haunting estate sales for antiques and fashioning each room around a poet. Michael, formerly in real estate, set about buying and restoring the 1913 Mediterranean-style house next door, which now hosts an enormous sitting room with a fireplace and four guest rooms, all under the spell of French Impressionist color schemes. In addition, he has just acquired a third house, across the street from the Amber House, which will have five additional guest rooms.

Situated not far from the State Capitol, Amber House is atmospheric, with lots of nooks and crannies. The main sitting room with its wood-beamed ceiling has plenty of comfortable chairs. In the late afternoons, guests snack here on cookies, coffee, and mineral water, or retreat to the smaller, front sitting room, with glass-fronted bookshelves and a window seat. Classical music wafts through all the public rooms.

The 14 guest rooms are floral and romantic, most with unusually luxurious bathrooms. They range from snug (Chaucer) to gloriously spacious (Renoir). The latter has leaded glass windows, a king-size bed, a sofa, and a bathtub built for two. Emily Dickinson, occupying a former sleeping porch, is bright and airy with a fireplace separating the sleeping area from the bathroom where there's a whirlpool bath with waterfall faucet and skylights that open. The sunny yellow van Gogh is arguably the most glamorous; it's dominated by a sybaritic greenhouse bathroom with a corner whirlpool and white wicker chaise longue.

Breakfast is served at a large antique Duncan Phyfe table in the dining room or at little tables in each guest room. Since guests often stay more than one night, the menus is never the same two days in a row. Quiche and potatoes with bell peppers is an Amber House specialty, as are waffles and strawberries. As a prelude to the meal, Michael sets early-morning coffee or tea on a tiny table outside each room.

🛏 *14 double rooms with baths. Robes; air-conditioning, phone, cable TV, cassette player and clock radio, whirlpool bath in 10 rooms, bicycles. $89–$219; full breakfast, afternoon refreshments. AE, D, DC, MC, V. No smoking, no pets.*

Hartley House

700 22nd St., Sacramento, CA 95816, tel. 916/447–7829 or 800/831–5806, fax 916/447–1820

Boulevard Park is one of Sacramento's less heralded historic treasures. Not far from the State Capitol, the area boasts several blocks of magnificent turn-of-the-century houses. The six little parks in the middle of 21st and 22nd streets form the district's centerpiece; each is a large, grassy, tree-shaded oval. This area was the site of the California State Fair between 1849 and 1900; the parks are remnants of the racetrack. Later, Boulevard Park became Sacramento's first residential subdivision, where houses cost $3,700 and no livestock was permitted. The genteel nature of Boulevard Park disappeared at the end of World War II, and by the 1960s, the area had become boardinghouse row.

A fourth-generation Sacramentan whose grandparents once operated a dormitory for young men in the 1920s and '30s, innkeeper Randy Hartley purchased this onetime boardinghouse in 1986 and brought new life into it. He restored the hardwood floors and stained-glass windows in the public rooms to their former glory and outfitted the five guest rooms with a cozy, chintz-free mix of antiques and amenities that evoke the crisp comforts of an Edwardian town house. The hitching posts that remain at curbside serve as reminders of the earlier era.

Brighton, set in what was once the sunporch, is arguably the prettiest and certainly the lightest guest room, with three walls of windows, a white wrought-iron bed, a ceiling fan, and a small TV. Dover flaunts the house's original bathroom fixtures, including a claw-foot tub.

Randy runs a comfortable, down-to-earth inn. The enormous white kitchen, the house's only blatantly 1990s touch, is outfitted with tall stools, where visitors nibble homemade cookies and chat with Randy until he shoos them out. Breakfast—omelets, blintzes, Belgian waffles—is served in the spacious dining room or, in good weather, in the flower-filled courtyard. Guests sometimes sit on the expansive front porch, often on the big porch swing, and sip fresh lemonade.

Games are piled high on the sitting-room shelves and the chessboard is always set up. More often, guests simply prefer to peruse a good book or the *Sacramento Bee*.

🏠 *5 double rooms with baths. Air-conditioning, modem ports, cable TVs, clock radios, robes, hair dryers; patio. $95–$150; full breakfast, afternoon refreshments. AE, D, DC, MC, V. No smoking, no pets.*

Johnson's Country Inn

3935 Morehead Ave., Chico, CA 95928, tel. and fax 916/345-7829

Countryish Chico, where agriculture is the main industry, would seem an unlikely spot to find a romantic Victorian bed-and-breakfast inn. But here is Johnson's, a big, bright-pink farmhouse with a wraparound veranda situated amid 10 acres of almond trees. Although a mere 2 miles from downtown Chico and the city's state university campus, the inn retains a feeling of quiet country elegance. There's even a lacy white gazebo tucked in among the trees, and the scent of roses fills the air.

Johnson's is the creation of David and Joan Johnson, incurable romantics who escaped the urban tangle of Los Angeles in 1992 for a quiet life in the country. They built the inn from the ground up using ideas from San Francisco's famed "painted ladies" and Petaluma's Victorians. While common rooms—parlor, dining room, sunny garden room—display the Victorian theme, guest rooms reflect the lives and interests of the innkeepers.

Two of the most interesting rooms contain artifacts of David's family history. The Jarrett, a corner room in the front of the house, is dedicated to the work and art of David's uncle, prominent 1930s illustrator Charles Dixie Jarrett. An art deco–style bed, boasting a classic waterfall design, dominates the room. Original drawings and poster art by Charles Jarrett grace the walls. Across the hall, the Harrison is dedicated to President Benjamin Harrison, who was David's great-great-grandfather. An 1860s Eastlake bed captures immediate attention in this room, which has black-and-pink paisley wallpaper and interesting mementos of the 23rd U.S. president; there's also a fireplace and whirlpool tub. Icart, done in burgundy and black, reflects the art nouveau period; a big double shower is wheelchair-accessible.

Guests awake to the aroma of coffee delivered to the bedroom. As one might expect in farm country, breakfast, served in a room overlooking the almond grove, is more than ample. A typical menu includes fruit salad, a selection of scones and muffins, and zucchini quiche accompanied by apple sausage.

🏠 *4 double rooms with baths. Air-conditioning, phones, robes; whirlpool bath and fireplace in 1 room, gardens, horseshoes, lawn games. $80–$125; full breakfast, afternoon wine, after-dinner dessert. AE, MC, V. No smok-*

ing, no pets, 2-night minimum on holiday weekends and for CSU/Chico graduation.

Wine & Roses Country Inn

2505 West Turner Rd., Lodi, CA 95242, tel. 209/334–6988, fax 209/334–6570

Wine & Roses Country Inn, located on 5 acres of rich farmland in Lodi, a grape-growing, wine-making community half an hour south of Sacramento, is an unexpected romantic surprise. A historic white farmhouse that's nearly 100 years old, the inn is prim and pretty and surrounded by acres of fragrant gardens and towering deodar trees. It's a popular setting for weddings and other romantic celebrations. And it serves as a home away from home for those doing business at the General Mills facility just up the street.

The inn, very much a family affair, is the creation of former realtor Kris Cromwell, her son Del Smith and his wife, Sherri, whom he met when she was hired as the inn's chef. Sherri, now a mother of two and the executive chef, supervises the inn's food service.

Comfort, coziness, and strong colors seem to have been Kris's priorities while decorating the guest rooms. Edelweiss, which overlooks the garden, is typical, with deep green walls, pale mauve carpeting, and a green and white floral print duvet on the big brass bed. The bathroom has a claw-foot tub with a shower. A clock radio awakens you if the chickens haven't. Moonlight and Roses is a melody in mauve and pink, with bouquets of roses adorning the walls and floral drapes framing the claw-foot tub; there's a small comfortable sitting area the room's bay window. Victorian touches abound: pots of potpourri, pink bows on the bathroom tissue, fresh flowers. Brides love the attic suite with its cathedral ceilings, French doors, rooftop deck, and sitting room furnished with two velvet wing-back chairs. All travelers appreciate the homelike ambience of the sitting room, which is set up with overstuffed sofas and chairs, a crackling fire in winter, and plenty of reading material filling library shelves.

Breakfast, Sunday brunch, lunch (Tues.–Fri.), and dinner (Wed.–Sat.) are served in the mauve dining room, overlooking the rosebushes. On warm days and nights, guests can eat outside on big round tables. In cooler weather, guests often sip coffee or wine in the sitting room while chatting with the innkeepers.

🛏 *9 double rooms with baths, 1 suite. Air-conditioning, TVs, phones, clock radios; restaurant, conference facilities, croquet, badminton, horseshoes, free use of health club off-site. $99– $165; full breakfast, afternoon and evening refreshments, wine dinners, dinner theater scheduled on weekends year-round. AE, D, MC, V. No smoking, no pets.*

Other Choices

Abigail's. 2120 G. St., Sacramento, CA 95816, tel. 916/441–5007 or 800/858–1568, fax 916/441–0621. 5 double rooms with baths. Air-conditioning, TVs, phones, radios, robes, hair dryers; whirlpool tub in 1 room, games in living room, garden hot tub, gift baskets available for special occasions. $95– $165; full breakfast, afternoon refreshments, evening snacks. AE, D, DC, MC, V. No smoking, no pets, 3-night minimum some holiday weekends.

Emma's Bed and Breakfast. 3137 Taylor Rd., Loomis, CA 95650, tel. 916/652–1392, fax 916/952–2254. 5 double rooms with baths. Air-conditioning, cable TV/VCRs, phones; whirlpool baths in 4 rooms, refrigerator in 1 room, gardens, fishing pond, llamas, horses, horse-drawn carriage rides. $120–$145; full breakfast, afternoon refreshments. D, MC, V. No smoking, no pets.

Lake Oroville Bed & Breakfast. 240 Sunday Dr., Berry Creek, CA 95916, tel. 916/589–0700 or 800/455–5253, fax 916/589–5313. 6 double rooms with baths. Air-conditioning, clock radios; whirlpool bath in 5 rooms, cable TV in parlor, stocked guest refrigerator, billiard room, outdoor barbecue, hiking trails. $75–$125; full breakfast, afternoon refreshments. AE, D, MC, V. No smoking, no pets, 2-night minimum on holiday weekends.

Reservations Services

B&B International (Box 282910, San Francisco, CA 94128, tel. 415/696–1690 or 800/872–4500, fax 415/696–1699). **Eye Openers B&B Reservations** (Box 694, Altadena, CA 91003, tel. 213/684–4428 or 818/797–2055, fax 818/798–3640).

Gold Country Along Highway 49

City Hotel

Main St., Columbia State Historic Park, Box 1870, Columbia, CA 95310, tel. 209/532–1479 or 800/446–1333, ext. 1280, fax 209/532–7027

In 1856, when Columbia was all ablaze with gold fever, George Morgan built the City Hotel in the heart of town. Intended as a lodging for gentlemen, this two-story brick storefront was refurbished by the state in 1975 and now welcomes all.

The City Hotel, inside Columbia State Historic Park, is part of a living museum. A stay here provides insight into gold-rush era life, particularly in the special re-creations of historic events that are scheduled throughout the year in the park and at the hotel.

The restoration and furnishings accurately reflect the gold-rush era, with only a nod to contemporary conveniences. Most furnishings predate 1875. The oldest is an antique writing desk from the 1820s. Although 14-foot ceilings make all rooms feel spacious, the best and largest are those that open onto the parlor. The two rooms across the front of the hotel are the most desirable of these; they have small balconies from which one can watch the Wells Fargo stagecoach pass by on the street below.

All rooms contain massive, carved wooden beds, marble-topped dressers, Oriental rugs, and Victorian-style floral wallpapers. Each room has a half-bath equipped with a wicker basket of "necessary items"—robe, disposable slippers, towels, et cetera—for the walk to the shower down the hall. A central sitting parlor scattered with Oriental rugs has a felt-topped poker table, books, magazines, and games.

The hotel, which serves as a training center for hospitality students at nearby Columbia College, routinely schedules Victorian-theme special events. Most popular is the annual Victorian Christmas Pageant and Feast, a typical holiday celebration of the 1860s, complete with costumed revelers. Other events include mystery weekends, a Victorian Easter Parade, a fireman's muster, and a re-creation of the argonauts at work in the mines.

The clubby restaurant at the City Hotel has long been considered among the best in the Gold Country. The prix-fixe menu includes an array of classic French and California selections and the wine list represents a who's who of California wine makers. The What Cheer Saloon next door may look like a knock-off of a western movie set, but as with everything else about Columbia, it's an accurate reflection of gold rush–era watering holes.

🏨 *10 double rooms with half-baths share 2 showers. Air-conditioning, robes and slippers; lobby phone, restaurant, saloon, theater-dinner packages. $75–*

$95; Continental breakfast, afternoon refreshments. AE, D, MC, V. No smoking, no pets.

Coloma Country Inn

345 High St., Box 502, Coloma, CA 95613, tel. 916/622–6919

It was in Coloma that California's gold-rush fever first erupted in 1848, with the discovery of gold at Sutter's Sawmill. Among the few remaining structures from that period, the Coloma Country Inn, a pretty farmhouse with a wraparound porch and gray shiplap siding, sits behind a long, white-picket fence in the verdant, 300-acre Marshall Gold Discovery State Park. The inn is also within easy walking distance of most historic sites.

Cindy and Alan Ehrgott first came to now-tranquil Coloma (population 250) in 1983 with the intention of expanding their Los Angeles–based adventure travel business, but ended getting bitten by the innkeeping bug. They still offer rafting trips and hot-air-balloon rides through the American River Canyon, where argonauts once panned for gold.

Coloma's history is represented by old photographs along the staircase on the inn's hand-stenciled walls, but the treasures in the house are not restricted to California's gold-rush era: Cindy has a fabulous collection of quilts from the 1880s to 1920s. Equally impressive is her collection of English and German blue-and-white delftware storage jars. An assortment of antique bric-a-brac is displayed in the living room, where guests can relax in wing-back chairs in front of the fireplace.

The guest-room furnishings are also eclectic, and each room is bright and tasteful. Rose has lots of windows, a private patio, and a bed and dresser made of New Mexico fruitwood. Eastlake boasts an oak Eastlake set with bed, dresser, and washstand. The Lavendar, one of two rooms on the second floor, is furnished with American antiques including a Duncan Phyfe secretary and a cherry chest of drawers with exquisite dovetail construction. The Geranium suite, a private hideaway popular with honeymooners, has its own trellised garden. The roomy, dreamy Cottage has delphinium-blue walls and sage-green trim, as well as a white Jenny Lind–style bed with turned spools. The lovely grounds include a gazebo, crab-apple trees, a small pond, and a formal rose garden.

Breakfast, served family-style on blue willow china in the dining room, is delightful here. There's a great view of the pond out back where ducks can be seen cruising and around which deer graze in the early morning haze. A typical ample menu features fruit—fresh in summer and compote in cool weather—blueberry muffins with cinnamon butter, and eggs scrambled with mushrooms and potatoes.

▦ *3 double rooms with baths, 2 doubles share bath, 1 suite, 1 double suite. Air-conditioning, kitchens in suites, bicycles, canoe, hot-air-balloon and white-water-rafting packages. $84–$170; full breakfast, afternoon refreshments. No credit cards. No smoking, no pets.*

Foxes Bed and Breakfast Inn

77 Main St., Sutter Creek, CA 95685, tel. 209/267–5882, fax 209/267–0712

The simple, pale gray two-story structure that houses the Foxes Bed and Breakfast Inn in Sutter Creek was built during the gold rush; although its 19th-century origins are certainly intriguing, this elegant seven-room inn owes its chief appeal to the late-20th-century pampering of its guests. Min Fox, who has owned the inn with her husband, Pete, since 1980, sits down with guests each evening and discusses the next day's breakfast. (There's an airy French toast made with apple juice and egg white for the cholesterol-conscious.) Breakfast is served in guests' rooms on an antique wooden table or at a private table in the garden shaded by a pink dogwood tree. An ornate silver pot holds coffee or tea. The place mats are crocheted, as are the little doilies that are slipped over the bases of the stemmed orange-juice glasses.

For years Pete and Min ran an antiques shop that specialized in Victorian pieces. When they decided to turn the house into an inn, they rearranged the unsold tables, armoires, and carved beds (one headboard is 9 feet tall) and—*voilà*—the place was practically furnished. Guest rooms have grown increasingly romantic over the years, particularly the three newer rooms in the carriage house out back.

The big Blue Room, with ice-blue floral-print wallpaper, has a large bed with a carved headboard. A wooden half-tester canopy with pale blue curtains is suspended overhead. A print of a red fox in winter repose hangs on one wall. (Every room here has a foxy touch, whether in pillow or print.) Appealing in a different way, the Anniversary Room in the front of the main house is tucked into a gable with light-filled windows on three sides; it has an elaborately carved 10-foot-tall armoire facing the bed.

The house has a peach-color front parlor, with a spool-based table and a couple of Rococo Revival sofas for curling up with a good book or flipping through the inn's collection of menus from local restaurants. Or guests may sit in the gazebo out back and admire the lush garden, particularly enticing in the spring when the big pink dogwood is in bloom.

🏨 *5 double rooms with baths, 2 suites. Air-conditioning, robes, radios, tape decks; fireplace, TV in 4 rooms. $100–$155, full breakfast. D, MC, V. No smoking, no pets, 2-night minimum on weekends.*

Groveland Hotel

18767 Main St., Groveland, CA 95331, tel. 209/962-4000 or 800/273-3314, fax 209/962-6674

Of all the gold-rush towns, Groveland wears its past most easily. Not a deserted ghost town like nearby Chinese Camp, or gentrified and upscale like Sutter Creek, Groveland remains what it always has been: a commercial center, home to miners and workers who built the Hetch Hetchy Dam, and a short drive from Yosemite National Park. The Iron Door Saloon here claims to be the oldest in the state still operating. And one of the two buildings that make up the Groveland Hotel, an adobe built in 1849, is considered among California's oldest and largest. Always a hotel, during the gold rush the adobe had a reputation among the miners as being the "best house on the hill, offering all the pleasures a man could want."

When Peggy Mosley discovered that the adobe and an adjacent Queen Anne Victorian were for sale and slated for demolition in 1990, she bought them and began the renovations that would make both buildings inviting to 20th-century guests without compromising their 19th-century history. Thus the adobe still displays its original facade, wraparound verandas, casement windows, and a central staircase. Likewise the Victorian has gingerbread and bay windows. Peggy looked to the past in decorating by installing floral wallpapers, antique French beds, wicker furnishings, and English armoires.

The three suites are the nicest accommodations; each occupies a pair of the original hotel rooms. Lilly Langtry on the second floor, a popular choice with honeymooners, is the prettiest of the suites, with soft pink sponge-painted walls surrounding a brass cannonball bed. There's a sofa opposite the fireplace and a spa tub in the bathroom. Two of the four upstairs rooms in the original adobe have stenciled decorations on the walls and French doors providing direct access to the veranda; they all open onto the guest lounge, where there's a TV and a selection of books and magazines.

The restaurant at the Groveland Hotel, open for dinner and Sunday brunch, has a classic menu (prime rib, roast duck, surf and turf), casual ambience, and good service.

Operating the Groveland Hotel is a new career for Peggy, a spunky woman who spent more than 40 years in the aerospace industry and has piloted her own airplane. Highlights of her life, she says, include knowing Elvis Presley and flying in the Powder Puff Derby.

▦ *14 double rooms with baths, 3 suites. Air-conditioning, radio, phones, robes; fireplace and whirlpool bath in suites, limited room service, restaurant, saloon. $95–$175; Continental breakfast, afternoon refreshments. AE, D, DC, MC, V. No smoking.*

Red Castle Inn

109 Prospect St., Nevada City, CA 95959, tel. 916/265–5135 or 800/761–4766

Dubbed the Castle as it rose on Prospect Hill in 1857, this four-story, brick Gothic Revival house still looks majestic. Set in a grove of cedars, chestnuts, and walnuts, the Red Castle Inn has a classic pitched gable roof dripping with icicle-shape gingerbread and a broad veranda shaded by white sail canvas curtains tied back with red sashes.

Mary Louise and Conley Weaver, who bought the house in 1985, were the perfect inheritors of this Sierra-foothills treasure: He was an architect in San Francisco, she specialized in interior design and historic preservation. Between them, the Weavers have transformed the inn into a virtual Vatican of Victoriana. The elegant parlor, its tall French doors draped in lace and framed by satin valances, boasts a growing collection of fine antiques, including a Renaissance Revival settee,

which Conley describes as "my new car."

Modern baths were installed in the former trunk-storage areas, but the guest rooms are all original to the house. On the first floor, one level below the main entrance, a private door leads to Forest View, where a large mahogany bed has a lighted canopy. On the main floor, the Garden Room's dramatic display of "Victorian clutter" includes a Renaissance Revival hall tree and a reproduction Chinese Chippendale canopy bed. Down the hall in the Gold Room, rust-and-gold drapes hang from a faux-burled cornice. Two diminutive suites on the third floor, formerly the children's quarters, have 7-foot ceilings. The fourth floor two-bedroom Garret suite has a great view through Gothic arched windows.

Gardens covering an acre and a half of hillside are cool and inviting on a warm summer day. Chairs, benches, and a porch swing hide in secluded corners amid the camellias and azaleas.

Mary Louise and Conley's breakfasts, served buffet-style on a sideboard in the main foyer, often include traditional American dishes such as Indian pudding or Dutch babies (a baked and fruit-filled pancake). Guests can eat in the parlor, outdoors in the terraced garden, or in the seclusion of their private sitting areas and verandas. On Saturday morning, guests can hire a horse-drawn carriage to tour the town's historic district.

▦ *4 double rooms with baths, 2 suites, 1 double suite. Air-conditioning in suites. $70–$140; full breakfast, afternoon refreshments. MC, V. No smoking, no pets, 2-night minimum on weekends Apr.–Dec. and holiday weekends.*

Other Choices

Amador Harvest Inn. 12455 Steiner Rd., Plymouth, CA 95669, tel. 209/245–5512 or 800/217–2304. 4 rooms with baths. Air-conditioning, 2 rooms share balcony, gardens, lake, winery tasting room adjacent. $85–$110; full breakfast, afternoon refreshments. MC, V. No smoking, no pets, 2-night minimum on special-event weekends.

Court Street Inn. 215 Court St., Jackson, CA 95642, tel. 209/223–0416 or 800/200–0416, fax 209/223–5429. 6 double rooms with baths, 1 double suite in cottage. Air-conditioning, TV, radio, tape player, robes; fireplace in 3 rooms, whirlpool bath in 1 room, outdoor whirlpool. $95–$135; full breakfast, afternoon refreshments. AE, MC, V. No smoking, no pets, 2-night minimum on holiday weekends.

Dunbar House, 1880. 271 Jones St., Box 1375, Murphys, CA 95247, tel. 209/728–2897 or 800/692–6006, fax 209/728–1451. 2 double rooms with baths, 2 suites. Air-conditioning, phone, TV/VCR, refrigerator, hair dryers; towel warmer, 2-person whirlpool bath in 1 suite, video library, gardens with gazebo, 2-person hammock. $115–$155; full breakfast, evening refreshments. AE, MC, V. No smoking, no pets, 2-night minimum on weekends.

Emma Nevada House. 528 E. Broad St., Nevada City, CA 95959, tel. 916/265–4415 or 800/916–3662, fax 916/265–4416. 6 double rooms with baths. Air-conditioning, TV, phones, robes; whirlpool bath in 2 rooms, fireplace in 1 room, gardens, fireplace in parlor, library. $100–$150; full breakfast, afternoon refreshments. AE, MC, V. No smoking, no pets, 2-night minimum on weekends August through December.

Flume's End. 317 S. Pine St., Nevada City, CA 95959, tel. 916/265–9665, 800/991–8118. 6 double rooms with baths. Air-conditioning, private deck outside 4 rooms, whirlpool bath in 2 rooms, sitting room with wet bar shared by 2 rooms, wood-burning stove in 1 room, stocked guest refrigerator. $75–$135, full breakfast. MC, V. No smoking, no pets, 2-night minimum on weekends Apr.–Dec.

Gold Quartz Inn. 15 Bryson Dr., Sutter Creek, CA 95685, tel.209/267–9155 or 800/752–8738, fax 209/267–9176. 24 double rooms with baths. Air-conditioning, TV, phone, alarm clock, hair dryer, ironing boards; guest laundry, soft drink machine, gardens, croquet. $75–$125; full breakfast, afternoon refreshments. AE, D, MC, V. No smoking, no pets.

Grey Gables. 161 Hanford St., Box 1687, Sutter Creek, CA 95685, tel. 209/267–1039 or 800/473–9422, fax 209/267–0998. 8 double rooms with baths. Air-conditioning, hair dryers; fireplace. $85–$125; full breakfast, afternoon tea, evening hors d'oeuvres. AE, D, MC, V. No smoking, no pets, 2-night minimum on weekends.

Indian Creek Bed and Breakfast. 21950 Hwy. 49, Plymouth, CA 95669, tel. 209/245–4648. 4 double rooms with baths. Air-conditioning, balcony and private entrances in 2 rooms, pool, outdoor hot tub, extensive gardens, creek. $90–$120; full breakfast, evening refreshments. D, MC, V. No smoking, no pets, 2-night minimum on holiday weekends.

M. L. Marsh House. 254 Boulder St., Nevada City, CA 95959, tel. 916/265–5709 or 800/874–7458, fax 916/265–8789. 5 double rooms with private baths, 1 suite. Air-conditioning, fireplace in suite, TV/VCR, phone on request, video library, gardens. $125–$150; full breakfast, afternoon refreshments. MC, V. No smoking, no pets, 2-night minimum Apr.–Dec. and holiday weekends.

Power's Mansion Inn. 164 Cleveland Ave., Auburn, CA 95603, tel. 916/885–1166, fax 916/885–1386. 11 double rooms with baths. Air-conditioning, TVs, phones, robes; fireplace in 2 rooms, whirlpool bath in 2 rooms, cable TV in parlor, German, Chinese, Dutch spoken. $79–$149; full breakfast, afternoon refreshments. AE, MC, V. No smoking, no pets.

Serenity, A Bed & Breakfast Inn.
15305 Bear Cub Dr., Sonora, CA 95370,
tel. 209/533–1441 or 800/426–1441. 4
double rooms with baths. Air-conditioning, fireplace in 2 rooms, guest parlor with books and games. $90–$115;
full breakfast, afternoon refreshments.
AE, MC, V. No smoking, no pets, 2-
night minimum on holiday weekends.

Reservations Services

B&B International (Box 282910, San
Francisco, CA 94128–2910, tel. 415/
696–1690 or 800/872–4500, fax 415/
696–1699). **Eye Openers B&B Reservations** (Box 694, Altadena, CA 91003,
tel. 213/684–4428 or 818/797–2055, fax
818/798–3640). **Gold Country Inns of
Tuolumne County** (tel. 209/533–1845).

High Sierra, Including Yosemite and Lake Tahoe

High Country Inn

*100 Green Rd. (at Bassets, HCR 2, Box
7), Sierra City, CA 96125, tel. 916/862–
1530 or 800/862–1530*

When you first drive up to the High
Country Inn, you become aware of the
ranchlike grounds, but you're still not
prepared for the well-kept secret that
awaits you. The craggy Sierra Buttes
in the background provide one of the
most stunning views in all of the Sierra.
More than 30 jewel-like lakes nestle
against those jagged mountains in the
remote Lakes Basin Recreation Area.

Owner Cal Cartwright, whose roots in
this region date from the 1850s, wanted
to settle here upon retirement. When
he and his wife Marlene found a ranch-
style mountain house on a 2½-acre corner, they snapped it up.

The house was built in 1961; a new section, added in 1981, offers the most private room, the second-floor Sierra
Buttes Suite. Tall cathedral windows
across one wall frame the buttes;
guests can laze in bed and watch the
morning sun creep down them and listen to the river that rushes through the
property. A wood-burning stove occupies one corner. The modern bath-
dressing room boasts a 6½-foot antique
tub. The Howard Creek Room is in the
older section, next door to Cal and Marlene's sleeping quarters, with a view of
the pond and two double beds and private bath. Though comfortable, it is
unsuitable as a romantic getaway.

The furnishings reflect Cal and Marlene's families' histories. The cane-seat
chairs in the Golden Pond Room came
from the East with Calvin's family in
1852. Marlene has decorated the inn
with antiques and quilts hand-sewn by
her mother.

The heart of the inn is a big, open living
room, dining room, and kitchen. Guests
can curl up in front of the large stone
fireplace with a book from the
Cartwrights' library (which focuses on
local history), or watch TV. Be prepared for a more likely alternative,
however, which is hearty conversation
with the chatty hosts. They'll share
local gossip, review recent newspaper
items, or discuss restaurant choices.

The inn has a special brand of entertainment in its trout pond. Marlene
invites guests to feed the fish—more
than 300 nibblers come right up to the
grassy shore to catch a bite.

Marlene sets up breakfast places at a
long table fronting the window wall; in
good weather she serves on the deck.
Guests can expect such delights as corn
bread and quiche spiced southwestern-
style, or zucchini-walnut waffles. A 7
AM wake-up tray of coffee or tea can
tide guests over till breakfast time.

🛏 *1 double room with bath, 2 doubles
share bath, 1 suite. Fireplace in suite.
Cable TV/VCR in living room, robes,
trout pond, river. $80–$125, full breakfast. MC, V. No smoking, no pets, 2-
night minimum on holiday weekends.*

Le Château du Sureau

48688 Victoria La., Box 577, Oakhurst, CA 93644, tel. 209/683–6860, fax 209/683–0800

Nestled in the Sierra Nevada foothills on 7 acres of wooded grounds and manicured gardens is an exquisite inn, Le Chateau du Sureau (Estate by the Elderberries). Viennese owner Erna Kubin modeled the château after those in southern France, evoking childhood memories of her visits to the houses of her well-to-do relatives.

Taking great care to provide authenticity wherever possible, Erna incorporated centuries-old tapestries, antique French furniture, and 15th-century tile into a structure built in 1991. With a bit of ingenuity, even the new became old: The carpenter who created the château's 40 wooden doors beat them with chains, and after the limestone floors were laid, they were cracked and chipped.

Each of the nine bedrooms is named for a plant or herb; all have a fireplace, a view of the Sierras, Provençal fabric, and an enormous bathroom with a deep tub. The Rosehip Room has an Empire-style queen-size bed and a 10-foot-high armoire. Elderberry is set in blue-and-white toile. The Napoleonic-era Saffron Room features ebony furnishings inlaid with ivory; the Lavender Room is a castle nook with a panoramic view of the Sierras.

Breakfast is the highlight of a stay at the château; guests can remain for five days without repeating a meal. The aroma of fresh breads, baked on the premises, is a wake-up call to a breakfast that may include corn cakes with fresh kernels, layered with lox and basil sauce, fresh fruit with homemade yogurt, and fresh-squeezed juice. Guests may eat in the dining room or the garden, among the flowers and a fountain.

Dinner is also served on the premises at Erna's Elderberry House, built in 1984, and just a short walk from the château along a winding path. Prix-fixe, six-course dinners change nightly.

▦ *9 double rooms with baths. Wood-burning fireplaces, CD sound systems in all rooms; restaurant, pool. $310–$410, full European breakfast. AE, MC, V. No smoking, no pets, 2-night minimum weekends, 3-night minimum holiday weekends.*

New England Ranch

2571 Quincy Junction Rd., Quincy, CA 95971, tel. and fax 916/283–2223

A beautiful drive 2 miles outside of Quincy brings you to 88 acres of pastureland and a white house that, as its name suggests, looks like a Vermont cottage. Built in the 1850s, the New England Ranch had fallen into disrepair by the time Barbara Scott purchased it in the late 1980s to pursue a dream. She left the comfortable life and social circles of Napa Valley in search of wide open spaces and the opportunity to someday own a horse. With this goal in mind, Barbara spent three years restoring the Ranch. Finally, in 1991, she opened this striking, intimate inn, furnished with beautiful family heirloom antiques and polished wood floors. Four years later she acquired her very first horse, an Arabian white mare.

Sunlight floods both upstairs guest rooms, which have an expansive view of the countryside. The pale apricot Vincent, with a lace-covered, brass step-up bed, shares a cozy sitting room with Chandler, which has a chenille bedspread and delicately patterned wallpaper. The bathrooms are especially cheery, with white-painted wood floors and bright floral wallpaper; one has an old English commode with a built-in sink, and the other features a large pedestal sink and claw-foot tub. The downstairs room is the largest and most deluxe, with a king-size bed. Those wishing to "rough it" a little can stay away from the main house in the "bunkhouse" trailer, which sleeps five.

Ideal for adults with children and/or horses, it has a complete kitchen and private bath and is near the barn, corrals, and riding area.

The exquisite pair of gold-leaf Czechoslovakian plates on the dining table are just for show, but Barbara does bring out her china and silver to serve the fresh ranch eggs, blintzes, and scones that she cooks on the house's original woodstove. The fresh herbs, vegetables, and fruits are all from her newly planted garden. In winter, if you're not up for nearby skiing or snowmobiling, you can retire after breakfast to the dusty-rose parlor and look out the bay window or into a blazing fire.

But in fine weather, you'll want to go out and explore the grounds. The outbuildings include an old creamery, which Barbara has converted into a country store. Some of the land is leased to neighboring ranchers, so cattle and horses graze the grounds. You can ride out into the rolling green hills on one of Barbara's mountain bikes or take a dip in one of the creeks on the property. Ask Barbara to introduce you to her pet llama Pierre and his sidekick donkey José, who might nibble carrots or alfalfa from your hand.

🏨 *3 double rooms with baths, 1 trailer with kitchen and bath. Robes; creeks, mountain bicycles, horse stables and corrals, airport pickup. $40–$95, full breakfast. MC, V. No smoking, no pets except for horses.*

Sorensen's

14255 Hwy. 88, Hope Valley, CA 96120, tel. 916/694–2203 or 800/423–9949

Those seeking a bona fide High Sierra atmosphere in rustic surroundings amid Douglas fir, piñon, and ponderosa, will want to consider this historic mountain resort alongside the Carson River at the 7,000-foot level. Sorensen's, just east of Carson Pass, is open year-round. It offers access to 600 square miles of

public land. Hiking, fishing, cross-country skiing, stargazing—you name it, you'll find it here.

The inn provides comfortable accommodations, ranging from the rudimentary to the classy, in bed-and-breakfast units and housekeeping cabins. One of the latter is a replica of a 13th-century Norwegian summer home shipped to Hope Valley piece by piece by Sorensen's former owner. Another, the Chapel, is a honeymooners' favorite. The log cabin has a steeple, church doors, vaulted ceilings, and a spiral staircase to heaven—well, to the bedroom, anyway.

Some of the cabins date from the turn of the century, when Martin Sorensen, an immigrant Danish shepherd, and his wife, Irene, began camping here. For more than 50 years, the place was primarily a hangout for family and friends, travelers, and wilderness folk. In 1970, the family sold the inn, which began a decade of decline; Sorensen's came to be known locally as the "Last Resort."

Then John and Patty Brissenden, community activists from Santa Cruz, purchased the place for 1,000 ounces of gold and set about to revitalize it, renovating some of the cabins and building others from scratch. The result is an eclectic collection of accommodations connected by a network of trails. Most of the cabins have kitchens; many have sitting areas and lofts. All cabins are offered on a housekeeping basis (breakfast not included), but small, simply furnished bed-and-breakfast rooms are available as well. Guests select breakfast from the menu at the Country Café, housed in a log cabin and open for all three meals.

Within walking distance of Sorensen's along the West Fork Carson River is a new acquisition of John and Patty's, called Hope Valley Resort. It offers camping, a convenience store, a prime fishing location, and llama rentals.

John and Patty enhance their guests' appreciation of the surroundings with classes in astrology, fly-fishing, nature, art, and other subjects. Guests can also hike along the fire trail that passes through the property, study the stars, and cross-country ski throughout the winter.

🏠 *1 double room with bath, 2 doubles share bath, 28 housekeeping cabins, each accommodating 2–6 persons. Restaurant, wood-burning stove in 18 rooms, convenience store, sauna, trout pond, picnic tables, barbecues, children's play area. $70–$275, full breakfast (for B&B guests). MC, V. No smoking, 2-night minimum on weekends, 3- or 4-night minimum on holidays.*

White Sulphur Springs

Hwy. 89, Box 136, Clio, CA 96106, tel. and fax 916/836–2387 or 800/854–1797

This big white farmhouse has welcomed travelers since the 1850s, when it was built as an overnight lodge for the Quincy Mohawk Stage Line. A tranquil charm surrounds the inn now; it's hard to imagine that thousands of prospectors once ranged over these tree-covered hillsides and gentle valleys. But if the magnificent view of Mohawk Valley, the airy elegance of the main house, the seclusion of the cottages, and the warmth of the innkeepers don't remind you that you've left the madding crowds far behind, the sounds of bullfrogs, cows, and distant coyotes surely will.

The ambience of the inn remains much the way it was when it was a stagecoach stop. Many of the furnishings are original to the inn: a pump organ in the parlor, an antique piano, brocade-covered Victorian settees, a pine bedroom set handcrafted by the inn's original owner. The inn also contains the original woodstove after which the town of Clio was named. The expansive windows of the parlor frame luscious green pastures dotted with cows, and on a large table in a corner sits a 136-year-old Christmas cactus. The attic has been converted to a museum where visitors can view collectibles from the stagecoach days.

There are guest rooms in the main house and in two cottages, the Dairy House and the Hen House (the original chicken coop). All have expansive views of meadows and mountains; a balcony across the front of the main house extends the view for guests on the second floor. The Victorian furnishings include a fainting couch, antique washstands, dry sinks, and rocking chairs.

Guests are served an elaborate ranch-style breakfast in the formal dining room. Breakfast is likely to consist of sausage-spinach frittata, home-style potatoes, homemade bread, and fruit.

The inn's warm (78 degrees year-round), spring-fed Olympic-size pool is used mainly in the summer, though heartier souls can jump into the steamy waters during other seasons. These same sulphur springs also help to cut down on heating bills—hot water has been piped under the floor of the main house and the cottages since 1974.

With five championship courses in the area, golf is popular with visitors, as are hiking, fishing, and cross-country skiing. Downhill skiing and snowmobiling are nearby at Johnsville. Concerts are sponsored by the Kentucky Mine in Sierra County during summer months. A schedule can be obtained by phoning the innkeepers.

🏠 *1 double room with bath, 5 doubles share 2 baths, 1 housekeeping cottage, 1 double housekeeping cottage with kitchen. Robes; outdoor pool, picnic area, barbecue. $85–$140, full breakfast. D, MC, V. No smoking, no pets, 2-night minimum on summer and holiday weekends.*

Other Choices

Busch and Heringlake Country Inn. Main St., Box 68, Sierra City, CA 96125, tel. 916/862–1501. 4 double rooms with baths. Whirlpool bath in 2 rooms, fireplace in 1 room, bar (seasonal). $90–

$130, full breakfast. MC, V. No smoking, no pets.

Chalfant House. 213 Academy St., Bishop, CA 93514, tel. 619/872–1790. 4 double rooms with baths, 3 suites. Air-conditioning, TV in parlor and suites, airport pickup, antiques shop. $65–$90; full breakfast, evening ice-cream sundaes. AE, D, MC, V. No smoking, no pets.

Clover Valley Mill House. Railroad Ave. and S. Mill St., Box 928, Loyalton, CA 96118, tel. 916/993–4819. 3 double rooms (1 with half-bath) share 1 full bath; 1 suite. Phone in rooms, TV/VCR in living room, horseshoes, volleyball, tetherball, croquet. $75–$130, full breakfast. MC, V. No smoking, no pets except for horses.

Norfolk Woods Inn. 6941 W. Lake Blvd., Box 262, Tahoma, CA 96142, tel. 916/525–5000, fax 916/525–6266. 2 double rooms with baths, 1 suite, 4 housekeeping cottages, 1 honeymoon cottage. Phones; fireplaces in all cottages, restaurant, beer bar, pool, spa, barbecue, badminton, volleyball, horseshoes, Ping-Pong. $90–$150, full breakfast (except for cottages). AE, MC, V. No smoking, pets in cottages only, 3-night minimum on holiday weekends, 2-night minimum on weekends in cottages.

Rainbow Tarns. Rainbow Tarns Rd. (off Crowley Lake Dr.), Rte. 1, Box 1097, Crowley Lake, CA 93546, tel. and fax 619/935–4556 or 800/935–4556. 3 double rooms with baths. Whirlpool bath in 2 rooms, trout ponds, horse stables and corral (for guests' horses). $95–$125; full breakfast, afternoon refreshments. No credit cards. No smoking, no pets (horses welcome), 2-night minimum on weekends, 3-night minimum on holiday weekends.

Shore House. 7170 North Lake Blvd., Box 343, Tahoe Vista, CA 96148, tel. 916/546–7270 or 800/207–5160, fax 916/546–7130. 7 double rooms with baths, 2 cabins with baths. Refrigerators; whirlpool bath in 1 room, private outdoor entrances to all rooms, kitchen in 2 rooms. $125–$165, full breakfast. MC, V. No smoking, no pets, 2-night minimum weekends, 3-night minimum holiday weekends.

White Horse Inn. 2180 Old Mammoth Rd., Box 2326, Mammoth Lakes, CA 93546, tel. 619/924–3656 or 800/982–5657. 4 double rooms with baths. Laundry facilities, pool table, fireplace, TV/VCR in common area, outside hot tub $75–$400; full breakfast weekends, Continental breakfast weekdays, afternoon refreshments. D, MC, V. No smoking, no pets.

Yosemite Peregrine. 7509 Henness Circle, Box 306, Yosemite, CA 95389, tel. 209/372–8517 or 800/396–3639, fax 209/372–4241. 3 double rooms with baths. Fireplace and refrigerators in all rooms, whirlpool bath in 1 room, TV room, private decks, outdoor hot tub. $100–$150; full breakfast, evening hors d'oeuvres. MC, V. No smoking, no pets.

Yosemite West High Sierra. 7460 Henness Ridge Rd., Yosemite West, CA 95389, tel. 209/372–4808. 3 double rooms with baths. Whirlpool bath in 1 room, hammock. $85–$150; full breakfast, afternoon refreshments. MC, V. No smoking, no pets.

Reservations Service

B&B International (Box 282910, San Francisco, CA 94128, tel. 415/696–1690 or 800/872–4500, fax 415/696–1699).

Colorado

The Boulder Victoria Historic Inn

Denver

Queen Anne Inn

*2147 Tremont Pl., Denver, CO 80205,
tel. 303/296-6666 or 800/432-4667, fax
303/296-2151*

The Queen Anne Inn, part of the nationally registered Clements Historic District, is just five minutes' walk from the
attractions of downtown Denver, whose
skyscrapers loom like the Rockies from
the front porch. A walking tour might
include various excellent art museums,
the ornate State Capitol and U.S. Mint,
the huge Tabor Center mall, and the
chic shops and restaurants of LoDo
(Lower Downtown), a converted warehouse district.

Two adjoining houses form the inn: One
is an 1886 High Victorian with a magnificent open 35-foot turret; the other is an
1879 Queen Anne mansion. Owner Tom
King converted the former, which had
served as the innkeeper's residence,
into two-room guest suites and added
the sweeping Victorian-style porch.
The Queen Anne was built for Edwin
Pierce, the brother of Augusta Tabor,
whose husband Horace was a flamboyant mining magnate. Both houses are
fitted with handsome oak wainscoting

and balustrades; vaulted 10-foot ceilings; bay windows; and period furnishings such as wrought-iron, brass, and
four-poster canopy beds, cherry or pine
armoires, oak rocking chairs, and elaborate cherry mantel top mirrors. Many
of the exquisite, creatively decorated
rooms and suites have soothing views of
Benedict Fountain Park.

Each of the four High Victorian gallery
suites is dedicated to a famous artist—
Remington, Audubon, Rockwell, and
Calder; all have exposed brick walls
and reproductions of the artists' representative works. The Calder Suite has
a jetted tub and gas fireplace, the Remington Suite has a hot tub on a small
porch that opens onto the garden, and
the Rockwell Suite has a 5-foot stained-
glass window and a casement opening
onto the turret. The decor of the bedrooms in the Queen Anne section is
even more unusual. The most spectacular touches are the mural of the home in
the Tabor Room, set during a typical
garden party in 1894, and a hand-
painted aspen grove snaking around
the turret of the Aspen Room.

After leaving his post as a promotion
and advertising executive for Braniff
Airlines, Tom King opened the highly
rated Babbling Brook Inn in Santa
Cruz, California. He sold the Babbling

Brook and then worked as a consultant, advising clients who were searching for that perfect inn. He fell in love with a Queen Anne he scouted for a client, so much so that he bought it. Many clients are businesspeople and foreign travelers, who appreciate Tom's profesionalism and expertise. He's always available during the evening beverage and cheese hour, which often includes tastings of the little-known but excellent Colorado wines (plus hot spiced cider in winter).

Breakfast is served either in bed or in the spacious dining room. Each morning, the buffet includes heart-healthy selections like all-natural granola, fresh fruits and juices, Tom's own blend of coffee (a Venezuelan–Costa Rican–Colombian mix), muffins, scones, croissants, oatmeal, and hot entrées like quiches, cheese strudels, and omelets.

🏨 *10 double rooms with baths, 4 suites. Air-conditioning, phones, cable TVs in all suites, some rooms with whirlpool baths or outdoor hot tubs, offstreet parking. $75–$155, full breakfast. AE, D, DC, MC, V.*

Other Choices

Castle Marne. 1572 Race St., Denver, CO 80206, tel. 303/331–0621 or 800/926–2763, fax 303/331–0623. 7 double rooms with baths, 2 suites. Air-conditioning, phones, ceiling fans, fireplaces and whirlpool tubs in suites, croquet, off-street parking. $85–$200, full breakfast. AE, MC, V.

Reservations Service

Bed & Breakfasts Innkeepers of Colorado (Box 38416, Dept. S-95, Colorado Springs, CO 80937-8416, tel. 800/265–7696).

High Rockies

Irwin Lodge

Box 457, Crested Butte, CO 81224, tel. 303/349–5308

The Irwin touts itself as the "best-kept secret in the Rockies," and it's no idle boast. Talk about seclusion: In winter you must take a thrilling snowmobile ride around several switchbacks to reach this aerie, nearly 1,000 feet above (and 8 miles from) Crested Butte. The lodge sits 10,700 feet above sea level on a remote ridge overlooking Lake Irwin and the Sangre de Cristo range. Built in 1976, this weathered wooden structure looks much older than it is. Manager Rich Curtis has created an informal, homey atmosphere: Several cozy lounge areas circle a magnificent stone fireplace in the expansive lobby, where guests mingle throughout the day, exchanging anecdotes about their adventures, playing pool, darts, and Foosball or watching videos on the big-screen TV.

The smallish, charmingly rustic rooms have pine walls and are tastefully appointed with mahogany furnishings. Due to its isolated nature, rates usually include all meals—a hearty breakfast and a fine Continental lunch and dinner, served family style—although rates including breakfast only are available. The predominantly repeat clientele knows this is the premier place in America for powder skiing, as the surrounding area boasts an average of 500 inches of fluffy white stuff a year. A Snowcat will take you up to 12,000 feet, accessing a 2,000-foot vertical drop. Summer activities include mountain biking, and fishing and canoeing on Lake Irwin.

With no phones, just a shortwave radio to civilization, the Irwin represents the ultimate in total isolation. If you crave a little shopping or nightlife, you can always make arrangements to head into Crested Butte, a carefully preserved Victorian mining town that is a National Historic District (chartreuse, hot pink, and powder blue facades attest to the locals' warmth and whimsy), or to the modern mountain village of Mt. Crested Butte, about 3 miles away, that sprouted around the increasingly popular ski area of the same name. It's considered the quintessential ski bum town: friendly and reasonably priced, with great bars, top galleries, and impressive restaurants for a town its size.

23 double rooms with baths, 1 suite. Lunch and dinner available, 2 hot tubs, Snowcat skiing, snowmobiling, fishing, canoeing. $230–$330 per person, all-inclusive, 3-night minimum Nov.– Apr.; $88–$160 per person, full breakfast, May–Oct. MC, V.

Sardy House

128 E. Main St., Aspen, CO 81611, tel. 303/920–2525 or 800/321–3457, fax 303/ 920–4478

The Sardy is a classic 1892 red sandstone-brick Queen Anne in downtown Aspen. One of the world's fabled resorts, Aspen is synonymous with glitz, glamour, and glorious skiing (the hiking, fishing, and mountain biking are equally superb from spring through fall). An exquisitely preserved Victorian mining town, its gracious mansions and lacy pastel-color gingerbreads today house one gourmet restaurant and stylish shop after another—an eye-popping display of conspicuous consumption.

The inn's two buildings are connected by an enclosed gallery: The original mansion has turrets, gables, and a striking black linseed roof; the carriage house was built in 1985 to duplicate the authentic Victorian attributes of the original house.

The tiny reception area gives little hint of the sumptuous interior. It opens onto an inviting parlor with bay windows that drip with lace and chintz. A narrow, winding staircase with a magnificent oak balustrade leads to the winsome bedrooms, individually decorated in aubergine, mauve, and rose, with Axeminster carpets from Belfast, cherry armoires and beds, wicker furniture, and such welcome touches as Laura Ashley bed linens, heated towel racks, and whirlpool tubs; many have stellar views of the ski slopes.

The Sardy (as well as the equally posh Hotel Lenado, *see below*) has been smoothly run for the last decade by co-owner Daniel Delano and general-manager Jayne Poss, who have crafted elegant yet homey surroundings. The staff's professional demeanor—friendly without being familiar—results in an ambience that is slightly more formal than at other similar B&Bs. Guests linger, chatting over the breakfasts that are served in the cozy dining room in winter and by the outdoor pool in summer. The fluffy blueberry pancakes are justly famous; other standouts include eggs Benedict, Brie omelets, and home-baked fruit breads. In the evenings, the dining room doubles as the Sardy House, one of Aspen's more select restaurants, emphasizing fresh indigenous ingredients like Colorado rack of lamb and flaky Rocky Mountain trout meunière.

14 double rooms with baths, 6 suites. Restaurant, ceiling fans, cable TVs, phones, whirlpool tubs, heated towel racks, VCRs, stereos, dry or wet bars in suites, pool, hot tub, sauna. Summer, $165–$450; spring and fall, $85–$195; winter, $265–$650; Christmas week, $365–$750; full breakfast. AE, DC, MC, V.

Williams House

*303 N. Main St., Breckenridge, CO
80424, tel. 303/453-2975*

Innkeepers Fred Kinat and Diane Jaynes spent a year restoring this intimate 1885 miner's cottage. It's perfectly situated for a walking tour of Breckenridge—one of Colorado's largest National Historic Districts and the oldest continuously occupied town (founded 1859) on the Western slope of the Continental Divide. The town's lovingly restored and repainted structures include log cabins, false-fronts, and Victorian gingerbreads.

The inn itself has a cream, chartreuse, and forest-green facade, framed by vaulting snowcapped peaks. From the cozy front parlor, done in pink and ultramarine, to the exquisitely detailed accommodations, the Williams House is a dream B&B. The rooms are romantic as can be, with chintz or lace curtains, Laura Ashley and Ralph Lauren linens, mahogany beds, walnut wardrobes or cherry armoires, Oriental rugs, old framed magazine covers, handblown globe lamps, fresh flowers and sachets, and footed tubs.

Fred and Diane have also restored the 1880 yellow-and-white–trim Willoughby Cottage next door. It has scalloped lace curtains, intricately carved Victorian doors and balustrades, elaborate mantel with hand-painted tiles, gas fireplace, whirlpool bath for two, kitchenette, and rustic antique fixtures and furnishings, including a graceful mirror and a tempting cherry love seat. In other words, it's ideal for a honeymoon or for a peaceful, undisturbed getaway.

Best of all are the affable hosts, who moved to the mountains from Houston in the 1980s. Avid skiers, they warn guests to expect cold cereal on powder days—a pity since Diane's muffins, quiches, kugel, and frittatas are addictive. Summit County is a year-round sports paradise, particularly noted for skiing: Breckenridge, Copper Mountain, Keystone, and Arapahoe Basin are all within minutes of one another. In the summer, Fred and Diane take guests on hikes.

▦ *5 double rooms with baths, 1 housekeeping cottage. Outdoor hot tub with views. $89–$225, full breakfast except on "powder days." AE.*

Other Choices

Apple Blossom Inn. 120 W. 4th St., Leadville, CO 80461, tel. 719/486–2141. 3 double rooms with baths, 4 doubles share 2 baths, 1 housekeeping suite. Alarm clocks, robes, fireplace in 1 room, pass to Lake County Recreation center with gym and pool. $59–$118, full breakfast. AE, MC, V.

Hardy House Inn. 605 Brownell St., Georgetown, CO 80444, tel. 303/569–3388 or 800/490-4802. 3 double rooms with baths, 1 2-bedroom suite. TV/VCRs, outdoor hot tub. $73–$120, full breakfast. MC, V.

Hotel Lenado. 200 S. Aspen St., Aspen, CO 81611, tel. 303/925–6246 or 800/321–3457, fax 303/925–3840. 19 double rooms with baths. Ceiling fans, cable TVs, phones, outdoor hot tub. $95–$440, Continental breakfast. AE, DC, MC, V.

Mary Lawrence Inn. 601 N. Taylor St., Gunnison, CO 81230, tel. 970/641–3343. 3 double rooms with baths, 2 suites. Fans, radios, TV in both suites. $69–$89, full breakfast. MC, V.

Ski Tip Lodge. Keystone Resort, Box 38, Keystone, CO 80435, tel. 970/468–4202 or 800/222–0188, fax 970/468–4343. 9 double rooms with baths, 2 doubles share bath. Restaurant, ski shuttle. $29–$204, full breakfast. AE, DC, MC, V.

Reservations Service

Bed & Breakfasts Innkeepers of Colorado (Box 38416, Dept. S-95, Colorado Springs, CO 80937-8416, tel. 800/265–7696).

North Central Colorado: Rocky Mountain National Park

Boulder Victoria

1305 Pine St., Boulder, CO 80302, tel. 303/938-1300

The Victoria sits in the heart of downtown, just off the Pearl Street Mall, an eye-catching array of trendy restaurants and boutiques where all Boulder hangs out. Owners Matthew Dyrofs and Jeff White, noted for their renovations of several historic Boulder homes, set out to create a model B&B when they restored this 1876 Classic Revival beauty, painted in muted blue, mauve, and beige. When it was redesigned in 1889, in addition to building a second floor, architects added unusual features for the time—bay and leaded glass windows, most of which descend from ceiling to floor, allowing light to stream in throughout the house. French doors open onto the formal Victorian gardens: Trumpet honeysuckles climb the entire west side of the building, rose bowers and banks of poppies and columbine adorn the walkways, and wisteria welcomes guests to the front porch.

The rooms, each named for a previous or present owner of the house, are individually decorated in similarly tasteful styles. Most have the Laura Ashley–English-country-home look, with brass beds, down comforters, lace curtains, dried flowers, rocking chairs, and other period antiques. Terry-cloth robes and TVs, discreetly placed in armoires, bring the picture up-to-date. Some rooms, such as the Nicholson, also offer stunning views of the Flatiron Mountains that ring the town.

Zoe Kircos is the capable innkeeper (the owners aren't involved in day-to-day operations but often stop by to chat). Zoe splits her time between the Boulder Victoria and their new property down the street, the Earl House (*see below*). Some of the Continental breakfast specialties that she and her staff serve in the small, dainty breakfast room are lemon-blueberry bread, spiced dried fruit compote, homemade muesli, and maple pecan granola. Cookies (ask for the sublime gingersnaps) and scones with lemon curd dress the informal afternoon tea; evening port in the parlor is another complimentary treat.

Boulder is one of the country's most progressive cities, a town of cyclists and recyclers obsessed with environmental concerns and physical fitness: A local joke is, "Even the dogs jog." There are more bikes than cars in this uncommonly beautiful and beautifully uncommon city. To the northeast of town is the alpine wonderland of Rocky Mountain National Park, which was sculpted by violent volcanic uplifts and receding glaciers. Its three distinct ecosystems, verdant subalpine (towering Ponderosa pines), alpine (silvery streams, turquoise lakes, emerald meadows woven with wildflowers), and harsh tundra (wind-whipped trees growing at right angles and microscopic versions of familiar plants) provide varied hiking experiences. The park teems with wildlife—beavers, bighorn sheep, majestic elk, soaring bald eagles.

🏨 *6 double rooms, 1 suite. Air-conditioning, cable TVs, phones. $94–$189, full breakfast. AE, MC, V.*

Other Choices

Briar Rose. 2151 Arapahoe Ave., Boulder, CO 80302, tel. 303/442-3007. 9 double rooms with baths. Air-conditioning and ceiling fans in 4 rooms, clock radios, fireplaces in 2 rooms, patios off 2 rooms, TV in common room. $75–$139, Continental breakfast. AE, DC, MC, V.

Coburn Hotel. 2040 16th St., Boulder, CO 80302, tel. 303/545–5200 or 800/585–5811. 12 double rooms with baths. Air-conditioning, ceiling fans, cable TVs, phones, off-street parking, afternoon refreshments. $134–$162, full breakfast. AE, MC, V. No smoking.

Earl House. 1305 Pearl St., Boulder, CO 80302, tel. 303/938–1400. 5 double rooms with baths; 1 suite with bath; 2 carriage houses with 3 bedrooms, 2 baths and kitchen. Air-conditioning, cable TVs, phones, afternoon refreshments. $94–$179 with 2-night minimum on weekends (carriage houses $90–$325 with 1-week minimum), full breakfast (except in carriage houses). AE, MC, V.

Pearl Street Inn. 1820 Pearl St., Boulder, CO 80302, tel. 303/444–5584 or 800/232–5949. 6 double rooms with baths, 1 suite with bath. Air-conditioning, cable TVs, phones, fireplaces, afternoon refreshments. $95–$125, full breakfast. AE, MC, V.

Reservations Service

Bed & Breakfasts Innkeepers of Colorado (Box 38416, Dept. S-95, Colorado Springs, CO 80937-8416, tel. 800/265–7696).

South Central Colorado Along I–25

Holden House

1102 W. Pikes Peak Ave., Colorado Springs, CO 80904, tel. 719/471–3980

Holden House has three separate buildings: The main house is a 1902 Colonial Revival Victorian in robin's-egg blue with off-white and burgundy trim; it has a porch with round pillars, a turret, and a steep roof. The carriage house is more High Victorian in style, with dual column pillars. Also a Colonial Revival, the third house is painted a light grayish-mauve with burgundy trim and has intricate fish-scale gingerbread adorning the main pillars.

Some rooms have period decor while others are furnished in a frillier style; many include heirloom quilts. A homey atmosphere prevails, with old family photos and keepsakes placed throughout. The Aspen Suite has an open-beam turret, see-through fireplace made of clear materials, and mountain views. The Goldfield has a 4-foot skylight above the bed, a marble tub, exposed brick walls, an oak fireplace, and antique waterfall furniture courtesy of Sallie's grandmother. The Silverton Suite is awash in Victorian elegance, with a mahogany four-poster bed, a mission oak fireplace, and a marble tub for two.

Owners Sallie and Welling Clark took their new careers as innkeepers seriously, enrolling in hotel management courses while they lived off Welling's Navy pension. In the more than a decade since they purchased the house (and spent a solid year renovating it), they've become bona fide B&B mavens, enthusiastically joining state and national associations, contributing to B&B cookbooks, and corresponding with fellow innkeepers throughout the world. That they love their work is evident. Among the little extras they provide is a 24-hour coffee, tea, and cookie bar. Sallie serves gourmet three-course breakfasts on a Queen Anne–style dining table that seats 10, in the antique- and heirloom-filled parlor. Her specialties include Holden House eggs goldenrod (puff pastry shell filled with eggs hollandaise) and Southwest eggs fiesta (a tortilla shell wrapped to form a hood on the back of a soufflé cup, then filled with eggs, cheese, bacon, salsa, and sour cream). Don't be deceived, however, Holden House is really run by house cats Ming Toy (a black beauty with gleaming gold eyes) and Muffin (part-Siamese). They've been written up in the Lifestyle section of *Cats* magazine but, swears Sallie, "fame hasn't gone to their heads—they were already spoiled."

Holden House is in downtown Colorado Springs, the state's second-largest city. Attractions include historic areas like Manitou Springs and Old Colorado City, the Pro Rodeo Hall of Fame and Museum of the American Cowboy, and the jutting spires and sensuously abstract red rock monoliths of the Garden of the Gods and the famed craggy Pikes Peak.

🎏 *5 suites. Air-conditioning, phones, fireplaces, oversize tubs. $105–$115, full breakfast. AE, D, DC, MC, V.*

Other Choices

Abriendo Inn. 300 W. Abriendo Ave., Pueblo, CO 81004, tel. 719/544–2703, fax 719/542–1806. 10 double rooms with baths. Air-conditioning, TVs, phones, off-street parking. $58–$110, full breakfast. AE, DC, MC, V.

Adobe Inn. 303 N. Hwy. 24, Buena Vista, CO 81211, tel. 719/395–6340. 5 double rooms with baths. Restaurant, ceiling fans, cable TVs, fireplace in 1 room, hot tub. $55–$89, full breakfast. MC, V.

Cottonwood Inn. 123 San Juan Ave., Alamosa, CO 81101, tel. 719/589–3882 or 800/955–2623. 2 double rooms with baths, 2 doubles with shared bath, 3 suites. Phones and TVs in some rooms, gallery, gift shop, art and cooking workshops. $64–$85, full breakfast. AE, D, DC, MC, V.

Hearthstone Inn. 506 N. Cascade Ave., Colorado Springs, CO 80903, tel. 719/473–4413 or 800/521–1885. 20 double rooms with baths, 2 doubles share one bath, 3 suites. Air-conditioning, radios, fans, fireplaces in 3 rooms, croquet, off-street parking. $78–$148, full breakfast. AE, MC, V.

Reservations Service

Bed & Breakfasts Innkeepers of Colorado (Box 38416, Dept. S-95, Colorado Springs, CO 80937-8416, tel. 800/265–7696).

Southwest Colorado: The San Juan Mountains and the Four Corners

San Sophia B&B

330 W. Pacific St., Telluride, CO 81435, tel. 970/728–3001 or 800/537–4781

This "contemporary Victorian," built in 1988 in downtown Telluride, has a handsome cream-color paint job with jade trim, whimsical gables, turrets, bay windows, and oddly angled nooks and crannies that personalize the interior. Owners Alica Bixby and Keith Hampton also run an advertising and promotion firm in town, put on the annual Wine Festival, and raise two young children, but they still manage to spend time mingling with guests.

Pristine mountain light streams into every room, warmly accented with whitewashed oak woodwork. Each cozy bedroom has contemporary brass beds with handmade quilts, elegant pine armoires, tables and nightstands handcrafted by Colorado artisans, skylights in their tiled bathrooms, and stained-glass windows over the oversize tubs. Color schemes favor desert pastels—terra cotta with teal accents, mint or purple with blue trim. Thoughtful extras include plush terry robes, ideal for heading downstairs to the six-person hot tub in the gazebo. The San Sophia Mercantile sells items such as fanny packs, water bottles, and signature sweatshirts.

The San Sophia embodies the concept of a room with a view: Vistas include the magnificent San Sophia ridge, gushing creeks and waterfalls, and spectacular sunrises over Telluride Peak. The third-story octagonal observatory offers smashing 360° panoramas. Fine photographs of the region that hang throughout the inn bring the views indoors.

The atmosphere is wonderfully convivial: Guests mingle in the hot tub, in the observatory, and over breakfast and complimentary afternoon wine and hors d'oeuvres. All repasts are served in the dining room, whose two-story picture windows look east over the San Juan Mountains. Vaulting floral arrangements and crisp apricot napery grace the tables. The menu for the bountiful breakfast buffet changes daily, but always includes yogurt, fresh fruit salads, cereals, muffins, and such treats as cream cheese and dill johnny cakes with smoked salmon and almond apple pan puff. A prix-fixe supper is offered nightly, followed by late-night ports and single-malt scotches.

Telluride, a valley caught between azure sky and gunmetal mountains, was once so inaccessible that it was a favorite hideout for desperadoes like Butch Cassidy, who robbed his first bank here in 1889: Some locals claim that it is named not for the mineral tellurium, but for the saying, "To Hell You Ride." Today the savage but beautiful terrain attracts mountain people of a different sort—alpinists, telemarkers, snowboarders, freestylers, mountain bikers, and freewheeling four-wheelers—who attack any incline with consummate abandon. One local quips, "The Wild Bunch is alive and well."

Gorgeously preserved, Telluride is full of cotton-candy colored Victorian gingerbreads and frontier trading posts. Every corner yields stunning prospects of the San Juan Mountains, which loom menacingly or protectively, depending on the lighting. Telluride deserves a prize for most annual festivals: wine, hot-air ballooning, and mushrooms are celebrated, in addition to film and music, both of which attract high-profile international industry folk.

▦ *16 double rooms with baths. Airconditioning, cable TVs, phones, fans, hot tub, ski lockers, underground parking. $114–$260, full breakfast. AE, MC, V.*

Other Choices

Pennington's Mountain Village Inn. 100 Pennington Ct., Telluride, CO 81435, tel. 970/728–5337 or 800/543–1437. 9 double rooms with baths, 3 suites. Private decks, refrigerators, cable TVs, phones, billiard room, hot tub, laundry, steam room, afternoon happy hour. $140–$300, full breakfast. No smoking. AE, D, MC, V.

St. Elmo Hotel. 426 Main St., Ouray, CO 81427, tel. 970/325–4951. 7 double rooms with baths, 2 suites. Restaurant, radios, TV in parlor, sauna, outdoor hot tub. $75–$98, buffet breakfast. AE, D, MC, V.

Wingate Guest House. 1045 Snowden St., Silverton, CO 81433, tel. and fax 303/387–5520. 5 double rooms share 2 baths. $54–$64, full breakfast. No credit cards.

Reservations Service

Bed & Breakfasts Innkeepers of Colorado (Box 38416, Dept. S-95, Colorado Springs, CO 80937-8416, tel. 800/ 265–7696).

Connecticut

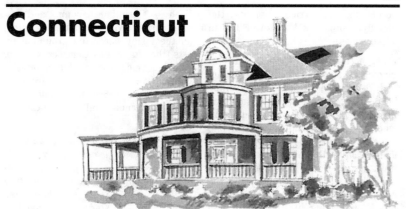

West Lane Inn

Southwestern Coast

Cotswold Inn

76 Myrtle Ave., Westport, CT 06880, tel. 203/226–3766, fax 203/221–0098

Westport has never been thought by travelers as a tourist destination, but thanks to the recent influx of trendy shops and restaurants, visitors are beginning to discover what this tony community has to offer. Honeymooners have for years been known to nest at the Cotswold Inn, a cute, gray cedar-shake cottage with a proliferation of gables and skylights. Nowadays you're also likely to encounter Europeans touring the Connecticut shoreline and New Yorkers looking for a short break from urbanity (Manhattan is just 50 miles away).

Though the steep gables, stone porches, and neatly manicured hedges and flower gardens recall England's Cotswold region, rooms capture the essence of 18th-century Connecticut, with reproduction Chippendale and Queen Anne furnishings—highboys, mule chests, wing chairs. Two rooms have canopy beds, one has a fireplace, and all are spruced up daily with fresh flowers, mints, and fine imported soaps. A common living room is made welcoming with about a dozen dried-flower arrangements and soft classical music filling the air. Here, each morning, a Continental breakfast of fresh cereals, fruit, yogurt, and gourmet coffees is laid out; wine and snacks are set out here early each evening. It's more museumlike than it is homey, but the Cotswold is perfect if you're looking for the efficiency and privacy of a small hotel but the intimacy of a bed-and-breakfast.

🏨 *3 rooms with baths, 1 suite. Air-conditioning, cable TVs, phones. $175–$225, Continental breakfast. AE, DC, MC, V. No smoking, no pets.*

The Inn at National Hall

2 Post Rd. W, Westport, CT 06880, tel. 203/221–1351 or 800/628–4255, fax 203/221–0276

The self-important name belies the whimsical and exotic interior of this towering redbrick Italianate on the downtown banks of the Saugatuck River. Built by Lee Tauck, the owner of the renowned tour company, Tauck Tours, the inn opened in 1993 as one of the two truly world-class luxury hotels in Connecticut, joining the equally sumptuous Mayflower Inn in Washington.

Each of the rooms here is a study in innovative restoration, wall-stenciling, and decorative design. The trompe l'oeil touches are evident from the moment you enter the lobby elevator, whose walls are painted to look like tome-filled bookshelves. A tour of the lounge and lobby reveal an exquisite furniture collection. Note the 300-year-old Swedish grandfather clock by the reception desk, and also the chandelier, which once hung in London's Savoy Hotel, looming above the table in the small, but elegant, conference room. Downstairs is a classic snooker table, imported directly from England. The hallways have fine hand-stenciling and delicate wood paneling.

Rooms and suites are magnificent—four of them have sleeping lofts and several have 18-foot windows. All of them are completely soundproof, modem- and fax-accessible, and have bathrooms of limestone, with sleek marble baths.

Every room has a theme or pattern that sets it apart from any other. Room 304 is probably the largest, with two-story floor-to-ceiling bookcases, tall windows overlooking the river below, and, behind the loft's bowfront balcony, an ornate four-poster bed. Room 306 has an armoire fitted with a custom-made kitchenette. Guests in this room (called the Equestrian thanks to its walls covered with horse stenciling) enjoy their own whirlpool bath, an enormous bathroom, and the inn's only fireplace. A smaller suite, Room 202, has French doors that separate the bedroom from the living area, making it perfect for entertaining friends or business clients. The Squirrel Room, so named for its antique squirrel lamp, is one of the smallest rooms, but it's still larger than what you'd find in a typical first-rate hotel.

With its Corinthian columns and tasseled curtain swags, Restaurant Zanghi, on the lushly decorated ground floor, sets the stage for Continental fare, including venison and rabbit. Exotic flavors show up across the menu, from the oysters with a Szechuan sauce, and sautéed peanut- and sesame-crusted calves' liver.

🛏 *8 double rooms with baths, 7 suites. Restaurant, air-conditioning, cable TV/VCRs, phones, refrigerators, kitchenette and fireplace in 1 suite, meeting facilities. $195–$450, full breakfast. AE, DC, MC, V. No smoking, no pets.*

Maples Inn

179 Oenoke Ridge, New Canaan, CT 06840, tel. 203/966–2927, fax 203/966–5003

The vast, sprawling, white-trimmed, yellow-clapboard Maples Inn reveals only a few of its 13 gables as it sits behind a deep lawn shaded by venerable maples on a street that's only a short drive from New Canaan's downtown shopping area. Its 12-over-12 and 9-over-9 windows that blink so invitingly at night have been welcoming guests with remarkable style since Cynthia T. Haas took over as owner 15 years ago.

Ms. Haas, a longtime New Canaan resident, had always wanted to run an inn. When her chance came, she made sweeping changes, rearranging rooms, bathrooms, closets, even walls. Totally refurbishing and redecorating each of the rooms, suites, and apartments made a dramatic difference, producing a subdued but elegant, highly individual, warm, and romantic atmosphere. There's even a completely equipped four-bedroom cottage that displays the same sensitivity to beauty and comfort.

All the bedrooms have canopied four-poster, queen-size beds and contain numerous antiques and furnishings from Ms. Haas's own collection. Yet the presence of such modern equipment as phones and TVs is never intrusive. Careful maintenance produces a gleam on mahogany chests, gilt frames, and brass lamps, and the imaginative use of fabrics and paper fans is an education in design. Even the red-white-and-blue theme in one suite is in good taste.

You can help yourself to breakfast each morning in the Mural Room, whose walls are painted with striking images of New Canaan during each of the four seasons. French doors open onto a wraparound porch, where you might eat in warm weather.

The small apartments and the cottage seem to encourage long-term stays by families, and youngsters, generally respectful of the premises, are made to feel at home in the friendly, informal atmosphere. A guest might well be asked to drop off some letters at the post office or offered a treat from a box of goodies in the front desk drawer. The Maple Inn is that kind of place.

▥ *6 double rooms with baths, 4 suites (1 with private screened-in porch), 9 apartments. Air-conditioning, cable TV and phones with voice mail, mini-refrigerators in most meeting rooms, working fireplace in 2 apartments. $65–$250, Continental breakfast. AE, MC, V. No pets.*

Silvermine Tavern

194 Perry Ave., Norwalk, CT 06850, tel. 203/847-4558, fax 203/847-9171

Silvermine was a pre-Revolutionary town that lies within the borders of Norwalk, New Canaan, and Wilton. The Tavern (part of which dates back to 1642), the Country Store, the Coach House, and the Old Mill are all clustered at the intersection of Silvermine and Perry avenues in Norwalk, a short distance north of the Merritt Parkway.

If he has a moment to spare in his busy schedule of keeping this large enterprise going, innkeeper Frank Whitman Jr. can fill you in on local history. His family has been running things here since 1955, and he grew up within the solid post-and-beam walls of the Colonial building at the heart of the present-day Tavern. Frank's eyes never seem to rest because he never lets up on the high standard he sets for every detail of the food and lodging.

Though it's best known as a restaurant, which overlooks the Silvermine River and the millpond, the inn also has wonderful guest rooms in the main building and across the road above the Country Store. The Tavern's common areas have unusual displays of primitive paintings, store signs, prints, and Early American tools and utensils; and the guest bedrooms, with their own complement of antique furnishings, have an equally pleasant atmosphere. The configuration of these rooms has evolved naturally over the ages, and the odd shapes only add to the charm. Room T-8 is entered through the bathroom, but is particularly cozy once you're inside. Some rooms have tubs but no showers because of the slanted ceilings. Wide-plank floors have hooked rugs to bridge the cracks of age, and starched white curtains grace the small, multipaned windows that glow invitingly at night, especially when there's snow on the ground.

Be sure to enjoy at least one meal here. The large low-ceiling dining room is romantic, with its Colonial decor and many water views. Traditional New England favorites are given some new slants: The duckling is semi-boneless and served in lingonberry sauce, and the preparation of the filet mignon and salmon change seasonally. Sunday brunch is a local tradition.

▥ *10 double rooms with baths. Restaurant, clock radios in rooms, air-conditioning in some rooms. $90–$110, Continental breakfast. AE, DC, MC, V. No pets. Closed Tues. year-round.*

Three Chimneys Inn

1201 Chapel St., New Haven, CT 06511,
tel. 203/789–1201, fax 203/776–7363

Running along the New Haven Green
and then into the heart of the Yale University
campus, Chapel Street appears
to be an infinite stretch of shops, old
hotels, bookstores, and restaurants
until you come to a surprise: Behind a
neatly kept garden stands a freshly
painted green, white, and pink Victorian
mansion, complete with gingerbread
trim and a carpeted stairway
flanked by potted geraniums. It's amazing
that this 1870 structure never fell to
the wrecker's ball as its neighbors
undoubtedly did; it's equally mind-boggling
that someone had the vision to
restore it to its present grandeur and
convert it into a thriving, much-needed
lodging in this vibrant college town.

Formally known as the Inn at Chapel
West, this mansion entered 1996 with
a new name, new ownership, and new
management. Under the extremely
competent management of new innkeeper
Fay Carrow, the guest rooms
never lack for bookings. The inn also
offers complete conference facilities
with catered meals—so a whiff or the
mere suggestion of something appetizing
wafting through its doors at mealtimes
is to be expected.

The guest rooms at the inn, though, are
the stuff on which it has built its following.
The owners were determined to
create a small hotel of uncommon luxury
and it is immediately evident that
they succeeded. Each room is decorated
individually, varying from Georgian
to Federal style. One room might
have a brass bed with a checkerboard
quilt, flanked by a French Provincial
writing table and chair. In another,
you'll come upon a four-poster canopy
bed, Oriental rugs, and a full-size desk.

The endless debate on family-owned
and -operated establishments versus
those professionally run will undoubtedly,
after a visit to Three Chimneys

Inn, turn in favor of the latter. The staff
here is delighted to guide you to the
best dining in New Haven or to go the
extra step and make arrangements for
theater tickets, a university tour, or
secretarial or baby-sitting services. It's
what makes the inn a bit of serendipity,
a true urban oasis.

🏠 *10 double rooms with baths. Air-*
conditioning, cable TVs, phones, free
parking. $150–$165, Continental buf-
fet breakfast. AE, D, MC, V. No smok-
ing, no pets.

Other Choices

Harbor House Inn. 165 Shore Rd., Old
Greenwich, CT 06870, tel. 203/637–
0145, fax 203/698–0943. 17 double
rooms with baths, 6 doubles share 2
baths. Full kitchen for guest use, air-conditioning,
TVs, phones. $89–$139,
Continental breakfast. AE, DC, MC, V.
No smoking, no pets.

Homestead Inn. 420 Field Point Rd.,
Greenwich, CT 06830, tel. and fax
203/869–7500. 14 double rooms and 3
singles with baths, 6 suites. Air-conditioning,
cable TV, phones, clock radios.
$95–$195, Continental breakfast. AE,
D, DC, MC, V. No pets.

Roger Sherman Inn. 195 Oenoke
Ridge, New Canaan, CT 06840, tel.
203/966–4541, fax 203/966–0503. 7 double
rooms with baths, 1 2-bedroom
suite. Restaurant and lounge with live
piano music, air-conditioning, cable
TVs, phones, dry cleaning available.
$100–$300, Continental breakfast. AE,
DC, MC, V. No pets.

Stanton House Inn. 76 Maple Ave.,
Greenwich, CT 06830, tel. 203/869–
2110, fax 203/629–2116. 23 double
rooms with baths, 2 doubles share 1
bath, 1 suite. Air-conditioning, phones,
cable TV in some rooms, copier, small
conference room, working fireplace in 2
rooms, wet bars in 7 rooms, pool. $80–
$135, Continental breakfast. AE, D,
MC, V. No smoking, no pets, 2-night
minimum on weekends.

Reservations Services

Bed & Breakfast, Ltd. (Box 216, New Haven, CT 06513, tel. 203/469–3260). **Covered Bridge Bed & Breakfast Reservation Service** (Box 447, Norfolk, CT 06058, tel. 203/542–5944). **Nutmeg Bed & Breakfast Agency** (Box 1117, West Hartford, CT 06207, tel. 203/236–6698).

Litchfield County South and Ridgefield

Boulders Inn

E. Shore Rd. (Rte. 45), New Preston, CT 06777, tel. 860/868–0541 or 800/552–6853, fax 860/868–1925

Built in 1895 as a private house, the stone and shingle Boulders Inn, with its carriage house and four guest houses, sits on a gentle slope with panoramic views of Lake Waramaug. The innkeepers, Kees and Ulla Adema, came from Holland and Germany, respectively, in the '60s, and now that their children are grown and away at school, they're able to devote themselves exclusively to the running of the inn. A bit of European charm seems appropriate to this hillside retreat.

The bedrooms are a curious mixture, with picture windows, Oriental rugs, antique Victorian furniture and bric-a-brac, as well as reproduction and overstuffed pieces happily coexisting. The eight rooms in the guest houses up the hill have private decks, recently enlarged baths, and working fireplaces. The Carriage House was opened in 1989, with three well-furnished rooms that have their own private entrances and fireplaces.

In the main inn building, the large living room and adjoining TV den welcome guests for relaxed reading and conversation. A recreation room in the basement offers a pool table, darts, and an assortment of games. Across the road, the inn has a private stretch of waterfront suitable for swimming and a beach house with a hanging wicker swing for passing peaceful moments. The more adventurous may set forth in a canoe, sailboat, rowboat, or paddleboat, all provided free to guests.

At dinner, which is included in the rates, you can choose from among several outstanding dishes, including pâté with pickled vegetables, shellfish risotto, venison cassoulet with cranberry beans and smoked sausage, and herb-grilled chicken with rosemary jus and garlic-mashed potatoes. The menu changes often, so be prepared for some imaginative specials.

Running the inn is a full-time job, but Kees and Ulla manage to squeeze in time for their hobbies. He is an avid stamp collector who exhibits internationally, and Ulla's specialty can be seen in the meticulously cut lamp shades used throughout the inn.

🏠 *15 double rooms with baths, 2 suites. Restaurant, air-conditioning in rooms, whirlpool baths in 4 rooms, mini-refrigerators and coffeemakers in Carriage House and guest houses, lake swimming, boating, tennis court. $250–$350, full breakfast; MAP available. AE, MC, V. No pets, 2-night minimum on weekends.*

The Elms

500 Main St., Ridgefield, CT 06877, tel. 860/438–2541

The impressive frame house that's The Elms inn on Main Street was once the home of a Colonial cabinetmaker, who built it in 1760, near the site of the Battle of Ridgefield. After the war, in 1799, it became an inn, which now includes an adjacent building erected in 1850. Since 1951 it has been operated by the Scala family, who in 1983 did a total renovation and have continued upgrading ever since.

By carefully combining antiques, re-productions, and modern fixtures, they've managed to produce an atmospheric but comfortable stopping-off place for weary, and hungry, travelers. The Elms prides itself on the award-winning Provence-influenced cuisine served in its dining areas. Specialties, such as local game and wild boar (served in January), have drawn the attention of appreciative "foodies" from all over.

Although the decorating approach to the guest rooms varies from "olde days" to modern hotel, each room is furnished with such appropriate Colonial-style touches as pineapple-stenciled wallpaper and hobnail spreads on lace-canopied four-poster beds. Most rooms have queen-size beds; good reading lights and comfortable Hitchcock armchairs are found throughout.

The most popular gathering spot is the lounge, where cocktails are served. Here, amid the settees, the upholstered wing chairs and cushioned Windsor chairs, beside a roaring fire, the inn's hearty Sunday brunch is also served.

The idea of lodging smack in the middle of town may not at first seem appealing, but The Elms is located on a broad avenue lined by tree-shaded mansions, close to pleasures such as band concerts in the nearby park and a short walk from antiques shops, boutiques, and historic sites. In fact, the antique map in the main dining room and the Revolutionary War relics scattered about the premises might even stir up your most patriotic sentiments.

🏠 *20 rooms with baths, 4 suites. Air-conditioning, TVs, phones, restaurant, room service. $105–$140, Continental breakfast. AE, DC, MC, V. No pets.*

Hopkins Inn

22 Hopkins Rd., New Preston, CT 06777, tel. 860/868-7295, fax 860/868-7464

This grand, 1847 Victorian, yellow and white frame building on a hill overlooking Lake Waramaug in New Preston has grown from a 19th-century boardinghouse to a delightful 20th-century country inn. As you drive up the short street that leads to both the inn and the Hopkins Winery, note the flag flying over the front entry, countless mullioned windows flanked by shutters, and gables, awnings, roofs, and porches. But presiding serenely over everything, the present-day innkeepers Franz and Beth Schober are the picture of efficiency.

At the inn, where dining has become celebrated, Franz is usually found in the kitchen, whence come the Austrian and Swiss dishes that form the centerpiece of the menu. His insistence on fresh ingredients extends to the maintenance of a fish tank stocked with trout, and he is also responsible for the extensive selection of wine that is carefully stored in the inn's cellar.

Beth's touch is seen just about everywhere else. She was a university librarian before taking over the inn in 1977, and her organizational skills show up in its smooth operation.

Guest rooms are all individual in shape and decor, though Colonial-print wallpapers and fabrics are used extensively. Furniture runs the gamut of country style, with emphasis on crisp, ruffled bed linens; sturdy, comfortable beds; good chairs for reading; and a variety of antique decorative pieces scattered about.

Although there's a cozy, somewhat Victorian living room, there are areas set up outdoors for sitting as well as for dining, under the shade of the trees and awnings.

This is possibly the only inn in Connecticut with vineyards and a winery at its doorstep. And even when the neighboring Hopkins Winery is technically closed, the inn will often arrange private tours for guests.

The Schobers have maintained the friendly, informal atmosphere the inn exhibited in its early days. Glancing through the guest book, you'll discover many names reappearing year after year—one indication of their success.

🏨 *8 double rooms with baths, 2 doubles share 1 bath, 1 double with hall bath, 1 housekeeping suite, 1 apartment. Restaurant, private lake beach. $61–$130, breakfast extra. No credit cards. No pets, 2-night minimum on weekends, closed Jan.–late Mar.*

Mayflower Inn

118 Woodbury Rd. (Rte. 47), Washington, CT 06793, tel. 860/868-9466, fax 860/868-1497

The countryside is abuzz these days with talk of this completely rebuilt inn in Washington, a picture-perfect country village perched high atop a mound of Litchfield County's old New England money. Certain suites at the Mayflower will set you back $495 a night, and one wonders how long folks will pay that sort of money out here in the sticks—even though we're talking about some awfully fancy sticks. Since Adriana and Robert Mnuchin opened the inn in March 1992, weekends have been booked solid. Of 24 families who celebrated the 1994 New Year's weekend at the inn, 20 slapped down deposits the next morning for the following year's festivities. On any given Saturday afternoon, you'll find the parking lot bumper to bumper with limos and sports cars. As one employee put it: "Each day seems to bring us a new famous face."

If you can stand the fact that the Joshua Reynolds portrait in the living room is a tad livelier than most of the guests, this opulent, if self-conscious, country inn is worth a splurge. The 28-acre grounds are replete with streams, trails, and a fitness center better suited to an NFL football team than a gaggle of bon vivants. And each of the 17 rooms and

seven suites, situated among three separate buildings, is decorated individually with fine antiques and four-poster canopy beds; the walls are hung with noteworthy prints and paintings, and papered in Regency stripes. The colossal mahogany-wainscoted bathrooms are marble throughout, and handmade Belgian tapestries are set importantly upon the bathroom floors.

If all that doesn't entice you, the mouthwatering cuisine of renowned chef, John Farnsworth, may. While you'll pay relatively more for dinner than for your room at most New England country inns, quite the opposite is true at the Mayflower, where dinner entrées range from $15 to $25—and the rooms cost 10 times that. If nothing else, come just to stare at this imposing compound.

🏨 *17 double rooms with baths, 8 suites. Restaurant, air-conditioning, cable TVs, phones, meeting facilities, tennis, heated pool, fitness center. $230–$550, breakfast extra. AE, MC, V. No smoking, no pets, 2-night minimum on weekends, 3-night minimum on holiday weekends.*

West Lane Inn

22 West La., Ridgefield, CT 06877, tel. 203/438-7323, fax 203/438-7325

Behind a broad expanse of carefully groomed lawn, this three-story Colonial-style mansion built in the late 1800s rises above a long columned sweep of porches that virtually demands relaxation. Only minutes from the center of Ridgefield and adjacent to the Inn at Ridgefield, the setting recalls a quieter time of small-town life in America.

Maureen Mayer, the owner-manager, has carefully reconstructed that atmosphere in the 18 years she has spent converting this former summer residence into a gracious country inn. As she sits on the porch sipping a cool drink, impeccably dressed and coifed, the former model and New York restaurateur is equally at ease supervising the efficient staff to maintain her high standards of comfort.

From the moment you step inside the oak-paneled lobby and (on cold days) feel the warmth of the cozy fire in the Victorian fireplace, you begin to get that "country inn" feeling. Guest rooms have well-chosen furnishings that are a slightly surprising contrast to the period style that predominates. But comfort is the byword; the queen-size and king-size beds, the upholstered barrel chairs, and the tables and lamps all seem to fit the oversize, high-ceiling rooms with their tall windows. Some of the rooms have working fireplaces that you're invited to light on chilly evenings. Several years ago, a former carriage house out back was converted to similarly furnished guest quarters, some with small kitchens. Most recently, cable TV and a personalized voice-mail system were added, to the joy of the West Lane's many business clients.

The lobby is a gathering place for guests when the weather prohibits sitting on the porches. A brightly wallpapered breakfast room directly off the lobby is again a contrast with its modern tables and chairs.

There's a cozy intimacy at West Lane Inn that makes it easy to strike up a conversation with fellow guests on the porch or in front of the fire. You can just stretch out and listen to the sound of the birds . . . or to the carillon concert from a nearby church.

▦ *14 double rooms with baths, 4 suites. Snacks, air-conditioning, cable TVs, phones, kitchenettes in some rooms, laundry and dry cleaning available. $120–$165, Continental breakfast; full breakfast extra. AE, DC, MC, V. No pets, 2-night minimum on holiday weekends.*

Other Choices

Curtis House. 506 Main St. S (Rte. 6), Woodbury, CT 06798, tel. 203/263–2101. 8 rooms with baths, 6 rooms share bath. Restaurant, TVs in some rooms. $40–$110, Continental breakfast extra. D, MC, V. No pets.

Homestead Inn. 5 Elm St., New Milford, CT 06776, tel. 860/354–4080, fax 860/354–7046. 14 double rooms with baths. Air-conditioning, cable TVs, phones. $74–$97, Continental breakfast. AE, D, DC, MC, V. No pets, 2-night minimum on weekends, May–Oct., and holidays.

Inn on Lake Waramaug. 107 N. Shore Rd., Lake Waramaug, CT 06777, tel. 860/868–0563 or 800/525–3466, fax 860/868–9173. 23 rooms with baths. 2 restaurants, air-conditioning, cable TVs, phones, boating equipment, tennis, game room, indoor pool. $209–$229, MAP. AE, MC, V. No smoking, no pets, 2-night minimum on weekends.

Stonehenge. Box 667, Ridgefield, CT 06877, tel. 203/438–6511, fax 203/438–2478. 14 double rooms with baths, 2 suites. Restaurant, room service, air-conditioning, cable TVs, phones. $120–$200, Continental breakfast. AE, MC, V. No pets.

Tucker Hill Inn. 96 Tucker Hill Rd., Middlebury, CT 06762, tel. 203/758–8334, fax 203/598–0652. 2 double rooms with baths, 2 doubles share 1 bath. Ceiling fans, cable TV/VCRs, air-conditioning in some rooms. $65–$95, full breakfast. AE, MC, V. No smoking, no pets.

Reservations Services

Bed & Breakfast, Ltd. (Box 216, New Haven, CT 06513, tel. 203/469–3260). **Covered Bridge Bed & Breakfast Reservation Service** (Box 447, Norfolk, CT 06058, tel. 203/542–5944). **Nutmeg Bed & Breakfast Agency** (Box 1117, West Hartford, CT 06027, tel. 203/236–6698).

Southeastern Coast

Antiques & Accommodations

32 Main St., N. Stonington, CT 06359, tel. 860/535–1736 or 800/554–7829

The British accent of this 1861 Victorian bed-and-breakfast in the center of North Stonington is no accident. Owner-managers Thomas and Ann Gray are avowed Anglophiles who travel twice yearly to England to buy things for the house. Their background as appraisers and liquidators of antiques has stood them in good stead; the place is teeming with them.

And, here's good news for guests: Everything is for sale. The Grays decided to combine their multiple interests by running an elegantly decorated small hostelry and at the same time offering many of the antiques for sale to their clientele. Do you like that pair of Ponty Pool sconces with the unusual George III seals? That painted pine 19th-century corner cupboard? How about the Massachusetts Sheraton four-poster in the Branscombe Room (named after an English B&B in Devon)? It could be yours . . . for a price.

Whether or not you buy the smallest trifle, the Grays welcome you to their home and go to great pains to provide for your comfort. The rooms are furnished, it should be noted, with *livable* antiques. In the Fireplace Room on the ground floor, you have your own stereo. The bridal suite is called Susan's Room after one of the first honeymooners to nest here. All the rooms are filled with bright Victorian touches: fresh flowers as well as dried arrangements, and gently scented candles everywhere. A four-course candlelight breakfast of fresh local eggs, sweet cider, and crumbly buttery muffins is served every morn-

ing to guests in the main house as well as those in the adjacent 1820 farmhouse, which has been adapted to guest lodging (though it has its own huge kitchen for "do-it-yourself" cooks).

The front parlor is a pleasant place to relax or have tea, and in warm weather, so is the stone terrace out front, shaded by a flowering crab-apple tree. You might also stroll through the fragrant herb and colorful edible-flower gardens. You can sit back in the early morning sun and savor the memory of breakfast, or, as you close your eyes, you can let your thoughts drift to the turned-down bedclothes and the candle burning on your night table awaiting you at the end of the day.

🏨 *5 double rooms with baths, 1 3-bedroom cottage. Air-conditioning, cable TV in 4 rooms, box lunches available. $149–$225, full breakfast. MC, V. Restricted smoking, no pets.*

Bee & Thistle Inn

100 Lyme St., Old Lyme, CT 06371, tel. 860/434–1667 or 800/622–4946, fax 860/ 434–3402

On a long a wide avenue in the Old Lyme historic district, behind a weathered stone wall, is a two-story 1725 Colonial house that has evolved gracefully into the Bee & Thistle Inn. On 5½ acres along the Lieutenant River, which joins the Connecticut to flow into Long Island Sound, the inn's broad lawns, towering trees, formal flower garden, and herbaceous borders form a perfect setting.

In the 14 years since Penny and Bob Nelson left behind the corporate world and academia in New York, they have realized a family dream here. A complete turnaround in their lifestyle occurred when they decided to become innkeepers while their two children were in the last years of school. But so successful were they and such was the lure of this special place that both kids now work here: son Jeff (a former sous-chef at Boston's Ritz-Carlton) in the kitchen and daughter Lori out front greeting, seating, and helping guests settle in.

Restoration has taken priority over renovation—which they have done only when comfort is at stake—and the result is the re-creation of a Colonial ambience in the best sense. The scale of rooms throughout is deliberately small and inviting, with fireplaces in the downstairs parlors and dining rooms, and light and airy curtains at the multi-paned bedroom windows. Almost all rooms have canopy or four-poster beds, with old quilts and afghans providing warmth when needed. Little touches change with the seasons—hanging on each door might be tiny beribboned straw hats or, at another time, sprigs of evergreen or holly. No slave to Colonial New England style, Penny brings to the rooms touches of Williamsburg and even Victoriana, with such oddities as a wing chair our Puritan forebears surely wouldn't recognize.

Breakfast can be brought to your room before or after a morning soak in an herbal bath (scented soap provided). And downstairs you might encounter a harpist one evening, or take high tea late some afternoon. The romantic atmosphere is created by working fire-places and candlelight that, coupled with high-class cuisine, can make for a memorable evening.

▥ *9 double rooms with baths, 2 doubles share 1 bath, 1 cottage. Restaurant, air-conditioning, phones. $69–$140, cottage $195; breakfast extra. AE, DC, MC, V. No smoking, no pets. Closed 2 weeks in Jan.*

Red Brook Inn

Box 237, Mystic, CT 06372, tel. and fax 203/572-0349

On the Gold Star Highway (Route 184), at the western outlet of Welles Road, you'll see one of the two buildings that make up the Red Brook Inn. The 1770 center-chimney Crary Homestead is set behind a stone wall, surrounded by a small garden on 7 acres of woodland. Innkeeper Ruth Keyes originally purchased the tavern at an auction when it was threatened at its previous site by a road-widening project. She then had it moved board by board, stone by stone, and reconstructed faithfully on its present site. She set about furnishing it with authentic Colonial-period antiques and installing the basic comforts of electricity and plumbing—judiciously modern though unobtrusive.

A transplant herself, the youthful and vigorous Ruth was a real-estate litigation appraiser in California before retirement. Today she's more at home pointing out the features of the property and cooking the hearty breakfasts served at the Red Brook. She has also mastered the intricacies of open-hearth cooking, and in November and December she prepares Saturday-night dinners for guests.

The Keeping Room, where meals are served, has a large granite fireplace and baking oven with an array of iron tools and utensils, including a rare "bottle jack" used to roast hanging game. The old stagecoach walls in the Tap Room have bare boards, which adds to the coziness of what is now a well-equipped game room, complete with Monopoly and Scrabble, dominoes, and checkers. Here guests are served complimentary afternoon tea and drinks.

Bedrooms in both buildings are furnished meticulously with Colonial antiques, including canopy and four-poster beds with rare period coverings. Most rooms have working fireplaces, with fires laid in winter, waiting to be lit when you arrive. Split wood is provided to keep them going during your stay. All rooms have private baths and two rooms even have whirlpool tubs.

The New England charm of these two buildings with their fine antiques and comfortable ambience makes a stay here an unqualified pleasure. The inn is only about 20 minutes from Mystic and the Foxwoods Casino.

 10 double rooms with baths. Fireplaces in 6 rooms, cable TV, refrigerator, phone in the Tap Room, extensive library. $95–$189, $375 for Colonial dinner package (offered only in winter); full breakfast and complimentary beverages. D, MC, V. No smoking, no pets, 2-night minimum on weekends and holidays.

Other Choices

Harbour Inne & Cottage. 15 Edgemont St., Mystic, CT 06355, tel. 860/ 572–9253. 4 double rooms with showers, 1 double with bath, 3-room cottage with fireplace, kitchen, whirlpool bath. Cable TVs, air-conditioning, gazebo by water, picnic facilities, kitchen privileges. $85–$250, no breakfast. No credit cards. 2-night minimum on weekends Memorial Day–late Oct.

Lasbury's Guest House. 41 Orchard St., Stonington, CT 06378, tel. 860/535– 2681. 3 double rooms share 2 baths. Cable TVs, mini-refrigerators, air-conditioning in 2 rooms. $85. No credit cards. No pets, 2-night minimum on summer and holiday weekends.

Old Lyme Inn. Box 787, 85 Lyme St., Old Lyme, CT 06371, tel. 860/434–2600, fax 860/434–5352. 5 doubles with baths, 8 suites. Restaurant, air-conditioning, cable TV, phones, clock radios, TV and working fireplace in library. $109– $158, Continental breakfast. AE, D, DC, MC, V. Closed Jan. 1–15.

Palmer Inn. 25 Church St., Noank, CT 06340, tel. 860/572–9000. 6 double rooms with baths. $115–$215, Continental breakfast. AE, D, MC, V. No smoking, no pets, 2-night minimum on weekends July–Oct.

Randall's Ordinary. Rte. 2, Box 243, N. Stonington, CT 06359, tel. 860/599– 4540, fax 860/599–3308. 14 double rooms with baths, 1 suite. Air-conditioning and whirlpool baths, fireplace in

suite. $115–$195, Continental breakfast. AE, MC, V. No pets, 2-night minimum on holiday weekends.

Talcott House. 161 Seaside Ave., Box 1016, Westbrook, CT 06498, tel. 860/ 399–5020. 4 double rooms with baths. Clock radios. $125–$135, full breakfast. MC, V. No pets, 2-night minimum weekends, July–Aug., closed Nov.–Mar.

Whaler's Inn. 20 E. Main St., Mystic, CT 06355, tel. 860/536–1506 or 800/ 243–2588, fax 860/572–1250. 41 double rooms with baths. 2 restaurants, air-conditioning, cable TVs, phones. $102– $135, breakfast extra. AE, MC, V. No pets, 2-night minimum on summer weekends.

Reservations Services

Bed & Breakfast, Ltd. (Box 216, New Haven, CT 06513, tel. 203/469–3260). **Covered Bridge Bed & Breakfast Reservation Service** (Box 447, Norfolk, CT 06058, tel. 203/542–5944). **Nutmeg Bed & Breakfast Agency** (Box 1117, West Hartford, CT 06207, tel. 203/ 236–6698).

Connecticut River Valley: Hartford to the Sound

Copper Beech Inn

46 Main St., Ivoryton, CT 06442, tel. 860/767–0330

Picture a rambling Victorian country cottage, complete with carriage barn and terraced gardens set behind spreading oaks and aged beech trees on 7 wooded acres in a small town not far from a river. You've just conjured up the Copper Beech Inn. Built in the 1880s as a residence for the ivory importer A. W. Comstock, it has happily evolved into a haven for dining and lodging in the quintessential Connecticut River Valley town of Ivoryton.

The current innkeepers, Eldon and Sally Senner, took over several years ago but have already made their mark on the guest rooms. There are four in the main house and they have been spruced up with a fresh infusion of antique furniture and bric-a-brac, creating a warm traditional ambience.

The renovated carriage house contains nine spacious guest rooms that were designed by the Senners. Architectural features, such as cathedral ceilings and exposed beams, give each room a distinctive character. While the rooms are essentially modern, the country theme of the main building is maintained in the furnishings and a sprinkling of appropriate antiques and graphics. The bathrooms here are most definitely contemporary, with large whirlpool tubs. Still, the combination of old and new, indoors and out, works to create the ambience of a country retreat, exactly what the Senners set out to do.

At one time the ground floor of the main house abounded with endless reception rooms so beloved by the Victorians. The larger rooms have been converted to a series of thematic dining areas that are elegant and very romantic in the evening when candlelight glows on the sparkling crystal and gleaming silver. The wine list here has a stellar offering of French and American vintages. In 1993 a Victorian-style conservatory was added to the main house—it's now the perfect spot to sip evening cocktails before the collection of neatly framed Audubon prints.

You won't find anything stressful here. The beautiful grounds, comfortable guest rooms, abundant lounge space, and welcoming dining rooms may well make your quest for a quiet country inn end at the Copper Beech.

🏨 *13 double rooms with baths. Restaurant (closed Mon. and Tues. Jan.–Mar.), air-conditioning and cable TV in carriage house. $105–$170, Continental breakfast. AE, DC, MC, V. No pets, 2-night minimum on weekends.*

Riverwind

209 Main St., Deep River, CT 06417, tel. 860/526-2014

As you approach the busy downtown area of Deep River, you can't miss the dark gray clapboard building with the gingerbread trim and the sign out front that identifies Riverwind as a country inn.

Innkeepers in residence, Barbara Barlow and Bob Bucknell, are always on hand to welcome guests with a cup of tea or something similarly soothing. Barbara came north from Virginia, where she'd taught school for a number of years, and fell in love with the Connecticut River Valley. When she found this 1830s Victorian, fallen sadly into disrepair, her preservationist instincts sensed a challenge. The process involved Bob, a local builder, who saw a different challenge, which he met by wooing and winning her. Barbara, who's also a justice of the peace, has filled the house with dozens of romantic touches—so if you're feeling inspired to marry, or perhaps just renew your vows, this is the place to be.

A combination of period charm and southern hospitality is felt throughout the house in the countless carefully placed antiques and bibelots and the decanter of complimentary sherry in the parlor, one of eight common rooms, four of which have fireplaces. In Champagne and Roses, the most spectacular guest room, a mahogany pencil-post bed under a fishnet canopy is surrounded by a vanity desk, a carved mirrored armoire, and rose-color wing chairs. You might drink the champagne that comes with this room on its private balcony at the level of the treetops.

Each room has a decorative theme, and all have antique furnishings and stenciling. The beds range from a country pine one with a painted headboard and a carved oak bed to an 18th-century bird's-eye maple four-poster bed with a canopy. The bathrooms have modern plumbing, but one has a Victorian claw-foot tub.

In the 18th-century-style keeping room that was added onto the original building just a few years ago, there's a huge stone cooking fireplace, where hot cider and rum are mulled all winter long. This is where you'll be served Barbara's hearty country breakfast, featuring Smithfield ham, her own baked goods, and several casseroles. Freshly brewed tea and coffee are always on hand, and in the front parlor a piano is ready for those inclined to play. Touches like these lift Riverwind out of the ordinary.

🏠 *7 rooms with baths (1 is a hall bath), 1 suite. Air-conditioning. $90–$155; full breakfast, tea, coffee, and sherry. AE, MC, V. Restricted smoking, no pets, 2-night minimum on weekends Apr. 15–Jan. 2.*

Simsbury 1820 House

731 Hopmeadow St., Simsbury, CT 06070, tel. 860/658–7658 or 800/879–1820, fax 860/651–0724

Perched on a hillside above the main road through the town of Simsbury is a classic country inn—a two-story brick mansion built in 1820, with an 1890 addition on its west side. The property had ended up in the hands of the town, which didn't know what to do with it, and in 1985, it was turned over to Simsbury House Associates, to rescue it from decay, restore it to its proper status, and operate it as a country inn and restaurant.

In just a few years, the Associates have wrought a remarkable, wonderful change. The restaurant has become recognized for the excellence of its cuisine, winning praise from leading food critics. The romantic candlelight setting elicits almost as much applause as the victuals.

The bedrooms were given just as much attention as the dining room in the ren-ovation, and the results are evident. They vary in configuration, as might be expected in a vintage building, and a judicious mix of antiques and modern furnishings works to the advantage of both. In the main house there are 19 rooms and two suites. Each has its special feature—a fireplace, a balcony, a patio, a wet bar, a dormer with a cozy window seat. If you walk under the porte cochere and cross the parking lot, you come to the old carriage house that now contains nine equally individual rooms and two suites. One, the split-level Executive Suite, has a private patio and entrance.

The room decor in the main house shows a designer's touch in the complementary use of colors—maroon, yellow, blue, green, and pink—and pattern to create a restful atmosphere. In the primarily brown and green decor of the carriage house, whimsy is added with well-chosen horse prints on bed coverings and curtains. Most rooms have imported English four-poster beds, but in one, old barn doors are used as a combination room-divider and king-size headboard. It works.

Although the common rooms in the main house are shared with restaurant patrons, there are lots of places to sit and read the paper or relax over a drink. The staff, supervised by innkeeper Kelly Hohengarten, seems to consist mostly of young people who take the time to be responsive to guests. Ms. Hohengarten should be proud.

🏠 *28 double rooms with baths, 6 suites. Restaurant, air-conditioning, cable TVs, phones. $95–$140, Continental breakfast. AE, D, DC, MC, V.*

Other Choices

Barney House. 11 Mountain Spring Rd., Farmington, CT 06032, tel. 860/674–2796, fax 860/677–7259. 6 double rooms with baths. Air-conditioning, cable TVs, phones, clock radios, 2 large and 4 small meeting rooms, tennis court. $89, Continental breakfast. AE, MC, V. No pets.

Bishopsgate Inn. Box 290, 7 Norwich Rd., Goodspeed Landing, East Haddam, CT 06423, tel. 860/873–1677. 5 double rooms with baths, 1 suite. Airconditioning, fireplaces in 4 rooms, sauna in suite. $85–$120, full breakfast. MC, V. 2-night minimum on holiday weekends.

Griswold Inn. 36 Main St., Essex, CT 06426, tel. 860/767–1776, fax 860/767–0481. 28 double rooms with baths, 10 suites. Restaurant, fireplaces in 7 suites. $90–$185, Continental breakfast. AE, MC, V. No smoking.

Reservations Services

Bed & Breakfast, Ltd. (Box 216, New Haven, CT 06513, tel. 203/469–3260). **Covered Bridge Bed & Breakfast Reservation Service** (Box 447, Norfolk, CT 06058, tel. 203/542–5944). **Nutmeg Bed & Breakfast Agency** (Box 1117, West Hartford, CT 06207, tel. 203/236–6698).

Northwest Corner

Greenwoods Gate

105 Greenwoods Rd. E (Rte. 44), Norfolk, CT 06058, tel. 860/542–5439

This neatly preserved Federal Colonial behind a 600-foot-long picket fence in secluded Norfolk appears unassuming enough. But what one suspects, from the exterior, may be a quiet antiques shop or even a private home is in reality Connecticut's foremost romantic hideaway. Owner George Shumaker, formerly an executive with the Hilton hotel chain, is a cheerful host with a penchant for playing cupid.

He's spared nothing in providing guests with all the trappings of a cozy

honeymooners' retreat—he's probably even gone a little over the top. Countless amenities greet guests: from chocolates and Cognac to soaps, fresh flowers, and powders to "situational" board games in every room; and champagne or a deep massage are available upon advanced request. The formal living room, with its wide-plank wood floors and authentic multipaned Federal windows, is decorated with period furnishings; it's a terrific place to meet other guests or chat with George. Most visitors, however, come here for one reason: romantic seclusion. It's possible to stay here three nights and never lay eyes on another soul.

Indeed, the rooms are among the most sumptuous around. Of the four suites, each with beds covered in starched white linens, the Levi Thompson Suite is the most interesting. Added later to the house, its entrance is marked by a short flight of stairs leading to a small sitting area with a cathedral ceiling. Then, two additional sets of stairs, both lined with solid cherry hand-tapered railings, lead to either side of an enormous master bed. If you haven't herniated a disk carrying your lover over the threshold, plenty of fun awaits you in the suite's oversize spa bath. Most recently, a spacious two-bedroom suite with its own den and library was added—this getaway has become probably the inn's most popular accommodation, so reserve well ahead.

George does his best to keep guests well fed, from offering a daily presentation of snacks and afternoon refreshments to preparing a huge two-part breakfast, basically a Continental spread of muffins and fresh fruit followed by a full and extremely hearty hot meal.

A short drive from Tanglewood in the Berkshires, and a moderate stroll to the Yale Summer Music and Art Festival, Greenwoods Gate is miles away from the headaches of urban living—and though the gruff and hard-hearted may find this setup a little too precious, couples looking to rekindle love's flame will probably be more than satisfied.

🏠 *4 suites with private baths, 1 2-bedroom suite. Whirlpool bath in 1 suite, TV in common room, liquor in rooms. $190–$225, full breakfast. No credit cards. No smoking, no pets, 2-night minimum on weekends.*

Manor House

Box 447, Maple Ave., Norfolk, CT 06058, tel. 860/542-5690

A pleasant stroll up a side street off the village green in Norfolk will bring you to the unique Bavarian Tudor residence that has been turned into a thriving bed-and-breakfast by its owner-managers Diane and Henry Tremblay (who own Covered Bridge Reservation Service).

After several years of working in Hartford's hectic insurance industry, they were both ready for a change in careers when they saw an advertisement for an unusual house for sale. Designed and built in 1898 by Charles Spofford, the architect of London's subway system, the house has 20 stained-glass windows designed and given by Louis Tiffany, a full Victorian complement of reception rooms, and extensive bedrooms.

The combination was irresistible. The Tremblays took over in 1985 and have gradually refurnished it and restored the Victorian atmosphere with a light touch. Henry devotes himself to the surrounding 5 acres of gardens, with beehives and a raspberry patch, whose yields find their way to the breakfast table.

The bedrooms are all furnished with antique and reproduction beds (with modern mattresses), Louis Nicole wallpapers, well-chosen bibelots, prints, mirrors, and carpets. In winter, flannel sheets and down comforters add to the warmth. The vast Spofford Room has windows on three sides, a king-size canopy bed with a cheery fireplace opposite, and a balcony. The intimate Lincoln Room still has space for an antique double sleigh bed, a white fainting couch, and a small upholstered rocking chair—along with the best view of the neighboring landscape. But the Balcony Room has the most remarkable feature—a private wood-paneled elevator (added in 1939) that works. It also has a private deck suitable for sunbathing or leisurely lolling.

In the roomy living room, with its mammoth raised fireplace, music lovers who have come to Norfolk for the annual Chamber Music Festival (within easy walking distance) may choose from the large collection of vintage recordings and compact discs. You may tickle the keys of the grand piano, which is kept in tune, or, in a quiet mood, seek the seclusion of the library and choose from its numerous volumes.

🏠 *8 double rooms with baths, 1 2-bedroom suite. Cable TV in common area, working fireplaces in 2 rooms, whirlpool bath in 1 room. $95–$175, full breakfast. AE, D, MC, V. No smoking, no pets, 2-night minimum on weekends, 3-night minimum on holidays.*

Under Mountain Inn

482 Undermountain Rd., Salisbury, CT 06068, tel. 860/435-0242, fax 860/435-2379

Driving north on Route 41 from Salisbury's Main Street, you cut through sweeping fields where horses graze and silos rise in the distance. After about 4 miles, a stone's throw from the Massachusetts border, stands a white clapboard farmhouse built in the early 1700s that has become the Under Mountain Inn.

The owners, Marged and Peter Higginson, bill themselves as Innkeepers and Chef, since the inn is also a popular restaurant. Peter's British origins emerge in the decor as well as the cuisine.

Their personal stamp is found all over, from the decor of the intimate dining rooms (each with a working fireplace) to the drawing room filled with antique knickknacks and Oriental and handmade American rugs. In the back of the house is The Pub, a faithful replica of a typical English taproom, whose paneling was found, during a restoration, hidden under the attic floorboards. Since Colonial law awarded all such lumber to the king of England, Peter reclaimed it in the name of the Crown.

Upstairs, the rooms are furnished individually in a manner dubbed "English country style." Thanks to a pruning of the property's dense foliage, all rooms have spectacular mountain views. Room names, such as Covent Garden and Drury Lane, recall favorite London haunts, and the decor will make Anglophiles weak in the knees. The spacious Queen's Room naturally has a queen-size bed; the King's Room opposite has its counterpart. A more contemporary room has a separate entrance.

Three surrounding acres have birch, fir, maples, and a thorned locust tree, rumored to be the state's oldest. Across the road is Fisher Pond. Guests may use its 1.8-mile footpath for a bracing stroll, that favored English form of exercise.

At dinner, which along with a full breakfast is included in the tariff, you may expect one of Peter's specialties: steak and kidney pie, roast goose, or bangers and mash—sausage and mashed potatoes to the uninitiated. Save room for the English trifle— dessert par excellence.

With the filling breakfast and dinner included in the rates, a stay here turns out to be one of the better values in the area.

🏨 *7 double rooms with baths. Restaurant, air-conditioning. $170–$205, MAP. 7% service charge. MC, V. No smoking, no pets, 2-night minimum on weekends.*

White Hart

The Village Green, Box 385, Salisbury, CT 06068, tel. 860/435–0030, fax 860/435–0040

Across from the village green at the eastern end of Main Street in Salisbury, the freshly painted white Colonial frame structure of the White Hart with its broad front porch clearly dominates the landscape. This venerable country inn has welcomed travelers since the 1860s and happily continues that tradition today.

In the 1980s it fell upon hard times and passed through a succession of owners until it was sold at public auction in 1989. The current owner-managers, Terry and Juliet Moore, have operated the celebrated Old Mill Restaurant in neighboring South Egremont, Massachusetts, for the past 17 years and are well seasoned in the art of local hospitality. Today they divide their time between the two establishments, and one of them is always on hand at the White Hart during the evening and busy weekends.

Before reopening in January 1990, the Moores decided to settle for nothing less than a total renovation inside and out. The visible results of their efforts show a respect for tradition combined with the finest in contemporary materials. The green and rose printed carpeting in the lobby is also found in the upstairs hallways along with shaded beige striped wallpaper and soft-white painted woodwork. Each of the bedrooms and suites is furnished with excellent Colonial reproductions. Upholstery, bedspreads, and curtains have been tailored with brightly contrasting fabrics in lively stripes, ribbons, and floral splashes. The configuration of each room is unique; instead of breaking down walls, quirks have been accommodated, giving the rooms a comfortable irregularity. Yet all have such conveniences as good lamps for reading, telephones with message lights, and modernized bathrooms. Several rooms on the eastern side have private entrances, and a few steps away, in the 1813 Colonial frame building called the Gideon Smith House, similar rooms and suites are available on two levels.

Dining in any of the White Hart's three restaurants, the bright and sunny Garden Court Room, the tavernlike Tap Room, or the elegant Julie's New American Seafood Grill, is a treat.

▥ *23 double rooms with baths, 3 suites. 3 restaurants, air-conditioning, cable TVs, phones, meeting facilities. $110–$190, breakfast extra. AE, DC, MC, V. 2-night minimum on weekends May–Oct., 3-night minimum holiday weekends.*

Other Choices

Country Goose. 211 Kent-Cornwall Rd. (Rte. 7), Kent, CT 06757, tel. 203/927–4746. 3 double rooms and 1 single share 2 baths. Hiking (Appalachian Trail) nearby. $90, Continental breakfast. No credit cards. No smoking, no pets, 2-night minimum on weekends, closed Mar.–Apr. 10.

Old Riverton Inn. Rte. 20, Riverton, CT 06065, tel. 860/379–8678 or 800/378–1796, fax 860/379–1006. 11 double rooms with baths, 1 suite. Restaurant, air-conditioning, cable TVs, tubing, fishing, and swimming nearby. $75–$160, full breakfast. AE, D, DC, MC, V. 2-night minimum on holiday weekends.

Toll Gate Hill Inn & Restaurant. Box 1339, Litchfield, CT 06759, tel. 860/567–4545 or 800/445–3903, fax 860/567–8397. 15 double rooms with baths, 5 suites. Restaurant, air-conditioning, cable TVs, phones, working fireplaces in 3 rooms and all suites. $110–$175, Continental breakfast. AE, D, DC.

Reservations Services

Bed & Breakfast, Ltd. (Box 216, New Haven, CT 06513, tel. 203/469–3260). **Covered Bridge Bed & Breakfast Reservation Service** (Box 447, Norfolk, CT 06058, tel. 203/542–5944). **Nutmeg Bed & Breakfast Agency** (Box 1117, West Hartford, CT 06207, tel. 203/236–6698).

Delaware

The Towers

Wilmington and Northern Delaware

William Penn Guest House

206 Delaware St., New Castle, DE 19720, tel. 302/328-7736

The historic marker stands on the streets of New Castle, a block from the banks of the Delaware River: "Near here October 27, 1682, William Penn first stepped on American soil. He proceeded to the fort and... we did deliver unto him 1 turf with a twig upon it, a porringer with river water and soil, in part of all." In the same year that Penn strode onto the shores of the New World, and on the same streets that he first trod, the William Penn Guest House appeared on the map, though perhaps not with quite the same historic significance. But Penn knew a good thing when he saw it; ask Irma Burwell, who runs the place now, she will tell you how the founder of Pennsylvania would bed down here.

Irma will also tell you what she and husband Dick charged when they started their bed-and-breakfast operation in 1956: $8 a night. Rates are still surpris-

ingly reasonable, and they're not likely to rise in the near future, since the hosts like the sensibilities and spending habits of their longtime clientele (repeat visitors account for two-thirds of their business). The Burwells welcome an international set of diverse ages and tastes—senior ambassadors who snooze and dewy-cheeked naturalists who cycle—all of whom appreciate a quiet, civilized atmosphere that doesn't cost them an unearthly sum.

The William Penn is a handsomely restored, impressively maintained Colonial structure that is modest in its air and amenities. Soft, wide-board Delaware-pine floors, a claw-foot tub, and an 18th-century chandelier in the dining room take guests back to an earlier era. The bedrooms—one with a king-size bed, another with one set of twins, and two with doubles—are carpeted blandly and furnished with pine antiques. If air-conditioning turns you off, there are ceiling fans to keep both second-floor units cool and ventilated in the summer.

You'll find the William Penn a perfect jumping-off point for touring Longwood Gardens, the Brandywine River Museum, Winterthur, the Hagley Museum, and Nemours Mansion. Cyclists in particular will delight in the area:

The house borders Battery Park, which runs right along the river and has a 2-mile biking path and promenade, as well as benches, picnic tables, tennis courts, and play areas for children.

🏨 *4 double rooms, 1 with private bath. Air-conditioning, TV in 3 rooms. $55–$80, Continental breakfast. No credit cards. No smoking in bedrooms, no pets.*

Other Choices

Boulevard Bed & Breakfast. 1909 Baynard Blvd., Wilmington, DE 19802, tel. 302/656–9700, fax 302/656–9701. 3 double rooms with baths, 1 double and 1 single share bath, 1 suite. Air-conditioning, cable TVs, phones, fireplaces in library and parlor, whirlpool in suite, off-street parking. $55–$75, full breakfast. AE, MC, V. Smoking restricted, no pets.

Cantwell House. 107 High St., Odessa, DE 19730, tel. 302/378–4179. 2 double rooms share bath, 1 suite. Air-conditioning in suite and 2nd-floor canopy bedroom, TV in suite, fireplace in living room. $55–$85, Continental breakfast. No credit cards. No smoking, no pets.

Reservations Service

Bed & Breakfast of Delaware (2701 Landon Dr., Suite 200 Wilmington 19810-2211, tel. 302/479–9500).

The Beaches

Eli's Country Inn

Rte. 36 Greenwood–Milford Rd., Greenwood 19950-0779, tel. 302/349–4265, fax 302/349–9340

The seven Shrock sisters never left home: They grew up on the 70-acre family farm midway between Dover and a half hour from Delaware's Atlantic beaches in the Mennonite community of Greenwood. Now they're hostesses at home. In 1992 they converted the farmhouse into Eli's, a six-bedroom B&B. Times have changed since they were growing up just 8 miles from the wealthy town of Milford; still, you can "hear the quiet" from the large wraparound front porch, while strolling the nature paths that surround the property or watching the sunsets from the garden. Ask about a hot-air balloon flight after breakfast with a launch from the front lawn.

The sisters enjoy their role providing hospitality to their guests and often provide a country dinner in the informal dining room. You may be invited to gather around for a sing-along or to play the family organ. The location and grounds make Eli's especially conducive for children. The large lawn is well suited for badminton, volleyball, or horseshoes, and Eli's Country Inn is one of three stops packaged in Delaware's Biking Inn to Inn (tel. 800/824–8754) program. If you're seeking countryside quiet and still enjoy the small towns and beaches of Delaware, this may be just the place for you and your family.

🏨 *6 bedrooms with private baths, 2 downstairs rooms accessible for guests with disabilities. Central air-conditioning, upstairs TV room, phones available. $50 single, $55 double per room. D, MC, V. No smoking.*

The Inn at Canal Square

122 Market St., Lewes, DE 19958, tel. 302/645–8499 or 800/222–7902, fax 302/645–7083

This decidedly upscale inn is in Lewes, a small, historic town that serves as both a gateway to the Atlantic beaches and a peaceful retreat for travelers along the Atlantic seaboard. This inn is special because of its waterfront location and unusual accommodation choices. Aside from 19 conventional rooms in the main building, travelers here can also opt for the *Legend of Lewes*, a houseboat with modern galley, two bedrooms, and two baths that floats peacefully at dockside (this arrangement is not recommended for families with children under 14). The inn is conveniently situated in a meandering complex of shops and a restaurant. Design purists may protest the stylistic mélange; the exterior looks like a developer's reproduction of a Nantucket village, yet the decor in the apartment resembles the interior of a typical Malibu hideaway. You might find it a bit incongruous, but are ceiling fans, bushy potted plants, a canal-front sundeck, and a baby grand piano really so hard to bear?

In the three-story main building, the rooms are large and furnished with Federal reproductions. You'll pay slightly more for those with porch access and water views and considerably more for the honeymoon suite (Room 305), which has a cathedral ceiling, Palladian windows, and private balcony. It may not be terribly spacious, but it's cozy, enjoys the best view in the inn, and has a queen-size bed. King-size-bed advocates have their pick of three rooms on the top floor.

The simple Continental breakfast can be eaten downstairs or taken back to the bedrooms on trays. Innkeeper Laurie Sergovic recommends Kupchick's as the best restaurant in Lewes; and Gilligan's, the restaurant next door, is open daily in season, from 11 AM to 1 AM.

Besides the Zwaanendael Museum and historic district, there are the beaches of Cape Henlopen State Park to keep you occupied; or you can try your hand at hooking a shark from a chartered fishing boat. In the summer, you can take your kids on the *Queen Anne's Railroad*, an old steam locomotive that now runs a 50-minute round-trip from Lewes.

▦ *17 double rooms with baths, 1 suite, 1 houseboat. Air-conditioning, cable TV and phones in bedrooms, confer-* *ence room. $115–$150, Continental breakfast; houseboat $225 ($1,200 a week). AE, D, DC, MC, V. No pets, 2-day minimum in houseboat on weekends, and in main building, weekends Memorial Day–Oct. and on some holiday weekends.*

New Devon Inn

2nd and Market Sts. (Box 516), Lewes, DE 19958, tel. 302/645–6466 or 800/824–8754, fax 302/645–7196

This hotel, with its striped awnings and lobby-level stores, opened in 1989 in the heart of Lewes's historic district and has fine views of St. Peter's Episcopal Church and historic cemetery. Built in 1926, the inn received a complete makeover in 1986, at the hands of its owners Dale Jenkins and Bernard Nash. Little remains of its past except the lustrous heart-of-pine floors. Its lobby is reminiscent of a Bloomingdale's window, with curious elephant chairs and an old-fashioned cage elevator.

The guest rooms are furnished in feminine elegance, with antiques and beds swaddled in designer linens. Though they're relatively small, they are warmly appointed, immaculately clean, and extremely comfortable. The corner rooms (108, for example) are the ones most requested. Room 101, with a double bed, receives buckets of early morning sunlight. And the inn offers special touches, such as turndown service, candy and cordials in the rooms, and morning coffee served in delicate antique cups. The inn has expanded its Continental breakfast and now offers an elegant presentation—on silver service, crystal, and china—of croissants, yogurt, sticky buns, cereal, and juice.

Of late the New Devon Inn has become known as a politician's hideout—Senators Simon and Biden have both stayed here to escape media frenzy—and business travelers can rely on a highly professional staff. Provisions for the disabled are also available.

Lewes, unlike Rehoboth and Bethany, is a year-round destination, so you won't barrel into locked doors at restaurants and crafts shops in the dead of winter. April heralds the Great Delaware Kite Festival at Cape Henlopen State Park; July is the month for the town's annual antiques show and sale; and the Christmas House Tour, sponsored by the Lewes Historical Society, precedes the Christmas Parade and a tree-lighting celebration in December.

🏠 *24 double rooms with baths, 2 suites. Air-conditioning, phones. $45–$170, Continental breakfast. AE, D, MC, V. No children, no pets.*

Pleasant Inn

31 Olive Ave., Rehoboth Beach, DE 19971, tel. 302/227–7311

In Rehoboth Beach, Peck Pleasanton's place is an anomaly, an inn with an adult air where you can imagine mature couples playing canasta on the porch until late and periodically ambling over to the wet bar to freshen their gin and tonics. Stylish, prettified, or even immaculately maintained it is not, though it does occupy one of central Rehoboth's most coveted properties: The big, foursquare Victorian with its widow's walk was built right on the boardwalk but was moved to its present location (a five-minute walk from the beach) following the Great Storm of 1918. There are 10 double rooms in the house plus a downstairs kitchen-apartment and studio. The guest rooms are furnished with well-worn items that may be old but are probably not antiques and have private baths that appear to have been last decorated in the '50s. A carriage house out back that sleeps four is rented by the week. Peck himself is a no-nonsense, slow-talking man who looks and acts as if he's seen it all. He doesn't provide breakfast for his guests, but he does make several bicycles available free of charge.

🏠 *10 double rooms with baths, 2 1-bedroom apartments, 1-bedroom carriage house. Air-conditioning, TV on porch, kitchenette in 2nd-floor hallway, limited off-street parking. $85–$110, no breakfast. No pets, 3-day minimum on holidays.*

Spring Garden Bed & Breakfast Inn

R.D. 5, Box 283A, Delaware Ave. Extended, Laurel, DE 19956, tel. 302/ 875–7015

This inn reveals its character slowly and subtly. It's an abundantly lived-in place that is deeply appreciated by its owner, Gwen North. She was raised by her parents in this half-Colonial, half-Victorian farmhouse on the outskirts of Laurel before she flew the coop for New York. During that absence she came to realize that her heart lay back at home. Says Gwen, "When you stay in the same place all your life, you stop seeing what's there."

What's here is a red-shutter country house that stands beside a creek lined with daylilies in spring. As pleasant as its exterior is, the inside is even better. The Colonial section, built between 1760 and 1780 by a Captain Lewis of Bethel, remained in the Lewis family for 100 years. Its front parlor and back kitchen have wood-plank floors and the snug, slightly off-kilter feeling of a boat. Breakfast, highlighted by Scotch eggs and homegrown fruit, is served beside a wood-burning stove.

A steep, narrow staircase takes guests to the inn's two Colonial rooms; the one called Naomi (for Gwen's mother) has a fireplace, a lace-canopy double bed, and a walnut rocker. Three bedrooms in the Victorian section, added in the late 1800s, have views of the garden and are filled with a soothing collection of antique furnishings, including a Victorian spool bed and Belgian cathedral chairs.

The Atlantic beaches are about 20 miles from the inn, but Gwen is quick to point out the other diversions to be found in this landlocked region of Delaware, such as canoeing and fishing at Trap Pond State Park and exploring the historic districts of Bethel and Laurel. An antiques dealer, Gwen sells collected pieces in a barn next to the inn.

Tops among the activities here is bicycling, a pastime Gwen has encouraged by organizing the Biking Inn to Inn program (tel. 800/845–9939), a three- to five-day stretch of cycling with stops at carefully selected inns—including a few on the Atlantic. The routes take bikers along the flat back roads of the Eastern Shore and offer opportunities for crabbing, bird-watching, and impromptu swims.

🏠 *2 double rooms with baths, 3 doubles share bath. Air-conditioning, TV in sitting room, 3 fireplaces. $65–$85, full breakfast. No credit cards. Smoking in designated areas, no pets.*

The Towers

101 N.W. Front St., Milford, DE 19963, tel. 302/422–3814, or, outside DE, 800/ 366–3814

Edgar Allan Poe's friend and fellow poet John Lofland lived at the Towers, which was once the Milford home of Lofland's stepfather, Dr. John Wallace. Lofland was an opium addict and Poe an alcoholic, but in their wildest hallucinations neither could have dreamed up a house like the Towers, a steamboat Gothic palace adorned with 10 varieties of gingerbread painted in 12 colors. Here flamboyant Victoriana radiates from the cherry, mahogany, and walnut finishings. Inside, the music room has a coffered sycamore ceiling and an 1899 Knabe grand piano. You're likely to find a record—perhaps Gene Autry's rendition of "Rudolph the Red-Nosed Reindeer"—spinning on the Victrola. The parlor is decorated with French antiques, and the dining room provides views of the gazebo, pool deck, and rose garden in back.

The warm but unobtrusive custodians of this more than 200-year-old marvel (it's on the National Register of Historic Places) are Rhonda and Daniel Bond, who bought it in January 1992 and now live on the premises in the old servants' quarters. They couldn't resist the ubiquitous stained glass, the carved garlands on the fireplaces, and the gold leaf peeking from behind the plywood walls. Rhonda can tell you about the Italian architect commissioned in the 1890s to transform the structure into the Victorian extravaganza you see today; the owner is said to have spent between $30,000 and $40,000 on the renovation.

The Tower room on the second floor is a favorite, with a turret niche and lots of rosy stained glass. The third floor's two suites are a bit more modern in character but still whimsically wonderful. All four doubles have their own bathrooms, but guests occupying the second-floor rooms must walk through a common area to enter theirs, and the third-floor facilities have showers only.

Rhonda fortifies her guests for a day of exploring or antiquing with a full breakfast—often her celebrated ricotta pancakes, served with fresh fruit or raspberry purée and ham. The inn is right across the street from one of Delaware's premier eating establishments, the Banking House, which is also an 18th-century-inspired bed-and-breakfast. Dinner at the Banking House and a stay at the Towers is a perfect combination.

🏠 *4 double rooms with baths. Air-conditioning, gas-log fireplaces in music room and dining room, pool. $95–$125, full breakfast. MC, V. No smoking, no pets.*

Wild Swan Inn

525 Kings Hwy., Lewes 19958, tel. and fax 302/645-8550

There's a pink Victorian house across from the library in Lewes where you can be serenaded with music from a 1914 player piano, an original 1906 Edison wax-cylinder phonograph, or an RCA Victrola. Originally the 1900s house was built and occupied by Captain Arthur Hudson, who ran the Fenwick Island Lightship. Inside the classic Queen Anne Victorian-style home are high ceilings, delicately carved scrollwork, lavish wallpaper, antique furnishings, lots of eclectic collectibles, and typical Victorian detail to pattern and color. Hope and Mike Tyler have attracted lots of media attention. That's because guests are pampered with a big formal breakfast in the dining room under brass chandeliers when the weather is crisp, or in a gazebo by the pool in summer. At the end of a busy day visitors look forward to a cool glass of sun tea or a cordial on the wide front porch. There's plenty of fine, fun dining in Lewes, just a walk away. When you return to your room at night, you'll find it's been freshened and a plate of cookies will be waiting at your bedside.

Nowadays Lewes is well known as the Delaware terminus of the Cape May–Lewes Ferry. It was first settled by the Dutch in 1631 as a whaling colony. Lewes's most famous attraction is the Zwaanendael (Valley of the Swans) Museum, a replica of the City Hall in Hoorn, The Netherlands, constructed to commemorate the 300th anniversary of the town. Inside, you'll find an interesting exhibit of artifacts from the British ship *DeBraak*, which sank off the Atlantic Coast in 1798.

▥ *3 rooms with baths. Air-conditioning, bikes, gazebo, pool. $85–$120, full breakfast. No credit cards. No smoking, no pets, 2-night minimum on weekends.*

Reservations Service

Bed & Breakfast of Delaware (2710 Landon Dr., Suite 200, Wilmington 19810-2211, tel. 302/479-9500).

Florida

Magnolia Plantation Bed & Breakfast Inn

St. Augustine

Casablanca Inn

24 Avenida Menendez, St. Augustine, FL 32084, tel. 904/829–0928 or 800/ 826–2626, fax 904/826–1892

Overlooking scenic Matanzas Bay, the Casablanca Inn is a charming base from which to explore the nooks and crannies of America's oldest city. Like nearly every other structure in St. Augustine, the Casablanca has stories to tell. Built in 1914 in the Mediterranean Revival style favored by architects of that era, the Casablanca was originally a residence hotel called the Matanzas. During Prohibition, the building's ideal location inspired rum-runners to use it as a signal house for contraband cargo. Eventually the building fell onto hard times, and then it remained unoccupied for decades.

Today, the only interior remnant of its colorful history is the word MATANZAS spelled out in the pale green-and-white entryway tiles, which were an inspiration for the celery-color, deep-pile carpet covering the floors and stairway. Rooms are gracefully furnished with antiques and reproductions. The Casablanca's Celebration Suite, with its private sundeck and double hammock overlooking Matanzas Bay, is a loafer's delight. An oversize whirlpool (terry-cloth robes are thoughtfully provided) will sooth tired muscles.

Innkeepers Anthony and Brenda Bushell serve the morning meal in either the sunny breakfast room or on the stately grand porch, a soothing spot to sip your coffee. At any time of the day, you can relax in one of the rocking chairs and drink in the sweeping view of the bay. Cooled by slowly rotating ceiling fans and ocean breezes, you'll enjoy watching the boats and tourists pass by.

10 suites, 2 rooms accessible for people who use wheelchairs and equipped for people who are hearing-impaired. Air-conditioning, whirlpool bath in rooms, bicycles available. $79–$179; full breakfast, beverages available in kitchen 24 hours, champagne and chocolates with weekend and holiday arrivals. AE, D, MC, V.

Other Choices

Carriage Way. 70 Cuna St., St. Augustine, FL 32084, tel. 904/829–2467 or 800/908–9832, fax 904/826–1461. 9 double rooms with baths. Air-conditioning, cable TV in parlor, fireplace in 1 room.

$69–$125; full breakfast, afternoon desserts. AE, D, MC, V.

Casa de la Paz. 22 Avenida Menendez, St. Augustine, FL 32084, tel. 904/829–2915 or 800/929–2915. 4 double rooms with baths, 2 suites. Air-conditioning, cable TVs, fireplace in 1 room, view of Matanzas Bay from 3 rooms. $79–$145, full breakfast. AE, MC, V.

Kenwood Inn. 38 Marine St., St. Augustine, FL 32084, tel. 904/824–2116, fax 904/824–1689. 10 double rooms with baths, 4 suites. Air-conditioning, some rooms with cable TV, pool. $75–$135; Continental breakfast, afternoon cookies and beverages. D, MC, V.

Old Powder House Inn. 38 Cordova St., St. Augustine, FL 32084, tel. 904/824–4149 or 800/447–4149, fax 904/825–0143. 8 double rooms with baths, 1 suite with whirlpool bath. Air-conditioning, TVs with cable on request, outdoor whirlpool bath, tandem bikes. $79–$150; full breakfast, afternoon tea, evening wine and hors d'oeuvres. D, MC, V.

Secret Garden Inn. 56½ Charlotte St., St. Augustine, FL 32084, tel. 904/829–3678. 3 suites with kitchenettes. Air-conditioning, cable TV, coffeemakers. $89–$109, Continental breakfast. MC, V.

Southern Wind. 18 Cordova St., St. Augustine, FL 32084, tel. 904/825–3623, fax 904/825–0360. 8 double rooms with baths, 1 suite. Air-conditioning, cable TV, 4 rooms with mini-refrigerators, fireplace in suite, 1 room with whirlpool bath. $69–$139, full breakfast. AE, D, MC, V.

Amelia Island

Hoyt House

804 Atlantic Ave., Amelia Island, FL 32034, tel. 904/277–4300 or 800/432–2085, fax 904/277–9626

Once inside Hoyt House, a 1905 Queen Anne residence, you'll find it hard to leave, despite its central location between the town of Fernandina Beach and the beaches of Amelia Island. Innkeepers John and Rita Kovatchavitch have re-created a gracious, turn-of-the-century Victorian home, successfully mixing fine period furniture with kitschy, one-of-a-kind accent pieces, such as the 5-foot-tall ceramic giraffe from Key West that stands guard near an emerald-green tile fireplace in one of three sitting rooms. An enormous wraparound porch, complete with wicker porch swing and rocking chairs, encourages relaxation. The formal parlor, decorated mostly in soft pinks, houses many of Rita's Lladro figurines and bone china collectibles. Breakfast is served in the formal dining room, which has warm purple walls, an elegant crystal chandelier, and many fine antiques.

Each of the nine guest rooms is tastefully appointed and individually decorated, with an eye to comfort as well as style. In a pale lavender room, for example, silver-framed photographs of a World War II–era couple rest on an étagère. While most rooms have a decidedly Victorian bent, one has a thoroughly modern flair, including an overstuffed black leather chair and a Tizio lamp. John and Rita named each room after the color of its walls: Blueberry, Sweet Lavender, Fire Coral, and Sea Foam Green, among others.

While the upstairs rooms invite guests to linger, patrons find themselves sooner or later in the Kovatchavitch's sleek, modern kitchen. It's here that Rita prepares not only the daily breakfast, but an assortment of cookies and other goodies that brings guests downstairs like a magnet. "It's just like our house back in Connecticut," John says. "Everyone used to congregate in the kitchen to watch Rita bake."

🖽 *9 double rooms with baths, some wheelchair accessible. Air-conditioning, cable TV in parlor. $95–$135; full* breakfast, afternoon cookies and beverages. AE, D, MC, V.

Other Choices

Elizabeth Pointe Lodge. 98 S. Fletcher Ave. (S.R. A1A), Amelia Island, FL 32034, tel. 904/277–4851, fax 904/ 277–6500. 24 double rooms with baths, 1 suite with kitchen, 1 room accessible for people who use wheelchairs. Air-conditioning, cable TV, some rooms with ocean views, FM radios, 2 rooms with mini-refrigerators and microwaves, 11 rooms with whirlpool baths. $100–$195; full breakfast buffet, evening wine and hors d'oeuvres. AE, D, MC, V.

Florida House Inn. 20–22 S. 3rd St., Amelia Island, FL 32034, tel. 904/261–3300 or 800/258–3301, fax 904/277–3831. 10 double rooms with baths, 1 suite. Restaurant, pub, air-conditioning, cable TVs, 6 rooms with fireplaces, 2 rooms with whirlpool baths. $70–$135, full breakfast. AE, D, MC, V.

1735 House. 584 S. Fletcher Ave. (S.R. A1A), Amelia Island, FL 32034, tel. 904/261–4148 or 800/872–8531, fax 904/261–9200. 5 suites. Air-conditioning, cable TV/VCR, mini-refrigerators, coffeemakers, microwaves, ocean view from all suites. $100–$160, Continental breakfast. AE, D, MC, V.

Williams House. 103 S. 9th St., Fernandina Beach, FL 32034, tel. 904/277–2328. 4 suites. Air-conditioning, cable TV/VCR, paddle fans, 3 rooms with fireplaces. $95–$135; full breakfast, private catered dinners can be arranged. MC, V.

Northwest Florida and the Panhandle

Josephine's French Country Inn

101 Seaside Ave., Seaside, FL 32459, tel. 904/231–1940 or 800/848–1840, fax 904/231–2446

With six stately columns supporting the front of its whitewashed facade, Josephine's has the air of a gracious antebellum plantation. Its location in the heart of Seaside—the carefully planned, award-winning, architectural gem of a beachfront community in the heart of Florida's Panhandle—makes it appealing at first glance. And after guests walk through the front gate of Josephine's white picket fence, cross the broad front porch with its comfortable wooden rocking chairs, and step into the parlor, they want to linger for a good while.

Guests stay in either the main house or in one of two separate buildings, each containing two suites. Rooms are individually decorated with antiques, balloon curtains, and a variety of guestroom furnishings, including four-poster and sleigh beds. Many have Battenburg lace–embellished comforters. All rooms have tub/shower combinations with extra-long tubs designed for luxuriant soaking. Kitchenettes in each room include mini-refrigerators, wet bars, and microwaves, and are stocked with the fixings for making coffee.

A full breakfast is served daily in the richly appointed Josephine's Dining Room. Over the fireplace, softly lit by crystal sconces, hang tasteful reproductions of Redouté flower prints originally commissioned by Napoleon's empress, the Josephine for whom the inn is named. The intimate restaurant also serves lunch and dinner Wednesday through Sunday with an eclectic menu of meats, poultry, and fish. Crab cakes are a house specialty.

With its overstuffed chairs and sofa, the parlor invites guests to stay awhile with a good book. But it's the lure of the sea and its breezes that bring most visitors to Seaside, and Josephine's guests can take advantage of the rocking chairs on either the downstairs porch or upstairs veranda. A true bonus for guests is to climb up to the inn's roof, where deck chairs are available for sunning, although most guests simply take in the superb view of Seaside's pastel cottages, emerald waters, and sugar-white sand beaches along the Gulf of Mexico.

🏨 *11 double rooms with baths, 4 suites. Air-conditioning, cable TV/VCR, fireplaces in all but 1 room, clock radios, kitchenettes, bicycles available; for $5 daily fee, guests have use of Seaside amenities, including community pool, tennis courts, croquet lawn, and shuffleboard courts. $130—$220, full breakfast. AE, MC, V.*

Other Choices

Dolphin Inn. 107 Savannah St., Seaside, FL 32459, tel. 904/231–1973 or 800/443–3146. 2 double rooms with baths. Air-conditioning, TV/VCR, fireplace in living room, mini-refrigerators, bicycles available, $5 daily fee for use of Seaside community amenities, including pool and tennis courts. $98, Continental breakfast. MC, V.

Henderson Park Inn. 2700 Hwy. 98, Destin, FL 32541, tel. 904/837–4853 or 800/336–4853. 18 double rooms with baths, 2 suites. Restaurant, air-conditioning, cable TVs, some rooms with fireplaces, refrigerators, microwaves, coffeemakers in most rooms, whirlpool baths in most rooms, gulf views, beachfront, pool. $89–$239, full breakfast. AE, D, MC, V.

Highlands House. Scenic Hwy. 30A, Santa Rosa Beach, FL 32459, tel. 904/

267–0110. 8 double rooms with baths. Air-conditioning, cable TV/VCR in parlor, welcome basket. $95–$125. D, MC, V.

Sugar Beach Inn. 3501 Scenic Hwy. 30A, Seagrove Beach, FL 32459, tel. 904/231–1577. 3 double rooms with baths. Air-conditioning, fireplace in 1 room, gulf views from 2 rooms. $95–$115, full breakfast. MC, V.

North Central Florida

Magnolia Plantation Bed & Breakfast Inn

309 S.E. 7th St., Gainesville, FL 32601, tel. 352/375–6653 or 800/201–2379, fax 352/338–0303

Right in the middle of one of Gainesville's Southeast historic districts, Magnolia Plantation is the result of a painstaking restoration undertaken by owners Joe and Cindy Montalto. The house, one of the South's few remaining examples of French Second Empire architecture, was built in 1886 by Emmet Baird, a local businessperson. According to legend, Baird built the mansion with profits from a pirate treasure that he uncovered on the Suwannee River. Rumors of the remaining treasure still persist, but when Joe and Cindy gutted the house, the only "booty" they found were a few old coins (one penny dates to the mid-1840s) that probably fell from the pockets of the mansion's original builders.

The tall, Italianate windows, mansard roof, and decorative moldings of the home pay tribute to a bygone era. Its focal point, a tall tower with decorative rooftop cresting, is a photographer's delight. Film buffs may notice a resemblance to the infamous house featured in *Psycho*, and Joe is quick to point out that the French Empire style is, in fact, characteristic of both structures; here, however, the similarities end. Painted in an inviting Covington blue, with dark red trim, Magnolia Plantation's enchanting exterior is a mere prelude to its interior delights.

The public rooms, which include both a "Gentlemen's" and "Ladies'" parlor, are liberally decorated with antiques and numerous photographs from Joe and Cindy's family albums. Leading to the second floor is a graceful mahogany staircase, accented with a garland of silk magnolia blossoms and tiny silver ornaments. "My Christmas decorations," says Cindy. "I liked the way they looked, so I've never taken them down."

Guest rooms, named after species of flowers, are individually decorated in a variety of styles. Gardenia, the bridal suite, has lace curtains brought to America from Germany by Joe's aunt. A white canopy and spread (crocheted by Joe's grandmother) accent the four-poster bed, which has a genuine feather-bed for deep slumber. The shower "curtain" around the in-room claw-foot tub is delicate white tulle. Jasmine, or the "Baby" room is delightfully decorated with memorabilia from Joe and Cindy's childhoods, such as her christening gown and his lederhosen. (Remember that crocheting German grandmother?) There's even a child's rocking chair, which was Cindy's mother's. A close look at the photos reveal baby Joe and baby Cindy, as well as other family members.

The Magnolia Plantation bears all the earmarks of a family operation. Cindy's mother, who lives in the carriage house behind the mansion, helps manage the inn. It was she who needlepointed the nameplates for each guest room. Joe's father, a landscape architect, helped design and install the delightful backyard garden, which has a pond, waterfall, and a gazebo that invites guests to sit a spell. Together, Cindy and her mother hand-painted the rose-tone floral accents that frame the windows of the Azalea Room.

On the back of each guest room door is an information card that expresses Joe and Cindy's philosophy as hosts: "You are here to relax, so relax. You do not have to pick up after yourself or make your bed." After a few days of that kind of pampering, it will be very hard to check out.

🏠 *5 double rooms with baths, 1 2-bedroom cottage with bath. Air-conditioning, clock radios with cassette players, cable TV in parlor, fireplaces in all rooms (except cottage), tandem bikes available. $75–$125; full breakfast; complimentary beverages, wine, and snacks served evenings. AE, MC, V. 2-night minimum in cottage.*

Other Choices

Clauser's Bed & Breakfast. 201 E. Kicklighter Rd., Lake Helen, FL 32744, tel. 904/228–0310 or 800/220–0310, fax 904/228–2337. 8 double rooms with baths. Air-conditioning, 2 rooms with whirlpool tubs, terry-cloth robes, complimentary port wine and sherry, outdoor hot tub and nature trail. $75–$120, full breakfast. AE, MC, V.

Herlong Mansion. 402 N.E. Cholokka Blvd., Micanopy, FL 32667, tel. 352/466–3322. 6 double rooms with baths, 4 suites, 2 cottages. Air-conditioning, cable TV in music room, 6 rooms with decorative fireplaces, clock radios, whirlpool bath in 1 suite, bicycles available. $50–$150; full breakfast, kitchen open 24 hours. AE, MC, V.

Lakeside Inn. 100 N. Alexander St., Mount Dora, FL 32757, tel. 352/383–4101 or 800/556–5016, fax 352/735–2642. 60 double rooms with baths, 16 parlor rooms, 11 lake-view rooms, 1 suite. Restaurant, bar, air-conditioning, cable TVs, mini-refrigerators in some rooms, terry robes, pool, tennis courts, boats available for rent. $95–$180, Continental breakfast. AE, D, MC, V.

Seven Sisters Inn. 820 S.E. Ft. King St., Ocala, FL 34471, tel. 352/867–1170, fax 352/867–5266. 6 double rooms with baths, 2 suites, 1 room accessible for people who use wheelchairs. Air-conditioning, cable TV in 3 rooms, fireplaces in 4 rooms, whirlpool bath in 1 room. $105–$165; full breakfast, complimentary beverages, afternoon tea. AE, D, MC, V.

Shady Oak Bed & Breakfast. 203 Cholokka Blvd., Micanopy, FL 32667, tel. 352/466–3476. 5 double rooms with baths. Air-conditioning, cable TV, whirlpool bath in 1 room. $75–$125; full breakfast, catered dinners on request. MC, V.

Central and East Central Florida

Live Oak Inn & Restaurant

444-448 S. Beach St., Daytona Beach, FL 32114, tel. 904/252–4667 or 800/881–4667, fax 904/239–0068

Set across the street from Halifax Harbor (guests with their own boats can use one of its slips), in the heart of the historic section of Daytona Beach, the Live Oak Inn & Restaurant seems worlds away from the gaudy glitz of the beachfront scene. Guests at the Live Oak travel through time to the early days of Daytona Beach's history. The two houses that comprise the inn date from 1871 and 1881, respectively, long before anyone in Daytona ever thought about a Speedway or driving on the beach. The historic air that permeates the inn is the mark of innkeepers Jessie and Del Glock, retired missionaries who spent a number of years in Japan. Many of the wall hangings in the guest rooms reflect the time they spent in the Far East.

The exterior of the inn is dominated by a wonderfully twisted century-old oak tree from which the inn takes its name. Gracefully draped with Spanish moss, the tree recalls a bygone era when genteel young women and their suitors courted beneath its branches. Diners seated by the front windows in the inn's candlelit restaurant get a view of the tree up close, as well as of the busy harbor across the street.

Each of the guest rooms is named after a prominent Floridian or a figure who was central to Daytona Beach history. Composer Stephen Foster is the inspiration for the Foster Room, painted a delicate shade of blue. In the peach-tone Audubon Room, guests will find an elaborate wicker birdcage on the dresser. Not all the rooms are named for famous people from the past, however. The Harley Room is decorated with motorcycle photographs and memorabilia. The Disney Room—with a stuffed Mickey and Minnie on the bed—is a tribute not only to Walt, but to the Glocks' status as ministers at Disney World's Wedding Pavilion. As a result of their missionary work in Japan, both are fluent in Japanese; many of the couples who tie the knot at Disney are from the Land of the Rising Sun, and the Glocks conduct the ceremony in Japanese.

Others thinking about getting hitched in Daytona can do so right at the inn. Del Glock will officiate, and the sweeping staircase in the 1871 house provides a dramatic entrance for any bride. Guests can stay at the inn, of course, and the reception can be held in either the restaurant or a lovely private room with carved wooden walls in the 1881 house or the sunny breakfast room in the 1871 house.

The Glocks have taken great pains to re-create the furnishings of the period. Rather than decorate each room solely with antiques, they carefully mixed old and new pieces to create a look that reflects the heyday of Daytona's pioneers. Many settlers could bring only a few precious heirlooms on the difficult trek to central Florida; they then made up for the lack of their "northern"-style furnishings by adding pieces produced by local artisans. Thus, in the Foster Room, guests will find a delicate oak antique secretary, as well as white wicker end tables; in the Audubon Room, a massive mahogany bed, more than 150 years old, and mahogany chest are complemented by a wicker chaise longue.

While the inn's furnishings reflect the Glocks' commitment to historic preservation, its amenities are thankfully late 20th century. Many rooms have tiled baths with whirlpools, and terry robes are thoughtfully provided. Should guests want to get away from it all, they have the option of using their in-room videocassette players. (Tapes are available.) However, those who want to forget about the present can lose themselves in one of the fine books available from a tea cart in the upstairs hallway. With most of the rooms having private porches, there's no finer way to experience old Florida.

🛏 *15 double rooms with baths. Restaurant, bar, air-conditioning, cable TVs, video and audiocassette players, clock radios, harbor views from some rooms, whirlpool baths in 6 rooms. $75–$200, Continental breakfast. No credit cards.*

Other Choices

Coquina Inn Bed & Breakfast. 544 S. Palmetto Ave., Daytona Beach, FL 32114, tel. 904/254–4969 or 800/805–7533, fax 904/254–4969. 4 double rooms with baths. Air-conditioning, fireplace in 1 room, bicycles available. $80–$175, full breakfast. AE, MC, V.

Courtyard at Lake Lucerne. 211 N. Lucerne Circle E, Orlando, FL 32801, tel. 407/648–5188 or 800/444–5289, fax 407/246–1368. 6 double rooms with baths in Norment-Parry Inn, 3 double rooms in I. W. Phillips House, 15 suites in Wellborn Suites. Bar, air-conditioning, cable TVs, some rooms with fireplaces, kitchenettes in Wellborn Suites,

whirlpool baths in 2 suites. $69–$165, Continental breakfast. AE, DC, MC, V.

Inn at Cocoa Beach. 4300 Ocean Beach Blvd., Cocoa Beach, FL 32931, tel. 407/799–3460 or 800/343–5307, fax 407/784–8632. 41 double rooms with baths, 9 junior suites. Bar, air-conditioning, cable TVs, most rooms with ocean view, whirlpool baths in 5 rooms, pool. $99–$195; Continental breakfast, wine and cheese hour. AE, D, MC, V.

Night Swan Intracoastal Bed & Breakfast. 512 S. Riverside Dr., New Smyrna Beach, FL 32168, tel. 904/423–4940 or 800/465–4261, fax 904/427–2814. 3 double rooms with baths, 3 suites. Air-conditioning, views of Intracoastal Waterway, guest refrigerator. $59–$129, full breakfast. AE, D, MC, V.

PerriHouse Bed & Breakfast Inn. 10417 S.R. 535, Lake Buena Vista, FL 32830, tel. 407/876-4830, fax 407/876–0241. 6 double rooms with baths (1 room can sleep 4). Air-conditioning, cable TVs, phones, private entrances, pool, outdoor spa, bird sanctuary. $85, Continental breakfast. AE, MC, V. 2-night stay required on weekends and holidays.

Key West

Gardens Hotel

526 Angela St., Key West, FL 33040, tel. 305/294–2661 or 800/526–2664, fax 305/292–1007

Although only one short block from the throngs of tourists on Duval Street—Key West's main drag—the Gardens Hotel is, quite literally, a tropical oasis. The hotel's main building, which dates from the 1870s, is one of Key West's oldest Bahama-style homes. The home and surrounding property were purchased in 1930 by Peggy Mills and her first husband. Mrs. Mills then spent the remainder of her life carefully cultivating the land, creating magnificent tropical gardens whose beauty guests can enjoy as they swim in the pool or take a leisurely walk around the grounds.

The gardens are filled with bromeliads, mango, balsa, breadfruit trees, and giant crotons. Flowering plants include lilies, hibiscus, bougainvillea, orange jasmine, and magnolia. Wrought-iron benches are strategically placed throughout the plantings, allowing for a contemplative stop. The garden's pathways are lined with 87,000 red bricks, which Mrs. Mills had imported from Cuba, Honduras, and England. Also interspersed with the flora and fauna are four enormous earthenware jars, or *tinajones*, used by Spanish settlers to catch rainwater for drinking. Mrs. Mills found them in Cuba about 1950, and persuaded then-president Batista to allow her to bring the 18th-century artifacts back to the United States.

After Mrs. Mills died in 1979, the property and buildings went through several owners and periods of great neglect. In 1992, Bill and Corinna Hettinger purchased the property and, after a 14-month, multimillion-dollar restoration, the Gardens Hotel welcomed its first guests.

There are two historic guest rooms upstairs in the main house; additional accommodations in the Gardens and Courtyard buildings are a short, delightful walk away. In addition, there are the Eyebrow Cottage, Carriage House, and Master Suite. All rooms are elegantly decorated with an eye for the telling detail: soft, floral prints in the bedspreads and matching curtains; gleaming hardwood floors; 12-foot ceilings with 10-inch moldings; pristine white marble baths with double sinks and whirlpool tubs. Each room contains an original Impressionist painting by New Zealand artist Peter Williams, whose style perfectly captures the island spirit.

Under the dining room's elaborate tin ceiling, the breakfast table is spread with fresh fruits, cheeses, chocolate croissants, and Key-lime pastries, a repast guests can enjoy in the nearby sunroom. An antique grandfather clock stands watch in the hallway, its hands permanently set at 11:20. (Since it's Key West, nobody cares what time it really is, anyway.) Guests can can also dine on the patio, where they will be entertained by Peggy, a very friendly macaw who will eat from guests' hands, if given the slightest encouragement.

With its pale blue walls, overstuffed striped couch, fireplace, and built-in bookcases, the living room invites guests to linger, whether over morning coffee or afternoon drinks. An inlaid-wood backgammon and checkers table is thoughtfully provided. But as Key West's tropical air circulates, guests find themselves drawn to the swimming pool with its mirrored bar, or to the fountains in the gardens and the courtyard. It's also the perfect spot for a moonlight swim, highlighted, perhaps, with the complimentary bottle of champagne that's provided whenever guests choose to imbibe.

🏨 *15 double rooms with baths, 2 suites. Air-conditioning, cable TVs, whirlpool baths, minibars in 13 rooms, pool. $155–$625, Continental breakfast. AE, MC, V.*

Other Choices

Curry Mansion Inn. 511 Caroline St., Key West, FL 33040, tel. 305/294–5349 or 800/253–3466, fax 305/294–4093. 24 double rooms with baths, 4 suites. Air-conditioning, cable TVs, VCR available, decorative fireplaces in 2 rooms, mini-refrigerators, whirlpools in some rooms, beach privileges at Marriott's Casa Marina and at Pier House, pool. $125–$275; Continental breakfast, evening cocktails. AE, D, DC, MC, V.

Heron House. 512 Simonton St., Key West, FL 33040, tel. 305/294–9227 or 800/294–1644, fax 305/294–5692. 23 double rooms with baths. Air-conditioning, cable TVs, phones, mini-refrigerators and wet bars, whirlpool bath in 1 room, weight room, pool, rooftop sundeck. $95–$249, Continental breakfast buffet. No children under 16. AE, DC, MC, V.

La Mer Hotel. 506 South St., Key West, FL 33040, tel. 305/296–5611 or 800/354–4455, fax 305/294–8272. 7 double rooms with baths, 4 double rooms with baths and sitting areas. Air-conditioning, cable TVs, ocean views from 4 rooms, kitchenettes in 5 rooms, bicycles available, pool (at sister hotel next door). $115–$270 ($10 extra person); Continental breakfast, afternoon tea. AE, MC, V.

Merlinn Guest House. 811 Simonton St., Key West, FL 33040, tel. 305/296–3336, fax 305/296–3524. 9 double rooms with baths, 1 single room with bath, 1 room accessible to people who use wheelchairs. Air-conditioning in all rooms except single, cable TVs, mini-refrigerators in some rooms, pool. $70–$160, Continental breakfast. AE, D, MC, V.

Pilot House. 414 Simonton St., Key West, FL 33040, tel. 305/294–8719 or 800/648–3780, fax 305/294–9298. 3 double rooms with baths; 2 suites; 1 penthouse with kitchen, private sundeck, and whirlpool bath; 1 room accessible to people who use wheelchairs. Air-conditioning, cable TVs, fireplaces in 3 rooms, kitchenette in 1 room, kitchens in 4 rooms, whirlpool baths in some rooms, pool. $80–$300, breakfast not included. AE, D, DC, MC, V.

Simonton Court. 320 Simonton St., Key West, FL 33040, tel. 305/294–6386 or 800/944–2687, fax 305/293–8446. 9 double rooms in inn, 2 poolside suites in manor house, 6 cottages, 6 double rooms in mansion. Air-conditioning, cable TV/VCR in some rooms, mini-refrigerators, kitchens in some rooms, 3 pools, outdoor hot tub. $110–$350, Continental breakfast buffet. AE, D, MC, V.

Watson House. 525 Simonton St., Key West, FL 33040, tel. 305/294–6712 or 800/621–9405. 3 suites in main house, 1 poolside cabana with living room and bedroom. Air-conditioning, cable TVs, outdoor whirlpool, pool, 2 suites with kitchens, coffeemakers. $125–$370, Continental breakfast delivered to room. AE, MC, V.

Southwest Florida and the Gulf Coast

Banyan House

519 South Harbor Dr., Venice, FL 34285, tel. 941/484–1385, fax 941/484–8032

If you know the lyrics to "Don't Sit Under the Apple Tree with Anyone Else but Me," you'll feel right at home at the Banyan House. Just change the type of tree from apple to banyan and you will have captured the flavor of the only bed-and-breakfast in Venice, Florida, a small but delightful Gulf Coast beach town.

Constructed in 1926 by railroad builders, the Banyan House has served as a museum, tearoom, USO Headquarters, and day nursery. Since 1981 it has been a bed-and-breakfast. Owners Suzie and Ian Maryan, a delightful British couple, are eager to accommodate their guests, offering a welcoming drink and conversation. Suzie and Ian have lived all over the world. Photographs documenting Ian's piloting career and the Maryans' many residences are scattered throughout the Banyan House's public areas.

Accommodations in the main house are three one-bedroom efficiency apartments. Continental breakfast and full maid service is included. Five additional apartments, with no maid service, are in two additional buildings on the property. Rooms in all buildings are spacious and elegantly appointed in bright, airy, Florida pastels. A common area downstairs has games and books available at no charge, along with tourist brochures. The Spanish-themed backyard patio area has a lovely pool and hot tub, which appropriately sits under the spreading branches of the banyan tree.

The Banyan House is very conveniently located within walking distance of the historic Venice shopping district. The beautiful Venice beach is just a short ride away; bikes are available at no charge. Sarasota is just 20 minutes away by car; the Banyan House's location also makes it easily accessible to major Central Florida attractions, such as Busch Gardens and Walt Disney World.

🏠 *3 1-bedroom efficiencies, 5 1-bedroom apartments. Air-conditioning, cable TVs, pool, outdoor hot tub, pool. $65–$105 daily, $315–$665 weekly; Continental breakfast. No smoking, no children. AE, D, DC, MC, V.*

Mansion House Bed & Breakfast

105 5th Ave. NE, St. Petersburg, FL 33701, tel. and fax 813/821–9391 or 800/274–7520

Just a few minutes' walk from the St. Petersburg waterfront on Tampa Bay, the Mansion House is a delightful hostelry in the city's historic district. Innkeepers Rosie and Robert Ray are the hosts, and they'll do just about anything to make you feel at home.

The house dates from 1904 and is decorated with an eclectic mix of Rob and Rosie's family heirlooms and lots of white wicker accented with peach and minty green cushions. Photos of the Rays' children—now college students—are much in evidence. A whimsical decorating touch in the dining room is the copper double boiler filled with Cabbage Patch dolls. A centerpiece of the parlor is the gleaming hardwood floor staircase, which leads to four upstairs guest rooms. (A fifth bedroom is downstairs, and there's also a separate carriage house behind the main house.) Guest rooms are cozily furnished with the same mix of antiques and wicker as the public rooms.

A sitting room upstairs has a large TV, antique writing desk, and lots of paperbacks and board games. It's a cozy spot to while away a few hours. A well-stocked mini-refrigerator is also here; guests are welcome to help themselves to its contents.

A unique advantage of the Mansion House is Rob's status as licensed boat captain. Guests can charter the 23-foot sport cruiser *Aussie Spirit* for a customized charter on the Gulf of Mexico that can range from an hour to a full day.

A highlight of a stay here is the morning meal, cooked by Rosie and served with charm and grace. Two popular items are her blueberry pancakes and orange French toast. If you want the recipe, it's yours, but Rosie does request that you provide her with a recipe in return. "But it's not a house rule," she emphasizes.

🏠 *6 double rooms with baths, including carriage house. Air-conditioning; cable TV/VCRs; terry-cloth robes; private label toiletries; toiletry basket; outdoor spa; complimentary wine, cheese, snacks, coffee, tea, and soft drinks. $85–$125, full breakfast. AE, MC, V.*

Other Choices

Bayboro House Bed & Breakfast on Old Tampa Bay. 1719 Beach Dr. SE, St. Petersburg, FL 33701, tel. and fax 813/823–4955. 4 rooms with baths, 1 suite with full kitchen and private sundeck. Air-conditioning, TV/VCRs, cordless phone shared by all rooms, off-street parking, views of Tampa Bay, beach towels and beach chairs available. $85–$145, Continental breakfast. MC, V.

Bay Gables Bed & Breakfast, Garden & Tea Room. 136 4th Ave. NE, St.

Petersburg, FL 33701, tel. 813/822–8855 or 800/822–8803, fax 813/822–8855. 5 rooms with baths, 4 suites, 1 room accessible for people who use wheelchairs. Air-conditioning, whirlpool bath in 1 room, kitchenettes in 4 rooms, terry robes. $85–$135, Continental breakfast. MC, V.

Gilchrist Bed & Breakfast. 115 Gilchrist St., Punta Gorda, FL 33950, tel. 941/575–4129. 2 double rooms with baths. Air-conditioning, cable TV and phone in common area, outdoor hot tub, patio with grill. $65–$95, Continental breakfast. MC, V.

Inn by the Sea. 287 11th Ave. South, Naples, FL 33940, tel. 941/649–4124 or 800/584–1268. 3 double rooms with baths, 2 suites. Air-conditioning, cable TV and phone in living room. $80–$165, Continental breakfast. AE, MC, V.

Inn on the Beach. 1401 Gulfway, St. Petersburg Beach, FL 33706, tel. 813/360–8844. 12 double rooms with baths. Air-conditioning, cable TV, phones. $45–$150, Continental breakfast Sat.–Sun. only. AE, D, DC, MC, V.

Sanibel's Song of the Sea. 863 E. Gulf Dr., Sanibel, FL 33957, tel. 800/231–1045. 22 rooms, 8 suites. Air-conditioning, cable TVs, phones, wine and flowers upon arrival, pool and outdoor hot tub, books and movies available, shared recreational facilities with Sanibel Inn next door. $154–$325, Continental breakfast. AE, D, DC, MC, V.

Georgia

The 1842 Inn

North Georgia and Atlanta

Glen-Ella Springs Country Inn & Conference Center

Bear Gap Rd. (Rte. 3, Box 3304), 8½ mi north of Clarkesville, GA, 30523, tel. 706/754-7295, fax 706/754-7295

Glen-Ella Springs Country Inn, a rambling 100-year-old hideaway just outside of Clarkesville, was lovingly renovated in 1987—after years of neglect—by Barrie and Bobby Aycock. The small hotel, listed on the National Register of Historic Places, sits by a gravel road on 17 acres of meadows and gardens.

At first glance the Glen-Ella, with its heart-pine floors, walls, and ceilings, appears down-home, but its uptown flair soon becomes evident. The front lobby, filled with chintz and antiques, serves as a parlor, and fires are lit here against the cool night air. From welcoming porches furnished with country-style rocking chairs you enter the guest rooms, where quilts, chintzes, original artwork, painted reproduction antiques, and Oriental and area rugs convey an English country feeling within naturally finished and painted pine-paneled interiors.

The hotel's dining room, with a fireplace, is the realization of Barrie's original dream: to own her own restaurant. Her kitchen is the source of the sweet baked goods—blueberry-granola pancakes and oat scones—served at breakfast and regional southern cuisine served at dinner. The food here has so enhanced the inn's reputation that it has become a culinary hot spot for Atlantans, who will drive the two hours for the sumptuous meals.

Special pursuits, such as mystery weekends and herb-gardening conferences, are listed at the lobby desk. Or you can relax by the pool on the large sundeck surrounded by flower gardens. Sports lovers will find excellent hiking at nearby Tallulah Falls. Golf (as well as tennis) is found at the Orchard, a championship course within a few miles of the inn. Kayaking and whitewater rafting on the Chattooga River are also popular, and the inn arranges horseback riding.

During the week, the conference center is frequently booked by Fortune 100 companies.

🏨 *14 double rooms with baths, 2 suites with fireplaces and whirlpool tubs. Air-*

conditioning, phones with voice mail; satellite TV in lobby, pool. $100–$175, full breakfast. AE, MC, V. No smoking, no pets.

Nicholson House

6295 Jefferson Rd., Athens, GA 30607, tel. 706/353–2200

Only about 15 minutes outside of Athens, Nicholson House is perfect for anyone attending functions at the nearby University of Georgia. The early 19th-century, 4,000-square-foot house rests majestically on 6 acres of a land grant originally awarded in 1779 to William Few, one of Georgia's two signers of the U.S. Constitution. Deer routinely parade across the front of the property. A portion of the old federal road, a system dating to the Andrew Jackson administration, runs through the lower front terrace.

Originally built by Ransom and Nancy Nichols as a two-over-two log house, the building was given a Colonial revival–style face-lift after 1947, totally concealing the log exterior. The Nicholsons, for whom the inn is named, purchased the property in that year and added a few rooms in addition to redesigning the appearance of the house. Within, random-width planking and uneven floors and ceilings reveal the original 19th-century structure. A wide front veranda offers restful rocking chairs from which to view the surrounding countryside and take in the sunset.

The bright, warm dining and living rooms are decorated in deep green and burgundy, with a paisley wall covering in adjoining spaces and gleaming white trim that ties the decorative elements together. They are furnnished with period reproductions and antiques, and along with the kitchen, they are both available to guests. The six bedrooms in the main house are furnished with period-style reproduction pieces. In addition to those in the main house, guest accommodations have been devel-

oped in a nearby hillside cottage and a carriage house.

The enhanced Continental breakfast, which focuses on healthy foods and often includes a fresh fruit entrée, yogurt, granola, juice, fresh muffins, and croissant, is served in the dining room. Innkeeper–owner Stuart Kelley, a former Eastern Airlines operations executive, lives on the property.

On the way to Nicholson House, via I–85, you'll find Jefferson, Georgia, where the Crawford Long Museum exhibits medical artifacts in tribute to the Georgia physician who first used ether to anesthetize patients. In Athens, the Georgia Museum of Art is not to be missed.

▦ *4 double rooms with baths. Air-conditioning, cable TVs, phones; trail to spring. $75, Continental breakfast. AE, D, MC, V. No smoking, no pets.*

Serenbe

10950 Hutcherson Ferry Rd., Palmetto, GA 30268, tel. 770/463–2610, fax 770/463–4472

Marie and Steve Nygren are not the kind of folks one expects to find in rural Fulton County, a short distance from Atlanta. This urbane, enterprising young couple with a professional history in the hospitality industry and a young family had been searching for a weekend retreat when they found this now almost 300-acre farm. They swapped an elegant in-town home and the urban corporate scene for life in the country. Marie named it Serenbe, combining the words serenity and being.

Now the family dog, Miz Scarlett, counts as her companions horses, cattle, chickens, rabbits, and pigs. The complex includes a carefully restored farmhouse, a barn and bungalow converted to bed-and-breakfast accommodations, and a painstakingly designed garden. No detail is spared: Classical music wafts over this pastoral setting through a cleverly hidden system of 30 speakers.

The weathered 1930s-vintage restored barn is a study in adaptive reuse. Beneath its rooms, a sheltered cabana looks out onto the carefully designed swimming pool, set with especially wide coping tiles. A common area, filled with fine art by local and national artists, opens onto a patio. Its fireplace burns on both sides, warming the large common living space and the outside patio. In the barn are three spacious rooms done with a "country modern" air. One features a whirlpool tub, another a reading nook. The barn also has its own kitchen. A separate, less dramatic bungalow holds two bedrooms and also has its own kitchen; it must be taken as a unit.

Serenity is indeed an apt name: Guests may stroll the expansive pastures; read in the cabana, where a full southern-style breakfast—grits and all—may be served; cool off in the pool; or meander through the geometric garden. If weather does not permit or a guest prefers, breakfast may be enjoyed in the family's home, where it is served in a large glassed-in porch. At a nearby facility, guests seeking a more active experience may rent horses and explore the farm's trails.

🛏 *3 double rooms with baths, including one with whirlpool tub, 1 cottage with 2 double rooms, living room and kitchen, large common area, satellite TV in common area, VCR and video library, fireplace, patio; pool and hot tub, canoeing, hiking, fishing, lake. $95–$145, full breakfast. No credit cards. No smoking, no pets.*

Other Choices

Beechwood Inn. Off GA 76 E, Beechwood Dr., Clayton, GA 30525, tel. and fax 706/782–5485. 4 double rooms with baths, 1 suite with living room, private balcony and kitchen. Air-conditioning, cable TV in suite, TV in living room for other guests. $95–$125, full breakfast. No credit cards. No smoking, no pets. Closed Nov.–May 1.

Gordon-Lee Mansion. 217 Cove Rd., Chickamauga, GA 30707, tel. 706/375–4728 or 800/487–4728. 4 double rooms with baths, 1 cabin with double room and sitting room. Air-conditioning, cable TV in rooms. $75–$100, breakfast buffet or menu. MC, V. No smoking, no pets.

Shellmont Bed & Breakfast. 821 Piedmont Ave., Atlanta, GA 30306, tel. 404/872–9290, fax 404/872–5379. 2 double rooms, 2 suites, 1 carriage house with a suite (steam shower). Air-conditioning, TVs, phones; VCR in carriage house. $84–$169; full gourmet breakfast, turndown service with gourmet chocolates. AE, DC, MC, V. No smoking, no pets.

Woodbridge Inn. 411 Chambers St., Jasper, GA 30143, tel. 706/692–6293, fax 706/692–9061. 12 double rooms with baths. Restaurant (limited lunch; dinner), air-conditioning, cable TVs, phones; swimming pool, gazebo, ponds. $65–$80, plus seasonal supplements; no breakfast. AE, D, MC, V. No smoking.

Reservations Services

Atlanta Hospitality Bed & Breakfast Reservations (2472 Lauderdale Dr., Atlanta, GA 30345, tel. 770/493–1930 or 800/484–2058 [code 1930]). Bed and Breakfast Atlanta (1801 Piedmont Ave., Atlanta, GA 30324, tel. 404/875–0525 or 800/967–3224, fax 404/875–9672). **Great Inns of Georgia** (tel. 404/843–0471 or 800/823–7787, fax 404/252–8886).

Middle Georgia

1842 Inn

353 College St., Macon, GA 31201, tel. and fax 912/741–1842 or 800/336–1842

Established in 1823, Macon is a virtual museum of fine antebellum and Victorian architecture, boasting 11 historic districts with more than 5,500 buildings on the National Register of Historic Places. This imposing Greek Revival mansion stands in the heart of Macon's historic Intown neighborhood, a few blocks from Mercer University and a five-minute drive from downtown. When Jefferson Davis came to Macon in 1887 for a grand confederate reunion ball, many members of the familiy stayed at the house, then still owned by its original builder, John Gresham, mayor of Macon. Various rooms in the inn are named for the important personages whose presence marks the house's history.

Named for the year its oldest portion was built, the inn was enlarged around the turn of the century, was professionally restored in 1986, and has earned many preservation awards. It was bought in 1991 by Phillip Jenkins, a Georgia native and fund-raising consultant, and his silent partner, Richard Meils, a Michigan physician. Phillip or one of the friendly staff members will show you to a spacious, well-appointed guest room in the main house or in the Victorian cottage, which was saved from demolition by being cut in half, moved to the property, and installed in back, past the brick courtyard.

The grand, white-pillared front porch—dramatically lit at night—opens to the traditional center hall found in many southern houses. The parlors are furnished with fine period antiques, including European tapestries, paintings, and a collection of period export porcelain. In the front parlor Phillip sometimes enjoys playing the Baldwin baby grand for guests, who often add their own musical acumen to the evening's cocktail hour.

In the quietly elegant bedrooms, ceiling fans whirl overhead. Brass or four-poster beds are featured in the rooms, some of which have period antiques, and breakfast is served along with the morning paper in your bedroom's sitting area or in the parlor. The outside courtyard also is pleasant for breakfast

in fine weather. Fresh flowers perfume the rooms, and evening turndown service includes gourmet chocolates. Six of the rooms have working fireplaces, and four have whirlpool baths.

Cocktails and hors d'oeuvres are available in the library after 5:30 each day. One of the events that makes a stay at the 1842 special is "Lights on Macon," a self-guided walking tour that guides visitors past more than 30 of the neighborhood's splendid homes. In a program structured in coordination with the National Trust for Historic Preservation, the selected homes are dramatically illuminated to focus on their architectural features.

▦ *12 double rooms with baths in house, 9 doubles with baths in cottage. Air-conditioning, cable TVs, phones. $95–$155; Continental breakfast (additional items available for an extra charge), afternoon refreshments. AE, MC, V. No pets.*

Parrott-Camp-Soucy Inn

155 Greenville St., Newnan, GA 30263, tel. 770/502–0676

Only an hour south of Atlanta, Newnan is an antebellum town with more than its share of preserved historic homes. It's an ideal stop for visitors seeking the Old South. This spectacular Second Empire Victorian house, one of the first of Newnan's homes developed as a bed-and-breakfast inn by innkeeper Sam Soucy, has been carefully restored.

The Parrott-Camp-Soucy house was originally built as a Greek Revival home in 1842. In 1884, as a bridal wedding gift, it was purchased by new owners and reconstructed with Victorian styling. The redesign may have been done by a northerner, as the vestibule and entry fireplace are cold-climate features.

Today the inn is owned and operated by a young couple, Helen and Rick

Cousins, and it bears their distinctive mark. Helen sewed the dramatic period-style hangings that adorn windows and frame passageways between rooms. In the kitchen, punched-tin cabinets, a Soucy legacy, add a dramatic period touch. Throughout the spectacular interior, Victorian styling is carefully maintained, but without sacrificing modern amenities. Guests may enjoy access to two stocked-bar refrigerators.

Four luxurious guest rooms make it difficult to choose among them. In the Regency Room, the bed is draped in lace and ribbons, and a claw-foot slipper tub awaits the guest in front of the fireplace. An 1890s-era rib-cage shower tempts the gentleman guest. The room's private veranda leads to the gardens. For reading, the Garden Room offers its own alcove, sitting area, and fireplace. Its oversize shower can easily accommodate two.

The Cousins, who live on the property behind the inn, are justifiably proud of their work. Breakfast is served on the veranda or in the dining room and features specially blended coffees and gourmet dishes. A well-stocked library contains books, music, and classic films. The 2 acres of beautifully maintained, rose-filled grounds, as well as a pool and hot tub, offer perfect opportunities for reading and relaxing.

🖼 *4 double rooms with baths. Air-conditioning, phones, TV/VCR in common room; pool–hot tub. $105–$165, full breakfast. MC, V. No smoking, no pets, no children.*

Other Choices

Crockett House. 671 Madison Rd., Eatonton, GA 31024, tel. 706/485–2248. 4 double rooms with baths, 2 double rooms share 1 bath. Air-conditioning, wood-burning fireplaces, cable TV in common area and in one guest room. $65–$95, full breakfast. AE, MC, V. No smoking, no pets.

Veranda. 252 Seavy St. (Box 177), Senoia, GA 30276, tel. 770/599–3905, fax 770/599–0806. 9 double rooms with baths, whirlpool bath in 1 room. Air-conditioning, TV in common area. $85–$105, full breakfast. AE, D, MC, V. No smoking, no pets.

Coastal Georgia

The Gastonian

220 E. Gaston St., Savannah, GA 31401, tel. 912/232–2869 or 800/322–6603, fax 912/232–0710

Two blocks from Savannah's Forsyth Park and 12 from River Street stands the Gastonian. A pineapple, symbolic of hospitality, is engraved on the brass sign at the entry, a hint of the comforts within. Californians Hugh and Roberta Lineberger bought the two adjacent Regency Italianate mansions that compose the inn in 1985. The couple has transformed the pair—constructed for two prosperous merchants after the Civil War—into one of the South's most captivating inns.

Roberta spent months selecting authentic Georgian and Regency-period antiques and original Savannah colors to recall the 19th-century ambience. In the front parlor and formal dining room, the antiques have the patina that comes from being well loved and from much polishing. Sideboards and tabletops are laden with heirloom crystal, silver, and fine china. Yet the inn doesn't have the museum feel that can make some historic homes uncomfortable. Guests are encouraged to lounge in the coral upholstered wing chairs on either side of the drawing-room fireplace or pick out tunes on the antique baby grand piano that dominates the front parlor. Scalamandre's Savannah-collection wallpapers adorn the hallways. Of the bedrooms, one is decorated in rustic country and contains ladder-back cane chairs and antique trunks; another is reminiscent of Colonial America, with crewel draperies and bedspreads; and still another is all British formality, dressed in chintz and damask upholstery. Most have rice poster or Charleston canopy beds. The baths are well lit and luxurious. Directly behind the main house is the carriage-house suite. Guests are greeted with fruit and a split of wine, and turndown service includes fresh pecan pralines and peach schnapps.

A sumptuous southern breakfast is served in the large country kitchen or the dining room. Late risers can opt for a Continental breakfast delivered bedside on a silver tray along with the local paper. An elevated sundeck with chaise longues, a wisteria- and jasmine-draped pergola, and a large hot tub makes for a pleasant spot to laze away the afternoon. The concierge has plenty of suggestions for terrific restaurants and will arrange for transport by horse-drawn carriage. March, April, May, and October are the inn's busiest times, so call well in advance.

🏨 *13 double rooms with baths, 3 suites. Air-conditioning, cable TV, phones, gas fireplaces. $125–$285; full breakfast, afternoon tea. AE, MC, V. No smoking, no pets.*

Greyfield Inn

Cumberland Island, GA (Box 900, Fernandina Beach, FL 32035), tel. 904/261–6408 (reservations and information), fax 904/321–0666

The only accommodations on Cumberland Island, Greyfield Inn is accessible only by ferry or other boat or by private plane, landing only by prior arrangement on a grass strip. Round-trip transportation aboard the *Lucy R. Ferguson* is free to inn guests. The imposing house with wide colonnade porches stands by itself in the primitive landscape. Built in 1901 by tycoon Thomas Carnegie for his daughter, the two-story, glinty white Victorian house retains much of its original glory. The inn is operated by Mitty Ferguson, Carnegie's great-great-grandson, and his wife, Mary Jo, who carefully preserve ties to the past. In September 1996 it was the site of John F. Kennedy Jr.'s small, unannounced wedding to Carolyn Bessette.

Greyfield is furnished with dark, heavy, late-19th-century furniture, some of it original to the house; family photographs; tabletop collections of seashore memorabilia; and antique rugs. Bedrooms are spacious, the linens crisp, and the hardwood floors burnished to a glossy shine. The spit-and-polished bathrooms (three baths are shared by eight guest rooms upstairs) have antique tubs, and there's an enclosed backyard shower house that is another full bath. Downstairs, the library bedroom has its own private bath. Recently completed, two cottages each contain two bedrooms with private baths and a common living area. These spaces are fully air-conditioned, whereas in the main house only the dining room is air-conditioned. Ceiling fans circulate air in the main-house guest rooms.

All meals are included in the rates. Breakfast is an informal but substantial affair. Hors d'oeuvres are served at the cocktail hour, and afternoon tea is a winter ritual. The ring of a bell announces the formal gourmet evening meal. The tradition of dressing for dinner (jackets on the gentlemen and dressy casual attire for women) transforms the nightly ritual into a festive occasion, but the inn's atmosphere is still relaxed. Lunches are left in picnic baskets in the old-fashioned kitchen. The Fergusons let you follow your own agenda or help plan a day's activities: shelling, fishing, clam digging, swimming, hiking, or beachcombing. Guests may also take guided Jeep tours of the island's historic ruins.

The best times to visit are in spring and early autumn, when the insect population and humidity level remain low.

🏠 *5 double rooms with baths, 7 doubles and 1 suite share 3 baths, outdoor shower house. Air-conditioning in dining room; shuttle to ferry, bikes, guided nature tours. $245–$350; American Plan, afternoon refreshments. MC, V. No smoking, no pets.*

Kehoe House

123 Habersham St., Savannah, GA 31401, tel. 912/232–1020 or 800/820–1020, fax 912/231–0208

Irish immigrant William Kehoe, who became wealthy in the ironworks business, built this imposing house to shelter his 10 children. Rich in classical and Italianate details, with typical Victorian elements, the 1892 Renaissance revival–style house sits imposingly on Columbia Square. Terra-cotta moldings, iron railings, and Corinthian columns are its most notable architectural details. The cost of construction was $25,000—a princely sum in that day.

Opened in 1993 as an inn after a $1.4 million renovation, it today is one of the star Consul Court properties and an important structure in the historic district. Kehoe House counts as its neighbor the famous Isaiah Davenport House, whose threatened demolition spawned the Historic Savannah Foundation.

Now restored and furnished with important period antiques, the inn boasts brass and marble chandeliers and a music room. Handwoven carpeting adorns the gleaming wood floors, which are made of pine, oak, and maple. Fine burnished woods enhance the building's sumptuousness. It contains 15 rooms, all with private baths. The honeymoon suite has access to a veranda and has a sitting room. The beamed, high-ceilinged attic space, decorated in period antiques and reproductions, features a large boardroom, making it ideal for meetings and banquets. Several small windows admit natural light, enhanced by track lighting and lamps.

The double parlor, featuring 14-foot ceilings and two fireplaces, is the ideal spot to enjoy the substantial breakfast and afternoon tea. Costing $15 per person, served at 3 or 3:30 PM, and available by reservation only, it features assorted tea sandwiches, scones, tartlets, or other baked goods made on the premises. Hors d'oeuvres are part of the cocktail hour, which begins at 6 PM. Chocolates, a Kehoe House robe, wine, and bottled water are the main ingredients in the Kehoe's turndown service.

Kehoe House is handy to all the fine restaurants and points of interest in the historic district. The Olde Pink House is only five minutes away for dinner. Bustling River Street is just a few blocks away.

🏠 *13 double rooms with baths, 2 suites. Air-conditioning, concierge, meeting, and banquet rooms. $150–$250, full breakfast. AE, D, DC, MC, V. No smoking, no pets.*

Open Gates

Vernon Square (Box 1526), Darien, GA 31305, tel. 912/437–6985

A brick and white-picket fence outlines the perimeter of Open Gates bed-and-breakfast, the home of Carolyn Hodges. The white-frame Victorian house with Italianate details, gray shutters, and a red front door was built in 1876. It is tucked beneath a canopy of Spanish moss cascading from live oaks and is on the corner of Vernon Square, a national historic district, three blocks from the Altamaha River, historic Darien's major thoroughfare.

Founded in 1736, the town was a shipping center for cotton and a busy lumber port. Plantation owners once based their economy on rice culture. It is now a jumping-off point for boat tours to Sapelo (a nearby barrier island), a shrimping port, and a center of domestic caviar production. Darien was profiled in the nonfiction best-seller *Praying for Sheetrock*, by Melissa Fay Green.

An avid preservationist and nature lover, Hodges eagerly shares her knowledge with interested visitors. She pulls her excursion boat, now powered by an ecologically friendly Honda four-stroke motor, behind her vintage Mercedes-Benz for the bird-watching expeditions she conducts.

In a sunny den, a game table is set for Chinese checkers and shelves are filled with books on coastal history, including the diary of the English actress Fanny Kemble, who recorded her stand against slavery while living in the area on one of the rice plantations owned by her husband, Pierce Butler of Philadelphia. Carolyn prepares a breakfast of plantation pancakes, served with an assortment of jams in her collection of fruit-shaped jam pots.

One guest bedroom, in Savannah blue, has a sleigh bed and a display of antique clothes and books; another, done in peach and blue, has twin beds and antiquarian children's books; and an upstairs room, painted light green, has wooden floors (cypress and heart-pine), pine furnishings, and botanical materials. A room above the garage with a private entrance has natural wood walls adorned with antique quilts.

The canoe standing on the back porch, the aquarium gurgling away in the den, and the baby grand, family portraits, and photographs in the Pompeiian-red front parlor remind you that this is a well-loved, lived-in family's home.

▦ *2 double rooms with baths, 2 doubles share 1 bath. Air-conditioning, cable TV in common area; large pool. $55–$63, full breakfast. No credit cards. No smoking, no pets.*

Statesboro Inn

106 S. Main St., Statesboro, GA 30458, tel. 912/489–8628 or 800/846–9466, fax 912/489–4785

This large cream-colored Victorian frame house with shaded verandas was built in 1905 by W. G. Raines. Renovated and opened as a B&B in 1985, it is equipped with such simple old-fashioned pleasures as rocking chairs on the front porch and such modern luxuries as whirlpool tubs.

Located in a quiet downtown area, the inn is 1 mile from Georgia Southern University and its botanical gardens. Visiting lecturers and professors are routinely housed at the inn during their stay in Statesboro. Savannah is an hour away via I–16.

The Garges family purchased the inn in 1993. Michele, Tony, and their daughter, Melissa, moving to Statesboro from Long Island, share the duties entailed in hosting guests. Bedrooms have brass beds, love seats, and country charm, and some have private porches. Four bedrooms and three common rooms have working fireplaces. In a restored cabin behind the house, so the story goes, Willie McTell wrote "Statesboro Blues," a hit song for the Allman Brothers Band. McTell, a renowned blind blues musician, hailed from Thomson, Georgia, near Augusta.

Added to the rear of the main house and discreetly attached to it is a wing of rooms—distant from the street—that are especially quiet. A banquet facility that accommodates 100 is part of this addition; wedding receptions and other special events frequently take place in this space and in the garden outside. An adjacent Craftsman-style bungalow containing four rooms, each with private bath and private porch and sharing a common living room, has just been developed. The Garges live on the property but in a separate space behind the inn.

The inn's public dining room is known for casual but elegant dining. The 50-seat, award-winning restaurant cooks up such regional specialties as crab cakes in tarragon cream sauce. The daily specials, such as a grilled duck breast with red-pepper glaze, are often particularly irresistible. The wine list is not lengthy, but it contains good selections. Breakfast is served in the same dining room and typically includes fresh fruit and an egg dish.

🏨 *13 double rooms with baths, 2 suites, 4 rooms with baths in adjacent bungalow, bungalow with common living room. Restaurant, air-conditioning, cable TVs, phones. $65–$90, full breakfast. AE, D, DC, MC, V. No smoking.*

Other Choices

Ballastone Inn. 14 E. Oglethorpe Ave., Savannah, GA 31401, tel. 912/236–1484 or 800/822–4553, fax 912/236–4626. 17 double rooms with baths, 9 suites (Ballastone); 5 suites (Manor). Air-conditioning, cable TV with VCR and phone in rooms, fireplaces and whirlpools in some rooms, video library, 24-hr concierge, elevator (Ballastone only); off-street parking. $105–$225; enhanced Continental breakfast, afternoon tea and nightcaps. AE, MC, V. No pets.

Olde Harbour Inn. 508 E. Factors Walk, Savannah, GA 31401, tel. 912/234–4100 or 800/553–6533, fax 912/233–5979. 24 suites with kitchens. Cable TVs, phones; concierge. $115–$175; Continental breakfast, afternoon refreshments. AE, D, DC, MC, V. Restricted smoking, no pets.

Presidents' Quarters. 225 E. President St., Savannah, GA 31401, tel. 912/233–1600 or 800/233–1776, fax 912/238–0849. 7 double rooms with private baths, 9 suites (4 baths of which have whirlpool tubs). Air-conditioning, cable TVs, phones; hot tub. $117–167, Continental breakfast. AE, D, DC, MC, V. No pets.

Reservations Services

Great Inns of Georgia (tel. 404/843–0471 or 800/823–7787, fax 404/252–8886). **RSVP Savannah** (9489 Whitfield Ave., Box 49, Savannah, GA 31406, tel.

912/232–7787 or 800/729–7787). **Savannah Historic Inns** (147 Bull St., Savannah, GA 31401, tel. 912/233–7660 or 800/262–4667).

Southwest Georgia

1884 Paxton House

445 Remington Ave., Thomasville, GA 31792, tel. 912/226–5197

Built, as the name suggests, in 1884, this elegant Victorian Gothic house has been well restored by Susie Sherrod, a retired army nurse (rank of colonel), who lives on the premises with her mother. The inn is located in the Tockwotton Historic District—one of Thomasville's two historic districts, where the houses date from the 1850s to the 1920s. The center of town is just a short stroll away.

One of only two Victorian Gothic homes left in Thomasville, the house boasts a splendid wraparound veranda set with rockers. The downstairs parlor, the former "women's parlor," features a molded plaster ceiling, original brass Victorian light fixtures, and a heartpine fireplace. The dining room, centered by a solid mahogany table, is illuminated by a shimmering Austrian crystal chandelier. The main house features four fine bedrooms, all with private bath. An adjacent cottage has two more rooms upstairs. Antiques fill the nooks and crannies in both public spaces and guest rooms. Decorations include splendid collections of Meissen porcelain, dolls, Lladró figurines and clocks, as well as hand-painted Russian lacquer boxes.

The 18th Century Suite is ideal for the business traveler: It has an 18th-century-style secretary good for working moments, as well as a separate sitting room. The deep antique tub in the bath is a perfect spot to unwind.

Susie is justifiably proud of her sumptuous breakfast, which often includes juice, an egg dish, stuffed French toast, and good coffee. She also usually adds an aromatic batter bread or jam-filled pastry to the breakfast table. Turndown service offers chocolates. An onsite gift shop specializes in handmade Victorian-style Christmas ornaments and gifts. Complimentary fresh fruit is always available in the kitchen, as are pastries, sodas, tea, and coffee.

Running the width of house in the back and halfway down the side, the garden room contains a sitting room and a breakfast space. The garden beyond includes rose arbors, beds of blooming flowers, and a swing under the tree.

▦ *6 double rooms with baths, air-conditioning, cable TVs, phones; VCRs in 3 rooms; garden. $75–$165, full breakfast. AE, MC, V. No smoking, no pets.*

Pathway Inn

501 S. Lee St., Americus, GA 31709, tel. 912/928–2078 or 800/889–1466

Americus is, in many ways, a classic country Victorian town. At its center lies the recently restored Windsor Hotel, linchpin for the well-done downtown redevelopment. In the heart of Americus's historic district, the Pathway Inn, a classic Victorian residence built in 1906 with a wide veranda, columned portico, and glorious stained-glass windows has been pristinely restored.

Resident innkeepers David and Sheila Judah have turned the upstairs spaces into the hub of the inn, with its large rooms, some with whirlpool tubs, and some with king-size beds. An upstairs hallway is furnished to serve as a sitting area; its entrance privatizes these guest rooms from the rest of the house.

One of three upstairs suites is the Carter Room, named for the nearby citizen who became president. It has a king-size bed, a desk for working, comfortable chairs, and a television with

internal VCR (there is a small video library). Carter portraits and memorabilia decorate the room. One of the two downstairs suites, the Roosevelt Room, is accessible to the disabled. Furnished with a queen-size bed, it has a private bath equipped with a marble shower.

Breakfast often features regional specialties, such as locally made sausage and syrup made from blueberries grown in neighboring Marion County. Hot dishes often include French toast à l'orange, blintz casserole topped with apricot preserves, and a western breakfast casserole. Wine and cheese are available upon arrival; daily afternoon tea is served.

▦ *5 double rooms with baths, some with whirlpool tubs, ceiling fans. Air-conditioning, cable TVs, phones. $65–$117, full breakfast. AE, D, MC, V. No smoking.*

Rothschild-Pound House

201 7th St., Columbus, GA 31901, tel. 706/322–4075 or 800/585–4075

The Rothschild-Pound House was carefully moved in 1993 to its current location on a lot in Columbus's historic district, where it is now nearby the restored downtown and the Chattahoochee Riverwalk, with its shops and restaurants. Built in 1870, the house, defined by a classic mansard roof, is one of two remaining Second Empire houses in Columbus. The Rothschild family made its fortune in the textile industry and remains prominent in Columbus.

Innkeepers Gary and Mamie Pound restored the home's hardwood floors and fireplaces and filled it with dramatic antiques. A working artist from a well-known family of artists, Gary has brought much of his work to show in the house. Fourteen-foot ceilings, a carved mahogany staircase, and marble and carved mahogany mantels in the rooms are among the house's architectural features. Two parlors frame either side of a generous entrance hall. The original address is etched into the cut glass above the doorway. A large veranda welcomes guests with its comfortable rocking chairs.

The four rooms in the main house all have antique beds (among them, mahogany and heart-pine four-posters) and private baths—two with whirlpools—and fireplaces. One guest room with a 1920s bath retains its original tile. Downstairs is a disabled-accessible guest room. Next door, on the other side of a cheerful landscaped garden, a renovated cottage, ramped for wheelchair access, offers four more rooms, also with antique beds. The cottage is excellent for business conferences; it features a large communal space, screened-in back porch, and full kitchen.

Breakfast is substantial, with fresh or curried fruit and a main course, such as quiche, French toast, or specialty pancakes. Wine and hors d'oeuvres are served in the evening in the handsome Victorian parlor. Mint juleps and peach daiquiris are specialties of the house. Guests can work out at a nearby health club.

🏨 *3 double rooms in the main house with baths, 1 with whirlpool tub; 4 double rooms in adjacent cottage with baths, 1 with whirlpool tub and common living room. Air-conditioning, cable TV/VCR in rooms, phones in cottage rooms; garden. $85–$125, full breakfast. AE, D, MC, V. No smoking, no pets.*

Reservations Service

Great Inns of Georgia (tel. 404/843–0471 or 800/823–7787, fax 404/252–8886).

Hawaii

Hale Ohia

Big Island of Hawaii: Kona

Adrienne's Casa del Sol B&B Inn

77–6335 Alii Dr., Kailua-Kona, HI 96740, tel. 808/326–2272

Perched on a hillside across from Lyman's Bay, the Casa del Sol looks out over Alii Drive to miles of ocean and a view up the coast to the promontory of Kailua, the commercial town center of the Big Island's Kona district. From the ocean-view lanais (porches) of the four suites or from the red-tile deck surrounding the swimming pool and spa, guests can watch cruise ships and fishing boats sailing in and out of Kailua, the Iron Man Triathlon in October, or, in winter, the surfers in Lyman's Bay. It's a five-minute drive to the fishing and diving boats, for those who can't resist the lure of the ocean. Disappearing Sands Beach, less than half a mile away, is a great spot for body or board surfing—except in winter, when it really does disappear.

Adrienne Ritz-Batty and her husband, Reggie, operated a popular B&B in the town of Captain Cook for eight years

before they bought the Casa del Sol in 1994. This Spanish Mission–style house is one of only three houses on the island with the red-tile-roof and graceful-arch detailing brought by Spaniards during the last century. There are wrought-iron banisters and lighting fixtures and the wide arches that surround the house let the sun shine in, brightening the rooms' pale-tone carpets and furnishings. Country accents adorn the couches and pillows that fill the spacious sitting room where guests sink into cool comfort after a day of sightseeing. Fresh island fruits, Kona coffee, and homemade breads—including Hawaiian coconut and macadamia nut—are served at breakfast.

Adrienne and Reg are fonts of information and advice on local restaurants, entertainment, and historic sites and are also familiar with the needs of business travelers so there are modem-capable phones with voice mail in all the guest rooms; fax and copying machines are available as well. All rooms have cable TV and guests may borrow a VCR and tapes from the house library for in-room use.

▦ *1 double room with bath, 4 suites. Ceiling fans, mini-refrigerators in room and 2 suites, kitchen in 2 suites, barbecue available. $100–$150, Conti-*

nental breakfast buffet served poolside. MC, V.

Hale Maluhia

76-770 Hualalai Rd., Kailua-Kona, HI 96740, tel. 808/329-1123 or 800/559-6627, fax 808/326-5487

Although the bed-and-breakfast is a business, Ken and Ann Smith, owners of Hale Maluhia (House of Peace) treat guests as if they are old friends, come to visit. With an abundance of space, Ken and Ann opened their Swiss Family Robinson–style home to guests in 1992. "It's acres of house—5,500 square feet," says Ann. The various levels of the property, which is set among the lush banyan and monkey-pod trees, gives you the feeling of living in a luxurious tree house. The landscaping and placement of the rooms also afford privacy.

The arrangement of the rooms fosters privacy, too. Both the Maile and Pikaki rooms each have their own bath. The kitchenette in Pikaki can make these two rooms into the stand-alone retreat called the Gate House. The Main House contains the Makua and Malia rooms, each with a private bath plus easy access to the dining room, living room, and breakfast lanai. The main house also has cable TV, stereo, and a piano. Away from those enclaves, the 800-square-foot Banyan Cottage looks out over the Kona Coast. Its king-size bed dominates a bay-windowed alcove, and stained-glass partitions surround the private marble whirlpool that has a spectacular view of the mountainside.

Inside and out, the sprawling house is surrounded by unique alcoves and lush flora. The eclectic mix of wicker and Victorian heirlooms—here an Oriental rug, there an antique cheval mirror—have the unmatched but loved look of the furnishings of *ohana* (extended-family) homes. Banana, mango, papaya, breadfruit, and banyan trees shade the compound, which is punctuated with streams, koi ponds, and waterfalls.

All guests have access to a Japanese stone-tiled spa with massage jets—as well as the game room and library, which are well stocked with books, videos, and games. Arts and crafts supplies are on hand as well, and the Smiths may direct guests in search of inspiration to the nearby artists' colony of Holualoa, a little farther up Hualalai Mountain.

For all its seclusion, Hale Maluhia is only minutes from the shops and beaches of Kailua-Kona. The ski slopes of Mauna Kea are less than an hour away. These slopes are not for beginners, but Ann can tell you where to get a "Ski the Volcano" T-shirt in Kailua-Kona even if you miss out on the slopes.

🏨 *5 double rooms with baths, 1 cottage that sleeps 5. Kitchenettes, library, game room, massage spa, office facilities, barbecues and beach/snorkeling equipment available. $65–$135, Continental buffet breakfast. AE, D, MC, V.*

Big Island of Hawaii: Volcano

Hale Ohia

11-3968 Hale Ohia Rd., Box 758, Volcano Village, HI 96785, tel. 808/967-7986 or 800/455-3803, fax 808/967-8610

Calm beauty and old-fashioned character will fill your senses as you come upon Hale Ohia. This is the house you wish your grandparents had lived in—and left you alone to play in—a mini-fortress of stone and cedar shakes, with red-shingle roof, hexagonal rooms, secluded spaces—and a turret! Your more mature tastes will fancy the leaded-glass windows and stone fireplace. The gardens are for connoisseurs of beauty—and who isn't?

In fact, says owner Michael Tuttle, the house did remind him of his grandmother's place, back in Kentucky, but what he really fell in love with was the landscape—"so lush, so green"—which is actually part of a rain forest. The house was built in 1931 by a Scottish sea captain who had come to the Big Island to manage Ohelo plantation, near Hilo. It was sold 10 years later to the Hawaiian Dredging Company and became the summer estate of the Dillingham family. It had been built for "living in a rain forest," says Michael, and loving care and diligence through the years has helped it stand up to the climate.

Four buildings on the Hale Ohia property have guest accommodations. The Dillingham Suite, in the main house, has its own entrance. Three more suites, one of which has a kitchen, are in a second building. Two cottages each have a fireplace, kitchen, and covered lanais filled with tropical plants. In the three-bedroom Ohia cottage, the decor and placement of the rooms suggest a turn-of-the-century lighthouse. (The feel of all the interiors reflects the builder's nautical tastes.) A curved stairway leads to the top two bedrooms, passing a bathroom on the stair landing, across from a stained-glass window. Other windows in Ohia cottage are of leaded glass. The focal point of the ground-floor living room is a game table.

The real star at Hale Ohia—the house (*hale*) is named for the ohia trees in the area—is the grounds. Tended for many years by the same landscape caretaker who had earlier laid out Hilo's beautiful Liliuokalani Gardens, these grounds include giant topiary, cymbidium orchids, kahili ginger, hydrangea, and five kinds of camellias, which provide a year-round show. Stone-lined walkways tempt guests to linger in the spectacular gardens even though one of nature's most spectacular shows is only a mile away: Volcanoes National Park.

▦ *4 suites, 2 cottages. Mini-refrigerators, Japanese furo (soaking) tub. $65–*

$95, Continental breakfast delivered to rooms. MC, V.

Kilauea Lodge

On Old Volcano Rd., Box 116, Volcano Village, HI 96785, tel. 808/967–7366, fax 808/967–7367

Ballyhooed by food critics and quietly hailed by local residents (who would like to keep it a secret) the Kilauea Lodge Restaurant will make you wish you had booked an extra week's stay. While dinner is open to the public, only those staying at the lodge have access to the full breakfast, which includes fresh island fruits and their most popular item, sweet bread French toast.

Owners Albert and Lorna Jeyte discovered this former YMCA camp when they honeymooned in 1986 at Volcanoes National Park. Two years later, the former *Magnum, P.I.* makeup artist and his wife turned the main building into a restaurant and the old bunkhouse into Hale Makua—four fireplace-warmed double rooms beautifully furnished with the light woods and snuggle-up fabrics that typify this Hawaiian mountain region as well as large skylights in the bathrooms. Tutu's Cottage, (Grandma's house), on a separate part of the property, has its own wide porch, a wood-burning stove, and large yard. In 1991 the Jeytes added the seven guest rooms of Hale Aloha, which are centered around a sitting room warmed by a stone fireplace. (Guests from the cottage and Hale Makua are also welcome to relax in the deep-cushioned comfort of the Hale Aloha sitting room, and it is spacious enough to accommodate all the guests at once.) Additional amenities include towel warmers in every bath, in-room coffee and tea servers, books, and sightseeing videos.

The Jeytes love this part of the Big Island, and are happy to share their knowledge of local lore and geography with their guests. Visitors who know his TV background press Albert for stories about the famous "faces" he has made up or ask whether celebrities ever stay at the lodge. (They do, and their privacy is respected, as is every guest's.)

Kilauea Lodge still has the air of a mountain summer camp—or enough of it, at least, to bring back youthful fantasies, such as afternoon dips and midnight trysts. There are, as well, hiking opportunities aplenty, either in the rain forest that surrounds the lodge or in the national park just five minutes away. These need be only as arduous as you wish; Devastation Trail and some other park "hikes" are actually on boardwalks, and the lodge is encircled by forests of tree ferns with well-marked paths suitable for easy strolling.

🏨 *11 double rooms with bath (1 unit accessible for people who use wheelchairs), 1 cottage. Restaurant open for dinner; chairlift can bring mobility-impaired guests to and from the restaurant. Library on Hawaiian culture, central heating. $95–$135, full breakfast. MC, V.*

Maui

Kula Lodge

On Haleakala Hwy., just past 5-mile mark on Rte. 377, ¼ mile from Crater Rd.; R.R. 1, Box 475, Kula, Maui, HI 96790, tel. 808/878–1535 or 800/233–1535, fax 808/878–2518

A Swiss-style chalet 20 minutes from Kahului Airport may sound improbable, but Kula Lodge, surrounded by farms and protea fields, sits 3,200 feet up on the side of Mount Haleakala, where the roads are winding and the terrain laced with hiking trails and bridle paths. Of course, once you spot the fine view of the island's west coast and, on a clear day, Lanai and Kahoolawe Islands sitting across the channel,

you'll know you're nowhere else but on Maui.

This is not the Maui with steamy tropical waterfalls or the one with crescents of white-sand beach or the one with paper umbrellas in improbably colored cocktails. This is Upcountry Maui, land of real cowboys, working farms and ranches, and mountain air—and less than an hour from the beaches of Wailea or the quirky whaling-town-turned-arts-center of Lahaina. Kula is a year-round home to many, and a great place to meet locals.

The lodge was built as a private home in the 1940s and has operated as a small inn since the 1960s. The current owner, Fred Romanchak, looks after business in the restaurant, the gift shop, the art gallery, and the guest rooms, and lives just up the street.

The lodge's restaurant—which offers unparalleled views from wraparound windows—serves hearty breakfasts, lunches, and dinners to sightseers heading to or from Haleakala's 10,000-foot summit. And the dining room's huge stone fireplace is a welcome sight to returning climbers who never dreamed it could be so cold on a volcano.

The mountain atmosphere extends to the lodge's wood-paneled sleeping quarters as well. The two largest units share a building to the right of the main lodge. Each has a queen-size bed, a sitting room, gas fireplace, and a loft with twin beds; the private decks look northwest, along the coast toward Lahaina. Another building has two units with queen beds, private baths, and smaller sleeping lofts (the twin-size futons are just right for kids who are old enough to enjoy the adventure of loft-sleeping, with mom and dad not too far away downstairs); the private decks here look southwest, toward the Wailea coastline. A fifth unit, dubbed a studio, is downstairs from the restaurant; it has a private bath and deck, but the owners don't brag about this view (it is not as spectacular as the one from upstairs). Space heaters are available when it gets chilly in the rooms without fireplaces.

🏨 *3 double rooms with baths, 2 suites. Restaurant, coffeemakers and supplies. $100–$150, breakfast extra. MC, V.*

Other Choices

Kamuela Inn B&B. Box 1994, Kamuela, HI 96743, tel. 808/885–4243. 31 rooms with baths, 2 executive suites (with kitchen), penthouse suite (with kitchen and sunset lanai). $54–$165, full breakfast. AE, D, MC, V.

Waimea Gardens Cottage B&B. Box 563, Kamuela, HI 96743, tel. 808/885–4550, fax 808/885–0559. 2 cottage units with baths. New England/Hawaiian antiques, cottages near stream. $110–$115, fully stocked kitchen with breakfast items. No credit cards.

Reservations Services

Affordable Paradise B&Bs (226 Pouli Rd., Kailua, HI 96734, tel. 800/925–9065). **All Islands B&Bs** (823 Kainui Dr., Kailai, HI 96734, tel. 800/542–0344). **B&B Hawaii** (Box 449, Kapaa, HI 96746, tel. 800/733–1632). **B&B Honolulu** (3242 Kaohinani Dr., HI 96817, tel. 800/288–4666). **Bed & Breakfast Maui-Style** (Box 98, Kihei, HI 96784, tel. 808/870–7865; Maui only). **Hawaii's Best B&Bs** (Box 563, Kamuela, HI 96743, tel. 808/885–4550). **Volcano Accommodations** (Box 28, Volcano, HI 96785, tel. 808/967–8662; volcanoes region only). **Volcano Reservations** (Box 998, Volcano, HI 96785, tel. 808/967–7244; volcanoes region only).

Oahu

Manoa Valley Inn

2001 Vancouver Dr., Honolulu, HI 96822, tel. 808/947–6019 or 800/634–5115, fax 808/946–6168

Thoughtfully and authentically restored in 1982 and listed on the National Register of Historic Places, Manoa Valley Inn is a find for anyone who wants to enjoy nearby Waikiki without trying to sleep amid its bright lights and bustle. Located in Manoa Valley, one of Honolulu's finest residential neighborhoods, the inn is just a short walk from the University of Hawaii's main campus, and from the bus to Waikiki (2 miles away), downtown Honolulu (4 miles), or Ala Moana beachside park and shopping center (2 miles). There is free parking (a rarity in Honolulu) for guests' cars.

Built in 1919, the house has many links to Hawaiian history. Guest rooms are named after such legendary families as Dole, Dillingham, Alexander, and Baldwin—and innkeeper Herb Fukushima, shares tales of earlier times with interested visitors.

Inside and out, the house is for time-travelers. Walls are papered with rose and Oriental-inspired florals; fringed apricot-silk lamp shades hover over reading chairs set around the living room's big stone fireplace; white crocheted doilies, table runners, and antimacassars are everywhere, from the billiard room's sideboard to the sunroom's card table: 20th-century accoutrements like color TV (in the living room) and in-room telephones are tucked out of sight when not in use.

A wicker-furnished lanai runs the entire length of the house and looks out across the back lawn to the high-rises of Waikiki. The Continental breakfast buffet and a late afternoon fruit and cheese tray are served here, and it's a popular spot for guests at any hour.

A suite and six double rooms are all upstairs, outfitted with exquisite beds made of antique iron or inlaid island woods, marble-top tables, and cut-glass lamps. The attention to authenticity banishes television for the most part (except in the suite and the cottage, which do have sets). The cottage—a double room with private bath in a separate building—offers the greatest privacy, but because it is built on ground slightly lower than the main house, it does not enjoy the mountain or ocean views that the upstairs guest rooms have. Still, the inn's own garden, full of croton, dracaena, delphinium, and plumeria, is just outside the cottage door.

🏨 *3 double rooms with baths, 3 doubles share 1 bath, 1 suite, 1 cottage. Ceiling fans, phones, terry-cloth robes, safes, piano, croquet. $99–$190, Continental breakfast buffet. AE, DC, MC, V.*

Idaho

Heritage Inn

Northern Panhandle

Clark House on Hayden Lake

E. 4550 S. Hayden Lake Rd., Hayden Lake, ID 83835, tel. 208/772-3470 or 800/765-4593, fax 208/772-6899

Pockets of sparkling blue water dot the gentle contours of deep green cedar and pine in Idaho's northern Panhandle. There are more lakes here than in any other region of the western states.

No doubt it was this verdant, remote setting that attracted the intensely private millionaire F. Lewis Clark to Hayden Lake. Here, Clark envisioned an elegant lakeside retreat of grand dimensions. Patterned after the summer palace of Germany's Kaiser Wilhelm II, this 33-room mansion with 10 fireplaces took 15 years to complete. Clark furnished it with the finest Europe had to offer—crystal chandeliers, French doors, deep molding. On 12 acres amid a cedar forest, it's hard to imagine that this palatial estate is just a few miles from Interstate 90, and 30 minutes from Spokane, Washington.

Four years after the estate's completion, in 1914, Clark disappeared—with all of his money. His wife, Winifred, was forced to sell the mansion to pay back taxes. After numerous incarnations—a boys' home, a naval hospital, various restaurants—the building sat vacant for 20 years. Just before it was to become a fireball (as a training exercise for the county fire department), Monty Danner and Rod Palmer took pity on what had been, in 1910, the most expensive house in Idaho.

In 1989, what is perhaps the most regal of all country estates in the Northwest became a gracious country inn. Danner and Palmer restored architectural details like Roman tiled bathtubs and ceiling moldings. The walls, rich cream and soft gold, complement polished wood floors and shiny white woodwork. Set against this subtle backdrop are sumptuous furnishings—Oriental carpets, Erté artwork, and Chippendale-style chairs. Natural and white wicker furniture coordinates nicely with reproduction Louis XIV and French provincial pieces. A mural in the parlor depicts the history of the house.

The bedrooms, like the public spaces, are expansive. Four of the five suites have fireplaces and several have lake views. Each has tall French doors, some of which open to terraces, decks, and garden nooks. The Hayden Lake

Suite, with natural wicker furniture and a ceiling fan, offers the best view. The F. Lewis Clark Suite, which also overlooks Hayden Lake, has a library and an extra-large bath with a double-head shower. The Winifred Clark Suite is distinguished by a white Louis XIV–style writing table trimmed in gold, a tall armoire, and a highboy. Beds have European-style feather bedding and down comforters in finely woven duvet covers.

For breakfast, sliced melon and strawberries might be followed by sausage and a stack of cinnamon pancakes with apple slices and chopped walnuts. Daily dinner service is also available: Sautéed Copper River salmon and chocolate cake are among the specialties.

🛏 *5 suites, 1 4-bedroom cabin. Ceiling fans in 3 suites, cable TV/VCR in common area, hot tub, nature trails, marina, meeting facilities, swimming, and snow skiing nearby. $100–$165, full breakfast. AE, D, DC, MC, V.*

Historic Jameson

304 6th St., Wallace, ID 83873, tel. 208/556-1554

The historic community of Wallace is midway between Spokane, Washington, and Missoula, Montana, in northern Idaho's Silver Valley—the world's largest silver mining district. Due to its colorful past and the preservation of many original buildings, the entire town is listed on the National Register of Historic Places. On a downtown street corner is a three-story redbrick building opened as the Theodore Jameson Steak and Billiard Hall in 1889. Today, the Historic Jameson houses a saloon and restaurant on the first floor, conference space on the second floor, and B&B accommodations on the third floor.

The Jameson's rooms are small yet charming. Furnishings include high-post beds, old-fashioned ceiling fans and luggage racks, side chairs, armoires, miniature dressers, and vanity tables with mirrors. Small brass reading lamps on doilies sit on petite bedside tables, vintage photographs and prints hang on the walls, and simple white woven bedspreads offset dark oak and walnut headboards. The late Victorian decor, in warm hues of brown, tan, and cream, is complemented by dainty floral wallpaper.

Maggie has been the Jameson's resident ghost since the 1930s. Manager Rick Shaffer says, "Legend has it that either she died here or thought it was such a nice place that she didn't want to leave." Fortunately, she has a playful spirit. Among her favorite ploys are hiding guests' keys, turning on ceiling fans, and turning off hot water as guests shower.

A Continental breakfast of juice, croissants, and coffee is served in guests' rooms or in the parlor. The restaurant also has an extensive breakfast menu if heartier fare is preferred. Serving classic American cuisine, the Jameson Restaurant is best known for its homemade bread and Irish coffee, made with the establishment's own brand of Irish whiskey. Ceiling fans, bentwood chairs, polished brass chandeliers, and a massive mirrored antique bar reveal its past as a fancy turn-of-the-century, Old West saloon.

🛏 *6 double rooms share 1 bath. Restaurant, air-conditioning in saloon and restaurant, indoor pool, sauna, hot tub nearby. $68; Continental breakfast included, full breakfast available. AE, MC, V.*

Other Choices

Berry Patch Inn. 1150 N. Four Winds Rd., Coeur d'Alene, ID 83814, tel. 208/765-4994. 3 double rooms with bath. On 2 acres of landscaped grounds on a mountainside, waterfall, stone fireplace, TV/VCRs, stereo in common area, private entrance through French doors into main-floor guest room. $115–$135, full breakfast. MC, V.

Blackwell House. 820 Sherman Ave., Coeur d'Alene, ID, tel. 208/664–0656. 3 double rooms with baths, 2 doubles share 1 bath, 1 suite. Air-conditioning in 4 bedrooms; cable TV in music room; fireplace in living room, morning room, and 1 suite. $75–$125, full breakfast. AE, D, MC, V.

Knoll Hus Bed & Breakfast. Box 572, St. Maries, ID 83861, tel. 208/245–4137. 1 cottage. Air-conditioning; phone in cottage; wood-burning stove; room service; terry-cloth robes; chocolates; bicycles; canoe; nature trails; picnic lunch, dinner, and transportation from Spokane International Airport available. $85–$135, full breakfast. No credit cards.

River Birch Farm Bed & Breakfast. Box 0280, Hwy. 2, Laclede, ID 83841, tel. 208/263–3705. 2 double rooms with baths, 4 double rooms share 3 baths. Ceiling fans, TV/VCR in common area, fireplace in living room, kitchen privileges, wood-burning stove in kitchen, barbecue on deck, terry-cloth robes, thongs, hot tub, swimming, fishing, canoes and mountain bikes available, downhill skiing nearby. $85–$95, full breakfast. MC, V.

Reservations Service

Idaho Department of Commerce (Box 83720, Boise, ID 83720, tel. 800/635–7820; listings only—call for brochure).

Central Rockies

Idaho Country Inn

134 Latigo La., Box 2355, Sun Valley, ID 83353, tel. 208/726–1019 or 800/250–8341, fax 208/726–5718

Railroad mogul William Averell Harriman dispatched Austrian Count Felix Schaffgotsch to find a site for a destination ski resort in the west "of the same character as the Swiss and Austrian Alps." What he came up with was Sun Valley, the grande dame of ski resorts in the central Idaho Rockies, which has been luring seekers of plentiful sun and snow with its Old World charm and Western hospitality since 1936.

The inn's site on a sun-washed saddle affords spectacular views of the nearby ski mountain and the Wood River Valley. Its location—midway between Ketchum and Sun Valley village—is convenient, yet removed and quiet.

It was ice and snow that attracted Terry and Julie Heneghan, proprietors of the Idaho Country Inn, to Sun Valley. Terry, from Massachusetts, and Julie, from Phoenix, were inspired to build an inn that would reflect Idaho's lore while providing first-class accommodations. Because this is a newer inn (built in 1990), it has a fresh, shiny look and special conveniences such as windows that open, thick towels, and mini-refrigerators and TVs hidden in armoires.

Here, rustic simplicity blends with contemporary sophistication. Peeled timber and smooth river rock from the area were used throughout, and local artisans built most of the furniture. Log beams, whitewashed walls, and a river-rock fireplace in the high-ceiling living room create a warm setting. In the afternoon, the Heneghan's two big Newfoundland dogs often amble in, hoping for neck scratches from guests.

Terry, a longtime fly-fishing guide, decorated the inn with a fish motif: Wall hangings depict trout and salmon, the tiles on the library's fireplace are decorated with fish, and a hand-painted headboard depicting central Idaho's famed fly-fishing hole, Silver Creek, is in the Angler Room. Terry's own artful fly-tying handiwork is also on display.

Natural twig furniture and a willow-and-wood poster bed set a romantic tone in the Willow Room. The Wagon Days Room pays tribute to the valley's mining heyday with a giant wagon wheel at the head of a heavy pine bed. Most of the rooms have patios or balconies.

For breakfast, Julie always makes something decadent and something healthy. Guests gather in the sunroom adjoining the living room to dine on chokecherry corn cakes with ham, potato crêpes with Basque filling (red and green peppers, yellow onions, tomatoes, and artichoke hearts), and piping-hot muffins. In the afternoon, Julie serves hot appetizers and homemade cookies fireside.

▦ *11 double rooms with baths. Airconditioning in 7 rooms, cable TVs, phones, 2 fireplaces in common rooms, mini-refrigerators, hot tub. $125–$185, full breakfast and afternoon snacks. AE, MC, V.*

Other Choices

Idaho Rocky Mountain Ranch. HC 64, Box 9934, Stanley, ID 83278, tel. 208/774–3544, fax 208/774–3477. 4 double rooms with baths, 8 duplex cabins, 1 honeymoon cabin. Fireplaces in cabins, lodge, and dining room; outdoor hot-springs swimming pool; hiking, cross-country skiing, horseback riding, white-water rafting, mountain biking nearby. June–Sept. $180, full breakfast and dinner; Nov.–Apr. $105–$125 (2 cabins only), full breakfast.

Knob Hill Inn. 960 N. Main St., Box 800, Ketchum, ID 83340, tel. 208/726–8010, fax 208/726–2712. 20 double rooms with baths, 4 suites. Café and gourmet restaurant, cable TVs, phones, minibars, VCR upon request, fireplaces in 4 rooms and 4 suites, indoor lap pool, hot tub, fitness room, sauna, ski lockers, transportation from municipal airport, masseuse available, downhill and cross-country skiing, nature trail nearby. $160–$350, full breakfast. AE, MC, V.

Boise Valley

Idaho Heritage Inn

109 W. Idaho St., Boise, ID 83702, tel. 208/342–8066, fax 208/343–2325

This stately home in a historic residential district of Idaho's capital was built by Henry Falk in 1904. Roughly 40 years later, then-governor Chase A. Clark acquired it and later passed it to his daughter and son-in-law, Frank Church, a senator and presidential candidate. The Churches used it as their Idaho residence until 1987, when Tom and Phyllis Lupher turned it into a gracious B&B inn.

Having renovated several historic properties and owned an antiques mall in Boise, the Luphers were well equipped to take on this inn, listed on the National Register of Historic Places. Period wall coverings, antique fixtures and furniture, diamond-pane glass windows, and Oriental rugs are found throughout. The dining room, beyond the large entryway, has a built-in walnut china cabinet with leaded-glass doors. The sunroom (with TV and VCR) combines with the living room to create a spacious common area with ample seating.

The Luphers have paid homage to the house's history by following a political theme in naming its rooms. Upstairs, the sunny Governor's Suite has mementos from Chase Clark's tenure as governor. Its color scheme is dark green and rose; white woodwork blends with the antique oak sleigh bed and dresser. Adding to its allure, the suite has a roomy bath with an art deco, tiled walk-in shower and separate tub, and French doors that open to an enclosed sunporch with white wicker rockers. The extra-large Judge's Chambers has Victorian walnut furnishings and a covered veranda; and the Carriage House has a wet bar, microwave, refrigerator, and privacy. In keeping with the political-history theme, the inn was proud to host former First Lady Barbara Bush, who stayed here in 1993.

Because it's in the Warm Springs district of Boise, this inn enjoys the luxury of never running out of hot water. Endless gallons of geothermal spring water in the bathrooms can be a spa-like experience.

Typical breakfast fare includes fresh-squeezed juice, fruit, baked German pancakes, apricot cream cheese–stuffed French toast, and apple skillet cake.

▥ *3 double rooms with baths. 2 suites, carriage house. Air-conditioning, cable TV in 2 rooms, cable TV/VCR in sunroom, fireplace in living room, wine in the evening, fax service, mountain bike rental. $60–$95, full breakfast. AE, D, MC, V.*

Other Choices

Idaho City Hotel. 215 Montgomery St., Box 70, Idaho City, ID 83631, tel. 208/392–4290, fax 208/392–4505. 5 double rooms with baths. Cable TVs, phones, clock radios. $37, breakfast not included. AE, D, DC, MC, V.

Reservations Service

Idaho Department of Commerce (Box 83720, Boise, ID 83720, tel. 800/635–7820; listings only; call for brochure).

Illinois

Magnolia Place

Galena

Felt Manor

125 S. Prospect St., Galena, IL 61036, tel. 815/777–9093

On a weekday afternoon in historic Galena, time passes slowly on its quiet Victorian-era streets. The scene changes, however, when thousands of visitors descend on this charming and best-preserved old river town of the Upper Mississippi region. In this world of here-today-and-gone-tomorrows, travelers cherish the locale as a picturesque getaway and historic center (the site of Ulysses S. Grant's home, among other attractions). With streets that are museums of mid-19th-century architecture—ranging from early Federal cottages to *Gone With the Wind*–style mansions—it's little wonder that Galena has become a B&B haven.

"Is it 1893 or 1993?" a visitor writes in the guest book of the Felt Manor. "After 15 minutes and a glass of sherry, it's hard for a harried Chicagoan to tell. Here in the parlor, there is no noise but the ticking of the clock." At Laura and Dan Balocca's B&B, guests often feel transported back to the golden era of 19th-century America, and no more so than during one of Laura's afternoon teas, highlighted perhaps by artichoke puffs and new potatoes stuffed with sour cream and caviar. Other old-time elements, such as gilt-framed Victorian lithographs, music on the square-box grand piano, and soft lighting from silk-fringed lamps, combine to make guests feel, as one eloquently put it, "enfolded within the inn's Victorian skirts."

Built atop Quality Hill, the town's tallest bluff, the Felt Manor is a four-story, orange brick, Second-Empire Victorian mansion with teal shutters: It sits next door to Ulysses S. Grant's first Galena home. The house was constructed in 1848 by dry-goods entrepreneur Lucius Felt, who became a millionaire despite an offer from Marshall Field's to merge companies. The inn has several entrances, but try climbing the imposing limestone staircase built into the steep slope leading up to the house: Listed with the Library of Congress as a national landmark, the 1850 staircase was then known as "Felt's Folly" because of its $40,000 cost.

There is also an underground ice house and a brick coach house. The inn's terraced grounds are being returned to the Victorian-era layout by a gardener from the Chicago Botanic Society. Once finished, masses of tea rose, black-night nasturtium, phlox, and foxglove will surround the veranda, which offers a panoramic view of the storybook town below.

Upstairs, five guest rooms are each furnished in period style. While Laura and Dan reside in the converted ballroom on the floor above that, they offer to spend evenings with guests in the entry-level parlors. At sunset, the town below becomes a sea of twinkling lights, and guests can often enjoy the free entertainment provided by the Northern Lights in the sky above.

▦ *3 double rooms with baths, 2 double rooms with shared bath. Fireplaces. $80–$160, full breakfast and Saturday afternoon tea. AE, D, MC, V.*

Hellman Guest House

315 Hill St., Galena, IL 61036, tel. 815/777-3638

A treasure trove of elaborate 19th-century mansions whose original owners had amassed fortunes from merchandising, mining, and steamboating operations, Galena has many houses built in the Greek and Italian revival styles popular in the 1840s and 1850s. As a town stocked with the type of houses that seem to inspire people to lay claim to and restore them, it has, not surprisingly, become a B&B boom town. Merilyn Tommaro, owner of the lovely Queen Anne Victorian that is now the Hellman Guest House, fell in love with the town and her Quality Hill house upon her first visit from the Chicago area.

Her five-year restoration project included researching original paint schemes, installing new plumbing and electrical systems, and remodeling bathrooms. To determine the exact appearance of the original wraparound porch and the second-story porch over the entry, vintage photographs and newspaper articles were unearthed. Today, guests can enjoy the fruits of Merilyn's arduous efforts. The sumptuous oak and pine woodwork in the guest rooms, the colorful ceramic tiles—reminiscent of those of 19th-century lavatories—that ornament the bathrooms, the hand-carved newel posts accenting the grand staircase, and the eye-catching turret room all bear witness to her dedication. An inviting parlor with a coal-burning fireplace beckons with the best seat in the house—a lovely 19th-century wingback chair, positioned by the picture window and an antique telescope focused on the craggy bluffs surrounding the town.

As to the four guest rooms, Merilyn will admit to no favorite. The Master Bedroom has a queen-size brass bed and tower alcove, while the others—named Pauline, Irene, and Eleanor, after the daughters of John V. Hellman, the original owner of the house—are cozy cocoons with antique beds and wicker rocking chairs. Offering a gracious welcome to guests is Merilyn's way, as she puts it, "to have days that are not only full, but fullfilling."

▦ *4 double rooms with private baths. Air-conditioning, fireplaces, off-street parking. $89–$129, full breakfast. MC, V.*

Inn at Irish Hollow

2800 S. Irish Hollow Rd., Galena, IL 61036, tel. 815/777-2010 or 815/777-6000

A turn onto Irish Hollow Road makes it immediately clear why 19th-century Irish settlers gave this charming countryside nook—five minutes outside the town of Galena—its name. Lushly green, with a winding stream and a misty haze that lingers through the morning, it resembles the idealized image many people have of Ireland. Once active in the 19th century as Galena's hub of the Great Western Railway (city fathers, many of whose fortunes were based on steamboating, fought against allowing the train to enter directly into the town), the Irish

Hollow dell attracted various services, one of which was a general store. Today, the store, exquisitely renovated, serves as a novel entrance for the Inn at Irish Hollow, which B&B connoisseurs now regard as one of the more unusual inns of the Midwest.

In 1989, Bill Barrick and Tony Kemp purchased the general store, its attached shopkeeper's house, and a nearby storybook cottage, and after extensive renovations to the property, began to welcome their first guests. The word quickly spread about the inn's gourmet kitchen, the luxurious modern amenities, and the charming parlor rooms, accented with antiques such as an old Steinway grand piano, a grandfather clock, and tapestry-covered chairs.

Acclaimed by *Glamour* magazine as one of the premier romantic getaways in the country, the French Maid Cottage—the legend is that it was built in the 1880s by a neighboring landowner as a discreet hideaway for his ladylove, a maid he had brought over from France—is very popular with honeymooners. This delightful cottage-for-two has a large whirlpool bath, a two-sided fireplace, and a four-poster bed.

The inn is noted for its weekend packages (two-night affairs, complete with candlelit dinner), its picture-book Christmas festivities, and its renovated general store, which has an antique coffee grinder, wooden scales, and old postal boxes. After feasting on stuffed French toast drizzled with the inn's fresh apple-orchard syrup, guests may choose to set off for Galena or nearby Chestnut Mountain Ski Resort, or to simply curl up in the inn's library to enjoy the comforting and warm haven that is the Inn at Irish Hollow.

🏨 *5 double rooms with baths, 1 cottage. Restaurant, air-conditioning, 2 rooms with private balconies. Cottage has double whirlpool bath, wet bar, microwave, mini-refrigerator. $110–$175 weekday; $315–$425 weekend packages, mandatory 2-night stay, with dinner; $295–$450 holiday packages (including Thanksgiving, Christmas, and Valentine's Day); full breakfast. DC, MC, V.*

Other Choices

Pine Hollow Inn. 4700 N. Council Hill Rd., Galena, IL 61036, tel. 815/777–1071. 7 double rooms with baths. Fireplaces in 5 rooms, whirlpool baths in 2 rooms, 120 acres. $75–$110, hearty Continental breakfast. D, MC, V.

Central Illinois

Old Church House Inn Bed & Breakfast

1416 E. Mossville Rd., Mossville, IL 61552, tel. 309/579–2300, fax 309/691–1834

"Sleeping in church is encouraged here," says Holly Ramseyer, innkeeper of the Old Church House Inn Bed & Breakfast. No need to ponder Holly's sense of good behavior, as she is the proud chatelaine of a hostelry converted from an 1869 Colonial-style Presbyterian church. After purchasing the structure—which had already been renovated into a private home—in 1988, Holly and husband, Dean, set about creating a bit of B&B heaven in Mossville, a quaint old river village on the north edge of Peoria.

Originally part of the church sanctuary, the formal living and dining rooms have tall, arched windows and 18-foot-high tongue-and-groove wood ceilings. The eye is caught by an aerie-level balcony-library, entered by means of a nearby ladder, which adds to the effect of the room's great height. The decor is a felicitous blend of eras—mixing classic heirloom pieces with reproductions—but a pulpit, altar table, and authentic vintage photographs and church bulletins attest to the fact that, as Holly puts it, "traveling pastors once led scores of souls to the Lord here."

Guests have a choice of two distinctive accommodations. Most noticeable upon entering the one called the Bedchamber is an 1860s carved-walnut bedstead whose handmade log cabin–motif quilt coordinates with the room's hunter-green and bordeaux-red color scheme. By contrast, the Garden Room is a lace-festooned boudoir: A sheer white canopy cascades over a white-iron and brass bed and traceries of roses and peonies adorn the papered walls. Feather-bed mattresses provide nights of pleasant dreams. The inn's top rate, called the Sweetheart rate, offers its guests the run of the entire inn.

At breakfast, a scattering of violets and nasturtiums over a fresh fruit medley is a delightful surprise, followed by frosted cinnamon rolls and a delicious porridge that would please even Goldilocks. After spending a day on the nearby Rock Island Bike Trail, you'll enjoy returning to the Old Church Inn for afternoon tea and a batch of Holly's chunky chocolate-chip cookies.

▦ *2 double rooms with shared bath. Afternoon tea. $69–$99, gourmet Continental breakfast. MC, V.*

Other Choices

Grandma Joan's Homestay. 2204 Brett Dr., Champaign, IL 61821, tel. 217/356–5828. 3 rooms with baths. Contemporary home, fireplaces, decks, hot tub. $50–$70; Continental breakfast, cookies and milk at bedtime. No credit cards.

Robert Frackleton House. 207 S. 12th St., Petersburg, IL 62675, tel. 217/632–4496. 2 rooms with baths. Pool. $60–$70, Continental breakfast. No credit cards.

Tiara Manor. 403 W. Court St., Paris, IL 61944, tel. 217/465–1865 or 800/531–1865. 4 rooms with baths. Restaurant, 7 fireplaces, gift shop, gazebo for weddings. $75–110, full breakfast. D, MC, V.

Southern Illinois

Magnolia Place Bed and Breakfast

317 S. Main St., Red Bud, IL 62278, tel. 618/282–4141

South of the state capital of Springfield, Illinois takes on a flavor far removed from that of much of the rest of the state. Called "Little Egypt" for its location between the river valleys of the Ohio and Mississippi rivers, southern Illinois has some of the most remarkable scenery in the country.

Along the Great River Road of Illinois Route 3, just 40 miles southeast of St. Louis, the quiet German farming community of Red Bud offers a peaceful retreat in a prosperous rural area. This is the town where Dolly Kramen was born and raised and where she opened Red Bud's first B&B in 1993. In the town's historic district, Magnolia Place is a stately three-story mansion designed by an English architect in the 1850s.

Dolly's love of all things blooming is apparent not only in the name of her inn and her four exquisite guest rooms, but also in the beautiful gardens. The gardens and the antebellum gazebo are often the site of weddings and, when weather permits, breakfast for overnight guests.

Guest rooms bear the names of Dolly's favorite flowers: magnolia, rose, wisteria, and gardenia. The Grand Magnolia Suite has an oversize whirlpool tub, big-screen TV/VCR, and movie library. Pocket doors, fireplaces, and curved-glass windows are highlights of the other three rooms.

Breakfast is an elaborate buffet featuring pastries, muffins, breakfast meats, and egg dishes.

🏨 *1 double room with bath, 2 rooms share bath, 1 suite. Air-conditioning, whirlpools, fireplaces. $60–$140, full buffet breakfast. MC, V.*

Other Choices

Isle View Bed and Breakfast. 205 Metropolis St., Metropolis, IL 62960, tel. 618/524–5838. 4 rooms with bath, 1 suite. Cable TVs, phones, fireplace in suite. $42.50–$115, full breakfast. AE, D, DC, MC, V.

Olde Squat Inn. Rte. 7, Box 247, Marion, IL 62959, tel. 618/982–2916. 14 original pioneer cabins with baths. Fireplaces, horseshoes, walking trails. $59, full breakfast. No credit cards.

Reservations Service

Illinois Bed and Breakfast Association (Box 82, Port Bryon, IL 61275, tel. 309/523–2406).

Indiana

Patchwork Quilt Country Inn

Southern Hills

Artists Colony Inn

Box 1099 (Van Buren and Franklin Sts.), Nashville, IN 47448, tel. 812/988–0600 or 800/737–0255

Fifty miles south of Indianapolis, the landscape swells and dips, spared by an ancient glacier that flattened much of northern Indiana. Amid this landscape of sweeping vistas, log cabins, and dense woodlands, a colony of Impressionist artists found the perfect subject matter for their canvases in the early 1900s.

Ever since the hamlet of Nashville in Brown County hosted the Hoosier School of Artists, arts and crafts have thrived here. Today, with more than 300 shops and 50 full-time crafters, Nashville bulges year-round with tourists.

Jay and Ellen Carter built this rectangular three-story wood-frame building off Nashville's busy main street in 1992 and surrounded it with gardens and trees. A redbrick walkway leads to a wide front porch that, weather permitting, hosts alfresco dining. Inside, the palette is dominated by deep blue, green, burgundy, and cream; and the simple early American furnishings draw from the Carter's own collection. Reproduction cherry and painted furniture, Windsor-style chairs, and woven coverlets furnish the spare, yet comfortable rooms. Shaker-style peg boards and tables, and graceful wrought-iron floor lamps further denote Colonial simplicity. Many of the furnishings, including the scatter rugs and runners that cover the stained pine floors, were made by local artisans. A longtime friend and furniture maker crafted the pencil-post beds, tables, cupboards, and all 224 of the chairs. The boulders in the massive stone fireplace were salvaged from local 19th-century homes.

Although they rely on a professional manager to oversee operations, the Carters are often on hand to greet guests, seat diners, and share a little history of the artists' colony. Ellen's father, Frederick W. Rigley, is the last living original art colony member. The large, airy dining room with beamed ceiling doubles as a gallery showcasing much of the couple's extensive collection of Hoosier School art. Each bedroom is named for one of the early artists and has both a photographic portrait and a short biography of the artist, in addition to a reproduction of one of his or her works.

In a town buzzing with tourists, this inn has a genial setting that complements the country-style food served for breakfast, lunch, and dinner (meals not included).

🏨 *20 double rooms with baths. Restaurant, air-conditioning, cable TVs, phones, outdoor hot tub. $69–$161, breakfast not included. AE, MC, V.*

Other Choices

Allison House Inn. 90 S. Jefferson St., Box 1625, Nashville, IN 47448, tel. 812/988–0814. 5 double rooms with baths. Air-conditioning, TV in lounge, fireplace in library. $85, full breakfast. No credit cards. No smoking. 2-night minimum stay.

Columbus Inn. 445 5th St., Columbus, IN 47501, tel. 812/378–4289. 29 double rooms with baths, 5 suites. Restaurant, air-conditioning, TVs, phones, clock radios, TV/VCR in game room, conference facilities, off-street parking. $86–$235, full breakfast. AE, D, DC, MC, V.

5th Generation Farm. R.R. 4, Bear Wallow Rd. (Box 90-A), Nashville, IN 47448, tel. 812/988–7553 or 800/437–8152. 2 double rooms share 1 bath, 2 suites. Air-conditioning, fireplace, hot tub, TV in suite and common area. $55–$95, full breakfast. MC, V.

Grant Street Inn. 310 N. Grant St., Bloomington, IN 47408, tel. 812/334–2353 or 800/328–4350, fax 812/331–8673. 22 double rooms with baths, 2 suites. Air-conditioning, cable TVs, phones, clock radios, fireplaces in 2 rooms and suites, whirlpool baths in suites. $80–$150, buffet breakfast. AE, DC, MC, V.

Ohio River Valley

Main Street Bed and Breakfast

739 W. Main St., Madison, IN 47250, tel. 812/265–3539 or 800/362–6246

Of all the Indiana towns born along the bustling water highway of the mighty Ohio River, perhaps the most notable is Madison. Roughly 60 miles downstream from Cincinnati, Madison is distinguished by a staggering array of architectural styles: ornate Steamboat Gothic, stately Federal, imposing Greek Revival, and gingerbread-perfect Victorian. Dubbed the "Williamsburg of the Midwest," Madison has more than 133 blocks listed on the National Register of Historic Places.

Main Street Bed and Breakfast, on a deep and narrow lot behind a wrought-iron fence and under a leafy canopy, is a short walk from the city's main historic district. The inn, built in 1843, was once the home of Madison's Civil War hero Colonel Alois Bachman. Dark green shuttered windows, a white-painted brick facade with Italianate details, and a modest front portico face Main Street. The building's understated presence belies its spaciousness: This Greek Revival–style home has 5,000 square feet of living space.

Owners/innkeepers Mark and Mary Balph, natives of the Ohio River valley, lived and traveled all over the world, returning to their hometown in 1992. Their experiences are reflected in a delightful mix of old and new traditional furnishings—English country antiques, Oriental rugs, comfortable wingback chairs, and light wall coverings. The most unusual piece, an 8-foot-tall stuffed giraffe, a remnant from the Balphs' days in the retail toy business, presides over the guest rooms in the second floor hallway.

The McIntyre Room, named for the building's architect, overlooks Main Street and is full of soft colors including floral Laura Ashley wallpaper; there are also a love seat, wingback chair, built-in bookcase, and shuttered windows. Pale yellow walls with white trim create a gentle backdrop for the bleached English pine furniture and rose comforter and wing back chairs in the Hennessey Room, named for longtime owners of the home. A daybed and twin bed tucked away in an adjoining room, reached only through the spacious bath, is perfect for children or singles traveling together.

The Lockridge Room, named for Mary's grandparents, has white walls trimmed in Wedgwood blue and a blue mottled rug covering the poplar floor. Two cozy wing chairs and a Queen Anne–style coffee table decorate its small sitting area. A fourth, slightly smaller room that joins the Lockridge, has wall-to-wall wheat-color carpeting and Wedgwood blue woodwork. Although each room has a fireplace, none are operational. Environmentally conscious, Mark and Mary discreetly placed tasteful recycling baskets in each room.

Morning coffee is served in the privacy of your room, but breakfast is a social event in the airy main floor dining room. Mark is the breakfast chef and will prepare anything according to your tastes and personal needs. The full breakfast always includes fresh fruit from local growers and homemade cream cheese–filled raspberry muffins. Be sure to smile before you leave. Mark and Mary fill photo albums of all their guests at Main Street B&B.

🖽 *4 double rooms. Air-conditioning. $89, full breakfast. MC, V.*

Other Choices

Cliff House. 122 Fairmount Dr., Madison, IN 47250, tel. 812/265–5272. 6 double rooms with baths. Air-conditioning, phones, cable TV/VCR in common area, mints, chocolate-chip cookies, fresh fruit. $87.50, hearty Continental breakfast. AE, D, MC, V.

Crescent House. 617 W. Main St., Madison, IN 47250, tel. 812/265–4251. 1 spacious guest suite. Phone, Egyptian cotton linens, fresh-cut flowers, bathrobes, refrigerator, private entrance. $110, Continental breakfast. MC, V. No children, no pets.

Jelley House Country Inn. 222 S. Walnut St., Rising Sun, IN 47040, tel. 812/438–2319. 1 double room with bath, 2 doubles share 1 bath, 1 housekeeping suite. Air-conditioning, TVs, clock radios, cable TV/VCR, fireplace in living room, hot tub, exercise equipment, bikes, picnic lunches, fishing expeditions, boat rentals available. $40–$65, full breakfast. V.

Kintner House Inn. N. Capitol and Chestnut Sts., Corydon, IN 47112, tel. 812/738–2020. 15 double rooms with baths. Air-conditioning, cable TV/VCRs, phones, fireplaces in 5 rooms. $39–$99, full breakfast. AE, MC, V.

River Belle Bed & Breakfast. State Rd. 66 (Box 669), Grandview, IN 47615, tel. 812/649–2500 or 800/877–5165, fax 812/649–2500. 1 double room with bath, 4 doubles share 2 baths, 1 cottage. Air-conditioning, TVs, fireplaces in common areas. $45–$65, hearty Continental breakfast. MC, V.

Indianapolis

Nuthatch Bed and Breakfast

7161 Edgewater Pl., Indianapolis, IN 46240, tel. 317/257–2660, fax 317/257–2677

This casual bed-and-breakfast is in a rustic setting, just minutes from downtown Indianapolis. The slow-paced White River provides a tranquil backdrop to this 1920s French country cottage in the village of Broad Ripple. The house was built by an amateur, which explains its eccentricities: the fireplace, half stone and half brick, is crooked ("nothing is straight," says Joan); the roof is highly peaked; and architectural details like arches and leaded glass French doors create a charming atmosphere.

The Nuthatch, appropriately enough, is named for an individualistic bird that frequents the area and eats upside down. There's a bird theme in the living room, which also has 13th- and 14th-century manuscripts on the walls and a mix of antique and modern furniture.

Hosts Joan and Bernie Morris have decorated the two guest rooms to reflect two important periods in Joan's childhood—her winters in Florida and her summers in New York's Adirondack Mountains. Barnwood paneling, antique hardware, and a working fireplace create a cozy retreat in the Adirondack Room on the lower level. Since the house is on a hill, the lower level isn't basementlike: Its windows are full size. A private terrace and greenhouse are inviting, with antique wicker furniture, remnants of Joan's childhood cabin.

Alternatively called the Wren's Nest or the Florida Room, this main level room has pale pink walls, sunny windows, and a small deck. With its own entrance through the herb garden, the Florida Room is a favorite for business travelers, who unwind in the tub and are soothed by the soft, tropical colors.

Joan often serves breakfast on the second-level deck that overlooks the river. Cooking is a passion—she teaches cooking classes—so be prepared for dishes such as scrambled eggs with fresh basil served on grilled portobello mushrooms, home-baked cranberry-raisin bread, Indiana cornmeal pancakes, or heart-shape waffles if you're celebrating a honeymoon or anniversary. Guests are encouraged to wander through Joan's flower and herb gardens or sit peacefully on the ground-level deck that also overlooks the river.

🛏 *2 double rooms with baths. Air-conditioning, TVs, phones, modems, off-street parking. $80–$95, full breakfast. AE, D, MC, V.*

Amish Country

Patchwork Quilt Country Inn

11748 County Rd. 2, Middlebury, IN 46540, tel. 219/825–2417

Just north of the toll road linking Illinois, Indiana, and Ohio, in the middle of 18 acres of corn and soybeans, is the matriarch of northern Indiana's legion of country inns. For more than a quarter of its existence, this century-old farmhouse has been welcoming guests for farm vacations. Although the heart of northern Indiana's Amish country now has more than 50 country inns, the Patchwork Quilt, under the watchful eyes of Ray and Rosetta Miller, still sets the standard begun more than 25 years ago.

True country comforts, like patchwork quilts and stick-to-your-ribs cooking, are offered within an immaculate, uncluttered setting. Throughout the inn, quilts adorn the beds, sofas, and walls. Mostly stitched by local Amish and Mennonite women, the brightly colored pieces of handiwork come in a variety of patterns like Lone Star, Wedding Band, and Flower Basket. The Cherry Basket pattern, the inn's logo, is replicated on linens, stationery, and wall hangings.

Inside the front door is a small parlor with a sofa, easy chairs, and piano. In the main dining room (The Keeping Room), a large Tree of Life pattern quilt hangs opposite a massive brick hearth. The Woodshed dining room has rustic decor accented by antique woodworking tools and a collection of plates from around the world.

The bedrooms, painted shades of blue, yellow, green, and red, have light-stained-pine and yellow-oak poster beds and bedside tables with low lamps. Just a few touches, like stenciled borders and woven rugs, dress them up. Many items found in the rooms can be purchased at the Country Gift Shed next door.

The good-eating tradition associated with the Amish is standard fare here as well. Generous portions of crunchy buttermilk pecan chicken, burgundy steak, baked ham, and homemade bread allow no one to leave the table hungry. There is no skimping; and the mashed potatoes and whipped cream are real.

Within a 150-mile radius is the nation's third-largest concentration of Amish and Mennonites. Few Amish families allow the English, as outsiders are known, to experience their lifestyle and culture firsthand. A tour guide tailors outings to guests' interests: quilts, crafts, farming, or harness and buggy making.

🛏 *9 double rooms with baths, 3 doubles share 1 bath, 1 suite. Restaurant, air-conditioning, TV in 6 rooms and in common area, whirlpool baths in suites, guided tours available. $55–$100, full breakfast. MC, V.*

Victorian Guest House

302 E. Market St., Nappanee, IN 46550, tel. 219/773-4383

In the heart of northern Indiana's "plain and simple" Amish country, the Victorian Guest House stands out like a polished gemstone. This gabled and turreted mansion, two blocks from Nappanee's historic town square, stands resplendent in its Victorian charm.

Listed on the National Register of Historic Places, this 1887 Queen Anne–style masterpiece was built for the Coppes family. Frank Coppes, whose company manufactured freestanding kitchen cabinets, insisted on expert craftsmanship, down to every exquisite detail: extensive wood paneling, stained-glass windows, brass hardware. Many locals were involved in the original construction of the house, and almost all of Nappanee had something to do with its transformation into an inn in 1986.

The etched-glass entryway leads through beveled-glass pocket doors into an expansive living room with polished hardwood floors and tall ceilings. Graceful Victorian upholstered chairs and tufted footstools are present here, and throughout the building. A wide doorway opens to the dining room where period wallpaper softens rich wood paneling. The massive 11-foot dining room table, with a servant buzzer hidden on the underside, is an original piece. Stained-glass windows made by Nappanee's renowned Lamb Brothers, whose work rivals that of Louis B. Tiffany, line the dining room and the crosscut golden oak staircase that leads to the bedrooms upstairs.

The Coppes Suite—originally the master bedroom—is paneled in light oak. Its bath has a large stained-glass window with a sinuous rose design set against a cobalt blue background, and a vintage bathtub made to comfortably accommodate its original occupant, who stood at 6 feet 3 inches: Fifty gallons of water are required for a soak. Catherine's Room—named for Coppes's wife, who was the epitome of elegance—is furnished with a brass bed and a rocking chair, among other vintage Victorian pieces. Although it's the smallest, the Sewing Room has a private rooftop balcony. Offering the most privacy, the Maid's Chambers, on the third floor, is an intimate space with an antique bathtub and pedestal sink.

Owners/innkeepers Vickie and Bruce Hunsberger had never stayed in a B&B when they happened on a for-sale sign in front of "The Old Coppes House" in 1992. However, their sensibilities about gracious accommodations, modern amenities, and personal service are evident. Guests are treated to an evening tray of assorted teas, hot chocolate, and cookies in their rooms. Breakfast, in the dining room, is an elegant affair, served on Depression-era glass dinnerware with crystal goblets and crisp cloth napkins.

▦ *6 double rooms with baths. Air-conditioning, cable TVs, phone in rooms on request, turndown service, airport transportation available. $49–$84, full breakfast. D, MC, V.*

Other Choices

Beiger Mansion Inn. 317 Lincolnway E, Mishawaka, IN 46544, tel. 219/256–0365 or 800/437–0131, fax 219/259–2622. 6 double rooms with baths, 1 suite. Gourmet restaurant with bakery, air-conditioning, cable TVs, clocks, phones, fireplaces in 2 rooms and common areas, conference facilities, crafts gallery. $75–$195, full breakfast. AE, D, DC, MC, V.

Checkerberry Inn. 62644 County Rd. 37, Goshen, IN 46526, tel. 219/642–4445, fax 219/642–4445. 12 double rooms with baths, 2 suites. Country-French restaurant with international menu, air-conditioning, phones, TVs, outdoor swimming pool, tennis courts, croquet. $96–$325, Continental buffet breakfast. AE, MC, V.

Market Street Guest House. 253 E. Market St., Nappanee, IN 46550, tel. 219/773–2261 or 800/497–3791. 4 double rooms with baths, 2 double rooms share 1 bath. Air-conditioning, TVs, fireplace in parlor, sunroom. $60–$75, full breakfast served in rooms. D, MC, V.

Varns Guest House. 205 S. Main St., Middlebury, IN 46540, tel. 219/825–9666 or 800/398–5424, fax 219/825–5839. 5 double rooms with baths. Air-conditioning, clock radios, cable TV in breakfast room, fireplace in living

room, whirlpool bath in 1 room, chocolates. $72, hearty Continental breakfast. D, MC, V.

North Coast

Hutchinson Mansion Inn

220 W. 10th St., Michigan City, IN 46360, tel. 219/879–1700

Built in 1876 by William Hutchinson—a lumber baron, world traveler, and former mayor of Michigan City—this stately, redbrick inn takes up an entire city block. Less than a mile from both the sandy stretches of Lake Michigan and the 18,000-acre Indiana Dunes National Lakeshore, this elegant Queen Anne–style mansion presides over the town's historic residential and commercial district.

History and antique buffs, the DuVals, Ben (a retired law professor) and Mary (a former teacher and realtor), acquired, restored, and redecorated the mansion in 1991. The home's charm and warmth reflects their roots. Both native Virginians, the DuVals are delighted to share the mansion's history, and to treat guests to their brand of Southern hospitality—fresh flowers, chocolates, and friendly conversation.

Although Queen Anne decor usually consists of dark interiors with heavy drapes, the DuVals have kept their inn surprisingly airy. The home is distinguished by stained-glass windows, tall beamed-and-molded ceilings, and dark-wood paneling; many of the massive antique pieces are familial heirlooms. There are many whimsical architectural details—private terraces, alcoves and nooks, and even a secret door hidden in the dining room's wood paneling. Oriental rugs cover polished hardwood floors. Above the wood paneling in the dining room is period wallpaper with a subtle rose motif; a pair of tall candle-sticks and a cut-glass punch bowl sit on a dark-wood sideboard, and a wide, matching mirror is hung above.

A massive 8-foot antique Renaissance Revival bed with inlaid burled wood is the focal point of the Hutchinson Room. A decorative marble fireplace, ceiling friezes, long lace curtains, and period light-colored wallpaper complete the refined setting. The Patterson Room has an 1820 museum-quality four-poster Southern Plantation bed with a canopy; high off the floor, it is reached by steps. In a corner overlooking the gardens and carriage house, the Jenny Lind Room has an unusual four-poster Jenny Lind bed with undulating spindles; it dates from the mid-1800s. The subdued Ser-vant's Quarters has a white-and-gold iron bed, private porch, and turn-of-the-century original bath. The redbrick car-riage house, topped with a white cupola and weather vane, has three luxurious suites with whirlpool baths and one with an extra-large soaking tub. One suite has a sitting room, garden room, and pri-vate terrace; another has a sitting room and a private porch with a two-seat swing.

In the library, filled with tall wood bookcases full of Ben's books, popcorn is served in the evening. A full break-fast might be served by candlelight (on dark or dreary mornings) on fine china and crystal with hand-crocheted place mats.

⊞ *5 double rooms with baths, 5 suites. Air-conditioning, phones with modem hookups, croquet. $82–$135, full break-fast. AE, MC, V.*

Other Choices

Creekwood Inn. U.S. 20/35 at I–94, Michigan City, IN 46360, tel. 219/872–8357, fax 219/872–8357. 12 double rooms with baths, 1 suite. Restaurant, air-conditioning, TVs, phones, clock radios, turndown service, conference facilities, horseshoes, paddleboat avail-able, boat and bike rentals, tennis courts, horseback riding nearby. $102–$156, full breakfast. AE, DC, MC, V.

Gray Goose Inn. 350 Indian Boundary Rd., Chesterton, IN 46304, tel. 219/926–5781 or 800/521–5127. 8 double rooms with baths. Air-conditioning, phones, cable TVs, 2 rooms with fire-places, boats available. $65–$75, full breakfast. AE, D, MC, V.

Reservations Service

Indiana Tourism Division, Depart-ment of Commerce (1 N. Capitol St., Suite 700, Indianapolis, IN 46204-2288, tel. 317/232–8860).

Iowa

Amana Colonies

Die Heimat Country Inn

Amana Colonies, Homestead, IA 52236, tel. 319/622–3937

Die Heimat Country Inn personifies all that makes the Amana Colonies region of east-central Iowa such an attraction for those who appreciate its simple beauty and the Old World culture of the Swiss and German immigrants who settled here. In 1855, members of the Amana Church Society settled on 26,000 acres of what is now just north of I–80, about an hour east of Des Moines. Seven small "colonies," or villages, display the history, culture, and religion of the Amana Church Society, which is often confused with the Amish.

Built in 1858, Die Heimat Country Inn has served the colonies as a stagecoach stop, a communal kitchen, a meeting room, and now as one of the most popular bed-and-breakfast inns in the state. Original samplers, calligraphy, and century-old photos are displayed throughout the inn, allowing visitors an opportunity to develop a deeper understanding of the history and culture of both the building and the community.

Owners Jackie and Warren Lock purchased the property in 1993 and have made only minor changes. Jackie serves breakfast on mismatched pieces of antique china she has picked up in antique stores around the world. The variety of serving pieces and patterns often spurs conversation, as guests remember similar patterns at their own family homes.

Jackie serves a full farm-style breakfast of scrambled eggs, homemade biscuits, French toast, and hot maple syrup. Because breakfast is served buffet style, guests can eat in the privacy of their rooms, on picnic tables outdoors, or in the large, yet comfortable dining room. Although Warren and Jackie are not members of the Amana Church Society, many of their employees are and are pleased to explain the history of the society and its culture.

Although small, guest rooms have walnut and cherry furniture made by local artisans. Each bed is queen-size and is covered with wool blankets made at the Amana Woolen Mill and Jackie's own handmade quilts and hand-loomed rugs.

Die Heimat Country Inn is on the National Register of Historic Places and in the heart of Main Amana. In January and February the inn hosts murder-mystery weekends. University of Iowa sporting events, Cedar Rapids, and the Amish community of Kalona are all less than an hour away.

🏨 *19 double rooms with baths. Air-conditioning, TVs, homemade sugar cookies, iced tea or hot cider upon arrival, large meeting facilities, perennial gardens, outdoor swing, picnic facilities. $45–$70, full buffet breakfast. D, MC, V.*

Other Choices

Lucille's Bett Und Breakfast. 2835 225th St., Williamsburg, IA 52361, tel. 319/668–1185. 2 double rooms with 1½ baths. Large fireplace, TV and piano in common room, croquet and lawn sports, snacks upon arrival. $55, full German-style breakfast. No credit cards.

Rawson House Bed and Breakfast. Box 118, Homestead, IA 52236, tel. 319/622–6035. 5 double rooms with baths, 1 suite with whirlpool. Air-conditioning, communal kitchen, formal parlor. $50–$72, full breakfast. MC, V.

Terra Verde Farm Bed and Breakfast. 1562 Derby Ave. NW, Swisher, IA 52338, tel. 319/846–2478. 1 double room with bath, 2 doubles share 1 bath. Air-conditioning; clock radios; wood-burning stove, grand piano, and TV in common room; refrigerator access; 40-acre orchard and grape arbor. $35, full country breakfast. No credit cards.

Mississippi River

Hancock House Bed and Breakfast

1105 Grove Terr., Dubuque, IA, 52001–4644, tel. 319/557–8989, fax 319/583–0813

The majesty and grandeur of the mighty Mississippi River–bluff region of northeastern Iowa befits the Victorian elegance of Dubuque's Hancock House Bed and Breakfast. Built in 1891 and now on the National Register of Historic Places, the Hancock House demonstrates Queen Anne architecture at its finest.

Meticulous renovations, begun in 1985, turned a poorly maintained apartment building into one of the Midwest's premiere B&Bs. After driving up the circular carriage drive and facing the inn's flower-lined birdbath and portico, guests are greeted with genuine enthusiasm by owners/innkeepers Chuck and Susan Huntley.

Each of Hancock House's nine guest rooms are furnished with feather ticks (mattress bolsters) and are named after members of the Hancock family, the Midwest's largest grocer/distributor at the turn of the century. Amenities to choose from include fireplaces and potbellied stoves, whirlpools and claw-foot bathtubs, iron and canopy beds, stained-glass windows and skylights. One choice you don't have to make is which room offers a better view of the convergence of Iowa, Wisconsin, and Illinois and the rivers that join these states.

Breakfast, served in the formal Victorian dining room on Victorian china, varies seasonally in order to feature local produce: An omelet may include Wisconsin Brie cheese and Iowa-grown apples. Coffee is roasted especially for the Hancock House in neighboring Galena, Illinois, and beer, stocked in the refrigerator, is brewed right in Dubuque.

🏨 *9 double rooms with baths, 4 with whirlpools. Individual heating/cooling controls, cable TVs, clock radios, locally made caramels, beverages, snacks, cribs and roll-aways available. $75–$150, full breakfast. D, MC, V.*

Other Choices

Bishop's House Inn of St. Ambrose University. 1527 Brady St., Davenport, IA 52803, tel. 319/322–8303. 5 double rooms with baths, 1 suite with fireplace and whirlpool. Air-conditioning, ceiling fans, claw-foot bathtubs, stained-glass windows, parquet floors, meeting facilities, library, laundry room. $65–$140, full breakfast. MC, V.

Monarch Bed and Breakfast. 303 S. 2nd St., LeClaire, IA 52753, tel. 319/289–3011 (inquiries), 800/772–7724 (reservations only). 2 double rooms share 1 bath, 2 suites. Air-conditioning, brass beds, fireplace in gathering room, French and Polish spoken. $45–$65, Continental breakfast or full breakfast. No credit cards.

River Oaks Inn. 1234 E. River Dr., Davenport, IA 52803, tel. 319/326–2629 or 800/352–6016, fax 319/324–1243. 5 double rooms with baths; carriage house with 3 rooms, 2 baths, and hot tub. Air-conditioning, fireplace, phone and cable TV in carriage house rooms, gazebo, copy machine and TV available. $59–$135; full breakfast served in formal dining room, on deck, or in suites. AE, D, MC, V.

North Central Iowa

Mrs. B's Bed and Breakfast

920 Division St., Garner, IA 50438, tel. 515/923–2390

A trip to the British Isles inspired Pat Buntenbach to return to her Colonial home in rural north-central Iowa and open a B&B she thinks is just as good or better than what the British have to offer. Inspired by the beautiful English gardens, Pat and her husband, Red, turned much of their 4 acres into a garden: They converted an old stone bar-

becue grill to a fountain surrounded by English tea roses, foxglove, and other "old-time" flowers. The gardens may be enjoyed from Pat's large back porch and gazebo, where she serves a full country breakfast of eggs, ham, home-made breads, and juice.

When Pat and her husband built their dream home more than 30 years ago, they selected green limestone from western Pennsylvania for the exterior. The massive fireplace that dominates much of the common room and kitchen, however, is made of clinker Dutch brick. That Pat and Red worked for years in the cattle business is reflected in the decor of what Pat calls the Cowboy and Indian Room. Photos and other items from century-old cattle drives they acquired and restored are displayed with their sons' old cowboy boots and hats and with Native American memorabilia accumulated on their frequent trips to reservations.

The other two guest rooms upstairs have more delicate decor: One room done in blue has family-heirloom quilts and samplers; the peach room with green accents, designed for guests staying more than a few nights—like the traveling professors who visit the nearby community college—includes a desk, telephone outlet, and a cozy reading area.

Some guests come for all-night quilting sessions at nearby Country Threads Quilt Shop while others enjoy the local gift shop, old-fashioned dry goods store, and the "Surf" Ballroom Dance Hall.

🏠 *3 double rooms with baths. Ceiling fans, color TVs, large fireplace in common room, gardens, bicycles. $55–$65, full breakfast. No credit cards.*

Other Choices

Antique City Inn. 400 Antique City Dr., Walnut, IA 51577, tel. 712/784–3722. 5 double rooms with baths, 1 suite with whirlpool bath. Early 1900s home with period decor one block from antiques shops. TVs, phones, organ in parlor. $50, full breakfast; dinner available. D, MC, V.

Large Pine Inn. 401 N. 3rd St., Clear Lake, IA 50428, tel. 515/357–7854. 3 double rooms with baths, shared kitchenette and parlor. TV and phone in parlor, antiques, claw-foot bathtubs, lake view, bicycles and Burley cart available. $75; full, healthy breakfast. AE, D, MC, V.

Kansas

Lyons' House

Northeast Kansas

Bednobs and Biscuits Bed & Breakfast

15202 Parallel Ave., Basehor, KS 66007, tel. 913/724-1540

Tucked away in the gentle rolling prairie of northeast Kansas in the little community of Basehor, Bednobs and Biscuits is hosted by the artistic and maternal Sonie Mance.

Sonie personalized the modern wood-frame farmhouse with the creative stenciling she added to each room. In the gathering room, she tastefully placed dried prairie flowers on the walls and above door frames, and has stenciled the windows and light switches with ivy. Large windows, accented by antique stained glass, have unencumbered views of the sprawling Kansas prairie, and the dark-wood beam ceiling is brightened by soft peach walls.

Stenciling also highlights the B&B's three spacious guest rooms and one bath upstairs. Stenciled dust ruffles and pillow shams decorate the Rose Room; and handmade quilts, samplers, and crochet work adorn each room. The decor of the Americana Room is more masculine, with a two-person saw, barbed-wire fence, American flag, and World War I memorabilia. The Orchid Room is traditionally feminine, with eyelet lace curtains, crocheted pieces, and ribbons on the dust ruffle. All rooms have skylights and ceiling fans. A tiny alcove at the end of the upstairs hallway has a built-in bookshelf with a variety of well-worn books that are free to wander home with guests.

Breakfast is made to order with attention paid to guests' special requests. Sonie's specialty, however, is a breakfast casserole of eggs, meat, and potatoes, served with chocolate-chip muffins and homemade jams and jellies.

Just beneath the strawberry-accented kitchen is "Grandma's Basement Gift Shop," where you may purchase Sonie's handmade quilts, napkins, place mats, jellies, and homemade apple butter in addition to crafts made by other local artisans.

Bednobs and Biscuits is just 30 minutes from downtown Kansas City, the International Airport, a winery, and the historic river communities of Parkville and Weston, Missouri. Under construction just 15 minutes away is the Land of Oz Theme Park, due to open in 1997.

▦ *3 double rooms share 1 bath. Gift shop, air-conditioning, cable TV/VCR in gathering room, skylights, herb garden, grape arbor. $55–$70; full breakfast, fresh-baked cookies upon arrival. No credit cards.*

Other Choices

Almeda's Inn. 220 S. Main St., Tonganoxie, KS 66086-0113, tel. 913/845-2295. 2 double rooms with baths, 2 singles share 1 bath, 1 suite. Air-conditioning, fireplace and TV in gathering room. $25–$65; Continental breakfast, snacks upon arrival. No credit cards.

Elderberry House. 1035 S.W. Fillmore St., Topeka, KS 66604, tel. 913/235-6309. 2 suites. Air-conditioning, TV/VCR, fireplace, antiques in common room, off-street parking. $45–$55; full or Continental breakfast, evening snacks. No credit cards.

Halcyon House Bed and Breakfast. 1000 Ohio St., Lawrence, KS 66044, tel. 913/841-0314. 4 double rooms share 2 baths, 4 suites with baths/phones. Air-conditioning, vaulted ceilings, fireplace in common room, cable TV/VCR in 4 suites, fireplace in 1 suite. $45–$85, full breakfast. AE, MC, V.

Fort Scott Area

Lyons' House

742 S. National St., Fort Scott, KS 66701, tel. 316/223-0779 or 800/784-8378

Just two hours south of Kansas City, Fort Scott offers visitors tours of the 1840s military post and the Victorian buildings downtown.

Pat Lyons came to the Fort Scott area from the East Coast and, much like original female pioneers, brings a feminine touch to the rugged prairie. The home's north parlor is still used for such Victorian pastimes as needlepoint and knitting: Pat encourages her guests to bring along their needlework and join her in the parlor for conversation and handwork. The house is filled with a large collection of looms and spinning wheels. Pat's favorite threads are silk, wool, and angora, and the results of her work can be found throughout the inn.

Original chandeliers, hardwood floors, and a massive native black-walnut staircase highlight the foyer. Parlors decorated in dark green with soft pink ceilings grace each side of the foyer and join the formal dining room through alcoves. The Lyons' House has four guest rooms with baths, sitting rooms, televisions, and fireplaces (only two fireplaces are in working order).

Southern breakfasts feature such treats as biscuits and gravy; broiled or fried green tomatoes; and ham, sausage, and bacon. Formal afternoon tea is served in the south parlor.

Pat's 1876 Victorian home is the focal point of many Fort Scott social events, especially around Christmas. Long before Thanksgiving, the house is elegantly trimmed for a Victorian holiday and the "Evening of Victorian Elegance," a nine-course dinner followed by historic vignettes reliving events in Fort Scott's history during the three weeks between Thanksgiving and Christmas. The Lyons' House also hosts mystery evenings, tea parties, weddings, and other social occasions limited only by the imagination.

▦ *4 double rooms with baths, 1 2-bedroom suite. Air-conditioning, phones, TVs, water bed in 1 room, library, laundry, antiques. $75–$135; full breakfast, afternoon tea. No credit cards.*

Other Choices

Bennington House. 123 Crescent Dr., Fort Scott, KS 66701, tel. 316/223-1837. 3 double rooms with private baths. Secluded location, air-conditioning, cable

TV/VCR in family room, clock radios, large deck with picnic tables. $45, full breakfast. No credit cards.

Chenault Mansion. 820 S. National St., Fort Scott, KS 66701, tel. 316/223–6800. 3 double rooms with private baths; 2 suites with telephones and TV; 4 fireplaces. Air-conditioning, stained-glass and leaded-glass windows, crystal chandeliers, parlor, cribs, porch swings, off-street parking. $70–$85, full breakfast. D, MC, V.

Central Kansas

Swedish Country Inn

112 W. Lincoln St., Lindsborg, KS 67456, tel. 913/227–2985, fax 913/227–3268

Central Kansas is an unlikely place to experience the European hospitality of a place like the Swedish Country Inn. A remote community of 3,000 Swedish-Americans, the town of Lindsborg is known throughout the Midwest as "Little Sweden on the Plains."

Built during the 1920s, the Swedish Country Inn became a hotel in the 1930s and a bed-and-breakfast in the 1970s. The spacious lobby has Swedish pine furniture, game tables, television, and a fire burning in the fireplace no matter the temperature outside. An adjoining gift shop sells many of the unique Swedish gift items made in the community, such as music boxes, linens, and the ever-present Dala Horse, a symbol of Swedish heritage. Swedish is spoken throughout the community and by several staff members at the Swedish Inn. Innkeeper Becky Anderson, a native of the area, knows a little Swedish and does her best to keep up with guests and others fluent in the language.

The inn's spacious rooms and suites are all furnished with Swedish pine and accented with handmade quilts and bold Scandinavian blues, greens, and yellows softened by Swedish lace curtains. Flower stenciling, native to the culture, is in most rooms.

A delightful Scandinavian buffet breakfast features Swedish tea rings, pickled herring, meats, cheeses, and Swedish meatballs. Imported coffees and teas round out a breakfast not found at any other B&B in the state of Kansas. If that doesn't fill you up, an in-house bakery offers baked goods to go.

To burn off a few of the calories consumed at breakfast, guests are welcome to borrow bicycles for a leisurely ride around town. Although this part of Kansas has no hills to speak of, any sore muscles you encounter after your bike ride can be pampered in the inn's private sauna.

In keeping with the Swedish culture, Lindsborg is the site of a much-celebrated Holy Week festival at Easter, the Svensh Hyllningsfest in October, and the St. Lucia Festival in December. Reservations are highly recommended at the Swedish Country Inn during these periods.

🏠 *19 double rooms with baths, 1 family suite, 1 bridal suite. Air-conditioning, TVs, phones, sauna, gift shop, bicycles. Disabled accessible. $50–$70, full breakfast. AE, D, MC, V.*

Other Choices

Balfour's House Bed and Breakfast. 940 1900 Ave., Abilene, KS 67410–6330, tel. 913/263–4262. 2 double rooms with private baths, 2 suites. Stone fireplace in living area, piano, stereo, satellite TV/VCR, indoor swimming pool, spa, bathrobes, grape arbor. $55–$150, full breakfast served poolside. AE, MC, V.

Hawk House. 307 W. Broadway, Newton, KS 67114, tel. 316/283–2045. 1 double room with bath, 3 doubles share 1 bath. Air-conditioning, antiques, library, stained-glass windows. $40–$60, Continental breakfast. MC, V.

Hedgeapple Acres. Box 247, Moran, KS 66755-0247, tel. 316/237–4646. 6 rooms with baths. Family room with cable TV/VCR, 2 fireplaces, whirlpool bath in 1 room, 80 acres of walking trails, excellent bird-watching, 2 fishing ponds. $65, full breakfast. AE, D, MC, V. No credit cards.

Plumb House. 628 Exchange St., Emporia, KS 66801, tel. 316/342–6881. 4 double rooms with baths; 2 suites, one with TV, refrigerator, and microwave. Bathrobes, off-street parking, garden swing, ponds and foot bridge. $65–$80, full breakfast. AE, D, MC, V.

Kentucky

Sandusky House

Louisville/Bluegrass West

Inn at the Park

*1332 S. 4th St., Louisville, KY 40208,
tel. 502/637-6930 or 800/700-7275*

The Inn at the Park is a splendid example of Richardsonian Romanesque architecture, with a turreted window bay, Dutch-style chimney, and onion-dome ornament. Depending on your taste, its rusticated stonework exterior might strike you as quirky or charming. The house makes a whimsical impression in a neighborhood dominated by staid Victorians.

Built in 1886, Inn at the Park was originally the home of Russell Houston, a well-known attorney and a co-founder of the Louisville & Nashville Railroad. The 7,500-square-foot stone mansion was restored to its original elegance in 1985, and opened as a bed-and-breakfast in December 1993. Innkeepers John and Sandra Mullins, who bought the property in early 1995, are native Louisvillians.

Modern-day Scarletts will love sweeping down the grand and graceful staircase of the entry foyer. Other period touches are rich hardwood floors, 14-foot ceilings, eight marble fireplaces, crown moldings, and second- and third-floor stone balconies overlooking the city's Central Park. The inn is furnished throughout with Victorian antiques and reproductions. Its largest and most elegant quarters, the Durrant Suite, has a four-poster bed and fireplaces in both bedroom and bath, along with a beautiful view of the park, a vista also seen from several other guest rooms.

Guests share several common areas, including living and dining rooms with magnificent carved fireplaces, a library, and a refreshment room where guests may enjoy beer, wine, and soft drinks without charge. Sandra also puts out wine and cheese for guests most evenings. In the morning, there's very little chance of going hungry: Breakfasts—which can be taken in either the elegant dining room or in your own room—include banana-walnut pancakes, grilled-ham omelets, and Belgian waffles.

▥ *4 double rooms with baths, 2 double rooms share bath, 1 suite with bath. Cable TVs, fireplaces, $79–$119, full breakfast. AE, MC, V.*

Old Louisville Inn Bed & Breakfast

*1359 S. 3rd St., Louisville, KY 40208,
tel. 502/635–1574, fax 502/637–5892*

After passing a welcoming five-globe lamppost out front, a guest entering the lobby of the Old Louisville Inn is apt to be struck, if not overwhelmed, by the heroic scale of the place, dramatized by a massive set of ornately carved mahogany columns. That's exactly the reaction John Armstrong desired in 1901 when he built the handsome Victorian structure as his private home; nothing less would do for the then-president of the Louisville Home Telephone Company. The 10,000-square-foot mansion was used as office space for several decades until a renovation in the early 1970s restored it to the splendor it had enjoyed as a monument to Armstrong's success as a business Titan.

The inn is tastefully decorated with furnishings bought from antiques shops or at local estate auctions. The breakfast room, which seats 20, has an original etched-glass chandelier and a built-in elaborately carved buffet. In the parlor is a fireplace and an eclectic lending library, as well as a collection of menus from nearby restaurants to help guests decide where to dine. The game room offers board games, including chess, backgammon, and a 1946 version of Monopoly. The most eye-catching features of the decor are the murals that adorn the inn's 12-foot ceilings; innkeeper Marianne Lesher will happily elaborate on the stories the murals tell.

Five of the guest rooms have marble baths with original fixtures, modernized to include showers; all guests sleep under antique quilts. Bay windows in some second-floor bedrooms have picturesque views of one of Louisville's best-preserved historic neighborhoods.

Old Louisville Inn is a hostelry suffused with romance. The third-floor Celebration Suite has a king-size arched-canopy bed, a sitting area, a fireplace, and a modern bath with whirlpool. If requested, Marianne will cater a private candlelit tête-à-tête dinner in your room. Your wake-up call the next morning will be the mouthwatering aromas of her muffins and popovers, and of the inn's signature blend of coffee.

🏠 *8 double rooms with baths, 3 double rooms share 1 bath. Air-conditioning, whirlpool bath in suite, exercise room, TV/VCR with video library in game room. $95–$195, full breakfast. MC, V.*

Rose Blossom Bed & Breakfast

*1353 S. 4th St., Louisville, KY 40208,
tel. 502/636–0295, 502/969–3923*

Old Louisville, just south of downtown, is the most elegant of this city's neighborhoods. Many streets are fascinating architectural smorgasbords: Richardsonian Romanesque, Queen Anne, Châteauesque, and Beaux Arts are just a few of the styles. One of the homes built in the Victorian Italianate manner is the Rose Blossom—an 18-room, three-story house listed on the National Register of Historic Places. It was built in 1884 as the residence of Vernon D. Price, who achieved fame as president of the *Saturday Evening Post*. When Mary Ohlmann purchased the property more than a century later, it was in need of total renovation. By 1992, she had completed a pumpkin-to-carriage transformation.

Mrs. Ohlmann went to great lengths to preserve the original appearance of the house: She cleaned and polished the hammered-brass hardware piece by piece; installed period-style windows and transoms to coordinate with the leaded-glass panes in the entrance hall and stairwell; restored the beautiful oak stairwell and the rear stairway to the original construction. Modern lighting systems now brighten what was probably a gloomy interior in the early days of gaslight. And in place of a dank cellar, the tireless chatelaine—mother of nine children—has opened a small but charming gift shop.

The house's 14-foot ceilings have been enhanced with crown moldings and medallions. The light fixtures, many of crystal and brass, are in keeping with the era and recapture the elegant feeling of the late 19th century, when this neighborhood was the most prestigious in Louisville.

The parlor rooms of the Rose Blossom have Victorian-era antiques and reproductions. Throughout the house, 10 original working fireplaces have carved mantels and ornate tile or metal decorations. The seven guest rooms share 4½ bathrooms.

A sunroom and solarium added at the rear offer quiet retreats. There are also a large, well-lighted breakfast room and a Victorian-style front porch—complete with a rare reversed-paint-on-glass ceiling—for guests who want to relax and look over the beautiful gardens.

The Rose Blossom is directly across the street from Central Park, part of a city park system designed by Frederick Law Olmsted, a co-designer of New York City's Central Park. Louisville's version is small and serene and is a happy haven for squirrels; here you can play tennis, take an evening stroll, or, in the summer, watch Shakespeare in the Park.

A full family-style breakfast is served by Mary herself with near-maternal devotion. Coffee, juice, and conversation are always available to guests.

🏠 *7 double rooms with shared baths. Air-conditioning, cable TVs, several fireplaces. $85, full breakfast. AE, D, MC, V.*

Other Choices

Bruntwood Inn. 714 N. 3rd St., Bardstown, KY 40004, tel. 502/348–8218. 4 double rooms with baths, 2 rooms share bath. Air-conditioning, grand parlor rooms. $65–$85, full breakfast. No credit cards.

Glenmar Plantation Bed & Breakfast. 2444 Valley Hill Rd., Springfield, KY 40069, tel. 606/284–7791 or 800/828–3330, fax 606/284–7791. 5 double rooms with baths, 2 doubles with shared bath, 1 suite, 1 cottage (sleeps 6). Air-conditioning, meeting room with antiques, working farm with horses, fishing pond. $85–$200; full breakfast, evening dessert. AE, MC, V.

Honeymoon Mansion. 1014 E. Main St., New Albany, IN 47150, tel. 812/945–0312. 6 suites with baths. 3 whirlpool baths, fireplace, stained-glass windows. $70–$140, full country breakfast. MC, V.

Linden Hill Bed & Breakfast. 1607 Frankfort Ave., Louisville, KY 40206, tel. 502/583–1400. 8 double rooms with baths. Air-conditioning, 10 working fireplaces. $75. No credit cards.

Mansion Bed & Breakfast. 1003 N. 3rd St., Bardstown, KY 40004, tel. 502/348–2586 or 800/399–2586, fax 502/349–6098. 8 double rooms with baths. Air-conditioning, period antiques. $85, hearty Continental breakfast. AE, D, MC, V.

Myrtledene. 370 N. Spalding Ave., Lebanon, KY 40033, tel. 502/692–2223 or 800/391–1721. 4 double rooms with shared baths. $65, full breakfast. MC, V.

Talbott Tavern/McLean House. Court Sq., Bardstown, KY 40004, tel. 502/348–3494, fax 502/348–0673. 8 double rooms with baths, 2 doubles with shared bath. Restaurant, air-conditioning, gift shop. $50–$89, Continental breakfast. MC, V.

Yellow Cottage. 400 N. Central Ave., Campbellsville, KY 42718, tel. 502/789–2669. 2 double rooms with baths.

Air-conditioning. $40–$50, Continental breakfast. No credit cards.

Reservations Service

Kentucky Homes Bed & Breakfast (1219 S. Fourth St., Louisville, KY 40203, tel. 502/635-7341) has about 40 properties scattered throughout Kentucky, most in the Louisville metro area.

Lexington/Bluegrass East

Boone Tavern Hotel

Main St. at Prospect St., Box 2345, Berea, KY 40404, tel. 606/986-9358 or 800/366-9358, fax 606/986-7711

Boone Tavern is a grand country inn managed and operated by students of a unique educational institution—Berea College—which charges no tuition, admits only low-income students, limits enrollment to 1,500, and requires all students to work in college jobs.

Berea, one of the first interracial colleges in the South, was founded in 1855 by John G. Fee and Cassius M. Clay to provide the needy youth of Southern Appalachia a high-quality liberal-arts education within the context of the Christian faith. For many years, enrollment was about half white and half black; African-American enrollment is now around 10 percent. Berea alumni include Harriette Simpson Arnow, author of *The Dollmaker*; former New York Yankee Earle Combs (1924–35)—the first Kentuckian inducted into the Baseball Hall of Fame; country-music songwriter Billy Edd Wheeler; and Juanita Kreps, Secretary of Commerce under President Jimmy Carter.

Boone Tavern was built at the suggestion of Nellie Frost, the wife of Berea's president, who, in 1908, understandably felt put-upon after providing lodging and meals at her home for about 300 summer guests. The stately, white-columned, three-story guest house that is now the Boone Tavern Hotel was begun the following year, and it has been renovated several times since. Inside, guests will find a traditional decor, with antique furniture reproductions (crafted by student woodworkers), bouquets of seasonal cut flowers, and a portrait of Daniel Boone greeting them in the main salon.

Service at the inn (where no alcoholic beverages are served, despite the word "Tavern" in its name; Berea is in dry Madison County) is provided largely by the students, many of them hotel-management majors. Since Boone Tavern opened, its dining room has become renowned for its Kentucky farm cuisine, notably its spoon bread (a cornbread soufflé) and corn sticks. Other specialties include chicken flakes in a bird's nest and cinnamon kites. Guests can take in the college's convocation series, music program, and art exhibits, which are open to the public.

🏨 *59 double rooms with baths. Restaurant, air-conditioning. $63–$87, breakfast not included. AE, D, DC, MC, V.*

Shaker Village of Pleasant Hill

3501 Lexington Rd., Harrodsburg, KY 40330, tel. 606/734-5411, reservations 800/734-5611, fax 606/734-5411

Considerably before Mies van der Rohe uttered the modernist rallying cry of "less is more," the Shakers perfected a style built from necessity: spare rooms, simple natural fabrics, plain wood furniture. Observers may think these are hardly the ingredients that constitute an extraordinary hostelry. But as many visitors to Pleasant Hill—the largest restored historic Shaker village in the United States—discover, the 80 guest quarters of this museum-like settlement offer the unique experience of living amid Shaker-style furnishings. In doing so, many guests come to truly appreciate the Shakers' timeless world of subtle and quiet beauty.

The Shakers were a utopian religious sect that flourished during the 19th century in villages in the eastern and midwestern United States, stretching from Maine to Indiana. They believed that "True Gospel simplicity . . . naturally leads to plainness in all things." Today, the Shaker belief that "utility is beauty" strikes a chord with visitors at Pleasant Hill who marvel at Shaker architecture, furniture, and textiles. The settlement was founded in 1805 by hardworking farmers, first- or second-generation descendants of the pioneers who settled the Kentucky River frontier in the early 1800s. Within 20 years there were nearly 500 members living on 4,500 acres. Over time, the Shakers built a total of 270 structures at Pleasant Hill—utilitarian buildings with little adornment but with classical lines, a sense of proportion, and a breathtaking simplicity.

Visitors have the choice of staying in rooms in 15 of the 33 original buildings, including the Old Stone Shop, the Old Ministers' Workshop, the Tan Yard House, and the Farm Deacon's Shop. Rooms (often on the second floors) are decorated in the best Shaker style, with reproduction drop-leaf tables, rockers, candle stands, ladder-back chairs, and pegboards offering distinctive touches. Modern-day comforts are not forgotten. Bathrooms have replaced water closets, and king-size beds offer spacious comfort (in lieu of the single beds celibate Shakers used). TVs in each room remind guests they haven't completely forsaken the 20th century. Outside, however, the clock has been magically turned back to 1850. When Pleasant Hill's historic restoration began in 1961, all utilities were buried, walks were repaired or replaced, U.S. 68 was rerouted around the village, and the village road was restored to its 19th-century condition.

Pleasant Hill offers six visitor services: touring, dining, lodging, meeting facilities, shopping, and riverboat excursions. The self-guided village tour includes 13 buildings. Costumed interpreters describe Shaker history and the Shaker way of life while working at 19th-century crafts, such as broom making and spinning. For meals, guests congregate in the old inn once used by Shakers to entertain "the world's people." Here, Kentucky's regional cuisine is served family-style; don't miss the justly famous Shaker lemon pie. After breakfast (which is not included in the room rate), you can shop for a wide variety of Kentucky crafts and handmade items. And if you're staying at Pleasant Hill from late April through October, riverboat excursions on the Kentucky River are available aboard *The Dixie Belle.*

🏠 *80 double rooms with baths. TVs, crafts shops. $50–$115, breakfast not included. MC, V.*

Other Choices

Canaan Land. 4355 Lexington Rd., Harrodsburg, KY 40330, tel. 606/734–3984. 4 double rooms with baths in main house (built 1795), 3 in separate rebuilt log house (1815). Air-conditioning, hot tub, swimming pool, 185-acre working sheep farm. $75–$105, full breakfast. No credit cards.

Cherry Knoll Farm Bed & Breakfast. 3975 Lemons Mill Rd., Lexington, KY 40511, tel. 606/253–9800. 2 double rooms with baths. Restaurant, air-conditioning, veranda overlooking horse farms. $75, full breakfast. AE, D, MC, V.

Gratz Park Inn. 120 W. 2nd St., Lexington, KY 40507, tel. 606/231–1777 or 800/227–4362, fax 606/233–7593. 38 double rooms with baths, 6 suites. Air-conditioning, cable TV, fax, copy machine, fitness center available. $120–$199, Continental breakfast. AE, D, DC, MC, V.

Rosehill Inn. 233 Rose Hill, Versailles, KY 40383, tel. 606/873–5957. 4 double rooms with baths. Air-conditioning, whirlpool bath in 1 room. $69–$89, full breakfast. AE, MC, V.

Sandusky House. 1626 Delaney Ferry Rd., Nicholasville, KY 40356, tel. 606/223–4730. 3 double rooms with baths, separate reconstructed log home (1820s) with 2 double rooms. Air-conditioning, fireplace and whirlpool tub in log cabin. $75–$95, full breakfast. MC, V.

Reservations Service

Bluegrass Bed & Breakfast (2964 McCracken Pike, Versailles, KY 40383, tel. 606/873–3208) has 18 properties in central Kentucky, ranging from cozy cottages, to big Victorian homes in urban settings, to manor houses on horse farms.

Northern Kentucky

Carneal House Inn. 405 E. 2nd St., Covington, KY 41011, tel. 606/431–6130, fax 606/581–6041. 6 double rooms with baths. Air-conditioning, terrace, private balconies. $80–$120, full breakfast. AE, MC, V.

Gateway Bed & Breakfast. 326 E. 6th St., Newport, KY 41071, tel. 606/581–6447. 1 double room with bath, 2 double rooms share a bath. Air-conditioning, rooftop deck, displays of antique musical instruments. $75–$85, full breakfast. AE, MC, V.

Ghent House. 411 Main St., Box 478, Ghent, KY 41045, tel. 502/347–5807. 3 double rooms with baths. Fireplaces, whirlpool bath in 1 room, outdoor hot tub, English walking garden. $60–$90, full breakfast. AE, MC, V.

Lamplighter Inn. 103 W. 2nd St., Augusta, KY 41002, tel. 606/756–2603. 9 double rooms with baths. Restaurant, tennis courts, pool, murder-mystery weekends. $65–$80, Continental breakfast. MC, V.

Eastern Kentucky

Blair's Country Living. Hwys. 80 and 421, R.R. 3, Box 865-B, Manchester, KY 40962, tel. 606/598–2854. 2 double rooms with baths. Air-conditioning, cable TV available. $50–$65, Continental breakfast. No credit cards.

Charlene's Country Inn Bed & Breakfast. Hwys. 7 and 32, H.C. 75, Box 265, Sandy Hook, KY 41171, tel. 606/738–5712, fax 606/738–4640. 3 double rooms with baths, 3 doubles share a bath. $65–$75, full breakfast. No credit cards.

Western Kentucky

Log House. 3239 Franklin Rd., Russellville, KY 42276, tel. 502/726–8483, fax 502/726–2270. 4 double rooms with baths. Air-conditioning, hot tub. $75–$85, Continental breakfast. AE, D, MC, V.

Round Oak Inn. U.S. 68 W, Box 1331, Cadiz, KY 42211, tel. 502/924–5850. 6 double rooms with baths. $45–$55, full breakfast. AE, D, MC, V.

Silver Cliff Inn. 1980 Lake Barkley Dr., Old Kuttawa, KY 42055, tel. 502/388–5858. 2 rooms with baths, 2 rooms share a bath (can be rented as a 2-bedroom suite). Air-conditioning, 7 fireplaces, swimming nearby. $70–$85, full breakfast. No credit cards.

Louisiana

Madewood Plantation

Greater New Orleans

Claiborne Mansion

2111 Dauphine St., New Orleans, LA 70116, tel. 504/949-7327 or 800/449-7327, fax 504/949-0388

Faubourg Marigny, adjacent to the French Quarter, was one of New Orleans's first suburbs. In the 1850s, the son of William C. C. Claiborne, Louisiana's first American governor, built this Greek Revival mansion for his family. Claiborne's descendants lived here until 1905; it was an apartment house when Cleo Pelleteri bought and restored it. The Bayou Ridge Cafe, also owned by Cleo, is among the area's several popular restaurants and nightclubs.

Cleo has created an elegant, secluded haven favored by many celebrities. Chastity Bono was a guest, and Larry Hagman stayed here while filming a TV pilot. In contrast to those in the area's Victorian B&Bs, the Claiborne's furnishings and objets d'art are contemporary. Crystal chandeliers hang from high ceilings, shining on polished hardwood floors and vases of fresh flowers. The sun-filled rooms and marble baths are spacious.

There are three suites and a room in the main house. Each suite has a large parlor and bedroom. One has a huge four-poster, curtained in an elegant white fabric. The room in the rear, overlooking the courtyard, has a canopy bed in delicious rose and white colors. The ground-floor room of the slave quarters, near the pool in the landscaped courtyard, has a wheelchair ramp; its bedroom–sitting room has slate floors, and twin red leather armchairs flank a fireplace. The two rooms above it, with whitewashed brick walls and white slipcovered sofas and chairs, can be combined for a suite.

For breakfast, Cleo does anything from croissants to waffles, depending on guests' individual preferences. In pleasant weather, guests like to eat beside the pool, but she says they often perch on stools in the kitchen.

🏠 *1 double room with bath and 3 suites in main house; 1 double with bath and 1 suite in slave quarters. Air-conditioning, phone with voice mail and cable TV/VCR in rooms, fax, pool. $125–$350; full breakfast, afternoon cocktails. AE, D, MC, V. Restricted smoking, no pets.*

House on Bayou Road

2275 Bayou Rd., New Orleans, LA 70119, tel. 504/945-0992 or 800/882-2968, fax 504/945-0993

In New Orleans's historic Bayou St. John area, near City Park, Cynthia Reeve's 18th-century West Indies-style home and its cottages provide a quiet, elegant retreat. Brad Pitt was a guest while filming *Interview with the Vampire*, and Dan Aykroyd stayed here during the opening of his New Orleans House of Blues.

The property sits on 2 landscaped acres, with flowering plants, shade trees, and brick patios. In pleasant weather, guests can enjoy the gourmet breakfast beside the pool and outdoor Jacuzzi. A pair of cats—Samson and Ping Pong—often play on the lawn.

The house and cottages are furnished with early Louisiana antiques; family heirlooms, such as an antique harp and oil portraits, are displayed throughout. Beautifully restored, the house features hardwood floors, Oriental rugs, old brick fireplaces, screened porches, and large windows that afford a light, airy ambience.

There are four guest rooms in the main house; each has its own distinct personality. One, with a four-poster rice bed, shelves filled with books, and a fireplace, has a polo motif, reflected in framed prints. Another, done in floral prints, has a large canopy bed and a stained-glass window and opens onto a porch. To the rear, there are three suites in a large Victorian cottage, one with a handsome antique sleigh bed, another an iron filigree bed. A real treasure is the private Creole cottage, with a skylight over the big four-poster, a wet bar, and stained-glass window in the Jacuzzi bath. Both cottages have front porches with rocking chairs and tinkling wind chimes.

A year-round cooking school is conducted here; packages are available.

Limousine service from the airport is available at an extra charge.

A full breakfast is served every morning, but on Saturday and Sunday, Cynthia prepares a champagne mimosa breakfast that may include eggs Benedict or a soufflé Florentine.

▥ *4 double rooms with baths in main house, 3 suites in cottage, 1 private cottage. Air-conditioning, phones, robes, sherry; cable TV in common room in main house, fax, modem. $155–$245, full breakfast. AE, D, DC, MC, V. Smoking only on porches, no pets, 5-night minimum for Mardi Gras and Jazz Fest.*

Lanaux Mansion

547 Esplanade Ave., New Orleans, LA 70116, tel. 504/488-4640 or 800/729-4640, fax 504/488-4639

The stately Italianate Lanaux Mansion stands on a quiet corner of Esplanade Avenue, between the French Quarter and Faubourg Marigny. Owner Ruth Bodenheimer, who is director of charters and incentives for the New Orleans Steamboat Company, says she fell in love with the house when she was 17; in 1989, she became its proud owner.

The house was built in 1879 for Charles Andrew Johnson, a wealthy bachelor. According to legend, Johnson was secretly in love with his business partner's wife. When Johnson died, he left the house and his entire fortune to her daughter. Marie Andry Lanaux then lived in the house, and her descendants occupied it until 1953.

The mansion boasts 14-foot ceilings both upstairs and down, as well as some of the original wallpaper, cornices, ceiling medallions, and mantels. A large oil portrait of Mr. Johnson gazes over a formal parlor, with its grand piano, objets d'art, and Renaissance-revival furnishings.

There is one suite in the main house, two in a wing, and a cottage in the rear courtyard. The Lanaux Suite, upstairs in the main house, and the "Enchanted Cottage," as Ruth calls it, are awash with Victoriana, right down to displays of high-button shoes and old-fashioned clothes. The Lanaux Suite boasts a four-piece rosewood bedroom set made by 19th-century cabinetmaker Prudent Mallard. In the wing, the Library Suite, with its plethora of books, and the Weiland Suite, with its huge open fireplace, were the original library and kitchen, respectively.

Each of the accommodations has a kitchenette, with coffeemaker, fridge, microwave, and supplies for a do-it-yourself Continental breakfast; all have an iron, ironing board, hair dryer, TV, and phone with private answering machine. Guests have maximum privacy; those in the wing and the cottage have private entrances, while those in the mansion are given a key to the front door.

🎏 *3 suites, 1 cottage. Air-conditioning, cable TVs, phones with answering machines. $122–$227, Continental breakfast. No credit cards. Restricted smoking, no pets.*

Melrose Mansion

937 Esplanade Ave., New Orleans, LA 70116, tel. 504/944–2255, fax 504/945–1795

This splendid Victorian Gothic on the fringe of New Orleans's French Quarter was built in 1884. It has a turret, dormers, stained-glass windows, a steeply pitched roof, Corinthian columns, and a guest list that includes Lady Bird Johnson. The former first lady attended the grand opening of the bed-and-breakfast in 1990 and was the first person to sign the register.

Each of the large, high-ceilinged rooms is furnished differently, but all feature handsome 19th-century Louisiana antiques, including four-posters. The usual amenities include down pillows, fine-milled soaps, monogrammed robes and towels, and small refrigerators

stocked with mineral water, soft drinks, and a split of complimentary champagne. Fresh flowers and a decanter of Courvoisier are placed in each suite, where there are also wet bars and whirlpool baths.

The star is the Donecio Suite, in the turret, with its 14-foot ceiling, chandelier of brass and etched glass, and ecru and ivory lace touches. All the mansion's baths are sumptuous affairs, but in this suite the whirlpool bubbles in the turret and a huge window overlooks the French Quarter.

Melrose's owners, Melvin Jones and Sidney Torres, bought the building in 1976 from New Orleans entertainer Chris Owens. It was an apartment house then and remained so for more than 10 years. Melvin, a general contractor, spent more than two years in extensive renovations, and his wife, Rosemary, did the interior decoration.

Guests can take breakfast in their room, around the heated pool, or in the formal dining room. An astonishing array of hors d'oeuvres is served with afternoon cocktails.

🎏 *4 double rooms with baths, 4 suites. Air-conditioning, library, meeting room, fitness center, turndown service; complimentary airport limousine service. $225–$425; full breakfast, afternoon refreshments. AE, MC, V. No pets; 4-night minimum during Mardi Gras, Jazz Fest, and Sugar Bowl.*

Salmen-Fritchie House

127 Cleveland Ave., Slidell, LA 70458, tel. 504/643–1405 or 800/235–4168, fax 504/643–2251

The little town of Slidell, on the Pearl River, about 35 minutes from downtown New Orleans, is home to one of the state's showplace B&Bs. Owners Sharon and Homer Fritchie live upstairs, and all 12 rooms on the main floor, as well as the restored 1895 carriage house, are for overnighters. Listed on the National Register of Historic Places, the white mansion (it also dates from 1895), which has a high-pitched roof, broad front porch, porte cochere, and beveled-glass door, basks on a spacious lawn. Immediately upon stepping inside the central hall, you'll notice a white Italian-marble sculpture on a table and an elaborate burgundy jardiniere, both original to the house. Nearby stands an 18th-century Chippendale long-case clock. A tour of the mansion and its priceless antiques is included.

The mansion features 12-foot ceilings, wood-burning fireplaces with intricately carved mantelpieces, expanses of cypress paneling, and an 85-foot-long by 25-foot-wide central hall. Within that ample space are a sitting area (with console TV an VCR) and a grand piano, on which are displayed miniature family photographs. The twin Queen Anne sofas flanking the fireplace in the library came from Linden in Natchez, Mississippi; the bookcase holds contemporary novels and volumes of the *Encyclopaedia Britannica*.

Each of the five guest rooms is furnished in period style. The Mallard Bedroom, for example, features the hand-carved work of Prudent Mallard, a well-known 19th-century New Orleans furniture maker. Three of the guest rooms have wood-burning fireplaces, and two can be combined to create a suite. Baths are spacious and modern. The carriage house, with contemporary furnishings, full kitchen, huge four-poster, and double Jacuzzi bath, has a large screened porch surrounded by greenery.

Early morning coffee can be brought to your room. Breakfast, served at a long table in a many-windowed breakfast room, may take the form of pecan waffles, French toast stuffed with fruits, or cheese, chive, and mushroom omelets with bacon.

🖼 *5 double rooms with baths, 1 cottage. Air-conditioning, phones, cable TVs; VCR in one room. $75–$150, full breakfast. AE, D, MC, V. No smoking, no pets. Closed Jan. 1, Thanksgiving, Dec. 25.*

Other Choices

Chimes. 1146 Constantinople St., New Orleans, LA 70115, tel. 504/488–4640 or 800/729–4640, fax 504/488–4639. 5 double rooms with baths. Air-conditioning; TV, phone, and stereo in rooms. $78–$106, full breakfast. No credit cards. No smoking.

Degas House. 2306 Esplanade Ave., New Orleans, LA 70119, tel. 504/821–5009, fax 504/821–0870. 4 double rooms with baths, 3 suites. Air-conditioning, clock radios, phones, cable TVs. $100–$200, Continental breakfast. AE, MC, V. Restricted smoking, no pets, 2-night minimum stay on weekends, 4-night minimum for Jazz Fest and Mardi Gras.

Duvigneaud House. 2857 Grand Route St. John, New Orleans, LA 70119, tel. 504/821–5009, fax 504/821–0870. 4 suites. Air-conditioning, clock radios, phones, cable TVs; dishwashers, washer/dryers in 3 suites. $135, Continental breakfast. AE, MC, V. Restricted smoking, no pets, 2-night minimum stay on weekends, 4-night minimum for Jazz Fest and Mardi Gras.

Josephine Guest House. 1450 Josephine St., New Orleans, LA 70130, tel. 504/524–6361 or 800/779–6361, fax 504/523–6484. 6 double rooms with baths. Air-conditioning, cable TVs. $85–$145, Continental breakfast. AE, D, DC, MC, V. Restricted smoking, 4-night minimum during Sugar Bowl, 5-night minimum for Mardi Gras and Jazz Fest.

Riverside Hills Farm. 96 Gardenia Dr., Covington, LA 70433, tel. 504/892–1794, fax 504/626–5849. 1 cottage. Air-conditioning, cable TV and phone in cottage; boat launch, fishing rods, nature trails. $90, Continental breakfast. No credit cards. Restricted smoking, no pets.

Robert Gordy House. 2630 Bell St., New Orleans, LA 70119, tel. and fax 504/486–9424, 800/889–7359. 1 double room with bath, 2 doubles share 1 bath. Air-conditioning, wood-burning fireplaces in parlor and 1 bedroom, washer/dryer for guests; 2 bikes. $95. AE, MC, V. Restricted smoking, 5-night minimum for Jazz Fest and Mardi Gras.

Sully Mansion. 2631 Prytania St., New Orleans, LA 70130, tel. 504/891–0457, fax 504/899–7237. 5 double rooms with baths. Air-conditioning, cable TVs, phones. $89–$175, Continental breakfast. AE, D, MC, V. 5-night minimum for Jazz Fest, Mardi Gras, and special events.

Woods Hole Inn. 78253 Woods Hole La., Folsom, LA 70437, tel. 504/796–9077. 2 cottages. Air-conditioning, cable TVs, phones in cottages. $95, Continental breakfast. No credit cards. No smoking, no pets.

Reservations Services

Bed & Breakfast, Inc. (1021 Moss St., Box 52257, New Orleans, LA 70152–2257, tel. 504/488–4640 or 800/749–4640). **New Orleans Bed & Breakfast** (Box 8163, New Orleans, LA 70182, tel. 504/838–0071, fax 504/838–0140).

Plantation Country

Butler Greenwood

8345 U.S. 61, St. Francisville, LA 70775, tel. 504/635–6312, fax 504/635–6370

Shaded by huge live oaks dripping tangled tendrils of Spanish moss, Anne Butler's home—a two-story frame house with a wraparound veranda, dormers, and gables—was built in the early 1800s. The 12-piece set of rosewood Victorian furniture in the parlor is original to the house. Still a working plantation, the property, about 2 miles north of St. Francisville, has been in her family since 1796. A tour of the house is included with an overnight stay.

The bed-and-breakfast accommodations are in six cottages sprinkled around the grounds. Each cottage has either a full kitchen or kitchenette—stocked with a coffeemaker, toaster oven, fresh juice and croissants in the refrigerator, cereal, and fruit—so you can prepare breakfast at your leisure, as well as remote-control cable TV, plenty of books and magazines, and good lamps for reading.

Anne found three 9-foot stained-glass church windows in an antiques shop and designed the Gazebo cottage around them. It has a king-size metal four-poster, wicker furnishings, and a kitchenette. The Cook's Cottage, which dates from the 1800s, has a working fireplace, brick walls, a porch with rocking chairs, and an old-fashioned bath with claw-foot tub. Another charmer is the Old Kitchen, built in 1796, which has exposed beams, old brick walls, skylights, and a Jacuzzi bath with a 115-foot floodlit well covered with heavy glass. The three-level windmill-shaped Dovecote has bedrooms on the first and third levels, with a parlor and full kitchen in between. Sunny and airy Treehouse has a wood-burning fireplace and a three-level rear deck overlooking lush bluffs. In each cottage is a copy of Anne's *Tourist Guide to West Feliciana Parish*. A writer and journalist for more than 25 years, Anne has written children's books, books on the criminal justice system, and a cookbook that includes vintage Feliciana photographs and anecdotes.

🏠 *6 cottages. Air-conditioning, cable TVs, clock radios in cottages; pool, guided nature/bird-watching walks. $80–$100, Continental breakfast. AE, MC, V. Restricted smoking.*

Cottage Plantation

10528 Cottage La., St. Francisville, LA 70777, tel. 504/635-3674

The country road to Cottage Plantation ambles across a wooden bridge and through a splendid wooded area thick with moss-covered live oaks, as well as dogwood, mimosa, and crepe myrtle trees. The plantation nestles in 400 such idyllic acres, far from traffic noises and other 20th-century distractions.

Built between 1795 and 1850, Cottage is one of only a handful of antebellum plantations that still have their original outbuildings. The office and one-room schoolhouse, kitchen, tiny milk house, barns, slave quarters, and other dependencies that made up the working plantation are intact, though weathered. One outbuilding is now a rustic restaurant called Mattie's House (open for dinner only); another is an antiques shop.

The well-maintained main building is a long, low yellow-frame structure; green shutters outline the gallery and dormer windows. The sloping roof is punctuated with chimneys and dormers from which window air-conditioning units jut anachronistically. A variety of dogs and cats nap or amble around the grounds.

Angling off from the main house is a similar structure—also original to the plantation—which houses the guest rooms. Downstairs rooms open onto the porch and get more light than those upstairs. All have four-posters and baths with modern plumbing and fixtures.

A tap on the door in the morning signals the arrival of a demitasse of coffee, accompanied by a flower. A serious breakfast is later served in the formal dining room, which, like the rest of the house (including guest rooms), is furnished with antebellum Louisiana pieces that might have been in the house when General Andrew Jackson called on the original owners after the 1815 Battle of New Orleans.

The plantation has been in the Brown family since 1951; Harvey and Mary Brown, the present owners, moved to St. Francisville from Miami to take charge in 1984. One of Mary's hobbies is apparent when you see the flower gardens that decorate the grounds near the main building.

▥ *5 double rooms with baths. Restaurant, air-conditioning, TVs; pool. $90, full breakfast. MC, V. Restricted smoking, no pets. Closed Dec. 24–25.*

Madewood Plantation

4250 Rte. 308, Napoleonville, LA 70390, tel. 504/369-7151 or 800/375-7151, fax 504/369-9848

In a lush country setting about equidistant from New Orleans and Baton Rouge, this handsome 21-room Greek Revival mansion offers a nostalgic glimpse of 19th-century life. Built in 1846 for Colonel Thomas Pugh, the house had fallen into a terrible state of disrepair when, in 1964, it was bought and restored by the Harold K. Marshall family of New Orleans. It is now owned by the Marshalls' son Keith and his wife, Millie, who will tell you, laughing, that the mansion became a bed-and-breakfast as the result of an exorbitant electric bill. Keith had just seen the bill when the phone rang and a caller asked if Madewood accepted paying guests. "Yes!" he replied. The Marshalls sometimes spend weekends at Madewood, but the resident managers are Janet Ledet and Dave D'Aunoy, who preside at the informal wine-and-cheese gatherings and candlelit southern dinners served to guests in the main mansion. Thelma Parker, the cook and housekeeper, who's been at Madewood for 25 years, makes a mean pumpkin casserole that's almost always served.

Madewood has spacious rooms with high ceilings, hardwood floors, handsome carved moldings, Oriental rugs, and sparkling crystal chandeliers. In addition to 18th- and 19th-century Louisiana antiques in the mansion and in Charlet House, there are English antiques collected by Keith when he was a Rhodes scholar.

There are four bedrooms upstairs and one downstairs; the latter has a handsome half-tester bed. Though all baths are private, those for the two back bedrooms upstairs can only be reached through the hall. Originally dressing rooms, these baths are much more spacious than those that were squeezed in when indoor plumbing became all the rage. The master bedroom, upstairs, has a large canopied four-poster; across the hall is a guest room decorated with antique children's toys. In addition, there are three suites in Charlet House, one of five outbuildings on the property. Its Honeymoon Suite has a working fireplace and a large screened porch. The house has served as a set for films, among them *A Woman Called Moses*, starring Cicely Tyson.

🏨 *5 double rooms with baths, 3 suites. Air-conditioning, turndown service, free tour of house and grounds. $175, MAP. AE, D, MC, V. Restricted smoking, no pets. Closed Thanksgiving Eve and Day, Dec. 24–25, Dec. 31–Jan. 1; rooms must be vacated for tours 10 AM– 5 PM in the main mansion and noon–3 PM in Charlet House.*

Other Choices

Garden Gate Manor. 204 Poydras St., New Roads, LA 70760, tel. 504/638–3890 or 800/487–3890, fax 504/638–4597. 4 double rooms with baths, 1 suite. Air-conditioning, cable TV in parlor, cable TV/VCR in suite. $80–$130; full breakfast, afternoon tea. AE, MC, V. No smoking, no pets, check-in between 3 and 6.

Green Springs Plantation. 7463 Tunica Trace, St. Francisville, LA 70775, tel. 504/635–4232 or 800/457–4978, fax 504/635–3355. 3 double rooms with baths. Air-conditioning; nature trails. $90, full breakfast. MC, V. Restricted smoking, no pets.

Nottoway. Rte. 1 (Box 160), White Castle, LA 70788, tel. 504/545–2730 or 504/346–8263 in Baton Rouge, fax 504/545–8632. 10 double rooms with baths, 3 suites. Restaurant, air-conditioning, phones in 11 rooms, free home tour; pool. $125–$250; wake-up Continental breakfast in rooms and full breakfast, sherry at check-in. AE, D, MC, V. Smoking on verandas only, no pets. Closed Dec. 24–25, Randolph Suite and Master Bedroom must be vacated for tours 9–5.

Tezcuco Plantation. 3138 Rte. 44, Darrow, LA 70725, tel. 504/562–3929, fax 504/562–3923. 1 suite in mansion, 16 cottages. Restaurant, air-conditioning, TV, clock radio, kitchen, tea- and coffeemakers in cottages, antiques-gift shop, Civil War museum. $60–$160; full breakfast, welcome glass of wine. AE, D, MC, V. No smoking in main mansion. Closed Thanksgiving Day, Dec. 25, and Jan. 1.

Reservations Services

Bed & Breakfast Reservations Services Worldwide, Inc. (Box 14841, Baton Rouge, LA 70898–4841, tel. 504/336–4035, fax 504/343–0672), a trade association, has international listings of B&B reservation services. **Bed & Breakfast Travel** (8211 Goodwood Blvd., Suite F, Baton Rouge, LA 70806, tel. 504/923–2337 or 800/926–4320, fax 504/926–4320) has B&B listings for Louisiana and parts of Alabama, Mississippi, and east Texas.

Cajun Country

A la Bonne Veillée

J. Alcee Road, off Rte. 339 (LeBlanc House, Rte. 2, Box 2270), Abbeville, LA 70510, tel. 318/937–5495

Off a country road between Lafayette and Abbeville stands A la Bonne Veillée, a two-story Acadian cottage. Moss-draped live oaks shade it, and ducks waddle about a nearby pond. Their quacking and the songs of birds are about the only sounds that can be heard.

Made of hand-cut cypress timbers, the house has a steeply pitched wood-shingled roof through which pokes a chimney made of old brick. Wood for the two fireplaces is stacked neatly on the front porch, where there are rocking chairs. American Empire antiques and plenty of books grace the parlor; adjacent is a master bedroom with a huge tiger-maple Sheraton canopy bed and scatter rugs on the cypress floors. The other downstairs rooms are a full kitchen and the only bath (it's almost as big as the bedroom). Steep, unfriendly stairs lead to an attic room with a brass bed, patchwork quilts, a trundle bed, and other pieces "from grandmother's attic," says owner Carolyn Doerle.

Carolyn and her husband, Ron Ray, who live in the historic LeBlanc House a stone's throw away, saved the cottage from demolition and had it moved to their 30-acre farm. Ron, a psychotherapist, also raises cattle. Carolyn is CEO of Doerle Food Services, her family's wholesale food concern. The two love restoring old houses, and the cottage was special. More than 100 years ago it was a *maison dimanche* (Sunday house)—it was customary for prosperous rural plantation owners to keep a town house to use on weekends.

The cottage is rented to singles, families, or to two couples traveling together. Breakfast is brought in, and there is an intercom to the main house, which guests may tour; apart from that, they have absolute peace and privacy. (Those who want to pick up the pace can drive to the Cajun dance halls in Lafayette, about 15 minutes away.)

The unusual name of the guest house derives from a Cajun phrase, "Let's go *veiller*." It means to make long evening visits after supper, chatting, gossiping, and telling stories.

▦ *1 cottage. Air-conditioning, TV, phone. $85–$140, Continental breakfast. No credit cards. No smoking, no pets.*

Camellia Cove

211 W. Hill St., Washington, LA 70589, tel. 318/826–7362

Herman and Annie Bidstrup's 1825 home, listed on the National Register of Historic Places, sits on 2 acres on a peaceful residential street in the little town of Washington. The large, white, two-story house has double porches and lacy Victorian trim. Rocking chairs on the upstairs porch are great for relaxing and enjoying the peace and quiet. On the broad side lawn, the scent of clover in the springtime is delicious.

The Bidstrups bought the house in 1982, spent a year and a half restoring it, and in 1986 moved into it. After living in Scotland and England, where they enjoyed staying in B&Bs, they decided to run one themselves. The two have traveled extensively, and the house is filled with mementos and artifacts, such as the African tribal masks that adorn the kitchen wall.

Camellia Cove has a wealth of wonderful memorabilia, in addition to its Louisiana antique furnishings. At the turn of the century, this was the home of Dr. Herbert Kilpatrick. His desk in the parlor remains much as it was when he lived in the house, and displayed on it is his license to dispense opium. In the central hallway, Herman's grandfather's handwritten marriage license, dated 1887, is pressed between the pages of the Bidstrup family Bible. (Herman is of Danish-German ancestry; Annie is French Acadian.)

Three of the upstairs rooms—all of them exceptionally large—are rented to overnight guests. A front room, just off the porch, has Victorian furnishings: a wood-carved bed, washstand, armoire, and dressing table. Its bath, almost as large as the bedroom, has a claw-foot tub with spray shower as well as a marble-topped dresser with a big mirror under a row of makeup lights. (Incidentally, part of the fun here is finding amenities, such as manicure scissors nestled in little porcelain potpourri-filled pots.) One of the guest rooms has two beds; its bath is across the hall. The third guest room does share that bath, but Annie only rents these two rooms to families or people traveling together.

Breakfast is served in the formal dining room. It always includes heaps of homemade biscuits and fig preserves.

🏨 *1 double room with bath, 2 doubles share 1 bath. Air-conditioning. $65–$75, full breakfast. No credit cards. Restricted smoking, no pets. Closed Jan. 1, Thanksgiving, and Dec. 25.*

Chrétien Point Plantation

665 Chrétien Point Rd., Sunset, LA 70584, tel. 318/233–7050 or 800/880–7050, fax 318/662–5876

In the early 1930s, a local photographer took pictures of this house and sent them to Hollywood. As a result, the stairway and the window above it were used as a model for those in Scarlett O'Hara's Tara. Then, too, there's the tale of the long-ago lady of Chrétien Point who shot a man on the steps, as Scarlett shot the Union soldier. Owners Jeanne and Louis Cornay will point out the very step on which the man was standing when he was killed.

Of solid brick construction, with six round white columns and double galleries across the front, the two-story house was built in 1831 for Hypolite Chrétien II and his wife, Félicité. During the Civil War, the house figured in a major battle. There is still a bullet hole in one of the front doors. The last Chrétiens lost the house a few years after the war, and it began to fall into a sorry state.

Louis found the deteriorated mansion while looking for a barn in which to keep his son's horse. Hay was stored in it; chickens, cows, and pigs roamed through it. The Cornays bought the house and restored it to its former grandeur.

The colors used in the house are those of nature's sunsets. Silk wall coverings are in vivid scarlets and pinks; one of the ceilings is painted a cool blue. There are six working fireplaces with imported French Empire marble mantels. The 19th-century Louisiana antiques include a carved armoire and four-poster by Mallard.

Three rooms have full-tester beds, one with a pale gold sunburst canopy and the others with canopy and spread in rich fabrics and bold colors. A downstairs room, formerly the wine cellar, has redbrick floors, blue velvet chairs, a New Orleans armoire, and a hand-carved bed. The bins that once held wine are now filled with books.

The only guest room with an adjoining bath is the master bedroom upstairs. Most other rooms have private hall baths.

There is no restaurant, but Louis says that in bad weather they'll rustle up something for hungry guests.

🏨 *3 double rooms with baths, 2 doubles share 1 bath. Air-conditioning, meeting room; pool, tennis court. $110–$200, full breakfast. AE, MC, V. Restricted smoking, no pets.*

Other Choices

Bois des Chênes. 338 N. Sterling St., Lafayette, LA 70501, tel. and fax 318/233–7816. 5 suites. Air-conditioning, cable TV, and mini-refrigerators in suites, wood-burning fireplace in 1 suite; fenced yard and kennel for small pets. $85–$175; full breakfast, wine. AE, MC, V. Restricted smoking. Closed Dec. 24–25.

Elter House Inn. 603 S. Main St., Washington, LA 70589, tel. 318/826–7362. 3 double rooms with baths. Air-conditioning, kitchen, washer/dryer. $70–$80, Continental breakfast. MC, V. No smoking, no pets.

Old Castillo Hotel/Place d'Evangeline. 220 Evangeline Blvd., St. Martinville, LA 70582, tel. 318/394–4010 or 800/621–3017, fax 318/394–7983. 5 double rooms with baths. Restaurant, air-conditioning. $50–$80, full breakfast. AE, MC, V. No smoking, no pets.

Seale Guest House. 123 Seale La. (Box 568), Eunice, LA 70535, tel. 318/457–3753. 5 double rooms with baths, 4 doubles share 2 baths, 5 suites. Air-conditioning, ceiling fans, clock radios; guest kitchen, TV in main house's common living area; access for people who use wheelchairs, camper hook-ups. $65–$150, Continental breakfast. MC, V. No smoking, no pets, 2-night minimum for Mardi Gras.

T' Frère's House. 1905 Verot School Rd., Lafayette, LA 70508, tel. and fax 318/984–9347 or or 800/984–9347. 4 double rooms with baths. Air-conditioning, cable TV, coffeemaker, alarm clock, and terry-cloth robes in rooms, fireplace in 1 room, parlor, and kitchen. $75–$90; full breakfast, afternoon cocktails. D, MC, V. Restricted smoking. Closed Thanksgiving week and Christmas week.

Reservations Services

Bed & Breakfast Reservations Services Worldwide, Inc. (Box 14841, Baton Rouge, LA 70898–4841, tel. 504/336–4035, fax 504/343–0672), a trade association, has international listings of B&B reservation services. **Bed & Breakfast Travel** (8211 Goodwood Blvd., Suite F, Baton Rouge, LA 70806, tel. 504/923–2337 or 800/926–4320, fax 504/926–4320) has B&B listings for Louisiana and parts of Alabama, Mississippi, and east Texas.

North-Central Louisiana

Cloutier Townhouse

8 Ducournau Sq., Natchitoches, LA 71457, tel. 318/352–5242, fax 318/352–0541

Adorned with filigreed cast-iron galleries that were assembled in France, the Cloutier (pronounced "*cloo*-chee") Townhouse sits smack in Natchitoches's historic district. Conna Cloutier's elegant home is one of the only bed-and-breakfasts that offer an unobstructed view of Front Street and Cane River Lake. This is the center of the town's famed Christmas Festival of Lights, when the trees, buildings, and bridges are ablaze. Conna opens her home for group tours (by appointment) during the month of December.

The town house occupies the top two floors of a three-story building that dates from the 1830s. In the European style, the first floor is a commercial establishment—in this case, the Open Hearth Deli & Pub. A carriageway leads from Front Street to a courtyard paved with old brick. From there, behind an iron gate, steps lead to the broad rear porches, where there are tables and rocking chairs. At both the front and back, French doors open onto the galleries.

In the large open area that contains the foyer, living room, and dining room, polished hardwood floors are covered with Oriental rugs and paneled walls reach to a 30-foot ceiling. A central staircase winds to the part of the third floor where Conna lives. Most of the furnishings are of the American Empire period. An Empire sideboard and a gold-leaf mirror supported by rosewood piano legs on a marble base were made for an early plantation nearby. Bookcases are filled with books, and the walls are hung with oil paintings, one a portrait of the wife of a 19th-century owner of the property.

The front guest room, which has a four-poster bed and other Louisiana antiques, opens onto the gallery and is somewhat noisy; its bath is private, but you have to go out into the hall to reach it. The master bedroom, which opens onto the foyer and the rear gallery, is both larger and quieter. Its focal points are a full-tester bed with an embroidered spread and old brick walls. Wing chairs and an upholstered settee (with good reading lamps) are tempting places to curl up and read the many books that lie about. Twin dressing areas, each with a spacious marble vanity and ample wall mirrors, are outside a large carpeted bath, which has a platformed whirlpool and a wood-paneled lighted shower stall.

▦ *2 double rooms with baths. Air-conditioning, cable TV in 1 room, 2 fireplaces in public rooms. $65–$90, full breakfast. M, V. No smoking indoors, no pets.*

Loyd Hall

292 Loyd Bridge Rd., Cheneyville (5119 Masonic Dr., Alexandria, LA 71301), tel. 318/776–5641 or 800/240–8135, fax 318/776–5886

Loyd Hall is a 640-acre working plantation that grows cotton, corn, and soybeans. Frank Fitzgerald's father bought the land in 1949, unaware that a deteriorated 19th-century mansion was buried beneath a tangle of trees and bushes. Frank and his wife, Anne, now live in the restored house. Frank is a veterinarian, and in addition to chickens, cattle, horses, and other farm critters, a small army of cats and dogs calls Loyd Hall home. A Catahoula hog dog, with one blue eye and one brown eye (a distinguishing feature of the breed), and a pudgy English bulldog make it a point to befriend guests.

Guests have a choice of four accommodations. The first B&B on the property—a replica of a rustic 19th-century Acadian cottage—has a sloping shingle roof, a front porch with rocking chairs, two bedrooms with four-posters and plump comforters, a washer and dryer, and a bath with claw-foot tub and shower and plenty of vanity space. A sleeper sofa in the parlor enables the cottage to sleep six; however, because of its small size, it's rented only to a family or to others who know each other well.

The ancient separate kitchen behind the mansion was transformed into an elegant Cinderella that houses the Camellia Suite and the Magnolia Suite, with a full-tester and a half-tester, respectively, brick floors, and wing chairs cozied up to an open fireplace. The suite in the restored 1800s Commissary has a four-poster and a back porch with a splendid view of rolling pasturelands.

All are furnished with 19th-century Louisianiana; three of the four have wood-burning fireplaces. Each has a kitchen with modern appliances, including dishwasher, toaster, and coffeemaker. Kitchens are stocked with a chilled decanter of wine, homemade muffins, milk, juice, and all the ingredients for a bacon-and-eggs breakfast, which guests prepare at their leisure and enjoy in privacy, wrapped in the cushy terry-cloth robes provided.

The plantation is in a quiet country setting, 16 miles south of Alexandria near the intersection of U.S. 167 and 71.

▦ *1 cottage, 3 suites. Air-conditioning, TV/VCR in cottage and suites, washer/dryer in cottage; pool, bicycles, fishing rods. $95–$125; full breakfast, wine. AE, MC, V. No smoking, no pets.*

Other Choices

Beau Fort Plantation. Rte. 494, Bermuda, LA (Box 2300, Natchitoches, LA 71457), tel. 318/352–5340 or 318/

352–9580. 3 suites. Air-conditioning, satellite TV in master suite, phone in 2 suites. $80, full breakfast. No smoking, no pets.

Fleur-de-Lis. 336 2nd St., Natchitoches, LA 71457, tel. 318/352–6621 or 800/489–6621. 5 double rooms with baths. Air-conditioning, cable TV/VCR in family room; wheelchair ramp. $60–$80, full breakfast. AE, MC, V. No smoking, no pets, 2-night minimum during Christmas Festival.

Hardy House. 1414 Weems St., Lecompte, LA 71437, tel. 318/776–5178 or 318/776–5896. 2 double rooms with baths, 2 suites. Air-conditioning, woodburning fireplace in kitchen, washer/dryer for guests; fishing poles, bikes. $85–$110, full breakfast. MC, V. No smoking, no pets.

Jefferson House. 229 Jefferson St., Natchitoches, LA 71457, tel. 318/352–3957 or 318/352–5756. 1 double room with bath, 2 double rooms with shared bath (available as a suite). Air-conditioning, cable TV in living room. $65–$100; full breakfast, afternoon cocktails. MC, V. Restricted smoking, no pets.

Levy-East House. 358 Jefferson St., Natchitoches, LA 71457, tel. 318/352–0662 or 800/840–0662. 2 double rooms with whirlpool baths. Air-conditioning, coffeemakers, cable TV/VCRs, phones, terry-cloth robes, turndown service with candy. $85–$150; full breakfast, sherry, complimentary champagne for guests celebrating their honeymoon or anniversary. MC, V. No smoking, no pets, no children, 2-night minimum for Christmas Festival. Closed Christmas week.

Tante Huppé House. 424 Jefferson St., Natchitoches, LA 71457, tel. 318/352–5342 or 800/482–4276. 3 suites. Air-conditioning, kitchen, coffeemaker, phone with 2 private lines, 2 cable TVs in each suite. $80, full breakfast. AE, MC, V. No smoking, no pets.

Reservations Services

Bed & Breakfast Reservations Services Worldwide, Inc. (Box 14841, Baton Rouge, LA 70898–4841, tel. 504/336–4035, fax 504/343–0672), a trade association, has international listings of B&B reservation services. **Bed & Breakfast Travel** (8211 Goodwood Blvd., Suite F, Baton Rouge, LA 70806, tel. 504/923–2337 or 800/926–4320, fax 504/926–4320) has B&B listings for Louisiana and parts of Alabama, Mississippi, and east Texas.

Maine

Cleftstone Manor

Southern Coast: Kittery to Portland

Captain Jefferds Inn

Pearl St., Box 691, Kennebunkport, ME 04046, tel. 207/967–2311

If you have a taste for the exquisite, and if your idea of beauty is heaps of precious, delicately crafted objects, then this is the inn of your dreams. (Those who find this style fussy and cluttered would be happier at the more stately and formal Captain Lord Mansion across the street.) Innkeeper Warren Fitzsimmons is an avid collector and antiquarian who once owned antiques shops in the posh Long Island resort of Southampton. He has put his passion to work in renovating and decorating the 1804 Captain Jefferds Inn and its carriage house. The white-clapboard black-shuttered sea captain's home, with its collections of majolica, American art pottery, and Sienese pottery, is clearly a labor of love, the realization of Fitzsimmons's dream of "serving people in gracious settings."

Public rooms include the exuberantly colorful parlor, where the extensive majolica collection resides, and the solarium, furnished with Art Deco rattan and copies of Della Robbia reliefs. Breakfast, served beneath the formal dining room's Venetian glass chandelier, or outdoors in fine weather, is as fancy as the decor, with frittatas, eggs Benedict, and blueberry crepes commonly on the menu.

Most of the rooms are done in Laura Ashley fabrics and wallpapers, with the addition of prize antiques: English curly maple chests, marble-top chests, old books (in all, the inn houses 10,000 volumes), and oil paintings and watercolors that would not look out of place in the Portland art museum. Among the bigger and better rooms are No. 2, with an English pine armoire and a second-floor corner location, and No. 12, which has its own little balcony, wicker furniture, and an airy, contemporary feel. No. 8 at the top of the house gives you lots of room, privacy, quiet, and a taste of the old-fashioned Maine look, with rag rugs and chenille bedspreads.

🏠 *12 double rooms with baths, 4 carriage-house suites. Cable TV in solarium, huge record library, croquet. $85–$165, full breakfast. MC, V. No smoking, no pets, 2-day minimum July–Oct. Closed early Dec.–Mar.*

Captain Lord Mansion

Box 800, Kennebunkport, ME 04046, tel. 207/967–3141

Of the mansions in Kennebunkport's Historic District that have been tastefully converted to inns, the 1812 vintage Captain Lord Mansion is hands down the most stately and sumptuously appointed. The three-story pale yellow house sits in the middle of a manicured lawn across the street from the Captain Jefferds Inn, from which it differs considerably in decor. While the Captain Jefferds hums, even riots, with color and clutter, the Captain Lord keeps an air of formal—but never stiff—propriety, seen to best advantage in the refined Gathering Room, which looks like a period room (Chippendale) in a museum, except for the guests lounging before the hearth.

Innkeepers Bev Davis and Rick Litchfield, former advertising executives in search of a career change, are far more laid-back in style than the house they meticulously restored. They chat and joke with guests over family-style breakfasts served informally at the two harvest tables in the cheery country kitchen. Bev and Rick rescued the Captain Lord Mansion from its Victorian gloom and refurbished it with crisp, authentic Federal decor.

Guest rooms, which are named after old clipper ships, are large and stately, though the formality relaxes as one ascends the elliptical staircase. The soberly elegant Brig Merchant, a desirable corner room on the ground floor, has a bed with a fishnet canopy, dark mahogany period furniture, and a maroon rug. Ship Lincoln, to many minds the finest room in the house, with a step-up four-poster bed and damask-covered walls, is also the room in which the inn's benign resident ghost appears (only women have ever seen her). Bark Hesper, on the third floor, is a whimsical, country-style room, quainter and smaller than the downstairs

rooms, with green dot-and-flower wallpaper and leafy views out the windows.

Bev and Rick have succeeded admirably in creating a pleasing base from which to venture forth on forays to Kennebunkport's architectural treasures, the shops of Dock Square, or the sand beaches lining the chill Atlantic.

▥ *16 double rooms with baths. 14 rooms with fireplaces and phones, gift shop, TV room. $149–$219, full breakfast and afternoon tea. D, MC, V. No smoking, no pets, 2-night minimum on weekends, 3-night minimum on holiday weekends.*

Dockside Guest Quarters

Box 205, York, ME 03909, tel. 207/363–2868

With the water views, seclusion, and quiet of its private 8-acre island in the middle of York Harbor, the Dockside has the best location of any small hotel in the Yorks. The Maine House, the oldest building on the site, is a classic New England turn-of-the-century clapboard house, kept in impeccable condition and set off with wide lawns and gardens. The four modern multiunit cottages tucked away behind lush trees have less character, but they feature slidingglass doors on the water and private decks; many come with kitchenettes.

David and Harriette Lusty have owned the place since 1953, and they have filled it with their personal warmth; colorful conversation; and their collection of nautical charts, ship models, and pictures. David, who has a background in the Navy, loves to sail, to take guests out on harbor tours, and to arrange charter-boat trips out to the Isles of Shoals. The Lustys' sons have since come aboard. Eric, a licensed merchant marine officer, keeps the tradition going as assistant manager.

Rooms in the Maine House are furnished with Early American antiques, some with white wicker and painted floors, and the ever-present marine motif. The effect is rather simple, spare, and airy. Cottage units are a logical choice for families and for those who insist on being right on the water. The inn's wraparound porch catches the ocean breeze, and a grandfather clock ticks sedately in the snug sitting room overlooking the ocean.

Loyal guests tend to settle in at the Dockside and stay put, spending their days strolling around Harris Island and down the dock, observing the parade of yachts on the harbor, and reading and lounging in the garden. You can walk to York's historic district, and the Kittery outlet shops beckon just a few miles to the south. The dining room, open to the public for dinner, is one of the finest in the area.

🏠 *3 double rooms in the Maine House and 10 cottage doubles, all with baths, 2 doubles share 1 bath, 7 apartment suites. Restaurant, TV in most rooms, private dock, motorboat and canoes, croquet, badminton, shuffleboard, horseshoes, fishing. $60–$150, breakfast extra. MC, V. No pets. Nov. 1– Memorial Day open Fri. and Sat. only; 2-night minimum July–Sept; 3-night minimum holiday weekends.*

Old Fort Inn

Box M, Kennebunkport, ME 04046, tel. 207/967–5353 or 800/828–3678, fax 207/967–4547

This inn at the crest of a hill on a quiet road off Ocean Avenue has a secluded, countryish feel and the welcome sense of being just a touch above the Kennebunkport action. Not that there is anything snooty about the Old Fort Inn. Innkeepers Sheila and David Aldrich, refugees from California, had jobs with an airline and in an antiques shop (she) and with an oil company (he). They have brought relaxed hospitality and clever interior design ideas to their new occupation, and Sheila's love of antiques shows up everywhere.

The front half of the former barn is now an antiques shop (specializing in Early American pieces); the rest of the barn is the reception area and a large parlor decorated with grandfather clocks, antique tools, and funny old canes. Here the Aldriches serve their guests a breakfast of homemade croissants and breads, granola, yogurt, and melon and berries.

To get to the guest rooms, you cross a lawn, skirt the bright flower beds that set off the ample pool (a rarity at an inn), and enter the long, low fieldstone and stucco carriage house that has been artfully converted to lodgings. Guest rooms vary in size and their decor reflects the Aldriches' witty and creative way with design and antiques: There are quilts on the four-poster beds; wreaths, primitive portraits, and framed antique bodices hang on the walls; the love seats are richly upholstered, some with blue-and-white ticking. Some rooms have hand stenciling, and several of the beds have fishnet canopies. Nos. 2 and 12 have choice corner locations.

During the day, when inn guests scatter to bike on Kennebunkport's shaded lanes, bask on the beaches, or drive up the coast to shop at L. L. Bean, the Old Fort's pool is an oasis of blissful solitude.

David remembers saying to himself, the first time he drove over the drawbridge into Kennebunkport, "This is where I want to be." More than a decade later, the enthusiasm that the Aldriches bring to living in Kennebunkport and running the Old Fort Inn is as apparent as ever.

🏠 *14 double rooms with baths, 2 suites. Air-conditioning, phones, cable TV, wet bars, whirlpool baths in some rooms and suites, laundry facilities, pool, 1 tennis court. $130–$260; buffet breakfast, cookies and candies in rooms. AE, D, MC, V. No smoking, no pets, 2-night minimum July–Labor Day and weekends year-round, 3-night minimum on holiday weekends. Closed mid-Dec.–mid-Apr.*

Other Choices

Bufflehead Cove. Box 499, Kennebunkport, ME 04046, tel. 207/967–3879. 3 double rooms with baths, 3 suites. Fireplaces in 4 rooms, robes, private dock for views and bird-watching. $85–$210, full breakfast and evening wine and cheese. D, MC, V. No smoking, no pets, 2-night minimum on weekends June–Oct. Closed weekends Jan.–Mar.

Green Heron. Box 2578, Kennebunkport, ME 04046, tel. 207/967–3315. 10 double rooms with baths, cottage sleeps 4. Air-conditioning, TVs, common TV/VCR. $85–$135, full breakfast. No credit cards. No pets on 2nd floor. Closed Jan.

Inn at Harbor Head. 41 Pier Rd., Kennebunkport, ME 04046, tel. 207/967–5564, fax 207/967–1294. 3 double rooms with baths, 2 suites. Fresh flowers in rooms, private dock, beach passes and towels, robes. $105–$250, full breakfast and afternoon refreshments. MC, V. No smoking, no pets, 2-night minimum.

Maine Stay Inn and Cottages. 34 Maine St., Box 500A, Kennebunkport, ME 04046, tel. 207/967–2117 or 800/950–2117, fax 207/967–8757. 4 double rooms with baths, 2 suites, 11 cottages. 5 cottages and 1 suite have fireplaces, cable TV and clock-radios in rooms, guest courtesy phone; jungle gym, croquet. $135–$215, full breakfast and afternoon tea. AE, MC, V. No smoking, no pets, 2-night minimum on weekends.

Pomegranate Inn. 49 Neal St., Portland, ME 04102, tel. 207/772–1006 or 800/356–0408, fax 207/773–4426. 6 double rooms with baths in main house; 1 double room with bath, 1 suite in carriage house. Air-conditioning, cable TVs, phones, fireplaces in some rooms. $105–$165, full breakfast. AE, D, MC, V. No smoking, no pets, 2-night minimum on weekends during busy season and on holidays.

White Barn Inn. Box 560 C, 37 Beach St., Kennebunkport, ME 04046, tel. 207/967–2321, fax 207/967–1100. 13 double rooms with baths in main inn, 4 double rooms in "gatehouse" cottages, 6 suites in carriage house, 1 cottage. Restaurant, lounge with piano bar, air-conditioning, fireplaces, cable TV, phones, fresh fruit, flowers, whirlpool baths in some rooms. $140–$350, Continental breakfast and afternoon tea. AE, MC, V. No smoking, 2-night minimum on weekends, 3-night minimum on holidays.

York Harbor Inn. Box 573, York Harbor, ME 03911, tel. 800/343–3869, fax 207/363–3545, ext. 295. 33 double rooms with baths, 4 suites. Restaurant, pub, air-conditioning, 3 no-smoking rooms, 6 rooms with whirlpool tubs, 3 fireplaces in carriage house, gift shop in lobby. $89–$195, Continental breakfast. AE, DC, MC, V. No pets.

Reservations Services

B&B Down East, Ltd. (Box 547, Macomber Mill Rd., Eastbrook, ME 04634, tel. 207/565–3517, fax 207/565–2076). **Peg Tierney B&B of Maine** (16 Florence St., Portland, ME 04103, tel. 207/775–7808).

Mid-Coast: Freeport to Port Clyde

East Wind Inn & Meeting House

Box 149, Tenants Harbor, ME 04860, tel. 207/372–6366, fax 207/372–6320

If you've read *The Country of the Pointed Firs,* Sarah Orne Jewett's charming sketches of coastal Maine, you may have an eerie sense of déjà vu as you drive the 10 miles down Route 131 into Tenants Harbor. The neat little white clapboard houses set in tangles of tall grass and beach roses, the narrow harbor from which the nearly black evergreens rise like sawteeth, the distant glimpse of islands and open water: All this is pretty much unchanged since Jewett wrote here at the turn of the century.

In the course of its 130 years set on a little knob of land overlooking the harbor and islands, the three-story white clapboard East Wind Inn has served as a sail loft and mason's hall. Today it's hard to imagine it as anything other than the perfect rustic inn, complete with wraparound porch. Innkeeper Tim Watts gave up his work as an accountant to buy the East Wind in 1974, and in his yearlong renovation, he was careful to leave its innocence and simplicity very much intact.

Guests lodge either in the inn or the Meeting House, a converted ship captain's house, just up the hill. The inn is a bit closer to the water, and its front rooms command a view of sunrise over the islands. The bedrooms are furnished with a hodgepodge of simple Early American–style brass bedsteads and pine chests; oak and mahogany furnishings give the rooms of the Meeting House more of a Victorian air. All the rooms are appealingly plain, as is the inn's living room, with its baby grand piano, nautical charts, and comfortable, well-worn sofas.

From the East Wind, you can drive (or bike) to Port Clyde for a picnic at the Marshall Point lighthouse or a day trip to Monhegan, or head up to Rockland for an afternoon with the Wyeths at the Farnsworth art museum.

▦ *Inn: 1 double room with bath, 14 doubles share 4 baths, 1 suite; Meeting House: 8 double rooms with baths, 2 suites, 1 apartment. Restaurant; phones; TV in suites, apartment, and living room; conference room; sailing seminars based at the premises. $78–$150, Continental breakfast. AE, D, MC, V. No smoking in dining room.*

Newcastle Inn

River Rd., Newcastle, ME 04553, tel. 207/563–5685 or 800/832–8669, fax 207/563–6877

This small, mid-19th-century white clapboard house has been transformed into one of Maine's friendliest, most impeccably run inns. Rebecca and Howard Levitan seem always to be around when you need to chat, get directions, or ask advice about sightseeing, yet they vanish discreetly when you prefer solitude. Rebecca comes from Maine and has a background in sales and marketing; Howard was a lawyer for 25 years.

Guest rooms, though not large, are decorated carefully with old spool beds, toys, and sofas; the effect is of minimum clutter and maximum light and river views. Room 6, located on the second floor in the back of the house, has a generous river view and a gas fireplace. In Room 17, you can relax in a two-person whirlpool bath or the king-size bed while watching a fire in the marble gas fireplace or gazing out at the river and garden beyond. Guests gather in the pub, which opens into the formal living room, with fireplace, overlooking the river.

The Levitans go all out for breakfast (a full meal that might include Santa Fe french toast, lobster crepes, eggs Benedict, or a frittata), and the five-course prix-fixe dinner (open to the public by reservation) makes a stay rewarding even if it rains the whole time.

Newcastle is a town with more charm than action; but the inn, set just off a picturesque winding road on a lawn that slopes down to the Damariscotta River, makes a convenient base for forays to Boothbay Harbor or Pemaquid Point, or a quiet afternoon of canoeing on the river. In the summer months, the inn's sunporch, with white wicker furniture and ice-cream-parlor chairs, makes a particularly appealing spot to contemplate the Damariscotta River and congratulate yourself for having found such a special place.

🏠 *15 double rooms with baths, 4 with gas fireplaces. Restaurant, pub, whirlpool bath. $95–$175, full breakfast; MAP rates available. MC, V. No smoking, no pets, 2-night minimum peak holiday weekends.*

Squire Tarbox Inn

Rte. 144 (R.R. 2, Box 620), Wiscasset, ME 04578, tel. 207/882–7693

As you drive the 8½ miles from Route 1, down Route 144, onto Westport Island, you may wonder if you made a wrong turn, for the signs of civilization peter out into lush rolling hills, woods, and a sprinkling of farmhouses. Then the reassuring champagne-yellow clapboard front of the Squire Tarbox looms into view, and you know just where you are: deep in the country at one of Maine's most serene inns.

"This is a really nourishing place," says innkeeper Karen Mitman with a soft smile, as she sits in a rocking chair, next to the fireplace, beside the grandfather clock. "People come here to reflect, to walk in the woods, to look at the birds." They also come to watch Karen and her husband, Bill, milk their goats and to sample their delicious goat cheese, served each night. For the Squire Tarbox is not only an inn, and on the National Register of Historic Places, but is also a working farm, with a small herd of 16 goats, a horse, laying hens, and a few donkeys. "We are goat missionaries who rent rooms," Karen says.

Karen and Bill had hotel experience in Boston, but none as goat farmers, when they bought the inn in 1981. Yet somehow they seem to have been in the rambling Federal house forever. Some of it dates from 1763 and some from 1820, and among the downstairs public rooms are a rustic dining room, where dinner is served beneath old ships' beams, and a music room with a player piano.

Of the bedrooms, No. 1 in the main part of the house is choice—a huge room with king-size bed, braided rugs on pumpkin-pine floors, and an antique footlocker. The attached barn has four rooms, more rustic in feel and smaller than the inn rooms, but also more private. No. 11 is the best for privacy, with gray-green woodwork, more space than the other barn rooms, and a view over the pasture.

When you tire of strolling around the property and bird-watching from the deck, ask the Mitmans to direct you to the shops of Wiscasset, the Maritime Museum at Bath, the lobster pier and scenic back roads of Five Islands (good for biking), and the beach at Reid State Park.

🏠 *11 double rooms with baths. Restaurant, fireplaces in 4 rooms, rowboat, farm animals. $85–$220; Continental breakfast, goat cheese in evening; MAP rates available. AE, D, MC, V. No smoking, no pets. Closed late Oct.–mid-May.*

Other Choices

Bradley Inn. Route 130, HC 61, Box 361 Pemaquid Point, New Harbor, ME 04554, tel. 207/677–2105, fax 207/677–3367. 12 double rooms with baths, 2 double rooms with bath and 1 suite in carriage house. Restaurant, pub, cable TV and phones in some rooms, croquet, bicycles, entertainment on weekends. $95–$200, Continental breakfast. AE, D, MC, V. Smoking permitted in pub only.

Briar Rose. Box 27, Rte. 32, Round Pond, ME 04564, tel. 207/529–5478. 2 double rooms with baths, 1 suite. Clock radios, antiques and country collectibles shop. $60–$110, full breakfast. No credit cards. No smoking, no pets.

Broad Bay Inn and Gallery. 1014 Main St., Waldoboro, ME 04572, tel. 207/832–6668 or 800/736–6769. 5 double rooms share 3 baths. Cable TV in common room, terry bathrobes. $45–

$75; full breakfast, tea, and sherry. MC, V. No smoking, no pets, 2-night minimum in Aug.

Fairhaven Inn. N. Bath Rd., Bath, ME 04530, tel. 207/443–4391. 8 double rooms with baths. Tavern, badminton, cross-country ski trail. $60–$100, full breakfast. MC, D, V. No smoking.

Flying Cloud. Box 549, River Rd., Newcastle, ME 04553, tel. 207/563–2484, fax 207/563–8640. 4 double rooms with baths, 1 suite. Guest library with TV/VCR. $65–$90, full breakfast. AE, D, MC, V. No smoking, no pets.

Marston House. Box 517, Wiscasset, ME 04578, tel. 207/882–6010 or 800/852–4137. 2 double rooms with baths. Terry-cloth robes in rooms. $75, Continental breakfast. AE, MC, V. No smoking, no pets. Closed Dec.–Apr.

Mill Pond Inn. 50 Main St., Nobleboro, ME 04555, tel. 207/563–8014. 6 double rooms with baths, 1 suite. Cable TV/VCR in game room, private beach, boats, canoes, bicycles, horseshoes, skating, swimming. $75, full breakfast. No credit cards. Restricted smoking, no pets.

181 Main Street. 181 Main St., Freeport, ME 04032, tel. 207/865–1226. 7 double rooms with baths. Cable TV in parlor, swimming pool. $85–$100, full breakfast. MC, V. No smoking, no pets.

Reservations Services

B&B Down East, Ltd. (Box 547, Macomber Mill Rd., Eastbrook, ME 04634, tel. 207/565–3517). **Peg Tierney B&B of Maine** (16 Florence St., Portland, ME 04103, tel. 207/775–7808). **Pineapple Hospitality** (Box F821, New Bedford, MA 02742, tel. 508/990–1696).

Penobscot Bay: Rockland to Blue Hill

Castine Inn

Main St., Box 41, Castine, ME 04421, tel. 207/326–4365, fax 207/326–4570

"We're the keepers of the flame," says Mark Hodesh of his role as innkeeper of the Castine Inn, a historic inn in a historic (and literary) seacoast town. The late Mary McCarthy, who summered up the street, used to drop in for dinner. The poet Philip Booth, McCarthy's next-door neighbor, told the Hodeshes that his grandfather stayed at the Castine Inn the night before he was married. Old Castine society wanted the inn to maintain the right style and tone—"Not high antique," as Mark puts it, "but comfortable, traditional Maine." He and his wife, the artist Margaret Parker, who come to Castine via Ann Arbor and New York City, have succeeded admirably.

The stately yellow-clapboard, 100-year-old inn mixes antiques, sturdily traditional new furniture, and paintings done by Margaret. The sitting room, in crimson velvet and old leather with well-worn Oriental rugs and books, is the kind of place in which you can let out a huge sigh and relax. Off the lobby there is a snug little pub, the perfect spot for an evening rendezvous.

Newer touches include Margaret's impressive mural of the town and harbor—which wraps around the spacious dining room—the big porch added to the east side of the inn, and the formal garden Margaret designed, with its arched bridge, roses, benches, gravel path, and arbor, where concerts are held in the summer.

Your rooms might have a dark-wood pineapple four-poster bed, white upholstered easy chairs, and oil paintings.

Spacious Room 1 on the second floor offers a glimpse of the harbor and has a superior corner location. The third-floor rooms are the biggest and command the finest views. From one side you see the harbor over the formal garden, from the other you overlook the town.

Castine is a perfect New England small town that invites you to linger, stroll along Main Street down to the harbor, or out along Perkins Street, past Federal, Greek Revival, and shingle-style houses to the lighthouse. The sea air and exercise will make the return to the Castine Inn and its hearty dinners all the more welcome.

🏨 *17 double rooms with baths, 3 suites. Restaurant, pub, sauna. $75–$125, full breakfast. MC, V. No smoking in dining room, no pets, 2-night minimum in July and Aug. Closed late Dec.–Apr.*

Eggemoggin Reach Bed and Breakfast

R.R. 1, Box 33A, Herrick Rd., Brooksville, ME 04617, tel. 207/359–5073, fax 207/359–5074

Approached by a long, wooded private drive, Eggemoggin Reach Bed and Breakfast stands on a wooded point with the waters of Eggemoggin Reach shimmering behind it. After summering in the area for years, Michael and Susie Canon built the house in 1988 as a family retreat, comfortably furnishing it with antiques, Oriental rugs, and simple decorative pieces, such as duck decoys and ginger jars. In 1993, they opened their home to guests. The house is built in the post-and-beam tradition of a Maine farmhouse, using an open plan so that every room overlooks the water. A large brick fireplace in the living room keeps the chill off on cool evenings and the smaller den, with woodstove, is an ideal retreat for a rainy afternoon.

Breakfast is served buffet-style in the living/dining room. It includes juices, muffins, and a hot entrée such as oven-baked apple pancakes, Charleston House French toast, or sour-cream breakfast cake. Most guests choose to take their breakfast outside on the large covered deck, part of which is screened in. The lovely view here, and from the upstairs guest rooms, is over the Reach to Little Deer Isle and out to Pumpkin Island lighthouse.

The Captain's Quarters room on the second floor is large, airy, and gets the early morning sun. It's attractively furnished with a braided rug, antiques, and a king-size bed. The Crew's Quarters suite, also on the second floor, has a queen-size bed and a den with a single bed. The third-floor Wheelhouse suite is the grandest in the house with a king-size bed. It's spacious and elegant in decor, with white-painted walls and off-white carpeting. The large, comfortable living room has a pull-out sofa bed and an extra single bed as well as a huge china cupboard.

There also are two one-room cottages, Port Watch and Starboard Watch, which face onto Deadman's Cove. Both have efficiency kitchens, woodstoves, bathrooms with cedar showers, and private screened porches overlooking the water. Each has a king-size bed and a small sitting area with a love seat, table, and chairs.

The Canons love to entertain, and if six or more guests desire, they often will arrange for a shorefront picnic, with lobster delivered right to the dock. There's plenty to explore nearby, including Deer Isle, Blue Hill, and Castine.

🏨 *1 double room with bath, 2 suites, 3 cottages. Fireplace and TV with VCR in living room, phone and woodstove in den, rowboat, canoe, dock, mooring. $134–$159, full breakfast. MC, V. No smoking, no pets, 2-night minimum on weekends June 15–Labor Day. Closed mid-Oct.–mid-May.*

Inn at Sunrise Point

Box 1344, Camden, ME, tel. 207/236-7716 or 800/237-8674

At Sunrise Point, just north of Camden in the town of Lincolnville Beach, travel writer Jerry Levitin found the perfect location to build his dream inn. The main inn and surrounding cottages are perched on the water's edge overlooking island-studded Penobscot Bay. The long driveway from Route 1 ensures privacy and quiet. Indeed, it's as if you discovered a romantic and remote location, yet it's only a few miles from downtown Camden. The Inn at Sunrise Point is the kind of place where, if you choose not to turn on the television, you can forget the rest of the world even exists.

Breakfast is served in the main house in the living room and adjoining glass conservatory, which both offer expansive water views. A fireplace in the living room keeps the chill off on inclement days. Afternoon refreshments are served outdoors on the porch, where guests can relax on white wicker furniture while listening to the waves crash, or, if the weather is poor, in the cherry-paneled library, in front of the stone fireplace. The library has an extensive selection of books and VCR tapes.

All rooms are named for and display works by Maine writers and artists, such as May Sarton and Winslow Homer. Each room has cable TV and VCR, a phone, and a working fireplace. The rooms are comfortably, although not fancifully, furnished. There are three rooms in the main house, all with water views. But the four cottages, each with a private deck, a whirlpool tub for two, a separate shower, and a minibar, offer the most privacy and luxury.

Although Jerry is in residence most of the time, he employs a full-time manager to run the inn. You can see his attention to detail in the little things— evening turndown service, choice of

feather or polyester pillows, Caswell-Massey toiletries and big fluffy towels in the rooms, and the stone paths lit with small lanterns that connect the cottages to the main house.

Camden, with its quaint harbor, shops, restaurants, and boating excursions, is less than 10 minutes away. The hiking trails of Camden State Park are also nearby, and the ferry to Islesboro leaves from the dock at Lincolnville Beach, just five minutes up the road. But you may find it hard to pull yourself away from the beauty and serenity at the inn, where you can watch windjammers sail on the bay and the loudest noise is the sound of the waves lapping at the shore.

🏨 *3 double rooms with baths, 4 cottages. Fireplaces, phones, cable TV/VCRs, terry-cloth robes, fans, individually controlled heat; whirlpool baths, private decks, and minibars in suites. $150–$325, full breakfast. AE, D, MC, V. No smoking, no pets, 2-night minimum on holiday weekends. Closed Nov.–Apr.*

John Peters Inn

Peters Point, Box 916, Blue Hill, ME 04614, tel. 207/374-2116

When you turn down the narrow lane and catch your first glimpse of this country inn, you may wonder whether your car has slipped into some bizarre wrinkle in the space–time continuum— for the John Peters, with its four colossal Doric pillars and open views over green fields to the head of Blue Hill Bay, looks like something out of Tidewater Virginia.

On closer inspection, you will see that it is actually a classic brick Federal mansion to which the columned porch was added in the 1930s. No matter. The John Peters is unsurpassed for the privacy of its location, the good taste in the decor of its guest rooms, and the whimsical informality of innkeepers Barbara and Rick Seeger. Rick gladly left an engineering job in Massachusetts for what the Seegers describe as their "fantasy utopia" just outside the town of Blue Hill.

More often than not, you will be greeted excitedly by the resident Welsh terrier, DOC (for disobedient canine), before Barbara or Rick escorts you into the living room with its two fireplaces, books and games, baby grand piano, and traditional furniture. Oriental rugs, which the Seegers collect, are everywhere. Huge breakfasts in the light and airy dining rooms include the famous lobster omelet, served complete with lobster-claw shells as decoration. After breakfast, you can lope down the hill to your boat or stroll into Blue Hill for a morning of browsing in the pottery and crafts shops.

The Surry Room, one of the best rooms (all are nice), has a king-size bed, a fireplace, curly-maple chest, gilt mirror, and six windows with delicate lace curtains. The Honeymoon Suite is immense, with wet bar and mini-refrigerator, Empire sofa and four-poster bed, deck, and a view of Blue Hill Bay. If you choose, you can have breakfast served to you in bed in this room. The large rooms in the carriage house, a stone's throw down the hill from the inn, have been completely renovated, with dining areas, cherry floors and woodwork, wicker and brass accents, and a modern feel. Four have decks, kitchens, and fireplaces, a real plus here. But nothing at the John Peters is a minus, except having to say good-bye.

🏠 *7 double rooms with baths, 1 suite in inn; 6 doubles with baths in carriage house. Phones in 4 carriage-house rooms, fireplaces in 9 bedrooms, swimming pool, canoe, sailboat, pond, 2 moorings. $95–$150, full breakfast. MC, V. No smoking, no pets. Closed Nov.–Apr.*

LimeRock Inn

96 Limerock St., Rockland, ME 04841, tel. 207/594–2257 or 800/546–3762

The city of Rockland is undergoing a quiet renaissance and the LimeRock Inn is well positioned for those wanting to be part of it. The turreted house was built in 1890 for congressman Charles E. Littlefield and is on the National Historic Register. Partners Captain Jerry and Kathleen Dougherty and Captain Thomas and Denise Perkins purchased the grand Queen Anne Victorian in 1994 and refurbished the property in time to open for the summer season. The inn's quiet residential location is a nice walk from downtown Rockland, where the Farnsworth Museum, the Maine State Ferry terminal, and a harbor full of boats await. And just up the street is the Lighthouse Museum.

Both the Doughertys and the Perkinses hail from Jackson, New Hampshire, where Jerry operates a furniture store, Kathleen is an interior decorator, and Thomas manages the Jackson Ski Touring Foundation, where Denise also works. Kathleen's attention to decorating detail and Jerry's furniture knowledge combined with the Perkinses' natural hospitality make the LimeRock both exquisite and welcoming. It has the elegance of the Norumbega, in Camden, without the solemnity and opulence, or the view.

The eight rooms are named after Maine islands and range in luxury from the small Petite Manan, with a tub hidden in the closet, to the Grande Manan, with a plantation rice carved four-poster king-size mahogany bed, a fireplace, and a whirlpool tub. Honeymooners prefer the Turret Room, with its metal wedding canopy bed and French country decor. The Island Cottage Room, located in the rear of the house, has a private deck opening onto the rear lawn and garden. It's done in a French country motif and has a whirlpool tub.

Guests gather for afternoon refreshments on the inn's wraparound porch. Breakfast is formally served in the dining room at private tables and may include wild Maine blueberry blintzes, crepes, eggs with Boursin, and homemade bread or scones.

Special touches here include evening turndown service complete with a rose and chocolates, Caswell-Massey toiletries, and iced spring water in the rooms. Captains Dougherty and Perkins always are eager to escape with their guests to the sea on *Dory Volante*, the inn's 36-foot yacht.

🛏 *8 double rooms with baths (2 can be made into suites). Afternoon refreshments, turndown service with rose and chocolates, iced spring water in rooms, sailboat cruises, bicycles, croquet. $85–$180, full breakfast. MC, V. No smoking, no pets.*

Norumbega

61 High St., Camden, ME 04843, tel. 207/236-4646

This sumptuous century-old turreted stone castle looks as if it blew in from some craggy corner of Bavaria. Though you may find the style a touch bogus and overpowering amid Camden's elegant clapboard houses, you may not be able to argue with the superb views of the bay and the luxurious splendor (for a price, of course) of the accommodations.

Designed and built in 1886 by Joseph B. Stearns, the inventor of duplex telegraphy, Norumbega was obviously the fulfillment of a deep-seated imperial fantasy. Current owner Murray Keatinge, who bought the inn in 1987, has updated the fantasy to a kind of Ralph Laurenesque environment of infinite leisure and seemingly old wealth. Members of his family now operate the inn along with a professional staff.

The public rooms have gleaming parquet floors, oak and mahogany paneling, richly carved wood mantels over the four first-floor fireplaces, gilt mirrors, and Empire furnishings. You feel as if you should dress in white linen or silk and languish in elegant repose over afternoon wine and cheese.

Sandringham (the rooms are named, appropriately, after castles and palaces), the former master bedroom, is in the turret and, though it lacks a water view, it is huge, airy, and ducal, with dark green wallpaper, a fireplace, and polished hardwood floors. At the back of the house, several decks and balconies overlook the garden, the gazebo, and the bay. The views from rear-facing rooms keep getting better as you ascend: The penthouse suite, with a small deck, fireplace, private bar, fabrics in tropical motifs, and a skylight in the bedroom, is nothing short of celestial.

Wine and cheese are served in the afternoon. Guests can have either a Continental or full gourmet breakfast delivered to their room, or dine family style in the formal dining room.

🛏 *12 double rooms with baths, 3 suites. Air-conditioning in penthouse, cable TV and pool table in game room, phones, 5 rooms with fireplaces, cable TV in some rooms, croquet, tennis privileges, murder mystery and wine-tasting weekends Jan.–Apr. $195–$345, penthouse $450; full breakfast, wine and cheese. AE, MC, V. No pets.*

Whitehall Inn

Box 558, Camden, ME 04843, tel. 207/236-3391 or 800/789-6565, fax 207/236-4427 in season

Camden's best-known inn started life in 1834 as a ship captain's home and sprouted another wing around the turn of the century when it began receiving guests. You will certainly feel the long history of civilized comfort as you cross the wide, flower-bright porch and walk through the decorous lobby on the soft, time-faded Oriental rugs. Penobscot Bay opens up across the road, and the inn's location midway between the shops, restaurants, and windjammers of Camden and the trails of Camden Hills State Park is ideal.

The Whitehall is dear to the hearts of literary folk, for it was here that Edna St. Vincent Millay, a Rockland girl, came in the summer of 1912 to recite her poem "Renascence" and launch her literary career. The Millay Room, just off the main lobby, contains Millay memorabilia.

Ed Dewing, a former Boston advertising executive, and Jean, his late wife, fell in love with the Whitehall in 1971; since then the inn has been very much a family affair, with son J. C. and his wife, Wendy, brother Chip, sister Heidi and her husband, Dane, and uncle Don Chambers all active in the day-to-day management of the inn.

The inn's loyal adherents cherish its high-toned, literary aura and the fact that everything looks the same year after year, down to the old-fashioned phones connected to an ancient switchboard with plugs, but newcomers may be a bit disappointed with the smallish, sparsely furnished rooms, with their old dark-wood bedsteads, Currier and Ives prints, claw-foot bathtubs, and not much else in the way of style.

Though the Whitehall has a countrified stateliness, you'll hear the traffic on Route 1 unless you get a garden-facing room in the rear wing. The rooms in the Victorian annexes, the Maine and the Wicker houses across Route 1, offer more seclusion and their quiet back rooms face the water. The dining room is open for dinner and breakfast.

▦ *35 double rooms with baths, 4 doubles share 2 baths, 5 singles with baths. Restaurant, cable TV in public room, phones, 2 large and 4 small meeting rooms, 1 all-weather tennis court, shuffleboard, golf privileges. $135–$170, full breakfast and dinner; B&B rates available. AE, MC, V. No pets. Closed mid-Oct.–mid-May.*

Other Choices

Blackberry Inn. 82 Elm St., Camden, ME 04843, tel. 207/236–6060, fax 207/236–4117. 9 double rooms with baths (2 rooms share shower), 1 suite with kitchen. Fireplaces and whirlpool tubs in some rooms, robes provided in garden rooms and rooms that share shower. $90–$150, full breakfast. MC, V. No smoking, no pets.

Blue Hill Inn. Box 403, Blue Hill, ME 04614, tel. 207/374–2844 or 800/826–7415, fax 207/374–2829. 11 double rooms with baths. Air-conditioning on 3rd floor, fireplaces in 4 rooms. $150–$185, MAP; B&B rates available. MC, V. No smoking, no pets, 2-night minimum on weekends July–Oct. Closed early Dec. and Jan.–mid-May.

Camden Maine Stay. 22 High St. (Rte. 1), Camden, ME 04843, tel. 207/236–9636. 5 double rooms with baths, 2 doubles share 1 bath, 1 suite. Cable TV/VCR with movies in common room. $75–$125; full breakfast, afternoon goodies. AE, MC, V. No smoking, no pets.

Edgecombe-Coles House. 64 High St., R.R. 1, Box 3010, Camden, ME 04843, tel. 207/236–2336. 6 double rooms with baths. Cable TV in den (in-room TV available), cross-country ski trails. $110–$185, full breakfast. AE, D, MC, V. No smoking, no pets, 2-day minimum mid-July–Aug.

Homeport Inn. Rte. 1, 121 E. Main St., Searsport, ME 04974, tel. 207/548–2259 or 800/742–5814. 6 double rooms with baths, 4 doubles share 1 bath, 2 2-bedroom cottages. Cable TV in living room, 3 rooms open to deck, croquet, badminton. $55–$85, cottages $500 per week; full breakfast. AE, D, MC, V. Restricted smoking, no pets.

Windward House. 6 High St., Camden, ME 04843, tel. 207/236–9656, fax 207/230–0433. 8 double rooms with baths. $80–$160, full breakfast. AE, MC, V. No smoking, no pets.

Reservations Services

B&B Down East, Ltd. (Box 547, Macomber Mill Rd., Eastbrook, ME 04634, tel. 207/565–3517). **Peg Tierney B&B of Maine** (16 Florence St., Portland, ME 04103, tel. 207/775–7808).

Down East: Deer Isle and Mount Desert Island

Claremont Hotel

Box 137, Southwest Harbor, ME 04679, tel. 207/244–5036 or 800/244–5036, fax 207/244–3512

Built in 1884 and continuously operated as an inn since then, the Claremont conjures up the atmosphere of the long, slow vacations of days gone by. The imposing yellow four-story clapboard inn, with its satellite guest houses and cottages, commands a spectacular view of Somes Sound, and there is croquet on the lawn (the August tournament is a highlight of the year) and cocktails at the boathouse from mid-July to the end of August. The Claremont's location at the end of a quiet road affords seclusion, though the busy harbor is a short stroll away.

Public rooms may look underfurnished to those whose taste in inns runs to the plush Victorian style of Bar Harbor's Cleftstone Manor or Holbrook House; but the stone fireplaces and the wicker and straight-back chairs in the Claremont's library and sitting room feel just right for Southwest Harbor, which has retained some of the rugged character of a fishing village. John Madeira Jr. has managed the inn for years for the McCue family, and a large, youthful staff joins him in summer.

The simple guest rooms are painted in mottled pastels. The water views from the inn rooms are unbeatable, and the sight of Somes Sound at dawn turning pale silver through the Claremont's gauzy white curtains is something to remember forever. There also are two guest houses on the property and 12 cottages with a more rustic feel, some of which have water views.

The large, rather formal airy dining room (open to the public for dinner), awash in sea light streaming through the picture windows, makes a fine setting in which to plan your day of hikes in the national park, bike rides on the network of carriage paths, sailing on Somes Sound, simply reading on the inn's cool lawn, or meditating on croquet. Modified American Plan (breakfast and dinner included) is required from mid-June through mid-September.

🏠 *24 double rooms with baths in main building, 5 double rooms with baths and 1 suite in Phillips House, 1 suite in Clark House, 12 cottages. Restaurant, library, cable TV in parlor, 1 clay tennis court, croquet, bikes, private dock, 3 rowboats, 10 moorings. $90–$155, full breakfast; MAP rates available. No credit cards. No smoking in guest rooms, no pets. Hotel and dining room closed mid-Oct.–mid-June, cottages closed late Oct.–mid-May.*

Cleftstone Manor

Rte. 3, Eden St., Bar Harbor, ME 04609, tel. 207/288–4951 or 800/962–9762

Attention, lovers of Victoriana! This inn was made in high Victorian heaven expressly for you. Ignore the fact that it is set amid sterile motels just off Route 3, the road along which traffic roars into Bar Harbor. Do not be put off by the unpromising, rambling, black-shuttered exterior. Inside, a deeply plush, mahogany and lace world of Victorian splendor awaits you.

An ornately framed portrait of Queen Victoria greets you as you enter the mansion, the former summer home of the Blair family (for whom Washington's Blair House is named). The parlor is cool and richly furnished with red velvet and brocade sofas trimmed with white doilies, grandfather and mantel clocks, and oil paintings hanging on powder-blue walls. In the imposingly formal dining room, Joseph Pulitzer's library table seemingly extends for miles beneath a crystal chandelier.

Of the guest rooms, the prize chamber (especially for honeymooners) is the immense Romeo and Juliet, once a section of the ballroom, which now has a pillow-decked sofa; blue velvet Victorian chairs; a lace-canopy bed; a massive, ornately carved Irish buffet that takes up most of one wall; and a handsome, dark-wood fireplace. There's more light in Hampton Court, a suite, with wicker furniture in its sitting room, a four-poster bed, and a working fireplace. Smaller and simpler is the Cambridge Room, with a brass and white-iron bed and green and rose wallpaper.

Innkeepers Pattie and Don Reynolds are far more youthful and far less formal than their surroundings. Don, originally from Louisiana, is an Air National Guard pilot. When the Reynoldses moved to Bangor in 1974, Don and Pattie had a great time renovating old homes, so getting involved with the Cleftstone seemed a logical next step.

The inn is convenient to Bar Harbor, 2 miles down the road, and to all the hiking, boating, biking, and beaching opportunities afforded by Acadia National Park.

▥ *14 double rooms with baths, 2 suites. 5 rooms with fireplaces. $100–$198; full breakfast, afternoon tea, refreshments. D, MC, V. No smoking, no pets, 2-night minimum in summer. Closed Nov.–Apr.*

Holbrook House

74 Mt. Desert St., Bar Harbor, ME 04609, tel. 207/288-4970

The Holbrook House offers a far more restrained (and more authentic)

approach to Victorian interior design than the Cleftstone Manor. William and Carol Deike bought the house in the spring of 1996.

Built in 1876 as a boardinghouse with a wraparound porch for rocking and big shuttered windows to catch the breeze, the lemon-yellow Holbrook House sits right on Mount Desert Street, the main access route through Bar Harbor. In 1876 it was no doubt pleasant to listen to the horses clip-clop past, but today, the traffic noise can be annoying, especially from the porch.

The downstairs public rooms include a lovely, formal sitting room with bright, summery chintz on chairs and windows, a Duncan Phyfe sofa upholstered in white silk damask, and an antique Victorian organ. China, crystal, and crisp linen add an elegant touch to the sunny, glassed-in porch, where a full formal breakfast is served.

The guest rooms are furnished with lovingly handled family pieces in the same refined taste as the public rooms. Room 6, on the second floor, has a corner location with four big windows, a four-poster bed, and oil paintings. Though smaller, Room 11, with its Laura Ashley fabrics, is the quietest room, and has a snug, country feel.

Right in town, Holbrook House is a short walk to the shops and restaurants of Bar Harbor, with the wonders of Acadia and the sea spread out all around. A stay at the Holbrook House is like a visit with your most proper (but by no means stuffy) relatives, the ones who inherited all the best furniture and have kept it in impeccable condition.

▥ *10 double rooms with baths in inn, 2 cottage suites. Cable TV in library and in cottages, croquet. $110–$225, full breakfast and afternoon tea. MC, V. No smoking, no pets, 2-night minimum. Closed late Oct.–Apr.*

Pilgrim's Inn

Deer Isle, ME 04627, tel. 207/348-6615

The pleasures of Deer Isle—back roads and tidal coves, pink granite and dark green spruce, sleepy villages and unspoiled fishing harbors—sink in slowly, and so does the special charm of the Pilgrim's Inn. The place looks pleasant enough at first sight—a barn-red, four-story, gambrel-roofed house, circa 1793, set just a few feet from the road, with a millpond out back and the harbor across the way. But a stay at the Pilgrim's Inn is more than pleasant. Its specialness has to do with the sweet aroma of bread and cakes baking that greets you at the door, with the way the light reflects off the water, with the simplicity and appropriateness of the furnishings, with the bright splashes of flower beds set in green lawns, and, of course, with its hospitable owners.

Innkeepers Jean and Dud Hendrick have lots of experience working with people. Dud was the lacrosse coach at Dartmouth for 13 years, and Jean has a background both in counseling and in working with food. When they got married they wanted a job they could do together, and they found it here. They have brought a spirit of ease, warmth, and unerring good taste to the Pilgrim's Inn.

The inn's formal parlor, just off the front entrance, is cool and stylish, with beige Oriental rugs and pale sofas, but guests tend to congregate downstairs in the rustic taproom with huge fireplaces, pine furniture, braided rugs, parson's benches, and a bay window overlooking the pond.

The water is visible from nearly all the guest rooms, which have English fabrics and generous proportions. Favorites include No. 8 on the second floor, with country pine furniture, a tall headboard, and three bright windows, and No. 5, with a cherry four-poster bed, cherry chest of drawers, and burgundy-and-white color scheme.

The attached barn has been converted to a dining room, a big open space that succeeds in being rustic and romantic at the same time, with original barn-wood walls, farm implements on display, and tiny windows overlooking the pond. Repeat guests to the inn are rewarded with a complimentary gift package of goodies, but one hardly needs that incentive to return.

▥ *10 double rooms with baths, 2 doubles and 1 single share 2 baths, 1 housekeeping cottage. Restaurant, gift shop. $140–$190, full breakfast and dinner. MC, V. No smoking in bedrooms, no pets. Closed mid-Oct.–mid-May.*

Other Choices

Inn at Canoe Point. Rte. 3, Hulls Cove (Box 216, Rte. 3, Bar Harbor, ME 04609), tel. 207/288-9511. 3 double rooms with baths, 2 suites. Air-conditioning in some rooms, guest phone, private beach. $135–$245, full breakfast. MC, V. No smoking, no pets.

Inn at Southwest. Box 593, Main St., Southwest Harbor, ME 04679, tel. 207/244-3835. 9 double rooms with baths. Common refrigerator. $65–$125, full breakfast and afternoon tea. AE, D, MC, V. No smoking, no pets.

Island House. Box 1006, Southwest Harbor, ME 04679, tel. 207/244-5180. 4 double rooms share 3 baths, 1 carriage-house suite. Cable TV in parlor and in carriage house. $50–$100, full breakfast. MC, V. No smoking, no pets.

Kingsleigh Inn. 373 Main St., Box 1426, Southwest Harbor, ME 04679, tel. 207/244-5302. 7 double rooms with baths, 1 suite. Cable TV in suite. $90–$175, full breakfast and afternoon refreshments. AE, MC, V. No smoking, no pets.

Manor House Inn. West St., Bar Harbor, ME 04609, tel. 207/288-3759 or 800/437-0088. 9 double rooms with baths in inn, 3 suites in chauffeur's cottage, 2 garden-cottage suites. TV in common room, fireplace or woodstove in 6 rooms, cable TV in garden-cottage suites. $50–$175, full breakfast. MC, V. No smoking, no pets, 2-night minimum July–Aug. Closed mid-Nov.–Mar.

Mira Monte. 69 Mt. Desert St., Bar Harbor, ME 04609, tel. 207/288–4263 or 800/553–5109, fax 207/288–3115. 13 double rooms with baths, 2 suites, 1 apartment. Air-conditioning, cable TVs, phones, VCR in library and suites. $120–$150, apartment $850 per week; full buffet breakfast and afternoon refreshments. AE, D, MC, V. Restricted smoking, 2-night minimum. Closed late Oct.–early May (suites open year-round).

Moorings Inn. Shore Rd., Box 744, Southwest Harbor, ME 04679, tel. 207/244–5523. 2 single rooms with baths, 3 double rooms with baths, and 4 double suites in inn, 3 motel rooms, 3 cottages (including 1 with 3 units). TV in living room and in cottages, kitchenettes in motel rooms, fireplaces in cottages, bikes, canoes, pier, outdoor gas grills. $50–$100; coffee, orange juice, and doughnuts. No credit cards. Smoking restricted, no pets. Closed Nov.–mid-May.

Penury Hall Bed 'n Breakfast. Box 68, Southwest Harbor, ME 04679, tel. 207/244–7102. 3 double rooms share 2 baths. TV in living room, washer and dryer, sauna, canoe. $50–$70, full breakfast. MC, V accepted; personal checks preferred. Restricted smoking, 2-night minimum June–Oct.

Reservations Services

B&B Down East, Ltd. (Box 547, Macomber Mill Rd., Eastbrook, ME 04634, tel. 207/565–3517). **Peg Tierney, Bed & Breakfast of Maine** (16 Florence St., Portland, ME 04103, tel. 207/775–7808).

Sebago Lake

Noble House

Box 180, Bridgton, ME 04009, tel. 207/647–3733

On a hill crest amid massive white pines, looking across Highland Lake to the White Mountains, this grand but utterly unpretentious house was built on a quiet residential street near town by a Maine state senator in 1903 and occupied for 40 years by the town dentist. In 1984 the Starets family, who had roots in Maine, left California to buy the place and convert it into one of the most refined, welcoming bed-and-breakfasts in the region.

Jane Starets runs the inn with her husband, Dick (when he isn't at work as a commercial pilot), and the summertime help of their four children. She is a soft-spoken woman whose good sense and good taste show up in the subdued, rather simple decor. You cross the wide porch to enter a simply appointed parlor with a comfortable sofa and wing chairs, dominated by a grand piano. Behind it is the dining room, where abundant breakfasts (fruit, eggs, blueberry pancakes, waffles, muffins, and breads) are usually served family style on china and linen, with the family's silver on the sideboard.

The guest rooms don't quite measure up to the elegance of the public rooms: Most are small and a bit spartan in their furnishings, with floral bedspreads, some quilts, and such corny touches as crossed skis hanging on the walls. The Honeymoon Room, however, has a good lake view, a whirlpool bath (as do three other rooms), white wicker furniture, and fresh flowers. The Staples Suite on the third floor offers the most space, privacy, and quiet, with white wicker furniture and fabrics in greens and browns.

A real asset of the Noble House is the dock across the street on Highland Lake, with chairs and a hammock and the view of Mt. Washington and the Presidential Range rising in the distance. "There is a certain magic about being on a lake," comments Jane, "and we've grown very partial to ours." Noble House is a fine place to develop your own partiality for Highland Lake and a good base for exploring the antiques shops of Bridgton and for day trips to Sebago or Long Lake, the nearby Oxford Hills, or even up to the White Mountain National Forest.

▥ *6 double rooms with baths, 3 doubles share 1 bath. TV in lounge, floating dock for swimming, croquet, canoe, paddleboat. $74–$119, full breakfast. AE, MC, V. No pets, 2-night minimum on weekends.*

Waterford Inne

Box 149, Waterford, ME 04088, tel. 207/583-4037

The tiny white-clapboard and green-shuttered villages known as the Waterfords boast a fine collection of country inns, but the Waterford Inne stands out for its breezy hilltop location and for its warmly convivial owners, Rosalie and Barbara Vanderzanden, a mother-and-daughter innkeeping team.

Back in the mid-1970s Barbara and Rosalie were schoolteachers in New Jersey and avid world travelers when they decided they wanted a change of lifestyle and geography. As Barbara tells it, they had been looking all over Maine when a real-estate agent showed them what was to become the Waterford Inne. They made an offer on the spot. "It was the feeling of the house that settled it," Barbara reminisces.

The property had been a dairy farm back in the 1820s, and 40 years later a prominent lumber family bought it. With open fields all around the house, huge pine trees fringing the fields, an orchard out back, and a big red barn off to the side, the place retains vestiges of its farming heritage and its decades serving as a wealthy family's hideaway.

Barbara and Rosalie have done a superb job of renovating the gold-painted, curry-trimmed house. The sitting room is cozy, with dried flowers hanging from exposed beams, a sofa facing the fireplace, and barnwood walls. In the more formal parlor they display china and antiques and a collection of Quimper plates.

The bedrooms, each furnished on a different theme, have lots of nooks and crannies. Nicest are the Nantucket Room with whale wallpaper and a harpoon, and the Chesapeake Room, with a private porch, fireplace, pumpkin-pine floors, a king-size bed, and ducks, ducks, ducks. A converted wood shed has five additional rooms, and though they have slightly less character than the inn rooms, four of them have the compensation of sunny decks.

The Vanderzandens enjoy trading travel tips with their guests and directing them to local lakes, ski trails, and antiques shops. They will prepare elaborate dinners by prior arrangement. Pets are welcome, but there is an extra charge.

▥ *6 double rooms with baths, 2 doubles share 1 bath, 1 suite. TV in common room, apple picking in orchard, cross-country ski trails, ice-skating pond, badminton. $74–$99, full breakfast. AE. No smoking in dining room.*

Hancock

Other Choices

Inn at Long Lake. Lake House Rd., Box 806, Naples, ME 04055, tel. 207/693–6226 or 800/437–0328. 14 double rooms with baths, 2 suites. Air-conditioning, TVs. $85–$130, Continental breakfast. D, MC, V. No smoking, no pets.

Kedarburn Inn. Rte. 35, Box 61, Waterford, ME 04088, tel. 207/583–6182, fax 207/583-6424. 2 double rooms with baths, 4 doubles share 2 baths, 1 suite. Pub, TV in parlor, crafts shop. $71–$125, full breakfast. AE, D, MC, V. No smoking.

Lake House. Rtes. 35 and 37, Waterford, ME 04088, tel. 207/583–4182 or 800/223–4182. 4 double rooms with baths, 1 cottage. Fireplace in sitting room, coffeemakers in guest rooms. $84–$130, full breakfast. MC, V. No smoking, no pets.

Quisiana. Point Pleasant Rd., Center Lovell, ME 04016, tel. 207/925–3500, fax 207/925–1004. 11 double rooms with private baths in 2 lodges, 32 cottages, some with fireplaces. Nightly musical performance, 3 clay tennis courts, 2 beaches, canoes, sailboats, rowboats, lake kayaks, Windsurfers, fishing guides, waterskiing, lake tours, and boat motors available at additional charge. $100–$145 per person; breakfast, lunch, and dinner. No credit cards. 1-week minimum in high season, closed Sept.–mid-June.

Crocker House Inn

Hancock Point Rd., Hancock, ME 04640, tel. 207/422–6806

Once one of 70 inns in the thriving summer community of Hancock Point, this century-old, shingle-style cottage amid tall fir trees sat abandoned for 20 years before Richard Malaby rescued it in 1980, and he's been restoring it ever since. The living room has a nice country feel to it. Guest rooms in the main inn are simply decorated with a mix of country furniture, oak and iron beds, oak washstands, white tie-back curtains, Martha Washington bedspreads, and stenciling. The carriage house has two additional rooms which have a more modern feel, as well as a TV room, small library, and large whirlpool bath.

The inn's dining room serves up a full breakfast and is also open for dinner.

Although none of the rooms has a water view, the Crocker House is only 200 yards from the water on either side, and 800 yards from the end of the point. It is a good jumping-off point for excursions to Acadia's Schoodic Point and spots farther up the coast.

🛏 *9 double rooms with baths in main house, 2 doubles with baths in carriage house. Restaurant, TV room, whirlpool bath. $100–$120, full breakfast; MAP rates available. AE, D, MC, V. Closed Jan.–Apr., part time Nov.–Dec.*

Le Domaine

Box 496, Hancock, ME 04640, tel. 207/422–3395 or 800/554–8498

Nine miles east of Ellsworth, standing on an otherwise rural stretch of Route 1, you will find a little slice of French sophistication that is as welcome as it is improbable. Although Le Domaine is known primarily for its restaurant, the French country-style rooms, done in chintz and wicker, with simple desks and sofas near the windows, are inviting.

Nicole L. Purslow, owner and chef, trained at the Cordon Bleu and apprenticed in Switzerland. Here in the Maine countryside she whips up classic haute cuisine dishes, the perfect accompaniments to which are bound to be hiding amid the more than 6,000 bottles of French vintage in the inn's wine cellar. Meals are served in an elegant dining room.

Though guest rooms are on the small side, the inn owns 100 acres with paths, and there's badminton on the lawn. Four rooms have balconies or porches over the gardens. The inn is situated halfway between Mount Desert Island and Schoodic Point, another part of Acadia National Park.

🛏 *7 double rooms with private baths. Restaurant, air-conditioning in 4* *rooms, radios and fruit in rooms. $200, MAP; 20% reduction for B&B. AE, D, MC, V. No pets. Closed Nov.–mid-May.*

Reservations Services

B&B Down East, Ltd. (Box 547, Macomber Mill Rd., Eastbrook, ME 04634, tel. 207/565–3517). **Bethel Area Chamber of Commerce** (Box 121, Bethel, ME 04217, tel. 207/824–2282). **Peg Tierney B&B of Maine** (16 Florence St., Portland, ME 04103, tel. 207/775–7808).

Off the Beaten Track

Country Club Inn. Box 680, Country Club Dr., Rangeley, ME 04970, tel. 207/ 864–3831. 19 double rooms with baths. Restaurant, TV in lobby, lounge, pool, public golf course next door. $110, full breakfast; MAP rates available. AE, MC, V. Closed mid-Oct.–Dec. 26, Apr.– late May.

Lodge at Moosehead Lake. Lily Bay Rd., Box 1167, Greenville, ME 04441, tel. 207/695–4400, fax 207/695–2281. 5 double rooms with baths, 3 suites. Game room, cable TV. $145–$295; full breakfast, dinner in off-season. D, MC, V. No smoking, no pets.

Weston House. 26 Boynton St., East-port, ME 04631, tel. 207/853–2907 or 800/853–2907. 4 double rooms share 2½ baths. Terry-cloth robes, TV in family room. $50–$70, full breakfast. No credit cards. No smoking, no pets.

Maryland

Spring Bank

Oxford/Eastern Shore

Ashby 1663

27448 Ashby Dr. (Box 45), Easton, MD 21601, tel. 410/822-4235

This is a manor house *magnifico*, or a Colonial estate with Italian dressing. The original foundation was laid in 1663 for a wealthy merchant family by the name of Goldsborough, who engaged the services of some 20-odd servants. The Italian influence entered the picture in the mid-19th century, when the villalike structure arose. If the setting looks familiar to you, it's because Ashby is a star—some scenes in the movie *Silent Fall*, starring Richard Dreyfuss, were filmed here.

Jeanie Wagner and Cliff Meredith, both Eastern Shore natives, purchased Ashby in 1986 and transformed it from ramshackle to technologized high-gloss. Cliff, who once presided over his own contracting company, engineered all the wiring, heating, air-conditioning, and plumbing. Under his direction, small, divided spaces were demolished and opened up. No sign of the former kitchen exists, for Cliff created (from scratch) a wall-to-wall white custom-equipped design, which has since appeared on the cover of a popular builders' magazine.

The pièce de résistance, however, is the Goldsborough Suite on the second floor. If you've never seen a fireplace in a bathroom, now's your chance: The room is exceedingly large and sumptuous, with marble surfaces, brass railings, a bidet, a whirlpool-rigged bath, and a two-headed shower separate from the honeymooners' tub. The sleeping chamber is dominated by a four-poster canopy bed (king-size, of course) adorned with garden-print ruffles, but its best feature is its walls of glass.

The list of perks here is endless. Warm, soft-spoken Jeanie will guide you through the downstairs fitness and tanning center, outdoors around the heated pool (with a river view) and lighted tennis courts, and back in to the screen porch. Some bed-and-breakfasts claim "full" morning meals and slap an egg on your plate. Not Jeanie. Request the California eggs with salsa and sour cream, or the Belgian waffles: Both presentation and quality are superior.

🏠 *15 double rooms with baths. Air-conditioning, TVs and phones in all manor house rooms, library, exercise* room, tanning bed, pool table, kitchens in cottage and carriage house, pool, boat dock, paddleboat, canoe, lighted tennis court. $185–$595; full breakfast, afternoon tea, evening cocktails. MC, V. No smoking, no pets, 2-night minimum on weekends.

Bishop's House

214 Goldsborough St., Box 2217, Easton, MD 21601, tel. and fax 410/820–7290 or 800/223–7290 outside MD

This handsome Victorian home (circa 1880) was built for former Maryland Governor Philip Frances Thomas and his wife. After the governor's death in 1892, the house was sold to the Episcopal Diocese and served as the Bishop's home, hence the name. Conveniently located near the heart of historic Easton, the Bishop's House has large first-floor rooms with a 14-foot ceiling and large plaster medallions. The first floor is centrally air-conditioned and offers facilities for social functions or business meetings. Second floor guest rooms have 12-foot ceilings and are decorated in romantic 19th-century oak, walnut, and mahogany; three guest rooms have working fireplaces and two have whirlpool baths. For socializing or for people-watching there's a wonderful wraparound front porch.

Golf packages, cycling tours, and sightseeing excursions are available to guests, and since the present owners are members of Biking-Inn-to-Inn on the Eastern Shore, Inc., they can assist with arrangements for staying at other member properties. Owner Diane Laird-Ippolito is proud of the inn's hot sumptuous breakfasts and knows Easton's restaurants well. She carefully matches her guests with what will be an appropriate dining experience.

Easton is in the heart of James Michener's *Chesapeake* country. It's just 10 miles to either Oxford or St. Michael's, both popular tourist villages on Maryland's Eastern Shore. The land is flat and ideal for bicyclists, because most of the country roads offer wide shoulder lanes exclusively for bicycles. With so much water nearby, in autumn you'll hear and see large numbers of Canada and snow geese overhead and in the nearby fields.

🏠 *6 guest rooms, 4 with attached baths, 1 with detached bath. Air-conditioning, fireplaces in 2nd-floor rooms, TV/VCR in common room, off-street parking, bicycle storage, complimentary transportation from local marinas and Easton Airport. $65–$110, full breakfast. No credit cards. No smoking, no pets.*

Brampton

25227 Chestertown Rd., Chestertown, MD 21620, tel. 410/778–1860

Brampton's charming character derives from both its house and its grounds. The inn is set in the fields south of Chestertown, framed by two towering, 120-year-old spruce trees at the end of a long drive. It's a three-story brick building with a white columned porch and 14 front windows, the perfect gentleman-farmer's country seat. The house is listed on the National Register of Historic Places, as are four of its surrounding 35 acres (the site of some famous experiments in crop rotation). Enter and pass through the airy foyer into a bookcase-lined living room, or climb the solid-walnut staircase. This front section of Brampton was built around 1860 by Henry Ward Carville, as a wedding present to his wife.

Upstairs in the six guest rooms the present owner's excellent taste becomes apparent. Michael Hanscom spent 10 years in San Francisco renovating old homes before moving here. His Swiss wife, Danielle, is responsible for the European atmosphere in the guest rooms. The bed linen and towels look and smell as if they'd been dried on a line in the Alps. Every room except the suite has a working fireplace or a wood-burning stove. The ceilings on the second floor are 11 feet high. The Yellow

Room at the front of the house is a favorite, a sunny paradise with an antique lace canopy above the bed. The two third-floor rooms are tucked under the sloping eaves and are decorated in country style, with locally crafted chairs and trundle beds.

Since Michael and Danielle arrived a decade ago, they've made many additions: a mammoth Vulcan commercial stove that enables the hosts to offer guests a choice of breakfast entrées; a TV room downstairs; and the Rose Room, outfitted with a king-size bed and a large bath (but reached by a staircase so narrow that Danielle advises no one over 6 feet to book this unit).

Danielle and Michael can suggest walks on the Brampton grounds to a pond or to the east fork of Langford Creek. There is something Old World about these unassuming hosts, both of whom are dedicated to perfecting every detail.

🖽 *8 double rooms with baths, 2 suites. Air-conditioning, TV in 1 suite. $95–$155; full breakfast, afternoon tea. AE, MC, V. No smoking, no pets, 2-night minimum on weekends.*

Gross' Coate 1658

11300 Gross' Coate Rd., Easton, MD 21601, tel. 410/819–0802 or 800/580–0802, fax 410/819–0803

If you respond to Walt Whitman's portrayal of Abraham Lincoln—"the sweetest, wisest soul," "head steady ... with proud and resolute spirit"—then envision that image as a place reflective of the same passionate but dogged thoughtfulness and integrity, a structure resounding with the same magnificent, melancholy stateliness of spirit. Gross' Coate is like an architectural realization of that great spirit. Since the first brick was laid in 1760, the creators and keepers—including Jonathan and Molly Ginn, who bought the estate in 1983—have stubbornly minded every aspect of the surroundings (63 secluded waterfront acres of the flat coastal plain that characterizes the DelMarVa peninsula). And they've remained sensitive through centuries of development to the importance of an integrated, dignified whole.

That sense of dignity begins on the steps of the large brick Georgian manor. The white wraparound porch is only slightly elevated—enough to offer a suggestion of ceremony—and distinguished by a unique double-columned arrangement topped by the graceful curves of a second-story balustrade. On the veranda is a soldiers' row of hunter-green rockers, which are there year-round.

Inside, the front foyer, sitting rooms, and upstairs chambers are large and light-filled, the appointments spare and discreet. Sixteen working fireplaces are distributed throughout the main house. Floor-to-ceiling windows downstairs shed floods of light over the dark black-walnut floorboards. Climb up the main staircase and walk out on the upstairs porch overlooking the water: The play of light over the Wye River at dusk is enough to produce mild heartache. Next to the main house, the Spring House Cottage with fireplace, two-person steam shower, soaking tub, and private terrace with 60-jet spa gets booked quickly.

If such grandeur suggests an intimidating ambience, it shouldn't. The Ginns want their guests—from business travelers to honeymooners to young children—to have fun and, if they desire, to be assured of absolute privacy. They offer uncommon attentions (an open bar, gourmet breakfasts, a dock, and two deepwater slips. Coffee, tea, and the daily paper are brought to your door each morning. Bring your boat, bring your dog, bring a camera, and drink champagne in the tree house: This is a gracious, friendly, happy environment.

🖽 *6 suites. Fireplaces, open bar, pool, golf range, dock, garden house, smoke-*

*house, complimentary bikes. $295–
$495; breakfast, afternoon tea. AE, D,
MC, V. Restricted smoking.*

Inn at Perry Cabin

*308 Watkins La., St. Michael's, MD
21663, tel. 410/745–2200 or 800/722–
2949, fax 410/745–3348*

The grand white frame house, much
enlarged from the original farmhouse,
sits serenely at the edge of the Miles
River, as it has since 1810. Much of the
decor of the Inn at Perry Cabin is pure
Laura Ashley, which is only fitting,
since this, the first Ashley Inn, is
owned by Sir Bernard Ashley, husband
of the late designer.

The reception rooms have been done à
la English country-house hotel, and
from time to time Sir Bernard and
Lady Ashley would swoop down on St.
Michael's, bringing new furniture and
decorations (not really new, of course,
but brought from their house in the
Bahamas or from the antiques empori-
ums of the world). Every object has
been chosen with care, and most of
them are antique—from the Colonial
American chests of drawers, highboys,
and bedside tables that came with the
house to the mirrors, lamps, pictures,
and the Oriental rugs spread everywhere you look. All of the bedrooms are
done in antiques, and all are completely
Laura Ashley—fabrics, wallpapers,
sprig-decorated tables, and beds with
spiral posts.

The main dining room, a soaring chamber two stories high, has an open wood-
burning fireplace at one end. The food is
excellent, and the silent, unobtrusive
service lives up to the British tone of
the place. Boat owners would find it a
welcome change from galley fare and
marina dining. The employees run the
inn impeccably. The only conceivable
drawback is the unfortunately situated
residential development across the harbor, but that's hardly reason for second
thoughts. Service, from the moment
you enter the reception hall, is exem-

plary. General manager Stephen Creese
sees to it that mineral water, ice, a plate
of fresh fruit, and homemade cookies
await guests in their rooms; the rate
also includes a daily newspaper, full
English breakfast, and afternoon tea.
The addition of swimming and exercise
facilities, a traditional English snooker
room, and a conservatory has extended
the house's pleasures, and nearby recreations are plentiful: The inn arranges
outings for everything from golf, fishing, and sailing to helicopter tours and
riding lessons. It's worth noting, for
business travelers, that the management accommodates any and all conference and meeting requirements.

🏨 *38 double rooms with baths, 3
suites. Air-conditioning, cable TVs,
phones, restaurant, indoor pool, steam
room, sauna, exercise room, snooker
room, conservatory, library, room service, croquet, short-term docking facilities, bikes. $195–$575; full breakfast,
afternoon tea. AE, DC, MC, V. No
smoking in dining room, no pets.*

Robert Morris Inn

*Box 70, on the Tred Avon, Oxford, MD
21654, tel. 410/226–5111, fax 410/226–
5744*

Although the town of Oxford and its
historic inn came vividly into the public
eye around the time of the American
bicentennial celebration, the Robert
Morris has managed to avoid being
spoiled by success. Built by Robert
Morris Sr. as a residence in 1710 and
run as an inn since the 1940s, it was
bought by Ken and Wendy Gibson in
1975 and is just what a country inn
should be.

The 18th-century section of the inn is
on Oxford's Morris Street, facing the
ferry dock, where there's always a line
of tourists waiting to board the tiny
Tred Avon Ferry, which tools between
Oxford and Bellevue. You might also
find a line at the Robert Morris restaurant, which occupies most of the inn's
first floor. Its Hitchcock chairs and

murals (actually 140-year-old hand-printed wallpaper samples) make it an attractive place to eat; crab cakes and Oxford coolers head the rather predictable menu. The slate-floor tavern beyond the dining room has a working fireplace and is reputedly where James Michener wrote the outline for *Chesapeake.*

Staying at the Robert Morris may prove more difficult than simply supping here. The Gibsons begin taking reservations on January 10 of each year and won't book a room more than a year in advance. Historic-minded souls should be adamant about claiming rooms in the 1710 section, where there's a rare, enclosed Elizabethan staircase and white-pine floors fastened with hand-hewn pegs. Top choices among the four guest rooms here are 2 and 15, the latter with a step-up poster bed and hand-stenciled borders on the walls. You might also request the room once occupied by Robert Morris Jr., a signer of the Declaration of Independence, or that of his father (who met a lamentable fate when he was hit by a cannonball fired in his honor).

The Gibsons know that some people are willing to dispense with history altogether in favor of luxurious quietude. To that end they've restored a roomy 1875 Victorian home, surrounded by mimosa and weeping copper-beech trees, just steps from the main house. Almost all the rooms in Sandaway Lodge are suites featuring screen porches, pine paneling, and immense claw-foot tubs (ask for 203, which has a chandelier over the bath; for 303, with its own staircase; or for one of the romantic River Rooms overlooking the Tred Avon).

🏨 *33 double rooms with baths, 2 efficiencies. Restaurant, air-conditioning, TV in 1 efficiency. $70–$220; Continental breakfast Tues., breakfast extra other days. MC, V. No smoking, no pets.*

Wades Point Inn

Box 7, St. Michael's, MD 21663, tel. 410/745–2500

Aside from a chartered yacht, there's no better place from which to appreciate the blue sweep of the Chesapeake than the Wades Point Inn. Halfway between St. Michael's and Tilghman Island, this rambling bed-and-breakfast on 120 acres is surrounded on three sides by the bay.

The oldest section of the inn was built in 1820 by shipwright Thomas Kemp, whose sleek Baltimore clippers were credited with winning the War of 1812. On the land side, this glowing white Georgian house has porches on two floors and chimneys at either end; an observation nook attached to one chimney was Thomas Kemp's lookout and is reached through a trapdoor in one of three rooms in the old portion of the house.

In 1890, later Kemps built an addition to the house on the bay side and opened the place as an inn. The present owners, Betsy and John Feiler, call this addition the Bay Room and have put it to use as a common area; it's large enough to hold a cotillion and is lined with windows and furnished with white wicker. Above the Bay Room is the Summer Wing, which holds six small chambers. These aren't air-conditioned, but given their proximity to the water, porches, and plentiful windows, they don't need it. There are washbasins in some of the Summer Wing rooms, as well as pastel prints and dancing white curtains that catch the rejuvenating breeze. Maybe that's why Mildred Kemp, the last of the family to occupy Wades Point, looked so hearty at age 90, when Betsy Feiler met her. "If living at Wades Point made her look like that," Betsy says, "I wanted to buy the place."

Building additions seems to be something of a tradition with the owners of Wades Point. There's a four-room summer cottage, and in 1989 Betsy and John completed a 12-room guest house about 200 yards from the main inn. These modern rooms have water views and balconies, and the two double beds and kitchenette in Number 423 make it a good choice for families. If you're looking for bona fide old Chesapeake Bay atmosphere, however, opt for a room in the main house.

🏨 *15 double rooms with baths, 9 doubles share 5 baths. Air-conditioning in new guest house, TV and fireplaces in common rooms, pond, private crabbing and fishing dock, walking and jogging trail, public boat ramp nearby. $74– $165, Continental breakfast. MC, V. Restricted smoking, no pets, 2-day minimum on weekends. Closed Jan.–Feb.*

Other Choices

John S. McDaniel House. 14 N. Aurora St., Easton, MD 21601, tel. 410/ 822–3704 or 800/787–4667. 6 double rooms with baths, 2 doubles share bath. Air-conditioning. $75–$110, Continental breakfast. AE, MC, V. No smoking, no pets.

Tavern House. 111 Water St. (Box 98 for mail delivery), Vienna, MD 21869, tel. 410/376–3347. 4 double rooms share 2 baths. Air-conditioning. $65–$70, full breakfast. MC, V. Restricted smoking, no pets.

White Swan Tavern. 231 High St., Chestertown, MD 21620, tel. 410/778– 2300, fax 410/778–4543. 4 double rooms with baths, 2 suites. Tearoom, air-conditioning, cable TV in sitting room. $100–$150, Continental breakfast. No credit cards. No pets.

Widow's Walk Inn. 402 High St., Chestertown, MD 21620, tel. 410/778– 6455 or 410/778–6864. 1 double room with bath, 2 doubles share bath, 2 suites. Air-conditioning, refreshments on arrival, sitting room with TV. $85– $110, Continental breakfast. MC, V. No smoking, no pets, 2-night minimum on holiday weekends.

Reservations Services

Amanda's Bed & Breakfast Reservation Service (1428 Park Ave., Baltimore 21217, tel. 410/225–0001 for information, 800/899–7533 for reservations, fax 410/728–8957). **Bed & Breakfast of Maryland/The Traveller in Maryland** (Box 2277, Annapolis 21401, tel. 410/269–6232, fax 410/263–4841). **Inns of the Eastern Shore** (1500 Hambrooks Blvd., Cambridge 21613, tel. 410/228–0575 for information, 800/373– 7890 for reservations).

Annapolis/ Western Shore/ Southern Maryland

William Page Inn

8 Martin St., Annapolis, MD 21401, tel. 410/626–1506, fax 410/263–4841

If your travels take you to Annapolis for Commissioning Week at the Naval Academy, for the December Parade of Lights, or simply to nose around the city's walkable historic district, there's rest for the weary explorer at the William Page Inn. Built in 1908, this brown-shingle Victorian is a youngster by Annapolis standards, but one with an accommodating style. Its wraparound porch has deep Adirondack chairs, and the boxwood in the William Paca House gardens perfumes the air. Somewhere over the high white wall at the end of Martin Street you might hear Naval Academy "middies" drilling, and four blocks away, at eateries around City Dock, crabs are being devoured, but on the William Page porch such distractions seem light-years away.

The genial innkeepers are Rob Zuchelli and Greg Page, a designer of theatrical lighting and a computer programmer. They took very early retirement to refurbish the inn, which had served as the First Ward Democratic Clubhouse for 50 years. They aired out the smoke-filled rooms; stripped 11 coats of paint from the massive staircase, to reveal oak, mahogany, and cherry wood; and filled the inn with Queen Anne and Chippendale reproductions. They also turned the third floor into one smashing suite, with a sleigh bed, skylight, window seats, and balloon shades that lift to reveal views of the Annapolis rooftops. Guests might take the presence of a whirlpool bath in the suite in stride, but they are likely to be surprised by the one attached to the little blue room on the second floor.

There's a wet bar stocked with setups, a working fireplace in the carpeted downstairs common room, and a discreet dog named Chancellor who is always happy to accompany guests on walks. Breakfast, served from the sideboard in the common room, consists of freshly baked muffins and breads, fruit-and-cheese trays, and perhaps an egg casserole or crepes—depending on chef Rob's mood. Greg earns his keep by running a side business, Bed & Breakfast of Maryland/The Traveller in Maryland reservations service, and he can bend your ear describing other choice places to stay.

2 double rooms with baths, 2 doubles share bath, 1 suite. Air-conditioning, cable TV in suite, wet bar, 2 whirlpool baths, robes for guests using shared bath, off-street parking. $85–$175, full breakfast. AE, MC, V. No smoking, no pets, 2-day minimum during special events, 5-day minimum during Boat Show and Commissioning Week.

Other Choices

Back Creek Inn. Calvert and Alexander Sts., Solomons, MD 20688, tel. 410/326–2022, fax 410/326–2946. 4 double rooms with baths. Air-conditioning, cable TV in common area and in cottage and suites, bikes, dock with 2 deepwater slips, access to nearby swimming pool. $65–$140, full or Continental breakfast. MC, V. Restricted smoking, no pets, 2-day minimum holiday weekends. Closed mid-Dec.–mid-Feb.

Gibson's Lodgings. 110 Prince George St., Annapolis, MD 21401, tel. 410/268–5555. 5 double rooms with baths, 13 doubles share 7 baths, 2 suites. Air-conditioning, TVs and phones in parlors and rooms with baths, conference room with kitchenette, free parking. $68–$125, Continental breakfast. AE, MC, V. No smoking, no pets.

St. Michael's Manor. 5200 St. Michael's Manor Way, Scotland, MD 20687, tel. 301/872–4025. 4 double rooms share 2 baths. Air-conditioning, 2 fireplaces in parlor, pool, bikes, canoe, rowboat. $65–$70, full breakfast. No credit cards. Smoking downstairs only, no pets, 2-day minimum on holiday weekends.

Reservations Services

Amanda's Bed & Breakfast Reservation Service (1428 Park Ave., Baltimore 21217, tel. 410/225–0001). **Annapolis Association of Licensed Bed & Breakfast Owners** (Box 744, Annapolis 21404). **Bed & Breakfast of Maryland/The Traveller in Maryland** (Box 2277, Annapolis 21404, tel. 410/269–6232).

Baltimore, Frederick, and Environs

The Inn at Antietam

220 E. Main St., Box 119, Sharpsburg, MD 21782, tel. 301/432–6601, fax 301/432–5981

Anyone who's ever visited a Civil War battlefield knows how haunting the site is, how the dawns seem to echo with the sound of bugles and gunfire, how at night the voices of soldiers rise like mist from the glades. Antietam, which surrounds the dusty little town of Sharps-burg, is surely one of the most stirring of such places, for it was here in September 1862 that one of the bloodiest battles of the Civil War claimed more than 23,000 lives in a single day.

Just north of town there's a national cemetery, with a statue by Daniel Chester French (who sculpted the statue of President Lincoln at Washington's Lincoln Memorial), called "The Private Soldier," which serves as the headstone for 5,000 Union dead. Adjoining the graveyard on a hillock facing the hazy Blue Ridge is the Inn at Antietam, a 1908 Queen Anne cottage with a wraparound porch, shaded by a giant silver maple and set amid fields. Owners Cal and Betty Fairbourn have restored the place in the style of the Civil War period, filling the parlor with Rococo Revival walnut furniture, the porch with rockers, and guest rooms with Eastlake dressers and beds.

The Fairbourns, who had restored another house in the area before moving into this one in 1987, enlisted the aid of a decorator here, which resulted in beautifully finished guest rooms. The converted smokehouse, at the rear, has a large brick fireplace, a sitting room lined with beaded paneling, and a loft bed. The master suite, another favorite, has an 1880s four-poster bed; matching spread, curtains, and wallpaper; and Battenberg lace.

After breakfast, served in the formal dining room on Royal Copenhagen china, Cal and Betty can offer tips on how best to see the battlefield—on foot, by bicycle, or even on cross-country skis. The surrounding area is also surprisingly rich in good restaurants, such as the Yellow Brick Bank, in nearby Shepherdstown, West Virginia, and Old South Mountain Inn in Boonsboro. During the first weekend in December the Valley Craft Network runs an annual Holiday Studio Tour; pottery, quilts, furniture, and natural fiberwear make ideal Christmas offerings. Shut-terbugs should ask Cal about local photo opportunities.

🏠 *4 suites. Air-conditioning, TV in smokehouse suite. $95–$105, full breakfast. AE. No smoking, no pets, 2-night minimum on weekends and holidays. Closed Dec. 22–Feb. 1.*

Mr. Mole

1601 Bolton St., Baltimore, MD 21217, tel. 410/728–1179, fax 410/728–3379

How did such an elegant town home in Baltimore's exclusive Bolton Hill neighborhood get such a name? It all goes back to the children's book, *The Wind in the Willows*, where Mole exclaims "Oh My" each time he encounters exceptional hospitality and accommodations. Mr. Mole is ideally situated for guests who want the convenience of a city inn and the comfort usually associated with large suburban properties. Mr. Mole is within walking distance of Baltimore's "Cultural Corridor" (including the Lyric Opera House, Myerhoff Symphony Hall, and Howard Street's Antique Row).

Co-owners and hosts Paul Bragaw and Collin Clarke have spared no effort to make their accommodations unique and comfortable. The first floor consists of a dining room with a large, lovely bay window and two sitting rooms full of color and elegant clutter. Guests can eat at individual tables or in the adjoining rooms. Typically, the Dutch-style breakfast consists of fresh fruits, Amish cheeses and meats, homemade breads, and coffee cake.

Each of the five guest suites has a private white bath, fresh flowers, a direct-dial phone, a clock radio, and a garage. The second floor Explorer Suite feels like a tented en-suite camp for African adventurers. Also on this floor is the Print Room, filled with prints and engravings, which is actually part of a two-bedroom suite with a marble fireplace, chairs and sofas, and loads of books on the shelves. A plant-filled sunroom on the third floor is probably the most romantic suite.

🏠 *5 rooms with baths. Air-conditioning, phones, fax, fresh flowers, Caswell-Massey toiletries. $80–$145, Continental breakfast. AE, D, MC, V. No smoking, no pets, 2-night minimum on weekends.*

Spring Bank

7945 Worman's Mill Rd., Frederick, MD 21701, tel. 301/694–0440, fax 301/694–5926 (call before faxing)

When you ask Beverly and Ray Compton why they bought their cavernous, 100-year-old farmhouse just north of Frederick in 1980, Beverly has a disarming answer: "We bought it to live and be happy in." And indeed it seems this warm couple is happy here, though the road to inhabiting the house was paved with hard work interspersed with joyful architectural surprises. While restoring the Italianate and Gothic Revival structure, the Comptons found details that seemed too good to be true: engraved designs in the glass of the front door, random-width hardwood floors, faux-marble mantels, antique William Morris wallpaper, and a wet-plaster fresco on the ceiling of the old billiard room—now a first-floor guest room. Some of these design points had been damaged over the years, but after a thorough cleaning, they stand as witnesses to another time and lifestyle. Ray is the son of a Chadd's Ford, Pennsylvania, antiques dealer, and perhaps his penchant for restoration is in his blood; in 1990 he received an award from the Historical Society of Frederick for the work he's done here. Beverly haunts local auctions and flea markets, and during the week she commutes to a federal job in Rockville.

The brick house is built in textbook-perfect telescoping style, with porches stretching across the front and along two stories on the side. The backyard gives way to farmland; the 20th century rarely intrudes at Spring Bank, despite its proximity to Highway 15. Choose your room upon arrival; the converted billiard parlor and the Sleigh Bedroom on the second floor are favorites, both sparely decorated with Eastlake-style antiques. In keeping with the 19th-century ethos, the baths have not been extensively modernized—no whirlpool tubs or French magnifying mirrors here.

For breakfast, the Comptons serve homemade breads with local jams and plenty of information on nearby auctions, held almost every day. One note of advice: If you have fears about booking a room with a shared bath, you should put them to rest. No one has to wait in line here, and if you were to pass up Spring Bank for this reason, you'd be missing out on one of the handsomest, best-run establishments in western Maryland.

🏠 *1 double room with bath, 4 doubles share 2½ baths. Air-conditioning, cable TV in parlor. $60–$95, Continental breakfast. AE, D, MC, V. No smoking, no pets, 2-night minimum on holiday weekends and weekends Apr.–mid-June and mid-Sept.–mid-Nov.*

Other Choices

Catoctin Inn. MD Rte. 85, 3613 Buckeystown Pike, Box 243, Buckeystown, MD 21717, tel. 301/874–5555 or 800/730–5550, fax 301/831–8102. 4 rooms with baths, 1 suite, 11 cottages. Air-conditioning, fireplaces, TVs, phones in cottages, whirlpool baths, robes, hair dryers, business facilities. $65–$125, full breakfast. AE, D, MC, V. Restricted smoking, no pets.

Inn at Buckeystown. 3521 Buckeystown Pike (General Delivery), Buckeystown, MD 21717, tel. 301/874–5755 or 800/272–1190. 3 double rooms with baths, 2 suites, 2 cottages. Air-conditioning, TV/VCR in Parson's Cottage and Far West Suite; fireplace, kitchen, outdoor hot tub, piano and TV/VCR in St. John's Cottage; fireplace in Winter Suite. $225–$275; $300 includes breakfast, dinner, and snacks. AE, MC, V. No smoking, no pets. Dining room closed Mon.–Tues.

National Pike. 9–11 W. Main St., Box 299, New Market, MD 21774, tel. 301/865–5055. 4 double rooms with baths, 1 suite. Air-conditioning, sitting room with TV. $75–$125, full breakfast. MC, V. No smoking, no pets, 2-night minimum during "New Market Days" (Sept.) and holiday weekends.

Tyler-Spite House. 112 W. Church St., Frederick, MD 21701, tel. 301/831–4455. 5 rooms with shared baths, 1 suite. Air-conditioning, 8 fireplaces, heated outdoor pool. $100–$200; full breakfast, high tea on weekends. AE, D, MC, V. No smoking, no pets.

Reservations Services

Bed & Breakfast Accommodations of Frederick and Western Maryland (7945 Worman's Mill Rd., Frederick 21701, tel. 301/694–5926). **Bed & Breakfast of Maryland/The Traveller in Maryland** (Box 2277, Annapolis 21404, tel. 410/269–6232).

Massachusetts

Harbor Light Inn

Southeastern Massachusetts

Foxglove Cottage

101 Sandwich Rd., Plymouth, MA 02360, tel. 508/747–6576 or 800/479–4746, fax 508/747–7622

Foxglove Cottage is easy to find: It's a few miles from downtown Plymouth on winding, tree-lined Sandwich Road, the original Colonial highway to Boston. Just look for the house painted pink, a color favored inside and out. Set on 40 acres of rolling fields and woods, the cottage has a spacious lawn bordered by holly, rhododendrons, and the remnants of an old stone wall. The front of the inn, an 1820 Cape-style clapboard home, faces a pasture with grazing horses; the gravel drive and entrance are at the side. You enter the inn by walking into the cheerful Common Room, a 1950s addition furnished with a geranium-print sofa and chairs, green wall-to-wall carpeting, a fireplace, and a late-Victorian oak rocking chair, chest, and armoire, which holds a TV/VCR for guests.

Michael Cowan and her husband, Charlie, originally bought the house in 1990 as a private home, and their love for

European B&Bs led them to convert it to an inn, removing shingles to restore the original clapboard look, exposing wideboard floors once hidden in attic space, and meticulously furnishing each room with matching antiques.

Michael favors the Victorian period, and every room in the original house is carefully decorated with coordinating fabrics, wallpapers, and collectibles, some of which are for sale. Lamps, tea sets, and china dogs and cats are set on tables; portraits of women on ivory and porcelain hang on the walls. The guest rooms, named the Marble Room and the Rose Room, are upstairs on either side of a landing. Each has beautiful wideboard floors, an English gas fireplace, two upholstered chairs with a lamp between them, and a private bath with tub and shower. The Marble Room has a rose-and-cream paisley comforter on the bed, and English floral wallpaper in the colors of lettuce-green, lavender, rose, and grape. There is a needlepoint chair, needlepoint pillows on the bed, and a marble-topped walnut dresser with a Palladian mirror. The Rose Room features two mahogany pineapple four-poster beds with white eyelet comforters and pillows. Framed silhouettes on the wall pick up on the black trim of fabrics and rose wallpaper.

A full breakfast of entrées—such as waffles with bananas and maple syrup, or sausage, egg, and cheese casserole—is served in the small, formal dining room, in front of a fireplace with an original beehive oven. In good weather, breakfast is served on the deck of the Common Room.

🏠 *3 double rooms with baths. Air-conditioning, fireplaces, common TV/ VCR, mini-refrigerators, croquet. $75, full breakfast. MC, V. No smoking, no pets, 2-night minimum on weekends in season.*

Jackson-Russell-Whitfield House

26 North St., Plymouth, MA 02360, tel. 508/746-5289

In the middle of town, steps from Plymouth Rock, the 1782 Jackson-Russell-Whitfield House is made of brick painted a striking brick red, with dark green shutters and white trim. Dr. Brian Whitfield originally bought the house for his chiropractic practice in 1987, but then decided it was too nice for an office. He is the first owner unrelated to Samuel Jackson, the ship captain and banker who built it.

The elegant common areas of the house were furnished by Brian as if still occupied by the original owners, who profited from Asian and European trade. Quarter-cut oak parquet floors and fluted moldings were added in 1847. The living room has inviting stuffed chairs, and a comfortable sofa beneath a 17th-century Japanese screen; there is a velvet ottoman, an Oriental carpet in deep pinks and blues, an aubergine velvet armchair, and a Chippendale sideboard with a decanter of spirits. Chinese portraits on scrolls frame the doorway to the music room, which houses a 1917 Steinway baby grand piano, gleaming against the deep green walls.

Upstairs, the pretty Blue Room has large windows and four Oriental car-pets. Russian-blue trim and wainscoting match the floral wallpaper, whose stylized birds complement the Spice Islands carving of the four-poster bed. There are tiger maple night tables with lamps on either side of the bed, and the room also has a working fireplace. Mirror-paned doors open to the adjoining Stenciled Room, where contemporary artist Carolyn Hedge has painted willow and other traditional motifs. This room has two four-poster twin beds with white spreads, ivory drapes, and a tiger maple dresser and night table. There is one bath for both rooms, but the two rooms are rented simultaneously only to parties traveling together, so that guests who occupy only one of the rooms are assured of a private bath. Next door is a room whose walls are entirely covered in murals of serene pale green trees and pastures overlooking a harbor. A row of teddy bears sits on the 1810 walnut four-poster canopy bed. Brian's mother, Phyllis, lives in this room during the summer, when she flies in from California to run the inn.

In summer, Phyllis presides over breakfast, baking scones, muffins, and a much-requested streusel coffee cake, served in the comfortably formal dining room. In the off season, Brian tends to guests in the afternoon and evening, and his friend Jay Hall bakes and serves breakfast.

🏠 *2 double rooms with 1 bath in summer, 3 double rooms with 1 bath in winter. Air-conditioning, fireplace in 1 room, off-street parking and fax available. $80, Continental breakfast. MC, V. No smoking, no pets, no children.*

Salt Marsh Farm

322 Smith Neck Rd., South Dartmouth, MA 02748, tel. 508/992-0980

On the historic Isaac Howland homestead farm at the quiet end of a harborside road in South Dartmouth, this two-story, mint-condition Georgian farmhouse (circa 1770) is run by Sally and Larry Brownell and has been in

Sally's family since World War II. In the back of the house lie 90 acres of grounds, where nature trails lead to maples, oaks, and hollies, a 40-acre salt marsh, and the sparkling waters of Little River.

The Brownells have turned over the front of their home to their bed-and-breakfast guests, who may lounge by the fireplace in the living room filled with books on local nature lore and history. A large gallery-type family room, where you'll probably see jigsaw puzzles laid out, runs the length of the house. The building is full of pewter, silver, and choice antiques, virtually all of which were passed down through Sally's or Larry's families. Some of the pieces date back for generations, such as the massive mahogany sideboard in the intimate dining room, where portraits of four of Sally's Colonial ancestors gaze down on the scene.

Each of the two small chambers has its own private hall and stairway; one offers twin four-poster beds, and the other a double bed. Sally's handmade quilts often cover the beds, and freshly picked flowers decorate the rooms. On the wall in the Rocking Horse Room is an unusual picture of a parrot made entirely of feathers. One of the bathrooms has an oversize, claw-foot tub and a tub-height window with a view of the grounds.

Sally is an accomplished cook who makes good use of her vegetable garden. Her breakfast repertoire includes five-grain pancakes (she buys the grain at a nearby gristmill); fresh eggs from the Brownells' henhouse, prepared in any number of ways; prizewinning blueberry muffins; and double-dipped French toast with a special orange sauce and what Sally calls "mystery" syrup. "I never tell the guests what it's made of until they've tried it," she says. "But they always ask for more."

The town beach is within biking distance, and New Bedford is about 6 miles away. Padanaram, the name of the local harbor village, is used on many signposts.

▦ *2 double rooms with baths. TV and phone in common areas, bicycles, private nature trails. $65-$85, full breakfast and afternoon tea. MC, V. No smoking, no pets, no children under 5, 2-night minimum on summer weekends and holidays.*

Other Choices

Windsor House. 390 Washington St., Duxbury, MA 02332, tel. 617/934–0991. 3 double rooms with baths. Restaurant, pub. $105–$125, $10 additional for each child; full breakfast. AE, D, MC, V. No pets.

Reservations Service

New England Hospitality Network (Box 3291, Newport, RI 02840, tel. 401/849–1298 or 800/828–0000).

Cape Cod

Captain Freeman Inn

15 Breakwater Rd., Brewster, MA 02631, tel. 508/896–7481 or 800/843–4664

This impressive Victorian facing Brewster's little town square was built in 1866 by a packet-schooner captain and fleet owner. Converted to an inn in the 1940s, it was bought in December 1991 by Carol Covitz, a former marketing director for a Boston computer company.

Carol has done a splendid job renovating the house. She restored the exterior's original Victorian greens, with contrast colors for the brackets and columns of the wraparound veranda. The veranda itself got a new floor of oiled mahogany, and has rockers and a screened section facing the pool. Inside, Carol had a jewel to work with. The ground floor is spacious and bright, with 12-foot ceilings and windows. Fine architectural details include the ornate Italian plaster ceiling medallions and marble fireplace brought back from the captain's travels.

Like the common areas, first-floor guest rooms feature 12-foot ceilings, grand windows, and ceiling medallions. Second- and third-floor front rooms offer 8½-foot ceilings and large windows with views of a white church and the square. In a 1989 addition are three "Luxury Suites"—spacious bedrooms with queen canopy beds, sofas, fireplaces, cable TV/VCRs, mini-refrigerators, and French doors leading to small enclosed porches with private whirlpool spas. Guest rooms have hardwood floors, local art, and individual heat controls; they are done in antiques and Victorian reproductions, with nice touches like crystal or brass lamps, eyelet spreads, and all-cotton sheets. Most beds have lace or fishnet canopies.

Carol's breakfasts showcase skills honed in professional cooking classes. (In winter she offers her own weekend cooking school.) Such dishes as potato-cheddar pie, Italian *stradas*, and compotes are served on the screened porch or by the fire in the dining room.

Out back, the 1½-acre lawn is bordered in wild grapes, blackberries, and highbush blueberries. Hurricane fencing surrounds the pool and its deck, which is edged in garden and set with lounge chairs. A bay beach is a five-minute walk away.

⊞ *9 double rooms with baths, 3 doubles share 1 bath. Common mini-refrigerator, ice machine, sink, movie library, outdoor heated pool, croquet, badminton, bikes. $90–$205, full breakfast and afternoon tea. AE, MC, V. No smoking, no pets, 2-night minimum in season, weekends.*

Captain's House Inn

371 Old Harbor Rd., Chatham, MA 02633, tel. 508/945–0127 or 800/315–0728, fax 508/945–0866

Finely preserved architectural details, superb taste in decorating, opulent baked goods, and an overall feeling of warmth and quiet comfort make this perhaps the finest of the Cape's small inns. Behind a high hedge about half a mile from the town center is a 2-acre estate comprising the main inn, a white Greek Revival built in 1839 by packet-boat captain Hiram Harding; the attached Carriage House, a three-quarter Cape; and the Captain's Cottage, a full Cape with a 200-year-old bow roof, set in its own yard with a lovely English garden.

Though the general style of the inn is Williamsburg—with historic-reproduction wallpapers, mostly king- or queen-size canopy or other antique beds, and upholstered wing chairs, as well as fluffy comforters and modern tile baths—each guest room has its own personality. Wild Pigeon is spacious and serene, with an antique canopied four-poster, tapestry-upholstered wing chairs in the sitting area, and cream Berber wall-to-wall carpeting under a high cathedral ceiling. In the Captain's Cottage, the spectacular Hiram Harding Room has 200-year-old hand-hewn beams and a wall of Early American raised walnut paneling centered by a large fireplace with wing chairs on each side, a sofa in front of wall-to-wall bookshelves holding many antique books, and a rich red Oriental carpet.

In the main inn, the variable-width pumpkin pine floors of the entry hall softly shine with age. Here and in the parlor, where a hearth fire sets a welcoming tone, impeccably chosen antiques are accompanied by luxurious Oriental carpets and oil paintings of sea captains. French doors lead to the white and bright glassed-in sunroom, where breakfast and a lavish English tea (with homemade scones, jams, and cream) are served on Wedgwood and crystal at individual tables.

Jan and Dave McMaster spent nearly two years in search of the "perfect inn" and became owners of the Captain's House in June 1993. Dave, a retired Navy commander and ex-CEO of a computer company, and Jan, a gracious Englishwoman with a knack for making you feel special, run the inn with a well-trained staff that includes English university students studying hotel management and catering. A full gourmet breakfast is now served, and there are honeymoon baskets, courtesy bicycles, and lawn croquet during the warmer months.

🏨 *14 double rooms with baths, 2 suites. Individual heat and air-conditioning. $130–$225, full breakfast and afternoon tea. AE, MC, V. No smoking, no pets.*

Chatham Bars Inn

Shore Rd., Chatham, MA 02633, tel. 508/945–0096 or 800/527–4884, fax 508/ 945–5491

Perched majestically atop a rise overlooking Pleasant Bay, just a stroll from the shops of Chatham, is this ultimate oceanfront resort in the old style. Once a kind of private club for the wealthy, Chatham Bars remains a traditionally classy inn. Built as a hunting lodge in 1914, the inn consists of the crescent-shape main building and 26 one- to eight-bedroom cottages (either in wooded groupings near the main inn or across the street on the bluff above the beach) on 20 landscaped acres. It has been completely restored as an elegant inn, where you'll feel free to dress in your best in season (no jeans or T-shirts in common areas after 6 PM).

Off the grand entry hall is the South Lounge, decorated with Victorian-style overstuffed chairs and comfortable couches in burgundy and beige, pots of eucalyptus, and an enormous fireplace; the brick terrace, with views out to the bay and the famous sandbars; and a year-round casual restaurant and bar. Simple elegance is the theme in the main dining room, with an expansive view of the sea from the window wall. The decor is bright and crisp, with a deep green rug setting off the white accents. A lavish breakfast buffet is served here each morning, with fresh fruits, sliced meats and smoked fish, finger pastries, and more; hot dishes are also available. The dinner menu centers on creative New England fare. A beachhouse grill has lighter meals and clambakes in summer.

Most rooms have decks. All the cottages have common rooms, some with fireplaces. Throughout, rooms are carpeted in shades of sand and sea and are attractively decorated with furnishings including traditional pine, more modern upholstered pieces, Queen Anne reproductions, gilt-framed art, and Laura Ashley touches.

An excellent time to sample the inn's offerings is from October through May, through inexpensive midweek bed-and-breakfast-by-the-sea getaway packages or romantic weekends.

🏨 *130 double rooms with baths, 20 suites, 2 master suites. 3 restaurants, phones, cable TVs, lending library, cottages with common mini-refrigerators, private beach, 4 tennis courts, lessons, putting green, heated outdoor pool, fitness room, volleyball, harbor cruises, movies, cocktail parties, shuffleboard, children's program (July–Aug.), newspaper, baby-sitting, launch service, adjacent golf course. $170–$1,000, no breakfast. AE, DC, MC, V. No pets.*

Inn at Fernbrook

481 Main St., Centerville, MA 02632, tel. 508/775–4334, fax 508/778–4455

When Boston restaurateur Howard Marstons built his mansion in this quiet village of Centerville, just outside Hyannis, he hired the best—Frederick Law Olmsted, designer of New York's

Central Park—to landscape it. Complete with man-made ponds, formal gardens, a vineyard, and hundreds of trees brought from all over the world by Marstons's sea captain father, the park they created made an elegant setting for the Queen Anne Victorian gem that is today the Inn at Fernbrook.

Though the original 17-acre estate has dwindled to 2, the eponymous fern-rimmed brook remains, as does part of Olmsted's design. Pebbled paths wind past a sunken, heart-shape sweetheart garden of red and pink roses, set in a heart-shape lawn; exotic trees (a Japanese cork, a weeping beech); a windmill; a vine-covered arbor; and two fishponds where Japanese koi swim amid water hyacinths and lilies.

The 1881 house itself, now on the National Register of Historic Places, is a beauty, from the turreted white exterior to the fine woodwork and furnishings within. All rooms have antique or reproduction beds, 1930s-style wood table radios, and decanters of sherry with antique glasses. Some have sitting areas with bay windows, fireplaces, canopy beds, Victorian sofas, and pastel Oriental carpets on floors of cherry, maple, or oak. The spacious third-floor Olmsted Suite has two bedrooms and a living room with a fireplace under cathedral ceilings, as well as a sundeck; there's also a cottage by itself across the lawns.

Breakfast is friendly and delicious, served in the formal dining room. Brian Gallo—who left the hotel business in 1986 to join his friend Sal Di Florio in converting the house into an inn—cooks the meals, and Sal serves. On Sunday Brian regales guests with tales of the house's past: Here, onetime owner Herbert Kalmus, inventor of the Technicolor process, hosted such Hollywood friends as Gloria Swanson and Cecil B. DeMille, and, in the 1960s, Cardinal Spellman (who was using the house as a summer retreat) entertained John F. Kennedy and Richard Nixon. In the afternoon, minted iced tea or hot tea can be taken (on request) in the living room or on the veranda, with its wicker furniture and hanging baskets of pink geraniums.

🏨 *4 double rooms with baths, 1 suite, 1 cottage (no kitchen). $125–$185, full breakfast. AE, D, MC, V. Restricted smoking, no children, no pets, 2-night minimum summer weekends.*

Moses Nickerson House

364 Old Harbor Rd., Chatham, MA 02633, tel. 508/945-5859 or 800/628-6972, fax 508/945-7087

Named for the whaling captain who built the house, this white Greek Revival with gray-blue shutters and large fan ornament (just across the street from the Captain's House Inn) has an atmosphere of simple elegance and romance. Rose bouquet-covered walls complement an overstuffed white sofa, Aubusson rug, and an antique lyre-base Duncan Phyfe table in the parlor, where guests can take tea in front of a fire. Throughout the inn are wide-board pine floors and original glass.

All guest rooms have firm queen-size beds with handmade quilts in summer and comforters in winter; most have pedestal sinks, and several have gas-log fireplaces. Room 7 is clubby and masculine, with Ralph Lauren fabrics, dark leathers and woods, and a fireplace; on the walls hang hunting hats and horns. In lovely Room 4, a high canopy bed is mounted by stepstool; a wood rack displays antique laces and linens, and a Nantucket hand-hooked rug complements the stenciled and whitewashed walls. Off the parlor is Room 1, with a romantic antique four-poster and armoire hand-painted with roses, and a blue velvet Belgian settee invitingly placed before a fireplace.

Your hosts, Linda and George Watts, met at the inn in June 1995 and married that November; Linda was in the insurance biz and George, a Canadian, was in politics and finance. The Watts serve breakfast in the glass-enclosed dining area that opens onto landscaped gardens (including a rose garden), a water fountain, and pond with goldfish.

▦ *7 double rooms with baths. Air-conditioning, croquet, double hammock, turndown service in season, TV available. $95–$169, full breakfast and afternoon tea or lemonade. AE, D, MC, V. No smoking, no pets, 2-night minimum summer weekends, 3-night minimum on major holidays.*

Other Choices

Augustus Snow House. 528 Main St., Harwich Port, MA 02646, tel. 508/430–0528; 800/320–0528. 5 double rooms with baths. Phones, cable TVs, 3 rooms with whirlpool tubs, tearoom. $145–$160, full breakfast. AE, D, MC, V. Restricted smoking, no pets, 2-night minimum weekends in season.

Bay Beach. 1–3 Bay Beach La., Box 151, Sandwich, MA 02563, tel. 508/888–8813. 6 double rooms with baths. Exercise facilities, newspaper, private beach, beach chairs. $150–$195; full breakfast, wine and cheese on arrival. No smoking, no pets, 2- to 3-night minimum on holidays. Closed Veteran's Day–May.

Beechwood. 2839 Main St. (Rte. 6A), Barnstable, MA 02630, tel. 508/362–6618 or 800/609–6618, fax 508/362–0298. 6 double rooms with baths. Air-conditioning in 1 room, fireplaces in 2 rooms, mini-refrigerators, bikes. $120–$150; full breakfast, afternoon tea. AE, MC, V. No smoking, no pets, 2-night minimum weekends in season.

Brass Key. 9 Court St., Provincetown, MA 02657, tel. 508/487–9005 or 800/842–9858, fax 508/487–9020. 12 double rooms with baths. Air-conditioning, phones, cable TV/VCRs, mini-refrigerators, hair dryers, bathrobes, videocassette library, turndown service, heated spa pool. $155–$220, Continental breakfast. AE, D, MC, V. Restricted smoking,

no pets, minimum stay required in season on holidays and during special events (number of nights varies).

Brewster Farmhouse. 716 Main St., Brewster, MA 02631, tel. 508/896–3910 or 800/892–3910, fax 508/896–4232. 3 double rooms with baths, 1 2-bedroom suite with bath. Cable TVs, air-conditioning, turndown service, fax, phones, VCRs available, heated pool, spa, beach towels and blankets, bikes. $95–$150, full breakfast and afternoon tea. AE, D, DC, MC, V. No smoking, no pets.

Honeysuckle Hill. 591 Rte. 6A, West Barnstable, MA 02668, tel. 508/362–8418 or 800/441–8418, fax 508/362–4854. 2 double rooms with baths, 1 suite. Air-conditioning, beach towels, chairs, umbrellas. $110–$150, full breakfast. AE, D, MC, V. No smoking. Closed Oct.–Apr.

Isaiah Clark House. 1187 Rte. 6A, Box 169, Brewster, MA 02631, tel. 508/896–2223 or 800/822–4001, fax 508/896–7054. 7 double rooms with baths. Air-conditioning, phones, cable TVs, common stereo, CDs, piano, turndown service, games, beach chairs and towels, airport or train-station pickup. $98–$120; full breakfast, afternoon tea, evening cookies and milk on request. AE, D, MC, V. No smoking, no pets, 2-night minimum weekends in season.

Isaiah Jones Homestead. 165 Main St., Sandwich, MA 02563, tel. 508/888–9115 or 800/526–1625. 5 double rooms with baths. 3 rooms with fireplaces. $95–$155, full breakfast, afternoon tea. AE, D, MC, V. Restricted smoking, no pets.

Liberty Hill. 77 Main St. (Rte. 6A), Yarmouth Port, MA 02675, tel. 508/362–3976 or 800/821–3977. 5 double rooms with baths. TVs, 3 rooms with air-conditioning, mini-refrigerator with mixers, train or airport pickup. $80–$135, full breakfast. AE, MC, V. No smoking in dining room, no pets, 2-night minimum on major holiday weekends.

Mostly Hall. 27 Main St., Falmouth, MA 02540, tel. 508/548–3786 or 800/682–0565. 6 double rooms with baths. Air-conditioning, common TV/VCR, piano, lending library, bicycles. $95–$125, full breakfast and afternoon refreshments. AE, D, MC, V. No smoking, no children, no pets, 2-night minimum usually in season and weekends year-round. Closed Jan.

Village Green Inn. 40 Main St., Falmouth, MA 02540, tel. 508/548–5621 or 800/237–1119, fax 508/457–5051. 4 double rooms with baths, 1 suite. Air-conditioning, fireplaces in 2 rooms, cable TV, common TV, piano, bikes. $95–$140, full breakfast. AE, MC, V. Restricted smoking, no pets, 2-night minimum in season, 3-night minimum on holiday weekends.

Wedgewood Inn. 83 Main St., Yarmouth Port, MA 02675, tel. 508/362–5157 or 508/362–9178, fax 508/362–5851. 4 double rooms with baths, 2 suites. Air-conditioning, common TV. $105–$160, full breakfast and afternoon tea. AE, DC, MC, V. Restricted smoking, no pets.

Reservations Services

Bed and Breakfast Cape Cod (Box 341, West Hyannis Port, MA 02672-0341, tel. 508/775–2772). **House Guests Cape Cod and the Islands** (Box 1881, Orleans, MA 02653, tel. 800/666–4678). **Orleans Bed & Breakfast Associates** (Box 1312, Orleans, MA 02653, tel. 508/255–3824 or 800/541–6226; covers Lower Cape, Harwich to Truro). **Provincetown Reservations System** (293 Commercial St., Provincetown, MA 02657, tel. 508/487–2400 or 800/648–0364; also shows, restaurants, and more).

Martha's Vineyard

Charlotte Inn

S. Summer St., Edgartown, MA 02539, tel. 508/627–4751, fax 508/627–4652

On a quiet street in the center of well-groomed Edgartown is an inn that stands out like a polished gem. Gery Conover, owner for more than 20 years, and his wife, Paula, oversee every detail with meticulous care and obvious pride to make sure their guests find everything fresh, pretty, welcoming—and perfect. From the original structure, an 1860 white clapboard home that belonged to a whaling-company owner, the Charlotte has grown into a five-building complex connected by lawns and a private courtyard. Ivy-bordered brick walkways lead past pockets of garden to flower-filled nooks perfect for reading or reflection. Across the street is the early 18th-century Garden House; one gorgeous room has French doors out to a private terrace looking onto a large English garden.

True Anglophiles, the Conovers have furnished the inn through antiquing trips to England—and continue to do so, since each room is redone completely every five years. Guest rooms feature mahogany furniture, brass lamps, original art, richly colored wallpapers, lush fabrics, and down-filled pillows, comforters, and chair cushions. One room in the veranda-wrapped 1850 Summer House has a fireplace and a baby grand piano.

The most exquisite accommodations on the island are here, in the Coach House. Set above a re-created estate garage lined with gleaming wainscoting, the suite features cathedral ceilings, a Palladian window, French doors, a green marble fireplace, and sumptuous furnishings. Everywhere you look, there's something wonderful: sterling silver lamps, Minton bone china, white cut-work-lace bed linens.

The main inn's ground floor is spacious and elegant, with the gallery's sporting and marine art and contemporary works displayed throughout. The mahogany-paneled common room with a fireplace draws guests for afternoon tea and cocktails. In winter breakfast is served there on white-cloth-covered tables.

The fine restaurant, L'étoile, in a glassed-in summerhouse with patio, serves dinner and Sunday brunch. It mixes luxuriant greenery, spotlighted oil paintings, and surprising antique accents, such as leather-bound books perched on the rafters. The contemporary French menu highlights native seafood and game.

🏠 *23 double rooms with baths, 2 suites. Restaurant, air-conditioning, TVs, phones, fireplaces in 5 rooms, common TV. $250–$650, Continental breakfast and afternoon tea. AE, MC, V. No pets. Restaurant closed Jan.– mid-Feb.*

Lambert's Cove Country Inn

Lambert's Cove Rd., R.R. 1, Box 422, West Tisbury, MA 02575, tel. 508/693– 2298, fax 508/693–7890

Approached via a narrow, winding road through pine woods, this secluded retreat is everything a country inn should be. The 1790 farmhouse is set amid an apple orchard, a large English garden bordered by lilac bushes, and woods that hide a tennis court. In spring, an ancient tree is draped in blossoms from 20-foot wisteria vines (photo spot for many weddings held here); in fall, a Concord grape arbor scents the air.

The inn's common areas are elegant, with rich woodwork and large flower arrangements, yet also make you feel at home. Most impressive is the gentleman's library, part of the additions made in the 1920s. This large, airy room features book-lined white walls, a fireside grouping of upholstered wing chairs, rich red Oriental carpets on a polished wood floor, and French doors leading out to the orchard. A cozier reading area on the second-floor landing offers a sofa and shelves of books and magazines.

The guest rooms are in the main house and in two adjacent buildings. Most main-house rooms have a soft, soothing country look, framed by Laura Ashley wallpapers; two at the back can convert to a suite with a connecting sitting room with sleep sofa and sliders opening onto a backyard deck. Rooms in the other houses have a bit more rustic feel. Two rooms upstairs in The Barn have exposed beams; downstairs, one large room with a sofa bed has sliders out to a deck. The Carriage House has camp-style decks and screened porches. Comfort is the focus, meaning unfussy furnishings, firm beds with country quilts, and bright, cheerful baths with extra-thick towels.

Fine dining is part of the experience, and the romantic restaurant serves unpretentious, excellent Continental cuisine in an intimate atmosphere of soft lighting and music. The popular Sunday brunch is served on a deck overlooking the orchard, weather permitting.

Innkeeper since summer 1992 is Russ Wilson, whose previous experience includes stints with Marriott and the Los Angeles Biltmore.

🏠 *15 double rooms with baths. Restaurant (dinner and Sun. brunch; off-season, weekends only), some rooms with air-conditioning, 1 room with fireplace, common TV, tennis court, beach passes. $125–$175, Continental breakfast. AE, MC, V. No smoking in common areas, no pets, 3-night minimum most weekends July–Aug.*

Oak House

Sea View Ave., Box 299, Oak Bluffs, MA 02557, tel. 508/693–4187, fax 508/696–7385

Among the summer homes along the coast road just outside Oak Bluffs center stands the Oak House bed-and-breakfast. Built in 1872 and enlarged and lavishly refurbished in the early 1900s, this wonderful Victorian beach house has a playful gingerbread-trimmed pastel facade and a wrap-around veranda with much-used rockers and even a swing or two.

Inside, the reason for the inn's name becomes clear: Everywhere you look, you see richly patinated oak, in ceilings, wall paneling, wainscoting, and furnishings. The two bedrooms that constitute the Captain's Room are fitted out like cabins in a ship, with oak wainscoting covering walls and ceilings. The best of the rooms with balconies (some just large enough for a chair) is the Governor Claflin Room, with French doors that open wide to let in a broad expanse of sea and sky. Unfortunately, cars whiz past on the road below, which some people may find distracting (a room at the back is one solution).

When the Convery family bought the Oak House in 1988, they created several tiny bathrooms out of existing closets. One spacious hall bath, with peach-painted pressed-tin walls and ceiling, a dressing table, and the inn's only tub, was turned into a private bath for the very feminine Tivoli Room. (Each room has a distinct personality.)

Alison Convery's island antiques shops provided much of the inn's superb furniture, brass lamps, sea chests, and such. The entrance hall evokes an elegant Victorian private home, with high ceilings, a baby grand piano, a hand-cranked organ, potted palms, and an impressive central staircase lined with sumptuous red Oriental carpeting. The glassed-in sunporch has lots of white wicker, plants, floral print pillows, and original stained-glass window accents.

In the afternoon, guests wander back from the beach (across the street) to meet and chat over tea. Homemade lemonade and iced tea, along with elegant tea cakes and cookies, are provided by Alison's daughter Betsi Convery-Luce, the warm and open innkeeper and a Cordon Bleu–trained pastry chef.

🏠 *8 double rooms with baths, 2 suites. Air-conditioning, TVs, common TV. $100–$250, Continental breakfast and afternoon tea. AE, D, MC, V. No pets, 3-night minimum most summer weekends. Closed mid-Oct.–early May.*

Outermost Inn

Lighthouse Rd., R.R. 1, Box 171, Gay Head, MA 02535, tel. 508/645–3511, fax 508/645–3514

In 1990, Hugh and Jeanne Taylor finished converting the sprawling, gray-shingle home they built 20 years earlier—and are raising their two children in—into a bed-and-breakfast. Hugh's redesign takes full advantage of the superb location, at the sparsely populated outermost western end of the island. Standing alone on acres of wide-open moorland, the two-story house is wrapped with picture windows that reveal breathtaking views of sea and sky in three directions; to the north are the Elizabeth Islands and, beyond, mainland Cape Cod. The sweeping red and white beams of the Gay Head Lighthouse, just over the moors on the Gay Head Cliffs, add an extra touch of romance at night.

White walls and polished light-wood floors of ash, cherry, beech, oak, and hickory create a bright, clean setting for simple contemporary-style furnishings and local art. Fabrics used throughout the inn are all natural—in the dhurrie rugs, the down-filled cotton comforters, and the all-cotton sheets. Several corner rooms have window walls on two sides.

The Lighthouse Suite has a private entrance, a skylighted bath, and a separate living room with a butcher-block dining table. The Oak Room has French doors that open onto a private deck with a great view of the lighthouse.

The wraparound porch, set with hammocks and rocking chairs, is ideal for relaxing and watching birds and deer. Breakfast is served there or in the dining room, with fireplace and window wall. In the afternoon complimentary hors d'oeuvres and setups for drinks are provided on request. In season, the inn operates a restaurant (by reservation only), offering a mix of gourmet and home cooking prepared by a Culinary Institute–trained chef—another excuse for guests not to wander far from the nest.

When you are ready to venture out, the owners are happy to help with arrangements for all kinds of activities. Hugh (of the musical Taylor clan) has sailed the local waters since childhood, and he will charter out his 50-foot catamaran to guests for excursions to Cuttyhunk Island. There's a privately accessed beach just a five-minute walk away.

▦ *6 double rooms with baths, 1 suite. Phones, 1 room with whirlpool bath, beach passes. $190–$285, full breakfast. AE, MC, V. Restricted smoking, no pets.*

Thorncroft Inn

460 Main St., Box 1022, Vineyard Haven, MA 02568, tel. 508/693-3333 or 800/332-1236, fax 508/693-5419

Set amid 3½ wooded acres about a mile from town and the Vineyard Haven ferry, the Thorncroft is like a little piece of English countryside. Beyond a manicured lawn bordered in neat boxwood hedges and flowering shrubs is the tidy Craftsman bungalow, graygreen with white shutters and a dormered second story, built in 1918 as the guest house of a large estate.

Since they bought the place in 1981, Karl and Lynn Buder have renovated it from top to bottom, furnishing it beautifully with a mix of antiques and reproductions to create an environment that is elegant yet soothing, somewhat formal but not fussy. In addition, they built a Carriage House out back with two rooms geared for romance, with large whirlpool baths (one backed by mirrored walls) and fireplaces. Two other irresistible inn rooms have attached private hot-tub rooms with screens just under the roof that let in fresh air for an Alpine effect.

Considering Lynn's master's degree in business administration and Karl's in public administration, it is not surprising that the Thorncroft—now their only business—is run as efficiently as it is.

The fine Colonial and richly carved Renaissance Revival antiques—including matched sets—are meticulously maintained. Beds are firm, floors thickly carpeted, tiled bathrooms modern and well lighted. Room fireplaces are piled with wood and kindling each day, ready for the touch of a match. Ice buckets, wineglasses, and corkscrews are provided in each guest room, as is a notebook of information on the area. The bedrooms are wired for computer modems—for those who just *can't* leave work behind. And for those who can, there's a bookcase full of magazines on an amazing range of subjects—and a wicker sunporch in which to read them, if you like.

Breakfast is an organized affair. You can order a Continental breakfast to be delivered to your room and set up elegantly on table-height trays, or sign up for one of two seatings the night before. A bell calls you to the table, where guests meet and exchange touring tips over such tasty entrées as almond French toast and Belgian waffles.

▦ *14 double rooms with baths. Airconditioning, cable TVs, phones, fireplaces in 10 rooms, bathrobes, hair dryers, ironing equipment, whirlpools,* *hot tubs, mini-refrigerators in some rooms, turndown service, newspaper, common mini-refrigerator. $150–$400, full breakfast and afternoon tea. AE, D, DC, MC, V. No smoking, no pets.*

Other Choices

Admiral Benbow Inn. 520 New York Ave., Box 2488, Oak Bluffs, MA 02557, tel. 508/693–6825. 6 double rooms with baths. TV in common area. $75–$150, full breakfast. AE, D, MC, V. No smoking, no pets, 2-night minimum weekends, 3-night minimum on holidays.

Aldworth Manor. 26 Mt. Aldworth Rd., Box 4058, Vineyard Haven, MA 02568, tel. 508/693–3203, fax 508/693–6813. 6 double rooms with baths, 1 suite. Phones with voice mail, common cable TV and mini-refrigerator, turndown service, beach chairs, towels, and coolers. $109–$219, Continental breakfast and afternoon tea. MC, V. No smoking, no pets.

Bayberry. Old Courthouse Rd., Box 654, West Tisbury, MA 02575, tel. 508/693–1984. 3 double rooms with baths, 2 doubles share 1 bath. Common refrigerator, croquet, beach passes and towels. $110–$150, full breakfast and afternoon tea. AE, MC, V. No smoking, no pets.

Beach Plum Inn and Cottages. Beach Plum La., off North Rd., Menemsha, MA 02552, tel. 508/645–9454 or 800/528–6616. 5 double rooms, 4 1- or 2-bedroom cottages, all with baths. Restaurant, air-conditioning, TVs, phones, turndown service, fax, baby-sitting, tennis, croquet, beach passes, bike rentals. $200–$300, full breakfast; rates that include all meals are available. AE, D, MC, V. No smoking, no pets. Closed Nov.–Apr.

Daggett House. 59 N. Water St., Box 1333, Edgartown, MA 02539, tel. 508/627–4600 or 800/946–3400, fax 508/627–4611. 21 double rooms with baths (1 with kitchenette), 4 housekeeping suites. Restaurant, phones, air-conditioning in 3 rooms, common TV, beach

towels. $90–$395, no breakfast. AE, MC, V. No smoking, no pets.

Sea Spray Inn. 2 Nashawena Park, Box 2125, Oak Bluffs, MA 02557, tel. 508/693–9388. 5 double rooms with baths, 2 doubles with shared bath. Common TV, refrigerator, and barbecue. $90–$140, Continental breakfast. MC, V. No smoking, no pets. Closed mid.-Nov.–mid.-Apr.

Shiverick Inn. Corner of Pease's Point Way and Pent La., Box 640, Edgartown, MA 02539, tel. 508/627–3797 or 800/723–4292, fax 508/627–8441. 10 double rooms with baths, 1 sitting room connects to 1 or 2 adjacent rooms to form a suite with sleep sofa. Most rooms with air-conditioning and fireplace, library with cable TV, stereo, and mini-refrigerator; bike rentals. $170–$260, Continental breakfast. AE, D, MC, V. No smoking, no pets.

Victorian Inn. 24 S. Water St., Edgartown, MA 02539, tel. 508/627–4784. 14 double rooms with baths. $125–$265, full breakfast and afternoon tea. AE, MC, V. No smoking, no pets in season.

Reservations Services

Accommodations Plus (R.F.D. 273, Edgartown, MA 02539, tel. 508/696–8880). **House Guests Cape Cod and the Islands** (Box 1881, Orleans, MA 02653, tel. 508/896–7053 or 800/666–4678). **Martha's Vineyard and Nantucket Reservations** (Box 1322, Vineyard Haven, MA 02568, tel. 508/693–7200; in MA, 800/649–5671).

Nantucket

Centerboard Guest House

8 Chester St., Box 456, Nantucket, MA 02554, tel. 508/228-9696

The look of this inn, a few blocks from the center of town, is unique on the island. In the high-ceilinged guest rooms, white walls (some with murals of moors and sky in soft pastels), blond-wood floors, white or natural wood furniture, white slatted shutters, and natural woodwork with a light wash of mauve tint create a cool, spare, dreamy atmosphere. There's more white still, in the lacy linens and puffy comforters on the featherbeds, each mounded with four pillows. Restrained touches of color are added by small stained-glass lamps, antique quilts, dishes of pink crystals, and fresh flowers.

No. 4 is the largest regular room, with a queen-size bed, a sofa, and an oversize shower; No. 2 has two antique brass and white-painted iron double beds. The small but pleasant studio apartment has a kitchen, two double beds in cabinetry-like berths on a ship, a separate twin bed in its own cubbyhole (fun for a child), a dining area, and a private entrance.

The first-floor suite is a stunner. Its large living room evokes the house's Victorian origins, with an 11-foot ceiling, the original parquet floor, a working fireplace topped by an elaborately carved oak mantel, and antique accents (a carved duck, a tapestry firescreen, lighting fixtures, and books). A nice modern touch is the wet bar. A lush hunter-green and rose Oriental carpet, sleep sofa, and upholstered chairs nicely complement the eggplant-color walls and the richness of the wood. Off the small separate bedroom, with a custom-built cherry four-poster bed

topped by a high fishnet canopy, is a well-appointed bath, whose highly polished darkwood cabinetry is set off by a rich green marble floor, double shower, and whirlpool tub.

Gerrie Miller, the inn's manager, sets out cold cereals, fruit, muffins, Portuguese bread, teas, and coffees in the sunny dining room amid such artistic touches as a sand-and-shell assemblage under glass and an 18th-century corner cupboard spilling antique-blue and purple dried hydrangeas.

🏨 *4 double rooms with baths, 1 studio apartment, 1 suite, 1 cottage. Air-conditioning, TVs, phones, mini-refrigerators, common TV/VCR, beach towels. $165-$285, Continental breakfast. AE, MC, V. No smoking, no pets, 2-night minimum most weekends.*

Jared Coffin House

29 Broad St., Nantucket, MA 02554, tel. 508/228-2400 or 800/248-2405, fax 508/228-8549

Amid the shops, restaurants, and activity of downtown stands this complex that is a perennial favorite because of its location, dependability, conveniences, and class. It consists of six structures dating from the 18th century to the 20th, and all are well maintained and landscaped. The landmark main inn is the most impressive.

In 1845, Jared Coffin, a wealthy shipowner, built this glorious three-story redbrick Greek Revival with Ionic portico, parapet, hip roof, and cupola (ask for a key to go up in it and check out the panoramic view). In 1847 it became a stopover for travelers, in 1961 the Nantucket Historical Trust restored it, and today it is watched over by Phil and Margaret Read—owners since 1976.

The first-floor public rooms are elegant, yet welcoming—with Oriental rugs and antique Sheraton and Chippendale furniture, portraits, clocks, and lace curtains. In cool weather, you can sit by the fire sipping drinks brought to you from the basement bar and restaurant, the Tap Room. Breakfast and dinner are served in the formal restaurant, Jared's, a lovely, high-ceilinged room with salmon walls, pale green swag draperies, Federal antiques, and chandeliers with frosted-glass globes.

The main house's 11 guest rooms are nicely furnished with Oriental carpets and a blend of 19th-century antiques and reproductions, including giltwood mirrors, upholstered chairs, and a carved four-poster pineapple bed. The second-floor corner rooms are the largest, with sitting areas, and the front corner room has more windows. The inexpensive single rooms—a rare commodity on the island—are small but tastefully done. Also lower priced are the small, clean, and comfortable rooms of the Eben Allen Wing, all with private baths and TV.

The Harrison Gray House, an 1842 Greek Revival across Centre Street, is the most popular part of the inn, offering bigger rooms, many with sitting areas, and large baths, as well as a common living room and a sunporch with TV; both it and the 1821 Henry Coffin House have queen canopy beds. The Daniel Webster House, built in 1964, with uninspired decor by Ethan Allen, is adjacent to the outdoor café and has a second-floor lobby and a small deck at the back, where guests can relax and have a drink or read the paper.

🏨 *52 double rooms with baths, 8 singles with baths. 2 restaurants, TVs, phones, some mini-refrigerators. $75–$200, full breakfast. AE, D, DC, MC, V.*

76 Main Street

76 Main St., Nantucket, MA 02554, tel. 508/228-2533

Built by a sea captain in 1883 as a private residence, 76 Main—now a gracious bed-and-breakfast inn—sits just above the bustle of the shops on quiet, mansion-lined upper Main Street. The original mansard roof has been obscured by an unfortunate Federal-style facade, with a fretted parapet and platinum gray shutters on the white wood siding; the mansard, however, is still visible at the sides.

A long, serpentine granite staircase leads to a beautifully restored Victorian entry hall, shining with rich woods—from the elegant patterned floor to the elaborately carved cherry staircase. Massive, dark-stained redwood pocket doors with bull's-eye moldings close the hall off from the very Victorian sitting room and the former dining room and parlor, now the two best guest rooms.

These two rooms share the hall's emphasis on fine wood, as well as its high ceilings. No. 3 has not only wonderful woodwork but also a two-tone wood floor, a carved armoire, and twin four-poster beds set off by Oriental-style blue-and-white wallpaper. The spacious No. 1 has three large windows, upholstered chairs, brass lamps, and a bed with eyelet spread and canopy.

The second- and third-floor hallways, with maple and oak flooring topped with Oriental rugs and runners, lead to rooms furnished less grandly but well, with Ethan Allen reproductions, braided rugs, handmade quilts over all-cotton sheets, country curtains, and light patterned wallpapers. Everything is sparkling clean. Some rooms on the dormer-punctuated third floor have skylighted baths, casement windows, or window seats.

In a single-story, motel-like annex out back (built in 1955, when the facade was added), you'll find six rooms with private entrances. Although they have low ceilings, the rooms are large enough for families of up to five and have been brightened with new plastering and white bedding. Furnished in a more Colonial style, with industrial carpeting, pretty wallpapers, and velour-upholstered armchairs, they are available in season only.

Owner Shirley Peters usually officiates over the inn's breakfast buffet, which is set out either in the breakfast room, on a long wood table over which guests get to know one another easily, or out back on the flagstone patio.

🏠 *18 double rooms with baths. Cable TV and mini-refrigerators in annex rooms. $125–$145, Continental breakfast. AE, D, MC, V. No smoking, no pets.*

Ten Lyon Street Inn

10 Lyon St., Nantucket, MA 02554, tel. 508/228–5040

In 1986, Ann Marie and Barry Foster opened this bed-and-breakfast on a quiet street about a five-minute walk from the town center. Barry's work—completely rebuilding the three-story Colonial-style house from its foundations—was pretty much done, but Ann Marie's had just begun. Since then, she has used her decorating skills, from upholstering to antiques restoration, to make this a most individual and eye-pleasing inn. Her touch is evident from the moment you pass through the gate into the small, flower-filled yard. Exotic bulbs, lilacs, and other perennials curve around the lawn, while during spring and summer pink and peach roses climb the trellises against the house's weathered gray shingles.

Barry, an electrical contractor, wanted to give the house something of a historic feel, so to the smooth, white plaster walls and ceilings and light-wood moldings he added such touches as new golden-pine floors in planks of variable widths, salvaged Colonial-era mantels, and hefty antiqued red oak ceiling beams.

Guest rooms have a spare, uncluttered look, yet are warmed by details. The white walls make a clean stage for exquisite antique Oriental rugs in deep, rich colors and some choice antiques, such as English pine sleigh beds and a tobacco-leaf four-poster bed; chairs upholstered in English florals; and such romantic fabrics as white lace curtains and a Battenberg lace canopy. The beds have hand-stitched quilts, down comforters, and all-cotton sheets (which Ann Marie actually irons). Bathrooms are bright white, with maize- and white-striped runners on the shiny floors and delicate wall hangings—white with a touch of color—brought from Ann Marie's native Austria. Several baths have separate showers; all have antique porcelain pedestal sinks and brass fixtures.

Room 1, the showpiece, has a 19th-century French country tester bed romantically draped in gauzy white mosquito netting. The large room is made lush with stunning red Turkish carpets, potted palms, gilt mirrors, and little antique gilt-wood cupids on either side of the bed.

Ann Marie provides a healthy Continental breakfast, served in the garden during summer; the muffins are low in sugar and fat, the jellies low in sugar, yet all are delicious. Common areas include a small upstairs sitting room and a newly decorated living room with a book-filled cabinet and an Oriental carpet.

🏠 *7 double rooms with baths. $135–$185, Continental breakfast. MC, V. No smoking, no pets. Closed mid-Dec.–mid-Apr.*

Westmoor Inn

Cliff Rd., Nantucket, MA 02554, tel. 508/228–0877

The tradition of gracious entertaining established when the Vanderbilts built their Nantucket summerhouse in 1917 continues today in its incarnation as a bed-and-breakfast.

After a day of exploring the island, guests gather for a predinner wine and cheese reception. Mornings, they meet again in the sunny, all-glass breakfast room over a buffet of yogurt, fruit salad, granola, croissants, home-baked scones or nut breads, juices, and more. Tables are set with white damask, flowers, and white china. Nice touches like ramekins of jams and butter, a bowl of ice around the milk pitcher on the buffet, a selection of daily newspapers, and soft classical music help make the experience especially enjoyable.

The entry, with sweeping staircase, has the air of the manor house. Off the entry is the living room, with a grand piano and a game table, as well as a glassed-in sunporch with white wicker chairs and a TV (for those inevitable rainy days). Outside the yellow Federal-style mansion with widow's walk and portico, a wide lawn set with Adirondack chairs and a garden patio secluded behind 11-foot hedges invite summer lounging.

Guest rooms are bright and white, with eyelet comforters and pillows, framed botanicals and old prints, and some very nice antiques; all have phones (only for outgoing calls). Third-floor rooms have lots of dormers and angles, with stenciling on the white eaves. The second floor has highly polished wide-board pine floors. Most baths are very nice and modern; a few need updating (old metal shower units and tile floors)—specify if it matters to you. One first-floor "suite" has a giant bath with extra-large whirlpool bath and French doors opening onto the lawn. The third-floor master bedroom, with a king bed and a queen sofa bed, has a broad view of moors and the ocean beyond to the north; to the east, it looks onto a neighbor's private baseball diamond.

A mile from the shops and restaurants, and just a short walk from an uncrowded ocean beach and the Madaket bike path, the inn is a good choice for those who prefer spaciousness and seclusion to the bustle and closeness of Nantucket town.

🏠 *14 double rooms, 3 housekeeping apartments. Bicycles, beach towels. $100–$245; Continental breakfast, wine*

and cheese. AE, MC, V. No smoking, no pets, 3-night minimum mid-June–mid-Sept. Closed early Dec.–Mar.

Other Choices

Century House. 10 Cliff Rd., Box 603, Nantucket, MA 02554, tel. 508/228–0530, fax 508/325–6068. 14 double rooms with baths. Common TV. $95–$195, Continental breakfast and afternoon happy hour. MC, V. No smoking, no pets. May close in winter.

Cliff Lodge. 9 Cliff Rd., Nantucket, MA 02554, tel. 508/228–9480. 10 double rooms and 1 single with baths, 1 apartment. Common refrigerator and coffeemaker, beach towels, barbecue grill. $100–$225, Continental breakfast. MC, V. No smoking, no pets.

Corner House. 49 Centre St., Box 1828, Nantucket, MA 02554, tel. 508/228–1530. 15 double rooms with baths, 2 suites. Fans, TVs and mini-refrigerators in some rooms, common TV, fax available, beach towels. $60–$175, Continental breakfast and afternoon tea. MC, V. Restricted smoking, no pets. Usually closed Jan.

Martin House Inn. 61 Centre St., Box 743, Nantucket, MA 02554, tel. 508/228–0678. 9 double rooms with baths, 2 doubles and 2 singles share 1 bath. Common TV and piano, 4 rooms with fireplaces. $55–$150, Continental breakfast. AE, MC, V. No smoking, no pets.

Seven Sea Street. 7 Sea St., Nantucket, MA 02554, tel. 508/228–3577, fax 508/228–3578. 10 double rooms with baths, 1 housekeeping apartment. Phones, cable TVs, mini-refrigerators, whirlpool room. $75–$245, Continental breakfast. AE, MC, V. No smoking, no pets, 2-night minimum most weekends, 3-night minimum on holidays.

Summer House. Ocean Ave., Box 880, Siasconset, MA 02564, tel. 508/257–4577. 8 1- and 2-bedroom cottages with baths. Restaurant, pool, poolside restaurant and bar, private beach. $175–$500, Continental breakfast. AE, MC, V. No pets. Closed Nov.–late Apr.

The Wauwinet. Wauwinet Rd., Box 2580, Nantucket, MA 02584, tel. 508/228–0145 or 800/426–8718, fax 508/228–6712. 29 double rooms with baths, 5 cottages. Restaurant, bar, air-conditioning, TV/VCRs, turndown service, room service, business services, concierge, videocassette library, 2 Har-Tru tennis courts, sailboard and Sunfish rentals and lessons, croquet, 18-speed mountain bikes, picnic cruises, Coatue Jeep tours, ferry pickup. $290–$450, full breakfast. AE, DC, MC, V. No smoking, no pets, 3- to 4-night minimum summer and holiday weekends. Closed Nov.–May.

White Elephant. Easton St., Box 1139, Nantucket, MA 02554, tel. 508/228–2500 or 800/475–2637, fax 508/325–1195. 48 double rooms with baths, 32 1- to 3-bedroom cottages. Restaurant, lounge with entertainment, room service, concierge, mini-refrigerators in cottages, fax, heated pool, croquet court, putting green, boat slips. $110–$595, breakfast extra. AE, D, DC, MC, V. No pets. Closed Nov.–Apr.

Reservations Services

House Guests Cape Cod and the Islands (Box 1881, Orleans, MA 02653, tel. 508/896–7053 or 800/666–4678). **Martha's Vineyard and Nantucket Reservations** (Box 1322, 73 Lagoon Pond Rd., Vineyard Haven, MA 02568, tel. 508/693–7200; in MA, 800/649–5671). **Nantucket Accommodations** (Box 217, Nantucket, MA 02554, tel. 508/228–9559).

Boston

A Cambridge House Bed-and-Breakfast

2218 Massachusetts Ave., Cambridge, MA 02140, tel. 617/491–6300 or 800/232–9989, fax 617/868–2848

Massachusetts Avenue is a busy, two-lane highway, but this 1892 yellow clapboard house, listed on the National Register of Historic Places, is set well back from the street. As you cross the wide front porch and enter the gorgeously decorated hallway, the outside noise and bustle vanish into a calm, well-ordered, Victorian glow.

In fact, the ground floor public rooms are the house's best features: They're dominated by gloriously carved cherry paneling and floor-to-ceiling fireplaces (the fireplace in the lobby is made of intricately carved African mahogany). The parlor and library show off hand-worked fire screens, elegant Victorian couches, bureaus, piano, and hardwood floors with Oriental rugs. A full breakfast is served in the handsome dining room, with its glass chandelier, Oriental rug, and corner china cabinet with silver coffee service.

A paneled staircase featuring portraits and a grandfather clock on the landing leads to the second floor and the best room in the house—the "suite" (actually, it's only one room). The room has thick carpets, a canopy bed, a working fireplace, a chaise longue, an alcove with a desk, and padded walls covered in fabric that complements the gray and pink of the bedskirts and drapes. Third-floor guest rooms have canopy or sleigh beds, fireplaces, and Victorian antiques. Most rooms in the carriage house, while tastefully furnished, are extremely small; despite wall-size mirrors installed in some to create a sense of space, you can only just walk around the bed.

Ellen Riley bought the house in 1985 and intended to use it as a private residence. She converted a couple of rooms into guest accommodations "just for fun," and got carried away by the bed-and-breakfast spirit. When she's not around, the inn is managed by polite and helpful innkeepers.

The house is just four blocks from the nearest subway station, and Harvard University is one stop away. There are plenty of shops and restaurants in the immediate vicinity, and 10 minutes on the subway will take you into the heart of Boston. And there's free parking.

▦ *11 rooms with baths, 5 rooms share 2 baths. Air-conditioning, cable TVs, phones, some rooms have fireplaces, parking. $79–$230, full breakfast and wine and cheese. AE, D, MC, V. No pets, no smoking, 2-night minimum on weekends May–Oct.*

82 Chandler Street

82 Chandler St., Boston, MA 02116, tel. 617/482–0408

In Boston's revitalized South End, on a quiet, tree-lined street of tall, redbrick row houses, this bed-and-breakfast is just a five-minute walk from the city center, a 10-minute taxi ride from the airport, and around the corner from Amtrak's Back Bay station. Constructed in 1863, the building sits on former tidal marshlands that were filled in to provide housing space for the city's growing middle class. Its mansard roof and redbrick, brownstone trim are trademarks of 19th-century Boston homes.

Owners Denis Coté and Dominic Beraldi bought the house in 1978, and after major renovation, turned it into apartments. In 1983, however, when one tenant moved out, they decided to try their hand at innkeeping. According to Denis, a social worker for 25 years, innkeeping is a positive kind of

social work, "but more enjoyable, since you're helping people to have a good time, rather than to survive!"

A full breakfast, including pancakes, French toast, or crepes is served family style in the big, sunny penthouse kitchen with exposed brick walls, plants, skylights, and a row of windows overlooking the city's rooftops. The bedroom across the stairwell is the "Room with a View": Its wide bay window looks out on downtown Boston and several landmark skyscrapers. The walls are exposed brick, the floors are polished pine with Oriental rugs, there's a working marble fireplace, and a skylight brightens the bathroom. Ask for this room first when making reservations (especially since all rooms cost the same).

Eighty-two Chandler Street is very much an "up and down" house: All other guest rooms open off the staircase and are "color coded" with green, red, blue, or yellow schemes. Front rooms have large bay windows and two have working fireplaces; all are spacious and sunny, with white enamel and brass headboards, pedestal sinks, Oriental rugs, plus a kitchen area with refrigerator and microwave oven.

Ever devoted to his guests' well-being, Denis provides a wealth of tourist information, directions, and advice on the best sights to see. Although guests can use two nearby parking lots (costing $12–$18 per day), parking is problematic throughout Boston and you're better off without a car.

▦ *5 double rooms with baths. Air-conditioning, phones, kitchen areas, fireplaces in some rooms, breakfast room, TV available. $75–$125, full breakfast. No credit cards. No smoking, no pets, 2-night minimum Apr.–Nov.*

Newbury Guest House

261 Newbury St., Boston, MA 02116, tel. 617/437–7666

This elegant, redbrick and brownstone row house was built in 1882 as a private home in Boston's fashionable Back Bay, still *the* place to live in Boston. A father and son team, Nubar and Mark Hagopian, bought the four-story house in 1990, and after extensive restoration and renovation, opened it as a bed-and-breakfast in January 1991. Not surprisingly, considering the location, the price, and the quality of the inn, business went well, and, in 1994, the Hagopians bought two neighboring buildings and converted those into B&Bs as well.

The location of this inn is perfect: Newbury Street—famous for its gas street lamps, broad sidewalks, leaded windows, and neat front gardens—is the city's smartest shopping street, home to a wide selection of clothing stores, antiques shops, art galleries, hair salons, and dozens of sidewalk cafés, restaurants, and trendy bars. It's also a short walk to the Public Garden, Boston Common, Copley Square, and many other attractions.

The first floor lobby has an arched stained-glass window, hand painted in the 1880s by an artist from Tiffany's. Guest rooms open off the beautifully carved oak staircase of this tall, narrow house. One suite has a cherry sleigh bed, nonworking fireplace, and intricately cut plaster moldings. A guest room on the same floor has a cherry bedroom set, carved wainscot paneling, and stained glass in the doors.

Throughout the rest of the house, "bay" guest rooms have couches and oriel windows overlooking Newbury Street; less expensive "traditional" rooms have wing chairs and are smaller—however, as Mark points out, they're not as small as the "small" rooms at Boston's famous Ritz-Carlton Hotel, just a few blocks away! Several rooms have cherry four-poster beds and nonworking fireplaces; all feature reproduction Victorian furnishings, dark-stained pine floors and rugs, queen-size beds, and prints from the Boston Museum of Fine Arts.

A Continental breakfast of breads and pastries is served in the dining room with its Victorian furnishings; in summer guests can eat outside on the brick patio.

There's metered street parking just outside, and the inn offers a limited number of spaces to guests for $10 per night. You don't need a car here, but if you will have one, consider reserving a space in advance.

▦ *32 double rooms with baths. Living room, air-conditioning, cable TV, phones, limited parking (extra). $75–$145, Continental breakfast. AE, D, DC, MC, V. No pets.*

Other Choices

Beacon Hill Bed and Breakfast. 27 Brimmer St., Boston, MA 02108, tel. 617/523–7376. 3 double rooms with baths. Air-conditioning, TVs, breakfast room. $150–$175, full breakfast. No credit cards. No smoking, no pets.

Beacon Inns. 1087 and 1750 Beacon St., Brookline, MA 02146, tel. 617/566–0088. 1087: 9 double rooms with baths, 2 rooms share 1 bath. 1750: 6 rooms with baths, 7 rooms share 3 baths. TVs, air-conditioning in some rooms. 1087: $39–$86; 1750: $39–$99; Continental breakfast. AE, MC, V. No pets.

Bertram Inn. 92 Sewall Ave., Brookline, MA 02146, tel. 617/566–2234. 13 double rooms, 11 with private baths, 2 share 1 bath. Phones, cable TVs, air-conditioning in some rooms, living room, porch, parking. $69–$164, Continental breakfast. MC, V. Restricted smoking, 2-night minimum on weekends May–Oct.

John Jeffries House. 14 Embankment Rd., Boston, MA 02114, tel. 617/367–1866, fax 617/742–0313. 22 rooms, 24 suites, all with baths. Air-conditioning, TVs, phones, kitchen facilities, parlor, reduced rates at local parking garage. $75–$130, Continental breakfast. D, MC, V. Restricted smoking, no pets.

Reservations Services

Bed & Breakfast Agency of Boston (47 Commercial Wharf, Boston, MA 02110, tel. 617/720–3540 or 800/248–9262, fax 617/523–5761). **Bed & Breakfast Associates Bay Colony Ltd.** (Box 57166, Babson Park Branch, Boston, MA 02157, tel. 617/449–5302 or 800/347–5088, fax 617/449–5958). **Bed and Breakfast Cambridge and Greater Boston** (Box 1344, Cambridge, MA 02238, tel. 617/576–1492 or 800/888–0178, fax 617/576–1430). **Bed and Breakfast Greater Boston** (Box 35, Newtonville, MA 02160, tel. 617/964–1606 or 800/832–2632, fax 617/332–8572). **New England Bed and Breakfast, Inc.** (1753 Massachusetts Ave., Cambridge, MA 02138, tel. 617/498–9819).

North Shore

Addison Choate Inn

49 Broadway, Rockport, MA 01966, tel. 508/546–7543

Rockport offers an excellent selection of inns, and the Addison Choate is one of the best. Shirley Johnson, an interior designer, bought the inn in 1992 with her husband, Knox, a landscape architect, and together they set about enhancing the historical character of an already attractive property.

Made of white clapboard, the long, narrow, two-story house, built in 1851, was the famed site of Rockport's first bathtub. The inn is a minute's walk from the town center and two blocks away from the Rockport-Boston railway station. Beyond the main building, the carriage house contains two one-bedroom apartments, and still farther is a large, fenced-in outdoor swimming pool. Spacious rooms in the main inn have big, tiled bathrooms and are individually decorated. The navy and white Cap-

tain's Room boasts a dark-wood four-poster bed with a net canopy, polished pine floors, handmade quilts, Oriental rugs, and paintings of ships. The Chimney Room has a white brick chimney passing through it, wide-board floors, a Victorian oak bureau with mirror, and rocking chair with a handwoven seat. Other rooms contain Hitchcock rockers and headboards, spool beds, filligree brass beds, quilts, local paintings, and wooden antiques. The "Room with a View" was converted from a loft, and its two huge windows have sea views over the rooftops. The bedroom has wide pine floorboards, patterned fabrics, white wicker furniture, a TV, and a refrigerator.

The large carriage-house apartments offer first-floor living space and kitchens; one contains an iron spiral staircase leading to a bedroom with cathedral ceilings, wooden beams, and a skylight; the other has stained-glass windows and a deck.

The living room has a Greek Revival mantelpiece, cozy reading nooks, and Classical antique and modern furnishings. An extended Continental breakfast with home-baked goods is served in the dining room; in summer, guests can sit on the porch overlooking the inn's perennial garden. Knox's hobby since childhood has been bird-watching, and he offers guided bird-watching tours around the greater Rockport area.

🏠 *7 double rooms with baths, 2 1-bedroom apartments. Air-conditioning in some rooms, gardens, parking, outdoor pool. $77–$124, Continental breakfast. D, MC, V. No smoking, no pets, 2-night minimum on weekends, 2-night minimum on holidays in season.*

Clark Currier Inn

45 Green St., Newburyport, MA 01950, tel. 508/465–8363

This three-story clapboard mansion is the newest inn in Newburyport—and the best. Built by shipping merchant Thomas March Clark in 1803, the lodging is a typical example of the Federal architecture for which Newburyport is famous. The interior has been completely renovated to reveal many period splendors, such as wide-board polished wood floors, window seats, original Colonial-style shutters, wood stoves, and a Federal "good morning" staircase—so-called because two small staircases join at the head of a large one, permitting family members to greet one another on their way down to breakfast.

Guest rooms, named after former owners or residents of the house, are all spacious and carefully decorated in period style, with Federal antiques. Some have pencil-post beds; one has a reproduction sea captain's bed complete with drawers below, and another contains a sleigh bed dating from the late 19th century. Many of the rooms have fireplaces with carved wood surrounds, but these are not in use. Typical of the Federal home, ceilings become lower as you reach the upper stories, so in first-floor rooms the ceilings are 11 feet high, but only 7 feet on the third floor, where guest bedrooms are converted from former servants' quarters; upstairs, the ambience is less formal, but still authentic.

Bob Nolan, an international banker and currency trader in New York City, and his wife, Mary, a political science teacher at Rutgers University in New Jersey, stepped out of their high-stress jobs back in 1990 to take on the Clark Currier. They wanted a more family-oriented lifestyle for themselves and their daughter Melissa, and believe they've found the perfect situation in Newburyport. Since taking over, they opened up the ground floor to create a large living room with working fireplace, antique desks, couches, and bookcases. A second-floor library has books and writing desks and a display of antique toys on the landing outside. The inn offers afternoon tea, and a buffet-style breakfast of breads and muffins in a recently converted kitchen, besides in-room extras like candy dishes, restocked daily by Melissa! In summer, guests can eat outside in the garden with its rocking chairs and gazebo.

▦ *8 double rooms with baths. Air-conditioning, TV in lounge. $65–$145, Continental breakfast. AE, MC, V. No smoking, no pets.*

Eden Pines Inn

48 Eden Rd., Rockport, MA 01966, tel. 508/546-2505

Built in 1900 as a private summer cottage, Eden Pines stands so close to the ocean that the whole place seems about ready to sail off to sea—in fact, two of the wood decks already did, which prompted owner-managers Inge and John Sullivan to build a storm-proof brick deck that has survived for many years. The house looks out to the twin lights of Thatcher's Island; below the deck lie rocks and the raging (or lapping) waves. The Sullivans bought the inn more than 25 years ago, and they utilize its location to the utmost. The large bedrooms have great ocean views, and five out of six have secluded private balconies. Rooms are eclectically furnished, with a mixture of modern rattan or wicker, some canopy beds, and a few older pieces picked up at antiques shops. A "fresh" look predominates, however, with pastel blue and yellow walls, modern floral fabrics, bright white moldings, and pastel-toned carpets; one room has a nonworking white-painted-brick fireplace. The large bathrooms have marble units and brass fixtures.

Downstairs, the living room features a stone fireplace with stone surround and dark-stained, pine-paneled walls. The breakfast room, with its white trellises, wood-plank walls, and straw matting, opens onto the oceanside deck; the room's huge windows provide excellent sea views.

For even better ocean vistas, take a look at the Sullivans' other property just down the street, the four-bedroom Eden Point House, which they rent by the week. It stands on a rock, surrounded by the sea on three sides, and is of a contemporary, open-plan design, with a semicircular living room; a stone, floor-to-ceiling fireplace surround; a high cathedral ceiling; and a large modern kitchen.

Eden Pines Inn and Eden Point House are a five-minute drive from Rockport center, and two minutes by car from the nearest beach.

🏠 *6 double rooms with baths. Air-conditioning, cable TVs, croquet lawn. $80–$130, Continental breakfast. MC, V. Restricted smoking, no pets, 3-night minimum on holiday weekends. Closed mid-Nov.–mid-May.*

Harbor Light Inn

58 Washington St., Marblehead, MA 01945, tel. 617/631–2186

On a bustling narrow street at the heart of Marblehead's historic district, this Federal-style inn is the best place to stay in town; it competes with the Clark Currier Inn in Newburyport as one of the classiest, most relaxing, and most authentic inns on the whole of the North Shore. If you take the Harbor Light Room and stand on tiptoe, you can see the lighthouse in the harbor; otherwise you'll only have an occasional glimpse of the sea. Nevertheless, you're bound to be impressed with the building's interior—wide-board hardwood floors, chintz chairs, silver ice buckets and candy bowls, original shutters that fold into the wall, and Chinese rugs. As for the beds, you can choose between a pencil-post bed and a hand-carved mahogany four-poster bed with a floral canopy. Bathrooms have huge mirrors and skylights, and some contain whirlpool baths as well.

The old building dates from the early 1700s, with one wing constructed in the 19th century. When innkeepers Paul and Suzanne Conway bought the place in a state of disrepair in 1986, they opened up the third floor and added a completely new section to the back of the house. They're veteran, energetic innkeepers, whose hard work and attention to detail have resulted in a luxurious inn with excellent amenities but undisturbed original features. The character of individual rooms varies tremendously—those in the earlier structure have more original features, such as unusual arched doorways, working fireplaces, and wideboard floors. On the third floor, however, rooms have skylights, exposed brick, cathedral ceilings, and wooden beams. In the new addition, rooms are modern in concept and in decor, and some offer private decks.

In 1992, the innkeepers bought the building next door and over the next year expanded the inn, adding seven more big, beautiful bedrooms with working fireplaces, four-poster beds, and painted wood paneling. One room has an old-fashioned bathroom with a claw-foot tub; the top floor room has exposed beams and a large, modern bathroom. The inn has two parlors with Chippendale furniture, wing chairs, and open fireplaces; Continental breakfast is served in the dining room.

🏠 *20 double rooms with baths, 1 suite. Air-conditioning, cable TVs, 2 parlors, dining room, conference room, outdoor pool. $90–$185, Continental breakfast. AE, MC, V. No pets, 2-night minimum on weekends July–Oct.*

Inn on Cove Hill

37 Mt. Pleasant St., Rockport, MA 01966, tel. 508/546–2701

This immaculate, well-maintained inn has an excellent location on a pretty hillside street, just two minutes' walk from the center of Rockport. The square, Federal-style house was built in 1791, reportedly with money from a cache of pirate gold discovered at nearby Gully

Point. Although some guest rooms are small (a few are really tiny), they're so carefully decorated in the Federal style, with white draperies and spreads, white wicker chairs, bright flowery print papers, and white painted brass headboards, that they can be called "cozy" with a clear conscience. Other rooms have such details as Laura Ashley floral-print wallpapers, patchwork quilts, unfinished wooden antiques, canopy and half-canopy beds, spool beds, iron door latches, wooden bathroom fixtures, wide-board floors, and pastel-toned Oriental rugs. Two rooms in an 1850s addition have been furnished in the Victorian style, with brass and wicker, and one bathroom contains an original claw-foot bathtub and bathroom set. The overall "country" style is executed with taste: You won't be ambushed by duck pillows or rag dolls at every turn.

The second and third floors are reached via two narrow spiral staircases (first-floor bedrooms are available), the front staircase has 13 steps, representing the original 13 Colonies. Both upper stories have decks, and the third floor affords a good view over the rooftops to Rockport Harbor and Bearskin Neck.

The guest lounge retains its original wide-board pine floors and dentil cornice moldings; furnishings include a mixture of Federal-style antiques, velvet wing chairs, rockers, and more modern, matching couches. There's no public breakfast room, so a rather scanty Continental breakfast (fresh muffin, juice, and coffee) is served on Wedgwood or Royal Doulton English bone china in the bedroom or outside in the garden at tables around an old pump.

Innkeepers John and Marjorie Pratt spent their honeymoon here and returned years later to buy the place. They've been running the inn since 1978, and in that time have done a good deal of restoration, removing 1950 cover-up features to expose original wood paneling and floors. The Pratts are excellent hosts with great senses of humor.

🏨 *9 double rooms with baths, 2 doubles share 1 bath. Air-conditioning, fans, TVs. $50–$105, Continental breakfast. MC, V. No smoking, no pets, 2-night minimum July–Aug. and on weekends May–June and Sept. Closed late Oct.–Apr.*

Yankee Clipper Inn

96 Granite St., Box 2399, Rockport, MA 01966, tel. 508/546–3407

The white Georgian mansion that forms the main part of this imposing, perfectly located Cape Ann establishment stands surrounded by gardens, challenging the waves from a rocky headland that juts out into the ocean. Constructed as a private home in the 1930s, this three-story oblong building with big square windows has been managed as an inn by one family for almost 50 years. Guest rooms in the mansion vary in size, but they're generally large; with the sea on three sides, all rooms (except one) have fabulous views. Many of them also offer weatherized porches, such as the one that wraps around the enormous suite where John and Jacqueline Kennedy stayed when the late president was still a Massachusetts senator. Furnished with Queen Anne- and Victorian-style reproductions, the rooms contain four-poster or canopy beds, chaise longues, and wicker porch furniture.

Across the lawns in a newer structure called the Quarterdeck, picture windows in all the rooms provide impressive ocean views. Modern and stylish, the spacious (some are huge) well-designed rooms have wood-paneled or blue/green painted walls, seascape paintings, wing chairs, and modern couches. The top-floor rooms are particularly attractive with their sloped ceilings, large bathrooms, and sitting areas.

On the other side of the street from the main inn is the Bullfinch House, an 1840 Greek Revival home, appointed with dark wood antiques, floral-print papers, lacy curtains, and pineapple four-poster beds.

Guests dine at the main inn, on a sunny porch with wrought-iron chairs, again overlooking the sea. Just behind the porch, the lounge has a huge fireplace with a mahogany surround and large floral stencils at either side. Dusky pink tones, pink velvet couches, and heavy-framed painted portraits re-create a Victorian atmosphere. Below the lounge, a conference center caters to business clientele. The well-managed inn has a friendly staff, and careful touches abound—the outdoor swimming pool, for example, is attractively landscaped and virtually invisible from the road. The Yankee Clipper is located more than a mile north of Rockport, so guests will need transport in and out of town.

🏠 *20 double rooms with baths, 6 suites. Restaurant, air-conditioning, outdoor pool. $99–$249, full breakfast. AE, D, MC, V. No smoking, no pets. Closed Dec. 20–26 and Jan.–Feb.*

Other Choices

Amelia Payson Guest House. 16 Winter St., Salem, MA 01970, tel. 508/744–8304. 3 double rooms with baths, 1 studio. Breakfast room, TV in rooms, 2 parlors, parking. $75–$95, Continental breakfast. AE, MC, V. No smoking, no pets.

Garrison Inn. 11 Brown Sq., Newburyport, MA 01950, tel. 508/465–0910. 24 double rooms with baths, 6 suites. 2 restaurants, air-conditioning, cable TV in rooms and lounge, live entertainment. $85–$165, no breakfast. AE, DC, MC, V. No pets.

Harborside House. 23 Gregory St., Marblehead, MA 01945, tel. 617/631–1032. 2 rooms share 1 bath. TVs, parking. $60–$80, Continental breakfast. No credit cards. No smoking, no pets.

Seacrest Manor. 131 Marmion Way, Rockport, MA 01966, tel. 508/546–2211. 6 rooms with baths, 2 rooms share 1 bath. Cable TVs. $84–$128, full breakfast. No credit cards. No smoking, no pets, 2-night minimum weekends, 3-night minimum holidays. Closed Dec.–Mar.

Seaward Inn. 62 Marmion Way, Rockport, MA 01966, tel. 508/546–3471. 38 double rooms with baths. Restaurant, putting green, bicycles, playground. $115–$150, full breakfast; rates including all meals available. AE, D, MC, V. No pets. Closed Dec.–Mar.

Tuck Inn. 17 High St., Rockport, MA 01966, tel. 508/546–7260. 10 double rooms with baths, 1 suite. Air-conditioning, cable TVs, living room, 2 dining rooms, outdoor pool, parking. $47–$107, Continental breakfast. MC, V. No smoking, no pets, 2-night minimum weekends May–Oct.

Reservations Services

Bed and Breakfast Associates Bay Colony Ltd. (Box 57166, Babson Park Branch, Boston, MA 02157, tel. 617/449–5302 or 800/347–5088, fax 617/449–5958). **Bed and Breakfast Marblehead and North Shore** (Box 35, Newtonville, MA 02160, tel. 617/964–1606 or 800/832–2632, fax 617/332–8572). **Greater Boston Hospitality** (Box 1142, Brookline, MA 02146, tel. 617/277–5430).

Pioneer Valley

Allen House

599 Main St., Amherst, MA 01002, tel. 413/253–5000

Dozens of bed-and-breakfast inns fall under the general term of "country-style"—a few have good antiques and interesting decor. But inns that are restored with historic precision and attention to every last detail are rare indeed: The Allen House, honored with a Historic Preservation Award from the Amherst Historical Commission in 1991, is one of them.

Alan Zieminski, a biochemist at the University of Massachusetts, has lived in the 1886 Queen Anne stick-style house since the late '60s. He bought it in 1988, and once he and his wife, Ann, began putting their vague ideas of restoration into practice, the project took on a life of its own. Along with Alan's brother Jonas, the family soon became experts in Aesthetic period—a Victorian movement heavily influenced by trade with Japan.

Guest rooms are museum-like representations of the Aesthetic era. Impressive period wallpapers decorate the walls. Sunflowers, the Aesthetics' emblem, are everywhere. Furnishings include some original Charles Eastlake pieces, such as the matching burled walnut bed head and dresser in the upstairs Eastlake room; other rooms have Eastlake reproductions, wicker "steamship" chairs, pedestal sinks, screens, carved golden oak or brass beds, goose-down comforters, painted wooden floors, and claw-foot tubs. Public rooms are just as impressive as bedrooms: The breakfast room has Anglo-Japanese reproduction wallpapers, an intricately carved fireplace, and its original grass reed matting, imported from Japan, on the floor. The sitting room floor also has its original covering—Victorian oilcloth, the forerunner of linoleum, and an 1880s Oriental hand-stitched rug.

When the Zieminskis bought the house, it was a kind of time capsule full of original, if faded, relics. The upstairs hallway is lined with pictures found stashed away in a locked room. Modern advantages are cable TV in the living room, tourist information, poetry books, afternoon tea, a hearty cooked breakfast, and free pickup service to guests from the nearby train and bus stations. It's a short walk from the center of Amherst, rates are reasonable, and the hosts—who seem a little overwhelmed by what they've achieved—are extremely pleasant company.

▦ *5 double rooms with baths. Airconditioning, living room with cable TV, breakfast room, afternoon tea, parking. $45–$135, full breakfast. AE, MC, V. Restricted smoking, no pets, 2-night minimum foliage and special college events weekends.*

Deerfield Inn

The Street, Deerfield, MA 01342, tel. 413/774-5587

Perfectly situated on the street that's really a string of museums, the peaceful Deerfield Inn, with its columned facade and white clapboard exterior, harks back to a gentler era. Built in 1884, it was substantially modernized after a fire in 1981, which explains the square, spacious guest rooms, reminiscent of more modern hotels. The style and grace of the light, airy interior owes much to the flair and imagination of the young, enthusiastic innkeepers, Karl Sabo and his English wife, Jane, who bought the place in 1987, leaving their fast-track lives in New York's Greenwich Village for "something different."

The couple has worked hard on redecoration, for example, having reproduction period wallpapers custom designed for the reception room, tavern, and many of the bedrooms. Guest rooms, with light floral themes, are furnished with sofas, bureaus, eclectic Federal-style antiques, and replicas of Queen Anne beds and Chippendale chairs. Some rooms have four-poster or canopy beds.

The large, sunny dining room on the first floor is elegantly decorated with silverware, Federal-style chairs, and antique side tables and is graced with candlelight in the evening. The cuisine is first-rate, and the inn has a well-deserved reputation for dining. Specialties on the menu include saddle of venison sautéed with chestnuts in blackcurrant sauce, rack of lamb with Dijon mustard and garlic, and salmon with scallops; several dishes are based on recipes from old cookbooks in the village museum. The inn is formal enough to make your stay a special event, but friendly enough to create a relaxed and welcoming atmosphere. From December to October, a cheerful café serves inexpensive sandwiches and salads during the day.

Just down the road are the dozen 17th- and early 18th-century house museums of Historic Deerfield, which provide year-round lectures and tours. The Barnard Tavern has a ballroom with a fiddlers' gallery, and several hands-on displays: You can climb into the rope bed and write on the slates. The Memorial Hall Museum displays tributes to the Native American Pocumtuck, as well as relics from the village's history.

🏠 *23 double rooms with baths. Restaurant, coffee shop, lounge, air-conditioning, TVs, phones. 2 rooms accessible for people who use wheelchairs. $145–$185, full breakfast. AE, DC, MC, V. Closed Dec. 24–26.*

Publick House and Colonel Ebenezer Crafts Inn

Rte. 131, On-the-Common, Sturbridge, MA 01566, tel. 508/347–3313 or 800/ 782–5425, fax 508/347–5073

These two inns operate under the same management and offer a wide variety of services with very distinct styles. The Publick House was founded (confusingly enough, by Ebenezer Crafts) in 1771, and recently underwent a major renovation. It's a big, sprawling old inn with extensive dining rooms lit by pewter chandeliers, and a menu emphasizing the same traditional Yankee meals that were served 200 years ago, from individual lobster pies to double-thick loin lamb chops. Four meals are served daily, year-round, and breakfasts are sometimes cooked on the open hearth. Accommodations at the Publick House consist of fairly small, "olde-worlde" bedrooms with uneven wide-board floors, some canopy beds, and plain wooden antiques. The Chamberlain House next door features suites in the same style, while contemporary accommodations are available at the new Country Lodge with its modern motel-style rooms.

Just over a mile away, the Crafts Inn is a quiet alternative to the hustle and bustle of the Publick House. A restored Colonial farmhouse built in 1786, it has eight spacious guest rooms with canopy or four-poster beds, antique desks, painted wood panels, and polished hardwood floors. Third-floor rooms have sloping gable roofs. Downstairs, guests share a library, sunporch, and a large lounge with Colonial furniture and an enormous brick fireplace; there's also an outdoor pool. Breakfast consists of baked goods, and afternoon tea is also served.

🏠 *17 rooms with baths (Publick House), 3 suites and 1 room with baths (Chamberlain House), 100 modern rooms with baths (Country Lodge), 8 rooms with baths (Crafts Inn). 3 restaurants, conference rooms, bar, tennis court, pool, shuffleboard, playground, bike rentals (Publick House); air-conditioning, library, living room, pool (Crafts Inn). $55–$155; breakfast extra (Publick House), Continental breakfast (Crafts Inn). AE, DC, MC, V. No smoking.*

Sturbridge Country Inn

530 Main St., Box 60, Sturbridge, MA 01566, tel. 508/347–5503, fax 508/347– 5319

Originally a farmhouse, this white 1840s building on Sturbridge's busy Main Road, and just a short walk away from Old Sturbridge Village, has an imposing Greek Revival facade that brings to mind a grand municipal edifice rather than a farmhouse. Guest rooms, all of which have working fireplaces, are furnished with Colonial reproductions that blend with the modern design. And every room has a whirlpool bath.

All rooms have impressive Colonial-style decor, but the small first-floor rooms are less desirable and can be noisy; the plumbing gurgles and the whirlpool tubs upstairs tend to reverberate downstairs. Upstairs, Rooms 7 and 8 are "theme rooms"—one features wicker furnishings, the other brass, and each offers a glass-enclosed sunporch. Both these rooms are grand, with exposed hand-hewn beams and steps that lead down from the whirlpool bath to the large bedroom. The best room of all, however, is the vast suite that occupies the whole of the third floor; it has cathedral ceilings, a large whirlpool bath in the living room, a wet bar, and big windows.

Guests are served a light Continental breakfast in the first-floor lounge, where innkeeper Patricia MacConnell, whose brother owns the inn, has succeeded in mixing old styles with modern comforts. The lounge has an open fireplace and Colonial-style furnishings and decor, but the open-plan architecture and cathedral ceilings lift the area into the 20th century and create a light and gracious ambience. In the summer, an adjoining garden area and gazebo are opened to guests.

The high-ceiling, post-and-beam barn adjoining the inn is now the Fieldstone Tavern. This restaurant serves traditional New England dinners like hearty stews, grilled chicken, and roast beef seven nights a week and lunchtime on weekends.

▦ *8 double rooms with baths, 1 suite. Restaurant, air-conditioning, cable TVs, fireplaces, whirlpool baths, live theater June–Oct. $59–$159, Continental breakfast. AE, D, MC, V. Restricted smoking, no pets.*

Yankee Pedlar Inn

1866 Northampton St., Holyoke, MA 01040, tel. 413/532–9494

The Yankee Pedlar has grown outward from a central yellow clapboard building, and now comprises several annexes of superbly decorated guest rooms, as well as an "opera house" for dances and banquets. Each annex has a different theme; rooms have four-poster beds, Currier and Ives prints, nightstands, desks, and other antiques. The spaciousness of the suites—some with fireplaces—make them worth the minimal extra cost. Although every room at this inn is unique, one of the best places to stay is the all-pink Victorian-style bridal suite. It's a wonderful extravaganza of deep carpets, dripping lace, draperies, mirrors, and birdcages, complete with Victorian valentines on the mantelpiece. If you prefer something simpler, the inn offers an alternative: the neighboring carriage house, with classic canopy beds, rustic antiques, cathedral ceilings, and exposed beams.

Antiques in the public rooms include a pre-Prohibition bar, decorative wood panels from the local (now demolished) Kenilworth Castle, a collection of copper pots, and dozens of old photographs of the region. Thursday through Saturday evenings there's live entertainment in the Oyster Bar, which is equipped with a popcorn machine in the shape of a street vendor's cart. The place feels like a popular London pub from the Victorian era, but with an added touch of class. The restaurant (J. J. Hilderth's, after the judge who first owned the house) serves good American fare with an emphasis on seafood and steak. Martin Clayton, the owner, purchased the inn in 1994.

The inn has only one disadvantage for vacationers—the location. Although it's convenient—only a short distance off I–91—it stands at a major intersection. Rooms near the road have triple-glazed windows, which keep out the noise, but either way, Holyoke is not an attractive city for tourists. On the plus side, the inn is a short drive from several colleges, including Mount Holyoke, Smith, Amherst, and the University of Massachusetts.

🛏 *20 double rooms with baths, 12 suites. Restaurant, 2 bars, air-conditioning, cable TVs, 4 banquet rooms. $65–$125, Continental breakfast. AE, D, DC, MC, V. No pets.*

Other Choices

Lord Jeffery Inn. 30 Boltwood Ave., Amherst, MA 01002, tel. 413/253–2576. 44 double rooms with baths, 6 suites. Restaurant, tavern, air-conditioning, phones, cable TVs. $78–$148, breakfast extra. AE, DC, MC, V. No pets.

Northfield Country House. 181 School St., Northfield, MA 01360, tel. 413/498–2692 or 800/498–2692. 3 double rooms with baths, 4 doubles share 2 baths. Lounge, pool, gardens. $50–$90, full breakfast. MC, V. Restricted smoking, no pets.

Sunnyside Farm Bed and Breakfast. 21 River Rd., Whately (Box 486, South Deerfield, MA 01373), tel. 413/665–3113. 5 double rooms share 2 baths. Pool. $45–$95, full breakfast. No credit cards. Restricted smoking, no pets.

Reservations Services

American Country Collection of B&B (4 Greenwood La., Delmar, NY 12054, tel. 518/439–7001, fax 518/439–4301). **The Greater Springfield/Berkshire Bed and Breakfast Homes** (Main St., Box 211, Williamsburg, MA 01096, tel. 413/268–7244).

The Berkshires

Apple Tree Inn

334 West St., Lenox, MA 01240, tel. 413/637–1477

This country inn has much to recommend it, particularly its setting on a gently sloping hillside with marvelous views over the Stockbridge Bowl and Laurel Lake, and literally across the street from Tanglewood's main gates. You're so close to the music festival that on a summer evening, you won't even need a ticket—you can listen to concerts from the inn's own gardens; because the inn is surrounded by 22 acres of land, planted with apple orchards and 450 varieties of roses, you may well decide to do just that.

Originally constructed in 1885, the main building features public areas furnished with Victorian antiques and the unexpected yet effective piece of modern art. Guests enter via the parlor, with its arches, Persian rugs, open fireplace, velvet couches, grand piano, hanging plants, and German nutcrackers on the mantelpiece. In the tavern room, oak-paneled walls support a collection of antique sleds, old tools, and a water buffalo head that stares out over the fireplace. The main restaurant, a circular 1960s addition, has a marquee-like ceiling with spokes of lightbulbs. Picture windows afford excellent views over the lawns and orchards.

Upstairs, guest rooms are furnished with a variety of antiques, including four-poster and brass beds, Victorian washstands, and wicker pieces. Four rooms have working fireplaces, and several have window seats with fabulous views over the hills and the lake. The generally spacious rooms come in unusual shapes with individual characters, especially the ones on the top floor, with eaves, gables, and skylights. However, there are some smaller rooms to avoid, especially No. 5 (the Blue Skylight Room), which is over the kitchen and can become hot and noisy, particularly in the busy summer season. The nearby lodge has 21 motel-like rooms.

The Apple Tree Inn has an interesting past, and belonged at one point to Alice of "Alice's Restaurant"—though she catered primarily to diners, not guests. Your hosts, Sharon Walker and Joel Catalano, are from New York City; they bought the inn in 1996.

▦ *Inn: 29 double rooms with baths, 2 doubles share 1 bath, 2 suites; lodge: 21 doubles with baths. Restaurant and tavern, air-conditioning, cable TV in suites and lodge rooms, pool, tennis court. Inn: $60–$300, lodge: $60–$150; Continental breakfast. AE, D, MC, V. No pets, 2-night minimum on weekends, 3-night minimum weekends July–Aug. and Oct. Closed mid-Jan.–Apr.*

Blantyre

16 Blantyre Rd. (off Rte. 20), Lenox, MA 01240, tel. 413/637-3556 or 413/298-1661, fax 413/637-4282

Lenox has many fine country inns, but the palatial Blantyre, on 85 magnificent acres, is outstanding. The service is superb. In 1989, Blantyre was voted best of the Relais et Châteaux group. Built in 1901, Blantyre's design is based on an ancestral Scottish home, and its castlelike Tudor architecture is unique to the region. Senator John Fitzpatrick and his family, who also own the Red Lion Inn in Stockbridge, acquired the estate in 1980, and with it the mammoth task of restoring a dilapidated giant to its proper stature. Some of the furnishings in the great hall are original, as are the plaster relief ceilings, the intricately carved oak paneling, and the leather-backed wallpaper.

While the hall, with its heavy carved wooden furnishings (and wooden rocking horse in full heraldic gear), appears imposingly solemn, the long, cream-tone music room next door evokes a lighter mood, with inlaid chess tables, an antique Steinway grand piano, a harp, antique Dutch and Italian cabinets, and exquisite chairs and couches. Doors open onto a terrace set with tables overlooking two large, perfectly manicured croquet lawns.

Staying at Blantyre is an expensive occasion, so make the most of it by reserving one of the five best rooms, all in the main house. Although the entire property is stylishly finished, the rooms in the carriage house and cottages can't compare with these spacious accommodations, which have hand-carved four-poster beds, bay windows, high ceilings, working fireplaces, chintz chairs, overstuffed chaise longues, boudoirs, walk-in closets, and Victorian bathrooms. The huge Paterson Suite has two bathrooms, a sitting room with fireplace, a pineapple four-poster bed, and matching wallpapers, linens, and draperies in pale green. If these rooms are booked, the smaller Ashley Suite or the carriage house's split-level suites beside the pool are next best.

The first-rate service rests in the hands of Scottish manager Roderick Anderson. The many extras include bathrobes, toiletries, newspapers, turndown service, and wine, cheese, and fruit.

▦ *16 Blantyre Rd. (off Rte. 20), Lenox, MA 01240, tel. 413/637-3556 or 413/298-1661, fax 413/637-4282. 13 double rooms with baths, 10 suites. Restaurant, air-conditioning, cable TVs, phones, 5 rooms have fireplaces, room service, heated pool, whirlpool bath, sauna, 4 tennis courts, 2 croquet lawns, walking trails. $250–$650, Continental breakfast. AE, DC, MC, V. No pets, 2-night minimum on weekends. Closed early Nov.–mid-May.*

Field Farm

554 Sloan Rd. (off Rte. 43), Williamstown, MA 01267, tel. 413/458-3135

Neither your average bed-and-breakfast, nor your typical Berkshire cottage estate, this former home of art collector Lawrence H. Bloedel has been owned by the Trustees of Reservations since 1984. The innkeepers are Sean and Jean Cowhig. The starkly geometric exterior of this 1948 American modern-style structure, its cedar walls painted in sickly brown, contrasts unromantically with the profusion of attractive period homes in the region. But consider its advantages: The 296 acres of private, wooded grounds contain a pond, a pool, a tennis court, and cross-country ski trails—and all this comes at a reasonable price. The place is not yet well known, and because it has only five guest rooms, staying here is like living on your own country estate.

The interior is unashamedly square, and the house, designed as a sort of display case for Bloedel's art collection (which went to the Williams College museum after his death), feels a bit like a modern museum. In 1994, the college returned eight pieces to the house on long-term loan, and they are now displayed in the public areas. Most of the 1950s oak, cherry, and walnut furniture in use was handmade by Bloedel, while other pieces were designed especially for the house—even the plastic doorknobs were custom made, quite a coup in the 1940s. Modern sculptures decorate the gardens. Guest rooms on the first floor are square and large (some are huge), with modern furnishings, painted brick walls, spotlighting, big picture windows, and expansive views over the grounds toward distant hills. Three bedrooms have private decks, and two have working fireplaces surrounded by custom-made tiles depicting animals, birds, and butterflies. Downstairs in the large public sitting room, you'll discover another working fireplace and more modern art. Incidentally, Bloedel, his wife, and their dog are buried in a private graveyard by the parking lot.

🏨 *5 double rooms with baths. Breakfast room, lounge, outdoor pool, pond, tennis, cross-country skiing. $85–$130, full breakfast. MC, V. No pets.*

Gateways Inn

51 Walker St., Lenox, MA 01240, tel. 413/637–2532

A formal, elegant, and expensive Lenox inn with a superb restaurant, Gateways was built in 1912 by Harley Proctor of Proctor and Gamble as a summer home he named Orleton. The oblong, white clapboard mansion, fittingly enough, resembles a bar of Ivory soap. When Proctor owned the house, it was surrounded by 7 acres of lawns and formal gardens and boasted a carriage house and a tennis court. The inn is on Walker Street, only steps away from the center of Lenox, which could be named "inn row" considering the number of establishments that line the road.

Upon entering Gateways, you step into an impressive entrance hall with oval windows; from here, a grand mahogany open staircase lighted by a skylight leads to the second-floor guest rooms. The best of these, in the east corner, is the huge Fiedler Suite, named after Tanglewood conductor Arthur Fiedler, who stayed here regularly. The suite has two working fireplaces, one each in the bedroom and the sitting room, and a pleasantly large dressing room off the bathroom. Several other rooms have fireplaces, and one suite features a quirky square pillar between the couch and the bed. All rooms have been individually decorated with light period reproduction wallpapers, and furnished with Colonial and Victorian antiques, four-poster or canopy beds, and rich Oriental rugs. The west corner room is furnished with an eight-piece maple and black-walnut Victorian bedroom set.

Public rooms downstairs include a small parlor with Colonial furnishings and a series of four dining rooms: The Rockwell Room is named after painter Norman Rockwell, who dined in a sunny corner here every week. These tastefully designed areas have chandeliers and tapestries on the walls. Entrées on the extensive (and fairly expensive) menu include rack of lamb, breast of chicken with crawfish, truffles, crepes in a honey liqueur sauce, and pheasant in a light game sauce; the chef's award-winning cuisine is one of the inn's major assets. In both the restaurant and guest services, the staff is suitably distant but very polite.

▦ *11 double rooms with baths, 1 suite. Restaurant, air-conditioning. $85–$295, Continental breakfast. AE, D, DC, MC, V. No pets.*

Merrell Tavern Inn

1565 Main St., Rte. 102, South Lee/Stockbridge, MA 01260, tel. 413/243-1794 or 800/243-1794

This Federal-style red clapboard building with a columned facade, listed on the National Register of Historic Places, remained uninhabited for almost 100 years, until the present owners bought it in 1981. They installed heat, running water, and electricity, and reopened the Merrell Tavern as one of the most beautifully authentic inns in the Berkshires. Innkeepers Charles and Faith Reynolds are retired schoolteachers who were honored with a Preservation Award from the Massachusetts Historical Commission in 1982. They are friendly, interesting, but unobtrusive hosts; Faith weaves and Charles likes working on the grounds.

Built about 1794 and turned into a stagecoach inn in 1817, the lodging is blessed with some good-size bedrooms that offer polished wide-board floors and area rugs, painted plaster walls, iron door latches, and mellow wood antiques. Most beds are pencil four-posters, some have simple white canopies, and three rooms contain working, Count Rumford–style wood-burning fireplaces. The necessity of abiding by a 500-year covenant that protects the building's historic aspect means small (but beautifully decorated) bathrooms—on the third floor, where rooms were built in the shell of the old ballroom, some bathrooms are housed in the former drovers' sleeping quarters.

The original keeping room, now the guest parlor, features a beehive oven and a large cooking fireplace with a Franklin stove. A breakfast of pancakes, French toast, or omelets is served in the original tavern room, which contains an open fireplace and the only complete "birdcage" Colonial bar in America. Look for the 19th-century detail: The wood grain on the bar and the doors is hand-painted, not natural; the pulley wheels on the ceiling were used to raise and lower the original candle chandelier (now in a Boston museum). The inn is about a mile east of Stockbridge, beside busy Route 102, but it's well back from the road. Behind the building, 2 acres of landscaped gardens with a gazebo descend gently to the Housatonic River.

▦ *9 double rooms with baths. Air-conditioning, breakfast room, TV room, parlor, phones. $65–$135, full breakfast. MC, V. No smoking, no pets, 3-night minimum on summer holiday weekends. Closed Dec. 24 and 25.*

River Bend Farm

643 Simonds Rd., Williamstown, MA 01267, tel. 413/458-5504 or 413/458-3121

One of the oldest buildings in the Berkshires, this property was constructed in 1770 by Colonel Benjamin Simonds, a founder of Williamstown and a commissioned officer of the Berkshire militia during the American Revolution. The restoration of River Bend Farm is totally authentic and it is listed in the National Register of Historic Places: A stay here takes you back to another era.

Guests enter through the kitchen and are greeted by an open range stove and an oven hung with dried herbs. Chairs hang on pegs on the walls Shaker style, and the room is filled with 18th- and 19th-century country antiques, from wood washtubs and spoon racks to flatirons and dozens of cooking implements. Also downstairs is a small formal sitting room with a fireplace, but "formal" only means the walls are plastered—upstairs it's another story. Bedroom walls consist of wide wood panels, some of them painted in their original colors (the owners, who restored the building before leasing it to the current management, scraped their way through layers of paper and paint to discover them); others are whitewashed, or made of simple scrubbed wide planks as are the floors and doors. Window draperies are "tab curtains" (no hooks, just cloth loops) of unbleached muslin. Accurate Colonial-style reproductions of candle chandeliers hang from the ceilings, and sconces with candles are fixed to the walls. Some rooms feature brick (nonworking) fireplaces. Beds are either four-posters with canopies or rope beds with feather mattresses, and antique pieces decorate the rooms—a spinning wheel here, a wing chair there, or a chamber pot in the corner.

Speaking of chamber pots ... the farm's only disadvantage is that five guest rooms share two bathrooms, one of which is located on the ground floor. It's an absolute Aladdin's cave of utilitarian antiques including washbowls, jugs, lamps, butter tubs, and hanging herbs.

Outdoors, guests have access to the river for canoeing, and can visit a warm spring pool ¼ mile up the river. Williamstown is about an eight-minute drive away.

🏨 *4 double rooms share 2 baths. $65– $80, Continental breakfast. No credit cards. Restricted smoking, no pets.*

Wheatleigh

Hawthorne Rd., Lenox, MA 01240, tel. 413/637–0610

Wheatleigh was built in 1893, a wedding present for an American heiress who brought nobility into her family by marrying a Spanish count. On 22 wooded acres, the mellow brick building, based on a 16th-century Florentine palazzo, is nothing short of baronial. Step into the great hall: The sheer style of the open staircase, the balustraded gallery, and the large Tiffany windows is breathtaking. Everything here is vast, including most guest rooms—and the beds! Rooms have high ceilings, intricate plaster moldings (more than 150 artisans were brought from Italy to complete the detailed decoration), and English antiques; eight have working fireplaces with big, elegant marble surrounds. Prices are vast as well, at almost $500 per night in high season, but for the clientele—most of whom look like they're escaping high pressure, big-city executive posts—it's no doubt worth the money.

Though it has much to recommend it, Wheatleigh has suffered from a mixed reputation over the years, with rumblings about the service and the unconventional—some said tasteless—mixture of antique and modern styles. The furnishings have been toned down to mostly classical pieces, the place has been repainted, and the rooms were refurbished in 1993 to give the inn an elegant new front. The service too seems up to scratch, and virtually anything is available to guests, from in-room massage to breakfast in bed.

The main restaurant, another huge room with elegant marble fireplaces and cut glass chandeliers, has an excellent reputation for its "contemporary classical" cuisine; the $55 or $68 prix-fixe menus (with 18% service charge) include roast antelope, pheasant, rabbit, and lobster; the Grill Room also serves full meals in a more casual setting.

🔢 *17 double rooms with baths. 2 restaurants, air-conditioning, limited room service, tennis, pool. $155–$535, breakfast extra. AE, D, DC, MC, V. No pets, 3-night minimum during Tanglewood and holiday weekends.*

Whistler's Inn

5 Greenwood St., Lenox, MA 01240, tel. 413/637-0975

Elegant, ornate, and somehow exotic, Whistler's Inn stands apart from its nearby competitors, with lavish Louis XVI antiques in the parlor; heavy, dark wood furniture in the baronial dining hall; and African artifacts in the office. Innkeepers Joan and Richard Mears, with their easy style, maintain an extraordinary ambience at this English Tudor mansion, built in 1820 by railroad tycoon Ross Wynans Whistler.

The Mearses, who have owned Whistler's since 1978, are widely traveled hosts, making for some interesting conversation. Richard, a published novelist, and Joan, formerly a teacher of art and English, continue to work on new writing projects.

Public rooms are impressive, with Chippendale furniture, ornate antiques (including Louis XVI palace mirrors, candelabra, clocks, and love seats), chandeliers, original artwork, Persian rugs, and marble fireplaces. A Steinway grand piano graces the music room/parlor, and next door is a well-stocked library, where complimentary sherry, port, or afternoon tea is offered to guests. The dining room or the sunporch provides a restful setting for breakfast. You may wish to take a look at the Mearses' first-floor office—it features many souvenirs brought back from their travels, including African pieces and a large wooden elephant puppet from a maharaja's palace.

Guest rooms are attractively decorated with designer draperies and bedspreads. They vary in size from the large master bedroom to two small chambers beneath the eaves, and all are furnished with antiques. One room features a Chippendale armoire, some rooms have working fireplaces, and most of them offer superb views across the small valley that includes 7 acres of private gardens, as well as a croquet lawn and a badminton court for guests. This peaceful place is only a short walk from the center of Lenox.

🔢 *4 double rooms with baths. Dining room, air-conditioning, phones in rooms, library, gardens, croquet, badminton. $70–$225, full breakfast and afternoon tea. AE, D, MC, V. Restricted smoking, no pets, 3-night minimum on weekends July, Aug., Oct.*

Other Choices

Brook Farm Inn. 15 Hawthorne St., Lenox, MA 01240, tel. 413/637-3013 or 800/285-7638. 12 double rooms with baths. Air-conditioning, ceiling fans, library, pool. $70–$185, full breakfast and afternoon tea. D, MC, V. No smoking, no pets, 3-night minimum weekends July–Aug., 2-night minimum weekends Sept.–June.

Candlelight Inn. 35 Walker St., Lenox, MA 01240, tel. 413/637-1555. 8 double rooms with baths. Restaurant, air-conditioning, bar. $80–$173, Continental breakfast. AE, MC, V. No pets.

Cliffwood Inn. 25 Cliffwood St., Lenox, MA 01240, tel. 413/637-3330, fax 413/637-0221. 7 double rooms with baths. Air-conditioning, outdoor and indoor pool. $73–$200; Continental breakfast (no breakfast winter weekdays), wine and cheese. No credit cards. No pets, 4-night minimum July and Aug. weekends, 3- to 4-night minimum holidays.

Dalton House. 955 Main St., Dalton, MA 01226, tel. 413/684-3854. 9 double rooms with baths, 2 suites. Air-conditioning, TVs, breakfast room, outdoor pool, picnic area, deck. $68–$115, Continental breakfast. AE, MC, V. No smoking, no pets, 2-night minimum on summer and fall weekends.

Gables Inn. 81 Walker St., Lenox, MA 01240, tel. 413/637-3416. 3 suites, 18 double rooms with baths. Air-conditioning, cable TV in 8 rooms, VCRs in suites. $80-$210, full breakfast. D, MC, V. No pets, 3-night minimum during Tanglewood, 2-night minimum fall and holiday weekends.

Ivanhoe Country House. 254 S. Undermountain Rd. (Rte. 41), Sheffield, MA 01257, tel. 413/229-2143. 9 double rooms with baths, 2 2-bedroom suites with kitchens. Air-conditioning in some rooms, individual refrigerators, outdoor pool. $55-$110, Continental breakfast. No credit cards. 2-night minimum on weekends July-Labor Day, 3-night minimum on holiday weekends.

The Orchards. 222 Adams Rd. (Rte. 2), Williamstown, MA 01267, tel. 800/225-1517; in MA, 413/458-9611, fax 413/458-3273. 47 rooms with baths. Restaurant, air-conditioning, cable TVs, room service, tavern, outdoor pool, sauna, whirlpool. $125-$225, full breakfast. AE, DC, MC, V. No pets.

Red Lion Inn. Main St., Stockbridge, MA 02162, tel. 413/298-5545, fax 413/298-5130. 108 rooms, 75 with baths, 10 suites. Restaurant, air-conditioning, exercise room, bar, meeting rooms, outdoor pool. $72-$350. Continental breakfast included for rooms without private bath. AE, D, DC, MC, V. No pets, 2-night minimum July and Aug. weekends.

Rookwood Inn. 11 Old Stockbridge Rd., Box 1717, Lenox, MA 01240, tel. 413/637-9750 or 800/223-9750. 19 double rooms with baths, 2 suites. Air-conditioning, breakfast room. $70-$250, full breakfast and afternoon tea. AE. No smoking, no pets.

Turning Point Inn. R.D. 2, Box 140, Great Barrington, MA 01230, tel. 413/

528-4777. 4 double rooms with baths, 2 rooms share 1 bath, 2-bedroom cottage. TV in lounge, fans, cross-country ski trail. $80-$100 (full breakfast); cottage $200 (no breakfast). AE, MC, V. No smoking, no pets.

Weathervane Inn. Rte. 23, South Egremont, MA 01258, tel. 413/528-9580. 11 double rooms with baths. Dining rooms, air-conditioning, TV in lounge, outdoor pool. $95-$195, full breakfast (rates including all meals are available Fri. and Sat.). AE, MC, V. No smoking, no pets, 3-night minimum during Tanglewood and holiday weekends. Closed Dec. 20-26.

Williamsville Inn. Rte. 41, West Stockbridge, MA 01266, tel. 413/274-6118. 16 double rooms with baths, 1 suite. Restaurant, bar, air-conditioning, pool, tennis. $105-$175, full breakfast. AE, MC, V. No smoking, no pets, 3-night minimum July-Aug. and holiday weekends.

Windflower Inn. 684 S. Egremont Rd., Great Barrington, MA 01230, tel. 413/528-2720 or 800/992-1993. 13 double rooms with baths. Air-conditioning, black-and-white TVs, piano, pool. $100-$170, full breakfast. AE. Restricted smoking, no pets, 3-night minimum during Tanglewood.

Reservations Services

American Country Collection of B&B (4 Greenwood La., Delmar, NY 12054, tel. 518/439-7001, fax 518/439-4301). **Berkshire B&B Homes** (Main St., Box 211, Williamsburg, MA 01096, tel. 413/268-7244, fax 413/268-7243). **New England Hospitality Network** (Box 3291, Newport, RI 02840, tel. 401/849-1298 or 800/828-0000). **Nutmeg B&B Agency** (Box 1117, West Hartford, CT 06127, tel. 203/236-6698 or 800/727-7592, fax 203/232-2989).

Michigan

Chicago Pike Inn

Southeastern Michigan, Including Ann Arbor and Detroit

Montague Inn

1581 S. Washington Ave., Saginaw, MI 48601, tel. 517/752–3939, fax 517/752–3159

Robert Montague was a respected businessman and civic leader when he built his 12,000-square-foot Georgian house—all of handmade brick—in 1929. He made his fortune developing ways to use sugar beet byproducts in the manufacture of hand creams and soaps, a process later sold to the Andrew Jergens Company.

Saginaw's historic Grove District was once an enclave of stunning residences. To help preserve important landmarks of the district, the city bought Montague's home in the early 1960s and demolished several of the more rickety surrounding properties. Then a group of five entrepreneurial-minded couples bought it from the city in 1985. Eight months later, they reopened the restored mansion and the adjacent carriage house as the Montague Inn. Not only has the three-story brick mansion

been named to the State Register of Historic Places, but it is also considered one of Michigan's best inns, a designation that's hard to dispute.

The inn's location on 8 gently rolling acres overlooking Lake Linton is a mixed blessing. There is usually a lot of activity on the grounds, and on days when the city park across the water is staging a concert or a raft race, there can be a large volume of traffic in the area. Caveat noted, the inn is still a champion. A winding staircase connects the three floors of guest rooms. The Georgian-style quarters typically contain four-poster beds and wing chairs and are tastefully decorated in subtle hues and patterns. The most compelling—and at $140 per night, the most expensive—is the elegant two-room Montague Suite, which features a fireplace, green Pewabic tile, and great views of the impeccably landscaped grounds. Other interesting accommodations are in the former chauffeur's quarters and the cleverly renovated five-car garage.

Guests enjoy a Continental breakfast of oatmeal, cereals, juice, and baked goods in either of two dining rooms, one of which has a welcoming fire on cold mornings. Lunches and candlelight dinners are first-class affairs, too, with an expansive (and expensive) menu and wine list. After meals—everything from asparagus ravioli with grilled portobello mushrooms to honey-marinated quail—logs are lighted in the fireplace of the main-floor library, and guests can look for the hidden cabinets inside the library walls, where Montague stashed his expensive liquor during Prohibition (by special request, you can even dine in a secret alcove behind a bookcase). Other guests choose to wander in the extensive herb and flower garden, participate in one of the inn's exciting events (Independence Day picnic, black-tie New Year's Eve dinner, or summer herb-garden luncheons), or just pen a postcard at the antique writing desk. Those who scrawl "Wish you were here" know what they're talking about.

▥ *16 double rooms with baths, 2 doubles share bath, 1 suite. Restaurant, air-conditioning, phones and TVs in rooms. $65–$140, Continental breakfast. AE, MC, V. Restricted smoking, no pets.*

Raymond House Inn

111 S. Ridge St., Port Sanilac, MI 48469, tel. 313/622–8800 or 800/622–7229

As the inn's owners, Shirley and Ray Denison, enjoy pointing out, there is no McDonald's in Port Sanilac. The retired couple do what they can to keep the golden arches at bay by heading a movement to have this old port village declared a Historic Maritime District, thereby limiting commercial development.

Port Sanilac sits halfway up the eastern edge of the Thumb region on Route 25, about 30 miles north of Port Huron and less than two hours from Detroit. It was one of Lake Huron's first ports of call during the heyday of steamship lines. Its colorful history includes lumberjacks, lake storms, rum-running, and forest fires that more than once destroyed the town. The port's history is honored in the newly opened shipwreck and maritime center.

The background of this comfortable, impressive Victorian house, which is listed on the State Register of Historic Places, is a little calmer but nevertheless significant. In 1850, Uri Raymond, the original owner, opened what is reputed to be the first hardware store in the state (Raymond Hardware, just a block down the road, is still in business). Raymond built his two-story brick residence in 1871, adorning it with classic Victorian touches: elaborate moldings and a winding oak staircase inside and outside a gingerbread facade with dripping white icicle trim. It stayed in the family for the next 112 years until Ray and Shirley—he's a retired Washington lobbyist for the AFL-CIO, she's an artist and conservation expert who in 1976 reframed the Constitution for the Bicentennial—bought it in 1983 and moved here from Washington, D.C.

The house, set on an acre planted with trees and gardens of wildflowers, was in good condition and is now full of family heirlooms, antiques, and numerous examples of Shirley's considerable artistic and restorative skills. She has recaned the chairs, restored the frames that hold a collection of old family photos in an upstairs hallway, and designed the clock in the dining room (she also designs and crafts artistic dolls). The upstairs quarters are authentically furnished, down to crocheted lacework on the window shades, handmade quilts, and hand-crocheted rugs. Lake Huron, a block away, can be spied from the upstairs.

▥ *7 double rooms with baths. Air-conditioning; fireplace, cable TV, and phone in parlor, radio/cassette players in rooms. $65–$75, full breakfast. AE, D, MC, V. No smoking, no pets. Closed Jan.–Mar.*

Stacy Mansion

710 W. Chicago Blvd., Tecumseh, MI 49286, tel. 517/423–6979

The story of one of the state's grandest homes can be gleaned from a quick look inside its first-floor library. On a desktop, the 1874 *Historical Atlas of Lenawee County* is opened to a sketch of the four-story brick mansion as it looked when Judge C. A. Stacy owned it. Directly above the open book hangs a buffalo head, provided by the current owners, Sonny and Joyce Lauber, who, among their other business interests, run one of the few bison farms in the country.

Stacy, newspaper publisher, business-man, and the first probate judge in the county, built the 8,000-square-foot house in the mid-1850s in anticipation of using it as the governor's residence. He lost the gubernatorial election but held on to the house, which has fine examples of 19th-century craftsman-ship such as a foyer with marbled wood and a rare cantilevered staircase.

"Sonny drove past the house for 25 years and always talked about buying it," says Joyce. When the badly neglected building on the outskirts of Tecumseh came on the market in 1988, the Laubers didn't think twice. The house had been stripped of nearly everything—from the furnishings to the brass doorknobs and gingerbread trim—so restoration has been a slow, expensive process. To their credit, they have taken time to research—and have spent the money necessary to recall its 19th-century ambience. They tore out the carpeting, restored the floors and woodwork, and replicated the plasterwork. They also researched historical wallpapers and were even able to buy back some of the furniture from former owners and area real-estate agents. All told, the house "is about 95% antiques," says Joyce. One bedroom has a double-mirrored wardrobe, another an 8½-foot-high, ornately carved walnut headboard. The only incongruous item is the water-filled mattress in the master bedroom. "We couldn't find a mattress that would fit the odd-sized mahogany full-tester bed," she explained.

During your stay, a morning "wake-up" tray of tea, coffee, juice, and homemade coffee cake is brought to your door, fol-lowed later by a full gourmet breakfast in the formal dining room.

The 1¼-acre site is expertly landscaped. Judge Stacy, who owned a local brick-yard, would certainly approve of the 45,000 bricks the Laubers used to cre-ate the paths that wind through the yards and gardens. A 150-year-old pine tree shades a formal garden often abloom with annuals and perennials and accented with wrought-iron garden fur-niture, while old-fashioned streetlamps and red maple trees flank the circular drive and help to make the outdoors an appealing retreat in itself.

▥ *5 double rooms with baths. Air-conditioning, phone in sitting room. $85–$120, full breakfast. MC, V. No smoking, small pets.*

Victorian Inn

1229 7th St., Port Huron, MI 48060, tel. 810/984-1437

Lynne Secory and Vicki Peterson were neighbors busily renovating their own homes when they got the impulse to breathe new life into what was once one of Port Huron's most magnificent houses, the old James A. Davidson res-idence. Davidson, founder of a large furniture and dry goods company that bore his name, had built the elaborate Queen Anne house in 1896 and lived in it until his death in 1911. In 1983, Lynne and Vicki persuaded their husbands to buy the property. Enlisting the aid of many preservation-minded friends, rel-atives, and craftsmen, and working from the architectural plans and spec sheets, they managed to accomplish their mission by the end of the year. Halfway through the project, the house was placed on the State Register of Historic Places. The result of their efforts is a harmonious combination of luxurious lodging and fine dining in a neighborhood of well-maintained Victorian-era buildings that has become a travel destination in itself.

Immediately to the right of the foyer as you walk in is the parlor. Its green velvet valances, antique lace window curtains, green-and-gold floral wallpaper, pincushion settee, and hurricane lamps are invitingly elegant. The second-floor guest rooms are similar blends of antique furnishings and little flourishes: a needlepoint headboard, a papier-mâché picture frame. Two rooms have modern private baths, while the Victoria and Edward rooms share a pedestal sink, claw-foot tub (no shower), and pull-chain toilet.

Guests can eat breakfast in the main-floor 50-seat restaurant, also open for lunch and dinner Tuesday through Saturday. The service is attentive, the staff is immaculately attired in crisp white uniforms, and the mainly American menu is well executed. The inventive soups and desserts are especially popular.

The inn is just a couple of blocks from the St. Clair River, which carries freighter traffic and cool breezes. The Museum of Arts and History is one block over, on Court Street, and houses one of the finest collections of marine lore in the state. Travel the dozen or so blocks to the Fort Gratiot Lighthouse, the first one on the Great Lakes, and return to the inn and wet your whistle at the stone-walled Pierpont Pub. Originally a cellar, it features an old red oak bar that used to be a dry goods counter.

▦ *2 double rooms with baths, 2 doubles share bath. Air-conditioning, room service, fireplace in parlor, restaurant, pub. $65–$75, Continental breakfast. AE, D, MC, V. No pets.*

William Clements Inn

1712 Center Ave., Bay City, MI 48708, tel. 517/894–4600, fax 517/895–8535

This gray Queen Anne–style mansion in Bay City is what eccentric Great-Aunt Emily's house always looked like, at least in the movies: Ornately carved staircases and ceilings, heavy oak furniture, and voluminous velveteen drapes establish the look. The house was built in 1886 for Willliam Clements, a local lumber baron and a collector of rare books who donated his impressive collection to the University of Michigan library in 1920.

Today, his love of books is still felt in the inn, where each suite is named after a writer or fictional character—from Louisa May Alcott and Emily Brontë to Henry David Thoreau and Charles Dickens. This is just one of the lovely touches the owners, Brian and Karen Hepp—a local couple with a great appreciation of history—brought to the inn when they purchased it in 1994. The two most lavish accommodations are the Ernest Hemingway Suite, a two-room whirlpool suite with a working fireplace, sitting area, French doors, a king-size bed and an in-room shower for two, and the Alfred Lord Tennyson Suite, which is actually the 1,200-square-foot former ballroom, now outfitted with a kitchen, living room, dining room, and queen-size bed. Second-floor guest rooms are spacious and filled with period furnishings, including iron or brass beds, marble-top tables, and oak armoires. One bathroom is particularly gracious, featuring china tiles bordered with hand-painted morning glories.

As the quintessential 19th-century man of industry and culture, Clements also exhibited a respect for music, equipping the music room with a magnificent Steinway grand piano. But Clements's true passion was books, and a few volumes from his former collection remain in the richly paneled main-floor library. Guests, however, are more likely to be found in the screened-in back porch, shaded by a 200-year-old beech tree. There they play cards and talk of the sea captains and lumber barons who built the other grand mansions that fill this historic district.

⚏ *4 double rooms with baths; 3 suites. Air-conditioning, TVs, phones; fireplace in 4 rooms, whirlpool bath in suites. $70–$175; Continental breakfast, evening refreshments. AE, D, MC, V. No smoking, no pets.*

Other Choices

Blanche House Inn and the Castle. 506 Parkview Dr., Detroit, MI 48214, tel. 313/822–7090. 13 double rooms with baths, 1 suite. Air-conditioning, cable TVs, phones; hot tubs in 4 rooms. $60–$125, full breakfast. AE, D, DC, MC, V. No smoking, no pets.

Botsford Inn. 28000 Grand River, Farmington Hills, MI 48336, tel. 810/474–4800. 14 historic double rooms; 49 modern rooms, all with baths. Phones; air-conditioning in some rooms, restaurant, cable TV, coffeemaker. $65–$75, full breakfast. AE, D, DC, MC, V. No pets.

Chicago Street Inn. 219 Chicago St., Brooklyn, MI 49230, tel. 517/592–3888, fax 517/592–9025. 3 double rooms with baths, 2 doubles share bath, 2 suites. Air-conditioning, cable TV in sitting room, phone in entranceway, fireplace in sitting room. $65–$165, full breakfast. MC, V. No smoking, no pets.

Clinton Inn. 104 W. Michigan Ave. (Box 457), Clinton, MI 49236, tel. 517/456–4151. 6 double rooms with baths, 4 double rooms share bath. Air-conditioning, cable TVs. $35–$45, Sunday brunch. D, MC, V. No pets. Closed Mon.

Dundee Guest House. 522 Tecumseh St., Dundee, MI 48131, tel. 313/529–5706. 1 double room with bath, 1 suite. Croquet and gazebo in backyard. $55–$95, Continental breakfast. MC, V. No smoking, no pets.

Southwestern Michigan, Including Battle Creek, Grand Rapids, Kalamazoo, Saugatuck

Chicago Pike Inn

215 E. Chicago St., Coldwater, MI 49036, tel. 517/279–8744

Parental love is the simple story behind this large yellow inn, which sits on U.S. 12 halfway between Detroit and Chicago. Looking to lure their daughter Becky back to Michigan, Harold and Jane Schultz dangled a carrot: They would buy one of Coldwater's most elegant mansions and convert it into a B&B if she would come home to run it. Becky, who had studied hotel management in college and was working at a plush Florida resort at the time, immediately agreed.

The 7,500-square-foot mansion was built in 1903 by local mercantilist Morris G. Clarke, who hired Asbury Buckley to design it. The Chicago architect was responsible for many of the fine homes built on Mackinac Island in the 1890s. Although the mansion was being used as a boarding house when the Schultzes bought it, it was still in remarkably fine condition. Today, such elegant touches as the built-in mirrored buffet in the cherry-paneled dining room, the double-mantel fireplace in the reception room, and the oak parquet floors can make you feel almost guilty about showing up in jeans and a T-shirt.

Guest rooms in the main house are appointed with period wall coverings and Victorian antiques such as marble-top tables. All but one are on the second floor; the exception is the Clarkes' Own Room (as it was labeled on the original architectural drawings). Off the library—a restful refuge with a marble fireplace and century-old tea table—this room is furnished with an ornately carved, lace-covered canopy bed. At the top of the stairs is Miss Sophia's Suite, the inn's most popular room, which has a yellow-tile fireplace with an oak mantel and a private balcony. The velvet sofa and large table make private breakfasts here a favorite option. A gambrel-roofed, two-story carriage house contains the two newest rooms. Decorated in the same style as the main house, these lodgings also include air-conditioning, whirlpool baths, refrigerators, and private balconies. All rooms reveal the innkeepers' attention to detail and include extra-nice touches such as individual thermostats and four pillows—two hard, two soft.

The antiques centers of Allen and Marshall are nearby, and northern Indiana—home to the famous Shipshewana auctions and a thriving Amish community—is just a half hour's drive away. Or you can hop on one of the inn's bicycles and explore Coldwater, a drowsy town filled with 19th-century statuary and Victorian-era homes.

▦ *5 double rooms with baths, 3 suites. Air-conditioning in 2 rooms, cable TV, fireplace, and phone in common area, fireplace in 1 room, refrigerator and whirlpool bath in 2 rooms, bicycles. $80–$165; full breakfast, afternoon refreshments. AE, MC, V. Restricted smoking, no pets.*

Greencrest Manor

6174 Halbert Rd., Battle Creek, MI 49017, tel. 616/962–8633

Finding a French Norman–style château on Battle Creek's St. Mary's Lake is an unexpected treat for bed-and-breakfast fans: The city is home to Kellogg and Post cereals and is known more for cereals than châteaus. Constructed of sandstone, slate and copper, the gracious 1935 inn sits on 15 acres adorned with formal gardens and European-style fountains. Open since 1989, it has drawn favorable reviews from numerous publications and has become known as one of the most romantic spots in the state.

Looking at the elegant marble floors, spiral staircase, ballroom-size living room, and paneled library, it's hard to imagine the inn's once-dilapidated condition. Originally built for a lumber baron, it served for almost two decades as a Roman Catholic monastery, then remained empty for more than seven years until 1987, when current owners Tom and Kathy Van Daff purchased it—Tom had actually grown up in the area and always admired the unusual structure. At the time the Van Daffs acquired it, the house was just a large concrete shell with no windows, doors, or interior light fixtures; there was a hole in the roof and several inches of water in the basement.

The Van Daffs were lucky enough to locate original blueprints of the house and garden, which guided them throughout the extensive renovation. Today, the 13,000-square-foot mansion is once again outfitted in the style it had been accustomed to, including spacious parlor rooms featuring elegant European antiques, soothing chintz fabrics, silk flowers, and a cosmopolitan country style. Spacious guest rooms decorated in the same manner also sport modern amenities including telephone and cable TV; suites have fireplaces and whirlpool baths. As for breakfast, your Rice Krispies will be served up in Wedgwood china—or you can opt for some delicious homemade muffins.

▦ *6 double rooms with baths, 2 double rooms with shared bath, 4 suites. Cable TVs, phones; whirlpool baths in suites. $75–$170, Continental breakfast. AE, MC, V. No smoking, no pets.*

Kingsley House

626 W. Main St., Fennville, MI 49408, tel. 616/561–6425

David and Shirley Witt tout their impressive Queen Anne house in tiny Fennville as being "as American as apple pie," an example of truth in advertising if ever there was one. It was built in 1886 by Harvey Kingsley, who introduced fruit trees to this area around Lake Michigan. Tipping their caps to Kingsley, the Witts have placed his picture in the living room and named each of the guest rooms after a variety of apple. An oak stairway leads to six second-story chambers, two of which are dubbed McIntosh and Golden Delicious. The most interesting is the Jonathan Room, formerly a stable boy's quarters, with a century-old bed and an 1850s platform rocker. Nestled in the tower is the Dutchess Room, which, with five windows, is the brightest, and is regally decorated in cranberry-hued wallpaper and antique lace. Immediately above it is Northern Spy, a honeymoon suite, which features an electric fireplace, a whirlpool bath, and a tower sitting room, with a calming view of miles of rolling countryside.

Shirley, who was born in the Netherlands, runs the household with smooth efficiency and simple elegance. The guest rooms and common areas are spacious and immaculately clean. The furnishings are a tasteful blend of oak and cherry antiques that harmonize with such family ornaments as the shadowboxes the Witts made.

A Continental breakfast buffet is served during the week. On weekends, breakfast is a fancy affair, served on linens and Royal Doulton china in the formal cherrywood dining room. The delftware and silver are typical of Dutch touches throughout the house. Five menus are rotated, but meals usually include country ham, farm-fresh eggs, hash browns, and homemade muffins and bread. Coffee and the morning paper are set out by 7:30, and tea, cold drinks, cookies, and snacks are available all day.

With busy Route 89 close at hand, traffic noise can be a problem in the front rooms. To escape, hop on one of the four 18-speed bikes the Witts provide and pedal 8 miles south to the Allegan State Game Area, famous as a rest stop for geese and other migrating waterfowl. Once there, you can hike, canoe, swim, cross-country ski, or pick wild blueberries, strawberries, and other fruit.

▦ *6 double rooms with baths, 3 suites. Air-conditioning, TVs, phones, fireplaces, and whirlpool tubs in suites, 2 phones in common areas. $65–$145; full breakfast on weekends, buffet breakfast weekdays, refreshments all day. AE, D, MC, V. No smoking, no pets.*

National House Inn

102 S. Parkview St., Marshall, MI 49068, tel. 616/781–7374, fax 616/781–4510

More than a smooth-running and magnificently preserved hostel from another period, the National House Inn is a centerpiece of what many consider the finest cross section of 19th-century architecture in the country. The oldest inn in the state opened as a stagecoach stop in 1835, two years before Michigan was admitted to the Union. For many years it served double duty as one of the final stops on the Underground Railroad, which spirited escaped slaves to Canada, 120 miles to the east. In 1878, it was converted into a wagon and windmill factory. The inn was drawing its final breath as an apartment house when a consortium of local businesspeople bought and restored it for the nation's Bicentennial.

For the past 12 years, innkeeper Barbara Bradley has watched a parade of tourists, business travelers, and honeymooners pass through the rustic entryway, which is warmed by a massive beam-and-brick open-hearth fireplace. The rough-hewn ceiling beams and aged plank floors are the framework for the particular selection of country antiques found in each room. There are punched-tin chandeliers; Windsor, ladderback, and herringbone wing chairs in the living room; spindle-leg tables and hurricane lamps in the dining room; and gilt-framed oil portraits throughout. Thanks to a unique fireplace set into handcrafted paneled cabinets, the upstairs lounge is comfortable and inviting, although in warmer weather guests prefer moving to the back porch and gardens.

Guest rooms are attractively wallpapered and carpeted, with the decor ranging from country style to the Victorian-era design of the Ketchum Suite, which overlooks a handsome garden and the village circle. There's plenty of elbow room in the dining room, where a Continental breakfast of boiled eggs, bowls of fruit, wheat bread, coffee, and a wide variety of fruit juices and teas is served.

Marshall is right off I-94, 10 miles east of Battle Creek. In 1991, the village—frequently referred to as "the Williamsburg of the Midwest"—was designated a National Historic Landmark District. The district encompasses some 850 structures (and nearly 50 historical markers), including striking examples of Queen Anne, Italianate, and Gothic Revival architecture.

▥ *16 double rooms with baths. Air-conditioning, cable TV, and phone in rooms. $66–$120, Continental breakfast. AE, MC, V. No-smoking rooms available, no pets.*

Pebble House

15093 Lakeshore Rd., Lakeside, MI 49116, tel. 616/469-1416

"Serenity is our goal," says Jean Lawrence, who, along with her husband, Ed, owns the relaxing Pebble House. Chicago expatriates, Jean was an art therapist and Ed a real estate investment analyst when they fell in love with the 1912 concrete-block and river-rock house on the shores of Lake Michigan. The Lawrences decided to furnish the inn in mission-style furniture because it seemed to fit and at the time, it was still relatively inexpensive. Today, the Pebble House is one of the few B&Bs faithful to the revolutionary early 1900s style that preached a return to handcraftsmanship. The Lawrences, who also own East Road Antiques in town, have meticulously furnished all the guest rooms and public areas with distinctive, clean-lined mission-style furniture and accessories, including hand-hammered copper bowls and green lead-glass lamps. Even Jean's Scandinavian-style breakfasts of baked Finnish pancakes and homemade coffee cakes are served on Roycroft Revival china.

The Lawrences work hard to make this a true retreat: There are no phones in the guest rooms and nary a television in sight. As an alternate pleasure to the electronic age, more than 2,000 books, including volumes of fiction, travel, and design, are tucked all about. Needless to say, their collection of books on the Arts and Crafts movement is a connoisseur's delight. If you're looking to explore the area's bountiful antiquing, you're in luck: Ed's even written a guidebook to the region's shops. For those who prefer more active relaxation, a tennis court and nearby beach also beckon.

▥ *3 double rooms with baths, 3-bedroom Coach House with bath, 2-bedroom Blueberry House with 2 baths. Air-conditioning, phones on request; kitchenette and wood-burning stove in Blueberry House. $90–$140, $220 for Blueberry House; full breakfast, refreshments. D, MC, V. No smoking, no pets. Closed Dec. 24.*

South Cliff Inn

1900 Lakeshore Dr., St. Joseph, MI 49085, tel. 616/983-4881, fax 616/983-7391

Seven years ago, Bill Swisher left behind a decade-long career as director of the Cassopolis, Michigan, Probate

Court and opened the South Cliff Inn. "I grew up in the area, and I suppose I was always looking for an excuse to come back," Bill says.

In the pre-air-conditioning days of the early 1900s, St. Joseph (or St. Joe, as it's sometimes called) and its sister city, Benton Harbor, were among the Midwest's most popular lakefront summer resorts. The collapse of the area's manufacturing base led to a decline of its fortunes in the 1970s, especially in Benton Harbor, always the more blue-collar of the two. South Cliff Inn, a salmon-colored brick English cottage, is a small but important representative of an economic renaissance that once again is capitalizing on the therapeutic breezes of Lake Michigan.

The 80-year-old inn is perched on a bluff, giving all but one of the seven guest rooms superb views of the water. The largest room, the Sunset Suite, is perhaps the most popular. The queen-size bed, sofa, and wing chair are dressed in complementary English chintz fabrics; the private bath features a custom-designed marble tub. In the Harbour Room, guests can lie back in a bubbling whirlpool bath and watch the sun melt into the lake in the evening. Two rooms now have balconies overlooking the lake. The entire place is decorated in English country style (not surprisingly, a perennial garden was added last year), with plenty of bold prints, chintz fabrics, and a large number of antiques. One of the guest rooms houses an imposing 150-year-old oak armoire that is so large it had to be hoisted through the windows.

The trouble was worth it: The inn is comfortable, sun-filled, and, with just one part-time staffer to assist Bill, commendably unhurried. The Continental breakfast includes juice, homemade bread, muffins, coffee cakes and—after all, this is orchard country—plenty of fresh fruit. That's enough carbohydrates to fuel a short walk to the downtown of this pleasant harbor town, whose turn-of-the-century storefronts

and monuments, landscaped brick streets, and Lake Michigan backdrop combine to make it perhaps the most picturesque in the entire state.

⊞ *7 double rooms with baths. Air-conditioning, cable TV in den, fireplace in 2 rooms, whirlpool bath in 2 rooms. $75–$150; Continental breakfast, refreshments all day. AE, D, MC, V. Restricted smoking, no pets, 2-night minimum on weekends, 3-night minimum on holidays.*

Stuart Avenue Inn

229 Stuart Ave., Kalamazoo, MI 49007, tel. 616/342–0230

The downtown Kalamazoo block that boasts the Stuart Avenue Inn has been likened to the exterior lot of one of those MGM musicals set at the turn of the century. Statuesque Queen Annes, Italianates, American Four-Squares, and other examples of high Victorian style form a colorful chorus line along tree-shaded Stuart Avenue. Modern civilization in the form of Kalamazoo College (a block away) and Western Michigan University (a half-mile walk), are nearby, but you'd never know it.

The Stuart Avenue Inn is actually a group of three houses, all adjacent to each other and grouped around a lovely garden. The showpiece is the spectacular 1886 Eastlake Queen Anne–style Bartlett-Upjohn House—built by newspaper publisher Edgar Bartlett and once home to Upjohn Pharmaceuticals cofounder James T. Upjohn. Next door is the 1902 Arts and Crafts–style Chappel House, site of the VIP suites. A few steps away is a small carriage house, with rooms as well as a mini-apartment perfect for extended stays.

Popular accommodations in the Bartlett-Upjohn House include the Mayor's Room, with elegant Bradbury and Bradbury wallpapers, burled walnut accents, and a queen-size bed. Others prefer the spacious VIP suites—complete with Jacuzzis, VCRs, and fireplaces—in the

Chappel House (if you opt to stay here, be sure to check out the "secret room" off the back staircase). Carriage-house rooms are more modest—but so is their room rate. All rooms are furnished with family antiques and photographs as well as what the staff charmingly calls "garage-sale relations."

A great place to relax is the adjacent gardens, a vacant lot turned into a city showcase. Formerly the site of a 1920s nationally recognized Shakespearean garden, it now features a gazebo, pergola, fountain, and lily pond and is a favorite spot for area weddings. Now under the stewardship of Mary Lou and Tom Baker, the Stuart Avenue Inn continues to offer a delightful range of options for weary travelers.

🏨 *12 double rooms with bath, 4 suites. Air-conditioning, TVs, phones. $49–$130, Continental breakfast. AE, D, DC, MC, V. No smoking, no pets, 5-day cancellation policy.*

Wickwood Country Inn

510 Butler St. (Box 1019), Saugatuck, MI 49453, tel. 616/857–1097, fax 616/857–4168

Guests at Saugatuck's oldest bed-and-breakfast are in for a treat, both figuratively and literally. The owner, Julee Rosso-Miller, is the coauthor of the *Silver Palate Cookbook*. With 2 million copies of her gourmet masterpiece sold, only the *Joy of Cooking* has kept it from being the best-selling cookbook of all time.

Julee came to her new career as innkeeper in much the same way she became a well-known gourmet writer: serendipity. Her mother's heart attack in 1986 forced her to reappraise her own hectic lifestyle as co-owner of one of the first-ever gourmet takeout shops in the country, New York's Silver Palate. She moved to Saugatuck and fell in love with the sunsets over Lake Michigan—and with Ray Miller, a local builder. They married, then persuaded

their neighbors to sell what has long been regarded as the best B&B in town. Of course, the location doesn't hurt: It's two blocks from downtown's many fine shops and restaurants and a short walk from the beach and other lakefront attractions.

With its brick floors, cedar walls, and vaulted ceilings, the circa-1940 inn resembles one of those small toasty hotels that dot the English countryside. The main-floor rooms, filled with overstuffed chairs, French and English antiques, fresh flowers, and original art, surround a courtyard blooming with perennials, roses, and herbs. The guest rooms have individual themes but are uniformly captivating, with plenty of antique lace, Ralph Lauren and Laura Ashley fabrics, and cabbage-rose patterns on the walls and beds.

Guests are pampered from daybreak to dusk. A buffet breakfast is served and a newspaper supplied weekday mornings on the old English pine buffet table in the dining area, which is filled with antique toy trains, boats, and trucks. On weekends, a hearty brunch is prepared. Hors d'oeuvres, which might include a light salmon mousse, bruschetta, Chinese ribs, and crudités with low-fat dip, are put out at 6 PM. As if this weren't enough, candies and jars of spiced nuts are placed in each room. Calorie counters can relax, though: Most items are selections from Julee's recent low-fat cookbook, *Great Good Food*.

🏨 *11 double rooms with baths, 2 suites. Air-conditioning, cable TV in library, fireplace in 1 suite. $140–$190; full breakfast, evening refreshments. MC, V. No pets, 2-night minimum on weekends. Closed Dec. 24–25.*

Other Choices

Fairchild House. 606 Butler St., Saugatuck, MI 49453, tel. 616/857–5985. 3 double rooms with baths. Air-conditioning, bathrobes; phone, TV, and fireplace in parlor. $125, full champagne breakfast. MC, V. No smoking, no pets, 2-night minimum on weekends.

Inn at Union Pier. 9708 Berrien St. (Box 222), Union Pier, MI 49129, tel. 616/469–4700, fax 616/469–4720. 16 double rooms with baths. Air-conditioning, cable TV and phone in Great House, fireplace in 12 rooms, hot tub, sauna, beach towels. $115–$185; full breakfast, afternoon and evening refreshments. D, MC, V. No smoking, no pets, 2-night minimum on weekends, 3-night minimum on holidays.

Maplewood Hotel. 428 Butler St. (Box 1059), Saugatuck, MI 49453, tel. 616/857–1771, fax 616/857–1773. 15 double rooms with baths. Air-conditioning, cable TV, phone, fireplace in 5 rooms, whirlpool bath in 5 rooms, lap pool. $85–$155, full breakfast. AE, MC, V. No smoking, no pets, 2-night minimum on weekends, 3-night minimum on holidays. Closed for 3 days at both Thanksgiving and Christmas.

McCarthy's Bear Creek Inn. 15230 C. Dr. North, Marshall, MI 49068, tel. 616/781–8383. 14 rooms with bath. Air-conditioning, TV on request. $65–$98, breakfast buffet. AE, M, V. No pets.

Mendon Country Inn. 440 W. Main St., Mendon, MI 49072, tel. 616/496–8132. 9 double rooms with baths, 9 suites. Cedar sauna, rooftop garden, picnic area, bikes, canoes available. $50–$159, deluxe Continental breakfast. AE, D, MC, V. Restricted smoking, no pets.

Parsonage 1908. 6 E. 24th St., Holland, MI 49423, tel. 616/396–1316. 1 double room with bath; 2 doubles share 1 bath. Air-conditioning, TV in sitting room. $90–$100; full breakfast, refreshments. No credit cards. No smoking, no pets. Closed last week in Feb.

Pine Garth Inn. 15790 Lakeshore Rd, Box 347, Union Pier, MI 49129, tel. 616/469–1642. 7 double rooms with baths, 5 2-bedroom cottages with baths. Air-conditioning, TV/VCRs; hot tub and fireplace in cottages. $115–

$150 double, $195–$225 cottage; full breakfast, afternoon refreshments (inn only). AE, MC, V. No smoking, no pets, 2-night minimum on weekends, 3-night minimum on holidays.

Twin Oaks Inn. 227 Griffith St., Box 867, Saugatuck, MI 49453, tel. 616/857–1600. 8 double rooms with bath, 3 suites, private cottage. Air-conditioning, cable TV/VCRs, phones. $65–$95; Continental breakfast weekdays, full breakfast weekends. D, MC, V. No smoking, pets in cottage only.

Victorian Villa Inn. 601 North Broadway St., Union City, MI 49094, tel. 517/741–7383 or 800/348–4552, fax 517/741–4002. 5 double rooms with baths, 5 suites. Restaurant, air-conditioning in most rooms, fireplace in 2 suites, bicycles built for two available. $75–$145; full breakfast, afternoon tea, dinner in adjacent restaurant available. D, MC, V. No smoking, no pets.

Yelton Manor. 140 N. Shore Dr., South Haven, MI 49090, tel. 616/637–5220, fax 616/637–4957. 17 double rooms with baths. Air-conditioning, cable TVs; fireplace in 7 rooms, whirlpool bath in 11 rooms. $95–$190; full or Continental breakfast, refreshments. AE, MC, V. No smoking, no pets.

Upper Peninsula

Big Bay Point Lighthouse

3 Lighthouse Rd., Big Bay, MI 49808, tel. 906/345–9957

Perched high on a rocky point 30 miles north of Marquette, this charming brick lighthouse and light keeper's home has had guided mariners on Lake Superior since 1896. Though the Coast Guard automated the light in 1941, it remains a working navigational aid and one of the few lighthouses open to the public as a bed-and-breakfast inn.

Owners Linda and Jeff Ganble and John Gale were active in historic preservation in Chicago when they discovered the lighthouse and its wooded property, then slated to become a condominium development, were for sale. In 1992, they purchased the lighthouse, several outbuildings, and 43 acres of woods and meadows. Today it houses a large living room with fireplace, dining area with warm exposed brick, and seven double rooms. Most impressive is the Sunset Suite, with cathedral ceiling and spacious sitting room—perfect for watching rosy orange sunsets fade into the lake.

Recreation begins right outside the door: The rugged Huron Mountains stretch to the west, offering hundreds of acres of superb hiking, mountain biking, and fly-fishing. Many guests are content to explore the lighthouse property itself, including 4,500 feet of shoreline. And everyone wants to climb the 60-foot tower for the 360-degree view. On a clear day, you can spot the U.P.'s Keweenaw Peninsula across 45 miles of open water. On rainy afternoons, there are plenty of lighthouse books, blueprints, and other memorabilia to peruse. Or cuddle up with a cup of hot cider and watch the fury of the Great Lake, just like the light keepers did a century ago.

▦ *7 double rooms with baths. Sauna. $115–$155 May–Oct., $85–$125 Nov.–April; full breakfast. No credit cards. No smoking, no pets.*

Laurium Manor Inn

320 Tamarack, Laurium, MI 49913, tel. 906/337-2549

Dave and Julie Sprenger were working as engineers in San Jose, California, when, as Julie describes it, they "decided to commit corporate suicide" and trade the Golden State's laid-back charms for the ruggedly isolated Keweenaw Peninsula. They shared a dream of owning a mansion they had visited in Laurium, a former copper boomtown. In 1989, they bought the vacant three-story neoclassical house and after three years of restoration work, reopened its heavy oak doors as a bed-and-breakfast.

The Upper Peninsula's largest (13,000 square feet!) and most opulent mansion was built in 1908 by Captain Thomas H. Hoatson, owner of the Calumet & Arizona Mining Company. At a time when miners were toiling 6,000 feet underground for 25 cents an hour, Hoatson spent $50,000 constructing the 40-room mansion and an additional $35,000 furnishing it. The copper magnate had impeccable taste, as lodgers and afternoon tour groups ($3 a head) quickly learn.

Every room is a marvel. Silver-leaf overlay draws your eye to the ceiling of the music parlor. The dining room boasts stained-glass windows and gilded elephant-hide wall coverings, and the kitchen includes a built-in icebox covering an entire wall and made of marble, tile, and oak.

While all the bedrooms were built on an extralarge scale, the Laurium Suite exhausts all superlatives; it covers a majestic 530 square feet and has a hand-carved oak fireplace and private balcony. All the guest quarters feature queen- or king-size beds, handmade flannel quilts, and period antiques.

The National Park Service has named the inn a "cooperating site" of the new Keweenaw National Historical Park, recognizing its significance in the area's mining heritage. Plan day trips to some of the national park's other historic sites, including the Calumet Theatre (where Sarah Bernhardt, Lillian Russell, and Douglas Fairbanks Jr. performed) or to one of the ghost towns sprinkled throughout the copper region. Lake Superior is just 4 miles away; Fort Wilkins State Park, a mid-19th-century army post on the northernmost tip of Keweenaw, is a short drive up U.S. 41.

🏠 *8 double rooms with baths, 2 doubles share bath, 2 suites. Phone and cable TV in den, fireplace in 2 guest rooms. $49–$109, breakfast buffet. D, MC, V. No smoking, no pets.*

Sand Hills Lighthouse Inn

Five Mile Point Rd, Box 414, Ahmeek, MI 49901, tel. 906/337–1744

Isn't it almost everyone's dream to live in a lighthouse? Well, Bill Frabotta decided to make this fantasy into a reality—and this inn is the result. Together with his late wife, Eve, Bill had searched for the perfect structure to acquire and renovate, and in 1960 they found just the place: the 1919 Sand Hills Lighthouse, a cream-colored brick building overlooking Lake Superior on wildly beautiful Keweenaw Peninsula. Today, guests can share the couple's dream with a stay in this remote outpost, where they can enjoy the best of both worlds—rugged scenery and refined lodging. It's more than refined, actually, thanks to a panoply of Victorian antiques that transform this inn into a warm and plush retreat.

Perched at the end of Five Mile Point about 25 miles northeast of Houghton, the Sand Hills Lighthouse was the last such manned building on the Great Lakes shore. Along with the rectangular-shaped light tower, it included housing for three keepers' families. Although the light was automated in 1939, the property remained active as a Coast Guard training site. During World War II, the property housed some 200 men, who bunked in the lighthouse and several outbuildings.

Bill spared no energy or expense outfitting the inn. While continuing to run his photography studio in Dearborn, Michigan, he and Eve spent whatever vacation time they could at the property. For three decades, they lived in the adjacent signal station (used for foggy weather) and planned the renovation work. While much of the original woodwork remains, most of the structure has been completely overhauled. The Frabottas also collected an impressive collection of antiques to furnish the inn, which finally opened as a B&B in 1995.

From the ornate crown molding to the velvet drapes in the common room, Sand Hills is bathed in Victorian splendor. Guest rooms feature Victorian dressing tables or chests, and the King Room and several others have massive four-poster beds. Other unique pieces are scattered throughout the inn; they include a lighthouse lens and the 5-foot-high turn-of-the-century coffee grinder tucked against the stairway in the light tower. Many of Bill's photographic portraits decorate the walls.

Still, it's hard to upstage Mother Nature and the majestic lake just outside the door. Guests are welcome to climb the 80 steps to the top of the light tower, which rises 90 feet above the water and offers magnificent views of unspoiled forest and the wide blue horizon of Lake Superior. Water lovers should opt for the Northeast Room or the Northwest Room, both with French doors that open onto private balconies overlooking the lake.

Downstairs, guests relax around the fireplace or curl up on the leather couch and sing along with Bill at the grand piano. Bill uses a late-1800s square grand piano as a sideboard in the dining room, where he serves up a full breakfast that might include "decadent" French toast, apple pancakes, and banana bread. After a hearty meal, guests can explore the rocky shoreline, hike, or ski the trails on the inn's 35 acres, or set off for a day of adventure in the Keweenaw.

🏠 *7 double rooms with baths (one room includes additional single day bed). Fireplace in 1 room and common room. $115–$175, full breakfast. No credit cards. No smoking, no pets.*

Thunder Bay Inn

Box 286, Big Bay, MI 49808, tel. 906/345-9376 or 800/732-0714

From the wide front porch of the gray clapboard Thunder Bay Inn, guests can gaze down on Lake Independence, picturesquely accented with the tower of an old sawmill peeking above the treeline. It's exactly the view Henry Ford—founding father of the automotive industry—wanted when he purchased the turn-of-the-century general store and warehouse in the 1940s. Ford owned vast holdings throughout the Upper Peninsula, including the old sawmill at Big Bay (not so incidentally, this mill produced the wooden panels for those beloved relics of the '50s and '60s, the Ford "Woody" station wagon).

In 1986, present owners Darryl and Eileen Small purchased and restored Ford's executive retreat and reopened it as the Thunder Bay Inn. They've collected a fascinating array of Ford memorabilia, displayed throughout this comfortable, unpretentious inn. Newspaper clippings in the dining room tell stories of the Ford company towns that peppered the peninsula as early as the 1920s, marvels of modernity with electric lights and indoor running water.

Guests today may not marvel at indoor plumbing, but they will appreciate Thunder Bay Inn's simple comforts and superb location. Guest rooms with period furniture line the wide second-floor corridor. The Henry Ford Executive Suite claims the prime front corner, with a fine lake view and ample sitting areas. Some double rooms have adjoining doors for conversion into suites. On the main floor, guests relax over Continental breakfast in the immense great room, where Ford held summer parties, or settle into wicker chairs on the porch.

But Henry Ford didn't provide the inn's only entry in the history books. The hotel was the setting for the 1959 classic *Anatomy of a Murder*, starring Jimmy Stewart and Lee Remick. Hollywood filmmakers even added the inn's north-woodsy pub, now a favorite among locals for its whitefish, steaks, and terrific homemade pizza. Although the hotel's name in the novel and movie—Thunder Bay Inn—is fictional, the story was based on a true crime, which took place in Big Bay in 1951. Today, Big Bay is a tiny resort area tucked against the Lake Superior shoreline and surrounded by the rugged and remote Huron Mountains. An avid outdoorsman, Darryl can direct guests to hiking trails, waterfalls, fishing spots, and other activities.

▥ *5 doubles with baths, 5 doubles with half baths and shared showers, 4 suites. TV in common room. $70–$105, Continental breakfast. MC, V. Restricted smoking, no pets.*

Other Choices

Celibeth House. Blaney Park Rd., M-77 (Rte. 1, Box 58A), Blaney Park, MI 49836, tel. 906/283-3409. 6 double rooms with baths, 1 quad. $48–$53, Continental breakfast. MC, V. No smoking, no pets.

Pinewood Lodge. Rte. 28 (Box 176), Au Train, MI 49806, tel. 906/892-8300. 3 double rooms with baths, 2 double rooms with shared bath, 2 suites. Hot tub, sauna. $75–$150, full breakfast. D, MC, V. No smoking, no pets.

Water Street Inn. 140 E. Water St., Sault Ste. Marie, MI 49783, tel. 906/632-1900 or 800/236-1904. 4 double rooms with baths. $75–$105, full breakfast. D, MC, V. No smoking, no pets.

Mackinac Island

Bay View at Mackinac

Main St. (Box 448), Mackinac Island, MI 49757, tel. 906/847-3295

Owner Doug Yoder's great-great-grandfather, Dr. John R. Bailey, a surgeon at Ft. Mackinac, would be pleased. Doug, who works in the music industry in Nashville during the winter, has painstakingly restored this 1890s house, which has been in his family for more than 100 years. The two-year renovation, which cost half a million dollars, has made the most of the home's elegance.

The sitting room's tin ceiling and fireplace and the refinished wood moldings throughout the house have kept their charm. The wraparound porch is decked out in green and white with skirted glass-top tables. Panoramic views of the water and abundant bright begonias and geraniums make this a perfect place to enjoy late afternoon refreshments.

Guest rooms feel more modern than Victorian as a result of the renovation, but bright new fabrics, skirted tables, and flower-garden wallpaper borders mixed with authentic period pieces, such as an antique inlaid-mahogany headboard, create a nice blend of old and new. Marble floors and ceramic tile in the bathrooms add a classic touch. All the curtains and bedspreads have been handmade for the inn, as was the carpeting in all the hallways and on all the stairs. Three different designs were cut and laid together to create a beautiful rose-colored and flowered carpet.

Newlyweds and chronic romantics will especially enjoy Doug's final additions—three suites, each luxuriously furnished with a whirlpool bath, a television, a CD and video library, a wet bar, and a private balcony overlooking the harbor. There have already been several weddings on those balconies.

Upon arrival you'll discover a sampling of fudge in your room in true Mackinac Island tradition. In the morning you'll awaken to the aroma of Doug's Bay View Blend Coffee and home-baked pastries. Take your breakfast up to the second-floor balcony snd start your day

off right—with a spectacular view of the Straits of Mackinac.

🏨 *17 double rooms with baths, 3 suites. Ceiling fans; TV in sitting room on request, conference room, gallery and marine supply store, short-term docking facilities. $95–$285, Continental breakfast. MC, V. No pets, 2-night minimum on weekends. Closed Oct.– Apr.*

Haan's 1830 Inn

Summer: Huron St. (Box 123), Mackinac Island, MI 49757, tel. 906/847–6244. Winter: 3418 Oakwood Ave., Island Lake, IL 60042, tel. 847/526–2662

The charm of Haan's 1830 Inn is not just in its appearance but in the owners themselves. Vernon and Joy Haan share business responsibilities at the inn with their son Nicholas and his wife, Nancy. Even their grandchildren lend a hand by folding napkins before breakfast at the 12-foot harvest table.

The house was built around the foundations of a log cabin that had been dragged over the ice from the mainland during the Revolutionary War. In the mid-1800s, it was the home of Ft. Mackinac officer and onetime island mayor Colonel Preston. The white columns in front give evidence the inn is the oldest Greek Revival home in what was the Northwest Territory; it was also the first B&B on Mackinac Island.

The Haans have turned what could have seemed old and shabby into someplace warm and inviting. Guest rooms are named after figures from the island's past and are tastefully decorated with a variety of antiques, including an elegant burled-walnut headboard. Taller guests should avoid the Reverend William Ferry and Pere Marquette rooms, since the ceilings in that part of the house are unusually low, probably to retain heat in the winter.

A fascinating centerpiece in the sitting room is a large black safe originally used by one of fur trader John Jacob Astor's agents. Original 1830 prints hang on the wall, and there is a large, dark cherry-wood desk that was built and used in Ft. Mackinac. The second-story porch, tucked under the trees, is a great place to hide out and absorb the island's atmosphere; for those looking for more excitement, the island's downtown is a mere three blocks away.

The Haans clearly enjoy running the inn. The marble-top breakfast buffet brims with delicious coffee cakes, muffins, and jams to be enjoyed at your leisure in front of a crackling fire in the dining room. Vernon is a history buff with a special talent for bringing history to life. In fact, you won't need to spend money on any of the island tours; Vernon is far more interesting and lively. The *Haan* in the inn's name, like the *1830*, is clearly not just for effect.

▥ *4 double rooms with baths, 2 doubles share bath, 1 housekeeping suite. Ceiling fans, chocolates, vouchers for cocktails at local restaurants. $80–$140, Continental breakfast. No credit cards. No smoking, no pets. Closed mid-Oct.–mid-May.*

Inn on Mackinac

Summer: Main St., Mackinac Island, MI 49757, tel. 906/847-6348 or 800/462-2546. Winter: Box 7706, Ann Arbor, MI 48107, tel. 313/665-5750

Trying to find all 13 colors on the inn's exterior, beyond the easier-to-identify hues of purple, pink, green, and peach, is a favorite pastime of guests. Assistant general manager Kelly Irby says most people can only identify five or six. The bright colors, inspired by Victorian homes like the so-called painted ladies of San Francisco, make the Inn on Mackinac one of the more eye-catching houses on the island.

Built in 1867, with the back section added later, the house used to be called the Chateau Beaumont in memory of the fort's famous army surgeon, William Beaumont. In 1988, the inn was remodeled to emphasize its quaint Victorian charm yet still provide a number of modern amenities.

The larger and more expensive rooms are in the front, which is the older section; they are charmingly furnished with cherry armoires, white shutters in the windows overlooking the street, and white lace swags over the beds. Although rooms in the back section are comfortable and also redecorated, they don't have as good a view and are smaller. Request a room with a bay window (found in both sections) since they add a sense of spaciousness to the room.

Although you are unlikely to meet up with owners Pat and Alice Pulte (they also own the Murray Hotel), a complete staff is on hand to answer any questions about the island or the inn. Because of its size, the inn may lack some intimacy found at other B&Bs, but it makes up for that in style and convenience. Although not right in the center of town, it is certainly close.

A sense of camaraderie is evident as soon as you step onto the expansive, second-floor wraparound porch, where guests gather throughout the day. In fact, the outdoor areas at the inn are as enjoyable as the rooms. At street level, a lattice-covered arch leads to a charming brick patio surrounded by gardens. This level, which includes the lobby and dining room, was created during the remodeling by digging out the home's basement and adding French doors all the way around. You can eat breakfast inside or on the patio or sample some of the Pultes' homemade fudge, made fresh daily and sold in the lobby.

▥ *44 double rooms with baths. Air-conditioning, TVs; wheelchair accessible. $74–$175, Continental breakfast. MC, V. No pets. Closed Oct. 15–May 15.*

Other Choices

Bogan Lane Inn. Bogan La. (Box 482), Mackinac Island, MI 49757, tel. 906/ 847–3439. 4 double rooms share 2 baths. Ceiling fans. $55–$65, Continental breakfast. No credit cards. No smoking, no pets.

Cloghaun Bed & Breakfast. Summer: Market St. (Box 203), Mackinac Island, MI 49757, tel. 906/847–3885. Winter: tel. 810/778–9311. 8 double rooms with baths, 2 doubles share bath. $70–$110, Continental breakfast. No credit cards. No smoking, no pets. Closed Oct. 15– May 15.

Murray Hotel. Summer: Main St. (Box 476), Mackinac Island, MI 49757, tel. 906/847–3361 or 800/462–2546. Winter: Box 7706, Ann Arbor, MI 48107, tel. 313/665–5750. 69 double rooms with baths. Air-conditioning, TVs; whirlpool bath in 2 rooms. $74–$175, Continental breakfast. MC, V. No pets. Closed Oct. 15–Apr.

1900 Market Street Inn. Market St. (Box 315), Mackinac Island, MI 49757, tel. 906/847–3811. 7 double rooms with baths. Ceiling fans, cable TVs; wheelchair accessible. $85–$140, Continental breakfast. MC, V. No pets, 3-night minimum during boat races. Closed Nov.–Apr.

Grand Traverse Region, Including Traverse City

Aspen House

1353 N. Manitou Trail W (Box 722), Leland, MI 49654, tel. 616/256–9724 or 800/762–7736, fax 616/256–2777

Owning a B&B was always a "someday thing" for Paula and Philip Swink. Someday arrived unexpectedly during a trip to northern Michigan in May 1995. After living on the West Coast for over 30 years, the Swinks fell in love with the northwoods region and within three months left a fast-paced San Francisco lifestyle, scouted a variety of B&Bs, moved into their new home, and opened for business.

The Swinks have transformed their 4,000-square-foot 1885 farmhouse into a spacious and elegant B&B reminiscent of old-world European charm. The dining room's dark oak table is elegantly set with antique china and silver. The large living room provides numerous overstuffed sofas and leather chairs, floor-to-ceiling bookcases, and a fireplace; a second-floor common room gives extra room to roam.

While two of the guest rooms are both inviting and very spacious—and feature ample sitting areas—each also offers unique amenities; the Pine Room has a small outdoor deck and the Aspen Room boasts a two-person Jacuzzi. The smaller but popular Victorian Room is elegantly decorated with marble-topped, Belgium walnut furniture, and 1920s artist Harrison Fisher's popular depictions of the Gibson Girls adorn the walls.

Two outdoor garden areas are charmingly set with tables and hammocks. Paula has created a lavish herb garden, and she uses all of the fresh herbs and edible flowers in her gourmet breakfasts. Refreshments are served each afternoon. When dining at night, guests may prefer to wait for the final course; Paula enjoys serving one of her dessert specialties—fruit torte, cheesecake, and peach dumpling—in the evenings. With the Swinks' penchant for spoiling their guests, don't be surprised if you are greeted some cold evening with a steaming bowl of homemade soup and Paula's renowned molasses bread.

A short stroll around the Swinks' property reveals remnants of earlier farming days—an aging cherry orchard and a potato patch—as well as a panoramic view of Lake Michigan. Guests may explore nearby trails owned by a local land conservancy, and the accessible beach—an easy climb down from a nearby bluff—is the perfect place to experience a spectacular Michigan sunset.

🖼 *3 double rooms with bath. Terrycloth robes; TV/VCR in living room, computer in small office. $100–$125, full breakfast. MC. V. No smoking, no pets.*

Linden Lea

279 S. Long Lake Rd., Traverse City, MI 49684, tel. 616/943–9182

A small and enchanting spot on the shore of a crystal-clear inland lake, Linden Lea is, as one of its owners describes it, reminiscent of scenes in the movie *On Golden Pond.* Country roads wind their way to the bed-and-breakfast, and, once you've found it, you won't want to leave.

In 1979, Jim and Vicky McDonnell bought a small summer cottage built around the turn of the century by three Civil War veterans. Vicky remembers, "The original cottage was a mess—rotting floors and everything—but I just kept looking at the view and saying, 'This is it. This is the place.'" Since then, Jim, a former teacher, has skillfully renovated the building and tacked on an addition; nine years ago the couple opened their multilevel, contemporary home as a B&B.

The living room, complete with a marble and cherry-wood fireplace from the late 1800s, expansive picture windows, high ceilings, and a large, comfortable sectional sofa, is an inviting place to unwind and enjoy the view. With that in mind, the guest rooms have cushioned window seats that overlook the lake. The rooms, separate from the family quarters, also offer a measure of privacy.

The mix of antiques and treasures creates a warm, eclectic atmosphere. Jim began collecting unusual paperweights on a trip to Scotland, and now more than 30 of the colorful glass pieces

adorn a table near the stairway. The handmade dolls and the decorative plates scattered throughout the house are gifts Vicky's mother received while serving as an army nurse. A player piano dating from 1871 is a favorite of guests.

The McDonnells and their children, Audrey and Wyatt, are a congenial family. They've been known to offer baby-sitting services and to invite guests to join the family for dinner on cold winter nights when the prospect of curling up in front of the fireplace seems more appealing than braving the elements to find a restaurant.

The breakfast menu varies, and guests may be treated to such delights as quiches, freshly baked peach puffs, chocolate-chip banana muffins, and stuffed French toast. After breakfast, guests can take the rowboat to explore one of Long Lake's many islands.

🖼 *2 double rooms with baths. Air-conditioning, TV/VCR in living room, private sand beach, rowboat and paddleboat available. $80–$95, full breakfast. No credit cards. No smoking, no pets, 2-night minimum on weekends May–Oct.*

North Shore Inn

12271 N. Northport Point Rd., Northport, MI 49670, tel. 616/386–7111

Originally part of an estate, this rambling, colonial-style home was built in 1946. Sue Hammersley, who has lived in the area for 24 years, bought the house in 1983, remodeled it, and turned it into her family home. Sue was a preschool teacher at the time, but a few years later, with her family's support, she left her job to convert the home on the shores of picturesque West Bay into a luxurious retreat.

The sit-down gourmet breakfast (Continental buffet if you miss the 9 AM meal) is an experience. Sue varies the menu according to the season, and the portions are generous. There is always a selection of muffins, coffee cake or cobblers, fresh fruit and juice, and a main dish such as pancakes, eggs, or a sausage casserole. Many of the herbs she uses in cooking and the fresh flowers found throughout the house are grown in Sue's English garden, whose colorful accent can be seen from the Wedgwood Suite.

The common room is filled floor to ceiling with books, games, and a collection of old movies for the VCR. A bay window stretches the full height of the room and looks out over the lawn and the beach. The musically inclined can tinkle on a grand piano and a Hammond organ. At the south end of the house, a screened-in porch is a marvelous place to enjoy the outdoors, even on an overcast or rainy day.

All the guest rooms are large; the popular Heritage Room, on the main floor, has a private entrance and a kitchen. Another favorite is the Country Rose Room, which has a pink marble fireplace and a private balcony overlooking the beach. Sue made the Whig Rose quilt that adorns the brass bed. All the guest rooms except the Bayshore Room, which is the smallest, have separate sitting rooms with sofa beds, so two couples may comfortably share a suite. The fireplace in each room has wood laid, ready to light when you arrive.

There is much to enjoy on the premises, but a bonus is the inn's location: only a few minutes' drive from either the restaurants and shopping in the quaint town of Northport or the rugged beauty of Northport State Park.

▦ *1 double room with bath, 2 suites, 1 housekeeping suite. Morning coffee and tea baskets left outside guest rooms. $135–$145; full breakfast, afternoon refreshments. No credit cards. No smoking, no pets. Closed Nov.–Apr.*

Omena Shores Bed and Breakfast

13140 Isthmus Rd. (Box 154), Omena, MI 49674, tel. 616/386-7313

Omena is one of the many quaint, sleepy villages that dot Northern Michigan's picturesque Leelanau County, and it just seems to attract special people. Tim Allen, the star of television's popular comedy *Home Improvement* recently purchased a large parcel of land there, and over 100 years ago, the noted Reverend Peter Dougherty came to establish the area's first Presbyterian Church near the shores of Omena Bay. Now, Mary Helen and Charlie Phillips—who, fans state, are truly special when it comes to gracious hospitality—have moved back to Omena for a third time to the renovated barn that was once part of that church's parsonage.

A warm complement to the careful renovation (which has nicely kept the barn's batten siding and hand-hewn beams intact) are Mary Helen's colorful, handmade quilts; they are everywhere—on the walls, over tables, and covering guest beds. A large outdoor deck overlooks the garden, expansive lawn, and shimmering Omena Bay.

The living room is smartly furnished with wing-back chairs and an overstuffed couch and love seat. Hummel figurines, family photos, and a menagerie of reading material round out this downstairs common area. Upstairs, the large Gathering Room is filled with games, books, menus from area restaurants, and unique collections—including birdhouses and antique toys—which all mingle together in a classy blend of country folk art and antiques.

A pencil-post bed adorned in a blue-and-crimson quilt is the focal point of the Colonial Room, which is accented with country samplers, an antique cabinet and dresser, and kerosene lamps. The more whimsical Teddy Bear Room, although smaller, is great for families with children who are sure to be delighted by the dozens of bears of varying shapes, sizes, and personalities.

The Bridal Room on the main floor is uniquely sentimental with an array of wedding photos next to the large picture window, the wedding portrait of Charlie's mother and father hanging above the bed elegantly covered in white, and an early 1900s wedding dress hanging in the corner against cream-and-rose-color wallpaper. A private outdoor entrance to the deck is an added amenity.

Hearty breakfasts are served on the Phillips's colorful collection of Fiestaware and often include Mary Helen's signature dish—spinach pie—as well as cherry pecan sausage, a fresh fruit cup, and a selection of homemade muffins and breads. A silver tray of coffee and tea is left early each morning outside every guest room, and a winter evening is often warmed by hot cider and popcorn.

🏨 *3 double rooms with baths, 1 double shares bath. Ceiling fans in rooms, TV and VCR in living room, terrycloth robes, croquet set outdoors. $70–$95, full breakfast. No credit cards. No smoking indoors, no pets, 2-night minimum on weekends May–Oct.*

Open Windows Bed & Breakfast

613 St. Mary's Ave. (Box 698), Suttons Bay, MI 49682, tel. 616/271–4300 or 800/520–3722

When an antique sampler in one of the guest rooms reads, "Give to the world the best you have, and the best will come back to you," and antique wooden alphabet blocks strategically placed along a stairway ledge spell out, "Have a great day," pleasant hospitality is sure to follow. And here, at the Open Windows, it certainly does. Although there aren't any vast open windows to speak of, the ambience and quaint setting—apart from the other neighboring homes on a small hill, the B&B is surrounded by a white picket fence and overlooks the charming village of Suttons Bay and its harbor—gives this intown B&B a relaxed, country feel that is quite appealing.

That appeal caught the attention of owners Don and Norma Blumenschine when they visited the B&B as guests several years ago. Shortly after that, in 1994, they decided to buy it and relocate from Toledo, Ohio, their home of 35 years.

The Blumenschines are a talented pair; Norma's culinary skills are recognized in the area, and she has conducted B&B cooking classes at the local college as well as hosted gourmet weekends. After relaxing in the Adirondack chairs on the porch, it's nice to discover they are custom made by Don, and he is more than happy to take custom orders for his handcrafted deck furniture.

Breakfast includes coffee cakes, stuffed French toast, fresh fruits from nearby orchards, and homemade jams and jellies, which along with Norma's special vinegars are available for purchase under the Open Windows label.

The three guest rooms are all upstairs and share a second floor common area, although guests are also welcome to enjoy the downstairs living room and dining area. The Rose Garden Room has a brass bed, a rose-covered Oriental rug, and a small sitting area. The largest room is Helen's Room, which is charmingly decorated with white wicker furniture, rich blue carpet, and country-style tab curtains. The Sunshine Room lives up to its name with yellow and white gingham, an antique white brass bed, and a marble-topped dressing table.

Open Windows' downtown location also puts guests within easy walking distance of Suttons Bay's unique shops, galleries, and restaurants.

⊞ *3 double rooms with baths. Air-conditioning in Rose Garden Room, ceiling fans in the others, TV/VCR in common room, croquet set. $75–$105, full breakfast. No credit cards. Restricted smoking, no pets, 2-night minimum on holidays and weekends May–Oct.*

Snowbird Inn

473 N. Manitou Trail W (Box 1124), Leland, MI 49654, tel. 616/256–9773, fax 616/256–7068

Everything about the Snowbird Inn is eclectic and romantic—the history, the decor, even the setting. The inn is shaded by ancient black walnut trees and situated on 18 acres consisting of both woods and open meadows, a secluded pond, private access to Lake Michigan, a working cherry orchard, and colorful flower gardens.

The entire estate first operated as a dairy farm in 1885, and the original outbuildings and barn still surround the farmhouse, which was built in 1917. Guests can explore a colorful piece of history by walking to a neighboring cottage used as a hideaway in the late 1920s by infamous gangster Scarface Al Capone; the 30-foot gun tower manned by his sentries also still stands.

Over the last five years, it is innkeepers Martha Sintz and Joe Psenka's penchant for the eclectic that has helped created the charm inherent in this country retreat. Guests enjoy browsing the unique collections displayed in the living and dining room areas, ranging from hat boxes, dolls, and oil lamps to candles, dishes, and folk art. A grapevine tree bathed in white lights stands in an upper hallway window overlooking the front wraparound porch and operates year-round as a festive nightlight.

The library adjacent to the living room is a book lover's dream—floor-to-ceiling bookshelves are literally overflowing with everything from Joseph Wambaugh thrillers and historical biographies to popular paperbacks, physics textbooks, and coffee-table art books. A cabinet next to the overstuffed couch is filled with an array of jigsaw puzzles and games, including a cute wooden cow and milk-can tic-tac-toe board, reminiscent of the inn's earlier days. Guests are also welcome to enjoy music from the owners' collection of over 300 compact discs.

Touted as Leelanau's "Grand Lady," it's not surprising that the Inn's four guest rooms are named after different women in the family and comfortably decorated in an array of flowered wallpaper, pinstriped curtains, and checkered comforters. In Thelma's Room—named after Joe's mother—the bird's-eye maple headboard and dresser are accented by a delightful custom-painted mirror and table, courtesy of Joe's daughter.

Martha's desire to "feed people well and make them feel comfortable" is augmented by her hearty breakfasts, which may include corn beef hash, egg casseroles, homemade bread, and fresh fruit.

⊞ *2 doubles with bath, 2 doubles share 1½ baths. Ceiling fans; fireplace in dining room. $85–$125, full breakfast. No credit cards. Restricted smoking, no pets, 2-night minimum on weekends Memorial Day–Oct.*

Other Choices

Brookside Inn. 115 N. Michigan Ave., Beulah, MI 49617, tel. 616/882–7271. 20 double rooms with baths. Saunas, steam baths, and tanning solariums in some rooms. $195–$250, full breakfast and dinner for two. AE, MC, V. No pets.

Chateau Chantal. 15900 Rue de Vin, Traverse City, MI 49684, tel. and fax 616/223–4110. 1 double room with bath, 2 suites. TVs, phones, individual heat and air controls; winery tours and wine tastings. $95–$125, full breakfast. MC,

V. Restricted smoking, no pets, 2-night minimum June 15–Oct.

Lee Point Inn. 2885 S. Lee Point La. (Rte. 2, Box 374B), Suttons Bay, MI 49682, tel. 616/271–6770. 1 double room with bath, 2 doubles share bath. Ceiling fans; picnic table, canoe. $85–$115, full breakfast. MC, V. No smoking, no pets.

Leelanau Country Inn. 149 E. Harbor Hwy., Maple City, MI 49664, tel. 616/228–5060. 4 single and 2 double rooms share 2 baths. Restaurant. $35–$55, Continental breakfast. AE, MC, V. Smoking in restaurant only, no pets. Open weekends only Nov.–Apr., closed Mar.

Neahtawanta Inn. 1308 Neahtawanta Rd., Traverse City, MI 49684, tel. 616/223–7315. 4 double rooms share bath, 1 double room with bath. Sauna, private beach. $70–$120, Continental breakfast. MC, V. No smoking.

Old Mill Pond Inn. 202 W. 3rd St., Northport, MI 49670, tel. 616/386–7341. 5 double rooms share 2½ baths. Bicycles. $70–$90, full breakfast. MC, V. No pets. Closed Nov.–May.

Victoriana 1898. 622 Washington St., Traverse City, MI 49684, tel. 616/929–1009. 2 double rooms with baths, 1 suite. Air-conditioning; fireplace in parlor. $60–$80, full breakfast, evening refreshments. MC, V. Restricted smoking, no pets.

Little Traverse Bay Region

Belvedere Inn

306 Belvedere Ave., Charlevoix, MI 49720, tel. 616/547–2251 or 800/280–4667

After 22 years of marriage, Tim and Karen Watters felt the time was right to act on what began as Karen's dream—to own an inn on the west shore of Michigan. Following a two-year search, they discovered this stately Victorian home, built in 1887 as a "cottage" in Charlevoix's elite summer colony; later it was operated as a hotel and then a boardinghouse. In three months the couple completely restored the house—adding everything from porcelain faucets and dual showerheads to new tile, carpet, and Victorian furniture—before opening in March 1994. They have more plans for the interior as well as outside, where they have started a multitiered flower garden and added a picnic area.

Their love of antiques is evident throughout the house. The upright grand piano in the parlor belonged to Tim's great-grandmother, and Karen's grandmother received the curved mahogany shelf, now holding brochures of area attractions and restaurant menus, as payment for cleaning rooms when she was 16 years old. A dining-room shelf sparkles with an eclectic collection of crystal and glassware that Karen purchased at auctions over the years. Tim laughingly explains, "I kept asking Karen why she was always buying this stuff, but now I realize that she had a plan."

Romantics will enjoy the king-size canopy bed in the Spring Room; it is completely surrounded by a floor-to-ceiling white lace curtain. One guest delightedly recalled, "It was like waking up in a cloud." Bathrooms for guests in the Spring and Autumn rooms are off the hallway, but bathrobes have been thoughtfully provided. The Rose Room has twin beds and is on the main floor. The noisiest room is probably the Winter Room; it faces the street and the Grey Gables Inn, a restaurant next door (where Belvedere Inn guests receive a special discount). The efficiency apartment boasts a private entrance and full kitchen, but it is the only area not decorated in the crisp, fresh style of the rest of the house.

Guests are served a complete breakfast that includes such specialties of Karen's as praline- or blueberry-stuffed French toast and sausage, or a strata of baked egg, ham, and cheese. An extra treat is the homemade dessert—which could be anything from cherry pie to strawberry shortcake to warm peanut butter cookies—served each evening in the parlor or living room, or on warm nights, on the spacious front porch.

🏠 *5 double rooms with baths, 1 suite, 1 efficiency. Ceiling fans; cable TV and fireplace in parlor. $60–$115, full breakfast. MC, V. Restricted smoking, no pets.*

Benson House

618 E. Lake St., Petoskey, MI 49770, tel. 616/347–1338

As a former Chamber of Commerce executive transplanted from downstate, Rod Benson knows how to make people comfortable; he and his charming wife, Carol, make an unbeatable team when it comes to hosting a bed-and-breakfast. The Bensons go out of their way to help you enjoy your stay by providing area restaurant menus, a travel planner, and chocolates in each guest room.

Set in a quiet, tree-filled neighborhood in Petoskey, the Benson House has an enviable location. As the locals tell it, when it opened in 1879 as the Ozark Hotel, people were aghast that anyone would put such an establishment so far from downtown. Nowadays, however, guests are only a few blocks' walk from the shopping and entertainment of the Gaslight District and minutes by car from first-class golf and skiing, but they still feel—what bliss!—miles away.

The two-story wood-frame house has been thoroughly renovated to provide modern amenities while still retaining elements of its Victorian history: high ceilings, wood moldings, pocket doors, old gas fixtures, floral prints, hardwood floors, and area rugs. The spacious guest rooms have individual themes, from the cathedral ceiling, dark wood,

and fruitwood four-poster bed of the Grand Master Suite to the white wicker and original wooden water closet in the bathroom of the Wicker Room.

Adjacent to the large living room is a game room, complete with an elegant parquet floor, entertainment center, backgammon and cribbage boards, puzzles, books, and a cozy couch, where the Bensons say they often discover guests relaxing and taking a short nap.

The most popular gathering spot is the 80-foot veranda, which wraps around two sides of the house and overlooks Little Traverse Bay. Furnished with white wicker and ablaze with colorful hanging plants, it is the perfect place to enjoy Carol's hearty breakfasts during the warmer months. Her menu varies and includes a shrimp quiche she calls Neptune's Delight, Irish Cream bread, and sticky-bun French toast. And, after a long day of shopping or recreation, you can return to the veranda, where the Bensons' afternoon hors d'oeuvres quell those hunger pangs and make you feel at home once again.

🏠 *4 double rooms with baths. Fireplace in living room, turndown service with chocolates. $89–$125, full breakfast. MC, V. No smoking, no pets, 2-night minimum on weekends, 3-night minimum on holidays.*

House on the Hill

9661 Lake St. (Box 206), Ellsworth, MI 49729, tel. 616/588–6304

As part of their early retirement plan, lifelong Texans Buster and Julie Arnim considered opening an art gallery in the Southwest, but after a tour of New England bed-and-breakfasts, they decided to open their own. Selling their Houston suitcase business in 1984, the Arnims moved north to see the turn-of-the-century farmhouse they had purchased, sight unseen, after an eight-state hunt for the perfect rural setting. A real-estate ad stated it was "near a gourmet restaurant"; Julie was convinced their B&B would be a success if good food was at hand. Indeed, two of northern Michigan's finest restaurants, Tapawingo and the Rowe Inn, are within two blocks.

After some hard work during the renovation process, the Arnims have made their House on the Hill a successful and elegant B&B. The carefully restored gray-and-white Victorian (including an addition used as their private quarters) sits on a hill near the little village of Ellsworth, overlooking 53 acres of countryside and the St. Clair Lake. Guests are free to hike or ski cross-country around the property and even borrow the boat docked at the lake. A spacious veranda wraps around the house and is filled with white wicker furniture and rocking chairs.

Inside, a curved staircase leads to the guest rooms upstairs. They are all spacious, immaculate, and pleasantly decorated. Each has its own thermostat, fresh flowers, candy, ice water, and bedside lights. A favorite is the Pine Room, with its cathedral ceiling, custom-built four-poster bed draped in white lace, and peaceful view of the woods behind the house. Antiques and such touches as a 200-year-old hand-carved ebony Oriental desk, Julie's rose-colored glass collection, and Japanese-style porcelain could make you nervous about kicking back and really relaxing, but the Arnims make you feel at home with a perfect blend of friendliness and reserve.

Julie and Buster serve a marvelous hearty breakfast on their large oak table, complete with fine china and silver. A culinary whiz, Julie rotates 65 different breakfast menus; for early risers, she puts out a basket filled with home-baked muffins, juice, and coffee, which goes beyond yum to yum-yum.

🏠 *7 double rooms with baths. Ceiling fans; cable TV in parlor. $115–$125, full breakfast. MC, V. Restricted smoking, no pets.*

Kimberly Country Estate

2287 Bester Rd., Harbor Springs, MI 49740, tel. 616/526–7646

The Greek Revival architecture and the gracious hospitality of the Kimberly Country Estate recall the genteel era of the Old South, but the interior is an elegant, gracious re-creation of an English country estate. Regardless of either impression, it's a treat to discover this 8,000-square-foot house in the heart of northern Michigan.

Owners Billie and Ronn Serba spent more than a year carefully remodeling this 30-year-old home in an effort to enhance its architecture while adding some modern conveniences. They put in new fireplaces, an updated kitchen, recessed lighting, and traditional mullion-style windows to take the place of the modern casements. In the living room, they replaced the sliding glass doors leading to the terrace with more graceful French doors. This attention to detail is evident throughout the house.

The Serbas moved from the Detroit area to Harbor Springs in the early 1980s, after owning a flower shop as well as restoring and decorating three homes together. Once in Harbor Springs, they first opened the shop Kimberly's Nest; the bed-and-breakfast followed in 1989. Throughout their 40-year marriage, they have been avid antiques collectors, acquiring such treasures as a Dutch pin armoire, a cast-iron chandelier, four-poster beds, and numerous chairs and accessories.

Floral chintz mixed with stripes and plaids creates a warm, romantic look, as do the fresh flowers, overstuffed sofas and chairs, Oriental rugs, and Battenburg lace bedspreads in the guest rooms. The B&B has become a very popular place for weddings; the entire house is often rented out on these occasions (or for the occasional executive retreat).

All the guest rooms are very spacious. The two largest rooms are the Lexington, with a fireplace, sitting area, and separate study, and the Verandah, which opens to a private terrace and has a fireplace and whirlpool bath. Guests are free to use the main-floor library; with its North Carolina black walnut paneling, fireplace, English-style armchairs, and paisley fabric–covered ceiling, it has the feeling of an old club—an old club founded on the grounds of a stately southern plantation.

⊞ *5 double rooms with baths, 1 suite. Baby grand piano in living room, swimming pool. $135–$250; Continental breakfast, afternoon tea. MC, V. No smoking, no pets, 2-night minimum on weekends, 3-night minimum on holidays. Closed Apr.*

Stafford's Bay View Inn

613 Woodland Ave., U.S. 31, Petoskey, MI 49770, tel. 616/347–2771 or 800/456–1917

It's hard to miss Stafford's Bay View Inn, set just off the main road running through Petoskey's historic Bay View District. A popular dining spot for both tourists and residents as well as a bustling inn, the imposing three-story Victorian was built in 1886; it served as lodging for summer visitors coming north via the now-defunct railroad to enjoy Bay View's cultural programs.

Owners Stafford and Janice Smith met and fell in love while working at the inn for the previous owner. They purchased it during the early 1960s and have now been joined in running the inn by their son and daughter-in-law, Reg and Lori, who are the day-to-day innkeepers. Over time, they have redecorated and added onto the inn—including five new suites—while retaining its comfortable charm. Furnishings in the second- and third-floor guest rooms include canopy and four-poster beds, richly colored wallpapers, antique dressers, wicker furniture, and such details as handmade eyelet and ribbon pillows.

The Smiths renovated the third floor in 1987, including adding a sitting room. Ever mindful of maintaining the house as a haven for young families, they provided this room so parents could enjoy stepping out without venturing too far from sleeping young ones. Children can often be seen happily romping in the first-floor common areas while parents finish their meal at a leisurely pace.

What the Bay View Inn may sometimes lack in quiet, it makes up for in its delicious food and the unending hospitality of its hosts. Open and airy, the main dining room is decorated with chandeliers, draped tables with fan-back chairs, fresh flowers and plants, and white lattice dividers between booths. Sometimes it may feel as though the restaurant crowd has taken over the inn, but a trip to the third floor or a stroll down to the water offers a good escape for overnight guests. The menus include such specialties as steaming bread pudding with raisins and cream. A splendid buffet awaits guests for Sunday brunch; selections may include ham, turkey, whitefish, chicken, biscuits, and scrumptious desserts. Although the inn does not serve alcoholic beverages, guests are invited to bring their own wine to dinner.

⊞ *17 double rooms with baths, 14 suites. Air-conditioning, cable TV in sun room and library, gas fireplace and whirlpool bath in 5 suites. $79–$195, full breakfast. AE, MC, V. Restricted smoking, no pets.*

Veranda at Harbor Springs

403 E. Main St., Harbor Springs, MI 48740, tel. 616/526–7782

Owners Doug and Lydia Yoder, from Georgia, brought a bit of their Southern hospitality north when they opened the Veranda in 1995. Window boxes overflowing with colorful blooms and the crisp yellow-and-white exterior first catch your eye, but it is the glass-enclosed veranda—for which this elegant B&B is named—that is truly the focal point. Here guests enjoy a glimpse of Little Traverse Bay while eating breakfast or an afternoon treat of pink lemonade and homemade cookies. Glass-top tables and armchairs upholstered in an array of peach and green florals mingle nicely with white wicker atop the ceramic-tile patio.

Decorated by Lydia in a distinct mix of garden-style fabrics and antique mahogany and oak furniture, each guest room boasts a private balcony and exudes a quiet, refreshing air. A true delight is the front suite, where a Jacuzzi is tucked into the Tudor-style window overlooking the water.

The Veranda's downtown location also puts guests within easy walking distance of Harbor Spring's upscale shops, galleries, and restaurants.

🏠 *4 double rooms with baths, 1 suite. TVs, phones; fireplace in sitting room, refrigerator and ice machine for guests. $95–$175, full breakfast. MC, V. Restricted smoking, no pets.*

Other Choices

Bear River Valley. 03636 Bear River Rd., Petoskey, MI 49770, tel. 616/348–2046. 3 double rooms share 2 baths. TV/VCR in common room, terry-cloth robes. $60–$75, Continental breakfast. No credit cards. No smoking, no pets, 2-night minimum on weekends.

Bridge Street Inn. 113 Michigan Ave., Charlevoix, MI 49720, tel. 616/547–6606, fax 616/547–1812. 3 double rooms with baths, 6 doubles share 3 baths. Ceiling fans in some rooms, baby grand piano in common area. $65–$115; full breakfast, afternoon and evening refreshments. MC, V. No smoking, no pets, 2-night minimum on weekends July–mid-Oct.

Gingerbread House. 205 Bluff St. (Box 1273), Bay View, MI 49770, tel. 616/347–3538. 3 double rooms with baths, 1 housekeeping double with bath, 1 housekeeping suite. Private outside entrances to guest rooms. $55–$100, Continental breakfast. MC, V. No smoking, no pets. Closed Nov.–Apr.

Torch Lake Bed & Breakfast. 10601 Coy St., Alden, MI 49612, tel. 616/331–6424. 1 double room with bath, 2 doubles share bath. ceiling fan in rooms. $65–$85, full breakfast. No credit cards. No smoking, no pets. Closed mid-Sept.–Memorial Day weekend.

Walloon Lake Inn. 4178 West Rd. (Box 85), Walloon Lake Village, MI 49796, tel. 616/535–2999. 5 double rooms with baths. Restaurant, beach and dock access on lake. $50–$70, Continental breakfast. MC, V. No pets.

Minnesota

The Mansion Bed & Breakfast Inn

Twin Cities Area

Ann Bean House

319 W. Pine St., Stillwater, MN 55082, tel. 612/430-0355 or 800/933-0355

The Ann Bean House was an eight-unit apartment building when proprietors Victoria and Bruce Brillhart bought it. Converting it to a country inn was a challenge, but they had a lot to work with. Their 1880 Victorian Stick–style house is a graceful one, with many bay windows and towers and turrets of varying heights. The interior is filled with woodwork that reflects Minnesota's lumbering past, including a beautiful carved oak banister and cherry, oak, and walnut parquet flooring in the vestibule. The abundance of large windows makes the house light and airy.

Two of the five bedrooms, the Guest Room and Ann and Albert's Room, measure a luxurious 400 square feet. The Guest Room has a brass sleigh bed, an enormous bay window, and a working fireplace with a carved oak mantel. Ann and Albert's Room has a north-facing bay window, as well as a new bath with a tempting whirlpool that fits into the shorter of the building's towers. Cynthia's Room has a whirlpool 6 feet in diameter and a fireplace embedded with teal-colored marble tiles.

Even more impressive, perhaps, is the whimsical pink Tower Room, with a slanted ceiling and a white cast-iron bed. A few stairs up, you'll find a delightful white wicker table for two, perfect for morning coffee or wine in the evening. Up another flight of stairs at the top of the tower is the star attraction—a spacious aerie with windows on four sides offering spectacular views of hilly Stillwater and the St. Croix River. On its way to becoming the most popular room, however, is the newest addition, Jacob's Room, with its carved-mahogany furniture and sunny window seat.

The house's charm is accentuated by the Brillharts' hospitality, especially Victoria's cooking. When you check in, you're offered homemade herb bread, cheeses, and hot artichoke dip, along with a glass of wine. Breakfast is a mélange of four or five of Victoria's fruit-and-yeast breads, fresh fruit, sausage rolls, hot dishes such as eggs Florentine—and some guests just can't wait for a helping of Victoria's homemade ice cream. After breakfast, your hosts can tell you about paddleboat trips, hot-air ballooning, and antiques hunting in the area.

⊞ *5 double rooms with baths. Air-conditioning, fireplace in 3 rooms, whirlpool tubs in 4 rooms. $79–$129 weekdays, $99–$159 weekends; full breakfast, afternoon refreshments. AE, D, MC, V. Restricted smoking, no pets.*

Asa Parker House

17500 St. Croix Trail N, Marine on St. Croix, MN 55047, tel. 612/433–5248 or 888/857–9969

On a rainy day, the Asa Parker House, in the tiny historic village of Marine on St. Croix, looks like something out of a British TV miniseries. Extensive grounds, elaborate flower gardens, a tennis court, and a gazebo make the setting of this Greek Revival B&B one of the finest in Minnesota. The house, built in 1856 by lumber-industry pioneer Asa Parker, was distinctive enough to tempt owners Connie and Chuck Weiss to venture into the B&B business, with the hope of providing a "romantic respite for people in love."

The public and guest rooms are all airy, bright, and predominately floral. The two downstairs parlors are done in a most attractive pink, with stylish accents of white wicker and chintz. The "receiving" music room has dried-flower wreaths, delicate furniture, and an organ, while the adjacent Gentlemen's Parlor offers plush leather reading chairs and a wooden chessboard.

If you can get past the frills, the guest rooms can be quite lovely—especially those bouquets of fragrant flowers. Truly luxurious is the rose-and-dusty-green Isabella Parker Room, with white wicker furniture, a claw-foot tub, and spectacular river valley views from its corner spot. The Alice O'Brien Suite, tucked under the eaves, has gabled windows, a large bath with a whirlpool tub, and a private deck with white Adirondack chairs and views of the flowering lawns—perfect for a reclusive weekend of romance or solitude. A screened porch downstairs overlooks a rock garden and fountain.

Connie uses the freshest fruits (her husband is in the produce business) to top off her hearty breakfasts, which include such favorites as baked peach pancakes and Grand Marnier French toast. She'll also encourage guests to reserve the screened gazebo for a private afternoon barbecue, or to enjoy a hike in William O'Brien State Park, just down the road. The park has miles of hiking, biking, and cross-country ski paths. There's also a marina a couple of blocks away, where you can rent canoes. But the sweeping views of the St. Croix River are so beautiful—particularly once the leaves begin to fall—that guests may just want to relax on the lawn.

⊞ *3 double rooms with baths, 1 suite. Air-conditioning, whirlpool bath in suite, stove in 1 bedroom, tennis court, screened gazebo. $99–$159, full breakfast, afternoon refreshments. D, MC, V. No smoking, no pets.*

Bluff Creek Inn

1161 Bluff Creek Dr., Chaska, MN 55318, tel. 612/445–2735 or 800/307–0019

Just 30 minutes south of the Twin Cities, this impeccable B&B serves as the perfect romantic getaway. While near most of the Twin Cities' major attractions—Mall of America, the Minnesota Renaissance Festival, and the Chanhassen Dinner Theater, to name a few—the Bluff Creek Inn stands amid a nature oasis of pastures, wildlife, and bounteous English gardens. Anne and Gary Delaney bought the quaint inn from a good friend in 1987 and have tended it as if it were a work of art: with great care and dedication.

The property was originally granted to a veteran of the War of 1812, but it wasn't developed until 1854, when Josef and Veronica Vogel emigrated from Germany and built their Prairie-style house using hand-kilned bricks made out of Mississippi River Valley clay and trees milled on the property. In the oldest building in Minnesota still in daily operation, guests will find several fascinating historical artifacts in the dining room, including the original property deed—signed by Abe Lincoln himself.

The downstairs parlor maintains a country-Victorian feel, with cornflower blue sofas, antiques, and dried-flower arrangements. There are also two appealing porches. The white one has plenty of rocking chairs; the screened-in side porch—originally an old-time summer kitchen—is where, in the summertime, of course, Anne and Gary serve their gourmet four-course breakfast on pleasantly decorated tables for two. They're particularly proud of their java, which they call "the best B&B coffee in the world."

It is difficult to describe the rooms in detail, for they alternate between no fewer than six different seasonal decorating themes. Anne has limited Gary to six, although he would prefer more. In the spring, guests may see a plenitude of stuffed or porcelain bunny rabbits in evidence, while in the wintertime, 134 Christmas trees of varying sizes decorate the house with holiday cheer.

Upstairs, Emma's Room, with hunter-green-and-red accents, has a hand-carved Norwegian pine bed. The Victorian Elizabeth's Room has an exposed-brick wall and richly hued green accents. Guests can soak in the antique claw-foot tub or gaze at the pasture from an adjoining deck. Perhaps the best room is Hollyhock Cottage, housed in the upper portion of an adjacent barn replica. The floors, walls, and ceiling of this bright L-shaped suite are knotty pine, and dormer eaves enclose a king-size bed. A two-side Italian marble fireplace looks onto the bed as well as onto the gigantic whirlpool tub—with terry-cloth robes provided as a gracious touch.

🏠 *5 double rooms with baths. Air-conditioning, whirlpool bath in 3 rooms, fireplace in 1 room. $75–$130 weekdays, $85–$150 weekends; full breakfast, afternoon wine and hors d'oeuvres. AE, D, MC, V. No smoking, no pets.*

Covington Inn

Pier One, Harriet Island, St. Paul, MN 55107, tel. 612/292–1411

On Harriet Island across from downtown St. Paul, this may be the only B&B with a true view of the Mississippi River. In fact, the inn is a towboat on the river itself. Wanting to provide people with an opportunity to experience life on the Mississippi, owners Tom Welna and Ann Reeves opened the No Wake Cafe on the boat in 1987. The success of the restaurant led to renovating the remaining portions of the towboat into an elegant B&B. The result might please even Mark Twain.

Originally from New Orleans, the 1946 towboat was built by the Nashville Bridge Company; it was their first commercial-use vessel built post–World War II. Originally named the *Codrington*, the boat's unique engine set the standard for the transport of liquid cargo, still in effect today. In 1997, however, little remains of its industrial past. Anne and Tom dry-docked the boat to restore the hull and gutted the interior before artfully rebuilding it using mostly recycled materials. The result is an elegant yet nautical B&B with pine wainscoting and unusual portholelike wall lamps.

The one common space is a bright salon on the main level of the boat; the salon is also a wine bar open to the public on weekend nights from 4 to 9. The salon's furniture is a mixture of antiques and clever touches, such as paddle-wheel ashtrays and boat-shaped cribbage boards. Plush couches and chairs surround a fireplace below a huge clearstory skylight. Guests can also stroll along the many outer decks, weather permitting.

The guest rooms are all creatively designed, with TV/VCRs hidden away in decorative wall cabinets and small—remember, this *is* a boat—but efficient, bathrooms. The two-level Pilot House Suite is the most spectacular. It has a bedroom with a corner fireplace made from hand-painted Portuguese tiles. A short climb up a private narrow staircase leads you to the original pilothouse, now the suite's comfortable sitting room. Completely encircled with windows, it has soft futon sofas and a large brass helm, which once controlled the rudders and engines. From here, or out on a private fir-wood deck, the entire St. Paul skyline can be seen aglow on a starry night. The bright and airy Master's Quarters also has a private deck, a fireplace, and pine and cedar woodwork.

A warm breakfast of fruit, coffee cake, an egg dish, and coffee is served in the salon, or you can have it brought to your room. Ann and Tom want their guests to feel like part of the crew—a boating etiquette manual can be found in each room—but there is no swabbing of the deck to be done here. Guests can just relax and enjoy the views and the gentle swaying of the mighty Mississippi.

🖽 *3 double rooms with baths, 1 suite. Air-conditioning, TV/VCR, phones; fireplace in 2 rooms. $95–$155 Oct.– Apr., $120–$180 May–Sept.; full breakfast. MC, V. Restricted smoking, no pets.*

Elephant Walk

801 W. Pine St., Stillwater, MN 55082, tel. 612/430-0359, fax 612/351-9080

Don't be surprised if you are summoned for breakfast at this delightful B&B by a gong—one that is attached no less to a beautiful and elaborately carved teakwood dragon embedded with glass and mica. From that first morning call, you'll know that Rita Graybill's Elephant Walk provides a refreshing alternative to the standard Victorian B&B. On the outside, one sees a stick-style pale-yellow-and-salmon Victorian home, complete with a cozy porch swing on a wraparound porch. One step inside, however, and you could almost believe you've made a magical detour to the Raffles Hotel in Singapore.

Rita spent 20 years traveling with her husband—he worked for the navy—mostly in Asian countries, and collected hundreds of spectacular and exotic items that now decorate the downstairs and guest rooms. In fact, the B&B's name comes from Rita's realization while unpacking boxes that the majority of her treasures were elephant keepsakes of various sizes and materials. She arranged them tastefully throughout the house, proceeded to add three bathrooms, three fireplaces, and four whirlpool baths, and opened for business in 1993.

Elephants are not the sole decor emphasis. There are other intriguing artifacts to discover, and better yet, there is an interesting story behind each and every one. The bright and soothing parlor houses a coffee table made from red and gold–leafed teakwood musical drums from Burma. Another table was constructed from a *hoc*, a device placed on elephant's backs to carry the rider's possessions.

Each of the bedrooms highlights a different country or region, and all are luxuriously fitted with whirlpool tubs and fireplaces. The Rangoon Room, done in cinnamon-and-gold tones, has mosquito netting over the four-poster teakwood bed, a hand-forged copper sink—formerly a candy kettle from Spain—and ornate Balinese masks. The Raffles Room has a unique whirlpool tub with an ivy trellis; the water trickles into the tub from the surrounding stone wall—reminiscent of a natural hot spring.

Most spectacular is the two-room Cadiz Suite, named for the city in Spain where Columbus set off to discover the new world. The spacious and bright window-lined suite is decorated with centuries-old hand-carved cathedral doors from Cadiz, a double-sided gas fireplace, a whirlpool surrounded by lush plants and hanging orchids, and an Indian rosewood sitting bench, which has hand-carved elephant armrests—of course. The suite leads to a private sundeck overlooking Rita's fish- and lily-filled water gardens.

Topping off this memorable experience are Rita's ample breakfasts and consistent hospitality. This B&B is as elegant as the more traditional Victorian fare but will fill you with dreams of travels to come.

▦ *3 double rooms with baths, 1 suite. Air-conditioning, gas fireplaces, whirlpool baths, ceiling fans, radios. $129– $189, full breakfast. MC, V. Restricted smoking, no pets.*

Le Blanc House

302 University Ave. NE, Minneapolis, MN 55413, tel. 612/379–2570

Le Blanc House is an elegant piece of the 19th century tucked into a modest and modern Minneapolis neighborhood. The 1896 Queen Anne is a striking structure with a delicate lavender exterior. In summer, its banks of petunias and walls of morning glories and nasturtiums are famous in the neighborhood. Add sparkling stained-glass windows and inviting front and back porches—the latter with the traditional swing—and you could be back in the days when the original owner, William Le Blanc, returned home each evening from the grain mills along the Mississippi.

Current owners Barb Zahasky and Bob Shulstad now run the inn full time, and have kept the decor faithful to the inn's period and named the three guest rooms after the daughters of its former

owners. Both Zofi's and Amelia's rooms have great views of the city skyline. Zofi's Room, a corner room with a bay window and a private bath—perfect for weekday business travelers—is furnished with a 19th-century high-topped walnut bed and matching marble-top dresser. Marissa's Room, the smallest of the three, is invitingly cozy. It has an antique brass bed, oak furnishings, handmade quilts and linens, and an unusual porthole window. All rooms have colorfully patterned Victorian reproduction wallpaper.

You'll awaken to the aroma of Bob's homemade breakfasts wafting from the dining room. Dishes include "heavenly" Belgian waffles, spinach-pistachio quiche, French toast stuffed with jelly and cream cheese, and filled crepes. Barb's sister owns a St. Paul bakery, and many mornings she brings over fresh muffins and pastries.

Le Blanc House is just blocks from the many attractions of the Minneapolis riverfront, where you'll find the restaurants of St. Anthony Main and Riverplace, as well as Boom Island Park, which offers paddleboat cruises, the River City Trolley, and an extensive riverfront walk. The area is quite culturally diverse, so you'll also find a wide variety of restaurants—Japanese, Italian, Lebanese, and Polish—within walking distance.

▦ *1 double room with bath, 2 doubles share bath. Air-conditioning, TV available. $85–$105, full breakfast. AE, MC, V. Restricted smoking, no pets.*

William Sauntry Mansion

626 N. 4th St., Stillwater, MN 55082, tel. 612/430–2653 or 800/828–2653

The William Sauntry Mansion is a meticulous restoration of an enormous 1890 Queen Anne home. The work done in the parlor—which was re-created down to the wall beading and corner ornaments—was so accurate that a visiting former resident remarked to owners Duane and Martha Hubbs on how well the wallpaper had held up. Some things *are* original: the parquet flooring laid in four woods and the parlor's oil-on-canvas ceiling, as well as light fixtures, fireplaces, and special stained-glass windows.

The Hubbses have restored houses in both Chicago and St. Louis. When they moved to Stillwater in 1988, they found the 25-room mansion converted to apartments and deteriorating. In 1991, after a two-year restoration in which the second floor was stripped down to the studs, they opened it as a bed-and-breakfast.

Aiming to remain true to the period not only in architecture and design, but in mood as well, the Hubbses provide such authentic touches as piano playing in the parlor during the afternoon social hour. The bedrooms, which have large windows and fireplaces, are also done in a Victorian style, with Asian and floral motifs and the richly hued paints favored by 19th-century builders.

Beltram's Room, with its south-facing tower bay window overlooking the gardens, green-tiled fireplace, spoon-carved cherry bedroom set, and private bath, is especially pleasant. For a Japanese ambience, try William's Room, which has crown dentil molding and is papered in an exotic pattern of gold, blue, and rust. Eunice's Room, in rose and blue, has an antique headboard, parquet floor, and a delicate oak fireplace ringed by the original rose-and-cream ceramic tiles. Its private bath, down the hall, has a galvanized-tin tub dating from the 1860s.

Sauntry, an Irish immigrant turned lumber baron, had maverick ideas about home construction: He sent his architects as far as the Alhambra Palace in Spain to gather details. Behind his home he built a recreation facility complete with ballroom, bowling alley, and swimming pool, and connected it to the house with Minnesota's

first skywalk. The skywalk is gone, and the building is owned by another family, but Sauntry's spirit lives on in his enormous house.

▦ *7 double rooms with baths (2 nonadjoining). Fireplace, double whirlpool in 4 rooms, bathrobes. $89–$149; full breakfast, early morning coffee, afternoon refreshments. AE, D, DC, MC, V. No smoking, no pets.*

Other Choices

Afton House Inn. 3291 St. Croix Trail S (Box 326), Afton, MN 55001, tel. 612/436–8883, fax 612/436–6859. 15 double rooms with baths, 1 guest cottage with 2 bedrooms. Air-conditioning, TVs, phones; restaurant, bar, gas fireplace in 8 rooms, double whirlpool bath in 10 rooms, private balcony in 4 rooms. $60–$140, Continental breakfast. AE, D, MC, V. Restricted smoking, no pets.

Chatsworth B&B. 984 Ashland Ave., St. Paul, MN 55104, tel. 612/227–4288, fax 612/225–8217. 3 double rooms with baths, 2 doubles share bath. Air-conditioning, whirlpool tub in 2 rooms, private deck in 1 room, Nordic Track, exercise bike. $65–$125; Continental breakfast on weekdays, full breakfast on weekends. D, MC, V. No smoking, no pets.

Elmwood House. 1 E. Elmwood Pl., Minneapolis, MN 55419, tel. 612/822–4558. 2 doubles share 1 bath, 1 suite. Air-conditioning, TV/VCRs; refrigerator, laundry facilities. $55–$85, Continental breakfast. AE, MC, V. Restricted smoking, no pets, 2-night minimum on weekends June–Aug.

Evelo's Bed & Breakfast. 2301 Bryant Ave. S, Minneapolis, MN 55405, tel. 612/374–9656. 3 double rooms share bath. Clock radios; refrigerator, coffeemaker, and phone on 3rd-floor landing, additional single bed in 2 rooms. $50, full breakfast. AE, D, DC, MC, V. Restricted smoking, no pets.

Garden Gate Bed and Breakfast. 925 Goodrich Ave., St. Paul, MN 55105, tel. 612/227–8430 or 800/967–2703. 3 double rooms and 1 suite share bath. $55–$75, Continental breakfast. No credit cards. Restricted smoking.

Harvest Restaurant and Inn. 114 E. Chestnut St., Stillwater, MN 55082, tel. 612/430–8111. 3 double rooms with baths. Double whirlpools and fireplaces. $129–$139, full breakfast. AE, D, MC, V. No smoking, no pets.

James A. Mulvey Residence Inn. 622 W. Churchill St., Stillwater, MN 55082, tel. 612/430–8008 or 800/820–8008. 5 double rooms with baths. Air-conditioning, fireplace in 3 rooms, whirlpool baths in selected rooms. $99–$159, full breakfast, afternoon refreshments, picnic lunches available. AE, D, MC, V. Restricted smoking, no pets.

Laurel Street Inn. 210 E. Laurel St., Stillwater, MN 55082, tel. 612/351–0031 or 888/351–0031, fax 612/439–0903. 3 double rooms with baths. Air-conditioning, whirlpool baths and gas fireplaces in two rooms. $105–$125 Nov.–Apr., $155–$175 May–Oct.; full breakfast. AE, D, MC, V. Restricted smoking, no pets.

Lumber Baron's Hotel. 101 Water St. S, Stillwater, MN 55082, tel. 612/439–6000, fax 612/430–9393. 16 double rooms with baths, 20 suites. TVs, phones, double whirlpool baths, gas fireplaces; restaurant, pub, air-conditioning, 5 conference rooms. $109–$229, full breakfast. AE, D, DC, MC, V. No pets.

Nicollet Island Inn. 95 Merriam St., Minneapolis, MN 55401, tel. 612/331–1800, fax 612/331–6528. 24 double rooms with baths. Cable TV/VCRs, phones, hair dryers, mineral water, cookies, newspapers; tubs in 2 rooms, 3 meeting rooms, restaurant, bar, movies for rent. $115–$150, breakfast extra. AE, D, DC, MC, V. Restricted smoking, no pets.

1900 Dupont. 1900 Dupont Ave. S, Minneapolis, MN 55403, tel. 612/374–1973. 4 double rooms with baths. Air-conditioning, TV available upon request. $85–$119, Continental breakfast. No credit cards. No smoking, no pets.

Rose Bed and Breakfast. 2129 Larpenteur Ave. W, Falcon Heights, MN 55113, tel. 612/642–9417 or 800/966–2728, fax 612/647–0954. 2 suites. Air-conditioning; phones, TV/VCRs, clock radios in suites; down comforter, bedtime snacks, and refrigerator in 3rd-floor suite; tennis court. $85, full breakfast. No credit cards. No smoking, no pets.

Schumacher's New Prague Hotel. 212 W. Main St., New Prague, MN 56071, tel. 612/758–2133, fax 612/758–2400. 11 double rooms with baths. Air-conditioning, whirlpool tub in some rooms, gas fireplace in 7 rooms, restaurant, gift shop. $137–$167, breakfast extra. AE, D, MC, V. Smoking only in restaurant, no pets.

Mississippi River Valley and Bluff Country

JailHouse Inn

109 Houston NW (Box 422), Preston, MN 55965, tel. 507/765–2181, fax 507/765-2558

Law-abiding citizens of the past century hurried past this 1869 Italianate redbrick building, which served as the Fillmore County Jail for more than 100 years. After then sitting empty for 15 years, the jail and the adjacent sheriff's quarters and offices were turned into a 13-room inn, after a renovation so extensive it is almost impossible to guess the structure's original use. Almost. One room provides an unforgettable reminder: The Cell Block Room still has its bars. Otherwise, it is much more comfortable than any inmate could have dreamed. Two queen-size beds with tufted bedspreads occupy separate cells, which are fitted with rag rugs, a whirlpool bath big enough for two, a sitting area, and the original toilet and basin.

Rest assured you won't feel the least bit incarcerated in the other bedrooms, all with beautiful pine or oak floors and many decorated with Eastlake furniture. The blue-and-rose Master Bedroom has a wood-burning fireplace, large windows, and a huge, old 1,000-pound china tub. The Oriental Room has a purple-and-black marble fireplace and a large, comfortable bathroom with a claw-foot tub. The pine-floored, maroon-and-rust Detention Room has access to the south-facing second-floor porch. The newest room, once the drunk tank, has the original oversize sheriff's tub. Even some of the JailHouse's smaller rooms—such as the bright yellow-and-white Sun Room or the blue-and-white Amish Room—are just as light and clean as the larger rooms.

There are plenty of public spaces, including the front parlor, which has a pine floor, marble fireplace, and grandfather clock; the larger and brighter oak-floored kitchen; and the first- and second-floor porches. Breakfast is served in a sunny, spacious basement dining area.

Owners Jeanne and Marc Sather, former restaurant designers from San Francisco, are accomplished cooks and veteran hosts, happy to lend their premises and their talents to special events or even to make impromptu trout dinners if you should find yourself lucky enough to catch one in the nearby Root River.

▥ *11 double rooms with baths, 1 2-bedroom suite. Air-conditioning, fireplace in 4 rooms, whirlpool bath in 3 rooms, breakfast room and parlor, meeting room, audiovisual equipment; near Root River trailhead. $40–$149; Continental breakfast weekdays, full breakfast weekends, afternoon refreshments. D, MC, V. No smoking, no pets.*

Pratt-Taber Inn

706 W. 4th St., Red Wing, MN 55066, tel. 612/388–5945

If you're interested in antiques, there are few better choices in this region than the Pratt-Taber Inn. Owners Jim and Karen Kleinfeldt fell in love with this house, not only for its location in historic Red Wing away from the bustle of big city life, but also for its potential as a historically authentic backdrop for their extensive antiques collection. The sturdy, white-trimmed brick Italianate Victorian inn is named after A. W. Pratt, a banker who built the house for his family in 1876, and his son-in-law, Robert Taber, who bought it in 1905. Ninety years later, it has become the Kleinfeldts' home, passion, and profession. Along with their gracious hospitality, they offer some of the best B&B breakfasts around.

The house, which is listed in the National Register of Historic Places, was restored in 1984. Old photographs guided much of the exterior work, including the replacement of the porches; one of them is embellished with a detailed star pattern honoring the United States' Centennial in 1876, the year the inn was built. Inside there are parquet floors, butternut and walnut woodwork, glass chandeliers, feather-painted slate fireplaces, and in the dining room, a large bay window. Throughout the house you'll find early Renaissance Revival and country Victorian antique furniture that dates from the late 1700s to the late 1800s, including a 112-year-old Murphy bed housed in a Victorian buffet and a stereopticon with a rare and complete *Tour the World* collection.

Three of the four upstairs rooms are corner rooms, and all are large and filled with impressive antiques. Polly's Room is particularly nice, with its queen-size brass bed, soft blue-and-ecru decor, black marble fireplace, and inviting claw-foot tub. Mary Lu's Room has views of Barns Bluff, and Beatrice's Room has an 1860s burled walnut Victorian dresser topped with Limoges china items, lending an aura of a time gone by.

Breakfasts—specialties include eggs Benedict with asparagus on homemade sourdough bread or cinnamon-orange French toast—are served in the dining room, on the porches, or in the guest bedrooms, all of which contain tables for two (Jim and Karen will serve from their collection of 1870 Limoges china upon request).

Being a bit of a town booster, Jim is also glad to provide guests with information on local activities, especially the summer trolley tours, which stop right at the inn's front door.

▦ *2 double rooms with baths, 4 doubles share 2 baths. Air-conditioning, clock radios; fireplace in 1 room, storage for bicycles, pickup service at airport, dock, or train station. $89–$110; full breakfast, afternoon refreshments. No credit cards. No smoking, no pets.*

Thorwood Historic Inns

315 Pine St., Hastings, MN 55033, tel. 612/437–3297 or 888/846–7966

If you want a luxurious bed-and-breakfast visit, as so many of the repeat guests do, the Thorwood Historic Inns—the 1880 Queen Anne Rosewood and the 1880 Second Empire–style Thorwood—are for you.

Pam and Dick Thorsen, a down-to-earth and friendly couple, fell in love with the river town of Hastings, 20 miles south of St. Paul, and opened Thorwood in 1983. The 6,600-square-foot house was built by a local lumber baron, William Thompson, and his wife, Sara, as their family home. Then, in 1989, the Thorsens opened the 10,000-square-foot Rosewood, six blocks away.

Interestingly, both inns had been hospitals, and occasionally people born in the buildings come back as guests to celebrate their birthdays.

Thorwood and Rosewood are not cozy, family-style bed-and-breakfasts. Thorwood has retained more of its original rooms and fixtures and because the Thorsens live there, is the homier of the two inns. It has a bay window and a fireplace in its main parlor, an interesting square bay in the front parlor, and maple-and-oak floors throughout.

Rosewood has a grand piano, a large fireplace, large ornate public rooms, and several bay windows big enough to park a Volkswagen in. Dark-green-and-rose wallpapers and carpets and white-and-oak woodwork, along with the building's great size, make Rosewood's parlors almost overwhelmingly formal.

Remodeling has given fireplaces and whirlpool baths to both inns' guest rooms. The largest and most ornate is a 900-square-foot suite called Mississippi Under the Stars, which has five skylights, a fireplace, a teakwood double whirlpool tub under a skylight, a round shower, a copper soaking tub, and a queen-size bed.

Thorwood's most elaborate rooms are Sara's Suite, a lavender-and-white three-level arrangement, with a skylight over the bed, a double whirlpool tub, and the best view; and the Steeple Room, with a built-in whirlpool bath set right into the steeple and a glass-domed fireplace dividing the bath area from the bedroom. Any of the other third-floor rooms at either inn are also bound to both intrigue and spoil even the hardest-to-please of people.

The Thorsens have taken to offering breakfast either in the public rooms or in baskets at your door.

▦ *13 double rooms with baths, 2 suites. Air-conditioning, TV/VCRs available, fireplace in 9 rooms, whirlpool bath in 12 rooms, gift shop; dinners available. $87–$217; full* breakfast, afternoon refreshments. AE, D, MC, V. No smoking, no pets.

Victorian Bed & Breakfast

620 S. High St., Lake City, MN 55041, tel. 612/345-2167

Wonderful views of Lake Pepin from each guest room make Lake City's Victorian Bed & Breakfast special. The lake, which many people claim is the most beautiful spot on the Mississippi, also dominates the perspective from the large windows in the downstairs public rooms.

Owners Ione and Bernie Link—originally from Wichita, Kansas—traveled far to settle in Lake City. One look at the grand view from the porch, and they decided on the spot to buy the inn.

The building, although an 1896 Stick-style Victorian, has a refreshing simplicity inside. Butternut wood on the staircase banisters and elsewhere is carved, but not elaborately so; small and simple stained-glass windows in rose, amber, and blue are set atop larger plain-glass windows.

Decorated with antiques and modern sofas, the Victorian is eclectic and comfortable, but not overstuffed. The most interesting items are the oak pump organ, made in 1905, and the many delicate glass lamps, some of which are handcrafted by Bernie himself.

The Redbud Room is best, with sweeping lake views from the huge bay window, a king-size bed, a private bath with a wide-plank pine floor, an oversize footed tub, and a rare antique pillbox toilet. The chaise lounge provides an excellent opportunity for getting lost in a book.

The sunny Magnolia Room is a large corner room at the front of the house with wonderful lake views, a canopy bed topped with a featherbed, and an antique claw-foot tub with brass fixtures. The Dogwood Room has carved oak furniture, a reading desk, and a unique stereopticon, but its bathroom is downstairs off the den.

Breakfast is served either in the sunny dining room, which also overlooks the lake, or in guest rooms. Wherever you partake your wake-up meal, you'll probably love Ione's baked apple pancakes, often made with just-picked apples from local orchards.

▥ *3 double rooms with bath (1 nonadjoining). Air-conditioning, ceiling fan, down comforters, featherbeds; TV/VCR in den. $65–$85; full breakfast, afternoon refreshments. No credit cards. Restricted smoking, no pets.*

Other Choices

Anderson House. 333 W. Main St., Wabasha, MN 55981, tel. 612/565-4524, fax 612/565—4003 or 800/535-5467. 18 double rooms with baths, 6 suites. Restaurant, bar, air-conditioning, TV available upon request, whirlpool bath in 4 suites, 17 rooms have river views, banquet/conference room. $50–$125, breakfast extra. D, MC, V. Closed Mon.–Thurs. Nov. 2–Mar.

Archer House. 212 Division St., Northfield, MN 55057, tel. 507/645-5661, fax 507/645-4295. 17 double rooms with baths, 19 suites with whirlpool baths. Air-conditioning, cable TVs phones; restaurants, complimentary champagne for rooms with whirlpool baths, ice and soft-drink machines, shops, 3 conference rooms. $45–$150, breakfast extra. AE, MC, V. No pets.

Bridgewaters Bed and Breakfast. 136 Bridge Ave., Wabasha, MN 55981, tel. 612/565-4208. 2 double rooms with baths, 3 doubles share 2 baths. Air-conditioning, stereo with CD player in common area. $68–$145; full breakfast on weekends, Continental breakfast on weekdays. MC, V. Restricted smoking, no pets.

Candle Light Inn. 818 W. 3rd St., Red Wing, MN 55066, tel. 612/388-8034. 4

double rooms with baths, 1 suite. Air-conditioning, fireplace in 2 rooms, whirlpool bath in 3 rooms. $85–$145; full breakfast, afternoon refreshments. MC, V. No smoking, no pets.

Carriage House Bed & Breakfast. 420 Main St., Winona, MN 55987, tel. 507/452–8256, fax 507/452–0939. 4 double rooms with baths. Air-conditioning, fireplace in 2 rooms, free bicycles, shuttle service from boat docks or train station. $70–$110, Continental breakfast. D, MC, V. No smoking, no pets.

Carrolton Country Inn. RR 2 (Box 139), Lanesboro, MN 55949, tel. 507/467–2257. 2 double rooms with baths, 2 doubles share bath. Air-conditioning, clock radios; phone in 2 rooms, piano, TV/VCR in parlor, picnic table. $60–$90, full breakfast. MC, V. No smoking, no pets.

Historic Scanlan House. 708 Parkway Ave. S, Lanesboro, MN 55949, tel. 507/467–2158 or 800/944–2158. 5 double rooms with baths. Air-conditioning, cable TV, chocolates, minibottle of champagne; whirlpool bath in 3 rooms, bicycle and cross-country ski rentals. $65–$130; full breakfast, coffee and baked goods all day. AE, D, MC, V. Restricted smoking, no pets.

Hungry Point Inn. 1 Old Deerfield Rd., Welch, MN 55089, tel. 612/437–3660 or 612/388–7857. 4 double rooms share 1½ baths, 1 2-bedroom log cabin with bath. Air-conditioning, fireplace in 2 rooms and cabin, whirlpool bath in cabin. $73–$135; full breakfast, afternoon herbal tea and cookies. MC, V. No smoking, no pets.

Martin Oaks. 107 1st St., Box 207, Dundas, MN 55019, tel. 507/645–4644. 2 double rooms and 1 single share 1½ baths. Air-conditioning, ceiling fan in 2 rooms, grand piano in living room. $55–$69; full breakfast, evening dessert. MC, V. No smoking, no pets.

Quill & Quilt. 615 W. Hoffman St., Cannon Falls, MN 55009, tel. 507/263–5507 or 800/488–3849. 3 double rooms

with baths (2 nonadjoining), 1 suite. Air-conditioning, coffeemaker, clock radios; whirlpool bath in suite, biking, hiking, cross-country skiing on nearby Cannon Valley Trail. $60–$130; full breakfast, evening dessert and coffee. MC, V. No smoking, no pets.

Red Gables Inn. 403 N. High St., Lake City, MN 55041, tel. 612/345–2605. 5 double rooms with baths. Air-conditioning, ceiling fans; bicycles, antiques store. $85–$95; full breakfast, all-season picnic boxes, mystery evenings. D, MC, V. Restricted smoking, no pets.

St. James Hotel. 406 Main St., Red Wing, MN 55066, tel. 612/388–2846 or 800/252–1875 or 612/227-1800 (metro line), fax 612/388–5226. 60 double rooms with baths. Air-conditioning, phones, cable TVs, clock radios; 2 restaurants, 2 bars, newspaper, whirlpool bath in 10 rooms, 11 meeting and banquet rooms, 11 shops, shuttle service from airport and dock. $80–$165; breakfast extra, complimentary champagne, coffee. AE, D, DC, MC, V. No pets.

Duluth and the North Shore

Bearskin Lodge

Box 275, Grand Marais, MN 55604, tel. 218/388–2292 or 800/338–4170, fax 218/388–4410

Dave Tuttle worked at Bearskin Lodge Resort when it was just an old lodge and several cabins 25 miles down the Gunflint Trail from Grand Marais and Lake Superior. Then in 1973, while still a senior in college, he bought it.

Today it remains low-key and woodsy, but a bit more ambitious. Since it's adjacent to the Boundary Waters Canoe area, you'll find hiking and cross-country ski trails; boat, ski, and mountain-bike rentals; and a naturalist program. There's even a masseuse. The new lodge, built in 1980, has four large town houses; there are also 11 new or spruced-up log or log-frame cabins. The multilevel town houses, though within a wing of the lodge, feel secluded, and each has a private deck. Some of the seven older cabins, built in the '20s, '30s, and '50s, have been remodeled to include room-brightening skylights above the beds. All are pleasant and have two or three bedrooms, woodstoves, and large, well-equipped kitchens. In addition, several have screened porches—critical during the buggy north-woods summers.

Rooms in both the town houses and the cabins are simple and comfortable, with chenille bedspreads and pine furniture. Each of the five two- or three-bedroom log cabins is charming, though cabins 9 and 10, built in 1990 of Engelmann spruce, are especially lovely. These cabins, although they're a bit far from the lake, have birch hardwood floors, braided rugs, brand-new kitchens as well-outfitted as any home's, and big, screened porches. The new pinewood cabin is wheelchair accessible.

One of the resort's most popular spots is the Hot Tub Hus, which sign up for in advance for private use. Its walls, benches, and ceiling are of pine, and it has a large deck and separate men's and women's changing rooms and showers.

Originally a summer-only resort, Bearskin now draws kudos from winter-sports lovers for its ice rink and 55 miles of cross-country ski trails (1 mile of which is lighted). Lodge-to-lodge skiing packages are available.

▦ *11 2- to 3-bedroom cabins and 4 1-to 3-bedroom lodge town houses. Woodstoves in cabins, kettle grill outside cabins; full meal service available in lodge dining room, wine and beer for sale, sauna, masseuse, spa house, baby-sitting, children's program, sand beach, boat and mountain-bike rental, 55 mi of hiking/cross-country ski trails, ski school, ski rental, ice-skating rink, broomball rink, naturalist program. $110–$231, breakfast extra. D, MC, V. Restricted smoking, no pets.*

Ellery House

28 S. 21st Ave. E, Duluth, MN 55812, tel. 218/724-7639 or 800/355-3794

If it's a comfortable family place you're looking for, Jim and Joan Halquist's beautiful 1890 Queen Anne is the place to stay. The house is on a fairly busy street yet feels rather removed because of its ¾-acre lot, hilltop location, and backyard ravine with creek.

The large, sunny rooms, lighted by large picture windows that face in three directions, are decorated in a trim, moderate Victorian style. The large bay window in the living room has a lake view that's best in winter (shade trees partially obscure the view in summer). In the adjoining dining room, a collection of turn-of-the-century tables and cabinets surround the dark oak dining table.

Breakfast is served in the dining room or in three of the four guest rooms. All are delightful. The Ellery Suite, at the front of the house, has a small private balcony and a 1920s-style bathroom. The Sunporch, a three-room suite, is composed of a cozy, floral-wallpapered bedroom with a brass bed, a large bath with oversize claw-foot tub, and a sunny, plant-filled porch with a wood-burning stove and treetop views. The Thomas Wahl Room is particularly nice, with a tiny table for two tucked into a large lake-view bay window; it also has an 1890s gas fireplace in the corner, a double marble shower, maple floors, and a cabbage rose–motif hooked rug.

Joan, a violinist with the Duluth-Superior Symphony Orchestra, encourages duets on the parlor's baby grand piano. Jim, whose background is in hotels, makes a point of offering comfort and relaxation to tired and stressed-out guests. The popular lake walk is just 2½ blocks from the inn, and the Halquists, both active, outdoorsy folks, can also recommend their favorite bike and cross-country ski trails; they even have a storage shed for any equipment you may bring. In addition, with two small children themselves, the Halquists don't mind accommodating the families of others. Their congeniality make the Ellery House very homey indeed.

🛏 *2 double rooms with baths, 2 suites. Ceiling fans and fresh flowers in rooms, fireplace in 2 rooms, balcony in 1 room. $69–$125, full breakfast. AE, MC, V. Restricted smoking, no pets.*

Finnish Heritage Homestead

4776 Waisanen Rd., Embarrass, MN 55732, tel. 218/984–3318 or 800/863–6545

About 1891, Finnish immigrant John Kangas nearly froze to death for lack of shelter in the wilds of northern Minnesota—the state's Mesabi Iron Range region. As a blizzard moved in, Kangas shot a moose and—so the legend goes—cut the animal open to crawl inside as protection against the elements. Having survived a night there, he decided this had to be the place the heavenly powers wanted him to build his family's home.

Almost 100 years after John began building his Embarrass, Minnesota, homestead, the area remains pretty wild, but the accommodations have improved considerably—thanks to Kangas's hard work and Finnish craftsmanship. He built nearly half a dozen log structures, including a rare 2½-story log building that served as a Finnish *poikatalo*, or boardinghouse, for loggers, miners, and railroad workers. Today, some of these buildings survive and can be explored, along with the fields and woods of the 32-acre farm.

In 1991, Buzz Schultz and his wife, Elaine Braginton, left the sweltering

heat of Arizona to be closer to their beloved Boundary Waters Canoe Area (just a half hour away from Embarrass). The new owners of the Kangas homestead learned Embarrass townfolk frequently advised visiting dignitaries to "go stay with Buzz and Elaine. They've got room." So it seemed natural to convert the multiple-dwelling grounds of the farm into what the Finnish immigrants called a *matka koit*—a house to stay in while on a journey.

The B&B offers five cozy, though somewhat small, upstairs rooms laid out in simple, comfortable farm style, with comforters on the beds and a few Norman Rockwell porcelain plates, photos, and memorabilia as wall hangings. All rooms share a bath, but guests are provided with terry-cloth robes and in winter, warm footies. The bathroom is almost as large as a guest room: One wall offers a bookcase stocked with everything from Garrison Keiller to guides on log-house restoration, and there's even an ironing board.

Three rooms have queen-size beds, one has two twin beds, and one has a single and a double bed. Each room has a handmade rug or quilt done by Grandma Kangas. Rooms are named with initials of Kangas family members. JJK Jr. (John Jr.) features an octagonal window, while the window in WWK (William's room) is in the closet; it's the only place the building's log structure is exposed. Downstairs, the parlor provides a place for guests to gather for a chat with Buzz and Elaine about the homestead and its history.

The best part of this B&B, though, may be its surrounding delights. A screened gazebo with ceiling fan offers a quiet place to rest or read and watch the geese and ducks wander about the lawn and vegetable and flower gardens. Elsewhere on the grounds are intriguing examples of log work—a towering 1907 hay barn and smaller outbuildings. Spike, the good-natured farm dog, gladly accompanies those wanting to hike the property (and can be a bear chaser if need be).

Short jaunts around the "neighborhood" can lead to skiing resorts in the winter or nifty places for fishing, swimming, canoeing, golfing, or hiking during warm weather. In Embarrass itself (the name derives from the term French voyagers gave the region's difficult-to-navigate rivers), townsfolk have revived the Finnish immigrant heritage with a gift shop, a heritage park, and the Heritage Pioneer Homestead Tour that, needless to say, includes the Kangas farm.

🏨 *5 double rooms with shared bath. TV/VCR in parlor, wood-fired sauna. $58.50–$87.50; full breakfast, bag lunch available for hikers, dinners available for extended-stay guests. MC, V. Restricted smoking, no pets.*

Mansion Bed & Breakfast Inn

3600 London Rd., Duluth, MN 55804, tel. 218/724–0739

Though imposing from the front, this 1928 rubble-stone and half-timbered Tudor mansion is really oriented toward its backyard. And what a backyard it is: Five hundred feet of Lake Superior shore provides the house with incredible views from almost every room. Who can resist sitting on the ample lawn in summer or fall to watch the many ships go by?

Built for mining executive Harry C. Dudley and his wife, Marjorie Congdon Dudley, daughter of Duluth lumber baron Chester Congdon, the Mansion is an inviting combination of grandeur and comfort. The main floor has a sunny dining room with a terrazzo floor, a wood-paneled library with a large fireplace and antique books, a large gallery with four window seats and three sets of French doors leading to a lakefront stone terrace, and a huge living room that opens onto a screened porch, a favorite spot for guests.

Sunny, lined with bear and wolf skins and mooseheads, guarded by a suit of armor, and fitted with a huge lake-view window seat, the third-floor Trophy Room is the inn's designated quiet room. Guests use it for reading and dreaming, and "fall asleep here all the time," says proprietor Sue Monson, who, along with her husband, Warren, bought the building in 1983. Warren is a busy physician, so Sue, who likes to cater to the guests, runs the Mansion herself with some help from her three grown children and a small part-time staff.

The bedrooms that belonged to members of the Dudley family, such as the Anniversary Suite and the Master Suite, are the largest, but the coziest are the former maids' quarters, now called the Peach and Beige rooms. The Master Suite can expand to an additional bedroom, while the carriage house offers one-, two-, or three-bedroom accommodations. Some of the bedrooms, all of which are carpeted and contain antiques and reproductions, do pale in comparison to the absolute splendor of the Mansion itself, but as one of the guests said, "I can't imagine anyone coming here and not being completely impressed and comfortable."

The 7-acre grounds are given over to lawns, gardens, and a forest of northern hardwoods, pine, and cedar; there's also a private beach, where guests often build bonfires on summer evenings.

🏨 *6 double rooms with baths, 4 doubles share 2 baths, 1-bedroom carriage-house suite. Large-screen TV and VCR in living room, kitchenette in carriage house, private beach. $105–$205, $165 for carriage house; full breakfast. MC, V. Restricted smoking, no pets.*

Olcott House

2316 E. 1st St., Duluth, MN 55812, tel. 218/728–1339 or 800/715–1339

At the turn of the century, William Olcott, president of Oliver Mining and onetime employee of John D. Rockefeller, and his wife, Fannie, traveled around the country, sketchbook in hand to record their favorite houses. In 1904, their dreams and sketches came together to create an impressive Georgian Colonial mansion, the Olcott House.

The white-columned mansion set on emerald green lawns was built with hospitality in mind—as visitors will note when they discover its small basement ballroom. Today, that tradition continues, since the Olcott is now a hostelry that fits comfortably into Duluth's East End, just four blocks from Lake Superior and minutes to Canal Park and downtown. Since 1994 the Olcott has been the cherished possession of Barb and Don Trueman (after running a travel business for 13 years, Barb wanted a slower pace), and they've appropriately furnished the 12,000 square feet of the house, plus a carriage house, for its new life as a B&B.

Their choices make the house lush but not cluttered. People who had lived, worked, or studied in the house during its incarnations as a family home and later as a school of music for the University of Minnesota-Duluth made contributions to the house collection, such as the photographs of the Olcott family that now grace several walls or the chapter about life in the house from an Olcott daughter's biography—charmingly copied for guests to peruse.

The Truemans revel in their historic dwelling and give interested guests a tour of the home on their first evening. The entryway is suitably elegant, with dentil work and a gracefully curved staircase. The music room, to the left of the entry, was built with coved corners for acoustic quality and now sports a baby grand piano. To the right, the library has a dark walnut mantel around a green marble–encased fireplace, one of eight fireplaces in the house. The side-by-side dining rooms, where breakfast is served, have tables set with all the crystal and china trim-

mings and matched-pattern mahogany sliding doors, wainscoting, and beams. Upstairs, the house has five suites and one double room, each with a special offering, such as the three-season porch and bay window with lake and harbor view from the Lake Superior Suite, or the charm of the blue-and-white Summer Suite with its inlaid-tile fireplace.

The separate carriage house has a small, equipped kitchen, a large living room with a fireplace (adorned with antique tiles that depict a forest and river scene), arched Palladian windows, and a queen-size bed beneath an overhead fan, along with white wicker furniture. Families will be pleased to know the Olcott House's gracious welcome also embraces children from toddlers on up.

🏨 *1 double room, 5 suites, 1 carriage house. Cable TV, phone, stereo in carriage house, TV in rooms on request, fireplaces in suites. $75–$155, full breakfast. MC, V. Restricted smoking, no pets, 2-night minimum stay on weekends June–Oct.*

Pincushion Mountain Bed & Breakfast

220 Gunflint Trail, Grand Marais, MN 55604-9701, tel. 218/387-1276 or 800/ 542-1226

After spending four snowless winters in Flagstaff, Arizona, Scott Beattie, a longtime cross-country skier and instructor, moved to a place where snow was guaranteed. He and his wife, Mary, checked out locations around the country and came to a spot 3 miles up the Gunflint Trail from Grand Marais. They built the Pincushion Mountain Bed & Breakfast in 1986. The almost unreal quiet here is broken only by the occasional birdcall.

The modern pine building sits on the Sawtooth Mountain ridgeline, 1,000 feet above Lake Superior. The woodsy inn has fir beams, pine and aspen paneled walls, and country-style furnishings and knickknacks.

Downstairs is a living room equipped with a woodstove and a dining room where a hearty breakfast is served. There are spectacular views of Lake Superior and the surrounding pine, aspen, and birch forest. This is the true north woods; don't be surprised if you see a deer, a moose, or even a bear passing by.

The four guest rooms upstairs are somewhat small but comfortable. The largest and probably most desirable is the corner Pine Room, which has a fold-out love seat, a comfortably sized bath, and a majestic view of Lake Superior in the distance. The Birch and Aspen rooms have tiny but adequate built-in baths with showers only; the latter has no lake view. The Maple Room has a private bath across the hall.

Scott, a certified ski instructor, gives skiing lessons, rents and repairs skis, and grooms Pincushion's own 15½ miles of trails. Although Pincushion accommodates skiers in particular, its 44 acres are equally attractive in summer and fall, when its ski trails are used for hiking. Because the inn's trails adjoin the 200-mile Superior Hiking Trail, Pincushion takes part in the north-shore lodge-to-lodge hiking program and in ski programs.

▦ *4 double rooms with baths. Fans, clock radios; sauna, mountain bikes and cross-country skis for rent, 15¼ mi of cross-country skiing and hiking trails, 1 mi of kerosene-lighted trails on winter Saturday nights, cross-country ski instruction, trail bag lunches available. $80–$100; full breakfast, afternoon refreshments. MC, V. No smoking, no pets, 2-night minimum stay on winter, late summer, and fall weekends. Closed Apr.*

Stone Hearth Inn Bed & Breakfast

1118 Hwy. 61 E, Little Marais, MN 55614, tel. 218/226–3020, fax 218/226–3466

In 1989, when Charlie Michels came to Little Marais, he wanted to buy some land on Lake Superior. Two years later he had a five-bedroom, 70-year-old inn, and a wife, Susan, who'd been one of his first guests.

The Stone Hearth Inn was the original homestead of the Benjamin Fenstad family. Benjamin built a log cabin on the site in 1893 and in 1924, built the home that Charlie owns today. An accomplished Twin Cities carpenter and contractor, Charlie did most of the renovation work himself. He made 10 rooms into six, stripped the narrow-plank maple floors, added beams and molding downstairs, and collected stones from the shores of Lake Superior to use in the construction of the large living-room fireplace.

Just 80 feet from the lake, the house has a wonderful long porch furnished with Adirondack chairs, perfect for relaxing in these serene surroundings. French doors open onto it from both the simple dining room, whose large handmade pine table sits in the center, and from the living room, where soft chairs and sofas flank the giant hearth and guests take turns playing the piano.

In all five guest rooms, you can fall asleep to the comforting sounds of the lake, but you'll get the best views from Rooms 2, 3, and 4. Room 2, a corner room in blue and white with a four-poster canopy bed, has a lake view even from its pink-and-white ceramic-tile bathroom.

An old boathouse just 30 feet from the lake was renovated in 1992 and rebuilt as a two-unit cottage. One unit is a suite with a bedroom, bathroom, living room with sofa bed, and kitchenette.

Both are upstairs and have gas fireplaces, whirlpool baths, and especially dramatic views from their picture windows. On the drawing board are two more double units with whirlpool baths and gas fireplaces, to be constructed in the carriage house.

Blueberry–wild rice pancakes, Austrian apple pancakes, lake trout sausage, and vanilla poached pears are perfect examples of Susan and Charlie's innovative cooking. On most clear nights, there is a bonfire down by the lake, with s'mores provided by the Michels and if you're lucky, northern lights provided by Mother Nature.

▥ *5 double rooms with baths, 1 suite with kitchenette. Gas fireplace, coffeemaker, and whirlpool bath in 1 room and suite, kitchen in suite, trail lunches available, lodge-to-lodge hiking program. $79–$130; full breakfast in inn, Continental breakfast in boathouse double room. AE, D, MC, V. No smoking, no pets.*

Other Choices

Fitger's Inn. 600 E. Superior St., Duluth, MN 55802, tel. 218/722–8826 or 800/726–2982 or 888/348–4377. 42 double rooms with baths, 18 suites. Airconditioning, phones, cable TVs, clock radios; room service, conference facilities including 160-seat theater, free valet parking, adjoining shopping and restaurant complex. $92–$250, breakfast extra. AE, D, DC, MC, V. No pets.

Inn at Palisade Bed & Breakfast. 384 U.S. 61, Silver Bay, MN 55614, tel. 218/226–3505, fax 218/226–4648. 4 double rooms with baths, 1 suite with kitchen. TV, clock radio, kitchen, and fireplace in 1 room. $80–$105; full breakfast, afternoon snack, coffee available all day. D, MC, V. No smoking, no pets. Closed mid-Oct.–Memorial Day.

Lindgren's Bed & Breakfast. County Road 35, Box 56, Lutsen, MN 55612-0056, tel. 218/663–7450. 3 double rooms

with baths, basement room with bunks and sofa beds. TVs; phones in 2 rooms, whirlpool bath in 1 room, fireplace in 1 room, Finnish sauna, bonfire pit, horseshoe pit, volleyball area, lodge-to-lodge ski and hiking program. $85–$125; full breakfast, trail lunches available. MC, V. No smoking, no pets.

Mathew S. Burrows 1890 Inn. 1632 E. 1st St., Duluth, MN 55812, tel. 218/724–4991 or 800/789–1890. 2 double rooms with baths, 3 suites. Alarm clock, radio/tape player, fireplace and unique full-body marble shower in 1 suite. $95–$118, full breakfast. AE, D, DC, MC, V. No smoking, no pets, 2-night minimum on summer weekends. Closed Dec. 24–25.

Naniboujou Lodge. U.S. 61 (Box 505), Grand Marais, MN 55604, tel. and fax 218/387–2688. 24 double rooms with baths. Restaurant, fireplace in 5 rooms, lake view from 12 rooms, basketball and volleyball courts. $50–$90; breakfast extra, afternoon tea. D, MC, V. No smoking, no alcohol in restaurant, no pets. Closed mid-Oct.–mid-Dec. and weekdays in winter, except for a Christmas-week package special.

Superior Overlook B&B. U.S. 61, Milepost 112 (Box 963) Grand Marais, MN 55604-0963, tel. 218/387–1571 or 800/858–7622. 1 double room with nonadjoining bath, 1 suite. TV/VCR, phone, and wood-burning stove in living room, kitchenette in suite, sauna. $95–$130, full breakfast. AE, D, MC, V. No smoking, no pets.

The Northwest and the Cuyana Iron Range, Including Brainerd and Detroit Lakes

Elm St. Inn

422 Elm St., Crookston, MN 56716, tel. 218/281–2343 or 800/568–4467, fax 218/ 281–1756

In the prairie town of Crookston, Minnesota, historic buildings are not a rarity: Thirty-five buildings in its business district alone are listed in the National Register of Historic Places. The architect of several of those buildings also designed this charming Arts and Crafts–era house in 1910. From lawyer to doctor to banker, the house served as a presentable, livable home for the town's professional families until it fell to the Crookston School Board, which had plans to demolish it.

John and Sheryl Winters, both involved in a local law firm, saved it from that fate in 1976. By 1992, their children had left home, and the Winters decided it was time to open their home to guests rather than ramble around in the suddenly all-too-ample space.

Downstairs, the small Grandmother's Room has a hunter green iron bed from the family's heirlooms as well as a maple antique vanity dresser with hourglass-shaped mirror. The room has beveled- and lead-glass windows with lace curtains, and the bed sports a handmade quilt; a private bath adjoins the room.

Upstairs, the maple-floored rooms "blossom." The Prairie Rose Room's sponge-painted walls are done in dusty rose and peach. A white wrought-iron bed with eyelet comforter and ruffles is accented with a hand-painted pillow, while a restored oak rocker cradles a teddy bear. The Morning Glory Room, done in pink-and-blue floral patterns, has a handmade "quilter's quilt" on the high queen-size bed (a wooden step is stowed below the bed for those needing a boost). The room features French provincial accents, a sweetheart boudoir chair, and eyelet curtains on the lead-glass windows.

The passionate purples of the Lilac Room have become a favorite with guests, according to the Winters. Pinks and purples dominate just about everything—even the hangars are purple. A hand-tied quilt covers the Pennsylvania cherrywood antique bed. The private bath next door is another reason so many guests lay claim to this room. Its delicate floral patterns of faded greens and peaches, a stained-glass window of greens and lavenders, and an assortment of bubble baths and an oversize claw-foot tub (big enough for two) make long soaks a luxurious temptation. For more acquatic relaxation, you can opt for a pass to the township's enclosed pool, just across the lawn from the inn.

Breakfast is served—charmingly by candlelight—on stylish china in the dining room, and guests benefit from John's upbringing in the family bakery. Wild rice–buttermilk pancakes with sunflower seeds top the favored fare. A music room, and a library room with a TV, a well-stocked bookcase, and a couch, and the airy upstairs screened porch with white wicker furnishings and a beguiling assortment of windchimes—all conspire to make the inn a hard place to leave.

▦ *4 double rooms with baths. Alarm clocks; air-conditioning in some rooms, TV/VCR in living room. $55–$65, full breakfast. AE, D, MC, V. No smoking, no pets.*

Hallett House

Hwy. 210 (Box 247), Crosby, MN 56441, tel. 218/546–5433

As you drive out of Crosby and approach the grand front lawn of Hallett House, you may feel you've stepped back in time. A driveway that curves beneath oaks and jack pines brings you to the front door of a pale Georgian Revival house with green trim and a small arched portico. Inside, painted Georgian paneling suggests grandeur, but the lush green wool carpeting somehow shrinks the large rooms to livable size. Sun streams through the windows of a porch that's been made into a wicker-furnished guest room. The library, with a fireplace and built-in bookshelves, has the air of a corner in an old-fashioned men's club.

Upstairs, past yellow-and-blue 1950s-era wallpaper with Early American scenes, the guest rooms give off that same feeling of luxury. The big, carpeted rooms, which have solid, often antique furniture and bay windows with venetian blinds, encourage the fantasy that you're staying in the home of some long-lost rich uncle. Here is the room of "the lady of the house," with its mirror-lined dressing area and vanity—you can almost smell the Chanel No. 5 and hear the faint tinkling of silver bracelets. Here is the master bedroom, with a baronial bed facing the bay window, or the maid's quarters, with her rather small bed and her own sitting room (and an up-to-date TV set). Down the hall, the eldest son's room seems to have been kept as it must have been before he left for college, all hardwood floors and a big oak bedstead.

In truth, the house was built in the early '20s by E. W. Hallett, a construction and real-estate magnate who was once one of the richest men in the county. Hallett was a fiscally conservative man—he didn't lose his shirt in the stock market crash—and his house, though large, is not ostentatious. He died in 1983 (at the age of 101!), and six years later a local couple, Kathy and Wes Pernula, bought the well-pre-served home and turned it into a bed-and-breakfast. They've had the sense to leave well-enough alone, adding only a few frills and figurines, most of them downstairs, so the delicious feeling of quiet privilege still prevails.

▦ *5 double rooms with baths. Ceiling fans; air-conditioning units available, cable TV in 2 bedrooms and in library. $55–$75, full breakfast. AE, MC, V. No smoking, no pets.*

Oakhurst Inn

212 S. 8th Ave., Princeton, MN 55371, tel. 612/389–3553 or 800/443–2258

It was perhaps the most prestigious house in the prosperous town of Princeton at one time, but when David and Suzie Spain bought Oakhurst in 1989, it was a cluttered near ruin. It took two years of hard work to return the house to something close to its days of glory. Unlike the original owner, banker John Skahen, the Spains aren't made of money, so Oakhurst today feels more like a family home than a ostentatious mansion. Still, much of the grandeur remains.

Built in 1906, the three-story house is one of those Victorians that borrowed from many styles, hence the Queen Anne wraparound porch and the magnificent Romanesque fireplace in the front parlor. The front door opens onto a grand vestibule, with ceilings nearly 10 feet high, oak floors and woodwork, and a long bench built into one wall. To the right are the front and back parlors (the Spains have added oak wainscoting to the back parlor and turned it into a library); to the left is the dining room, complete with plate rail. The Spains hope to make the decor more consistent with one period: At present, an Eastlake chair, a mission rocker, and a reupholstered camelback couch sit incongruously near one another. An air of homey middle-class nostalgia is perpetuated by Norman Rockwell plates, small stuffed bears, and braided area rugs.

Upstairs, the tasteful, comfortable guest rooms do better at creating a period look. The John J. Skahen Room, for instance, features a velvet fainting couch and a pencil-post four-poster queen-size bed covered with reproduction quilted lace. The smaller Sterling Room has a bathroom with such 1906-type features as a pedestal sink, a clawfoot tub, and wainscoting. The sunny Lucy Room has a white iron bed with lace coverlet and lace curtains at the windows, making for a pleasant mixture of frill and simplicity.

The Spains and their children live on the third floor of this big house, and perhaps their presence has something to do with the down-to-earth family atmosphere of the place. Guests are welcome to visit Suzie in the kitchen, where they may be offered a chocolate-chip cookie or two while she talks of the horrors of renovation. While the remodeling was no doubt hard to live through, the result is a cozy success.

🛏 *3 double rooms with baths. Air-conditioning, TV/VCR in library. $70–$85; full breakfast on weekends, Continental on weekdays, evening refreshments. MC, V. No smoking, no pets.*

Park Street Inn

Rte. 1 (Box 254), Nevis, MN 56467, tel. 218/652–4500 or 800/797–1778

This little jewel box sits on a little street in a little town you'd miss if you drove too fast. Nevis, once a prosperous logging town, now makes a bid for tourism with the nearby Heartland Bike Trail and Lake Belle Taine. The Park Street Inn represents this newer Nevis, although it is also rooted in the town's history.

Built in 1912 by Justin Halvorson, a well-to-do banker and local land developer, the house is more of a bungalow than a mansion, but it was done up in style—or more accurately, all kinds of styles, for Halvorson apparently was no purist. The compact oak stairway

and banister were constructed out of state and brought to town by train. Other Midwestern craftsmen contributed a beveled-glass fan window and exquisite entry arches of carved oak in a French Empire style, with acanthus-topped fluted columns and flower-basket bas-reliefs. In contrast, an oak mantel sports the clean, simple lines of mission-style design.

Halvorson lost his money in the Depression and moved to California. Given that Nevis, too, was declining, it's surprising so many of the original treasures in the house remained. Irene and Len Hall bought the place in 1996 after it had already been a B&B for several years. Many of the house furnishings are original, but the Halls added their own personal touches to the rooms so tactfully that returning guests felt sure several new pieces had been there all along.

In the living room and dining area, subdued wallpaper and matching valances complement lace-curtained windows. The Halls decided to make a major statement in the living room; they adorned it with a bubbling fountain, and dominating one corner is a striking backlit stained-glass window whose original home was a Methodist church.

The upstairs is a bit less restrained, but still interesting. The largest guest room, which has a wicker-furnished sleeping porch facing Lake Belle Taine, also features a built-in cupboard bed whose oak arch came from a Lutheran church altar—a nice ecumenical touch given the stained-glass window below, Len likes to note. Each room has its own wallpaper pattern and quilt—a handmade double wedding-ring quilt in one bedroom, a bright star pattern in another. The Halls also restocked the numerous built-in bookshelves (with both new and antique vintage editions) and added many more, making the house a sort of BBB—Bed, Book, and Breakfast.

🏨 *3 double rooms with baths, 1 suite. TV in sitting room. $55–$90; full breakfast, evening refreshments. MC, V. Restricted smoking.*

Peters' Sunset Beach

2500 S. Lakeshore Dr., Glenwood, MN 56334, tel. 320/634–4501 or 800/356–8654 in MN

One look inside the main lodge's dining room gives you the flavor of this classic lakeside resort: knotty-pine paneling, fish trophies, paintings of scenes from a Hiawatha-like Native American legend, light fixtures done up like painted drums, and a broad porch overlooking Lake Minnewaska.

The lodge, a gorgeous example of Craftsman-style design, is one of the resort's three buildings on the National Register of Historic Places. The place has changed a bit since train conductor Henry Peters jumped off the Soo Line in Glenwood and opened his summer hotel in 1915. It has grown from a small hostelry to a resort, complete with its own 18-hole golf course, accommodating up to 175 guests in a variety of up-to-date rooms, cottages, and luxury town houses. But it's still run by the Peters family, and they have restored the historic 1923 Annex to its old-fashioned appearance—making it, in the words of Henry's grandson Bill Peters, "our country inn."

From the outside, the Annex looks a lot like the main lodge, almost like a wing that detached itself and settled several steps away.

The Peterses have installed antique bedsteads, tables, and dressers, many of them from the turn of the century, to fit in with the refinished original woodwork. Quilts, made by a local artisan, grace each bed; the wallpaper is quietly floral. The whole building has an agreeable, unpretentious air about it, although there are some discordant touches left over from the Annex's pre-restoration interim years.

Still, the Annex has a certain charm, and there are other compensations: The restaurant serves some of the best food in the area. The nearby town of Glenwood is pretty, the resort's grounds are gracious, and Lake Minnewaska itself is lovely. You can certainly see why Henry Peters made this the end of his line.

🏨 *20 double rooms (12 in Court Bldg., 8 in Annex) with baths; 3 suites in Main Lodge, 10 town houses sleep 4–9 people; 2 1-bedroom cottages, 5 2-bedroom cottages, 3 3-bedroom cottages, 1 4-bedroom cottage, 1 7-bedroom housekeeping cottage. Restaurant, snack bar, air-conditioning, cable TVs, meeting room, beach, boat rentals, tennis, golf, racquetball. $65–$250, full breakfast and dinner. MC, V. No pets, 2- to 4-night minimum. Closed Oct.–Apr.*

Spicer Castle

11600 Indian Beach Rd. (Box 307), Spicer, MN 56288, tel. 320/796–5870 or 800/821–6675

If you somehow missed the opportunity to live in an old country mansion circa 1913, here's your chance. This imposing house, now on the National Register of Historic Places, was built in 1895 by farm developer John Spicer, one of the founders of Minnesota's branch of the Democratic Party. According to current owner Allen Latham, Spicer's grandson, the last renovations on the house were done in 1913, shortly after it was wired for electricity, and the building hasn't been changed since. Set on the wooded shores of Green Lake, the Tudor-style half-timbered house was originally called Medayto Cottage, but in the 1930s fishermen on the lake started referring to it as "the Castle," perhaps because of its crenellated tower. Though it's otherwise not particularly castlelike, the name stuck.

However beautiful its exterior, it's the interior that makes the Castle distinctive. The furnishings, rugs, china, and

Craftsman-style lamps and clocks are all antiques and have been in place since the 1913 redecoration. Walking across the gleaming maple floors, through the living and dining rooms, the well-stocked library, and the grand porch overlooking the lake, you get the sense you are not just viewing the past, but actually participating in it.

The first floor, with dark furniture and burlap wall coverings (a typical period Craftsman touch), might seem dark, but it's not oppressive—rather, it encourages quiet reflection and talk. In winter, it becomes downright cozy, as the fireplaces throw their flickering light on the ceiling beams.

Upstairs, it's almost like a different house. White beaded paneling and large windows give the place the bright air of a Nantucket summer cottage. Some renovation has been done up here, primarily in the bathrooms, but Allen and his wife, Marti, have kept to the period, with pedestal sinks and claw-foot tubs (some in the rooms themselves). The bedsteads and dressers are in various styles, but all belonged to the Lathams' forebears. Two equally well-preserved cottages offer more privacy.

Breakfast is served in the dining room in cool months, on the lakeside porch in summer. There are no TVs, telephones, or air-conditioning. This is pure 1913—they won't be missed.

🎴 *8 double rooms with baths, 2 cottages. Ceiling fans in some rooms, whirlpool bath in 1 bedroom and 1 cottage. $60–$130; full breakfast, afternoon tea. AE, D, MC, V. No smoking, no pets. Closed weekdays Sept.–Apr.*

Other Choices

Carrington House. 4974 Interlochen Dr., Alexandria, MN 56308, tel. 320/846–7400 or 800/806-3899. 4 double rooms with baths, 1 cottage. Air-conditioning, cable TV on porch, ceiling fans in commons area, whirlpool bath in cot-

tage and 1 room. $85–$130, full breakfast. No credit cards. No smoking.

Heartland Trail Inn. Rte. 3 (Box 39), Park Rapids, MN 56470, tel. 218/732–5305. 6 double rooms share 3 baths. Air-conditioning, ceiling fans in some rooms. $45–$60, full breakfast. MC, V. No smoking, no pets.

Log House on Spirit Lake and Homestead. Ottertail Rte. 4 (Box 130), Vergas, MN 56587, tel. 218/342–2318 or 800/342-2318. 5 double rooms with baths. Air-conditioning, terry-cloth robes and fresh flowers, fireplace and whirlpool bath in 3 rooms. $85–$135; full breakfast, welcome tray. D, MC, V. No smoking, no pets.

Nims' Bakketopp Hus. R.R. 2 (Box 187A), Fergus Falls, MN 56537, tel. 218/739–2915 or 800/739-2915. 3 double rooms with baths. Air-conditioning, phones; cable TV available on request, oversize whirlpool bath in 1 room. $65–$95; full breakfast, evening refreshments. D, MC, V. No smoking.

Peace Cliff. HCR 73 (Box 998D), Walker, MN 56484, tel. 218/547–2832. 3 double rooms with baths, 1 single with bath, 1 suite. Cable TV/VCR in common room. $42–$100; full breakfast, evening refreshments. AE, D, MC, V. No smoking, no pets, 2-night minimum summer weekends.

Prairie View Estate. Rte. 2 (Box 443), Pelican Rapids, MN 56572, tel. 218/863–4321 or 800/298-8058. 1 double room with bath, 2 doubles share bath. Air-conditioning, TV in parlor. $50–$65; full breakfast, evening refreshments. D, MC, V. No smoking, no pets.

Stonehouse Bed and Breakfast. HCR 2 (Box 9), Pequot Lakes, MN 56472, tel. 218/568–4255. 1 cottage with double bed and queen-size bed. TV/VCR, kitchen. $80–$125, full breakfast. MC, V. No pets.

Tianna Farms. Box 968, Walker, MN 56484, tel. 218/547–1306. 4 double rooms with baths, 1 suite. Air-conditioning, cable TV in living room and library, swimming dock, tennis. $45–$125, full breakfast. D, MC, V. No smoking.

Walden Woods. 16070 Rte. 18 SE, Deerwood, MN 56444, tel. 612/692–4379. 4 double rooms share 2 baths. $55–$75, full breakfast. AE, MC, V. No smoking, no pets.

Whistle Stop Inn. Rte. 1 (Box 85), New York Mills, MN 56567, tel. 218/385–2223 or 800/328-6315. 2 double rooms with baths, 1 suite, 1 caboose with whirlpool bath. Cable TV in suite and 1 bedroom, ceiling fans in suite, sauna. $39–$69; full breakfast, evening refreshments upon request. AE, D, MC, V. Restricted smoking, no pets.

Southwestern Prairie

Park Row Bed and Breakfast

525 W. Park Row, St. Peter, MN 56082, tel. 507/931–2495

Like many of the older large houses in rural Minnesota, Ann Burckhardt's bed-and-breakfast, a few blocks from St. Peter's Main Street, is two houses fused together. The larger of the two, a Carpenter Gothic, was built in 1874 with wooden gingerbread trim on its porch railings and eaves. In 1903, the house was purchased by a probate court judge, who added what was tantamount to another building, a Queen Anne–style wing with an apron porch and a turreted circular staircase. After the judge's death in the 1930s, his home suffered the fate of many such big houses: It was turned into a duplex. A local professor bought it in 1971, returning it to its eclectic late-Victorian grace.

It's this combination of styles that Ann, who bought the house in 1989, has maintained in her decor. The interior is as eclectic as the exterior, but its Victo-

rian look is homey, not dark and heavy as this style sometimes is. The downstairs is light and spacious. In the dining room, where a huge bay window draws in daylight from three directions, late-Victorian antiques blend with modern reproductions. Small-scale furnishings, bright stained-glass windows, and lace curtains reinforce the sense of sunshine and fresh air.

Each of the four guest rooms is furnished with period antiques and has its own country theme. But Ann is not heavy-handed about it and is simply out to create a *feeling* of England (or France or Germany). There's a Norwegian-style painted floor in the Scandinavian Room. In other rooms, bright colors and fabrics project the same decorative frilliness as the exterior gingerbread. It never gets cutesy, however.

"I want my guests to feel as if they're stepping back into 1910," Burckhardt says. Granted, it's a somewhat modernized 1910—there's wall-to-wall carpeting, done in a Victorian pattern—but the shower you take will be in a clawfoot tub with its original oak rim, and there will be no TV in your bedroom.

Expect an exceptional breakfast. The indefatigable Burckhardt commutes 66 miles to Minneapolis three days a week to work as a food journalist, so food is a passion with her. She gets to try out new, and usually delicious, recipes on her guests. And since she is a writer, reading is another passion: Books and magazines, mostly of local and regional interest, are displayed throughout the house. Pleasures here are quiet ones, but never unrewarding.

🏠 *4 double rooms share 2 baths. Air-conditioning, cable TV in living room. $58–$73, full breakfast. AE, D, MC, V. No smoking, no pets. Closed Jan.*

Sod House on the Prairie

Rte. 2 (Box 75), Sanborn, MN 56083, tel. 507/723–5138

When Stan McCone was growing up, older relatives told him tales of his forebears—sodbusting white settlers of the Great Plains, just like those that Willa Cather and Laura Ingalls Wilder wrote about. Since few trees sprouted on the grasslands, pioneers literally built their houses out of the earth. These sod houses, made of blocks of cut turf, were held together by the dense root systems of the prairie grass.

McCone dreamed of re-creating this lost type of architecture. After working for several years as a cattle buyer, he got a chance to make his dream come true when he learned one of his neighbors in rural Sanborn had a patch of virgin prairie on his land. Soon Stan set to work, with the same kind of grit and sweat as his pioneer ancestors, cutting massive blocks of sod (he describes the sound as "the ripping of a giant canvas"). The result is two buildings set amid acres of (reseeded) prairie grass: a rudimentary "poor man's dugout" and a larger "rich man's soddy," both open to the public as a museum. For those who want a full dose of pioneer experience, the larger is a snug, rustic bed-and-breakfast. Just recently, the McCones renovated an authentic 19th-century log cabin, which guests delight in touring.

The house's furnishings—antique bedsteads and buffets, kitchen and farm implements hanging on the walls and beams—are practical and sturdily beautiful. The only piece that could be considered at all fancy is the leather fainting couch that doubles as a bed, across which is spread a heavy, shaggy buffalo-hide blanket.

Authenticity is the key word here. There are no wires or pipes running through the soddy's turf walls—heating comes from a potbellied stove, air-conditioning from open windows, light from oil lamps. The bathroom is a two-seat outhouse steps away; to wash, guests must pour water from a jug into the 100-year-old pitcher and bowl.

Virginia and Stan McCone provide a simple, hearty country breakfast incorporating high-quality meats, which is Stan's other line of business. If you want to cook your other meals, throw some logs into the mighty Monarch stove. One family spent a prairie Christmas here, cooking up a feast on the Monarch, with the soddy so snug the kids padded about in shorts. Though few of us today would want to live day to day with the rigors of pioneer life, we can still savor a sample of it, thanks to the McCones. Needless to say, Laura Ingalls Wilder fans welcome!

▥ *1 house with 2 double beds and outhouse. Wood-burning stove. $75–$125, full breakfast. No credit cards.*

Other Choices

Fering's Guest House. 708 N. Main St., Blue Earth, MN 56013, tel. 507/526–5054. 1 double room with bath, 2 doubles share bath. Air-conditioning, cable TV in rooms. $36–$45, Continental breakfast. No credit cards. No smoking, no pets.

Prairie House on Round Lake. R.R. 1 (Box 105), Round Lake, MN 56167, tel. 507/945–8934. 1 double room with bath, 1 double with half-bath, 2 doubles share bath. Air-conditioning, lakeside beach, tennis court. $55, full breakfast. No credit cards. No smoking.

Mississippi

Dunleith

North Mississippi Hill Country

Caragen House

1108 Hwy. 82 W, Starkville, MS 39759, tel. 601/323-0340

Though this most unusual steamboat Gothic–style Victorian house was built in 1890 in downtown Starkville, it got a new lease on life in 1981 when it was cut in half and moved in two parts to its present site on 22 acres, still in the city limits. The Caragen House is as grand today as it must have been in the 1890s; it resembles a steamboat, with its oval-shape wraparound porches on the first and second story and spindle railings helping to create the illusion. Either porch offers a an excellent view of the adjoining fields and woods.

Owner Kay Shurden—a caterer who stays busy with weddings and other special events—says that "Caragen" means "beloved spirit" in Italian. The Caragen House is a popular place for parents of nearby Mississippi State University students; since Southeastern Conference sports draw thousands of fans, call early for reservations during peak football season.

For furnishings, Shurden chose to stay within the period of the home's construction. She found very good reproductions and selected nice fabric and paint that enhanced the original floors, windows, and ornate Italian mantels.

Each room has an entertainment center cleverly tucked away in a massive piece of furniture, and a wet bar is also hidden from view. Rooms are named according to color: the Yellow Room, for instance, is light and airy, with wickerlike furniture and a daybed for children. Each room has special elements of the period, such as leaded beveled glass. Bathrooms are new and modern, though Shurden had to do some creative planning to add two bathrooms upstairs without altering the basic design of the house.

Guests tend to gather in the breakfast area, which was originally a screened porch. Adjoining it is a big back porch complete with a swing, fans, ferns, and view. Hearty breakfasts feature homemade breads and sweets.

🏨 *5 double rooms with baths. Air-conditioning, cable TV, wet bar, full-service catering available. $85–$100, Continental breakfast. MC, V. No smoking.*

Highland House

810 Highland Circle, Columbus, MS 39701, tel. and fax 601/327-5577

Once known by locals as the Lindamood House, this imposing Greek Revival mansion has dominated Highland Circle in Columbus since the early 1900s, when it was rebuilt after a disgruntled housekeeper purportedly set fire to the original 1862 wood structure. Now Jim Holzhauer, a physician, and his wife, Celeta, are the proud owners-innkeepers of this 9,000-square-foot showplace B&B. The house boasts a widow's walk, 78 windows, 13 working fireplaces, 14-foot ceilings, two parlors, and three dens.

Downstairs to the left, two parlors are separated by faux marble columns. To the right are two festively decorated dining rooms, with a huge brick fireplace directly ahead. The fireplace is a replica of a brick kiln once used by brick maker Mr. Lindamood. Above it all is a hand-painted ceiling that took two years to complete. Jim's chess-set collection is displayed throughout the house.

One guest room is downstairs, near the wide staircase behind the fireplace that winds up to the second story, where three more guest rooms await. Antiques and Asian pieces are used in the colorful guest rooms, giving them an eclectic but interesting feel. Even amid the architectural excellence and expensive furnishings, the Highland House is quite comfortable, and guests are made to feel as though they've "come home." Upon arrival, Celeta offers a wonderful minted lemonade and a tour of the house. She's from a small town in Alabama and is a soft-spoken southern belle who gives guests her undivided attention.

Other amenities include a pool, a hot tub, and a video library of 3,000 movies, plus mint juleps on the veranda, Bailey's and coffee in the evening, and a breakfast extravaganza prepared by the resident chef. Among the menu items are orange-poached pears with white chocolate and raspberries, baked apples, homemade breads, jams, and casseroles.

🏠 *4 double rooms with baths. Fireplace, phone, TV/VCR in rooms; pool, exercise room, tanning bed. $100-$160; full breakfast, champagne brunch on Sun. MC, V. Restricted smoking, no pets.*

Mockingbird Inn

305 N. Gloster St., Tupelo, MS 38801, tel. 601/841-0286, fax 601/840-4158

Jim and Sandy Gilmer decided to leave the corporate world and strike out on their own. So in addition to starting a recycling business, they found a spacious old two-story home on a shady street corner and transformed it into a B&B. In researching the home's history, the Gilmers found that the original builders from 1925 loved to entertain and, interestingly enough, had theme parties relating to various countries. The globe-trekking Gilmers named their B&B the Mockingbird Inn, after the state bird—a symbol of hospitality. It's only fitting that a mockingbird appears at the porch windows periodically.

It's also only fitting that people who have seven favorite places in the world and seven rooms to decorate should recreate those places in the decor of the rooms and the bathrooms. You can almost hear gondolas gliding across a canal in the Venice Room, where rich Venetian tapestry and old lace make it more authentic. The Mackinac Island Room resembles a wonderful white-washed lakeside cottage, light and airy, with pickled wood. A pewter wedding canopy bed and chaise longue are two of many elements that leave no doubt as to the inspiration for the Paris Room. Greek columns are perfectly at home in the large Athens Room; a plus is the L-shape whirlpool for two. Even Isak Dinesen would feel at home in the

Africa Room, where faux jungle-animal skins and mosquito netting around the bed set the scene. Pastels and seashells make the Sanibel Island Room as authentic as possible; add the verdigris iron bed and wicker furniture, and it's Florida revisited. Finally, in the Bavaria Room, lots of knotty pine, a sleigh bed, antique skis, and typical lace-trimmed windows bring southern Germany to northern Mississippi.

Guests linger on the indoor porch, with its wicker furniture and coffee and tea makings. The inn is popular with businesspeople who attend one of the two Tupelo furniture markets and with tourists of the rock-and-roll persuasion, who like to look across at the school where Elvis Presley attended sixth and seventh grades.

▥ *7 double rooms with baths. Air-conditioning, cable TVs, phones; fireplace in 1 room, Jacuzzi in 1 room. $65–$125; full breakfast, afternoon refreshments. D, MC, V. No smoking, no children under 13.*

Spahn House

401 College St., Senatobia, MS 38668, tel. 601/562–9853 or 800/400–9853

Senatobia, just 30 minutes south of big, bustling Memphis, is a pretty-as-a-picture-book small town, the home of what's quickly becoming one of the state's most popular B&Bs: the Spahn House. Owners are Joe and Daughn Spahn. He's a building contractor, and she's a former partner in a brokerage firm who came "back home" to the Magnolia State via Chicago, New York City, and Miami after she met and married Joe. Their 15-room southern mansion, built in 1904, is on a tree-canopied street in a quiet, historic neighborhood.

The grand old house was a true Victorian until its renovation in 1948, which left it bearing a slight resemblance to the Greek Revival style. When the Spahns bought the house in 1994, they began a careful re-renovation into a

B&B. The parlor's recessed arches give the first inkling that this is no ordinary house. High ceilings, original pine floors, and rich woods add to the turn-of-the-century ambience. Throughout the house, window treatment may be lace left over from a wedding or vines carefully crafted as valances. A wide staircase leads to the second-story common area, which connects to all the guest rooms. Antiques were purchased in Memphis and New Orleans and "all in between," according to Daughn. Each room has a different theme, including the Gentlemen's Room, where antique clothing and hats are casually displayed. Quaint old chests have been converted to vanities; this utilitarian use of odd pieces of furniture adds to this B&B's appeal.

Daughn is now a caterer with a staff of 12, and guests can arrange a private gourmet dinner. Breakfasts are elegant: Expect a soufflé that may be filled with ham and cheese, strawberries and whipped cream, or perhaps one with a pumpkin center folded into an omelet, fresh fruits, and an assortment of other gourmet offerings, all served with the panache of a businesswoman turned master chef.

▥ *4 double rooms with bath. Jacuzzi in 2 baths, TV in common area. Private candlelight dinner available with advance reservation. $75–$110, full breakfast. MC, V. No smoking, no pets.*

Other Choices

Alexander House. Anderson and Green Sts. (Box 187), West, MS 39192, tel. 601/967–2266 or 800/350–8034. 3 double rooms with baths, 2 doubles share 1 bath. TV in two rooms and upstairs common area. Full dinner available with advance reservations. $65, full breakfast. D, MC, V. No smoking.

Amzi Love House. 305 7th St. S, Columbus, MS 39701, tel. 601/328–5413. 3 double rooms with baths, 1 suite. Air-conditioning, robes, phones. $85–$100; full breakfast, welcoming refreshments. MC, V. Restricted smoking, no pets.

Backstrom B&B. 4567 Hwy. 182 E (Box 2311), Columbus, MS 39704, tel. 601/328–0222 or 800/698–3983. 1 double room with private bath, 2 doubles share 1 bath. Air-conditioning, TV/VCRs, phones. $55–$65, full breakfast. MC, V. No smoking, no pets.

Carpenter Place. 1280 Rte. 25 S, Starkville, MS 39759, tel. 601/323–4669. 2 double rooms with baths in main house, 1 suite in carriage house. Air-conditioning, TV in suite and kitchen, phone in suite. $65–$150, full plantation breakfast. MC, V. No smoking, no pets.

Cartney Hunt House. 408 7th St. S, Columbus, MS 39703, tel. 601/329–3856. 3 double rooms with baths. Air-conditioning, TVs, phones. $85, full breakfast. AE, MC, V. No smoking, no pets.

Liberty Hall. Armstrong Rd., Columbus, MS 39701, tel. 601/328–4110. 3 double rooms with baths. Air-conditioning; pool, walking trails. $85, full breakfast. MC, V. No smoking, no pets.

Puddin Place. 1008 University Ave., Oxford, MS 38655, tel. 601/234–1250. 2 suites. Air-conditioning, cable TVs. $85–$125, full breakfast. No credit cards. Restricted smoking, no pets.

Sassafras Inn. 785 Hwy. 51 (Box 612), Hernando, MS 38632, tel. 601/429–5864 or 800/882–1897, fax 601/429-4591. 3 double rooms with baths, 1 cottage-suite with microwave and mini-refrigerator, TVs, phones; indoor pool and hot tub. $80–$175, full breakfast. AE, D, MC. No smoking, no pets.

Near the Natchez Trace and the Mississippi Delta

Balfour House

1002 Crawford St. (Box 781), Vicksburg, MS 39181, tel. 601/638–7113 or 800/294–7113

Civil War historians will surely be familiar with the Balfour House (circa 1835), for it was the home of diarist Emma Balfour, who kept a daily account of the Siege of Vicksburg in 1863. The diary is now part of the Emma Balfour Collection of the Mississippi Department of Archives and History. After the fall of Vicksburg, the Union army used the house, an outstanding example of the Greek Revival, as their local headquarters.

The Balfour House was the scene of a festive Christmas dance in 1862, where Confederate officers and their ladies had come for a bit of R&R. The dance, however, was interrupted when a Confederate courier rushed into the ballroom to announce that Yankee gunboats had been sighted on the nearby Mississippi River. The festivities quickly ended, as the men dashed out the door to defend the Confederacy. Each year, the Reenactment of the 1862 Christmas Ball at the Balfour House is a much-anticipated event in Vicksburg.

Bob and Sharon Humble are relatively new owners of the house. It was meticulously restored in the early 1980s by previous owners and won the 1984 Award of Merit from the Mississippi State Historical Society. (The house is also listed on the National Register of Historic Places, is featured at the Smithsonian, and is a designated Mississippi Landmark.)

Period purists will be pleased to know that the Balfour House remains as authentic and "of the period" as possible. The graceful, elegant redbrick structure, with bold white trim, has a rare, three-story elliptical spiral staircase. In the four guest suites, the antique—predominantly Empire—furnishings reflect the age and style of the house. One room contains a massive 7-by 8-foot canopied "family bed." Guestroom colors range from dark green to mauve and pale green to pale pink, each with matching color schemes in the adjoining bath.

Breakfast menus vary, but guests can expect fare such as quiche Lorraine and fruit or an egg-and-cheese casserole with fruit and bread.

🛏 *4 suites in main house. Air-conditioning, TVs, phones. $85–$150, full breakfast. AE, D, MC, V. No smoking, no pets.*

Canemount Plantation

Rte. 552 W (Rte. 2, Box 45), Lorman, MS 39096, tel. 601/877-3784 or 800/423-0684

This 6,000-acre working plantation near Port Gibson, just off the Natchez Trace, is nestled quietly among vast forests and fields, flowing streams, and hills, welcoming guests to an idyllic escape. Canemount was built in 1855 in the Italianate revival style. The house is almost unchanged, except that the butler's pantry has been converted to a small kitchen for the owners, Ray John and Rachel Forrest and their son John.

Canemount, in all its Spanish moss–draped glory, is a haven for wildlife. The Forrests, formerly of Morganza, Louisiana, purchased it in 1981 as a hunting retreat, but according to Rachel, they "fell in love with the place and decided to stay permanently." White-tailed deer are so plentiful that Canemount was selected for a Mississippi State University study of their life span. Meandering paths and trails offer opportunities to see deer, Russian boar, and wild turkey. Certain areas are designated for wildlife photography,

and a guided Jeep wildlife safari is offered every afternoon.

Guests are invited to have dinner with the Forrests at no extra charge and to tour the antiques-filled main house. Accommodations are in nearby, private, restored antebellum structures: Rick's Cottage, with brick walls, original wood floors, and a tester bed; the Grey Cottage, which has a Jacuzzi; and the Pond House, with a whirlpool tub. Each cottage is furnished with antiques and contemporary pieces and is wonderfully quiet except for the sounds of birds and an occasional deer.

The plantation acreage includes the historic Windsor Plantation, where the haunting ruins—23 towering Greek columns—still stand, though the massive house was destroyed by fire in 1890. The Persnickety Pig dining area, also on the plantation, is in a converted dairy. It's where festive Cajun pig roasts are held, as well as catered parties and group dinners, by reservation.

🛏 *3 cottage suites. Air-conditioning, TV in rooms and common area; heated pool, ponds. $145–$165; full breakfast, dinner. MC, V. No smoking, no pets.*

Cedar Grove

Rte. 2, Box 298, Church Hill, MS 39120, tel. 601/445-2203, fax 601/445-2372

The imposing Cedar Grove gets lots of attention among B&B aficionados, perhaps because of its history, certainly because of its bold color schemes and lush furnishings. Built in 1840, the massive mansion has an eclectic architectural pedigree, though it is predominantly Greek Revival. There's still a Union cannonball lodged in a parlor wall from when Vicksburg was under siege during the Civil War. Federal troops later used it as a hospital. Cedar Grove is also a National Historic Landmark and on the National Register of Historic Places. Amazingly, after all this time, the original heavy furniture made for the house remains in the master bedroom and the children's rooms, along with a few pieces attributed to Prudent Mallard, a prominent New Orleans furniture maker of the day.

The house sits on 4 acres, with contoured lawns, fountains, pool, croquet, gazebos, and a playable, smaller-than-average "Victorian-style" tennis court on the back grounds. Tennis rackets and balls and croquet mallets are available at the front desk. The Mississippi River is just across the street, and sometimes the sound of riverboat calliopes can be heard in the distance.

The main house boasts an array of wall colors, including gold, red, violet, deep yellow, and, in some rooms, festive combinations of two colors. The woodwork and molding in the ballrooom and parlor is ornate and elaborate, with heavy window treatments. The guest rooms in the main house are colorful and spacious, with gaslit chandeliers, pier mirrors, Italian marble mantels, and other elements of the house's earlier eras.

Breakfast is served inside the mansion, at the restaurant, which overlooks the garden. The plantation breakfast consists of eggs, sausage, grits, fruit, and breads. The restaurant at Cedar Grove opens at 6 PM for dinner; walk-ins are welcome.

▦ *15 double rooms with baths in main house and dependencies, 12 suites, 4 cottages. Restaurant, air-conditioning, TVs, phones; pool, croquet, Victorian-style tennis court, gift shop. $85–$165, full breakfast. AE, D, MC, V. Restricted smoking, no pets.*

Cedars Plantation

2200 Oak St. (Box B), Vicksburg, MS 39180, tel. 601/636–1000 or 800/862–1300

The Cedars Plantation was built as a one-story planter's cottage around 1830, with four big rooms surrounded by porches. In the 1850s, the elegant Greek Revival portion was added, blending amazingly well with the original struc-

ture. Now the stately, columned, two-and-a-half-story house sits atop a slight incline, surrounded by a seemingly endless white picket fence, mirrorlike ponds, old oak trees laden with lazy Spanish moss, and colorful flowers of the season.

Once a working plantation, the Cedars adorns the lush green rolling hills about 20 miles north of Natchez, just off the scenic Natchez Trace Parkway on Route 553 and within walking distance of the historic Christ Episcopal Church, thought to be the oldest Episcopal parish in the Southwest.

Prominent Natchezians have owned the Cedars, as well as Hollywood actor George Hamilton (at which time it was featured in *Architectural Digest*). It is now owned by Glenda and Dick Robinson of Chicago, who have restored the Cedars to its former grandeur. A resident staff manages this National Register property.

A parlor is situated to the right of the foyer, a formal dining room to the left. Look upward from the center of the foyer, and see the staircase spiraling up to the third floor. Fine period antiques, some imported from Europe and some southern, decorate each room. The airy house is painted in lights pastels; it has numerous tall jib windows that also serve as doors. Some of the original decorative painting is still intact, as are plaster cornices, center medallions, and ornate moldings. Guest rooms are spacious and "of-the-period" perfect.

The pale yellow suite on the third floor was once an attic and is now a treetop perch from which to view the grounds through Palladian arched windows. The suite also has a working fireplace, wet bar, and a Jacuzzi by the windows.

Special big, fluffy biscuits complement the ham, eggs, grits, fruit, or casserole. Breakfast can be served in the breakfast room, the formal dining room, or weather permitting, on a porch for an outstanding view of the gently rolling hills and lovely trees.

🏨 *3 double rooms with baths, 1 3-room suite. Mini-refrigerator, ice-maker, robes, TVs, phones. $135–$175; full plantation breakfast, complimentary beverage. MC, V. No smoking, no pets, no children under 12.*

Dunleith

84 Homochitto St., Natchez, MS 39120, tel. 601/446–8500 or 800/433–2445

Dunleith is one of the South's most beautiful houses, from the colonnaded galleries that encircle it to the superior antiques within and the 40 acres of landscaped grounds, wooded bayous, and green pastures without. It is constantly photographed, often written about, and occasionally appears in films. Dunleith is also a National Historic Landmark on the National Register of Historic Places.

The palatial mansion (circa 1856) is owned by William Heins III of Natchez. A resident manager and staff run the business of daily tours and lodging, and it is, quite noticeably, a business. Fortunately, the magnificence of Dunleith's architecture and interiors neutralizes the regimented recitations of the staff and the grandeur of the place prevails.

Among the elegant furnishings are the dining room's French Zuber wallpaper, printed from woodblocks circa 1855 that were hidden in a cave in France during World War I. The V'Soske carpet in the front parlor determined the color scheme for the room's walls, draperies, and upholstery; the greenish-gold walls and draperies perfectly complement the peachy pinks and gold tones in the carpet. A Louis XV ormolu-mounted mahogany Linke table is in a prominent place in the front parlor.

Three of the guest rooms at Dunleith are in the main house, and eight are in the former servants' wing, built in 1856. The rooms are quiet and private and are well decorated in mid-19th-century style, with a mixture of reproduc-

tions and antiques. A Victorian color scheme with peaches, blues, and pastels is used throughout. Each guest room has a working fireplace, original from the era of construction.

Another nice feature: The grounds are subtly lighted at night so that guests can stroll in the "moonlight" or enjoy the romantic views from wicker rockers on the galleries.

Old brick and warm woods set the stage for the big plantation breakfast served in the restored poultry house. Exposed beams, lots of windows, and wooden floors add a homey touch that guests may have pined for in the elaborate, museumlike main house.

🏨 *11 double rooms with baths. Air-conditioning, TVs; phones in 8 rooms. $85–$130, full breakfast. AE, D, MC, V. Restricted smoking, no pets, no children under 18.*

Fairview

734 Fairview St., Jackson, MS 39202, tel. 601/948–3429

The Colonial-revival Fairview, built in 1908, was designed by the architectural firm of Spencer & Powers of Chicago for local lumber baron Cyrus G. Warren. It occupies an enviable tract of land in Jackson's Belhaven historic district, not too far from downtown, yet far removed from the hustle and bustle. Innkeeper–owners Carol and William Simmons have been B&B proprietors since 1993, though the house has been in William's family since 1930.

The three-story facade sets the scene for what's inside, such as the oak-paneled library, with its ornate molding, leather sofa and chairs, and extensive Civil War book collection. When they decided to transform their private residence into a public house, the Simmonses adapted and redecorated family bedrooms into guest rooms, converted a parking area to a versatile ballroom, and found a use for every nook and cranny. The result is a well-planned, elegantly decorated, beautifully furnished showplace. The French furniture looks particularly elegant paired with polished marble floors and mantels, as in the foyer.

The suites and guest rooms feature deep, rich reds or soft, gentle golds and cream pastels, and outstanding fabric choices for beds and window treatment. Antiques and reproductions are used in conjunction with contemporary pieces. All the beds are either king or queen, some rooms have Jacuzzis, and the third-floor suite features two queen beds and a Jacuzzi.

The Simmonses keep the sprawling house filled with B&B guests, weddings, and business meetings, which also keep their full-time chef and catering staff busy. Guests rave about the French toast served with dressed-up grits, bacon, fresh fruit, and the special blend of Louisiana's own Community coffee. Dinner, available with advance reservations, is generally a pasta with beef, seafood or veal, salad, seasonal vegetable, and luscious dessert.

▥ *3 double rooms with baths, 2 doubles with Jacuzzis, 5 suites. Dinner with advance arrangements; air-conditioning, TVs, phones. $80–$150, full breakfast. AE, D, MC, V. No smoking, no pets.*

Glen Auburn

300 S. Commerce St., Natchez, MS 39120, tel. 601/442-4099 or 800/833-0170

In a town that's world-renowned for its antebellum mansions, the Victorian Glen Auburn is hard to miss. The house, built in 1875, is a rare example of French Second Empire architecture. It has included among its owners the actor George Hamilton. In 1988 Carolyn and Richard Boyer "retired" to Natchez from Baton Rouge, Louisiana, where he was a physician, and bought the house.

They have since fully restored it. The result is an almost perfect example of Victorian elegance, from the Eastlake chandeliers, outstanding millwork, ornamental plaster, and elaborately stenciled ceiling to the original floors. The exterior color is now a shade lighter than eggplant, with creamy white trim.

There's a special quality to the house, which one begins to notice with the sweet scent of roses on the veranda. Drinks are served at the main house each afternoon after check-in; weather permitting, the veranda or the area by the pool is a lovely place to enjoy the refreshments. Perhaps it's sanctioned by higher powers, for it is close to three houses of worship—Trinity Episcopal, St. Mary's Catholic, and the Jewish Synagogue.

Glen Auburn's interior is elegant, its accommodations deluxe. All antiques have been carefully selected and are appropriate to the age and style of the house. In the main house, the luxurious Josephine suite is on the first floor, complete with Gothic king-size bed and grand marble bath with double Jacuzzi and separate shower. There are four other suites in the house and three bedrooms in the Garden House, all tastefully done but not stiff and formal. Ralph Lauren wallpaper sets the scene for the color scheme, which includes romantic rose, aubergine, and soft moss. Fine art and fresh flowers lend a gracious sparkle to each room.

Breakfast is always an occasion. Banana-stuffed French toast and egg casserole with mushrooms, peppers, and ham are two customary offerings, augmented by an assortment of fresh fruit and breads and pear or peach preserves made from trees on the lawn. If you're looking for Victorian splendor rather than ersatz frills, this is the place.

▥ *3 double rooms with baths, Jacuzzi, and shower, 5 suites. Air-conditioning, gas fireplaces in suites, wet bar in common area in main house, TV/VCR in suites and 2 rooms, phones,* *terry-cloth robes, hair dryers; pool, off-street parking at 307 S. Pearl St (behind the house). $110–$175, full breakfast. No smoking, no pets, no children under 12. AE, MC, V.*

Millsaps Buie House

628 N. State St., Jackson, MS 39202, tel. 601/352–0221 or 800/784–0221, fax 601/ 352–0221

The Millsaps Buie House's location on the busiest street in Jackson, Mississippi, sets it apart from the Magnolia State's many plantation-like bed-and-breakfast inns. An elegant Victorian mansion, built in 1888 in the heart of downtown, it is grand, historic, and filled with antiques. Everything about the house says "quality," from exterior construction to interior details like the hand-molded plaster frieze work, bay windows, and other elements representative of the Queen Anne style.

Once the home of Major Reuben Webster Millsaps of the Confederate army—as well as a banker, financier, and founder in 1892 of the distinguished Millsaps College—the house has been in the same family for five generations. It has been a B&B since 1987 and is described as "a 19th-century urban retreat for the 20th-century traveler." One might add "business traveler," for although the house contains priceless heirlooms, each room has a telephone with computer data-port and a small, unobtrusive bedside radio, and TVs are concealed in old armoires. For health-conscious guests, a fitness center is nearby.

Guests are encouraged to relax in the drawing room, parlor, or library before retiring to their room for the evening. Pier mirrors in the parlor reflect the grand piano, and the house as a whole reflects the style and taste of the distinguished interior designer, Berle Smith, who also refurbished the Governor's Mansion, the New State Capitol, and Florewood Plantation in Greenwood.

Bedrooms are furnished in a pleasing mixture of period antiques and reproductions, including canopy beds, rosewood chairs, and marble-top tables. Original mantelpieces add detail and interest, while old family portraits add authenticity. The rich, pleated draperies in one of the rooms are a soft-green fabric and match the carpet and the dominant color in the flowered wallpaper.

A hearty southern breakfast is served, with specialties such as homemade banana bread, cheese grits, bran muffins, and hot biscuits. Whether serving or giving directions to Jackson attractions, the staff members are at all times hospitable.

▦ *11 double rooms with baths. Air-conditioning, cable TV and phone with data-port in rooms. $85–$155, $15 for second person; full breakfast. AE, D, DC, MC, V. Restricted smoking, no pets, no children under 12.*

Monmouth

36 Melrose Ave., Natchez, MS 39120, tel. 601/442–5852 or 800/828–4531

The massive Monmouth (circa 1818) is not only one of Mississippi's best-known B&Bs, it's also the state's unofficial Hollywood connection. Monmouth appears to be the choice of the movie industry, according to reports from members of the Hollywood press corps who often accompany filmmakers to this most photogenic part of the sunny South. Actors and crew stayed here while in Natchez filming John Grisham's *A Time to Kill.*

Owners Ron and Lani Riches live in Los Angeles but stay at Monmouth as much as possible. The Richeses (he's a land developer) bought Monmouth about 20 years ago and have worked hard at restoring the grand old house. Monmouth's Greek Revival portico was added in 1853, at which time the original brick was covered with eggshell stucco and scored. The grounds, all 26 acres, are immaculate, and there's always something in bloom.

The interior mood is formal, with the blue-silk-covered Rococo-revival furniture in the double parlor made even prettier by the glow of a Waterford crystal chandelier. The windows are done with fanciful swags, valances, fringes, and lace.

The bedrooms in the main house are a decorator's dream. The peach bedroom, a favorite, features peach walls and fabrics made into magnificent draperies on the windows and the canopy bed. Other grand accommodations include the four garden cottages, the carriage house, the former servants' quarters, and the six new Plantation Suites. The suites have fireplaces, Jacuzzis, and period furnishings. The Quitman Retreat, a new house on the property, is richly decorated in blues and creams and is the most exquisite of all. There's also a conference center to accommodate up to 120 for meetings. Those suites farthest away from the main house are the most elaborate in style.

Monmouth is the only property in Mississippi that's listed in the the National Trust's Historic Hotels of America, and it is a National Historic Landmark.

Upon arrival, guests are greeted with delicious pralines and beverages, followed later by the cocktail hour, when fresh mint juleps and complimentary hors d'oeuvres are served. In the morning, the full southern breakfast takes on a special elegance: It's served on fine china in a formal setting.

🏨 *6 double rooms with baths and 1 suite in main house, 11 doubles with baths and 7 suites in outbuildings. Restaurant (dinner only, 1 seating nightly), air-conditioning, TV and phone in rooms, robes and luxury bath products in rooms; croquet course. $115–$220; full breakfast, hors d'oeuvres during cocktail hour. AE, D, MC, V. No smoking, no pets, children over 14 welcome.*

Mount Holly

Box 140, Chatham, MS 38731, tel. 601/ 827-2652

The address for this Italianate mansion is Chatham, a very small town near the Mississippi River where there are a couple of stores and a tiny post office, but it is pure Mississippi Delta, about 20 miles south of Greenville. It's situated on the beautiful Lake Washington—an oxbow lake of the Mississippi River—and near the Great River Road, which runs along the mighty Mississippi. Built in 1856, this grand plantation house, with all the trappings of Old South money, overlooks the lake and its moss-adorned cypress trees.

The 30-room Mount Holly, built circa 1856, was the center of social life for prominent Delta planters, and in the 1880s, it came into the possession of the great-grandfather of Civil War historian and writer Shelby Foote. The Foote family, though no longer in residence, still congregates at Mount Holly for reunions.

When Ann and T. C. Wood (she's an interior designer, he an educator) bought Mount Holly in 1979, they knew that restoring the house would be a challenge, for it had enjoyed little TLC as a rental property. They continue to meet the challenge with unobtrusive but ongoing projects.

The house was built of handmade red brick, measuring 24 inches thick on the exterior walls, 18 inches thick on the inside. Though not documented, it is believed that the noted architect Samuel Sloane designed the house. The foyer has two oval niches on each side of the entrance; throughout the house arched windows look out onto the grounds. Notable antiques, including pieces from southern cabinetmakers, among them Prudent Mallard of New Orleans, are at Mount Holly.

Mount Holly's ornamental plaster is a work of art, from the four-tiered moldings to the decorative medallions in the center of the 14-foot ceilings. Rich earth colors accent the furnishings and style of the home. The former ballroom upstairs, now a common room for guests, is painted cinnamon. The arched jib windows open onto a balcony that overlooks the lake to the front and cotton fields to one side. Every room at Mount Holly offers a lake view. Guest rooms feature high ceilings, antique furnishings, and a sense of what it must have been like on this plantation in the late 1850s.

Because of its prime location in "hunt country," Mount Holly attracts serious duck hunters in December and January, all of whom relish the hot and ample southern breakfast served before the hunt.

🖼 *6 double rooms with baths, 2 doubles share 1 bath. Air-conditioning; private pier. $75–$150, full breakfast. D, MC, V. No smoking, no pets.*

Other Choices

Anchuca. 1010 First East St., Vicksburg, MS 39180, tel. 601/631–6800 or 800/469–2597. 6 double rooms with baths, 1 suite. Air-conditioning, TVs, phones; Jacuzzi in some rooms, microwave, mini-refrigerator in guest cottages; pool. $85–$190, full breakfast. AE, D, MC, V. Restricted smoking.

Annabelle. 501 Speed St., Vicksburg, MS 39180, tel. 601/638–2000 or 800/791–2000, fax 601/636–5054. 6 double rooms with baths, 1 suite. Air-conditioning, phones, cable TVs; pool. $80–$125, full breakfast. AE, D, DC, MC, V. No smoking, no large pets.

Burn. 712 N. Union St., Natchez, MS 39120, tel. 601/442–1344 or 800/654–8859. 2 double rooms with baths in main house, 1 suite, 4 doubles with baths in dependency. Air-conditioning, TVs; pool. $95–$130, full breakfast. AE, MC, V. No smoking, no pets.

Corners. 601 Klein St., Vicksburg, MS 39180, tel. 601/636–7421 or 800/444–7421, fax 601/636–7232. 14 double rooms

with baths, 1 suite, 1 2-bedroom cottage. Air-conditioning, TVs, phones; Jacuzzis in 8 rooms. $85–$120, full breakfast. AE, MC, V. Restricted smoking.

French Camp Bed and Breakfast Inn. 1 Bluebird La., French Camp, MS 39745, tel. 601/547–6835 (recorder). 5 double rooms with baths. Air-conditioning. $60, full breakfast. MC, V. No smoking.

Governor Holmes House. 207 S. Wall St., Natchez, MS 39120, tel. 601/442–2366, fax 601/442–0166. 4 suites. Air-conditioning, TVs. $85–$115, full breakfast. AE, D, MC, V. No pets, no children under 12.

Guest House Historic Inn. 201 N. Pearl St., Natchez, MS 39120, tel. 601/442–1054, fax 601/442–1374. 16 double rooms with baths. Air-conditioning, cable TVs, phones, small refrigerators, coffeemakers. $95, Continental breakfast. AE, D, DC, MC, V.

Linden. 1 Linden Pl., Natchez, MS 39120, tel. 601/445–5472 or 800/647–6742. 7 double rooms with baths. Air-conditioning. $85–$100, full breakfast. No pets, no children under 10.

Lucas Hill. 500 N. Huntington St., Kosciusko, MS 39090, tel. 601/289–7860. 2 double rooms with baths. Air-conditioning, fireplace in 1 room. $65–$95, gourmet Continental breakfast. AE, D, MC, V. No smoking, no pets, no children under 12.

No Mistake Plantation. 5602 Hwy. 3, Satartia, MS 39162, tel. 601/746–6579 or 888/283–1390. 4 double rooms with baths in main house, 1 cabin. Air-conditioning. $140–$160, full breakfast. AE, MC, V. No smoking, no pets.

Oak Square. 1207 Church St., Port Gibson, MS 39150, tel. 601/437–4350 or 800/729–0240. 10 double rooms with baths. Air-conditioning, TVs, phones. $75–$95, full breakfast. AE, D, MC, V. No smoking, no pets.

Ravenna. 8 Ravenna La., Natchez, MS 39121, tel. 601/445–8516 or 800/647–

6742. 2 double rooms with baths, 1 cottage. Air-conditioning, TV and fireplace in cottage; pool. $85–$100, full breakfast. AE, MC, V. Restricted smoking, no pets.

Redbud Inn. 121 N. Wells St., Kosciusko, MS 39090, tel. 601/289–5086 or 800/379–5086, fax 601/289–5086. 4 double rooms with baths. Restaurant, air-conditioning, TVs, phones. $75–$100, full breakfast. MC, V. Restricted smoking, no pets.

Wensel House. 206 Washington St., Natchez, MS 39120, tel. 601/445–8577, fax 601/442–2525. 3 double rooms with baths. Phones, TV/VCRs. $75, $15 additional for third person; full breakfast. No smoking, no pets.

Weymouth Hall. 1 Cemetery Rd. (Box 1091), Natchez, MS 39121, tel. 601/445–2304. 5 double rooms with baths. Air-conditioning. $85; full breakfast, welcoming beverage. MC, V. No smoking, no pets, arrive by 5.

Reservations Services

Lincoln, Ltd. Bed & Breakfast Mississippi Reservation Service (Box 3479, Meridian, MS 39303, tel. 601/482–5483 or 800/633–6477). **Natchez Pilgrimage Tours Bed & Breakfast Reservations** (Box 347, Natchez, MS 39121, tel. 601/446–6631 or 800/647–6742).

Mississippi Gulf Coast Region

Bay Town Inn. 208 N. Beach Blvd., Bay St. Louis, MS 39520, tel. 601/466–5870 or 800/467–8466. 7 double rooms with baths. Air-conditioning. $75–$85, full breakfast. AE, MC, V. No children under 14, no pets, no smoking.

Father Ryan House. 1196 Beach Blvd., Biloxi, MS 39530, tel. 601/435–1189 or 800/295–1189, fax 601/436–3063. 11 rooms with baths, some whirlpools, 3 suites. TVs, phones, robes; laundry facilities, gift shop; pool. $85–$130, full breakfast or Continental breakfast for early-risers. AE, MC, V. No smoking, no pets.

Inn at the Pass. 125 E. Scenic Dr., Pass Christian, MS 39571, tel. 601/452–0333 or 800/217–2588. 4 double rooms with baths, 1 cottage. Air-conditioning, TVs, phones. $55–$125, full breakfast. AE, D, MC, V, personal checks. No smoking.

Tally House. 402 Rebecca Ave., Hattiesburg, MS 39401, tel. 601/582–3467. 4 double rooms with baths. Air-conditioning. $50–$75; full breakfast, welcoming beverage. MC, V. No smoking, no pets.

Reservations Service

Lincoln, Ltd. Bed & Breakfast Service (Box 3479, Meridian, MS 39303, tel. 601/482–5483 or 800/633–6477).

Missouri

Branson Hotel

Branson

Branson Hotel

*214 W. Main St., Branson, MO 65616,
tel. 417/335–6104*

Teri Murguia and husband, Jim, renovated the 1903 hotel in 1991, with help
from Teri's mother, Opal Kelly, who
runs the nearby Branson House Bed
and Breakfast. The whole family is into
providing peaceful getaways from the
cookie-cutter hotels and motels of this
music boomtown. From the white-
painted antique wicker rockers and
Adirondack chairs on the shady front
porch to the glass-walled dining room
overlooking the yard's perennials and
birdbath, the Branson Hotel seems
miles away from Branson's famed
"strip." But the gridlock of tourists
(and their exhaust-spitting cars and
buses) begins on the street below.

Peach walls, blue-and-peach floral carpeting, and soft classical music greet
guests inside the front door, where Teri
offers sherry, tea or coffee, and butter
cookies and English shortbread. Fresh
flowers from the garden—peonies in
spring—add to the relaxing ambience.
Teri keeps ice and soda in a hall refrigerator near the unusual back-to-back

staircases. She provides complimentary champagne for special occasions.

Rooms have a mix of reproduction
antiques—for instance, new queen- and
king-size iron, brass, and oak beds—
and antique accents, such as Victorian
prints and Tiffany-style reading lamps.
Teri's favorite is the Honeymoon Suite,
dressed in romantic pinks and blues,
and decorated with an oak four-poster
bed with New England–style fishnet
canopy, wing chairs, and an antique
walnut dresser. The Wicker Room's
white iron bed is matched up with
antique white wicker chairs and soothing white and lavender linens. More
masculine are the Duck Club and the
Fox's Den, the latter designed around a
large fox print Teri found in a gallery
near her part-time home in Kansas
City, where she formerly worked in the
construction and engineering fields.

Guests gather around a large harvest
table for breakfasts that may include
banana-walnut pancakes and cheddar-
cheese muffins, or blueberry-stuffed
French toast and sourdough bread.

🏨 *9 double rooms with baths. Air-
conditioning, cable TVs, phones, clock
radios, off-street parking. $75–$95; full
breakfast, afternoon refreshments. No
credit cards.*

Other Choices

Apple Bed & Breakfast Inn. 5517 State Highway T, Branson, MO 65616, tel. 417/334–5690. 3 double rooms with private baths. Air-conditioning, hot tub, private patio. $65–$75, full breakfast. No credit cards.

Cameron's Crag. 738 Acacia Rd., Box 295, Branson, MO 65616, tel. 417/335–8134 or 800/933–8529, fax 417/336–2238. 2 double rooms with baths, 1 suite. Air-conditioning, indoor hot tub and refrigerator in 1 room, outdoor hot tub on deck adjoining 1 room, whirlpool and kitchen in suite, phones and cable TV/VCR, private entrances, wooded location. $75–$95, full breakfast. AE, D, MC, V.

Emory Creek Bed and Breakfast. 143 Arizona Dr., Branson, MO 65616, tel. 417/334–3805. 7 double rooms with baths and Jacuzzis. Air-conditioning, clock-radios, TVs, TV/VCR in sitting room, wooded location, nature trails. $75–$95, full breakfast. D, MC, V.

Kansas City

Southmoreland on the Plaza

116 E. 46th St., Kansas City, MO 64112, tel. 816/531–7979, fax 816/531–2407

Within walking distance of the Country Club Plaza shopping mecca is this 1913 12-room Colonial Revival mansion that Penni Johnson and Susan Moehl have transformed into the city's busiest B&B.

The innkeepers' attention to detail is evident in the fresh flowers, apples, sherry, and chocolates placed in each room, many of which have fireplaces or decks. The living room, decorated in rich Colonial colors (as are a number of the bedrooms), is stocked with books, jigsaw puzzles, and 162 "happy ending"

movies for watching on the TV/VCR tucked into the 1865 Austrian armoire.

Chalkboard menus are updated each day in the dining room, where guests delve into gourmet breakfasts featuring such fare as French toast stuffed with brown sugar–cured ham and Lorraine Swiss, batter fried, and topped with slivers of toasted almonds. Guests dine either at the 1800s pine harvest table in the dining room or on the side veranda, overlooking the shady lawn where Baby, the cat, sometimes lounges. A deck with views of the waterfall and goldfish pond has a gas grill that Susan sometimes uses for unusual breakfast creations.

Off the dining room is the solarium, decorated with cool white wicker and blue and white pillows. The innkeepers keep plenty of newspapers, including the *Wall Street Journal*, for business travelers or vacationers who don't want to get away from quite everything.

Penni, a lawyer, and Susan, a former executive at Kansas City–based Hallmark Cards, left the corporate life after Susan fell in love with B&B's while bicycling in Cape Cod. When they stumbled onto this gray-stucco mansion set back from the street in the Southmoreland neighborhood of apartment buildings and condominiums, they knew they had found their spot. They built a carriage house in the rear for themselves.

Each room is named for a Kansas City notable and has a copy of the book displayed, left open to the page with the biography of the room's namesake. For instance, the Leroy "Satchel" Paige room, named for the Kansas City baseball legend, is paneled in knotty pine and made to look like a tiny northwoods fishing cabin. Baseball memorabilia, antique skis, and snowshoes grace the walls, and a queen-size log bed is the centerpiece.

🏨 *12 double rooms with baths. Air-conditioning, fireplaces in 3 rooms, Jacuzzis in 2 rooms, phones, off-street parking, business services including fax and copier, airport shuttle, sports and dining privileges at nearby private club. $105–$150; full breakfast, complimentary wine and cheese. AE, MC, V.*

Other Choices

Behm's Plaza Carriage House. 4320 Oak St., Kansas City, MO 64111, tel. 816/753–4434. 5 double rooms with baths. Air-conditioning, Jacuzzi in 1 room, hot tub on private deck attached to 1 room, fireplace in 1 room, TV/VCR in living room, off-street parking. $95–$125; full breakfast, complimentary wine and cheese. AE, MC, V.

Doanleigh Wallagh Inn. 217 E. 37th St., Kansas City, MO 64111, tel. 816/753–2667, fax 816/531–5185. 5 double rooms with baths. Air-conditioning, phones, computer modem access, cable TV, fireplace, Jacuzzi and refrigerator in 3 rooms, off-street parking, fax and copier, VCR in solarium, grand piano and pump organ in parlor, park and tennis courts nearby. $90–$135; full breakfast, afternoon snacks. AE, D, MC, V.

St. Genevieve

Inn St. Gemme Beauvais

78 N. Main St., St. Genevieve, MO 63670, tel. 573/883–5744 or 800/818–5744

Originally constructed in 1848, this magnificent home with a brick facade and two-story white columns is in a quaint French community about 50 miles south of St. Louis.

Just three blocks from the great river, the three-story Inn St. Gemme Beau-

vais has an elegant dining room with marble fireplace and a banquet room among its common rooms. Innkeeper Janet Joggerst, a lifelong native of St. Genevieve, will prepare your breakfast to order, taking special consideration for any dietetic needs. However, her specialty is a French recipe for pancakes that includes oats and apples.

The upstairs guest rooms are filled with period antiques and handmade quilts, although updated with modern conveniences: In the Governor's Room, the television is tastefully hidden in the cabinet of an old Victrola. Each room, some with either canopy beds or Murphy beds, has its own theme. The Memories Room is filled with antique toys, dolls, and children's books.

After a wonderful day exploring the countryside in and around St. Genevieve or riding the Mississippi River ferry to Illinois and back, guests may relax in the outdoor dining area for wine and hors d'oeuvres. If additional relaxation is needed, try the outdoor hot tub or a massage from the certified massage therapist on call. With these special amenities, it is no wonder that the Inn St. Gemme Beauvais is known as a romantic hideaway.

🏨 *7 double rooms with baths, 5 suites. Air-conditioning, lounge and dining area, cable TV, exercise room, banquet facilities, off-street parking. $70–$125; full breakfast, complimentary tea, wine, and hors d'oeuvres. MC, V. No smoking.*

St. Louis

Boone's Lick Trail Inn

1000 S. Main St., St. Charles, MO 63301, tel. 314/947–7000

The state's first permanent settlement on the Missouri River, historic old St. Charles—25 minutes west of downtown St. Louis—retains the leisurely charm of an 1800s river town. Here was the last outpost of civilization, where Lewis and Clark launched their 1804 expedition and the state of Missouri assembled its first legislature in 1821. Visitors stroll along cobblestone Main Street with its gaslights and restored brick buildings housing dozens of restaurants, cafés, and antiques and crafts shops. Others come for the hiking and biking along Missouri's Katy Trail, which begins here and travels west along an abandoned railroad right-of-way. One of the state's first riverboat casinos, the *Casino St. Charles*, is a few steps away.

The Boone's Lick Trail Inn, which dates to around 1850, sits at the edge of this commotion behind a hedge of pink Simplicity roses. But V'Anne and Paul Mydler purchased it in 1981 and renovated the brick, three-story Federal-style building, salvaging some of the original windows and pine plank flooring.

Guests may stay in the third-floor room with its tiny walk-out balcony and view of the Missouri River and the *Goldenrod Showboat* docked there. The attic room has sloping ceilings, a double bird's-eye maple bed, and an 1840s slave bed that can be pulled out to make a double. There's a large bathroom with a modern shower, old marble sink, a small makeup table, and plenty of thirsty towels.

Four smaller rooms are in a wing at the back of the house and have private entrances. The two upstairs open onto a porch that overlooks a historic gristmill and Boonslick Road—named, as was the inn, for an old trail Daniel Boone's sons used to take to a natural salt lick. Rooms have a mix of Early American antiques and family heirlooms, lace curtains, folk-art stenciling, and dried flowers.

V'Anne collects antiques, such as the 8-foot-long oak and walnut "textile table" from an old general store, on which she now sets her simple, but filling buffet breakfasts. A hot dish, such as cheese-stuffed French toast or a baked egg casserole, is served with fresh fruit and pastries or muffins, with locally made jams and jellies. Paul has taken over the baking of a guest favorite—lemon "sandbag" biscuits. The "sandbag" was added during the Great Flood of 1993, when much of downtown St. Charles was sandbagged against the rising river, which stopped short of the inn by about 60 feet.

▥ *5 double rooms with baths. Air-conditioning, phones, TV in 2 rooms, off-street parking. $85–$120, full buffet breakfast. AE, D, MC, V.*

Other Choices

Eastlake Inn. 703 N. Kirkwood Rd., Kirkwood, MO 63122, tel. 314/965–0066. 3 double rooms with baths. Air-conditioning, TV and fireplace in living room, turndown service, off-street parking, breakfast on patio. $65–$85, full breakfast. MC, V.

Winter House. 3522 Arsenal St., St. Louis, MO 63118, tel. 314/664–4399. 2 double rooms with baths. Air-conditioning, clock-radios, off-street parking. $60–$75; hearty Continental breakfast, afternoon refreshments. AE, D, DC, MC, V.

Reservations Services

B&B Inns of Missouri (Box 775294, St. Louis, MO 63177, tel. 800/213–5642). **B&B–Kansas City** (Box 14781, Lenexa, KS 66285, tel. 913/888–3636). **Ozark Mountain Country B&Bs** (Box 295, Branson, MO 65616, tel. 417/334–4720). **River Country B&Bs** (1900 Wyoming St., St. Louis, MO 63118, tel. 314/965–4328).

Montana

Emily A. Bed & Breakfast

Gold West Country

Barrister Bed & Breakfast

416 N. Ewing St., Helena, MT 59601, tel. 406/443–7330 or 800/823–1148, fax 406/442–7964

Across the street from lovely St. Helena's Cathedral stands the Barrister, a Queen Anne house built between 1874 and 1880. The Barrister once served as the rectory for the Helena diocese; today, the innkeeper, Nick Jacques, displays a photo of himself as a young altar boy who once served Mass at the cathedral. "The first time I saw the inside of the house," Nick confesses, "was when I was being scolded by the Monsignor."

The former altar boy, a fifth-generation Montanan, is also a former public defender: The B&B's name is about all that remains of Nick's former life. In 1993, when the house opened as a B&B, it was placed on the National Register of Historic Places.

The Barrister has an unusually large amount of public space: The parlor, formal dining room, den, TV room, library, office, and enclosed sunporch are all available for guests to use and enjoy. Incorporating six ornate fireplaces, four original leaded stained-glass windows, high ceilings, and carved staircases, the Barrister provides guests with an elegant return to the gracious living of the late 19th century.

Guest rooms are spacious and reflect a variety of moods. The very masculine Captain's Quarters is decidedly nautical; a deep red carpet and paisley bedspread complement the theme. The Lilac Room has a clearly more feminine air, with frilly hats and a purse displayed on the wall. The Barrister Suite, the most elegant of all the rooms, has an elaborate armoire, lace curtains, and large bathroom.

▦ *2 double rooms with baths, 3 rooms have private baths across the hall. Air-conditioning, rooms with baths across the hall have terry-cloth robes, business center with computer data ports. $85–$100; full breakfast, evening social at 5:30 with wine and hors d'oeuvres. AE, MC, V.*

Goldsmith's Bed & Breakfast Inn

809 E. Front St., Missoula, MT 59802, tel. 406/721–6732

Goldsmith's Bed & Breakfast Inn welcomes travelers with a unique brand of hospitality. Unlike most bed-and-breakfasts, in which the morning meal is served in a common dining room, Goldsmith's serves its guests next door at Goldsmith's Ice Cream Parlor and Restaurant, which is a favorite with students and other locals. Guests can choose from any item on the extensive breakfast menu.

Upon crossing the front porch (where breakfast may also be served), guests enter Goldsmith's B&B and find a startling photograph that shows the early 20th-century house up on blocks and rolling down one of Missoula's main streets. Owners Jeana and Richard Goldsmith moved the house from its original location to its present one on the banks of the Clark Fork River, across a footbridge from the University of Montana. The house, a 1911 brick jewel, was formerly the residence of Clyde Duniway, the university's second president. The Common Room has a lovely bay window that overlooks the river. Fresh flowers, a fireplace, a library, and maple and oak hardwood floors add to the ambience.

Guest rooms have Oriental carpets and period antiques and reproductions, including some sleigh beds. Bathrooms are hand-tiled and have oversize bath towels. Two of the rooms (Room 1, the Parlor Room, and Room 4, the Red River Room) have delightful views overlooking the Clark Fork River. But even without a river view, guests will find themselves happily ensconced in the comfort and privacy of this homey inn.

🏨 *7 double rooms with baths, Rooms 1, 2, 6, and 7 may be rented as suites. Air-conditioning, phones, cable TV in common room, nook with library. $69– $129, full breakfast served next door at Goldsmith's Ice Cream Parlor and Restaurant. AE, D, DC, MC, V.*

Sanders–Helena's Bed & Breakfast

328 N. Ewing St., Helena, MT, 59601, tel. 406/442–3309, fax 406/443–2361

In the heart of Helena's historic district, just a few short blocks from the Old Governor's Mansion is the Sanders, an 1875 home that was one of the first houses in what is now Montana's capital city. Set on a tree-lined street just three blocks from the lovely cathedral of St. Helena, the Sanders provides its guests with a gracious return to the days of the Montana Territory.

The house was built as a home for Wilbur and Harriet Sanders, who arrived in Montana in 1863 with the Sidney Edgerton wagon train. (Edgerton, the first governor of the Montana Territory, was Sanders's uncle.) Sanders, who in 1889 became one of Montana's first two senators when statehood was granted, was a founder of the Montana Historical Society and put much of his extensive mineral collection on display in the vestibule of his home. Glass-fronted cases show a large number of the rocks Sanders uncovered in his mines. Many are dated, including a jar with stones collected during the summer of 1863 by young Harriet Sanders during her crossing of the Great Plains with the Edgerton wagon train from Omaha, Nebraska, to Bannack, Montana. Not surprisingly, this B&B attracts many geologists.

Hosts Bobbi Uecker and Rock Ringling have preserved much of the Sanders's historic past. Various pieces of the furniture in the guest rooms are original, including several antique beds and bureaus. The public rooms are delightfully decorated with items such as an upright piano and a built-in buffet of warm, golden crosscut oak and beveled glass. Guests staying on the upper floors might be startled by the sight of "Chili Bean," a star bovine on the rodeo circuit who died of natural causes. Mounted above the staircase, Chili

Bean gazes down upon all who pass under her. It's hard to take her terribly seriously, however, since her considerably large horns are adorned with a variety of unusual hats.

Guest rooms, named after members of Bobbi and Rock's families, are filled with delightful touches such as a mimeographed "Sanders Quiz" that guests can take at their leisure. Because of the Sanders's location in Montana's capital city, it receives its fair share of business as well as leisure travelers. Several rooms have been designed with corporate guests in mind. There are alarm clocks in every room; radios are thoughtfully labeled with stations and their formats; and in Teddy's Buckaroo, the 8-foot ceilings allow an extra-roomy stall shower. Beth's Room, painted a cheerful yellow, has a stunning view of the Continental Divide. Althea's Room is perhaps the most historically accurate; almost all of its furniture is original to the house. Although its private bathroom isn't attached to the sleeping area, a terrycloth robe is thoughtfully provided for the short walk down the hall.

▦ *6 double rooms with baths, 1 room with bath down the hall. TVs, phones, hair dryers. $55–$95; full breakfast, afternoon cookies, sherry, fruit, and beverages. AE, D, MC, V.*

Yellowstone Country

Gallatin Gateway Inn

Rte. 191, Box 376, Gallatin Gateway, MT 59730, tel. 406/763–4672 or 800/676–3522, fax 406/763–4672, ext. 313

Opened in 1927 by the Chicago, Milwaukee, and St. Paul Railroad as one of the grand railroad hotels of the Rocky Mountain West, the 42,000-square-foot Gallatin Gateway Inn has high arched windows, Spanish-style corbels, and carved beams. The original railroad

clock in the high-ceiling lobby still keeps accurate time, and the checkerboard-square tile floor and gleaming Polynesian mahogany woodwork looks exactly as it did during the heyday of railroad travel.

The glorious Spanish Peaks form a picture-postcard-perfect backdrop to the inn's outdoor pool and tennis court. Its location 12 miles south of Bozeman and 80 miles north of Yellowstone National Park makes it an ideal stopping point for travelers. Fly fishermen take note: The Gallatin River is a five-minute walk away. In addition, there's a casting pond on the inn's property, giving folks an opportunity to practice before heading out to the real thing.

The inn's superb dining room is an experience in itself. Knowing locals from Bozeman head here on weekends, so reservations—even for inn guests—are essential. The extensive menu features a fresh catch of the day, of course, but there are also tempting beef, veal, lamb, and chicken entrées with unique presentations.

Although guests may want to curl up with a good book in front of the massive fireplace in the lobby, there are plenty of activities in and around the inn in both winter and summer. Gallatin Gateway is close to two of Montana's premier ski areas: Bridger Bowl and Big Sky. In the summer, horseback rides through the Lee Metcalf wilderness area in the Spanish Peaks can be arranged.

▦ *35 double rooms and suites, some accessible to people who use wheelchairs. Air-conditioning, pool, tennis court, casting pond, fly-fishing school during certain weeks, massages by appointment. $60–$115, Continental breakfast. AE, D, MC, V.*

Other Choices

Lindley House. 202 Lindley Pl., Bozeman, MT 59715, tel. 406/587–8403 or 800/787–8404, fax 406/582–8112. 3 double rooms with baths, 1 double room and 1 single room share 1 bath, 3 suites. Terry-cloth robes; hair dryers; amenity baskets; cable TV/VCRs, phones, and coffeemakers in some rooms; balcony, fireplace, and 2-person bathtub in 1 suite; full kitchen and washer/dryer in penthouse; exercise room with sauna. $65–$250, full breakfast. MC, V.

Sacajawea Inn. 5 N. Main St., Box 648, Three Forks, MT 59752, tel. 406/285–6515 or 800/821–7326, fax 406/285–4210. 33 double rooms with baths. Air-conditioning in some rooms, Cable TVs, phones, dining room. $59–$99, Continental breakfast. AE, D, MC, V.

Sportsman's High Bed & Breakfast. 750 Deer St., West Yellowstone, MT 59758, tel. 406/646–7865. 5 double rooms with baths. Satellite TV and phone in common area, hot tub. $65–$115, full breakfast. AE, MC, V.

Torch & Toes Bed & Breakfast. 309 S. Third Ave., Bozeman, MT 59715, tel. 406/586–7285 or 800/446–2138. 2 double rooms with baths, 1 double room with private bath across hall, 1 suite (carriage house). $70–$90, full breakfast. MC, V.

Voss Inn. 319 S. Willson St., Bozeman, MT 59715, tel. 406/587–0982. 6 double rooms with baths. Phone and cable TV in parlor. $85–$95, full breakfast. AE, MC, V.

Glacier Country

Emily A. Bed & Breakfast

Box 350, Seeley Lake, MT 59868 (mile marker 20, 5 miles north of Seeley Lake on Montana Rte. 83), tel. 406/677–3474 or 800/977–4639, fax 406/677–3474

In the heart of the scenic Seeley-Swan Valley, one of Montana's premier outdoor recreation areas, lies the Emily A. Bed & Breakfast. On 160 acres of the Circle Arrow Ranch, as well as an 8-acre lake and the Clearwater River, the Emily A. offers a spectacular outdoor setting and an equally commanding interior. Built of locally harvested larch logs from the nearby hills that provide the lodge with a warm, soft golden glow, the Emily A. provides its guests with a true Western experience with all the modern amenities.

The B&B is the brainchild of Marilyn and Keith Peterson. Keith, the retired team doctor for baseball's Seattle Mariners, has baseball memorabilia (including original wool jerseys worn by Pete Rose and Johnny Bench) on display in one of the downstairs common rooms. Marilyn, who handles the day-to-day operations of the inn, is a registered dietitian. The Emily A. represents the realization of their dream to share the Montana hospitality and lifestyle they know and love with their guests.

The Emily A. is named for Marilyn's grandmother, Emily Alvis Stinson Shope, who came to Montana in 1893 to help found the Boulder School for the Deaf Mute. When her husband died, the young widow supported her seven children by running one of Missoula's first board and rooming houses. That family tradition of hospitality lives on today, as her granddaughter hosts guests from near and far.

There is plenty for guests to see and do in and around the Emily A. The headwaters of the Columbia River are close at hand, so fishing is a popular pastime. Or, you might want to spend some quality time on the back porch with binoculars: Ospreys, eagles, loons, ducks, geese, deer, and other wildlife contribute to an ever-changing view.

Evenings at the Emily A. are ideal for gathering around the huge two-story, 25-foot fireplace. As Marilyn says, "The stones of our two-story fireplace have their own stories to tell. They are geological specimens gathered by the

Peterson family over several lifetimes." The Peterson family is evident in just about every room of the house, public or private. Cozy guest rooms are named after the Peterson's children; there's a Grandparents' Room as well. Family photographs are displayed throughout the house, as well as keepsakes and other family heirlooms.

▦ *2 double rooms with private baths, 3 double rooms with shared baths, 2-bedroom suite with kitchen. Cable TV in upstairs common area, fishing, sled-dog rides, horseback riding by arrangement. $95–$150, full or Continental breakfast. D, MC, V.*

Other Choices

Bad Rock Country B&B. 480 Bad Rock Dr., Columbia Falls, MT 59912, tel. 406/892–2829 or 800/422–3666, fax 406/892–2930. 7 double rooms with baths. Whirlpool, some rooms with steam bath. $85–$95, full breakfast. AE, D, DC, MC, V. No smoking.

Burggraf's Countrylane Bed 'n Breakfast. Rainbow Dr. on Swan Lake, Bigfork, MT 59911, tel. 406/837–4608 or 800/525–3314, fax 406/837–2468. 5 double rooms with baths. Whirlpool bath in 1 room, free canoes, rental boats, croquet court. $85–$100, full breakfast. No credit cards.

Garden Wall Inn. 504 Spokane Ave., Whitefish, MT 59937, tel. 406/862–3440. 3 double rooms with bath, 1 suite. Crabtree & Evelyn toiletries, evening turndown service, complimentary morning newspaper, morning coffee served in room. $85–$115; full breakfast, afternoon hors d'oeuvres and beverages. AE, MC, V.

Glacier River Ranch. Box 176, Coram, MT 59913 (Rte. 2 E, 7 miles west of Glacier National Park), tel. 406/387–

4151. 5 double rooms with baths, guest house with 2 bedrooms. Air-conditioning, TV room with cable TV/VCR, cable TV in guest house, hot tub, fishing at on-site trout pond, horseback riding, cross-country skiing. $65–$125; full breakfast, evening appetizers. MC, V.

Good Medicine Lodge. 537 Wisconsin Ave., Whitefish, MT 59937, tel. 406/862–5488, fax 406/862–5489. 9 double rooms with baths. Some rooms with balcony and mountain views, outdoor spa, guest laundry, ski room. $75–$105, full breakfast. MC, V. Closed Apr. 7–May 16 and Oct. 14–Dec. 12.

Mountain Timbers Lodge & Cross Country Ski Area. 5385 Rabe Rd., Box 94, Columbia Falls, MT 59912, tel. 406/387–5830, fax 406/387–5835. 7 double rooms with shared bath. Whirlpool, croquet. $55–$125, full breakfast. MC, V.

O'Duach'ain Country Inn. 675 Ferndale Dr., Bigfork, MT 59911, tel. 406/837–6851, fax 406/837–4390. 2 suites with bath, 3 rooms with shared bath. Outdoor spa. $55–$95, full breakfast. AE, MC, V.

Plum Creek House. 985 Vans Ave., Columbia Falls, MT 59912, tel. 406/892–1816 or 800/682–1429, fax 406/892–1876. 5 double rooms with baths, 1 suite. Views of Glacier National Park, cable TV/VCRs, phones, robes, slippers, coffee service, video library, barbecues, fire pit, heated pool, hot tub, catered gourmet dinners available. $115, full breakfast. AE, D, DC, MC, V.

Turn in the River Inn. 51 Penney La., Columbia Falls, MT 59912, tel. 406/257–0724 or 800/892–2474, fax 406/756–0725. 3 double rooms with baths, 1 suite (sleeps 4). 1 room accessible for people who use wheelchairs; hot tub, canoe. $95–$115; full breakfast, evening hors d'oeuvres. AE, MC, V.

Nebraska

Plantation House

Elgin

Plantation House

401 Plantation St., Elgin, NE 68636, tel. 402/843-2287

Guests arriving at the Plantation House might well feel they've taken a detour into antebellum Mississippi. With four imposing columns on its facade, this 28-room Greek Revival–style mansion resembles a classic southern plantation. The grandly scaled inn offers an enjoyable mix of comfort, history, and relaxation says Barbara Clark, who with her husband, Merland, renovated this town landmark for its operation as a B&B.

The Clarks enjoy recounting the house's history, which begins in the 1880s when George Seymour, Elgin's first banker, built the house for his bride. With the addition of several small workers' dwellings on its estate of 640 acres and, later, in 1916, the four cypress-wood columns framing the front entrance, local people began calling it "the Plantation."

There are many architectural charms to savor and most of the rooms are accented with antiques. Among the guest quarters, Mrs. Butler's Room is a

suite of turn-of-the-century Empire-style furniture (a legacy of the Seymour era), the Old Guest Room has attractive rose-strewn wallpaper, and there is also the Stained Glass Room. In winter, guests may enjoy the warmth of the cozy wood-burning stove in the family room or the five working fireplaces throughout the public areas of the house. The second-floor salon contains a TV/VCR, board games, and a phone.

Out back stands an antique gazebo and one of the original workers' houses, now used as a guest cottage. All white trim, pink shutters, and white wrought-iron furniture, the cottage is favored as a nuptial-night hideaway. Breakfast is served family-style in the formal dining room, where French toast with locally cured bacon is often on the menu.

Directly across the street, the Elgin City Park has an outdoor swimming pool, tennis, and volleyball courts. You can take a day trip to Ashfall State Park, where the prehistoric remains of three-toed horses and rhinos are being excavated from volcanic ash.

🏨 *3 double rooms with baths, 3 double rooms share 1 bath. Air-conditioning, computers available for business professionals, TV/VCR and phones in common area. $35–$60, full breakfast. No credit cards.*

Hastings

Grandma's Victorian Inn

1826 W. 3rd St., Hastings, NE 68901, tel. 402/462-2013

In the heart of Nebraska's famed Sandhill Crane region, Grandma's Victorian Inn is a tribute to innkeeper Robin Sassman's great-grandmother. Photos of five generations of Krueger women greet guests in the lobby and throughout the two-story Victorian home. Built as the family home for railroad executive George H. Lamont, the house was featured in an 1880s handbill to entice Easterners "out West" to south-central Nebraska.

More than 100 years later, the Kreuger family was also enticed by the long-neglected house. After two years of renovation, family members returned the home to its original Victorian charm. Today, a path of brick from long-ago local brick yards leads to an ornate cream-colored exterior accented by contrasting green and cranberry latticework trim. White wicker furniture on the covered porch and the ice-cream-parlor table and chairs on the second-floor balcony encourage travelers to unwind.

When you step beyond grandma's 1880s carved-wood and stained-glass front door, you'll appreciate the detailed research by Robin's mother for period wallpaper and other furnishings that create such a nostalgic and restful environment. Much of the original woodwork was saved during the renovation of the house. Some, such as a unique curio cabinet built into the staircase, was added. Gleaming wainscoting, trim, floors, and pocket doors to the dining room create touches of warmth throughout the house.

Antiques and handcrafted Battenberg-lace coverlets ornament the five spacious guest rooms, three of which commemorate Grandma Krueger's given name— Margret Henrietta Selma. All have queen-size beds and family rocking chairs and there's a lavender fainting couch in Margret's room and an heirloom wedding gown hanging inside Henrietta's Victorian-period armoire. The Heritage Room is notable because even with antique furnishings, it (and its bath) complies with the American Disabilities Act for accessibility. The other four baths have period claw-foot tubs and raised tank toilets.

Breakfast may be served in bed upon your request. However, the inviting aroma of Belgian waffles, French toast, and homemade muffins draw guests from their rooms to the sunny bay windows and glistening china of the dining room. Cozy tables for two are all the more pleasurable because of the nearby warmth of a working potbellied stove and flower- and candle-laden buffet.

One-half mile from the many antiques shops of downtown Hastings, Grandma's Victorian Inn is in a comfortable residential area. Guests arriving after dark can appreciate a detail: Colorful stained-glass windows on all levels of the home have been specially lighted to enhance the warmth of an already charming bed-and-breakfast inn.

Hastings, a growing community of 25,000, is the home of the National Square Dance Festival each September, a pioneer museum, and an impressive IMAX theater.

▥ *5 double rooms with baths. Air-conditioning, dining room, TV upon request, off-street parking. $50–$60, full breakfast. D, MC, V.*

Capital Area

Heart of Dannebrog Bed and Breakfast

121 E. Elm St., Dannebrog, NE 68831, tel. 308/226-2303

The warmth of candles glowing in each window and a cheery hello from innkeeper René Simdorn welcome you to the Heart of Dannebrog Bed and Breakfast. Officially registered as the Danish Capital of Nebraska, the small town of 300 residents is also made famous as the focus of many "Postcards from Nebraska," a regular feature by Dannebrog writer Roger Welsch on *CBS Sunday Morning*.

A lifelong resident of the Dannebrog area, René grew up next door to the house she turned into the town's first bed-and-breakfast. Built in 1905, the house sat empty for several years, wherein it acquired the dubious honor of being the Dannebrog's haunted house. Soon after opening the inn in 1994, René did notice the chocolate mints in each guest room mysteriously disappearing. Not a believer of ghost legend, she soon traced the mystery to Freckles, her cocker spaniel.

During the renovation, René and her family took pains to save all the original woodwork in the house. The beautiful natural wood in the open stairway and the impressive door trims were well worth the effort. Guests are invited to play the family piano in the parlor or watch television in the living room. Football fans will appreciate the University of Nebraska football memorabilia on display, a tribute to René's son's career as a Cornhusker defensive back.

Two guest rooms atop the stairs share a bath and a cozy reading area. The larger of the two rooms, the Spring Room, has Battenberg lace tablecloths, a white rocking chair, and airy window coverings dappled with pansies. A quilted wall hanging and matching bed cover and pillows feature fruit and flowers in pastel blue and yellow. Across the hall, the Autumn Room has a comfortable double iron bed with an inviting green and rust comforter and matching pillows tucked into the eave.

Breakfast is a unique Danish treat. Just a few blocks from René's home is Harriett's Danish café, where guests are treated to Danish pancakes, eggs, coffee, and Medisterpolse, a Danish pork sausage made just across the street at the Steakmaster. Much of the charm at Harriett's are the locals who walk in, pick up their own coffee cup, serve themselves, and chat.

Dannebrog is small-town America at its best. Whether you're swinging in René's front porch swing or walking or biking the trail just two blocks away, the residents of Dannebrog greet you with a hearty wave and sincere hello. Just 20 minutes north of Grand Island, the town hosts a popular Grundlovs Fest the first weekend in June and a Danish Christmas the first weekend in December.

🏨 *2 guest rooms share 1 bath. Air-conditioning, cable TV/VCR, phone in common area, piano in parlor. $40-$45, full breakfast. No credit cards. No smoking, no pets.*

Other Choices

Carriage House. Box 136B, Rte. 1, Beatrice, NE 68310, tel. 402/228-0356. 1 double room with bath, 5 double rooms share 3 baths. Air-conditioning, phones, TV/VCR in living room, fireplace in parlor, kennels available. $45-$60, full breakfast. MC, V.

Crow's Nest. 503 Grant St., Holdrege, NE 68949, tel. 308/995-5440. 3 double rooms share 1 bath. Air-conditioning; sunporch; hot tub; fishponds; phone, TV/VCR, and fireplace in common area. $40-$50, full breakfast. MC, V.

Home Comfort. 1523 N. Brown St., Minden, NE 68959, tel. 308/832–0533 or 800/318–0533. 5 double rooms with baths, 1 guest house that is accessible for persons with disabilities. Air-conditioning, dining room, phone, TV, grand piano in common room, horses and petting zoo, walking distance to Pioneer Village, transportation to Sandhill Crane blinds. $50–$60, full breakfast. No credit cards.

Hotel Wilber. 203 S. Wilson St., Wilber, NE 68465, tel. 402/821–2020. 10 double rooms share 2 shower rooms. Restaurant, beer garden, air-conditioning, cable TVs, phones near lobby, TV/VCR in downstairs pub, kennels available. $42–$65, full breakfast. MC, V.

J.C. Robinson House. 102 E. Lincoln, Waterloo, NE 68069, tel. 402/779–2704 or 800/779–2705. 1 double room with bath, 3 doubles share 1 bath. Air-conditioning; clock radios; phone, cable TV/VCR, CD player in two common areas; 4 fireplaces; kennels available. $50–$75, full breakfast. No credit cards.

Kirshke House Bed & Breakfast. 1124 W. 3rd St., Grand Island, NE 68801, tel. 308/381–6851 or 800/381–6851. 4 double rooms share 2 baths, 1 suite with waterbed, honeymoon cottage. Air-conditioning; TV/VCR, phone, and fireplace in parlor; wooden hot tub in lantern-lit brick washhouse. $45–$100, full breakfast. AE, D, MC, V.

Offutt House. 140 N. 39th St., Omaha, NE 68131, tel. 402/553–0951. 7 double rooms with baths, 2 suites. Air-conditioning, phones and clock radios in most rooms, 5 fireplaces, library, TV in sunporch and smaller ones available in rooms, small bar. $65–$125; Continental breakfast weekdays, full breakfast weekends. AE, D, MC, V.

Parson's House Bed & Breakfast. 638 Forest Ave., Crete, NE 68333, tel. 402/826–2634. 2 double rooms share 1 bath; common whirlpool tub. Air-conditioning, cable TV/VCR, phone in den, fireplace in living room. $40, full breakfast. No credit cards.

Whispering Pines Bed & Breakfast. 21st St. and 6th Ave., Nebraska City, NE 68410, tel. 402/873–5850. 2 double rooms with private baths, 3 double rooms share 1 bath. Air-conditioning, phones in 2 rooms, cable TV/VCR, whirlpool in outdoor gazebo, water garden with 4 goldfish ponds. $50–$75, full breakfast. D, MC, V.

Reservations Services

Nebraska Association of B&Bs (R.R. 2, Box 17, Elgin, NE 68636, tel. 402/843–2287). **Nebraska Division of Travel & Tourism** (Box 94666, Lincoln, NE 68509, tel. 402/471–3794; listings only).

Nevada

Gold Hill Hotel

Carson City and Environs

Deer Run Ranch

5440 Eastlake Blvd., Washoe Valley, Carson City, NV 89704, tel. 702/882-3643

After an extended search for the perfect spot to build their bed-and-breakfast, David and Muffy Vhay ended up building right on the Washoe Valley ranch where Muffy grew up. Deer Run, opened in 1984, is a working alfalfa ranch in the Virginia Range, permeated by the pungent smell of wild sage. The idyllic location at the southern end of the Quarter Circle J. P. Ranch has a small pond and large cottonwoods. The eastern escarpment of the Sierra Nevada mountains and Washoe Lake in all its shimmering glory (after disappearing for several years due to drought) are also in view.

That David Vhay is an architect is reflected not only in the house—which is bermed on two sides to compensate for the climate extremes of the high desert—but also in the layout of the grounds. Site and structure form a perfect union, creating a spacious, secluded, and sensuous B&B experience.

Both guest rooms have handmade quilts, wall-to-wall window seats with built-in magazine racks, and western decor. The two baths, across the hall from the rooms, have handmade pottery sinks and polished cedar vanities. In the common sitting room are a fireplace, mini-refrigerator, and crammed bookshelves. In the winter, guests skate on the pond and fly down the long sled run (equipment provided); in warmer weather, splashing in an 18-foot aboveground pool and bird-watching round out the recreation. There's also a potter's studio where Muffy turns out all the plates and containers (and even a couple of sinks!) used on the premises. The eponymous deer graze in the fields.

A large garden and small orchard feed the guests year-round. In addition to seasonal fruits, vegetables, and pancakes (such as pumpkin), breakfast, served in the sitting room, consists of frittatas, Dutch babies, and home-baked bread.

🏠 *2 double rooms with baths. TV/ VCR in sitting room; welcome basket of fruit, wine, and snacks. $80–$95, full breakfast. AE, MC, V.*

Genoa House Inn

180 Nixon St., Box 141, Genoa, NV 89411, tel. 702/782-7075

Genoa is the oldest town in Nevada, its location chosen by Latter-day Saint settlers in 1851 for its scenery and its agricultural and commercial potential. Today, commerce and agriculture have moved to neighboring communities, leaving the scenery and, of course, the history. Within walking distance of the Genoa House Inn, at the bottom edge of the sheer eastern escarpment of the Sierra Nevada mountains, are the rebuilt Mormon stockade and Nevada's oldest bar; on the B&B grounds is a giant oak, believed to be the oldest oak in the state.

The inn was built in 1872 and is listed on the National Register of Historic Places. It's a compact, two-story Victorian, which has withstood almost continual renovation for the last decade. One of the previous owners remodeled the second floor into a cross-gable two-bedroom addition, full of unusual angles, corners, nooks, and crannies. One of the two rooms has mahogany antiques and a private whirlpool bath; the other has antique Gothic stained-glass windows from New Zealand, an antique Turkish fainting couch, and a bi-level tile shower. Both have balconies, reached by giant lilacs in the spring.

The latest reconstruction was designed by Deer Run Ranch architect David Vhay and engineered by the current owners, Linda and Bob Sanfilippo. A third-generation Tahoan and a former business traveler, Linda stayed in her first B&B in the early 1970s and immediately became a hotel refugee. She and Bob, the town's maintenance man, bought the Genoa House in 1986 and furnished it with antiques, converted the garage into their quarters, and added a third guest room, downstairs, with a private entrance and bath (with a 1906 Wolf tank toilet).

A coffee tray at the door greets guests in the morning, and breakfast is usually coddled eggs, homemade cinnamon rolls, and fresh fruit. Use of the facilities at Walley's Hot Springs (mineral baths, heated swimming pool, sauna, and exercise equipment) is included in the rates.

▦ *3 rooms with baths. No air-conditioning, refreshments served on arrival, fitness facilities nearby. $105-$130, full breakfast. AE, MC, V.*

Gold Hill Hotel

Box 710, Virginia City, NV 89440, Hwy. 342, Gold Hill, NV, tel. 702/847-0111

Gold was discovered on Gold Hill in 1859, when what was soon to become western Nevada was still the far western edge of Utah. Although its sister town, Virginia City, is far more famous, Gold Hill predates it. The Gold Hill Hotel harkens all the way back to the first days of the Comstock Lode—making it the oldest operating inn, and one of the oldest buildings, in Nevada.

The hotel is just below Greiner's Bend, a steep and narrow S-curve in the 1-mile stretch of road that connects Virginia City with Gold Hill. The steepness is reflected in a noticeable tilt to the floors in the original wing, lending its foundation authenticity. The Great Room on the main floor (now the lounge) has a stone floor and fireplace, stucco walls with exposed brick, period furniture, and an antique piano and organ. The cozy bar was added in 1960, built to look original; the Crown Point Restaurant, serving dinner and Sunday brunch year-round and also lunch in summer, was added in 1987 and is decorated with black-and-white photographs of the area's mining heyday.

The four guest rooms in the original building are small; two of the four share a bathroom, which has brick walls, wood fixtures, and a high-sided porcelain tub. Of the seven rooms in the new wing, built in 1987, all have air-conditioning.

Four are spacious and have stone fire-places, wet bars, TVs, balconies, and large modern baths. The all-wood Guest House across the road from the inn has two one-bedroom suites with full kitchens and sofa beds in the living room.

Proprietors Bill and Carol Fain have owned the Gold Hill Hotel for 10 years, and in keeping with the historical status of the inn, they present lectures on a variety of aspects of the Comstock experience every Tuesday evening. Adjoining the hotel is Western Books, a big specialty bookstore with a good selection of titles on the Comstock, Nevada, Western explorers, railroads, and Native Americans.

🏨 *9 double rooms with baths, 2 rooms share 1 bath, 2 1-bedroom suites. Restaurant, TVs and phones in newer wing, 4 rooms with fireplaces, clock radios. $35–$135, Continental breakfast. MC, V.*

Haus Bavaria

593 N. Dyer Circle, Box 3308, Incline Village, NV 89450, tel. 702/831–6122 or 800/731–6222, fax 702/831–1238

Built by a German couple in 1980 as a bed-and-breakfast, this alpine stucco-and-wood chalet was designed to be conducive to comfort, quiet, and privacy. One mile from Lake Tahoe and the only bed-and-breakfast on the Nevada side of the lake's north shore, Haus Bavaria sits at 6,300 feet with a view of the ski runs at Diamond Peak. It is a welcome alternative to the impersonal condos and cacophonous casinos of the resort towns on the east side of the lake.

The two-level inn has five guest rooms upstairs with Danish-style dressers and headboards, heavy quilts, and sliding glass doors that open onto wraparound balconies. Also upstairs is a large sitting room with leather sofas, sling chairs, a wood-burning stove, and maps and photographs of the lake.

A full breakfast is prepared by proprietor Bick Hewitt, a transplanted San Diegan who acquired Haus Bavaria in 1990. The day's first meal might consist of eggs, French toast, cornmeal pancakes (from his Texan grandmother's recipe), or waffles, along with fruit, muffins, and fresh-ground coffee. The dining room is paneled with tongue-in-groove knotty pine and decorated with a collection of German mugs and teapots. A swinging door and louvered shutters connect to the kitchen, where guests can sit in an Art Deco chair at the kitchen worktop that Bick calls the "newspaper nook." Doors open onto a comfortable patio.

Guests are provided with passes to Incline Village's private beaches and recreation center; also nearby are two golf courses, tennis courts, downhill and cross-country skiing, hiking, and casino nightlife.

🏨 *5 double rooms with baths. No air-conditioning, TV in sitting room, ski closet, beaches, skiing nearby. $110–$145, full breakfast. AE, D, MC, V.*

Nenzel Mansion

1431 Ezell St., Gardnerville, NV 89410, tel. 702/782–7644

This three-story, 8,000-square-foot mansion built in 1910 is surrounded by ranch land on three sides and faces downtown Gardnerville and the Sierra Nevada beyond. Its exterior would be reminiscent of a Southern Colonial plantation big house if it weren't for New England–style dormers on the upper floors and a Nantucket-type widow's walk at the top.

The mansion's strength is in its details: The large foyer has four archways; its original wallpaper has been lovingly preserved; and its custom rounded double doors have the original mortise lock hardware. The Great Room is just that: 40 feet long and 18 feet wide, with contemporary couches and easy chairs, marble (gas) fireplace, and antique player piano. It seats 100 comfortably for wedding ceremonies or 40 for sit-down dinners. Twelve-foot ceilings enhance the house's already open, airy feel.

The four guest rooms are up 21 stairs. Two share a bath, which has an antique porcelain tub. The suite has honeymoon decor in white and blue florals, a sitting area, a walk-in closet, and an unusual bathroom with raspberry-color tiles and a bidet. The other rooms have wicker, brass, and antiques, with feather comforters, wooden rockers, and armoires.

The centerpiece of the formal dining room is the 19-bulb crystal and cutglass chandelier: The mansion's other chandeliers have all been fabricated to match it. Soufflés, breakfast meats, Texas toast, biscuits, and fruit are served by your hosts, local administrators Chris and Virginia Nenzel and whichever of their four grown children and large extended family happen to be on the scene.

▦ *1 double room with bath, 2 doubles share 1 bath, 1 suite. No air-conditioning, laundry facilities. $80–$110, full breakfast. MC, V.*

Wild Rose Inn

2332 Main St., Box 256, Genoa, NV 89411, tel. 702/782–5697

The Wild Rose Inn is a three-story, 4,000-square-foot Queen Anne Victorian built by Sandi and Joe Antonucci in 1989. The Wild Rose is as modern as the Genoa House down the street is historic, and spacious as the Genoa House is cozy. With its wraparound porch, cupola tower, and bay windows, there's not a square room in the house.

The guest room on the first floor below the cupola has five windows, hand-stenciled walls, and an antique trunk. The second floor has three rooms in a unique circular floor plan: None of the bedrooms shares a common wall, and all are thus utterly private; interiorwall insulation further ensures the quiet. The bright room with floral wallpaper in the top of the cupola has a sweeping panorama of the valley and mountains, an iron bed, and antique oak furnishings. Another room's bath has a separate dressing room with built-in wardrobe and vanity.

The third floor contains the Wild Rose's suite, a sprawling affair that sleeps four, with an iron bed in the main room, a twin bed in the dormer alcove, and a trundle bed in the anteroom. The suite also has two skylights; cream with lace trim sheets, bedspreads, and curtains; a wet bar with a mini-refrigerator in the sitting room; and a large bathroom with his-and-her shell-shape pedestal sinks and an oversize tub.

Breakfast is served buffet-style in the guest parlor on the ground floor: eggs, cereals, fruit, scones, French toast, plentiful cinnamon rolls, muffins, coffee. Like the Genoa House, rates include admission to Walley's Hot Springs. Within walking distance of the Wild Rose are two dinner houses, a historic bar, and an old-fashioned country store.

▦ *4 rooms with baths, 1 suite. Air-conditioning, use of Walley's Hot Springs. $95–$130; buffet breakfast, afternoon wine. AE, MC, V.*

Reservations Service

Nevada Commission on Tourism (Capitol Complex, Carson City, NV 89710, tel. 800/638–2328; listings only; call for brochure).

New Hampshire

Snowvillage Inn

The Seacoast

Moody Parsonage Bed and Breakfast

15 Ash Swamp Rd., Newmarket, NH 03857, tel. 603/659-6675

Moody Parsonage, built in 1730 for John Moody, the first minister of Newmarket, is the oldest and perhaps most welcoming residence-turned-bed-and-breakfast in New Hampshire. Today's world and worries seem far away in a red clapboard house where a spinning wheel sits on the landing, and you can still see the original paneling, staircases, and wide pine floors. Five fireplaces—one is always going in the dining room on chilly mornings—are cozy reminders of days when even the seacoast was on the edge of the wilderness.

Owner Deborah Reed grew up in the Parsonage, returning to it after 35 years of marriage and residences that spanned the globe, from Germany to Washington state. A retired registered nurse, she eased into innkeeping by first opening her house to University of New Hampshire students. Now she says she has "discovered that a B&B is definitely in the caregiving category."

One bedroom and bath are on the first floor. The other three rooms are upstairs and share a bath, making a good arrangement for a family. Though one of these is comparatively small, the other bedrooms are very large and have working fireplaces. The house is decorated with family portraits and furnished with family antiques, rushseat and wing chairs, electrified oil lamps, iron-bound wood footlockers, and copper kettles. A fluffy white down comforter covers a queen-size canopy bed.

Fresh flowers are everywhere. "With 2 acres to care for, I guess you could say my hobby is gardening, and I enjoy every minute of it," Deborah says. She also refinishes furniture when time permits.

Great Bay, the magnificent estuary and wildlife sanctuary for migrating waterfowl, is within 2 miles, and across the road is a golf course. You can sit on the Parsonage lawn and watch the golfers tee off. Other options include a shopping mall or two, the facilities of the Great Bay Athletic Club, and a ballroom that plays big-band music. You are only a 15-minute drive from the museums and restaurants of Durham, Exeter, and Portsmouth, or the beaches and boardwalk of Rye and Hampton; Newmarket itself is only 2 miles south.

🛏 *1 double room with bath, 3 doubles share 1 bath. Air-conditioning, fireplaces. $55–$65, Continental breakfast. No credit cards. No smoking, no pets.*

Rock Ledge Manor

1413 Ocean Blvd. (Rte. 1A), Rye, NH 03870, tel. 603/431–1413

Rock Ledge Manor was built between 1840 and 1880 as part of a major seaside resort colony so the style is Victorian gingerbread. The white mansard gambrel-roofed house, replete with the black shutters and wraparound porch, overlooks the Atlantic at Concord Point just south of Rye State Beach. The islands you see in the distance are the Isles of Shoals.

The owners, Norman and Janice Marineau, turned their oceanfront home into a bed-and-breakfast in 1982. Norman had been in catering, which may be why breakfast here is such a major event. It could be crepes, or Belgian waffles, or omelets and homemade sweet rolls.

The meal is served in a breakfast room with a view of the sea. The table is set formally with china and linens, the way breakfast was served a century ago. Off the breakfast room, a delightfully old-fashioned sunroom full of plants is just the place to retire to with the morning papers. Or you might prefer to let the breeze ruffle your pages on the wide porch.

Two bedrooms are on the ground floor and two on the second, all with sea views. Marble-top sinks and dressers are part of the authentic Victoriana, as are the brass-and-iron beds and the languidly turning paddles of the ceiling fans.

You may have to reserve well in advance in summer, when many returning guests come for a week or more, and the seacoast is gloriously uncrowded in the spring and fall. You are only 5 miles

from historic Portsmouth with its museums, galleries, restaurants, and all-year schedule of special events. From May to October, cruises to the offshore islands and whale-watching trips leave from Rye Harbor. A few miles south in North Hampton is the Factory Outlet Center, where you can shop seven days a week at more than 35 stores, tax free.

The two Seacoast State Parks are both in Rye. Rye Harbor Park has picnic areas and saltwater fishing. Odiorne Point was the site of the first European settlement in New Hampshire (1623) and has an Interpretive Center with programs offered by the Audubon Society and University of New Hampshire. Its tide pools are wonderful.

🛏 *2 double rooms with baths, 2 doubles with ½ baths, shared shower. $70–$90, full breakfast. No credit cards. No smoking, no pets, 2-night minimum on weekends June 15–Oct. 15.*

Other Choices

Exeter Inn. 90 Front St., Exeter, NH 03833, tel. 603/772–5901 or 800/782–8444, fax 603/778–8757. 46 double rooms with baths, 1 suite with fireplace. Restaurant, air-conditioning, cable TV, phones, fitness room with sauna, meeting and reception rooms. $75–$175. AE, D, DC, MC, V.

Governor's House Bed and Breakfast. 32 Miller Ave., Portsmouth NH 03801, tel. 603/431–6546, fax 603/427–0803. 4 double rooms with baths. Air-conditioning, cable TV in library, ceiling fans, tennis court, off-street parking. $75–$140, full breakfast. AE, MC, V. No smoking, no pets.

Governor's Inn. 78 Wakefield St., Rochester, NH 03867, tel. 603/332–0107, fax 603/335–1984. 8 double rooms with baths. Restaurant, air-conditioning, cable TV, wide-screen cable TV/VCR in recreation room, conference room that seats 150. $58–$108, full breakfast. AE, MC, V. No smoking, no pets.

Highland Farm Bed and Breakfast.
148 County Farm Rd., Dover, NH
03820, tel. 603/743–3399. 2 double rooms
share 1 bath. Cable TV/VCR in library.
$75–$87, full breakfast. MC, V. No smoking, no pets.

Inn at Christian Shore. 335 Maplewood Ave., Portsmouth, NH 03801, tel.
603/431–6770. 3 double rooms with
baths, 1 double room with ½ bath, 1
double and 1 single with shared bath.
Air-conditioning and cable TV in all
rooms. $35–$85, full breakfast. MC, V.
No smoking, no pets.

Inn at Elmwood Corners. 252 Winnacunnet Rd., Hampton, NH 03842, tel.
603/929–0443 or 800/253–5691. 5 double rooms share 3 baths, 2 housekeeping suites. TV, books, games in library.
$65–$90, full breakfast. MC, V. No
smoking, no pets, 2-night minimum on
holidays May–Oct.

Martin Hill Inn. 404 Islington St.,
Portsmouth, NH 03801, tel. 603/436–
2287. 4 double rooms with baths, 3
suites. Air-conditioning, off-street parking. $85–$110, full breakfast. MC, V. No
smoking, no pets.

The Oceanside. 365 Ocean Blvd.,
Hampton Beach, NH 03842, tel. 603/
926–3542, fax 603/926–3549. 9 double
rooms with baths. Air-conditioning,
guest refrigerator, beach chairs and
towels. $90–$125, Continental breakfast. AE, D, MC, V. No smoking, no
pets, 3-night minimum. Closed mid-
Oct.–mid-May.

Sise Inn. 40 Court St., Portsmouth,
NH 03801, tel. 603/433–1200 or 800/
267–0525 (reservations only), fax 603/
433–1200. 25 double rooms with baths,
9 suites. Air-conditioning, cable TV/
VCR, phones, some rooms with whirlpool baths, fireplaces, stereos, 3 meeting rooms, off-street parking. $99–
$175, Continental breakfast, AE, DC,
MC, V. No pets.

Victoria Inn. 430 High St., Hampton,
NH 03842, tel. 603/929–1437. 3 double
rooms with private baths, 3 doubles
share 1 hall bath. Air-conditioning,
cable TV, phones, off-street parking,
public beach nearby. $95–$115, full
breakfast. MC, V. No smoking, no
pets.

Lakes Region

Nutmeg Inn

*80 Pease Rd., Meredith, NH 03253, tel.
603/279–8811, fax 603/279–7203*

All the rooms are named after spices
and decorated accordingly. The walls of
Sage, for example, are just *that* shade
of green, and should you wonder how
the innkeepers, Kathleen and Horst
Sieben, managed to find a shower curtain to match the squares of the quilt,
the answer is that the quilts are handmade.

The Cape-style house was built in 1763
by a sea captain who dismantled his
ship to get the timber for the beams
and paneled what is now a dining room
with illegal "king's boards," those
extra-wide cuts reserved for royal
needs. An 18th-century ox yoke, said to
have been used during the original construction, is bolted to the wall over a
walk-in-size fireplace, and the wideboard floors are also original.

The Nutmeg has been a stagecoach
tavern, a working farm, part of the
Underground Railroad, and, in the
recent past, a private school. Kathleen
has a love for old houses and has made
a full-time job out of managing and renovating this one, doing much of the
work herself.

The Nutmeg is located on a rural side
street off Route 104, the main road that
runs between I–93 and Lake Winnipesaukee. Annalee's Doll Museum and
showroom are nearby. Two miles away
is Meredith village, where there are
galleries, shops, and the dock for lake
cruise ships. Gunstock ski and recre-

ation area is about 10 miles away, and there is easy access to the White Mountains as well. However, the Nutmeg has a 20- by 40-foot swimming pool and more than 7 acres of lawn and gardens. You might just want to stay right here and take it easy.

🏨 *8 double rooms with baths, 2 doubles share 1 bath, 1 suite. Air-conditioning, some rooms with working fireplaces, 3 rooms for private parties and meetings, swimming pool. $65–$85, full breakfast. MC, V. No smoking, no pets, 2-night minimum on weekends and holidays. Closed Nov.–Apr.*

Red Hill Inn

R.F.D. 1, Box 99M, Center Harbor, NH 03226, tel. 603/279–7001 or 800/573–3445, fax 603/279–7003

An amiable clutter of memorabilia from the first half of the 20th century makes this redbrick mansion on Overlook Hill an unusual country inn. A high school yearbook from the '40s; puzzles and board games from the '30s; mysterious gewgaws and whatnots from the '20s are what a fortunate houseguest in an old movie might discover.

When Rick Miller and Don Leavitt found Red Hill, it was a complex of vandalized buildings on the 60-acre campus of a defunct college. Happily they did not heed the advice to tear it down, but began the salvation and restoration of the main house, farmhouse, and stone cottage, which had, in 1904, been a grand summer estate and working farm. Outdoor porches were converted into bathrooms and sitting rooms, the latter with sweeping views of meadows, mountains, and Squam Lake. Period furniture and even books popular when the inn was a private house were acquired and set in place. If you ever wondered what happened to that old Philco radio, look in the Chocorua Suite. Surprise!

In the inn's dining room, guests quickly discover that Chef Elmer Davis loves dessert. On any given night, the wait staff must recite close to a dozen choices, including his famous vinegar pie (which is sweeter than it sounds), his windswept chocolate torte, and his Kentucky High Pie. But before you get that far, try one of his special appetizers, maybe the baked brie wrapped in phyllo, or any one of two dozen entrées featuring seafood, lamb, and duck. Many of the fresh herbs are grown on the premises. The large, hearty herb garden on the inn's east side features everything from the ordinary (parsely, thyme, chives) to the extraordinary (hyssop, Egyption onion, winter savory, and sweet woodruff). In each room guests find a map of the garden and a history of each of the herbs grown in it.

After dinner guests head for the popular Runabout Lounge in which a 1940 Chris Craft speedboat has been halved to form the bar. This is the same model boat featured in the 1981 movie, *On Golden Pond*, much of which was shot on Squam Lake. But the best way to end a day at the Red Hill Inn is to grab a book and a cup of tea and simply watch the sun set over Squam Lake from the great bay window in the common room.

🏨 *16 double rooms with baths, 5 suites. Restaurant, lounge, phones, TV/VCR in living room, many Franklin stoves, some whirlpool baths, tennis courts and cross-country skiing nearby. $85–$165, full breakfast. AE, D, DC, MC, V. No pets, 2-night minimum on weekends.*

Tamworth Inn

Box 189, Main St., Tamworth, NH 03886, tel. 603/323–7721 or 800/642–7352

Tamworth village is synonymous with the Barnstormers Playhouse, summer-night entertainment no one—visitor or resident—would think of missing. Just down the street, the tower of the venerable Tamworth Inn is nearly as well known.

Phil and Kathy Bender, who bought the rambling 1830s Victorian a few years ago, have achieved a rare balance. This haven for rest and refreshment since stagecoach days is now where townspeople come for a wedding in the gazebo, new American cuisine in the dining room, or a casual evening in the pub.

Behind the inn, gardens and lawn taper to Swift River. Here Kathy has put her former profession of landscape architect to work, making the most of the romantic gazebo setting with plants and flowers indigenous to New England. Phil, a former banker, manages and co-hosts the inn.

The Benders have reduced the total number of rooms in favor of all private baths and four suites. Some rooms are large enough for a third person, and all are furnished with a mixture of 19th-century country antiques and 20th-century pieces.

In winter, fires crackle on the hearths of the dining room, library, and living room, and pots of potpourri in water sit over warming candles. In the pub, there's time for conversation around the Franklin stove as cross-country skiers drop in, and regulars swap ice-fishing stories.

In summer, diners sit in the main dining room and in the screened porch, and the 20-by-40-foot outdoor swimming pool becomes the center for relaxation as well as a hangout for the theater cast and crew. You can also carry a good book down to the hammock by the river and just forget the world completely.

Morning coffee will be brought to your bedroom, if you like. When you amble at leisure to the cheery corner breakfast room you can help yourself to juice, cereal, home-baked breads and muffins, Kathy's special eggs, or French toast.

🏠 *11 double rooms with baths, 4 suites. Restaurant, partial air-conditioning, TV/VCR (with movie collection), swimming pool, fly-fishing in stream. $95–$115, full breakfast; $120–$140, MAP for 2. MC, V. No smoking, 2-night minimum on holidays.*

Wakefield Inn

2723 Wakefield Rd., Wakefield, NH 03872, tel. 603/522–8272 or 800/245–0841

When you turn off Route 16 and drive east to the historic district of Wakefield Corner, time and traffic vanish. A New England miracle? Well, no, but the Wakefield Inn is listed on the National Register of Historic Places for good reason. It is a gem of Federal architecture, as square and substantial as a fully rigged ship, which is precisely what its seagoing builder demanded. He also insisted it be an unconventional three stories high, so he could have the tallest house in the village, and he originally built two houses side by side. Soon the two were joined as one, and later on, a wraparound porch was added.

All this and more you learn from Harry Sisson, who shares innkeeping and ownership with his wife, Lou. The Sissons came to New Hampshire from Connecticut. "We moved in, and the first thing I had to do was cater a wedding reception," Lou recalls. Wedding receptions are numerous here (the village church is across the street). Two doors away is the Museum of Childhood. Inn guests receive free passes.

Inside the inn there are surprises: a three-sided fireplace in the dining room; the freestanding spiral staircase (no supporting center pole) is one of the few in the United States. Indian shutters and wide pine floors are typical of the late-Colonial era. Upstairs, the guest rooms are named after important 19th-century visitors, such as John Greenleaf Whittier. Throughout the inn are framed tintypes of unsmiling New

Englanders. Some pictures the Sissons found in the attic; some are the gifts of inn guests. Many of the subjects are unknown, the "instant ancestors" of the flea market.

All the bedrooms are large—several have an extra bed, ideal for a family—with views of the mountains and countryside or of the historic village. Forget your toothbrush? No matter. Baskets of "most likely to be forgotten" items sit on hall stands inviting you to help yourself.

Lou's handmade quilts provide the decorative center for the bedrooms. She also holds special "quilting weekends" at the inn, assuring guests they will return home with completed (or nearly so) quilts of their own.

▦ *7 double rooms with baths. Dinner by advance reservation only. $65–$75, full breakfast. MC, V. No smoking in bedrooms, no pets, 2-night minimum on holidays.*

Wolfeboro Inn

90 N. Main St., Box 1270, Wolfeboro, NH 03894, tel. 603/569–3016 or 800/451–2389, fax 603/569–5375

A landmark lakeside inn with the amenities of a complete resort and the warmth of a bed-and-breakfast, the Wolfeboro is one block from town and a stroll from the galleries, shops, and sights of the historic village. The original white clapboard house with green shutters faces Main Street, but extensions overlook Wolfeboro Bay.

The rooms and suites are furnished in well-polished cherry and pine, flowered chintzes, with no kitsch whatsoever. The baths have heating lamps, and TVs are mostly tucked out of sight in armoires. Some rooms have quilts and folk art, but the general feeling is one of controlled elegance: Blue, mauve, and maroon are the principal colors.

Structural additions have been made since the inn's beginnings in the 1800s: Rooms in the newest wing are a tad brighter than the older ones, and many have balconies or decks. The oldest part of the inn includes some original (1812) bedrooms with fireplaces, as well as the venerable Wolfe's Tavern. The main dining room has Windsor chairs, a working fireplace, and paneling from the 1760s.

Things get a bit more rustic in the old tavern, where there is an oven fireplace, and the serving staff can offer 40 brands of beer from all over the world. On the menu of hearty hot and cold specialties is Montcalm's Revenge, a sandwich big enough for six hungry people.

Guests at the inn are multigenerational and many are lake regulars (and remember coming here as children) as well as first-timers and honeymooners. It would be a shame to come just for overnight and not take advantage of the full span of facilities. Everything is available for a prolonged lake holiday, from the inn's excursion boat (no charge to guests for boat trips or any other amenity) to many other sports facilities. Tennis and golf are nearby.

In winter you can try skiing, skating, ice fishing, and ice boating while taking advantage of low off-season package rates. The tavern is handy for hot mulled cider between events.

▦ *38 double rooms with baths, 5 suites, 1 1-bedroom apartment. Restaurant, tavern, air-conditioning, cable TV, phones, elevator, room service, private lake beach, excursion boat (operated seasonally), conference facilities in inn or on boat. $79–$169, Continental breakfast. AE, MC, V. No pets.*

Other Choices

Inn on Golden Pond. Rte. 3, Box 680, Holderness, NH 03245, tel. 603/968–7269. 7 double rooms with baths, 1 suite. Cable TV in common room, game room in summer. $95–$135, full breakfast. AE, MC, V. No smoking, no pets.

Inn on Newfound Lake. 1030 Mayhew Turnpike (Rte. 3A), Bridgewater, NH 03222, tel. 603/744–9111. Main inn: 6 double rooms with baths, 4 doubles with private hall baths, 8 doubles share 4 baths; Lilac House (open May–Oct.): 8 doubles with baths (4 can be made into suites). Restaurant, badminton, croquet, recreation room in barn. $55–$195, Continental breakfast. AE, D, MC, V. No smoking in large dining room, no pets, 2-night minimum on weekends June–Oct.

Kona Mansion Inn. Moultonboro Neck Rd., Moultonboro, Box 458, Center Harbor, NH 03226, tel. 603/253–4900, fax 603/253–7350. 9 double rooms with baths, 4 housekeeping cottages, 2 3-bedroom chalets. Restaurant, TVs in rooms, air-conditioning in main building, 3 meeting rooms, swimming, golf, tennis free to guests. $65–$140, breakfast extra. MC, V. No pets in main building. Closed Nov.–Apr.

Tuc' Me Inn. 118 N. Main St., Wolfeboro, NH 03894, tel. 603/569–5702. 3 double rooms with baths, 4 with shared baths. Cable TV in parlor, air-conditioning in bedrooms, cross-country and hiking trails nearby. $65–$85, full breakfast. MC, V. No smoking, no pets.

Reservations Services

Bed and Breakfast Inns of New England (33 Red Gate La., Meredith, NH 03253, tel. 603/279–8348). **Lake Sunapee Business Assoc.** (Box 400, Sunapee, NH 03782, tel. 603/763–2495 or 800/258–3530).

White Mountains

Inn at Thorn Hill

Thorn Hill Rd., Jackson, NH 03846, tel. 603/383–4242 or 800/289–8990, fax 603/383–8062

Romantic is a word you hear a lot at Thorn Hill, the mansion designed by Stanford White, the Gilded Age's most famous architect. Staying here, you are within walking distance of shops, galleries, and sports, but still in your own special place, and the view of Mount Washington from here is superb.

Jim and Ibby Cooper, owners and proprietors, came to Thorn Hill from hospitality and education careers in California, Texas, and Florida. Their older children—excited to be involved—fit right in with a lifestyle that seems less a business than a constant round of entertaining good friends. Yet the elegant past is never far away. In the drawing room you are greeted by two mannequins wearing 1870s wedding and wedding reception dresses. In one bedroom, a blue velvet fainting couch is an invitation to swoon; spectacular Oriental rugs and electrified Victorian oil lamps are everywhere.

While the main house is unabashedly romantic-traditional, the carriage house has been done in the country style of the same period. Here the open fireplace and overstuffed sofas of the Great Room suggest you can sprawl, and the Steinway baby grand piano of the main-house drawing room is balanced with the Carriage House's outdoor hot tub. Three cottages—beloved by honeymooners—are done in an eclectic blend best described as, well, romantic.

Thorn Hill is a year-round retreat. In spring, summer, and autumn, there are wildflowers and pine forests, swimming, hiking, fishing, and the like. In winter, you can step directly from the inn's waxing room onto the 150-kilometer Jackson Ski-Touring cross-country trail network or ski downhill at five major areas nearby. You can toboggan on the property, and a horse-drawn sleigh will pick you up at the door.

Thorn Hill's dining room is becoming known throughout the valley for its contemporary New England cuisine and its wine list—as well as the candlelight.

🖽 *13 double rooms with baths, 3 suites, 3 cottages. Restaurant, pub, air-conditioning in main house and cottages, cable TV/VCR in parlor, small meeting room in carriage house, swimming pool, badminton, shuffleboard, croquet, horseshoes, cross-country ski trails, tobogganing. $110–$220, full breakfast; $140–$275, MAP. AE, D, DC, MC, V. No smoking, no pets, 2-night minimum on foliage, Christmas, and holiday weekends. Closed Apr.*

Notchland Inn

Rte. 302, Hart's Location, Bartlett, NH 03812, tel. 603/374–6131 or 800/866–6131, fax 603/374–6168

In the barn of Notchland Inn there are llamas. Yet these rare animals are only part of the surprises of this highland estate overlooking the Saco River Valley at the entrance to Crawford Notch. The mountain lodge, built of locally quarried granite and native timbers, is equally unexpected. It was constructed in 1852 by Samuel Bemis, a Boston dentist. The lifetime bachelor bequeathed it to his loyal caretaker, whose children began to take in summer guests. Notchland became a year-round inn in 1983.

Since then, innkeepers have added such renovations as a new wing with a gourmet restaurant, and a gazebo by the duck pond. An old schoolhouse has become a two-suite guest house, with working fireplaces and early photographs of the mountains on the walls. The main house has not changed much since the 19th century. The bedrooms have armoires, wing chairs, and afghans as well as fireplaces. Guests gather in the Stickley Room for apéritifs or cocktails before dinner.

Les Schoof and Ed Butler, the current owners, bought the inn in 1993 when they moved here from Manhattan. They have brought their own touches, such as the award-winning perennial gardens out back.

The accessories are as predictable as dried flowers and as unusual as the slate grave marker that reads "1788. Nancy Barton died in a snowstorm in pursuit of her faithless lover."

The seasons unfold from this mountainside vantage point. You can try whitewater canoeing in springtime, hiking and trout fishing in summer. There is ice-skating on the inn pond in winter and miles of trails for cross-country skiing. The barn houses a pair of draft horses who draw hayrides in autumn and sleigh rides in winter. Notchland is surrounded by a National Forest, and while there is much to do outdoors at Hart's Location, it's an early-to-bed sort of place.

🖽 *7 double rooms with baths, 4 suites. Fireplaces, 2 meeting rooms, outdoor hot tub, river swimming, hiking and cross-country ski trails. $130–$190, full breakfast; $170–$230, MAP. AE, D, MC, V. No smoking, no pets, 2- to 3-night minimum on weekends and some holidays.*

Snowvillage Inn

Stuart Rd. (Fire La. 37), Snowville, NH 03849, tel. 603/447–2818 or 800/447–4345

From 1,000 feet up on the side of Mt. Foss, the span of the Presidential Range at sunset appears hand colored. No wonder Barbara and Kevin Flynn find it ideal for their own country inn. For hikers, skiers, readers, and environmentalists as well as lovers of good food, Snowvillage was, and is, irresistible.

The guest rooms (including one with 12 windows) are in the main house, in an old carriage barn/library, and in a new lodge, where every room has a working fireplace. Each has been named for a writer or literary genre and contains appropriate bedside reading. Although many of the fascinating pictures and accessories are Tyrolean, the architecture is New England farmhouse, and the buildings are a cheerful cranberry red with white trim.

Oriental rugs, wing chairs, good reading lights, knotty pine paneling, and welcoming homemade chocolate chip cookies will make you feel not only cared for, but right at home. Breakfast might include eggs Benedict, pumpkin pancakes, vegetable omelets, or French toast stuffed with cream cheese and apricot preserves. Packed lunches and special guided hikes with gourmet food can be arranged, right down to a five-course champagne lunch. Cooking classes are held at the inn three times a year: spring, fall, and winter.

In winter, there's professional instruction in cross-country skiing, and at any time of year Kevin is ready to point out a trail through the blueberry barrens or map out the way to the area's numerous antiques and discount-shopping meccas. Guests have resident beach privileges at Crystal Lake, minutes away.

The four-course candlelight dinner might begin with the chef's specialty, Mediterranean fish soup or homemade pâté, although the bulk of the menu relies on such country French mainstays as duck à l'orange and rack of lamb. Save room for the silk pie that regulars rave about or even some pumpkin cheesecake.

🏛 *18 double rooms with baths. Restaurant, 3 small conference rooms, resident privileges at lake, tennis court, volleyball, horseshoes, cross-country skiing (equipment rental, lessons), hiking trails, sauna, cooking school. $118–$210, full breakfast. AE, D, MC, V. No smoking, no pets.*

Sunset Hill House

Sunset Hill Rd., Sugar Hill, NH 03585, tel. 603/823-5522 or 800/786-4455, fax 603/823-5738

In 1882, in the era of the grand hotel, a magnificent inn was built in Sugar Hill.

It was perched on a 1,700-foot ridge that gave guests a stunning view of both the Presidential Range to the east and Vermont's Green Mountains to the west. This prize location was best known for the fiery glow that played out over the White Mountains at the end of each day, and so the hill and the inn were both named for these beautiful sunsets. Although the great hotel is now gone, a more modest Sunset Hill House continues to serve guests as a country inn.

Innkeepers Michael and Trisha Coyle renovated, redecorated, and opened this second empire Victorian house in 1993. The interior is done in bright country floral patterns, without seeming frilly or precious. Each of the inn's three large common areas has its own feel: a formal sitting parlor, a lively music parlor, and a very informal game room with a TV/VCR. Outside, the 30-by 30-foot deck looks out to the Presidential Range. Many of the rooms have nonworking fireplaces. Although every room has a view of some distant mountains, some have bay windows that make perfect reading nooks. Two larger rooms are Jacuzzi suites. The best room in the inn, the innkeeper's favorite, is No. 201, which has two bay windows that look onto the Presidential Range.

Expect homey, friendly service. Guests who stay during Thanksgiving weekend usually take part in the holiday work bee to ready the inn for the Christmas season. The Sunset Hill House has a Valentine theme weekend, a Maple Sugaring weekend in March for tapping trees and boiling sap, and a lupine festival held each June when the hillside is awash in lavender blooms.

The multicourse breakfast includes items such as banana-stuffed French toast, vegetable quiche, and sweet potato and roast beef hash. The Sunset Hill has both a restaurant and a tavern. The restaurant menu is quite fancy and favors such complex dishes as roast rack of lamb with a granola-mustard crust, split and finished with port wine–peppercorn sauce; or sesame sugar-crusted chicken breast, while the lighter tavern menu features sandwiches, nachos, and pizza.

🎫 *27 double rooms with baths, 3 suites. Restaurant, tavern, cable TV in common areas, informal room service, ceiling fans in rooms, heated swimming pool. $75–$145, full breakfast. AE, D, MC, V. No smoking, no pets, 2-night minimum during foliage season and holiday weekends.*

Other Choices

Franconia Inn. Easton Rd., Franconia, NH 03580, tel. 603/823–5542 or 800/473–5299, fax 603/823–8078. 31 double rooms with baths, 3 suites. Restaurant, cable TV in lounge, movie room, game room, hot tub, swimming pool, 4 tennis courts, sleigh rides in winter, cross-country skiing, bicycles, croquet, riding stable (8 horses), soaring center, golf privileges at nearby 9-hole course. $75–$113, full breakfast; MAP rates available. AE, MC, V. No pets. Closed Apr.–mid-May.

Horse & Hound Inn. 205 Wells Rd., Franconia, NH 03580, tel. 603/823–5501. 8 double rooms with baths, 2 double suites. Restaurant, cable TV in lounge, cross-country ski trail. $65–$115, full breakfast. AE, D, DC, MC, V. Closed Apr. and Nov.

Inn at Crystal Lake. Rte. 153, Box 12, Eaton Center, NH 03832, tel. 603/447–2120 or 800/343–7336, fax 603/447–3599. 11 double rooms with baths. Canoes, lake swimming. $60–$100, full breakfast. AE, D, MC, V. Restricted smoking, no pets, 2-night minimum on holidays.

Lavender Flower Inn. Box 328, Main St., Center Conway, NH 03813, tel. 603/447–3794 or 800/729–0106. 3 double rooms with baths, 4 doubles share 2 baths. Cable TV in living room. $50–$93, full breakfast and snacks. AE, D,

MC, V. No smoking, no pets, 2-night minimum on holiday weekends.

Mulburn Inn. Main St., Bethlehem, NH 03574, tel. 603/869–3389 or 800/457–9440. 7 double rooms with baths. TV in common room, 2 18-hole golf courses nearby. $55–$90, full breakfast and afternoon tea. AE, D, MC, V. No smoking, no pets.

1785 Inn. Box 1785, Rte. 16, North Conway, NH 03860, tel. 603/356–9025 or 800/421–1785, fax 603/356–6081. 12 double rooms with baths, 5 doubles share 2 baths, 1 suite. Restaurant and bar, air-conditioning, cable TV in bar and suite, cable TV/VCR in guest living room, 4 fireplaces in public rooms, room service, swimming pool, cross-country ski and hiking trails, volleyball, shuffleboard, tennis. $60–$159, full breakfast. AE, D, DC, MC, V. No smoking in main dining room or in bedrooms, no pets, 2-night minimum during foliage season.

Sugar Hill Inn. Rte. 117, Box 954, Franconia, NH 03580, tel. 603/823–5621 or 800/548–4748. 10 double rooms with baths in main house, 6 doubles with baths in 3 cottages. Restaurant, air-conditioning in dining room, fireplaces in 2 cottages. $100–$135, full breakfast and afternoon tea. AE, MC, V. No smoking, no pets, 2-night minimum in foliage season.

Whitneys' Inn. Rte. 16B, Jackson, NH 03846, tel. 603/383–6886 or 800/677–5737. 20 double rooms with baths, 8 suites, 2 2-bedroom cottages. Restaurant; air-conditioning and TV in some rooms; 3 meeting rooms with catering; cable TV in lounge, pub, and game room; fireplaces in cottages; swimming pond; tennis. $64–$166, breakfast; MAP available. AE, D, MC, V. No smoking in dining room; 2-night minimum on holidays and on some weekends, Jan.–Mar., July–Aug., mid-Sept.–mid-Oct.

Reservations Services

Jackson Resort Association (tel. 800/866–3334). **Mt. Washington Valley Central Reservation Service** (tel. 800/367–3364). **Mt. Washington Valley Chamber of Commerce** (tel. 603/356–5701 or 800/367–3364). **Reservation Service of the Country Inns in the White Mountains** (tel. 603/356–9460 or 800/562–1300). For referrals (not direct reservations) in communities around Berlin, contact the **Northern White Mountains Chamber of Commerce** (tel. 800/992–7480).

Fitzwilliam

Amos A. Parker House

Rte. 119, Box 202, Fitzwilliam, NH 03447, tel. 603/585–6540

"Oh, what's this?" are words Freda Haupt hears a lot from her guests. Great bunches of her own dried flowers hang in the barn sitting room of the Amos A. Parker House, only one of the hobbies of the creative and energetic owner. An eye-stopping garden slopes to the river behind the house, and on the roadside, a genuine liberty pole attests to its history as a meeting place for Revolutionaries. Today's kitchen and Great Room were the original cabin in 1700, but by 1780, the shelter had grown to a family home requiring six (still working) fireplaces.

You stroll downhill to the Fitzwilliam Green with its ring of 18th-century houses and overflowing antiques stores. Minutes away are Rhododendron State Park and the all-faith outdoor Cathedral of the Pines.

▦ *2 double rooms with baths, 2 suites. Tennis courts and cross-country trails nearby. $80–$90, full breakfast. No credit cards. No smoking, no pets, 2-night minimum on holidays.*

Hannah Davis House

186 Depot Rd., Fitzwilliam, NH 03447, tel. 603/585–3344

The fragrance of baking bread sets the mood for this 1820 Federal house only steps from the Monadnock village green. Kaye Terpstra occasionally helps out her neighbor at the Amos A. Parker House. In Kaye's kitchen-hearth room, the old beehive oven no longer functions, but elsewhere in the house, four fireplaces all work, and the oversize bathrooms have tubs with cat's-paw feet and brass fittings. The enormous hanging scale in the kitchen is a memory of the country store the Terpstras owned elsewhere before deciding to open their bed-and-breakfast. Kaye, a former social worker, and Mike, who was an engineer, now pursue cooking and carpentry. Kaye describes her mouthwatering breakfasts: omelet stuffed with bacon, cream cheese, tomato, and herbs; crepes with parsley sauce; homemade granola, applesauce, and breads. In returning the house to its original form, Mike has managed to save much of the old glass as well as the T-over-T doors and chair-rail wainscoting. And he has thoughtfully added a deck so guests can enjoy Fitzwilliam's picture-book spires and rooftops just beyond the trees.

▦ *3 double rooms with baths, 3 suites. Cable TV/VCR in common area. $60–$95, full breakfast. MC, V. No smoking in bedrooms, no pets.*

New Jersey

Chimney Hill Farm

Jersey Shore

Hollycroft

506 North Blvd. (Box 448, Spring Lake, NJ 07762), tel. 908/681-2254

One of the people who built this summer house in 1908 wanted a place at the shore; the other wanted a mountain retreat. The resulting compromise is this Adirondack-style lodge nestled among the trees on a bluff above Lake Como, at the northern edge of Spring Lake. It's a little out of the way and hard to find, but it's well worth the effort.

Architect Mark Fessler and his wife, Linda, who loves crafts and collecting, bought Hollycroft in 1985 and maintained its North Country mood throughout. The house was constructed of white cedar and ironstone with a half-timbered stucco-and-stone exterior. Inside, exposed log-and-stone walls peek out here and there among the knotty pine, while beamed ceilings add a sturdy exclamation point. In the living room, a 16-foot ironstone fireplace between two staircases faces a sunken, brick-floored area, where guests can sip sherry while looking out a wall of windows at Lake Como. The

breakfast buffet is set out in the adjacent dining area or in the glassed-in breakfast room. In warm weather, guests eat on the patio.

If the common areas haven't completely won you over, the guest rooms will. They are individually decorated and all but one has a view of the lake. Most have iron and brass beds, though some are made of wood. Stenciling is everywhere, as is evidence of the Fesslers' artful collecting.

The Pomeroy Room, in cool white and green, is like a garden. A side table is built of twigs, and the bed is made under a blanket of leaves. Windsor Rose is, not surprisingly, awash in roses. Its adjacent glassed-in porch with white wicker furniture serves as a private sitting area. Upstairs, where Linda and Mark added warm mahogany floors, are four rooms. Grassmere has a striking custom-made, cast-iron canopy bed and a gas fireplace with tile surround (one of two in bedrooms). (In addition, there are three wood-burning fireplaces in public areas, which suffuse the house with smells of a real fire.) Next door, Somerset has a dark-wood four-poster bed. It would have a completely masculine English-country air if not for the birdhouse and miniature furniture hanging in a corner. Lords of Manor, the honeymoon suite, comprises 650 square feet of luxury. It has a sitting room with TV/VCR, refrigerator, and bar and 7-foot French glass doors lead out to a screened porch that overlooks the lake. The bedroom, which has a cathedral ceiling and exposed log beams, has a queen-size canopy feather bed.

The inn is four blocks from the beach, and its proximity to Lake Como attracts anglers and bird-watchers. In the cooler months the Fesslers host mystery weekends.

🏨 *6 double rooms with baths, 1 suite. Air-conditioning, bicycles, beach towels, chairs, transportation to and from train and bus. $95–$150, full breakfast. AE. No smoking in bedrooms, no pets, 2-night minimum on weekends, 3-night minimum on holiday weekends.*

Normandy Inn

21 Tuttle Ave., Spring Lake, NJ 07762, tel. 908/449-7172, fax 908/449-1070

This huge Italianate villa with Queen Anne touches was built for the Audenreid family of Philadelphia around 1888 and became a guest house in 1909. It still had the feel of a guest house in 1982, when Michael and Susan Ingino, who had had an ice-cream business in nearby Toms River, bought the inn and slowly began transforming it into a textbook of high-Victorian furnishings.

The Normandy, on the National Register of Historic Places, has become the standard against which the other bed-and-breakfasts in Spring Lake are measured. The inn's museum-quality furnishings create a formal atmosphere that the Inginos deliberately undercut, urging guests to relax. "To see a guest curl up on a sofa with a book is just what I want," Mike explains.

With the exception of rattan furniture in the casual enclosed side porch, there are no reproductions or modern pieces here. Everything is genuine American Victorian, from the first floor's formerly gaslit chandeliers and Renaissance Revival parlor set with women's faces carved on the arms to the Rococo Revival and Eastlake bedroom sets found in the guest rooms upstairs.

Rooms are individually decorated down to the wallpaper and carpeting. Two are particularly spectacular, but for very different reasons. A room in the front half of the second floor, where 11-foot ceilings are rimmed with plaster moldings, has a very impressive four-piece burled-wood bedroom set. Much less formal is the Tower Room, which has windows on four sides. Though its bathroom is down the stairs and down the hall (bathrobes are provided), it's only a minor inconvenience when you consider the bright sunlight, cool breezes, and views over the rooftops to the ocean.

For families (well-behaved children are very welcome here), there are two suites, each with a gas fireplace. One of them, above a 1930s garage, has a full kitchen and green marble whirlpool bath for two. It's done in a contemporary style but is still dotted with turn-of-the-century antiques.

The four-course hot breakfasts make it easy to skip lunch and spend the day at the beach, a two-minute walk away.

🏨 *14 double rooms and 1 single with baths, 2 suites. Air-conditioning, phones, cable TV on side porch and in rooms upon request, fireplace in parlor, bicycles, beach tags, towels and chairs, transportation to and from train and bus. $108–$270, full breakfast. AE, D, DC, MC, V. Restricted smoking, no pets, 2-night minimum on weekdays July–Aug. and on weekends Mar.–Nov., 3-night minimum on weekends July–Aug. and on holiday weekends.*

Pierrót by the Sêa

101 Centre St., Beach Haven, NJ 08008, tel. 609/492-4424

Innkeepers Jane Loehwing and her daughter Jennifer had lived in North Jersey all their lives. In 1994, in search of peace and quiet and to take on the challenge of running their own business, they bought this ivory-colored B&B on Long Beach Island.

The restoration of the 1865 inn is accurate to the high-Victorian era, with the exception of a 12-foot-tall mahogany reproduction of a bedroom set that a previous owner, a professional Victorian restorer, made to see how closely he could match the style. (He matched it perfectly.) There's Queen Anne fireside chairs in the first-floor parlor and intricately carved walnut bedroom sets, Oriental rugs, and multiple wallpapers in the bedrooms—but oh, the stained glass.

There are a handful of original stained-glass windows remaining, but the showstoppers, all over the house, were made by the previous owner. The glass in the front door has a beautiful palette of vibrant colors, in the dining room window is a stained-glass tree, and the glass in the bedrooms blends with each color scheme. One window in a front bedroom glows at daybreak, and even the outside shower has its own stained glass.

Looking beyond the windows, you can see (and hear) the ocean from the majority of the rooms. The inn is just a half block from the dune-backed beach and is within walking distance of restaurants, the movies, outdoor amusements, and theater. Unfortunately, the modern motels across the street generate noise on Saturday nights in summer that, according to Jane, makes it seem like "42nd Street in a bathing suit." Air conditioners, when turned on, mask the sound.

An elaborate multicourse breakfast is served in the dining room in winter, while in warmer months guests and lighter fare move out to the wraparound veranda, where two rooms have private entrances. Other activities on your not-so-busy agenda might include walking, cycling, rollerblading, or taking the brick path to the gazebo for some serious seaside relaxation.

▦ *6 double rooms with baths, 3 doubles share bath. Air-conditioning in 4 bedrooms, cable TV and fireplace in parlor, bicycles, beach tags, tennis badges. $75–$160; Continental breakfast Memorial Day–Labor Day, afternoon tea. No credit cards. No smoking, no pets, 2-night minimum on weekends, 3- to 4-night minimum on holiday weekends.*

Other Choices

Ashling Cottage. 106 Sussex Ave., Spring Lake, NJ 07762, tel. 908/449–3553 or 888/274–5464. 8 double rooms with baths, 2 doubles share bath. Air-conditioning in most rooms. cable TV/VCR and gas fireplace in parlor, bicycles, beach tags, towels, chairs, transportation to and from train and bus. $75–$160, full breakfast. No credit cards. Restricted smoking, no pets, 2-night minimum on weekends, 3-night minimum on holiday weekends. Closed Jan.–Apr.

BarnaGate Bed & Breakfast. 637 Wesley Ave., Ocean City, NJ 08226, tel. 609/391–9366. 1 double room with bath, 1 double with ½ bath, 3 double rooms share 2 baths. Cable TV in parlor, beach tags, transportation to and from train and bus. $70–$120, Continental breakfast. AE, MC, V. No smoking, no pets, 2-night minimum on weekends in season.

Bayberry Barque. 117 Centre St., Beach Haven, NJ 08008, tel. 609/492–5216. 5 double rooms with baths, 3 doubles share bath. Cable TV in living room, mini-refrigerator in hall, outdoor shower, beach tags and chairs. $70–$135; Continental breakfast, Sat. afternoon wine-and-cheese parties in summer. MC, V. No smoking, no pets, 2-night minimum on weekends mid-June–mid-Sept., 3-night minimum on holiday weekends.

Candlelight Inn. 2310 Central Ave., North Wildwood, NJ 08260, tel. 609/522–6200, fax 609/522–6125. 7 double rooms with baths, 3 suites. Air-conditioning in 4 bedrooms, cable TV in parlor and 1 suite, fireplaces in parlor, one bedroom, one suite, and 2nd-floor foyer, hot tub on sundeck, whirlpool baths in one room and one suite. $100–$250; full breakfast, afternoon refreshments. AE, D, MC, V. No smoking, no pets, 3-night minimum on weekends July–Aug.

Chateau. 500 Warren Ave., Spring Lake, NJ 07762, tel. 908/974–2000, fax 908/974–0007. 30 double rooms with baths, 6 suites, 2 housekeeping units. Air-conditioning, phones, TV/VCRs, 17 rooms have wet bars, 12 rooms have fireplaces, 10 rooms have soaking tubs, bicycle rentals, beach tags. $62–$215, Continental breakfast extra (except in Winter, Sun.–Thurs.). AE, D, DC, MC, V. No pets. 2-night minimum on weekends July–Aug.; 3-night minimum on weekends June–Sept.; 2-, 3-, or 4-night minimum on holiday weekends.

Conover's Bay Head Inn. 646 Main Ave., Bay Head, NJ 08742, tel. 908/892–4664 or 800/956–9099, fax 908/892–8748. 12 double rooms with baths. Air-conditioning in bedrooms, guest refrigerator, fireplace in parlor, beach tags, towels and chairs, on-site parking, transportation to and from train and bus. $100–$210; full breakfast, afternoon tea. AE, MC, V. No smoking, no pets, 3- or 4-night minimum on holiday and summer weekends.

Henry Ludlam Inn. 1336 Rte. 47, Dennisville, NJ 08270, tel. 609/861–5847. 5 double rooms with baths. Air-conditioning, cable TV in parlor and on porch, fireplaces in 3 bedrooms and common room, beach tags. $85–$120; full breakfast, afternoon refreshments. AE, MC, V. No smoking, no pets, 2-night minimum on weekends May–Nov., 3-night minimum on holiday weekends.

Sea Crest by the Sea. 19 Tuttle Ave., Spring Lake, NJ 07762, tel. 908/449–9031 or 800/803–9031, fax 908/974–0403. 10 double rooms with baths, 2 suites. Air-conditioning, TV/VCRs, phones, mini-refrigerators in suites and hall, fireplaces in 8 rooms and parlor, croquet, bicycles, beach tags, towels and chairs. $159–$259; full breakfast, afternoon tea. AE, MC, V. Restricted smoking, no pets, 2-night minimum on weekends Sept.–June and on weekdays July–Aug., 3-night minimum on weekends July–Aug. and on holiday weekends.

Seaflower. 110 9th Ave., Belmar, NJ 07719, tel. 908/681–6006. 5 double rooms with baths, 1 suite. TV/VCR and games in parlor, mini-refrigerator in hall, bicycles, beach tags, transportation to and from train. $70–$140, full breakfast. AE. No smoking, no pets, 2-night minimum on weekends Memorial Day–Labor Day, 3-night minimum on holiday weekends.

Studio. 102 Cedar Ave., Island Heights, NJ 08732, tel. 908/270–6058. 3 double rooms share 2 baths. Air-conditioning, cable TV in sunroom, fireplaces in studio and library, bicycles, bay and river beach tags, beach towels. $85, full breakfast. AE. No pets.

Victoria Guest House. 126 Amber St., Beach Haven, NJ 08008, tel. 609/492–4154. 17 double rooms with baths. Air-conditioning in 10 bedrooms, guest refrigerators, bicycles, beach tags and chairs, tennis badges. $95–$145; Continental-plus breakfast, afternoon lemonade and iced tea. No credit cards. No smoking, no pets, 2½- or 3½-day minimum on weekends. Closed Columbus Day–mid-May.

Reservations Service

Bed & Breakfast Adventures (2310 Central Ave., Suite 132, North Wildwood 08260, tel. 609/522–4000 or 800/992–2632 for reservations, fax 609/522–6125).

Along the Delaware

Chimney Hill Bed and Breakfast

207 Goat Hill Rd., Lambertville, NJ 08530, tel. 609/397–1516, fax 609/397–9353

Owners Terry and Richard Anderson have big plans for this inn on a rolling ridge above the quaint town of Lambertville. The original 1820 fieldstone building was enlarged in 1927 by Margaret Spencer, one of the first female architects to graduate from MIT. The Andersons' proposed additions include converting the carriage house, barn, and greenhouse with an eye to boosting corporate business and reclaiming the formal gardens, raspberry bushes, and boxwood maze, which had fallen on hard times. The couple has even started occasional "seasonal gatherings," in which an actor in period costume entertains guests with facts and folklore.

It's hard not to want to curl up by the fire on one of the wicker chaises in the beamed sunroom, where windows on two sides bathe the stone room in light. A full breakfast is served at candlelit tables in the low-ceilinged dining room, lined with hunt prints, and the adjacent guest pantry stocks sherry and snacks for other hours. Echoing the landscaping outside, flora is the dominant motif in the bedrooms, from the rose-covered bed and ivy stenciling of the Ivy Room to the sunflowers of Vincent's Hideaway (named for Van Gogh).

▦ *8 double rooms with baths. Air-conditioning in bedrooms, fireplaces in 3 public areas and 5 bedrooms, on-site parking, balloon trips from inn arranged. $75–$150, full breakfast. AE, MC, V. No smoking, no pets, 2-night minimum on weekends in season, 3-night minimum on holiday weekends.*

Inn at Millrace Pond

313 Johnsonburg Rd., Rte. 519 (Box 359), Hope, NJ 07844, tel. 908/459–4884, fax 908/459–5276

In the historic Moravian village of Hope, an old millrace leaves a small millpond and flows through a chasm of slate toward a 1769 stone gristmill, which once supplied flour to Washington's troops and is now an inn. When you enter its gorgeous foyer, you can look down a story and a half at the skeleton of the old wheel and walk downstairs between stone walls to see where the millrace once ran (in summer, a little water still flows in the channel). Though the inn complex also includes two other Colonial buildings used for lodging, as well as antiques and gift shops, the focus is on the gristmill with its guest rooms, a tavern, and a gourmet restaurant. Its architecture is stunning, from the bottom-floor tavern, with its huge walk-in fireplace, cage bar, and flour chute, to the top floor's bedrooms, where cathedral ceilings reveal the enormous timbers of the roof. The building's beams and wide-board floors have been preserved throughout.

The gristmill bedrooms have Shaker reproductions; elsewhere there are regional antiques—made in New York, Pennsylvania, and New Jersey. The six-bedroom Millrace House, a frame building that was the miller's dwelling, has more formal furnishings and a parlor with a fireplace. Its bedrooms and the two in the Stone Cottage have collections of Queen Anne, Chippendale, and Sheraton pieces. Each of the Stone Cottage bedrooms (one upstairs and one down) has its own entrance, and they are prized for romantic seclusion. Previous inn guests have included Nick Nolte, Barbra Streisand, Dustin Hoffman, and Michael Feinstein.

Innkeepers Cordie and Charles Puttkammer took over in 1993 and have been sprucing up the place since. She is a professor of childhood development, and he runs his own consulting business—that is, when he isn't collecting things or taking guests for a summer spin in his 1921 Cadillac touring car. The Puttkammers are ably assisted by general manager Dirck Noel, who is about as happy in his work as a person can be.

🏨 *15 double rooms with baths, 1 suite. Restaurant; tavern; air-conditioning; phones; cable TV in 10 bedrooms and parlor; fireplaces in 1 room, parlor, and tavern; tennis; $85–$165, Continental breakfast. AE, DC, MC, V. No smoking, 2-night minimum with Sat. reservation.*

Stewart Inn

708 S. Main St. (Box 6), Stewartsville, NJ 08886, tel. 908/479–6060, fax 908/479–4211

More than a decade ago attorney Brian McGarry and his wife, Lynne, an antiques collector and needlework-kit manufacturer, became the latest occupants of this rambling 1770 fieldstone manor house. It was originally built for the owner of Stewartsville's gristmill, which ground flour to feed George Washington's troops during the Revolutionary War. Between 1800 and 1967, it was added to countless times and passed between countless owners, among them Broadway producer Harry Bannister and his wife, actress Ann Harding, whose friends in the entertainment industry—among them Clark Gable—used the house as a retreat. Although the stars left nothing behind, the inn has retained a dramatic atmosphere.

About a 25-minute drive from the many fine restaurants of Lambertville, Stewart Inn has 16 acres of lawns; formal perennial gardens; a stocked trout stream; and a meandering pasture that leads to a working farm with ducks, sheep, goats, and peacocks. The eggs served at breakfast are provided by the farm's chickens. Lynne has a wild-game license, and it's not unusual for there to

be a wounded animal in residence that she's nursing back to health. More animals, in the form of knickknacks, make their home in the common areas downstairs.

The best times to visit the inn are summer, when the swimming pool offers a respite from the heat, and fall, when the maple and apple trees show off their bright colors. (Unfortunately, the hum from nearby I–78 mars the otherwise bucolic setting.) In the winter, the house is filled with plants brought in from the outside.

Inside, off-white walls bring out the richness of the dark cherry and mahogany furnishings and the colorful tapestries and rugs. Many rooms have antique jam cupboards, and all have brass oil lamps on night tables beside the beds. Needlework is displayed throughout the house, and Lynne sells kits for those who are inspired. Long-term guests, often businesspeople in transit, frequently stay at the inn, taking breakfast in the cozy kitchen. Short-term visitors eat at individual tables in the dining room and enjoy such standbys as Jack's Flaps, named for a former longtime guest who loved to cook pancakes.

🏨 *7 double rooms with baths, 2 doubles share bath, 3 suites. Air-conditioning, cable TVs, phones, fireplaces in 2 rooms and 5 common areas, badminton. $95–$150, full breakfast. AE, MC, V. Restricted smoking, no pets, 2-night minimum on weekends May–Oct.*

Other Choices

Cabbage Rose Inn. 162 Main St., Flemington, NJ 08822, tel. 908/788–0247. 5 double rooms with baths. Air-conditioning, phones, cable TV in parlor, guest pantry. $80–$120; Continental-plus breakfast on weekdays, full breakfast on weekends. AE, D, MC, V. Restricted smoking, no pets, 2-night minimum with Sat. reservation.

Chestnut Hill on the Delaware. 63 Church St., Milford, NJ 08848, tel. 908/995–9761. 3 double rooms with baths, 2 doubles share bath, 1 housekeeping suite. Air-conditioning, phones, cable TV in 3 bedrooms and parlor, fireplace in parlor, transportation to and from bus. $85–$140, Continental breakfast. No credit cards. No smoking, no pets, 2-night minimum on weekends and at all times for cottage.

Holly Thorn House. 143 Readington Rd., Whitehouse Station, NJ 08889, tel. 908/534–1616, fax 908/534–9017. 4 double rooms with baths, 1 suite. Air-conditioning, phone jacks, fireplace in suite, mini-refrigerators and wet bars in gathering and billiard rooms, pool, cabana. $100–$115, full breakfast. AE, D, MC, V. No smoking in bedrooms, no pets.

Hunterdon House. 12 Bridge St., Frenchtown, NJ 08825, tel. 908/996–3632 or 800/382–0942, fax 908/996–2921 (call before faxing). 6 double rooms with baths, 1 suite. Air-conditioning; fireplace in parlor, dining room, and 1 room. $85–$145, full breakfast. AE, MC, V. Restricted smoking, no pets, 2-night minimum on weekends.

Isaac Hilliard House. 31 Hanover St., Pemberton, NJ 08068, tel. 609/894–0756 or 800/371–0756. 3 double rooms with baths, 1 suite. Air-conditioning, cable TV/VCR in suite and parlor, mini-refrigerator in suite, fireplace in suite and in parlor, bicycles, pool. $55–$130; full breakfast, welcoming refreshments. AE, MC, V. No smoking, no pets, 2-night minimum on holiday weekends.

Jerica Hill. 96 Broad St., Flemington, NJ 08822, tel. 908/782–8234. 5 double rooms with baths. Air-conditioning, phones, TVs, fireplace in living room. $85–$110, Continental-plus breakfast. AE, MC, V. No smoking, no pets, 2-night minimum on most weekends.

Peacock Inn. 20 Bayard La., Princeton, NJ 08540, tel. 609/924–1707, fax 609/924–0788. 15 double rooms with baths. Restaurant, bar, air-conditioning, cable TV in lounge and 6 rooms, phones in 6 rooms, fireplaces in restaurant. $100–$135, Continental breakfast. AE, MC, V.

Stockton Inn. 1 Main St. (Box C), Stockton, NJ 08559, tel. 609/397–1250. 3 double rooms with baths, 8 suites. Restaurant, air-conditioning, TVs, fireplaces in 7 suites and 1 room, mini-refrigerators in some rooms. $60–$165, Continental breakfast. AE, D, MC, V. No pets, 2-night minimum on weekends, 3-night minimum on holiday weekends.

Whistling Swan Inn. 110 Main St., Stanhope, NJ 07874, tel. 201/347–6369, fax 201/347–3391. 9 double rooms with baths, 1 suite. Air-conditioning, cable TV in parlor, fireplaces in foyer and parlor, bicycles. $85–$135, full breakfast. AE, D, MC, V. Restricted smoking, no pets, 2-night minimum on holiday weekends.

Reservations Services

Bed & Breakfast Adventures (2310 Central Ave., Suite 132, North Wildwood 08260, tel. 609/522–4000 or 800/992–2632 for reservations, fax 609/522–6125). **Bed and Breakfast of Princeton** (Box 571, Princeton 08542, tel. 609/924–3189, fax 609/921–6271).

Cape May

The Abbey

34 Gurney St. at Columbia Ave., Cape May, NJ 08204, tel. 609/884–4506

The Abbey never was an abbey. Built in 1869 as a summer home for Philadelphia coal baron John B. McCreary, it is one of Cape May architect Stephen Button's best works and the finest example of Gothic Revival architecture in town. Current owners Jay and Marianne Schatz gave it the name because they thought the facade resembled a house of worship.

Actually, like many local B&Bs, the Abbey comprises two buildings. Jay and Marianne, who were both chemists before their love of old houses and antiques brought them to Cape May, opened the main house, known as the Villa, in 1979. In 1986 they bought and renovated the 1873 Second Empire house next door. The addition, now called the Cottage, was built by McCreary for his son's family. Though each house has two parlors and bedrooms named for cities with Victorian architecture (there's usually something from the respective city in each room), the buildings have their own feel, befitting their varying styles. The Villa, with its impressive 65-foot tower, is formal and dramatic. On the first floor are ruby-color, stenciled-glass windows, an 1860 walnut-and-chestnut sideboard with a carved wolf's head, and massive 11½-foot-tall matching bookcases in the back parlor, perfect for a room with 12-foot ceilings. Upstairs, the San Francisco Room is the most opulent, but the Newport Room in the tower three stories up has a remarkable bath that makes it a popular guest quarter. In contrast, the Cottage, its parlor furnished in wicker, feels like a light, bright summer house.

There's more to recommend the Abbey than the quality of its restoration and period antiques, however. There's a touch of whimsy, courtesy of Jay and Marianne. Many Cape May B&Bs have a rack in the foyer adorned with vintage hats, but Jay, who admits he suffers from "achapeauphobia" (the fear of being without a hat) doesn't stop in the front hall. Crammed in a closet in the back parlor is an assortment of helmets and other military hats. Those that don't fit, such as sombreros and pith helmets, are stashed elsewhere, but there's no sign of a cowl or wimple at this abbey.

🏠 *12 double rooms with baths, 2 suites. Air-conditioning in 10 bedrooms, mini-refrigerators, croquet, beach tags, towels and chairs. $90–$200; full breakfast, afternoon refreshments. D, MC, V. Restricted smoking, no pets; 2-, 3-, or 4-night minimum on weekends. Closed Jan.–Mar.*

Mainstay Inn

635 Columbia Ave., Cape May, NJ 08204, tel. 609/884–8690

An 1872 men's social club formerly called Jackson's Clubhouse, the Mainstay is one of Cape May's best bed-and-breakfasts. Many a gambler whiled away the hours under these 14-foot ceilings and on the lofty veranda, which, more than 100 years later, is the city's most ostentatious spot for doing nothing.

In 1976, the property was purchased by Tom Carroll, who came to Cape May to serve at the nearby Coast Guard Training Center, and his wife, Sue, an antiques and Victorian-costume collector. The Carrolls renovated the building with an astonishing attention to detail, and the Mainstay became a focal point in the move to revive Victorian Cape May as a resort town. Included in this magnificent restoration are the house's original chandeliers as well as most of the original furniture. Rooms are named for famous Cape May visitors, such as the General Grant and Stonewall Jackson suites, which coexist as harmoniously as the elegant antiques, some of them museum quality.

For more privacy, there's the Officers' Quarters, the "new" building across the street. Built to house military personnel during World War I and renovated into four one- or two-bedroom suites, this addition offers all the modern amenities lacking in the carefully preserved Mainstay and adjacent Cottage. Each suite here has its own cable TV/VCR, phone, whirlpool bath, gas fireplace, private porch, and snack bar;

and breakfast is delivered to each unit. Despite the modern comforts, however, there are enough old touches, such as antique mantels in the sitting areas and back-lit stained glass in the bathrooms, to add vintage charm.

The Carrolls socialize actively with guests, some of whom have been inspired to open B&Bs of their own, and turn breakfast and tea into friendly occasions. "We like guests to feel as if they're not just staying with us, but that they're part of the Mainstay's atmosphere," says Tom.

In addition to being active in Cape May historic preservation and the city's Victorian Week festivities, the Carrolls are enthusiastic fans of Victorian culture and games, the more whimsical the better. Tom races sailboats, so you might see him on the ocean, from the cupola, which has a distant ocean view.

🏠 *9 double rooms with baths, 7 suites. Air-conditioning, microwaves, and mini-refrigerators in 4 suites; gas fireplace in main-house drawing room. $140–$195; Continental breakfast June–Sept. (Officers' Quarters, full breakfast Oct.–May), full breakfast is served in the main house at all times. No credit cards. Restricted smoking, no pets, 2-night minimum on weekends, 3-night minimum June–Sept.*

Queen Victoria

102 Ocean St., Cape May, NJ 08204, tel. 609/884–8702

A Union Jack flying from an inviting front porch full of rockers is the first sign of what the Queen Victoria is all about. Dane Wells and his elegant wife, Joan, who is active in the restoration and preservation of Victoriana nationwide, have created a private and genteel country inn in the center of the historic district. It's an homage to the queen, her family, and the period named for her.

Three restored seaside villas make up the property. The 1881 Second Empire–style Queen Victoria and Stick-style Prince Albert Hall are the two main buildings. They have similar facilities, such as outfitted guest pantries, and are open to all guests, who are encouraged to move between them freely. Breakfast is served in both elegant dining rooms, while a proper afternoon tea, with sweet and savory treats, is poured on the porch of one house in summer and in the other's parlor with fireplace in cooler months. Adorning the walls are historic wallpapers, one dotted with Victoria's imperial crown, and pictures of the ubiquitous queen. Furnishings are carefully researched period pieces.

All guest rooms have appropriate items of decor, such as a beautifully framed scarf of Victoria and her court in the Mayfair Room. Accommodations range from small rooms to large luxury suites, and furnishings include white wicker, brass and iron, and the dark woods of high Victorian. Cable TV is found in suites and a parlor, and many of the rooms have whirlpools. Regent's Park, a small cottage with fireplace adjacent to the Prince Albert, is fully accessible to guests with disabilities.

Across Ocean Street is the elaborately painted (try counting its colors) Queen Anne–style Queen's Cottage. Rented to families or others traveling together, it is not open to guests in the other buildings. The two rooms, one of which has a gas-log fireplace, have whirlpools for two and TVs.

Despite the adherence to period details, the Queen Victoria lacks the antiques-cluttered spaces and stiff formality of other Victorian inns. In the cozy Arts and Crafts–style parlor, with its brick fireplace, player piano, and mountain of scrolls, is a basket of *Madeleine* books, a signal that children are welcome. (A crib, high chair, trike, and blocks are also available.) In fact, all guests will feel comfortable and royally treated here.

🏨 *17 double rooms with baths, 6 suites. Air-conditioning, phones in 2 suites, mini-refrigerators in all bedrooms, bicycles, beach tags, towels and chairs, on- and off-site parking. $90–$250; full breakfast, afternoon tea. AE, MC, V. No smoking, no pets; 2-, 3-, or 4-night minimum on weekends and holidays.*

Other Choices

Albert Stevens Inn. 127 Myrtle Ave., Cape May, NJ 08204, tel. 609/884–4717 or 800/890–2287. 7 double rooms with baths, 2 suites. Air-conditioning, TV in 1 suite, gas fireplaces in dining room and parlor, hot tub Oct.–Apr., beach tags and towels. $85–$155; full breakfast, afternoon tea, dinner 3 times a week late Feb.–Apr. AE, D, MC, V. Restricted smoking, no pets, 2-night minimum on weekends, 3-night minimum Aug. and holidays. Closed Jan.–Presidents' Day.

Barnard-Good House. 238 Perry St., Cape May, NJ 08204, tel. 609/884–5381. 3 double rooms with baths, 2 suites. Air-conditioning, beach tags, towels and chairs. $90–$137, full breakfast. MC, V. Restricted smoking, no pets, 2-night minimum on weekends, 3-night minimum mid-June–mid-Sept., 4-night minimum on holiday weekends. Closed Nov.–Apr.

Captain Mey's Inn. 202 Ocean St., Cape May, NJ 08204, tel. 609/884–7793. 7 double rooms with baths, 1 suite. Air-conditioning, TV in 2 rooms, whirlpool tub in 1 room, mini-refrigerator in hall and 3 rooms, fireplace in dining room, beach tags, towels, and chairs. $75–$210; full breakfast, afternoon tea. AE, MC, V. Restricted smoking, no pets; 2-, 3-, or 4-night minimum July–Aug. and on weekends.

Carroll Villa. 19 Jackson St., Cape May, NJ 08204, tel. 609/884–9619, fax 609/884–0264. 22 double rooms with baths. Restaurant (closed Jan.), air-conditioning, phones, cable TV in lobby, fireplace in restaurant, beach tags. $60–$150, full breakfast. AE, MC, V. Restricted smoking, no pets, 2-night minimum on weekends and July–Aug., 3-night minimum on holiday weekends. Closed 2 weeks in Jan.

Columns by the Sea. 1513 Beach Dr., Cape May, NJ 08204, tel. 609/884–2228, fax 609/884–4789. 11 double rooms with baths. Cable TV in sitting room or in bedrooms on request, mini-refrigerators in rooms, bicycles, beach tags, towels, and chairs. $140–$197; full breakfast, afternoon refreshments. MC, V. Restricted smoking, no pets, 2-night minimum Memorial Day–Sept., 3-night minimum on weekends.

Inn at 22 Jackson. 22 Jackson St., Cape May, NJ 08204, tel. 609/884–2226 or 800/452–8177, fax 609/884–0055. 5 suites. Air-conditioning, gas fireplace in foyer, bicycles, beach tags, towels and chairs. $95–$300; full breakfast, afternoon refreshments. AE, MC, V. Smoking on porches only, no pets, 2-night minimum on weekends.

Manor House. 612 Hughes St., Cape May, NJ 08204, tel. 609/884–4710. 7 double rooms with baths, 2 doubles share bath, 1 suite. Air-conditioning, hair dryers, whirlpool bath in suite, beach tags, towels and chairs. $90–$174; full breakfast, afternoon tea. D, MC, V. Restricted smoking, no pets, 2-night minimum on weekends, 3-night minimum on holiday weekends. Closed Jan.

Springside. 18 Jackson St., Cape May, NJ 08204, tel. 609/884–2654. 4 double rooms share 2 baths. Beach tags and chairs. $60–$75, Continental breakfast on weekends. MC, V. Restricted smoking, no pets, 2-night minimum on weekends June–Sept., 3-night minimum on holiday weekends.

Victorian Rose. 715 Columbia Ave., Cape May, NJ 08204, tel. 609/884–2497. 5 double rooms with baths, 2 doubles share bath, 2 housekeeping suites, cottage. Air-conditioning in 4 bedrooms and cottage, cable TV in suites and cottage, mini-refrigerator on each floor, beach tags. $85–$137; full breakfast, afternoon refreshments. No credit cards. No pets, 2-night minimum on weekends mid-Oct.–May, 3-night minimum on weekends June–Sept. Closed Dec.–Mar.

Virginia Hotel. 25 Jackson St., Cape May, NJ 08204, tel. 609/884–5700 or 800/732–4236, fax 609/884–1236. 24 double rooms with baths. Restaurant, bar, air-conditioning, cable TV/VCRs, phones, videotape rentals, modem hookups, beach tags, towels and chairs. $190–$250, Continental breakfast. AE, D, DC, MC, V. No smoking in restaurant, no pets, 2-night minimum on weekends off season, 3-night minimum on weekends in season.

Wooden Rabbit. 609 Hughes St., Cape May, NJ 08204, tel. 609/884–7293. 2 double rooms with baths, 2 suites. Air-conditioning, TVs, beach tags and chairs. $60–$190; full breakfast, afternoon tea. D, MC, V. No smoking, no pets, 2-night minimum on weekends, 3- or 4-night minimum July–Aug.

Reservations Services

Bed & Breakfast Adventures (2310 Central Ave., Suite 132, North Wildwood 08260, tel. 609/522–4000 or 800/992–2632 for reservations, fax 609/522–6125). **Cape May Reservation Service** (1382 Lafayette St., Cape May 08204, tel. 609/884–9396 or 800/729–7778).

New Mexico

Adobe and Roses

Santa Fe and Environs

Alexander's Inn

529 E. Palace Ave., Santa Fe, NM 87501, tel. 505/986–1431

Owner Carolyn Lee, the daughter of a foreign service diplomat, traveled all over the world while she was growing up. But when it came time to raise her son, Alexander, she decided to settle in Santa Fe and launch a B&B. Santa Fe is the richer for it, and Carolyn hasn't done badly either since opening in 1986. Her charming establishment, only six blocks from the Plaza on historic Palace Avenue, sees a lot of repeat business and is often booked solid.

A self-described fitness buff who loves to ski, mountain bike, dance, whitewater raft, and play tennis, Carolyn and her B&B exude a refreshing wholesomeness and youthful vitality: "You can shop anywhere in the world; I try to interest my guests in getting out and participating in some of the wonderful outdoor sports available here."

Of course, leaving the premises might be a problem, as they are conducive to laziness. The Craftsman-style two-story residence, built in 1903, is fronted by a deep veranda and covered with wooden shingles. Its spacious rooms are furnished with antiques as well as American country–style furniture. Fine woodworking is found throughout, as is pretty floral-patterned wallpaper. The upstairs rooms feature walk-in-size dormer windows that flood the rooms with light and produce odd and delightful nooks, crannies, and angles. A downstairs bedroom, perhaps the best room, has a fireplace and original stained-glass windows.

Across a small backyard, which bursts in summer with flower gardens under the shade of some immense old trees, are two cottages. The front unit has a loft-style bedroom up a spiral staircase, a kitchen, a fireplace, and a double whilpool tub in a Mexican tiled bathroom. The rear unit has a raised kiva fireplace and Saltillo-tile floors.

In keeping with her healthy lifestyle, Carolyn's homemade granola, muffins, yogurt, sumptuous fruit salads, coffee, juice, and tea make for a hearty and delicious start for the day. In warm weather you can eat out on the rear deck; in spring an apricot tree bends its fragrant boughs over your table.

▦ *3 double rooms with baths, 2 doubles share bath, 3 cottages. TVs, fresh* flowers, hot tub, complimentary health club membership and mountain bikes. $75–$140, cottages $140–$150; Continental breakfast, afternoon snacks. MC, V. No smoking.

Grant Corner Inn

122 Grant Ave., Santa Fe, NM 87501, tel. 505/983–6678

This is the bed-and-breakfast that innkeepers talk about when they get together over potluck dinners. It's one of the best run and most successful in the state. Owners Pat and Louise Walter couldn't be more suited to their job. He's a designer-builder who engineered the structural changes in the 1915 East Coast Colonial-style manor, the only one like it in Santa Fe; she's the daughter of Jack Stewart, who founded the renowned Camelback Inn in Scottsdale, where she grew up. Louise later studied at the Cornell hotel school. Donning chef's hat and apron, Pat now runs the kitchen while Louise runs the rest of the show.

And what a production. Only two blocks from the Plaza in a small tree-filled lot, surrounded by a veranda and garden, the house originally belonged to the Winsor family, wealthy New Mexican ranchers. The rooms and public areas are appointed with antiques and treasures collected from around the world by the Walters. Hand-stitched quilts, brass and four-poster beds, armoires, and artwork make each room unique. The undisputed star is Room No. 8, a visual treat with its antique wood-burning stove, white brass bed, love seat, quilted bedspread, Oriental rugs, and Old World touches. The downstairs public rooms also hearken back to grander days, with overstuffed couches, ceiling fans, and crystal chandeliers.

The breakfast menu includes such treats as banana waffles, eggs Florentine, and green-chili-laden New Mexican soufflé, all accompanied by fresh-ground European coffee, fruit juice, fruit, and homemade rolls and jellies. Small wonder the public comes clamoring on weekends when the dining room is open to one and all. Meals are served in front of a crackling fire in the dining room or, in summer, on the veranda. Guests get a complimentary glass of wine in the evening. Elaborately prepared picnic baskets are available, too.

The Grant Corner Inn also operates the Grant Corner Inn Hacienda, a Southwestern-style condominium five blocks away; it's available for parties of up to four. Rates ($105–$130 double room per night) include breakfast at the inn.

🏠 *7 double rooms with baths, 2 doubles share bath, 1 single with bath. Cable TV, phones, in-house massages available, lounge with dining nook, microwave, refrigerator, privileges at nearby tennis club. $70–$155, full breakfast. MC, V. No smoking.*

Inn on the Alameda

303 E. Alameda, Santa Fe, NM 87501, tel. 505/984–2121 or 800/289–2122, fax 505/986–8325

Alameda means "tree-lined lane," befitting its location alongside the Santa Fe River, which gurgles virtually through the center of town. This setting, between the historic Santa Fe Plaza and gallery-filled Canyon Road, is both tranquil and convenient: Even without a car, guests have easy access to shopping, museums, and restaurants.

Opened in 1986, this lodging was originally intended to be a bed-and-breakfast with resident managers. However, it soon blossomed into one of Santa Fe's most prestigious small hotels, combining the relaxed atmosphere of a New Mexico country inn with the amenities of a world-class hotel.

Rooms, in a contemporary adobe complex with a network of enclosed courtyards and *portales* are decorated in Southwestern colors, down to the accessories, beds, wall hangings, and wood-frame mirrors. Handmade armoires, oversize chairs, headboards, ceramic lamps, and colorful tiles all exemplify the best of local craftsmanship. Prints and posters by Armado Peña, R. C. Gorman, and other renowned local artists grace the walls. All of the inn's eight individually designed suites are appealing, some more opulent than others. Room 140, for example, features two kiva fireplaces, two TV sets, and two phones. Here and there you'll find a bleached cattle skull mounted on the wall or over a door.

Although the inn has no full-service dining room, its complimentary gourmet breakfast buffet is a wonder, with homemade muffins, bagels, creamy pastries, cinnamon rolls, fruit and fresh-squeezed fruit juices, teas, and Kona coffee, all served up by a friendly team of young Native Americans. Guests may eat at tables in the lobby's spacious library or in the Agoyo Room lounge; room service is also an option. A number of fine restaurants are nearby. The inn helps with tickets and reservations for evening entertainment and has a number of attractive package arrangements with spas, tours, and ski resorts.

▦ *58 double rooms with baths, 9 suites. Cable TV; robes; wet bars, refrigerators, kiva fireplaces, and patios with some rooms; massage room; exercise center; guest laundry; 2 outdoor hot tubs; patio dining; full bar; pets welcome. $140–$350, Continental breakfast. AE, D, DC, MC, V.*

Preston House

106 Faithway St., Santa Fe, NM 87501, tel. 505/982–3465

This 1886 Queen Anne Victorian home, the only one of its kind in Santa Fe and with all of its angles and turrets intact, is the elegant restoration of noted artist-designer Signe Bergman, who moved from Santa Barbara to Santa Fe in 1974 to pursue a painting career. It wasn't until she was commissioned to do a large hotel mural in 1978 that she began to think of opening an inn of her own. She purchased Preston House

that year and set about restoring it, later adding an adobe guest house and two Queen Anne–style garden cottages to the property.

Preston House is tucked away in a quiet garden a few blocks from the Plaza. Its guest house is just across the dead-end street, and the cottages are in the back. The main house is on the National Register of Historic Places.

The public rooms are open and sunny; fruit bowls, original and fantastically futuristic stained glass, lace curtains, and fresh-cut flowers add to the appeal. Books in the well-stocked library shed light on some of Preston House's former owners, among them three colorful characters: land speculator George Preston, who operated with a band of other charlatans in divvying up the Southwest territories after the Civil War; a man who exposed the gigantic Peralta-Reavis land-grant fraud; and a cure-all doctor.

Guest rooms in the main house are furnished in ornate late 19th-century fashion. Some have Edwardian fireplaces, ceiling fans, stained-glass windows, brass beds, Queen Anne chairs, and fringed lace tablecloths. Room 1, off the dining room, is for early risers. Rooms in the adobe guest house, in contrast, are done in the traditional Southwestern mode. Room 15, with a king and sofa bed, fireplace, and sitting room, has its own entrance. The Queen Anne–style garden cottages, with queen beds, single-size window seats, and fireplaces, couldn't be cozier.

An elaborate Continental breakfast is served at two large tables in the common areas. Full afternoon tea and dessert are offered as well. The owner's paintings, which hang in galleries and private collections all over the country, are displayed throughout the house and may be purchased.

▦ *4 double rooms with baths, 2 doubles share bath in main house; 7 double rooms with baths in adobe guest house; 2 garden cottages. TVs, phones. $75–*

$160; Continental breakfast, afternoon tea. AE, MC, V. No smoking.

Rancho de San Juan

Box 4140, Espanola, NM 87533, tel. 505/753-6818, fax 505/753-6818

Mountains, mesas, and the Ojo Caliente River valley make up the stunning vista from Rancho de San Juan, set beneath the petroglyph-dotted Black Mesa, 35 miles north of Santa Fe. Out in the middle of nowhere there is a stunning silence under a huge sky. Yet here is a spanking new, incredibly elegant Pueblo-style structure.

Conceived, owned, and run by David Heath and John Johnson, this enchanting B&B is their dream come true. David, formerly in real estate and retail—at Saks Fifth Avenue, among other fine stores—and John, a registered architect who worked extensively in the Far East, spent 10 years planning this career move. Searching for the perfect location, they stumbled upon this isolated valley and immediately knew they had found it. They bought a 225-acre tract.

When you enter the main building, an eye-dazzling painting of Navajo yeis (gods) greets you. To your left is the refined but relaxing living room, its 14-foot-high ceiling spanned by hand-peeled vigas centered by an immense fireplace. Oriental rugs, tile floors, wonderful Southwestern and Native American art and artifacts, carved-wood corbels, and antique doors are indicative of meticulous attention to detail and finely honed design sensibilities.

To your right is the 16-seat dining room, open to the public Wednesday through Saturday nights and for Sunday lunch, and to guests any night of the week with prior notice. Haviland china, silver, and linen create a graceful impression, highlighted by the antique wooden fireplace mantel. Here John serves up full breakfasts to guests and

exquisite dinner delicacies, focusing on northern Italian and French cuisine, or local specialties. A private dining room, seating up to 14, is off to one side.

The four accommodations cluster around a pretty courtyard. Each room has a different theme but all are finely finished. The San Juan room has a Victorian motif with a crocheted lace bedspread and raw silk drapes. The Acoma and Santa Clara suites both have king-size beds. The Black Mesa room has a Territorial-style fireplace, a faux canopy bed, and a small flower garden. A new addition is a two-bedroom casita.

🛏 *5 double rooms with baths, 1 suite. Private entrances and patios; individual heating; ceiling fans; terry-cloth robes; sherry in decanters on silver trays; massage, facials, and herbal wraps by appointment; public dining room; private dining room with VCR and slide machine for meetings; outdoor patio dining with fountain, whirlpool bath, hiking paths. $150–$250. AE, MC, V. No smoking, no pets.*

Territorial Inn

215 Washington Ave., Santa Fe, NM 87501, tel. 505/989-7737, fax 505/986-9212

The last of the private homes along tree-lined Washington Avenue in the heart of downtown Santa Fe—just off the Plaza—the Territorial Inn was built in the 1890s by Philadelphian George Shoch. A stylish blend of New Mexican stone-and-adobe architecture, this pitched-roof structure is surrounded by large cottonwoods, a front lawn, and a private rose garden.

In recent years, the building was occupied by a law firm. Legal secretary Lela McFerrin acquired the property in 1989, and she preserved or restored much of the century-old building. Now the inn has the gracious feel of the days when it was home to Levi A. Hughes, a well-known Santa Fe merchant who, with his wife, graciously entertained high society and visiting celebrities of the day.

The reception area and living room are large and comfortable, with overstuffed couches and chairs, fireplaces, a large bowl of jellybeans, and a set of encyclopedias. An eye-catching turn-of-the-century brick stairway leads to the upstairs guest rooms.

The 10 bedrooms range from large and luxurious to cozy and quaint; all are individually furnished with period pieces; canopy, brass, or four-poster beds; handmade quilts; and down comforters. Many of the ceilings have canopy linings, traditionally found in early adobe homes with viga beams. (They originally helped to keep dirt, twigs, and insects from falling into the soup; here, they cover the fluorescent lighting fixtures used in the legal offices of the former occupants.) The best rooms are No. 9, with its canopy bed and Victorian fireplace, and No. 3, with its private patio; the most claustrophobic is No. 7.

Breakfast—fresh pastries, strawberries and cream, juice, and coffee—is delivered to the bedrooms or, in summer, served in the rose garden. There's afternoon tea and cheese, and brandy turndowns with cookies at night. Pets aren't allowed, but Mr. Shumway, a collie, keeps the guests from being lonely for four-legged companions.

▥ *8 double rooms with baths, 2 doubles share bath. Cable TV, ceiling fans, down comforters, fireplace in 2 rooms, gazebo-enclosed hot tub, off-street parking, laundry service available. $80–$160, Continental breakfast. MC, V. No smoking, no children under 10, no pets.*

Other Choices

Adobe Abode. 202 Chapelle St., Santa Fe, NM 87501, tel. 505/983–3133, fax 505/986–0972. 6 double rooms with baths. Cable TV, phones, coffeemakers, terry-cloth robes. $100–$155; full gourmet breakfast, sherry and cookies

always available. D, MC, V. No smoking, no pets.

Casa del Rio. Box 702, Abiquiu, NM 87510 (19946 U.S. 84), tel. 505/753–2035. 1 double room with bath, 1 casita. Fireplaces in both rooms, wake-up tray, fresh flowers, outdoor pool, water garden. $85–$95; full breakfast, afternoon tea. No credit cards. No smoking, no pets.

Casa Escondida. Box 142 (off NM 76 at Road Marker 0100), Chimayo, NM 87522, tel. 505/351–4805 or 800/643–7201. 8 double rooms with baths, 1 1-bedroom cottage. Kitchen in casita, wildflower gardens, hot tub. $75–$130; full breakfast, afternoon snacks. AE, MC, V. No smoking.

Dos Casas Viejas. 610 Agua Fria St., Santa Fe, NM 87501, tel. 505/983–1636. 2 double rooms with baths, 2 minisuites, 2 suites. Cable TV, ceiling fans, fireplaces, private entrances, robes, hair dryers, fresh flowers, mini-refrigerators, outdoor pool. $165–$275; Continental breakfast, afternoon wine. MC, V.

Dunshee's. 986 Acequia Madre, Santa Fe, NM 87501, tel. 505/982–0988. 1 casita, 1 2-bedroom suite. TV, stereo CD/tape player, microwave in each room, fresh flowers, art by leading local artists. $110; full breakfast in B&B, Continental in casita. MC, V. No smoking, no pets.

El Paradero. 220 W. Manhattan Ave., Santa Fe, NM 87501, tel. 505/988–1177. 8 double rooms with baths, 4 doubles share 2 baths, 2 suites. Air-conditioning, cable TV and fireplaces in suites, fireplaces in 4 rooms, color TV in sitting room, two fireplaces in public areas. $70–$130, full breakfast. MC, V. No smoking.

Guadalupe Inn. 604 Agua Fria St., Santa Fe, NM 87501, tel. 505/989–7422, fax 505/989–7422. 11 double rooms with baths, 1 suite. Cable TV, phones, whirlpool tubs in 4 rooms, gas fireplaces in some rooms, covered parking. $125–$175, full breakfast. AE, D, MC, V. No smoking, no pets.

Inn of the Animal Tracks. 707 Paseo de Peralta, Santa Fe, NM 87501, tel. 505/988–1546. 5 double rooms with baths. Air-conditioning, cable TVs, fireplace in 1 guest room and in common room. $90–$130; full breakfast, afternoon tea. AE, MC, V. No smoking.

Inn on the Paseo. 630 Paseo de Peralta, Santa Fe, NM 87501, tel. 505/984–8200 or 800/457–9045, fax 505/989–3979. 18 double rooms with baths, 1 2-bedroom suite. Air-conditioning, cable TVs, phones, fax service. $75–$155, Continental breakfast. AE, DC, MC, V. No smoking, no pets.

La Posada de Chimayó. Box 463, Chimayó, 87522, tel. and fax 505/351–4605. 2 double rooms with baths, 2 suites. Fireplaces, spacious grounds, walking trails. $80–$100; full breakfast, afternoon wine. No credit cards. No smoking, no children under 12.

Orange Street Inn. 3496 Orange St., Los Alamos, NM 87544, tel. 505/662–2651 or 800/662–3180. 2 double rooms with baths, 4 doubles share 2 baths, 2 suites. Private entrance to suite, cable TV/VCR in common area, guest use of kitchen and laundry, ski packages available. $50–$85; full breakfast, afternoon wine and snacks. D, MC, V. No smoking.

Pueblo Bonito. 138 W. Manhattan Ave., Santa Fe, NM 87501, tel. 505/984–8001, 800/461-4599, fax 505/984–3155. 11 double rooms with baths, 7 suites. Cable TVs, fireplaces, laundry facilities. $85–$140; Continental breakfast, afternoon refreshments. MC, V. No smoking, no pets.

Water Street Inn. 427 Water St., Santa Fe, NM 87501, tel. 505/984–1193. 11 double rooms with baths. Cable TVs, fireplaces, voice mail. $135–$170; Continental breakfast, evening wine and snacks. AE, MC, V. No smoking, no pets, no children under 7.

Reservations Services

Bed and Breakfast of New Mexico (Box 2805, Santa Fe, NM 87504, tel. 505/982–3332). **New Mexico Bed and Breakfast Association** (Box 2925, Santa Fe, NM 87504; write for brochure, and contact participating inns directly).

Taos

American Gallery Artists House

132 Frontier Rd., Box 584, Taos, NM 87571, tel. 505/758–4446 or 800/532–2041, fax 505/758–0497

The 7-foot-tall, flat, black iron sculpture in front of the American Artists Gallery House isn't Kokopelli, whose flute-bearing image can be seen in every gift shop between San Diego and Santa Fe, but the *Goddess of Bed and Breakfasts,* a special creation of artist Pozzi Franzetti. And it's not for sale—perhaps the only piece among the 500 or so works of art here that doesn't have a price tag. Although almost all B&Bs in northern New Mexico sell works by regional and nationally known artists—"It's a way to get paintings to hang on your walls without paying for them," says one wry innkeeper—this establishment is serious about its artistic endeavors. Owners LeAn and Charles Clamurro, who purchased the B&B in July 1994, are happy to discuss the array of art found in every room. The B&B frequently hosts art openings for featured artists; at other times, artists are invited to breakfast with the guests.

Another passion of the owners is their fine lodging. Charles is a graduate of the Cornell hotel program, and his experience includes a three-year stint running La Fonda Hotel in Santa Fe; LeAn has a similarly impressive background in hotel management and currently heads the New Mexico Bed

& Breakfast Association's marketing committee. The inn is adjacent to a field where the Taos July 4th fireworks and the October Hot Air Balloon Festival take place, providing ringside seats for both.

Its seven rooms are spread throughout the adobe compound: three in the main house, two in an adjacent guest house, and two in separate garden cottages; three suites with whirlpool baths were added in the summer of 1996. All accommodations have kiva fireplaces, colorful Mexican tiles in the bathrooms, Native American rugs covering tile or wooden floors, leather drum tables, and carved furniture.

Breakfast is served promptly at 8 AM around a large table in a glass-enclosed greenhouse-style dining area. One of 10 or so breakfast entrées—chili egg frittata, blue corn pancakes with fresh blackberries, pecan-stuffed French toast—is accompanied by fresh fruits, home-baked breads, and fresh-brewed coffee or a variety of teas.

🛏 *7 double rooms with baths, 3 suites. Kitchens in suites, fax, outdoor hot tub. $75–$150; full breakfast, afternoon beverages and hors d'oeuvres. AE, MC, V. No smoking, no pets.*

Casa Europa

840 Upper Ranchitos Rd., HC 68, Box 3F, Taos, NM 87571, tel. 505/758–9798, 888/758–9798

There's a marvelous, ornate, 200-year-old brass bed in the French Room at the Casa Europa that must take an army of maids weeks to keep polished. But gleaming and polished it is, and you'll feel a little like Louis XIV or Catherine the Great as you drift off to sleep with sounds of crickets and field frogs wafting through the partially opened French windows above the courtyard of this 200-year-old adobe farmhouse. Casa Europa is run with care and precision by Marcia and Rudi Zwicker, the owner and chef of the pop-

ular Greenbriar Restaurant in Boulder, Colorado, for 16 years.

Current zoning laws prohibit the Zwickers from expanding, but they've purchased the property across the street, so the pastoral and mountain views—horses grazing, massive cottonwoods, wooden fences, and clouds you can almost reach out and touch—will never be obscured. When they restored the inn in 1983, the couple left all its adobe bricks and wood viga ceiling beams intact. Among Casa Europa's many artistic treasures is the oldest door in Taos, discovered years ago in the basement of the Guadalupe Church.

The rooms, whose whitewashed walls are splashed with sunlight, are furnished with an eclectic collection of European antique and traditional Southwestern pieces. Paintings, arranged gallery style, feature Native American and other contemporary artists; there are also three signed etchings by Salvador Dalí. Each of the rooms is based on a theme. In the central sitting room of the spacious Southwest Room is a Swedish porcelain woodstove; there's a large white marble bath with a whirlpool and—one of those rarest of creatures in the American Southwest—a bidet.

At breakfast, German-born Chef Rudi pulls out all stops—fluffy popovers, eggs Florentine, quiche, fresh-baked Danish pastries, blue corn pancakes, cheese blintzes, sautéed trout with tomato cups filled with scrambled eggs—but not all at once, of course. The astounding pastry selection includes chocolate mousse cake, truffles, fresh fruit tarts, and Black Forest tortes. Steaming coffee is served in individual decanters.

🛏 *6 double rooms with baths. Fireplace in 5 rooms, cable TV in public rooms, Swedish sauna, hot tub. $85–$135; full breakfast, afternoon tea in summer, hors d'oeuvres in ski season. MC, V. No smoking, no pets.*

El Rincón

*114 Kit Carson Rd., Taos, NM 87571,
tel. 505/758-4874*

If you're looking for something unique, you've found it here. With its maze of rooms and hallways upstairs and down and its kitchens and courtyards, El Rincón looks like a cross between a set for a melodrama and a Western museum. Up front is the oldest trading post in Taos, still flourishing. Piled high with Western artifacts, feathered Indian headdresses, Navajo rugs, beads, drums, *santos* (saints) carvings, buckles, and pots, it has a one-room museum whose prized possession is a pair of Kit Carson's leather pants.

It's difficult to tell where the store and museum end and the bed-and-breakfast begins. Nina Meyers, daughter of Ralph Meyers, an old-time Taos resident, artist, and trader, has followed in her father's footsteps. Her own work and photographs, paintings, and other art, both contemporary and historic, fill the walls of the B&B.

El Rincón has the look of an organic building that's grown over the century, and now that Taos real estate prices have skyrocketed, the B&B has begun to grow up, instead of out. Paul "Paco" Castillo, who owns the B&B along with his mother, Nina, is installing a rooftop deck with hot tub, barbecue, and picnic table above the already luxurious Rainbow Room (it also has a kitchen, washer and dryer, and dining area). The decor in the Santiago Room evokes images of Old World Spain, and it is only when you open a cabinet to find a TV/VCR or locate the whirlpool bath that you realize it's better appointed than most any room found in times past. Unit 12 has a canopy bed with a handmade wedding-ring quilt, heavily embellished with Spanish lace; there's a tiled floor-to-ceiling mural of the Garden of Eden in the bath. Unit 8, which has beautiful old corbels, murals, and woodwork created by local artisans,

also has a kitchenette, hot tub, fireplace, stereo, and TV/VCR. Peek through the lace curtains on the windows and you'll see Kit Carson's house across the street.

The B&B is in the heart of bustling Taos, just a quarter-block from the plaza, and the thick adobe walls provide respite from noise and light. Guests who tire of roaming the plaza or skiing the mountains can retire to the cool depths, choose a movie from an extensive video library, and watch it in their room. They might also wander through the house and get Paco to take a break from his continual building projects and recount a bit about the building's history, such as why there is an old stone well sunk in the floor adjoining the kitchen (it is, of course, grated so you needn't worry if you have intrepid children).

🏨 *16 double rooms with baths, 3 suites. Refrigerators, whirlpool tubs, color TVs, VCRs, stereos, kitchens and hot tubs in suites, video library. $59–$125, Continental breakfast. AE, D, MC, V.*

Hacienda del Sol

109 Mabel Dodge La., Box 177, Taos, NM 87571, tel. 505/758-0287, fax 505/751-0319

The Hacienda del Sol, which borders 95,000 acres of Pueblo land and overlooks some of the most spectacular scenery in northern New Mexico, was acquired in the 1920s by art patron Mabel Dodge Luhan. She and her fourth husband, Tony Luhan, a Taos Pueblo Indian, lived here while building their main house, Las Palomas de Taos, now the Mabel Dodge Luhan House (*see below*). They kept the Hacienda del Sol as a private retreat and a guest house.

Although it's only about a mile from the Plaza and just off a main roadway, the inn remains secluded. Innkeepers John and Marcine Landon, who bought the property in 1990, make sure everything runs like clockwork. The house, a model of adobe construction built in 1810, has viga ceilings, arched doorways, and large, quiet rooms.

Author Frank Waters was living in the Tony Luhan room when he saw a young Taos Indian being arraigned by three police officials for killing a deer; the incident was the inspiration for his classic novel of Pueblo life, *The Man Who Killed the Deer*. Containing a kiva fireplace, sheepskin rug, and a desk at the window shaded by what's believed to be the oldest cottonwood tree in Taos, the room has undoubtedly changed little. The more contemporary Los Amantes Room adjoins a private room with a double-size black whirlpool bath on a mahogany platform, amid a jungle of potted plants; there's a skylight above, and the attached bathroom is a celebration of decadence with its jet-black sink, tub, shower, and toilet, all with gleaming silver hardware. In the bedroom bookcase are *Edge of Taos Desert*, *Taos, A Memory*, and *Winter in Taos*, all by Mabel Dodge Luhan, and, of course, *The Man Who Killed the Deer*. Most of the rooms have kiva fireplaces, Spanish antiques, Southwestern-style handcrafted furniture, and original artwork, much of it for sale. There's also an adobe casita with three guest rooms, three baths, and fireplaces, which can be rented as a suite.

Breakfast is served in front of the dining room fireplace or, weather permitting, on the patio. Entrées might include a blintz soufflé or blue corn pancakes with blueberry sauce, complemented by a superb house-blend coffee.

▦ *9 double rooms with baths, 1 suite. Cable TV in public room, outdoor hot tub, gift shop. $70–$130; full breakfast, afternoon snacks. MC, V. No smoking, no pets.*

Mabel Dodge Luhan House

240 Morada La., Box 3400, Taos, NM 87571, tel. 505/758-9456 or 800/846-2235, fax 505/751-0431

This classic, rambling, pueblo-style structure, formerly the home of heiress Mabel Dodge Luhan and classified as a National Historic Landmark, is a combined B&B and conference center. Owners George and Susan Otero acquired the property in 1978 from actor Dennis Hopper, who stayed here while editing his film *Easy Rider* and liked it so much that he bought it. There are 10 guest rooms in the main house, parts of which are more than 200 years old; eight more rooms are in a separate guest house built in the same pueblo style in 1989.

Luhan bought the house in 1915, and she and her husband, Tony Luhan, spent the next seven years enlarging and remodeling it. The three original rooms grew to 17; the main part of the house rose from one story to three. Upon its completion in 1922, Mabel Dodge Luhan took the lead in promoting the Southwest as a utopia, offering her literary and artistic friends an antidote to civilization. Her guests here included D. H. Lawrence, Georgia O'Keeffe, Willa Cather, Mary Austin, and John Marin.

The creative spirit nurtured so lovingly by Luhan, who died in the house in 1962 at the age of 83, still exists today. The inn is frequently used for literary workshops, educational conferences, and cultural seminars.

A living room, sitting room, and separate library are at the center of the main house, joined by a string of bedrooms furnished with turn-of-the-century pieces. The master suite on the second floor still contains Luhan's magnificently carved double bed, as well as a kiva fireplace and entrance from the patio. And in the bathroom is a mural painted on the window glass by D. H.

Lawrence, who was shocked that the bathroom had no curtains and anyone could see in when Mabel bathed. In the separate guest house, all the rooms are decorated in Southwestern style, with carved, hand-painted furnishings.

If you crave crisp service and linen, designer soaps, and a lot of pampering, don't look for them here. The walls beg for paint, the floors creak, and you have to be part mountain goat to maneuver the loftlike stairs leading to the Solarium bedroom at the top of the house. But if you want to soak up the magic days of the past that made Taos what it is today, this is the place to come.

▦ *18 double rooms with baths, 2 doubles share bath, 2 suites. Extensive grounds, lunch and dinner available for groups of 10 or more, conference facilities. $75–$200, full breakfast. MC, V. No smoking, no pets.*

Taos Country Inn at Rancho Rio Pueblo

Box 2331, Upper Ranchitos and Karavas Rds., Taos, NM 87571, tel. 505/758–4900 or 800/866–6548

Yolanda Deveaux opened the Taos Country Inn after her children left for college, and in many ways the inn still feels like a family home. Yolanda resembles a hummingbird as she flits through spacious and well-lit rooms ensuring that guests' needs are met and adding thoughtful touches along the way, such as preparing fires in the rooms of guests returning from a day of skiing. In the morning, the aroma of strong coffee and good things cooking wafts through the rooms and hallways of this sprawling Spanish hacienda, parts of it built nearly two centuries ago. Yolanda is from an old-line Taos family that acquired the hacienda more than 20 years ago. Her father, Dr. Reynaldo Deveaux, "delivered half the people in Taos," she says.

The inn is on 22 acres of pastureland and cultivated orchards and gardens, 1 mile north of town adjoining the Rio Pueblo. Guests can wander about in the fields, marveling at the distant mountain horizons, still snowcapped in the spring; chat with a field hand burning off sections of grass; and photograph the horses and sheep in a neighbor's farmyard.

The house reflects the talents of skilled local craftspeople—doors by Leroy Mondragon and Roberto Lavadi, abstract paintings in huge swatches of shocking red by James Mack, and fireplaces by Carmen Velarde, the Leonardo of fireplace makers. The public rooms, whose large windows bring the outdoors in, are filled with handcrafted furnishings, couches upholstered in textured desert tones, and glass-topped saguaro or cholla cactus-rib tables.

The guest rooms are spacious and sunny. All have white stuccoed fireplaces, sitting areas, leather sofas, Native American artifacts, Southwestern artwork, and king- or queen-size beds with fluffy down comforters and a mountain of pillows.

At breakfast—served at natural wood tables, one long and formidable, others smaller and more intimate—Yolanda unsuccessfully urges a second plate of Belgian waffles, piled high with whipped cream and strawberries, on a guest who could hardly manage the first. Her entrées might include cream cheese and salmon omelets or *huevos rancheros* or other regional specialties, all accompanied by a buffet of fruit dishes, yogurt, pastries, and breads. A small refrigerator contains juices and other soft drinks to which guests may help themselves at any time.

▦ *9 suites. Phones, cable TVs, VCRs and massage available. $110–$150; full breakfast, afternoon refreshments. MC, V. No smoking, no pets, no children under 12.*

Other Choices

Adobe & Pines. U.S. 68 and Llano Quemado, Box 837, Ranchos de Taos, NM 87557, tel. 505/751–0947 or 800/723–8267, fax 505/758–8423. 4 double rooms with baths, 3 cottages. Jet tubs in 4 rooms, fireplaces in all rooms. $95–$150, full breakfast. MC, V. No smoking, no pets, no children under 12.

Blue Door. 64 La Morada Rd., Box 2953, Taos, NM 87571, tel. 505/758–8360 or 800/824–3667. 2 double rooms with baths. Cable TVs. $85; full breakfast, afternoon snacks. MC, V. No smoking, no pets.

Brooks Street Inn. 119 Brooks St., Box 4954, Taos, NM 87571, tel. 800/758–1489. 6 double rooms with baths. Kiva fireplaces, espresso machine. $75–$105; full breakfast, afternoon snacks. AE, MC, V. No smoking, no pets.

Casa de las Chimeneas. 405 Cordoba Rd., Box 5303, Taos, NM 87571, tel. 505/758–4777, fax 505/758–3976. 3 rooms with baths, 1 suite. Cable TVs, phones, bars, mini-refrigerators, hot tub. $120–$150; full breakfast, afternoon hors d'oeuvres. AE, MC, V. No smoking, no pets.

Casa de Milagros. 321 Kit Carson Rd., Box 2983, Taos, NM 87571, tel. 505/758–8001 or 800/243–9334, fax 505/758–0127. 6 double rooms with baths, 1 2-bedroom suite. Cable TV, wood-burning fireplaces in most rooms, kitchenette in one room, full kitchen in suite, hot tub, courtyard garden. $70–$160, full breakfast. MC, V. No smoking.

Harrison's Bed and Breakfast. 1134 Millicent Rogers Rd., Box 242, Taos, NM 87571, tel. 505/758–2630. 2 units (up to 4 people each) with private baths. TV and pool table in family room. $20–$70, full breakfast. No credit cards. No smoking, no pets.

Inn on La Loma Plaza. 315 Ranchitos, Box 4159, Taos, NM 87571, tel. 505/758–1717 or 800/530–3040. 5 double rooms with baths, 2 4-person studios.

Cable TV; phones; fireplaces, kitchenettes, and hot tubs in studios. $95–$195; full breakfast, afternoon refreshments. AE, MC, V. No smoking.

La Posada de Taos. 309 Juanita La., Box 1118, Taos, NM 87571, tel. 505/758–8164 or 800/645–4803, fax 505/751–3294. 5 double rooms with baths, 1 cottage. Library, TV in common room. $80–$117, full breakfast. No credit cards. No smoking, no pets.

Little Tree. 226 Honda Seco Rd., Box 960, El Prado, NM 97529, tel. 800/334–8467. 4 double rooms with baths. Clock radio, down comforters, cookies, and fruit in all rooms, TV/VCR in 3 guest rooms, library. $80–$95; Continental-plus breakfast, afternoon refreshments. AE, D, MC, V; checks preferred. No smoking, no pets.

Old Taos Guesthouse. 1028 Witt Rd., Box 6552, Taos, NM 87571, tel. 505/758–5448 or 800/758–5448. 6 double rooms with baths, 2 suites, hot tub. $60–$115, Continental-plus breakfast. MC, V. No smoking, no pets.

Orinda Bed and Breakfast. 461 Valverde, Box 4451, Taos, NM 87571, tel. 505/758–8581 or 800/847–1837. 3 double rooms with baths. cable TV in common room, video library, refrigerators, kiva fireplaces. $70–$85, suite $155 for 4 people; full breakfast, afternoon refreshments. AE, D, MC, V. No smoking, no pets.

Ruby Slipper. 416 La Lomita Rd., Box 2069, Taos, NM 87571, tel. 505/758–0613. 7 double rooms with baths. Outdoor hot tub. $79–$114; full breakfast, in-room coffee. AE, D, MC, V. No smoking, no pets.

Salsa del Salto. Hwy. 150, Box 1468, El Prado, NM 87529, tel. 505/776–2422 or 800/530–3097. 10 double rooms with baths. Some rooms have fireplaces and jet bathtubs. Outdoor heated pool, hot tub, tennis court. $85–$160, full breakfast. MC, V. No smoking, no pets.

Reservations Services

Bed and Breakfast of New Mexico (Box 2805, Santa Fe, NM 87504, tel. 505/982–3332). **New Mexico Bed and Breakfast Association** (Box 2925, Santa Fe, NM 87504; write for brochure, and contact participating inns directly). **Taos Bed and Breakfast Association** (Box 2772, Taos, NM 87571, tel. 800/876–7857). **Traditional Taos Inns** (Box 2117, Taos, NM 87571, tel. 505/758–8245 or 800/525–8267).

Albuquerque

Adobe and Roses

1011 Ortega St. NW, Albuquerque, NM 87114, tel. 505/898–0654

A blue mailbox marked "1011" is the only indication that you've arrived at Dorothy Morse's place in Albuquerque's North Valley, a rural enclave 15 minutes from downtown; there's literally no sign of a commercial establishment on gravel-lined Ortega Street. And the sense that you're visiting a friend—one who respects your privacy and has unusually attractive guest quarters—lasts throughout a stay at Adobe and Roses.

Dorothy originally rented out an extra suite in her home as a onetime favor to an overbooked innkeeper but later decided, what with her daughters off in college, that running an inn might not be a bad idea. In 1988, she began building a separate two-unit guest cottage, laying the floors and tile herself. After more than three decades on the premises, she has a lovely and comfortable establishment.

The pueblo-style main house and guest cottage are indeed made of adobe, and, yes, there are roses everywhere, but they don't dominate among the wildly colorful blossoms on the 2-acre grounds. Most outstanding, maybe, are the rich purple irises that grow along the banks of a tranquil fishpond, so large they look like orchids. At sunset, all colors are transformed as the clouds behind the Sandias, off to the east, turn brilliant shades of pink.

The guest rooms fulfill every Southwest fantasy, with Mexican-tile sinks, terra-cotta pottery, equipale (pigskin) chairs, tinwork mirrors, wood-beam ceilings, Saltillo-tile floors, exposed brick walls, and kiva fireplaces. All are light, airy, and large—the suite in the main house easily fits a baby grand piano in the sitting room and an attached full kitchen—with individual cooling and heating units. Down comforters also help keep things cozy at night, when the 5,000-foot altitude can send the mercury dipping.

You can choose to eat breakfast in the dining room, on the portale, or in your room. Freshly ground coffee, homemade breads, muffins, and coffee cakes are staples; for those who like hot meals, Dorothy will prepare such specialties as a grits, chili, cheese, and asparagus casserole made with eggs laid by the chickens that wander the grounds. Best of all, because you're not *really* at a friend's house, you don't have to offer to do the dishes.

🛏 *1 double room with bath, 2 suites. Kitchen in cottage units, TV in 1 suite, kiva fireplaces, private entrances, laundry facilities, barbecue grill, horse boarding, outdoor fountains. $50–$79, full breakfast. No credit cards. No smoking, 2-night minimum.*

Bottgër Mansion

110 San Felipe NW, Albuquerque, NM 87104, tel. 505/243–3639

This elegant, light blue American Foursquare–style B&B, built in 1912 by German-born Charles Bottgër, was once called "The Pride of Old Town." Under owners Patsy and Vince Garcia, who took control in 1992, it is returning to its former glory. The beauty salon that used to occupy the second floor is now four double bedrooms, and an upstairs deck overlooking the tree-shaded courtyard will be added. With Old Town right out the door, bus and Sun Tran Trolley stops steps away, the Albuquerque Country Club just a few blocks away, and the downtown area a 15-minute walk, one of the most appealing aspects of this B&B is its location.

Another is the character of the residence. Professional fixer-uppers, the Garcias acquired a real gem in this National Historic Landmark. Many interesting people have passed through its gate, among them Machine Gun Kelly and his cohorts. This and many other stories tumble from the cheerful Patsy, who grew up in the area. Vince's family was one of the 12 families that founded Old Town in 1706, so the Garcias really know this intriguing section of Albuquerque.

The three downstairs suites—each named after a family grandmother—have wonderful features. The Sofia room has an ornate, delicately imprinted pressed-tin ceiling, a brass bed, and an adjoining sunroom with twin beds, tea table, and view of the courtyard. The Mercedes room has a black marble whirlpool tub, wood shutters, and pink marble floors. Lola has a mural painted by one of the residence's former owners (George Gallegos), a ceiling frieze, a bathtub and shower flanked by marble columns, and a separate sitting room.

The living room has a striking marble fireplace, white pressed-tin ceiling, and antique chairs and couches with ornately worked wood trim. Breakfast burritos smothered in green chili, Russian crepes, stuffed French toast, or whatever's for breakfast is served in your room, outdoors in the courtyard, or in the sunny dining room with white wrought-iron tables and chairs. A refrigerator is well stocked with refreshments, and guests are welcome to it day or night.

▦ *4 double rooms with baths, 3 suites. Ceiling fans and radios, mobile phone, TV in living room. $79–$139, full breakfast. AE, D, MC, V. No smoking, no pets.*

Casa del Granjero

414 C de Baca La. NW, Albuquerque, NM 87114, tel. and fax 505/897–4144 or 800/701–4144

Casa del Granjero means the "farmer's house," but don't start thinking rustic. It's the rare field hand who hangs his hat in a place that has a glass-enclosed hot tub building and 52-inch stereo TV; business office with copier and fax; and plush white terry guest robes. Some mighty sophisticated folks have stayed here, among them, actor Mickey Rourke.

There *is* a rural quality to the inn's 3-acre North Valley property. But the B&B's Spanish appellation plays on the name of owners Butch and Victoria Farmer, who bought the Territorial-style adobe in 1987. More than 100 years old, the house was in rather sad shape when they acquired it. Butch, a contractor, converted the courtyard to a great room and added three baths, three sitting rooms, a portale, and an outbuilding.

The Farmers hadn't intended to operate a B&B, but when friends began urging them to open up their lovely home to guests, they decided to give it a go. It was such a success that Butch recently added a gazebo, bathhouse, hot tub, waterfall, built-in barbecue, and four more guest rooms in a separate ranch-style home across the street: the Bunk House.

Butch's construction skills can also be seen in many of the touches in the seven guest rooms: Santa Fe–style pine beds, carved wood corbels and beams, bright Mexican tiles inset into the kiva fireplaces. Victoria combs yard sales and auctions for treasures, coming up with an antique trastero (combination closet and bench) or perhaps one of the colorful kilims or Navajo rugs scattered throughout the house. Even Butch's mother contributes to the cause, stitching pretty quilts for the rooms. Of all the accommodations, the Allegre Suite, with its lace-curtained canopy bed, is the most romantic and spacious.

Victoria cooks up a serious breakfast feast, everything from Italian to New Mexican specialties; one morning you might be served a breakfast burrito with avocado, fresh fruit, and flan. You can indulge, with peer support, at the long dark-wood table in the huge central dining room, or pig out in the privacy of your own patio.

▥ *3 double rooms (2 with baths), 4 suites. Desks and kiva fireplaces, private entrances to suites, VCR and video library in common room, washer/dryer. $69–$149, full breakfast. MC, V. No smoking.*

Casas de Sueños

310 Rio Grande SW, Albuquerque, NM 87104, tel. 505/247–4560 or 800/242–8987, fax 505/842–8493

Houses rarely determine their own fate, but that's just one of the many ways in which Casas de Sueños (Houses of Dreams) is exceptional. In 1979, lawyer Robert Hanna commissioned Albuquerque architect Bart Prince to design an office above the entry to his low-slung adobe complex. So many people came by to gape at the result that Hanna spent half his time inviting them in to look around. In 1990 he decided to turn this pleasant but distracting activity into a business—and thus a B&B was born.

The artistic inclinations of this inn, one block from Old Town, aren't limited to its recent addition. Casas de Sueños was designed as an artists' community in the 1930s by painter J. R. Willis; at the perimeter of his house and studio he built a group of rental cottages, which now house guests. Little inspira-

tional paths and niches, some with waterfalls, abound in the complex, and a profusion of blossoms climbs up walls and spills out onto a lush lawn. There are more than 50 rosebushes and a dozen varieties of grapevines on the acre of grounds.

In addition, the inn's dining room, where a gourmet hot and cold buffet is set out each morning, doubles as a gallery for local artists. With its French doors, lace tablecloths, viga ceilings, and kiva fireplace, the room is warm and cheerful. On nice days, you can head out to the lovely adjoining patio.

The guest rooms, most with private entrances and courtyards, are decorated in different styles, each more attractive than the last. All have fresh flowers and luxurious bedding; many boast kitchens, fireplaces, Oriental rugs, and ornate wood furnishings acquired from the estate of a Spanish nobleman. The La Cascada suite lets out onto its own private waterfall; the Porter features a Willis mural and private patio with outdoor hot tub; and the wonderfully over-the-top Rio Grande has a skylight, florid gilt mirror, and brass Cupids holding the toilet paper roll.

Oh yes, and Bart Prince's fantastic creation is now used for massages instead of a law practice. Officially named the Dream Space, the loft is a kind of architectural Rorschach test: Locals have dubbed it "the snail," but others have sworn it's anything from a ram's head to an ancient fertility symbol.

▥ *3 double rooms with baths; 4 1-bedroom suites, 4 2-bedroom suites, 8 casitas. Phones, voice mail, cable TV, modem jacks in some rooms, kitchens in most casitas, fireplaces in some rooms, library, off-street parking. $85–$250, full breakfast. AE, D, DC, MC, V. No smoking, no pets.*

Casita Chamisa

850 Chamisal Rd. NW, Albuquerque, NM 87107, tel. 505/897–4644

The first B&B in Albuquerque, Casita Chamisa is also historic in other ways. Originally an adobe farmhouse dating back to 1850, it sits atop the ruins of five successive Pueblo and pre-Pueblo village sites, the oldest dating from around 720 BC! Jack Schaefer, previous owner of the home and author of *Shane*, used to find pottery shards from time to time. The mother lode was hit when current owners Kit and Arnold Sargeant began construction of the B&B's 30-foot pool. Kit, an author and archaeologist, enlisted the help of the University of New Mexico to conduct a thorough excavation. More than 150,000 pottery shards and artifacts were eventually recovered. Some remain on view at the home, along with part of the excavation.

In the pastoral North Valley, which was settled in the 1600s by the Spanish colonialists, this B&B has everything you associate with the region. It is shaded by massive river cottonwoods, which keep the place cool on even the hottest days. Chickens, roosters, beehives, herb and vegetable gardens, horses (not for riding), fruit trees, and winding *acequias* (irrigation ditches) retain the former farm's character.

There are only two accommodations, so tranquility is the order of the day. The ivy-covered guest house has a small sitting room with a corner kiva fireplace, a queen bed, a private patio, and a greenhouse where you can sit and read or write. The kitchenette and a separate bedroom with twin beds covered with French knot bedspreads make this an ideal place for a small family. Animals, a sandbox, swing set, and pool are real attractions for kids. A charming bedroom in the main house is decorated with a Mexican tin mirror and a hand-carved Mexican headboard. It also has a kiva fireplace and private entrance onto the covered portale that wraps around two sides of the home.

The home has a great library and a baby grand piano and is filled with wonderful arts and crafts from around the world, including a basket collection, Mexican textiles, and odds and ends gathered by Arnold during his worldwide travels with the U.S. Army.

A country Continental breakfast is served on a plant-filled, enclosed, glass-covered patio, in the dining room before a small fireplace, or out on the portale. It includes fruit, juices, coffee and tea, as well as coffee cakes and muffins, or another slice of history: some of Arnold's fresh sourdough bread, made from a 200-year-old Basque starter.

🛏 *1 double room with bath, 1 2-bedroom casita. Fireplaces in both rooms, library, enclosed pool, hot tub, greenhouse, gardens, sundeck. $80–$135, Continental breakfast. AE, D, MC, V. No smoking.*

Elaine's

Box 444, 72 Snowline Estates, Cedar Crest, NM 87008, tel. 505/281–2467 or 800/821–3092

It might be hard to decide which you like better, Elaine O'Neil or her house, but then the two are inextricably intertwined. One of the nicest building contractors you're ever likely to meet, Elaine supervised the construction of her rough-hewn stone-and-log cabin down to the last interesting detail—for example, the ornate iron braces that anchor the joints of the ceiling beams, which are at once decorative and functional.

A winding dirt road leads up to Elaine's, set in the heart of the Sandia Mountains in Cedar Crest, 15 miles east of Albuquerque on the historic Turquoise Trail to Santa Fe. But the bed-and-breakfast's rustic setting and structure belie its elegant interior. If the Victorians had slalomed, they doubtless would have headed to just such a retreat for après-ski sherries.

Although there are fine antiques all around the house, this is a cheerful, unpretentious place. Light from huge windows in the two-story-high cathedral ceiling streams into an upstairs common area, where an enormous stone fireplace is fronted by comfortable couches. Guests often just flop down on the plush hunter-green carpet and play one of the board games stocked in the rooms, read, or stare into the flames.

One of the second-level rooms has a whirlpool tub, while the third-level room has dramatic views of mountains and plains in three directions. Fresh flowers and soft, downy bedding help make all three accommodations, which mix sturdy wood furnishings and more delicate antiques, very appealing. One disadvantage: Because the romantic top-floor bedroom was built loft style, its occupants can overhear late-night revelers on the lower level—but it is still Elaine's most popular room.

Breakfast here, served in a new airy and plant-filled breakfast room, is simple but hearty; large helpings of fresh fruit, pancakes or waffles, and sausage are standard, but guests can get pretty much what they like. Afterward, many find that the crisp mountain air inspires them to take a long walk. Charlie, a fat golden retriever who likes to laze on "his" front porch bench, will happily accompany guests on a hike through the Cibola National Forest, abutting the inn's 4 acres. Eliot, part wolf, part German shepherd, disdains Charlie's friendly doggie ways but always condescends to come along for the exercise.

🏠 *3 double rooms with baths. Private balcony in 2 rooms, wraparound deck, hiking trails on property, skiing and horseback riding nearby. $77–$85, full breakfast. AE, MC, V. No smoking, no pets.*

Other Choices

Enchanted Vista. 10700 Del Rey NE, Albuquerque, NM 87122, tel. 505/823–1301. 1 double room shares bath, 2 suites with baths. TVs, refrigerators, coffeemakers, dining table, whirlpool

tub in 1 room, basketball court and tetherball. $62–$74, Continental breakfast. No credit cards. No smoking, no cats.

Hacienda Vargas. 1431 El Camino Real, Box 307, Algodones, NM 87001, tel. 505/867–9115 or 800/261–0006. 2 double rooms with baths. 5 suites with double whirlpool baths. Kiva fireplaces throughout house, library, art gallery, barbecue, outdoor gazebo, meeting facilities. $79–$139, full breakfast. MC, V. No smoking, no pets.

Old Town Bed & Breakfast. 707 17th St. NW, Albuquerque, NM 87104, tel. 505/764–9144. 1 double room with shower, 1 suite. Off-street parking, fountain. $65–$80. No credit cards. No smoking, no pets.

Sarabande. 5637 Rio Grande Blvd. NW, Albuquerque, NM 87107, tel. 505/345–4923. 3 double rooms with baths. Library, fireplace in sitting room, hot tub, all-terrain bicycles. $85–$110, full breakfast. MC, V. No smoking, no pets, no children.

W. E. Mauger Estate. 701 Roma Ave. NW, Albuquerque, NM 87102, tel. 505/242–8755, fax 505/842–8835. 8 double rooms with baths, 1 2-room suite. Coffeemakers, hair dryers, irons, clock radios, and TVs, refrigerators in most rooms, balcony in one room, fireplace, TV in sitting room, sunporch, patio, off-street parking. $75–$115; full breakfast, snacks, evening wine and cheese. AE, MC, V. No smoking.

Yours Truly. 160 Paseo de Corrales, Box 2263, Corrales, NM 87048, tel. 505/898–7027. 3 double rooms with baths. Guest robes, TVs, radios, kiva fireplaces in 2 rooms, clerestory windows, large music selection, fireplace in living room, hot-air balloon rides ($200 for 2 people). $75; full breakfast, afternoon wine, snacks and morning coffee. AE, MC, V. No smoking in bedrooms.

Reservations Services

Albuquerque Bed & Breakfast Association (Box 7262, Albuquerque, NM 87194; write for a pamphlet detailing participating inns). **Destination Southwest** (121 Tijeras Ave. NE, Albuquerque, NM 87125, tel. 800/466–7829).

Southern New Mexico

Eaton House

403 Eaton Ave., Socorro, NM 87801, tel. 505/835–1067

Unlike other adventurers who headed west to seek their fortune but built homes in familiar East Coast–style when they arrived, Colonel E. W. Eaton—Civil War hero, founder of a smelter, and, later, mayor of Socorro—constructed a thick-walled Territorial adobe for his young New Mexican bride in 1881. This is not to suggest the wealthy Eatons did not indulge in "civilized" Eastern touches: leaded-glass windows and a built-in classical-revival colonnade bookcase grace their elegant home, which remained in family hands for nearly 100 years.

Innkeepers Anna Appleby and Tom Harper have retained the original blend of New Mexican and Victorian styles in their upscale B&B. Their seven guest rooms—all offering private entrances—are decorated with impeccable taste. The Vigilante Room features a Santa Fe–style bed and trastero (combination closet and bench) crafted by a local artisan, as well as a colorful Mexican-tile sink. Matching carved wooden beds built for twin girls more than 80 years ago are set in Daughters' Room, which also has a fluted-glass light fixture original to the house. The Colonel Eaton Room has a queen-size pencil-post bed so high you need a stool to climb in, flowered imported Dutch tile in the bath, and

delicate English lace curtains. The Marcellina Chavez Casita, named for the wife of Colonel Eaton, is a spacious suite with a king-size bed, a Pueblo-style fireplace, and massive vigas that cross the ceiling; the Bosque Casita, similarly roomy, has a Mexican-tile bath. All rooms have luxurious European-goose-down blankets.

The B&B is an extremely popular spot for bird-watchers, largely because it's near the Bosque del Apache, a wildlife refuge on the banks of the Rio Grande. The Sevilleta National Wildlife Refuge and Cibola National Forest are also nearby. Both Tom and Anna are avid bird-watchers, and Anna will prepare a light "Early Birder" breakfast basket for guests who want to set off first thing in the morning. They can return to a full gourmet breakfast in the high-ceiling dining room. Main dishes are sinful—soufflés topped with chopped bananas, banana cream liqueur, whipped cream, and homemade pomegranate sauce, for example—but all the fruits used are organic, and the meats are made without nitrates or preservatives.

🏠 *1 single room with bath, 6 double rooms with baths. Ceiling fans, fireplaces and whirlpool tubs in 2 rooms, library, fireplace, binoculars and field guides available. $75–$120; full breakfast, afternoon tea. AE, MC, V. No smoking, no pets, no children under 14.*

Ellis Store & Co. Bed and Breakfast

Hwy. 380, mile marker 98, Box 15, Lincoln, NM 88338, tel. 505/653–4609 or 800/653–5460, fax 505/653–4610

This lodging's history dates from 1850, when it was a modest, two-room adobe in territory where the Mescalero Indians still posed a threat to settlers. During the Lincoln County War, the building's thick walls provided refuge for members of the McSween faction, and Billy the Kid was kept here pending his trial. Today, the house looks out on a peaceful lawn where deer graze in the evening.

In 1993 David and Jinny Vigil ended their 10-year search for a B&B with this one. David, a former engineer whose family has been in New Mexico for nearly 300 years, has done a lot of work on the building, adding bathrooms and meticulously restoring the front portale to include its historic sag. Guests sit under it in the quiet of the morning while enjoying Jinny's gourmet cooking. In the evenings, her culinary skills draw people from as far away as Carlsbad. They come to enjoy such delicacies as veal Madeira as part of a six-course meal served in the spacious depths of a dining room glowing with light from the fireplace.

Three of the guest rooms in the main house have wood-burning stoves; the fourth, Nancy's Room, has a fireplace. Each is named for a former resident of the house (though Billy the Kid only needed to stay a few days to get one named after him) and is decorated with antiques. The accommodations are interesting but not necessarily private, as many rooms have adjoining doors, and a pair share a bath. Behind the building sits the Mill House, which contains four rooms sharing a bath and a large family den.

However, it would be hard to imagine a guest staying indoors when there is so much to see in the surrounding area. David leases 6,400 acres nearby and offers horseback hunting trips for ruggedly inclined guests, and there is fishing in the creek that runs through the property. Guests also have the option of hiking or taking a historical tour of Lincoln.

🛏 *2 double rooms with baths, 2 doubles share bath, 4 doubles share 1 bath in Mill House. Wood-burning stove or fireplace in 4 rooms, 6-course dinners served by reservation, fishing, hunting, hiking. $$69–$99, full breakfast. D, MC, V. No smoking, no pets.*

The Lodge

1 Corona Pl., Box 497, Cloudcroft, NM 88317, tel. 505/682–2566 or 800/395–6343, fax 505/682–2715

Cloudcroft's Lodge embodies the yin and yang of late-Victorian design in a singularly appealing fashion. Built in 1899 by the Alamogordo and Sacramento Mountain railway to house its workers, this ornate but imposing structure has a lobby where any hunter would be proud to rest a gun: A stuffed bear stands snarling in the corner, and a long-horned eland stares down from over the copper fireplace at deep-maroon leather couches and chairs. But pink-floral carpets lead down the hallway to individually decorated rooms with chenille bedspreads, period antiques, pastel-flocked wallpaper, ceiling fans, and, in many cases, four-poster beds.

Some of the accommodations are rather small, but they're accordingly less expensive. And if you get one with a view, it'll open up the space immeasurably. If you don't, you can always climb up to the hotel's copper-covered bell tower, which Judy Garland visited with Clark Gable. On a clear day, you can see White Sands National Monument in the distance. Those who really want to hide away with friends can rent the Retreat, a four-bedroom cottage with a kitchenette, just across the front parking lot from the main building.

The pool on the lush back lawn is inviting in warm weather, but winter is as delightful as summer in this mountain retreat. A gently sloping, pine-shrouded golf course on the grounds becomes a playground for cross-country skiers; downhill runs at the Cloudcroft Ski Area are only 2 miles away; and lift-line tubing can be arranged through the front desk.

Any time of year, it's a treat to visit Rebecca's, the Lodge's elegant American-Southwestern dining room, named after the putative resident ghost. A

Continental breakfast at Rebecca's is included in room rates for those who stay at the Pavilion: A Bed and Breakfast, about ½ mile to the south of the main building, but also part of the Lodge. This single-level structure is rustic in style—rooms have beamed ceilings, knotty-pine walls, and, in some cases, enormous stone fireplaces.

▦ *10 single rooms with baths, 30 doubles with baths, 7 suites in hotel, 11 doubles with baths in B&B, 1 4-bedroom cottage. Phones, cable TVs, sauna, spa, bar, 2 gift shops, conference facilities. $59–$299; breakfast not included for Lodge or Retreat guests, Continental breakfast for B&B guests. AE, D, DC, MC, V. No pets.*

Lundeen Inn of the Arts

618 S. Alameda Blvd., Las Cruces, NM 88005, tel. 888/526–3326, fax 505/647–1334

You'll think you've died and gone to Santa Fe when you wake up at this arty, upscale bed-and-breakfast, but you'll be paying Las Cruces prices for the experience. Owned and designed by architect Gerald Lundeen and his wife, Linda, whose art gallery is on the premises, the inn is designed to nurture aesthetic impulses in its visitors.

Gerald seamlessly joined two 1895 adobe houses, Mexican Colonial style, in order to create the B&B; what was once the patio between them became the 18-foot-high Marienda Room, where most of the inn's activity takes place. Guests attend art classes, conferences, and performances in this unusual space, which is decorated in an eclectic (and ecumenical) fashion: The ornate wood balustrade is from a synagogue in El Paso and the pressed-tin ceiling frieze is from a Methodist church in Lordsburg. Huge Palladian windows let in lots of light at breakfast, when guests enjoy elaborate meals

here—at least one hot entrée as well as a tempting variety of baked goods.

Reading niches and comfortable sitting areas abound in both wings of the house. Guest rooms are named for Western artists such as Georgia O'Keeffe and Frederic Remington. The one dedicated to Native American painter R. C. Gorman has a kiva fireplace, viga beams, and a curved seating nook with built-in bookcases. The connection between artist and decor is occasionally mysterious—one wonders, for example, how cowboy painter Gordon Snidow might feel about being represented by a room with a bidet in it—but never mind: All the accommodations are beautifully furnished with a whimsical mix of antiques and newer, handcrafted pieces. And, naturally, the walls are decked with fine art and reproductions. A newly restored adobe in the back of the inn adds three casitas with full baths to the rooms available. In fact, the Lundeen Inn offers long-term residence if you find you just can't separate yourself from Las Cruces.

The inn offers courses in silversmithing, ceramics, coil pottery, and architecture, all of which are taught monthly. Most of the classes last a week, and people sign up months ahead for them, but guests can sign up for single classes. There is also a course on breadmaking, and to this end the Lundeens have installed an Indian *horno*, a lumpy adobe oven that can bake up to 18 loaves at a time.

▦ *20 double rooms with baths, 6 suites. Phones, TVs, fireplaces, balconies, kitchenettes in some rooms, exercise room and massages available, off-street parking, $68–$105, full breakfast. AE, D, DC, MC, V. No smoking.*

Other Choices

Bear Mountain Guest Ranch. Box 1163, Silver City, NM 88062, tel. 505/538–2538. 11 double rooms with baths, 2 3-room suites, 1 2-person cottage, 1

4-person cottage. Electric blankets, kitchenettes in 2 cottages, sunporch, nature classes available. $95–$105, all meals included. No credit cards. No smoking in indoor common rooms.

Black Range Lodge. Star Rte. 2, Box 119, Kingston, NM 88042, tel. 505/895–5652, fax 505/895–3326. 4 double rooms with baths, 3 suites. 2 rooms have private balcony, patio, greenhouse, piano, Ping-Pong, Foosball, pool, TV/VCR room, video library. $55 first night, $45 each additional night (except holidays); Continental breakfast. D, MC, V. Smoking outside or on balconies only.

Carter House. 101 N. Cooper St., Silver City, NM 88061, tel. 505/388–5485. 4 double rooms with baths, 1 suite. Clock radios, ceiling fans, newspaper, free local calls, library, TV room, off-street parking, horseback riding, massage. $58–$69, full breakfast. MC, V. No smoking, no pets.

Casa de Patrón. Box 27, Lincoln, NM 88338, tel. 505/653–4676, fax 505/653–4671. 5 double rooms with baths (1 adjoining). 1 1-bedroom casita, 1 2-bedroom casita. Kitchenette in 1 casita, coffeemaker and refrigerator in other, clocks in rooms, fireplaces in 2 rooms, whirlpool bath in 1 room, pipe organ and piano in common areas, patio, off-street parking. $79–$107; full breakfast for rooms, Continental breakfast for casitas. MC, V. No smoking, no pets.

Enchanted Villa. Box 456, Hillsboro, NM 88042, tel. 505/895–5686. 3 double rooms with baths, 2 double rooms with shared bath. Fireplace, TV/VCR room, video library, dog run. $60, full breakfast. No credit cards. No smoking in guest rooms.

Mesón de Mesilla. 1803 Avenida de Mesilla, Box 1212, Mesilla, NM 88046, tel. 505/525–9212 or 800/732–6025. 3 single rooms and 6 double rooms with baths, 4 suites. In-room phones available, suites have kiva fireplaces, 1 has private balcony, pool, free Las Cruces airport pickup, off-street parking, picnic baskets available, banquet room. $45–$82, full breakfast. D, DC, MC, V.

Sierra Mesa Lodge. Fort Stanton Rd., Box 463, Alto, NM 88312, tel. 505/336–4515. 5 double rooms with baths. Clocks, kimonos, TV available, hot tub, hiking trails. $95–100; full breakfast, afternoon tea. D, MC, V. No smoking, no pets, no children under 14.

Reservations Services

Bed & Breakfast of New Mexico (Box 2805, Santa Fe, NM 87504, tel. 505/982–3332). **New Mexico Bed and Breakfast Association** (Box 2925, Santa Fe, NM 87504; write for a list of member inns).

New York

The Huntting Inn

Lake George

Balsam House

Atateka Dr., Friends Lake, Chestertown, NY 12817, tel. 518/494-2828, fax 518/494-4431

A forest preserve, mountain views, a private beach on Friends Lake, comfortable rooms, and sophisticated fare—you'll find all these at Balsam House. Built in 1845 as a farmhouse, the building became a vacation lodge in 1891; in 1982 owner Frank Ellis turned it into a year-round, full-service inn. Innkeepers and new co-owners Josef and Maggie Roettig, assisted by an able and knowledgeable staff, make sure guests lack nothing during their stay.

Guests have access to all the offerings of the Adirondacks, but they're certainly not roughing it in the wilderness. Though differing in layout, all the guest rooms have a light decor with white lace Duvet curtains and Victorian touches. The original floorboards have been sanded and glazed and all the bathrooms have been modernized, some with Italian marble. Room 30 has a skylight and a view of nearby Gore Mountain.

The inn's restaurant, Le Papillon, is now under the illustrious hand of chef Josef. The room has been redone and is "elegant, but with a touch of Adirondack spirit and a fireplace in the center," says Josef. Formerly executive chef at the Four Seasons in California, Josef calls his fare "International Viennese" and says his baby rack of lamb wrapped in pastry is a favorite. The extensive wine list has won numerous awards.

The inn's beach on Friend's Lake, a few minutes' walk down the hill, has its own dock, canoes, and rowboats.

The actress Mary Frann, from TV's *Newhart*, stayed at the inn to soak up atmosphere and pick up pointers before assuming the role of innkeeper on that long-running show. Rumor has it that the three backwoods brothers on the show—Larry, Darryl, and Darryl—were inspired by a couple of colorful locals who stop in here from time to time.

🏨 *16 double rooms with baths, 4 suites. Restaurant; air-conditioning; TV in some rooms; canoes, rowboats, and mountain bikes available; hiking trails nearby. $85–$210, full breakfast. AE, DC, MC, V. No pets.*

Bent Finial Manor

*194 Main St., Warrensburg, NY 12885,
tel. 518/623-3308*

The Bent Finial, definitely among the
most elegant bed-and-breakfasts in the
area, is certainly one of the most opulent. The stunning 1904 Queen Anne
Victorian mansion opened in 1989.

The mansion was built by cattle baron
Lewis Thomson. During the Civil War,
Thomson made his fortune supplying
beef to Union troops. Like many of the
other nouveaux riches of his era, he
wanted his home to duplicate the opulent excesses of the European nobility—
and he succeeded. Twenty-three kinds
of wood—including oak, birch, hemlock,
pine, and several varieties of cherry—
make up the floors, moldings, wainscoting, and the impressive staircase.
You enter the front parlor and music
room between Corinthian columns and
capitals. All the rooms have their original beveled, etched, or stained-glass
windows.

It's to the credit of owners Dr. Allen
and Therese Axenfield that the period
antique furnishings do justice to this
magnificent house. Before you leave,
make sure the Axenfields tell you the
peculiar story of how the house got its
name. And if you have back pain, Dr.
Axenfield offers holistic chiropractic
health care on the ground floor.

▦ *5 double rooms with baths, 2
housekeeping suites. Air-conditioning,
phones, 1 room with fireplace and private porch. $85–$135, full breakfast.
MC, V. Restricted smoking, no pets.*

Lamplight Inn

*231 Lake Ave., Box 70, Lake Luzerne,
NY 12846, tel. 518/696-5294 or 800/
262-4668*

In 1890 the Lamplight Inn, a grand Victorian Gothic in the village of Lake
Luzerne, was built by a wealthy bachelor lumberman as his summer playhouse. One can only guess at the
romantic trysts of this 19th-century
playboy, but adjoining doors (no longer
used) to two other bedrooms from
the master bedroom hint at the possibilities.

Today, the Lamplight is a romantic bed-
and-breakfast for 20th-century guests,
thanks to innkeepers Gene and Linda
Merlino. In 1984 they were still dating
when they bought this mansion on a
whim. Within a year they were husband
and wife; they spent their honeymoon
painting the front porch. Honeymooning guests and couples who may or may
not be considering a wedding in the
future love the Lamplight, as room-
diary accolades attest: "Our privacy
was respected and our newness as a
couple treated with gentleness and
humor," one newlywed wrote, and there
have been quite a few proposals uttered
on bended knee under this romantic
roof.

The decor helps considerably. The
downstairs sitting room has its original
chestnut molding, wainscoting, and
unusual keyhold staircase. On cool
evenings the room is lit by two fireplaces. Wicker chairs beckon visitors to
the comfortable front porch, and the
airy dining room provides the perfect
backdrop for Linda's granola and
muffins and Gene's peach crepes and
three-egg omelets.

Guest rooms are Victorian in the
romantic sense of the word—they are
flowery and lacy. One of the nicest
places to stay is the Canopy Room,
with an original carved-oak mantel,
hearth tiles, and a gas fireplace. In a
newly constructed wing is a unique
room that perfectly matches the rest of
the house: The Skylight Room has a
carved-oak, high-back Victorian bed
covered in an antique patchwork quilt,
with a skylight overhead. It's hard to
choose a room here, because so much
love and attention to detail have gone
into each one.

A guest entry in the Canopy Room
diary probably sums up the Lamp-

light experience best: "Your rocking chairs, soft quilts, and warm hospitality have transformed us back into human beings."

🏠 *17 double rooms with baths. Air-conditioning, 12 rooms with fireplaces, 7 rooms with TV, 4 rooms with whirlpool baths, 1 room is accessible for people who use wheelchairs, beach across street. $89–$165, full breakfast. AE, MC, V. Restricted smoking, no pets, 2-night minimum on weekends, 3-night minimum on holidays and during special events.*

Other Choices

Chester Inn. Box 163, Main St., Chestertown, NY 12817, tel. 518/494–4148. 2 double rooms with baths, 2 suites. Air-conditioning in most rooms, dinner available upon request. $65–$110, full breakfast. MC, V. No smoking, no pets, 2-night minimum on holiday weekends.

Crislip's Bed and Breakfast. 693 Ridge Rd., Queensbury, NY 12804, tel. 518/793–6869. 3 double rooms with baths. TV in 2 rooms and in common room. $55–$75, full breakfast. MC, V. No smoking.

Friends Lake Inn. Friends Lake Rd., Chestertown, NY 12817, tel. 518/494–4751. 14 rooms, 10 with baths. 6 rooms with whirlpool baths, 7 rooms with pull-out couches, restaurant, wine bar, beach. $105–$250; full breakfast, lunch and dinner available. AE, MC, V. Restricted smoking, no pets.

Hilltop Cottage Bed and Breakfast. Box 186, Rte. 9N, Bolton Landing, NY 12814, tel. 518/644–2492. 1 double room with bath, 2 doubles share bath. Piano and wood-burning stove in living room. $50–$60, full breakfast. MC, V. No smoking indoors, no pets, 2-night minimum on holiday weekends.

Merrill Magee House. 2 Hudson St., Warrensburg, NY 12885, tel. 518/623–2449. 10 double rooms with baths, 1 suite. Restaurant, tavern, air-condi-

tioning, pool, whirlpool. $95–$115, full breakfast. AE, D, MC, V. No smoking in dining room, no pets, 2-night minimum on summer and holiday weekends. Closed Mar.

Sanford's Ridge Bed & Breakfast. 749 Ridge Rd., Queensbury, NY 12804, tel. 518/793–4923. 3 double rooms with baths. TV in common room, pool. $65–$95, full breakfast. MC, V. No smoking, no pets, 2-night minimum on holiday weekends.

Saratoga Rose. 4274 Rockwell St. (Box 238), Hadley, NY 12835, tel. 518/696–2861 or 800/942–5025. 3 double rooms with baths, 2 suites. Restaurant, bar, whirlpool bath in 1 room and both suites. $65–$165, full breakfast. D, MC, V. Restricted smoking, no pets, 2-night minimum Aug. and on holiday weekends.

Reservations Service

American Country Collection (1353 Union St., Schenectady, NY 12308, tel. 518/370–4948).

Saratoga and Albany

Adelphi Hotel

365 Broadway, Saratoga Springs, NY 12866, tel. 518/587–4688

If Kublai Khan had decreed that his stately pleasure dome be built in late 19th-century Saratoga instead of in Xanadu, he might have come up with the Adelphi Hotel. This lodging is nothing like home, unless home is an Italian palazzo, with the requisite piazza and ornamented by a maze of Victorian fretwork. The opulent lobby is done in a style so reminiscent of La Belle Epoque that one could picture the Divine Sarah Bernhardt holding court amid its splendor. It's hard to believe that not too long ago the Adelphi stood empty, evidence of fortune gone sour. Saratogans shook their heads and laughed at what they took to be the foolhardiness of Gregg Siefker and Sheila Parkert when they bought the place in 1988, but no one's laughing anymore: The hotel is one of Saratoga's showpieces, its lobby bar and café a gathering place for natives and visitors alike (in July it's a favorite hangout of members of the New York City Ballet).

No two rooms are the same: All the furnishings are eclectic—and recherché. If you seek accommodations that hark back to the Adirondack camps enjoyed by some of America's wealthiest families, ask for Room 16, the Adirondack Suite, with mission-style furniture manufactured in upstate New York, a twig settee, Papago Indian baskets on the wall, and a wood-paneled bathroom. If you yearn for the south of France but can't afford to go there, the Riviera Suite (Room 12) may lessen the pangs somewhat. Its sitting area, furnished with rattan, is graced with a Mediterranean mural; an amusing Casbah painting hangs on the bedroom wall; and the bathroom is decorated in apricot tones. Other rooms are furnished with Tiffany lamp shades, brass-and-iron beds with crocheted bedspreads, wicker settees, and Victoriana.

The Adelphi was built when Saratoga was known as the Queen of the Spas. Today the city is still the center of a lively and elegant social scene, especially in August, when the raceway is open—but keep in mind that Saratoga has a lot to offer during the other 11 months of the year, when hotel reservations are easier to come by.

▥ *19 double rooms with baths, 18 suites. Restaurant (open July and Aug.), bar, air-conditioning, cable TV, phones, room service, pool. $90–$310, Continental breakfast. AE, MC, V. No pets, 3-day minimum on weekends in Aug. Closed Nov.–Apr.*

Inn on Bacon Hill

200 Wall St., Schuylerville, NY 12871, tel. 518/695–3693

Some B&Bs are a labor of love, and such is the case for the Inn on Bacon Hill. The 1862 Italianate Victorian farmhouse sits in near isolation on a country road, though it's less than a 15-minute drive to Saratoga Springs. Inside and out are signs that somebody competently and with great care has restored and maintained this place. The somebodies in this case were Andrea Collins-Breslin and her mother, Millie. In 1986 they bought this 16-room, former home of a state senator and gentleman farmer, and they got to work.

Take the beautifully gleaming chestnut bannister: The 56 spindels took Andrea and Millie 31 full days to refurbish the inlaid mahogany on the newel posts. Additional touches are the result of hours mother and daughter spent researching the history and telling the story of the house in the 56 hand-sewn squares of a quilt that lies on the bed in the Queen Anne's Lace Room. Any stay at Bacon Hill will reveal many more such pleasures.

When you close the doors to the downstairs Victorian Parlor Suite, it feels like the house is all yours. You can play the baby grand piano by the light of the original gas chandelier, now converted to electricity. Upstairs are the Morning Glory and Tulip rooms, which share a bath. Also, there's an arched alcove that makes an intimate setting for tea and conversation.

The original yellow and pink floribunda rosebushes (documented by the century-old paintings hanging in the parlor suite) please the eyes of guests relaxing under the corbelled front porch. Oceans of waving corn are replaced in winter by fields of snow extending to the Green Mountains of Vermont, visible in the distance.

Andrea, a former specialist in employee relations, left the corporate world to spend more time with Millie and get involved in a more people-oriented job. Andrea is the perfect hostess, having mastered that elusive combination of seeing to her guests' needs while leaving them their privacy. Many of the original artworks around the house are by Millie, the artist-in-residence. Vicki, the golden retriever, serves as greeter. Twice a year, for guests considering going into the business, Andrea teaches a course at the inn called "Innkeeping: The Facts and Fantasies."

🏠 *2 double rooms with baths, 2 doubles share bath. Air-conditioning. $65–$135, full breakfast. MC, V. No smoking, no pets, 2-night minimum on Aug. weekends.*

The Mansion

Rte. 29, Box 77, Rock City Falls, NY 12863, tel. 518/885-1607

Rock City Falls, a 19th-century mill town 7 miles west of Saratoga Springs, seems an unlikely destination for travelers. The Kayaderosseras Creek still flows, but the mills and factories are quiet. Aside from a few antiques shops, there doesn't seem to be much that would draw visitors to this sleepy village . . . not much, that is, until one spots the Mansion, one of the most elegant and romantic bed-and-breakfasts you'll encounter anywhere. The Venetian villa-style residence, soon to be listed on the National Register of Historic Places, was built in 1866 as a summer home for George West, a prominent industrialist and inventor of the folding paper bag. No expense was spared in the construction of the 23-room mansion; it has 12-foot etched-glass doors, marble fireplaces with inlaid mantels, copper and brass lighting fixtures, and Tiffany chandeliers.

It is a credit to proprietor Tom Clark and innkeeper Alan Churchill, who restored the mansion, that this bed-and-breakfast is both sumptuous and friendly. The art books stacked invitingly in the library are for browsing, perhaps while sipping iced tea or Saratoga water on the side porch. Classical music wafts through the house. The art, which Tom collects on his travels, invites close inspection. The antique parlor organ is there for playing. All the guest rooms are enticing, but the Four-Poster Room, with its queen-size carved bed, and the Queen Room, with garden views, are particularly handsome.

And there are the flowers. Baskets of fuchsia hang from the porches; roses, peonies, and delphiniums fill the gardens; and bouquets of fragrant Casablanca lilies and foxglove may greet you in the front hall or parlors. Throughout the year floral arrangements brighten every guest room. Alan of the green thumb even grows orchids.

Alan nurtures his guests the way he nurtures his flowers—you are made to feel like a treasured friend in this hospitable house. Everything here—from the Victorian furnishings to the homemade fruit breads served with breakfast—is in excellent taste. As Alan says, "The house demands it. It's so special."

🏠 *4 double rooms with baths, 1 suite. Air-conditioning, pool. $95–$165, full breakfast. No credit cards. No smoking indoors, no pets, 2-night minimum in Aug. and on holiday weekends. Closed Thanksgiving and Dec. 25.*

Sedgwick Inn

Rte. 22, Berlin, NY 12022, tel. 518/658-2334

The Sedgwick Inn, a rambling New England farmhouse with Victorian additions, was built in 1791 as a stagecoach stop. It sits on 12 verdant acres at the foot of the Berkshires, in Berlin; it was once a favorite getaway of New York politicos and their cronies and later became a popular tavern. It is said that Cole Porter once performed here. Today the inn combines all three of its earlier incarnations: It's a way station, where vacationers and second-home owners stop to refresh themselves on their journeys to points north; New York City residents come to get away from it all; and the inn's renowned restaurant (with live piano music on Friday and Saturday nights) draws visitors and locals alike.

Another major draw is innkeeper Edie Evans. Fourteen years ago Edie and her late husband, Bob, bought the then-defunct inn—she had been a psychiatric social worker—and spent a year restoring it. You can sense her presence throughout the establishment, from her original sculptures in the living room to her blueberry muffins at breakfast.

If the bedrooms could talk they might say, "Lincoln could have slept here." Of course, there's no record that the 16th president ever did pass through Berlin, but if he had he might have felt right at home in Room 9, with its four-poster bed and Oriental rug; and he probably would have been delighted with the king-size bed in Room 7 and the book-lined shelves in Room 11.

Edie is particularly proud of her restaurant. It's not just the food and drink that soothe the soul here but also the innkeeper's attitude: "We only have one sitting a night for each table," she notes. "We don't want our guests to feel rushed."

Behind the inn there's a six-unit motel annex. The rooms there, decorated with Cushman Colonial furnishings, are less expensive than those in the main house. Edie has transformed an old carriage house behind the inn into a gift shop; there you can find antique jewelry, crafts, and one-of-a-kind items.

🏠 *10 double rooms with baths, 1 suite. Restaurant, TV with VCR in some rooms, limited room service, gift and gourmet shops. $65–$120, full breakfast. AE, D, DC, MC, V. Restricted smoking, 2-night minimum on holiday and summer weekends.*

Other Choices

Chestnut Tree Inn. 9 Whitney Pl., Saratoga Springs, NY 12866, tel. 518/ 587–8681. 7 double rooms with baths, 3 doubles share 2 baths. Cable TV in parlor, off-street parking. $55–$200, Continental breakfast. MC, V. No smoking, no pets, 3-night minimum on special-event weekends. Closed Nov.–mid-Apr.

Gregory House. Rte. 43, Box 401, Averill Park, NY 12018, tel. 518/674– 3774. 12 double rooms with baths. Restaurant, air-conditioning, phones, cable TV in common room, pool. $80–$90, Continental breakfast. AE, DC, MC, V. No pets.

Inn at Saratoga. 231 Broadway, Saratoga Springs, NY 12866, tel. 518/ 583–1890, fax 518/583–2543. 34 double rooms with baths, 4 suites. Restaurant, banquet facilities, air-conditioning, cable TV, use of nearby YMCA pool and gym. $65–$345, Continental breakfast. AE, D, DC, MC, V. No pets, 2-night minimum in Aug., 3-night minimum on the Traver's Stakes weekend.

Mansion Hill Inn. 115 Philip St., Albany, NY 12202, tel. 518/465–2038. 8 double rooms with baths. Restaurant, air-conditioning, cable TV. $105–$155, full breakfast; dinner available. AE, D, DC, MC, V.

Mill House Inn. Rte. 43, Stephentown, NY 12168, tel. 518/733–5606. 7 double rooms with baths, 5 suites. Air-conditioning, pool. $80–$145; Continental breakfast, afternoon tea. AE, MC, V. No smoking, no pets, 2-night minimum July and Aug. weekends.

Saratoga Bed and Breakfast. Church St., Saratoga Springs, NY 12866, tel. 518/584–0920. 8 double rooms with baths. Air-conditioning, cable TV in common room. $65–$210, full breakfast. AE, D, MC, V. No smoking, no pets, 2-night minimum on Aug. weekends.

Six Sisters. 149 Union Ave., Saratoga Springs, NY 12866, tel. 518/583–1173, fax 518/587–2470. 3 double rooms with baths, 1 suite. Air-conditioning, refrigerators, whirlpool bath in one room. $60–$250, full breakfast. AE, MC, V. No smoking, no pets, 2-night minimum on weekends Apr.–Nov., 5-night minimum in Aug.

Westchester House. 102 Lincoln Ave. (Box 944), Saratoga Springs, NY 12866, tel. 518/587–7613 or 800/581–7613. 7 double rooms with baths. Air-conditioning. $75–$250, Continental breakfast. AE, MC, V. Restricted smoking, no pets, 4-night minimum in Aug., closed Jan.

Reservations Service

The American Country Collection (1353 Union St., Schenectady, NY 12308, tel. 518/370–4948).

The Catskills

Beaverkill Valley Inn

Lew Beach, NY 12753, tel. 914/439–4844

"I have laid aside business, and gone a-fishing," wrote Izaak Walton in *The Compleat Angler;* Walton would probably have loved the Beaverkill, America's most famous fly-fishing stream. Although the Beaverkill Valley Inn, built in 1893 as a boardinghouse at Lew Beach, never played host to Walton, Jimmy Carter, Robert Redford, Sigourney Weaver, Gary Trudeau, Jane Pauley, and assorted Kennedys have all been guests here. Owned and developed by Laurance Rockefeller and managed by able innkeeper Christina Jurgens, the inn caters to those who cherish privacy. Its surrounding forests and nearby fields, preserved as "forever wild," are protected from development.

This is not to say that accommodations are rustic—not by a long shot. A comfortable, old-money look enhances the place. White-painted rocking chairs line the wide porch, a welcoming fire warms the living room on frosty days, and the dining-room windows offer a panoramic view of the grounds. The card and billiard rooms, with their green-shade lamps, have a clubby, masculine atmosphere; they call to mind an era when men took leave of their female companions to enjoy their after-dinner brandy and cigars.

The fare that precedes that post-prandial brandy is sumptuous, with such offerings as poached Norwegian salmon with watercress sauce, and fillet of beef with blue-cheese sauce. All baked goods are made on the premises, and the inn uses homegrown herbs and salad greens.

Guest rooms are simply furnished with brass-and-iron beds, comfortable chairs, handmade quilts, and good reading lamps. Many of the rooms have twin beds.

Although fishing is the main draw here (the inn has a package arrangement with the Wulff Fly Fishing School nearby), it's certainly not the only attraction. A converted barn with a cathedral ceiling houses a heated swimming pool, a help-yourself ice-cream parlor, a theater, and a children's playroom. Sports enthusiasts also have access to tennis courts, hiking, and cross-country ski trails, and skating in winter.

🏠 *13 double rooms with baths, 8 doubles share 5 baths. Restaurant, bar, conference facilities, game rooms, stocked pond, Beaverkill fishing. $260–$330; breakfast, lunch, afternoon tea, dinner. AE, MC, V. No smoking indoors, no pets, 2-night minimum stay on weekends, 3-night minimum on holiday weekends.*

Captain Schoonmaker's Bed-and-Breakfast

913 State Route 213 (Box 37), High Falls, NY 12440, tel. 914/687-7946

You'll find it easy to lose yourself in the past at this meticulously restored 1760 Hudson Valley stone house. Americana is everywhere. The place at High Falls even claims its own Early American ghost, Captain Fred. The hosts, Sam and Julia Krieg, also very friendly, are quite knowledgeable about local history. Julia teaches third grade, and Sam is a retired biology professor who taught animal behavior and ornithology.

Captain Schoonmaker's is, actually, four different places: the stone house, with four bedrooms (one with a fireplace), a living room, dining room, library, solarium, and canopied decks; the 1840 Towpath House, a half mile from the main house; Krum House, an 1876 Victorian in town; and the 1820 Carriage House, in front of the main house.

In the days when mules towed barges through New York State's canals, the Towpath House was the home of the lock tender for the Delaware and Hudson Canal. Guest rooms here (one with a fireplace) have four-poster, cannonball, or Victorian beds; pine cupboards; blanket chests; and wing chairs.

The Krum House has two large rooms with private baths. The Carriage House rooms, the most sought-after and romantic, overlook a trout stream with a private waterfall. The two upstairs were once a hayloft, and the original beams have been left exposed. One downstairs room has a brass bed and a tree growing through the middle of a private deck. A Lone Star quilt covers the canopy bed in the other.

Probably only the Kriegs' famous breakfasts could tear guests away from their waterfall rooms—it's hard to ignore seven courses of such culinary delights as lemon poppy-seed cake, cheese soufflé, and blueberry strudel. Guests breakfast at an antique black-walnut table by the dining-room fireplace. Against the wall stands an antique printer's cabinet. The living room has another fireplace and an Early American cupboard used to display quilts and coverlets. Nearby is the De Puy Canal House, a highly touted restaurant with an international menu.

▥ *2 double rooms with baths, 12 doubles share 5½ baths. Cable TV in library-den, swimming and trout fishing in stream. $80–$90, full breakfast. No credit cards. No pets, 2-night minimum on weekends mid-Sept.–Thanksgiving. Closed Christmas week.*

Redcoat's Return

Platte Cove (Dale La.), Elka Park, NY 12427, tel. 518/589-9858 or 518/589-9895

Up a twisting mountain road in the Catskill Game Preserve, you'll encounter a little bit of the spirit of England at the Redcoat's Return. Once the center of a potato-and-dairy farm, the 1860 home at Elka Park was later a summer boardinghouse. Now this lodging is known in the area for its Saturday-night prime rib and Yorkshire pudding and for its English country hospitality.

Tom (the Redcoat) and Peg Wright have owned the inn since 1973; he was once a chef on the *Queen Mary* and she was an actress. The inn features extensive art and antiques collections that bring together mementos of trips abroad—and there's a moose head, named Basil, over the fireplace. Tom, who has a quirky sense of humor, says that he plays golf in his spare time and that "Peg is interested in metaphysics." Both are practiced conversationalists. Tom is full of stories about his objets d'art, which include a cricket bat and a framed antique scarf commemorating the first boxing match between an Englishman and an American, in 1860. Winston and Zoe, the

Wrights' Bernese mountain dogs, can also be charming hosts.

The Wrights have chosen to preserve the atmosphere of the old boarding-house, so rooms are small but pleasantly cozy. All the mattresses are new, but the antique iron beds and oak dressers are part of the original decor. Third-floor bedrooms have eaved ceilings, and one large room offers two double beds. The eight guest rooms that share four baths are all supplied with bathrobes for guests.

Hikers should enjoy the numerous trails that lead from the inn onto nearby Overlook, Indian Head, Twin, and Hunter mountains. There are cross-country trails and three alpine ski areas close by. Spring anglers have access to a trout stream on the property, and golfers will find several fine courses a short drive away.

Antiques shops and galleries are available for the less athletic, and for those who really want to sit and do nothing it's hard to beat the view from the inn's porch. It's also hard not to gain weight after sampling Tom's chocolate mousse, English-sherry trifle, and apple pie à la mode.

▦ *6 double rooms with baths, 8 doubles share 4 baths. Restaurant. $70–$95, full breakfast. AE, MC, V. No pets, 2-night minimum in Feb. and Oct. weekends, 3-night minimum on holiday weekends.*

Other Choices

Albergo Allegria. Rte. 296, Windham, NY 12496, tel. 518/734–5560. 12 double rooms with baths, 4 suites. TV in rooms, swimming hole. $45–$175, full breakfast. MC, V. Restricted smoking, no pets, 2-night minimum on weekends.

Deer Mountain Inn. Rte. 25 (Box 443), Tannersville, NY 12485, tel. 518/589–6268. 7 double rooms with baths or showers. Restaurant. $95–$135, full breakfast. AE, MC, V. Restricted smoking, no pets.

Eggery. County Rd. 16, Tannersville, NY 12485, tel. 518/589–5363. 13 double rooms with baths, 1 suite. Cable TVs, phones. $75–$120, full breakfast. AE, MC, V. No pets, 3-night minimum on holiday weekends, 2-night minimum on peak weekends.

Greenville Arms. R.D. 1 (Box 2), Greenville, NY 12083, tel. 518/966–5219. 12 double rooms with baths, 1 suite. Restaurant, 1 room with air-conditioning, pool. $80–$145, full breakfast. D, MC, V. No smoking, no pets, 2-night minimum on holiday weekends.

Inn at Lake Joseph. 400 St. Joseph's Rd., Forestburg, NY 12777, tel. 914/791–9506. 10 double rooms with baths. Restaurant, pool, lake. $158–$258; breakfast, afternoon tea, dinner. AE, MC, V. No smoking in dining room, no pets, 2-night minimum on weekends.

Mountainview Inn of Chandelee. 913 Shandelee Rd., Livingston Manor, NY 12758, tel. 914/439–5070. 8 double rooms with baths. Restaurant, tap-room. $72–$76, full breakfast. AE, D, DC, MC, V. No pets, 2-night minimum on holiday weekends.

Point Lookout Mountain Inn. The Mohican Trail, Rte. 23, East Windham, NY 12439, tel. 518/734–3381. 13 double rooms with baths. Restaurant, TVs, recreation room with hot tub. $60–$115, Continental breakfast. AE, DC, MC, V. 2-night minimum on winter weekends.

Scribner Hollow Lodge. Rte. 23-A, Hunter, NY 12442, tel. 518/263–4211 or 800/395–4683, fax 518/263–5266. 28 double rooms with baths, 10 suites, 26 condos. Restaurant, fireplaces in 22 rooms, air-conditioning, conference facilities, indoor and outdoor pools, tennis. $144–$450; full breakfast, dinner. Condos (without meals) $200–$350. AE, D, MC, V. No pets, 2-night minimum on weekends during winter and summer high season, 3-night minimum on holiday weekends.

Hudson River Valley

Anthony Dobbins Stagecoach Inn

268 Main St., Maplewood Terr., Goshen, NY 10924, tel. 914/294-5526

Since 1740, only three families have owned the Anthony Dobbins Stagecoach Inn. The present proprietor, Margo Hickok, takes pleasure in imagining what the original inn—complete with common room and bundling boards—must have been like. In its present incarnation as a bed-and-breakfast, the inn is no doubt a great deal more comfortable than its 18th-century predecessor. It even has an elevator.

The house is charmingly furnished with English antiques, some of which are family heirlooms. "Nothing matches, but everything fits," says Margo, a former fashion model who once ran a spa for the Gabor sisters and now guides aspiring young models.

Even the furnishings are steeped in history. Margo's family is descended from both Wild Bill Hickok and William Penn, and the room named for Mr. Penn boasts a bed that belonged to the founder of the Crown Colony of Pennsylvania. (The shaded area on the headboard may very well be where he rested his head.) The Hickok Room has an antique brass bed and a fainting couch; the adjoining Green Room has a fireplace. The William Penn room, with flowered wallpaper and Williamsburg-blue trim, has an antique four-poster bed, fireplace, sundeck, and private bath, and can be transformed into a double suite with the Roosevelt room next door.

Among the many artful touches are all-cotton sheets, and homegrown flowers are placed in each room throughout spring and summer. You can breakfast on the terrace by the reflecting pool, in the sunroom by the fountain, with a pink flamingo, or at the Heplewhite table with Windsor chairs in the formal dining room. A collection of Currier and Ives prints and paintings of horses adorns the inn's spacious entry hall, but for the real thing, visitors need only walk half a block to the racetrack. Goshen is known as the Cradle of the Trotters, and the harness track here is the nation's oldest. Tennis courts are also a short walk away, and hot-air-balloon rides can be arranged at a nearby airport.

🏠 *2 double rooms with baths, 1 double suite. Air-conditioning in 2 rooms, TV in common rooms, fruit and candy in each room. $85–$150; Continental breakfast, afternoon tea. AE, MC, V. Restricted smoking, no pets, 2-night minimum on weekends.*

Inn at Shaker Mill

Cherry La., off Rte. 22, Canaan, NY 12029, tel. 518/794-9345 or 800/365-9345, fax 518/794-9344

The Inn at Shaker Mill, 10 miles from Tanglewood and from skiing at Jiminey Peak, is an unusual establishment for two reasons: its Shaker decor and its gregarious host, Ingram Paperny.

As befits a converted 1823 Shaker mill, the rooms are simply furnished in a comfortable but utilitarian style. Pegboards hang from the plaster walls, and in the Shaker tradition the common room has a barrel roof—though it also boasts a glass wall that looks out on the mill's picturesque brook and waterfalls.

After more than 25 years in the business, Mr. Paperny has been called the doyen of New England innkeepers. A stay at the inn is like spending time in the home of a fascinating new friend. As might be expected of a former consultant to the United Nations, Ingram is an internationalist; he speaks four languages and relishes playing host to an eclectic bunch of visitors. During summer he brings European hiking and cultural groups to the United States, acts as their tour leader and host, and encourages them to mix with the American guests at the inn. He is also a woodworker and is responsible for all the carpentry done in the building.

The inn is unique in another way: It charges per person, so singles who want to get away from the city can retreat to a place that doesn't put the emphasis on couples (which isn't to say that a room overlooking the waterfalls wouldn't serve as a romantic retreat for two). Also, several of the rooms are large enough to accommodate families: The stone-wall, wood-beam suites on the third floor can sleep six.

The inn's hospitality extends to meals as well. Breakfasts include juice, fresh fruit, cereals, yogurt, cheese, bagels, muffins, breads, and eggs. Dinners vary with the whim of the chef. On Saturday nights in summer there are outdoor barbecues.

🏠 *20 double rooms with baths. Restaurant, swimming pond, sauna. $80– $150, full breakfast and dinner. MC, V. No smoking in dining room.*

Le Chambord

2075 Rte. 52, Hopewell Junction, NY 12533, tel. and fax 914/221–1941 or 800/274–1941

Although it is housed in an 1863 Georgian mansion one minute from the Taconic Parkway, Le Chambord could easily be the focal point of an antebellum southern plantation. In fact Scarlett O'Hara would feel right at home on its pillared veranda. The mansion's involvement with things southern is more than skin-deep, however: The trapdoor under the inn's bar leads to a former stop on the Underground Railroad.

Miss O'Hara was not far from the mind of innkeeper Roy Benich when he named the latest additions to Le Chambord: Tara Hall, containing 16 rooms;

and Butler Hall, which has corporate and banquet facilities. Both structures are in keeping with the genteel traditions of the opulent dining and banquet rooms and the nine handsome bedrooms in the main building.

Roy, a former art-and-antiques dealer, has designed Le Chambord for aesthetic appeal and treats it as his home. "It's my wife and children," he says. He lives on the premises and laments that he works up to 19 hours a day on the inn and the restaurant. (You'll know that he's a bachelor as soon as you see him in one of the outrageous neckties for which he is renowned.) He chooses all the art and antiques for the inn, and his taste is impeccable (and nothing like his taste in neckties). Not many dining rooms can boast a $20,000 antique Chinese breakfront, and not many bedrooms and sitting rooms have sofas and wing chairs covered in imported floral tapestries. For the cost of each of these chairs, "you can furnish two Holiday Inn rooms and have $200 left over," Roy laughs. No expense has been spared in selecting food and wine, also.

The owner's focus on visual delights is shared by his chef, Leonard Mott, a Culinary Institute of America graduate. For more than 10 years the two have collaborated on an elegant menu that satisfies both the palate and the eye.

Despite such luxuries, the inn is quite affordable. True, the wine list offers a 1929 Château Lafite Rothschild for $1,500—but there are also good wines in the $15 range.

🏠 *25 double rooms with baths. Restaurant, air-conditioning, cable TVs, meeting facilities, fitness room. $115, Continental breakfast. AE, DC, MC, V. No pets. Closed Dec. 25.*

Simmons Way Village Inn

33 Main St., Millerton, NY 12546, tel. 518/789–6235

Simmons Way Village Inn, set on a wide expanse of lawn in the middle of Millerton, was built by the village's first merchant in 1854 and was transformed into a handsome country inn in 1983.

Current owners Richard and Nancy Carter (he is a management consultant and educator, she is a bank vice-president) bought Simmons Way in 1987 with the idea of running an inn that combined "European civility and American comfort" and served the best in international cuisine.

There are two common rooms on the first floor, one of which opens onto the inviting front porch, where guests may eat breakfast in the warmer months. The second room is home to Max the parrot, who may say hello if he's feeling sociable. The main dining room was added in 1986 but is hard to distinguish from the original structure.

The bedrooms (six on the second floor and three on the third) are furnished with English and European country antiques. Each has its own charm; but Room 5, with its rose-floral wallpaper, queen-size antique iron bed, embroidered bedspread, wicker love seat, and 6-foot French bathtub with handheld shower, is perhaps the most romantic. Room 2, the Bridal Suite, offers a private covered porch, marble fireplace, and queen-size crown-canopy bed; and Room 4 has peach walls, an English brass canopy bed, swag curtains, and a stripped-pine armoire.

If one can bear to leave these lovely rooms (where breakfast may be taken, if desired) and venture beyond the inviting front porch, the surrounding area is well worth exploring. A swimming pool is 3 miles away, golf courses are close by, and the inn offers special weekday packages that include tickets to the nearby Lime Rock (auto) Race Track—where you might just catch a glimpse of Paul Newman, who frequently races there.

"We strive for a full country-inn ambience," says Richard, "—rooms, spirit, and cuisine." Regional game and specialties can be found at the highly rated restaurant, where the extensive wine list goes all the way up to a $350 Lafite Rothschild.

🏠 *9 double rooms with baths, 1 suite. Restaurant, air-conditioning, banquet facilities, cable TV and phone in common room, complimentary sherry. $145–$175; full breakfast, afternoon tea or wine. AE, DC, MC, V. Restricted smoking, no pets, 2-night minimum on weekends May 1–Nov. 1, 3-night minimum on holiday weekends.*

Troutbeck

Leedsville Rd., Amenia, NY 12501, tel. 914/373-9681, fax 914/373-7080

This Tudor-style manor house set amid 442 gracious acres outside the hamlet of Amenia figured prominently in American literary and political history. It was once home to Myron B. Benton, whose circle of friends included Emerson, Thoreau, and John Burroughs. The estate served as a gathering place for the likes of Sinclair Lewis, Teddy Roosevelt, and Lewis Mumford in the early 20th century, and black leaders formed the NAACP under its roof.

Today Troutbeck also serves the movers and shakers of the corporate world as a conference center during the week. On weekends, however, it is transformed into one of the area's most romantic country inns, the vision of genial innkeeper Jim Flaherty and his partner, Bob Skibsted.

Guests lack nothing here. The Troutbeck package includes three gourmet meals a day, an open bar, and access to all sorts of recreational activities, ranging from tennis, swimming (indoor and outdoor), fishing, and cross-country skiing to strolling through walled gardens and watching video movies or major sports events on cable TV.

Most guest rooms are suitably romantic, although the rooms in the main house seem more so. For the premium prices charged by Troutbeck, guests might prefer a canopied, fireplaced, sunporched room in the manor house (with its leaded-glass windows, 12,000-book oak-panel library, and comfortable English country appointments) or the Garden House (overlooking the walled gardens) to the Americana offered in the neighboring Century Farmhouse rooms. Of course, guests in any of the buildings have access to all the inn's amenities.

If you can tear yourself away from the estate, the surrounding area is prime antiquing territory, and guests can take elegant prepared picnics with them on excursions. The inn will also arrange transportation to concerts at Tanglewood, dance performances at Jacob's Pillow, and Shakespeare at the Mount.

🛏 *37 double rooms with baths, 4 double rooms share baths. Restaurant, air-conditioning, banquet facilities, fireplaces in 9 rooms. $375–$475; breakfast, lunch, dinner, wines, and spirits. AE, MC, V. No smoking in dining rooms, no pets. Closed weekdays for conferences.*

Other Choices

Bird and Bottle Inn. Old Albany Post Rd., Rte. 9 (R.R. 2, Box 129), Garrison, NY 10524, tel. 914/424–3000, fax 914/424–3283. 2 double rooms with baths, 1 suite, 1 cottage. Restaurant, air-conditioning. $210–$240, breakfast and dinner. AE, DC, MC, V. No pets, 2-night minimum on weekends with Sat. reservation.

Hudson House, A Country Inn. 2 Main St., Cold Spring, NY 10516, tel. 914/265–9355. 12 double rooms with baths, 1 suite. Restaurant, air-conditioning. $105–$180, full breakfast. AE, MC, V. No smoking, no pets.

Martindale Bed and Breakfast Inn. Rte. 23, (Box 385), Claverack, NY 12513, tel. 518/851–5405. 2 double rooms with baths, 2 doubles share bath. TV/VCR in

parlor, dinner available with 24 hours' notice. $65–$75, full breakfast. No credit cards. Restricted smoking, 2-day minimum on weekends June–Labor Day and Oct.

Pig Hill Inn. 73 Main St., Cold Spring, NY 10516, tel. 914/265–9247. 4 double rooms with baths, 4 doubles share 2 baths. Air-conditioning, fireplaces in some rooms. $100–$150, full breakfast. AE, MC, V. No smoking, no pets.

Plumbush Inn. Rte. 9D, Cold Spring, NY 10516, tel. 914/265–3904. 2 double rooms with baths, 1 suite. Restaurant, air-conditioning, cable TV in sitting room. $95–$125, Continental breakfast. AE, MC, V. Closed Mon. and Tues.

Swiss Hutte. Rte. 23, Hillsdale, NY 12529, tel. 518/325–3333. 12 double rooms with baths, 1 double suite. Restaurant, air-conditioning, phones, cable TVs, pool, tennis. $160–$180, MAP. MC, V. 2- or 3-night minimum on holiday weekends, depending on season. Closed mid-Mar.–mid-Apr.

Reservations Service

American Country Collection (1353 Union St., Schenectady, NY 12308, tel. 518/370–4948).

Eastern Long Island

Huntting Inn

94 Main St., East Hampton, NY 11937, tel. 516/324–0410, fax 516/324–8751

Huge elms and maples surround the Huntting Inn, a pre-Revolutionary landmark set on 2½ acres in the midst of East Hampton Village. The 1699 house, originally a saltbox, was built by the Church of England for the Reverend Nathaniel Huntting. In 1751 Huntting's widow, probably short of cash, turned her home into a public house, and it's been an inn ever since. During the American Revolution it became the only neutral meeting ground in the area.

Innkeeper Linda Calder (who also manages Hedges' Inn, owned by the same corporation) has been here since 1980. Her degree from the Fashion Institute of Technology in New York City comes in handy in matters of inn decor. Her warmth, boundless energy, and good humor are evident as she tends to the needs of guests in the two inns.

The inn's dining room will look familiar to Manhattan's restaurant cognoscenti—it's run by the Palm Restaurant and has similar decor, including a pressed-tin ceiling, oak wainscoting, wide-board floors, bentwood chairs, a brass-rail bar, and drawings of celebrities lining the walls. As at the Palm, steaks and lobsters come in colossal proportions.

Guest rooms have cotton-chintz floral-print wall coverings. A number of antique beds are brass, iron, or a combination of both. One of the most charming rooms here is also the smallest, with a single brass-and-iron bed, a hand-crocheted bedcover, and lace curtains. The suite, done in a white-and-green scheme, has antique oak furnishings and lace curtains on the windows. It also offers a king-size bed and a queen-size pull-out couch to accommodate families.

Across the street you'll find public tennis courts, and there's a golf course nearby. The inn provides guests with town stickers for parking in beach areas. The main village beach features a pavilion with lifeguards and refreshments. Other beaches in the area are more secluded but have few or no amenities. The inn lies within walking distance of all of East Hampton's shops, theaters, and museums.

▦ *17 double rooms with baths, 2 single rooms with baths, 1 suite. Restaurant, air-conditioning. $150–$350, cold buffet breakfast. AE, DC, MC, V. No pets, 2-night minimum on weekends May–June and Sept.–Oct., 3-night minimum on weekends July–Aug., 5-night minimum July 4 and Labor Day weekends.*

Ram's Head Inn

108 Ram Island Dr., Shelter Island, NY 11964, tel. 516/749–0811

Ospreys nest atop the telephone poles by this inn on Shelter Island. A yellow and white awning shelters the patio, and a beached rowboat sits in a children's play area on the wide front lawn. The voice of Billie Holiday is often heard in the dining room. The 1929 center-hall Colonial-style building is all weathered shakes, white trim, and green shutters. Guests can walk to a gazebo by the tennis courts, and a grassy path leads down to 800 feet of beachfront on Coecles Harbor. Summer guests are cooled by bay breezes.

In June 1947, the nuclear physicists Enrico Fermi, J. Robert Oppenheimer, and Edward Teller attended a conference here on the foundations of quantum mechanics. The event is remembered with a framed document hanging in the entrance hall. Today guests will find the Ram's Head a serene setting for a meeting, an executive getaway, a family retreat, or a romantic weekend à deux.

Owners James and Linda Ecklund and innkeeper Brian Moorehead collaborate in running the place, and each fills in wherever necessary to make sure guests are taken care of. In 1980 the Ecklunds bought the inn in a rather "decayed state," as they put it, and have spent the intervening years restoring it.

The common rooms are often flooded with natural light. The lounge, decorated in a nautical theme, features ships' lanterns and a model sloop on the mantel. Green wicker couches have flowered cushions, and the library is the perfect spot for a rainy-day read. Here framed sheet music lines the walls, and a piano occupies an honored place. Every Sunday from 7 to 11 PM, a local jazz group livens up the atmosphere. The dining-room menu stresses fresh seafood creatively prepared and presented. Specialties include shellfish bisque garnished with caviar and lobster, and braised red snapper accompanied by oyster mushrooms and artichokes.

Guest rooms are simple, bright, and airy; some have porches. Those with a water view are often requested, but in summer the harbor can be glimpsed only through the leaves of majestic oak trees.

🏨 *5 double rooms with baths, 4 doubles share 2 baths, 4 suites. Restaurant, free use of boats and tennis court. $110–$230, Continental buffet breakfast. AE, V. Restricted smoking, no pets, 3-night minimum on holiday weekends, 2-night minimum other weekends.*

1770 House

143 Main St., East Hampton, NY 11937, tel. 516/324–1770

At various times in its history the 1770 House, actually a 1740 Colonial built for one of East Hampton's earliest families, has been a general store; a dining hall for students at the Clinton Academy next door; and, finally, an inn that had its heyday in the 1940s and '50s. When Miriam and her late husband, Sidney, Perle bought it, in 1977, it had been in a state of decline for several years. The Perles—joined by their daughter Wendy and son Adam—were undaunted by the formidable restoration needed to return the building to its former glory.

Guest rooms have been furnished with fine antiques of various periods and origins. One room has a fireplace and an English-style carved canopy bed. Another has an Early American highboy. The inn's elegant library features English-pine paneling and a fireplace. The dining room holds the owners' extensive collection of clocks and apothecary jars. "The kitchen," jokes Miriam, "is painted smoked salmon."

Behind the main house sits a converted carriage house fit for four. All rooms are furnished with antiques, including the master bedroom with queen-size, canopy bed and the combination living room and library. An elegant hand-carved staircase leads to an auxilliary loft bedroom with double bed.

🏨 *7 double rooms with bath, 1 suite. Restaurant, air-conditioning. $120–$250, full breakfast. AE, MC, V. No smoking, no pets, 3-night minimum on summer weekends, 2-night minimum other weekends.*

Village Latch Inn

101 Hill St. (Box 3000), Southampton, NY 11968, tel. 516/283–2160 or 800/545–2224

The theatrical air to the 5-acre compound that makes up the Village Latch Inn is no accident. Owner Marta White spent her life in the theater, and she revels in setting a stage. Her husband and fellow innkeeper, Martin, is a photographer who used to work in commercial films. The main house is "old Southampton, turn-of-the-century, Gatsby-style," says Marta. The circa-1900 building, once the annex to Southampton's most opulent hotel, may have been a Sanford White design. Near the main house are what Marta refers to as the "outbuildings," which were part of the old Merrill Lynch estate. These include the Terry Cottage, which features a comfortable living room, with flowered wallpaper, and Victorian dining room; the Potting Shed, where the first American locomotive was built and which is now used for corporate meetings; six modern duplexes with private decks; and two other large houses connected by a Victorian greenhouse. One of these houses has a distinguished collection of Mexican folk art.

The living room in the main house could be the set of a movie—perhaps *Auntie Mame.* Plush leopard-print cushions and gold- and silver-threaded pillows are tossed artfully on the couches. Balinese marionettes hang from the walls. It's all eccentric, eclectic, and artsy—and it works.

No guest room resembles another, and Marta is always changing things. "If I'm not creating space, then it's boring," she comments. The rooms are decorated with a collection of antiques from different periods. Despite its lavishness, the inn is cozy—the sort of place where guests can help themselves to coffee or a cold drink any time of the day, even if the sign says KITCHEN CLOSED.

A number of the buildings can be rented to groups, and the facilities have been used for everything from fashion shoots to family reunions. The greenhouse is the perfect setting for an intimate wedding. The inn is a five-minute walk from town and a mile from the beach.

▦ *50 double rooms with baths, 11 suites, 6 duplexes. Lunch catering on request, air-conditioning, cable TV and phones in rooms on request, pool, tennis courts. $99–$350, Continental breakfast. AE, D, DC, MC, V. 3-night minimum July and Aug. weekends, 2-night minimum other weekends.*

Other Choices

Basset House Inn. 128 Montauk Hwy., East Hampton, NY 11937, tel. 516/324–6127. 7 double rooms with baths, 1 double and 2 singles share 2 baths, 2 suites. Air-conditioning, cable TV in some rooms. $75–$195, full breakfast. AE, MC, V. 2-night minimum on summer weekends, 4-night minimum some holidays.

Hedges' Inn. 74 James La., East Hampton, NY 11937, tel. 516/324–7100.

11 double rooms with baths. Restaurant, air-conditioning. $165–$250, cold buffet breakfast. AE, DC, MC, V. No pets, 3-night minimum on July and Aug. weekends, 5-night minimum July 4 and Labor Day weekends.

Hill Guest House. 535 Hill St., Southampton, NY 11968, tel. 516/283–9889 or 718/461–0014 (Nov.–Apr.). 1 double room with bath, 2 doubles share bath, 3 doubles share 2 hall baths. $65–$80, breakfast extra. No credit cards. No pets, 2-night minimum on weekends June and Sept., 3-night minimum on weekends July–Aug. Closed Nov.–Apr.

Maidstone Arms. 207 Main St., East Hampton, NY 11937, tel. 516/324–5006, fax 516/324–5037. 12 double rooms with baths, 4 suites, 3 cottages. Restaurant, air-conditioning, cable TV in rooms, car service from jitney, train, and East Hampton airport. $165–$325, Continental breakfast. AE, MC, V. No pets, 4-night minimum on holiday weekends, 3-night minimum during peak weekends.

Mill House Inn. 33 N. Main St., East Hampton, NY 11937, tel. 516/324–9766. 8 double rooms with baths. Beach passes. $125–$195; full breakfast, afternoon beverages. AE, MC, V. No smoking, no pets, 3-night minimum on holiday weekends.

Old Post House Inn. 136 Main St., Southampton Village, NY 11968, tel. 516/283–1717. 7 double rooms with baths. Air-conditioning. $80–$175, Continental breakfast. AE, MC, V. No pets, 2-night minimum on weekends June–Sept., 3-night minimum on holiday weekends.

North Carolina

Granville Queen Inn

Carolina Coast

Catherine's Inn

410 S. Front St., Wilmington, NC 28401, tel. 910/251-0863 or 800/476-0723

As a young girl, Catherine Ackiss traveled with her family to Virginia's Skyline Drive, where they stayed in primitive tourist homes. She thought then that the accommodations—and the atmosphere—could stand a little southern hospitality. At Catherine's Inn, she has created that atmosphere in a sterling setting, an 1883 Italianate mansion in Wilmington's historic district. Ackiss operated Catherine's Inn on Orange from 1988 to 1994 before buying the Forshee-Sprunt House overlooking the Cape Fear River. The home is painted a crisp white and has a brick and wrought-iron fence. Though Catherine lost some trees in 1996's devastating Hurricane Fran, she otherwise survived unscathed.

Guests can pass the time in one of the twin parlors at the front of the house. Catherine's mother's grand piano made the move, along with many other family items that give the inn warmth and charm. If the weather is good, most guests congregate in rockers on the wraparound porch. Another big attraction is a lush sunken garden. Once planted with strawberries and scuppernong grapevines, it's now a beautifully landscaped retreat where guests can watch the big ships come into port and enjoy the smell of magnolia blossoms spilling over the stone wall.

Guests of Catherine's former inn will feel right at home, since she has duplicated much of the decor. The twin room is once again painted a striking dark purple, while other rooms feature four-poster and canopy beds. Crocheted bed covers and hand-tied canopies add romance to the guest rooms. Fresh flowers and glasses of sherry in the evenings give the inn a personal touch.

Walter Ackiss, a retired chemist, is in charge of storytelling and helps out with breakfast; pancakes with orange or blueberry syrup are served alongside homemade sausage on family silver and china. Conveniences include a stocked refrigerator and library.

🛏 *5 double rooms with baths. Air-conditioning, ceiling fans, phones; cable TV in parlors, turndown service. $75–$98; full breakfast, evening refreshments. MC, V. Restricted smoking, no pets.*

First Colony Inn

6720 S. Virginia Dare Trail, Milepost 16, Nags Head, NC 27959, tel. 919/441-2343 or 800/368-9390, fax 919/441-9234

The last of Nags Head's old shingle-style inns was scheduled for demolition when two generations of a Lexington family pooled their resources, mortgaged their homes, and bought the First Colony Inn in 1988. Richard and Camille Lawrence had two things going for them: a piece of land where the inn could be relocated and children with expertise, including a preservation architect, an engineer, an accountant, and a designer. The whole town lined the streets the night the inn (sawed into three pieces) was moved away from the ocean's grasping fingers and down the road to its new home.

Today the inn is listed on the National Register of Historic Places and is far more luxurious than it was in 1932, when it was first constructed. In all, nine of the Lawrences own and operate the inn, and they all helped to restore it with their own hands. The exterior has been returned to its original beauty, complete with two-story, continuous wraparound porches and a brown-shingled roof. The whole interior was reconfigured; now the 26 rooms have private baths and lots of extras, such as heated towel bars, English toiletries, an iron and ironing board, and refrigerators. Luxury rooms also have wet bars or kitchenettes, as well as whirlpool baths and private screened porches. White walls give the inn a fresh feeling, and each room is furnished differently. Some have cherry beds and dressers, others feature white wicker with floral-print cushions, and still others have canopy beds with crocheted lace.

An enhanced Continental breakfast including a hot entrée, croissants, pastries, and fruit is served in the first-floor dining room, which contains antique buffets, enormous old mirrors, and vintage photos of Nags Head. The second-floor library is a cozy enclave where guests can read or play games. One of the most delightful bits of reading is a framed letter about a classic Nags Head vacation on letterhead stationery, circa 1934, when it was called LeRoy's Seaside Inn. There's a 50-foot pool with a roomy wooden deck in back, and the ocean is a short walk across the street.

The inn is also convenient to *The Lost Colony* outdoor drama in Manteo, hang gliding at Jockey's Ridge, first-flight history at the Wright Brothers National Memorial, and the many attractions of the Cape Hatteras National Seashore.

🛏 *26 double rooms with baths. Air-conditioning, cable TVs, phones. $145-$250; Continental breakfast, afternoon tea. AE, D, MC, V. No smoking, no pets, 2-night minimum summer weekends, 3-night minimum holidays.*

Granville Queen Inn

108 S. Granville St., Edenton, NC 27932, tel. 919/482-5296

Guests get to live out their fantasies at this bed-and-breakfast inn in the heart of Edenton. The ornate sign with its elaborate crown is the first clue to what's inside, and the peach paint on the neoclassic 1907 house hints at the romance to be found within. For Marge and Ken Dunne, it was love at first sight. After staying at the inn themselves, they sold their chain of gourmet cheese shops on Long Island, New York, and bought the inn in 1991. They've retained the unique character that has charmed guests since the inn was first created in 1989.

The first thing you encounter after entering the front door is a sculpture of a pair of cranes, their feet planted in a square white marble fountain and their heads pointed upward to a dark ceiling made of plaster squares hand-molded with Cupid faces and then gilded. There's a formal dining room with a crystal chandelier; a side porch sporting white wicker, glass-top tables, and ceiling fans has been enclosed as another dining area.

Each of the guest rooms provides an ambience you might find by taking a trip to a foreign country or stepping into the pages of a storybook. In the Egyptian Room, the most exotic and most requested, guests go to sleep under a leopard coverlet, watched over by two huge black sphinxes flanking a pair of thronelike chairs draped with the same sheer gold-shot fabric that's at the windows. In the Queen of Italy bathroom, the water spouts from a cherub's mouth. All the oversize tubs have waterfalls. The Queen Victorianna Room is bright and airy and has window seats, a canopy bed, and a claw-foot tub. The Captain's Quarters is furnished in dark mahogany, with a decorated, lacquered dinghy suspended over the bed. The Queen of Queens Room has a massive bed with a bronze plaque of the Blessed Mother set into the headboard. Some rooms have gas-log fireplaces and private patios.

Dining at the Granville Queen is just as lavish. The five-course gourmet breakfast includes grilled chicken breast or filet mignon with eggs and potatoes. Wine and cheese are served on weekend afternoons.

▦ *9 double rooms with baths. Air-conditioning, cable TV/VCRs, phones. $95–$105, full breakfast. No credit cards. No smoking, no pets.*

Harmony House Inn

215 Pollock St., New Bern, NC 28560, tel. 919/636–3810 or 800/636–3113, fax 919/636–3810

The low and melodious chime of an ornate Italian clock marks the hours at this Greek Revival house in New Bern's historic district. The house was built in the early 1850s and enlarged three times. It was even sawed in half as part of one enlargement around the turn of the century and converted to apartments in the '70s. It was made whole again in 1985, converted to a bed-and-breakfast inn that's elegant and homey at the same time.

The double front doors and hallways are the only hint of its strange architectural past. Its history can be seen in framed photos from *Harper's Weekly* depicting the Battle of New Bern. The town fell to Union forces and served as their base of operations in eastern North Carolina for the duration of the war. The Harmony House was occupied by Company K of the 45th Massachusetts Regiment, who posed for a picture in front of the house in 1863.

Ed and Sooki Kirkpatrick, who bought the inn in 1994, added a new suite and extra amenities but retained the homey touches. Harmony House is furnished with family photos, handcrafted local furniture, and antiques, including an 1875 pump organ. The soft pastel colors of the walls set off the canopy beds and colorful comforters. Sooki's needlepoint flowers and "HH"-crocheted coasters give the house a personal touch.

Breakfast is a time for socializing in the formal dining room, where the Kirkpatricks lay out a different hot dish on the Empire sideboard each day: pancakes stuffed with cottage cheese, quiche, Scotch eggs, ham Strata, or bacon and eggs, plus fruit, homemade granola, and coffee cake. There's also fresh-ground coffee and an assortment of teas.

The Kirkpatricks have brochures on local attractions and restaurants; many are within walking distance. Ed has also mapped out suggested bike routes for visitors. The inn has long been a favorite overnight stop for bike tours from all over the country.

▦ *9 double rooms with baths, 1 suite. Air-conditioning, ceiling fan, cable TV. and phone in rooms. $85–$130; full breakfast, complimentary beverages. AE, D, MC, V. No smoking, no pets.*

Island Inn

Lighthouse Rd. (Box 9), Ocracoke, NC 27960, tel. 919/928-4351, fax 919/928-4352

This historic inn, the oldest one on the Outer Banks, has stood for nearly a century. It got its name because it sat on Ocracoke's highest point, with a creek on either side. Built in 1901 of old ship timbers, it served as an Odd Fellows Lodge, public school, and officers' club before becoming an inn in 1945. It may not be as polished as a modern hotel, but the inn also has the character and atmosphere you won't find in a contemporary lodging. It even has a ghost, Mrs. Godfrey, the wife of a former innkeeper; she opens the kitchen door from time to time and leaves things out of place. People have such a good time here, they don't miss luxury; they do find good food and very caring, hospitable hosts. Bob and Cee Touhey, formerly of Winston-Salem, gave up careers in marketing and teaching and are renovating the inn in stages. With basic improvements behind them, they've now added cosmetic touches such as blue-and-white striped awnings, new interior doors, and new carpeting throughout.

The best rooms, with panoramic water views, are in the Crow's Nest, up some steep stairs. These rooms feature light-gray natural-wood walls and ceilings, new bathrooms, and contemporary furnishings with a beach motif. The ocean breeze pours in from sliding glass doors on two sides. In the main inn, rooms have antique furnishings and vintage photographs and feel like Grandma's house. Families prefer the modern annex, where extra-large rooms open on the heated pool.

The dining room, the oldest Outer Banks restaurant, has also gotten a face-lift with fresh white walls, new windows, and new wood ceilings with track lighting. The prints on the walls—including one of the inn itself—were done by an Alabama artist who stays at the inn every summer. A no-smoking area is on the enclosed sunporch. Many cooks are children of people who cooked here decades ago; they use the same recipes for such trademark dishes as oyster omelets, crab cakes, clam chowder, and scrambled eggs with herring roe. A new chef has added dinner delights such as grilled shrimp with Aunt Annie's green chili cheese grits.

The village of Ocracoke is on the island of the same name, accessible only by ferry. The laid-back, casual atmosphere seems a little like that of Cape Cod. The pirate Blackbeard was killed close to where the Ocracoke Lighthouse is. At the British Cemetery, the Union Jack flies over the graves of British sailors killed offshore, and everyone loves Ocracoke's wild ponies.

📏 *35 double rooms with baths. Air-conditioning, cable TV; phones in annex rooms. $45-$110, breakfast extra. D, MC, V. No smoking in the inn, no pets, 3-night minimum holidays.*

Langdon House

135 Craven St., Beaufort, NC 28516, tel. 919/728-5499

Langdon House, a block from the Beaufort waterfront and across the street from the Old Burying Ground, is just about as old as that historic cemetery. It's built of hand-hewn heart-pine timbers and put together with hand-forged nails, and owner Jimm Prest is fairly sure the ballast-stone foundation was laid in 1733. (The cemetery was deeded to the town in 1731.)

A Colonial–Federal-style house with a Bahamian roof line, Langdon House is painted white with dark green shutters and has upstairs and downstairs porches across the front. The floor plan is very simple—a central hall and stairway running down the middle, a parlor on the left side, a bedroom to the right (the largest and sunniest), and three to the rear. All the rooms have queen-size beds (with no headboards but with lots of comfy pillows) and are named for different guests. The dining room, upstairs over the parlor, resembles an 18th-century tavern; an Edwardian oak table takes up most of the room. The kitchen is also upstairs—an arrangement already in place when Prest renovated the house in 1985. Furnishings are an assortment of antiques, some on loan from local residents. The parlor contains an Estes pump organ, an 1840s Empire secretary, and other treasures—all furniture that is friendly and familiar, not museum pieces you wouldn't dare touch.

What really sets Langdon House apart is Prest himself. Having spent 365 days a year on the road for Coca-Cola before he became an innkeeper, he knows what it is to be a traveler, and he's accommodating to a remarkable degree. He'll arrange excursions, make sure guests are fishing with the right lure, and furnish beach baskets with towels and suntan lotion; complimentary beverages are always available. To top it off, he's just plain friendly, the kind of innkeeper who likes to share a glass of wine and good conversation with guests on the rocking-chair-dotted verandas.

Prest encourages his guests to sleep late and will cook a full breakfast for them anytime after 7:30 AM. He describes the food as wholesome but not without sin, such as too-pretty-to-eat orange-pecan waffles or omelets. And he describes his business—aptly—not just as the renting of rooms but rather as the fine art of innkeeping.

▦ *4 double rooms with baths. Air-conditioning; bicycles, fishing rods, ice chests. $88–$120, full breakfast. No credit cards. No smoking, no pets, 2-night minimum summer weekends and holidays.*

Pecan Tree Inn

116 Queen St., Beaufort, NC 28516, tel. 919/728-6733

On Joe and Susan Johnson's first visit to Beaufort, they sat in a waterfront restaurant and watched wild ponies graze on nearby Carrot Island. When dolphins swam up the river to complete the scene, the Johnsons took it as a sign they were now where they belonged. Joe, who ran a chain of hardware stores, and Susan, who sold auto insurance, left New Jersey and bought a Victorian home less than a block from the waterfront. The home was actually built in 1856, and Victorian embellishments, including porches, turrets, and gingerbread trim, were added in the 1890s. Now restored to its original splendor, it's a charmer that lures 20–30 people a week just for a tour.

Rooms are bright and airy, with light floral wallpapers and bedcovers. The furnishings are a mix of antiques and reproductions from different periods. The Blue Room, for example, features a white wrought-iron bed with a wicker wardrobe and dresser. The Country Room has a pine pencil-post canopy bed and an antique trunk. The Green Room was renamed the Wow Room for the response it inevitably provokes. Here, deep-green carpeting and fabrics provide a dramatic contrast to the white walls. The Bridal Suite is pure romance. The four-poster canopy bed is accented with a brocade coverlet, and the rose-and-white tile bath includes a two-person Jacuzzi.

A small library is outfitted with books, games, and a guest refrigerator stocked with complimentary beverages. Other favorite places for relaxing are the porches, where breakfast is often served in fair weather. The fare includes homemade muffins, cereals, fresh fruit, and, of course, pecan sticky buns.

Named for two ancient pecan trees that grow on the property, the inn is beautifully landscaped. There's a small yard in front and a huge garden in back, planted with more than 1,000 flowers, shrubs, and trees. (The local chefs also stroll back here to pluck some of Susan's herbs.) The city's best restaurants are all within walking distance, as are the historic district and the water-front.

🏨 *7 double rooms with baths. Air-conditioning. $80–$120, Continental breakfast. MC, V. No smoking, no pets.*

White Doe Inn

319 Sir Walter Raleigh St., Manteo, NC 27954, tel. 919/473–9851 or 800/473–6091, fax 919/473–4708

The white Victorian on the corner of Sir Walter Raleigh Street has been a Manteo icon for generations. The Meekins family of Rodanthe moved to the island and built the house in 1896 as a 1½-story frame structure. Years later, Rosa Meekins saw a picture in the Sears catalog and had her husband built an addition modeled on the Victorian home in 1910.

Bebe Woody grew up wondering what lay behind the lace curtains of the majestic Queen Anne. In 1993 she and husband Bob Woody bought the house, now on the National Register of Historic Places, and spent two years renovating the home into an inn. They were uniquely suited to the job: Bebe retired from 31 years with the National Park Service, specializing in historic preservation and restoration, and Bob still works in visitor services.

The study, tastefully furnished in antiques, has a fireplace with built-in bookcases on either side. A baby grand dominates the parlor, where chamber-music concerts are sometimes held. Breakfasts of French toast or pancakes, fresh fruit and old-fashioned hash browns is served in the downstairs dining room.

The Garret Bedchamber, on the third floor, is one of the most unusual rooms. A two-way fireplace serves the bedroom and the bath, which features a Jacuzzi. The Virginia Dare room is the most romantic, with a four-poster queen-size rice bed and a bath with Jacuzzi. Light pours in through the windows of the Turret room, located in the turret on the corner of the house. The Old Towne Bedchamber has two wicker double beds and a stained-glass window. The Scuppernong has 9-foot sloped ceilings and an antique cast-iron claw-foot tub.

The inn takes its name from an old Indian legend that Virginia Dare, the child who disappeared with the Lost Colony, was turned into a white doe that still roams the island to this day.

🏨 *7 double rooms with baths. Air-conditioning, fireplace, ceiling fan, and phone in rooms, whirlpool tubs in 2 rooms. $113–$175; full breakfast, afternoon refreshments. MC, V. Smoking on porches only, no pets, no children under 12, 2-night minimum on weekends Easter–Thanksgiving.*

Worth House

412 S. 3rd St., Wilmington, NC, 28401, tel. 910/762–8562 or 800/340–8559, fax 910/763–2173

This picture-perfect Queen Anne home stands out, even in a historic district full of beautiful homes. Its twin turrets, trimmed with shingles, their windows lined with lace curtains, promise an intriguing interior—and deliver. Built by merchant Charles Worth in 1893, it was a private home for many years before being converted to a boarding house during World War II, when shipbuilding boomed in the port city. Abandoned in the late 1970s and restored in the mid-'80s, it was purchased by Francie and John Miller in 1994.

Francie likes to say that while you might find more elegant accommodations, you won't find any more comfortable. The Worth House is, in fact, beautiful without being fussy or intimidating. It's furnished with antiques from the period, with the exception of a big-screen TV in one of the downstairs parlors. Mirrors, tables, and other pieces come from France, Baton Rouge and New Orleans. There's a sitting room on each floor, as well as a garden with a decorative pond in back, and a screened porch on the second floor.

Guest rooms have antique wood beds, including four-posters. Favorite rooms include the Azalea and Rose suites, both of which have private sunporches. The Azalea suite is located inside the big turret and boasts two large bay windows. The third-floor rooms are not for the tall. Conforming to the roof and turret lines, they have sloping ceilings and unusual shapes. But for some guests, that just adds to the charm.

Breakfast is served in the formal dining room, and Francie will accommodate most any schedule. Special amenities include a modem line for business travelers and a laundry available for guests.

🛏 *5 double rooms with baths, 2 suites. Air-conditioning, ceiling fans, phones; cable TV in parlors, fireplaces in some rooms, laundry. $75–$115, full breakfast. MC, V. No smoking, no pets, 2-night minimum on holiday and special weekends.*

Other Choices

King's Arms Inn. 212 Pollock St., New Bern, NC 28560, tel. 919/638–4409 or 800/872–9306, fax 919/638–2191. 7 double rooms with baths, 1 suite. Air-conditioning, cable TVs, phones. $85–$125; Continental breakfast, afternoon refreshments. AE, MC, V. Restricted smoking, no pets.

Roanoke Island Inn. 305 Fernando St., Manteo, NC 27954, tel. 919/441–5511, fax 919/473–3282. 6 double rooms with baths, 2 suites. Air-conditioning, cable TVs, phones. $88–$118; Continental breakfast, refreshments. AE, D, MC, V. Restricted smoking, no pets, 2-night minimum weekends.

Tranquil House Inn. 405 Queen Elizabeth St. (Box 2045), Manteo, NC 27954, tel. 919/473–1404 or 800/458–7069, fax 919/473–1526. 23 double rooms with baths, 2 suites. Air-conditioning, cable TVs, phones; bicycles. $129–$169; Continental breakfast, evening refresh-

ments. AE, D, MC, V. No pets, 2-night minimum summer weekends, 3-night minimum holiday weekends.

Reservations Service

North Carolina Bed & Breakfast Assn. (Box 1077, Asheville, NC 28802, tel. 800/849–5392).

The Piedmont

Arrowhead Inn

106 Mason Rd., Durham, NC 27712, tel. and fax 919/477–8430 or 800/528–2207

The large arrowhead monument from which this inn draws its name designates an old Native American trading route called the Great Path, which once stretched from eastern Virginia to the North Carolina mountains. It's a proper frame of reference for this house, which, like the path, predates the United States. The manor house was built about 1775 on a 2,000-acre land grant purchased from Joseph Brittain, and for more than 100 years, slaves worked the land. The original house had four rooms—two upstairs and two down—but several were added over the years. Situated on 4 acres, it is a two-story Colonial-style house with brick chimneys and tall Doric columns that support the long front porch. The house is painted white with black shutters. The boxwood, magnolias, and flower beds around it are about 150 years old, and more than 40 species of birds live on the property.

After a succession of owners, Jerry and Barbara Ryan bought the house in 1985 and turned it into a bed-and-breakfast, winning an award from the Durham Historic Preservation Society for adaptive reuse. Jerry had worked as a publisher of business magazines, and Barbara, a former editor and ghostwriter, continues to write magazine articles.

Guest rooms are decorated with an assortment of antiques and collectibles from the Colonial through the Victorian period. The front rooms of the house look out on the flower beds, while the back view is dominated by an enormous magnolia. For those wanting more privacy, there are two rooms in an adjacent carriage house. The Land Grant Cabin, which has a downstairs sitting room and a loft bedroom, is a favorite. In addition to families and couples, the inn is quite popular with traveling businesswomen and recently started a "frequent guest" program for business travelers.

The Ryans greet arriving guests with complimentary refreshments and are always available in the evening when everyone gathers in the keeping room to work puzzles, read, or talk. Barbara promises guests a different breakfast every day. They range from hearty country breakfasts with bacon, eggs, fruit, and muffins to more exotic fare. Lower-fat alternatives are prepared on request.

▥ *5 double rooms with baths, 2 suites, 1 cabin. Air-conditioning, phones, coffeemakers; ceiling fans in public rooms, TV in keeping room, cabin, and suite, guest refrigerator. $95–$180; full breakfast, afternoon tea. AE, D, DC, MC, V. Restricted smoking, no pets.*

Fearrington House

Fearrington Village Center, U.S. 15– 501, Pittsboro, NC 27312, tel. 919/542– 2121, fax 919/542–4202

If you didn't know better, you'd think a click of the heels had transported you to the Cotswolds of England. Actually, this bucolic setting is Fearrington Village, a 200-year-old farm remade into a residential community just off U.S. 15– 501 between Chapel Hill and Pittsboro. The village is the creation of R.B. and Jenny Fitch, who studied inns and

restaurants all over Europe before they began the 1,100-acre project in 1974. It consists of the inn and private homes, a restaurant (in the former farmhouse), a bank, pharmacy, pottery, jewelry store, bookstore, and garden shop.

The inn's guest rooms are clustered around a charming courtyard with a central fountain and look out over the gardens and the pasture, where Galloway cows and Tunis sheep graze. The rooms are furnished in English pine that matches the flooring from a London workhouse; they are complemented by polished floral-print fabrics and dried arrangements. The luxurious bathrooms have towel warmers. The Fitch children now help run the business, from decorating the rooms to overseeing the restaurant and gardens.

Breakfast is served in the restaurant, comprising different rooms done up in the elegant country style that is Fearrington's hallmark. Green ivy stenciled on the walls provides a natural complement to the real vines and boughs that peek through the many windows overlooking the gardens. Dinner draws not only inn guests but diners from Chapel Hill and Durham. Entrées include sautéed halibut with roasted fennel; rare yellowfin tuna with white-wine ginger sauce and fried leeks; and grilled beef tenderloin on a Parmesan disk with peppercorn sauce. Most guests eat lunch in the Market Café or go for a picnic, which can be ordered from the deli. Then they gather for afternoon tea in the Garden Room.

One of the most pleasant things about the Fearrington is its low-key country atmosphere. You won't be subjected to a schedule here, but you might try a round of croquet or ride one of the bikes to the swimming pool and tennis courts. Of course, there are plenty of diversions nearby—the Morehead Planetarium at Chapel Hill, Duke Chapel, and the Duke Homestead. The inn is affiliated with Relais & Chateaux.

🏨 *17 double rooms with baths, 12 suites. Air-conditioning, TV and phone in rooms. $165–$275; full breakfast, afternoon tea. AE, MC, V. No smoking in bedrooms, no pets.*

Henry F. Shaffner House

150 S. Marshall St., Winston-Salem, NC 27101, tel. 910/777–0052 or 800/952–2256, fax 910/777–1188

The Henry F. Shaffner House was built between 1907 and 1909 by Henry Fries Shaffner, one of the founders of Wachovia Bank. The house was saved twice, the first time from fire by Shaffner himself, who went onto the rooftop with buckets of water. He later replaced the cedar shingles with copper, which helped to preserve the mansion through the next 70 years, even after it was abandoned and neglected. The house was saved again in 1990 by Henry and Betty Falls, who spent two years renovating it. Henry, who owns the insurance agency across the street, initially had designs on the overgrown back lot, which he needed for parking. But once he stepped inside the home, he saw past the layers of paint and dirt to the treasure underneath.

The house was built using the finest materials and workmanship. Tiger-oak paneling covers the walls of the entry hall and adorns the doors, windows, and exposed ceiling beams. Many of the brass fixtures remain, as do the tile fireplaces and a huge ornate radiator in the library. The Queen Anne detailing on the exterior, with large wraparound porches and a wrought-iron fence, is stunning enough to stop traffic, even on the busy main thoroughfare that now runs past it. It was the coming of the interstate, which cuts alongside the house, that moved Shaffner's widow to sell it in 1949. For today's travelers, the location provides easy access from downtown to any Winston-Salem attraction.

Rooms are beautifully appointed with rich fabrics, comfortable sofas and chairs, and gleaming reproduction furniture. Each room is different. The Winston Room is decorated in English Regency—deep sapphire-blue carpet, stucco walls, and a queen-size sleigh bed. The Reynolda is bright and feminine, the Bethabara darkly masculine. The Piedmont Room is a remarkable penthouse suite, with whirlpool bath and wet bar, in the 18th-century Biedermeier style. The king-size canopy bed is covered with a leopard-print comforter, and leopard-print accents are echoed tastefully in the wallpaper and bolster pillows. Throughout, the inn combines the charm of the past with modern amenities. Special touches such as chocolates, turndown service, and gift baskets for special occasions make the inn a popular spot for weddings, honeymoons, and anniversaries. The Fallses also hold murder-mystery weekends several times a year.

🏨 *5 double rooms with baths, 3 suites. Air-conditioning, cable TVs, phones; passes to nearby fitness center. $99–$189; Continental breakfast, afternoon wine and cheese. AE, MC, V. No smoking, no pets.*

Homeplace

5901 Sardis Rd., Charlotte, NC 28270, tel. 704/365–1936

The Homeplace, a well-preserved remnant of the past, has somehow survived modern development in the bustling Sunbelt city of Charlotte. The almond-colored house, on 2½ wooded acres with profuse plantings of flowers, is located at the corner of a busy residential intersection but is so quiet inside, you might just as well be at the top of Walton's Mountain.

Frank and Peggy Dearien had admired the 1902 country Victorian farmhouse for several years before the chance arose in 1984 for them to buy it and turn it into a bed-and-breakfast. Frank took early retirement from his accounting job, and the inn is now their full-time occupation. They furnished the house in Victorian period pieces, quilts, cross-stitch pictures, and family memorabilia. Peggy made all the curtains. The most cherished artwork in the house is a collection of primitive paintings reminiscent of Grandma Moses's work that Peggy's father did during the last years of his life.

The Victorian Lady Room, done in mauve and green, was planned around a cross-stitch picture made by their daughter Debra Moye. The largest room in the inn, it has a four-poster rice bed. The blue and white English Country Room overlooks the garden and the gazebo. The Pewter Rose Suite is great for families or honeymooners. The bedroom is particularly romantic; it has a queen-size canopy bed draped with a rose-print fabric. When honeymooners stay here, Peggy will serve a private breakfast in the sitting room. A daybed here can accommodate a third person for family groups. All the rooms have little personal touches, such as a purse or hand mirror that belonged to Frank's mother.

The Deariens, who live on the property, are great believers in practicing southern hospitality. There's always hot water for tea or coffee, as well as ice and soft drinks. Breakfast, served in the dining room, might be poached pears with raspberry sauce, scrambled dill eggs with cheese sauce, or waffles and cinnamon cream.

▦ 2 double rooms with baths, 1 suite. Air-conditioning, ceiling fans, cable TV in common areas, irons and ironing boards in rooms. $98–$120, full breakfast. AE, MC, V. No smoking, no pets, 2-night minimum holiday weekends.

Pilot Knob Inn

Box 1280, Pilot Mountain, NC 27041, tel. 910/325-2502

The two-story log tobacco barns that dot this rural landscape aren't usually the kind of places you'd consider spending the night. Here, however, they have become a one-of-a-kind B&B. The property adjoins Pilot Mountain State Park, and the knob that crowns the 1,500-foot mountain is within view. (If the names ring a bell, it's because they inspired the place-names in Andy Griffith's mythical Mayberry.)

Five small barns and a slave cabin, all at least 100 years old, were moved to the 50-acre wooded site by innkeeper Jim Rouse, who added decks and porches to the barns while keeping their rustic look and enlarged the slave cabin. Jim's father, Don, who is also involved in the operation, can always find something that needs fixing or changing. Norman Ross, a silent business partner from Chicago, owns the collection of 6,000 records in the library. The barns are furnished in a mix of 18th-century reproductions, southern primitive, and country English antiques, in addition to Oriental and dhurrie rugs. Each has a whirlpool tub for two and a fireplace and is equipped with such amenities as bathrobes, hair dryers, fresh fruit, and flowers. Some of the barns have massive "Paul Bunyan" beds, handmade of juniper logs by a local craftsman. The common room, downstairs in the bilevel central barn—where guests gather to read and listen to music—features a 300-year-old Italian-marble fireplace, a William and Mary love seat, and a coffee table made of parquet flooring from Versailles (really!). There's a dry sauna and a pool, and a 6-acre lake and gazebo are ideal for fishing. A contemporary building overlooking the pool and the mountain beyond houses the office, kitchen, a conference room, and a gift shop that sells community crafts. Guests can also while away the evening at a new gazebo with a ceiling fan and picnic tables.

Privacy and isolation are the main attractions at Pilot Knob. It's tucked away with no signs or billboards to point the way and is the perfect place to commune with nature, slow down, and rekindle romance. Guests usually get together at breakfast, which is served in the central barn and prepared by Jim's mother, Pat. Her specialties are chocolate-chip sour-cream coffee cake, waffles and sausage, poached pears, and a peach and cream-cheese concoction called Peach Pilot—all served with fresh berries in season.

🏠 6 cabins. Air-conditioning, TV and phone in cabins. $110–$130, Continental breakfast. MC, V. Smoking in cabins only, no pets, no children, 2-night minimum Oct. and holidays.

Other Choices

Blooming Garden Inn. 513 Holloway St., Durham, NC 27701, tel. 919/687–0801, fax 919/688–1401. 2 double rooms with baths, 2 suites. Air-conditioning, ceiling fans, cable TV in library and 1 suite, whirlpool bath in suites, refrigerator. $85–$160, full breakfast. AE, D, DC, MC, V. No smoking, no pets.

Magnolia Inn. Magnolia St. and Chinquapin Rd. (Box 818), Pinehurst, NC 28374, tel. 910/295–6900 or 800/526–5562, fax 910/215–0858. 12 double rooms with baths. Restaurant, air-conditioning, cable TV in rooms and pub. $130, breakfast only; $160, MAP. AE, MC, V. Restricted smoking, no pets, 2-night minimum spring and fall weekends.

Reservations Service

North Carolina Bed & Breakfast Assn. (Box 1077, Asheville, NC 28802, tel. 800/849–5392).

The Mountains

Balsam Mountain Inn

Box 40, Balsam, NC, 28707, tel. 704/456–9488 or 800/224–9498, fax 704/456–9298

Half past nine on spring nights, the moon rises on Balsam, perfectly placed between two mountain peaks, as if a painter set it there for the benefit of the folks sitting in rocking chairs at the Balsam Mountain Inn. Actually, it wasn't the moon but the inn that was strategically placed so that the sun, which warmed the porches in the morning, would leave them in shade during hot summer afternoons and so guests could watch the moonrise nightly year-round.

At one time, the North Carolina mountains were full of rambling wood-frame inns like this one, but the Balsam Mountain Inn is one of only a handful remaining. Built at what was then the highest elevation of the Western North Carolina Railroad, it offered a cool escape from the summer heat when it opened in 1908 as the Balsam Mountain Springs Hotel. It operated into the 1980s but was condemned, boarded up, and had 125 broken windows when Merrily Teasley bought it in 1990 and began restoration. Plumbing, wiring, and heat are all new, but the inn retains virtually all of its vintage charm. Beadboard paneling covers all the walls, and the heart-pine floors have a comforting creak.

A huge mansard roof with more than 100 dormer windows covers the inn, which is fronted by a two-story porch lined with rockers and hanging plants. Everything about this inn says "relax," from the library, stocked with 2,000 volumes, to the chairs gathered around the lobby fireplaces.

Some of the guest rooms have ornate iron beds, while others have "twig" beds—headboards fashioned from boughs and twisted vines by a local craftsman. Bathrooms have either showers or Victorian claw-foot tubs, as well as corner-mounted sinks with separate taps for hot and cold water.

The large dining room is painted gray with lavender, green, and burgundy trim for a charming effect. The full-service restaurant serves three meals a day, and a lavish breakfast is included in the room rate. French toast with a caramelized syrup coating, topped with fresh fruit, is representative of the breakfast fare.

🏨 *42 double rooms with baths, 8 suites. Restaurant. $90–$160; full breakfast, tea and hot chocolate in lobby. D, MC, V. Restricted smoking, no pets, 2-night minimum some weekends and holidays.*

Cedar Crest Inn

674 Biltmore Ave., Asheville, NC 28803, tel. 704/252–1389 or 800/252–0310, fax 704/253–7667

The Cedar Crest Inn, its yellow paint and high-pitched roof exuding warmth and cheer, sits on a hill overlooking Biltmore Village. The Victorian inn has close ties to Vanderbilt's 250-room French château. Built in 1891 by the craftsmen who worked on the famous mansion, Cedar Crest has the same hand-carved mantels, beveled glass, and other fine detailing found in Biltmore.

Innkeepers Jack and Barbara McEwan, former residents of Racine, Wisconsin, looked for a year and a half before finding Cedar Crest, which in 1930 had been converted into a tourist house. The McEwans restored it in 1984, removing 13 layers of wallpaper and adding several bathrooms. Barbara did the decorating herself, using family heirlooms and antiques and filling in with pieces found at estate sales; Jack drew upon the management skills he had learned as a hotelier.

Dark, rich paneling and wide, ornate window frames are set off with white lace curtains in the common rooms downstairs. Each of the guest rooms has its own Victorian character, accomplished with lace and silk fabrics, soft colors, and wallpapers. The Queen Anne Room, which has shirred fabric on the ceiling, is a favorite; another is the Garden Room, with a brass bed, mosquito netting, and white linen bedding. Honeymooners and anniversary

couples love the guest cottage, a 1915 bungalow furnished with mission-style furniture in the Arts and Crafts style. The Celebration Suite has a large bedroom, sitting room, and whirlpool. Four of the bedrooms have a gas fireplace.

Visitors enjoy gathering around the fire in the parlor; in the formal dining room, where the McEwans serve breakfast; or in the study, which has a coffee table made by Spanish ironsmiths. Depending on the season, iced tea, lemonade, pressed cider, hot chocolate, or wassail is served in the parlor or library. When the weather is warm, guests often team up for croquet; otherwise, indoor activities include reading and playing cards and board games. In addition to visiting the Biltmore estate, guests can explore the sights and shops in the village, including All Souls' Episcopal Church, which George Vanderbilt had built in 1896 for his daughter's wedding.

🏨 *8 double rooms with baths, 1 suite, 1 cottage with two suites and a common kitchen. Air-conditioning, cable TV in study and suites, phones. $120–$210; Continental breakfast, afternoon tea. AE, D, DC, MC, V. No smoking, no pets, 2-night minimum weekends and holidays.*

Greystone Inn

Greystone La., Lake Toxaway, NC 28747, tel. 704/966–4700 or 800/824–5766, fax 704/862–5689

In the early 1900s, the rich arrived in their private railcars to vacation at secluded Lake Toxaway. Modern travelers head for the Greystone Inn, a Swiss-style mansion at the edge of the lake that's on the National Register of Historic Places. Built in 1915, the house was converted to an inn in 1985 by Tim Lovelace, a retired financial consultant, who later added Hillmont, a 12-room annex.

Guests can choose between staying in the historic house, which has casement windows, glass doorknobs, and antique beds, and enjoying the modern luxury of the Hillmont Annex, whose rooms contain fireplaces with gas logs, king-size beds, and private balconies overlooking the lake. These contemporary rooms are quite spacious. There are wing-back chairs by the fireplace and leather chairs by the window, and the huge bathrooms have large whirlpool baths and separate, freestanding glass showers. The Presidential Suite, the former library, is the most impressive of the mansion rooms, highlighted by soaring 25-foot ceilings, built-in oak bookcases, a huge floor-to-ceiling stone fireplace, and a bay window overlooking the lake. The Firestone Room, formerly the kitchen, still has a wood-burning stove, a stone fireplace, and exposed beams.

In the dining facility, open only to guests, vast windows frame the mountains and the lake. Chef Chris McDonald serves southern cuisine with a modern twist, such as trout Pontchartrain and delicate baby-corn fritters. The six-course gourmet dinner and lavish breakfast are included.

Greystone guests can play tennis and golf at the adjoining Lake Toxaway Country Club and go swimming, waterskiing, windsurfing, sailing, and canoeing on the lake from the inn's private dock. Many guests hike to Mills Creek Falls or Deep Ford Falls for a picnic. Rainy days are devoted to playing bridge and reading or pampering oneself at the spa.

After tea, a social highlight of the day, Tim conducts animated lake tours on the Mountain Lily II. Everyone gathers in the library lounge for hors d'oeuvres and cocktails before dinner.

▦ *30 double rooms, 3 suites with whirlpool baths. Air-conditioning, ceiling fan, cable TV/VCRs, phones; turn-down service, morning newspaper; airport transportation available. $245–$495; MAP, afternoon tea, hors d'oeuvres, all sports (complimentary tee times for golf unavailable at certain times of the year). AE, MC, V. No pets, 2-night minimum weekends. Open weekends only Jan.–Mar.*

Richmond Hill Inn

87 Richmond Hill Dr., Asheville, NC 28806, tel. 704/252–7313 or 800/545–9238, fax 704/252–8726

As a young man, Thomas Wolfe used to look up at the Richmond Hill mansion and wonder what kind of people lived in such a glorious place. Years later he would meet members of the Pearson family and write that they were as grand as the house itself. The Queen Anne–style mansion was built in 1889 as the home of Richmond Pearson, a diplomat and statesman, and his wife, Gabrielle. It had long since fallen into disrepair when Jake and Marge Michel of Greensboro bought the home in 1987 and invested $3 million to restore it. The Richmond Hill Inn opened in 1989, and Denise Maluck is now the general manager.

The Michels retained not only the elegant architecture but also the gracious ways of the past, from valet service at the carriage entrance to afternoon games of croquet on the manicured lawn. Afternoon tea is served in the sweeping oak-paneled entry hall, where leather and tapestry-print Victorian chairs are grouped around the fireplace under the benevolent gaze of Gabrielle herself. The restored portrait is one of many Pearson family items that the Michels have recovered. Guests can relax on the porches or in a cozy oak-paneled library.

The 12 guest rooms in the mansion are named for historic figures of the era and North Carolina writers with Asheville ties and are furnished in antiques, such as canopy beds and claw-foot tubs. The most popular is the romantic Gabrielle Pearson Room, where the canopy bed is draped in peach-colored fabric and lace curtains grace the windows of the eight-sided room. The Chief

Justice Suite has a whirlpool bath, wet bar, and fireplace with gas logs. In a more contemporary style, the Croquet Cottages also have fireplaces with gas logs as well as pencil-post beds and private porches with rocking chairs. A new addition includes the Garden Rooms, the most spacious rooms the inn has to offer, and an additional restaurant.

Gabrielle's, located inside the mansion and one of Asheville's best restaurants, serves new American cuisine with southern regional influences. Breakfast, featuring fresh fruit crepes and exotic omelets, is served in this elegant cherry-paneled dining room. And just to make sure you really feel pampered, the turndown service includes chocolates and a gift to take home.

12 double rooms with baths, 9 cottages, 5 Garden Rooms. Air-conditioning, cable TVs, phones. $135–$375; full breakfast, afternoon tea. AE, MC, V. No smoking, no pets, 2-night minimum weekends. Closed 2 weeks in Jan.

Other Choices

Inn at Taylor House. Rte. 194 (Box 713), Valle Crucis, NC 28691, tel. 704/963–5581, fax 704/963–5818. 5 double rooms with baths, 3 suites. Air-conditioning on 3rd floor, ceiling fans in rooms, day spa with massage therapist. $120–$235; full breakfast, afternoon tea. MC, V. No smoking, no pets, 2-night minimum weekends, closed mid-Dec.–Mar.

Lodge on Lake Lure. Charlotte Dr. (Rte. 1, Box 519), Lake Lure, NC 28746, tel. 704/625–2789 or 800/733–2785. 12 double rooms with baths, 2 suites. Air-conditioning, ceiling fans; cable TV in library; boats, canoes, and sea cycles. $95–$200, full breakfast. AE, D, MC, V. No smoking, no pets, 2-night minimum weekends, 2- or 3-night minimum holidays.

Maple Lodge Bed & Breakfast. 152 Sunset Dr. (Box 1236), Blowing Rock, NC 28605, tel. 704/295–3331, fax 704/295–9986. 10 double rooms with baths, 1 suite. Ceiling fans; cable TV in 4 rooms, and jacks for phones or modems in 2 rooms. $78–$120, full breakfast. AE, D, MC, V. No smoking, no pets, no children under 12, 2-night minimum some weekends. Closed Jan.

Waverly Inn. 783 N. Main St., Hendersonville, NC 28792, tel. 704/693–9193 or 800/537–8195, fax 704/692–1010. 13 double rooms with baths, 1 suite. Air-conditioning, ceiling fan in most rooms, cable TV in parlors and all rooms. $89–$195, full breakfast. AE, D, MC, V. Restricted smoking, no pets, 2-night minimum holidays.

Reservations Service

North Carolina Bed & Breakfast Assn. (Box 1077, Asheville, NC 28802, tel. 800/849–5392).

North Dakota

Volden Farm

Mid-State North Dakota

Country Charm Bed & Breakfast

R.R. 3, Box 71, Jamestown, ND 58401, tel. 701/251-1372

This inn invites you to savor the bounty of its setting: the song of wild birds, great fields of wheat, the nearness of friendly hills, the sight of a chipmunk peering through the tall grass. Curious deer are frequent visitors to the 12 acres surrounding Tom and Ethel Oxtoby's country-farm bed-and-breakfast. Rabbits, squirrels, and other wildlife are also frequent sights on the beautifully manicured grounds, along with the occasional fox or coyote. And, since the farmstead is on one of America's busiest migratory flyways, numerous birds are attracted to the Oxtobys' feeders. You might say the Country Charm B&B has a certain animal magnetism.

The 1897 farmstead sits on a gentle knoll just 1½ miles off Interstate 94. Pine, spruce, cottonwood, and fruit trees surround it on three sides while the prairie stretches as far as the eye can see to the south. As the favored gathering spots of most guests, the redwood deck and glassed-in sunporch—prettily stenciled with vine motifs—afford the pleasantest views. On clear nights, guests often gather on the front porch to watch the stars twinkle above the lights of Jamestown, 6 miles away. Or, they'll ask Tom to go for a ride along the country roads in his classic 1958 Ford Skyliner convertible (one of his five antique Ford vehicles); with its trademark hardtop down, it's a delightful way to go in search of the Big Dipper.

"Our inn is really peaceful," says Ethel Oxtoby. "That's why a lot of people come here. And if you want a quiet stay, visit during our North Dakota winters, which can last from Thanksgiving to early May. Twenty inches of snow, three-day blizzards, and hot-chocolate weather can really do the soul right." Ethel is a quilter (a big regional activity), and you'll find her "double wedding rings," "cathedral windows," and "fan patterns" throughout the guest rooms, which are also adorned with lace, country tins, hearts and sheep motifs, and North Dakota wheat wreaths and sculptures.

Full breakfasts are served on the round oak table in the dining area or on the walnut table on the sunporch. Fresh orange juice and an apple-raisin puffed pancake can be a delicious way to start the day while you count the pheasants that fly past the window, trying to get a word in edgewise among the chattering bluejays. After a second cup of aromatic coffee or tea, head for the nearby Arrowwood Wildlife Center or historic Frontier Village.

🏠 *3 double rooms and 1 single room share 1 bath. Air-conditioning, antique car rides, sunporch. $40–$50, full breakfast. No credit cards.*

North Dakota Heartland

Beiseker Mansion

1001 N.E. 2nd St., Box 187, Fessenden, ND 58438, tel. 701/547–3411

This imposing 15-room mansion stood vacant for a number of years, and probably would have for many more if Paula and Jerry Tweton hadn't made a wrong turn in 1989 onto the residential street where it sits. The couple had already traveled to California, Illinois, and Wisconsin in their search for an inn to buy when Jerry, then a professor of history at the University of North Dakota, was asked to speak in the small community of Fessenden. They were elated to find only 143 miles from their home in Grand Forks what they had been looking for all along. Shortly thereafter, they purchased the National Register–listed property and began restoring it.

The Queen Anne–style home was built in 1899 by T. L. Beiseker, a wealthy land speculator who owned 27 banks. He lived in the Victorian mansion until his death in 1942. From then until the mid-1970s it was used as a women's retirement home by the Order of the Eastern Star and then remained mostly vacant until the Twetons bought it.

Beiseker Mansion is one of only two Victorian homes in North Dakota with twin turrets. The cedar-wood structure has a wraparound veranda of Pennsylvania sandstone, stained- and leaded-glass windows, golden oak wainscoting, and alabaster light fixtures. It is on several heavily treed acres within walking distance of most of the rest of the community. Hundreds of persons pay a small fee to tour the home each year.

Four of the six air-conditioned bedrooms on the mansion's second floor are available for guests. Furnished with antiques and twin-, double-, and queen-size beds, all rooms have cable TVs and VCRs. A third-floor special-occasion suite has Victorian-era Turkish decor, king-size bed, and whirlpool bath for two.

Guests often relax in wicker chairs on the veranda; join Jerry, a respected scholar, for an impromptu lesson on North Dakota history; or comb through the extensive library of books, magazines, and videocassettes.

The Twetons serve a full breakfast of freshly ground coffee, fruit, eggs, and other dishes made from scratch. Their family-recipe pancakes and special sausage are favorites with guests. Evening meals are also available at extra charge. The limited dinner can include a well-aged tenderloin steak Madeira, chicken in wine sauce, and a platter of Bohemian pot roast with all the trimmings.

🏠 *4 double rooms share 2 baths, 1 suite. Fireplace in common area, central phone. $45–$95, full breakfast. MC, V.*

Luverne

Volden Farm

R.R. 2, Box 50, Luverne, ND 58056, tel. 701/769–2275

As the *Grand Forks Herald* charmingly put it, JoAnn and Jim Wold's inn is "the kind of place where guests can go to bed in Czarist Russia and wake up in Scandinavia—there are twin motifs at work." Icons and pre-revolutionary and dissident Russian art, acquired by the couple while Jim was a U.S. Air Force military attaché in Moscow, contrast with decorations reflecting the Wolds' Norwegian roots. Maple floors and furnishings add to the decidedly European look.

The original part of the house, built in 1926, includes the parlor, music room, library, and two guest bedrooms. The newer part was added in 1978 and is a light and airy space containing a fireplace in the conversation pit. Redwood siding, which grays and weathers over time, was purposely chosen for the exterior for its ability to blend in with the surrounding trees, giving the home the look of a Russian dacha.

Forty-one miles north of Valley City and I–94, Volden Farm sits on a hilltop overlooking the Sheyenne River and the fertile farmland beyond. Natural stands of oak, virgin prairie, sparkling springs, and nature trails make this a wonderful place for lovers of the outdoors. Inside, there is an antique billiard table and equipment for other games in the basement.

Furnishings in the guest bedrooms include family heirloom quilts, linens, and antiques from all over the world. One bedroom overlooks pastures and an orchard. A separate building that once served as Jim's law office is a short distance from the main house and has been transformed into a quaint guest cottage. It has a bath with shower and a kitchenette. In the main floor bedroom, two Norwegian sleigh beds have been joined together and topped with a feather bed to make a king-size bed. Upstairs are twin beds, a built-in Swedish bed, and 1930s-style bed. From two nearby window seats, you can enjoy the sunrise. An outside deck is built onto the second story.

JoAnne serves a full Scandinavian breakfast beginning with fresh fruit juice, Swedish pancakes served with chokecherry-raspberry syrup, Norwe-gian cheese and flat bread, vegetables and fruits in season, and freshly ground coffee and herbal or Earl Grey tea. Other meals are available at an additional charge.

🛏 *1 double room with bath, 2 double rooms share 1 bath. Bottled water in rooms, robes, evening snack, toiletries. $40–$75, full breakfast. No credit cards.*

Other Choices

Bohlig's Bed & Breakfast. 1418 3rd Ave. S, Fargo, ND 58103, tel. 701/235–7867. 3 double rooms share 2 baths. Clock radios, central phone, TV in sitting room. $40–$45, full breakfast. No credit cards.

Dakotah Rose Bed & Breakfast. 510 4th Ave. NW, Minot, ND 58701, tel. 701/838–3548. 2 suites with king-size beds and baths, 2 doubles with private baths, 2 doubles share 1 bath. Tearoom open seasonally, air-conditioning in some rooms, central phone, TV/VCR, ballroom serves as common area for guests. $45–$65, full breakfast. MC, V.

Farm Comfort Bed and Breakfast. R.R. 2, Box 71, Kenmare, ND 58746, tel. 701/848–2433. 2 double rooms share 1 main floor bath. Clock radio in bedrooms. Phone and TV in living room and basement; snack kitchen in basement. $30–$35, full breakfast. No credit cards.

511 Reeves Bed & Breakfast. 511 Reeves Dr., Grand Forks, ND 58201, tel. 701/775–3585. 1 double room with bath, 2 double rooms share 1 bath. Air-conditioning, central phone, cable TV/VCR in family room, fireplace in living room. $55–$75, full breakfast. AE, MC, V.

Historic Jacobson Mansion Bed and Breakfast. R.R. 2, Box 15A, Scranton, ND 58653, tel. 701/275–8291. 3 double rooms share 2 baths. Air-conditioning, phone in 1 room and kitchen. $50–$60, full breakfast. No credit cards.

House of 29. 215 7th St. S, Oakes, ND 58474, tel. 701/742–2227. 1 double room with bath, 2 doubles share 1 bath, 3 singles with detached baths. Air-conditioning, TV/VCR, phone in common area. $40–$50, full breakfast. No credit cards.

Logging Camp Ranch Bed & Breakfast. H.C. 3, Box 27, Bowman, ND 58623, tel. 701/279–5702. 2 double rooms share 1 bath. Clock radios, phone, TV/VCR in large living/dining area. $50, full breakfast. No credit cards.

Lord Byron's Bed & Breakfast Inn. 521 S. 5th St., Grand Forks, ND 58201, tel. 701/775–0194. 2 double rooms share 1 bath, 1 double room with private ½ bath. Air-conditioning, central phone, evening snack. $75, full breakfast. No

credit cards. No smoking, no pets, no children under 15.

White Lace Bed & Breakfast. 807 N. 6th St., Bismarck, ND 58501, tel. 701/258–4142. 1 double with bath. Air-conditioning, phones, TV/VCRs, clock radios, close to capitol grounds. $60, full breakfast. AE, D, MC, V.

Reservations Service

North Dakota Tourism Promotion Division (604 E. Blvd., Bismarck, ND 58505, tel. 701/328–2525; listings only).

Ohio

White Oak Inn

Northern Ohio

Baricelli Inn

2203 Cornell Rd., Cleveland, OH 44106, tel. 216/791-6500, fax 216/791-9131

Nestled in Cleveland's Little Italy, a neighborhood of restaurants, bakeries, and art galleries, the Baricelli Inn offers European elegance in an urban American setting.

Four-poster Amish-built king- and queen-size beds dominate the inn's seven suites, where cable televisions are tucked away in authentic 1860s armoires of mahogany or oak. Rooms 3 and 6 are the most popular due to their spaciousness and views of the courtyards. Originally built in 1896, the inn was once the private residence of an academic and her physician husband.

The inn honors the memory of the Baricellis by serving fine European cuisine prepared by chef Paul Minnillo, Jr., who opened the inn and its restaurant in 1984 with his father. The chef is proud to tell visitors the inn's restaurant has no freezer: Everything he serves is fresh. In addition to fine dining, the restaurant serves bistro fare on its shaded garden patio on summer evenings.

While Paul Jr. trolls Europe a couple of times a year for recipes and ideas for the kitchen, Paul Sr. collects bits and pieces of local history to decorate the five dining parlors and the bedrooms. His finds include brass-sill windows from a historic downtown Cleveland building that was demolished, stained-glass windows from an old church, and a statue of St. Thomas Aquinas that presides peacefully over an outdoor cocktail patio. This local color mixes well with the Villeroy and Boch china and silk-shaded crystal candleholders that adorn the dining tables in this turn-of-the-century brownstone.

Visitors to the inn find themselves within walking distance of a treasure trove of cultural and academic institutions, including Severance Hall, home to the celebrated Cleveland Orchestra; the world-renown Cleveland Museum of Art; Case Western Reserve University; the Museum of Natural History; Crawford Auto-Aviation Museum; and a host of others. The neighborhood, wedged into a hill leading to Cleveland Heights, is crisscrossed with redbrick streets and crammed with small houses, boutiques, and a wide variety of restaurants—all Italian.

🏨 *7 rooms with bath. Phones, cable TVs. $125–$150, European breakfast. AE, DC, MC, V.*

Bogart's Bed & Breakfast

62 W. Main St., New Concord, OH 43762, tel. 614/826–7439 or 614/872–3514

Jack and Sharon Bogart bought this exquisite 1830s landmark home the minute it was available. Good thing, too: They were running out of room at their antiques store, 4 miles away. The Bogarts opened their B&B on the quiet historic main street in 1994. It is within walking distance to Muskingum College, shops, and restaurants.

The exquisitely decorated house has both a comfortable sitting room and dining room with fresh flowers in abundance. Outside there is a spacious, screened, wraparound porch, ideal for relaxing with a book or eating breakfast.

The Bogarts' five guest rooms are named after people who have owned the house. Downstairs, off the kitchen, and with private access to the porch, is a room that was added to the house in the 1930s. The wallpaper, an intricate design of small flowers, gives the room, which has twin beds, a homey feel. The front room has a double bed and an 1880s rosewood armoire. The rich color scheme (teal with wine trim) would make it an ideal choice in winter. The three upstairs rooms each have one double bed and a twin day bed. One has a sunflower motif and is a favorite among guests. Another has a country theme, with a beautiful tiger maple bed and a matching chest of drawers. The largest room is awash in lilacs and has a small kitchenette and eating area.

Guests can use the college's gym, which is within easy walking distance. Also, golf courses, museums, and a state park are just a few miles away.

Sharon cooks breakfast to order each morning and is happy to fulfill special requests.

🏨 *5 double rooms with bath. Air-conditioning, TV/VCR in sitting area. $65–$75, full breakfast. MC, V. No smoking.*

Inn at Honey Run

6920 Rte. 203, Millersburg, OH 44654, tel. 330/674–0011 or 800/468–6639, fax 330/674–2623

If every B&B owner's dream is to have the perfect setting where the inn blends with its surroundings to create a pleasant ambience, then Marge Stock succeeded admirably. The design is modern, but the use of wood, especially oak, gives the impression that this inn is also part of nature's bounty.

Built in 1982, the inn consists of a main house with floor-to-ceiling windows, outside decks, and bird feeders everywhere; a guest house called the "Honeycombs," an earth-sheltered building burrowed into a hillside with 12 guest rooms that, from the outside, do indeed look like a honeycomb; and two cabins each with two bedrooms, a small kitchen, a living room, and a private deck.

The inn is decorated simply, in deference to the plain-living Amish who reside in the area. At Christmastime, instead of lights, the inn hangs red-and-green-pattern quilts and scatters poinsettias throughout common areas. A Christmas tree, placed on a large outdoor deck off the inn's main floor, has decorations for the birds—literally. Carved-out gourds and halved grape-fruits stocked with seeds hang from the branches, and strings of popcorn and cranberries draw brilliantly colored cardinals, along with a wide variety of other birds.

One wall of the inn has 43 planks of different kinds of wood culled from area trees; many of the inn's guests make a sport of trying to identify each one (a cheat sheet is kept on a nearby coffee table). Hickory rocking chairs and fireplaces make two common areas ideal spots for relaxed contemplation. In the inn's rooms, televisions and telephones are hidden in cabinets, and field guides for wildflowers and birds sit atop simple wooden end tables. Although several rooms are decorated in plain Shaker style, every room is different. About half of them have stunning views of the wooded hillside, and all have good light for reading.

The Honeycombs, set below the crest of a hill buried under a lush carpet of grass and wildflowers, appears cavelike and dark from the outside. Inside, however, glass-panel doors leading to stone-wall back patios look out on a series of rolling hills, where sheep and goats graze. The six rooms of the top floor have large sandstone fireplaces, and four of the Honeycomb rooms have secluded patios.

Simplicity reigns as well in the two guest houses, which are atop the hill. One is called Trillium, the other Cardinal, and the decor, from bedspreads to wall hangings, reflects these names. Each guest house has two bedrooms with double beds, along with a sofa bed and a bed hidden in the wall, making sleeping space for six in each house. The houses are outfitted with microwave ovens, dishwashers, and washer-dryer units.

The Inn at Honey Run doesn't prohibit children, but it doesn't encourage parents to bring them, either. The relaxed pace and pastoral setting are engineered to please adults and don't offer much to active children. This is a place, says Marge, where people who lead stressful lives come to rest and recharge. For this reason, and because Marge likes to keep things immaculate, children are allowed to stay in the main building, but not in the Honeycombs and guest houses. Marge says young parents are frequent guests here, taking time away from their children to get reacquainted.

Meals are reflective of the inn—excellent, simple food. The menu changes daily and often features baked tenderloin of beef, panfried trout caught locally, and fresh, healthy, steamed vegetables. Out of respect for the Amish, the inn serves no alcohol and its restaurant is open only to inn guests on Sunday. Also, the resident pets, including Honey the cat and a few dogs, are very territorial; therefore, no other pets are allowed here.

Marge is planting a large orchard, and she serves produce and preserves from the inn's property in the dining room. In fact, guests can watch the preserves being made at the Milkhouse Café. On the top of a hill, a short walk from the main inn, the café is a great place for visitors and guests to sample the preserves out on the deck (or by the fireplace), while drinking in the serene landscape.

Marge is constantly seeking guests' suggestions and criticism, and she seems to think of everything to make a stay here special—from leaving walking sticks outside all of the buildings, to stocking shelves with books that guests can take home and send back when they finish reading them.

🎁 *37 double rooms with bath, 2 cabins sleep 8. Restaurant, café, air-conditioning, phones, TVs, radio-and-cassette alarm clocks, exercise machines, meeting rooms. $79–$280, Continental breakfast. AE, MC, V. Minimum 2-day stay in cabins.*

White Fence Inn

8842 Denman Rd., Lexington, OH 44904, tel. 419/884–2356

When Bill and Ellen Hiser saw this breathtaking 70-acre farm 6 miles outside of Mansfield in 1987, their search for their dream inn was over. The Hisers left Phoenix, Arizona—where Bill had been teaching for 10 years—and threw himself into the innkeeping business with a determination that has paid off. The setting is idyllic: a woods; apple orchard; dairy barn; fishing pond with bass and blue-gill; and a full barn with chickens, cows, ducks, and turkeys, all set around a 107-year-old country farmhouse on 70 acres of tillable soil.

Inside the house, the seven guest rooms—four upstairs, two downstairs, and one in the basement—are decorated according to different themes. Upstairs, the Amish room has authentic Amish oak furniture and chairs, shaker pegs with Amish clothes and hats hanging from them, and a high oak bed with an Amish handmade quilt. The Southwestern room is decorated with adobe items from Bill's days in Arizona: furniture and pottery, adobe-tile floor, Navajo rug, and Southwestern wallpaper. A third guest room is decorated in classic Victorian style; it has a sleigh bed with a tall cherry headboard, a cherry chest of drawers, and lots of blue and pink color to complement the Victorian wallpaper. The fourth room has a pre-Civil War brass bed and a stenciled wood floor in the traditional Country style. These last two share a bath.

The most luxurious guest room in the inn is downstairs; it has a king-size four-poster bed, a cathedral wood ceiling, a sunken tub for two, a large fireplace, a private deck, a TV/VCR, and a refrigerator. The second downstairs room is smaller and is decorated in the turn-of-the-century Primitive style, with stenciled walls, a wood floor, and simple furniture.

Additionally, there is a large family room, with its own entrance, in the finished basement. This room has two double beds, a twin bed, and a Ben Franklin stovepipe fireplace. Also, the Hisers are converting the carriage house into a deluxe room; it is due to be completed in 1998.

Guests can relax by the fire in the comfortable sitting room that has a TV/VCR and a large bookshelf stacked with books and assorted reading material; or, they can choose the parlor, which also has a large fireplace, and where there is a chest of drawers full of games. The large windows to the east allow for floods of light in the morning, as well as wonderful views of the farm and the surrounding countryside. And not to be missed is the secluded hot tub—just steps from the inn—in the converted chicken coop.

The White Fence is near the Amish country and there is an 18-mile bike trail close by: The Hisers can arrange for a pick-up truck to meet you at the end of the trail. There is also a playground on the premises and children under 6 stay free. On summer weekends, the nearby Mid-Ohio Racetrack hosts race meets—rooms fill up fast, so book well in advance.

🏠 *4 double rooms with baths, 2 doubles share bath, 1 family room that sleeps 5, with bath, ground-floor rooms are accessible for people who use wheelchairs. Ceiling fans, TV/VCR and refrigerator in 1 room, TV/VCR in sitting room, games in parlor, fishing pond. $57–$104, full breakfast. No credit cards. Closed Mar.*

White Oak Inn

29683 Walhonding Rd. (Ohio Rte. 715), Danville, OH 43014, tel. 614/599–6107

The White Oak Inn was built in 1915 from white oak trimmed on the property. It was converted into an inn in 1985 and was bought by current owners Yvonne and Ian Martin in 1992. Tired of the drill of corporate life in Toronto, the Martins threw themselves into their dream with gusto, and the result is an inn of great charm along a two-lane scenic route near Danville, 55 miles northeast of Columbus.

A beveled-glass front door leads into the house, where downstairs you will find a comfortable living room furnished in an eclectic—but thoroughly comfortable—style: sofas, rocking chairs, a large brick fireplace, a square grand piano, and an antique games table. As Yvonne says, "I want people to be able to sit down and relax with their feet on the coffee table." And guests do relax in here, or, if the weather is clement, in a rocker or oak swing on the 50-foot-long front porch.

The 10 guest rooms are divided between the main house and a separate guest house. The seven guest rooms in the main inn are tastefully furnished with antique high beds covered with hand-sewn quilts from the nearby Amish community, ruffled curtains, and fresh flowers. Every room is named after the wood used in its design: the Ash Room, the Cherry Room, the Maple Room, the Oak Room, the White Oak Room, the Poplar Room, and the Walnut Room. The White Oak Room downstairs was once the family dining room and study; it is so big you could literally throw a party in the bathroom, so long as you move the single bed that the Martins have put into it to accommodate groups of three. Originally a chicken barn, the guest house has three comfortable guest rooms: Two have brick wood-burning fireplaces, and one of these and the other have oak-beam cathedral ceilings. One even has a whirlpool tub. They all have oak antiques, and the headboards on the queen-size beds are reproductions of originals that were once in the main house.

Dinner in the inn's dining room, where guests sit at common tables, might include such entrées as apricot peppercorn pork loin, herb-stuffed chicken breast, and penne pasta with Italian sausage and chicken in a jalapeño sauce, followed by a dessert with an indulge-yourself name like chocolate decadence—a chocolate cake with chocolate chunks and chocolate, marshmallow, and pecan frosting, all covered with hot fudge sauce; or you could go for a less threatening peach cobbler.

The Martins host special events throughout the year such as a Naturalist's Weekend and a Country Inn Cooking Class Weekend. Otherwise, the pace is very relaxed. The inn is surrounded by several hundred acres of conservation land and the Amish country is close by as well—that is if you can nudge yourself off of the hammock to go exploring.

▦ *10 double rooms with baths. Air-conditioning, radios, alarms, bicycles, outdoor games, phones and TVs upon request. $75–$130; full breakfast, complimentary soft drinks and fresh-baked cookies. No children under 12. D, MC, V. Minimum 2-day stay during peak season.*

Other Choices

Michael Cahill Bed & Breakfast. 1106 Walnut Blvd., Ashtabula, OH 44004, tel. 216/964–8449. 2 double rooms with baths, 2 doubles share 1½ baths. Air-conditioning, terry-cloth bathrobes in rooms, phone and TV in living room, tennis courts and beach within 2 blocks. $35–$55, full breakfast. No credit cards.

Mulberry Inn Bed and Breakfast. 53 N. 4th St., Martin's Ferry, OH 43935, tel. 614/633–6058. 3 double rooms share 2 baths. Air-conditioning, books, TV/VCR, fireplace in parlor. $40–$60, full breakfast. AE, D, MC, V.

Whitmore House. 3985 Ohio Rte. 47 W, Bellefontaine, OH 43311, tel. 513/592–4290. 2 double rooms and 1 single room share 1 bath. Restaurant, air-conditioning, library, garden, phone in 1 room, TV in library. $35–$50; full breakfast, complimentary evening snacks. No credit cards.

Oklahoma

Montford Inn

Northeastern Oklahoma

Graham-Carroll House

501 N. 16th St., Muskogee, OK 74401, tel. 918/683–0100

Before Oklahoma was made a state, in 1906, Muskogee was far grander than "Tulsey Town" (Tulsa), 50 miles northwest. Muskogee was the center for commerce (cotton and oil) and the government policy headquarters for the five Native American tribes that were moved to Oklahoma from the southeastern United States 100 years previously. Today the old sandstone Agency building in Honor Heights Park houses the Five Civilized Tribes Museum, which exhibits artifacts and art from the Cherokee, Chickasaw, Choctaw, Seminole, and Creek tribes.

Sixteenth Street was once more commonly known as "Silk Stocking Avenue," where Muskogee's most fashionable and venerable citizens lived. Although paint now peels from some homes in this downtown neighborhood, the Graham-Carroll House, an 11-room mansion built with oil money, has been well maintained.

During the two years it took to build the house, the interior was thoroughly embellished. If a surface can be carved, polished, fluted, or scalloped, it is. Rooms with dark moldings and burnished hardwood floors hold carved mahogany furniture and plum upholstery. The sheer ornateness of this 1935 Gothic Victorian causes innkeeper Linda Feickert to assure her guests that they needn't tiptoe around.

Hand-cut marble fashions the foyer floor, and overhead, a chandelier sparkles with ropes of crystal. The Carroll Suite on the second floor is awash with '30s glamour, with green walls and a lavender bathroom; a 6-foot marble whirlpool tub set under stained-glass windows in the Honeymoon Suite overlooks roses and dahlias. Well-tended English gardens entice guests outdoors.

Linda serves breakfast in a glassed-in porch she calls the conservatory, in the light from the stained-glass windows she bought from the First Baptist Church. Her specialties are blueberry pancakes, omelets, and crepes. On weekends she prepares entrées such as Jamaican grilled shrimp, grilled salmon, and Chateaubriand, for an extra charge, for guests and the general public.

🏨 *3 double rooms with baths, 2 suites with whirlpool baths. Air-conditioning, cable TVs, phones, elevator. Lunch for* groups of 6 or more, dinner for 6 or more on weekdays; dinner always available on weekends. *$80–$95, full breakfast. AE, D, DC, MC, V.*

Inn at Woodyard Farms

Rte. 2, Box 190, Pawhuska, OK 74056, tel. 918/287–2699

The Tallgrass Prairie Preserve in Osage County is one of the largest remnants of the bluestem prairie that once stretched from the Gulf Coast through the Midwest. Cattle driven up the Chisholm Trail from Texas once grazed here; now bison nose through the wildflowers. The Inn at Woodyard Farms sits less than 6 miles away, on 75 acres of rolling hills dotted with yellow coreopsis, pale purple coneflowers, and cows ambling under the blackjack oaks. The agenda here, says Carol Maupin (who owns the inn with her sister, Nancy Woodyard), is to have no agenda other than watching the sun come up in a rocking chair on the porch, possibly visiting the sandstone Osage Tribal Museum, and then watching the sun go down from the porch's other side.

Carol can be a bit grand. Nothing ticks her off quite so much as to have someone assume that because she lives in rural Oklahoma, she's a hick. "Honey," she says, "I've taken care of two presidents and a king." She also boasts of her culinary expertise: She was an apprentice to Helen Corbett, who in the 1950s and '60s reigned over the Zodiac Room at Neiman-Marcus in Dallas.

Like Helen, Carol makes food look and taste wonderful and pays no regard to fat and calories (unless requested to do so in advance). Breakfast may be ham steaks, eggs and green-chili grits, or eggs Benedict, and Carol's justly applauded biscuits.

The inn was built in vintage farmhouse style by a local high school carpentry class (Nancy is the school's superintendent) with wide-plank floors, a sand-stone fireplace, and fanlight windows. The interior looks as if Carol refined not only her cooking but her decorating sense at Neiman-Marcus: The chairs are upholstered in lemony florals, the plaid sofas are deep, and the pumpkin-color breakfront holds a collection of majolica tureens, platters, and bowls. The four bedrooms upstairs are fairly small, but everything is top drawer—silky sheets, bright floral bedspreads, antique armoires, and footed bowls holding chocolates. There are stacks of spy thrillers, novels, photography books, and everything Martha Stewart has touched. Only about an eighth of Carol's cookbook collection is on display in the baker's rack in the kitchen: Guests have been known to lug armfuls upstairs (followed by the inn's three cats) to read in bed like novels. A cautionary note: Summer can be searing in Oklahoma, especially on the prairie.

🏠 *4 double rooms with baths. Air-conditioning, TV/VCR in public area. $65, full breakfast. MC, V.*

Other Choices

Candlewyck Inn. 594600 E. 307 La., Grove, OK 74344, tel. 918/647–8221, fax 918/786–3573. 12 suites, 1 cottage. Air-conditioning, fireplaces, whirlpool tubs, balconies and terraces, TVs/VCRs, boat and swimming dock. $99–$275; full breakfast, lunch and dinner available. MC, V.

Jarrett Farm Country Inn. Rte. 1, Box 1480, Ramona, OK 74061, tel. 918/371–9868. 5 suites. Wet bars and kitchens in 2 suites, double whirlpool baths in 3 suites. Air-conditioning, TV/VCRs, swimming pool, outdoor spa, solarium, walking trails on 230-acre horse farm. $125–$185; full breakfast, dinner available. AE, MC, V.

Reservations Service

Oklahoma Bed and Breakfast Association (766 DeBarr, Norman, OK 73069, tel. 800/676–5522; listings only).

Central Oklahoma

Montford Inn

*322 W. Tonhawa, Norman, OK 73069,
tel. 405/321-2200 or 800/321-8969*

When Phyllis and Ron Murray built the Montford Inn in 1994, they intended the sprawling wooden house to have the feel of an early Oklahoma prairie-style farmhouse. But even Oklahoma Territory's most pampered residents didn't have switch-on gas fireplaces, king-size beds, in-room coffee bars, or bathtubs with water jets.

The inn is named for Phyllis's ancestor, Montford Johnson, a Chickasaw cattle rancher who was a chum of Jesse Chisholm. Family heirlooms are everywhere—Johnson's framed license to operate in Indian Territory hangs in the library and a Kiowa headdress, a gift to Johnson, hangs over the stairs. Much of the needlework was done by Ron's Danish grandmother.

Phyllis has a gift for imaginitive juxtaposition: Upstairs, snowy curtains float from curtain rods made from elm and hackberry branches; and a collection of kachina dolls are displayed in a Victorian curio cabinet in the living room, where Oriental rugs mix with Navajo blankets, wingback chairs, and overstuffed sofas piled with pillows.

The inn's east wing has four eclectically furnished rooms, including two with private outdoor hot tubs and decks. Alma Mater pays homage to nearby University of Oklahoma, with a framed letter sweater, pennants, and vintage team photos; other rooms have sunny wicker and an 8-foot walnut headboard.

Upstairs, a Ponderosa pine canopy bed, a lace covered bonnet bed, and English hunting prints are among the varied furnishings. More secluded is the sole guest room on the west wing or two cottage suites with kitchenettes, living rooms, and two-person whirlpool baths.

Breakfast is served around Phyllis's grandmother's walnut dining room table or on tiny tables for two. Tonhawa Smoothies, a blend of yogurt, fruit, and juices, appear daily, along with such dishes as the Montford Sunrise, a savory blend of chilies, eggs, cheese, and grits, garnished with pansies.

🏨 *10 rooms and 2 guest cottages with baths. Cable TVs; guest office with photocopying, fax machines, and modem. $70–$165. AE, D, MC, V.*

Victorian Rose

*415 E. Cleveland, Guthrie OK, 73044,
tel. 405/282-3928 or 800/767-3015*

To say that the Victorian Rose Bed and Breakfast in Guthrie is surrounded by history is no exaggeration: The 1894 Queen Anne–style house sits in the middle of 400 blocks of Victorian storefronts and residences (the largest urban area on the National Register of Historic Places).

The history of Guthrie is more aptly called a saga: The town became the territorial capital in 1889, when a land run opened the area to settlement. It was the most progressive city in the territory—the first to have lights and a Carnegie library—until statehood in 1910, when voters moved the state capital to Oklahoma City. For decades many local business owners and residents were too strapped for cash to properly remodel, so they simply covered things up—much to the delight of 1980s developers and preservationists, who found hundreds of stained-glass windows beneath plywood and original handblown light fixtures hanging above false ceilings.

The Victorian Rose, three blocks from the downtown business district, has its own treasures, like a working gaslight fixture, polished oak floors, and beveled windows. In the evenings, the inn literally glows—owner Foy Shahan makes

Tiffany-style stained-glass lamp shades and dozens of them light the inn, along with candles and oil lamps. Foy also makes the glass kaleidoscopes that rest on the marble-topped table in the parlor.

All three of the inn's guest rooms are on the second floor. The most popular room, Victorian Dream, has a private balcony, a queen-size wrought-iron bed piled high with champagne-colored brocade bed coverings and pillows, and a huge rosy tiled bath with brass fixtures and a dressing table. Guests in the Victorian Promise room use a bath across the hall with a claw-foot tub. This room also has access to a private screened porch outfitted with a reading lamp and ceiling fan. Guests relax, too, on the patio in the side yard, where flowers and herbs bloom around a fountain, or on the wicker porch swing or rockers on the wraparound porch.

As a foil to the carved mahogany and wicker are intriguing works of art, like a local artist's colored pencil drawing of Cavalry soldiers and a Plains Indian scout.

But visual treats aren't the specialty of the house, according to Linda Shahan. "Guests come back for the breakfasts," she says. Linda once got a call from a bed-and-breakfast owner in Kentucky, who said one of her guests, who had stayed at the Victorian Rose, was craving Linda's banana crepes, and could she share the recipe. Also popular are gingerbread waffles, cheese muffins,

and coddled eggs. Says Linda, "My guests leave here and go downtown to the antiques stores to look for antique egg coddlers."

▦ *3 doubles with baths. Air-conditioning, TV/VCRs, turndown service. $69–$79, full breakfast. AE, D, DC, MC, V.*

Other Choices

Arcadian Inn Bed and Breakfast. 328 E. 1st St., Edmond, OK 73034, tel. 405/ 348–6347 or 800/299–6347. 2 double rooms with baths, 3 suites. Air-conditioning, whirlpool bath in 1 suite, fireplace in 1 suite. $65–$120, full breakfast; dinner available. AE, D, MC, V.

Cutting Garden Bed and Breakfast. 927 W. Boyd St., Norman, OK 73069, tel. 405/329–4522. 3 double rooms with baths. Air-conditioning, cable TVs, phones. $55–$75, full breakfast. AE, D, MC, V.

Holmberg House. 766 Debarr St., Norman, OK 73069, tel. 405/321–6221. 4 double rooms with baths. Air-conditioning, cable TV; across street from University of Oklahoma campus. $65–$85, full breakfast. AE, MC, V.

Reservations Service

Oklahoma Bed and Breakfast Association (766 DeBarr, Norman, OK 73069, tel. 800/676–5522; listings only).

Oregon

Williams House

South Coast

Chetco River Inn

21202 High Prairie Rd., Brookings, OR 97415, radio tel. 541/469-8128 or 800/327-2688

By the time you reach the Chetco River Inn, 17 slow miles inland from Brookings along a twisting, single-lane forest service road that runs beside the Chetco River, you'll feel that you have left the busy world far behind. The large, cedar-sided, contemporary inn was designed over the phone by owner Sandra Brugger and the architect, who has never actually visited the property! While it fits well into the rugged surroundings, the inn is thoroughly modern rather than rustic.

Broad covered porches, cross-ventilation windows, and deep-green marble floors keep the inn cool during those occasional hot days of summer, when you can lounge in shaded hammocks, cast a fishing line (the Chetco is just outside the front door), or bob in the river in inner tubes. During the evenings, everyone gathers to talk in the airy, vaulted-ceiling common room furnished with Oriental carpets, leather couch, caned captain's chairs, and Chippendale dining ensemble. A collection of wreaths adorns the walls of the open kitchen at the end of the room.

Upstairs are tall shelves of books and games on the banistered landing leading to the guest rooms. A fishing motif dominates the River View Room, with cedar-paneled ceiling, red-and-black plaid bedspread, wicker furnishings, and a collection of antique creel baskets and duck decoys. The other rooms, which look out on the lush trees surrounding the house, are slightly larger, furnished with Oriental rugs, eclectic antiques, and reproduction brass and iron bedsteads. All rooms have vanity areas and robes. An overflow room that opens onto a private bath can be used by families or a group of friends.

Your best dining option is Sandra's five-course dinners, which are available by advance notice. Featuring fresh local ingredients, the menu might include smoked salmon pâté, orange-carrot soup with Grand Marnier, grilled game hen, and homemade ice cream. It's a good bet that you'll want to skip lunch after indulging in the multicourse breakfast (included in the tariff), but Sandra can also pack a lunch for your outing if you prefer.

If you have a raft or kayak, bring it along to take full advantage of the river. Inflated inner tubes provide another fun mode of transit.

🏨 *4 double rooms with baths. Badminton, darts, horseshoes, swimming holes, nature trails, deep-sea charters or fishing guides by arrangement, fishing packages. $95; full breakfast, afternoon refreshments, lunch and dinner available. MC, V. No smoking, no pets.*

Cliff House

Yaquina John Point, Adahi Rd., Box 436, Waldport, OR 97394, tel. 541/563-2506, fax 541/563-4393

This large, 1930s gable-on-hip-roofed house, perched on Yaquina John Point in the coastal town of Waldport, is perhaps the closest you'll come on the Oregon coast to the Smithsonian's attic, with pieces by Steuben, Lalique, Tiffany, Dresden, and Rosenthal among the amazing abundance of objects here. Elaborate lead-glass chandeliers contrast—not unpleasantly—with knotty pine and cedar paneling, modern skylights, and an enormous river-stone fireplace. Window seats on the banistered, wraparound landing above the living room provide a cozy spot for sitting and taking in the sights, both inside and out. The setting is spectacular, a green headland jutting into the sea, with endless white beaches, shore pines, cliffs, and green surf.

Each of the four guest rooms reflects the romantic whims of owners Gabrielle Duvall and D.J. Novgrod. In the bedrooms, you will find potbellied woodburning stoves; a profusion of fresh-cut flowers; trays of sherry and chocolates; fluffy down comforters; and mounds of pillows on brass, sleigh, or four-poster rice beds. The Bridal Suite, with a positively royal 15th-century French gilt and ice-blue velvet Louis XV bedroom set, and mirrored bathroom with two-person shower and whirlpool tub overlooking the ocean, is by far the most opulent chamber. Terry robes and sandals are supplied for the short trip from your room to the large hot tub or sauna on the broad sundeck overlooking the ocean and the Alsea Bay and bridge.

A run on the beach below or a vigorous game of croquet is a good way to work off the large morning meal, an elegant affair served at the black lacquer table on fine china with silver or gold flatware and plenty of fresh flowers. Gabby is happy to arrange a variety of romantic interludes—including catered dinners, sunset horseback rides, or champagne limousine drives into the nearby mountains.

🏨 *4 double rooms with baths, 1 2-bedroom housekeeping cottage. Phones, cable TV/VCRs, individual heat control, wood-burning stoves in some rooms, Jacuzzi in suite, masseuse available, hot tub, sauna, rental bicycles. $120–$245; full breakfast, catered meals available. MC, V. No smoking, no pets, 2-night minimum on weekends, 3-night minimum on holidays. Limited service Nov.–Mar.*

Johnson House

216 Maple St., Florence, OR 97439, tel. and fax 541/997-8000

Entering Ron and Jayne Fraese's simple Italianate Victorian in Old Town Florence, dating from 1892, you will pass into a different era, accompanied by the sounds of Jack Benny, Fred Allen, and Fibber McGee and Molly emanating from a 1930s Philco radio in the living room. Antique sepia photographs and political cartoons adorn the walls, and vintage hats hang from the entryway coat tree. Furnishings throughout the house date from the 1890s to the mid-1930s, and include marble-top tables and dressers, Queen Anne– and Chippendale-style chairs, walnut armoires, cast-iron beds, and a sprinkling of ornate Victorian pieces.

The guest bedrooms have lace curtains, crocheted doilies, and eyelet-lace-trimmed percale duvet covers on goose-down comforters and pillows. Sadly, the old hardwood floors have been covered over in industrial-brown paint. The best room in the house isn't actually in the house but in the tiny garden cottage, with a claw-foot tub in the sunny bedroom. Although the porch with whitewashed Adirondack chairs out front is billed as private, you'll probably find yourself sharing the porch with a friendly cat or two napping in the sun.

Jayne's green thumb is evident in the delightful gardens surrounding the cottage, producing the fresh herbs, fruits, and edible flowers that garnish her bountiful, beautifully presented breakfasts. Among the more popular main courses she serves are wild mushroom and cheese soufflé, Swedish sour cream waffles with lingonberries, and salmon crepes in mushroom sauce.

The Johnson House is a five- to 10-minute drive from ocean beaches and only a block from the quaint antiques shops, crafts boutiques, and eateries on the bay dock. A bowl of chowder at Mo's on the dock will do for a casual meal, but for seafood in a more refined atmosphere, head to the Windward Inn Restaurant (3757 Hwy. 101 N, tel. 541/997–8243), a few miles to the north. Also nearby are the Sea Lion Caves, Oregon Dunes National Recreation Area, and the strange carnivorous lilies at the Darlingtonia Botanical Wayside.

For those who want to reside smack on the ocean, the Fraeses have a romantic vacation rental 9 miles north on Highway 101. Moonset, a stunning octagonal cedar cabin for two, sits on a high meadow with a spectacular view of the coastline.

▦ *2 double rooms with baths, 3 doubles share 2 baths, 1 cottage suite. Individual heat control, croquet, boccie. $95–$105, full breakfast. D, MC, V. No smoking, no pets. Limited service Dec.–Feb.*

Sea Quest

95354 Hwy. 101, Yachats, OR 97498, tel. 541/547–3782 or 800/341–4878, fax 541/ 547–3719

When Elaine Ireland and George Rozsa bought this contemporary cedar-shingle-and-glass home on a low coastal bluff outside Yachats, they remodeled it to create a romantic seaside retreat. They installed five guest rooms, a lounge, and a rounded entry on the ground floor and a roomy kitchen open to the main living area on the second floor. A round gravel driveway was added to the property, but otherwise the grounds have been left in their natural state, providing a good habitat for the many birds in this area.

Elaine describes the decor as "eclectic, early garage sale," but her treasure trove of fine antique furniture and accent pieces would be the envy of any antiques hound. A pair of wooden skis and a weathered snowshoe hang over the driftwood mantel of the massive fireplace, competing for attention with the intriguing geodes, coral, and polished stones used as accents in the brickwork.

Wall colors coordinate with valances, bed linens, and mounds of pillows on queen-size beds in the guest rooms, each equipped with ocean-view Jacuzzi. Room 2, with twig furnishings and dried flower arrangements, and Room 4, with a telescope and book-filled secretary desk, are particularly popular, but a private entrance also makes Room 1 an appealing choice.

The hosts are friendly and cheerful. Their L-shaped kitchen island becomes a buffet each morning, filled with platters of seasonal fruit, fresh-baked goods, hot entrées such as sautéed apples and sausages, fluffy quiches, and a large bowl of Elaine's homemade granola. You can dine out on the deck or at smartly set tables in the great room, protected from ocean breezes.

Both the deck and the large picture windows inside the house are excellent vantage points from which to experience one of this inn's special attractions: It's not at all surprising to see whales pass by fairly close to shore during their twice-yearly migrations between Baja California and Alaska. Winter (Nov.–Feb.) brings tremendous waves and high tides and presents the most dramatic storm-watching possibilities.

▥ *$125–$245; full breakfast, evening snacks and beverages. D, MC, V. No smoking, no pets, 2-night minimum on weekends, 3-night minimum on holidays.*

Tu Tu Tun Lodge

96550 N. Bank Rogue, Gold Beach, OR 97444, tel. 541/247-6664, fax 541/247-0672

Fine-dining options in the tiny coastal town of Gold Beach are few, but follow the Rogue River 7 miles inland and your culinary prayers will be answered at Tu Tu Tun (pronounced "to toot in") Lodge. Owners Dirk and Laurie Van Zante, an exceptionally friendly young couple, preside over cocktails and hors d'oeuvres as you relax on the piazza, enjoying the breathtakingly beautiful river scenery. Then it's on to a multicourse, fixed-price dinner that often features barbecued Chinook salmon or prime rib accompanied by a superior selection of wines. During the busy high season (May–Oct.), there are only four spaces at the table for nonguests at breakfast and dinner (lunch is for guests only), so reservations are highly recommended.

Tu Tu Tun, named after the peaceful tribe of riverbank-dwelling Indians, is an ideal retreat. Surrounded by an abundance of wildlife dwelling in the old-growth timber and the rugged river, you'll quickly get back in touch with nature. In the evenings, you might sit near the big stone fireplace in the modern, open-beam cedar inn watching

for the pair of bald eagles that fly down over the river at sunset. At "O'dark hundred" (the Van Zantes' expression for daybreak), avid anglers are down at the dock raring to tackle the Rogue's mighty steelhead and salmon.

The two-story wing of riverside guest rooms is motel-like in structure only. Named after favorite fishing holes on the Rogue River, each room features individual artwork and appointments; some have fireplaces, other have outdoor soaking tubs, but all have wonderful river views from a balcony or patio and thoughtful touches such as binoculars for wildlife viewing, fine toiletries, and fresh flowers. The cedar-lined, two-bedroom River House shares the great view and is equipped with a kitchen, as are the spacious suites in the main lodge and the charming, three-bedroom Garden House next to the orchard.

Deeply discounted off-season rates include a breakfast tray of goodies delivered to your room each morning. Storm-watching and steelhead fishing are activities you can enjoy here in the winter.

▥ *16 double rooms with baths, 2 housekeeping suites, 1 2-bedroom housekeeping unit, 1 3-bedroom housekeeping unit. Restaurant, bar, phones, TV in suites, conference facilities, heated lap pool, 4-hole pitch-and-putt, horseshoe court, nature trails, jet-boat tour pickup from dock, guided fishing, complimentary use of fishing gear. $130–$310, breakfast extra; dinner available May–Oct. MC, V. No smoking, no pets. Main lodge and restaurant closed last Sun. in Oct.–last Fri. in Apr.*

Ziggurat

95330 Hwy. 101, Yachats, OR 97498, tel. 541/547-3925

Like some fanciful dream of ancient Babylon, Ziggurat rises out of the tidal grasslands of the Siuslaw River. Seven miles south of Yachats, this terraced, step-pyramid-shaped inn, hand-built with native salt-silvered cedar siding, is without question the most unusual member of Oregon's B&B fraternity. Owner Mary Lou Cavendish soon realized that the interest the pyramid generated would bring a steady stream of visitors and that she and partner Irving Tebor had more than enough room to share, so she opened her amazing home as a bed-and-breakfast after construction was completed in 1987. Come here for the uniqueness of the structure, not for the company of the innkeepers who prefer to leave guests to themselves.

Inside, an eclectic collection of original artwork—from Indonesian *wayang* puppets to Buddhist paintings from Nepal—and specially commissioned wooden furniture complement the house's sleek, ultramodern lines, stainless-steel trim, black carpeting, slatelike tiles, smooth white walls, and tinted triangular windows. On the ground floor, a narrow solarium surrounds two guest suites that share a living room–library, complete with microwave, sink, and refrigerator. The East Room has a modern canopy bed in elm and a sauna in the bathroom. The West Room has a 27-foot-long glass wall, slate tile floor, mirrored ceiling above the bed, and a glass-block shower separating the bedroom from the bathroom. A library nook, living room with grand piano and wood-burning stove, and dining room, kitchen, and bathroom with steam shower share space on the second floor. Forty feet up and tucked under the eaves of the pyramid is another guest room, with two balconies and parallelogram windows overlooking the ocean and the arched bridge that spans the Yachats River. Guests residing here have exclusive use of the steam shower two floors below.

A brisk walk to the beach below the house is a good follow-up to the large breakfast served on one of the two glass-enclosed sunporches. Irv's home-made breads are often the highlight of the morning repast. Ziggurat is within easy reach of the area's many coastal pleasures, including Cape Perpetua, Sea Lion Caves, Strawberry Hill Wayside, and the boutiques and restaurants of tiny Yachats. Those interested in shells should make a stop at the Sea Rose Gift Shop (95478 Hwy. 101, Yachats, tel. 541/547–3005) to see the displays of rare, exotic, and common shells from around the world.

▦ *1 double room with detached bath, 2 suites. Piano, library. $110–$125, full breakfast. No credit cards. No smoking, no pets, 2-night minimum on holidays.*

Other Choices

Coos Bay Manor. 955 S. 5th St., Coos Bay, OR 97420, tel. 541/269–1224. 3 double rooms with baths, 2 doubles share bath. Bicycles. $65–$75, full breakfast. No credit cards. No smoking.

Floras Lake House by the Sea. 92870 Boice Cope Rd., Langlois, OR 97450, tel. and fax 541/348–2573. 4 double rooms with baths. Sauna, windsurfing classes and equipment, boats, bicycles. $95–$130, extended Continental breakfast. D, MC, V. No smoking, no pets. Closed mid-Nov.–mid-Feb.

Home by the Sea. 444 Jackson, Box 606-F, Port Orford, OR 97465, tel. 541/332–2855, fax 541/332–7585. 2 double rooms with baths. Cable TV. $75–$85, full breakfast. MC, V. No smoking, no pets, 2-night minimum on summer weekends.

Kittiwake. 95368 Highway 101, Yachats, OR 97498, tel. 541/547–4470. 3 double rooms with baths. Beach wear and gear, beach trail. $110–$125; full or Continental breakfast, complimentary coffee, tea, and cookies. AE, D, MC, V. No smoking, no pets, 2-night minimum on weekends and holidays.

Lighthouse. 650 Jetty Rd., Box 24, Bandon, OR 97411, tel. 541/347–9316. 4 double rooms with baths. TV in 1 room, cable TV in common area. $90–$110, full breakfast. MC, V. No smoking, no pets. Closed July 4.

Sea Star Guest House. 375 Second St., Bandon, OR 97411, tel. 541/347–9632. 2 double rooms with baths, 2 housekeeping suites. Cable TV. $55–$80, breakfast extra. MC, V. No smoking, no pets.

Serenity. 5985 Yachats River Rd., Yachats, OR 97498, tel. 541/547–3813. 3 suites. Refrigerators, nature trails. $99–$145, full breakfast. MC, V. German and Italian spoken. No smoking, no pets.

Reservations Services

Bed & Breakfast Reservations— Oregon (2321 N.E. 28th Ave., Portland, OR 97212, tel. 503/287–4704 or 800/786–9476). **Northwest Bed and Breakfast** (1067 Hanover Ct. S, Salem, OR 97302, tel. 503/370–9033, fax 503/316–9118).

Southern Oregon, Including Ashland

Jacksonville Inn

175 E. California St., Box 359, Jacksonville, OR 97530, tel. 541/899–1900 or 800/321–9344, fax 541/899–1373

Gold flecks still sparkle in the mortar of the locally made bricks and quarried sandstone used to construct this two-story building in 1863. On the main street of Jacksonville, this historic building has served as a general store, bank, hardware store, office complex, and furniture repair shop. Purchased in 1976 by Jerry and Linda Evans, it is now an inn and dinner house, with a well-deserved reputation for the best wining and dining around.

Of the eight guest rooms on the top floor, the best and largest is the Peter Britt room, with a whirlpool tub, canopy bed, antique desk, and comfy wing chairs. All the rooms have wood trim salvaged from buildings of the same period, and frontier American antiques including bedsteads, dressers, and chairs. Telephones, minifridges, and TVs hidden away in specially constructed armoires that match the period furnishings are standard features. Tall brass-and-oak bedsteads have been lengthened to accommodate queen-size mattresses. Seven of the rooms have been redecorated and now feature cheerful floral wallpapers and linens, upgraded bathroom fixtures, and double-pane windows.

For breakfast, you choose from a gourmet menu; entrées might include a chef's choice omelet, spinach and mushroom *gâteau* in Mornay sauce (scrambled eggs with cream cheese and sherry in a puff-pastry cup), or brioche French toast with maple butter and cinnamon sugar, preceded by fresh-squeezed orange juice and a fruit platter. The dining room is open to inn guests and the general public for breakfast, lunch, dinner, and Sunday brunch. There's also a quiet bar–lounge and a bistro in the basement that features a lighter and less formal menu.

A one-room wood-frame cottage two blocks away is another part of the inn's growing choice of accommodations. With a canopy pencil-post bed across from a marble fireplace, wet bar, stocked kitchenette, and whirlpool tub and sauna shower in the spacious bathroom, it is a romantic little hideaway. The cottage proved so popular that two more cottages were added in 1996 to meet demand. Ashland and its Oregon Shakespeare Festival activities are about 20 minutes away by car.

🏠 *8 double rooms with baths, 3 housekeeping cottages. Restaurant, bar, air-conditioning, phones, TVs, kitchenette and whirlpool tub in 1 cottage, wine shop, conference facilities, bicycles. $90–$225, full breakfast. AE, D, DC, MC, V. No smoking.*

Winchester Country Inn

35 S. 2nd St., Ashland, OR 97520, tel. 541/488-1113 or 800/972-4991, fax 541/ 488-4604

Of the many Victorian bed-and-breakfasts in Ashland, this 1886 Queen Anne is the only one with a restaurant, and it's the closest to the Shakespeare Festival theaters as well. Painstakingly renovated by Michael and Laurie Gibbs during the early 1980s and listed on the National Register of Historic Places, the Winchester has established a reputation as one of the finer dining spots in Ashland. Open to the public for dinner and Sunday brunch, it offers a seasonal menu plus favorites such as French Vietnamese *teng dah* beef (broiled fillet marinated in a lemon-peppercorn sauce) and duck with caramelized brandy sauce and seasonal fruits. The outstanding food makes up for the fact that the small guest sitting room just beyond the gift shop is almost entirely overshadowed by the restaurant.

The decor of the guest chambers maintains the period style of the house without the Victorian clutter. A mixture of American Colonial reproductions and antiques, as well as Rococo Revival and Eastlake reproductions, including tall mirrored wardrobes and brass-and-iron or heavy, carved wooden bedsteads, add distinction, while contemporary cushioned chairs and wall-to-wall carpeting make it comfortable. There are many nice touches in the main house, such as a hand-painted porcelain sink set into an antique dresser, which serves as a vanity in the bedrooms, and scented salts in the attached bathroom for luxurious soaking in the deep claw-foot tub. A crystal decanter of sherry and sinfully rich truffles on a tray on the dresser make a late-night snack irresistible.

Favorite rooms include the Sylvan Room, in sunny shades of peach, and the creamy blue Garden Room, both of which have delightful bay sitting areas overlooking the terraced gardens. The Sunset Room has its own balcony view of the treetops of downtown Ashland. Rooms at the basement level have garden patios or small decks as compensation. The private cottage has two beautiful luxury suites, and the Victorian and its carriage house next door have a large guest library, four more suites, and five double rooms (one of which is accessible to wheelchair users), to add to Winchester's array of accommodations.

In winter and spring, the Gibbses offer a variety of special packages, from murder-mystery weekends to a popular Dickens Christmas Festival tie-in.

▦ *12 double rooms with baths, 6 suites. Restaurant, air-conditioning, fireplaces, phones, TV, VCR, and stereo in suites, whirlpool tubs, library, gift shop. $95–$180; full breakfast, late-night snacks. AE, D, MC, V. No smoking, no pets.*

Other Choices

Antique Rose Inn. 91 Gresham St., Ashland, OR 97520, tel. 541/482-6285. 3 double rooms with baths, 1 2-bedroom housekeeping cottage. Fireplace in 1 room; fireplace, whirlpool tub, sauna, and kitchen in cottage. $109–$159; full breakfast, afternoon refreshments. AE, MC, V. No smoking, no pets, 2-night minimum weekends June–Sept. and holidays.

Arden Forest Inn. 261 W. Hersey St., Ashland, OR 97520, tel. 541/488-1496 or 800/460-3912. 4 double rooms with baths, 1 2-bedroom suite. Air-conditioning, horseshoe court. $78–$85, Continental breakfast. AE, MC, V. No smoking, no pets.

Bayberry Inn Bed and Breakfast. 438 N. Main St., Ashland, OR 97520, tel. 541/488-1252. 5 double rooms with baths. Air-conditioning. $100; full breakfast, afternoon refreshments. MC, V. No smoking, no pets.

Chanticleer Inn. 120 Gresham St., Ashland, OR 97520, tel. and fax 541/482–1919 or 800/898–1950. 6 double rooms with baths. Phones, individual climate control, stocked refrigerator in kitchen. $125–$165; full breakfast, evening refreshments. AE, MC, V. No smoking, no pets, 2-night minimum on weekends June–Sept.

Chriswood Inn. 220 N.W. "A" St., Grants Pass, OR 97526, tel. 541/474–9733 or 800/457–9733. 3 double rooms share 2 baths. Air-conditioning, vanity sinks, robes, cable TV, conference facilities. $55–$70, full breakfast. No credit cards. No smoking, no pets.

Country Willows Bed and Breakfast Inn. 1313 Clay St., Ashland, OR 97520, tel. 541/488–1590 or 800/945–5697, fax 541/488–1611. 5 double rooms with baths, 3 housekeeping suites, 1 2-bedroom housekeeping cottage. Air-conditioning, robes, TV, VCR, video library, gift shop, pool, hot tub, mountain and street bikes. $90–$175; full breakfast, evening refreshments. AE, MC, V. No smoking, no pets.

Flery Manor. 2000 Jumpoff Joe Creek Rd., Grants Pass, OR 97526, tel. 541/476–3591, fax 541/371–2303. 2 double rooms with baths, 1 suite, 1 room without bath available as an extra room. Air-conditioning, nature trails, croquet, horseshoes. $75–$125; full breakfast, afternoon refreshments. MC, V. No smoking, no pets.

Lithia Springs Inn. 2165 W. Jackson Rd., Ashland, OR 97520, tel. 541/482–7128 or 800/482–7128, fax 541/488–1645. 5 double rooms with baths, 9 suites. Fireplace, wet bar, mini-refrigerator, CD-player in suites, 2-person whirlpool tub in suites and 2 rooms, bicycles, bicycle storage, bicycle trail. $75–$135, Continental breakfast. AE, MC, V. No smoking, no pets, 2-night minimum on weekends.

Morical House Garden Inn. 668 N. Main St., Ashland, OR 97520, tel. 541/482–2254. 5 double rooms with baths, 2 housekeeping suites. Air-conditioning,

phones, badminton, croquet. $103–$150; full breakfast, afternoon refreshments. MC, V. No smoking, no pets, 2-night minimum on weekends Mar.–Oct.

Mt. Ashland Inn. 505 Mt. Ashland Rd., Box 944, Ashland, OR 97520, tel. and fax 541/482–8707 or tel. 800/830–8707. 2 double rooms with baths, 3 suites. Whirlpool tub and fireplace in 2 suites, TV, VCR, and wet bar in meeting room, ski storage room, snowshoes, sleds, mountain bikes, cross-country skis. $100–$170, full breakfast. AE, D, MC, V. No smoking, no pets, 2-night minimum on weekends June–Sept. and holidays.

Peerless Hotel. 243 Fourth St., Ashland, OR 97520, tel. 541/488–1082. 4 double rooms with baths, 2 suites. Air-conditioning, phones, TV on request, whirlpool baths in 2 rooms, health club access, after-theater shuttle. $95–$175; Continental breakfast, evening refreshments. AE, MC, V. No smoking, no pets.

Pine Meadow Inn. 1000 Crow Rd., Merlin, OR 97532, tel. and fax 541/471–6277 or tel. 800/554–0806. 4 double rooms with baths. Turndown service. $80–$110; full breakfast, afternoon refreshments. No credit cards. No smoking, no pets.

Romeo Inn. 295 Idaho St., Ashland, OR 97520, tel. 541/488–0884 or 800/915–8899, fax 541/488–0817. 4 double rooms with baths, 1 suite, 1 housekeeping suite. Air-conditioning, phones, piano, library, pool, hot tub. $120–$180; full breakfast, afternoon refreshments, bedtime treats. MC, V. No smoking, no pets, 2-night minimum June–Oct. and weekends Mar.–Oct.

Touvelle House. 455 N. Oregon St., Box 1891, Jacksonville, OR 97530, tel. 541/899–8938, fax 541/899–3992. 3 double rooms with baths, 2 suites. Whirlpool bath in 1 suite, cable TV in library, conference facilities, pool, hot tub, bicycles. $80–$155, full breakfast. No credit cards. No smoking, no pets.

Willowbrook Inn Bed and Breakfast. 628 Foots Creek Rd., Gold Hill,

OR 97525, tel. 541/582–0075. 2 double rooms with baths, 1 suite. Air-conditioning, pool, hot tub. $60–$70, full breakfast. MC, V. No smoking, no pets.

Wolf Creek Tavern. 100 Front St., Box 97, Wolf Creek, OR 97497, tel. 541/866–2474. 8 double rooms with baths. Restaurant, air-conditioning, gift shop, conference facilities. $55–$75, Continental breakfast extra. D, MC, V. Closed 2 weeks in Jan.

Woods House. 333 N. Main St., Ashland, OR 97520, tel. 541/488–1598 or 800/435–8260, fax 541/482–8027. 6 double rooms with baths. Air-conditioning. $100–$115; full breakfast, afternoon refreshments. MC, V. No smoking, no pets, 2-night minimum June–Oct.

Reservations Services

Ashland's B&B Clearinghouse (Box 1376, Ashland, OR 97520, tel. 541/488–0338). **Ashland's B&B Reservation Network** (Box 1051, Ashland, OR 97520, tel. 541/482–BEDS or 800/944–0329). **Ashland/Jacksonville Reservations** (tel. 800/983–4667). **Bed & Breakfast Reservations—Oregon** (2321 N.E. 28th Ave., Portland, OR 97212, tel. 503/287–4704 or 800/786–9476). **Northwest Bed and Breakfast** (1067 Hanover Ct. S, Salem, OR 97302, tel. 503/370–9033, fax 503/316–9118).

Willamette Valley, Including Eugene

Campbell House

252 Pearl St., Eugene, OR 97401. tel. 541/343–1119 or 800/264–2519, fax 541/343–2258

For years you could only see the chimney of this 1892 mansion, which once belonged to a timber baron. Shrubs, trees, and Oregon's ubiquitous blackberry vines obscured the rest of the vacant 8,000-square-foot Queen Anne Victorian. But now Campbell House shines on a hill just above Eugene's bustling downtown. Within blocks are brew pubs, fine cafés, urban markets with smart shops, and the Hult Center of the Performing Arts.

Innkeepers Myra and Roger Plant first saw the house on a bike ride. It was years, however, before they could convince the heirs of the original owner to sell; and then came months of remodeling. They remade the place from the inside out, adding new oak floors, brass fittings, and turn-of-the-century–style mouldings. The dining room and the library were refurbished and the delightful corner sinks in each bathroom saved.

A long drive brings you past green grounds dotted with rhododendrons, to the entrance, at the back of the house. The back patio and gazebo, where complimentary local wine is served in the afternoon, is lined with hanging, flowering plants. It's a lovely spot, although the scene deserves better than the white plastic lawn furniture provided.

The guest rooms, though, make you quickly forget about lawn furniture. Each of the 14 rooms is unique, although most have a vaguely English Country look. The best suite is the Dr. Eva Johnson, named after a Campbell family member who became one of Eugene's first female doctors. The view of the city and the Cascade Mountain foothills is inspiring and the whirlpool tub built for two, romantic. Original oak floors, high ceilings, and gentle colors—evergreen, melon, and beige—complete the portrait of turn-of-the-century elegance. The finest view is from the small, burgundy and gray Three Sisters. Facing east, you get startling morning light and a superb view of the trio of Cascade peaks called the Three Sisters, all over 10,000 feet high.

One drawback of the Campbell House is its proximity to the train tracks, which are a few blocks downhill.

Evenings can be a bit noisy, but the Plants provide colorful earplugs.

Mornings begin with coffee on a tray outside your room and evolve into a full meal downstairs. Favorite entrées include Belgian waffles and crustless quiches. If possible, sit in the sunny library overlooking town.

▦ *14 double rooms with baths. Phones, modem lines, TV/VCRs, fax and photocopying machines, conference facilities. $65–$235, full breakfast. AE, MC, V. No smoking, no pets.*

Hanson Country Inn

795 S.W. Hanson St., Corvallis, OR 97333, tel. 541/752–2919

In 1928 Jeff Hanson built this rotund Dutch Colonial on a high knoll overlooking the rolling Willamette Valley as the headquarters for his prospering poultry-breeding ranch. Here, in the egg house opposite the main house, he developed his world-famous strain of White Leghorn chickens. After Hanson died, the house stood empty for 13 years. In 1987 it was purchased by Patricia Covey, a friendly Californian looking for escape from the Bay area, who had seen Corvallis listed in Best Cities to Live in in America. With plenty of polish and elbow grease, Patricia was able to restore the original grandeur of the house's unique features, including the carefully laid honeycomb tile work in the bathrooms and the intricately carved spindle room divider and sweeping spindle staircase, both made of New Zealand gumwood carved by local craftsmen.

A baby grand piano, 1920s American furniture, assorted sculptures, and a selection of Patricia's own paintings bring understated elegance to the great living room with its massive central fireplace. Sun pours through tall windowpanes, brightening the cozy reading nook where a plump easy chair sits beside floor-to-ceiling bookcases. The sunporch, with sparkling stained-glass windows and casual rattan furniture, looks onto a terraced garden with a stone fountain and a white vine arbor.

The suite, in shades of peach and seafoam green, has a lovingly polished four-poster bed, an attached sitting room, and a private veranda overlooking a gentle slope to the valley below. The largest double room, a favorite of wedding couples because of its romantic box-canopy bed, has a sitting alcove and windows on three of its sides—providing views of the valley, the terraced garden, and the quiet pasture behind the house. All rooms are appointed with 1920s American furniture and soft bed linens imported from England. The two-bedroom cottage with hardwood floors, iron bedsteads, and down comforters is perfect for families needing space and privacy.

You can get acquainted with resident cats, chickens, and sheep, explore the unrestored egg house, or take walks in the gardens and orchards on the 5-acre grounds. Wine tasting at nearby vineyards or a visit to Oregon State University's Horner Museum are other entertainment possibilities.

▦ *1 double room with bath, 2 doubles share bath, 1 suite, 1 2-bedroom housekeeping cottage. Phone and cable TV in 2 rooms. $65–$125, full breakfast. AE, D, DC, MC, V. No smoking, no pets.*

Oval Door Bed and Breakfast

988 Lawrence St., Eugene, OR 97401, tel. 541/683–3160 or 800/882–3160 , fax 541/485–5339

This 2½-story, pitch-roofed house with a wraparound porch was built in 1990 but matches the surrounding homes from the '20s and '30s in this centrally located, older neighborhood near the University of Oregon and the Hult Center for the Performing Arts in Eugene. A whimsical purple door hints at the unconventional things to come.

Inside, a collection of modern art by Pacific Northwest artists is a counterpoint to centuries-old antiques and comfortable, modern American furniture. The dining room has an 1860 Eastlake walnut dining table and floral prints filling one wall; another wall has glass doors that open onto a broad wraparound porch with cushioned chairs and a swing for resting beneath the rustling leaves of the shade trees.

Guest rooms are furnished with a mixture of contemporary and antique pieces; an open steamer trunk that serves as a dresser in one room is especially striking. Extra touches include Perrier and water glasses on doily-covered trays, fresh and dried flower arrangements, candles and books of poetry, a choice of pillows (down, poly, or orthopedic), thick terry robes, and a selection of current paperbacks that you are free to take when you leave. The cozy, two-person whirlpool tub room is adorned with candles, flower arrangements, mirrors, a stereo, and a selection of scented bath salts and oils. The heated towel rack is a rare joy to find in the United States.

Hostess Judith McLane dropped out of the California corporate fast lane to run the inn. She uses a large tile set on the dining room buffet as a blackboard to announce the breakfast menu of the day; her specialties include Popeye's Morning (creamed spinach) and Idaho Sunrise (a twice-baked potato stuffed with a poached egg).

▦ *4 double rooms with baths. Phones, ceiling fans, individual heat control. $70–$93, full breakfast. AE, MC, V. No smoking, no pets.*

Steamboat Inn

Steamboat, OR 97447, tel. and fax 541/498–2411 or tel. 800/840–8825

Deep in the Umpqua National Forest, 38 winding miles east of Roseburg, this 1955 river-rock and pine lodge sits alongside the luminous blue North Umpqua River. Fisherfolk from around the globe come here to test their skills against the elusive steelhead and trout. Owners Jim and Sharon Van Loan were themselves frequent visitors and worked as members of the inn's summer crew for three years before buying it in 1975.

While its fishing tradition is still much in evidence—rehabilitated fly-tying cabinets serving as the reception desk and an unobtrusive fly shop—the Steamboat has seen a shift toward a more refined country inn. The rough edges of this fishing camp have been delicately hewn down with coordinated pastel bedding, draperies, and carpets, as well as thoughtful decorative touches of dried flowers, botanical prints, and hand-quilted comforters in the refurbished riverside cabins. Knotty pine paneling and rustic Americana furnishings in the guest rooms echo the decor of the main lodge.

Recent additions to the property include two detached suites along the river and five roomy, lofted chalets a half-mile up the road. A king-size bed in the master bedroom, twin beds in the loft, a fireplace in the living room, deep-soaking tub in the roomy bathroom, and a kitchenette stocked with dishes and cookware make the chalets perfect for families or small groups. The riverside suites offer intimate seclusion, with large wood-burning fireplaces, two-person Japanese-style soaking tubs, and large private decks looking onto the river.

The Steamboat's famous candlelit "fisherman's dinner" might include Northwest wines, salad spiced with roasted local nuts or garden-fresh herbs, fresh bread, a vegetable dish, and roasted lamb or fresh spring salmon steamed, poached, or grilled. Wine-tasting dinners are available on winter weekends.

Nonfishing activities in the area include backpacking and hiking on the trails of the surrounding Umpqua National Forest, soaking in swimming holes, picking wildflowers, or making a day trip to cross-country ski at Diamond Lake or to admire the breathtaking, crystal-blue waters of Crater Lake.

🏠 *8 cabins with baths, 2 suites, 5 2-bedroom housekeeping cottages. Air-conditioning, library, conference facilities. $95–$225, breakfast extra; dinner available. MC, V. No smoking. Closed Jan.–Feb.*

Westfir Lodge

47365 1st St., Westfir, OR 97492, tel. 541/782–3103

Anchoring the tiny community of Westfir, just west of the crest of the Cascade Mountains, Westfir Lodge was long the hub of activity in the town, which had a population of several thousand in its heyday a half-century ago. However, you can't tell by looking at the two-story clapboard Arts and Crafts–style building that it was formerly the main office of the Westfir Lumber Company.

Gerry Chamberlain and Ken Symons, who bought the building in 1990 after a search across six states for a suitable place to open a B&B, added bathrooms to the building and converted the offices, which ring the first floor, into bedrooms. Over the years, four additional guest rooms were added on the second floor. The large central space became a living area, kitchen, and formal dining room. Antiques—some family heirlooms, others procured in Southeast Asia, and some purchased at local estate auctions—as well as heavy formal drapes on the windows and a wood-burning stove create a kitschy English country ambience in the public spaces.

The 10-foot ceilings almost make the accommodations seem spacious. Two adjoining bedrooms on the north side of the lodge have views of the woodpile, trees, and a neighbor's home, and are quieter than those on the east side, which face a road traveled by logging trucks that often leave town before daylight; in addition, the many logging trains that whistle past Westfir can be heard from here. However, the Willamette River is just across the road from the lodge, and if you're a sound sleeper, the river views and larger room size are inducements to opt for the accommodations on the east side of the building.

Full English breakfasts are offered, a result of the fact that Ken hails from Australia. He gets English bangers at a butcher shop in Portland, three hours to the north, and serves the traditional British sausage with fried potatoes, eggs, and a broiled half-tomato topped with cheese, mushrooms, and bits of vegetables. Accompaniments include scones, other English breakfast breads, and Australian biscuits, as well as fresh fruit. You can eat on the patio looking out at pink hedge roses, daisies, poppies, and varied annuals; the garden also offers a view of the recently renovated, 180-foot-long Office Bridge, the longest covered bridge in Oregon.

🏠 *7 double rooms with baths. Reception facilities, nearby kennel for pets. $65, full breakfast. No credit cards. No smoking, no pets.*

Other Choices

Apple Inn Bed & Breakfast. 30697 Kenady La., Cottage Grove, OR 97424, tel. 541/942–2393 or 800/942–2393. 2 double rooms with baths. TVs; hot tub, RV parking. $65–$75; full breakfast, afternoon snacks. No credit cards. No smoking, no pets.

Beckley House. 338 S.E. 2nd St., Oakland, OR 97462, tel. 541/459–9320. 2 double rooms share bath, 1 suite. Horse and carriage rides. $65–$80, full breakfast. No credit cards. No smoking, no pets.

Eagle Rock Lodge. 49198 McKenzie Hwy., Vida, OR 97488, tel. 541/822–396. 2 double rooms with baths, 6 suites. Masseuse available, conference facilities, guided trips. $85–$109; full breakfast, dinner and catering available. AE, DC, MC, V. No smoking, no pets.

House of Hunter. 813 S.E. Kane, Roseburg, OR 97470, tel. 541/672–2335 or 800/540–7704. 2 double rooms with baths, 2 doubles with basins share bath, 1 2-bedroom suite. Air-conditioning, TV/VCR in living room, video library, laundry facilities. $50–$75, full breakfast. MC, V. No smoking, no pets.

McGillivray's Log Home Bed and Breakfast. 88680 Evers Rd., Elmira, OR 97437, tel. 541/935–3564. 2 double rooms with baths. Air-conditioning. $60–$70, full breakfast. MC, V. No smoking, no pets.

Reservations Services

Bed and Breakfast Innkeepers (711 W. 11th Ave., Eugene, OR 97202, tel. 541/345–7799). **Bed and Breakfast Reservations—Oregon** (2321 N.E. 28th Ave., Portland, OR 97212, tel. 503/287–4704). **Country Host Registry** (901 N.W. Chadwick La., Myrtle Creek, OR 97457, tel. 541/863–5168). **Northwest Bed and Breakfast** (610 S.W. Broadway, Suite 606, Portland, OR 97205, tel. 503/243–7616).

Wine Country, Including Salem

Flying M Ranch

23029 N.W. Flying M Rd., Yamhill, OR 97148, tel. 503/662–3222, fax 503/662–3202

The mysterious red "M" signs begin in downtown Yamhill—a somnolent town of 700 or so in the very press of the wine country—and continue west for 10 miles into the Chehalem Valley, in the rugged foothills of the Coast Range. Following them alertly will bring you to the 625-acre Flying M Ranch, perched above the Yamhill River.

The centerpiece of this rough-and-ready, Wild West–flavored amalgam of motel, campground, dude ranch, timber camp, and working ranch is the great log lodge, decorated in a style best described as Paul Bunyan Eclectic and featuring a bar carved from a single, 6-ton tree trunk. On weekends, this is *the* happening place; the adjoining restaurant serves thick steaks and prime rib, and there are even a few fish dishes on the menu now. Sensitive souls may notice the accusing eyes of dozens of taxidermied trophies watching while they eat.

You have a choice of eight secluded cabins and 28 motel units. (Ask about special packages: The Retreat package includes dinner for two with wine, wine and fruit in the room, a full breakfast, and horseback riding.) The motel is modern and clean, but lacks personality. The cabins, a better choice, are equipped with kitchens, living rooms, wood-burning stoves, and decks overlooking the river. All are spacious, and evoke a rustic, log-cabin charm. The cozy Honeymoon Cabin has a huge stone-and-brick fireplace and a double whirlpool tub. The two-story Wortman Cabin sleeps up to 10 and has the newest furnishings.

Be sure to book ahead for a longtime Flying M specialty, the Steak Fry Ride. Participants ride a tractor-drawn hay wagon to the ranch's secluded creekside elk camp for a barbecued steak dinner with all the trimmings, including a crooning cowboy. The more adventuresome can ride horses from the ranch's stables, one of the Flying M's many countrified amenities. There are horseshoe pits, a big swimming hole, and good fly-fishing. As if this weren't enough, the wineries are a half-hour drive away over backcountry gravel roads. Be sure to make it back by dusk, because finding the Flying M in the dark can be a real challenge.

▦ *28 double rooms with baths, 1 suite, 5 housekeeping cabins, 1 2-bedroom housekeeping cabin. Restaurant, bar,*

TV in 2 cabins, live entertainment, conference and catering facilities, swimming hole, tennis court, fishing, hiking trails, horseback riding, horseshoe pits, campsites, airfield. $60–$200, breakfast extra. AE, D, DC, MC, V. Closed Dec. 24–25.

Mattey House

10221 N.E. Mattey La., McMinnville, OR 97128, tel. 503/434-5058

Mattey House is a sprawling Queen Anne mansion nestled behind its own little vineyard a few miles north of McMinnville. Its tasteful, distinctively western Victorian ambience and its experienced hosts make Mattey House the area's most consummate B&B.

The house itself was built in 1892 by Joseph Mattey, a prosperous local butcher and cattle rancher. Jack and Denise Seed, originally from England, bought it in 1993 and have lavished considerable time and expense on the guest rooms, public areas, and grounds. Their affable English sheepdog, Emma, is happy to show you around.

To wine-country visitors tuckered out by a long day's slurping, Mattey House is an oasis of welcoming warmth. Entering the living room, which is framed by Ionic columns and fretwork, you'll find a beckoning fire in the old carved-wood-and-tile hearth, soothing classical music on the compact-disc player, reproduction William Morris wallpaper, and a cheerful mix of period furnishings and more informal modern pieces, such as deep, comfy couches and wicker tables. There's a porch swing overlooking the vineyard and 10 acres of largely unlandscaped grounds for those in a strolling mood.

Upstairs are the four guest rooms, all named for locally grown varieties of grapes. The Chardonnay Room, with its tall windows and crisp white decor, is bright and sunny; so is the Blanc de Blancs Room, with white wicker, antique brass bed, and soothingly pas-

toral artwork. Chardonnay has a connecting door to the burgundy-hued Pinot Noir Room; it's possible to reserve them as a two-couple suite. These three rooms share two baths, but the Seeds have approval to add two more, so each may have a private bath by 1997. All bathrooms come with wine-glycerine soaps. The Riesling Room, with a private bath, is furnished with an antique pine dresser and a 6-foot-long claw-foot tub. Beds are covered with homemade quilts and a mint is placed on your pillow at turndown.

The Seeds fortify you before launching you on a morning's wine touring. Breakfast features fresh local fruit—perhaps a baked apple or peach in raspberry sauce—followed by fresh-baked scones and the house specialty, an Italian-style frittata, or Dutch apple pancakes. At the end of your tour, you are rewarded with hors d'oeuvres and one last cheering glass of the Oregonian grape.

🏠 *1 double room with bath, 3 doubles share 2 baths. Robes, clocks. $70–$85; full breakfast, afternoon refreshments. MC, V. No smoking, no pets, 3-night minimum during Pinot Noir Festival (late July) and holiday weekends.*

Steiger Haus

360 Wilson St., McMinnville, OR 97128, tel. 503/472-0821 or 503/472-0238

"Zsa Zsa Gabor slapped here," proclaims the plaque in Steiger Haus's hallway, covered with hundreds of pictures of guests. Well, actually it says "slept." These little mementos aren't just there for show; they're an illustration of the genuine affection innkeepers Susan and Dale DuRette, who purchased the property in 1996, feel for their guests. After a weekend at Steiger Haus, you feel like family.

On a quiet residential street near downtown McMinnville, the modern, cedar-sided structure was built in 1984 as a B&B. Linfield College, the site of

Oregon's annual International Pinot Noir Celebration, is just across the creek at the back of the property.

Steiger Haus is a warm, homey sort of place, thanks largely to Susan's affinity for sewing. Many of the inn's colorful quilts and place mats were created in her cedar-walled solarium-studio. The inn's public areas have a country-contemporary charm. On the main level are an open kitchen with breakfast bar, brick fireplace, an antique deacon's bench, and oak dining suite with Windsor-style chairs built by an Oregon craftsman. There are comfortable, modern TV rooms upstairs and downstairs. In summer and fall, most of the action shifts outdoors to the inn's four decks and parklike, oak-shaded grounds.

Steiger Haus's five unfussy guest rooms are cool, and contemporary, enlivened with dried floral arrangements, fresh paint, and sunlight. (Two of them can be linked to form a suite.) Handmade quilts in many of the rooms provide a warming touch. The downstairs room, which opens onto one of the decks, has a brick fireplace, a small, cozy sitting area, and a large private bath. The Treetop Room upstairs features a mission-style pine slat bed, tall windows, and a huge skylighted bath. An adjacent room is equipped with two single beds and a delicately carved oak armoire.

Breakfast, served between 8 and 9 AM, is a hearty affair; Susan garners particularly rave reviews for her fresh-fruit crepes.

▥ *5 double rooms with baths. Fireplace in 1 room, cable TV/VCR, phone on each floor, conference facilities, bicycle storage, horseshoe pit. $75–$110, full breakfast. MC, V. No smoking, no pets, 2-night minimum during college events and holiday weekends.*

Youngberg Hill Vineyard

10660 Youngberg Hill Rd., McMinnville, OR 97128, tel. 503/472–2727, fax 503/472–1313

Like ghostly twilight sentinels, the deer come down to greet you at Youngberg Hill Farm. They have free run of this 700-acre estate, high in the hills west of McMinnville. Well, nearly free run—you must remember to close the gate of the deer fence that surrounds the house itself and its 10 acres of young Pinot Noir vines, a favorite midnight snack for these graceful stags.

This rural bed-and-breakfast, owned by Martin Wright (originally from Britain) and his wife, Jane (originally from South Africa), is a monster-size replica of a classic American farmhouse commanding breathtaking views over mountain and valley from atop a steep-sided hill. Early spring evenings at Youngberg Hill, a working farm and vineyard, means dozens of tiny white-faced lambs wobbling through the lush pastureland on knobby knees. These are watched keenly by the Wright's young sons, Richard and Michael, who also appreciate having playmates visit (children over six are welcome here).

Youngberg Hill is a comfortable place that has a proper, lived-in warmth. The common areas are spacious, modern, and high-ceilinged, with Victorian belly-band molding and bull's-eye corners. The furnishings are largely golden oak period reproductions; the sitting room's deep sofa and settee, upholstered in an unusual grapevine-patterned chintz, are a welcoming touch, as are the suede-covered armchairs and wood-burning stove. Big windows make the most of the hilltop estate's romantic views. The five guest rooms are small to medium in size; furnished with golden oak and Victorian Cottage reproductions, they have a cozy modern ambience. Fresh flowers in the room and truffles on the pillow add a touch of romance.

Guests rave about Jane's breakfasts. Her specialties—scrambled egg in puff pastry with crab fondue or eggs Benedict, preceded by freshly baked muffins or bread and a fruit course—keep tummies full and happy well into an active day. Among the inn's special attractions are a nicely stocked, reasonably priced wine cellar, including older vintages and small high-quality producers.

🏠 *5 double rooms with baths. Air-conditioning, fireplace in 2 rooms, conference and wedding facilities. $120; full breakfast, afternoon refreshments. MC, V. No smoking, no pets, no children under 6, 2-night minimum over holidays.*

Other Choices

Kelty Estate. 675 Hwy. 99W, Lafayette, OR 97127, tel. 503/864–3740 or 800/867–3740. 2 double rooms with baths. Cable TV in living room, billiards table, coin laundry. $65–$75, full breakfast. No credit cards. No smoking, no pets.

Main Street Bed & Breakfast. 1803 Main St., Forest Grove, OR 97116, tel. 503/357–9812, fax 503/359–0860. 3 double rooms share bath. Phones. $55–$65; full breakfast, afternoon refreshments. AE, MC, V. No smoking, no pets.

Marquee House. 333 Wyatt Ct. N.E., Salem, OR 97301, tel. 503/391–0837 or 800/949–0837. 3 doubles with baths, 2 doubles share bath. TV, VCR, and video collection in living room. $55–$90, full breakfast. MC, V. No smoking, no pets, 2-night minimum during holidays and university events.

Orchard View Inn. 16540 N.W. Orchard View Rd., McMinnville, OR 97128, tel. 503/472–0165. 2 double rooms with baths, 2 doubles share bath. Laundry facilities. $70–$80, full breakfast. MC, V. No smoking, no pets, 3-night minimum during Pinot Noir Celebration (late July).

Partridge Farm. 4300 E. Portland Rd., Newberg, OR 97132, tel. 503/538–2050. 1 double room with bath, 2 suites. TV/VCR in library, nearby kennel for pets. $80–$100, full breakfast. MC, V. No smoking, no pets.

Springbrook Hazelnut Farm. 30295 N. Hwy. 99W, Newberg, OR 97132, tel. 503/538–4606 or 800/793–8528. 4 double rooms share 2 baths, carriage-house with bath and kitchen. TV in parlor, library, tennis court, pool, trout pond. $90–$135. No credit cards. No smoking, no pets. Carriage house open year-round, main inn closed Nov.-Mar.

State House. 2146 State St., Salem, OR 97301, tel. 503/588–1340 or 800/800–6712, fax 503/585–8812. 2 double rooms share bath, 2 housekeeping suites. Air-conditioning, phones, TV in suites, TV in common room. $50–$70, full breakfast. D, MC, V. No smoking, no pets, 2-night minimum during university graduation in May.

Reservations Services

Bed & Breakfast Reservations—Oregon (2321 N.E. 28th Ave., Portland, OR 97212, tel. 503/287–4704 or 800/786–9476). **Northwest Bed and Breakfast** (1067 Hanover Ct. S, Salem, OR 97302, tel. 503/370–9033, fax 503/316–9118).

Portland

Heron Haus

2545 N.W. Westover Rd., Portland, OR 97210, tel. 503/274–1846, fax 503/248–4055

A long flight of wooden stairs leads down from the driveway of this West Hills mansion. At the bottom is a tiny, secluded orchard of pear, apple, and cherry trees. This is just one of the many hidden charms of Heron Haus, one of the most accomplished B&Bs in the Rose City.

The house itself is a sturdy Tudor built in 1904 from stucco and Port of Portland ballast stone. It sits high in the hills above Northwest Portland, handy to the hiking trails and old-growth stands of gigantic Forest Park as well as to the shopping and restaurants of the Pearl District. Its effervescent owner, Julie Keppeler, worked in investment real estate, publishing, convention planning, and adult education before settling into the B&B business. She's also a weaver, potter, and photographer.

Keppeler renovated the 10,000-square-foot house in 1986 with assurance and charm. The modern touches, such as Southwestern artwork and Scandinavian-flavor furnishings, subtly complement the house's existing features. There's a huge breakfast room with herringbone-patterned oak floors and fireplace; a warm, carpeted sunroom overlooking the backyard pool; and a sophisticated entertainment room with a big-screen TV/VCR and deep couches. Most beguiling of all is the mahogany-accented library, its leaded-glass cabinets filled with selections ranging from Isak Dinesen to Audubon, its furnishings sturdy Victorian Eastlake.

Each of the six huge, impeccably decorated guest rooms has a private bath, a comfortable sitting area, a phone, a work desk, and, particularly convenient for business travelers, a modem jack. The most splendid of the five rooms is the Kulia Suite, modern and airy with a queen-size bed and a romantic, flower-shaped hot tub overlooking the downtown skyline. The Ko Room, just down the hall, is distinguished by its antique seven-headed shower, king-size brass bed, and two well-appointed sitting areas. (These two rooms can be converted into a $250-per-night suite.) At the top of the house, the Manu Room and the Mahina Room sprawl over a space so large that four average

B&B rooms would easily fit into the space allotted for these two sunny rooms.

Breakfast is a luxury Continental affair, with fresh fruits, croissants, pastries, and cereal. The trendy Nob Hill shops, galleries, and restaurants that line N.W. 23rd Avenue are within comfortable walking distance of the B&B.

🛏 *6 suites. Air-conditioning, phones, modem lines, cable TV, pool. $125–$300. MC, V. No smoking, no pets.*

Lion and the Rose

1810 N.E. 15th Ave., Portland, OR 97212, tel. 503/287–9245 or 800/955–1647, fax 503/287–9247

When it was built in 1906 for Portland brewing magnate Gustave Freiwald, this startlingly ornate, Queen Anne–style mansion was one of the city's showplaces. Its grounds, occupying nearly a full city block, featured park-like gardens, a stable for Freiwald's matched team of Clydesdale horses, and, later, a garage for one of Portland's first horseless carriages, a splendid white Packard with red leather interior.

The house's current owners, Kay Peffer, Sharon Weil, and Kevin Spanier—kindred spirits, indeed—include among their possessions a unique 1955 Oldsmobile Super 88 stretch limo, whose tail-finned red-and-white contours would surely have brought a tear to old Gustave's eye. It's equally certain that he would have approved of their stewardship of his house, now restored to all its pre-Prohibition splendor.

Since its opening in 1993, The Lion and the Rose has been one of Portland's premier B&Bs. From the gleaming floors of inlaid oak and scrubbed fir to the ornate period light fixtures (many original to the house), The Lion and the Rose has set a new standard of formal elegance among Portland inns.

The public areas offer an expanse of polished wood, antique silver, and delightful turn-of-the-century touches. The Freiwalds' original carved mahogany sofas were identified from historical photographs of the house's interior and restored to their original opulence. For the musically inclined, an 18th-century Miller pump organ and a 1909-vintage Bush & Lane piano in exquisitely grained walnut face one another across a lush Oriental carpet. The overall feel is substantial and ornate, but just short of florid.

The same maniacal attention to detail is evident throughout the six guest rooms, of which Lavonna is arguably the nicest; it features a round, sunny sitting area in the mansion's cupola, with a king-size iron canopy bed and cheerful white wicker furniture. This room is also one of the most affordable because it shares a bath (across the hall) that has a sunny window seat, an Eastlake dressing table, and a deep claw-foot tub swathed in lace curtain.

A breakfast as opulent as the surroundings is served in the dining room from 7:30 to 9:30 AM. The inn is just a short saunter from Broadway Street, an area filled with fine restaurants and splendid shopping.

▥ *4 double rooms with baths, 2 doubles share bath. Air-conditioning, phones, TVs and VCRs on request. $90–$130; full breakfast, afternoon tea. AE, MC, V. No smoking, no pets.*

McMenamins Edgefield

2126 S.W. Halsey, Troutdale, OR 97060, tel. 503/669–8610, fax 503/665–4209

It's fair to say that you've probably never encountered an inn quite like the Edgefield complex. A sort of pastoral, self-contained English village 15 minutes east of downtown Portland and five minutes west of the magnificent Columbia River Gorge National Scenic Area, Edgefield is the brainchild of Portland brew pub moguls Mike and Brian McMenamin.

The 25-acre estate includes its own vineyard, winery, brewery, bustling village pub, meeting facilities, restaurant, movie theater, and gardens. Everywhere are signs of the McMenamins' cheerful eccentricity: in the whimsical artwork adorning the pub, theater, and brewery; in menu items with names like Jack's Stratogroover and The Vondrak (two types of French-bread pizza); and in freshly brewed house ales like Terminator Stout and Invisibility Ale.

Most of the guest rooms are in the complex's huge, four-story Colonial Revival centerpiece, Edgefield Manor, built in 1911 as the dormitory for the Multnomah County Poor Farm. When the McMenamin family bought it in 1990, it was in an advanced state of dilapidation, having stood empty for more than 10 years. A major renovation, completed in 1993, added 91 more guest rooms to the original 14, as well as dormitory space for 24 guests and a fine-dining restaurant and bar.

The quietest accommodations are in the former administrator's colonial-style house, set about 100 yards from the main building; party-animal types might opt to stay in the pub/theater building or main lodge; families might want to stay in the family room that sleeps six. All rooms are sunny and eschew Victorian opulence for a clean Old Western simplicity. They have scrubbed wood floors and are furnished with a few simple antiques and bright Southwest-style fabrics. There are no telephones or TVs, but the admission price for the movie theater on the property is very reasonable.

A hearty breakfast, designed to fortify you for long hikes in the gorge or swims in the nearby Sandy River, is served in the Black Rabbit Restaurant. Choices might include omelets, crunchy French toast, corned beef hash, fresh local fruit, and, on special occasions, eggs Benedict with Dungeness crab.

▥ *3 suites, 2 hostel rooms with 24 dormitory beds, 100 rooms share 55 baths.*

Restaurant, bar, brewery, pub, winery, outdoor beer garden (in summer), cinema, conference facilities. Single $45–$115, family room (sleeps 6; breakfast $15 extra for more than 2 guests) $180; full breakfast. AE, D, MC, V. No smoking, no pets.

Portland Guest House

1720 N.E. 15th Ave., Portland, OR 97212, tel. 503/282–1402

Northeast Portland's Irvington neighborhood used to be full of neatly kept working-class Victorians just like this one, with its flower-filled yard and window boxes, and its mocha-colored paint and graceful wrought-iron fence. Most of them fell to the wrecking ball when the prosperous 'teens and '20s transformed Irvington into a neighborhood for the nouveau riches.

This house endured decades of neglect until longtime neighborhood residents Susan and Dean Gisvold brought it back to life in 1987. Now, rebuilt from the studs outward, the house oozes a comfortable sense of place and history, from its scarred oak floors to the haunting photographs of once-resident families on the walls. It's not as grand as The Lion and the Rose (*see above*) or the nearby White House (*see below*), but it's hardly a poor relation, and it has a fresh, sunny authenticity all its own.

Each of the seven smallish, high-ceilinged guest rooms has some special and memorable touch: an ornately carved walnut Eastlake bed or armoire, an immaculately enameled claw-foot tub, or a shady deck overlooking the back garden. A large, simply decorated suite in the sunlit basement is configured with families in mind, and the absence of Victoriana breakables throughout the house makes this the best family-friendly B&B in town.

Outside the four second-floor rooms is a lace-curtained window seat that's perfect for reading or postcard writing. The tasteful mauve and gray walls of the downstairs living and dining rooms are finished with white bull's-eye molding; a gorgeous Oriental carpet cushions the hardwood floor. The ponderous Eastlake living room suite has been reupholstered in pretty rose satin.

Fifteenth Avenue, which runs by the etched-glass front door, can be busy in the mornings and afternoons, but this is barely noticeable in the soundproofed house. The conveniently central Northeast Portland neighborhood, with its broad tree-shaded avenues lined with stately old homes, offers plentiful charms of its own. The MAX light-rail line is a 10-minute walk to the south. Closer to home, the shops on Broadway Street offer Oregon wines and produce, imported cheeses, and fresh-baked breads for picnics in the landscaped yard.

The Gisvolds don't live on the premises, but they're often around, and a full-time manager occupies a downstairs apartment. Breakfast is served in front of the cheerful dining room fireplace or alfresco on the back porch when it's nice out.

▥ *5 double rooms with baths, 2 doubles share bath. Air-conditioning, phones, bicycle storage. $55–$85, full breakfast. AE, DC, MC, V. No smoking, no pets.*

Portland's White House

1914 N.E. 22nd Ave., Portland, OR 97212, tel. 503/287–7131

The splash of falling water provide a melodious welcome at this memorable Northeast Portland B&B. Listed on the National Register of Historic Places, the house was built in 1912 in Southern Federal style. Except for the tiled roof, it bears an uncanny resemblance to its District of Columbia namesake—a resemblance indicative of the chief-executive personality of its builder, timber tycoon Robert Lytle. Its sweeping circular driveway, carriage house, and Greek columns all whisper of bygone elegance. "I always tell guests to go ahead and make a speech from the balcony if they want to," says innkeeper Mary Hough.

This White House's neighborhood, Irvington, may lack the grandeur of Pennsylvania Avenue, but its location makes it handy to downtown, Memorial Coliseum, the MAX light-rail line, and the Oregon Convention Center. Owners Larry Hough, an electrician by profession, and his Dublin-born wife, Mary, a former antiques dealer, bought the house in 1984 and have since lavished more than 10,000 hours on its restoration. The public areas gleam with hand-rubbed Honduran mahogany and ornately inlaid oak. (Even the old servants' quarters are finished with mahogany.) The sweeping hand-carved stairway is lit by exquisite Pulvey stained-glass windows. Buckets of detergent and hours of patient scrubbing revealed hand-painted scenic murals, commissioned in the '20s, lining the walls of the foyer. Outside, the sunny rose-hung decks make fine places for relaxing with a spot of summer tea. Downstairs is a cavernous ballroom.

The six spacious, high-ceilinged guest rooms are furnished with a tasteful mix of antiques, period pieces, and reproductions. The Canopy and Baron's rooms feature ornate canopy beds and huge claw-foot soaking tubs. In the Garden Room, French doors open onto a private veranda trellised with flowers. The Balcony Room has an ornate brass bed, tiled Art Deco bathroom, and a small balustraded balcony overlooking the courtyard fountain.

The Houghs are hardworking resident innkeepers who attack their duties with charm and zest. When Mary was a child in Ireland, her mother kept boardinghouses; Mary's blood ties to the lodging business are evident in her immaculate housekeeping and hearty breakfasts. She refers to the morning repast as "Blarney Surprise" (plenty of blarney to accompany the hot entrée, be it eggs Benedict or a fruit-slathered waffle). The tea kettle is always on the hob, and the pantry is well stocked with fresh-baked chocolate chip cookies and a brimming basket of local apples.

▦ *6 double rooms with baths. Airconditioning, phones, TV on request, library, TV room. $98–$116; full breakfast, afternoon tea. MC, V. Restricted smoking, no pets.*

RiverPlace Hotel

1510 S.W. Harbor Way, Portland, OR 97201, tel. 503/228–3233 or 800/227–1333, fax 503/295–6161

The downtown Portland skyline towers above the rotunda roof and turrets of the RiverPlace Hotel on the banks of the Willamette River. A forest of sailboat masts crowds the complex's marina; the green ribbon of 2-mile-long Waterfront Park begins almost at the hotel's front door. The RiverPlace anchors a crescent of shops, restaurants, condominiums, and offices that went up in 1985 and breathed new life into downtown Portland's front door.

Observers disagree on the overall feel of the hotel, thoroughly modern though it is. Some say it looks vaguely Dutch; to others it has a clean Cape Cod ambience. One thing they all agree on, however, is its elegance; since the hotel opened its doors, it has become a residence of choice for visiting celebrities and CEOs.

Inside, the RiverPlace has the feel of an intimate European hotel. The subtle luster of teak as well as green Italian marble is everywhere, and the staff provides a level of service seldom seen in this casual western city. (The 150 employees outnumber the guest rooms nearly two to one.) The lobby, bar, and restaurant are handsome spaces, luxuriously appointed with wood-burning fireplaces, rich fabrics, and Oriental carpets.

The 84 guest rooms overlook river, skyline, and courtyard, but they lack some of the elegance of the public areas. Thick carpeting and well-soundproofed walls are a given; the paint is a subtle pale yellow that makes the most of Portland's often wan sunlight. Furnishings are modern and comfortable, but they have a cookie-cutter uniformity. The rooms are medium in size and spare. Junior suites have huge tiled bathrooms and comfortable sitting areas. Fireplace suites are larger, with marble-top wet bars, king-size beds, small whirlpool baths, and two color TVs each. At press time, plans were in the works to redecorate the rooms.

Dinner at the Esplanade Restaurant off the lobby is an experience to savor. The nightly menu may include such delicacies as spinach with smoked salmon and shrimp wontons in hazelnut vinaigrette and grilled steelhead with berry vinegars and pepper oils.

▦ *39 double rooms with baths, 35 suites, 10 apartments. Restaurant, bar, air-conditioning, phones, cable TV, voice mail, 24-hr room service, sauna, valet parking. $125–$700, Continental breakfast. AE, D, DC, MC, V.*

Other Choices

Clinkerbrick House. 2311 N.E. Schuyler St., Portland, OR 97212, tel. 503/281–2533. 1 double room with bath, 2 doubles share bath. Kitchen, phone, and TV in common room. $55–$65, full breakfast. MC, V. No smoking, no pets.

General Hooker's B&B. 125 S.W. Hooker St., Portland, OR 97201, tel. 503/222–4435 or 800/745–4135, fax 503/295–6410. 2 double rooms with baths, 2 doubles share bath. Air-conditioning, cable TV, VCR, modem lines, ½-price YMCA passes. $75–$120, vegetarian Continental breakfast. AE, MC, V. No smoking, no pets, 2-night minimum Apr.–Oct.

Georgian House. 1828 N.E. Siskiyou St., Portland, OR 97212, tel. 503/281–

2250, fax 503/281–3301. 1 double room with bath, 2 doubles share 1½ baths, 1 suite. Air-conditioning in 3 rooms, TV in 2 rooms, TV/VCR and phone in common room. $65–$85, full breakfast. MC, V. No smoking, no pets.

Hotel Vintage Plaza. 422 S.W. Broadway, Portland, OR 97205, tel. 503/228–1212 or 800/243–0555, fax 503/228–3598. 82 double rooms with baths, 19 suites. Restaurant, piano lounge, no-smoking room, air-conditioning, room service, phones, TVs, 2-person whirlpool tubs in suites, concierge, valet parking. $155–$245. No pets.

MacMaster House. 1041 S.W. Vista Ave., Portland, OR 97205, tel. 503/223–7362. 5 double rooms share 2½ baths, 2 suites. Air-conditioning, cable TV, bicycle storage. $80–$120, full breakfast. AE, D, DC, MC, V. No smoking, no pets.

Reservations Services

Bed & Breakfast Reservations—Oregon (2321 N.E. 28th Ave., Portland, OR 97212, tel. 503/287–4704 or 800/786–9476). **Northwest Bed and Breakfast** (1067 Hanover Ct. S, Salem, OR 97302, tel. 503/370–9033, fax 503/316–9118).

North Coast

Grandview Bed & Breakfast

1574 Grand Ave., Astoria, OR 97103, tel. 503/325–0000 or 800/488–3250

Seen from the quiet residential street in Astoria that it faces, the Grandview Bed & Breakfast doesn't stand out, but once you're inside the nearly 100-year-old shingle-style house, you'll know what's special about it.

Because the Grandview rises so precipitously from a hill that falls away steeply, the views from the inn are spectacular and the sensation of floating can be intense. Innkeeper Charlene Maxwell quickly brings you back to earth, however. She has steeped herself in local lore and shares it with you in an easygoing but authoritative manner.

The guest rooms upstairs are eccentrically decorated with a mixture of period furnishings and odd modern touches (for example, plastic patio furniture table and chairs). A few rooms have canopy beds, and all are outfitted with faux fireplaces that serve to heat the rooms of this cavernous home. In one room, fluffy clouds scud across sky-blue walls. In brightly painted bookcases, tiny artificial birds perch on bookends. Indeed, with unobstructed vistas of the Columbia River and the Coast Range of southern Washington and of the dozens of church steeples of Old Astoria, you'll feel as if you're in an aerie. As if this weren't enough, the Refuge Room features birdcall recordings (the real thing is right outside the window), bird-flocked wallpaper, and a bookcase filled with books on birdwatching. The favorite, though, is the Tree Tops; it has a curtained reading nook, clock tables by the bedside, and a telescope for distance viewing from the private balcony.

For those who prefer to be earthbound, there is a very plain two-bedroom suite in the lower level of the house, with a separate entrance that's perfect for families. The motif here is zoo animals and jungle prints (stuffed animals hang from the window and from the directors chairs, covered in a leopard spot print).

The arrangement of some of the guest rooms is flexible: Seven double rooms on the second and third floors can be divided into two suites or rented separately. Prices depend on whether you have a private bath.

The entrance hall is a bit cluttered with Charlene's work desk, which is only a few feet from the main door. The dining area, however, is very inviting, positioned in a light-filled turret that offers views of the river and town. For more privacy, you might opt to dine in a smaller bullet turret on the other side of the kitchen, ideal for a twosome. Muffins, fresh fruit, and juice round out what Charlene calls a "Continental plus" breakfast. She also includes lox and bagels whenever she can get good smoked salmon.

▦ *4 double rooms with baths (or 6 doubles share 2 baths, depending on bookings), 1 suite. $39–$146, Continental breakfast buffet. D, MC, V. No smoking, no pets, no alcohol on premises.*

Sandlake Country Inn

8505 Galloway Rd., Cloverdale, OR 97112, tel. 503/965–6745, fax 503/965–7425

Sandlake Country Inn is a peaceful place on an old cranberry farm on the road to Sandlake Park. On Christmas morning in 1890, the Norwegian schooner *Struan* was wrecked off Cape Lookout, leaving tons of heavy bridge timbers strewn on the beach. Storm-weary homesteaders with few building materials hauled the timbers off and made sturdy homes. Only a few of these are still standing, the most notable of which is the weathered-shingle Sandlake Country Inn, where innkeepers Femke and Dave Durham preside.

Besides restoring the natural woodwork, part of the dining room ceiling was removed to reveal the old bridge timbers. The sitting room is a cozy creation, with velvet-covered Victorian settees, a stone fireplace, and views of flowering rosebushes outside.

From the sitting room, French doors open onto Rose, an L-shaped guest room furnished in white wicker, set off by ecru netting that sweeps from the ceiling to the corners of the rose-print-comforter-covered bed. The room overlooks the rose garden. Upstairs is the honeymoon suite, taking up the entire floor and opening onto a deck that surveys the 2½-acre property; keep a look out for deer and elk.

Just off the dining room is The Timbers, a wheelchair-accessible guest room with an outdoorsy feel, complete with a 1920s wicker fishing creel slung over the sturdy timber bedposts, a timber-framed fireplace, a deck in the garden, and a fragrant cedar-lined bathroom. There is also a charming cottage outside about 100 feet from the main house: Inside the feeling is plush, with thick carpeting and huge throw pillows on the floor before a black marble fireplace. A large hot tub is strategically located between the bed and the deck. As in the suites, Arts and Crafts oak period pieces and reproductions predominate.

Homemade baked apple oatmeal is a breakfast staple, as are fruit parfaits, soufflés, and eggs Florentine. The Durhams like to focus on providing a romantic retreat, so they see to it that you are treated to breakfast in bed: Every morning a tray with the multicourse repast elegantly presented on Royal Doulton china is delivered to your room.

🛏 *2 double rooms with baths, 1 suite, 1 housekeeping cottage. Radio/cassette players, TV/VCR in most rooms, closed-captioned TV in suite, bicycles. $80–$125, full breakfast. AE, MC, V. No smoking, no pets, 2-night minimum on weekends May–Oct. Closed Christmas week.*

St. Bernards

3 E. Ocean Rd., Box 102, Arch Cape, OR 97102, tel. and fax 503/436–2800 or tel. 800/436–2848

Imagine having an extra million dollars and several years to travel the world collecting antiques and art that would one day fill your fantasy inn. That, and years spent visiting B&Bs and inns to see what worked and didn't work, was what gregarious innkeepers Don and Deanna Bernard did before building

their enormous shingled sand castle, complete with turret and drive-through tunnel, on the scenic Oregon coast a few miles south of Cannon Beach.

Together, the charmingly humorous and well-versed Bernards designed and constructed the sprawling, chateaulike structure, from the foundation to the ingeniously carved scenes depicted in the exterior shingles. Now they are content to stay at home, traveling vicariously through their many guests.

As one would expect of a fantasy castle, the guest rooms are quite grand. Decorated by Deanna with an artist's eye, they are appointed with every amenity for comfort and romance— down duvets on firm beds, plush robes, super-soft cotton sheets, large soaking tubs with ocean views, and gas fireplaces. A spacious workout room with sauna rounds out the well-thought-out amenities of this adult-oriented inn. Ginger, appointed with ornate Austrian bedsteads dating from the 1860s takes it's palette from a collection of ginger jars, while Gauguin uses the muted pastels of the painters work hung on the walls. Tower, with it's incredible Louis XIV Bombay bed, has an attached sitting room in the turret, while Provence, on the garden level with a private patio overlooking the ocean, features terra-cotta floors, antique pine furniture, Pierre Deux fabrics in country French yellow and blue, and a two-person whirlpool bath.

Breakfast, served in the rounded dining room beneath the inn's cupola, is also a grand affair, with fresh juice, coffeecakes, seasonal fruits, and a hot entrée served on Deanna's fine collection of china and crystal. The Bernard's background as restaurateurs shines through in the morning repast. In the evenings, they gather with you before the fireplace in the large living room to chat over wine and hors d'oeuvres.

🛏 *6 double rooms with baths, 1 suite. Phones, TVs, VCRs, individual heating system, sauna, exercise room.*

$129–$189; full breakfast, evening refreshments. AE, MC, V. No smoking, no pets.

Sylvia Beach Hotel

267 N.W. Cliff St., Newport, OR 97365, tel. 503/265–5428

For years, what is now the Sylvia Beach Hotel was known as a flophouse with a view. In Newport, once the state's honeymoon capital, the 1911 hotel overlooking the sea was for decades a low-rent residential hotel before Portland restaurateur Goody Cable and Roseburg partner Sally Ford decided to make it a kind of literary lodging—or a library that sleeps 40.

The plain green clapboard hotel takes its name not from the beach (actually, it's on a bluff on Nye Beach) but from the renowned patron Sylvia Beach, who in the 1920s and '30s ran the Shakespeare & Co. bookstore in Paris, a haven for American literati. Each room is dedicated to a famous writer, with appropriate books and decorating scheme. The Hemingway Room, for example, is all the manly Papa could have hoped for: a bed made out of tree limbs beneath a mounted antelope head, and an old Royal typewriter in the corner. The Agatha Christie Room is all green, with clues from her books lurking everywhere (the three bullets embedded in the wall are particularly menacing).

Down the hall is the Oscar Wilde Room, a smallish place resembling a Victorian gentleman's lodgings. The view, which faces a roof from the other side of the hotel, is far from awe-inspiring. But the managers are way ahead of you. Right next to the window is a framed Wilde quote: "It's altogether immaterial, a view, except to the innkeeper who, of course, charges it in the bill. A gentleman never looks out the window."

The most popular rooms are the Poe Room, a scary place in black and red, complete with raven and pendulum suspended over the bed, and the Colette Room, a sexy French suite with lace canopies, velvet window seat, and peach-colored headboard. The upper reaches of the hotel are turned over to a large library (some 1,000 books), with plenty of nooks and crannies and comfortable armchairs for book lovers.

The food at the hotel's restaurant— Tables of Content—is excellent. Breakfast is selected from a wide range of offerings on the menu, including frittatas and German-style pancakes served in the pan. But the best meal is dinner, an eight-course gourmet feast served family style.

🏠 *20 double rooms with baths; separate dormitory with 8 bunks for women and 4 bunks for men. Restaurant, fireplace in 3 rooms. $61–$129, dormitory bed $20; full breakfast, evening refreshments. AE, MC, V. No smoking, no pets, 2-night minimum on weekends. Closed 1st week in Dec.*

Whiskey Creek Bed & Breakfast

7500 Whiskey Creek Rd., Tillamook, OR 97141, tel. 503/842–2408

On Three Capes Scenic Loop about 10 miles west of Tillamook, Whiskey Creek Bed & Breakfast offers quietude in rustic surroundings.

Built in 1900 by the operator of a custom sawmill, the cedar-shingled Whiskey Creek is paneled inside with rough-hewn spruce. Originally, the mill operator made spruce oars and used the odd pieces of leftover wood for the main floor. For years, the home and the mill were powered by a small hydroelectric turbine on Whiskey Creek, about 100 feet away and the southern boundary of the property.

The house is split into two separate apartments—one upstairs and one downstairs—with private entrances; these can be rented for a night or a week. Upstairs, the two-bedroom apartment is paneled with the original rough-hewn spruce and has two terraces overlooking Netarts Bay; the cathedral-ceilinged dining area is decorated with owner Allison Asbjornsen's rabbit *objet d'art* collection. A fabulous wood-burning stove keeps the smallish rooms warm and cozy when it's cold. Adorning the white walls of the one-bedroom downstairs apartment, which also offers a view of the bay and the lawn, are Allison's oil paintings, watercolors, collages, and sculptures. Both units have queen-size futon beds and overstuffed chairs, a living room, a bathroom, and a kitchen for cooking your own meals.

Basically you are on your own here. Allison no longer lives on the premises, but Karen Foote, another artist, cheerfully manages the B&B. Karen will happily answer questions about the area and will deliver a Continental breakfast to you in the morning. Otherwise she leaves you alone to enjoy the beautiful natural surroundings. Bear, elk, and deer still roam this area, and salmon make their way up Whiskey Creek to a state fish hatchery just across the creek from the inn. Blue herons are a common sight. Tillamook means "land of many waters," and there are streams everywhere for exploring. Plans are in the works to make the inn a retreat in winter, with yoga and other types of courses.

▦ *2 apartments. $100, Continental breakfast for 1-night stays only. MC, V. No smoking.*

Other Choices

Anderson's Boarding House. 208 N. Holladay Dr., Seaside, OR 97138, tel. 503/738–9055 or 800/995–4013. 6 double rooms with baths, 1 housekeeping cottage. TVs, bicycle storage. $75–$120, full breakfast (guests in main house only). MC, V. No pets, 2-night minimum on weekends.

Astoria Inn. 3391 Irving Ave., Astoria, OR 97103, tel. 503/325–8153. 4 double rooms with baths. Cable TV, VCR, and karaoke machine in living room; bicycle storage. $70–$85; full breakfast, afternoon refreshments. D, MC, V. No smoking, no pets.

Benjamin Young Inn. 3652 Duane St., Astoria, OR 97103, tel. 503/325–6172 or 800/766–6482. 4 double rooms with baths, 1 2-bedroom suite. Fireplace and whirlpool bath in suite. $75–$125, full breakfast. MC, V. No smoking, no pets, 2-night minimum on holiday weekends.

Channel House. 35 Ellingson St., Box 56, Depoe Bay, OR 97341, tel. 503/765–2140 or 800/447–2140, fax 541/765–2191. 5 double rooms with baths, 4 suites, 3 housekeeping suites. Cable TVs, binoculars; kitchen in 3 rooms, hot tubs. $60–$200, Continental breakfast. D, MC, V. No smoking, no pets.

Columbia River Inn Bed and Breakfast. 1681 Franklin Ave., Astoria, OR 97103, tel. 503/325–5044 or 800/953–5044. 4 double rooms with baths. Refrigerators, clock radios; fireplace and whirlpool tub in 1 room. $75–$125, full breakfast. MC, V. No smoking, no pets, 2-night minimum on holiday weekends.

Franklin St. Station. 140 Franklin Ave., Astoria, OR 97103, tel. 503/325–4314 or 800/448–1098. 3 double rooms with baths, 2 suites. Fireplace, cable TV, VCR, and stereo in 1 suite; wet bars in 2 suites. $63–$115, full breakfast. MC, V. No smoking, no pets.

Gilbert Inn. 341 Beach Dr., Seaside, OR 97138, tel. 503/738–9770 or 800/410–9770, fax 503/717–1070. 8 double rooms with baths, 2 suites. Phones, TVs, conference facilities. $79–$95, full breakfast. D, MC, V. No smoking, no pets, 2-night minimum on weekends. Closed Jan.

Hudson House. 37700 Hwy. 101 S, Cloverdale, OR 97112, tel. 503/392–3533, fax 503/392–3533. 2 double rooms with baths, 2 suites. CD- players, coffee and tea in rooms, TV/VCR in library, bicycles. $65–$75; full breakfast, evening refreshments. AE, D, MC, V. No smoking, no pets.

Inn at Manzanita. 67 Laneda St., Box 243, Manzanita, OR 97130, tel. 503/368–6754, fax 530/368–7656. 13 double rooms with baths. Wet bars, TV/VCRs, hot tubs; kitchen in 2 rooms; masseuse available. $100–$145, no breakfast. MC, V. No smoking, no pets, 2-night minimum on weekends and July–Aug.

Stephanie Inn. 2740 S. Pacific Rd., Cannon Beach, OR 97110, tel. 503/436–2221 or 800/633-3466, fax 503/436–9711. 40 double rooms with baths, 6 suites. Wet bars, phones, TV/VCRs, whirlpool baths; library, video library; masseuse available; free shuttle into town. $119–$360; full breakfast buffet, evening refreshments, dinner available. AE, D, DC, MC, V. No smoking, no pets, 2-night minimum in Aug. and all weekends and holidays.

Tyee Lodge. 4925 N.W. Woody Way, Newport, OR 97365, tel. 541/265–8953 or 800/553–8933. 5 double rooms with baths. Fireplace in 1 room, bicycles, beach trail. $100–$110, full breakfast. MC, V. No smoking, no pets.

Reservations Services

The Bed & Breakfast Register (tel. 503/249–1997 or 800/249–1997). **Bed & Breakfast Reservations—Oregon** (2321 N.E. 28th Ave., Portland, OR 97212, tel. 503/287–4704 or 800/786–9476). **Northwest Bed and Breakfast** (1067 Hanover Ct. S, Salem, OR 97302, tel. 503/370–9033, fax 503/316–9118).

Columbia River Gorge and Mt. Hood

Auberge des Fleurs

39391 S.E. Lusted Rd., Sandy, OR 97055, tel. 503/663-9449, fax 503/663–1129

You'll be bathed in color if you approach this inn during spring and summer. In the heart of an active nursery specializing in lilies, Auberge des Fleurs (Inn of the Flowers) is surrounded by 60 acres of flourishing bulbs.

Even if you have only a passing interest in flowers, this Dutch Colonial–style home is worth visiting. Polished walnut floors, gray marble fireplaces, bleached woodwork, and a brick patio create an elegant yet relaxing atmosphere. Just 40 minutes from Portland and 30 minutes from either windsurfing or skiing, the inn is a convenient, stylish base for exploring the Portland area and the scenery to the east.

The house was originally built by Jan de Graaf, a Dutch botanist who found the Northwest a perfect place to develop his hybridized lilies. The current owners, Molli and Don Flynn, have several nurseries along the West Coast. Although they are often at the property, day-to-day management is done by friendly local folk.

A huge living-room area has been overly modernized, but other elements—such as the original imported tile in the kitchen—are either intact or restored. Two sunny sitting rooms overlook the canyon and have excellent views of Mt. Hood's rugged northwest face. The dining room is almost too formal, with its high-back chairs and four large windows that look out on the trellised garden. A Continental breakfast, with an emphasis on fresh fruit, is served.

It's surprising to find that this large house holds only two guest rooms, both upstairs. The larger, with views of the garden, continues the bleached-wood theme, although the spare look is tempered somewhat by modern carpeting. The second room, although a bit smaller, has a more expansive feeling because of its good light and its view of the grounds.

Perhaps the most interesting part of Auberge des Fleurs to stay in is the old caretaker's cottage about 200 yards from the main house. The small house, about 300 feet directly above the confluence of the Sandy and the Bull Run rivers, is rustic and has its own kitchen and bath. The bleached-wood bed and wardrobe seem a little out of place here, but the smell of fresh air is ample compensation.

▦ *2 double rooms with baths, 1 housekeeping cottage. Conference facilities, horseback riding. $75, cottage $115; Continental breakfast. No credit cards. No smoking in house, no pets.*

Bridal Veil Lodge

Box 87, Bridal Veil, OR 97010, tel. 503/695-2333

In 1921, Virgil Amend hauled timbers from the mill down the hill to an empty spot beside the Historic Columbia River Highway, in the tiny gorge community of Bridal Veil. There, within the sound of delicate Bridal Veil Falls, he built a lodge.

After years of functioning as a lodge, years of being a family residence, and years of being not much of anything, the old rustic Bridal Veil Lodge has reverted to its original purpose. Amend's great-granddaughter Laurel Slater and her husband have created a country-style bed-and-breakfast within 20 minutes of Portland's bustling waterfront.

But if Portland's lights are visible just to the west, it's what lies to the east that makes Bridal Veil's location spe-

cial. The log structure is on the edge of the Columbia River Gorge National Scenic Area, a 90-mile-long preserve of trails, dizzying waterfalls, rock formations, high cliffs, and wilderness. Trails going through this region can be found within a mile of the lodge.

Inside, the inn is warm and the sense of family is unmistakable. Old photos adorn the shelves in the dining area, which is dominated by a large, 1920s-vintage harvest table and a huge wrought-iron cookstove. In the main common area, a player piano holds sway beneath high, exposed fir beams.

The two rooms upstairs feature hand-tied quilts on the walls. Grandpa's Room looks out into dense forest; knotty pine walls and a hand-carved oak headboard and matching dresser evoke the rough-hewn days when the lodge was built. Across the hall, the larger Grandma's Room is far more feminine, with table skirts, curtains, and plenty of light to keep the pine walls from dominating. A sitting area overlooks the front of the lodge: Though the view's immediate foreground is the highway and the parking lot for the state park across the road, the road isn't busy, and the lot gives way to rolling fields down to the Columbia.

Perhaps the inn's greatest asset is Laurel Slater, who grew up in the house and can answer questions about local history. Laurel's breakfasts tend to be healthy and hearty, since a good portion of her guests are either heading out to hike the gorge's notoriously steep trails or to embark on other outdoor activities, including windsurfing. German-style pancakes, fresh fruit, and plenty of sausage and bacon are regular fare.

▦ *2 double rooms share 1½ baths. TV in common area. $58–$65, full breakfast. No credit cards. No smoking, no pets.*

Fernwood at Alder Creek

54850 Highway 26 E, Sandy, OR 97055, tel. 503/622–3570

Nestled in the foothills just west of Mount Hood, this prosaically named B&B is impressive looking. Built in pieces between 1910 and 1924, this large, vintage log home would qualify as old growth if it were a tree.

Although just off busy U.S. 26, which zips to mountain recreation areas from Portland, Fernwood feels miles away from anything noisy or modern. A huge, multipaned window set into one log wall seems vaguely Bavarian, but the atmosphere is purely Northwest. The highway's hum is washed away by Alder Creek, about 100 feet below the inn and in a major hurry to meet up with the Sandy River just beyond the highway bridge. Some of the area's best steelhead fishing holes can be found at the confluence of the creek and the river.

Inside, a warm and rustic feeling pervades with a collection of local handmade furniture and some antiques from the families of innkeepers Margo and Darrell Dempster. Surrounded by trees and ferns, this side of the house is a bit dark. But the spacious dining room–library, with an immense, supporting pole running vertically through it, is filled with natural light from a large window. Books and a collection of *Life* magazines dating back to the 1930s are displayed on the walls of this grand room, which has a loft that's perfect for reading or sleeping.

Both of the inn's two suites have decks and creek views. The Red Huckleberry Suite, downstairs, also features a private entrance and a small kitchen. But you might not bother to use it, since with a only a little hint you can convince the Darrells to whip up raspberry pizza and other delicious treats. After indulging in their tasty snacks, you can relax in the suite's knotty pine bath, with its bucolic view of the creek and canyon. One disappointment, though, is that while sitting in the whirlpool tub the creek is not visible.

The Curly Willow Suite upstairs lacks the independent feel of the suite below. The deck is accessed through the front door of the inn and the suite's sitting room doubles as a reception area during the day. But the furnishings are more distinctive, especially the wrought-iron bed and the oak, American Empire rocking chair. The whirlpool tub is away from the window and in its place is a fine window seat for reading or just sighing at the peaceful scenery.

The hearty and creative family-style breakfasts served in the dining room on the main floor might include raspberry puffed pastries or blueberry waffles with homemade syrup. You might even get leftover raspberry pizza.

🏨 *2 suites. Kitchenette, whirlpool tub in 1 suite. $65–$75, full breakfast. MC, V. No smoking, no pets.*

Hood River Hotel

102 Oak St., Hood River, OR 97031, tel. 541/386–1900, fax 541/386–6090

Although Hood River now bills itself as a kind of rustic Riviera for windsurfers, the newly restored Hood River Hotel is a reminder of the town's older character. True, Hood River's fresh identity as a recreational center is the reason the hotel was worth fixing up, but the hotel existed as a simple railroad stopover as early as 1910.

The 38-room brick-faced structure sits just off Main Street. At the front desk is Pasquale Barone, a veteran of the European hospitality industry, who came to the United States to bring a little Continental flair to Hood River. The rooms are furnished with Georgian reproductions; the beds add a much-needed touch of individuality, be they brass, four-poster, or canopy. The main appeal of the hotel is the two-story-high lobby, bar, and restaurant, which flow into one another.

You might enter past a string duo performing classical riffs before a giant hearth, the flames crackling away. To the left of the lobby, divided into several sitting areas with Chippendale and Queen Anne reproductions, is an imposing wooden bar serving local beers and wines in a classy yet laidback atmosphere. (Windsurfers are often big spenders, but they hang around in wet suits or Lycra shorts.) The bar and the dining room, which extends up to the mezzanine over the lobby, are immense, featuring the building's original pine woodwork.

The food continues the hotel's theme of being at once traditional and trendy. Dinners can get pricey, but the perfectly done seafood is worth it. Breakfasts are not included as part of the room rate, but they are worth the money with specials such as chili rellenos with spiced hash-brown potatoes.

The hotel is close to Hood River's antiques shops and also near the town's liveliest nightspots. A few blocks away is the White Cap Brew Pub (tel. 541/386–2247), home of the Hood River Brewery. Besides serving up its Full Sail Ale, one of the Northwest's most popular local ales, the pub has a panoramic view of the mile-wide Columbia as it rips through the gorge. Closer to the hotel is the Brass Rail, a hopping dance club that features bands from the Portland and Seattle club scene.

▥ *32 double rooms with baths, 6 housekeeping suites. Restaurant, ceiling fans, TVs, phones, kitchen in 2 rooms, 24-hour room service. $49–$145. AE, MC, V. No smoking, no pets.*

Lakecliff Estate Bed & Breakfast

3820 Westcliff Dr., Box 1220, Hood River, OR 97031, tel. 541/386–7000

From the front room of the stately Lakecliff Estate Bed & Breakfast, the Columbia River gorge is like a three-dimensional postcard. Framed by a window that stretches the width of the large, oak-beamed room, the river view is nothing short of transfixing. The mile-wide river, about 200 feet below, with forests down to its edge and high cliffs topped by small farms, is visible on the Washington side of the gorge. When the wind cooperates, legions of little specks with colorful sails—the gorge's latest fun seekers, windsurfers—dot the water.

While all that plays out down below, more worldly pleasures await in the Lakecliff. Sitting by the huge native stone fireplace on the west wall of the main room, even nonsmokers might feel the urge to light up the old briar pipe and tell a story of the hunt. Over the fireplace is a six-point deer, and in the hall a moose head serves as a humorous hat rack.

The estate, now on the National Register of Historic Places, was designed by A.E. Doyle, a turn-of-the-century Portland architect who also designed the Multnomah Falls Lodge and several public buildings in Portland, as well as Portland's charming downtown drinking fountains. Originally built for a Portland merchant family as a country getaway, the large home is something of a grand bed-and-breakfast by Northwest standards. Three of the four guest rooms feature rugged fireplaces made with rocks found on the property when it was built in 1908. Three also have views of the gorge, while the fourth looks back on the woods between the estate and the highway. All are done in country-French style, with oak beams and down comforters on the beds.

Innkeepers Bruce and Judy Thesenga have created an impressive place to relax while taking in the sights of the gorge. In the dining area, Judy's collection of antique milk bottles rings an upper shelf. Bruce, who runs a horse ranch in the hills across the river from the Lakecliff, often takes a turn in the kitchen, where he produces Lakecliff bacon, a sweet, crunchy bacon served cold. Other breakfast mainstays are huckleberry pancakes, frittatas, Dutch babies, and oven-baked French toast.

▥ *2 double rooms with baths, 2 double rooms share bath. Shuffleboard court. $85–$100, full breakfast. No credit cards. No smoking, no pets. Closed Oct.–Apr.*

Old Welches Inn

26401 East Welches Rd., Welches, OR 97067, tel. 503/622–3754

During the days of the Oregon Trail, wagons frequently stopped in Welches on the Salmon River, well below the glaciers of Mt. Hood and its steep passes. Below spread the fertile Willamette Valley, the goal of the weary pioneers. By 1890 the valley had become civilized, and Welches Hotel lured the carriage trade from Portland with the promise of hiking, fishing, and relaxation.

A simple, white clapboard house is all that remains of the hotel, whose dining room once seated 120. The inn combines the atmosphere of a laid-back ski lodge and an old country estate. Bleached woodwork accentuates the sunny, airy feel of the place.

Much of that feeling comes from Judi Mondun, who operates the inn with her husband, Ted. The couple, both of whom were involved in finance in Miami, happened upon the Mt. Hood area during the late 1980s when their customary ski slopes in Colorado lacked snow. While Ted maintains his accounting practice in the Sunshine State, Judi tends to the Old Welches Inn.

A large wood-burning stove on a base of rounded river rocks lends a rustic look to the living room, which overlooks the river through French doors. The covered patio, with a floor of hand-fitted river stones and lattice walls, features an 8-foot-high stone fireplace that was originally part of the old hotel.

The three upstairs rooms share two baths. The largest, which overlooks Resort at the Mountain's 27-hole golf course and has views of Hunchback Mountain, has a sleigh bed, Georgian hunting scenes on the raw silk-covered walls, and a floral upholstered rocking chair. A second room lacks a dramatic view, but the rich cedar paneling and ornate iron bedstead more than compensate. The remaining room on that level has a cannonball-style headboard and is festooned with duck decoys.

An outlying cabin is even closer to the river and the golf course—it overlooks the first hole. The 1901 structure has its own kitchen, two bedrooms, and a river-rock fireplace.

▥ *3 double rooms share 2 baths, 1 2-bedroom housekeeping cabin. $75, cabin $130; full breakfast (except for cabin). AE, MC, V. No smoking, 2-night minimum on holiday weekends.*

Williams House

608 W. 6th St., The Dalles, OR 97058, tel. 541/296–2889

The family of innkeeper Don Williams can be traced to The Dalles area as far back as 1862. The B&B he runs with his wife, Barbara, is a link to that past, when The Dalles was just a few years removed from being a simple trading post frequented by French and English trappers. A noted local historian who has been active in preserving several old buildings in The Dalles, Don is a font of information on the region.

Williams House sits halfway up a steep slope above the town's business district. Directly below is a small creek that meanders through the estate's arboretum. Built in 1899, the house is textbook Queen Anne, with spindle-work porch supports and friezes, a round tower, gables aplenty, decorated verge boards, and enough gingerbread for a decade of Christmases.

The grand style continues inside with a broad, open staircase of Nicaraguan mahogany. Two sitting rooms provide ample space for lounging on Victorian settees—one with Roman heads carved on the back—and chairs while you thumb through the Williamses' eclectic book collection. The Chinese plates, bowls, and artifacts displayed throughout the main floor lend an imperial touch to the house.

A suite on the main floor features a four-poster bed and a private sitting room that face the creek. The bathroom has the original Italian marble and a 6-foot-long claw-foot tub. An unusual feature of the suite is the Victorian intercom system.

Upstairs are two guest rooms that share one modern bath. The larger room has an English canopied four-poster bed from the 1750s, a late 18th-century English Adamesque leather-top desk, an American Queen Anne maple high-boy, and a private deck with views to the Klickitat Hills across the Columbia River. The other room is furnished largely with Victorian pieces from New England, but the hand-carved headboard with central walnut burl panel dates from 1775.

Breakfast—coddled eggs, cherry-tinted honey, and jam from the fruits of the Williamses' orchard—is served on Spode china. In good weather, which occurs often in this, the driest part of the gorge, breakfast is served in a gazebo on the back patio.

🏠 *2 double rooms share bath, 1 suite. Air-conditioning, cable TV. $65–$75, full breakfast. AE, D, MC, V. No smoking, no pets.*

Other Choices

Beryl House. 4079 Barrett Dr., Hood River, OR 97031, tel. 541/386–5567. 4 double rooms share 2 baths. VCR, CD player in common room, video and CD library, equipment storage. $55–$65, full breakfast. MC, V. No smoking.

Chamberlin House. 36817 E. Crown Point Hwy., Corbett, OR 97019, tel. 503/695–2200. 2 double rooms with baths. $60–$70; full or Continental breakfast, champagne splits in evening. No credit cards. No smoking, no pets.

Columbia Gorge Hotel. 4000 W. Cliff Dr., Hood River, OR 97031, tel. 541/386–5566 or 800/345–1921. 46 double rooms with baths. Restaurant, bar, lobby lounge, TVs, phones, fireplace in 2 rooms, conference facilities. $150–$270; full breakfast, catering available. AE, D, MC, V. No smoking in restaurant.

Doublegate Inn. 26711 E. Welches Rd., tel. 503/622-4859. 2 double rooms with baths, 2 suites. Guest kitchenette, VCR in common room, video library. $80–$115; full breakfast, complimentary hot and cold beverages. D, MC, V. No smoking, no pets.

Hackett House. 922 State St., Hood River, OR 97031, tel. 541/386–1014. 3 double rooms and 1 suite share 2½ baths. Robes, conference facilities, equipment storage, free parking. $65–$75; full breakfast, evening refreshments, dinner available. AE, D, MC, V. No smoking, no pets.

State Street Bed & Breakfast. 1005 State St., Hood River, OR 97031, tel. 541/386–1899. 4 double rooms share 2 baths. Recreation room, storage area for sports equipment. $60–$80, full breakfast. MC, V. No smoking, no pets.

Reservations Services

The Bed & Breakfast Registry (tel. 503/249–1997 or 800/249–1997). **Bed & Breakfast Reservations—Oregon** (2321 N.E. 28th Ave., Portland, OR 97212, tel. 503/287–4704). **Northwest**

Bed and Breakfast (610 S.W. Broadway, Portland, OR 97205, tel. 503/243–7616).

Central and Eastern Oregon, Including Bend

Cascade Country Inn

15870 Barclay Drive, Box 834, Sisters, OR 97759, tel. 541/549–4666 or 800/316–0089

Cascade Country Inn may be the only bed-and-breakfast in America where you can fly in and park your plane in the yard. On the high desert plain of eastern Oregon, this country inn offers commanding vistas of the snowcapped Cascade Mountains in a quiet, rural setting close to the town of Sisters.

Flying is a passion for the owner, Judy Tolonen, which is why the inn has its own runway for small private aircraft. One part of the hanger where Judy keeps her own plane has been made into a two-level studio guest room filled with an intriguing collection of flying memorabilia, including a coffee table made from a Continental radial aircraft engine, an antique aircraft gas pump, and photos of aviators.

Built in 1994, the inn is modeled after a large country house with a porch and dormers. A double staircase leads up from the reception area to the guest rooms on the second floor. The hemlock used for floors, doors, and trim throughout the house softens its newness. In the first-floor living area, with blue overstuffed chairs and sofa and a love seat of floral fabric, there is a commanding view of the three peaks known as the Sisters. Both the living area and the open dining area beside it are furnished with reproduction antiques and papered in a country plaid design.

Each of the individually decorated guest rooms has a queen- or king-size bed and a private bath with floral-relief ceramic tiles painted and hand-fired by Judy. One wall in My Heart's Desire, on the first floor, has been constructed of old boards painted a soft yellow. On the second floor, the two spacious rooms on either end of the house feature gas fireplaces, cathedral ceilings, and enormous windows. The other two second-story rooms have built-in seating areas tucked in under mountain-facing windows. Furnishings in all the rooms are new, but have a country look.

Breakfasts typically consist of quiche or French toast filled with cream cheese and whipped cream, baked apples, sausage, and fresh fruit. Part of the morning's pleasure is to sit and talk with Judy, whose whirlwind energy and sense of humor add a lively spark to the solitude of the surrounding desert landscape.

🏠 *6 double rooms with bath, 1 suite separate from house. Air-conditioning, TV in 2 rooms, VCR in upstairs den, mountain bikes, runway for private aircraft. $100–$125, full breakfast. MC, V. No smoking, 2-night minimum Memorial Day–Labor Day.*

Elliott House

305 W. 1st St., Prineville, OR 97754, tel. 541/416–0423

In 1908, when Elliott House was built, Prineville was a booming cattle center on the edge of the frontier. Ranching is still big in Crook County, but Prineville is now best known for rockhounding (within a few miles are huge agate beds where the curious can easily pick up "thunder eggs" and petrified wood). Despite its rough-hewn reputation, Prineville has always been the most genteel town in central Oregon. Elliott House, a Queen Anne Victorian, keeps that tradition of class in the outback alive.

With its thick green lawns, wraparound porch, Tuscan columns, and bay windows, the house—on the National Register of Historic Places—stands out like a well-groomed dowager in an otherwise undistinguished neighborhood. Re-creating the past has become a fulltime occupation for the innkeepers, Andrew and Betty Wiechert. Once they found their "dream house," they moved up from the Bay Area and began carefully restoring it.

Fueled by their lifelong passion for antiques, the Wiecherts have filled Elliott House with a marvelous collection of turn-of-the-century furnishings, most of it oak. There is an interesting piece wherever you look. The comfortable parlor, for instance, has a 1916 Wurlitzer piano.

The two guest rooms on the second floor are also filled with vintage pieces and accessories. A 100-year-old mahogany side table and English oak commode with black marble graces one of them. In the second room, which has cabbage-rose wallpaper, there's a double cast-iron bed with a high mattress and an embroidered quilt that came by wagon train, as well as an 1890 oak "potty chair" (decorative, of course). The rooms share a large sumptuous bathroom with floral-print wallpaper, original brass fixtures, and a marbletopped sink.

Betty custom designs breakfasts. Served by candlelight on antique china, the morning's repast might include a bowl of fresh fruit or homemade applesauce, Swedish waffles or crepes with raspberries, or eggs with sausage rolls. To accompany it all, Betty cranks up the Edison cylinder phonograph and fills the dining room with period music.

🛏 *2 double rooms share bath. Cable TV/VCR in attic lounge. $70; full breakfast, afternoon refreshments. No credit cards. No smoking, no pets, no children under 12.*

Frenchglen Hotel

Frenchglen, OR 97736, tel. 541/493-2825

It's almost impossible to miss the Frenchglen Hotel—that is, once you *find* Frenchglen, a tiny spot on the map deep in the eastern Oregon desert. The town consists of a school (most of the families live on ranches sprinkled across a 1,000-square-mile area), a store, and the hotel.

Built in 1920, still pioneer days in this remote region, the state-owned hotel resembles a simple prairie church, with a gabled roof that's visible from miles away as you approach from the north. Manager John Ross spent years as a cook on Alaskan fishing boats, so remoteness is nothing new to him. At least here, at the foot of Steens Mountain, he gets a fresh supply of faces every few days.

Inside, the hotel is simple and rustic. A huge camp-type coffeepot is always on the hob in the combination lobby–dining room. You can absorb local history and whet your appetite for touring with a collection of picture books in the lobby. The dining room, really two long pine tables, serves as a gathering place for ranchers and visitors.

The food here has long been a standout. Every evening a large, hearty familystyle dinner is served for overnight guests and the general public. A typical group might include a ranching couple who have driven 60 miles to celebrate their anniversary, a pair of bird-watchers, and a local mechanic. John whips up huge salads, rich casseroles, homebaked rolls, and a main meat dish for à la carte dining. Breakfast is also bountiful, although it's served individually from a menu and isn't included in the room rate.

All the rooms are upstairs off a single hallway. The five rooms in the original part of the hotel have plain white walls and wooden bed frames handmade by John. The three rooms at the back of the hotel, added during the 1930s, have knotty pine walls. Views sweep eastward across the broad Blitzen Valley up the gradually sloping shoulders of

Steens Mountain. All eight rooms share two bathrooms midway down the long hall.

Most of the people who stay at the hotel, which is on the National Register of Historic Places, are devoted bird-watchers who are attracted by the nearby Malheur National Wildlife Refuge. In the fall, however, Steens teems with hunters. The mix of hunters, ranchers, and conservationists can make for some lively conversations over breakfast.

🏠 *8 double rooms share 2 baths. Restaurant. $45–$49, breakfast not included. MC, V. No smoking, no pets. Closed mid-Nov.–mid-Mar.*

Lara House

640 N.W. Congress St., Bend, OR 97701, tel. 541/388–4064 or 800/766–4064

Staying at Lara House, a cross-gabled Craftsman house built in 1910, gives you a glimpse of what life was like in Bend when it was a four-day trip to Portland instead of the present-day three-hour drive. Beside peaceful Drake Park on the Deschutes River near downtown, Lara House stands out; it's on a huge lot with a sloping lawn atop a retaining wall of native lava rocks.

The house's original woodwork can be seen in the trim and door frames and in the alderwood-coffered ceiling of the living room. There a massive, lodge-size fireplace dominates, to be enjoyed from two cream-and-blue patterned camelback love seats or from the ladder-back chairs about the gaming table. The walls here are heavily stuccoed. Walk through the double French doors and the atmosphere changes radically. Restored to its original style, the huge sunroom with a glass table, overlooking the 11-acre riverside park, is an airy, light-filled haven.

The large, carpeted guest rooms, all on the second floor, have seating areas and private bathrooms. The L-shaped Drake Room, furnished in dark oak, has a duck theme: wallpaper borders swimming with them, framed prints of them, and a wall unit displaying knickknacks of these fine-feathered friends. The black claw-foot tub in the bathroom is the original. Softer and more romantic is the Shevlin Room with its alcoved, lace-covered bed, Queen Anne–style couch and chair, and Cupid prints. A masculine tone predominates in the Cascade Room, which has handsome black-striped wallpaper.

There is a choice of venues for breakfast: the formal dining room, sunroom, or terraced redwood deck that surrounds the house. Innkeepers Doug and Bobbye Boger not only arrange rafting tours on the Deschutes, but Doug, a part-time ski instructor, also leads ski tours that include lessons at nearby Mt. Bachelor.

🏠 *5 double rooms with baths. Baby-sitting available, hot tub, rafting and skiing tours arranged. $55–$95; full breakfast, afternoon and evening refreshments, dinner and catering available. D, MC, V. No smoking, no pets.*

Sather House Bed-and-Breakfast

7 N.W. Tumalo, Bend, OR 97701, tel. 541/388–1065

Bend is booming, and its recent "discovery" has inevitably led to a great deal of undistinguished, fast-track development along its peripheries. Luckily, the quiet charm of Bend's older neighborhoods can still be savored at the Sather House, a spacious historic home on the northwest side of town.

Built in 1911 for the Sather family, who occupied it for 75 years, the sturdy-looking Colonial Revival house occupies a prominent location at the intersection of three wide, tree-lined streets. The exterior, glistening white with green trim, has a wraparound veranda and overhanging eaves. Like the other homes in this immaculately maintained residential neighborhood, three blocks from the Deschutes River and walking distance to downtown, Sather House evokes a feeling of calm, comfortable dignity.

The owner, Robbie Giamboi, totally renovated the house and her meticulous taste is evident the moment you step inside. Period furnishings, old-fashioned without being oppressive, are used throughout. Original woodwork, all of it Douglas fir, has been beautifully restored. Robbie sponged and rag-rolled the walls herself. The light-filled living room, with lace-curtained windows, has wing-back chairs and a comfortable sofa gathered near a fireplace. Built-in benches in the parlor are used for a games area. There is also a big, airy kitchen and a butler's pantry, where you can get an early morning coffee.

Of the four guest rooms, all on the second floor, the largest and lightest is the Garden Room. It has a sofa and a rocking chair; Battenburg and lace are used for curtains and the comforter. The English Room, done in paisleys, blues, greens, and burgundies, is darker and more traditionally masculine. The Victorian Room is decorated in blues and pinks with a canopied bed and a 1910 claw-foot tub in the bath. The Country Room features a picket-fence headboard and hand-painted desk.

Robbie says her goal is to "pamper the women and feed the men." Breakfast, served in the formal dining room, typically consists of French toast with raspberries and almonds, or pecan pancakes. She serves fireside tea in winter and lemonade and cookies on the veranda in summer.

▦ *2 double rooms with baths, 2 doubles share bath. Cable TV. $75–$85; full breakfast, afternoon tea or refreshments. D, MC, V. No smoking, no pets, no children.*

Shaniko Hotel

Shaniko, OR 97057, tel. 541/489–3441

Bed-and-breakfasting in a ghost town may not strike everyone as a good bet. But here on the high dusty plains south of The Dalles, the Old West feel of the restored Shaniko Hotel is palpable.

Guest rooms at the hotel, which first opened in 1901, are spare and perhaps a bit too antiseptic with their period reproduction furniture. (The mock old-fashioned wooden iceboxes acting as night tables *are* clever, however.) The only special room is the pink-and-white Bridal Suite, which features a small sitting room and a two-person whirlpool tub. Still, there's plenty of atmosphere just outside; you need only peek out of the window to see a town falling down as the wind wails through the old buildings and shutters flap eerily.

Shaniko has been a ghost town since the 1940s, when the last rail line leading to town washed out. Yet in 1900, the town's population numbered in the thousands and it was the world's biggest shipper of wool. Stagecoach lines spoked into the frontier of eastern Oregon, and Shaniko was the railhead for the only line that then penetrated the high plains.

Despite the slightly sterile feel, owners Jean and Dorothy Farrell give a personal warmth to the hotel and to their guests. Of course, that's easy to do in this town of 19, where all except two work either in the hotel or at its adjoining restaurant. Jean, a retired plumbing contractor, is also the mayor of Shaniko, a delicate job that involves keeping the town looking rundown without allowing it to collapse completely.

Breakfasts are copious, geared to a day of shearing sheep or baling hay, and dinners are mammoth, with huge wads of sweet homemade bread complementing mashed potatoes and gravy with hunks of meat.

Those calories can be partially walked off with a stroll through Shaniko. The old firehouse has been kept up to house ancient horse-drawn fire rigs. The blacksmith shop is run by a small company that makes reproduction carriages. For real culture shock, you can tour the tiny, false-fronted Shaniko Post Office. Across the lonesome highway is the old, creaking water tower, the tallest building in town. The first new structure to be built in Shaniko in decades—a combination ice-cream parlor, meeting place, and photo studio—is right next to the hotel, which also has a highly browsable antiques store.

🏠 *17 double rooms with baths, 1 suite. Restaurant, whirlpool tub in suite. $56–$66, suite $96; full breakfast. D, MC, V. No smoking in rooms, no pets.*

Stange Manor

1612 Walnut St., La Grande, OR 97850, tel. 541/963–2400 or 800/286–9463

When Marjorie McClure was growing up during the late 1930s in La Grande, the Stange mansion, just a few blocks away, seemed a place of unattainable glamour. Owned by lumber baron August Stange, the richest man in the county, the house on the western edge of this small college and ranching town was an obligatory stop for any political figure and celebrity passing through.

Marjorie left La Grande in 1956 for California. It wasn't until 1992, when she and her husband Pat returned for her father's 100th birthday, that Marjorie finally got her chance to stay at the elegant manor. Three months later, the McClures had closed the deal to buy the place that Bing Crosby and Guy Kibbe had visited during Marjorie's childhood.

Built in 1926, the imposing Georgian Revival home sits on huge grounds in an otherwise unspectacular residential neighborhood. Stang Manor's interior is full of stylish details from the 1920s. You can enjoy the large Italian stone fireplace in the living room from a semi-

circular sectional couch upholstered in a rose-print tapestry fabric.

Throw open the French doors of the sunroom, complete with a working wall fountain of teal-colored Italian tiles, and the years quickly melt away. Built-in benches line the perimeter of the window-filled room, affording views of the property. White rattan furniture adds to the Jay Gatsby aura of the room.

As you ascend the grand staircase to the upstairs guest rooms, you'll pass a large Georgian hunting tapestry purchased by Stange and a plaster bust of Aphrodite at the top. The master suite boasts a turn-of-the-century-mahogany-turned-four-poster bed and matching dresser with tilting mirror. The bathroom features the original "foot washer," fed with running water. But extraordinary features are found in every room of this historic house, which has remained unmodified except for its wall coverings.

Breakfast is a lavish affair served in the dining room beneath a pewter and crystal chandelier original. Built-in floor-to-ceiling china display cabinets, flocked wallpaper, and full-length balloon curtains contribute to the formal ambience of the room. Usually Pat and Marjorie will join you for breakfast, which might be considered an intrusion if they weren't so cordial, informative, and easygoing.

🏠 *2 double rooms with baths, 2 2-bedroom suites. Fireplace and cable TV in 1 suite. $75–$90; full breakfast, afternoon tea. D, MC, V. No smoking, no pets.*

Other Choices

Bed-and-Breakfast by the River. Rte. 2, Box 790, Prairie City, OR 97869, tel. 541/820–4470. 1 double room with bath, 2 doubles share bath. TV/VCR, pool table in game room. $35–$50, full breakfast. No credit cards. No smoking, no pets, no alcohol.

Chandlers Bed, Bread & Trail Inn. 700 S. Main St., Joseph, OR 97846, tel. 541/432–9765, 800/452–3781. 3 double rooms with baths, 2 doubles share 1½ baths. TV/VCR in common area, computer available, free shuttle to nearby trailheads. $50–$80, full breakfast. MC, V. No smoking, no pets.

Clear Creek Farm Bed-and-Breakfast. Rte. 1, Box 138, Halfway, OR 97834, tel. 541/742–2238 or 800/742–4992, fax 541/742–5175. 4 double rooms share bath, 2 2-room bunkhouses share 3 outdoor bathhouses. Library, conference facilities, hot tub. $60, single bunkhouses $40, $30 per person for parties of 2 or more; full breakfast. MC, V. Bunkhouses closed Nov.–Apr.

Hotel Diamond. 10 Main St., Diamond, OR 97722, tel. 541/493–1898. 1 double room with bath, 5 doubles share 2½ baths. Deli next door, air-conditioning, mountain bikes. $45–$65; breakfast not included, dinner by reservation. MC, V. No pets, no children.

Pine Valley Lodge and Halfway Supper Club. 163 N. Main St., Halfway, OR 97834, tel. 541/742–2027. 2 double rooms share bath, 2 suites share bath. Restaurant, bicycles. Double rooms $60–$65, suites $90; full breakfast. No credit cards. No smoking.

Reservations Services

Bed and Breakfast Reservations—Oregon (2321 N.E. 28th Ave., Portland, OR 97212, tel. 503/287–4704).

Northwest Bed and Breakfast (1067 Hanover Ct. S, Salem, OR 97302, tel. 503/243–7616 or 503/370–9033, fax 503/316–9118).

Pennsylvania

Limestone Inn

The Poconos

French Manor

Huckleberry Rd. (Box 39), off Rte. 191, South Sterling, PA 18460, tel. 717/676–3244 or 800/523–8200, fax 717/676–9786

The 40-acre setting is aristocratic and the views exquisite. Rolling hills and mountain ranges reveal themselves periodically as you drive up the winding, wooded road toward the crest of Huckleberry Mountain to the fieldstone manor house with a slate roof, cooper-mullioned windows, and arched oak door.

It was built between 1932 and 1937 as a summer residence for mining tycoon and art collector Joseph Hirschorn, who modeled it after his château in southern France. After changing hands several times, the house became an inn in 1985 and in 1990 was bought by Ron and Mary Kay Logan, who own and manage the nearby Sterling Inn.

The 40-foot-high Great Room, with a vaulted cherry-wood ceiling and a mammoth plastered-stone fireplace at each end, makes a spectacular restaurant. French doors with leaded glass open onto a slate terrace that has a sweeping view of the countryside. The guest rooms, named after European cities, have cypress and cedar walls and ceilings and are decorated in a mix of contemporary style and French antique reproductions. "Venice" has an ornate headboard on its king-size bed. Baths have old-fashioned tile with pedestal sinks. The carriage-house has two suites with fireplace and whirlpool bath and is furnished like the manor house but with smaller rooms. Though it is secluded, its feeling of newness makes it not nearly as nice as the larger house.

A full-service, no-smoking dining room with a full liquor license treats guests to an à la carte menu that changes about every two months and features highly touted French cuisine. A recent selection included grilled beef tenderloin nestled on a roasted garlic and tomato *concassée* cream; and fresh salmon baked in a sauce of champagne, white peppercorn, and asparagus.

With panoramic views as a backdrop, you can take peaceful walks or go cross-country skiing. Golf, horseback riding, and other recreations are nearby. The medieval atmosphere of the house—and the thoughtful service of the Logans and their staff—create the timeless feeling that you have really gotten away from it all.

⊞ *6 double rooms with baths, 3 suites. Restaurant open daily for breakfast and dinner, air-conditioning in bedrooms, TV in lounge, croquet. $120–$225, full breakfast. AE, D, MC, V. No smoking, no pets.*

Inn at Meadowbrook

Cherry Lane Rd. E (R.D. 7, Box 7651), Stroudsburg, PA 18301, tel. 717/629–0296 or 800/249–6861, fax 717/620–1754

Guests who arrive at the Inn at Meadowbrook after dark are often relieved to find they aren't lost. On the long and winding 4½ wooded miles from Tannersville you may begin to think you've missed it, but suddenly, around a corner, there it is, blanketed by soft light and trees and chirping night sounds: a white clapboard manor house with green trim. And just across the road is a white mill house that's part of the inn. If you're going to get pleasantly lost anywhere in the Poconos, this is the place to do it.

For many years the 1867 house and its 43 acres were a horse farm, and in 1985 Kathy and Bob Overman bought the estate and turned it into a bed-and-breakfast. Kathy, an artist who loves to garden, has given each of the guest rooms a distinctive decor. Bob, the resident gourmet chef, has mastered the celebrated raspberry-cinnamon-raisin pudding recipe you may be lucky enough to sample for breakfast.

You can curl up with a book on the leather sofa in the light-flooded parlor or in wing chairs that face the fireplace, or you can simply gaze out the windows at the pond, gazebo, and mill house. The spacious hunter-green dining room, added in the '20s, is a setting out of *The Great Gatsby*, with 15-foot ceilings, arched columns, and tall Palladian windows on three sides framing the gardens, the rushing brook with footbridge, and a pond. French doors open onto the terrace for dining in warm months.

The guest rooms are furnished with English and American antiques and country pieces. There are patchwork quilts, lots of books, wicker chairs, and convenient reading lamps. Room 9, a favorite of guests, has rich burgundy paisley draperies, hunter-green walls, an antique brass bed, and a view of the stables. Room 10 overlooks the pond and has a white birch four-poster bed that Bob built.

On the inn's own grounds you can swim, fish, play tennis, ice-skate, and take leisurely walks with a picnic lunch. Bob and Kathy can arrange horseback riding and carriage and sleigh rides. The area also has its share of antiques shops and flea markets.

⊞ *10 double rooms with baths, 6 doubles share 2 baths. Restaurant, TV/VCR in recreation room, pool, 2 tennis courts, shuffleboard, pond. $60–$95, full breakfast. AE, D, DC, MC, V. Restricted smoking, no pets, 2-day minimum on weekends.*

Inn at Starlight Lake

Starlight, PA 18461, tel. 717/798–2519 or 800/248–2519, fax 717/798–2672

The hamlet of Starlight, nestled in the foothills of the Moosic range, was once a railroad stop, and in 1909 this Adirondack-style lodge was built on the lake nearby to serve passengers. Today the sprawling white-and-green clapboard inn looks much as it did around the turn of the century, and it's just as peaceful. Jack and Judy McMahon have been innkeepers here since 1974. Before that they lived in New York City and worked in the theater, where they met while performing.

The rambling parlor, with its wood-burning stove, stone fireplace, and baby-grand piano, sets the homey, lodgelike mood. There's a comfortable mixture of antiques, Mission oak furniture, and well-lived-in pieces, with numerous Tiffany-style lamps for reading. In winter you might expect Bing Crosby to step out and warble "White Christmas."

Guest rooms on the second and third floors are simple and unpretentious, with framed prints on floral-papered walls, crocheted doilies, and lots of magazines. You'll find iron beds and marble-top dressers, but mostly a hodgepodge of old and not-so-old furniture. A row of recently renovated cottages is furnished with antique reproductions. The suite has a king-size bed and a whirlpool bath for two; above it is another charming room with an iron bed and a fieldstone fireplace.

Chef David Giles presides in the dining room. Everything served is made on the premises, including breads, pastas, ice cream, and pastries. You can work off a little of David's duck with orange sauce with a game of pool, Ping-Pong, or tabletop shuffleboard in the inn's game room.

No motors are allowed on the 45-acre lake, so it's quiet and crystal clean for swimming and fishing. On occasional murder-mystery weekends, whodunits are performed by the Starlight Players. In winter there's ice-skating, and the McMahons' son, a certified ski instructor, can take you down the property's slopes or show you the best trails for cross-country skiing. On crisp autumn mornings you are likely to see deer or flocks of wild turkeys through the early mist.

🏨 *20 double rooms with baths, 2 doubles share bath, 1 suite, 3-bedroom Family House. Restaurant, bar, TV/VCR in sunroom, baby-sitting arranged, tennis court, canoes, bicycles. $115–$200; full breakfast, dinner. MC, V. No smoking in dining room, no pets, 2-day minimum in season, 3-day minimum on holidays. Closed first 2 weeks in Apr.*

Settlers Inn

4 Main Ave., Hawley, PA 18428, tel. 717/226–2993 or 800/833–8527, fax 717/226–1874

This rambling Tudor-style grand hotel built in 1927 has been restored as a country inn. It's on a well-traveled bend of Route 6, five minutes from Lake Wallenpaupack, but once you enter the high-ceilinged living room, with its chestnut beams and massive stone fireplace, you'll forget about the location. Antique marble-top tables, Victorian chairs and sofas evoke the atmosphere of an English country hotel. The rooms, furnished with "early attic" antiques, also have Early American memorabilia.

The popular dining room is the domain of Grant Genzlinger, who's not only chef-innkeeper but also a student of ancient Chinese languages. He and his wife, Jeanne, share innkeeping duties with their partner, Marcia Dunsmore, and distinguish themselves mightily in the kitchen arts. The flavorful, amply portioned dinners testify to the proprietors' assiduous search for locally grown ingredients as well as to their loyalty to regional specialties. Dishes reflect the joy of a year-round pursuit of the best and brightest in the Pennsylvania agricultural community. Witness the cheddar pasta supper dish, composed of fettuccine, leeks, and spinach tossed in a sauce of Up Country Pennsylvania sharp cheddar and Forest Home Dairy fresh cream; or the chicken schnitzel, a scallop of chicken dipped in a light lemon and thyme batter, scented with nutmeg, sautéed, and served with fettuccine and roasted zucchini, peppers, yellow squash, onions, and tomatoes. You'll dine sitting in one of the more than 100 Gothic, church-school chairs brought from the Bryn Athyn Cathedral near Philadelphia.

If you detect a sometimes whimsical, sometimes earnest voice in the menu descriptions, trust it for its very contradictions. The trio in charge does it all with a winning combination of dead seriousness and an insouciant aptitude for gustatory lucky strikes. Where else would you find garlic additions to an entrée honored on the menu as the "errant lily"?

The location is ideal for getting to winter or summer sports, and the town has enough antiques shops to keep you browsing for days.

▥ *15 double rooms with baths, 4 suites. Restaurant, air-conditioning, TV in sitting room, 2 meeting rooms, large banquet room. $83–$143, full breakfast. AE, D, MC, V. Restricted smoking, no pets.*

Sterling Inn

South Sterling, PA 18460, tel. 717/676–3311, 717/676–3338, or 800/523–8200

Ron Logan, owner of the Sterling Inn, has put together a 10-page document tracing the site's history, from its occupation by the Nini subtribe (a branch of the Leni–Lenape) all the way up to his and his wife's proprietorship. "There is little wonder why the Indians would choose this particular site for their village," he observes. "Mountains on either side, the Wallenpaupack Creek with an abundance of trout, level fertile land, bubbling springs, and plenty of deer, bear, and other game."

It's still lovely here today, and this in itself is testimony to Ron and Mary Kay Logan's talent, energy, and restraint. The inn consists of an inviting white clapboard main house with hunter-green rooftop, built in 1857, and a cluster of cottages. It all sits on the road, nestled in a forested valley traversed by nature trails and winding waterways. The couple provides once-a-week lectures and guided nature walks, conducted by local author John Serrao, so that guests can absorb more than a glimpse of the 105 surrounding acres of birch, hemlock, and American beech, not to mention the wildflowers and bird life.

A fresh, countrified air prevails inside the inn, notwithstanding a few modern embellishments—a heated indoor pool, a poolside bar, and a spa. The dining room, open to guests and nonguests alike, is dominated by a large stone fireplace and decorated with a delicate floral-patterned wallpaper, pink tablecloths and woodwork, and bright blue cotton curtains over broad window valances. Resident chef George Pelepko Filak, a graduate of the Culinary Institute of America, is happy to accommodate special diets, but each standard menu is lavished with entrées like medallions of veal lombardi; scampi with scallops, garlic, and wine; and steamed red snapper.

The rooms, accented by playful ruffles and flounces, echo the clean, bright-eyed ingenuousness of the downstairs dining room. They all have phones and private baths; fireplace suites and cottages are available. The Logans offer several discount package rates. Romance and privacy give visitors here a true escape. Winter delights include horse-drawn sleigh rides and cross-country skiing; in the summer diversions such as swimming, hiking, horseback riding, and fishing abound.

▥ *38 double rooms with baths, 16 suites. Restaurant, phones, indoor pool, spa, 9-hole putting course, cross-country ski trails, nature trails. $140–$220; full breakfast, dinner. AE, D, MC, V. No smoking in dining room, no pets.*

Other Choices

Beach Lake Hotel. Main and Church Sts. (Box 144), Beach Lake, PA 18405, tel. 717/729–8239 or 800/382–3897. 6 double rooms with baths. Restaurant, air-conditioning in bedrooms, pub with TV. $95, full breakfast. MC, V. Restricted smoking, no pets, 2-day minimum on holiday weekends.

Brookview Manor. Route 447 (R.R. 1, Box 365), Canadensis, PA 18325, tel. 717/595–2451. 9 double rooms with baths, 1 suite. Whirlpool baths in 2 rooms, fireplace in 1 room, TV in den, pool table, Ping-Pong, games room. $100–$150, full breakfast. AE, D, MC, V. No smoking indoors, no pets, 2-night minimum on holiday weekends.

Cliff Park Inn. Cliff Park Rd. (R.R. 4, Box 7200), Milford, PA 18337, tel. 717/296–6491 or 800/225–6535, fax 717/296–3982. 19 double rooms with baths. Restaurant, air-conditioning, conference facilities, TV/VCR in meeting rooms, 9-hole golf course, pro shop, stable. $128–$205 (full breakfast and dinner), $93–$155 (breakfast only). AE, D, DC, MC, V. No pets. Closed Dec. 24–25.

Overlook Inn. Dutch Hill Rd. (Box 680), Canadensis, PA 18325-9755, tel. 717/595–7519. 18 double rooms with baths, 2 suites. Restaurant, air-conditioning available, phones, TV in library, conference facilities, pool. $75–$100; breakfast, high tea, dinner. AE, MC, V. No smoking in dining room or guest rooms, no pets.

New Hope/Bucks County

Barley Sheaf Farm

Rte. 202 (Box 10), Holicong, PA 18928, tel. and fax 215/794–5104

Turn off well-traveled Route 202 10 minutes from New Hope, and you'll see sheep grazing in the pastures on either side of a sycamore-flanked lane. At the end is Barley Sheaf Farm, the 1740 mansard-roofed fieldstone house that in the '30s was the hideaway of playwright George S. Kaufman. Today this charming 30-acre farm, though just around the bend from the bustling antiques shops of Peddler's Village, manages to retain the quiet gentility that prevailed when Lillian Hellman, Alexander Woollcott, and Moss Hart visited here.

The swimming pool, a duck pond, and the bank barn add texture and a relaxed appeal to the house and grounds, which have been designated a National Historic Site. On a visit to the States in 1994, Peter and Veronika Suess, two businesspeople from Switzerland, saw Barley Sheaf and fell in love with it. They quit their jobs, bought the property via international fax, and arrived the first night to a full house of guests.

The house and adjacent cottage are furnished in a mixture of English and American antiques, with rich Oriental rugs scattered over the wide-plank floors. Guests gather in the common room, by the fire, for chess, checkers, and conversation.

The bedrooms on the second and third floors have elegant views. The rooms are decorated with floral prints and brass-and-iron beds. Peter and Veronika have brought with them furniture, antiques, and traditions including breakfast *grittibaenz* (little men made of bread with raisin eyes).

The cottage is cozy, and in winter months there's always a crackling fire. The three bedrooms here are decorated with American folk art, both antique and reproduction. Each room has sloping eaves, hooked rugs, and antique pine furniture. Though the rooms are small, the cottage is perfect for families.

You should expect to hear noises in this rural setting—the noises of a working farm: the baaing of sheep, the buzzing of bees (which manufacture 300 pounds of honey annually), and the occasional rumble of a tractor. But that means you can count on the abundant breakfasts (which include eggs, bread, jams, and honey) to be farm fresh.

🏠 *8 double rooms with baths, 4 suites. Air-conditioning, TV in study, pool, badminton, croquet, meeting room in barn. $105–$255; full breakfast, afternoon tea. AE, MC, V. No smoking, no pets, 2-day minimum on weekends, 3-day minimum on holidays.*

Evermay-on-the-Delaware

River Rd., Erwinna, PA 18920, tel. 610/294-9100, fax 610/294-8249

Thirteen miles north of New Hope is Evermay-on-the-Delaware, a romantic country hotel with a carriage house and cottage set on 25 parklike acres between the river and the canal. Here Victorian elegance is still very much in fashion.

The mansion, which is on the National Register of Historic Places, was built in 1790 and had a third floor added in 1870. From 1871 through the early 1930s, it was a popular country hotel. It was the Stover family home for many years and then bought by innkeepers William and Danielle Moffly. After meticulous restoration, they reopened it in March 1982. You will find Fred and Ron to be unobtrusive, genteel hosts; their style is in keeping with the hotel's tradition of understated elegance.

In the stately double parlor you can meet for afternoon tea or for an aperitif in the evening. The fireplace is inset with Mercer tiles, and there are crystal chandeliers, tapestry rugs, a Victorian grandfather clock, and brocade camel-back settees. Breakfast is served in a conservatory off the back parlor. The bedrooms, carefully decorated with Victorian antiques and named after Bucks County notables, have wide-plank squeaky floors; some retain their original fireplaces. Carved walnut beds, massive headboards, marble-top dressers, Victorian wallpaper, and fresh fruit and flowers are everywhere. Ask for one of the six bedrooms in the main house that face the river. The carriage house may be preferable for groups traveling together. It has a two-bedroom suite with sitting room and bath on the second floor and two double rooms on the ground floor.

The Evermay is ideally located for enjoying the countryside in any season. If you venture out into the meadows or into the old barn, you will run across sheep, chickens, and pheasants.

🏨 *14 double rooms with baths, 1 suite. Restaurant, air-conditioning and phones in bedrooms, hookups for modem. $85-$170; Continental breakfast, afternoon tea. MC, V. No smoking in dining room, no pets, 2-day minimum with Sat. reservation, 3-day minimum on holidays. Closed Dec. 24.*

Inn at Fordhook Farm

105 New Britain Rd., Doylestown, PA 18901, tel. 215/345-1766, fax 215/345-1791

The Inn at Fordhook Farm, set on 60 acres a mile and a half from the center of Doylestown, is the Burpee family estate. There's a bank barn and a carriage house, surrounded by the fields and meadows where W. Atlee Burpee first tested seeds for his company before the turn of the century. The oldest part of the fieldstone-and-plaster house with a mansard roof dates from 1740. Through the years, additions were carefully made to blend architecturally with the original structure. Burpee's grandchild, Jonathan Burpee, grew up here. Thinking that a bed-and-breakfast would be a good way to preserve the family home, Jonathan and his wife, Carole, opened it to guests in 1985.

The house, furnished throughout with a mixture of English and American family antiques, is a living legacy of photographs, china, furniture, grandfather clocks, and other Americana. In the dining room, the mantel is inlaid with Mercer tiles, and the long mahogany table is set with heirloom china each morning for breakfast. French doors open to a large terrace shaded by a 200-year-old linden tree, with a view of the broad, sweeping lawn. In the bedrooms, you will find floral prints, quilts, 19th-century four-poster beds, window seats, and family photographs and portraits.

The carriage house is a spacious two-bedroom suite not quite as carefully decorated as the main house, but ideal for a family or for two couples. The chestnut-paneled Great Room there, once a study, has a vaulted ceiling and Palladian windows, and children's books, photographs, and other Burpee memorabilia everywhere.

The style at Fordhook Farm is a quiet, casual elegance. Carole serves an elaborate Saturday tea—by the fire during the winter, outdoors on the generous terrace in warm months.

▦ *5 double rooms with baths, 2 doubles share bath. Air-conditioning, conference room. $93–$300, full breakfast. AE, MC, V. No smoking, no pets, 2-day minimum on weekends, 3-day minimum on holidays.*

Inn at Phillips Mill

N. River Rd., New Hope, PA 18938, tel. 215/862–2984

Perched at a bend in the road, in a tiny hamlet on the Delaware Canal near New Hope, is a 1750 stone inn that looks like an illustration from Grimms' Fairy Tales. There may be no country inn with a setting more romantic than the Inn at Phillips Mill. Built as a barn and a gristmill, it once stood next to the village piggery—a copper pig with a wreath around its neck now welcomes you from just above the deep-blue door.

For 70 years the gristmill has been the September home of the Phillips Mill Community Art Show. In the early 1970s, the main building and its walled garden caught the imagination of Brooks and Joyce Kaufman. Thinking it had the look of a European village, they bought it; Brooks, an architect, started the renovation, and Joyce began doing the interior. They opened in 1977.

The guest rooms are small, but they will enchant you. Some are tucked imaginatively into nooks and under eaves, and each is whimsically furnished. There are brass and iron and late 19th-century four-poster beds, and an eclectic mix of antiques, wicker, quilts, dried bouquets, hand-painted trays, embroidered cloths on night tables, Provençal fabrics, floral wallpapers, and oil paintings. The cottage, also decorated in a mix of French country and American antiques, has a bedroom, a bath, and a living room with a stone fireplace. If you wish, breakfast will be delivered to your bedroom door in a big basket. When you lift the blue-and-white checkered cloth, you will find muffins and a pot of coffee or tea.

Phillips Mill is famous for its restaurant, and rightly so. The candlelit tables in the three dining rooms are intimately nestled into nooks and crannies under low, rough-beamed ceilings. The menu is French and may feature garlic-encrusted swordfish in a beurre blanc sauce, or smoked breast of moulard duck with herbed lentils. Two pastry chefs, Roz Schwartz and Thomas Millburn, prepare *les délices de la maison* (house delights).

The winding back roads are perfect for hiking, bicycling, or driving to see the fall foliage.

▦ *4 double rooms with baths, 1 suite, 1 cottage. Restaurant, air-conditioning, pool. $80–$125, Continental breakfast extra. No credit cards. No pets, BYOB, 3-night minimum on holiday weekends. Closed early Jan.–early Feb.*

Wedgwood Inn

111 W. Bridge St., New Hope, PA 18938, tel. 215/862–2570

You can't miss the Wedgwood Inn. This hip-gabled 1870 Victorian clapboard house on a tree-lined street is only two blocks from the center of New Hope, and it's painted bright Wedgwood blue. It has a large veranda loaded with pots of flowers and hanging ferns, a gazebo. The companion property next door, called Umplebey House, was built of plaster and stone about 1830 in the Classic Revival tradition. It has walls that are 26 inches thick, brick walkways through flowering gardens, and a carriage house in back. Across the street is another companion property, the Aaron Burr House, a six-bedroom Victorian with a maximum capacity of 18 guests, popular for business conferences. It has two suites, one with a stone fireplace and one with gas.

Innkeeping seemed a logical profession for owners Nadine Silnutzer and Carl Glassman, 15-year veterans of the B&B game. They like gardening, and they delight in finding antiques at auctions and flea markets. Carl, with his colleague Ripley Hotch, has published a book, *How to Start and Run Your Own Bed & Breakfast Inn* (Stackpole Books), and teaches innkeeping at New York University.

Wedgwood pottery, oil paintings, handmade quilts, and fresh flowers are everywhere in the sunny interior. The parlors in both houses have coal-fed fireplaces and plush Victorian sofas and chairs. The windows are covered with lace swag curtains. Persian rugs lie on hardwood floors. Both houses have bedrooms with bay windows and Victorian antiques, brass beds, and four-posters. The circa-1890 carriage house has a small sitting room and a glass-enclosed porch, a kitchenette, and a four-poster in the loft that overlooks a small deck. It's a private retreat that's ideal for reading a novel, or maybe writing one.

Days begin casually with a "Continental-plus" breakfast, served in the sunporch, the gazebo, or if you prefer, in bed. If you ask, Carl and Dinie will get you theater tickets, make dinner reservations, and arrange picnics, dinner in the gazebo, or a moonlight carriage ride.

🏠 *12 double rooms with baths, 2 suites. Air-conditioning in bedrooms, TV in parlors, concierge services, swimming and tennis privileges for nominal fee at nearby club. $75–$195; Continental breakfast, afternoon tea. AE, MC, V. No smoking, 2-day mini-* mum on weekends, 3-day minimum on holiday weekends.

Whitehall Inn

1370 Pineville Rd., New Hope, PA 18938, tel. 215/598–7945 or 888/379–4483

Ten minutes southwest of New Hope and five minutes from Peddler's Village is the Whitehall Inn, a white plaster-over-stone manor house, circa 1794, set on 12 rolling acres, with a huge white barn and stables at the side. It is one of the most peaceful and secluded inns in Bucks County.

Two transplanted Oklahomans, Mike and Suella Wass, are responsible for elevating the business of innkeeping to a fine art. No guest will feel neglected here; from the moment you cross the threshold, the Wasses convince you with seeming effortlessness (or perhaps it's hard work) that your visit is important to them. Some establishments have lost this gift—the host greets you with a "you're on your own" dispatch—but this couple encourages your interest in the area, engages you in conversation, and ultimately earns your compliments. After years in their niche, the Wasses continue to stand above the rest.

Inside the house, past the sunroom, are high ceilings, Oriental rugs on wide-plank floors, and windows with deep sills. The parlor has a fireplace, a late 19th-century pedal organ, comfortable contemporary sofas with lots of Victorian lamps, and the soothing sounds of antique clocks ticking everywhere. The bedrooms (four with fireplaces) are furnished in a mixture of late Victorian and American country antiques. You will find a basket of apples, a bottle of mineral water, and Crabtree and Evelyn soaps, colognes, and shampoos. The linens are imported, and in winter you sleep between flannel sheets.

Heirloom china and ornate Victorian sterling flatware are used for breakfast, a sybaritic and beautifully orchestrated four-course feast, with lighted tapers on the table and sideboards. The Wasses keep your menu on file, so you'll never get a repeat unless you make a special request.

High tea is served at 4 each afternoon with crystal, china, and silver. In summer, you can relax by the pool, play tennis, or go horseback riding nearby. In October, you can walk in the gardens or fields, enjoy the foliage, and spend evenings by the fire in the candlelit parlor. Lovers of chocolate and/or chamber music should inquire about special-event weekends in the spring.

🏨 *4 double rooms with baths, 2 doubles share bath. Air-conditioning, pool. $130–$180; full breakfast, high tea. AE, D, MC, V. No smoking, no pets.*

Other Choices

Ash Mill Farm. Rte. 202 (Box 202), Holicong, PA 18928, tel. 215/794–5373. 3 double rooms with baths, 2 suites. Air-conditioning, breakfast in bed on request. $90–$145; full breakfast, afternoon tea, complimentary brandy. No credit cards. Restricted smoking, no pets, 2-day minimum with Sat. reservation, 3-day minimum on holiday weekends.

Bridgeton House. River Rd. (Box 167), Upper Black Eddy, PA 18972, tel. 610/982–5856. 6 double rooms with baths, 2 suites, garret, penthouse. Air-conditioning, fireplaces in dining room and in suites. $89–$225; full breakfast. MC, V. No smoking, no pets, 2-day minimum on weekends, 3-day minimum on holiday weekends. Closed Dec. 24–25.

Bucksville House. 4501 Durham Rd. and Buck Dr., Kintnersville, PA 18930, tel. 610/847–8948. 4 double rooms with baths, 1 suite. Air-conditioning; cable TV in den; fireplaces in 3 bedrooms; garden with waterfall, deck, and gazebo. $100–$130, full breakfast. AE, D, MC, V. No smoking, no pets.

Highland Farms. 70 East Rd., Doylestown, PA 18901, tel. 215/340–1354. 2 double rooms with baths, 2 doubles share bath. Air-conditioning, cable TV/ VCR, pool, tennis court. $135–$195, full breakfast. AE, MC, V. No smoking, 2-day minimum on weekends, 3-day minimum on holidays.

Logan Inn. 10 W. Ferry St., New Hope, PA 18938, tel. 215/862–2300. 16 double rooms with baths. Restaurant, tavern, air-conditioning, cable TVs, phones, meeting room. $95–$150, Continental breakfast. AE, D, DC, MC, V. No pets, 2-day minimum on weekends May–Dec., 3-day minimum on holiday weekends.

Pinetree Farm. 2155 Lower State Rd., Doylestown, PA 18901, tel. 215/348–0632. 2 double rooms with baths, 2 doubles share bath. Air-conditioning, cable TV in study, pool. $145–$165, full breakfast. No credit cards. No smoking, no pets, 2-day minimum on weekends, 3-day minimum on holiday weekends.

1740 House. River Rd., Lumberville, PA 18933, tel. 215/297–5661. 23 double rooms with baths, 1 suite. Pool. $75–$125, Continental breakfast. No credit cards. No smoking in dining room, no pets, 2-day minimum on weekends in season.

Brandywine River Valley

Duling-Kurtz House & Country Inn

146 S. Whitford Rd., Exton, PA 19341, tel. 610/524–1830, fax 610/524–6258

On a country road midway between Valley Forge and the Brandywine Battlefields is the Duling-Kurtz House & Country Inn. Down a driveway lined with converted gas street lamps are formal gardens, a Victorian-style gazebo, and a footbridge that crosses a stone-lined brook. The 1830s farmhouse and the adjacent barn, both white plaster over fieldstone, were elegantly restored and opened in 1983. Raymond Carr and David Knauer, who did the restoration, named the property after their mothers. The new owner, Michael Person—who hails from Vienna, Austria, and has a background in hotel management—has orchestrated a massive upgrading since taking over in 1992, and he is a decidedly hands-on operator. He staunchly defends the concept of fine dining and lodging at affordable prices, and he runs an intimate, service-oriented inn.

The guest rooms (in the barn) have been restored and furnished in Williamsburg period reproductions. You will find marble-top sinks; Oriental rugs; writing desks; and canopied, brass, and four-poster beds. One suite has its own courtyard. Rooms are named for historic figures: Honeymooners often request the George Washington Room, with its king-size, cherrywood canopy bed and a step-down bathroom with a claw-foot tub. A Continental breakfast is served on china in the parlor.

A sheltered brick walkway connects the barn and the farmhouse restaurant, which is also furnished with Colonial reproductions. Near the entrance you'll discover an unusual 18th-century beehive bread oven. Four of the dining rooms have stone fireplaces, and richly mullioned windows detail the dining areas. The *Philadelphia Inquirer* has praised chef David Robinson. Michael insists that fine cuisine needn't mean breaking the bank; dinner entrées average $22.

You can stroll through peaceful wooded areas adjoining the inn, and when it's warm you can enjoy tea in the gazebo. Museums and battlefields are not far away, and Michael and his staff will point you to the best antiquing and shopping.

▦ *15 double rooms with baths, 3 suites. Restaurant, air-conditioning, cable TVs, phones, room service, 3 con-* *ference rooms with catering. $55–$120, Continental breakfast. AE, D, DC, MC, V. No pets.*

Fairville Inn

Rte. 52 (Box 219), Fairville, PA 19357, tel. 610/388–5900, fax 610/388–5902

In the heart of Andrew Wyeth country, on the road between Winterthur Museum and Longwood Gardens, this country-house inn set on 5½ acres behind a split-rail fence is surrounded by estates, beautiful gardens, and miles of country back roads. The hub of the inn is a cream-colored 1826 Federal plaster-over-double-brick house with black shutters. A Victorian-style veranda across the front makes an open porch on the second floor. In back are the barn and carriage house, smaller clapboard and fieldstone buildings that were recently constructed by an Amish family who live nearby.

Swedish-born Ole Retlev and his wife, Patricia, both former ski instructors, owned two different inns in Mt. Snow, Vermont. But, as Ole explains, "There's more to draw travelers here on a year-round basis." So, in 1986, they moved to the Brandywine River valley and opened the Fairville Inn.

The rooms are bright and airy, appealingly furnished with Queen Anne and Hepplewhite reproductions. Before the fireplace in the living room are two blue settees, with a large copper-top coffee table between them. The flowered draperies and potted plants give the room an understated "relaxed formal feel," as Ole calls it. The bedrooms in the main house, all of quirky size and shape, are done in light, elegant country colors and are carpeted. You will also find four-poster beds, canopy beds, settees, writing desks, floral wallpapers—and fresh flowers. The four rooms in the barn are somewhat smaller, but all have working fireplaces. Siding from the old barn has been used for mantels and paneling, and some of the sinks have copper drainboards.

Two suites in the carriage house have private terraces and balconies that overlook a pond and rolling farmland; four units have fireplaces. They are at the back of the property and away from traffic noise. With cathedral ceilings and old barn timbers for beams and mantels, they are also the most architecturally interesting.

Canoeing, hiking, antiquing, and museum-browsing are only some of the area's pastimes. Or why not attend a polo match during one of the warmer months?

🏨 *13 double rooms with baths, 2 suites. Air-conditioning, cable TVs, phones. $125–$185; Continental breakfast, afternoon tea. AE, D, MC, V. No smoking, no pets.*

Hamanassett

Rte. 1 (Box 129), Lima, PA 19037, tel. 610/459-3000

Meet Evelene Dohan, the proprietor of Hamanassett: She has taught, run a catering business, and gone home a multiple champion from the Philadelphia Flower Show. Her gifts are evident both on the grounds and in the interior buildings of this secluded estate.

The hilltop residence overlooks 48 acres of woods and meadow, shaded garden pathways, and stone-walled ponds. In April and May, approaching guests pass through a fragrant lane of rhododendrons and azaleas, blossoming in profusion along the ellipse that fronts the main house. Inside, the innkeeper's cut-flower arrangements grace each room; potted plants and hanging ferns flood the light-filled solarium. Mrs. Dohan, who came as a bride in 1950 and raised her children here, has appointed her rooms with four-poster canopied beds, Oriental rugs, and handsome antiques. And she single-handedly serves up delectable country breakfasts with homemade jams, compotes, and freshly baked confections.

Hamanassett was built in 1856 for Dr. Charles Meigs, a Philadelphia pioneer in obstetrics, but what you see today bears little resemblance to the doctor's summer retreat. As Mrs. Dohan will tell you, the little farmhouse then consisted of just "three rooms down, and three rooms up." But in 1870 her late husband's grandfather purchased the estate. His son—her father-in-law— didn't like the sensation of enclosure, and so he added onto and redefined the original structure (including the pumpkin pine flooring). He installed arched passageways instead of doors between rooms on the first floor, so the main body of the house feels united, allowing fluid movement from room to room and a less obstructed flow of light. Before ascending the main staircase, note the blue-and-white delft tile depiction of human history encased in the broad white arch to your right: The story begins with the expulsion from the Garden of Eden.

You may find yourself so seduced by the beauty this proficient innkeeper has created that you won't want to venture outside it. But if you do, all the most popular points of interest are only minutes away. Hamanassett sits just off well-traveled Route 1, but its acreage makes an ample buffer between the estate and the roadway.

🏨 *6 double rooms with baths, 2 doubles share bath. Solarium, TVs in all rooms, air-conditioning in some. $90–$125, full breakfast. No credit cards. No smoking, no pets, 2-night minimum.*

Scarlett House

503 W. State St., Kennett Square, PA 19348, tel. 610/444-9592

It's been around only since October 1990, but Scarlett House has risen quickly to the top with its comfort, beauty, and professionalism. The house sits right in the heart of Kennett Square's historic district. While the rough granite exterior may not seduce you, the minute you walk through the front door (flanked by leaded glass panes and twin inglenooks) you'll pledge allegiance to this residence. It was built in 1910 by a prominent Quaker businessman for his son, Robert Scarlett, who lived here until the 1960s.

Much of this inn's allure has to do with the innkeepers, Sam and Jane Snyder, who are avid admirers of Victoriana. Many of the furnishings were part of a collection procured from house sales and auctions by the previous proprietor, Susan Lalli Ascosi. She also acquired enough knowledge and decorative sense to take some license with Victorian tradition by manipulating color schemes. Where Victorians would have stayed with darker tones, Susan splashed pastels on the wooden walls of the bedchambers and strictly limited the figurine-filled shelves. The entire interior, embellished by the eclectic collection that Sam and Jane brought with them, is striking for its ambience of polished order and marked lack of "stuff."

The walls in the second-floor master suite are pink, trimmed at the top with a light floral border. But the Victorian walnut bed is the room's decided cynosure. It's a stunner, with a huge Renaissance headboard looking down on all-cotton, hand-ironed sheets. Walnut reappears in a more ornately carved dresser with a framed full-length mirror; an exquisite plain-faced corner cupboard of the same wood, crafted by an Amish man in 1820, sits directly opposite.

Business travelers have closed deals in this place; women have completed theses; amorous young couples have basked in its charms. All guests eventually gravitate to the sitting room on the second floor: It faces south, so it's engulfed by light. This is a perfect place to leaf through all the local literature (including restaurant listings, with current menus) that Susan keeps.

▦ *1 double room with bath, 2 doubles share bath, 1 suite. Cable TV, fireplace,*

and newspapers in downstairs parlor. $75–$125, full breakfast. AE, D, MC, V. No smoking, no pets, 2-night minimum on some weekends. Closed Dec. 24– Jan. 1.

Sweetwater Farm

50 Sweetwater Rd., Glen Mills, PA 19342, tel. 610/459–4711, fax 610/358– 4945

Fifteen minutes east of Chadds Ford, at the end of a circular driveway, is a stately 1734 Georgian fieldstone manor house with shutters the color of lemon custard. Sweetwater Farm once sheltered wounded Revolutionary War soldiers and the Marquis de Lafayette and was a refuge for slaves on the Underground Railroad.

In the fields around the 16-room house, thoroughbreds and goats graze amid wildflowers. From each window there are views of majestic maples on the 15 lush acres, and of the 50 undeveloped acres beyond. Proprietors Grace Le Vine and Richard Hovespian couldn't help but be drawn to this bucolic charm.

Inside you will find tall, deep-set windows and a sweeping center-hall staircase. Almost every room has a wood-burning fireplace, random-width floors of oak and pine, and original paintings. Rustic Pennsylvania primitive pieces are mixed with authentic 18th- and 19th-century antique furnishings and reproductions. The six guest rooms have handmade quilts and fine linens on canopy beds and four-posters, embroidered spreads, dried-flower wreaths, and hidden nooks containing odd collectibles.

There are a library, with a fireplace and wall of books, a living room, and a sunroom with TV, which becomes a "boardroom" for small business meetings and luncheons. In warm weather, the broad back veranda overlooking the fields and the swimming pool is a favorite spot.

Breakfast, served in the dining room in front of the fireplace, features everything from sweet-potato waffles or puff pancakes with brown-sugar syrup to home-fried potatoes with sausage and bacon. Five cottages, also furnished in American antiques, are the ultimate romantic hideaways, with fireplaces, kitchens, and four-poster canopied beds. Museums, historic houses, and antiques shops are all nearby.

🏠 *7 doubles with bath, 5 cottages. Air-conditioning, conference room, pool. $150–$275, full breakfast. AE, MC, V. No smoking.*

Other Choices

Bankhouse Bed and Breakfast. 875 Hillsdale Rd., West Chester, PA 19382, tel. 610/344–7388. 2 double rooms share bath. Air-conditioning. $65–$85, full breakfast. No credit cards. No smoking, no pets.

Bed and Breakfast at Walnut Hill. 541 Chandlers Mill Rd., Avondale, PA 19311, tel. 610/444–3703. 2 double rooms share bath. Air-conditioning, fireplaces, TV in 1 room, cable TV/VCR in family room, hot tub. $65–$80, full breakfast. No credit cards. Restricted smoking, no pets.

Lenape Springs Farm. 580 W. Creek Rd. (Box 176, Pocopson), West Chester, PA 19366, tel. 610/793–2266 or 800/793–2234. 5 double rooms with baths. Air-conditioning, pool table. $70–$94, full breakfast. MC, V. Restricted smoking, no pets.

Meadow Spring Farm. 201 E. Street Rd. (Rte. 926), Kennett Square, PA 19348, tel. 610/444–3903. 4 double rooms with baths, 2 doubles share bath. Air-conditioning, TVs, game room with pool table and table tennis, hot tub, kitchen privileges, pool, carriage rides. $75–$85, full breakfast. No credit cards. No pets.

Pace One. Thornton and Glen Mills Rds. (Box 108), Thornton, PA 19373, tel. 610/459–3702, fax 610/558–0825. 6 double rooms with baths. Restaurant, air-conditioning and phones in bedrooms, 3 conference rooms with catering, free use of nearby tennis and racquetball courts. $65–$85, Continental breakfast. AE, DC, MC, V. No pets. Closed Dec. 25.

Reservations Services

A Bed & Breakfast Connection/Bed & Breakfast of Philadelphia (Box 21, Devon 19333, tel. 610/687–3565 or 800/448–3619, fax 610/995–9524). **Association of B&Bs in Philadelphia, Valley Forge, and Brandywine** (Box 562, Valley Forge 19481-0562, tel. 610/783–7838 or 800/344–0123, fax 610/783–7783). **B&B of Chester County** (Box 825, Kennett Square 19348, tel. 610/444–1367).

Lancaster County/ Amish Country

Churchtown Inn

Rte. 23, Churchtown (2100 Main St., Narvon, PA 17555), tel. 717/445–7794

Across from the historic church in this tiny Pennsylvania Dutch village is the Churchtown Inn, a circa-1735 Georgian fieldstone inn and carriage house that are listed on the National Register of Historic Places. From 1804 to 1853 the inn was the home of Edward Davies, a member of the 25th Congress and a state legislator. Once you enter the restored mansion you will know it was built for the gentry.

To the right of the entryway are two parlors with Victorian antiques and original ornate mantels. Here each evening, innkeepers Jim Kent and Stuart and Hermine Smith entertain guests with music and conversation. Before opening their bed-and-breakfast in April 1987, the three stayed at 150 B&Bs in six states to pick up ideas. Back in New Jersey Hermine was a health-food retailer, Stuart was a choral director whose choirs appeared at Lincoln Center and Carnegie Hall, and Jim was an accountant and ballroom-dancing teacher. (He'll gladly give you a quick lesson.) Stuart is known to delight guests with a concert on the grand piano, or he might wind up an antique music box from the inn's fine collection.

The 15-room center-hall mansion is decorated throughout with European and American antiques. The glassed-in garden room, where breakfast is served, overlooks farmland and a distant mountain range. A onetime summer kitchen with a walk-in fireplace has been converted into a den with a TV/VCR. Guest rooms have antique marble sinks, and brass or iron, sleigh or carved, or four-poster canopy beds. You'll find wardrobes, washstands, and TV cabinets handmade by an Amish craftsman. Each room has a sitting area. The dormer rooms on the third floor are cozy but have low ceilings.

On many weekends special packages are offered that include scheduled events. These vary from Victorian balls, carriage rides, and murder mysteries to authentic Amish wedding feasts, barbecues with music, cabaret, classical string quartets, and festive holiday dinners. The inn is close to antiques and crafts markets, the Reading outlets, and Amish farms. You can bike, hike, fish, or cross-country ski in nearby French Creek State Park.

🛏 *6 double rooms with baths, 2 doubles share bath, 1 suite in carriage house. Air-conditioning and TV in rooms. $55–$135; full, 5-course breakfast. MC, V. No smoking, no pets, 2-night minimum on weekends, 3-night minimum on holiday weekends.*

Clearview Farm Bed and Breakfast

355 Clearview Rd., Ephrata, PA 17522, tel. 717/733–6333

Up a winding road along the base of a mountain ridge in northern Lancaster County is a beautifully restored three-story limestone farmhouse built in 1814. It sits on 200 acres of peaceful Pennsylvania farmland, and there's a huge bank barn nearby. There's also a pond out front that's the domain of two swans. The setting of Clearview Farm is elegantly pastoral; it's the kind of place you want to keep secret. Mildred and Glenn Wissler bought the house when they married more than 30 years ago. Glenn is a farmer who also has a good eye for color, and Mildred is a talented decorator who grew up learning about her father's antiques business. After working together to choose the right furnishings and decorations, they opened the bed-and-breakfast in 1989.

Country antiques and collectibles are mixed with exquisite Victorian furnishings throughout. You'll find a fireplace in the den, and there are hooked rugs on the original random-width floors. Exposed beams and limestone walls give the kitchen a homey feel. Guest rooms are lushly textured with lots of colors and patterns. The Royal Room has an ornately carved walnut Victorian bed, a Victorian mirrored étagère displaying turn-of-the-century knick-knacks, Victorian chairs, and marble-top tables. The Princess Room is lavished with lace and fitted with a canopy bed, a Victorian marble-top dresser, and a washstand. The French Room has a highly carved antique bed in a curtained alcove, a matching armoire, and French upholstered chairs. In the rooms on the third floor, hand-pegged rafters and limestone walls are exposed. Here you'll find homemade quilts, country antiques, and a doll collection.

Breakfast is served in the formal dining room that overlooks the fields.

The dining room has elegant draperies and Victorian-print wallpaper. Every morning Mildred prepares a full country breakfast.

The mountain ridge behind the house is great for hiking or quiet walks. In autumn, you can enjoy the fall foliage by car or by bike—just follow Clearview Road; it's one of those scenic back roads you always hear about. Nearby are Wahtney's Inn (an excellent restaurant), farmers' markets, and five antiques malls.

▦ *5 double rooms with baths. Air-conditioning, TV in family room. $95–$125, full breakfast. D, MC, V. No smoking, no pets.*

Limestone Inn

33 E. Main St., Strasburg, PA 17579, tel. 717/687–8392 or 800/278–8392

In the very heart of the Amish country, in Strasburg's historic district, is the Limestone Inn. This elegant bed-and-breakfast, listed on the National Register of Historic Places, was built about 1786 as a merchant's residence. From 1839 to 1860 the principal of the noted Strasburg Academy boarded about 50 boys here. After the Civil War, the house served as an orphanage.

The 16-room house, based on a symmetrical five-bay Georgian plan, has a central hallway. The building also has some Germanic overtones, and details like the pent roof and the decorative stonework called "tumbling" between the second-floor windows give the inn a distinctive architectural sense.

Innkeepers Jan and Dick Kennell are both natives of New Hampshire. Friends who ran a B&B gave them the idea of establishing their own, and they opened the Limestone in May 1985. Dick was with the Department of Agriculture and Forestry in Washington, DC, for 30 years; and Jan, who is versed in Colonial history, was a tour guide in Annapolis.

Though antique clocks in the elegant rooms tick away, time stands still. The inn is furnished with Colonial and primitive family antiques and reproductions, and you'll find whitewashed walls, wide-planked wavy floors, and Williamsburg colors in every room. In the keeping room there are woven woolen rugs, lots of books and folk art, and settees in front of the fireplace. A spinning wheel stands in the corner. There are old family photographs and a player piano in the living room. Up the steep, narrow stairs you'll find the guest rooms, with old pegged doors, quilts, trunks, and complementary chocolates. On the third floor, the original numbers on the doors show where boys from the academy once slept.

For the multicourse breakfast, served in the dining room at a long table set with a lace cloth, Dick, an excellent chef, may whip up his French toast or sourdough pancakes. He and Jan often serve their guests in period costumes.

The Limestone Inn is quiet and homey, and it's close to antiques stores. The Kennells have Amish friends nearby who have quilts for sale for less than you'd pay in commercial centers. With advance notice, they will set you up for dinner at an Amish home.

▦ *6 double rooms with baths. Air-conditioning. $75–$95, full breakfast. AE, V. No smoking, no pets, 2-night minimum on holiday weekends.*

Smithton Country Inn

900 W. Main St., Ephrata, PA 17522, tel. 717/733–6094

Twelve miles north of Lancaster is one of the best inns in all of Pennsylvania Dutch country: the Smithton Country Inn, which began taking in lodgers in 1763. It was built by Henry and Susana Miller, who were householders of the Ephrata Community, an 18th-century Protestant monastic sect. Stone walls and flower gardens surround the fieldstone building on a hill overlooking the

Ephrata Cloister. Innkeeper Dorothy Graybill is Pennsylvania Dutch. She bought Smithton in 1979, attentively restored it down to the most minute detail, and reopened it in 1982.

At dusk, lamps are lit in each window. The first floor has a Great Room and library to the right, and a dining room, where breakfast is served, to the left. Upstairs, guest rooms are individually decorated, but in each you'll find a working fireplace, antique or hand-made reproduction furniture, hand-made quilts, reading lamps, stenciling, mini-refrigerators, and chamber music. Feather beds are kept in trunks for guests who request them. Flannel nightshirts, coordinated to the color scheme of the room, hang on wooden pegs behind the doors. Many rooms have canopy beds; some have whirlpool baths.

The attached duplex suite has its own entrance. Inside there are a living room, a snack area, a queen-size bed, a twin cupboard bed, and a whirlpool bath. In 1992, Dorothy added a new unit, the Purple Room, on the second floor facing the back gardens. It includes hand-planed cherry woodwork and floors, an exposed-stone wall, a fireplace, a king-size canopied bed, an all-ceramic bathroom, and a whirlpool.

Numerous decorative influences come from the nearby Ephrata Cloister. The hand-hewn doors are pegged and have wooden hardware. Dorothy's partner, Allan Smith, hand-planed the old floor-boards and made the clay tiles for the bathrooms and a Cloister-inspired buffet for the dining room.

Guests enjoy Smithton's breakfast, served by candlelight—usually a plate of fresh fruit, juice, Pennsylvania Dutch waffles, and pastry. Afterward, Dorothy gives tips on the proper etiquette when meeting the Plain People of Lancaster County. This is the place to find out how to avoid the tourist traps and spend your time at authentic preserves of the area's heritage.

🏠 *7 double rooms with baths, 1 suite. Air-conditioning. $75–$170, full breakfast. AE, MC, V. No smoking, 2-night minimum with Sat. reservation and on holidays.*

Other Choices

Adamstown Inn. 62 W. Main St., Adamstown, PA 19501, tel. 717/484–0800 or 800/594–4808. 4 double rooms with baths. Air-conditioning; cable TV in 3 bedrooms; morning coffee, tea, or hot chocolate; off-street parking. $70–$105, Continental breakfast. MC, V. No smoking, no pets, 2-night minimum on weekends Apr.–Dec.

Cameron Estate Inn. 1855 Mansion La., Mount Joy, PA 17552, tel. 717/653–1773. 17 double rooms with baths. Restaurant, air-conditioning, TV/VCR in sitting area, conference facilities in restaurant; bicycles, access to pool and tennis courts. $65–$115, Continental breakfast. AE, D, DC, MC, V. No pets.

Doneckers. 318–324 N. State St., Ephrata, PA 17522, tel. 717/738–9502, fax 717/738–9554. 24 double rooms with baths, 2 doubles share bath, 12 suites. Restaurant (open Thurs.–Tues.), air-conditioning, cable TV in common room. $69–$185, Continental breakfast. AE, D, DC, MC, V. No pets, 2-night minimum on holiday week-ends. Closed Dec. 24–25.

General Sutter Inn. 14 E. Main St., Lititz, PA 17543, tel. 717/626–2115, fax 717/626–0992. 8 double rooms with baths, 2 suites. Restaurant, coffee shop, air-conditioning, TVs, phones, library, 2 conference rooms. $75–$100, no breakfast. AE, D, MC, V.

King's Cottage. 1049 E. King St., Lancaster, PA 17602, tel. 717/397–1017. 9 double rooms with baths, 1 carriage house suite. Air-conditioning, cable TV in library, off-street parking. $69–$180; full breakfast, afternoon tea. D, MC, V. No smoking, no pets, 2-night minimum on weekends, 3-night minimum on holiday weekends.

Patchwork Inn. 2319 Old Philadelphia Pike, Lancaster, PA 17602, tel. 717/ 293–9078 or 800/584–5776. 1 double room with bath, 2 doubles share bath, 1 suite. Air-conditioning, bike storage, off-street parking. $65–$85, full breakfast. D, MC, V. No smoking, no pets, 2-night minimum on holiday weekends.

Swiss Woods. 500 Blantz Rd., Lititz, PA 17543, tel. 717/627–3358 or 800/ 594–8018, fax 717/627–3483. 6 double rooms with baths, 1 suite. Air-conditioning, TV in suite and in common room, whirlpool baths, kitchenette for guest use. $88–$128, full breakfast. D, MC, V. No smoking, no pets, 2-night minimum on weekends, 3-night minimum on holidays.

Reservations Service

Hershey Bed & Breakfast Reservation Service (Box 208, Hershey 17033, tel. 717/533–2928).

Gettysburg/York

Bechtel Mansion Inn

400 W. King St., East Berlin, PA 17316, tel. 717/259–7760

In 1897 the leading local businessman built this 28-room Queen Anne mansion in the center of town as a residence for his family. It's such a fanciful, through-the-looking-glass place that you'll know it at once. The yellow-brick-and-white-trim building has a high pointed turret, a long curved porch, and lush Victorian gardens.

Owners Charles and Mariam Bechtel live in Fairfax, Virginia, but every weekend they are resident hosts. Charles grew up on a nearby farm and will give you inside tips on touring the countryside. Innkeeper Ruth Spangler, who is always on hand, is knowledgeable about local history and customs.

The Bechtel, which became an inn in 1983, has been carefully furnished with American and European 19th-century antiques. It's on the National Register of Historic Places. Guests with a love of art and architecture will appreciate the intricate artisanship that went into the building and restoration of the house. Many rooms have original brass chandeliers. The Victorian parlor has vertical shutters, sliding pocket doors, and a handsome mantel—all in elegant cherry wood. The dining room has etched-glass windows and a large window seat. The breakfast room was the original kitchen, and you'll find French windows in the chimney corner and handmade furniture, pottery, and paintings by local artists throughout the house.

Each bedroom is furnished in antiques, with handmade Pennsylvania quilts, lace curtains, and a brass chandelier. In many you will find built-in wardrobes with full-length mirrors, and two have private balconies. Bathrooms retain their original ornate Victorian decor (though the plumbing is new). One of the most popular is the Sara Leas Room, with its turret-shaped bay window and view of East Berlin's National Historic District.

You can easily spend a weekend exploring the Bechtel's nooks and crannies. Its location—almost equidistant from York, Gettysburg, and Hershey—makes it an ideal base for touring the area.

🛏 *8 double rooms with baths, 1 suite. Air-conditioning, TV/VCR in common areas, gift shop in carriage house. $85– $145, full breakfast. AE, D, DC, MC, V. No smoking, no pets, 2-night minimum on holiday weekends in Oct.*

Beechmont Inn

315 Broadway, Hanover, PA 17331, tel. 717/632–3013 or 800/553–7009

This 1834 Federal redbrick town house, with black shutters and window boxes overflowing with flowers, is on a tree-lined street in Hanover, about 13 miles south of Gettysburg and York. In 1994 William and Susan Day bought the Beechmont, after having worked here for three years. Bill was the handyman and Susan served the breakfast; they live in the carriage house out back. The inn is furnished with elegant Federal-period antiques and replicas. In the library are 18th-century books and a collection of Civil War memorabilia. One suite has a marble fireplace, and one has a whirlpool. Up the winding staircase, guest rooms have four-poster beds, writing desks, and lace curtains. During warmer months you can relax in the old-fashioned glider in the landscaped courtyard.

🛏 *4 double rooms with baths, 3 suites. Air-conditioning, phones, off-street parking. $80–$135; full breakfast, afternoon tea. AE, D, MC, V. No smoking, no pets, 2-night minimum on weekends for suites.*

Brafferton Inn

44 York St., Gettysburg, PA 17325, tel. 717/337-3423

A stay at the Brafferton Inn may be the most pleasant way to get a full sense of Gettysburg's historical richness. The 10-room stone house built in 1786, the first residence in town, faces a mid-19th-century street and has an adjacent six-room pre–Civil War clapboard addition. On the first day of the battle, a bullet shattered an upstairs window. It lodged in the mantel and is still there today. During the war, services were held here while the church was being used as a hospital. And just down the street is the house where Lincoln completed his Gettysburg Address.

In 1993 Jane and Sam Back purchased the inn, which is listed on the National Register of Historic Places. Sam has a master's degree in history and was interested in the Civil War, and Jane worked in the admissions office of a boarding school in Connecticut. Both were ready for a midlife change.

The inn has high ceilings, oversize doors, and odd nooks, turns, steps up and steps down that will constantly surprise you. It glows with Colonial colors. In the living room is the original fireplace and an 18th-century grandfather clock bracketed by portraits of Sam's ancestors dating from before the Civil War. Here you'll also find a pre–Revolutionary War mirror hanging over an 18th-century lowboy. Guests breakfast in the dining room encircled by a folksy mural on four walls that depicts the area's historic buildings.

An atrium connects the stone house to the carriage house. This area, with brick floors and walls, is decorated with primitive pieces and pottery. Farm implements are displayed on the walls, and opened antique cupboards are filled with antique toys. Down a wooden walkway is a deck and small garden, where dahlias, zinnias, petunias, and marigolds grow.

The guest rooms, with 18th-century stenciling on whitewashed walls, are furnished with country antiques and family pieces. You'll also find oil paintings, prints, and drawings. A local potter made the basins for washstands and dressers that have been transformed into sinks.

After a candlelight breakfast set to classical music, you can relax in the atrium while you plan the day. The inn is an easy walk from the battlefield, shops, and restaurants.

🛏 *11 double rooms with baths, 5 doubles share 2 baths, 2 suites. Air-conditioning, off-street parking. $90–$125, full breakfast. MC, V. Restricted smoking, no pets.*

Doubleday Inn

104 Doubleday Ave., Gettysburg, PA 17325, tel. 717/334-9119

You don't have to be a Battle of Gettysburg buff to enjoy a stay at the Doubleday Inn; but the Doubleday is the only

B&B that is actually *on* the Gettysburg Battlefield. Upon Oak Ridge, with a view of the town of Gettysburg a half mile away, the inn nestles in a grove of trees on a monument-lined road, with the Railroad Cut, the Peace Light Memorial, and an observation platform all just a few steps from the door.

In 1994 Charles Wilcox, a financier in the futures industry, and his wife, Ruth Anne, a registered nurse, gave up their jobs and moved from Illinois to pursue their dream of owning and operating an inn. They bought the Doubleday, named after Abner Doubleday, the man who "invented" baseball and who also, as Brigadier General, commanded the Union forces the first day of the battle on what is now the site of the inn.

Charles and Ruth Anne brought with them loads of Colonial country furniture and scoured Pennsylvania and Ohio for suitable period antiques. The recently redecorated bedrooms are a mix of four-posters, brass beds, iron beds, and an oak pineapple bed. Two rooms are what Ruth Anne calls "Grandma's rooms," with thick quilts and old-fashioned fabric prints. Another room has a Laura Ashley look. The third-floor attic room is more masculine, with dark greens and reds, bookcases, and both a double and a twin bed.

Every morning a full, hot breakfast is served by candlelight, on china and crystal. Civil War literature is available to read, and every Saturday night throughout the year and Wednesday nights during the busy season, a licensed battlefield guide comes to lecture and answer questions about the battle. Breakfast discussions the following mornings are especially spirited.

🏠 *5 double rooms with baths, 4 doubles share 2 baths. Air-conditioning, picnics available. $84–$104; full breakfast, afternoon tea. D, MC, V. No smoking, no pets, 2-night minimum on holiday weekends.*

Mercersburg Inn

405 S. Main St., Mercersburg, PA 17236, tel. 717/328–5231, fax 717/328–3403

Mercersburg, at the foot of the Blue Ridge Mountains, is a historic village off I–81, an hour and a half from Washington, DC. This country inn, on the outskirts of town, is an impressive Classic Revival redbrick structure with white trim, adorned with numerous porticoes, porches, and terraces.

It's the kind of place where you expect something romantic has either already happened or will. In the entrance hall, twin staircases wind dramatically to the second floor, and rose and green Scaglioli columns accent the chestnut wainscoting. The classic Arts and Crafts sunroom has a tiled floor and fireplace, high beamed ceilings, and a wall of broad windows. It's done in peach and blue, with flowered upholstery and curtains. You can sit back on the deep window-seat cushions and admire the stately grounds.

Owners Walter and Sandy Filkowski have filled the spacious guest rooms with restored antiques and pieces handmade locally. You will find four-poster, canopy, and king-size beds. Some rooms have fireplaces; others have private balconies with views of the mountains. Three rooms have tiled, high-ceilinged bathrooms with antique needle showers, pedestal sinks, and freestanding tubs. Each bathroom has been meticulously restored to its turn-of-the-century grandeur.

In the formal mahogany-paneled dining room, there are a deep green marble fireplace, leaded-glass built-in cabinets, Tiffany stained-glass light fixtures, and parquet floors. Here the award-winning restaurant serves six-course dinners of regional new American cuisine.

A bit farther north is a pocket of Amish country that most tourists never hear about. Innkeepers Sally Brick and John Mohr will fill you in on the area's touring, antiquing, fishing, and hiking opportunities.

▦ *15 double rooms with baths. Restaurant (open weekends), air-conditioning, phones, TV/VCR in game room, conference room. $135–$200, full breakfast. D, MC, V. No smoking indoors, no pets, 2-night minimum on fall-foliage and ski-season weekends and holidays.*

Other Choices

Emig Mansion. 3342 N. George St. (Box 486), Emigsville, PA 17318, tel. 717/764–2226. 3 double rooms with baths, 4 doubles share 2 baths. Air-conditioning in rooms, off-street parking. $85–$110, full breakfast. MC, V. Restricted smoking, no pets.

Fairfield Inn. Main St., Fairfield, PA 17320, tel. 717/642–5410. 2 double rooms share bath. Restaurant, air-conditioning in common areas and bedrooms, meeting room. $50–$75, Continental breakfast. AE, MC, V. No smoking in dining room, no pets. Closed Sun., Mon., 1st week Feb., and 1st week Sept.

Historic Farnsworth House Inn. 401 Baltimore St., Gettysburg, PA 17325, tel. 717/334–8838, fax 717/334–5862. 5 double rooms with baths. Restaurant, air-conditioning in bedrooms, TV in sunroom. $75–$85, full breakfast. AE, D, MC, V. Restricted smoking, no pets, 2-night minimum on some weekends.

Old Appleford Inn. 218 Carlisle St., Gettysburg, PA 17325, tel. 717/337–1711 or 800/275–3373, fax 717/334–6228. 9 double rooms with baths, 1 suite. Air-conditioning, off-street parking. $80–$138; full breakfast, afternoon tea. AE, D, MC, V. No smoking, no pets, 2-night minimum on special event weekends.

Tannery Bed and Breakfast. 449 Baltimore St., Gettysburg, PA 17325, tel. 717/334–2454. 9 double rooms with baths, 1 suite. Air-conditioning, TV in sitting room, off-street parking. $85–$125, Continental breakfast. MC, V. No smoking, no pets.

Rhode Island

The 1661 Inn & Guest House

Newport

Cliffside Inn

2 Seaview Ave., Newport, RI 02840, tel. 401/847-1811 or 800/845-1811, fax 401/ 848-5850

Consistently ranked among the top inns in New England, the Cliffside has been superbly appointed by owner Winthrop Baker of Connecticut, and it is tenderly watched over by young innkeeper Stephan Nicolas.

On a quiet side street, the inn overlooks the ocean and is close to Newport's Cliff Walk. Originally a summer cottage called Swann Villa, the house was built in 1880 for Governor Thomas Swann of Maryland. In another incarnation, it housed the prestigious St. George's prep school. Now restored to mint Victorian condition, the inn has come into its own as a special hideaway filled with cozy nooks and crannies and flooded with daytime sunlight from its many bay windows.

A veranda arrayed with comfortable wicker furniture makes a good lounging spot in summer. The large center hallway, with its original gleaming hardwood floor, leads to a spacious parlor, which has a Victorian fireplace bedecked with an ornate antique mirror.

Each guest room is unique, but all are decorated with Victorian furniture and Laura Ashley fabrics. The rooms have names recalling past residents or referring to the various decors. Miss Beatrice's Room is a large room with a window seat and an antique "Lincoln-style" queen-size bed, with its massive carved headboard and footboard in cherry wood. The bathroom, with marble and raised wood paneling, has a whirlpool bath. The Governor's Suite—the inn's most luxurious quarters—has a king-size four-poster bed, a whirlpool bath, an antique Victorian birdcage shower, and an unusual two-sided fireplace (one side is in the bedroom, the other in the bathroom).

🏨 *8 double rooms with baths, 7 suites. Air-conditioning, cable TVs, phones, 9 rooms with fireplaces, 9 rooms with whirlpool baths, 5 rooms with both. $145-$305, full breakfast and afternoon tea. AE, D, DC, MC, V. No smoking, no pets, no children.*

Francis Malbone House

392 Thames St., Newport, RI 02840, tel. 401/846-0392, fax 401/848-5956

Colonel Francis Malbone made a sizable fortune as a shipping merchant, succeeding well enough at his trade to build, in 1760, a most impressive yellow-brick mansion and countinghouse just across Thames Street from the harbor where he kept his boats at anchor. His home, restored over the past 15 years, opened to guests in 1990, becoming Newport's only Colonial mansion operating as an inn. It's only a 10-minute walk from Washington Square, a plus for visitors interested in historic Newport.

The design of the house is attributed to the great architect Peter Harrison, who also designed Newport's Touro Synagogue, Brick Market, and Redwood Library. A pair of formal parlors occupy the front of the house; the present dining room, once the kitchen, features an authentic Colonial brick fireplace with a beehive oven. Here, a full gourmet breakfast is offered to guests, with a main dish served family-style and other dishes available from a buffet table. Typical entrées are eggs Florentine, poached pears in raspberry melba sauce, crepes, or pumpkin waffles with cinnamon syrup. Afternoon tea at the inn may feature lemon squares or walnut brownies, or a variety of savory hors d'oeuvres. All the foods served at the inn are made on the premises. Will Dewey, one of the innkeepers, is a culinary-school graduate of Providence's Johnson & Wales University.

All the public rooms are tastefully furnished with Colonial reproduction pieces and antiques. Innkeepers Dewey and Mary Frances Brophy offer a wonderfully warm, personal welcome. Repeat guests rave about the highly professional service and the elegant, gracious atmosphere.

A grand staircase with hand-carved balusters leads to the guest rooms, which are spacious and full of natural light, with views of either the garden or the harbor. Guests may rent the Counting House next door, a lovely self-contained suite with distinctive, tall

windows, a whirlpool bath, a four-poster bed, its own sitting area, and private entrances.

Though the Malbone house stands on busy Thames Street, it is set well back from the sidewalk behind its white picket fence. The large, lushly landscaped garden in the back, with a gurgling ornamental fountain and wrought-iron furniture, makes a green retreat where breakfast is served in the summertime.

🏠 *18 double rooms with baths. Whirlpool bath, fireplaces in most rooms, parking. $135–$325, full breakfast. AE, MC, V. No smoking, no children.*

Inn at Castle Hill

Ocean Dr., Newport, RI 02840, tel. 401/849–3800

The Inn at Castle Hill is perched in jaunty isolation, far from the madding crowd of downtown Newport, on a 40-acre peninsula with its own private beach. Built as a summer home for scientist and explorer Alexander Agassiz, the inn is a rambling shingled structure of curves, gingerbread woodwork, turrets, and jutting porches, imitating the chalets of Dr. Agassiz's native Switzerland. Outbuildings dot the grounds, including Agassiz's former laboratory (which may be rented as a suite), a series of waterside cottages (rented by the week), and Harbor House, where Grace Kelly lived while filming *High Society*.

Inside the inn, many original furnishings reflect Agassiz's fondness for Chinese and Japanese art, particularly bronzes and porcelain. The lounge, with Oriental rugs and richly patterned period wallpaper, has two small Victorian sofas nestled next to an unusual hand-carved fireplace, its design similar to a stained-glass rose window in a Gothic cathedral. Three water-view dining rooms include the professor's original study; the Sunset Room; and the original dining room, whose carved sideboard conceals two safes designed for silver and other valuables. The dining rooms attract nonguests, particularly for Sunday brunch, and on summer Sunday afternoons the inn offers a top-notch outdoor barbecue with music.

The six spacious oceanside rooms in the main house, which must be booked months in advance, are furnished with Victorian antiques and comfortable chairs, decorated with bright floral fabrics, and have enormous bathrooms. Room 6, with a large bay window, was built for Mrs. Agassiz; Room 7, Dr. Agassiz's bedroom, has walls and a ceiling of inlaid oak and pine; Room 8, decorated with white wicker furniture, features an old claw-foot bathtub in which you can relax with a view of the bay and the Newport Bridge. In Room 9, novelist Thornton Wilder wrote *Theophilus North* while listening to the distant ringing of the bell at the Castle Hill Lighthouse. An upstairs suite combines a large living room and a bedroom. The six-unit Harbor House is, like the rest of this classic old inn, shabbily chic—not the place for those who equate luxury with such modern amenities as Jacuzzis, oversize beds, and in-room TVs. But for many repeat guests, the inn's antique and somewhat creaky charms, along with its fabulous views and private beach, make it the genuine article, the essence of Newport.

🏠 *12 double rooms with baths, 3 doubles share 1 bath, 1 suite. Restaurant, private beach. $50–$200, Continental breakfast. AE, MC, V. No pets, no children, 2-night minimum stay on summer weekends. Closed Dec. 24–25, restaurant closed early Nov.–mid-Apr.*

Ivy Lodge

12 Clay St., Newport, RI 02840, tel. 401/849–6865

Behind the front door of this elegant Queen Anne Victorian, designed by Stanford White, waits an amazing sight: a 33-foot-high Gothic-style oak-paneled entry, with a three-story turned-balus-ter staircase. Tucked in at an angle at the foot of the staircase is a brick fireplace, built in the shape of a Moorish arch, where a welcoming fire burns on fall, winter, and spring afternoons.

Veteran innkeepers Maggie and Terry Moy live at Ivy Lodge. Their manner is low-key and gracious; they know how to make guests very comfortable. The sumptuous breakfast served here might include such delicacies as smoked fish, bananas flambé, bread pudding, or fresh strawberries and popovers with whipped cream.

Ivy Lodge, which was built in 1886 for a prominent New York physician, has eight guest rooms, all of which have been newly carpeted, painted, and wallpapered and are tastefully decorated with a combination of Victorian antiques and good-quality reproductions; rooms are spacious and give a sense of privacy. The Moys are on a continual campaign of improvement. Recently, the inn's exterior has been repainted, and two large bedrooms—the Turret Room and the Ivy Room—have been added. The Turret Room, decorated in peach and green, has a king-size bed and a private bath with a Victorian claw-foot tub. The Ivy Room has a queen-size four-poster bed with French cut white linens, Waverly ivy wallpaper, and a private bath. A new set of Herend dishes for the dining room has an ivy pattern.

A 20-foot-long mahogany table that seats 18 dominates the long dining room, with floor-to-ceiling bay windows at one end. Also on the main floor, a bright sitting room with floral wallpaper and wicker furniture is invitingly filled with books and magazines. The airy living room features pink-and-white-striped Art Deco sofas, thick carpeting, and a huge fireplace. A wraparound porch opens onto a lovely garden filled with many specimen plants.

While Ivy Lodge is neither as large nor as opulent as the fabled mansions on nearby Bellevue Avenue, it is every bit as gracious. Fantasies of living in Newport in its 19th-century heyday may well be realized here.

🏨 *8 double rooms with baths. $100–$165, full breakfast. AE, MC, V. No smoking.*

Victorian Ladies

63 Memorial Blvd., Newport, RI 02840, tel. 401/849–9960

At first glance, the location of the Victorian Ladies may give pause, for this bed-and-breakfast is on a busy thoroughfare, Memorial Boulevard. But once you're inside, double-pane windows and air-conditioning muffle the street noise, and the sumptuous furnishings and the friendly attention of hosts Don and Helene O'Neill fully compensate.

Don and Helene bought their home in 1985 after a B&B trip to California convinced them that they would enjoy being hosts at their own establishment. They found a fairly run-down property built about 1840 consisting of a private home and an accompanying carriage house. Don was able to restore the place himself, thanks to his years of experience as a carpenter for the Newport Restoration Foundation.

The mansard exterior of the Victorian Ladies is now painted slate gray and burgundy; the two buildings are connected by a flower-filled latticed courtyard that serves as an outdoor breakfast area in the summer. Inside, the inn is splendidly decorated, each room reflecting Helene's creativity and eye for design.

The living room, mauve and light blue, has a crystal chandelier, cozy fireplace, floral wallpaper, several plump-pillowed couches, and many ornamental objects from the Far East. The adjoining dining room reflects the color scheme of the living room but has more of a country feeling, with a large, simple pine table and sideboard where ample traditional breakfasts of eggs and bacon or ham are served.

Each guest room is different, though the general look is frilly: Flounces and lace are brightened by house plants and fresh flowers. A favorite of many guests is the honeymoon suite: Its romantic four-poster bed is festooned with chintz, echoed at the windows by matching balloon shades. As in so many other rooms in the inn, the bed here is heaped with ruffled pillows handmade by Helene. Another guest room features children's lace dresses on the walls, set off by a black background with a rosebud print; all the furnishings and accessories are carefully coordinated to this color scheme. The rooms are furnished with an eclectic collection of antiques, reproductions, and modern pieces, which coexist in harmony.

🏨 *11 double rooms with baths. Air-conditioning, TVs, off-street parking. $135–$175 May 15–Nov. 1, $85–$105 Nov. 2–May 14; full breakfast. MC, V. No smoking, no children.*

Other Choices

Admiral Fitzroy Inn. 398 Thames St., Newport, RI 02840, tel. 401/848–8000 or 800/343–2863, fax 401/848–8006. 18 double rooms with baths. Air-conditioning, phones, hair dryers, elevator, 2 rooms with private decks, off-street parking. $85–$175, full breakfast and afternoon tea. AE, DC, MC, V. 2-night minimum on summer weekends, 3-night minimum on holiday weekends and during the Newport festivals.

Elm Tree Cottage. 336 Gibbs Ave., Newport, RI 02840, tel. 401/849–1610 or 800/882–3356, fax 401/849–2084. 6 double rooms with baths. Air-conditioning, fireplaces in most rooms. $135–$325, full breakfast. AE, MC, V. No smoking, no pets, no children, 2-night minimum on weekends, 3-night minimum on holiday weekends. Closed Dec. 24–26.

The Inntowne. 6 Mary St., Newport, RI 02840, tel. 401/846–9200 or 800/457–7803, fax 401/846–1534. 26 double rooms with baths. Phones, kitchen facilities in some rooms, small patios off some rooms, 24-hr front desk, access to health club facilities at the nearby Marriott. $95–$179, Continental breakfast. Parking in municipal lot costs $12.25 per day. AE, MC, V.

Sanford-Covell Villa Marina. 72 Washington St., Newport, RI 02840, tel. 401/847–0206. 6 double rooms, 3 with shared baths. Outdoor pool with heated salt water. $65–$225, Continental breakfast and afternoon refreshments. No credit cards. 2-night minimum in summer.

Reservations Services

Anna's Victorian Connection (5 Fowler Ave., Newport, RI 02840, tel. 401/849–2489 or 800/884–4288). **Bed and Breakfast Newport Reservation Service** (33 Russell Ave., Newport, RI 02840, tel. 401/846–5408). **Bed and Breakfast of Rhode Island, Inc.** (Box 3291, Newport, RI 02840, tel. 401/849–1298).

The Coast

The Richards

144 Gibson Ave., Narragansett, RI 02882, tel. 401/789–7746

Imposing and magnificent, this English manor–style mansion, built of granite quarried on the site, was the brainchild of Joseph Peace Hazard, scion of one of the founding families of Rhode Island. There's a mysterious story of how Hazard came to build his summer home; ask the current owner, Nancy Richards, and she'll be delighted to share it with you. Nancy and Steven Richards and their two daughters, who bought the house in 1987, are only the third family to own it since its construction more than a century ago, so the legends have been passed along intact.

Meticulously restored and listed on the National Register of Historic Places, the Richardses' home has a broodingly Gothic mystique that is almost the antithesis of a summer home. From the wood-paneled common rooms downstairs, French windows look out onto a lush landscape, with a grand swamp oak the centerpiece of a handsome garden. The library, its shelves lined with interesting books, often has a fire crackling in the fireplace on chilly late afternoons. Each morning, in the baronial dining room, equipped with an early 19th-century English sideboard, Nancy serves a breakfast consisting of fresh fruit, strudel, cereal, coffee, and muffins as well as such main courses as eggs Florentine and oven pancakes.

Although only six of the 12 bedrooms are open to guests, they are in a separate wing, so you never have the sense of intruding upon the family. Each guest room is furnished with 19th-century English antiques; the brass bed, two 19th-century sleigh beds, and a canopy bed are particularly interesting. Four of the rooms have private baths, in one of which is a linen press original to the house. Each room has a working fireplace (which visitors are welcome to use), down comforters, and tasteful furniture upholstered in floral fabrics, as well as cut-glass decanters of sherry for a late-afternoon sip.

Nancy and Steven know their stuff, having operated bed-and-breakfasts in the Narragansett area for the past two decades, and their manner is welcoming yet unobtrusive. They've found a property worthy of their talents with this superbly restored house, offering visitors luxurious accommodations in a quiet rural setting.

🏠 *2 double rooms with baths, 2 doubles share 1 bath, 1 2-bedroom suite. $60–$160, full breakfast. No credit cards. No smoking, no pets, 2-day minimum on summer weekends, 3-day minimum on holidays.*

Shelter Harbor Inn

*10 Wagner Rd., Westerly, RI 02891, tel.
401/322–8883*

Though it's set beside busy Route 1
(with neither sea nor harbor in sight),
the Shelter Harbor Inn is surprisingly
peaceful, buffered from the highway by
a rolling lawn. On the grounds you'll
find the main building, a two-story
farmhouse built from 1800 to 1810, and
the original coach house and barn,
where more guest rooms have been
quietly tucked away.

The lobby, library, sunporch, and
restaurant are decorated with a quirky
choice of antiques. For instance, there's
an enormous Hoosier hutch and a Sim-
plex wall clock, which many guests cite
as their favorite antique in the place.
Each guest room is furnished differently, with a combination of Victorian
antiques and reproduction pieces; bedspreads and curtains are in muted
floral patterns. Purists may be disappointed that the working fireplaces in
some rooms are modern and somewhat
tacky in design—not in the style of the
inn's original construction—but this is
one of the few inns in the area that
allows visitors to light fires in their
rooms. Several of the rooms with fireplaces also have decks (the corner
room, No. 9, is a particular favorite),
and if you climb to the roof there's
another deck, with a hot tub and barbecue, open to guests. Some of the furnishings in the guest rooms show signs
of wear and could be replaced.

The inn's restaurant serves three meals
a day and receives rave reviews from
locals despite prices that range a little
on the high side; lighter fare is served
in the veranda bar. A breakfast worth
getting up for is included in the room
rate. One breakfast specialty is ginger
blueberry pancakes; fresh seafood is
frequently featured on the dinner
menu.

This efficiently run inn is a good choice
for a romantic getaway. The management is friendly, unobtrusive, and
professional. Owner Jim Dey, a self-
described "Wall Street exile," bought
the inn in 1976, and has masterminded
many of its renovations himself. Though
he and his wife, Debbye, no longer live
on the property, they are here most of
the time. If you arrive on a summer or
fall afternoon, you are likely to see Jim
rolling around the inn's front lawn on
his ride-on mower, a job he reserves for
himself, he says, because it gives him
time to think.

🏠 *23 double rooms with baths. Restaurant, bar, air-conditioning, TV,
phones, paddle tennis, croquet. $92–
$126, full breakfast. AE, D, MC, V. No
pets, 2-day minimum on weekends
Memorial Day–Thanksgiving, 3-day
minimum on holidays.*

Stone Lea

*40 Newton Ave., Narragansett, RI
02882, tel. 401/783–9546*

A mile south of the town of Narragansett, just off winding Ocean Drive,
Stone Lea is a large shingle-covered
house that offers panoramic ocean
views. Built in 1884, it was designed by
the famous architectural firm of McKim,
Mead and White, who were also responsible for Narragansett's most classic
buildings, the Coast Guard House, Towers, and Casino. Rotundas and bay windows sprout all over this handsome
summer house, and inside you'll find big
windows, lots of light, and elaborate
detail, such as the carved wood paneling
in the main entrance hall and stairway.
A favorite perch for many guests is the
window seat on the stair landing.

Converted to a bed-and-breakfast in
the early 1980s, Stone Lea has been
operated since May 1995 by the Lancel-
lotti family. Guy, a Rhode Island surgeon, is the new owner and his parents,
Guy and Lucy, offer a big hand in summer. The rooms are quiet and spacious,
although the most memorable feature
of the place is the glorious ocean view.
Every guest room offers a glimpse of

the water, and some face directly onto the sea. The interior is "getting more Victorian all the time," according to the Lancellottis, who consistently add period antiques. Another homey addition is wallpaper throughout the house.

The living room is a friendly spot, furnished with a player piano and a reproduction of an antique pool table. In the dining room, lined with shelves bearing antique china, chef John Erwin surprises guests daily with his full breakfasts. These also include homemade muffins, coffee cake, coffee breads, and fresh fruits. The air of tranquillity here is a real plus, and this is, overall, one of the nicest places to stay in Narragansett.

🏨 *7 double rooms with baths. Cable TV in common area. $100–$150, full breakfast. MC, V. No smoking, no pets, 2-day minimum on weekends in summer, 3-day minimum on holidays. Closed Thanksgiving, Christmas.*

Weekapaug Inn

25 Spring Ave., Weekapaug, RI 02891, tel. 401/322-0301

At the end of curving Ninigret Avenue, past a line of gracious, well-maintained vintage beachfront homes, waits an enchanting inn where time seems to have stood still since 1939. The Weekapaug Inn has been operated by the Buffum family every summer since 1899, with only one interruption—when it was destroyed by the hurricane of 1938. Even in the face of that catastrophe, the family acted quickly, rebuilding the inn from scratch several hundred yards away from its former waterside site and reopening just one week late in the summer of 1939.

The building seems more a mansion than an inn, with a peaked roof, stone foundation, and huge wraparound porch. It's perched on a peninsula surrounded on three sides by salty Quonochontaug Pond; just beyond a barrier beach is Block Island Sound (the inn

rents boats to interested guests). Like a set from the old TV series *Father Knows Best*, there's a comfy tidiness about the furnishings in the common rooms and bedrooms, where every surface looks freshly painted, waxed, or varnished. The decor of the bedrooms is cheerful, if not particularly remarkable, and each room is big and bright, with wide windows offering impressive views.

Many guests have been regulars here for several summers—some as many as 45 or 50 years—although newcomers are more than welcome ("We like to see fresh faces here," comments caretaker Horst Taut). Standards in the restaurant are very high; a new menu every day features four to six entrées, emphasizing seafood, and a full-time baker makes all the desserts, breads, and rolls. Thursday-night cookouts feature swordfish, steak, and chicken, as well as seasonal vegetables.

The Weekapaug Inn is a complete summer vacation spot, offering a full range of diversions: access to a nearby private golf course, tennis, lawn bowling, sailing, windsurfing, rowing, fishing, access to a private beach, shuffleboard, croquet, Ping-Pong, billiards, and weekly movies. Though many of its guests are middle-aged and older, the inn's children's program has made it a favorite of families, too. A full-time children's program director runs two daily sessions, with special excursions and projects that make even the youngest feel welcome.

🏨 *33 double rooms with baths, 21 singles with baths. Restaurant. $165–$175 per person, MAP. No credit cards. No pets, 2-day minimum on weekends, 3-day minimum on holidays. Closed Labor Day–mid-June.*

Other Choices

Admiral Dewey Inn. 668 Matunuck Beach Rd., South Kingstown, RI 02879, tel. 401/783-2090. 10 double rooms, 8 with baths. $60–$125, Continental breakfast. MC, V. No smoking.

Ocean House. 2 Bluff Ave., Watch Hill, RI 02891, tel. 401/348–8161. 56 double rooms with baths, 3 single rooms with baths. Restaurant, cocktail lounge. $185–$210, breakfast and dinner. MC, V. No pets, 2-night minimum on weekends, 3-night minimum on holidays. Closed Labor Day–late June.

Reservations Service

Bed and Breakfast of Rhode Island, Inc. (Box 3291, Newport, RI 02840, tel. 401/849–1298).

Block Island

Atlantic Inn

High St., Box 188, Block Island, RI 02807, tel. 401/466–5883 or 800/224–7422

When rocking in a comfortable chair on the wide, shady porch of this classic summer hotel, you may feel a sense of déjà vu, for planted at the bottom of the rise is a small building that looks disconcertingly similar to the Atlantic Inn. "It's a miniature of the hotel that the previous owners built for the children who visit here," explains innkeeper Brad Marthens, who with his wife, Anne, bought the inn in 1994. The two had vacationed on the island for years. "We both love the ocean, so this place is perfect for us," says Marthens.

Built in 1879, the Atlantic Inn is a long, white Victorian inn with a slate-blue roof, bravely fronting the elements on a hill above the ocean. Big windows, high ceilings, and a sweeping staircase contribute to the breezy atmosphere. Guest rooms, which are capacious though not huge, are lined up on long, straight hallways. The inn is furnished with turn-of-the-century furniture, much of it golden oak. The generally austere feel of the

place is softened by predominantly pastel colors, and homey touches abound: There are handmade boat models in the dining room. The overall effect is refreshingly unfrilly, creating a restful ambience that accords well with the bracing effect of the clean ocean air.

Continental breakfast is served, and breads are fresh-baked on the island. The restaurant is open for dinner June–mid-September. The 6-acre grounds are carefully maintained, and boast large wildflower, herb, and vegetable gardens (the produce of which is used in the kitchen); two all-weather tennis courts; and a smooth green croquet lawn, allowing for a game of mallets and wickets at a moment's notice.

And then there are the views. Isolated from the hubbub of the Old Harbor area, at the Atlantic Inn it's possible to perch on a hillside and muse on the patterns the wind makes in the long grasses, on the rippling of waves across the many small ponds within sight, or on the sparkle of the not-too-distant ocean.

21 double rooms with baths. Restaurant; phones; electric fans; common area with large-screen TV, games, and books. $99–$195, Continental breakfast. AE, MC, V. No smoking, no pets, 2- or 3-night minimum on weekends June–Aug. Closed Nov.–Mar.

Hotel Manisses

1 Spring St., Block Island, RI 02807, tel. 401/466–2063 or 800/626–4773, fax 401/466–3162

As you stroll along Spring Street on a foggy night, your eye might be caught by a translucent glow in the sky. Continue down the street and you'll discover the source: the magnificent brass chandelier suspended inside the cupola of the Manisses, like a beacon of welcome from a bygone era.

The Manisses is an 1870 Victorian gem, restored with loving care and constant diligence by its owners and operators—

Joan and Justin Abrams, their daughter Rita Draper, and her husband, Steve. (The family also owns and operates the nearby 1661 Inn and Guest House; *see below.*) No expense has been spared in the inn's renovation and decoration, but what's perhaps more important, the Drapers and Abrams families work hard to make their guests feel comfortable, relaxed, and pampered. While not intruding on guests' privacy, the hosts have refined to a high art the successful innkeeper's usual attention to detail. As Rita Draper escorts guests to their rooms, her eye constantly sweeps over the territory, checking to make sure that every plant has been watered and that every lace doily and antimacassar is neatly in place.

Furnishings were clearly chosen with care. Many of the guest rooms, named after famous shipwrecks, are filled with unusual Victorian pieces painstakingly restored, such as the many-leveled bureau in the Princess Augusta Room. Even more intriguing are the knickknacks occupying every available bit of space, such as the ivory toilet set on the bureau in one room. Afternoon tea and bedside decanters of brandy show an extra level of thoughtfulness. The restaurant, too, is a standout, with inventive cuisine drawing upon local seafood, homemade bread, and fresh vegetables grown in the Manisses garden. Breakfast for guests at the Manisses, which is served at the 1661 Inn, a one-minute walk up the road, is copious: eggs, sausage, cornbread, smoked bluefish, muffins, and much more.

🏨 *17 double rooms with baths. Restaurant; phones; ceiling fans; whirlpool baths in some rooms; petting farm next door featuring llamas, goats, and black swans. $90–$255, buffet breakfast served at nearby inn. AE, MC, V. No children.*

1661 Inn & Guest House

Spring St., Block Island, RI 02807, tel. 401/466-2421, 401/466-2063, or 800/ 626-4773, fax 401/466-3162

If your island vacation fantasy includes lounging in bed while gazing at swans on the marshes and a roiling sea, consider booking an oceanside room at the 1661 Inn and Guest House. For that matter, any room here is comfortable and relaxing. Owners Joan and Justin Abrams and operators Rita and Steve Draper (*see* Hotel Manisses, *above*) are noted for their attention to detail. Even if your room doesn't face the water, you can loll on the inn's expansive deck or in a lounge chair on the gentle oceanside slope and enjoy the panorama of the water below.

In the front hallway, there's a wall full of pictures of the inn contributed by former guests, suggesting what a special experience staying here has been for many people. Recently refurbished from top to bottom, the inn has fewer rooms than it once did, which gives guests larger bedrooms with more luxurious appointments. Many rooms offer whirlpool baths, often accompanied by Victorian "fainting couches" that allow the whirlpool-induced glow to linger. Each room is different, each decorated with an eye to detail. For example, the floral wallpaper in one room matches the colors of the hand-painted tiles at the top of that room's antique bureau. Another room features a collection of handmade wooden ship models. Yet another, a duplex looking out to sea, has an antique canopy bed.

No matter how lost you may get in the comfort of your surroundings, be sure to get up in time for breakfast, a splendid experience in any season but especially so in summer, when guests can sit outdoors on the canopied deck. The ample buffet may consist of fresh bluefish, corned-beef hash, Boston baked beans, sausage, Belgian waffles, roast potatoes, French toast, scrambled eggs, hot and cold cereal, fruit juices, and fresh muffins. Afternoon cocktails are also served, with such hors d'oeuvres as bluefish pâté and super-spicy nachos.

Adjacent to the inn is the Guest House, with smaller rooms and some shared baths. Though the atmosphere here is slightly more spartan, the prices are quite reasonable, and all the inn's amenities remain available.

▦ *9 double rooms with baths in inn; in guest house, 5 doubles with baths, 4 doubles share 1 bath. Phones, 4 rooms accessible to people who use wheelchairs. $60–$325, full buffet breakfast. AE, MC, V. No pets.*

Other Choices

Barrington Inn. Box 397, Beach and Ocean Aves., Block Island, RI 02807, tel. 401/466–5510. 6 double rooms with baths, 2 apartments. Ceiling fans, TV/VCR in common room. $50–$149, Continental breakfast. MC, V. No smoking, no pets, no children. Closed Dec.–Mar.

Blue Dory Inn. Dodge St., Box 488, Block Island, RI 02807, tel. 401/466–

5891 or 800/992–7290. 13 double rooms with baths, 3 suites, 4 cottages. Cable TV in lobby. $65–$350, Continental breakfast. AE, D, MC, V. No smoking, no pets, 2-night minimum on weekends.

Rose Farm Inn. Roslyn Rd., Box E, Block Island, RI 02807, tel. 401/466–2034. 17 double rooms with baths, 2 doubles share 1 bath. Cable TV in common room, refrigerator and ice machine available. $75–$179, Continental breakfast. AE, D, MC, V. No smoking, no children; 3-night minimum in July and Aug., 2-night minimum on June, Sept., and Oct. weekends.

Surf Hotel. Dodge St., Box C, Block Island, RI 02807, tel. 401/466–2241. 20 double rooms and 20 singles; all share 9 baths. Barbecue grill in backyard for guests. $45–$130, Continental breakfast. MC, V. No pets, 6-night minimum in July and Aug. Closed Columbus Day–Memorial Day.

Reservations Service

Bed and Breakfast of Rhode Island, Inc. (Box 3291, Newport, RI 02840, tel. 401/849–1298).

South Carolina

Two Meeting Street

Myrtle Beach and the Grand Strand

Sea View Inn

Myrtle Ave., Pawleys Island, SC 29585, tel. 803/237-4253, fax 803/237-7909

In the morning you can put your feet on the lye-washed hardwood floor and rush to the window to catch a breath of the fresh air that filters through the starched curtains. You might wander out to drink your early morning coffee on the big screened-in porch, or you may take it into the living room, where there's always a fire on cool days. This is the seaside as it was meant to be— unadulterated by air-conditioning, neon, and such citified comforts as wall-to-wall carpeting. Built in the 1930s and rebuilt in the 1950s after being devastated by Hurricane Hazel, the Sea View is a no-frills two-story beachside boardinghouse with long porches. There is also a six-room air-conditioned cottage on the marsh.

Page Oberlin, who once ran a large restaurant, took over as innkeeper about 20 years ago. A stay at her "barefoot paradise," though certainly not for everyone, is a special experience (in high season, the minimum stay is a week). Don't expect any programming, unless you're attending one of the semi-annual painting workshops or wellness retreats (which feature meditation, yoga, massage, organic foods, and guest speakers). Meals, served family style— with grits, gumbo, crab salad, pecan pie, and oyster pie—are really the only scheduled events. (Mexican and Thai nights are inspired by Page, who brings back authentic menus from her extensive travels.) The time is yours—to read, collect shells, walk on the beach, or just do nothing. This is life on Pawleys Island.

Each guest room has pickled cypress walls and is simply furnished with a hand-painted dresser, a double bed and a twin covered with handmade bedspreads from Guatemala, and art from the spring workshop. Each room has a half-bath; showers are down the hall (and also outside for ocean swimmers). All the rooms have a view of the ocean or the marsh, and the design of the building guarantees a cross breeze. Your program for getting your life in order won't be disturbed here; though the inn has a well-stocked library, the tube is nonexistent, and there's only one phone. There are sailing, golf, and tennis nearby, plus arts-and-crafts shops. And you can always go ghost hunting among the moss-draped live oaks; you might encounter Alice, searching for her engagement ring in the marshes, or the Gray Man, who warns people about approaching storms.

🎏 *19 doubles and 1 single share 6 showers. $140–$170, AP. No credit cards. No pets, 2-night minimum May and Sept.–Oct., 1-week minimum June–Aug. Closed Nov.–Apr.*

Other Choices

Brustman House. 400 25th Ave. S, Myrtle Beach, SC 29577, tel. 803/448–7699 or 800/448–7699, fax 803/626–1500. 4 double rooms with baths. Air-conditioning, phone and ceiling fan in rooms, TV/VCR in lounge and suite; badminton, croquet. $65–$80; full breakfast, afternoon refreshments. No credit cards. No smoking, no pets.

Chesterfield Inn. 700 N. Ocean Blvd. (Box 218), Myrtle Beach, SC 29578, tel. 803/448–3177 or 800/392–3869, fax 803/626–4736. 31 double rooms with baths in old section, 26 doubles with baths in new section (6 with kitchenettes). Restaurant, air-conditioning, cable TVs, phones; pool, shuffleboard, croquet. $74–$105, breakfast extra; $112–$140, MAP. AE, D, MC, V. No pets. Closed Dec.–Jan.

King's Inn at Georgetown. 230 Broad St., Georgetown, SC 29440, tel. 803/527–6937 or 800/251–8805. 7 double rooms with baths, TV in lounge; lap pool. $75–$115, full breakfast. AE, MC, V. Restricted smoking, no pets.

Litchfield Plantation. River Rd. (Box 290), Pawleys Island, SC 29585, tel. 803/237–4286 or 800/869–1410, fax 803/237–8558. 4 suites. Air-conditioning, cable TVs, phones. $155–$190, Continental breakfast. AE, MC, V. No smoking, no pets.

Mansfield Plantation. U.S. 701 N (Rte. 8, Box 590), Georgetown, SC 29440, tel. 803/546–6961 or 800/355–3223. 8 double rooms with baths. Air-

conditioning. $95; full breakfast, afternoon wine, cold drinks. No credit cards. No smoking.

Serendipity, An Inn. 407 71st Ave. N, Myrtle Beach, SC 29572, tel. 803/449–5268 or 800/762–3229. 12 double rooms with baths, 2 suites. Air-conditioning, TVs, refrigerators; pool, outdoor hot tub, Ping-Pong, shuffleboard. $77–$129, Continental breakfast. AE, MC, V. No smoking in breakfast room, no pets, 2-night minimum July–Aug. 15. Closed Dec.–Jan.

1790 House. 630 Highmarket St., Georgetown, SC 29440, tel. 803/546–4821 or 800/890–7432. 4 double rooms, 1 suite, 1 cottage. Air-conditioning, TV in rooms on request; bicycles, Ping-Pong. $75–$125; full breakfast, afternoon refreshments. AE, D, MC, V. Restricted smoking, no pets, 2-night minimum holiday weekends.

Charleston and the Low Country

Kings Courtyard Inn

198 King St., Charleston, SC 29401, tel. 803/723–7000 or 800/845–6119, fax 803/720–2608

It is easy to overlook the small doorway that leads into the shady courtyard of this European-style inn, wedged between the city's best antiques shops and fashionable boutiques on King Street, one of Charleston's oldest shopping thoroughfares. Just a stone's throw from the new Saks Fifth Avenue and a block from the Old City Market's souvenir shops, restaurants, and crafts vendors, you can shop-till-you-drop, then return to this soothing oasis. But you don't have to be a shopper to enjoy the inn's universal appeal. Guests will quickly recognize the ambience, service, and respect for privacy that are characteristic here.

Designed by architect Francie D. Lee and built in 1853, the two structures that compose the Greek Revival inn have the appearance of being only one because of their exterior stucco, which was added after the great earthquake of 1886. The buildings were restored in 1983 by Richard T. Widman and converted into an inn, which had been their original use. Prior to the Civil War, plantation owners and shipping magnates stayed here when they did business in Charleston. The rooms are furnished with 18th-century reproductions, including French armoires and beds hung with hand-tied fishnet canopies, and decorated in elegant, traditional fabrics, with Oriental rugs accenting the original heart-pine floors. There are guest rooms on all three stories: Two have pressed-tin ceilings, 14 have gas-burning fireplaces, and one has a private balcony. Most of the rooms open onto one of the two inner courtyards with fountains; the rest overlook King Street. A large whirlpool bath is the center of a rear garden area.

In a small formal room off the main courtyard, a fire burns in winter and guests can relax and have cocktails—complimentary wine and sherry are always available, as is brandy after dinner. Guests may have breakfast here, in one of the courtyards, the breakfast room, or their bedroom; a full meal is available upon order. Breakfast comes with a morning newspaper, and the nightly turndown service includes chocolates.

▦ *37 double rooms with baths, 4 suites. Air-conditioning, cable TVs, phones, small meeting room; outdoor whirlpool bath. $105–$210, Continental breakfast. AE, MC, V. Restricted smoking, no pets.*

Rhett House Inn

1009 Craven St., Beaufort, SC 29902, tel. 803/524–9030, fax 803/524–1310

This 1820 Greek Revival mansion in Beaufort's historic district was the home of Thomas Rhett, a rich planter, who summered here with his wife, Caroline Barnwell, and their children. The house exemplifies the rich and lavish lifestyle of prosperous southern planters prior to the Civil War. (Nowhere in the South was wealth flaunted more than in Beaufort.) The three-story square, white building has black shutters and double-decker verandas on the second and third floors, supported by 14 fluted Doric columns. It stands on the edge of Craven Street, with a huge live oak dripping with Spanish moss directly in front and gardens to the side and the rear.

The mansion was looking somewhat sad when Steve and Marianne Harrison, executives in New York's garment industry, first spied it on a vacation in 1986. But it was love at first sight. Steve quit his job as president of Anne Klein, and Marianne gave up her knitwear company so they could move to Beaufort and become innkeepers. The Harrisons completely renovated the mansion and filled it with their own antiques and art. Though elegant, the inn is warm and friendly with a French country-cottage look; guests feel comfortable in sweaters and tennis shoes, and boaters on the Intracoastal Waterway (only a block away) often drop in. Famous guests have included Barbra Streisand and Nick Nolte (when they were filming *Prince of Tides*), Dennis Quaid, and Demi Moore; Steve says he brushes with more celebrities in this town, popular with filmmakers, than he did in New York City.

There's a great variety of accommodations. Some rooms have private entrances and are accessible to persons with disabilities. Two rooms have working fireplaces, and the honeymoon suite has a private porch and a whirlpool bath. Amenities in the rooms include fresh flowers and miniature African violets, a CD player (there's a CD library in the sitting room), a full-length mirror, and four pillows.

The inn recently remodeled its restaurant, Caroline's at Craven, into a sophisticated, black-and-white affair with shaded candles, gilt-framed photos, and a chef's table. Dinner is served Tuesday through Saturday to both guests and the public. Highlights are spicy collard greens stuffed with chicken and goat cheese, roasted barbecue duck, and apple-wood-smoked pork. Guests can eat breakfast in the restaurant, in the garden, or on the porch. Picnics can be arranged on request.

▦ *9 double rooms with baths, 1 suite. Restaurant, air-conditioning, ceiling fan, cable TVs, phones, CD players, robes; turndown service, bicycles. $125–$225; full breakfast, afternoon refreshments. AE, MC, V. Restricted smoking.*

Two Meeting Street

2 Meeting St., Charleston, SC 29401, tel. 803/723–7322

This Queen Anne Victorian, built in 1892, is one of the most beautiful houses in the city's historic district and is usually included in spring and fall house tours. You know this is a special place the minute you step through the iron gates onto a walk lined with flowers and shrubs. The landscaped gardens are manicured to perfection; the curved verandas, with their arched columns and balustrades, are freshly painted. The sparkle of the beveled glass and the polished brass on the heavy wooden door add to the welcome of the innkeeper's official greeting.

Its location, overlooking the Battery and the harbor, makes it convenient to all of Charleston's pleasures. In 1931, it was turned into an inn, and it eventually passed to Jean and Pete Spell. Together with their daughter, Karen Spell Shaw, the Spells have made the house a showplace, one of the city's most popular lodgings, and raised innkeeping to an art. All three are locals with insider's advice—Pete is a Citadel grad, and Jean is a licensed city guide who will enthusiastically help guests tailor a day of sightseeing around their interests. The Spells' fascination with Charleston and the Low Country is evident in the many books around the house.

You enter the foyer, a large open room with richly carved English oak paneling, stained-glass windows, and a heavy stairway over which hangs a huge crystal chandelier. The reception rooms are also paneled, and the house has nine stained-glass windows in all, two of them Tiffanys. The formal parlors, off the foyer, are furnished with Victorian reproduction love seats, 18th-century chairs, family heirlooms, and photos; the formal dining room has a dazzling crystal chandelier and highly polished silver. Guests can enjoy a fire-lit breakfast here in winter.

Each guest room has its own personality, and all are furnished with antique four-poster or canopy beds and Oriental rugs. The two honeymoon suites have working fireplaces and French doors that open to the outside, creating a feeling of privacy. The rooms on the first and second floors are the most sought after, but those on the third floor are just as appealing except that you must climb the stairs.

The staff members at Two Meeting Street go out of their way to make each stay memorable. Guests can enjoy afternoon tea with homemade cakes, Low Country sweets, cheese, and crackers. Breakfast is a treat, too, with fresh fruit salad and oversize "Texas" muffins.

▦ *9 double rooms with baths. Air-conditioning, TVs. $135–$250; Continental breakfast, afternoon tea. No credit cards. No smoking, no pets, 2-night minimum weekends. Closed Dec. 24–26.*

Other Choices

Battery Carriage House Inn. 20 South Battery, Charleston, SC 29401, tel. 803/727–3100 or 800/775–5575, fax 803/727–3130. 10 double rooms with baths, 1 suite. Air-conditioning, cable TVs, phones, robes; turndown service, complimentary newspaper. $99–$199; Continental breakfast, afternoon snacks. AE, D, MC, V. No smoking, no pets.

Beaufort Inn. 809 Port Republic St., Beaufort, SC 29902, tel. 803/521–9000, fax 803/521–9500. 15 double rooms with baths. Restaurant, air-conditioning, ceiling fans, TVs, phones, refrigerators, honor bars; small conference room. $110–$185; full breakfast, afternoon tea. AE, MC, V. Restricted smoking, no pets.

Cassina Point Plantation. Box 535, Edisto Island, SC 29438, tel. and fax 803/869–2535. 4 double rooms share 2 baths. Air-conditioning, ceiling fans; TV and refrigerator in guest lounge; canoes, croquet, fishing poles. $105; full breakfast, afternoon refreshments. No credit cards. Restricted smoking, no pets. Open Wed.–Sun., weekends only Jan.–Feb.

Fulton Lane Inn. 202 King St., Charleston, SC 29401, tel. 803/720–2600 or 800/720–2688, fax 803/720–2940. 22 double rooms with baths, 5 suites. Air-conditioning, cable TVs, phones, refrigerators, honor bars; turndown service. $95–$240, Continental breakfast. MC, V. No smoking, no pets.

Jasmine House Inn. 64 Hasell St., Charleston, SC 29401, tel. 803/577–5900 or 800/845–7639, fax 803/577–0378. 10 double rooms with baths. Air-conditioning, cable TVs, phones, ceiling fans; outdoor whirlpool. $150–$180, Continental breakfast. AE, D, DC, MC, V. No pets.

John Rutledge House Inn. 116 Broad St., Charleston, SC 29401, tel. 803/723–7999 or 800/476–9741, fax 803/720–2615. 16 double rooms with baths, 3 suites. Air-conditioning, cable TVs, phones, refrigerator; turndown service, concierge. $150–$310; Continental breakfast, afternoon tea. AE, MC, V. Smoking in 1 carriage house only, no pets.

Middleton Inn. Ashley River Rd., Charleston, SC 29414, tel. 803/556–0500 or 800/543–4774. 52 double rooms with baths. Air-conditioning, TVs, phones, refrigerators; large meeting room; pool, bicycles, tennis, croquet, free admission to Middleton Place. $99–129, full breakfast. AE, D, DC, MC, V. Restricted smoking.

Twenty-Seven State Street Bed & Breakfast. 27 State St., Charleston, SC 29401, tel. 803/722–4243. 2 double rooms with baths, 3 suites for long-term visitors. Air-conditioning, kitchenettes, cable TVs, phones; bicycles. $95–165, Continental breakfast. No smoking, no pets.

TwoSuns Inn Bed & Breakfast. 1705 Bay St., Beaufort, SC 29902, tel. and fax 803/522–1122 or 800/532–4244. 5 double rooms with baths. Air-conditioning, ceiling fan, phone in rooms, cable TV/VCR in parlor; bicycles, croquet, horseshoes. $105–$135; full breakfast, afternoon refreshments. AE, MC, V. No smoking, no pets.

Reservations Services

Historic Charleston B & B (60 Broad St., Charleston, SC 29401, tel. 803/722–6606 or 800/743–3583). **RSVP Reservation Service** (9489 Whitefield Ave., Box 49, Savannah, GA 31406, tel. 800/729–7787). **Southern Hospitality B&B Reservations** (110 Amelia Dr., Lexington, SC 29464, tel. 803/356–6238 or 800/374–7422).

Thoroughbred Country and the Old Ninety Six

Annie's Inn

U.S. 78 E (Box 300), Montmorenci, SC 29839, tel. 803/649–6836

You won't be a stranger at this inn long. Before you know it, you'll be sipping coffee by the wood cookstove and getting acquainted with the other guests (usually businesspeople during the week and couples on weekends). The experience is a lot like going to Grandma's because of the friendly, at-home atmosphere that pervades Scottie Peck's kitchen.

Scottie and her late husband bought the house several years ago, and after his death, she turned it into a bed-and-breakfast inn, the oldest B&B in town. The nearly 200-year-old farmhouse in the rural community of Montmorenci, just outside Aiken, stood at one time on a 2,000-acre cotton plantation. The crop is still grown nearby, but only 2 acres of the original tract remain with the house.

There were originally three floors, but the top floor was hit by a cannonball during the Civil War and subsequently removed. A doctor had his practice in the house for a time and used it as a hospital; the resident ghost is a child who cries.

The house's most distinguishing features are its big front porch and second-floor balcony. It has a central hallway, with formal rooms on either side, the kitchen to the back, and bedrooms upstairs. Scottie has furnished it in French and English country style, combining antiques, handmade quilts, area rugs, and lace. Small bathrooms with showers were carved out of existing space so that each guest room has one. Guests who are staying for a long time usually choose one of the two completely equipped housekeeping cottages behind the house.

Scottie serves breakfast in the kitchen or in the dining room (when she has a full house). Because she is from Colorado, she doesn't serve grits but offers such entrées as waffles with fresh steamed apples on top, popovers served with locally produced honey, and eggs Benedict.

On nice days, guests gather at the swimming pool, play croquet, or pitch horseshoes, and Scottie always has plenty of books, magazines, and games on hand for rainy days.

🏠 *5 double rooms with baths, 2 cottages. Air-conditioning, ceiling fans, TVs, phones. $55–$95, full breakfast. AE, D, DC, MC, V. Restricted smoking, no pets.*

Belmont Inn

Court Sq., 106 E. Pickens St., Abbeville, SC 29620, tel. 864/459-9625 or 888/251-2000

This three-story hotel, with its long, arched double veranda, planted on one corner of Court Square, has played a prominent role in the history of the town. Built in 1903 and called the Eureka, it was the resort of famous statesmen, lawyers and judges during court sessions, drummers, and vaudeville actors in its heyday. The hotel went through hard times, eventually closed in 1974, opened in 1984 after a complete restoration, then closed again in a tattered state. Three college chums from nearby towns bought the place in 1996 and reopened after giving the inn a major sprucing-up.

Since its rebirth, the Belmont has developed quite a following. Its guests like to combine a visit with a couple of nights at the Opera House, following the example of stars like Jimmy Durante, Fanny Brice, Sarah Bernhardt, and Groucho Marx, who made overnight stops in Abbeville. The town calls itself the "birthplace and deathbed of the Confederacy," and there is a Confederate memorial in the town square.

Guest rooms are furnished in Victorian reproductions, with four-poster beds and armoires; the bathrooms are strictly functional, and only rooms facing the town square have a noteworthy view. Though the heart-pine floors are original, the fireplaces are now only decorative. The best lodging in the house, the John C. Calhoun Room, has a four-poster bed and opens onto the second-floor balcony. The fancy Lafayette

Room is accessorized completely in red and gold. Public rooms are also furnished in Victorian reproductions, some period antiques, wicker, and rich hunting colors. The lobby exudes a turn-of-the-century atmosphere; a registration desk is in the middle of the room, and sitting areas and separate parlors are off to the side.

Timothy's restaurant, serving regional cuisine, offers all meals plus Sunday brunch. Guests help themselves to a Continental buffet breakfast served here and may take it out to the veranda overlooking the square. Light fare is served in the Curtain Call Lounge on the basement level. The meeting rooms, also on this level, were originally used by traveling salesmen to display their merchandise.

🏨 *25 double rooms with baths. Air-conditioning, cable TVs, phones. $69–$129; Continental breakfast, afternoon refreshments. AE, D, DC, MC, V. Restricted smoking, no pets.*

Other Choices

Brodie Residence. 422 York St. SE, Aiken, SC 29801 tel. 803/648–1445. 2 double rooms share 1 bath. Air-conditioning, cable TVs, phones, ceiling fans; turndown service with chocolates; pool, indoor Jacuzzi. $50; Continental breakfast, afternoon refreshments. No credit cards. No smoking, no pets.

Greenleaf Inn. 1308 N. Broad St., Camden, SC 29020, tel. 803/425–1806 or 800/437–5874. 8 double rooms with baths, 3 suites, 1 cottage. Phones; free use of nearby health club. $55–$75, full breakfast. AE, D, MC, V.

New Berry Inn. 240 Newberry St. SW, Aiken, SC 29801, tel. 803/649–2935, fax 803/642–5840. 5 double rooms with baths. Cable TVs, phones, meeting room; free use of nearby health club. $60; full breakfast, afternoon refreshments. AE, D, DC, MC, V. No smoking, no pets.

Rosemary Hall. 804 Carolina Ave., North Augusta, SC 29841, tel. 803/278–6222 or 800/531–5578. 8 double rooms with baths. Air-conditioning, cable TVs, phones, turndown service with robes, concierge. $125–$250; full breakfast, afternoon refreshments. AE, D, DC, MC, V. Restricted smoking, no pets.

Vintage Inn. 909 N. Main St., Abbeville, SC 29620, tel. 864/459–4784. 1 double room with bath, 2 double rooms share 1 bath. Air-conditioning, ceiling fans; refrigerator in sitting area. $65–$125, full breakfast. AE. Restricted smoking, no pets.

Willcox Inn. 100 Colleton Ave., Aiken, SC 29801, tel. and fax 803/649–1377 or tel. 800/368–1047, fax 803/643–0971. 24 double rooms with baths, 6 suites. Restaurant, air-conditioning, cable TVs, phones, meeting room; free use of nearby health club. $75–$115, breakfast extra. AE, DC, MC, V. No pets.

Reservations Services

Southern Hospitality B&B Reservations (110 Amelia Dr., Lexington, SC 29464, tel. 803/356–6238 or 800/374–7422).

South Dakota

Willow Springs Cabins

Black Hills

Eighth Street Inn Bed & Breakfast

735 8th St., Spearfish, SD 57783, tel. 605/642-9812

Nestled among tall pines in a historic residential neighborhood, this bed-and-breakfast, with its flower-lined front walk and inviting porch, makes you feel as if you've gone home for a visit.

This Queen Anne home was built by entrepreneur Eleazer Dickey in 1900 for his wife, Wynne. Almost every piece of lumber was hand picked, including the original fir woodwork and open staircase that accent the entrance. If relaxing among the antiques, brass beds, and handmade quilts isn't enough, there is a hot tub on the back deck that overlooks the garden and gazebo and is available to guests.

Five bedrooms with different styles of beds, framed quilts, old-style black-and-white photographs on the walls, and heirlooms will remind some guests of their childhood visits to the old homestead.

Breakfast includes a variety of eggs, turkey bacon, fresh fruit juices, and fresh-baked tomato-stuffed bread.

▦ *1 double room with bath, 4 doubles share 1 bath. Phones in 2 rooms; TV/ VCR, stereo, fireplace in living room; hot tub. $40–$70, full breakfast. MC, V.*

Villa Theresa

801 Almond St., Hot Springs, SD 57747 tel. 605/745-4633

The ambience of this bed-and-breakfast will make you feel as if Buffalo Bill Cody could walk through the front door any minute. The Poker Room, a wonderful place to relax and dream of days gone by, retains much Old West charm. Since gambling is not legal in Hot Springs, it's used primarily as a reading room today.

Each guest room has its own theme: The Old West Room has an antique wire-frame bed, handmade comforter, and old-fashioned claw-foot tub; depictions of parrots and exotic flowers surround the whirlpool bath and mosquito netting is draped around the bed in the Tropical Suite; a tepee encircles the bed in the American Indian Room, which also has authentic Sioux artwork and a double whirlpool bath; the Music Room is for those with an interest in classical music; and the Royal Room, with the best view in the house, has elegant decor including a crystal chandelier and a brass shower rise. Its view from atop Villa Theresa is of the bluffs and of downtown Hot Springs.

The name Villa Theresa is a tribute to the wife of Fred Evans, founder of Evans Plunge, which is still this town's major attraction. Evans Plunge is a swimming pool, sauna, hot tub, and health spa complex that is fed by natural hot springs. Villa Theresa was a gentlemen's club until Evans turned it into a private residence in the 1920s. Decorated by interior designer Marshall Field, founder of Marshall Field's department stores, the house has an 18-foot, intricately hand-painted green and peach floral ceiling. Some of the original furnishings are still part of this exquisitely decorated home.

▦ *6 doubles with baths. Cable TV available. $60–$129. D, MC, V.*

Willow Springs Cabins

11515 Sheridan Lake Rd., Rapid City, SD 57702, tel. 605/342–3665

These two simple cabins, on a 160-acre piece of land that was originally a gold mine, are surrounded by the Black Hills National Forest, rich in native Ponderosa pine. The owners are Joyce and Russell Payton; Russell's grandparents homesteaded this area, a secluded spring-fed valley 11 miles southwest of Rapid City.

Although built in 1991 by Joyce and Russell, the Frontier Cabin (for adults only) seems older due to its pine exterior and tin roof. Inside, rustic western decorations include a woven Lakota dream catcher (a traditional Indian ornament used to filter bad dreams) above the bed's headboard, which Russell fashioned from the same wood as the cabin frame. Lamps with metal cutout bison silhouettes hang from both sides of the headboard. The small bathroom has a claw-foot tub.

Willows Cabin, a log structure built for the Forest Service in the 1950s and later moved to the Payton place, is decorated with the Paytons' heirlooms—dark wood-frame bed, entry bench, and great-grandmother's wooden rocker. A more modern pull-out couch accommodates family stays. The log walls display Russell's mother's eyelet lace baptismal gown, and large, ornately gilded framed photographs of his grandparents. The small bathroom off the main room has a shower, no bath.

A short walk from the cabins is the historic Flume Trail. If you have the time (and energy) you can walk the 6 miles to Sheridan Lake, enjoying the many varieties of wildflowers and wildlife along the way, or meander to a replica log cabin built alongside an abandoned railroad bed. Also nearby is an old-fashioned swimming hole near a fishing creek.

A full breakfast of freshly ground gourmet coffee or tea, fresh fruit and juices, egg dishes or waffles, and homemade breads is served on your private porch, in bed, or in a basket to take to the creek.

▦ *2 cabins with baths. Cable TVs, cassette players, mini-refrigerators, microwaves, coffeemakers, 2 outdoor hot tubs. $95–$120, full breakfast. MC, V. No pets.*

Other Choices

Abigail's Garden B & B. 13137 Thunderhead Falls La., Rapid City, SD 57702, tel. 605/343–6530. 2 double rooms with baths. Air-conditioning, TV and fireplace in common room, bicycles, hammock, garden gazebo, hiking, trout fishing, $115–$125, full gourmet breakfast and afternoon snack. MC, V.

Black Hills Hideaway. U.S. Highway 385, 7 miles south of Deadwood, SD 57732, tel. 605/578–3054. 8 rooms planned; 2 available at press time, each with detached bath. TV/VCR and/or air-conditioning available. Quiet, built in 1976 on 67 acres near the Black Hills National Forest. Whirlpool baths, gas fireplaces, bicycles available. $89–$139, full breakfast. MC, V.

Bunkhouse B & B. 14630 Lower Spring Creek Rd., Hermosa, SD 57744, tel. 605/342–5462. 1 double room with bath, 2 rooms share 1 bath. Air-conditioning, TV/VCR in recreation room, woodstove in family room, gift shop, nearby hiking and riding trails (bring your own horse). $75–$95, full ranch breakfast. MC, V.

Carriage House. 721 West Blvd., Rapid City, SD 57701, tel. 605/343–6415. 2 double rooms with baths, 3 rooms share 1 bath. Library and living room with TV/VCR and stereo. $50–$89, full breakfast. MC, V.

Custer Mansion. 35 Centennial Dr., Custer, SD 57730, tel. 605/673–3333. 4 double rooms with baths, 1 double room and 1 single room share 1 bath. Color TV in the library. $75–$120, full breakfast. MC, V.

Flying B Ranch B & B. R.R. 10, Box 2640, Rapid City, SD 57701, tel. 605/342–5324. 2 double rooms share 1 bath, 2 suites. Air-conditioning, TV/VCR and hot tubs in suites, fireplace in 1 suite, TV and pool table in recreation room, heated outdoor pool. All the work of a ranch—calving, branding, herding—available for viewing or participation. $55–$100, full ranch breakfast. MC, V.

H-D Lodge B & B. 23101 Triangle Trail-Hisega, Rapid City, SD 57702, tel. 605/341–7580. 9 double rooms with baths, 2 suites. Hiking, fishing, tubing. $55–$90, Continental breakfast. D, MC, V.

Tennessee

McEwen Farm Log Cabin Bed & Breakfast

East Tennessee

Adams Edgeworth Inn

Monteagle Assembly, Box 340, Monteagle, TN 37356, tel. 615/924-4000, fax 615/924-3236

Adams Edgeworth Inn is located atop the Cumberland Plateau inside a Victorian community nicknamed the Chautauqua of the South. It is a southern hotel in the grand, old-fashioned sense, with a broad wraparound porch and screen doors. Every summer, the Monteagle Assembly, the 96-acre community surrounding the inn, hosts an eight-week program of events that range from literary seminars to classical music concerts. Most of the assembly is used infrequently during the rest of the year, and guests at the inn are free to wander the enclave of 160 Victorian houses and scenic paths. Originally a boardinghouse, the inn was built in 1896 but was renovated and reopened in 1977; none of its authenticity seems to have been lost in the remodeling. The entire compound is listed on the National Register of Historic Places.

David and Wendy Adams, the owner-proprietors, retired from prominent jobs in Atlanta. Wendy was director of fund-raising for the city's opera and ballet, and David headed the research department at a brokerage firm. They are an outgoing, articulate couple who know the area well. They operate both this country inn and a European-style small hotel in Chattanooga. The Edgeworth library boasts some 2,000 volumes, and its art collection ranges from Old Master paintings to contemporary art and items of antiquity picked up during the Adamses' extensive travels.

A gentle quiet pervades the Edgeworth, where guests read, talk, or play board games. The rooms, which have 12-foot ceilings and border on the luxurious, are decorated in country cottage style, with lots of chintz in warm colors. Some rooms have fireplaces and four-poster beds; others have twin brass beds. The bridal suite has an oversize tub. In warm weather, the porch is the perfect place to spend an evening in a rocking chair; in the afternoon, the hammocks are irresistible. Breakfast is served in a cozy dining room, and five-course, candlelit dinners (by reservation) are served on antique china and silver. Wendy graduated from the Culinary Institute of America.

Nearby attractions include the University of the South at Sewanee, a small, well-respected school, and the South

Cumberland State Recreation Area, which has some trails. The Monteagle Winery produces a nice selection of sweet German wines.

▦ *13 double rooms with baths, 1 suite. Air-conditioning, cable TV in some rooms, library, dining room, gift shop; pool, tennis courts on the Assembly grounds. $75–$175, full breakfast. AE, MC, V. No smoking, no pets, 2-night minimum weekends and during summer assemblies.*

Big Spring Inn

315 N. Main St., Greeneville, TN 37745, tel. 423/638–2917

Up a long drive shrouded by walnut, maple, pecan, and magnolia trees sits Big Spring Inn, a Greek Revival house built in 1905 as a wedding present. Since 1993, it has been owned by Nancy and Marshall Ricker, who worked as a manager of a speech pathology department and an architect, respectively, and traded the beauty of Bend, Oregon, for this dream.

The expansive front porch, outfitted with a white wicker porch swing and other wicker pieces, is welcoming. Inside, the Rickers have filled the rambling inn with English and American antiques and good reproductions, some purchased from a nearby antiques store, one of many. The 1790 Hepplewhite dining table seats 12 at reservation-only dinners for inn guests. The Rickers' taste runs to Laura Ashley prints and accessories, which nicely complement the oak floors; beveled, leaded-glass windows; and original chandeliers. Six chimneys punctuate the unusual roofline, and metal shingles produce a soothing rhythm in the rain. Of the bedrooms, a favorite is the Felice Noell Austin Room, a light, airy room with Victorian Rose wallpaper and a white wrought-iron bed. Its spacious bath has original black and white tiles, a walk-in shower, and a large tub. The Hassie Hacker Doughty Room, the original owners' master bedroom,

has a fireplace with mantel, large bay window, king-size antique brass bed, and oversize bathroom.

The Rickers are gracious yet unobtrusive hosts and provide many special touches. At 7 AM a tea cart appears on the second-floor landing for early risers. Rooms have robes, Caswell-Massey toiletries, and homemade cookies in the evenings, and croquet and other lawn games are often played in the well-kept yard.

The inn is in historic Greeneville, a New England–style village settled in 1783, and is a short walk from the burial site and birthplace of President Andrew Johnson. The village is close to plenty of attractions—the brilliant fall colors of the Cherokee National Forest and the Great Smoky Mountains; white-water rafting; the Dixon-Williams Mansion, a pre–Civil War showplace that housed troops from both sides; and storytelling in Jonesborough—but it's far from the crowds and mini traffic jams that plague Gatlinburg.

▦ *2 double rooms and 2 singles with baths, 1 suite. Air-conditioning, cable TVs, phones; pool. $76–$120, full breakfast. AE, MC, V. No smoking, no pets.*

Blue Mountain Mist Country Inn

1811 Pullen Rd., Sevierville, TN 37862, tel. 423/428–2335 or 800/497–2335, fax 423/453–1720

The Blue Mountain Mist Country Inn sits high on a hill amid a 60-acre farm at the foot of the Great Smoky Mountains, and the owners of this Victorian-style inn, Sarah and Norman Ball, have played their vantage point to the hilt. A wraparound porch is well equipped with wicker furniture and rockers. In spring, flowers blossom in the yard; by summer, the pond, a short distance from the porch, is abloom with water lilies. Of course, fall, with its brilliant foliage, is the busiest season.

The Balls have deep roots in the area: Their parents grew up in the rugged terrain that is now Great Smoky Mountains National Park (one set lives on another farm across the road), so they know the history and geography of the area. Both were educators by profession—Sarah was an elementary school teacher, and Norm was principal at a vocational center.

Built in 1987, the inn is modeled after local, Victorian-style farmhouses. It's bright and airy and is furnished with family heirlooms, locally made quilts, and country crafts. Old photographs and paintings of the area, by the Balls' daughter and a local artist, hang on the walls, and two rooms are equipped with claw-foot tubs. The Bridal Room has a two-person whirlpool bath in the inn's turret, which has windows on three sides. It shares a balcony and the mountain view with the Rainbow Falls Room, which has its own hot tub tucked behind a stained-glass partition, and with the LeConte Suite, the most spacious of the rooms. All bedrooms are carpeted.

Common areas upstairs and down have fireplaces and shiny hardwood floors. Each of the five small wooden cottages has a fully equipped kitchen, fireplace, TV and VCR, porch, and large whirlpool tub in the main room.

The inn, near Little Pigeon River, is on a country road that serves as a back door into both the park and the Great Smoky Mountains Arts and Crafts Community, circumventing much of the local traffic. Pigeon Forge, known for its outlet shopping, is just 4 miles away.

🏨 *12 double rooms with baths, 5 cottages. Meal service for groups, cable TV/VCR in parlor. $95–$135; full breakfast, evening dessert. MC, V. No smoking, no pets, 2-night minimum holidays and Oct. Inn closed Dec. 23–25.*

Buckhorn Inn

2140 Tudor Mountain Rd., Gatlinburg, TN 37738, tel. 423/436–4668, fax 423/436–5009

The lobby of the Buckhorn Inn, which is on a wooded hillside at the edge of Great Smoky Mountains National Park, commands one of the best views of the local peaks, and several of the rooms have good views as well. Designed to blend in with its surroundings, the inn has a rustic flavor much as it must have had when it was built in 1938. The Buckhorn is in the middle of a lush, 35-acre estate surrounded by pine trees; comfortable fireside chairs in the sitting and dining rooms invite guests to relax with a glass of wine and look out on Mt. LeConte, one of the highest peaks in the Smokies. A Steinway grand piano rests in one niche of the lobby, and a library dubbed the "hikers' corner" is in another spot. With its "well-loved shabby" decor, this inn appeals to the old-money crowd.

Rooms are small—almost to the point of being cramped—but all are carpeted and furnished with simple but understated grace. The most interesting bedroom is in the inn's original water tower, where bath facilities are on one level and the bedroom is above. It has the feel of a tree house. On all but the warmest days of the year, the scent of wood smoke lingers in the air. In the dining room, breakfast and a six-course gourmet dinner (by reservation only) are served on small tables with green tablecloths. Four cottages and two relatively spacious guest houses are on the grounds, but the cottages are a cut or two below the inn rooms. Each is equipped with a fireplace and a screened-in porch with a good view, but the carpets are worn, the beds are on the soft side, and the buildings themselves are made of cinder blocks, with concrete decks. The two-bedroom guest houses, one of which can accommodate conferences, have much more room but are not much more comfortable than the cottages.

Nonetheless, this secluded inn with its own ½-mile nature trail and fishing pond remains one of the best in the Smokies. It's 1 mile from the entrance to the national park and about 6 miles northeast of Gatlinburg and its myriad activities. It is in the midst of some 70 shops, galleries, and eateries of the secluded Great Smoky Mountains Arts and Crafts Community.

🏨 *6 double rooms with baths, 4 cottages, 2 guest houses. Air-conditioning, cable TV in cottages. $95–$250, full country breakfast. MC, V. Restricted smoking, no pets; 2-night minimum holidays, weekends, and Oct.*

Von-Bryan Inn

2402 Hatcher Mtn. Rd., Sevierville, TN 37862, tel. 423/453–9832 or 800/633–1459, fax 423/428–8634

The Von-Bryan Inn commands what may well be the best mountaintop bed-and-breakfast view in the Smokies. A crooked road climbs to the inn, situated on a knoll with a 360-degree vista of the surrounding mountains. Morning mist typically blankets the patchwork farmlands in Wears Valley below and the wooded dales beyond.

Jo Ann and D. J. Vaughn bought the house from the original owner, who built it in 1986 as a private retreat, and they now run the place with their sons, David and Patrick. Jo Ann, who operated a telephone-answering service in Knoxville, and D. J., a retired corporate accountant, opened the Von-Bryan after traveling extensively in surrounding states to research country inns. They are quiet but amicable people who offer plentiful advice on the area. D. J., a woodworker by hobby, made many of the pendulum clocks in the house and some of the furniture. The inn's builder emphasized wood surfaces and soaring, cathedral-like ceilings. Bright skylights filter in the sunshine, and big windows frame the view.

Every room, furnished in a blend of traditional and country antiques, has a view. The honeymoon suite—one of two with a whirlpool—is appropriately decorated in passionate red hues. A tri-level suite has a canopy bed draped with silk wisteria on the second floor, a bath with a steam shower on the first, and a reading loft on the third. Three skylights and wraparound windows with a view of the English country garden add to the romance. A plush canopy bed graces another room, two brass beds from the Middle East are in another, and a queen-size spool bed anchors yet another room. Soft jazz is usually on the stereo in the common area upstairs, and a fireplace blazes in the downstairs living room. In summer, the pool and its nearby hot tub are good places to bask in the sun. The inn is aptly equipped with a telescope for a closer look at distant sights. The log-cabin chalet, designed for families, has a full kitchen and a television room as well as a living room with a fireplace, three bedrooms (one with a balcony), and two bathrooms. It has a wraparound screened-in deck, too, and a whirlpool bath. Gatlinburg, Pigeon Forge, Dollywood, and the entrance to the national park are within 30 minutes.

🏨 *5 double rooms with baths, 1 suite, 1 chalet. Air-conditioning, TV in living room. $90–$180, full buffet breakfast. AE, D, MC, V. No smoking, no pets.*

Other Choices

Adams Hilborne. 801 Vine St., Chattanooga, TN 37403, tel. 423/265–5000, fax 423/265–5555. 11 double rooms with baths. Restaurant. $95–$275, Continental breakfast. AE, MC, V. Restricted smoking, no pets.

Bluff View Inn. 412 E. 2nd St., Chattanooga, TN 37403, tel. 423/265–5033. 7 double rooms with baths. Air-conditioning, cable TVs, phones. $125–$175, full breakfast. DC, MC, V. No smoking, no pets.

Hale Springs Inn. 110 W. Main St., Rogersville, TN 37857, tel. 423/272–

5171. 9 double rooms with baths. Restaurant, air-conditioning, cable TVs. $40–$90, Continental breakfast. AE, MC, V. No pets. Closed Dec. 25.

Hippensteal's Mountain View Inn. Grassy Branch Rd. (Box 707), Gatlinburg, TN 37738, tel. 423/436–5761 or 800/527–8110, fax 423/436–2354. 9 double rooms with baths. Air-conditioning, ceiling fans, TV and phone jacks in rooms. $120; full gourmet breakfast, evening dessert. AE, D, MC, V. No smoking, no pets. Closed Dec. 24–25.

Richmont Inn. 220 Winterberry La., Townsend, TN 37882, tel. 423/448–6751. 10 double rooms with baths. Air-conditioning; gift shop, nature trail. $90–$140; full breakfast, evening dessert. No credit cards. No smoking, no pets.

Tennessee Ridge Inn. 507 Campbell Lead Rd., Gatlinburg, TN 37738, tel. 423/436–4068. 4 double rooms with baths, 1 suite. Air-conditioning, cable TV in rooms on request; pool. $98–$135, full breakfast. D, MC, V. Restricted smoking, no pets, 2-night minimum weekends, 3-night minimum holidays. Closed Jan.

Wayside Manor. 4009 Old Knoxville Hwy. 33, Rockford, TN 37853, tel. 423/970–4823 or 800/675–4823, fax 423/981–1890. 4 double rooms with baths, 1 2-bedroom cottage, 1 5-bedroom lodge. Air-conditioning, TV/VCRs, phones; whirlpool in some rooms, business center; pool. $90–$135, full breakfast. AE, D, MC, V. Restricted smoking, no pets.

Reservations Services

Bed & Breakfast Adventures (Box 150586, Nashville, TN 37215, tel. 615/383–6611 or 800/947–7404). **Tennessee Bed & Breakfast Innkeepers Association** (Box 120428, Nashville, TN 37212, tel. 615/321–5482 or 800/820–8144).

Middle Tennessee

Falcon Manor Bed & Breakfast

2645 Faulkner Springs Rd., McMinnville, TN 37110, tel. 615/668–4444, fax 615/815–4444

McMinnville offers an out-of-the-way base at the center of the Nashville-Chattanooga-Knoxville triangle. Twenty-five miles east of I–24's Manchester exit 111 or 33 miles south of I–40's Smithville exit is Falcon Manor, an historic Victorian mansion lovingly cared for by George and Charlien McGlothin. For nature lovers, Rock Island State Park is 10 miles away; Fall Creek Falls, 35 miles; Old Stone Fort, 25 miles; and Savage Gulf State Natural Area, 15 miles away.

The house was built in 1896 by entrepreneur Clay Faulkner for his wife, Mary. Faulkner had a woolen mill nearby and produced "gorilla pants," so labeled because their strength kept even a gorilla from tearing them apart. Strength is evident here, too, as the house sits on a 17-foot concrete foundation with walls three bricks thick. From 1946 to 1968, the property was used as a hospital and nursing home. George McGlothlin bought the house at auction in 1989 (sight unseen by Charlien), but by then, it required massive renovation. Charlien left her job at NASA and joined George in four years of restoration; they estimate they did 95 percent of the work themselves.

Guests will find rooms filled with massive period antiques. Red velvet settees and chairs, with marble-top tables, fill the common living room. Bedrooms have an almost overpowering amount of authenticity. On some occasions, George and Charlien dress in Victorian costumes and offer carriage rides for newlyweds.

A full breakfast is an additional charge; if you do not opt for this, breakfast is not otherwise included in the rate. If you have a hankering for Victoriana, a Victorian Gift Shop offers stationery, potpourri, mugs, calendars, and a host of other items embellished with roses and other Victorian emblems.

▦ *6 double rooms, 2 with baths; 4 rooms share 2 baths. Cable TV in common areas. $75–$85, full breakfast extra. MC, V. No smoking, no pets.*

Hachland Hill Dining Inn

1601 Madison St., Clarksville, TN 37043, tel. 615/647–4084, fax 615/552–3454

This inn is a treat for the traveler in search of a rustic evening beside a fireplace. Forty-five minutes north of Nashville in rural Clarksville, it is surrounded by an 80-acre park full of raccoon, deer, and other wildlife. Trails wander into the woods, and guests wake up to the sound of birds.

Phila Hach is an extraordinary hostess, a worldly woman who was a flight attendant before settling down with her late husband, Adolph Hach, and founding the inn in 1955. She appears on local television shows and is the author of eight cookbooks. The dinner menu is laden with fried chicken, Tennessee country ham, and surprises like Moroccan leg of lamb (pricey but worth the splurge), or indulge in the decadent, full southern breakfast (extra charge). Phila's specialty is catering large events; the grand ballroom seats 300.

Phila designed the inn after Federal-style Cape Cod homes, and on winter nights, soup bubbles in a pot dangling on a fireplace crane. The bedrooms are neat and comfortable, with historic touches: One has a spool bed with a wedding-ring quilt, and many of the furnishings throughout are Early American. Some have Germanic touches, heirlooms from the time when Phila's family emigrated

from their North Sea environs. The mantel keystone over the main fireplace is from the long-since-demolished local tobacco exchange (Adolph was a tobacconist). A 150-year-old, 2,000-piece "postage-stamp" quilt hangs from a wall. The Hachs traveled widely, and items from their sojourns are in evidence: a Japanese print here, a Swiss vase there.

The 1790 House, a cabin connected to the inn by a breezeway, has been transformed into a dormitory space for those taking part in a wedding or reunion. Out back sit a pair of cabins, perfect for either romantic solitude or family lodging. Each cabin has two levels and modern bathrooms and comes with a guarantee of tranquillity; though the cabins are equipped with phones on which guests can dial out, the phones do not ring. The cabins are on a wide, shady terrace, where warm-weather cookouts are held, overlooking a wooded ravine.

▦ *7 double rooms with baths, 3 cabins. Air-conditioning, TV/VCR in 2 rooms, nonringing phones in rooms, office facilities. $65, Continental breakfast. AE, MC, V. Closed Dec. 24–25.*

McEwen Farm Log Cabin Bed & Breakfast

Bratton La. (Box 97), Duck River, TN 38454, tel. 615/583–2378

The McEwen Farm Log Cabin Bed & Breakfast features a trio of buildings for rent on a farm 2 miles from the Natchez Trace, hidden away on a back road. No signs point the way, but it's easy enough to find: just north of the communities of Shady Grove and of Duck River, named for the slow-moving waterway known for smallmouth bass and catfish as well as canoeing. Bill and Helen McEwen run the place from their house on a hilltop pasture several hundred yards from the well-spaced lodgings, evidently situated with privacy in mind. The farm is a popular stopover for bicyclists traveling the Natchez Trace Parkway, and it attracts visiting joggers and walkers as well to its big, quiet fields.

Helen is a homemaker, and Bill, a community college administrator, raises hunting dogs; the hounds are kept in pens near the barn, their howls occasionally piercing the otherwise quiet night. The McEwens began hosting guests in 1987, after restoring a log cabin that dates back to the 1820s. They designed the cabin on the back of a paper sack with the intention of turning it into a guest house for family and friends, but passersby were drawn to it immediately. The original structure belies its age; its floors and walls are rugged but clean, and the main room, which has a fireplace, leads into a modern kitchen. Outside there is a porch swing; upstairs are three beds. Cabin No. 2—next to a railroad sign that says MCEWEN CROSSING, ELEVATION 607—is much like No. 1.

Downhill in an adjacent dale is No. 3, which is not a cabin at all but a restored 1879 Victorian passenger train depot from nearby Centerville, where it served the Nashville, Chattanooga, and St. Louis railways. The most secluded of the lodgings, it is completely wrapped by a wooden deck generously furnished with rocking chairs that face a tiny stream. It has two bedrooms, one bath, and a kitchen beneath its original 14-foot ceilings, where fans turn lazily. The ticket window has been turned into a reading nook. Family antiques—country-style tables and sideboards—furnish the cozy cabins.

Guests at McEwen Farm are welcome to meet the hunting dogs or wander the grounds at will. Nashville is 45 minutes away, and—as this is Tennessee walking horse country—stables abound.

▥ *3 cabins. Air-conditioning; canoe rental. $85, Continental breakfast. MC, V. No smoking.*

Old Cowan Plantation

126 Old Boonshill Rd., Fayetteville, TN 37334, tel. 615/433-0225.

The Old Cowan Plantation captures some of the genteel charm of the Old South in an 1886 Colonial home beside a country road. Hostess Betty Johnson's ambition was to open an antiques shop in the house, but after deciding there was a glut of such businesses in nearby Fayetteville, she turned the house into an inn, filling a void in local lodging. Though it was modernized in 1985, the place clings tenaciously to its farmhouse ambience. Betty's hobbies show up around the house in various handicrafts, quilts, and cross-stitch items.

One upstairs room has a brass bed and a spacious bath and shower; the other is equipped with a pair of twin beds and uses a bath downstairs with a pedestal tub. The home's original staircase leads to a narrow landing with an antique pie safe that now serves as a linen closet. Breakfast is served at a lace-covered table with a view of the neighboring pasture.

The inn's rural setting is one of its biggest draws. In spring, the yard is full of wildflowers, and a rose garden blooms in June. When snow covers the ground, oak and magnolia trees frame the house in a striking winter scene. Guests usually gravitate to the front-porch rocking chairs, particularly in the early evening, when deer graze across the road and sometimes even wander into the yard.

The Old Cowan Plantation is 2 miles from Fayetteville's town square and 15 miles from the Jack Daniel Distillery at Lynchburg. It is 30 miles from the Space and Rocket Center in Huntsville, Alabama, where you can tour NASA labs and space-shuttle test sites and roam through a park full of rockets, visit the center's hands-on museum, or view an Omnimax space film. Fifteen minutes away is Tims Ford Lake, with waterskiing in summer and fishing year-round. The inn is just north of U.S. 64, which has been designated an official scenic highway east almost to Chattanooga and as far west as Shiloh National Military Park, site of a bloody Civil War battle.

🏠 *2 double rooms with baths, 1 apartment. Air-conditioning, TV in common area. $45, Continental breakfast. No credit cards. No smoking, pets in fenced backyard only.*

Other Choices

Bird Song Country Inn. Sycamore Mill, 1306 Rte. 49 E, Ashland City, TN 37015, tel. and fax 615/385–0196. 3 double rooms with baths. Air-conditioning; heated spa. $90–$150, full breakfast. AE, MC, V. Restricted smoking.

Evins Mill Retreat. 1535 Evins Mill Rd. (Box 606), Smithville, TN 37166, tel. 615/597–2088, fax 615/597–2090. 14 double rooms with baths. $120 ($170 with dinner); theme weekends $350–$400, full breakfast. AE, D, MC, V.

Lynchburg Bed & Breakfast. Mechanic St. (Box 34), Lynchburg, TN 37352, tel. 615/759–7158. 2 double rooms with baths. Air-conditioning, cable TVs. $55–$60, Continental breakfast. MC, V. No pets.

Lyric Springs Country Inn. 7306 S. Harpeth Rd., Franklin, TN 37064, tel. 615/329–3385 or 800/621–7824, fax 615/329–3381. 4 double rooms with baths. Air-conditioning; pool. $125, full breakfast. AE, MC, V. No smoking.

Reservations Services

Bed & Breakfast Adventures (Box 150586, Nashville, TN 37215, tel. 615/383–6611 or 800/947–7404). **Tennessee Bed & Breakfast Innkeepers Association** (Box 120428, Nashville, TN 37212, tel. 615/321–5482 or 800/820–8144).

West Tennessee

Magnolia Manor

418 N. Main St., Bolivar, TN 38008, tel. 901/658–6700

Well off the beaten path in southwest Tennessee, Magnolia Manor creates an imposing presence along Main Street in tiny Bolivar, a historic burg that boasts the oldest courthouse in West Tennessee. It is one of two dozen or so antebellum homes in the neighborhood that were spared from Union torches during the Civil War; tours of the area can be arranged.

The two-story house is built in the Georgian Colonial style, its 1849 construction date noted on a bronze eagle mounted onto one corner. The walls, made of sun-dried red brick laid by slaves, are 13 inches thick. It was constructed as a symmetrical rectangle, with center halls upstairs and down separating the spacious rooms.

Elaine and Jim Cox, a reserved but polite couple, were inspired to open the inn in 1984 by the bed-and-breakfasts they'd stayed in on a long trip through Europe. Elaine is a former cosmetology instructor; Jim is a retired hospital administrator. Beyond travel, the Coxes' hobbies are interior decorating and cooking, both of which are evident at the manor. The house is ornately restored, and portraits of the four Union generals who occupied the house were commissioned by the couple and now hang in the entry hall. Downstairs, the inn's 14-foot ceilings provide space that mitigates the heavy furnishings and a lingering, musty scent reminiscent of old houses in distant childhood memories. The downstairs suite, a double parlor, is furnished opulently with early Victorian, museum-quality pieces: a big rosewood headboard, a rosewood gentleman's chair, and others adorned with hand-carved roses. Upstairs are two double rooms and a spacious suite. One bed is graced with a massive walnut canopy; another is made of the same wood, its construction dated from plantation timbers. The suite has a walnut-and-rosewood Victorian bed and matching furniture, shipped upriver by steamboat years ago from New Orleans. All bedrooms have working fireplaces.

For history buffs in particular, Bolivar makes for a pleasant day trip from Memphis, 90 minutes away. An hour away is Shiloh National Military Park. Also of interest are the nearby Pinson Mounds, where there is a Native American museum. Historians believe Hernando de Soto passed through the area on his epic search for the Mississippi River, a journey noted by various markers.

▥ *2 double rooms share 1 bath, 2 suites. Air-conditioning, cable TV on sun porch. $75–$85, full breakfast. No credit cards. No smoking, no pets.*

Other Choices

Highland Place Bed & Breakfast. 519 N. Highland, Jackson, TN 38301, tel. 901/427–1472. 4 double rooms with baths. $85–$135, full breakfast. MC, V. Restricted smoking, no pets.

Reservations Services

Bed & Breakfast Memphis Reservation Service (Box 41621, Memphis, TN 38174, tel. 901/726–5920). **Tennessee Bed & Breakfast Innkeepers Association** (Box 120428, Nashville, TN 37212, tel. 615/321–5482 or 800/820–8144).

Texas

Charnwood Hill

East Texas, Including Dallas and Fort Worth

Annie's Bed & Breakfast

106 N. Tyler St., Big Sandy, TX 75755, tel. 903/636–4355 or 800/BB–ANNIE, fax 903/636–4744

Annie's is more than the only bed-and-breakfast in Big Sandy; Annie's is an industry—and, for most people, the only reason to come to Big Sandy.

"Annie" is Annie Potter, whose multi-million-dollar mail-order needlecraft and pattern business, Annie's Attic, Inc., got started with a $100 investment in 1973. When mail-order customers began to trickle into Big Sandy (population 1,200), Annie would serve them tea but had no real means of entertaining them. So, in the mid-'80s, she began assembling the Victorian Village, a cluster of three brightly painted, converted Victorian homes. In addition to the B&B, the complex now includes a restaurant and tearoom and a needlecraft gallery and gift shop.

The bed-and-breakfast is a large, gray-and-white, seven-gabled house, which

had only one story when it was constructed in 1901 for the former mayor and postmaster G. A. Tohill. Potter had a second floor and attic added and filled virtually every corner of every room with antique Victorian furnishings. They are often draped with quilts or other craft works, including many crocheted by Potter.

The 12 guest rooms are designed for two people, but many can sleep more because they include sitting areas with sofa beds. The best of them all, the Queen Anne Room, has a queen bed, a sofa bed, and a spiral staircase that leads to twin beds in a loft. And, like the Garret and Balcony rooms, it has a private balcony.

Needlecraft festivals, crochet seminars, and other events are often held on the village grounds. Annie's guests receive a complimentary breakfast in the tearoom; choices range from New York strip steak and eggs to several low-fat gourmet entrées. Saturday breakfast is served in the home.

Innkeepers Clifton and Kathy Shaw will organize a barbecue for your group, chat with you on the front porch—or leave you alone if you crave privacy. For those not interested in crochet and needlepoint, there are precious few attractions in Big Sandy itself. This is especially true on Saturday, when the town pretty much shuts down in deference to the Sabbath of the Worldwide Church of God, headquartered in the area. Still, given the quality of rooms and service, Annie's is one of the best B&B bargains in the region.

🏨 *7 double rooms with baths, 5 doubles share 3 baths. Phones, mini-refrigerators, TV in some rooms. $50–$115, full breakfast. AE, D, MC, V. No smoking, no pets.*

Charnwood Hill

223 E. Charnwood, Tyler, TX 75701, tel. 903/597–3980, fax 903/592–6473

In the city that hosts the famed Texas Rose Festival, you can pay no greater compliment to a residence than to say that a Rose Queen lived there and that the Queen's Tea was held on the lawn. Tyler's Charnwood Hill, converted to a B&B in 1993, has housed not one but two queens. Margaret Hunt, daughter of the late oilman H. L. Hunt, was crowned in 1935; Jo Anne Miller received the honor in 1954.

As much as the yellow rose of Texas, the name Hunt is the stuff of Lone Star legend. And the Charnwood Hill estate, where the Hunt family lived before moving to Dallas in 1938, does not disappoint. Built in the 1860s by the headmaster of a school for girls, the three-story structure housed both a college and a hospital during the 19th century. The elegant, Greek Revival–influenced residence was bricked in 1901 by J. B. Mayfield, who raised a family here before selling the home to Hunt.

Hunt added his own touch to the home: a third-floor Art Deco suite constructed for daughters Margaret and Caroline. The suite's stark whites, barely-there pastels, and indirect lighting combine to stamp an indelible air of *Great Gatsby*–era privilege on the accommodation, and they contrast sharply with the frilly, floral guest bedrooms that dominate the first and second floors.

Male business travelers tend to favor the sprawling Millers' Trophy Room, named for H. C. Miller, who bought the house from Hunt. The blue-and-burgundy room has a full bar, gun cabinet, and bed that can be folded into the wall to make room for a small conference area.

Throughout the high-ceiling home, the furnishings are extravagant. The Walker family purchased the residence from the Millers in 1978, and in a four-year restoration, they have spared no expense to create a regal atmosphere, with crystal chandeliers, 100-year-old Oriental rugs, and antique pieces.

Common areas include a library and TV room, two second-floor balconies, and a screened swing porch. Guests enjoy a breakfast that might feature eggs Benedict or French toast in the formal dining room. And, more than 50 years after it served as the setting for Hunt's Queen's Tea, the west garden is as lovely as ever.

🏨 *5 double rooms with baths, 2 suites. Phones, TV/VCR in most rooms, free airport transportation in Tyler. $95–$270; full breakfast, complimentary beverages. D, MC, V. No smoking, no pets.*

Excelsior House

211 W. Austin St., Jefferson, TX 75657, tel. 903/665–2513

The Excelsior House is the remarkably restored centerpiece of Jefferson, a town sometimes called the "Williamsburg of Texas." Built in the 1850s by riverboat captain William Perry, the historic hotel has remained in continuous operation since then, although by the middle of this century, the brick-and-timber structure had slowly deteriorated and was largely forgotten.

Its rebirth began in 1954, when Estella Fonville Peters purchased the inn and undertook its renovation. Opening the building to public tours, filling the drawing room with the music of noted orchestras, and hosting elaborate balls, she revived interest in the hotel—and, in the process, sowed the seeds of Jefferson's commercial future. The Jessie Allen Wise Garden Club bought the hotel when Peters died in 1961 and has maintained and operated the facility with care ever since.

With iron columns and a lacy ironwork gallery that lend flourish to the simple rectangular edifice, the Excelsior House looks like it came to the Wild West by way of New Orleans. The ballroom features a French chandelier, Oriental rugs, antique marble mantles, and a pair of period pianos. The dining room includes a glassed-in patio, where guests can enjoy a Plantation Breakfast of orange blossom muffins, country ham, scrambled eggs, and biscuits.

Each of the inn's 13 guest rooms and suites has a story to tell. Past guests have included William Vanderbilt and Oscar Wilde; both Ulysses S. Grant and Rutherford B. Hayes slept in what is now the Presidential Suite. Lady Bird Johnson was a frequent visitor and donated a good deal of the furniture in the room that bears her name. All the rooms are furnished with antiques, including marble-topped dressers, spool beds, and mahogany, cherry, and maple pieces.

Spurned railroad tycoon Jay Gould had predicted doom for Jefferson in the Excelsior House lobby in the 1870s, so it's fitting revenge that one of the hotel's most popular rooms is named after him. Across the street from the hotel, "Atalanta," Gould's decadently ornate private railroad car, is open to public tours.

🏨 *11 double rooms with baths, 2 suites. Air-conditioning, TVs. $55–$90, no breakfast. No credit cards. No smoking, no pets.*

Hotel St. Germain

2516 Maple Ave., Dallas, TX 75201, tel. 214/871–2516, fax 214/871–0740

In a city known for glitziness, the Hotel St. Germain is perhaps the definitive lodging. Nestled amid some of Dallas's most exclusive restaurants and shops, the boutique hotel, opened in 1991, offers visitors the chance to indulge in the high life of a different time and place: 19th-century France.

A Victorian prairie mansion built in 1906, the inn was purchased in 1989 by Claire Heymann, who set out to reclaim the structure's noble origins while paying tribute to her own French-Creole roots. From the moment the hotel's front doors are opened, revealing the large entry hall embellished with crackle-back moldings and crystal chandeliers, the visitor is swept into a lavish, self-contained universe.

Heymann's secret is painstaking authenticity. A New Orleans native whose mother was an antiques dealer, she has been assembling French collectibles almost since her childhood. Her acquisitions are complemented by her knowledge of French design, developed through frequent trips abroad and study at the University of Paris.

The entry hall gives way to a pair of sitting rooms, a parlor, and a library, each housing its own treasures—such as the library's grand piano, bedecked with ancient, marbled candelabras. The dining room, which looks out onto a New Orleans–style walled courtyard with a fountain, is perhaps the most evocative of Gaul: The long table, draped in a burgundy damask tapestry, is topped by a rose-filled centerpiece that rests on a silver Alsatian platter; a mid-19th-century French basket chandelier hangs from the room's ceiling. Breakfast—which typically includes fresh fruit compote, croissants, quiche, and café au lait—is served on a rare, century-old set of Limoges china. Dinner, which could be lamb tenderloin or game hen, is served Thursday, Friday, and Saturday nights.

Upstairs, the seven spacious guest suites have plush, canopied feather beds. All have wood-burning fireplaces, sitting rooms, and baths with soaking tubs or whirlpool baths. Although rates are prohibitive, and the hotel has a reputation for boarding the glitterati, Heymann promotes her inn as a place where common folk can come for that once-in-a-lifetime splurge.

▦ *7 suites. Cable TVs, robes, VCRs available, room service, concierge, valet parking, nightly turndown service, privileges at nearby fitness club, limited restaurant. $225–$600, full breakfast. AE, MC, V. No smoking, no pets.*

McKay House

306 Delta St., Jefferson, TX 75657, tel. 903/665–7322

In 1877, when Jefferson was a worldly river port, it was rocked by the brief visit of "Diamond Bessie"—the stage name of Annie Stone Moore Rothchild, a popular entertainer. While in town with her husband, a wealthy Cincinnati gambler named Abe Rothchild, the pair walked alone into a field. A gunshot was heard, and Abe returned alone, claiming his wife had shot herself by accident. After three trials over seven years, Rothchild was a free man, but the people of Jefferson never accepted the "not guilty" verdict.

One of the attorneys who successfully defended Rothchild was Hector McKay, the first of two generations of McKays that lived in this 1851 Greek Revival. In the early 1980s, the McKay House was purchased by Dallasites Tom and Peggy Taylor, who, through extensive renovations, transformed it into the city's most luxurious B&B.

The inn is furnished almost entirely with antiques, mostly Eastlake, many of them quite valuable. But this place is anything but stuffy. Innkeepers Joseph and Alma Anne Parker know how to help folks break the ice, from the funny period hats distributed for visitors to wear at breakfast, to Victorian gowns and nightshirts provided in the rooms, and, in one room, his-and-hers claw-foot tubs that offer an opportunity for simultaneous scrub-downs. An ancient Packard pump organ is played to call guests to the hearty "Gentleman's Breakfast," which is served in period dress and may consist of honey-cured ham, cheese biscuits, and homemade pineapple zucchini bread and strawberry preserves. Afterward, guests can relax on the wide front porch, outfitted with a swing and white wicker chairs.

The guest rooms are individual in personality but uniform in elegance; each offers such furnishings as a canopy bed and antique armoire. The two downstairs rooms have coal-burning fireplaces; the two upstairs suites feature a balcony, skylight, and his-and-hers tubs; and a downstairs suite includes two bedrooms, each with its own fireplace. But perhaps the most memorable rooms are the two set off from a central, dog-trot hall in the tin-roofed Victorian garden cottage located behind the main house. The Keeping Room, in particular, is amusingly authentic: a claw-foot tub sits exposed in a bay window, next to a transplanted outdoor privy, fully equipped with a lantern and a Sears Roebuck catalog.

▦ *4 double rooms with baths, 3 suites. Phones, cable TVs. $85–$145, full breakfast. MC, V. No smoking, no pets, 2-night minimum on holiday weekends.*

Miss Molly's Bed & Breakfast

109½ W. Exchange Ave., Fort Worth, TX 76106, tel. 817/626–1522 or 800/996–6559, fax 817/625–2723.

As the drovers on the street below brought in herd after herd of longhorns, hitting every saloon and dance hall on the way to the stockyards, the guests in the second-floor walk-up gazed down, primly elevated from the fray. In the early 1900s, the eight rooms that now make up Fort Worth's best bed-and-breakfast housed the guests of Miss Sylvia Marquis's Furnished Rooms, an oh-so-proper hotel.

By the 1930s, however, the wild ways of the stockyard district had had their influence; the hotel had become an infamous brothel named for its madam, Miss Josie. When Mark and Susan Hancock renovated and reopened the abandoned space as Miss Molly's in 1989, they decided to name adjacent rooms after Miss Josie and Miss Sylvia—provoking the guest to wonder whether either, or both, of the former proprietors might be turning in their graves.

Located over the Star Cafe steak house in the Fort Worth Stockyards Historic District, Miss Molly's may be the most mythically Texan of Texas's bed-and-breakfasts. The rooms, which form a circle around the registration desk at the top of the stairs, are chock-full of saddles, stirrups, cowboy hats, buckskin, and other western paraphernalia. What keeps the whole thing from being hokey is that the artifacts are authentic: The rope that dangles from the wall mirror in one room, for example, is the actual one used to win the Fort Worth rodeo in 1928.

The rooms have been furnished to appear as they did in the 1920s: iron beds draped with colorful quilts; ceiling fans; a washstand with a bowl and pitcher. With the exception of Miss Josie's room, none of the rooms have private baths. Three bathrooms with pedestal sinks, claw-foot tubs, and pull-chain toilets stand side by side in one corner of the establishment.

The Hancocks encourage folks to mingle; they say they measure success by the number of friends they and their visitors have made here. Guests are given custom-made blue-and-white ticking robes to wear to the copious

Continental breakfast buffet, which typically includes coffee cakes, muffins, strawberry bread, and a fruit cup.

🏠 *1 double room with bath, 7 doubles share 3 baths. Fans, air-conditioning. $85–150, Continental breakfast. AE, D, DC, MC, V. No smoking, no pets.*

Other Choices

Caddo Cottage. 1 2-bedroom cabin. Air-conditioning, TV, kitchen. $85, Continental breakfast. No credit cards. No pets, 2-night minimum on weekends.

Cleburne House. 201 N. Anglin St., Cleburne, TX 76031, tel. 817/641–0085. 2 double rooms with baths, 2 doubles share bath. Whirlpool bath in 1 room, 2 rooms share balcony sitting area, TV. $55–$85, full breakfast. No credit cards. No pets, no children under 12.

House of the Seasons. Box 686, 409 S. Alley St., Jefferson, TX 75657, tel. 903/665–1218. 3 suites. Whirlpool baths, cable TV in suites. $125, full breakfast. MC, V. No smoking, no pets.

Inn on the River. 205 S. Barnard St., Glen Rose, TX 76043, tel. 214/424–7119, fax 214/424–9766. 19 double rooms with baths, 3 suites. Climate control in each room, heated outdoor pool. $115–$165, full breakfast. AE, D, DC, MC, V. No smoking, no pets, no children under 18.

Maison-Bayou. 300 Bayou St., Jefferson, TX 75657, tel. 903/665–7600, fax 903/665–7383. 10 double rooms (some accommodate up to 6 people) with baths. Air-conditioning, games, TVs and kitchenettes in 5 rooms, flatbottom boat with one cabin, fishing, horseback riding. $85–$125, full breakfast. MC, V. No smoking.

Mansion on Main. 802 Main St., Texarkana, TX 75501, tel. 903/792–1835 or 214/348–1929. 5 double rooms with baths, 1 suite. Phones, cable TVs. $60–$99, full breakfast. AE, MC, V. Smoking on balconies and veranda only, no pets.

Oxford House. 563 N. Graham St., Stephenville, TX 76401, tel. 817/965–

6885 or 817/968–8171, fax 817/965–7555. 4 double rooms with baths. Climate control, tearoom-gift shop. $65–$85; full breakfast, afternoon tea or candlelight dinner by reservation. MC, V. No smoking, no pets, no children under 6.

Pride House. 409 E. Broadway, Jefferson, TX 75657, tel. 903/665–2675. 10 double rooms with baths. Ceiling fans, climate control, stained-glass windows, some TVs. $75–$110, full breakfast. MC, V. No smoking, no pets, 2-night minimum on weekends.

Seasons. 313 E. Charnwood, Tyler, TX 75701, tel. 903/533–0803. 4 double rooms with baths, 1 suite. Air-conditioning, ceiling fans. $85–$125, full breakfast. AE, D, MC, V. No smoking, no pets, no children under 13.

Stillwater Inn. 203 E. Broadway, Jefferson, TX 75657, tel. 903/665–8415, fax 903/665–8416. 3 double rooms with baths. Air-conditioning, cable TVs, phones, refrigerator in common area. $85–$95, full breakfast. AE, MC, V. No smoking, no pets, 2-night minimum on weekends.

Reservations Services

A & L Reservations (603 E. Elizabeth St., Jefferson, TX 75657, tel. 903/665–1017 or 903/665–1019). **Bed and Breakfast Texas Style** (4224 W. Red Bird La., Dallas, TX 75237, tel. 214/298–8586 or 800/899–4538). **Book-A-Bed-Ahead** (Box 723, Jefferson, TX 75657, tel. 903/665–3956 or 800/468–2627). **Jefferson Reservation Service** (124 W. Austin, Jefferson, TX 75657, tel. 903/665–2592 or 800/833–6758).

San Antonio, Austin, and the Hill Country

Austin Street Retreat

231 W. Main St., Fredericksburg, TX 78624, tel. 210/997–5612, fax 210/997–8282

Tucked only a block from Main Street and minutes from Fredericksburg's shopping district, this B&B is actually a compound of five historic homes. Owned by a couple and managed by a local reservations service, these stylish retreats have created a new standard for area properties. The luxurious whirlpool tub for two found in each structure is your tip-off that hedonistic luxuries are emphasized here.

From the outside, you might wonder how Annie's Cabin could be one of the top guest houses in Fredericksburg, requiring reservations months in advance. The answer comes as soon as you walk in the room: over-the-top decadence, handcrafted for honeymooners. With smoky-rose-color walls in the bedroom, the cabin is dominated by a king-size bed made from a fence reconfigured by a craftsman Cupid to resemble hearts and arrows; it's covered with a thick layer of linens, a tapestry duvet, and a sumptuous pile of pillows.

In Kristen's Cabin, a king-size iron bed overlooks a fireplace in the front bedroom. An Italian tapestry sofa and chair complete the look, and a painting of the owner's grandmother in her wedding dress lends a romantic air. Connected to the bedroom by a Saltillo-tiled hallway is the bath, its focal point a whirlpool on a limestone pedestal. The bars on the windows are there because the room served as a cell in 1885 when the town jail burned. Outside, a private flagstone courtyard with a three-tiered fountain offers a quiet, private retreat.

Eli's Cabin is less frilly, starting with the cast-iron mantle saved from a Philadelphia mansion. A pencil-post bed, Mexican tin mirror, and a staghorn chandelier add a southwestern touch. This cabin also has a private courtyard with a double hammock.

The oldest structure of the five is Maria's Cabin, a log cabin built in 1867. Its two bedrooms preserve its historic flavor with plank floors, twig furniture, chinked log walls, and historic paintings, but pamper visitors with extras the pioneers never enjoyed: two queen-size beds with down comforters and a whirlpool bath.

But none of the other getaways shares the aged elegance of El Jefe (The Boss). Decorated in 1900s Southwestern style, this two-story cottage has beamed ceilings and appointments that range from frayed sombreros to well-worn leather chairs to antique suitcases. Upstairs, the whirlpool bath overlooks the complex through French doors.

🏠 *4 1-bedroom guest houses, 1 2-bedroom guest house. Air-conditioning, whirlpools, fireplaces in 4 homes, cable TV in 2 homes, CD players in 2 homes, phones, coffee bar with microwave. $95–$100, Continental breakfast. D, MC, V. No smoking, no pets.*

Crystal River Inn

326 W. Hopkins St., San Marcos, TX 78666, tel. 512/396–3739, fax 512/353–3248

Crystal River Inn hosts Mike and Cathy Dillon might have been content to rely on their proximity to the rivers San Marcos, Blanco, and Guadalupe to attract visitors to San Marcos, a small city 51 miles north of San Antonio. But the Dillons are more creative than that: They offer guests murder mystery weekends, "ladies' escape" weekends, gourmet picnics, and other diversions to make a visit to their inn a special experience.

Mike, a manager of high-rise office buildings in Houston, and Cathy, a nurse, were shopping for a peaceful place to live when they fell in love with this 1883 mansion, which mixes Greek columns with Victorian gables and has a double-decker porch. The Dillons opened it as a B&B in 1984 and have since added two buildings to the property.

The houses are decorated, as the Dillons put it, "with furniture we like"; the emphasis is not on antiques but on casual elegance. The guest rooms—each named for a Texas river—have themes that range from Victorian to southwestern. The four suites are luxurious: The Blanco, which overlooks the main house's second-floor veranda, has 12-foot ceilings and unusual fabric-upholstered walls; the San Marcos, in the Rock Cottage, features a marble garden tub with 24-carat gold fixtures, fireplace, and skylight.

As part of the popular murder mystery weekend, where the foul deed that costumed guests work to unearth is based on people and events in San Marcos history, guests enjoy a welcoming party and dessert buffet on Friday and a sunset cruise at Aquarena Springs and a multicourse dinner on Saturday. During the summer, a tubing trip down the San Marcos River is also included. Year-round, the owners put together packages including treats as diverse as massages, European facials, and carriage rides.

🏠 *7 double rooms with baths, 4 2-bedroom suites. TV in most rooms, phones in some rooms, mini-refrigerator and microwave in cottage. $70–$120, full breakfast. AE, D, DC, MC, V. No smoking, no pets, 2-day minimum most weekends.*

Inn on the Creek

Box 858, Salado, TX 76571, tel. 817/947–5554, fax 817/947–9198

Suzi Epps is a picky one. Ask her about most any bed-and-breakfast in Texas and she's been there—and found it lacking. That kind of perfectionism, along with Epps's experience as a professional architect, has helped turn the Inn on the Creek into a reason to stop in Salado, a little town 45 miles north of Austin known mostly for its well-preserved 19th-century Main Street.

Inn on the Creek is a collection of five houses, three of which were salvaged from condemnation and brought to a shady spot on Salado Creek from elsewhere in Texas; all were painstakingly restored by Suzi, along with parents, Bob and Sue Whistler, and husband, Lynn. The oldest of the houses, an 1892 woodframe Victorian imported from Cameron, is connected to another house by a covered wooden walkway to form the inn's main complex. The second building, a two-story, wood frame, includes a large dining room that on weekends opens for dinner as a full-service restaurant. The breakfasts served here tend toward the exotic, ranging from German puff pancakes to Italian frittatas.

The furnishings throughout the main complex are anything but exotic; they run toward the simpler, more understated pieces of the Victorian age. The rooms exude a quiet elegance, each furnished with Victorian antiques, family photographs, and antique dresser sets. White wrought iron and wicker fill the Tyler Room. The most impressive is the spacious, third-floor McKie Room, which has a king-size bed as well as a library nook with a window seat that overlooks the creek.

Directly across the street is the Holland House, built circa 1880, and up the block the Reue House, a Civil War–era farmhouse with four guest rooms. Its highlight is the Kiowa Room, which has a bed made from a 300-year-old loom. Sally's Cottage, a one-bedroom hideaway with an adjoining living room, rounds out the inn's facilities.

🏨 16 double rooms with baths, 2 cottage suites. Cable TVs, phones, ceiling fans and small refrigerators in some rooms, limited restaurant, golf privileges. $100–$125, full breakfast. MC, V. No smoking, no pets.

Ogé House on the Riverwalk

209 Washington St., San Antonio, TX 78204, tel. 210/223–2353 or 800/242–2770, fax 210/226–5812

A classic plantation house built during the Greek Revival craze that spread across the South in the years before the Civil War, the Ogé (pronounced OH-jhay) House is the crowning glory of San Antonio's historic King William neighborhood. Owners Patrick and Sharrie Magatagan have created an understated tribute to the antebellum South, complete with a veranda from which one can look out over the pecan-shaded estate. But it has all the modern amenities: From the registration desk to the in-room premium cable TV and the state-of-the art telephone system, their inn has the ambience of a luxury hotel.

Built in 1857 by pioneer Texas ranger and cattle rancher Louis Ogé, the three-story manse sits on 1.5 acres of landscaped lawns and gardens overlooking the Paseo del Rio. It had been a boardinghouse before the Magatagans purchased it in 1991 and set out to transform it into San Antonio's brightest B&B. Kitchenettes were turned into lovely vanities; walls were painted in creamy whites; bathrooms were overhauled; and pine floors were polished and draped with fine Oriental rugs.

Patrick, who had lived with San Antonio native Sharrie in Connecticut for eight years before returning to the Alamo City, fell in love with antiques while living in the Northeast, and—ironically, in this antebellum southern mansion—purchased many of the furnishings for the inn there. Even one of the home's tributes to things Texan—a bullhorn sofa in an upstairs lounging area—was purchased "up nawth." Texas-theme furnishings are also found in the Bluebonnet Room, complete with a rolling-pin bed and a West Texas judge's desk. Otherwise, early American Victorian furniture dominates the guest rooms and suites.

The house's second floor is the main floor, with an entryway, sitting room, library, kitchen, dining room, and two guest rooms. The first floor is an English basement, which houses a guest room and suite as well as the Magatagans' living quarters. The three third-floor suites are the most impressive: Each has access to the wide veranda or, in one case, a small private balcony.

Sharrie prepares a full breakfast, which may consist of eggs, Southwest sausage gravy and biscuit, French toast, scones, croissants, sweet rolls, popovers, and hot and cold cereals. It's served in the formal dining room or on the front veranda.

🏨 *5 double rooms with baths, 4 suites. Air-conditioning, cable TVs, phones, refrigerators, fireplace in 7 rooms and in all suites. $135–$195, Continental breakfast. AE, D, DC, MC, V. No smoking, no pets, no children under 16, 2-night minimum on weekends.*

Settlers Crossing

231 W. Main St., Fredericksburg, TX 78624, tel. 210/997–5612, fax 210/997–8282

Ever wondered what it was like for German settlers on the American frontier in the 19th century? You and your clan can spend the weekend in your own "Little Haus on the Prairie" at Settlers Crossing, a 35-acre tract located in the rolling countryside between Luckenbach and Fredericksburg. Dotted by log cabins, mesquite trees, and friendly farm animals, this is easily the best family-oriented B&B in the Hill Country.

Of course, the German settlers didn't have a whirlpool bath—a feature of the luxurious Von Heinrich Home, one of four guest houses on the estate of hosts David and Judy Bland. The structures are close enough to one another to be convenient for groups or family reunions, but far enough apart to allow for private getaways.

The Pioneer Homestead, a stone-and-log cabin original to the property, was constructed in the 1850s by the Kusenberger family, German immigrants who were among Fredericksburg's first settlers. The modern appliances in the full kitchen of the two-bedroom house are skillfully tucked away to preserve a feeling of authenticity. The most striking feature is a robin's-egg-blue stenciled ceiling, painted when the house was built. Also original to the grounds, the Baag Farm House was built in the 1920s as a wedding gift for a Kusenberger descendant. The simple, blue wood-frame house has a wood-burning stove and antique dining room table that seats eight.

You may well encounter bleating sheep, grazing goats, and braying donkeys, who like to approach the split-rail fence surrounding the Indian House. The mood of the living room is set by an antique camelback sofa; the high-ceiling master bedroom features a queen-size, four-poster bed with acorn finials. The hosts live in a nearby three-story house imported from Kentucky.

But the most remarkable guest home on the property is the Von Heinrich Home, a two-story German *fachwerk* cottage built in Pennsylvania in 1787. Inside is an outstanding collection of 19th-century folk art, including an antique horse sculpture and an old hooked rug over the fireplace.

🏨 *3 2-bedroom guest houses, 1 3-bedroom guest house. Air-conditioning, TV/VCRs, phones, fireplaces or wood-burning stoves, full kitchen in 3 homes, whirlpool bath in 1 home. $85–$119,*

Continental breakfast. D, MC, V. No smoking, no pets.

Ziller House

800 Edgecliff Terr., Austin, TX 78704, tel. 512/462-0100 or 800/949-5446, fax 512/462-9166

The premier host home in Texas's capital city is the perfect antidote for those weary of formal, frilly Victorian B&Bs. Ziller House owners Sam Kindred and Wendy Sandberg-Kindred offer a unique brand of contemporary sophistication that has drawn such famed visitors as Dennis Quaid, Meg Ryan, and Linda Ellerbee. Sam and Wendy nonetheless remain prime examples of the unaffected Austin spirit; they love to sit around the living room with their guests and shoot the breeze.

A gated, secluded estate on the cliff above the south bank of Town Lake, the 1938 Italian-style mansion is at the very center of Austin, a stone's skip from the Texas capitol. The entryway leads to an eclectic living room with Eastern accents, including a Chinese lacquered screen and artificial bonsai trees. The room, which has contemporary furnishings, is dominated by a stone fireplace that was cut from a fossil bed.

The four guest rooms, three of which are upstairs, have their own personalities. The Library Room, for example, is lined with bookshelves and offers a pretty view of the lake. The balcony that gives the Balcony Room its name is surrounded on all sides by live oaks; the room's bathroom, with its dynamic black-and-saffron-yellow color scheme, is also striking. The Sun Suite has a canopy bed and a separate sitting area with a sleeper sofa.

There are plenty of places to relax on the grounds, from the stone patio, to the cliffside gazebo, to the spa. A masseur lives on the property, and guests can schedule a massage any time. Visitors with children are welcome; those who

want to get away from the kids for an evening can leave them with the hosts' baby-sitter, who also takes care of Sam and Wendy's two children. And Sam, a wine dealer and gourmet chef, knows all the best restaurants in Austin.

Sam—who will prepare dinner for guests on request—usually cooks breakfast in the afternoon on an enormous Wolf stove in the kitchen. Arriving visitors find the meal—usually an egg dish, breakfast meat, pastry, and fresh fruit—tucked away in the small refrigerator that is in each room's service cabinet, along with a microwave oven. The self-contained quality of the guest rooms (each also has a cordless cellular phone) is especially appealing to business travelers, who are welcome to use the hosts' 18-chair dining room table for meetings.

🎈 *3 double rooms with baths, 1 suite, 1 carriage house. Cable TV/VCRs, CD player in living room, 2,000 video library, outside dog run, hot tub. $120, full breakfast. AE, MC, V. No smoking, pets in runs only, 2-night minimum on weekends.*

Other Choices

Beckmann Inn And Carriage House. 222 E. Guenther St., San Antonio, TX 78204, tel. 210/229-1449 or 800/945-1449, fax 210/229-1061. 3 double rooms with baths, 2 suites in carriage house. Cable TVs, turndown service, guest refrigerator, mini-refrigerators in carriage house rooms, trolley stop. $90-$130, full breakfast. AE, D, DC, MC, V. No smoking, no pets, no children under 12, 2-night minimum on weekends.

Bonner Garden. 145 E. Agarita St., San Antonio, TX 78212, tel. 210/733-4222 or 800/396-4222, fax 210/733-6129. 5 double rooms with baths. TV/VCRs, phones, CD player in sitting room, videotape library, outdoor pool. $85-$125, full breakfast. AE, D, DC, MC, V. No smoking, no pets, 2-night minimum on weekends.

Bullis House Inn. 621 Pierce St., Box 8059, San Antonio, TX 78208, tel. 210/223–9426, fax 210/299–1479. 2 double rooms with baths, 5 doubles share 4 baths. Individual climate control, phone in 1 room, outdoor pool. $49–$69, Continental breakfast. AE, D, MC, V. Smoking in guest rooms only, no pets, 2-night minimum on weekends.

Carrington's Bluff. 1900 David St., Austin, TX 78705, tel. 512/479–0638. 6 double rooms with baths, 2 doubles share bath. Cable TVs, phones. $59–$99; full breakfast, tea. AE, D, DC, MC, V. No smoking.

Comfort Common. 717 High St., Box 539, Comfort, TX 78013, tel. 210/995–3030, fax 210/995–3455. 5 double rooms with baths, 2 suites, 2 cottages. TVs and fireplaces in some rooms. $60–$95, full breakfast. AE, D, MC, V. No smoking, no pets, no children under 12, 2-night minimum on holiday and special-event weekends.

Das Kleine Nest. 231 W. Main St., Fredericksburg, TX 78624, tel. 210/997–5612, fax 210/997–8282. 1 double room with bath. Cable TV, air-conditioning, ceiling fans, phone, coffeemaker, small refrigerator, stove, microwave. $68, no breakfast. D, MC, V. No pets.

Delforge Place. 231 W. Main St., Fredericksburg, TX 78624, tel. 210/997–5612, fax 210/997–8282. 4 suites. Cable TVs, refrigerator. $85–$95, full breakfast. D, MC, V. No smoking, no pets, no children under 6 unless family rents entire house.

Fredericksburg Bed and Brew. 245 E. Main St., Fredericksburg, TX 78624, tel. 210/997–1646, fax 210/997–8026. 12 rooms with baths. $79–$89, beer sampler (no breakfast). AE, MC, V. No smoking, no pets, no children.

Herb Haus. Drawer 927, 402 Whitney St., Fredericksburg, TX 78624, tel. 210/997–8615 or 800/259–4372. 1 2-bedroom guest house. Cable TVs, phones, ceiling fans, air-conditioning, kitchen. $105, Continental breakfast and evening snacks. AE, D, DC, MC, V. No smoking, no pets, no children under 12.

Nagel House. 231 W. Main St., Fredericksburg, TX 78624, tel. 210/997–5612, fax 210/997–8282. 1 3-bedroom cottage. Cable TVs, phones, microwave, refrigerator, stove. $85, Continental breakfast. D, MC, V. No smoking, no pets, no children under 10 except infants.

Schmidt Barn. 231 W. Main St., Fredericksburg, TX 78624, tel. 210/997–5612, fax 210/997–8282. 1 1-bedroom guest house (sleeps 4). Phone, air-conditioning, ceiling fan, CD and tape player, microwave, coffeemaker. $79, full breakfast. D, MC, V.

Woodburn House. 4401 Ave. D, Austin, TX 78751, tel. 512/458–4335. 4 double rooms with baths. Desks, phones, TV and VCR in living room, exchange library. $79–$89, full breakfast. AE, MC, V. No pets, no children under 10.

Yellow Rose. 229 Madison St., San Antonio, TX 78204, tel. 210/229–9903 or 800/950–9903. 5 double rooms with baths. Cable TV, Caswell and Massey toiletries, trolley stop one block away. $90–$125, full breakfast. AE, D, MC, V. Smoking on porches only, no pets, no children under 9, 2-night minimum on weekends.

Reservations Services

Be My Guest Travel Services (402 W. Main St., Fredericksburg, TX 78624, tel. 210/997–7227). **Bed and Breakfast Hosts of San Antonio** (1777 N.E. Loop 410, Ste. 600, San Antonio, TX 78217, tel. 210/824–8036). **Gastehaus Schmidt Reservation Service** (231 W. Main St., Fredericksburg, TX 78624, tel. 210/997–5612).

Utah

Green Gate Village

Southwestern Utah

Bard's Inn

150 S. 100 West, Cedar City, UT 84720, tel. 801/586–6612

Now pillars of the Utah Shakespearean Festival Guild in Cedar City, Jack and Audrey Whipple got hooked on the bard during their first visit to town. Their 1900s-era golden shingle-and-brick bungalow reflects their passion for the playwright, from dolls in Elizabethan costumes to guest rooms named after the characters in Shakespeare's plays.

The well-traveled Whipples have acquired scores of unique antiques and decorations for their inn. Audrey designed and created the stained-glass panels—some reassembled from discarded church windows—seen throughout the house. A salvaged oak banister follows the slow curl of the stairway from an enclosed porch to the three upstairs guest rooms.

It is the unexpected touches—creamy crocheted gloves lying across a dropleaf desk in the upstairs sitting room, a Chinese checkerboard in a bathroom—that make this such a fascinating place

to stay. Everything in the house seems to have a story; ask Audrey to tell you how she rescued the claw-foot stool from a sheep pasture in northern Idaho.

The Katharina Room has a turn-of-the-century high-back walnut bed with spring-colored linens, and a big braided runner on the floor; its small alcove hosts a twin walnut sleigh bed. Across the hall, the Olivia Room has cranberry carpeting, antique oak furnishings, and a collection of ceramic figures on an intricately carved wall shelf. A strawberry border trails around the ceiling of the Titania Room, and stained-glass circles are suspended in two windows. On the main floor is the sophisticated Mistress Ford suite, with a sunny private library. The Beatrice Suite, in the basement, is fitted with matching twin oak beds and a double bed. Thoughtful items in all the rooms include night lights and plump pincushions bristling with needles and thread.

The inn has a refrigerator and sink for guest use and a small dining area with a festive collection of marbles centered on the table. Audrey's healthy but delicious breakfasts might include her home-baked Boston raisin bread, poppyseed rolls, almond cherry zucchini bread, and Jack's personal favorite, made from an old recipe passed down verbally—dainty, frosted *colachis* filled with apricots.

🏨 *3 double rooms with baths, 2 suites, 1 duplex cottage. Kitchen in cottage and 1 suite, off-street parking. $65–$80, full breakfast. MC, V. No smoking indoors, no pets. Open June–Sept. only (other dates by prior arrangement).*

Greene Gate Village

76 West Tabernacle St., St. George, UT 84770, tel. 801/628–6999 or 800/350–6999

Diagonally across from the historic adobe Mormon Tabernacle, Greene Gate Village looks like a tiny pioneer settlement, and, in a way, it is. This unusual complex brings together seven pioneer-era structures—among them adobe homes, a rock granary, and spruced-up wooden cabins—moved from sites scattered across the St. George Valley. In most cases, an entire house can be rented, making this an excellent place to stay with family or a group of friends. The spacious interior yard is a perfect group common area, with its flower beds, tidy lawns, and postcard-pretty swimming pool.

Built in the mid-1800s and the only village structure original to this site, the tan stucco Orson Pratt House sports a gingerbread-trimmed porch. The first-floor Shanna suite of rooms has brass and oak furniture and hand-quilted floral bedspreads. Next door, in the Lindsay Room, the paper-white cutwork shams and bedspread stand in crisp contrast to the royal blue carpet; photographs of Orson Pratt, a counselor to Brigham Young, hang over the fireplace. The bathroom is tiny, but there's a large Jacuzzi tub in a separate room.

Creaking wicker chairs sit on the rustic porch of the weathered two-room Tolley cabin, which looks out toward the swimming pool. Inside, where a family of 13 once lived, are two simply decorated rooms, each with a fireplace.

Village founders Mark and Barbara Greene had to reconstruct the two-bedroom Morris House, originally located several blocks away: On moving day, the axle on the house trailer broke, and the two-story home suddenly became a pile of shattered glass, adobe brick, and broken door and window frames.

Breakfast, served in the garden room of the Bentley House, usually includes omelets, bacon, sausage, juices, and either pecan waffles, homemade bread, or croissants.

🏨 *Village: 3 double rooms; 2 triples, and 5 quads, all with baths. Off-site: 4 doubles and 1 quad room with baths; Greene House complex (house and carriage house), which can sleep 22. Phones, TVs, kitchens in 5 rooms, fireplaces in 6 rooms, whirlpool tub in 5 rooms, pool, walking tour, off-street parking, 5-course dinners served Thurs.–Sat. by reservation. $50–$125, full breakfast. AE, DC, MC, V. No smoking, no pets, 2-night minimum for Greene House complex.*

Harvest House

29 Canyon View Dr., Springdale, UT 84767, tel. 801/772–3880

When native Bostonians Steve and Barbara Cooper first visited Zion Canyon, they were determined to find a way to come back permanently. Barbara, a gourmet chef and former co-owner of Boston's Harvest Catering Company, also wanted to be able to use her culinary and decorating skills. Luckily for their guests, the Coopers found the ways and means to bring their plans to pass.

Just off Springdale's main drag, Harvest House is a modern, two-story ranch-style structure, built of mottled tan-and-brown brick and buttery stucco. Best of all, practically every window in the house lets in a personal slice of Zion Canyon.

Shades of black and gray dominate in the living room, including a nubby charcoal sofa and many black-and-white photographs; splashes of color come from a collection of cups and saucers and brightly painted wooden animals romping on the hearth. A stained-glass cactus bloom set above the front door sends prisms of light sparkling across the walls, and French doors lead to a flagstone patio.

The main-floor guest room sports lacy curtains on windows that have a view of the cactus garden Steve created; blue-and-green linens look refreshing, and Barbara's handmade paper collages accent the walls. Upstairs, one west-side room is done in stylish pink and black, with a wicker chaise longue for reading or dreaming. A snug love seat highlights another room decorated in rose and ferny green. Sunsets bathe both rooms in colorful light. The pastel-toned master bedroom has a wide window looking out on the apple orchard next door, which attracts deer each evening. On warm summer nights, the sound of the Virgin River is a soft counterpoint to conversations on the private deck.

Breakfast at Harvest House is both festive and delicious. Colorful place settings and butter sculptures formed in a collection of Victorian-era pewter molds are all part of the glamorous presentation of such entrées as poached eggs with basil hollandaise or cheese blintzes with rivers of fresh fruit topping. Fresh muffins, pastries or breads, and Steve's stout coffee help round out the morning meal.

▥ *3 double rooms with baths, 1 triple with bath. Air-conditioning, TV/VCR, video library, wet bar in living room, outdoor hot tub, fishpond, off-street parking. $75–$95; full breakfast, afternoon refreshments. D, MC, V. No smoking, no pets.*

Nine Gables Inn

106 W. 100 North, Kanab, UT 84741, tel. 801/644–5079

Jeanne Bantlin was visiting her brother in Kanab when she and her husband, Frank, discovered on an evening walk that the home they had been admiring throughout their stay was suddenly for sale. Both former U.S. West Communications employees, the Bantlins promptly bought this 1890s, two-story ranch house and set about turning it into a bed-and-breakfast.

White stucco now covers the red sunbaked adobe brick, the building material used for most of the houses in the area. A pert white picket fence encloses a yard blooming with myrtle and vinca and a vegetable garden twined with perennial blooms.

The completely remodeled living room has shining new hardwood floors that reflect light from tall, narrow windows. Many of the furnishings in this room, and throughout the inn, are family treasures. But by far the most inviting common area is the upstairs sitting room, with its large circle rug, ceiling fan, rocking chairs, surprisingly comfortable dignified courthouse bench, wood-burning stove, and Victrola with a cabinet full of board games.

A small, sunny guest room at the front of the house has textured gray carpet and matte white walls; a first-edition Zane Grey novel on the nightstand is a reminder that the author was a guest in this home while researching some of his books. In a medium-size room down the hall are a honey-colored oak-slatted bed and the most comfortable chair in the inn: a reupholstered horsehair rocker found in an old milk house.

The long, quiet bedroom at the back of the house features a curly maple rolltop desk that invites letter writing; a firm bed covered with a blue-and-pink "Briar Rose"–patterned quilt; a framed crocheted collar and a colorful old Certificate of Baptism on the wall; and the trunk that carried Jeanne's grandfather's belongings when he emigrated from Norway.

Frank's breakfasts are served in what was once the front parlor; boasting the original bay window and a working fireplace, it's now a very pleasant dining room. Hot or cold cereal shares the board with pastries or muffins, juices, and fresh fruit. A summer treat to hope for is a bowl of huge raspberries from the backyard berry patch.

▦ *3 double rooms with baths. Air-conditioning and ceiling fans in all rooms, TV in common area, off-street parking. $80, full breakfast. MC, V. No smoking, no pets. Closed Nov.–mid-May.*

O'Toole's Under the Eaves

980 Zion Park Blvd., Box 29, Springdale, UT 84767, tel. 801/772–3457

It's easy to see why construction of this two-story mock-Tudor cottage, begun in 1935, took five years: Under the Eaves is made of buff sandstone blocks cut from the walls of Zion Canyon. Fronted by a lovely flower-filled square porch, the inn is a pleasantly incongruous sight on Springdale's motel-lined main street.

Owners Rick and Michelle O'Toole bought the already established property in the spring of 1993. Their first step toward making the guest house their own was to plant favorite flowers in the small backyard, a delightful oasis where pecan, almond, and fruit trees blend with flourishing perennials, lilacs, and lavender.

The parlor and dining room are filled with cozy, worn antiques, and shelves are stocked with books and games. Beyond the kitchen lie two guest accommodations. The cheerful south room has a polished hardwood floor and crisp country linens. The small blue-and-white north room is decorated with a springy hand-loomed rug and a simple ladder-back chair. Both rooms are illuminated by antique light fixtures taken from the "upstairs rooms" of an old saloon in Pioche, Nevada.

A popular suite nestled "under the eaves" encompasses the entire second floor. Its kitchen and sitting area overlook the gardens, and additional windows face Zion Canyon. A claw-foot tub adds an element of fun to the bathroom.

A separate Garden Cottage holds three small rooms. Two have fanciful linens and stained-glass windows in their compact bathrooms. A mahogany sleigh bed is the focal point of the antiques-filled third room, set in the large, well-lighted basement. This room also boasts a whirlpool tub.

Guests can enjoy sunrise coffee service on the front porch of the main house, and then eat family-style in the dining room. Breakfast highlights include fresh breads, egg-and-cheese casseroles with homemade salsa, and the occasional breakfast tostada with chilies and beans.

▦ *3 double rooms with baths, 2 doubles share bath, 1 suite. Air-conditioning, kitchenette in suite, garden gazebo, off-street parking. $69–$125, full breakfast. D, MC, V. No smoking, no pets, no children under 10.*

Seven Wives Inn

217 N. 100 West, St. George, UT 84770, tel. 801/628–3737 or 800/600–3737

In the heart of St. George's Historic District, two neighboring homes compose Seven Wives Inn, named for an ancestor of one of the owners, who indeed had seven wives. The larger two-story house, built in 1873, features a double-tier veranda and a wood-shingled roof projecting gables in three directions; its attic was the occasional hiding place of die-hard polygamists fleeing federal marshals after multiple marriages were outlawed in 1882. The adjacent President's House, a modified two-story Renaissance Revival cube built in 1883, often provided lodging for visiting presidents of the Mormon Church.

Innkeepers Jay and Donna Curtis and Jon and Alison Bowcutt are always keeping their eyes open for antiques to add to those collected in the parlors of both houses and throughout the guest rooms. Jon is a popular local artist and his pencil drawings and oil paintings hang in the inn's common areas.

In the main house, the Lucinda Room is a study in pastels, with an elaborate antique brass bed, soft, gray hooked rugs, a rose-colored velvet sofa and chair, and a green French ceramic stove; small children can be accommodated in a Murphy bed that descends from an antique armoire. The romantic, high-ceiling Melissa Room on the second floor has a lace minicanopy over the bed and a private balcony. The notorious attic room is brightened by a skylight and an art deco pewter chandelier; a high, floral-painted bed sits against a wall of exposed adobe brick.

The four rooms in the President's House are accessed by a steep, narrow staircase. The Caroline Room has dark green walls lightened by large windows, and a kaleidoscopic "Nine Patch" quilt on the bed. Spring is eternal in the small Rachel Room, where the walls are papered with pastel tulips. The furnishings are white wicker, and floral swags arch over white wooden blinds.

The high-ceiling dining room in the main house has tables set for two or four. In addition to homemade granola, breakfast choices might include German apple or apple pecan pancakes; bread pudding; sausage *en croûte*; or bacon, eggs, and cheese in a nest of hash browns.

🏠 *10 double rooms, 2 triples, 1 single, all with baths (4 rooms can be combined as suites). TVs, phones, fireplaces or stoves in 4 rooms, private balconies in 4 rooms, outdoor pool, off-street parking. $55–$125, full breakfast. AE, D, DC, MC, V. No smoking, no pets.*

SkyRidge
Bed and Breakfast

Box 750220, Torrey, UT 84775, tel. and fax 801/425–3222

SkyRidge Bed and Breakfast is near the western boundary of Capitol Reef National Park. The house's design echoes territorial style, and the exterior is an unusual greenish brown—close in color to blooming rice grass, one of the native plants that surround the inn.

Owners Karen Kesler and Sally Elliot relocated from Mendocino, California, in 1993 to design, build, and decorate SkyRidge. Above all, the women wanted a visual feast. Seventy-five windows bring the outside beauty inside. Art furniture fashioned by Karen accents every room, and works by other local artists add visual interest and are available for purchase.

In the cozy living room, guests can relax around a central fireplace with a patterned facade made from more than 30 pounds of roofing nails. Built-in shelves are filled with books, from dog-eared Mother Goose to lush art tomes, and small pieces of African art. The walls here, as elsewhere in the inn, are hand textured and sponge painted neutral colors.

All of SkyRidge's guest rooms are comfortable and intriguing. On the first level, the Buffalo Berry Room mixes Oriental rugs with plump cactus-strewn pillows piled on the bed. Mannequin hands holding crystal door knobs further the room's funky feel. Across the front porch, the Tumble Weed Suite has antique walnut furnishings.

Upstairs, in the large Sagebrush Room, cream and jewel-toned quilts accent two beds perched on gray Berber carpet. Seven windows look across a valley to aspen-covered slopes. The Pinyon Room has heavily textured walls, a pitched roof line, and an oddly appealing jumble of furniture including a match stick four-poster bed, and an art deco floor lamp. A small hot tub is on an enclosed deck. From the high-back bed in the Juniper Room, a bay of six windows provides views of peaks and cliffs silhouetted against the sunrise.

In the main floor dining room, seven tall narrow windows share wall space with Mexican masks and a vivid canvas of a cactus in bloom. Sturdy wicker chairs provide comfortable seating for Sally's culinary specialties—croissant French toast, Mexican frittata with fresh tomatillo salsa, or apple spice pecan waffles—all accompanied by yogurt, granola, and fruit harvested from Capitol Reef National Park.

3 double rooms with baths, 1 quad with bath, 1 suite. Ceiling fans and individual heat controls, TV/VCRs, video library, guest refrigerator, horseshoe pits, picnic area, barbecue, off-street parking, activity and trip planning. $72–$102, full breakfast and afternoon refreshments. MC, V. No smoking, no pets, 2-night minimum on holiday weekends.

Other Choices

Blue House. 125 E. Main, Rockville, UT 84763, tel. 801/772–3912. 1 double room and 1 triple with bath, 2 doubles share bath. TV in common area, trampoline, outdoor patio. $65–$75, full breakfast. MC, V. No smoking.

Bryce Point Bed and Breakfast. 61 N. 400 West, Box 96, Tropic, UT 84776, tel. 801/679–8629. 2 double rooms and 3 triples, all with baths, 1 cottage. Ceiling fans, TV/VCRs, outdoor hot tub, guest barbecue, off-street parking. $55–$90, full breakfast. MC, V. No smoking, no pets.

Francisco Farm Bed & Breakfast. 51 Francisco La., Box 3, Tropic, UT 84776, tel. 801/679–8721 or 800/642–4136. 3 double rooms with baths. TVs, hot tub, farm animals, off-street parking. $55–$70, full breakfast. No credit cards. No smoking, no pets.

Grandma Bess' Cottage. 291 W. 200 South, Box 640, Parowan, UT 84761, tel. 801/477–8224. 3 double rooms share bath. Air-conditioning, TV in common area. $45, full breakfast. No credit cards. No smoking, no pets, no alcohol.

Morning Glory Inn. 25 Big Springs Rd., Springdale, UT 84767, tel. 801/772–3301. 2 triple rooms with baths, 1 quad with bath, 1 3-person cottage. Hot tub in cottage; volleyball, basketball, and badminton courts; playground equipment; picnic area; off-street parking. $60–$85, full breakfast. MC, V. No smoking, no pets.

Paxman's House Bed & Breakfast. 170 N. 400 West, Cedar City, UT 84720, tel. 801/586–3755. 3 double rooms, 1 triple, all with baths. TVs, off-street parking. $65–$75, full breakfast. MC, V. No smoking, no pets.

Smith Hotel. Hwy. 89, Box 106, Glendale, UT 84729, tel. 801/648–2156. 5 double rooms, 1 single, 1 triple, all with baths. Off-street parking. $45–$65, Continental breakfast. MC, V. No smoking, no pets. Closed Nov.–Mar.

Snow Family Guest Ranch. 653 E. Hwy. 9, Box 790190, Virgin, UT 84779, tel. 801/635–2500 or 800/308–7669. 9 double rooms with baths. Big screen TV, swimming pool, outdoor hot tub, gazebo, garden, pond. $75–$135; full breakfast, afternoon refreshments. MC, V. No smoking, no pets, no infants.

Theater Bed & Breakfast. 118 S. 100 West, Cedar City, UT 84720, tel. 801/586–0404. 1 double room with adjoining bath, 2 doubles share bath. Hot tub, exercise equipment, off-street parking, guest bicycles, ski storage, free airport shuttle. $65; full breakfast Mon.–Sat., Continental breakfast Sun. No credit cards. No smoking, no pets, no alcohol.

Zion House. 801 Zion Park Blvd., Box 323, Springdale, UT 84767, tel. 801/772–3281. 1 double room with bath, 2 doubles share bath, 1 suite with bath. Air-conditioning, kitchen and private entrance in suite, off-street parking.

$70–$95, full breakfast. No credit cards. No smoking, no pets.

Zion's Blue Star. 28 W. State Rte. 9, Virgin, UT 84779, tel. 801/635–3830. 2 double rooms share bath, guest cottage. Air-conditioning in rooms, kitchen in cottage, TV in common room. $65, full breakfast. MC, V. No smoking, no pets.

Reservations Services

There are no bed-and-breakfast reservations services in the area. Write to the statewide **Bed and Breakfast Inns of Utah, Inc.** (Box 3066, Park City, UT 84060) and the **Utah Travel Council** (Council Hall/Capitol Hill, Salt Lake City, UT 84114, tel. 801/538–1030 or 800/200–1160), both of which publish free directories.

Southeastern Utah

Castle Valley Inn

CVSR Box 2602, Moab, UT 84532, tel. 801/259–6012

Although it feels as though it's way out past nowhere, stunning Castle Valley is only about 20 miles from Moab; it's reached via S.R. 128, a designated Scenic Byway that winds along the Colorado River. A road marked by buildings ranging from a red rock-colored geodesic dome to a western movie set leads to the Castle Valley Inn, a wooden rambler home with a native-stone chimney and sparkling geodes set into the foundation.

When you arrive, you'll be surrounded by 360° of ragged-topped cliffs—and a lot of silence. There is a tendency to want to linger outside in the 11-acre yard and orchard, and new innkeepers Robert Ryan and Hertha Wakefield have made this easy with balconies on bungalows, a large patio adjacent to the main house, lighted paths, and benches scattered about to take advantage of the vistas. A sheltered hot tub is magical at night.

The main-house guest rooms, some upstairs, some down, are decorated in a simple, contemporary Southwestern style, with striking color combinations such as variegated shades of lavender and green. Each bathroom includes a hair dryer, robe, and shower-massage head in a stall artistically tiled. Three separate bungalows have private decks and porches. Baskets from Africa and a handcrafted chest decorate the Fremont Bungalow.

Breakfast, which might include green chili quiche, mango yogurt, muesli, and fresh-ground coffee, is served on the patio whenever possible. A sumptuous fixed-price dinner is offered five nights a week.

🏠 *5 double rooms with baths, 3 double bungalows. Air-conditioning, kitchens in bungalows, VCR, video library in common room, outdoor hot tub. $90–$155; full breakfast, afternoon refreshments. MC, V. No smoking indoors, no pets, no children under 15, 2-night minimum.*

Grist Mill Inn

64 S. 300 East, Box 156, Monticello, UT 84535, tel. 801/587–2597 or 800/645–3762

There was a lot of head-shaking among Monticello locals when Dianne and Rye Nielson announced their plans to gut a vacant mill and redesign and rebuild it, but doubt changed to admiration by the time the project was completed in 1988: More than 900 people showed up to tour the inn before its opening. Now a place worth staying in an otherwise passing-through kind of town, the Grist Mill Inn is also distinctive for its reasonable rates.

The portions of the huge three-story flour mill that were wooden clapboard when the mill was constructed in 1933 have been sheathed in light-gray aluminum siding. Bright blue tin roofs top both sections of the structure. The entire renovation is documented in a photo album.

A multicolored firebrick hearth in the lobby sitting room is the focal point for a conversation area, with plush purple wing chairs and soft lamplight. If you look up you'll see the driveshaft for a grain sacker that sits a few feet away—one of the many original pieces of mill equipment left throughout the inn. Other lovely common areas include the second-floor Blue Goose TV room (named after an old saloon in town), which also has a pump organ. A bank of high, square windows in the third-floor library provides sufficient light to enjoy reading materials ranging from magazines, remodeling books, and contemporary novels to a complete collection of Hardy Boys and Nancy Drew mysteries.

The Corbin Room, named for Dianne's grandfather, who owned the first telephone company hereabouts, has phones everywhere; one wall and the ceiling are horizontally paneled with rosy stained wood, and an antique armoire holds a Murphy bed. The three-level Bailey Room has two sleeping areas and several antique sewing machines; the bathroom sink is in a treadle machine cabinet. Behind the inn a wooden railroad caboose holds a snug Victorian-style bedroom and a kitchen; its observation tower has a sitting room.

Breakfast is served in the dining room; you can see the Abajo Mountains through glass doors and windows. The Nielsons' morning specialties include French toast stuffed with sweet peaches or served with a clove-tinged maple syrup, and scrambled eggs and cheese piled on cubed potatoes.

▥ *8 double rooms, 2 triples, all with bath. TVs, indoor hot tub, gift shop. $60–$90, full breakfast. AE, D, DC, MC, V. No smoking indoors, no pets.*

Sunflower Hill

185 N. 300 East, Moab, UT 84532, tel. 801/259-2974

Once a bare adobe-brick farmhouse surrounded by nothing but crop land, Sunflower Hill was enlarged and renovated, and the crumbling adobe was fortified and covered with pale stucco. A separate cottage was added to the original late 19th-century structure and the farm field became a spacious wooded lot with a hedge of white roses lining the split-log fence.

The main common area, which doubles as the dining room, is as cheerful as innkeepers Aaron and Kim Robison. Mismatched antique chairs are pulled up to several small tables covered with blue-and-white-checked cloths; a century-old Austrian sideboard with dishes peeking through its heavy glass-pane doors sits between windows curtained in crisp white ruffles; and a tall umbrella stand and coat tree are topped with a bright-red hatbox. Across the hall, a small office area known as the Welcome Room contains copious information on the Moab area. An antique cash register is a reminder, perhaps, that this is where reservations are taken and accounts are settled.

The guest rooms are varied in size, but each has a distinctive character. In truth, there's not a bad choice among them. Accessed from the enclosed porch opposite the dining room door, the Sun Porch Room has been fitted with ceiling-to-floor windows covered in vertical miniblinds for privacy. Up a step is a painted metal bed; a woven sunflower throw draped on a quilt stand echoes a ceiling border blooming with golden sunflowers. The Rose Room has stenciled roses twining along the walls, a graceful four-poster bed, and an antique dressing table. The blue-and-white Morning Glory Room has a private garden entrance with morning glory vines growing around the door.

Across the yard, the Garden Cottage has a stenciled tulip border high on the sitting room walls. A whimsical flower garden is painted on the wall of the sunny bedroom.

Sunflower Hill's breakfasts are a variety of sturdy homemade breads, fruity muffins, yogurt, honey granola, and lots of fresh fruit, or hot entrées like fruit-filled pancakes, southwest eggs, or whole wheat waffles with tangy berry patch syrup.

🏨 *4 double rooms, 1 single, 6 suites, all with baths. Air-conditioning, TVs, outdoor hot tub, guest kitchenette, bicycle storage, barbecue. $70–$140, full breakfast. MC, V. No smoking, no pets, no children under 8.*

Other Choices

Bankurz Hatt. 214 Farrer St., Green River, UT 84525, tel. 801/564–3382. 1 double room with bath, 3 doubles share bath. Ceiling fans in rooms, outdoor hot tub, guest bicycles, off-street parking. $75–$125, full breakfast. AE. No smoking, no pets.

Bluff Bed and Breakfast. Box 158, Bluff, UT 84512, tel. 801/672–2220. 2 double rooms with baths. TV in common area, off-street parking, hiking. $75, full breakfast. No credit cards. No smoking, no pets.

Desert Chalet. 1275 E. San Juan Dr., Moab, UT 84532, tel. 801/259–5793 or 800/549–8504. 1 triple room with bath, 2 doubles and 2 triples share 2 baths. Ceiling fans; TV/VCR, stereo in common area; outdoor hot tub; kitchen,

laundry, and storage available; barbecue. $45–$75, Continental breakfast. MC, V. No smoking, no pets, no children under 4. Closed Dec.–Feb.

Grayson Country Inn. 118 E. 300 South, Blanding, UT 84511, tel. 801/678–2388, 800/365–0868. 7 double rooms with baths. 1 cottage with kitchen. TVs, air-conditioning in some rooms. $32–$52, full breakfast. AE, MC, V. No smoking, no pets.

Pack Creek Ranch. LaSal Mountain Loop Rd., Box 1270, Moab, UT 84532, tel. 801/259–5505, fax 801/259–8879. 9 cabins, ranch house (sleeps 12) with 1½ baths. Gift shop, masseuse, hot tub, sauna, outdoor pool, trail rides. $125 per person including all meals; Nov.–Mar., $56 per person without meals. AE, D, MC, V.

Valley of the Gods Bed and Breakfast. Box 310307, Mexican Hat, UT 84531, tel. 970/749–1164 (cellular). 4 double rooms with baths. Raft trips, pack horse or llama trips, and archaeological tours available. $82, full breakfast. MC, V. No smoking.

Reservations Services

There are no bed-and-breakfast reservation services in the area. Write to the statewide **Bed and Breakfast Inns of Utah, Inc.** (Box 3066, Park City, UT 84060) or the **Utah Travel Council** (Council Hall/Capitol Hill, Salt Lake City, UT 84114, tel. 801/538–1030 or 800/200–1160), both of which publish free directories.

Vermont

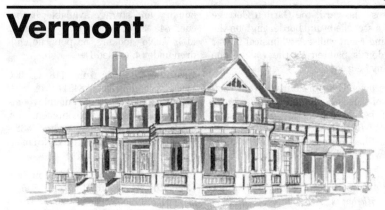

Inn at Montpelier

Southeastern Vermont

Governor's Inn

86 Main St., Ludlow, VT 05149, tel. 802/228-8830 or 800/468-3766

The atmosphere at this formal little retreat just 10 minutes away from the Okemo Mountain ski area is high Victorian. Everything from the vest-pocket lobby, where afternoon tea is served, to the innkeepers' collection of antique teacups and chocolate pots evokes a turn-of-the-century elegance. As visitors learn during Deedy Marble's orientation tour, the governor in question is Vermont Governor William Wallace Stickney, who in 1890 had the house built as a wedding present for his wife; the bridegroom's portrait still stands on the mantel over the painted slate fireplace in the living room. These romantic beginnings haven't been forgotten by innkeepers Charlie and Deedy Marble, who have created an appealing hideaway for honeymooners and couples celebrating anniversaries. The Marbles' thoughtful attention to detail is evident everywhere: The inn's wide-plank pine floors gleam; puffy lace-trimmed floral chintz duvets on the beds match the sheets; arriving guests find glasses and miniature cordials in their rooms, and the inn's special chocolates appear every evening when the beds are turned down.

The hosts take as much pleasure in entertaining their guests as in providing a restful atmosphere. It was partly because they had become so proficient at orchestrating elaborate dinner parties for friends that they finally left management jobs in 1981 to open an inn. Before welcoming their first guests, however, they decided to hone their skills at Roger Verge's famed cooking school in the south of France. As a result of the Marbles' training (and their flair for presentation), the five- or six-course dinners at the Governor's Inn border on the theatrical. Fresh-faced teenage waitresses in floral skirts, white high-neck blouses, and mob caps announce each course. Guests dine by candlelight with table settings of antique bone china and sterling silver and often linger over meals that might include hot wine broth, Cornish hens with cinnamon glaze and apple and pâté stuffing, and Edwardian cream with raspberry sauce. The apple pie is especially recommended. Charlie is in charge of breakfast, which often includes his signature rum-raisin French toast.

Although Ludlow isn't the most charming town, the innkeepers' hospitality makes this place worthwhile. Also, Chester, Grafton, and Weston are all nearby.

🏠 *8 double rooms with baths, 1 suite. Restaurant, air-conditioning, fireplace in public area, game room, afternoon tea. $95–$140, MAP; B&B rates available. MC, V. No smoking, no pets, 2-night minimum on weekends, 3- to 4-night minimum on holidays and at Christmastime.*

Inn at Long Last

Main St., Box 589, Chester, VT 05143, tel. 802/875–2444

Innkeeper Jack Coleman made national headlines in the 1970s when he took a sabbatical from his post as president of Haverford College in Pennsylvania to work in a variety of blue-collar jobs. In 1986, when he finally decided to leave the world of academia and foundations for good, he moved north and opened this Victorian country inn. The result mirrors the diversity of his interests and his puckish wit. Bookshelves in the large wood-paneled library hold volumes in literature, science, biography, music, history, and labor economics (Coleman's field); one entire shelf is devoted to George Orwell. An army of toy soldiers fills a glass case beside the enormous fieldstone fireplace in the pine-floor lobby, where guests like to gather for after-dinner drinks, lounging on one of the large couches in front of the fire.

Although not overly warm, this grand old inn, like its innkeeper, invites respect. Individual rooms are named after people, places, and things important to Coleman and are decorated simply with personal memorabilia; a pamphlet in each room explains the significance of the room names. The Dickens Room, with a high carved headboard, is the most spacious, and the Audubon and Tiffany rooms offer access to the second-story porch. The quietest section of the house is at the back.

The eclectic dinner menu might include Mediterranean fish stew with tomato, saffron, and garlic; shredded pork quesadillas with sour cream and lime; and Shaker lemon pie. The wine list is, surprisingly, less diverse: All the wines are from California. The spectacular mahogany bar with its marble countertop and silver chafing dish gives the dining room a turn-of-the-century opulence that in the candlelight blends beautifully with abstract pastel prints on the walls. Breakfast is served in a sunny room filled with the sounds of Gregorian chants.

The town of Chester is fairly sleepy, necessitating a certain resourcefulness from its visitors. Guests with an interest in history enjoy strolling through the nearby "stone village," a cluster of privately owned Civil War–era stone houses that town legend says may have been part of the Underground Railroad. The pharmacy right next door to the inn has also been around since those days. There are numerous good bike routes in the area.

🏠 *27 double rooms and 3 singles with baths. Restaurant, TV in public area, 2 tennis courts. $160, MAP. MC, V. No smoking, no pets, 2-day minimum on foliage weekends. Closed Apr., 2 weeks in Nov.*

Inn at Sawmill Farm

Rte. 100, West Dover, VT 05356, tel. 802/464–8131, fax 802/464–1130

Staying at this aristocratic inn in the Haystack Mountain/Mt. Snow ski region is like being a guest at the country home of a British lord whose family fortune is still intact. The decor here may be country, but it's the kind of country featured in glossy home-and-garden magazines: There's a polished copper milk tank used as a table base, plaid carpet, a brick foyer decorated with a horse collar and farm tools, and chamber music piped into the low-ceilinged reception area. Guests like to congregate around the huge fireplace in the living room in winter with their afternoon tea, or stroll by one of the two ponds when it's warm.

In 1968 architect Rodney Williams and his wife, Ione, an interior designer, bought an old dairy farm that dated back to 1897, but don't expect a rugged rural retreat. The atmosphere is on the formal side—men must wear jackets in the public areas after 6 PM—and the owners cater to a select clientele.

Wallpaper in the guest rooms matches the bedspreads and upholstery; one room might be all soft pastels, another bright with vibrant hues. The carpet is thick enough to swallow high heels. The bed might be decorated with a tiny lace pillow, or a wall might display a framed quilt sample. The 10 cottages have larger rooms (some are suites) with working fireplaces.

The Williamses' son Brill, who is now the innkeeper, presides as chef in the two restaurants. One is a formal dining room with six tables, an antique sideboard, Early American portraits, Queen Anne furniture, and a baby grand piano. The second has a greenhouselike area and simple whitewashed timber pillars that contrast nicely with silver napkin rings. The menu features such entrées as roasted free-range chicken stuffed with shallots and mushrooms, lobster, and baby frogs' legs in Riesling sauce with truffles.

The Inn at Sawmill Farm is comparable to a city sophisticate who has retreated to the country—reserved, perhaps, but with impeccable taste.

🏠 *20 double rooms with baths. Restaurant, air-conditioning in some rooms, TV in public area, swimming pool, tennis court, 2 trout ponds. $320–$400, MAP. AE, MC, V. No smoking in dining room, no pets, 2-night minimum on weekends.*

Inn at Weathersfield

Rte. 106, Weathersfield, VT 05151, tel. 802/263–9217 or 800/477–4828, fax 802/263–9219

When Ron and Mary Louise's home in Thornburn, Ohio, was bought as part of a historic preservation project in 1979, they decided to move to New England and restore this rambling Colonial farmhouse, originally built in 1795. Visitors are greeted in the entry by hot apple cider simmering in an iron kettle over an open hearth. On Thanksgiving and Christmas, Mary Louise uses the hearth, its brick beehive oven, and antique utensils to cook dinner for the guests. Her authentic 18th-century recipes are only slightly modified for modern taste. She cooks on ordinary days as well, but then she sticks with more modern appliances; visitors often see her coming out of the kitchen dressed in her chef's whites. A former sales executive turned amateur entertainer, Ron provides dinner music on the dining room's grand piano, singing Cole Porter or Gershwin tunes with enthusiasm.

The nine rooms and three suites are each distinctly decorated, all with period antiques that complement the Colonial atmosphere; several rooms were renovated in 1994 and most have fireplaces. In the Otis Stearns Room, for instance, swaths of lace over the iron bedstead form a canopy anchored by a bouquet of dried flowers. A camelback trunk sits at the foot of a four-poster bed in one room, a stenciled Windsor chair and hardwood floors lend a simple grace to another. A bowl of nuts and apples in each room greets guests; Colonial spareness doesn't preclude such modern comforts as electric blankets and telephones in the rooms. Some bathrooms are on the small side and have 1940s-style fixtures, although one of the suites does have a two-person whirlpool. The inn has several gathering areas, including the tavern, library, formal parlor, and Willow Wood sunroom.

In the afternoon, a lavish English tea, complete with homemade pastries and hors d'oeuvres served from silver chafing dishes, is only a warm-up for Mary Louise's five-course dinner, which might include escargots, farm-raised partridge, and lemon-champagne sorbet. At breakfast, guests are often treated to a poetry reading by Harold Groat, an eighth-generation Vermonter.

▦ *9 double rooms with baths, 3 suites. Restaurant, sauna, exercise equipment, pool table, afternoon tea. $175–$225, MAP. $5 charge for use of fireplace. AE, D, MC, V. No smoking, no pets, 2-night minimum on most weekends, 3-night minimum on holiday weekends.*

Kedron Valley Inn

Rte. 106, Woodstock, VT 05071, tel. 802/457–1473, fax 802/457–4469

A strong sense of family strikes visitors as soon as they step into Max and Merrily Comins's inn; in 1985 they moved from New York and began the renovation of what in the 1840s had been the National Hotel, one of the state's oldest hotels. Mannequins in the entry hall wear the antique wedding dresses of Merrily and her grandmother, the couple's collection of family quilts is scattered throughout the inn, and framed antique linens deck the walls.

But the dresses and quilts are not the only reason for the inn's familial flavor. This is one of the rare antiques-filled inns that welcomes children, who are encouraged to build sand castles on the pond's small beach and make friends with Blondie, the dog, or Max, the cat, and the Comins' son, Drew. Many rooms have either a fireplace or a Franklin stove, and each is decorated with a quilt. Two rooms have private decks, another has a private veranda, and a fourth has a private terrace overlooking the stream that runs through the inn's 15 acres. Families often are housed in one of six units in a one-story log building at the back of the property, where

the rooms, lined up ski-lodge style, are more rustic than the rooms in the main inn. They're decorated in similar fashion, with a mix of antiques and reproductions.

Refugees from the Big City will find the country charm they're looking for in such features as the hand-stenciled walls, Franklin stoves and working fireplaces with pewter dishes on the mantels, and four-poster canopy beds with white chenille bedspreads and peony-patterned pastel sheets.

The dining room, where Max serves as host in the evenings, specializes in French dishes with a nouvelle twist, such as fillet of Norwegian salmon stuffed with herb seafood mousse, in puff pastry; or shrimp, scallops, and lobster with wild mushrooms, sautéed in shallots and white wine and served with Frangelico cream sauce.

The bustling town of Woodstock is nearby for strolling or shopping as is Kedron Valley Stables—an operation not affiliated with the inn—which offers trail rides and lessons.

▦ *27 double rooms with baths. Restaurant, lounge, ½-acre swimming/skating pond with sand beach, riding center. $120–$195, full breakfast; $160–$241, MAP. D, MC, V. 2-night minimum on weekends, mid-Sept.–late Oct., and Dec. 24–Jan. 1; 3-night minimum on holiday weekends. Closed Apr.*

Old Tavern at Grafton

Rte. 121, Grafton, VT 05146, tel. 802/843–2231 or 800/843–1801, fax 802/843–2245

The white-columned porches on both stories of the main building wrap around a structure that dates back to 1801 and has been an inn for most of that time. Today's guests can still take a look at the register that bears the signatures of such prominent visitors as Daniel Webster and Nathaniel Hawthorne. Despite its long and distinguished career, the inn hardly shows its age, largely because of the efforts of the Windham Foundation, which in 1963 began buying and restoring historic homes like this one in and around Grafton. Thanks to the foundation, visitors can now enjoy whiling away the hours in a perfectly preserved white-clapboard town that encourages creative idleness: strolling down to the stream that flows through the center of town; spending long mornings on the Old Tavern's porch watching a car go by every half hour or so; taking a horse-drawn carriage tour; or reading the notices posted on the bulletin board in front of the general store.

The main building has 14 rooms, the oldest just above the lobby. There are 22 rooms in the restored Windham and Homestead houses across the street, and seven rental cottages. The rooms in the main building evoke New England's 18th-century frontier days. Each is decorated with country antiques; some have crocheted canopies or four-poster beds that could easily be as old as the inn itself. The newer rooms are generally sunnier and sport bright pastels. There's a well-stocked library off the lobby, and the old barn in the back houses a comfortable tavern with authentic English pub furniture, where guests can partake of afternoon tea. Both spots have brick fireplaces that invite guests to linger long after dinner. Two dining rooms—one with Georgian furniture and oil portraits, the other with rustic paneling and low beams—serve traditional, hearty New England dishes, such as venison stew or grilled quail; some offerings feature cheddar cheese made just down the road at the Grafton Village Cheese Factory.

▦ *35 double rooms with baths. Restaurant, lounge, game room, TV in public area, swimming pond, platform tennis and tennis courts. $95–$165, Continental breakfast. AE, MC, V. Pets allowed in some buildings, 2-night minimum during foliage season, 3-night minimum on some holidays. Closed Apr., Dec. 24–25.*

Other Choices

Four Columns. West St., Box 278, Newfane, VT 05345, tel. 802/365–7713. 15 double rooms with baths. Restaurant, tavern, air-conditioning, TV in public area, swimming pool, hiking trails. $110–$175, full breakfast; $210–$275, MAP (mandatory during foliage season). AE, D, DC, MC, V. No smoking, no pets, 2-night minimum on weekends, 3-night minimum on holiday weekends.

Hermitage. Coldbrook Rd., Box 457, Wilmington, VT 05363, tel. 802/464–3511. 29 double rooms with baths, 4 doubles share 2 baths. Restaurant, TV in common area, fireplaces, 3 common rooms, phones, sauna, swimming pool, tennis court, cross-country ski center and trails, sporting clays. $225, MAP; B&B rates available. AE, DC, MC, V. No pets, 2-night minimum on most weekends.

Hickory Ridge House. Hickory Ridge Rd., R.D. 3, Box 1410, Putney, VT 05346, tel. 802/387–5709. 3 double rooms with baths, 4 doubles share 3 baths. TV in public area. $50–$90, full breakfast. MC, V. No smoking, no pets, 2-night minimum on holiday weekends.

Juniper Hill Inn. Juniper Hill Rd., Box 79, Windsor, VT 05089-9703, tel. 802/674–5273 or 800/359–2541. 16 double rooms with baths. Restaurant, TV in public area, pool, ceiling fans, hiking trails nearby. $90–$140, full breakfast. D, MC, V. No smoking, no pets. Closed Apr., 2 weeks in Nov.

Parker House. 16 Main St., Box 0780, Quechee, VT 05059, tel. 802/295–6077. 7 double rooms with baths. Restaurant, air-conditioning, TV in public area. $100–$125, full breakfast. AE, MC, V. No pets, 2-night minimum during foliage season, graduation, Christmas, and holidays. Closed Mar. and 2 weeks in Nov.

Whetstone Inn. South Rd., Marlboro, VT 05344, tel. 802/254–2500. 8 double rooms with baths, 4 doubles share 1 bath. Restaurant, fireplaces in living and dining rooms, kitchenettes in 3 rooms, skating pond. $55–$95, breakfast extra. No credit cards. No smoking in public areas, 1-week minimum July–Aug. during music festival, 3-night minimum on holiday weekends.

Windham Hill Inn. Windham Hill Rd., West Townshend, VT 05359, tel. 802/874–4080 or 800/944–4080, fax 802/874–4702. 18 double rooms with baths. Restaurant, fireplaces in 9 rooms, whirlpool bath, skating pond, cross-country ski trails. $175–$245, MAP. AE, D, MC, V. No smoking, no pets. Closed Apr.–mid-May.

Reservations Services

Manchester Lodging Referral Service (tel. 802/824–6915). **Vermont Bed & Breakfast** (Box 1, East Fairfield, VT 05448, tel. 802/827–3827).

Southwestern Vermont

Arlington Inn

Rte. 7A, Arlington, VT 05250, tel. 802/375–6532 or 800/443–9442

The Greek Revival columns at the entrance to this carefully restored railroad magnate's home give the building an imposing presence. The rooms, however, are anything but intimidating. Their cozy charm is created by clawfoot tubs in some bathrooms, linens that coordinate with the Victorian-style wallpaper, and the original moldings and wainscoting. The main section of the inn was built in 1848 by Martin Chester Deming, and rooms here are named after members of his family. The decor features Victorian antiques, massive headboards that tower over sleepers, and etched-glass shades on curving bronze Victorian oil lamps. The carriage house, built at the turn of the century and renovated in 1985, blends country

French and Queen Anne period furnishings with folk art. The inn is separated from the road by a spacious lawn, so all guest rooms are fairly quiet.

New innkeepers Deborah and Mark Gagnon traded their life in the financial world (he was in banking, she is a CPA), for this quiet New England town in 1994. While emphasizing the mansion's gracious social and historical significance, they have upgraded the rooms with such modern conveniences as queen- and king-size beds; rooms in the carriage house have become more inviting with their new overstuffed chairs. Their efforts are also commendable in the dining room, where they strive to uphold the inn's reputation of having one of the best restaurants in the region. In addition to using local products from Vermont farms whenever possible, such as buffalo raised right in Arlington and pheasant from Dorset, the chef also prepares raised game, including antelope from Texas. Polished hardwood floors, green napkins and walls, candlelight, and soft music complement the elegant food. The Gagnons put on a full country breakfast, which is served in a solarium at the back of the inn.

Arlington is Norman Rockwell country—the faces in many of his illustrations are those of Arlington townfolk—and the inn is within walking distance of a small exhibit devoted to his work.

🏠 *16 double rooms with baths, 3 cottages. Restaurant, lounge, air-conditioning, TV/VCR in public area, fireplaces in public areas and 9 guest rooms, tennis court. $70–$160, full breakfast. AE, D, MC, V. No pets, 2-night minimum on weekends. Restaurant closed Christmas Eve, New Year's Day.*

1811 House

Rte. 7A, Manchester, VT 05254, tel. 802/362–1811 or 800/432–1811

Parts of this rambling inn date from 1770, and when one walks through the door into the low-ceilinged entryway, the first impression gathered is of entering a typical Colonial building. The experience of staying here, however, is more like visiting an elegant English country home, without having to pay the transatlantic airfare. The inn's genteel air is in keeping with Manchester's traditional role as a summer getaway for the rich. This hostelry has been in operation since 1811 (the only break in service was when it was owned by Abraham Lincoln's granddaughter). The current owners are James and Elaine Nelson-Parker.

The decor is basically Federal with a relaxed touch. A veritable stable of horse paintings give a distinctly Windsoresque atmosphere to many of the public rooms, and the Waterford crystal, stenciled floral borders along the ceilings, and ornately carved chairs in the dining room all contribute to an inn worthy of a British princess. The pub-style bar (open only to guests) is suitably dark and cozy, decorated with horse brasses and exposed rafters, and boasts the largest collection of single malt scotches in Vermont.

English floral landscaping, extensive gardens, terraces, and a pond all decorate the 7½ acres surrounding the inn. Both public and guest rooms contain elegant English and American antiques from the family's own collection; six guest rooms have working fireplaces, and many are quite spacious. Some bathrooms in the main inn are a bit old-fashioned but serviceable; the ones in the three cottages are the most modern. The Robinson Room has a marble-enclosed tub, not to mention a terrific view of the lawn from its own porch. The Mary Lincoln Isham Room has a canopy bed covered with white chenille and matching floral wallpaper and drapes.

Breakfast is often in the hearty English tradition, with potatoes, mushrooms, bacon and eggs, and scones.

▦ *14 double rooms with baths, 3 cottages. Lounge, air-conditioning. $160–$200, full breakfast. AE, MC, V. No smoking, no pets, 2-night minimum on weekends and holidays and during foliage season.*

West Mountain Inn

River Rd., off Rte. 313, Arlington, VT 05250, tel. 802/375–6516

Everywhere you turn at the West Mountain Inn are reminders of owners Wes and Mary Ann Carlson's idiosyncratic enthusiasms. Just for starters, take the llama ranch on the property, which started as a hobby. The small African violets in the rooms, which guests are invited to take home with them, come with instructions for care. The white Adirondack chairs on the front lawn are perfect for contemplating a spectacular view of the surrounding countryside, and in winter the sloping lawn practically cries for a sled.

All of which is to say that the Carlsons, both former educators, have created a place that has the feeling of being a world apart; that's part of what lured movie stars Michael J. Fox and Tracy Pollan to get married here (Wes still tells stories about tabloid reporters' efforts to bribe employees). This 1840s farmhouse, restored over the past 13 years, sits on 150 secluded acres where squirrels come up and feed outside guests' windows. Plush carpet, quilted bedspreads, chocolate llamas on the bedside stands, and copies of the books of local author Dorothy Canfield Fisher lend an air of simple, comfortable luxury to the guest rooms. Rooms 2, 3, and 4 in the front of the house afford the same panorama as the front lawn (though there are almost no bad views in the place); the three small nooks of Room 11 resemble railroad sleeper berths and are perfect for children.

At happy hour, guests gather in the library to nibble on complimentary hors d'oeuvres, such as chicken fingers and fruit, and get acquainted before moving into the low-beamed, paneled, candlelighted dining room. The menu offers hearty New England specialties with interesting little twists, such as veal tenderloin topped with sun-dried tomatoes and Asiago cheese. Aunt Min's Swedish rye and other flavorful breads, as well as desserts, are made on the premises. Tables by the windows offer a splendid view of the mountains, which goes a long way to promote inner peace.

▦ *13 double rooms with baths. Restaurant, library/pub, bar, air-conditioning in dining room, TV and phones in public area, fireplaces in 4 rooms, trail maps in rooms, walking and cross-country ski trails. $155–$180, MAP. AE, D, MC, V. Smoking in pub only, no pets, 2-night minimum on weekends.*

Other Choices

Battenkill Inn. Box 948, Manchester Village, VT 05254, tel. 802/362–4213 or 800/441–1628. 11 double rooms with baths. Air-conditioning, fireplaces in common areas and some rooms. $85–$150, full breakfast. AE, MC, V. No smoking, no pets.

Hill Farm Inn. R.R. 2 (just off Rte. 7), Box 2015, Arlington, VT 05250, tel. 802/375–2269 or 800/882–2545. 6 double rooms with baths, 5 doubles share 3 baths, 2 suites, 4 cabins (in summer only), 1 suite. Restaurant, TV and fireplaces in public area. $70–$160, full breakfast. AE, D, MC, V. Restricted smoking, 2-night minimum on most weekends, 3-night minimum on holiday weekends.

Inn at Westview Farm. Rte. 30, Dorset, VT 05251, tel. 802/867–5715. 9 double rooms with baths, 1 suite. Restaurant, tavern, air-conditioning, TV in public area and suite, Rumford fireplace, terrace. $85–$140, full breakfast; $155–$205, MAP. AE, MC, V. No pets, 2-night minimum on holiday weekends.

Closed late Mar.–late Apr., late Oct.–mid-Nov.

Molly Stark Inn. 1067 E. Main St., Bennington, VT 05201, tel. 802/442–9631 or 800/356–3076. 6 rooms with baths, 1 cottage. Ceiling fans, wood-burning stove and TV in public area, air-conditioning in some rooms. $75–$150, full breakfast. AE, D, MC, V. No smoking, no pets, 2-night minimum on weekends June–Oct. and holidays.

Reluctant Panther. West Rd., Box 678, Manchester, VT 05254, tel. 802/362–2568 or 800/822–2331, fax 802/362–2586. 16 double rooms with baths. Restaurant, lounge, air-conditioning, phones, cable TVs. $138–$325, MAP. AE, MC, V. No smoking, no pets.

South Shire Inn. 124 Elm St., Bennington, VT 05201, tel. 802/447–3839, fax 802/442–3547. 9 double rooms with baths. Air-conditioning, TV in public area, fireplaces and whirlpool baths in some rooms. $95–$145, full breakfast. AE, MC, V. No smoking, no pets.

Wilburton Inn. River Rd., Manchester, VT 05254, tel. 802/362–2500 or 800/648–4944. 34 double rooms with baths. Restaurant, air-conditioning, TV in some rooms and in lobby, pool, 3 tennis courts. $95–$195, full breakfast and afternoon tea. AE, MC, V. No smoking, no pets, 2-night minimum on holidays.

Reservations Services

Bennington Area Chamber of Commerce (Veterans Memorial Dr., Bennington, VT 05201, tel. 802/447–3311). **Chamber of Commerce-Manchester and the Mountains** (Adams Park Green, Box 928, Manchester, VT 05255, tel. 802/362–2100). **Vermont Bed and Breakfast** (Box 1, East Fairfield, VT 05448, tel. 802/827–3827).

Northern Vermont

Inn at Montpelier

*147 Main St., Montpelier, VT 05602, tel.
802/223-2727, fax 802/223-0722*

Until 1988, if you had wanted to stay in
the state capital, you had your choice of
large chain hotels or small motels. But
then came Maureen and Bill Russell,
who decided to renovate a spacious yellow Federal brick house only a short
walk from the center of town. The inn,
built in 1828, was designed with the
business traveler in mind, but the
architectural details, the antique four-
poster beds and Windsor chairs, and
the piped-in classical music also attract
visitors whose most pressing business
in town is deciding how late to sleep.
The formal sitting room, with a large
marble fireplace, cream-color woodwork, and stately tapestry-upholstered
wing chairs, has an elegant Federal feel
to it, as though the original owners
were about to glide down the polished
staircase in rustling taffeta and black
knee breeches. The wide wraparound
Colonial Revival porch, with its octagonal corner section, is especially conducive to relaxing, and is one of the
inn's most notable features.

The guest rooms in the frame building
across the driveway are just as elegant
as the ones in the main inn, and there
are small pantries in each building
where guests can prepare coffee, store
food, and find snacks for late-night nibbling. The smallest rooms are in the
main inn. All the rooms are done in a
mix of antique and reproduction furniture, with rich floral decorator fabrics.
Maureen's Room has a private sundeck,
others have separate sitting rooms, and
many of the walls are hung with original art.

The soft rose-color decor and a marble
fireplace contribute to an elegant dining

room where inspired, skillfully prepared fare is served; some people in the
area drive an hour to experience the
delicate flavors and superior attention
to detail at the inn's restaurant. Specialties include truffled chicken sausage
served over hand-rolled fettuccine; a
shiitake, portabella, and cremini mushroom tart; roasted loin of venison with
dried cranberries, chestnuts, and a
Madeira sauce; and Vermont rabbit
served with red peppers, sun-dried
tomatoes, and a champagne-butter
sauce.

As a destination, Montpelier has much
to recommend it; it's centrally located
for exploring the state's rural northern
section. Guests of the inn can walk the
few short blocks to the state capitol
with its vest pocket–size legislative
chambers or the Vermont Museum
next door, which contains artifacts of
early Vermont life. Despite the inn's
proximity to town—it's in Montpelier's
National Historic District—it is nestled on a quiet street and is quite tranquil. The moral of the story: This inn is
a relatively undiscovered gem.

▥ *19 double rooms with baths. Air-
conditioning, TVs, phones, fireplaces
in 6 bedrooms, 2 shared kitchenette
areas, 2 large and 2 small meeting
rooms, restaurant. $99–$169, full
breakfast. AE, D, DC, MC, V. No pets.*

Inn at the Round Barn Farm

*E. Warren Rd., R.R. 1, Box 247, Waits-
field, VT 05673, tel. 802/496-2276*

Wedding parties have replaced cows in
the big round barn here, but the
Shaker-style building still dominates
the farm's 85 acres of quiet countryside.
The process of restoring the 1910 12-
sided barn involved jacking up the
entire structure and putting in a new
foundation. The result is one of the 12
remaining round (at least dodecagonal)
barns in the state; it's used for summer
concerts, weddings, and parties and is

on the National Register of Historic Places.

The inn's rooms are not in the barn but in the 1806 farmhouse, where books line the walls of the cream-color library, and breakfast is served in a cheerful solarium that overlooks a small landscaped pond and rolling acreage. The florist's touch is evident in the abundance of fresh flowers scattered throughout the inn, and the collection of pig memorabilia. The rooms are plush with eyelet-trimmed sheets, new quilts on four-poster beds, brass wall lamps for easy bedtime reading, and floral drapes that match the wallpaper. Two of the larger rooms have whirlpool tubs and the three most recently renovated rooms in the north wing of the house have fireplaces, but many guests ask for the Palmer Room, which has a bed with a carved headboard of burled mahogany, a marble-top nightstand, and a spectacular view. Anne Marie DeFreest does the cooking at breakfast—her favorites appear to be French toast or cottage-cheese pancakes with a maple-raspberry sauce.

The inn is only a short drive to either Waitsfield or Warren, two low-key towns well-equipped for outdoor activities; skiing, good bike routes, sleigh and carriage rides, hiking, and canoeing opportunities abound. Your hosts are Shari-Lynn and Chris Williams.

▥ *11 double rooms with baths. TV in public area, fireplaces and whirlpools in some rooms, swimming pool. $115– $195, full breakfast. AE, MC, V. No smoking, no pets.*

Inn on the Common

N. Main St., Craftsbury Common, VT 05827, tel. 802/586-9619 or 800/521- 2233, fax 802/586-2249

If you're looking for a serious getaway, you can't get much farther away than Vermont's Northeast Kingdom. The rolling farmland has an out-of-time quality that gives a glimpse of the way most of the state used to be: The area's sheer distance from civilization and its rugged weather have kept most of the state's development farther south. When Penny and Michael Schmitt decided in 1973 to leave New York's Fifth Avenue and investment banking behind to renovate the early 19th-century Federal building, they spared no expense; that means that behind the white picket fence are Scalamandré reproductions of historic wallpapers, Crabtree and Evelyn toiletries, thick plush carpets, and a 250-label collection of vintage wines.

One of the inn's three white clapboard buildings is directly on the common; the other two, the main building and the south annex, are just off it. Each building has no more than six rooms, so the feeling is intimate. Families often are housed in the south annex, which has a kitchenette with a microwave and refrigerator and a VCR with a large selection of films. Though each room is different (some are on the small side), all are beautifully detailed, with quilts on the beds, swag draperies with trim that coordinates with the wallpaper, bathrobes in the closets, and flowered champagne glasses at the ready. Dinner is served only to inn guests at communal tables, and Penny and Michael greet guests beforehand for hors d'oeuvres and cocktails.

Breakfast, which might include bacon, muffins, pancakes, and French toast, is served overlooking the rose garden in summer. Afterward, guests may visit the 140-acre Craftsbury sports center nearby, where, in addition to facilities for cross-country skiing in winter and water sports in summer, they find a staff of naturalists eager to offer information on local wildlife.

This is one of the most highly regarded inns in the state, and may be booked as much as a year in advance for peak seasons. But if you can get there and get a room, it's well worth it.

🏨 *16 double rooms with baths, 1 suite. TV/VCR and fireplace in living room, fireplace or wood stove in 5 bedrooms, swimming pool, tennis court. $220–$270, MAP. MC, V. No smoking in dining room, 2-day minimum on foliage and holiday weekends, 3-day minimum Christmas–New Year season.*

Rabbit Hill Inn

Rte. 18, Lower Waterford, VT 05848, tel. 802/748-5168 or 800/76-BUNNY

When the door swings open and you are welcomed—often by name—into a warmth that will melt away even the most stressful of journeys, you'll know you've found the place. The Rabbit Hill Inn, on 15 wooded acres, has been receiving guests since its days as a stagecoach stop on the route between Montreal and Portland, Maine, 200 years ago, and innkeepers John and Maureen Magee are dedicated to upholding its long-standing tradition of gracious hospitality. Maureen's knack for details and talent for bestowing just the right amount of attention on her guests somehow enables her to lure people into refocusing their priorities—at least for the time being.

The Magees' obvious fondness for the gentility of days past is expressed in the formal, Federal-period parlor where mulled cider from the fireplace crane is served on chilly afternoons. The low wooden beams and cozy warmth of the Irish-style pub right next door, where John tends bar and shares his knowledge of the area, create a comfortable contrast that is carried throughout the rest of the inn. The individually decorated rooms are as stylistically different as they are consistently indulgent: The Loft, with its 8-foot Palladian window, king canopy bed, double whirlpool bath, and corner fireplace, is one of the most requested; the abundant windows, Victrola, and working pump organ with period sheet music make the Music Chamber another favorite. Rooms toward the front of the inn get views of the Connecticut River and the White Mountains in New Hampshire. Rooms in the Carriage House, although more private, tend to be smaller and less lush—particularly the downstairs section, but they will eventually be renovated to be on a par with the rest of the inn.

In the elegant dining room chef Russell Stannard prepares an eclectic, regional cuisine that might include grilled sausage of Vermont pheasant with pistachios, or smoked chicken and red lentil dumplings nestled in red pepper linguine. The bountiful country breakfast begins with a buffet overflowing with home-baked coffee cakes and muffins, quiches, and fresh fruits.

🏨 *21 double rooms with baths, 7 suites. Restaurant, pub, TV in public area, whirlpools in some rooms, fireplaces in many rooms, walking/cross-country ski trails on property, canoes. $189–$259, MAP. AE, MC, V. No smoking, no pets, 3-night minimum stay Christmastime and holiday weekends. Closed Apr. and 1st 3 weeks in Nov.*

Swift House Inn

25 Stewart La., Middlebury, VT 05753, tel. 802/388-9925, fax 802/388-9927

Andrea and John Nelson didn't exactly intend to open an inn when they did; they were looking at inns with the idea of buying something in 10 years, after John retired from IBM's finance department. But on the way to the airport to go home to New Jersey one day in 1985, they stopped by the big white Federal home set atop a sweeping expanse of lawn, and their decision was made. Since then they've made the Swift House Inn one of the most elegant in the state—the kind of place that gives new meaning to the line about having a silver spoon in one's mouth.

The patrician air here is no coincidence; the inn was the private home of two of Middlebury's most prominent families:

the Swifts, who built the oldest section of the house in 1814, and the Stewarts, one of whom married the grandson of the original owner and lived in the home until 1943. As a result of the long private ownership, elegant Gilded Age detailing has been well preserved. The richly ornamented cherry paneling and trim glow in the dining room, where the bright purple and green grape–clustered wallpaper is an exact reproduction of the pattern installed in 1905. Rooms have the same luxurious feel. The Emma Willard Swift Room not only has a private porch but also retains the built-in brass wall phone Mrs. Swift installed so she could listen to church services. White eyelet-trimmed sheets, gathered lace curtains at the windows, floral chintz draperies that match a wing chair, a fresh carnation in a bedside bud vase—the attention to detail gives the impression that this is still an affluent family's private home.

The carriage house was converted in 1990 and is recommended for families, although the more-than-spacious rooms and the enormous new bathrooms with whirlpool baths would lure any guest looking for luxury. One of the rooms has French doors that open onto its own patio. Rooms in the gatehouse are closer to the road and therefore a bit noisier. In the dining room, an attentive staff serves an adventurous menu that might include angel-hair pasta with imported mushrooms in macadamia pesto sauce, or smoked pheasant salad with vinaigrette.

🏠 *21 double rooms with baths. Phones, restaurant, air-conditioning, TV in public area, fireplaces in common areas and in some rooms, sauna, steam room, conference room. $90–$165, Continental breakfast; MAP rates available. AE, MC, V. No pets. Restaurant closed Tues.–Wed.*

Other Choices

Beaver Pond Farm Inn. R.D. Box 306, Golf Course Rd., Warren, VT 05674, tel. 802/583–2861. 4 double rooms with baths, 2 double rooms share 1 bath. Golf, hiking, ski trails. $40–$60, full breakfast. MC, V. No smoking, no pets.

Black Lantern Inn. Rte. 118, Montgomery Village, VT 05470, tel. 802/326–4507 or 800/255–8661. 10 double rooms with baths, 6 suites. Restaurant, TV/VCRs in some rooms, fireplaces in 6 suites, whirlpools in suites. $75–$125, full breakfast; MAP rates available. AE, D, MC, V. No pets.

Edson Hill Manor. Edson Hill Rd., Stowe, VT 05672, tel. 802/253–7371 or 800/621–0284. 25 double rooms with baths. Restaurant, fireplaces in 22 rooms, pool, stables, pond. $100–$160, MAP. AE, D, MC, V. No pets, 5-night minimum at Christmastime, 3-night minimum Presidents' Day weekend.

Fox Hall Inn. Rte. 16, Barton, VT 05822, tel. 802/525–6930. 4 double rooms with baths, 4 double rooms share 3 baths. 2 fireplaces in public areas, hiking and cross-country ski trails, canoes. $60–$90, full breakfast and afternoon snacks. MC, V. No smoking, no pets, 2-night minimum during fall foliage.

Gables Inn. 1457 Mountain Rd., Stowe, VT 05672, tel. 802/253–7730 or 800/422–5371. 17 double rooms with baths, 2 suites. Restaurant, air-conditioning and TV in some rooms, TV in public area, fireplace in living room, pool, hot tub. $75–$150, mid-Apr.–mid-Dec.; $120–$240. AE, MC, V. No smoking, no pets.

Green Trails Inn. Main St., Brookfield, VT 05036, tel. 802/276–3412 or 800/243–3412. 14 double rooms (8 with private baths, 6 share 3 baths). $75–$125, full breakfast; MAP rates available in winter. MC, V. No smoking, no pets.

Lareau Farm Country Inn. Route 100, Box 563, Waitsfield, VT 05673, tel.

802/496–4949. 11 double rooms with baths, 2 double rooms share 1 bath. Whirlpool bath in 1 room, fireplace and TV in sitting room, swimming, sleigh rides. $75–$100, full breakfast. D, MC, V. No smoking, no pets.

Waybury Inn. Rte. 125, East Middlebury, VT 05640, tel. 802/388–4015 or 800/348–1810. 14 double rooms with baths. Restaurant, pub, TV in public area, ceiling fans. $80–$115, full breakfast. D, MC, V.

Wildflower Inn. Darling Hill Rd., Lyndonville, VT 05851, tel. 802/626–8310 or 800/627–8310. 12 double rooms with baths, 10 suites. Game room, children's playroom, outdoor pool, hot tub, sauna, cross-country ski trails, sleigh rides, skating and fishing pond, tennis court, petting barn. $89–$220, full breakfast.

MC, V. 2-night minimum on weekends. Closed Apr. and Nov.

Ye Olde England Inn. 433 Mountain Rd., Stowe, VT 05672, tel. 802/253–7558 or 800/477–3771, fax 802/253–8944. 17 double rooms with baths, 9 suites, 3 cottages. Restaurant, pub, air-conditioning, TVs, fireplaces, and whirlpools in some rooms; swimming pool. $115–$295, full breakfast. AE, MC, V. 2-night minimum on weekends.

Reservations Services

Stowe Area Association (Box 1230, Stowe, VT 05672, tel. 800/247–8693). **Sugarbush Lodging** (tel. 800/537–3333). **Vermont Bed and Breakfast** (Box 1, East Fairfield, VT 05448, tel. 802/827–3827).

Virginia

North Bend Plantation

Northern Virginia

Ashby Inn & Restaurant

692 Federal St., Paris, VA 22130, tel. 540/592-3900, fax 540/592-3781

West of Middleburg and Upperville along U.S. 50, the turnoff for minuscule Paris may surprise unwary motorists; half the travelers looking for this hamlet in a hollow below the road probably miss it completely and end up crossing Ashby Gap or the Shenandoah River. At the Ashby's restaurant, visitors are treated to some of rural Virginia's most sophisticated food, masterminded by innkeepers Roma and John Sherman. The menu changes seasonally; crab cakes and New England mussel chowder with pumpkin-smoked bacon and spicy oil reign as favorites. Dinner runs about $70 for two.

Perhaps the only danger in staying at the inn is that dinners leave many guests too blissfully comatose to appreciate their rooms. There are six in the main building, all furnished with a spareness that is a calming contrast to the rich food. Quilts, blanket chests, rag rugs, and the occasional cannonball bed set the country tone, though in every case, the views are the chief enhancement. As morning light shines through the windows, some guests may feast anew upon the garden, Blue Ridge foothills, lowing cows, and other pastoral delights. The coveted Fan Room has two skylights and a glorious fan window opening onto a balcony.

The four expansive rooms in Paris's former one-room schoolhouse are top-of-the-line and excellent values. Each has a private porch that opens onto those splendid countryside views. The Glascock Room has deep red walls, a canopied four-poster bed, and an antique trunk with extra towels. Oriental rugs cover the hardwood floors, and there are two sinks in the large bathroom. Two wing chairs facing the fireplace and a window seat are inviting places for curling up with a book.

Roma, an avid equestrian, and John are generally too busy during dinner to chat, but at breakfast—featuring fresh eggs cooked to order and succulent muffins—guests might get to know their hosts. Roma left advertising for innkeeping, and John, once a House Ways and Means Committee staffer, still writes speeches for politicians and CEOs between stints as the Ashby Inn's maître d'.

🏨 *8 double rooms with baths, 2 doubles with sinks share 1½ baths. Restaurant, air-conditioning; TVs, phones, and fireplaces in schoolhouse rooms. $100–$220, full breakfast. MC, V. Restricted smoking, no pets. Closed Jan. 1, July 4, Dec. 25.*

Inn at Little Washington

309 Middle St., Washington, VA 22747, tel. 540/675–3800, fax 540/675–3100

In 1978, in a village of 160, an hour and a half west of (Big) Washington, D.C., in the eastern foothills of the Blue Ridge, master chef Patrick O'Connell and his partner, Reinhardt Lynch, opened a restaurant that grew into a legend, attracting guests from all over the world. From the outside, the three-story white-frame building looks like any other quiet southern hotel; only the Chinese Chippendale balustrade on the second-floor porch suggests the decorative fantasy within. The rich interior is the work of British designer Joyce Conwy-Evans, who has designed theatrical sets and rooms in English royal houses. The settees in the inn bear as many as 13 elegantly mismatched pillows each; the garden, with crab-apple trees, fountain, and fishpond, cries out to be used as a stage backdrop. One bedroom has a bed with a bold plaid spread, shaded by a floral-print half-canopy—and, amazingly, the mélange works. In the slate-floor dining room with William Morris wallpaper, a fabric-swathed ceiling makes guests feel like pashas romantically sequestered in a tent. (A room and a suite in the Guest House, across the street, are good for two couples traveling together, but they lack the sumptuousness of the main building.)

Chef O'Connell's food appears to have cast a spell over almost all of those who have sampled it, as the abundant positive reviews testify. Now, with plans to expand the kitchen, the pro-prietors seem intent on adding to the ranks of the bewitched. The menu, which changes nightly, makes compelling reading itself, and the six-course dinner costs $98 per person on Saturday, $88 Friday, and $78 Sunday and weekdays, not including wine and drinks. Some rare vintages rest in the 10,000-bottle cellar.

Breakfast, served overlooking the courtyard garden, is far above the usual Continental fare. Miniature pastries and muffins are tucked in a basket alongside tasty croissants; raspberries glisten in large goblets. Those not still sated from dinner can order, at extra cost, a full breakfast—a lobster omelet with rainbow salsa and a bourbon-pecan waffle.

Clearly the inn, with its staff of 50, is a place for indulgence, and anyone unwilling to succumb to it—both psychologically and financially—should opt for humbler digs. But the waiting list alone suggests there are plenty of hedonists out there.

🏨 *9 double rooms with baths, 3 suites. Air-conditioning, phones, robes; room service, turndown service, whirlpool baths and separate double showers in suites, fireplace in entrance lobby; bicycles. $270–$675; Continental breakfast, afternoon tea. MC, V. No smoking in dining room, no pets. Closed Dec. 25 and Tues. except in May and Oct.*

L'Auberge Provençale

Rte. 340 (Box 119), White Post, VA 22663, tel. 540/837–1375 or 800/638–1702, fax 540/837–2004

Fourth-generation chef Alain Borel and his wife, Celeste, have brought the romance, personal touches, and fine dining of a French country inn to tiny White Post, an hour and a half west of the Beltway. The 1753 stone house is set on 8½ acres and is surrounded by rolling pastureland. Inside are the Borels' special accents: Alain's great-grandmother's copper pots in the dining room, provincial prints in the guest rooms, whimsical carved carousel animals, painted tiles, and art by Picasso, Buffet, and Dufy.

Visitors might be advised not to fill up on the plate of fresh fruit, chocolate, and homemade cookies that welcomes them to their rooms, saving their appetites instead for the five-course dinner ($38–$55). The meal may commence with tempura-style shrimp and saffron sauce or fried plantains, continue with Bahamian conch chowder, then culminate with rack of lamb and black beans, roasted garlic, and rosemary or pompano in parchment and citrus with papaya and tarragon. Celeste, who handles the wine, has assembled a 250-selection list, plus the Captain's List, with rare vintages for the connoisseur. Breakfast in the sunny, bay-windowed, peach-colored dining room starts with a mix of tangerine and orange juice and is followed by such delicacies as fresh fruit, rich croissants, poached egg in phyllo cups, applewood smoked bacon, and house-cured smoked salmon.

For guests who request it, a bit of Borel magic can accompany them in the form of a picnic basket (tablecloth, fruit, cheese, sandwiches, salads, chocolates, and wine) to be savored in some nook along Skyline Drive or at one of the local wineries. Alain's particularity extends to his gardens, where he fusses over herbs and vegetables grown from seeds imported from France or one of the 54 fruit trees, including such exotics as Asian pears, persimmons, and kiwis.

Celeste is as deft a decorator as she is a wine selector. The three rooms in the new wing are furnished with the fabrics and colors of Provence, accented by hand-painted Spanish tiles; they have fireplaces and private entrances opening onto the gardens. Room 9, the Chambre des Amis, features a canopy bed, cheery yellow and blue prints, and windows facing two directions. For lazy hours with a book or for just viewing the countryside, the large private deck off Room 7 in the main house is perfect.

🏨 *8 double rooms with baths, 3 suites. Restaurant, air-conditioning, TV in suite, phone jacks in 3 rooms, fireplaces in 5 rooms, living room, and dining room. $125–$250, full breakfast. AE, D, DC, MC, V. No pets, no children under 10. Restaurant closed Mon.– Tues., inn closed Dec. 25–Jan.*

Morrison House

116 S. Alfred St., Alexandria, VA 22314, tel. 703/838–8000 or 800/367–0800, fax 703/684–6283

Under new ownership since early 1996, the inn, led by managing partner Peter Greenberg, retains the charm instilled by its previous proprietors, whose name it still bears. Most visitors continue to assume that the handsome property, with its reddish brown brick laid in a Flemish bond, white-pillared portico and double-hung windows, is another of the renovated Federal structures that abound in Alexandria. But the five-story Morrison House was built in 1985, under the watchful eye of a curator from the Smithsonian.

All guest rooms are different but have the Federal look about them, with camelback sofas, Chippendale-style chairs, swagged draperies, and a few decorative fireplaces. Still prominent, too, is the Morrisons' handiwork, which includes the customized armoires, with TVs, drawers, and room for hanging clothes. Little luxuries abound, including Italian marble bathrooms with scales and lighted, magnifying makeup mirrors, big towels, and double sinks in most rooms.

The pastel-colored Elysium, the hotel's restaurant, features American cuisine with some American twists. There's also seating in the more casual Elysium Grill, with its cherrywood floors, red-leather chairs, and, on several evenings, piano entertainment.

The Morrison House is a six-block walk from the Metro station, making a jaunt to D.C. just minutes away. Guests can ramble through the shops and galleries of Old Town Alexandria, or they can just unwind here, savoring the inn's tranquillity and polished service. (There is 24-hour room service and concierge, and a multilingual reception staff.)

🖼 *42 double rooms with baths, 3 suites. Restaurant, air-conditioning, cable TV and phone in rooms, robes, turndown service; fireplace in parlor. $150–$295. AE, DC, MC, V. Smoking on 1 floor and in Elysium Grill only, no pets.*

Other Choices

Bailiwick Inn. 4023 Chain Bridge Rd., Fairfax, VA 22030, tel. 703/691–2266 or 800/366–7666, fax 703/934–2112. 13 double rooms with baths, 1 suite. Restaurant, air-conditioning, phone jacks; fireplaces in parlors and 4 rooms, turndown service, whirlpool baths in 2 rooms, TV in sitting room. $130–$295; full breakfast, afternoon tea. AE, MC, V. No smoking, no pets.

Bleu Rock Inn. 12567 Lee Hwy., Washington, VA 22747, tel. 540/987–3190 or 800/537–3652, fax 540/987–3193. 5 double rooms with baths. Restaurant, air-conditioning, fireplaces in dining rooms and lounge, turndown service. $125–$150, Continental or full breakfast. AE, MC, V. No smoking in dining rooms, no pets. Closed Mon.–Tues. and Dec. 24–25.

Norris House Inn. 108 Loudoun St. SW, Leesburg, VA 20175, tel. 703/777–1806 or 800/644–1806, fax 703/771–8051. 6 double rooms share 3 baths. Air-conditioning, phone jacks, robes; fireplace in 3 rooms, turndown service. $75–$140; full breakfast, evening refreshments. AE, D, DC, MC, V. Restricted smoking, no pets, 2-night minimum Apr.–May and Sept.–Oct. weekends.

Pink House. 40174 Main St., Waterford, VA 22190, tel. 540/882–3453, fax 540/882–3559. 2 suites. Air-conditioning, phone jack in suites; private outdoor sitting areas. $100, full breakfast. No credit cards.

Richard Johnston Inn. 711 Caroline St., Fredericksburg, VA 22401, tel. and fax 540/899–7606. 7 double rooms with baths, 2 suites. Air-conditioning, cable TV in living room and 3 rooms. $90–$130, Continental breakfast. AE, DC, MC, V. No smoking, no pets.

Sycamore Hill. Rte. 1 (Box 978), Washington, VA 22747, tel. 540/675–3046. 3 double rooms with baths. Air-conditioning, TV in living room and 1 room, fireplace in living room, turndown service. $110–$150; full breakfast, afternoon refreshments. MC, V. No smoking, no pets, 2-night minimum holiday and May weekends and Oct.

Welbourne. Welbourne Rd. (Rte. 1, Box 300), Middleburg, VA 22117, tel. 540/687–3201. 5 double rooms with baths, 3 cottages. Air-conditioning; TV in living room, fireplaces in 4 rooms and 2 cottages. $88–$100; full breakfast, evening cocktails. No credit cards. No cigars, no cats, 2-night minimum spring, fall, and holiday weekends.

Reservations Services

Blue Ridge Bed & Breakfast Reservation Service (Rocks & Rills Farm, Rte. 2, Box 3895, Berryville, VA 22611, tel. 540/955–1246). **Princely Bed & Breakfast Reservation Service** (819 Prince St., Alexandria, VA 22314, tel. 703/683–2159). For a copy of the **Bed and Breakfast Association of Virginia's directory,** describing more than 100 establishments, call the Virginia Division of Tourism's B&B line (tel. 800/262–1293). The Division of Tourism's Washington, D.C., office also operates a **B&B and small-inn booking service** (tel. 202/659–5523 or 800/934–9184 outside D.C.).

Eastern Shore

Garden and the Sea Inn

4188 Nelson Rd., New Church, VA 23415, tel. 757/824-0672 or 800/824-0672 outside VA

The Garden and the Sea Inn sits on a quiet lane near Route 13, the main thoroughfare along the Eastern Shore, in tiny New Church, just 1½ miles south of the Maryland border and 15 minutes from Chincoteague. The main house of the inn is composed of the 1802-built Bloxom's Tavern and its 1901 addition. A few years ago New Church's oldest farmhouse, dating from the mid-19th century, was moved onto the property. It's now the Garden House, with a parlor where guests can relax with sherry, apples, and brownies, an inviting wide porch, and three guest rooms.

In 1994 Sara and Tom Baker bought the inn because they wanted to be in business together. After looking at properties from Pennsylvania to Florida, the newly married couple visited this property, and Sara said, "Let's do it."

Although it has less of the feel of a little French inn than the previous owners imparted (mainly because of a more American slant on the menu), the Garden and the Sea is still a sophisticated, inviting place to stay. The decor mixes antique furnishings, French wicker, Oriental rugs, ballooning fabrics, Victorian moldings and detail, and bay windows. From the multicolored gingerbread trim on the wide front porch to the sunny, rose-hued dining room, it's exceptionally appealing. Guest rooms are spacious. In the main house, the Chantilly Room, with a wicker sleigh bed and painted dresser, and the Giverny Room, with floral prints and dark-green lacquered wrought-iron furniture, have large baths with double sinks and bidets. The large, private Champagne Room in the Garden House has a two-person whirlpool tub and shower and a wrought-iron canopy bed.

Tom, who has been the chef at top Washington hotels, creates dinners featuring produce from local farms and fresh fish from nearby waters in menus that change every three weeks. There are two fixed-price menus, as well as à la carte choices (entrées run about $18–$24). Specialties include a sea scallop, shrimp, and oyster dish and Tom's outstanding soups. The serve-yourself buffet breakfast, a bit of a letdown after the excellent dinner, is available in the dining room or—when weather permits—in the garden patio beside the lily pond and fountain.

🛏 *6 double rooms with baths. Restaurant, air-conditioning, ceiling fans, robes, whirlpool bath in 4 rooms; sheltered outdoor area for small pets. $75–$155; Continental breakfast, afternoon refreshments. AE, D, MC, V. Restricted smoking, 2-night minimum weekends. Closed Dec.–Mar.*

Miss Molly's Inn

4141 Main St., Chincoteague, VA 23336, tel. 757/336-6686 or 800/221-5620

In stark contrast to the high-priced, high-rise resorts up the coast, Chincoteague's Miss Molly's Inn instills visitors with a sense of place that for some may prove indelible. Like the small island on which it sits, whose isolation and thin soil have never sustained caved in to the various booms that threatened to consume it, the inn reflects persistence in the face of change. It lies on the island's main drag, which is orderly and navigable even on holiday weekends, just over the causeway bridge from the wisp of the mainland. While the island as a whole may once again be undergoing something of a rediscovery, Miss Molly's is a quiet retreat, an enclave of simple hospitality and respectful company.

A chief reason is innkeeper Barbara Wiedenheft, who makes the most of this low, unobtrusive 1886 Victorian whose woody gray color makes it blend with the seacoast sky. Flanked by a series of porches and sitting just off Main Street, it is named after builder J.T. Rowley's daughter, who lived there until she was 84. In a previous incarnation as a rooming house, the inn played host to Marguerite Henry, author of *Misty of Chincoteague.* Barbara will point out the downstairs room where Henry stayed while writing the book, which has helped produce a constant stream of guests since its publication in 1947. The upstairs rooms, which feature reading lights and copies of the text especially for insomniacs, are cozy, and guests may wander onto the inn's various porches to enjoy the Atlantic breeze. Styles of the furnishings span the century, from mission to modern, and share a simple understatedness.

However versed they may happen to be with the island's habits, Barbara and her husband, David, are actually expatriates from the Washington, D.C., area. (It was work for the British embassy there that facilitated Barbara's fluency in three languages.) Weather permitting, she may be found out back serving tea in the screened-in gazebo, which faces the channel and its fishing traffic, or just around the corner at the Channel Bass Inn, which the Wiedenhefts also operate and where guests of both inns mingle with patrons from the public over Barbara's scrumptious scones.

▦ *5 double rooms with baths, 2 doubles share 1 bath. Air-conditioning, clock radios, woodstove in dining room, beach towels. $59–$145; full breakfast, afternoon tea. D, MC, V. No smoking, no pets, 2-night minimum weekends, 3-night minium holiday weekends. Closed Jan.–Feb.*

Other Choices

Cape Charles House. 645 Tazewell Ave., Cape Charles, VA 23310, tel. 757/331–4920, fax 757/331–4960. 5 double rooms with baths. Air-conditioning, ceiling fans, whirlpool tub in 1 room, cable TV in parlor; beach chairs, bicycles. $80–$105; full breakfast, afternoon refreshments. AE, D, MC, V. Restricted smoking, no pets.

Channel Bass Inn. 100 Church St., Chincoteague, VA 23336, tel. 804/336–6148, fax 804/336–6599. 8 double rooms with baths, 2 suites. Air-conditioning. $79–$175, breakfast extra. Restricted smoking, no pets, 2-night minimum weekends, 3-night minimum during holidays and Pony Penning.

Inn at Poplar Corner and the Watson House. 4248 Main St. (Box 905), Chincoteague, VA 23336, tel. 757/336–6115 or 800/336–6787, fax 757/336–5776. 10 double rooms with baths. Air-conditioning, whirlpool tubs in 4 rooms, 1 room with private balcony. $55–$139; full breakfast, afternoon refreshment. MC, V. Restricted smoking, 2-night minimum weekends. Closed Dec.–Mar.

Island Manor House. 4160 Main St., Chincoteague, VA 23336, tel. 747/336–5436 or 800/852–1505. 6 double rooms with baths, 2 doubles share 1 bath. Air-conditioning; bicycles. $70–$120; full breakfast, afternoon tea. MC, V. Restricted smoking, no pets, no children under 10, 2-night minimum weekends, 3-night minimum holidays.

Nottingham Ridge. 28184 Nottingham Ridge La. (Box 97-B), Cape Charles, VA 23310, tel. 757/331–1010. 3 double rooms with baths, 1 suite. Air-conditioning, TV/VCR in den and suite; beach. $85–$130; full breakfast, afternoon refreshments. No credit cards. No smoking, no pets.

Pickett's Harbor. 28288 Nottingham Ridge La. (Box 97AA), Cape Charles, VA 23310, tel. 804/331–2212. 2 double rooms with baths, 4 doubles share 2 baths. Air-conditioning, TV/VCR in family room, fireplaces in family and dining rooms; bicycles. $75–$125, full breakfast. No credit cards. Restricted smoking, 2-night minimum holiday weekends.

Spinning Wheel Bed and Breakfast. 31 North St., Onancock, VA 23417, tel. 804/787–7311. 5 double rooms with baths. Air-conditioning, wood-burning stove in living room, turndown service; bicycles. $85–$95; full or Continental breakfast, afternoon refreshments. MC, V. No smoking, no pets. Closed Thanksgiving.–Apr.

Reservations Services

Amanda's Bed & Breakfast Reservation Service (1428 Park Ave., Baltimore, MD 21217, tel. 410/225–0001). **Bed & Breakfast of Tidewater Virginia Reservation Service** (Box 6226, Norfolk, VA 23508, tel. 804/627–1983). **Inns of the Eastern Shore** (1500 Hambrooks Blvd., Cambridge, MD 21613, tel. 800/373–7890). For a copy of the **Bed and Breakfast Association of Virginia's directory,** describing more than 100 establishments, call the Virginia Division of Tourism's B&B line (tel. 800/262–1293). The Division of Tourism's Washington, D.C., office also operates a **B&B and small-inn booking service** (tel. 202/659–5523 or 800/934–9184 outside D.C.).

Williamsburg and the Peninsula

Edgewood

4800 John Tyler Memorial Hwy., Charles City, VA 23030, tel. 804/829–2962 or 800/296–3343

Says frothy innkeeper Dot Boulware in her liquid southern accent, "I have to tell you, I am a romantic." And so is Edgewood—three marriage proposals were made in one week here. But before she and her husband, Julian, bought Edgewood Plantation, on scenic Route 5 approximately half an hour from Colonial Williamsburg, in 1978, she didn't care a bit for Victoriana. Fortunately tastes change, and when she became the mistress of an 1850s Carpenter Gothic house, she began collecting Victorian antiques like a woman possessed.

Dot's eight-bedroom house, visible from Route 5, looks on the inside like Miss Havisham's dining room, minus the cobwebs. It is full to bursting with old dolls, antique corsets and lingerie, lace curtains and pillows, love seats, baby carriages, stuffed steamer trunks, mighty canopied beds, highboys, Confederate caps—the list goes on and on. At Christmastime she professionally decorates 18 trees and festoons the banister of the graceful three-story staircase with bows. Clearly, more is better at Dot Boulware's Edgewood.

In her hands, Victoriana is thoroughly feminine, even though in one chamber, the Civil War Room, she's tried to cater to the opposite sex, decorating with intimate details of men's 19th-century apparel. Large people of either sex will have a hard time moving freely in this wildly crowded bed-and-breakfast. Lizzie's Room, the favorite, has a king-size pencil-post canopy bed and a private bath with a double marble shower and claw-foot tub. The room enshrines the memory of a teenager who, Dot says, died of a broken heart when her beau failed to return from the Civil War. Prissy's Quarters, upstairs in the carriage house, has a kitchen area.

Breakfast is served in the dining room by candlelight. The brick-walled, beam-ceilinged downstairs tavern is a cozy sitting area with a fireplace, backgammon board, TV, and popcorn machine. There are also fireplaces in the dining room, a kitchen, a tea room, and two bedrooms. Outside there's an unrestored mill house dating from 1725, an antiques shop, gazebo, swimming pool, and formal 18th-century garden (which makes a delightful wedding setting). Edgewood is centrally located for touring the James River plantations.

▦ *6 double rooms with baths, 2 suites. Tearoom, air-conditioning, turndown service; pool. $118–$178; full breakfast, light afternoon refreshments. AE, MC, V. Restricted smoking, no pets, 2-night minimum holiday weekends.*

Liberty Rose

1022 Jamestown Rd., Williamsburg, VA 23185, tel. 757/253–1260 or 800/545–1825

Bed-and-breakfast keepers in Williamsburg are in something of a bind. Because all the historic buildings in town are owned by either the Williamsburg Foundation or the College of William and Mary, they can't offer travelers authentic Colonial accommodations. Some have Colonial-style decoration anyway, but others, like Sandy and Brad Hirz, owners of the Liberty Rose, have come up with different, imaginative solutions to the dilemma.

Besides sheer ingenuity, Sandy and Brad have romance going for them. They were just friends when Sandy decided to leave the West Coast to open a B&B in Williamsburg. Brad was helping Sandy house-hunt when they looked at a 1920s white clapboard and brick home a mile west of the restored district (on the road to Jamestown). Sandy bought it in five minutes. Then Brad started seriously courting her, but it was Sandy, and not the B&B, who inspired him. Now they run Williamsburg's most beguiling B&B, decorated à la nouvelle Victorian with turn-of-the-century touches.

Sandy, a former interior designer, has a special talent for fabrics and is responsible for the handsome tieback curtains, many-layered bed coverings, and plush canopies. The patterns are 19th-century reproductions. Brad has held up his end of the business by managing remodeling details. The bathrooms are particularly attractive: One has a floor taken from a plantation in Gloucester, a comfortable claw-foot tub, and an amazing freestanding, glass-sided shower. The sumptuous Suite Williamsburg has an elaborate carved-ball and claw-foot four-poster bed and a fireplace. (The parlor, too, has a fireplace.) All rooms have a TV with VCR and a collection of films, and an amenities basket bulging with everything the traveler might need, from bandages to needle and thread. The furnishings are a fetching mix of 18th- and 19th-century reproductions and antiques. The latest romantic touch is two tree swings (one a two-seater) by the new courtyard.

Liberty Rose sits on a densely wooded hilltop, and the lake on the William and Mary campus is within easy walking distance. A stroll at dusk may be hard to resist, since romance sets the tone here all year round.

▦ *1 double room with bath, 3 suites. Air-conditioning, phone and TV/VCR in rooms, turndown service. $125–$195; full breakfast, afternoon refreshments. AE, MC, V. No smoking, no pets, no children under 12.*

North Bend Plantation

12200 Weyanoke Rd., Charles City, VA 23030, tel. 804/829–5176 or 800/841–1479

Routinely, a stay at this Charles City County plantation begins with a tour of the house and grounds conducted by Ridgely Copland, a farmer's wife and a nurse (several years ago named Virginia nurse of the year). Along the way Ridgely points out Union breastworks from 1864, wild asparagus, herds of deer, a swamp, and the wide James River. Only one other Virginia bed-and-breakfast—Welbourne near Middleburg—is so strikingly authentic, but North Bend differs from that slightly gone-to-seed mansion in that it's a well-maintained working farm. The Coplands are salt-of-the-earth people striving to keep their 850 acres intact in the face of modern agricultural dilemmas.

North Bend, on the National Register and also a Virginia Historic Landmark, was built for Sarah Harrison, sister of William Henry Harrison, the ninth president, who died in office having served just one month. It's a fine example of the Academic Greek Revival style, a wide white-frame structure with a black and green roof and a slender chimney at each corner. Built in 1819 with a classic two-over-two layout, large center hall, and Federal mantels and stair carvings, it was remodeled in 1853 according to Asher Benjamin designs. But beyond its architectural distinctions, North Bend is drenched in history. The Sheridan Room, the premier guest bedroom, represents both sides of the Civil War. It contains a walnut desk used by the Union general Philip Sheridan, complete with his labels on the pigeonholes. A copy of his map was found in one of its drawers and is now laminated for guests' viewing. The room's tester bed belonged to Edmund Ruffin, the ardent Confederate who fired the first shot of the war at Ft. Sumter. The headboard is a reproduction; a Yankee cannonball in 1864 splintered its predecessor.

Above all, though, at North Bend history means family. George Copland is the great-great-nephew of Sarah Harrison and the great-great-grandson of Edmund Ruffin. Family heirlooms are everywhere, as is the amazing collection of Civil War first editions, which make fascinating bedtime reading. There's an inviting upstairs wicker-furnished sunporch and a one-of-a-kind children's area with vintage toys.

▦ *4 double rooms with baths, 1 suite. Air-conditioning, TV in rooms, robes, fireplace in 1 room; pool, tandem bicycles, croquet, horseshoes, badminton, volleyball. $105–$135; full breakfast, welcoming refreshments. MC, V. Smoking on porches only, no pets, no children under 6. Closed Thanksgiving, Dec. 25.*

Other Choices

Applewood. 605 Richmond Rd., Williamsburg, VA 23185, tel. 757/229–0205 or 800/899–2753, fax 757/229–9405. 3 double rooms with baths, 1 suite. Air-conditioning, cable TV and fireplace in parlor, turndown service; bicycles. $85–$130. AE, D, MC, V. No smoking, no pets, 2-night minimum holiday and special-event weekends.

Colonial Capital. 501 Richmond Rd., Williamsburg, VA 23185, tel. 757/229–0233 or 800/776–0570, fax 757/253–7667. 4 double rooms with baths, 1 suite. Air-conditioning, cable TV/VCR in parlor and suite, turndown service; bicycles. $95–$135; full breakfast, welcoming drink. AE, MC, V. No smoking, no pets, no children under 8, 2-night minimum during peak weekends.

Newport House. 710 S. Henry St., Williamsburg, VA 23185, tel. 757/229–1775. 2 double rooms with baths. Air-conditioning, TV/VCR and videos, fireplace in living room. $120, $110 subsequent nights; full breakfast. No credit cards. No smoking, no pets, 2-night minimum weekends and holidays.

War Hill Inn. 4560 Longhill Rd., Williamsburg, VA 23188, tel. 757/565–0248. 5 double rooms with baths. Air-conditioning, cable TVs; fireplace in parlor, whirlpool bath in cottage. $75–$120, full breakfast. MC, V. No smoking, no pets, 2-night minimum weekends.

Reservations Services

Bensonhouse (2036 Monument Ave., Richmond, VA 23220, tel. 804/353–6900). For a copy of the **Bed and Breakfast Association of Virginia's** directory, describing more than 100 establishments, call the Virginia Division of Tourism's B&B line (tel. 800/262–1293). The Division of Tourism's Washington, D.C., office also operates a **B&B and small-inn booking service** (tel. 202/659–5523 or 800/934–9184 outside D.C.).

Piedmont

Clifton

1296 Clifton Inn Dr., Charlottesville, VA 22911, tel. 804/971-1800 or 888/971-1800, fax 804/971-7098

From the warm, paneled library and the comforter-covered beds to the sunny terrace and the languid lake, there are reasons aplenty to settle in here at one of the state's top inns.

Clifton stands in quiet Shadwell, near Jefferson's birthplace. No wonder it's a National Historic Landmark—the handsome white-frame, six-columned manse was once home to Thomas Mann Randolph, governor of Virginia, member of Congress, and husband of Jefferson's daughter, Martha. It's now owned by a Washington attorney but ably administered by innkeepers Craig and Donna Hartman. As chef, Craig also oversees Clifton's wonderful meals (the applewood-smoked loin of veal with Vidalia-onion marmalade has lots of takers). Midweek dinners are $38. Saturday's five-course, prix-fixe dinners ($48) include entertainment.

There are guest rooms in the manor house, the carriage house, the livery, and Randolph's law office. All have wood-burning fireplaces, antique or canopy beds, and large baths; they may also feature French windows, lake views, and antique bedcoverings. Rooms in the dependencies have a fresh, cottagey feel: whitewashed walls, bright floral prints, lots of windows. Suites in the carriage house boast shutters, windows, and other artifacts from the home of the explorer Meriwether Lewis.

The grounds spread through 48 acres of woods. The 20-acre lake offers good fishing (the inn provides rods and tackle boxes) and lazy floats on inner tubes. Vines and slate stonework blend the swimming pool and heated spa tub into the bucolic setting. There's also a clay tennis court, as well as croquet, volleyball, horseshoes, and badminton. For pure loafing, there are gardens off the dependencies, wooden chairs scattered across the lawns, and a small gazebo. The extensive gardens are carefully tended: The estate grows its own flowers, lettuce, and herbs.

Clifton offers a magical combination of elegance and hominess. Common areas, too, have fireplaces. A corner of the big butcher-block island in the kitchen is for guests, who often sit and chat with Craig as he cooks. A jar of cookies is always there, and sodas are in the refrigerator.

▦ *10 double rooms with baths, 4 suites. Restaurant, air-conditioning; lake, pool, spa tub, tennis court. $175–$235; full breakfast, afternoon tea. MC, V. No smoking, no pets, 2-night minimum weekends.*

High Meadows and Mountain Sunset

High Meadows La. (Rte. 4, Box 6), Scottsville, VA 24590, tel. 804/286-2218 or 800/232-1832

High Meadows, which stands on 50 acres in Scottsville, is above all a bed-and-breakfast inn done by hand. The hands in question are those of Peter Shushka, a retired submariner, and his wife, Mary Jae Abbitt, a financial analyst.

In this unique B&B, Federal and late-Victorian architecture exist side by side, happily joined by a longitudinal hall. It wasn't always so. The Italianate front section was built in 1882 by Peter White, who had intended to level the older house several paces behind it. But bearing in mind her growing family, his wife refused to give up the old place, built in 1830, and for a time a plank between the two was the tenuous connector that kept the marriage intact. Today High Meadows is on the National Register.

Peter and Mary Jae have decorated the place with great originality, keeping intact the stylistic integrity of each section. They've also used fabrics on the bed hangings and windows imaginatively. Fairview, in the 1880s portion, is the quintessential bride's room, with a fireplace, flowing bed drapery, a three-window alcove, and a claw-foot tub. The Scottsville suite, upstairs in the Federal section, has stenciled walls lined with antique stuffed animals, a fireplace, and rafters across the ceiling. A two-person whirlpool sits in the middle of the Music Room.

The Carriage House, also called Glenside, is a contemporary building of cedar, glass, and slate on the site of the original; this two-room suite has a kitchen, deck, and two-person outdoor hot tub. The property also includes the Mountain Sunset (named for its view), a 1910 Queen Anne manor house with two suites, two rooms, fireplaces, decks, and plenty of privacy.

Breakfast consists of Shushka specialties like cranberry-almond muffins and ham-and-egg cups laced with tomatoes and Gruyère cheese. During the week, dinner here runs $20–$30 per person and includes wine. Saturday, the MAP policy includes a six-course dinner. And to cap all this off, there are 5 acres of vineyards, which produce pinot noir grapes for the inn's own private-label wine.

🏨 *7 double rooms with baths, 6 suites. Air-conditioning, cable TV in 1 suite, fireplace in 11 rooms and 4 common areas, robes, turndown service, whirlpool baths in 3 rooms. $79–$175; full breakfast, evening hors d'oeuvres and wine tasting. MC, V. No smoking, 2-night minimum all spring, fall, and holiday weekends. Closed Dec. 24–25.*

Inn at Meander Plantation

U.S. Rte. 15 (Rte. 5, Box 460A), Locust Dale, VA 22948, tel. and fax 540/672–4912

Even those already versed in the treasures of the Piedmont region may be guilty of a gasp when they visit the Inn at Meander Plantation, just off Route 15 about 10 miles north of Orange. The simple sign and whitewashed brick markers give little hint of the architectural jewel that comes into view at the top of the driveway. Located on an estate settled in 1727 by Joshua Fry, a mapmaking partner of Thomas Jefferson's father, the inn bears faithful testament to its Colonial origins, replete with slave quarters and summer kitchen.

Innkeepers Suzanne Thomas and Suzie Blanchard, who along with Blanchard's husband, Bob, run the establishment, offer a reliably warm welcome that has kept a host of visitors coming back regularly to this historic hilltop residence.

An ample parlor and dining area, an occasional low-slung hallway, and bedrooms notable for their high, roomy beds and large windows, recall the days before electric light and central air, when natural assets had to be exploited. The series of outbuildings, including a stable, recalls the role that equestrian expertise has played in the area's history, both military and economic. The owners still keep horses on the property.

Another dependency, the summer kitchen, separated from the main house by a shaded brick walkway decked out with nodding fuchsia buds in the milder months, features a two-story suite with a claw-foot tub and shower in the sunny bathroom upstairs. Here, as in any of the other spacious rooms, visitors can revel in the immense solitude this venue affords or contemplate the nearby attractions, a list of which the hosts provide on parchment-style paper at check-in. Located far beyond the reach of city lights and sounds, the inn provides a wide back porch for those who want to savor the dusk, and brick paths for others who want to take the property's name at face value and wander off to enjoy the pristine view of the constellations.

🏠 *5 double rooms with baths, 1 suite. Fireplaces, piano, conference facilities, TV; hiking, fishing, tubing, pony rides, stabling for horses, lawn games. $95– 185, full breakfast. No smoking.*

Keswick Hall

701 Country Club Dr. (Box 68), Keswick, VA 22947, tel. 804/979–3440 or 800/274–5391, fax 804/977–4171

A visit to Keswick Hall is like spending a weekend with friends in the English countryside—that is, if those friends are very wealthy and live in a vast house with armies of antiques, plump chairs and couches, a butler to serve drinks, and a golf course in the backyard. Keswick sits on 600 acres in the wooded, rolling countryside east of Charlottesville. It's owned by Sir Bernard Ashley, who was married to the late Laura Ashley, so fabrics and furnishings from the company are used throughout. Tiny floral prints, though, do not dominate the place. Instead, fabrics, none of which are repeated, run the gamut from crisp stripes to elegant brocades. Sir Bernard's personal collection of antiques, century-old books, paintings, and silver-framed family photos gives the house the lived-in-for-generations look. One innkeeping colleague of Ashley's recently said, somewhat in awe, that each interior door alone contains $1,000 worth of hardware.

Bedrooms are individually decorated in color schemes ranging from soft beige and white to crisp blues to cozy dark green. All have comfy chairs, couches, or cushioned window seats. Baths have extra touches, such as whirlpool tubs in six rooms, extra-long tubs in several others, heated towel racks, hair dryers, an abundance of thick towels, terry-cloth robes, and dishes with cotton balls. Some rooms have private terraces with golf-course views, and several have decorative fireplaces.

Visitors want to loaf here, perhaps in front of a roaring fire on chilly days, lingering over coffee and the paper in the sunny morning room, having afternoon tea with delicate madeleines and scones in the yellow Crawford Lounge, or penning a letter at Sir Bernard's desk in the library. The all-red snooker room is the spot for predinner drinks and canapés and a late-night brandy, served by the friendly butler.

There's a full country breakfast with a wide range of choices in the garden room. Dinner in the elegant white-and-pastel dining room is a three-course affair ($55).

Guests have access to the Keswick Club, a private facility whose crowing asset is an Arnold Palmer–designed 18-hole golf course, along with fitness facilities, an indoor-outdoor pool, tennis courts, a croquet lawn, and a wood-paneled casual dining room.

🏠 *43 double rooms with baths, 3 suites. Restaurants, air-conditioning, cable TV and phone in rooms, turndown service, conference facilities; golf course, fitness facility, bicycles, pool. $195–$645; full breakfast, afternoon tea. AE, DC, MC, V. No smoking in dining rooms, no pets.*

Prospect Hill

2887 Limetrack Rd., Trevilians, VA 23093, tel. 540/967–0844 or 800/277–0844, fax 540/967–0102

For elegance and luxury, Prospect Hill is one of Virginia's finest inns, lying just east of Charlottesville in the 14-square-mile Greensprings National Historic District. It's the oldest continuously occupied frame manor house in Virginia. But except for the obligatory dependencies and impressive boxwood hedges, Prospect Hill doesn't look like a plantation, because it was rebuilt in the Victorian era, when a columned facade and decorative cornices were added. The innkeepers have painted it lemony yellow.

Fresh flowers, a basket of fruit, and just-baked cookies welcome guests to their rooms. There are four nicely furnished rooms in the main house, but the big treat is the six refurbished dependencies. Sanco Pansy's cottage, 100 feet from the manor, has a sitting room and whirlpool tub for two. The Carriage House, lit by four Palladian windows, offers views of ponies in the meadow nibbling the green Virginia turf. Surrounded by such *luxe, calme, et volupté*, it's strange to consider that in the last century, the dependencies were filled with hams, ice blocks, and livestock.

Dinner at the inn is a marvelous production, not so much for the cuisine (French-inspired and well above average) as for the ceremony. This begins with complimentary wine and cider a half hour before supper—outdoors in good weather. When the dinner bell rings, guests file in to hear the menu recited by innkeeper Bill Sheehan or his son, Michael. Then come an earnest grace and five excellent courses.

A hot breakfast arrives on a tray for guests wishing to stay ensconced in the dependencies. Some, however, crawl out of the soothing whirlpool tub and into the dining room. As splendid as the inn is, it hasn't become too smoothly professional. Even the most low-profile guest is liable to meet the gregarious innkeepers and appreciate the way they've put their stamp on Prospect Hill.

▥ *5 double rooms with baths in manor, 5 doubles with baths and 3 suites in dependencies. Air-conditioning, TV/VCR in meeting room, fireplaces in rooms, whirlpools in 8 rooms, clock radios; pool. $240–$325; MAP. D, MC, V. No pets, 2-night minimum with Sat. stay. Closed Dec. 24–25.*

Other Choices

1817 Antique Inn. 1211 W. Main St., Charlottesville, VA 22903, tel. 804/979–7353 or 800/730–7443, fax 804/979–7209. 4 double rooms with baths, 1 2-bedroom suite. Air-conditioning, cable TVs; bicycles. $89–$199; Continental breakfast, lemonade and tea on arrival. AE, MC, V. Restricted smoking, no pets, 2-night minimum on UVA-event weekends, 3-night minimum at graduation.

Holladay House. 155 W. Main St., Orange, VA 22960, tel. 540/672–4893 or 800/358–4422, fax 540/672–3028. 5 double rooms with baths, 1 suite. Air-conditioning, cable TV in 2 rooms and recreation area. $95–$185, full breakfast. AE, D, MC, V. No smoking, no pets, 2-night minimum weekends Oct.–Nov. and during UVA graduation. Closed Thanksgiving, Dec. 24–25.

Inn at Monticello. 1188 Scottsville Rd., Charlottesville, VA 22902, tel. 804/979–3593, fax 804/296–1344. 5 double rooms with baths. Air-conditioning, fireplaces in 2 rooms. $115–$135; full breakfast, afternoon refreshments. MC, V. No smoking, no pets or children under 12, 2-night minimum some high-season weekends. Closed Dec. 25.

Shadows. 14291 Constitution Hwy., Orange, VA 22960, tel. 540/672–5057. 4 double rooms with baths, 2 cottage suites. Air-conditioning, gas-log fireplace in 1 cottage, turndown service. $80–$110; full breakfast, afternoon refreshments. MC, V. No smoking, no pets, 2-night minimum some fall weekends and holidays.

Silver Thatch Inn. 3001 Hollymead Dr., Charlottesville, VA 22911, tel. 804/978–4686, fax 804/973–6156. 7 double rooms with baths. Restaurant, air-conditioning, clock radios, cable TV in bar. $110–$150, Continental breakfast. AE, DC, MC, V. No smoking, no pets, 2-night minimum weekends Apr., May, and Nov. Closed Dec. 24–25.

Sleepy Hollow Farm. 16280 Blue Ridge Turnpike, Gordonsville, VA 22942, tel. 540/832–5555 or 800/215–4804, fax 540/832–2515. 3 double rooms with baths, 1 housekeeping suite with full kitchen and whirlpool, 2 suites. Air-conditioning, TV in 3 rooms, whirlpools in 2 rooms, TV/VCR in sitting room, 3 fireplaces and 2 stoves in common rooms and suites; swimming pond, riding arranged. $65–$125; full breakfast, afternoon refreshments. MC, V. No smoking in dining room, 2-night minimum some weekends.

Tivoli. 9171 Tivoli Dr., Gordonsville, VA 22942, tel. 540/832–2225 or 800/840–2225. 4 double rooms with baths. Phones; TV/VCR in reading room. $75–$125, full breakfast. MC, V. Restricted smoking, no pets, 2-night minimum preferred on weekends.

200 South Street. 200 South St., Charlottesville, VA 22901, tel. 804/979–0200 or 800/964–7008, fax 804/979–4403. 17 double rooms with baths, 3 suites. Air-conditioning, phones; cable TV in 3rd-floor lounge, fireplaces in 9 rooms, turndown service, whirlpool baths in 7 rooms. $100–$185; Continental buffet breakfast, afternoon tea and wine. AE, DC, MC, V. No smoking in public rooms, no pets, 2-night minimum weekends Apr.–May and Sept.–Oct.

Reservations Services

Guesthouses Bed & Breakfast, Inc. (Box 5737, Charlottesville, VA 22905, tel. 804/979–7264) can arrange entrée to private houses that are otherwise closed to the public. For a copy of the **Bed and Breakfast Association of Virginia's directory,** describing more than 100 establishments, call the Virginia Division of Tourism's B&B line (tel. 800/262–1293). The Division of Tourism's Washington, D.C., office also operates a **B&B and small-inn booking service** (tel. 202/659–5523 or 800/934–9184 outside D.C.).

Blue Ridge/ Shenandoah Valley

Jordan Hollow Farm Inn

326 Hawksbill Park Rd., Stanley, VA 22851, tel. 540/778–2285 or 888/418–7000, fax 540/778–1759

As anyone who's traveled much in rural America knows, farms aren't always the idyllic-looking places about which city folk fantasize. However, this one comes close. Jordan Hollow Farm is situated on 150 acres in the middle of the scenic Shenandoah Valley at the base of the Blue Ridge range, with great views of the Massanutten Mountains. It is a restored Colonial working horse farm that has been given new life as a cozy, beautiful, and serene country inn. At the heart of the farm amid maple trees sits a 200-year-old farmhouse incorporating two hand-hewn log cabins and now known as the Farmhouse Restaurant.

Proprietors David and Gail Kyle and assistant Joan Nichols run the place, whose reincarnation as a stopover began in 1981. Guests can choose from the low-ceilinged Farmhouse Room in the main house, 16 more in the Arbor View Lodge, and four upscale rooms in the Mare Meadow Lodge, which is built of hand-hewn logs. The last are carpeted and have fireplaces, quilts and matching curtains, cedar furniture, and whirlpool tubs. The old carriage house and corn crib have a new life as a gathering lounge, whose antique couches and chairs, game tables, and a small library put guests at ease.

Half the guests come for to ride, half to savor the tranquillity. Every day, several equestrian groups (including beginners) leave the farm to wander over the foothills; youngsters go on pony rides. Guests can even bring their own horses; a stall is $10. Beautiful hiking trails crisscross the property, and folks at the farm can direct guests to even more in Shenandoah National Park or George Washington National Forest. Canoeing on the Shenandoah, caving, swimming, and golf are also nearby.

The Farmhouse Restaurant, whose specialties are served inside and in two other dining rooms, has built a considerable reputation with locally grown ingredients. Chefs Joann Cubbage and Julia Slye, experts at regional American recipes, also ensure that Virginia wines and local microbrews remain staples of the menu.

▦ *21 double rooms with baths. Restaurant, phones, air-conditioning; cable TV in 9 rooms and lounge, fireplace in lounge and 4 rooms; horseback riding. $110–$150. AE, D, DC, MC, V. No pets, except horses.*

Trillium House

Wintergreen Dr., Wintergreen (Box 280, Nellysford, VA 22958), tel. 804/ 325–9126 or 800/325–9126 (reservations only), fax 804/325–1099

Guests from near and far alike have to hand it to Ed and Betty Dinwiddie. For the pair, building a bed-and-breakfast on the grounds of Wintergreen resort may have seemed the most natural thing in the world; after all, their family had vacationed there for years. But to skiers, refugees from the Blue Ridge Parkway, wildflower enthusiasts, and all-round mountain devotees, the idea was a stroke of genius. The fact that Trillium House lies across the road from the gargantuan sports complex, with its indoor pool, tennis courts, ski slopes, hiking trails, golf course, and stables, should give prospective visitors a clue as to the activities available.

From Wintergreen's gate, a roller-coasterish road brings guests 3½ miles to the doorstep of Trillium House. The beige frame building fronted by a porch and a Palladian window, surrounded by trees and stylish condominiums owned by Wintergreen residents, was built in 1983. Entrance is through the Great Room, which is two stories high, near a staircase at the side leading to a loft library. The front sitting area has a wood-burning stove, above which hang several organ pipes; by the front door, a canister holds a collection of walking sticks. Breakfast is served in the dining rooms, with views of bird feeders and the backyard gazebo, and Friday and Saturday dinners (by reservation) are cooked by chef Ellen, who formerly worked in one of Wintergreen's restaurants. The 12 guest rooms at Trillium House lie in two wings off the Great Room. Their architectural tone is slightly motelish, but decorative touches add some personality—here a quilt or a framed picture that could only have been created by one of the Dinwiddie brood, there a writing desk from the Homestead or a bed with a lace canopy.

The odds are that guests will spend most of their stay here pursuing varieties of R&R on the resort or ensconced in the Great Room, chatting with other guests or Ed and Betty, who manage to seem amazingly relaxed despite their demanding housekeeping duties. The single disappointment is that Trillium House doesn't have mountain views; those after such scenery will have to grab a stick and walk.

▦ *10 double rooms with baths, 2 suites. Air-conditioning, phones; TV in rooms on request, cable TV/VCR and movie collection in sitting room, turndown service. $90–$150, full buffet breakfast. MC, V. No smoking in dining room, no pets, 2-night minimum weekends, 3-night minimum some holidays.*

Other Choices

Ashton Country House. 1205 Middlebrook Ave., Staunton, VA 24401, tel.

540/885–7819 or 800/296–7819. 4 double rooms with baths, 1 suite. Air-conditioning, ceiling fans in rooms, fireplace in dining and living room. $90–$125, full breakfast, afternoon refreshments. MC, V. No smoking, no pets, no children under 10.

Belle Grae Inn. 515 W. Frederick St., Staunton, VA 24401, tel. 540/886–5151, fax 540/886–6641. 9 double rooms with baths, 5 suites, 2 cottages. Air-conditioning, cable TV and phone in 11 rooms, fireplace in 13 rooms and 3 common areas, turndown service, 2 restaurants; nearby health club. $85–$150, full breakfast. AE, MC, V. No smoking, no pets.

Chester House. 43 Chester St., Front Royal, VA 22630, tel. 540/635–3937 or 800/621–0441 (reservations only), fax 540/636–8695. 5 double rooms with baths. Air-conditioning, robes, clock radios; cable TV in TV lounge, fireplace in 2 rooms and public rooms. $85–$120, Continental breakfast, afternoon refreshments. AE, MC, V. Restricted smoking, no pets, 2-night minimum some weekends.

Fassifern. Rte. 39 W (R.R. 5, Box 87), Lexington, VA 24450, tel. 540/463–1013 or 800/782–1587. 5 double rooms with baths. Air-conditioning, fireplace in living room. $84–$92, full breakfast. MC, V. No smoking, no pets. Closed Thanksgiving, Dec. 24–25, Dec. 31.

Fort Lewis Lodge. Rte. 625 (HCR3, Box 21A), Millboro, VA 24460, tel. 540/925–2314, fax 540/925–2352. 9 double rooms with baths, 3 suites, 2 cabins. TV/VCR in game room; bicycles, hot tub. $135–$190, MAP. MC, V. Restricted smoking, no pets. Closed mid-Oct.–mid-Apr.

Inn at Gristmill Square. Rte. 619, Court House Hill Rd. (Box 359), Warm Springs, VA 24484, tel. 540/839–2231, fax 540/839–5770. 16 double rooms with baths, 1 apartment. Restaurant, bar, air-conditioning, cable TV, phone and mini-refrigerator in rooms, fireplaces in 8 rooms. $85–$100, Continental breakfast; MAP available. D, MC, V. Restricted smoking, no pets.

Inn at Narrow Passage. U.S. 11 S (Box 608), Woodstock, VA 22664, tel. 540/459–8000, fax 540/459–8001. 12 double rooms with baths. Air-conditioning, TV/VCR in sitting room, clock radios in rooms. $85–$110; full breakfast, afternoon refreshments. MC, V. No smoking, no pets; 2-night minimum in spring, fall, and holiday weekends. Closed Dec. 24–25.

Joshua Wilton House. 412 S. Main St., Harrisonburg, VA 22801, tel. 540/434–4464. 5 double rooms with baths. Restaurant, café, air-conditioning, phones; fireplace in 1 room; bicycles. $95–$105, full breakfast. AE, MC, V. Restricted smoking, no pets, 2-night minimum some weekends. Closed Dec. 24–25.

Lavender Hill Farm. Rte. 631 (R.R. 1, Box 515), Lexington, VA 24450, tel. 540/464–5877 or 800/446–4240. 2 double rooms with baths, 1 2-bedroom suite. Air-conditioning, ceiling fans, satellite TV/VCR in living room. $64–$74, full breakfast. D, MC, V. No smoking, no pets, 2-night minimum holidays and special-event weekends.

Sampson Eagon Inn. 238 E. Beverley St., Staunton, VA 24401, tel. 540/886–8200 or 800/597–9722. 3 double rooms with baths, 2 suites. Air-conditioning, phones; turndown service, fax, photocopying. $89–$105; full breakfast, afternoon refreshments, beverages. AE, MC, V. No smoking, no pets; 2-night minimum May, Oct., and some holiday weekends.

Seven Hills Inn. 408 S. Main St., Lexington, VA 24450, tel. 540/463–4715, fax 540/463–6526. 6 double rooms with baths, 1 suite. Air-conditioning. $80–$125, Continental breakfast. MC, V. Restricted smoking, no pets, 2-night minimum some weekends.

Thornrose House. 531 Thornrose Ave., Staunton, VA 24401, tel. 540/885–7026 or 800/861–4338. 5 double rooms with baths. Air-conditioning, cable TV in sitting room, fireplaces in dining and living rooms, turndown service; bicycles. $60–$80; full breakfast, afternoon tea. No credit cards. No smoking, no pets, 2-night minimum Oct. and May weekends.

Reservations Services

Bed & Breakfasts of the Historic Shenandoah Valley (402 N. Main St., Woodstock, VA 22664, tel. 540/459–4828). **Historic Country Inns of Lexington** (11 N. Main St., Lexington, VA 24450, tel. 540/463–2044). **Virginia's Inns of the Shenandoah Valley** (Box 1387, Staunton, VA 24401). For a copy of the **Bed and Breakfast Association of Virginia's directory,** describing more than 100 establishments, call the Virginia Division of Tourism's B&B line (tel. 800/262–1293). The Division of Tourism's Washington, D.C., office also operates a **B&B and small-inn booking service** (tel. 202/659–5523 or 800/934–9184 outside D.C.).

Washington

Sun Mountain Lodge

Columbia River and Long Beach Peninsula

Scandinavian Gardens Inn

1610 California St., Long Beach, WA 98631, tel. 360/642-8877

When you step into this spacious bed-and-breakfast in the heart of Long Beach, be prepared to get a taste of Scandinavian culture. Before you enter, innkeepers Rod and Marilyn Dakan, who are not Scandinavian, will ask you to take off your shoes.

If this request is based on the observance of Scandinavian custom, you can immediately see a more practical reason for it—the white wool carpeting that covers the ground floor. The house is immaculate; there doesn't seem to be a single corner where even the most fastidious person wouldn't feel comfortable eating *lutefisk* off the floor.

The main common area, with its white carpet and blond-wood furnishings, is somewhat intimidating, but the colorful guest rooms easily compensate for it. On the main floor is the Icelandic Room, done in plums and greens, with an antique armoire and love seat and rose-maling on wall cabinet doors. The Danish Room, all blue and cinnamon tones, is decorated with hearts and nautical knickknacks. The Norwegian Room features greens and golds and a simple pine bed.

Upstairs, the teal and red Finnish Room offers such special touches as a skylight in the bath and an antique vanity. The main attraction here, however, is the Swedish Suite. Done in soft pinks and light blues, both rooms in the suite have dormer windows. Although the view is pedestrian—guests look out on the surrounding residential area— inside there's a hot tub for two with an overhead skylight, as well as a sitting area that includes a small refrigerator. The bedroom has a teakwood bed set, antique vanity, and a half bath.

But even if you haven't booked the honeymoon suite, you need not go without a hot soak: The recreation room offers a hot tub, sauna, and exercise equipment. You can also enjoy the game tables in the social room, which doubles as the dining area. Rod and Marilyn serve breakfast—a feast including traditional creamed rice, fruit soup, or blueberry French toast—wearing Scandinavian costumes.

🏠 *3 double rooms with baths, 1 suite. Hot tub and mini-refrigerator in suite;*

exercise equipment, hot tub, and sauna in recreation room. $75–$125, full breakfast. D, MC, V. No smoking, no pets, 2-night minimum on holiday and local festival weekends.

Shelburne Inn

4415 Pacific Way, Box 250, Seaview, WA 98644, tel. 360/642–2442, fax 360/642–8904

Sitting along the peninsula's main thoroughfare, behind a white picket fence enclosing rose and other gardens, is a green wood-frame building that is the oldest continuously run hotel in the state. Opened in 1896, the Craftsman-style inn joined to a late Victorian building is owned by Laurie Anderson and David Campiche.

The inn has a homey, country atmosphere. The lobby is somewhat cramped, with a seating area around a fireplace, a church altar as a check-in desk, a large oak breakfast table, and more. The original beaded-fir paneling, as well as large panels of Art Nouveau stained glass rescued from an old church in England, are found throughout the inn. A new section, built in 1983, is quieter than the older sections, though the latter have been soundproofed and carpeted.

Fresh flowers, original artwork, and fine art prints adorn the guest rooms, most of which have decks or balconies. Some rooms feature country pine furnishings, others mahogany or oak. Beds have either handmade quilts or hand-crocheted spreads. Some rooms are rather small, but the suites are spacious. Suite No. 9, in rose and cream, features large stained-glass panels between the bedroom, highlighted by a brass bed and a richly carved oak armoire, and a sitting room, furnished with natural wicker and an Arts and Crafts secretary. The large bathroom includes a roomy tub with gold-plated ball-and-claw feet.

The Shelburne's breakfast is one of the top three, if not *the* best, in the state. David makes use of regional produce from wild mushrooms to local seafood, and Laurie does all the baking. You can choose from among five or six entrées, which may include an asparagus omelet or grilled oysters with salsa.

The highly regarded Shoalwater Restaurant, housed in the enclosed front porch, is owned by Tony and Ann Kischner and offers such elegant entrées as duck with dried cherry sauce. The wine list has more than 400 titles. The Heron and Beaver Pub serves light meals, along with the best concoctions from the Northwest's microbreweries.

🏨 *13 double rooms with baths, 2 suites. Restaurant, pub. $99–$165, full breakfast. AE, MC, V. No smoking, no pets, 2-night minimum on weekends and holidays.*

Sou'wester Lodge

Beach Access Rd., Box 102, Seaview, WA 98644, tel. 360/642–2542

Just behind the sand dunes on the peninsula is this red-shingled, three-story inn. Make no mistake about it: The Sou'wester is not for everyone. Perhaps more than any other B&B in the state, it is an experience weighted as much by the unique character of the innkeepers as it is by the setting, a big old lodge built in 1892 as the country estate of Senator Henry Winslow Corbett of Oregon.

Len and Miriam Atkins left their native South Africa in the early 1950s to work in Israel, then moved to Chicago to work with the late child psychologist Bruno Bettelheim. With the idea of establishing a treatment program on the West Coast for emotionally disturbed children, they spent six months in 1981 in a camper, scouting potential sites. Instead, they opted to help adults unwind from the stresses of daily life.

The lodge is strewn with the acquisitions of a lifetime of world travels, including a hand-carved parlor set inlaid with mother-of-pearl from the Middle East. This is one of several sitting areas in the living room, which has a large fireplace, tongue-and-groove fir paneling, ceiling with massive beams, and Persian rugs.

An unusual aspect of the Sou'wester is that it bills itself not as a B&B but as a B&MYODB (make your own darn breakfast), with kitchen access provided (but not food). Second- and third-story accommodations are suites with full kitchens and views of the Pacific. Guest rooms are furnished with the occasional antique but more often Salvation Army furniture, with marble-ized linoleum floors; nicer touches are the handmade quilts or chenille bedspreads and artwork done by various artists while staying in that room.

Another slightly offbeat note that adds to the Sou'wester's charm is the collection of guest cabins and trailers scattered among the firs. The cabins are a bit more rustic than the guest rooms. Trailers feature handsome blond-wood interiors with lots of 1950s rounded corners. Tent and RV spots are also available.

▦ *3 double rooms share bath, 6 suites, 4 cabins, 15 trailers. Kitchens in suites, cabins, and trailers; cable TV on request in some units. $40–$104, no breakfast. D, MC, V. No smoking, pets in outdoor units only.*

Trout Lake Country Inn

15 Guler Road., Trout Lake, WA 98650, tel. 509/395–2894

In 1904, pioneers in the upper Trout Lake Valley built a large hall for community meetings. Since then the rustic, western building with its distinctive false front has been everything from a post office in the 1930s to a bowling alley in the 1950s to a public bath house.

Whatever the incarnation, the building has always been the center of the small community of ranchers and farmers wedged up against the bulk of Mt. Adams about 25 miles north of the Columbia River. Since 1988, it has been a charming bed-and-breakfast run by Gil and Milly Martin. Besides catering to guests who may be on their way to a rigorous hike in the wilderness or a breezy drive around the northeast side of Mt. St. Helens, the Trout Lake Country Inn offers a restaurant, country store, soda fountain, dinner theater, and small video store for locals.

At the end of a dead-end road, the inn is welcoming, if a little hard to find in this community of 300. More often than not, the lanky fellow on the front porch will be Gil, ushering you in casually, yet efficiently. Inside, the front room is a bit dark, but lovingly strewn with artifacts speaking to the building's age and importance in the community. There's a section of post office boxes, and there are photos of the area covered in ash from the 1980 eruption of Mt. St. Helens, a reminder that while the Trout Lake Valley is mainly known for its proximity to Mt. Adams, it is also close to the more volatile mountain about 50 miles northwest.

Straight past the soda fountain cum cash register cum registration desk, lies the main hall. Across the stage up front is a hand-painted drop curtain emblazoned with "Trout Lake Art Players" in the style of old vaudeville acts. Gil writes his own plays, usually comedy revues or melodramas starring Milly.

Accommodations—two rooms upstairs and one in a nearby cabin—are simple and rustic. The pine walls are original, cut by a local mill at the turn of the century. The creekside cabin is a treat, built on top of the icehouse that once served the whole settlement. The cabin's deck provides perhaps the best view of Mt. Adams in the valley and is just above a swimming hole in the creek.

Served in the main hall, breakfast is a tasty collection of fresh fruit, huckleberry pancakes, and baked egg dishes. Besides the dinner theater, meals and snacks are also available to you from a small, but diverse menu.

🏨 *2 double rooms share 1 bath, 1 cabin. Restaurant, soda fountain, dinner theater, gift shop, hot tub. $55–$90, full breakfast. MC, V. No smoking, no pets.*

Other Choices

Bingen Haus. Box 818, Bingen, WA 98605, tel. 509/493–4888; 6 double rooms share 2 baths. Hot tub. $65–$85, full breakfast. MC, V. No smoking, no pets.

Bradley House Country Keeper Bed & Breakfast Inn. 61 Main St., Cathlamet, WA 98612, tel. 360/795–3030 or 800/551–1691. 2 double rooms with baths, 2 doubles share bath. $75–$90; full breakfast, afternoon refreshments. MC, V. No smoking, no pets. Closed Dec. 25.

Farm Bed and Breakfast. 490 Sunnyside Rd., Trout Lake, WA 98650, tel. 509/395–2488. 2 double rooms share bath. Robes, bicycles, area tours. $65–$75; full breakfast, box lunches available. No credit cards. No smoking, no pets.

Flying L Ranch. 25 Flying L La., Glenwood, WA 98619, tel. 509/364–3488. 8 double rooms with baths, 3 doubles share 2 baths, 2 cabins. 2 common kitchens, bicycles, hot tub. $70–$110, full breakfast. AE, MC, V. No smoking, no pets in lodge.

Gallery Bed & Breakfast at Little Cape Horn. 4 Little Cape Horn, Cathlamet, WA 98612, tel. 360/425–7395. 3 double rooms with baths, 2 double rooms with private WC and shared shower. Hot tub. $50–$135, Continental or full breakfast. No credit cards. No smoking.

Gumm's Bed & Breakfast. 3310 Hwy. 101, Box 447, Seaview, WA 98644, tel. 360/642–8887 or 800/662–1046. 2 double rooms with baths, 2 doubles share bath. Cable TV, hot tub. $70–$85, full breakfast. MC, V. No smoking, no pets.

Chick-a-Dee Inn at Ilwaco. 120 Williams St., Ilwaco, WA 98624, tel. 360/642–8686. 9 double rooms with baths, 2 doubles share bath. $85–$155, full breakfast. AE, MC, V. No smoking, no pets, 2-night minimum for summer weekends and holidays.

Inn at White Salmon. 172 W. Jewett St., White Salmon, WA 98672, tel. 509/493–2335 or 800/972–5226. 16 double rooms with baths. Air-conditioning, TVs, phones, hot tub. $89–$115, full breakfast. AE, D, DC, MC, V. Restricted smoking.

Kola House Bed & Breakfast. 211 Pearl Ave., Ilwaco, WA 98624, tel. 360/642–2819. 4 double rooms with baths, 1 suite, 1 cabin. Sauna in suite. $60–$75, full breakfast. MC, V. No smoking, no pets.

Land's End. Box 1199, Long Beach, WA 98361, tel. 360/642–8268. 2 double rooms with baths. Phone on request, cable TV. $95–$120, full breakfast. MC, V. No smoking, no pets.

Moby Dick Hotel and Oyster Farm. Sandridge Rd., Box 82, Nahcotta, WA 98637, tel. 360/665–4543, fax 360/665–6887. 1 double room with bath, 9 doubles share 5 baths. Phone and TV in common area. $65–$90, full breakfast. AE, MC, V. No smoking, no pets, 2-night minimum on weekends June–Aug.

Reservations Services

Pacific Bed & Breakfast Agency (701 N.W. 60th St., Seattle, WA 98107, tel. 206/784–0539). **Travelers Bed & Breakfast** (Box 492, Mercer Island, WA 98040, tel. 360/232–2345). **Washington State Bed & Breakfast Guild** (2442 N.W. Market St., Seattle, WA 98107, tel. 206/548–6224).

Olympic Peninsula

Ann Starrett Mansion

744 Clay St., Port Townsend, WA 98368, tel. 360/385-3205 or 800/321-0644, fax 360/385-2976

This improbably ornate Queen Anne in Port Townsend, painted in cream, teal, and rose, was built in 1889.

You may find the almost museum quality of the Ann Starrett Mansion off-putting, but hosts Bob and Edel Sokol are low-key and friendly. Bob is a retired Air Force pilot and was navigator on *Air Force One* for President Jimmy Carter. Edel, a native of Germany, is an avid collector and baker.

The foyer—with a front desk hand-crafted in Port Townsend when Washington was a territory—opens to a dramatic free-hung, three-tier spiral staircase of Honduran and African mahogany, English walnut, oak, and cherry. At the top is the eight-sided tower dome, frescoed by George Chapman with allegorical figures of the four seasons and the four virtues. The dome was designed as a solar calendar: Sunlight coming through small dormer windows on the first days of each new season shines onto a ruby glass, causing a red beam to point toward the appropriate seasonal panel.

Other ceiling frescoes are found in the adjacent dining room and parlor, whose decor is a paean to the period. Elaborate carved moldings are featured throughout the house. The absence of fireplaces shows that this antiquated heating method was eliminated by modern central heating.

The Master Suite looks like a museum period room. Once the Starretts' master bedroom, it features Persian rugs, a Brussels tapestry tablecloth, an 1880 mahogany Eastlake bedroom suite, and

a floral tapestry canopy that extends from the floor to the 12-foot ceiling. The Drawing Room has a little antique tin tub painted with cherubs, and an 1860 Renaissance Revival mahogany bed. The contemporary Gable Suite offers a view of Puget Sound and the Cascades, as well as a two-person hot tub.

Breakfast includes champagne, stuffed French toast, homemade muffins, and juice, and is served in the elegant dining room.

🏨 *8 double rooms with baths, 2 doubles share bath, 2 suites. Hot tub in 1 suite. $70–$185, full breakfast. AE, D, MC, V. No smoking, no pets, 2-night minimum on holiday and festival weekends.*

James House

1238 Washington St., Port Townsend, WA 98368, tel. 360/385-1238

The picture-perfect location—high atop a bluff, with sweeping views of Port Townsend's waterfront, the Cascade and Olympic mountains, and Puget Sound—is only one of the many striking features of the 1889 James House.

The gray wood-frame Queen Anne house, with gables, dormers, porches, and five redbrick chimneys, is the grandest of all Port Townsend's Victorian accommodations.

An atmosphere of elegance and contemplation prevails. The entrance hallway, dominated by a hand-carved cherry staircase made from logs that came around Cape Horn, is a monument to fine woodworking. Like the two front parlors, the hall features original parquet floors in elaborate patterns of oak, walnut, and cherry. Breakfast is served in the large dining room or in the homey kitchen by the Great Majestic cookstove.

Years of restoration work preceded the house's 1973 opening as one of the first Northwest bed-and-breakfasts. It is furnished with period antiques (some original to the house), Oriental rugs, an antique player piano, and many beveled- and stained-glass windows. Four of the house's nine original fireplaces remain, with carved mantels and Minton tile framing.

Guest rooms are on three floors of the house and in the cottage out back. The house's master or bridal suite offers unsurpassed views, its own balcony, a sitting parlor, a fireplace, a private bath, and the original late Victorian bed, armoire, and fainting couch. The cottage, which sleeps four, has lots of windows and a more contemporary feel.

Innkeeper Carol McGough, a health care professional, moved here from Boston in 1990. She enjoys tending the roses, daisies, geraniums, herbs, and other plants that spill out of the James House's gardens, as well as making potpourris for her guests. Breakfast includes fruit, scones or muffins, and soufflés or quiches, all made from fresh ingredients.

▦ *7 double rooms with baths, 2 doubles with detached baths, 3 suites, 1 cottage. $65–$145, full breakfast. AE, MC, V. No smoking, no pets, 2-night minimum on holiday and festival weekends.*

Manor Farm Inn

26069 Big Valley Rd. NE, Poulsbo, WA 98370, tel. 360/779–4628

The silver trout rises from the dark waters of the rock-lined pool to lunge at the proffered lure. It is dusk, and the setting sun plays over the deep Oxfordshire greens of lush fields and forests. Shaggy-headed scotch cattle low softly through the gloom as the fairy-light effect from the inn's structures glows into life. The only other sound is the whistling of a sheepdog trainer as her canine student puts a flock through its paces in an adjoining field.

Such is the dinner hour at Manor Farm Inn, an oasis of elegance and country charm just across Puget Sound from Seattle. Here, a classic 1886-vintage white clapboard farmhouse is the centerpiece of a 25-acre "gentleman's farm," complete with sheep, chickens, pigs, and other animals.

Some inns are popular because of their convenience to business districts, tourist attractions, and universities. Others, however, attract a devoted clientele because they are special places, where the pressures of modern life seem half a planet away. Manor Farm Inn, which isn't particularly convenient to anything, falls into the latter category.

Innkeeper Jill Hughes, a former teacher, provides rods, flies, even floppy fishing hats for those who want to try their luck in the well-stocked trout pond. Bicycles, the best way to explore the inn's extensive grounds, are also available.

The interior of the Manor Farm Inn is filled with special touches. White walls, oatmeal-colored carpets, rough-hewn beams, and wide, sunny windows give the spacious guest rooms a clean and soothing simplicity. They're furnished with French and English pine armoires and writing desks and tables; eiderdown comforters warm the king-size beds.

The kitchen is another special feature at Manor Farm. A gourmet four-course dinner is served nightly; a sonorous old brass bell summons you to the comfortable drawing room, where a crackling wood fire and predinner sherry await. The farm-style breakfast, which begins with warm scones and coffee delivered to each room, includes oatmeal, fresh eggs from the farm chickens, oven-roasted potatoes, bacon, and sausage. Be sure to save a slice or two of home-baked bread for the inn's friendly goats, Tammi and Pepe, who occupy a fenced pasture down by the trout pond.

🏨 *7 double rooms with baths, 2-bedroom Farm Cottage, 2-bedroom Beach House. Restaurant, bicycles, croquet, fly fishing, horseshoes. $110–$160, full breakfast. MC, V. No children under 16, no pets.*

Old Consulate Inn

313 Walker St., Port Townsend, WA 98368, tel. 360/385–6753, fax 360/385–2097

Another of Port Townsend's Queen Anne Victorians—like the James House (*see above*), on the bluff overlooking the water—this brick-red beauty comes complete with conical turret, dormers, an unusual sloping "wedding cake" porch with a bay-view swing, well-tended gardens, and lots of white Adirondack chairs for lounging. Also known as the F.W. Hastings House, the inn was built as a private home in 1889 by the son of the town's founder and was the German consulate from 1908 to 1911.

It was a quirk of fate that brought the inn's present owners to innkeeping. Rob and Joanna Jackson had planned to celebrate their 25th anniversary with a large reception in their California home and a trip to Tahiti. Preparation for the event included refinishing their hardwood floors, but in the process, workmen set the house afire. The Jacksons changed their plans: They had a quiet dinner for 10, chucked the Tahiti trip, took a drive up Highway 101, and fell in love with Port Townsend and the Hastings House. Later that year, when they learned that the house was for sale, Rob gave up his contracting job and Joanna her post as corporate controller, and they became innkeepers.

The oak-paneled front parlor features its original chandelier, with large bunches of green glass grapes, and a fireplace framed in Italian tile. A large sitting room is comfortable for reading and conversation, with a fireplace, Queen Anne sofas and chairs, a baby grand piano, a pump organ once owned by England's royal family, and a chinoiserie chest original to the house and inlaid with mother-of-pearl. In the evening, the Jacksons serve complimentary port and sherry by the fire. A smaller anteroom off the dining room offers cable TV, a VCR, and lots of books. The doll, beer stein, and other collections displayed throughout the house can get a bit overwhelming.

Guest rooms on the second and third floors have a Victorian ambience, with floral wallpapers, custom-made comforters, dolls placed on bureaus, and a picture hat here and there on the walls. From the Tower Room there is a sweeping view of the bay. All suites have claw-foot tubs.

Joanna is one of the friendliest innkeepers and best cooks around. A cookbook featuring her recipes is being published. Her breakfasts are leisurely seven-course affairs; Greek puffed eggs with lemon cream is a house specialty.

🏨 *5 double rooms with baths, 3 suites. Air-conditioning, billiards, hot tub. $79–$185; full breakfast, afternoon refreshments. AE, MC, V. No smoking, no pets.*

Other Choices

Annapurna Inn. 538 Adams St. Port Townsend, WA 98368, tel. 360/385–2909 or 800/868–2662. 6 double rooms with baths. Sauna, steam room, massage and reflexology services, yoga instruction, accommodations for groups up to 18, conference facilities. $70–$110, full vegan breakfast, treatments extra; 2-night retreat with massage treatments $250. MC, V.

Domaine Madeleine. 146 Wildflower La. (8 mi east of town), Port Angeles, WA 98362, tel. 360/457–4174, fax 360/457–3037. 3 double rooms with baths, 1 suite, 1 cottage. Air-conditioning, kitchen in cottage, TV/VCRs, CD players, phones, video library. $125–

$165, full breakfast. AE, MC, V. No smoking, no pets, no children under 12.

Heritage House. 305 Pierce St., Port Townsend, WA 98368, tel. 360/385–6800 or 800/335–4943, fax 360/379–0498. 4 double rooms with baths, 2 doubles share bath, 1 suite. Hot tub, tennis nearby. $77–$140, full breakfast. AE, D, MC, V. No smoking, no pets.

Lake Crescent Lodge. HC 62, Box 11, Port Angeles, WA 98362, tel. 360/928–3211. 47 double rooms with baths, 5 doubles in lodge share bath. Restaurant, lounge, gift shop, rowboats. $67–$170, breakfast and box lunches extra. AE, D, DC, MC, V. Closed late Oct.–late Apr.

Lake Quinault Lodge. South Shore Rd., Box 7, Quinault, WA 98575, tel. 360/288–2571 or 800/562–6672, fax 800/288–2415. 89 double rooms with baths, 3 suites. Restaurant, no-smoking rooms, indoor pool and hot tub, sauna, pool tables, gift shop, fishing, hiking, boat rentals. $62–$130, suites $100–$250, breakfast extra. AE, MC, V. Restricted smoking.

Lizzie's Victorian Bed & Breakfast. 731 Pierce St., Port Townsend, WA 98368, tel. 360/385–4168 or 800/700–4168. 7 double rooms with baths. $70–$135, full breakfast. D, MC, V. No smoking, no pets, 2-night minimum on holiday and festival weekends.

Quimper Inn. 1306 Franklin St., Port Townsend, WA 98368, tel. 360/385–1060. 3 double rooms with baths, 2 doubles share bath. $65–$130, full breakfast. MC, V. No smoking, no pets.

Ravenscroft Inn. 533 Quincy St., Port Townsend, WA 98368, tel. 360/385–2784, fax 360/385–6724. 8 double rooms with baths, 2 suites. Fireplaces in 3 rooms. $65–$135, suite $165; full breakfast. AE, D, MC, V. No smoking, no pets, 2-night minimum on holiday and festival weekends.

Tudor Inn. 1108 S. Oak St., Port Angeles, WA 98362, tel. 360/452–3138. 5 double rooms with baths. Cable TV in one room. $75–$120, full breakfast. MC, V. No smoking, no pets, 2-night minimum on summer weekends and holidays.

Reservations Services

Pacific Bed & Breakfast Agency (701 N.W. 60th St., Seattle, WA 98107, tel. 206/784–0539). **Travelers Bed & Breakfast** (Box 492, Mercer Island, WA, 98040, tel. 206/232–2345). **Washington State Bed & Breakfast Guild** (2442 N.W. Market St., Seattle, WA 98107, tel. 206/548–6224).

Seattle and Environs

Bacon Mansion/ Broadway Guest House

959 Broadway E (corner of Broadway and Prospect), Seattle, WA 98102, tel. 206/329–1864

On a quiet tree-lined street in the Harvard-Belmont Historical District, only five minutes from downtown, the zestfully run Bacon Mansion/Broadway Guest House was a welcome addition to the Seattle bed-and-breakfast scene. Owners Daryl King and Tim Avenmarg-Stiles opened the doors of this huge, imposing 1909 Edwardian-style Tudor in February 1993.

The house had been operated as an inn for several years when King and Avenmarg-Stiles bought it; they added seven guest rooms to the original three, installed new bathrooms and furnishings, and in the process created an ambience of comfortable luxury. The inn's public areas are tasteful, with wool carpets in shades of rose, cream, and indigo laid over glossy hardwood floors. Headlining the decor of the main sitting room is a black concert grand piano adorned with a Liberace-style candelabra. French doors overlook the garden courtyard, complete with fountain, out back. Flowers in every room make it feel like June all year around.

One of the most inviting of the public rooms is the library, with its dark wood wainscoting, oak floor edged with a mahogany inlay, leaded-glass book-cases, carved-oak-and-tile fireplace, and rare bronze-and-alabaster chande-lier. The room has a comfy sleigh couch upholstered in cream and blue, as well as several deep chairs for reading.

Guest rooms at the Bacon Mansion run the gamut from the floral motifs of the Garden Suite and Iris Room to the more masculine confines of the Clipper Room and the Capitol Suite. The latter is the largest and most impressive of the in-house accommodations, with a pine four-poster bed, carved oak fire-place, wet bar, original tiled bath (with two-person soaking tub), and a fine view of the Space Needle. There's a nice view of Mt. Rainier from the top-floor Iris Room at the opposite end of the house.

Out back, past the fountain, is the two-story Carriage House. On the main floor is the spacious Carriage Suite with white plaster walls, forest-green carpeting, and a queen-size brass bed; on the second floor is the Carriage Loft, another, smaller suite. The full-size liv-ing-room hide-a-bed on the first floor makes this the best choice for families or other large groups.

▦ *6 double rooms with baths, 2 dou-bles share bath, 2 suites. Phones, TVs. $69–$129, Continental breakfast. AE, MC, V. No smoking, no pets.*

Bombay House

8490 Beck Rd. NE, Bainbridge Island, WA 98110, tel. 206/842–3926 or 800/ 598–3926

In a quiet, rural setting just a 30-minute ferry ride from Seattle, Bom-bay House is a three-story Victorian mansion owned by Bunny Cameron, a former caterer, and her husband, Roger Kanchuk, who ran a business

that served legal papers. The couple pulled up stakes in Anchorage, Alaska, looking for a better climate. One might question whether Puget Sound is an improvement, but in 1986, after scour-ing various western locations, Bunny and Roger landed on Bainbridge Island and bought the Bombay House.

The house, which has a widow's walk and wraparound porch, was built in 1907 by a master shipbuilder from Port Blakely (famous for its four-masted schooners built in the heyday of the tall ships). Today it houses comfortable country antiques with a few contempo-rary pieces. The entrance opens to a spacious, sunny living room with 10-foot-high ceilings, stained-glass win-dows from Europe, and contemporary sofa and easy chairs facing the massive brick fireplace. A century-old rock maple loom from Maine stands against one wall; a 1912 upright piano stands against another. One guest room, which has a functioning old tin bathtub in the center, is on the main floor, and an open staircase leads up to the others. The Captain's Suite is a large, airy room decorated in forest green and white, with a wood-burning parlor stove, large bird's-eye maple bed, sofa bed, and claw-foot soaking tub with hand-held shower.

In the glass-enclosed dining area, you can munch on Bunny's special fruit-bran muffins, quick breads, cakes, pas-tries, and homemade cereals while you watch the large white ferries plying the waters of Rich Passage between Bain-bridge Island and the Kitsap Peninsula.

The half-acre yard contains a rough cedar gazebo and informal gardens of roses, daisies, peonies, and lilies exploding with color.

▦ *2 double rooms with baths, 2 dou-bles share 1 bath, 1 suite. $59–$149; Continental breakfast, complimentary beverages. AE, MC, V. No smoking, no pets, no children under 5.*

Gaslight Inn

1727 15th Ave., Seattle, WA 98122, tel. 206/325-3654, fax 206/324-3135

The three-story, teal-colored Gaslight Inn atop historic Capitol Hill was always a showplace. A developer built the Arts and Crafts foursquare-style home in 1906 to show prospective customers the kind of home they could build after they had bought their lot from him.

Owners Stephen Bennett and Trevor Logan bought the dilapidated building in 1980, and after four years of painstaking restoration, opened it as a bed-and-breakfast. Those who reject the excesses of Victorians will love the more austere aesthetic.

The inn, named for its original gaslight fixtures, also retains the original beveled and stained-glass windows on all three floors, oak millwork, graceful fluted columns, and oak-paneled wainscoting with egg and dart detailing. All the oak and the muted color schemes lend a warm feel to the inn, while large windows and unfussy furnishings—authentic Arts and Crafts, mission, and Eastlake—give it a bright, clean look.

The charcoal-gray living room to the south features a glossy green-tiled fireplace with an oak mantel, Stickley rocker, rare oak and green-glass mission library lamps, wing chairs, and an Arts and Crafts sofa. The parlor, painted hunter green, contains three Arts and Crafts rocking chairs, sofa, and circa 1900 Victrola with a wooden horn. Mounted heads of elk and antelope hang in the three downstairs sitting rooms, and beautiful and delicate blown glass pieces, by local artist Jim Nowak, add colorful accents.

Each of the guest rooms is unique, with its own distinctive and well-executed decor; every one is equipped with remote-control TV and a small refrigerator. Some rooms have views of downtown, only a short bus ride away. Room 1 has a crisp, hardy appeal, with its ivory-and-blue mattress-ticking wallpaper and lots of wood. It features two Eastlake walnut chests and table, a walnut headboard, a hand-pieced quilt, and a bathroom with dark-stained wainscoting and a small Eastlake mirror. Despite dark taupe walls, Room 2 is warm and sunny, with white millwork, an elaborately carved golden oak bed and dresser, and an Arts and Crafts armoire. Another room is rustic, with a log bed made in the San Juan Islands and pine furniture. The five suites in the house next door, including a very spacious third-floor suite with kitchen, desk, fireplace, and expansive view of the Puget Sound, are elegant, comfortable, and particularly ideal for those planning an extended stay.

▦ *6 double rooms with baths, 3 doubles share 2 baths, 5 suites. Fireplace in 1 room and 3 suites, cable TV, refrigerators, pool. $66-$148, Continental breakfast. AE, MC, V. No pets, 2-night minimum Memorial Day-Labor Day and on weekends.*

M.V. Challenger

1001 Fairview Ave. N (park at the Yale St. Landing shopping center and marina), Seattle, WA 98109, tel. 206/340-1201, fax 206/621-9208

In a city that's defined by water, what could be more appropriate than a stay on a tugboat? Doing the improbable, owner Jerry Brown, a real-estate appraiser from the Midwest, bought the 96-foot working tug, built in 1944 for the U.S. Army, renovated it, and opened the *M.V. Challenger* as a bed-and-breakfast. It's certainly not hyperbole to call it unique.

Moored on the south end of Lake Union, a small lake 10 blocks from the heart of Seattle and filled with sailboats, cruisers, and charter boats, the *Challenger* is not for the claustrophobic. Common areas inside the vessel are open and fairly spacious, but some cabins are very snug.

You are asked to remove your shoes as you enter the main salon, built over the former cargo hatch, now decorated in ivory, blue, and beige with wood trim, brass candlesticks, and nautical gauges. The check-in area at the bar includes a TV, VCR, stereo, and small aquarium. Walls are covered with nautical maps, and two contemporary couches flank the granite fireplace in an adjoining carpeted conversation pit. The aft-deck solarium, which affords panoramic views of the waterfront, can be opened to the sky on sunny days but is more typically enclosed with canvas and vinyl.

Staterooms, some no bigger than a walk-in closet, are papered with nautical maps. Two cabins have bunks, the others double or queen-size beds. All come equipped with radios and phones. The red-striped comforter and matching pillowcases and curtains, towels, and a small painted radiator, also in red, make the Captain's Cabin cozy and bright. If you've been assigned to the Master's Cabin, you might be tempted to take to your bed, from which you can observe the busy comings and goings on the lake. A tub conveniently sits behind the bed.

Two new boats were recently added to the "Challenger fleet": A modern trawler, which has wooden boat charm and a newer power boat, which is more spacious but lacks the personality that the tug and trawler offer. These boats give families or small groups suite-style, private, accommodations.

Most of the staff is very friendly, but you might want to steer clear of the owner Jerry, who plays the part of the crotchety old salt to perfection.

▥ *9 double rooms with baths, 3 doubles share bath, 1 suite. Phone, radio, and sink in all rooms; TV/VCR, stereo, and refrigerator in some rooms; solarium. $60–$165, full breakfast. AE, MC, V. No smoking, no pets, no shoes indoors.*

Roberta's Bed & Breakfast

1147 16th Ave. E, Seattle, WA 98112, tel. 206/329–3326

For a quarter century Roberta Barry has ruled the roost at her eponymous bed-and-breakfast in Seattle's elegant, tree-shaded Capitol Hill neighborhood, luring repeat customers with a mix of humor, energy, and genuine warmth. "People come here to have a good time," she says, explaining her innkeeping philosophy. "I just want them to be comfortable."

Roberta's freshly painted, flower-trimmed, square-frame house, built in 1903, sits in a quiet residential neighborhood across 15th Avenue from green Volunteer Park and its sumptuously restored conservatory. One small drawback is that Capitol Hill, which contains several of the city's most enjoyable B&Bs, can be a little hard for first-time Seattle visitors to find. Calling for directions will save headaches later. Note, too, that because of local zoning laws, there's no sign out front; look sharp for the address when you arrive.

Arriving at Roberta's, you'll make your way past a broad, covered sitting porch. Inside, the common areas are bright and sunny, personalized with a piano of antique oak, a beautifully tiled gas fireplace, and an ornate cast iron and nickel wood-burning stove. The gregariously natured Roberta loves to read, and there are books everywhere.

The five guest rooms are on the small side, with bright sunlight filtering through white lace curtains. The rugs on the hardwood floors and the comforters on the queen-size beds are modern and unpretentious. The third-floor Hideaway Suite, decorated in pale green and ivory, is the most spacious. Tongue-and-groove walls and a crazily angled ceiling enliven the space, which also includes a big claw-foot bathtub, oak chairs and tables, a queen-size brass bed, and a futon couch. Window seats in one alcove offer a view of the Cascade Mountains.

Seattle, a great restaurant town, offers a bewildering array of choices, particularly for fanciers of the Pacific Rim cuisines. Roberta is happy to make both recommendations and reservations, a thoughtful bonus for out-of-town guests. Her own tasty breakfasts—served in the dining room with wood-burning stove—are vegetarian affairs, featuring such specialties as baked eggs, Dutch babies (baked pancakes drizzled with lemon juice and powdered sugar), and fluffy omelets.

▦ *3 double rooms with baths, 1 double with bath in hall, 1 suite. Tennis nearby. $85–$110, full breakfast. MC, V. No smoking, no pets.*

Shumway Mansion

11410 99th Pl. NE, Kirkland, WA 98033, tel. 206/823–2303, fax 206/822–0421

East of Seattle, across Lake Washington in Kirkland, is the Shumway Mansion, a gray Shingle Style mansion with two-story bay windows, dating from 1909–10. Built by the progressive Shumways, whose daughter Carrie Holland Shumway was the first woman in the state to sit on a city council, the 10,000-square-foot house was saved from demolition by Richard and Salli Harris and their oldest daughter, Julie Blakemore. Backed by investors, the Harrises rescued the 24-room mansion, moved it 2½ miles to its present location, and renovated it to the tune of some $500,000.

A formality pervades the house, which is decorated largely with 18th- and 19th-century European pieces, Oriental rugs, lace curtains, and silk floral arrangements. The living room features the original fireplace, with two parlor sets, one a blue upholstered walnut spindle-style suite from Austria,

the other French Victorian, covered in burgundy mohair. The sunroom is particularly charming, tiled in black and white with white wicker furniture, pink-and-white-striped wallpaper, and pink hanging lamps.

You can enjoy the grounds from two rear verandas linked by a long deck. Downstairs is a ballroom with four sets of French doors leading to a patio and gazebo. A recently opened guest room on the same level has a private garden, fireplace, and—an oddity in the bed-and-breakfast industry—a Murphy bed.

Guest rooms on the second floor share a tiny reading alcove on the same floor. Richard, a retired stockbroker, can't abide froufrou (although he does admit tolerating the odd straw hat with dried flowers here and there) and is proud of the soft easy chairs with ottomans, soundproofing, extra pillows, and good reading lights in every room. Each room mixes late-19th-century European and American furnishings with traditional-style modern pieces, old prints on the walls, Laura Ashley–style print wallpaper and bed linens, and resident stuffed animals—five or six per room.

Julie's candlelight breakfasts, served on crystal and china, include a variety of egg dishes or blueberry pancakes, as well as homemade muffins, scones, and coffee cake.

▦ *7 double rooms with baths, 1 suite. Individual heat control, TV available, access to nearby health club. $75–$105; full buffet breakfast, afternoon refreshments. AE, MC, V. No smoking, no pets, no children under 12.*

Sorrento Hotel

900 Madison St., Seattle, WA 98104, tel. 206/622–6400 or 800/426–1265, fax 206/625–1059

The wings of this venerable hotel enfold its fountain courtyard like the covers of an open book. Arriving, you will run a gauntlet of palm trees, valet parking, and doormen, finally winning access to the hushed interior of the ornate Sorrento Hotel, an Italianate throwback to a more gracious time, perched high on Seattle's Pill Hill.

Since 1909, visiting dignitaries ranging from President Harding and the Vanderbilt family to Debbie Gibson and David Bowie have made the Sorrento their lair while in the Emerald City. With good reason: The Sorrento provides a level of European luxury small-hotel service rarely encountered in the laid-back Northwest. Crackling fireplaces, hand-burnished Honduran mahogany, elaborate flower arrangements, and a hyperattentive staff make a memorable first impression.

In the guest rooms, the amenities and service successfully walk the line between gracious attentiveness and overkill. The home-baked butter cookies and miniatures of Dow's Port on the book-lined entertainment complex are warming touches; the Sorrento Hotel matchboxes, gold-embossed with the guest's name, are a flicker of Trumpian excess. There's plenty of space; no two rooms are exactly alike, although rose-colored carpets, cream walls, down pillows, and tasteful antique furnishings of teak, brass, oak, and walnut are consistent features. The vast, $1,200-per-night Penthouse Suite, popular with reclusive rock and movie stars, has a deck with an outdoor soaking tub and a view of the memorable Seattle skyline, as well as a wood-burning fireplace, four-poster bed, and its own library.

Downstairs, in the octagonal, mahogany-paneled Fireside Room, cocktails are served beside a huge green-tiled fireplace. The hotel's restaurant is a hallowed temple of gastronomic excess thronged with healthy-looking Seattleites who come to smack their lips in guilty pleasure over chef Eric Lenard's richly sauced renditions of regional specialties: timbale of oyster mushroom with smoked duck and hazelnuts, for example, and sautéed filet mignon with smoked tomatoes and elephant garlic. Breakfast is on your own (but the room service is excellent).

🏨 *34 double rooms with baths, 42 suites. Restaurant, bar, air-conditioning, cable TV, phones, on-premises shiatsu masseur, concierge, access to health club, complimentary downtown limousine service. $145–$1,200, breakfast extra. AE, D, DC, MC, V. No pets.*

Other Choices

Chambered Nautilus. 5005 22nd Ave. NE, Seattle, WA 98105, tel. 206/522–2536. 4 double rooms with baths, 2 doubles share bath. TV on request. $79–$105, full breakfast. AE, DC, MC, V. No smoking, no pets, 2-night minimum on weekends mid-Apr.–mid-Oct., 3-night minimum on holiday weekends.

Inn at the Market. 86 Pine St., Seattle, WA 98101, tel. 206/443–3600 or 800/446–4484, fax 206/625–1059. 56 double rooms with baths, 9 suites. Room service, rooftop deck, access to athletic club, conference facilities. $130–$325; no breakfast, complimentary morning coffee. AE, DC, MC, V. No pets.

Salisbury House. 750 16th Ave. E, Seattle, WA 98112, tel. 206/328–8682. 4 double rooms with baths. $70–$115; full breakfast, afternoon refreshments. AE, DC, MC, V. No smoking, no pets, 2-night minimum holiday and summer weekends.

Villa Heidelberg. 4845 45th Ave. SW, Seattle, WA 98116, tel. 206/938–3658 or 800/671–2942, fax 206/935–7077. 1 double room with bath, 4 doubles share 2 baths. Cable TV, phones. $70–$110, full breakfast. AE, MC, V. No smoking, no pets.

Reservations Services

Pacific Bed & Breakfast Agency (701 N.W. 60th St., Seattle, WA 98107, tel. 206/784–0539). **The Seattle B&B Association Hotline** (Box 24244, Seattle, WA 98124, tel. 206/547–1020). **Washing-**

ton State Bed & Breakfast Guild (2442 N.W. Market St., Box 355-FD, Seattle, WA 98107, tel. 800/647–2918).

Whidbey Island

Cliff House and Sea Cliff Cottage

5440 Windmill Rd., Freeland, WA 98249, tel. 360/331–1566

High on a cliff above Admiralty Strait, on 400 feet of waterfront, stand the Cliff House and the more secluded Sea Cliff Cottage. The natural beauty and tranquillity of the location led owner Peggy Moore to build her incredible home on Whidbey Island. She's proud of what she created, and rightly so, since the 1981 Cliff House—a contemporary statement in glass, wood, and stone—has brought awards to its architect, Arne Bystrom.

A large open kitchen and dining area stands on one side of a 30-foot glass atrium; a study and seating area is on the other side. The sunken living room has a fireplace and a sea foam–green sectional with a perimeter of tiny lights that make it appear to float at night. The floor-to-ceiling windows in the dining and living rooms allow glorious views of Admiralty Strait, Puget Sound, and the Olympic Mountains.

The two spacious loft bedrooms are upstairs. Because guests share living and dining facilities, Peggy will only rent the two rooms to acquainted parties; the innkeepers themselves have separate quarters. The larger room, decorated in shades of peach and ecru, opens out over the living area. Amenities that have attracted the rich and famous include a king-size feather bed, a whirlpool bath, and two upholstered chairs that swivel so guests can fully appreciate the view of the sun setting over the mountains.

The second bedroom—decorated mostly in white, with whitewashed pine furniture, Battenberg lace, pink glass lamps, and a pink chintz folding screen—overlooks the kitchen and dining area to the forest beyond. There's a skylight in the dark blue tile bathroom. Comprehensive music and video libraries can keep you entertained on chilly evenings.

Sea Cliff Cottage is as romantic and cozy as Cliff House is airy and elegant. The porch has a bit of gingerbread among the driftwood railing, and Adirondack chairs. There's a country French feel to the living room: whitewashed pine walls, pine armoire, wicker chairs and love seat with pale green and pink cushions, and a brick fireplace. The bedroom is pink, with a wicker headboard and Ralph Lauren linens on the bed, and a cushioned window seat overlooking the trees and the water. There is also a fully equipped kitchenette and a dining area, as well as a bathroom.

🛏 *2 double rooms with baths in house, 1 cottage. Kitchen and fireplace in cottage; hot tub. House $385, cottage $165; Continental breakfast. No credit cards. No smoking, no pets, 2-night minimum most of the time.*

Colonel Crockett Farm

1012 S. Fort Casey Rd., Coupeville, WA 98239, tel. 360/678–3711

Colonel Walter Crockett, a relative of Davy Crockett, built this house in 1855. It was derelict in 1984 when Robert and Beulah Whitlow found it; today the house is listed in the National Register of Historic Places. Robert, a former banker and personnel director, and Beulah, a retired teacher, spent 18 months and $235,000 transforming the old farmhouse into an inn, which stands amid 3 acres of lawn and flower gardens.

The Victorian cross-gabled structure has Doric pilasters on pedestals, which lend an incongruous formal grandeur to an otherwise modest house. The entry hall and small solarium have stained- and leaded-glass windows and white wicker furniture. The main public room is a comfortable and well-stocked library with red oak paneling, a slate fireplace, an English brass rubbing, and a collection of bulldogs in an antique glass case. The furniture includes a mirror-back English settee and matching chairs, an upholstered Eastlake chair and matching rocker, and another hand-carved rocker.

The five guest rooms have been individually decorated. The Crockett Room, the inn's bridal suite, is furnished with a draped and canopied queen-size four-poster, a marble-top washstand, and a Belgian field desk; its bathroom has an extra-long tub with lion's-head feet. The Edwardian fainting couch in the sitting area is a particularly rare piece. The Alexander Room, with a tiger maple bed and dresser, overlooks meadows, Crockett Lake, and Admiralty Bay.

The dining room has a fireplace and a telescope for you to use. The small tables are dressed up with pink and white linens, and are surrounded by the Whitlows' collections of antique porcelain plates; Royal Copenhagen, Wedgwood, and Belleek pieces; and gleaming English silver. There is a view out to the iris gardens and Crockett Lake. Breakfast specialties include eggs California, generous platters of fruit, and homemade muffins with seasonal ingredients (ask and Beulah may share some of her original recipes).

The farm is on a major flyway, so many migrating birds stop over on Crockett Lake, making this a haven for bird-watchers. It's within close proximity to 9 miles of beach with public access (most beaches in the area are private property), and very near Fort Casey State Park and the Port Townsend ferry terminal.

▥ *5 double rooms with baths. $75– $105, full breakfast. MC, V. No smok-ing, no pets, 2-night minimum on holiday weekends.*

Inn at Langley

400 1st St., Box 835, Langley, WA 98260, tel. and fax 360/221–3033

This contemporary structure at the edge of the Langley business district is a contemplative melding of earth, sky, water, wood, and concrete. The two cedar-shake, mission-style buildings—inspired by Frank Lloyd Wright—are surrounded by quiet gardens of herbs, berries, flowers, and fruit trees.

An archway leads to a long, rectangular reflecting pond, which connects with the Country Kitchen, a restaurant that serves Continental breakfast to guests and opens to the public for dinner on Friday and Saturday. Behind the dining room lies a longer building with the same lines and a lot of glass and wood. This structure includes the office, 22 guest rooms, and two suites trailing down the bluff to the beach.

Lawyer–developer Paul Schell discovered Langley when he and his wife, Pam, moved from New York to Seattle during the early 1970s. After doing several redevelopments in Seattle, Paul opened the 13,000-square-foot, $1 million Inn at Langley in June 1989.

The interior, with an almost Asian sense of space and understatement, was designed to be restorative. Neutral colors—black, taupe, gray, beige—form a quiet background. The waterside wall in the common area is nearly all glass, affording a staggeringly beautiful view past the deck to Saratoga Passage, Camano Island, and the Cascade Mountains. The room's fireplace and its maple, fir, cherry, and pine appointments seem to meld with the outdoors.

The Country Kitchen might be a wealthy friend's dining room. You'll find no maître d' standing at an official podium, no coat check, and no cash register. A huge river-rock fireplace rises before you; tables for two line the walls unobtrusively. The restaurant, a veritable gallery of local crafts, has a locally made, Wright-inspired "great table" for 10 on the far side of the fireplace.

Steve and Sandy Nogal, the inn's managers, have seen it happen again and again: "People arrive here all aggressive," Steve says. "They're keyed up after having to wait for a ferry. Slowly, they unwind and blossom." Steve is the creative force behind the incredible dinners served here each weekend. He builds menus around Whidbey Island foodstuffs, and has a ready group of suppliers that bring in salad greens, eggs, baby vegetables, jams and jellies, and freshly harvested mussels to be used in his artful culinary presentations.

🏨 *22 double rooms with baths, 2 suites. Restaurant, phones with voice mail, TVs, VCRs, mini-refrigerators, whirlpool baths, conference facilities. $179–$269; Continental breakfast, dinner available Fri. and Sat. AE, MC, V. No smoking, no pets, 2-night minimum on weekends.*

Other Choices

Anchorage Inn. 807 N. Main St., Coupeville, WA 98239, tel. 360/678–5581. 5 double rooms with baths. Air-conditioning, cable TV. $75–$90, full breakfast. AE, D, MC, V. No smoking, no pets. Closed mid-Dec.–mid-Feb.

Captain Whidbey Inn. 2072 W. Captain Whidbey Inn Rd., Coupeville, WA 98239, tel. 360/678–4097 or 800/366–4097, fax 360/678–4110. 12 double rooms with baths, 10 doubles and 2 suites share 2 baths, 7 cottages. Restaurant, bar; phone in some rooms; kitchen in some cottages; conference facilities. $95–$205, Continental breakfast. AE, D, DC, MC, V. No pets, 2-night minimum on weekends, 3-night minimum on holiday weekends.

Country Cottage of Langley. 215 6th St., Langley, WA 98260, tel. 360/221–8709 or 800/713–3860. 5 double rooms with baths. TV/VCRs, stereos, refrigerators, coffeemakers; Jacuzzi in 2 rooms; video library. $105–$159, full breakfast. AE, MC, V. No smoking, no pets, 2-night minimum on summer weekends and holidays.

Eagles Nest Inn. 3236 E. Saratoga Rd., Langley, WA 98260, tel. and fax 360/221–5331. 4 double rooms with baths. Cable TV/VCR, hot tub. $95–$115; full breakfast, complimentary beverages. D, MC, V. No smoking, no pets, 2-night minimum on holiday weekends.

Fort Casey Inn. 1124 S. Engle Rd., Coupeville, WA 98239, tel. 360/678–8792. 1 suite, 1 2-bedroom cottage, 8 2-bedroom units. Wood-burning stoves and kitchens in most units, bicycles. $75–$125, Continental breakfast. AE, MC, V. No smoking, no pets.

Guest House Cottages. 3366 S. State Hwy. 525, Greenbank, WA 98253, tel. 360/678–3115. 6 cottages, 1 suite. Air-conditioning in 1 cottage, TV/VCRs, whirlpool tubs, exercise room, video library, pool, hot tub. $110–$285, Continental breakfast. AE, MC, V. No smoking, no pets, 2-night minimum on weekends, 3-night minimum on holiday weekends.

Home by the Sea Cottages. 2388 E. Sunlight Beach Rd., Clinton, WA 98236, tel. 360/321–2964, fax 360/321–4378. 1 suite, 2 cottages. Kitchens, phones, TV/VCRS, whirlpool tubs. $155–$175, Continental breakfast delivered 2 mornings only. MC, V. No smoking, 2-night minimum on weekends.

Inn at Penn Cove. 702 N. Main St., Box 85, Coupeville, WA 98239, tel. 360/678–8000 or 800/688–COVE. 3 double rooms with baths, 2 doubles share bath, 1 suite. Fireplaces in 3 rooms; whirlpool tub in suite; air-conditioning, cable TV, VCR, video library in Kineth House. $60–$125; full breakfast, complimentary beverages. AE, D, MC, V. No smoking, no pets.

Log Castle Bed & Breakfast. 3273 E. Saratoga Rd., Langley, WA 98260, tel. 360/221–5483, fax 360/221–3822. 4 double rooms with baths. Wood stoves in 2 rooms, nature trail. $90–$115; full breakfast, afternoon refreshments. D, MC, V. No smoking, no pets, 2-night minimum on holiday weekends. Closed 5 days during Christmas.

Lone Lake Cottage and Breakfast. 5206 S. Bayview Rd., Langley, WA 98260, tel. 360/321–5325. 1 houseboat with detached bath, 1 suite, 2 cottages. Kitchens, TV/VCRs, CD players, whirlpool tubs, video library, bicycles, canoes, paddleboat, rowboat, fishing gear. $125, Continental breakfast for 1st 2 days. No credit cards. No smoking, no pets, 2-night minimum on weekends.

Whidbey Inn. 106 1st St., Box 156, Langley, WA 98260, tel. 360/221–7115. 3 double rooms with baths, 3 suites. Fireplace in suites. $110–$160, full breakfast. AE, MC, V. No smoking, no pets.

Reservations Services

Pacific Bed & Breakfast Agency (701 N.W. 60th St., Seattle, WA 98107, tel. 206/784–0539). **Washington State Bed & Breakfast Guild** (2442 N.W. Market St., Box 355–FD, Seattle, WA 98107, tel. 800/647–2918). **Whidbey Island Bed & Breakfast Association** (Box 259, Langley, WA 98260, tel. 360/679–2276).

San Juan Islands

Inn at Swifts Bay

Port Stanley Rd., Rte. 2, Box 3402, Lopez Island, WA 98261, tel. 360/468–3636

"There'll always be another boat, but there may never be another property like this," said Robert Herrman when he and Christopher Brandmeir decided to sell the sailboat they had been grooming for a round-the-world adventure and buy the 1975 mock-Tudor building, 2 miles from the Lopez Island ferry landing, that is now the Inn at Swifts Bay. The inn is surrounded by rhododendrons, madronas, and firs amid 3 acres of woods, with another acre of beach a four-minute walk away.

Robert and Chris give the inn its heart. These two California transplants have woven themselves into the island community over the years. Sadly, at press time the inn was on the market; even if it remains a bed-and-breakfast when sold, it won't be the same without Chris and Robert who were the glitter in this shining star.

The inn's decor is sophisticated, but the rooms feel lived-in and loved. The sunny living room has large bay windows, a fireplace, a chintz sofa and chairs on an Oriental rug, and shelves of books. The raised dining room, pale yellow with hand-stenciled ivy around the ceiling, is the setting for breakfast, which might include hazelnut waffles with fresh island berries and crème fraîche, or eggs with just-caught Dungeness crabs. The den/music room behind the living room features burgundy Laura Ashley wallpaper, a large brick fireplace, two Queen Anne upholstered wing chairs, a TV/VCR with more than 150 tapes, and French doors that open onto the deck and the woods.

The individually decorated guest rooms are spacious and airy. Room 2 has hunter green walls with cream accents, window swags of patterned fabric, an Arts and Crafts headboard on the queen-size bed, a gateleg desk, and a large dark-cherry mirror and chest. In the attic, a large room with a sitting area has pale peach walls, a queen-size sleigh bed, and an English armoire and chest; three long, narrow skylights have been cut into the sloping ceiling, and there's a private entrance and small deck. The adjacent attic suite has a separate sitting room and large private deck. In 1994, Chris and Robert added a private cottage on Hunter's Bay, the perfect escape for romantic private retreats.

▦ *2 double rooms with baths, 2 doubles share bath, 1 suite, 1 cottage. Fireplaces and mini-refrigerators in suites and 2 rooms, TV/VCR in den, video library, exercise room, hot tub. $75–$195; full breakfast, afternoon refreshments. AE, D, MC, V. No smoking, no pets, 2-night minimum in cottage.*

Orcas Hotel

Box 155, Orcas, WA 98280, tel. 360/376–4300, fax 360/376–4399

On the hill overlooking the Orcas Island ferry landing sits a three-story red-roofed Victorian with a wraparound porch and a white picket fence. The Orcas Hotel was built as an inn between 1900 and 1904 by Canadian landowner William Sutherland. Today the hotel is listed on the National Register of Historic Places; even the flower gardens—drifts of daffodils, wisteria vines, irises, and roses—have been restored. The hostelry is managed by Craig and Linda Sanders, Brad Harlow, and Amy McGinnis—four active young people who, when they aren't bicycling, hiking, or playing volleyball or softball, are likely to be in the kitchen cooking gourmet meals.

The hotel has a colorful past. A bullet hole through a veranda post recalls the Prohibition-era escape of a bootlegger who foiled his pursuers by leaping to freedom over the porch railing. Some islanders claim that liquor was smuggled in by small boats and stored in the woodpile and the attic. During the hotel's restoration in 1985, loose planks were discovered in the attic, with enough space underneath to store dozens of bottles of booze. The ghost of Octavia, one of the original managers, was seen as recently as 1985, by two of the workmen who were doing the restoration. (Don't worry—the building has been exorcised.)

The main floor has a bakery–espresso café, a dining room, and a parlor furnished with Queen Anne settees, marble-top tables, and Oriental rugs. The dining room (open to the public) overlooks the ferry landing as well as part of the garden. All public rooms have splendid harbor views, and showcase works by Orcas artists, such as a stained-glass mermaid in the cocktail lounge.

Two romantic guest rooms at the front of the inn have French doors opening onto a wrought-iron-furnished sundeck with views of the waterfront. Both rooms feature fluffy feather beds and duvets and marble-top tables, and the Blue Heron Room has an Eastlake parlor set. Each has a large bathroom with a double whirlpool bath. The innkeepers readily admit that temperatures in the building are idiosyncratic, so they've supplied each room with a fan and a space heater.

▦ *2 double rooms with baths, 2 doubles and 1 triple with ½-baths share 2 full baths, 5 doubles and 1 triple share 4 baths. Restaurant (June–Sept.), bakery, cocktail lounge, conference facilities, bicycle rentals. $69–$170, full breakfast. AE, D, MC, V. No smoking, no pets, 2-night minimum on holiday weekends.*

Turtleback Farm Inn

Crow Valley Rd., Rte. 1, Box 650, Eastsound, WA 98245, tel. 360/376–4914 or 800/376–4914, fax 360/376–4914

Bill and Susan Fletcher abandoned suburban life in the San Francisco Bay area (he was a real-estate broker, she a homemaker) for 80 acres of meadow, forest, and farmland on Orcas Island, where they now herd French geese and occasionally deliver a baby lamb by flashlight. Forest green with white trim, the renovated, Folk National–style farmhouse stands in the shadow of Turtleback Mountain, with Mt. Constitution to the east, a 10-minute drive from the Orcas Island ferry landing.

Don't expect to spend a lot of time chatting with the innkeepers; the Fletchers appear for breakfast but generally spend the evenings in their own home down the hill. A framed Seattle newspaper clipping by the front door—a 1933 ad for *Tarzan the Fearless*—pays homage to the movie's star and Susan's father, Buster Crabbe.

The inn itself is spacious and airy but spare. The cream-colored sitting room, with a beamed ceiling and peach-and-green accents, includes a Rumford fireplace, a pilgrim-style trunk, a cabbage-rose upholstered sofa, and a corner game table. The salmon-colored dining room has fir wainscoting and five small oak tables.

The guest rooms are decorated with Cape May Collection wallpaper. All have reading lamps, comfortable seating, cream-colored muslin curtains, and meadow and forest views. The Meadow Room has a private deck overlooking the pasture. The light fixtures and crystal doorknobs in most rooms and the claw-foot tubs and bathroom mirrors were rescued from Seattle's old Savoy Hotel before it was razed, and the sinks and beveled-glass bathroom shelves above them come from Victoria's grand old Empress Hotel. The comforters on the beds are stuffed with wool batting from the Fletchers' own sheep. In the works is a new building to house four deluxe guest rooms with fireplaces and steam showers.

Breakfast is served in the dining room or, in nice weather, on the deck overlooking the valley, on tables set with bone china, silver, and linen. If you want the recipes, you can buy Susan's cookbook. Full meal service is available by reservation for groups.

▦ *7 double rooms with baths. Walking paths. $80–$160; full breakfast, complimentary beverages. D, MC, V.*

No smoking, no pets, 2-night minimum on holidays and weekends Apr.–Oct.

Other Choices

Blair House. 345 Blair Ave., Friday Harbor, WA 98250, tel. 360/378–5907, fax 360/378–6940. 1 double room with bath, 2 doubles with ½-bath share full bath, 4 doubles share bath, 1 cottage. Kitchen in cottage, pool, hot tub, barbecue grill. $75–$125, full breakfast. AE, D, MC, V. No smoking, no pets or children in main building.

Deer Harbor Inn. Deer Harbor Rd., Box 142, Deer Harbor, WA 98243, tel. 360/376–4110, fax 360/376–2237. 8 double rooms with baths. Restaurant, gift shop, hot tub. $99, Continental breakfast. AE, MC, V. No smoking, no pets.

Duffy House. 760 Pear Point Rd., Friday Harbor, WA 98250, tel. 360/378–5604 or 800/972–2089, fax 360/378–6535. 5 double rooms share 2 baths. Private beach. $85–$95; full breakfast, afternoon refreshments. MC, V. No smoking, no pets, 2-night minimum on weekends July–Aug. and on holidays.

Edenwild Inn. Box 271, Lopez Island, WA 98261, tel. 360/468–3238. 8 double rooms with baths. Restaurant, bicycle rentals, ferry, seaplane, and airport pickup. $85–$140; full breakfast, afternoon aperitif. MC, V. No smoking, no pets, 2-night minimum on holiday weekends.

Friday Harbor House. 130 West St. (Box 1385, Friday Harbor, WA 98250), tel. 360/378–8455, fax 360/378–8453. 20 double rooms with baths, 1 suite. $185, suite $325; Continental breakfast. Restaurant, fireplaces, refrigerators, phones, modem lines, TVs, VCR in suite, conference facilities. No smoking, no pets, 2-night minimum July–Sept. and all holidays.

Hillside House. 365 Carter Ave., Friday Harbor, WA 98250, tel. 360/378–4730 or 800/232–4730, fax 360/378–4715. 7 double rooms with baths. Robes, aviary. $80–$170, full breakfast. AE, D, MC, V. No smoking, no pets.

Kangaroo House. 5 N. Beach Rd., Box 334, Eastsound, WA 98245, tel. 360/376–2175. 1 double room with bath, 3 doubles share 1½ baths, 1 suite. Guest refrigerator, game room, hot tub. $70–$110, full breakfast. MC, V. No smoking, no pets.

MacKaye Harbor Inn. Rte. 1, Box 1940, Lopez Island, WA 98261, tel. 360/468–2253, fax 360/468–3293. 2 double rooms with baths, 3 doubles share 2½ baths. Kayak instruction and rental, mountain bikes, boat buoy, airport and ferry pickup. $69–$139; full breakfast, afternoon refreshments. MC, V. No smoking, no pets, 2-night minimum July–Sept.

Mariella Inn & Cottages. 630 Turn Point Rd., Friday Harbor, WA 98250, tel. 360/378–6868 or 800/700–7668, fax 360/378–6822. 7 double rooms with baths, 4 suites, 6 cottages, 1 studio cottage with detached bath. Restaurant, kitchen in 6 cottages, hot tub, volleyball court, tennis court, boat dock, private beach, fishing pond, bicycle and kayak rentals, sailing and cruise charters. $125–$375, Continental breakfast buffet or basket. MC, V. No smoking, no pets, 2-night minimum on weekends July–Aug. and on holidays. Closed 1st 2 wks in Jan.

Old Trout Inn. Horseshoe Hwy., Rte. 1, Box 45A, Eastsound, WA 98245, tel. 360/376–8282. 2 double rooms share bath, 2 suites, 1 cottage. Fireplace in 2 suites, kitchen in cottage, sauna in housekeeping suite, robes, hot tub, bicycles, nature trail, binoculars, ferry pickup. $80–$160; full breakfast, afternoon refreshments. D, MC, V. No smoking, no pets.

Olympic Lights. 4531-A Cattle Point Rd., Friday Harbor, WA 98250, tel. 360/378–3186, fax 360/378–2097. 1 double room with bath, 4 doubles share 2 baths. Croquet, boccie, horseshoes. $70–$105, full breakfast. No credit cards. No smoking, no pets, 2-night minimum July–Sept. and on holiday weekends.

Sand Dollar Inn. Horseshoe Hwy., Box 152, Olga, WA 98279, tel. and fax 360/376–5696. 4 double rooms with baths. Guest refrigerator and phone. $88–$120, full breakfast. AE, MC, V. No smoking, no pets.

San Juan Inn. 50 Spring St., Box 776, Friday Harbor, WA 98250, tel. 360/378–2070 or 800/742–8210, fax 360/378–6437. 5 double rooms with baths, 6 doubles share 3 baths, 1 suite. Kitchen in suite, hot tub. $80–$140, Continental breakfast. AE, D, MC, V. No smoking, no pets.

Spring Bay Inn. Obstruction Pass Park Rd., Box 97, Olga, WA 98279, tel. 360/376–5531, fax 360/376–2193. 4 double rooms with baths. Guest refrigerator, hot tub, barbecue, nature trails, kayak and hiking tours, binoculars. $165–$195; full breakfast, evening refreshments, dinner available. AE, D, MC, V. No smoking, no pets, 2-night minimum Apr.–Oct.

States Inn. 2039 W. Valley Rd., Friday Harbor, WA 98250, tel. 360/378–6240, fax 360/378–6241. 7 double rooms with baths, 2 doubles share bath. Bicycle storage, horseback riding, ferry and airport pickup/drop off. $80–$110; full breakfast, afternoon refreshments. MC, V. No smoking, no pets, 2-night minimum on holiday weekends.

Trumpeter Inn. 420 Trumpeter Way, Friday Harbor, WA 98250, tel. 360/378–3884 or 800/826–7926, fax 360/378–8235. 5 double rooms with baths. TV, games, hot tub, bicycle storage, ferry and airport pickup. $90–$125; full breakfast, afternoon refreshments. MC, V. No smoking, no pets.

Wharfside Bed & Breakfast. K-Dock, Slip 13, Port of Friday Harbor Marina, (Box 1212, Friday Harbor, WA 98250), tel. 360/378–5661. 1 double room and 1 triple share bath. Robes, fishing and crabbing gear, rowboat. $90–$95, full breakfast. MC, V. No smoking indoors,

2-night minimum June–Sept. and holidays.

Windsong. 2 Deer Harbor Rd. (Box 32, Orcas, WA 98280), tel. 360/376–2500, fax 360/376–4453. 4 double rooms with baths. Guest phone, TV on request, library, hot tub, barbecue, kayak storage, ferry and airport pickup. $115–$140, full breakfast. MC, V. No smoking, no pets.

Reservations Services

Orcas Island Chamber of Commerce Accommodation Hotline (tel. 360/376–8888). **Pacific Bed & Breakfast Agency** (701 N.W. 60th St., Seattle, WA 98107, tel. 206/784–0539). **San Juan Island Central Reservations** (tel. 360/378–6670). **Washington State Bed & Breakfast Guild** (2442 N.W. Market St., Box 355-FD, Seattle, WA 98107, tel. 800/647–2918).

Whatcom and Skagit Counties, Including Anacortes, Bellingham, and La Conner

Channel House

2902 Oakes Ave., Anacortes, WA 98221, tel. 360/293–9382 or 800/238–4353, fax 360/299–9208

Midway between downtown Anacortes and the ferry terminal is the Channel House, a 1902 shingled Craftsman bungalow with awe-inspiring views of Guemes Channel and the ferry landing that can be seen from most rooms. Innkeepers Dennis and Patricia McIntyre, who once owned a restaurant, dreamed of acquiring a smaller business when their daughter went off to college, but when she turned 15, they thought, "Why wait?" An ad in the *Los Angeles Times* turned up the Channel House.

The dining room, certainly the most spectacular room in the house, features lush ferns and other potted plants that stand against dark blue–and–peach floral-print wallpaper, white painted wainscoting, and the original glazed terra-cotta tile floor with cobalt-blue borders. A window with the original stained glass depicts lily pads in shades of green and pink. As you dine on the house specialty—French toast stuffed with cream cheese, pineapple, and pecans—you can watch the ferries plying Rosario Strait.

Ten steps up are the living room, with exposed beams and a 10-foot-high ceiling, and a cozy study. Both rooms display porcelain dolls made by Dennis's mother from antique molds, complete with hand-painted features and hand-sewn costumes.

Each guest room has its own style, but all are spacious and light, with high ceilings, hardwood floors, and Oriental rugs. Grandma's Room is furnished with an antique four-poster bed with Laura Ashley bedding, and a turn-of-the-century Eastlake-type oak dresser; the walls are covered with old family photos and little china collectibles. The more formal Canopy Room has a canopy bed covered with the same antique lace that dresses the window and an early 19th-century fainting couch upholstered in cream-colored damask. The walls are covered with a cream and green striped paper with a floral border. In a separate cottage, the Victorian Rose room seems a perfect spot for reverie; its window seat is crowded with soft throw pillows, and the fireplace has cream tiles with hand-painted pink roses that are echoed in the pale-pink walls and ceiling border of roses against a black background.

The McIntyres are wonders at promoting their little corner of the world as more than just a convenient stopover for the San Juan Islands ferries. They point out to guests that there are 2,500 acres of forest and seven freshwater lakes to explore, regularly scheduled whale-watching trips, and sea kayak rentals all in the vicinity.

🏨 *4 double rooms with baths, 2 doubles with baths in cottage. Whirlpool baths and fireplaces in cottage rooms, hot tub. $69–$95, full breakfast. AE, D, MC, V. No smoking, no pets.*

La Conner Channel Lodge

205 N. 1st St., Box 573, La Conner, WA 98257, tel. 360/466–3101, fax 360/466–1525

One of only a handful of waterside inns in the Puget Sound area is this shingled, Northwest contemporary structure with rose-entwined lattice fences. It is ideally located on Main Street, a short walk from the many restaurants and boutiques lining the waterfront.

Twig furniture, bark bowls, hand-woven baskets, and dried and fresh flower arrangements impart a lodgelike feeling to the lobby lounge. A towering stone fireplace and a cozy adjacent library help create a relaxed, homey atmosphere. Weekend evenings, entertainers tickle the ivories of the shiny grand piano between the lounge and library. Fir doors just behind the piano open onto a terraced stone deck leading down to the pier. There is a Native American reservation opposite the hotel; you can occasionally hear the songs and drums of a tribal meeting floating across the narrow waterway.

In the guest chambers, fish prints on the walls and shell-motif pillow shams and duvets reflect the inn's waterfront location. There are loads of extras: gas fireplaces; cushioned lounge chairs; coffeemakers; minifridges and cable TVs discretely hidden in cabinets; chocolate truffles on the bedside table; soft terry robes; and roomy, slate-tiled bathrooms with two-person Jacuzzi tubs. Each of the rooms has a deck or balcony; those on the second and third floors offer the best views of the channel. The Captain's Suite, perfect for families, has a small second bedroom with twin beds, porthole windows, and a nautical door. Couples seeking romance and privacy might opt for the gatehouse with a Jacuzzi in the bedroom (but no view of the channel).

A Continental breakfast buffet with trays of fruit, fresh-baked goods, and bowls of yogurt and granola is served in the small second-floor dining room. Cozy tables are set up near the corner fireplace and on the open balcony across the hallway, which overlooks the lounge below and the Swinomish Channel just outside. If you prefer, the congenial staff will deliver breakfast to your room.

🏨 *29 double rooms with baths, 12 suites. Phones, cable TV, refrigerators, moorage and charter boats available. $140–$210; Continental breakfast, afternoon refreshments. AE, DC, MC, V. No smoking, no pets.*

Majestic Hotel

419 Commercial Ave., Anacortes, WA 98221, tel. 360/293–3355 or 800/588–4780, fax 360/293–5214

Many of the guests who use the Majestic Hotel merely as a stopover on the way to the nearby San Juan Islands end up wishing they could linger. Dominating the historical district of Anacortes, the Majestic is one of the Northwest's premier small hotels.

Standing in the two-story-high lobby filled with 19th-century English leather sofas and wing chairs, an elegant brass chandelier, a white marble mantelpiece flanked by engaged columns, and copious flower arrangements, it's difficult to believe that this space was part of a meat market until 1954. Happily, Jeff and Virginia Wetmore, restaurant and inn developers from northern California, recognized this diamond in the rough, built in 1889. After six years of restoration, which included stripping away everything except the original framework, they opened the hotel in

1990. Two years later they added a charming English garden, an oasis of greenery and flowers where you can relax over a cup of coffee or play with your children.

The Wetmores take particular pride in the Rose & Crown Pub behind the lobby, where you can enjoy light meals and draft beers from local microbreweries amid 200-year-old English mahogany wainscoting, a backbar from a Victorian ice-cream parlor, and beveled- and stained-glass doors from a London pub. More substantial fare is served in Janot's Bistro, where cuisine such as Dungeness crab cake on seasonal greens with goat cheese vinaigrette and Northwest bouillabaisse in a saffron broth features the freshest ingredients available in the area. The convenient downtown location also puts you within easy reach of an array of other dining and shopping options.

Each of the hotel's 23 guest rooms is individually decorated and furnished with antiques from around the world, collected by the Wetmores. The Scottish Highland Room sports fishing rods, baskets, and old shotguns mounted on the walls, and there is a Scottish military chest from the 1880s. In the Asian Room the walls have been marbleized, and Japanese, Korean, and Chinese furniture and art are featured. An oakpaneled cupola affords a 360-degree view of Puget Sound, the marina, the San Juan Islands, and the Cascade and Olympic mountains.

🖼 *23 double rooms with baths. Restaurant, pub, phones, cable TV, minibars, refrigerators, VCRs in some rooms, conference facilities. $89–$177, Continental breakfast. AE, D, MC, V. Smoking on 2nd floor only, no pets.*

Other Choices

Albatross. 5708 Kingsway W, Anacortes, WA 98221, tel. 360/293–0677 or 800/662–8864. 4 double rooms with baths. Cable TV/VCR, library, airport and ferry pickups on request, sailing charters available. $85–$95, full breakfast. MC, V. No smoking, no pets.

Hasty Pudding House. 1312 8th St., Anacortes, WA 98221, tel. 360/293–5773 or 800/368–5588. 4 double rooms with bath. TV/VCR in 1 room. $60–$85, full breakfast. AE, D, MC, V. No smoking, no pets.

Heron Inn. 117 Maple Ave., La Conner, WA 98257, tel. 360/466–4626. 9 double rooms with baths, 3 suites. Phones, TVs, clock radios, 2-person whirlpool tub in 1 suite, hot tub. $69–$88, suites $110–$155; Continental breakfast. AE, MC, V. No smoking.

Hotel Planter. 715 1st St., La Conner, WA 98257, tel. 360/466–4710 or 800/488–5409, fax 206/466–1320. 12 double rooms with baths. Phones, TVs, hot tub. $75–$120, no breakfast. AE, MC, V. No smoking, no pets.

Ridgeway House. 1292 McLean Rd., Box 475, La Conner, WA 98257, tel. 360/428–8068 or 800/428–8068, fax 360/428–8880. 2 double rooms with baths, 3 doubles share 2 baths, 1 cottage. Kitchen in cottage, cable TV in lounge. $70–$90; full breakfast, evening refreshments. AE, D, MC, V. No smoking, no pets, 2-night minimum late Mar.–early Apr.

Schnauzer Crossing. 4421 Lakeway Dr., Bellingham, WA 98226, tel. 360/733–0055 or 800/562–2808, fax 360/734–2808. 1 double room with bath, 2 suites. CD players; fireplace, wet bar, cable TV/VCR, and whirlpool tub in 1 suite; hot tub. $115–$185; full breakfast, afternoon refreshments. MC, V. No smoking, 2-night minimum on weekends and holidays.

White Swan Guest House. 1388 Moore Rd., Mt. Vernon, WA 98273, tel. 360/445–6805. 3 double rooms share 2 baths, 1 cottage. Kitchen in cottage. $80, cottage $140; Continental breakfast. MC, V. No smoking, no pets.

Reservations Services

Anacortes Bed and Breakfast (tel. 360/293–5773). **Bed & Breakfast Service** (Box 5025, Bellingham, WA 98227, tel. 360/733–8642). **Fidalgo Island Bed & Breakfast Guild** (1312 8th St., Anacortes, WA 98221, tel. 360/293–5773). **Northwest Bed and Breakfast** (1067 Hanover Court S, Salem, OR 97302, tel. 503/370–9033, fax 503/316–9118). **Pacific Bed & Breakfast Agency** (701 N.W. 60th St., Seattle, WA 98107, tel. 206/784–0539). **Washington State Bed & Breakfast Guild** (2442 N.W. Market St., Box 355-FD, Seattle, WA 98107, tel. 800/647–2918).

Cascade Mountains

Mazama Country Inn

42 Lost River Rd., HCR 74/Box B9, Mazama, WA 98833, tel. 509/996–2681 or, in WA, 800/843–7951, fax 509/996–2646

East of the North Cascades National Park, nestled in a valley laced with cross-country skiing trails, is this serenely rural, rustic mountain lodge. Owned by George Turner and Bill Pope, the Mazama is a sprawling 6,000-square-foot, two-story wood-sided building with a front entry of stone and log posts, dormer windows, and a brick-red roof set against a backdrop of pine trees and mountains.

The spacious dining and living room features a massive Russian stone fireplace, vaulted ceiling, peeled-log furniture, and floor-to-ceiling windows that look out at the valley floor and the mountains beyond. Glass doors lead to the deck, furnished with umbrella tables for picnic lunches. Watercolor landscapes by a local artist are displayed throughout.

Most guest rooms are comfortable, but certainly not opulent. Some of the rooms on the second floor have two levels, with a queen-size bed on the upper and a child-size bed tucked under the staircase. Four larger rooms, connected to the lodge via covered walkway, have decks. Also available are five cabins, ideal for families.

The inn attracts guests who want a mountain experience. In summer, the area offers mountain biking, hiking, horseback riding, river rafting, llama trekking, and fishing. In winter, the inn itself provides ski rentals and lessons and arranges for heli-skiing, inn-to-hut ski touring, and dogsled rides. One of the hedonistic experiences you can enjoy after a day of cross-country skiing is slipping into the outdoor hot tub, surrounded by snowbanks, and gazing at the stars.

Winter breakfasts include hearty oatmeal, eggs, biscuits, coffee cake, and fruit; in summer, the main dish might be a vegetarian omelet or a whole-wheat sesame-seed waffle. Makings for sandwiches are set out after breakfast for you to fix your own brown-bag lunches. In winter, dinner is served family style and includes appetizer, entrée, and dessert. In summer, dinners are offered from the restaurant menu and may include seafood Provençale, mushroom fettucine with prosciutto and garlic, or pork loin piccata; a favorite dessert is chocolate mousse cake.

🏨 *14 double rooms with baths, 5 cabins. Restaurant, kitchen in cabins, sauna, gift shop, hot tub. Summer $60–$85, breakfast not included; winter $140–$175, including all meals; cabins (year-round) $95–$120, no meals. MC, V. No smoking, no pets, 2-night minimum in cabins.*

Run of the River Inn

9308 E. Leavenworth Rd., Box 285, Leavenworth, WA 98826, tel. 800/288–6491, fax 509/548–7547

On the Icicle River a half mile from Leavenworth, with a bird refuge on two sides, is this bed-and-breakfast in a classic log structure. It was built in 1979 to take advantage of extraordinary views of the river, Tumwater and Icicle canyons, and the towering Cascades.

A second story with cathedral ceilings was added by innkeepers Karen and Monty Turner, who moved here in 1987 from Las Vegas, where they both taught fifth grade. Karen still teaches, while Monty runs the inn and maintains his collection of classic and antique bicycles.

You have the entire fireplace-warmed living area downstairs to yourself because the Turners live in a small house adjacent to the inn. The country breakfast may include yogurt with fruit or a fresh fruit plate, hash browns, cinnamon rolls, and a cheese and sausage strata.

A guest sitting room is at the top of the circular staircase; supported by hand-peeled logs fashioned by a local craftsman, the staircase is one of the inn's many hand-hewn log features custommade for the Turners. Like the rest of the inn, the sitting room has an upscale country look, with handmade willow furniture and a stenciled pine dry sink. Beverages and fresh cookies are set out to make you feel at home.

Bedrooms have high cathedral ceilings of pine, hand-hewn log furniture, and locally made hand-embroidered quilts on queen-size beds. Each room has a commanding view of the natural surroundings, along with an old fly rod, ski pole, or snowshoe on one wall as a reminder of the diversions the area offers.

The inn overlooks 70 acres of wetlands, including a small island in the river. The Turners' own landscaping includes a small pond with a log bench, a wildflower meadow with a few trails, and aspen and alpine fir trees.

In winter, the area affords the opportunity for sleigh rides drawn by thorough-bred Belgian draft horses, and plenty of cross-country skiing and snowmobiling. Summer activities include hiking, whitewater rafting, bicycling, horseback riding, fishing, golfing, and harvesting fruit at peach, apple, and plum orchards.

▦ *4 double rooms with baths, 2 suites. Cable TV, hot tub, bicycles. Double rooms $95–$120, suites $130–$150; full breakfast. AE, D, MC, V. No smoking, no pets, 2-night minimum on weekends and during festivals.*

Salish Lodge

6501 Railroad Ave. S.E., Box 1109, Snoqualmie, WA 98065, tel. 206/888–2556 or 800/826–6124, fax 206/888–2533

At the crest of Snoqualmie Falls is the lodge whose authentic Northwest look and dramatic site made it the choice for exterior shots of the Great Northern Hotel in the TV series "Twin Peaks." Rebuilt in 1988 to follow the style of the original roadway inn built here in 1916, with dormers, porches, and balconies, the lodge added, in 1995, a stunning new Japanese-style spa where you can relax in hydrotherapy pools and sauna and steam rooms or arrange for a professional facial or mud wrap.

Run with the professional flair of a small elegant hotel, the entire inn is decorated in a sophisticated Pacific Northwest theme, with warm red-hued woods; rusticated stone; and fabrics and wallpapers in rich shades of rust, blue, and cream. Northwest art and Native American crafts complement the decor.

The library is an inviting room, with a hardwood floor, hefty maple beams, and rows of maple bookshelves; coffee is always available here, and tea and cookies are set out in the afternoon. Comfortable armchairs, a sofa, and a game table are arranged around the large stone fireplace. Although the lodge is used for meetings and the restaurant is open to the public, access to this room, as well as to the enclosed hydrotherapy and sauna rooms and fitness center, is restricted to overnight guests.

Guest rooms have stone fireplaces, mini-bars, natural wicker and Shaker-style furniture, either a balcony or a window seat, and goose-down comforters. All baths feature double whirlpool tubs, with French doors that open for fireplace viewing (candles are provided); each comes with thick, hooded terry robes. The four corner suites all offer spectacular views of the waterfalls.

Lighted paths leading to the top of the falls make for romantic evening walks. Walking trails lead to the bottom of the falls, and bike paths connect with extensive country roads. A sports court (for pickleball, volleyball, and badminton) is across the road.

The dining room serves excellent regional cuisine and has the largest wine cellar in the state. The country breakfast is legendary, with course upon course of oatmeal, eggs, bacon, trout, pancakes, hash browns, and fresh fruit.

🏨 *91 double rooms with baths, 4 suites. Restaurant, lounge, air-conditioning, TVs, phones, whirlpool tubs, VCR and video rentals, steam room, sauna, hydrotherapy pools, exercise room, 3 lighted courts for tennis and basketball, bicycles, spa services. $180–$575, breakfast extra. AE, D, DC, MC, V.*

Sun Mountain Lodge

Patterson Lake Rd., Box 1000, Winthrop, WA 98862, tel. 509/996–2211 or 800/572–0493, fax 509/996–3133

Perched high on a mountaintop above the former gold-mining town of Winthrop, this grand resort offers panoramic vistas of the 3,000 acres of wilderness surrounding the resort, 500,000 acres of national forest, the North Cascades, and the Methow Valley below.

In keeping with its mountain setting, the lodge is constructed from massive timbers and local stone. In the lobby of the main building—a busy place, with restaurants, meeting rooms, and many other guest facilities—sitting areas include hand-hewn furniture, stone floors, and large picture windows. The huge circular wrought-iron chandelier was created by a local artisan, as were most of the handsome, lodge-style fixtures.

Guest rooms feature hand-hewn birch furniture, hand-painted bedspreads, original regional art, and, of course, fine views. The best vistas are from the Gardner Wing, actually a separate building adjacent to the lodge. All rooms there are equipped with lava-rock gas fireplaces, private decks, wet bars. (Some main-lodge rooms also feature fireplaces and wet bars.) Housekeeping cabins, with kitchenettes, brick fireplaces, and walls of natural pine, are available on Patterson Lake, about a mile from the main lodge. A new addition, the Mt. Robinson Building, scheduled for completion by Christmas 1996, offers equally panoramic views from its double rooms and suites.

The restaurant is renowned for its superb cuisine and wines. Dinner is served in the main dining room, which has expansive views, and might include smoked Kahlua Hoisin Chinese duckling, autumn-run salmon, or pork with cilantro and red chili butter.

An interpretive center offers a full program of nature activities, including slide shows and guided walks. Trail rides, riding lessons, hayrides, and cookouts are available; rowboats, sailboats, canoes, and mountain bikes are for hire. In winter, the lodge offers sleigh rides, ice skating, ski lessons, and cross-country skiing on the second-largest ski trail system in the United States.

🏨 *94 double rooms with baths, 8 suites, 13 cabins. 2 restaurants, room service, phones in lodge rooms, kitchen* *in cabins, exercise room, gift shop, athletic shop, meeting rooms, heated pool, 2 outdoor hot tubs, 2 tennis courts, horseback riding, ice-skating rink, 2 playgrounds. $95–$270, breakfast extra. AE, MC, V. No smoking in main dining room, no pets.*

Other Choices

Alexander's Country Inn. 37515 State Rd. 706 E, Ashford, WA 98304, tel. 360/569–2300 or 800/654–7615, fax 360/569–2323. 8 double rooms with baths, 4 suites, 2 guest houses. Restaurant, hot tub. $69–$125, full breakfast. MC, V. No smoking, no pets.

All Seasons River Inn Bed & Breakfast. 8751 Icicle Rd., Box 788, Leavenworth, WA 98826, tel. 509/548–1425 or 800/254–0555. 5 double rooms with baths, 1 double with bath. Air-conditioning, cable TV, whirlpool baths, game room, bicycles. $95–$125, full breakfast. MC, V. No smoking, no pets, 2-night minimum stay on weekends, festivals, and holidays.

Cashmere Country Inn. 5801 Pioneer Dr., Cashmere, WA 98815, tel. 509/782–4212 or 800/291–9144. 5 double rooms with baths. Pool, hot tub, ski packages. $75–$80; full breakfast, dinner by arrangement. AE, MC, V. No smoking, no pets, 2-night minimum preferred on weekends.

Haus Rohrbach Pension. 12882 Ranger Rd., Leavenworth, WA 98826, tel. 509/548–7024 or 800/548–4477, fax 509/548–5038. 5 double rooms with baths, 2 doubles share bath, 3 suites. Air-conditioning, hot tub, pool. $75–$160, full breakfast. AE, D, DC, MC, V. No smoking, no pets, 2-night minimum on weekends Sept.–mid-Mar. and on festival weekends.

Maple Valley Bed & Breakfast. 20020 S.E. 228th St., Maple Valley, WA 98038, tel. 206/432–1409, fax 206/413–1459. 2 double rooms share bath. $75, full breakfast. No credit cards. No smoking, no pets.

Moore House Bed & Breakfast. 526 Marie Ave., Box 629, South Cle Elum, WA 98943, tel. 509/674–5939 or, in OR, WA, and Canada, 800/228–9246. 3 double rooms with baths, 6 doubles share 2 baths, 3 suites. Air-conditioning, mini-refrigerator, coffeemaker, and TV in suites; hot tub. $45–$115; full breakfast, full meal service for groups by prior arrangement. AE, MC, V. No smoking, no pets, 2-night minimum mid-Dec.–Feb.

Mountain Home Lodge. Box 687, Leavenworth, WA 98826, tel. 509/548–7077 or 800/414–2378, fax 509/548–5008. 10 double rooms with baths, 1 cabin. Air-conditioning, pool, hot tub, tennis court. Summer $90–$175, full breakfast (lunch and dinners by reservation); winter $185–$305, all meals included; cabin $350 for 2 plus $75 for each additional person, meals optional. AE, D, MC, V. No smoking, no pets, no children, 2-night minimum Dec.–Mar.

Mountain Meadows Inn. 28912 State Rte. 706 E, Ashford, WA 98304, tel. 360/569–2788. 3 double rooms with baths, 1 suite, 3 housekeeping units in separate building. Access to sauna and hot tub. $75–$95, full breakfast. MC, V. No smoking, no pets.

Old Honey Farm Country Inn. 8910 384th Ave. SE, Snoqualmie Falls, WA 98065, tel. 206/888–9399 or 800/826–9077. 9 double rooms with baths, 1 suite. Restaurant. $75–$125, full breakfast. D, MC, V. No smoking, no pets.

Silver Bay Lodging. Box 85, Stehekin, WA 98852, tel. 509/682–2212. 2 double rooms with bath, 1 suite, 2 cabins. Kitchen and wood-burning stove in cabins, croquet, lake swimming. $75–$120, full breakfast; cabins $95–$135, no breakfast. No credit cards. No smoking, no pets, 2-night minimum in suite (closed mid-Oct.–mid-May), 5-night minimum in cabins July–mid-Sept.

Reservations Services

Bed & Breakfast Association of Seattle (Box 31772, Seattle, WA 98103–1772, tel. 206/547–1020). **Pacific Bed & Breakfast Agency** (701 N.W. 60th St., Seattle, WA 98107, tel. 206/784–0539). **A Traveler's Reservation Service** (Box 492, Mercer Island, WA 98040, tel. 206/232–2345).

Spokane and Environs

My Parents' Estate

719 Hwy. 395, Box 724, Kettle Falls, WA 99141–0724, tel. 509/738–6220

This inn, nestled in the Selkirk Mountains less than two hours from Spokane, has both a scenic setting and a unique history. Opened as a mission in 1873, its 43 acres were home to the Sisters of Providence and later to a convent for Dominican nuns who ran a school on the site. The main house was once the Mother Superior's quarters and office. It also contained a chapel, now the two-story-high living room reserved for guests. Reminders of the property's history abound, including religious statues once used in services and intricate linen handwork done by the nuns.

Owners Al and Bev Parent bought the property after a preliminary round of remodelling had already been carried out. Bev then spent four years restoring the grounds, which contain everything from century-old "Crown of Thorn" trees to a peaceful little cemetery, where the nuns were buried, to a charming gazebo built in the 1930s. Some of the outbuildings were demolished, others moved. A professional artist, Bev set up a winter studio beneath the gymnasium, built when the place was a boys' ranch.

The large, square, wood-frame house, painted white and surrounded by white rail fences, is as pristine as the grounds. It's been completely modernized, but still has the second-story porch where the Mother Superior would greet visitors. Inside, it's warm and refreshingly uncluttered. Bev's collections of handmade quilts and antique tools, toys and historical memorabilia are unobtrusively displayed in the second-story sitting area. She's painted designs on several old pieces in the guest rooms. One room has a rare hand-painted bedroom suite of cottage furniture from the 1890s. All of the rooms have queen-size beds with Laura Ashley–style linens and wonderful views of surrounding pastureland and mountains. The Suite, in a separate outbuilding, has a white iron bed, fireplace, antique armoire, and claw-foot tub in the bathroom. The 1,200-square-foot Cottage, with mellow knotty-pine walls and Western-style furnishings, is available by the week or month.

Breakfast, a stylish affair served in the dining area just off the kitchen, typically features homemade muesli, muffins, and quiche. Several feeders are set up right outside the windows so that you can bird-watch as you dine.

🏠 *3 double rooms with baths, 1 suite, 1 2-bedroom cottage by week or month. Air-conditioning, kitchen in suite, pool table in upstairs lounge, half basketball court in gymnasium. $65–$100, full breakfast; cottage $40/day for month, $75/day for week, no meals. MC, V. No smoking, no pets, no children under 15. Closed mid-Dec.–early Jan.*

The Portico

502 S. Adams St., Ritzville, WA 99169, tel. 509/659–0800

Travelers between Spokane and Seattle can pull off the freeway and find respite at the Portico, a beautifully restored historic landmark in an unlikely place—Ritzville, a farming town 60 miles southwest of Spokane. At first glance, there seems to be little to see or do here, but this unassuming little town is home to a 1937 Art Deco movie house, a nine-hole golf course, a bowling alley, and a park, which, coupled with Ritzville's clean, safe streets, evoke a simpler time.

The Portico was originally built in 1902 as the home of Nelson H. Greene, a prominent merchant, financier, and wheat broker. When the town burned down in 1889, Greene financed its reconstruction, encouraging the use of brick; hence the Portico's unusual mating of material—buff-colored brick—and Queen Anne, Classical Revival, and Craftsman styles.

Innkeepers Bill and Mary Anne Phipps are passionate about architecture and period furnishings; their attention to detail is evident, starting with the entrance hall, whose parquet floor bears a pattern of unstained dark and light oak, bordered with serpentine work in bird's-eye maple. In the parlor the wallpaper, in rich reds and golds, is a reproduction of a turn-of-the-century design. The fireplace is framed by oak spindle work supported by Ionic columns. The ceiling, which resembles pressed tin, was actually produced by anaglyph, a process favored at the turn of the century for creating a design in relief.

The restoration has created two guest rooms, one very large and the other fairly small. The bigger one is decorated with rich paisley wallpaper and mid- to late-19th-century English furniture. A carved walnut bed sports a two-tailed mermaid at its head and an angel protecting a child at its foot, both symbols of good luck. A settee covered in crewelwork is shaped to allow two ladies to sit comfortably without wrinkling their gowns. The other room is bright and cheerful, with a white wrought-iron bed topped with a quilt handmade by Mary Anne.

Breakfast is fresh and generous. In season, Mary Anne serves raspberries and blackberries fresh from her garden;

homemade cinnamon rolls, eggs with a cheese sauce, delicious yeasty waffles, and homemade granola are often on the menu.

▦ *2 double rooms with baths. Air-conditioning, cable TV. $59–$74, full breakfast. AE, D, MC, V. No smoking.*

Waverly Place

W. 709 Waverly Pl., Spokane, WA 99205, tel. 509/328-1856

Waverly Place offers lodgings in a quiet old neighborhood just five minutes from downtown Spokane. The turreted Queen Anne house sits across the street from Corbin Park, whose 11½ acres encompass tennis courts, a jogging track, a baseball diamond, and a playground. Waverly Place, built in 1902, is one of several turn-of-the-century houses bordering the park; the neighborhood is listed on the state's Register of Historic Places.

Innkeepers Marge and Tammy Arndt are a mother-and-daughter team whose love for rambling Victorian houses led them to buy the building over a decade ago. With distinctive late Victorian pieces—many of them from Marge's mother-in-law's attic—they've created an environment in which the furnishings seem truly at home amid the graceful architecture of the house. Guests have exclusive use of two parlors, where the gleaming fir woodwork includes intricate beading around the mantelpiece and Grecian columns that separate the rooms. Most of the original light fixtures are intact, including the dining room chandelier. Victorian lamps throughout the house sport fringed shades handmade by Tammy. Both women enjoy researching the house; in painting its exterior they consulted old photographs and the builder's grandson in order to remain faithful to the original look: bright white with green and red trim.

Although they both have other jobs—Tammy is a meeting coordinator and Marge is a consultant for a church directory service—one of the women is always on hand. The guest rooms on the second floor are airy and comfortable, with queen-size reproduction beds and Oriental carpets and dhurrie rugs over shiny hardwood floors. The attic has just been converted into a spacious new suite.

Breakfast is, in Tammy's words, "decadent, delicious, and high in fat and cholesterol," although Waverly Place is quick to accommodate special diets. Served in the dining room on Haviland china, the fare reflects the innkeepers' Swedish heritage. Menus feature puffy Swedish pancakes with huckleberry sauce and almond-flavored pastries called *kringla*, as well as egg dishes, sausages, and fresh fruits and juices.

🏨 *2 double rooms share 2 baths, 1 suite. Air-conditioning, pool, Jacuzzi. $70–$95, full breakfast. AE, D, MC, V. No smoking, no pets, 2-night minimum 1st weekend in May.*

Other Choices

Fotheringham House. 2128 W. 2nd Ave., Spokane, WA 99204, tel. 509/838–1891. 1 double room with bath, 3 doubles share 2 baths. Tennis. $75–$90; full breakfast, afternoon tea. MC, V. No smoking, no pets, no children under 12.

Love's Victorian Bed and Breakfast. 31317 N. Cedar Rd., Deer Park, WA 99006, tel. 509/276–6939 or 888/929–2999. 2 double rooms with baths. Air-conditioning, robes, TV/VCR, indoor hot tub, bicycles, cross-country skis. $85–$110; full breakfast, evening refreshments. MC, V. No smoking. Closed 1st weekend in Dec.

Marianna Stoltz House. 427 E. Indiana Ave., Spokane, WA 99207, tel. 509/483–4316 or 800/978–6587, fax 509/483–6773. 2 double rooms with baths, 2 doubles share bath. Air-conditioning, cable TV. $55–$80; full breakfast, evening refreshments. AE, D, DC, MC, V. No smoking, no pets.

Reservations Service

Spokane Bed & Breakfast Reservation Service (627 E. 25th Ave., Spokane, WA 99203, tel. 509/624–3776).

The Palouse

Green Gables Inn

922 Bonsella St., Walla Walla, WA 99362, tel. 509/525–5501

In a business where location is often everything, Green Gables Inn has everything. One block from the Whitman College campus, the Arts and Crafts–style mansion is in a picturesque historic district: Trees nearly a century old line the peaceful streets, and most of the homes in the area have been carefully restored.

Rowland H. Smith and Clarinda Green Smith, for whom the house was built in 1909, took the lead in developing the neighborhood. For nearly four decades after 1940, their place housed the nurses and offices of the Walla Walla General Hospital; it didn't return to being a private residence until 1978. Margaret Buchan and her husband, Jim, the sports editor at the local newspaper, bought the mansion in 1990 and converted it into a B&B and reception facility.

A broad porch, tucked under the overhanging eaves, sweeps across the front of the mansion and around one side, an ideal setting for relaxing on a warm afternoon, lemonade and book in hand. The Buchans filled the yard with flowering plants, bulbs, and shrubs. Inside the front vestibule, a large foyer is flanked by two sitting areas, both with fireplaces and one with a TV.

The five guest rooms, whose names are derived from the novel *Anne of Green Gables*, are on the second floor; the hallway between them is lined with floor-to-ceiling bookshelves, and a love seat tucked into a corner creates a cozy library. All of the rooms feature baths with claw-foot tubs. The only room with a fireplace, Idlewild, also has a private deck and a Jacuzzi. Dryad's Bubble is sufficiently spacious to accommodate a reading area with an overstuffed chair and ottoman, a dresser and dressing table, and a king-size bed with striped comforter; French doors open to a small private balcony. The smallest room, Mayflowers, was once the maid's quarters; now the picture of Victorian femininity, with floral wallpaper, an antique quilt, and plenty of pillows with lace shams, it affords lots of privacy.

Margaret serves breakfast, which might include sausage quiche and seasonal fruit, in a formal dining room. An Arts and Crafts–style sideboard displaying her collection of china and serving pieces from the early 1900s runs the length of one wall.

▦ *5 double rooms with baths, 2 suites. Air-conditioning, kitchen in 1 suite, cable TV. $75–$160, full breakfast. AE, D, MC, V. Children under 12 welcome in carriage house. No smoking, no pets.*

Purple House Bed and Breakfast

415 E. Clay St., Dayton, WA 99328, tel. 509/382–3159

Although only a block off Highway 12—which is also the main street through Dayton—The Purple House Bed and Breakfast is quiet; perhaps because Dayton isn't on the way to anywhere, traffic is never too bad here. Owner Christine Williscroft spent five years remodeling and decorating the Queen Anne–style home, built in 1882 by a pioneer physician in what is now one of Dayton's oldest neighborhoods, before opening it to guests in 1991.

A native of southern Germany, Christine brought European touches to her B&B. The main floor guest room, which she calls the master bedroom, has a bidet in the bathroom, and French doors open to the patio and swimming pool that comprise the entire backyard of the house. Christine's real passion, however, is for things Chinese. Her formal living room is filled with Chinese antiques and appointments: Oriental rugs, an antique screen, a wedding kimono, and a hutch. Two carved wooden temple dogs guard the room's grand piano, and two shih tzus guard the house.

Privacy was a priority in the design of the guest rooms. The carriage house suite has a freestanding fireplace, a kitchenette, and a sunken Japanese soaking tub. The master bedroom has a pink sunken tub, color-coordinated with the rest of the room, which includes a rose-print bedspread. Two accommodations upstairs share not only a bath with a marble shower, floor, sink, and counter, but also a small sitting area at the top of the stairs. An antique oak sleigh bed and forest-green paisley wallpaper make the smaller of the rooms feel snug. The other room, facing the front yard, lacks antiques but is cheerful and sunny.

Strudel and huckleberry pancakes often turn up at breakfast along with local bacon or sausage. Christine will pack a picnic lunch for you, and she offers afternoon pastries and tea in the parlor. Dinner, served family style, is available at $25 per person for guests (minimum six people). A typical entrée might be Hungarian goulash, pork roast, or standing rib roast.

▦ *1 double room with bath, 2 doubles share bath, 1 suite. Air-conditioning, kitchen in suite, cable TV in common room, pool May–Sept., ski equipment and bicycle storage. $85–$125; full breakfast, afternoon refreshments, dinner and picnic lunches available. MC, V. No smoking.*

Stone Creek Inn

*720 Bryant Ave., Walla Walla, WA
99362, tel. 509/529–8120, fax 509/529–
8120*

When it was built in 1883, the Moore
mansion was a home in the country;
now it's a 4-acre oasis in a modest residential neighborhood. The house has a
distinguished history: Original owner
Miles Moore was the last governor of
the Washington Territories and later
the mayor of Walla Walla. Stone Creek
still runs through the estate and century-old trees tower over the lush
lawns, punctuated by flower beds near
the mansion. The pond in which
Moore's three sons splashed has been
replaced by a swimming pool, but otherwise the estate has been carefully
restored to its original splendor. A
thick wall of trees and foliage shields
the house and grounds from the street.

Patricia Johnson, an innkeeper from
Portland, bought the three-story Queen
Anne structure in 1995. Little renovation was required, so Patricia directed
her energies toward decorating the
first and second floors of the mansion
and landscaping the grounds. Her
antique furnishings lend an air of
graceful sophistication to the enormous
rooms (the ceilings on the first floor are
12 feet high). Collecting dolls is an obvious passion for her—a glass-fronted
showcase filled with them greets you as
you enter the vestibule.

Elements of the Eastlake style can be
found throughout the house, which has
an abundance of spindle work and
ornate bracketing. Governor Moore's
lawbooks are still in the bay-windowed
library, which also contains an 1828
Chickering piano. A 1925 Steinway sits
in the grandly proportioned living
room, where you can relax by the fireplace. There's a parklike view of the
grounds from every one of the windows.

The afternoon sun brightens the first-
floor Garden Room, which features an
opulent bath with a marble counter,
gold-plated faucets, and crystal lighting fixtures. A fireplace graces the second-floor Veranda Suite, with sunny
yellow wallpaper, a turn-of-the-century
high oak bed, and access to a private
screened porch overlooking Stone
Creek and the swimming pool. The
Governor's Room, done in terra-cotta
and cream with Venetian lace on the
windows, opens onto a study and Governor Moore's dressing room. It shares
a bath with the Terrace Room, which
has a private balcony.

Breakfast—which may include fresh
local fruit, home-baked muffins and biscuits, French toast, waffles, or ham and
eggs—is served in a formal dining room
with a fireplace.

🏠 *2 double rooms with baths, 2 doubles share bath. Air-conditioning, fireplace in 2 rooms, pool, hot tub,
limousine service from Walla Walla
airport. $85–$125, full breakfast. MC,
V. No smoking, no pets.*

West Virginia

The General Lewis Inn

Eastern Panhandle

Boydville

601 S. Queen St., Martinsburg, WV 25401, tel. 304/263–1448 or 202/626–2896

The story always told about Boydville, Martinsburg's grandest house, concerns its near destruction by Union troops during the Civil War. One often hears how some pretty southern belle pleaded with roughshod Federals to spare her family manse, but in the case of Boydville, the tale is documented. Mary Faulkner, of the clan that has resided in Boydville for 150 years, wired Abraham Lincoln, whose decision to let Boydville stand arrived just before northerners lit the torch.

A later Faulkner served as U.S. senator, commuting to the nation's capital by train (just as present owner LaRue Frye does today). When the six o'clock train from the District hooted over nearby Bull's Eye Bridge, the Boydville servants began crushing ice for the senator's mint julep. And when he arrived on the wide front porch and reclined in a green rocker (the very one there today), his drink was waiting.

Boydville, a limestone manor house covered with white stucco, was completed in 1812 by General Elisha Boyd, a hero of the War of 1812 and a friend of Martinsburg's founder, Adam Stephen. The mansion, with its ivy-covered walled patio, is surrounded by 10 park-like acres of lawn and garden. Guests are shown the case locks stamped with the imprimatur of the locksmith to King George IV, the English molding in the downstairs parlors, and English hand-painted wallpaper dating from 1812 in the foyer. The rooms are enormous, the most desirable being the Adam Stephen Room; it has hand-painted mural wallpaper imported from France in the early 1800s and the first tiled bathroom in Martinsburg.

Confederate general Stonewall Jackson retreated to Boydville for physical and emotional renewal many times during the Civil War. Thanks to LaRue and the other three working professionals who lovingly tend Boydville, the mansion still has that power to soothe.

🏠 *6 double rooms with baths. Air-conditioning, fireplace and cable TV in common area, fireplaces in 2 bedrooms. $100–$140, Continental breakfast. MC, V. No smoking, no pets, 2-night minimum Memorial Day weekend and on Oct. weekends.*

Hillbrook

Rte. 2 (Box 152), Charles Town, WV 24514, tel. 304/725-4223, fax 304/725-4455

Would Hillbrook, hidden along a country lane outside Charles Town, be such a special place without its innkeeper, Gretchen Carroll? One tends to think not, although the house itself is spectacularly eccentric, splayed in six stages along a hill, never more than one room wide or one room deep. The house has 13 sharply peaked gables, half-timbered white-stucco walls, and mullioned windows—the one in the living room has 360 panes. Ann Hathaway would feel right at home. Gretchen calls the style "Norman Tudor" and explains that during World War I a civil engineer by the name of Bamford fell in love with an inn in Normandy and determined to re-create it in the wilds of West Virginia. Erratically, he chose to start with two ancient log cabins. The logs and mortises of one of these are still apparent in the dining porch.

Gretchen was a foreign-service brat who grew up in the far corners of the world, including Turkey, Thailand, and the Ivory Coast; and Hillbrook is full of exotic curios and objets d'art. The living room holds pottery and a Senegalese fertility statue; in bedrooms you'll find Oriental rugs, an antique Vuitton steamer trunk, and a Thai spirit house. Richly patterned wallpaper, upholstery, and pillows; randomly angled ceilings; potted plants; and architectural cubbyholes complete the Hillbrook picture. The Cottage guest room, with its private entry overlooking an ancient springhouse (from which Hillbrook gets its water), has paisley-pattern wallpaper and a wood-burning stove backed with Italian tile. Locke's Nest overlooks the living room from 20 feet up and has brass double and single beds and a lavender bathtub.

The inn's seven-course dinners feature stuffed quail or grilled rosemary lamb chops; feta-cheese-and-pome-granate salad; and chocolate "decadence" cake. Breakfast specialties are sherried mushroom omelets, home-baked grilled fruit breads, and a delightful "egg blossom" dish.

Bullskin Run Creek trickles away at the bottom of the Hillbrook lawn, the haunt of ducks, inn guests, and a cat named Princess Fuzzy Butt. There are, of course, attractions to visit in the surrounding area, but nothing that would keep one away from idyllic Hillbrook for long.

🏠 *6 double rooms with baths. Tavern, air-conditioning, fireplaces in 2 rooms, high tea on Sun. Nov.–Apr. $240–$380 (including all meals; lunch $20; dinner $60 weekdays, $68 weekends). D, MC, V. No smoking in dining area, no pets.*

Other Choices

Aspen Hall. 405 Boyd Ave., Martinsburg, WV 25401, tel. 304/263-4385. 5 double rooms with baths. TV in library, hammock on porch, fireplace in breakfast room. $95–$110, full breakfast. MC, V. No smoking, no pets. Closed Jan.–Feb. 10.

Bavarian Inn and Restaurant. Shepherd Grade Rd., Rte. 480 (Rte. 1, Box 30), Shepherdstown, WV 25443, tel. 304/876-2551, fax 304/876-9355. 72 double rooms with baths. Restaurant, TVs, phones in rooms, private balconies, 26 rooms with fireplaces and jetted tubs, 3 conference rooms, tennis courts, exercise room, pool. $75–$145, breakfast extra. AE, DC, MC, V. Smoking restricted, no pets, 2-night minimum on holiday weekends.

Carriage Inn. 417 E. Washington St., Charles Town, WV 25414, tel. 304/728-8003, fax 304/725-3810. 5 double rooms with baths. Air-conditioning, fireplaces in 4 rooms. $65–$95, full breakfast. MC, V. No smoking in bedrooms, no pets.

Cottonwood Inn. Rte. 2 (Box 61-S), Charles Town, WV 25414, tel. 304/725-3371. 7 double rooms with baths, 1 suite. Air-conditioning, TVs, fireplace in suite. $85–$105, full breakfast. AE, D, MC, V. Restricted smoking, no pets.

Country Inn. Berkeley Springs, WV 25411, tel. 304/258–2210 or 800/822–6630, fax 304/258–3986. 58 double rooms with baths, 12 doubles share 4 baths, 1 suite. Restaurant, pub, room service, air-conditioning, cable TV in rooms, phones in hall and in annex rooms, spa, 2 conference rooms. $37–$145, breakfast extra. AE, D, DC, MC, V. No smoking in suite, no pets, 2-night minimum on weekends May–Oct. and major holiday weekends.

Gerrardstown's Prospect Hill. Box 135, Gerrardstown, WV 25420, tel. 304/229–3346. 2 double rooms with baths, 1 cottage. Air-conditioning, TV in apartment and living room, phones and fireplaces in rooms. $85–$95, full breakfast. MC, V. No smoking, no pets, 2-night minimum on Oct. weekends and holidays.

Highlawn. 304 Market St., Berkeley Springs, WV 25411, tel. 304/258–5700. 9 double rooms with baths, 1 suite. Air-conditioning, TV in bedrooms. $70–$98, full breakfast. AE, MC, V. No pets, 2-night minimum most weekends.

Thomas Shepherd Inn. Box 1162, Shepherdstown, WV 25443, tel. 304/876–3715. 7 double rooms with baths. Air-conditioning, TV in library, dinners and picnic lunches on request. $85–$115, full breakfast. AE, D, MC, V. Smoking on porch only, no pets.

The Mountains

Cheat Mountain Club

Box 28, Durbin, WV 26264, tel. 304/456–4627, fax 304/456–3192

Standing 3,800 feet above sea level, on the shoulder of the colossal Cheat Mountain and surrounded by nine of West Virginia's 10 highest precipices and the 901,000-acre Monongahela National Forest, the Cheat Mountain Club has a setting that will always be enough to make it special among inns. Lovers of the outdoors are sure to appreciate the changing seasons here, whether the lodge is buried in snow, blanketed with wild rhododendrons, or enveloped in a fog so thick that no one bothers to step outside the front door. The grounds include 188 acres, across which the trout-rich Shavers Fork River flows. Five miles of trails within the club's boundaries, along which shy black bears are often spied, are groomed for hiking, mountain biking, and cross-country skiing.

Resident manager Libbo Talbott, a native West Virginian, brings to the lodge warmth, good humor, a knowledge of the outdoors, and three excellent meals that are included in the club's daily rate. Fly-fishing–pro Frank Oliverio is called in to teach his delicate art and to share his knowledge of local streams.

The pine-paneled guest rooms on the lodge's second floor are functionally decorated and immaculately kept. Only one has a private bath, but the large, multiple shared bathrooms (one for women, another for men) are extremely comfortable and outfitted with tubs, showers, and piles of fresh linen; there's also a sink in each guest room. The third floor holds a dormitory-style room. Downstairs is a large gathering hall, and dining room with self-serve bar. There is almost always a crackling fire in both of the stone hearths. The room is full of topographical maps, magazines, and books and is a meeting place where guests enjoy predinner drinks.

1 king-size room with bath; 7 doubles, 1 single, and dormitory (sleeps 6) share 2 baths. Box lunches available, fishing, mountain biking, cross-country skiing, canoeing, horseshoes, snowshoes, games room, and 2 meeting rooms. $80–$110 per person, including all meals and use of recreational gear. No credit cards. No smoking in bed-

rooms, no pets, 2-night minimum on weekends. Closed Dec. 25.

General Lewis Inn

301 E. Washington St., Lewisburg, WV 24901, tel. 304/645-2600 or 800/628-4454, fax 304/645-2600

This is a country hostel of perfect proportions (just 25 rooms), run by the Hock family since 1928. It lies in a shady residential section of Lewisburg, a National Register town with a historic academy, stone church, and Confederate cemetery. Down the street from the inn are pleasant shops selling West Virginia quilts, ladies' dresses, and antiques. You can see everything Lewisburg has to offer in an easy afternoon, leaving you lots of time to sit on the veranda at the General Lewis. Out front there's a restored carriage, which used to rumble over the James River and Kanawha Turnpike (now Route 60), and in the back garden is owner Mary Hock Morgan's large old dollhouse.

Mary's parents started the General Lewis in the original house, built in the early 1800s; the architect who designed the West Virginia governor's mansion in Charleston later supervised a 1920s addition to the building, which blends flawlessly with the older section. The Hocks were great antiques collectors, and the inn is full of their prizes, including farming implements and a nickelodeon that still plays "The Man in the Moon Has His Eyes on You." The front desk came from the Sweet Chalybeate Springs Hotel and was reputedly leaned on by Patrick Henry and Thomas Jefferson.

Though the inn is ably managed by Nan Morgan, granddaughter of Randolph and Mary Hock, Mary Hock Morgan is usually around to show children where to find the checkers. She lived in the General Lewis until the age of 15 and is dedicated to keeping it retrogressive. The inn has some newfangled touches, such as central heat and air-conditioning with individual room controls.

All the rooms on the first and second floors are different, and when unoccupied, the doors are left open so that guests can nose around. Because the same rate can apply to rooms of radically varying size, guests might want to ask for the largest in any given category. But even if you wind up in a cozy chamber, you won't be disappointed.

🏠 *23 double rooms with baths, 2 suites. Restaurant, room service during restaurant hours, air-conditioning, cable TV, phones. $60-$88, breakfast extra. AE, MC, V. No smoking.*

James Wylie House

208 E. Main St., White Sulphur Springs, WV 24986, tel. 304/536-9444

The James Wylie House may not be the biggest or poshest lodging in White Sulphur Springs, but it's the only true bed-and-breakfast in this resort town. It's also one of the oldest buildings in Greenbrier County, predating the town of White Sulphur Springs and the Federal Fish Hatchery (still open), which were once part of the original 107-acre Wylie estate. Listed on the National Register, this historic house was built in 1819 by a local surveyor whose 1794 log cabin still stands out back. The main house was Victorianized at a later date, giving it its single-gable brick facade and broad, white front porch. The lawn stretches down to Route 60, just south of the business district. On the second floor are three high-ceilinged bedrooms decorated in country style by owners Cheryl and Joe Griffith. There's a large porch perfect for reading or snoozing, a croquet setup on the lawn, and bikes for those who wish to explore White Sulphur Springs. When the sun goes down, guests gather in two parlors for board games, piano playing, or the more conventional TV/VCR.

The log cabin, one of the oldest structures in Greenbrier County, still has musket holes in its walls; it's ideal for guests seeking privacy. There's a stone fireplace and small kitchenette on the first floor, and a double bedroom and private bath with the original claw-foot bathtub on the second. The cabin is charmingly decorated in country red and blue and hung with prints.

The Wylie House is a convenient headquarters for excursions into the mountains to the north or to the wet and wild New River, about an hour's drive west. Just down the street is the famous Greenbrier Resort, offering golf, tennis, swimming, riding, and elegant dining. There are local festivals, museums, battlefields, and shopping; and you can trust the Griffiths to have the latest information on nearby hiking, fishing, canoeing, rafting, caving, golfing, and skiing.

🎛 *3 double rooms with baths, cabin with double bedroom and convertible sofa. Air-conditioning, TVs. $70–$120, full breakfast. AE, MC, V. No smoking, no pets.*

Other Choices

Cardinal Inn. Rte. 219 (Rte. 1, Box 1), Huttonsville, WV 26273, tel. 304/335–6149. 9 double rooms share 3 baths. TV with VCR in sitting room, phones on each floor. $50, full breakfast. MC, V. No smoking, no pets.

Current. Denmar Rd. (Box 135), Hillsboro, WV 24946, tel. 304/653–4722. 4 double rooms share 3½ baths. TV in sitting room, hot tub, kennel. $50, full breakfast. MC, V. No smoking.

Hampshire House 1884. 165 N. Grafton St., Romney, WV 26757, tel. 304/822–7171. 5 double rooms with baths. Fireplaces in 2 rooms, air-conditioning, TV in all rooms, TV with VCR in music room. $60–$85, full breakfast. AE, D, DC, MC, V. No smoking, no pets.

Henderson House. 54 College Ave., Buckhannon, WV 26201, tel. 304/472–1611 or 800/225–5982. 6 double rooms with shared baths. Air-conditioning, phone jacks in rooms, TV and board games. $35, full breakfast. AE, D, MC, V. No smoking, no pets.

Hutton House. Box 88, Huttonsville, WV 26273, tel. 304/335–6701. 6 double rooms with baths. Parlor, recreation room, TV. $60–$70, full breakfast. M, V. No smoking, no pets.

Inn at Elk River. Elk River Touring Center, Slatyfork, WV 26291, tel. 304/572–3771. 5 double rooms with baths, 5 suites share 3 baths, 2-bedroom cottage. Restaurant with adjacent pub, hot tub, swimming hole, Nordic ski trails. $35–$115, full breakfast. MC, V. No smoking in farmhouse, inn, or restaurant; no pets, 2-night minimum on weekends in ski season.

Lynn's Inn. Rte. 4, Box 40, Lewisburg, WV 24901, tel. 304/645–2003 or 800/304–2003. 4 double rooms with baths. Ceiling fans in rooms, cable TV and phones in the two sitting rooms. $50–$60, full breakfast. MC, V. No smoking, no pets.

Wayside Inn. 318 Buffalo St., Elkins, WV 26241, tel. 304/636–6120. 2 double rooms with baths, 2 doubles share bath. $55, full breakfast. AE, MC, V. No smoking, no pets.

Woodcrest. Rte. 2, Box 520, Beckwith, WV 25840, tel. 304/574–3870. 5 rooms, 4 with baths, 4-bedroom cabin with 2 baths. Air-conditioning, phones, TV room, library, room service, shelter by pond for picnics. $60 (cabin: $100 for 4 people, $15 per additional person), full breakfast. AE, D, MC, V. No smoking, no pets. Closed Nov.–Mar.

Wisconsin

Allyn Mansion Inn

Milwaukee and Southeast Wisconsin

Allyn Mansion Inn

511 E. Walworth Ave., Delavan, WI 53115, tel. 414/728-9090

When Alexander Allyn, along with Milwaukee architect E. Townsend Mix, built this palatial mansion in 1885, his motto may well have been "If you've got it, flaunt it—and do it in good taste." Current owners Joe Johnson and Ron Markwell followed that dictum when restoring Allyn's home, which had spent decades as a furniture store and then a nursing home. The house, listed on the National Register of Historic Places, is considered Wisconsin's best-preserved example of the Queen Anne–Eastlake style.

The duo filled the mansion's 23 rooms with American antiques that, along with six original gasoliers, French walnut woodwork, parquet floors, and 10 Italian marble fireplaces—four topped with grand Eastlake mirrors—create the very picture of late-19th-century elegance. The high, coved ceilings in each of the three parlors have been repainted with floral scrollwork, as in

Allyn's day, following the designs uncovered during restoration. The front room glitters with gold French wallpaper, and green velvet portieres dangle from walnut rings over the doorway. Shutters on the tall windows shield from sunlight the room's stately grandfather clock, Victorian tufted-silk sofa, and matching chairs, and a cribbage board made from a walrus tusk stands ready on the marble coffee table. In another parlor is an 1890 Steinway grand piano, originally from a convent (and now the focus of the inn's musicales). The dining room displays English china from Chicago's 1893 Columbian Exposition. In the library, floor-to-ceiling bookshelves accommodate a collection of books about the Windy City. The bathroom beyond has a galvanized tin tub dating from the 1880s, and the kitchen, anchored by a regal cream enamel stove manufactured in 1930, displays a calendar clock and a complete set of Flow Blue china. Bathrooms, at one end of each floor, are shared.

The Empire Room is furnished completely in that period's antiques and dazzles guests with an 1830 tester bed with a slipper sofa at its foot, a mirror, fireplace clock, game table, curvy settee, and marble-topped table. In the

Mary Elizabeth Room, guests can relax on the chaise lounge before bedding down on the 9½-foot-tall full-tester.

Enormous trees and colorful flower beds surround the house, and the grand porte cochere, a replica, will have you looking for carriages to drive up and complete the picture.

▦ *8 double rooms share 7 baths. Air-conditioning. $60–$100, full breakfast, evening refreshments. MC, V. No smoking, no pets.*

Eagle Centre House

W370 S9590 Hwy. 67, Eagle, WI 53119, tel. 414/363–4700

Riene and Dean Herriges were so intrigued with an 1846 Greek Revival–style stagecoach inn in a nearby town that they decided to create a replica. Dean, a master carpenter, spent a year directing the construction that cloned a twin but with the most modern amenities down to central heating and air-conditioning. After all, they were building the house to serve as a B&B.

While the conveniences are modern, the inn is decorated entirely with period furnishings. Riene picked out a fetching Whitman's Sampler of antiques from the 1830s to the 1880s. Most notable are the two melodeans—a forerunner of the pump organ—which grace the parlor and dining room. On winter nights, wood-burning stoves in the parlor and tap provide a comforting ambience. In the dining room, guests enjoy a hearty breakfast of fresh fruit, pastries, and quiche or French toast, all under the gaze of a cheerful portrait of Abe Lincoln. Upstairs, one guest room has a burled walnut bedstead; another has an Eastlake bedroom set. One room even has an antique rope bed—not to worry, there's another bed in that room. Outside, walking trails on 20 acres of woodland and restored prairie beckon.

▦ *5 double rooms with baths. Air-conditioning, radios; double whirlpool*

bath in 2 rooms. $95–$145; full breakfast, evening refreshments, AE, MC, V. No smoking, no pets.

Hitching Post

N88 W16954 Main St., Menomonee Falls, WI 53051, tel. 414/255–1496, fax 414/255–4552

There really is a stone hitching post next to this inn. The original was used to tether the horse belonging to Dr. William Hoyt, a distinguished doctor who began the home for his family in 1869. Dr. Post died in 1870, and the house was completed by his wife, Nancy, who took over her husband's practice, although she had no medical training, and kept the household together until her son George completed medical school and took over both the practice and the home. The Colonial Revival home, now owned by Holly Smith, sits on a large, shaded, 1-acre suburban lot at the edge of Menomonee Falls, a half hour from downtown Milwaukee. Holly has landscaped the yard with lilac bushes, a wildflower garden, and 2,000 daylilies. Every spring, she adds to the garden color with hundreds of annuals.

The bright and airy living room, painted white and accented with floral stenciling, contains a number of Smith family antiques, including a mirror over the fireplace, which belonged to Holly's great-grandfather, and a large table clock. There are more antiques in the family room, where a comfortable sofa and easy chairs surround the fireplace. "In the winter, guests always find their way in here because it's so warm and embracing when we light a fire," Holly says.

Upstairs are two guest rooms. Dr. William's Room is furnished with an antique cedar chest, an antique rocker, and a king-size canopy bed with a cabbage-rose pattern in pinks and greens on both the canopy and comforter. Dr. George's Room is decorated with blue-and-yellow sponge-painted designs and is furnished with a maple double bed that belonged to Holly's grandfather; the quilt covering the bed was sewn by Holly's grandmother. Just down the hall from the guest rooms, Holly keeps a guest library of hundreds of best-sellers, mysteries, and classics. Both guest rooms share the 1930s bathroom, which still contains a 6-foot tub, ideal for a long, relaxing soak, as well as the original sink, now topped by an antique mirror.

Holly serves her breakfast of homemade pastries and muffins, eggs, fresh fruit, juice, and gourmet coffee either in the dining room, with its cabinet displaying Smith family china and silver, outdoors on the deck overlooking the wildflower garden, or in the guest rooms.

🎫 *2 double rooms share bath. Air-conditioning, newspapers, robes, pool, nearby bike trail, tennis courts. $60–$75; full breakfast, evening refreshments. MC, V. No smoking, no pets.*

Inn at Old Twelve Hundred

806 W. Grand Ave., Port Washington, WI 53074, tel. 414/268-1200

When Stephanie Bresette and her husband Ellie bought this magnificent Victorian home in 1990, they almost felt like they were the original owners. Built in 1890 by a wealthy local widower, it was purchased in 1920 by a Chicago bachelor. In 1945, it was acquired by a childless couple, who then sold it to the Bresettes. Because it had only a few owners—none of whom wanted to "modernize" it—the 6,000-square-foot home retains many original light fixtures, its original oak woodwork, lead and stained glass, and such period fixtures as pocket doors and quaint fireplaces.

Happily, Stephanie had an extensive antique collection, which fit perfectly into the home. The parlor and living room are now furnished in shades of Victorian plum, rose, and cranberry, with velvet-upholstered wing chairs and matching sofa. Two of the home's many Oriental rugs cover the floors. The dining room, where Stephanie serves breakfast on cool days, has oak paneling and a beamed ceiling and is furnished with two antique oak sideboards and a china cabinet that houses Stephanie's collection of Waterford crystal and antique cut glass.

Upstairs, the original master suite has a private porch and is furnished with a king-size brass-and-iron bed. The sitting area has two comfy wing chairs facing a fireplace. Another suite has a four-season enclosed porch, complete with fireplace. That suite is furnished in a light and informal 1920s cottage style.

Stephanie and Ellie completely refurbished the third floor, which was unfinished when they purchased the home. They removed 6 tons of original plaster and created two luxury suites. While decked out with whirlpool baths, the rooms retain the character of the house because the Bresettes reused original woodwork and custom-ordered new woodwork to match the old. The two suites have cable TV and VCRs as well as fireplaces; one also has its own tree-top-level porch.

The Inn's annex, just 50 feet from the main house, includes two suites and a double room. One suite has a whirlpool bath as well as an oversize shower with two showerheads. It is furnished with an antique walnut bed and matching dresser. The second suite has Oriental rugs and antique oak furniture. All three rooms in the annex have a refrigerator, microwave, and coffeemaker.

🎫 *1 double room with bath, 6 suites. Air-conditioning, cable TV/VCRs in suites, fireplace in rooms, whirlpool bath in 4 rooms, bathrobes, refrigerator for guests. $95–$175, full breakfast. AE, MC, V. No smoking, no pets.*

Manor House

*6536 3rd Ave., Kenosha, WI 53143, tel.
414/658-0014*

When auto executive James Wilson
became vice president of the Nash
Motor Company, headquartered in
Kenosha, he built this grand estate.
Wilson's stately 1924 French Renaissance Revival mansion, its brick-and-
stone walls, covered with ivy and
topped by a slate roof, is designed in
the style of the great English manor
houses. In the city's Lakeshore Historic District, surrounded by other
opulent homes and just across the road
from Lake Michigan, the Manor is
listed in the National Register of Historic Places. Encircled by landscaped
grounds with towering trees and a
wonderful formal English garden that
includes some 40 species of carefully
tended ornamental trees and shrubs, a
sunken pool with a fountain, and a
gazebo and arbor, the house could easily be the setting for a *Masterpiece Theater* presentation.

Guests enter the grand hall, with its
ornate oak paneling, slate floor, and
thick rugs. A wide central stairway
leads to the upstairs rooms. To the left
down a wide hallway is the living room,
which occupies one end of the first floor.
A fireplace and a grand piano are the
center of attention here. The library is
paneled in mahogany and contains a
fireplace with marble and mahogany
facing. The more informally decorated
sunroom provides a view of the formal
gardens. The grand dining room, with
oak paneling, also has a fireplace. When
guests eat there, they sit at a massive
table under the room's elaborate crystal chandelier.

Upstairs, the mansion's third-floor ballroom has been converted to a luxury
suite that retains the original dark oak
beams and coffered ceiling. A private
balcony affords a view of Lake Michigan. Four large rooms and one suite on
the second floor—three with lake views
and all with private baths—are mainly

furnished in Queen Anne antiques and
reproductions. The lovely Rose Room,
with a view of the garden, has a brass-
and-iron bed and a huge walk-in dressing room.

Lest guests feel the Manor really is a
stuffy English country house, owner
Laurie Novak-Simmons puts everyone
at ease with snacks in the kitchen,
piano playing in the living room, and
friendly conversation everywhere. She
serves breakfast in the guest rooms,
the garden, or in the dining room.

🏨 *4 double rooms with baths, 2 suites.
Air-conditioning, phones, cable TVs;
whirlpool bath and fireplace in 2
suites, honor bar in library, snacks and
ice in kitchen, bike trails, access to tennis courts, fishing wharf, marina.
$100–$199, full breakfast. AE, MC, V.
Restricted smoking.*

Stagecoach Inn

*W61 N. 520 Washington Ave., Cedar-
burg, WI 53012, tel. 414/375-0208 or
888/375-0208*

After careful restoration by historian
Brook Brown and his wife, Liz, this compact Greek Revival limestone inn once
again welcomes travelers, as it did when
stagecoaches stopped in Cedarburg on
their journey between Milwaukee and
Green Bay in 1853, when the house was
built. Restoring the corner pub was the
Browns' first project. They uncovered
the tin ceiling, set up a long, well-used
wooden bar where the original had
stood, refinished the rough plank floors,
brought in some handsome tavern
tables, and—in a place of honor behind
the bar, next to the vintage silver cash
register and grandmother clock—installed the original pub's wooden sign-
post depicting a fleet of white steeds.
This is where the inn's guests gather for
breakfast every morning and where,
in the evenings, they congregate for
draughts of Sprecher, a local root beer.

A prize wallflower bench from an old-
time dance hall sits in the front-hall cor-

ridor, at the bottom of the steep, narrow cherry-wood staircase that leads to the guest rooms on the second and third floors. The rooms' sunny nooks and low dormers host a collection of rustic furniture, much of it 100-year-old pine. Braided rugs and Oriental carpets warm the rough pine floors.

One suite has an exposed limestone wall, an antique oak dresser, and a whirlpool bath. Another, one of three that overlook Cedarburg's beautifully preserved old main street, has a hand-stenciled frieze on the walls and a cherry-wood country Victorian bed, wardrobe, and dresser. The walls of the third-floor rooms are also stenciled, and the furniture is antique pine; two rooms have whirlpool baths, and another has two sleigh beds and is brightened by a skylight. The only guest room on the ground floor is a suite. In it are an 1860 four-poster bed, a sturdy immigrant chest that still looks capable of transporting all your worldly possessions, and a well-worn Oriental carpet.

The 1847 frame house across the street now houses three of the Stagecoach's whirlpool suites, all furnished with antiques. Guests return to the main building in the morning to join other guests for a breakfast of freshly ground coffee, juice, cereals, croissants, and homemade muffins.

🏨 *6 double rooms with baths, 6 suites. Air-conditioning, cable TV in most rooms, fireplace in 2 suites, whirlpool bath in suites, pub, chocolate shop. $65–$130; Continental breakfast, afternoon refreshments. AE, D, DC, MC, V. No smoking, no pets.*

Other Choices

American Country Farm. 12112 N. Wauwatosa Rd., Mequon, WI 53092, tel. 414/242–0194. 1 double room with bath. Air-conditioning, TV, kitchen, fireplace. $75 midweek, $95 weekends; Continental breakfast. MC, V. No pets.

Elizabethan Inn. 463 Wrigley Dr., Lake Geneva, WI 53147, tel. 414/248–9131. 10 double rooms with baths. Air-conditioning, TV in living room and available in all rooms, fireplace in 1 room, whirlpool bath in 4 rooms, private pier. $85–$155, full breakfast. MC, V. No smoking, no pets, 2-night minimum on weekends and holidays.

Lakeside Manor Inn. 1809 S. Shore Dr., Delavan, WI 53115, tel. 414/728–5354. 4 double rooms with baths, 2 doubles share bath; 1 suite, 1 2-bedroom cottage. Air-conditioning, cable TV/VCRs; fireplace in suite and living room, private pier and beach. $89–$189; full breakfast weekends, Continental breakfast weekdays, afternoon refreshments. MC, V. No smoking, no pets.

Lawrence House. 403 S. Lake Shore Dr., Lake Geneva, WI 53147, tel. 414/248–4684 or 800/530–2262. 5 double rooms with baths. Air-conditioning, cable TV, whirlpool baths, video library. $120–$175; full breakfast, afternoon refreshments. AE, D, DC, MC, V. No pets, 2-night minimum on weekends in summer.

Lazy Cloud Lodge. N2025 N. Lake Shore Dr., Fontana, WI 53125, tel. 414/275–3322. 9 double rooms with baths. Air-conditioning fireplace and whirlpool bath in rooms. $125–$195, Continental breakfast. AE, MC, V. No smoking, no pets.

Pederson Victorian Bed & Breakfast. 1782 Hwy. 120 North, Lake Geneva, WI 53147, tel. 414/248–9110. 1 double room with bath, 3 doubles share bath. Air-conditioning, ceiling fans, hammocks, porch swing. $45–$80, full breakfast. MC, V. No smoking, no pets.

Roses. 429 S. Lake Shore Dr., Lake Geneva, WI 53147, tel. 414/248–4344 or 888/767–3262. 4 double rooms with baths. Air-conditioning, cable TV. $65–$120; full breakfast, afternoon tea and sherry. Restricted smoking, no pets.

Washington House Inn. W62 N573 Washington Ave., Cedarburg, WI 53012, tel. 414/375–3550 or 800/554–4717. 34 double rooms with baths. Air-conditioning, phone, cable TV, and HBO in 29 rooms, whirlpool bath in 31 rooms, gas fireplace in 14 rooms, social hour with locally made wine and cheese, elevator, sauna. $59–$179, Continental breakfast. AE, D, DC, MC, V. No pets.

Water's Edge. W4232 West End Rd., Lake Geneva, WI 53147, tel. 414/245–9845. 4 double rooms with baths, 1 suite, 2 2-bedroom apartments. Air-conditioning, cable TV, fireplace in 2 rooms, whirlpool bath in 1 room, private pier. $105–$140, full breakfast. AE, MC, V. No smoking, no pets, 2-night minimum on holidays.

Madison and Environs

Arbor House

3402 Monroe St., Madison, WI 53711, tel. 608/238–2981, fax 608/238–1175

This handsome Greek Revival building began life in the 1830s as a one-room pioneer home. That original structure, the oldest residence in Madison, is preserved as the living room of the Arbor House. In 1854, an inn was attached to the front of the small house, which became a stagecoach stop on the route from Madison to the west. The building began to deteriorate after the stagecoach gave way to the railroad, but was saved in the 1940s when an art professor at the nearby University of Wisconsin purchased the historic structure and restored it, adding a rear wing that contained his studio.

The home has been a B&B since 1986, and today, thanks to careful restoration, the entire building retains its pioneer feel, with original pine-and-oak floors, stone fireplaces, and narrow hallways. But innkeepers Cathie and John Imes are not only preserving a venerable building. They're also developing an environmentally friendly

B&B, with organic cotton sheets and towels, wool carpets and rugs, organic soaps and bath products, and water- and energy-saving plumbing and lighting—all while providing a quiet, luxurious retreat in the city.

The front rooms of the building, which served as the tavern in the 1850s, are now luxurious quarters called the Tap Room. Brass fixtures, a fish tank, and an old porthole window create a nautical theme, while a wet bar reminds guests of the room's original purpose. The antique brass bed in the Cozy Rose Room is made up with floral-patterned linens; one of the original stone fireplaces and a double whirlpool bath add to the relaxing, romantic mood. A view of the wooded yard and two skylights in the vaulted ceiling betray the origins of the top-floor suite called the Studio. Once the professor's atelier, it's now dominated by a brass bed with a lively Southwestern-design quilt; there's a separate dressing room, and another skylight crowns the cedar-paneled whirlpool room.

The adjoining annex features a two-story great room with beamed ceiling of massive Douglas fir timbers salvaged from a Sears building in Chicago. The annex's three rooms are furnished in comfortable style; one has a pine sleigh bed and plaid linens, another a four-poster bed with wildflower-patterned linens.

Breakfast is served either on an enclosed pine-paneled porch that overlooks the flower garden or in the Annex great room.

▦ *7 double rooms with baths, 1 suite. Air-conditioning, radios, robes; TV in 6 rooms, refrigerator in 2 rooms, whirlpool bath in 5 rooms, phone, TV, fax, and computer available in common room, croquet, badminton, bird-watching, bike path across street. $84–$180; Continental breakfast weekdays, full breakfast weekends, evening refreshments. AE, MC, V. No smoking, no pets.*

Collins House

704 E. Gorham St., Madison, WI 53703, tel. 608/255–4230

This sturdy brick Prairie-style house, built for a lumber magnate in 1911, was divided into apartments, then used as an office building, and then abandoned. But it was on a prime corner lot in Madison's historic district, next to a small city park and overlooking Lake Mendota. So in 1985, Barb and Mike Pratzel bought it and dismantled its "modernizations," revealing ceilings with oak and mahogany beams, decorative lead-glass windows, and the clean geometric lines of Prairie design. Then they polished the rare red-maple floors, filled the house with a collection of vintage mission and Arts and Crafts furnishings that complement the exquisite woodwork, and opened it as a bed-and-breakfast.

In the living room, a hassock and armchairs are grouped in front of a fireplace bordered in large, unglazed, moss green tiles, which are surrounded by a massive mahogany frame and mantel. The ceiling has beams, and an oak-leaf frieze is stenciled on the cream-colored walls; moldings are dark mahogany. Twin lead glass–fronted bookcases mark the entry to the library, whose frieze is in the Arts and Crafts style; inside, a plump upholstered armchair and sturdy rockers ring a well-worn Persian rug. Outside the library are three lakefront sunporches. Breakfast is served on one of the porches, where guests can watch the sailboats and crew teams, and, in winter, ice skaters and ice fishermen. Barb and Mike, who also own a gourmet catering firm, often serve Swedish oatmeal pancakes in the morning.

The light and airy guest rooms upstairs have handmade quilts, soothing color schemes, and striking mission and Arts and Crafts furniture. The largest room affords views in two directions, over Lake Mendota and the capitol building's dome. A tea cart filled with begonias and an immense oak breakfront and matching secretary give the room, which stretches the entire width of the house, a turn-of-the-century feel. Another suite, created by removing a wall between two small bedrooms, has its own balcony facing Lake Mendota.

The Collins House is only a short walk from the capitol, the university, State Street shops, a park on Lake Mendota, and Lake Monona.

🏠 *2 double rooms with baths, 3 suites. Phones; TV in 1 room, TV/VCR in common room, double whirlpool bath in 2 suites, whirlpool tub in 1 room, video library. $85–$140, full breakfast. D, MC, V. No smoking.*

Fargo Mansion Inn

Mailing address: 211 N. Main St., Lake Mills, WI 53551, tel. 414/648–3654; inn address: 406 Mulberry St., Lake Mills

The Wells Fargo Company was doing rather well in 1890, so when E. J. Fargo bought himself this grand house, he made it even grander. To the already stately Queen Anne building, Fargo added a gabled third floor, the cupola atop the showpiece octagonal turret, and an elaborate, gabled porte cochere. Over the years, however, the house fell into disrepair and sat empty and condemned until it caught the eye of a developer who drove past it after making a wrong turn; Barry Luce decided then and there to buy it. He completely renovated it, and the house became an inn, furnished with antiques from the town's Opera Mall Antiques Center, which the developer and his partner, Tom Bolks, also operate.

The sunny, spacious living room, a popular spot for weddings, is a Victorian confection full of sculpted moldings and other architectural furbelows. The focal point is the fireplace of laurel wreath–patterned tiles framed by an ornately carved wood mantelpiece; the shelves above are crammed with figurines and antique clocks. The music room holds a huge Federal dining table, two matching side tables, and two movable cabinets. The everyday dining room, wainscoted in oak, is no less elaborate, from its mirrored Victorian buffet and sideboard to the Corinthian columns that frame the doorway to the adjoining solarium. The small library contains a Victorian pump organ, a sled filled with antique dolls and teddy bears, and a vintage toy ironing board.

Of the guest rooms upstairs, the Master Suite is the most popular because of its private balcony and its size—large enough to dwarf a bed with an 8-foot-tall headboard and to accommodate a teardrop chandelier and the plump velvet sofa by the white marble fireplace. A "secret" doorway, disguised as a bookcase, opens to reveal one of the inn's signature modern marble bathrooms; this one also has a whirlpool tub. The other rooms, of varying sizes, are decorated in late-Victorian style and filled with antiques.

On the house's double lot, lovely gardens of shrubbery and banks of daffodils have replaced the bear pit in which Mr. Fargo staged battles between bruins for the entertainment of his guests.

🏠 *8 double rooms with baths. Air-conditioning, TV in living room, whirlpool bath in 5 rooms, conference facilities. $79–$160, full breakfast. MC, V. No smoking, no pets.*

Jamieson House

407 N. Franklin St., Poynette, WI 53955, tel. 608/635–2277 or 608/635–4100

Local merchant Hugh Jamieson was really prospering in the late 1870s, so in 1878 he decided not only to keep up with the Joneses, but to outdo them. Not content with commissioning an opulent brick home for himself—to reflect his new standing in the community—he then ordered the construction

of a home even more opulent, if that were possible, to accommodate his son and heir.

Today, they are a single B&B, thanks to innkeeper Heidi Hutchison, who has added (and renovated) a turn-of-the-century schoolhouse to the site and come up with a hostelry with a 19th-century feel and 20th-century amenities. The site encompasses a lovely 2-acre wooded and landscaped park on the edge of a small town 30 miles north of Madison.

All three buildings are furnished in late-19th-century antiques or reproductions. The Main House contains three guest rooms as well as the inn's common areas—two parlors, a formal dining room, and the conservatory. Upstairs, the Main Room is furnished with a brass bed with a crown canopy, an Italian painted armoire, and an 1876 marble-top dresser—the finishing touch is a settee upholstered in gold velvet, which occupies the bay window. Step in the bathroom, however, and you'll skip a century: A nifty double whirlpool bath awaits. Down the hall, cozy Lucy's Room has a brass bed and a brass daybed, a wicker settee, and a sunken tub in the bathroom. The Maid's Room actually incorporates the *Upstairs/Downstairs* back steps leading to the kitchen. This room is furnished much better than the Jamieson's maid ever dreamed—a king-size brass bed with half-canopy, a set of dark green wicker chaise longues and settee, and another double whirlpool bath.

The son's residence, now called the Guest House, includes the Master Suite, with a magnificent antique bed of burled walnut and oak. The second room of the suite contains a comfortable leather-upholstered couch and easy chair. Upstairs, the Pierce Room is decorated in elegant colors of light blue and dusty rose, including the blue half-canopy over the bed.

Nearby, the School House includes two suites, both with a fireplace, a TV, and a

VCR. Heidi serves a full breakfast in the formal dining room of the Main House, with its wonderfully ornate gothic Victorian dining set, or in the bright and airy conservatory. She's famous for her asparagus quiche, her homemade muffins and croissants, and her baked apple pancakes. After breakfast or later in the day or evening, guests gather in one of the two parlors of the Main House to watch TV and— keeping in step with the Victorian grace of Jamieson House—enjoy afternoon tea and conversation.

🏠 *11 double rooms with baths. Air-conditioning, TV/VCR in 2 rooms and in common area, fireplace in 2 rooms, double whirlpool bath in 5 rooms. $70–$140, full breakfast. AE, D, MC, V. No smoking.*

Mansion Hill Inn

424 N. Pinckney St., Madison, WI 53703, tel. 800/798–9070, fax 608/255–2217

Considered by Madisonites to be the height of opulence when it was built in 1858, this ornately carved sandstone Romanesque Revival mansion still upstages its neighbors in the historic district. Swagged with double tiers of delicate wrought-iron balconies, it would be more at home in New Orleans. Inside, a spiral staircase anchored by an immense, intricately carved newel post rises four stories from the jewel-box foyer to a turreted belvedere with sweeping views of the city. The tawny marble floor, flamboyant floral arrangements, elaborate gilt moldings, friezes, rich detailing, and three hand-carved Italian marble fireplaces create the atmosphere of a small European hotel and set the tone for the entire inn.

The small front parlor is arranged with conversational groupings of rococo revival–style furniture: settees upholstered in rose damask, side chairs with velvet ottomans. Guests can warm up at the elegant marble fireplace or

sashay over to the Emerson square grand piano for a musical interlude. The carved walnut dining table, original to the mansion, holds plates and pitchers of refreshments and newspapers from near and far to which guests are welcome to help themselves.

Each of the guest rooms is individually and lavishly decorated, and most are embellished with ornate cornices and ceiling medallions and elegant, modern marble baths. In nine of the rooms, French doors open onto pleasant terraces. The Lillie Langtry Room has a white marble fireplace, a veranda, wallpaper hand-painted in neo-Grecian patterns, Renaissance Revival furniture, and a bed draped in lace. The room known as the Turkish Nook recalls the 1890s craze for Orientalia: The wallpaper depicts a stylized lotus blossom design, and the bed, whose spread is a Near East–style tapestry, sits under a lacy sultan's tent. Velvet pouf ottomans complete the look. Rooms on the lower levels are smaller and not as elaborately decorated, but have their own patios.

You can have breakfast delivered to your room on a silver tray, along with your choice of morning newspaper, or arrange to partake in the parlor.

🏠 *11 double rooms with baths. Air-conditioning, phones, TVs, stereos; fireplace in 4 rooms, 6 rooms with sitting areas, 9 rooms with terrace, whirlpool bath in 8 rooms; private wine cellar, teleconference facilities; 24-hour valet service and valet parking, access to health club. $120–$290, Continental breakfast. AE, MC, V. No smoking, no pets.*

Other Choices

Cameo Rose. 1090 Severson Rd., Belleville, WI 53508, tel. 608/424–6340. 4 double rooms with baths, 1 suite. Air-conditioning, ceiling fans; TV/VCR in 2 rooms, whirlpool bath in 1 room, fireplace in living room, hiking and cross-country ski trails. $79–$139; full breakfast, afternoon refreshments. MC, V. No smoking, no pets.

Canterbury Inn. 315 W. Gorham Street, Madison, WI 53703, tel. 608/258–8899 or 800/838–3850. 2 double rooms with baths, 4 suites. Air-conditioning, phone, TV, CD player, robes, and refrigerator in rooms, whirlpool bath in suites, VCR available, gift certificate for bookstore. $80–$300; Continental breakfast, evening refreshments. AE, MC, V.

Enchanted Valley Garden. 5554 Enchanted Valley Rd., Cross Plains, WI 53528, tel. 608/798–4554. 2 double rooms share bath. Air-conditioning, TV in den, hiking in adjoining woods. $50–$70; full breakfast, evening refreshments. No credit cards. No smoking, no pets.

Past and Present Inn. 2034 Main St., Cross Plains, WI 53528, tel. 608/798–4441. 1 2-bedroom suite, 2 1-bedroom suites. Restaurant, air-conditioning, phones, TVs; whirlpool bath in 1-bedroom suites, gift shop. $75–$150, full breakfast (in restaurant). MC, V. No smoking, no pets.

University Heights Bed and Breakfast. 1812 Van Hise Ave., Madison, WI 53705, tel. 608/233–3340. 2 double rooms with baths, 1 suite. Air-conditioning, TV in common area, whirlpool bath in suite. $65–$125, full breakfast. AE, D, MC, V.

Victoria-on-Main. 622 W. Main St., Whitewater, WI 53190, tel. 414/473–8400. 1 double room with bath, 2 doubles share bath. TV in sitting room, kitchen available for guests' use. $48–$75, full breakfast. MC, V. No smoking, no pets.

Wisconsin River Valley, Including Wausau, Baraboo, and Spring Green

Crystal River Inn

E1369 Rural Rd., Waupaca, WI 54981, tel. 715/258–5333 or 800/236–5789

With its white clapboard walls and green shutters, Crystal River Inn is one of the first buildings visitors to Rural see as they turn off busy Highway 22. It is in perfect keeping with the history-rich heritage of its town. And it's quite a town: The entire community is listed on the National Register of Historic Places. Settled by New Englanders in the 1850s, the tiny hamlet has the white clapboard–green shutter look often found along the Eastern seaboard. Fortunately, Rural was bypassed by the railroad early on, and it has a preserved-in-amber air to it. The few dozen Rural residents work diligently to maintain the unique character of their town—and two of the hardest working are Lois and Gene Sorenson, owners of this inn.

They have furnished the inn with a tactful eye for its enduring appeal. The oldest part of the inn was built in 1853 by Andrew Potts, one of Rural's first settlers. Additions followed, the most recent being a sunroom and indoor gazebo built by the Sorensons to provide additional space to serve guests. An antique press-back rocker and wood-burning stove anchor the living room, while the sitting room has a picture window looking out on the Crystal River and the shaded backyard with its gazebo. An indoor gazebo is furnished with casual patio tables and chairs—not Victorian perhaps, but comfortable; guests gather here to eat breakfast, as well as play cards and board games. A nearby sunroom holds an antique feed chest Lois found in the barn.

The bedrooms are furnished in an eclectic mixture of country Victorian and contemporary styles. The Canopy Room has a four-poster bed Gene made from boards and pillars of the porch of a house about to be demolished. The Attic Room has a window seat overlooking the woods and an antique brass bed. Andrew's Room has an iron bed, behind which is hung a decorative filigreed gable peak from a 19th-century church. Helen's Summer Room features a tiny porch overlooking the river as well as a gas fireplace.

Many guests come to the inn to enjoy not only the town but the neighboring river, which winds through the community and is crossed by four bridges. The Crystal is popular for canoeing because it is cool, clear, fast, and shallow—if paddlers tip over, they just stand up and climb back into the canoe. Bicyclists also like the area because there's plenty of scenery and—even better— lots of lightly traveled paved roads.

🏠 *5 double rooms with baths, 2 double rooms share 1 bath. Air conditioning, ceiling fans; TV in common room, double whirlpools in 2 rooms, fireplaces in 4 rooms. $65–$115; full breakfast, evening refreshments. MC, V. No smoking, no pets.*

Dreams of Yesteryear

1100 Brawley St., Stevens Point, WI 54481, tel. 715/341–4525

Designed in 1901 by architect J. H. Jeffers (who was also the architect of the Wisconsin Pavilion for the 1904 St. Louis World's Fair), Dreams of Yesteryear was singled out from among its Victorian peers by Bonnie and Bill Maher, a couple determined to save the attractive, grand, old Queen Anne from destruction. Bonnie, an antiques collector, recognized the value and aesthetic potential in the oak woodwork, hardwood floors, leaded-glass windows, and footed tubs that remained in the house. She replaced a rotting roof with wooden shingles and restored the Queen Anne lines of "a chimney you could watch the sunset through." Then, with the major overhaul complete, she began "gathering" Victoriana. The voluptuously carved parlor sofa became theirs when a stranger telephoned to say, "Aunt Minerva just died at 93—could you use it?"

Today that sofa, along with a revolving library table discovered at a church bazaar, faces the fancy fireplace with its Victorian cascade decorations and surrounding tools. Sheet music for "Lola" sits on the vintage upright piano, alongside a 1904 phonograph that still has its wooden needles. Bonnie's lavish breakfasts, which feature local cranberry juice and pecan-stuffed French toast, are served on the inn's original dining room set.

Upstairs, it's hard to choose: Gerald's Room, done in French blue with a pineapple-post bed, is next to a tiny balcony; Isabella's Room, with an elaborately carved headboard, has an ivy-filled bay window, and a cozy reading nook; Florence Myrna's Room, with gardenia wall coverings comes with its own deep-green ceramic-tiled bathroom lit by antique wall sconces; and the cozy Maid's Quarters offers telephone access and a desk, making it appealing to business travelers.

The two suites on the third floor each has a bedroom and sitting room. One is furnished with a white wrought-iron bed and has a whirlpool bath, while the other is done in brown wicker and has a black wrought-iron bed.

🏠 *2 double rooms with baths, 2 doubles share bath, 2 suites. Air conditioning, fans in rooms, whirlpool in 1 room, fireplace in common room, TVs in suites and 1 room. $55–$129; full breakfast, afternoon refreshments. AE, D, MC, V. No smoking, no pets.*

Historic Bennett House

825 Oak St., Wisconsin Dells, WI 53965, tel. 608/254-2500

Historic Bennett House is a pleasant alternative to the many hotels and resorts in the Wisconsin Dells. A handsome 1863 Greek Revival mansion, the inn helps guests recall a gentler era. It was here that Civil War veteran Henry Hamilton Bennett became a pioneer photographer; his stop-action pictures, the first ever taken, are displayed today in the Smithsonian Museum. Gail and Richard Obermeyer, a former stage actress and a university communications professor, are running the inn in their retirement years. "We wanted the change of seasons. We'd visited relatives in the Dells and loved it." The couple knew exactly what they wanted: the intimate atmosphere of a European bed-and-breakfast and a "historic home with warmth and charm," Gail says.

First they found the perfect house, complete with a white picket fence, only a block from downtown and the Wisconsin River. Then they waited for it to come on the market—which it soon did.

Guests from as far away as Germany and South Korea have come to this casually elegant inn. Before dinner, visitors relax with a glass of wine on the floral-patterned sofa or in a pair of wing chairs drawn up to the white, woodburning fireplace in the living room. Breakfast is served at the communal table in the other half of the long room, which has a walnut-toned china cabinet and buffet and, on cool days, an open fire. Here Gail brings out the house specialty, eggs Bennett, or another favorite, toast Bennett (a variation on stuffed French toast). There's also a small, cozy den with a TV and comfortable sofa.

The ground-floor suite has a bedroom with Eastlake furniture, a parlor furnished with a love seat, antique table and chairs, and a framed antique tapestry; there's also a VCR and video library. Upstairs, the English Room has the original black floors, a walnut canopy bed, and an antique armoire from Britain. It shares a bathroom with the snug Garden Room, fitted with a brass bed and wicker furniture. The bathroom, with its gold fixtures, hand-painted Italian sinks, and claw-foot tub, is so seductive that some guests call it a therapeutic environment.

▥ *2 double rooms share bath, 1 suite. Air-conditioning, TV in suite and common room, fireplaces in common rooms. $70-$99; full breakfast, evening refreshments. No credit cards. No smoking, no pets.*

Oakwood Lodge

365 Lake St., Green Lake, WI 54941, tel. 414/294-6580

Guests at Oakwood Lodge are part of a long tradition. This graceful "cottage" is the sole survivor of a once-famed resort built on the shores of Green Lake in 1866. In what was then the Wisconsin wilderness, it was the first full-scale vacation resort west of Niagara Falls, intended to cater to well-to-do families of Midwest metropolises such as Chicago and Milwaukee. The resort eventually went out of business and all buildings save this one were eventually razed to make way for modern homes. The shores of Green Lake are still a playground, though, and the relaxed ambience remains, lingering along the lakeshore under the verdant oaks.

Because Oakwood Lodge itself was built as a cottage there are no stained-glass windows, no ornate woodwork or other elaborate decorations. What makes up for all that are the lake views from nearly all the rooms—and to take advantage of the site, there are balconies and windowed cupolas galore, a wraparound porch on three sides, a shaded lawn sloping down to the lake, and a private dock.

Guests are warmly greeted by innkeepers Bob and Mary Schneider, who maintain the place as a traditional lake cottage with modern amenities. The parlor now holds a TV/VCR in addition to a pair of floral print sofas and two wing chairs. The dining room has been converted into an informal gathering room for guests, with an antique dresser holding a coffee and tea service. The porch is chock-full of wicker rockers, settees, and easy chairs, while Adirondack-style chairs are scattered throughout the shaded yard. Serious sun worshipers head for the deck.

The guest rooms are similarly informal, with high ceilings, white lace curtains, and white chenille bedspreads. Furnishings are of the summer-cottage variety—simple, casual, not always perfectly matched. Room 3, which is on first-floor corner, has an entrance from the front porch, four large windows, pink floral print wallpaper on two walls, and a white wicker bed; Room 4 also has a separate porch entrance. Oakwood remains a favored spot for families, who particularly cotton to the accommodating layouts of the double rooms.

Breakfast is served on the four-season porch. Mary acts as a "short-order cook" for breakfasts, offering guests several breakfast menu options at a time of their choosing. She gets raves on her omelets—but don't dare miss her apple cake.

🏨 *12 double rooms with baths, 2 double rooms share a bath. Ceiling fans, private pier, TV/VCR in parlor. $62– $108; full breakfast, coffee, and snacks. MC, V. No smoking, no pets.*

Rosenberry Inn

511 Franklin St., Wausau, WI 54401, tel. 715/842-5733

This 1908 Prairie schoolhouse built for Judge Rosenberry, in what is now Wausau's Andrew Warren Historic District, was divided into efficiency apartments back in the 1940s. Fortunately, two enthusiastic devotees came

along and returned the old home to life as a B&B. By the time Fred and Laurie Schmidt bought the Rosenberry in 1995, it had a well-established reputation. The Schmidts haven't rested on the inn's laurels, however. They turned one of the downstairs rooms into a dining room for guests. They painted and refurnished and generally improved the rooms and the historic feel of the Rosenberry House. They also own the DeVoe House across the street; it's the oldest home in the historic district, dating from 1868.

Today, each guest room in the Rosenberry House contains a tiny kitchen (a remnant of its efficiency apartment days), eating nook, bath, and rustic Victorian furnishings—patchwork quilts, wooden rockers, and braided rugs. The three first-floor bedrooms still have tiled working fireplaces; rooms with western exposure are the sunniest and most spacious.

An imposing staircase with a breathtaking stained-glass window on the landing leads to the second floor. Here, four rooms evoke a comfortable and Victorian setting. The Rosenberry Room, in the corner overlooking the street and gardens, has a bird's-eye maple bed, wicker armchairs, and a tiled fireplace. In one corner is a china cabinet showcasing a collection of antique tea sets. Decorations in other rooms include a calliope horse, a stenciled bed, and a wicker settee. The Schmidts have mixed antiques and contemporary furniture in pleasing combinations.

Across the street, the DeVoe House has been divided into two guest suites; both the downstairs and upstairs accommodations contain whirlpool tubs, fireplaces, and open-to-view kitchen appliances, all in one large room with partitions. Throughout the house are collections of antique hope chests, patchwork quilts, and, in the room under the rafters, a rope-suspended porch swing.

Both establishments on this quiet, almost aristocratic residential street have porches and gardens for relaxation. Fred serves breakfast on the spacious porch of the Rosenberry House in warm weather, and, in cooler days, in the dining room, accented with its antique lace tablecloth. Hustle and bustle aren't too far away: The inn is only a quick walk from downtown.

▥ *7 double rooms with baths, cottage has 2 double rooms with baths. Air-conditioning, fireplace in 4 rooms. $65–$125, full breakfast. MC, V. No smoking, no pets.*

Other Choices

Bettinger House. 855 Wachter Ave., Hwy. 23, Plain, WI 53577, tel. 608/546–2951. 2 double rooms with baths, 3 doubles share 2 baths. Air-conditioning, ceiling fans in 2 rooms. $50–$65, full breakfast. No credit cards. No smoking, no pets, 2-night minimum summer weekends.

Breese Waye. 816 MacFarlane Rd., Portage, WI 53901, tel. 608/742–5281. 4 double rooms with baths. Air-conditioning, ceiling fans, TV/VCR in common room, fireplace in living room. $60–$75, full breakfast. No credit cards. No smoking.

Candlewick Inn. 700 W. Main St., Merrill, WI 54452, tel. 715/536–7744 or 800/382–4376. 4 double rooms with baths. Air-conditioning, fireplace in 2 rooms and common rooms. $55–$95; full breakfast, afternoon refreshments. MC, V. No smoking, no pets.

Hill Street. 353 W. Hill St., Spring Green, WI 53588, tel. 608/588–7751. 4 double rooms with baths, 1 triple with bath, 2 doubles share bath. Air-conditioning, ceiling fans. $65–$75; full breakfast, evening refreshments. MC, V. No smoking, no pets, 2-day minimum weekends June–Oct.

Nash House. 1020 Oak St., Wisconsin Rapids, WI 54494, tel. 715/424–2001 or 800/429–6834. 3 double rooms with baths. Air-conditioning, ceiling fans; fireplace in common room, tandem bike. $45–$65; full breakfast, afternoon refreshments. AE, MC, V. No smoking, no pets.

Parkview. 211 N. Park St., Reedsburg, WI 53959, tel. 608/524–4333. 2 double rooms with baths, 2 doubles share bath. Air-conditioning, ceiling fans; fireplace in common room, refreshments on arrival. $60–$75, full breakfast. AE, MC, V. No smoking, no pets.

Pinehaven. E13083 Rte. 33, Baraboo, WI 53913, tel. 608/356–3489. 4 double rooms with baths, 2-bedroom cottage with kitchen. Air-conditioning, candy in rooms, fireplace in common room; small private lake with paddleboat and rowboat, whirlpool in cottage. $65–$125, full breakfast (no breakfast in cottage). MC, V. No smoking, no pets.

Sherman House. 930 River Rd., Box 397, Wisconsin Dells, WI 53965, tel. 608/253–2721. 3 double rooms with baths, 1 suite. Air conditioning. $55–$70, Continental breakfast. No credit cards. No pets. Closed Nov.–Mar.

Swallow's Nest. 141 Sarrington St., Box 418, Lake Delton, WI 53940, tel. 608/254–6900. 4 double rooms with baths. Air-conditioning, fireplaces in common rooms, pool table, TV in common room. $70–$75, full breakfast. MC, V. No smoking, no pets.

Ty-Bach. 3104 Simpson Lane, Lac du Flambeau, WI 54538, tel. 715/588–7851. 2 double rooms with baths. Swimming, boating, private pier, bikes, outdoor hot tub, hiking and cross-country ski trails, kitchen for guests, TV/VCR in common area. $65–$70, full breakfast. No credit cards. No smoking.

Victorian Swan on Water. 1716 Water St., Stevens Point, WI 54481, tel. 715/345–0595. 3 double rooms with baths, 1 suite. Air-conditioning, fireplace in parlor and in suite, whirlpool in suite. $55–$120, full breakfast. AE, D, MC, V. No smoking, no pets.

Hidden Valleys, Including La Crosse and Prairie du Chien

Duke House

618 Maiden St., Mineral Point, WI 53565, tel. 608/987–2821

Even though it is in the Midwest, this 1870 Federal-style house—one of the oldest in Mineral Point—feels like a New England Victorian. Darlene Duke and her husband, Tom, packed up their antiques collection and left the East Coast fast lane in search of a more pleasant way of life.

One of the reasons Darlene loves the light and airy house is the many windows that enable her to indulge in her needlework, even on a gloomy day. The focus of the creamy white living room is the working fireplace; a plush pastel Chinese rug warms the broad-planked floor. An old brass trunk serves as a coffee table, and there's a Colonial drum table beneath the newel post. These and a few reproduction pieces give the room a lived-in, homey atmosphere, perfect for the early evening social hour the Dukes feel is the best time of the day.

The house is built on the area's highest point of land, so the views from the upstairs bedrooms capture most of the small city, which seems almost untouched by time. The four-poster bed in the Canopy Room is covered with a crocheted string spread and a canopy, and the finials are in the form of pineapples, the symbol of hospitality. With its pierced-tin lamp, its low, wooden Colonial-era rocker, the steamer trunk in the huge walk-in closet, and the copper warming pan hanging on the wall, the room is comfortable without being precious.

Across the hall, in Grandma's Room, more pineapples appear on the four-poster bed, complemented by floral wallpaper, a white rug covering well-polished floorboards, a decorative kerosene lamp, and bookcases filled with tomes of area history and lore. Other pieces find their way here from Duke's Antiques, which is only a short stroll away, close to the artisans' shops that occupy the former miners' dwellings.

▦ *2 double rooms share bath. Air-conditioning, fireplace in common room. $48–$58; full breakfast, morning coffee, and Cornish appetizers delivered to guest rooms. MC, V. No smoking, no pets. Closed Mar.*

Franklin Victorian

220 E. Franklin Pl., Sparta, WI 54656, tel. 608/269–3894

W. G. Williamson, a prominent Sparta banker, personally inspected every piece of wood that went into the interior of this raspberry red clapboard Victorian. His meticulous standards are evident the minute you cross the white-columned front porch. The floors are of glowing maple complemented by black ash and quarter-cut oak. Pocket doors of curly birch lead to a parlor with russet ceramic tiles, a beveled-glass window, and a double-manteled fireplace with fluted Corinthian columns—elegant reminders of the late 1800s, when Sparta, with its spas and mineral waters, was a hub of social activity.

Cordial innkeepers Jane and Lloyd Larson have integrated their family heirlooms into the house. In the dining room, which has an elaborate parquet floor with a "braided" border, is a built-in buffet with floor-to-ceiling glass doors showcasing china that's been in Jane's family for three generations. In the parlor is the Civil War–era miniature pump organ that belonged to Jane's grandfather. The portable instrument, which he played at funerals, keeps company with a boxy Victorian velvet sofa trimmed in mahogany and its honor guard of stuffed velvet chairs that belonged to Jane's great-grandparents. The intricate sunset-motif stained-glass window faces west, providing a vivid late-afternoon glow to the stairway landing.

Guests love the Wicker Room, with its white wrought-iron bed and wicker furnishings, which contrast with the dark blue floral-design wallpaper. Most requested, however, is the Master Bedroom, which has a grand titled fireplace with decorative columns, an immense oak headboard crafted by Lloyd Larson from the the wall of a judge's chamber, and a tall highboy of bird's-eye maple that belonged to Jane's parents. Its bathroom, with tongue-and-groove wainscoting, still boasts the original marble-top sink.

Guests can enjoy a private chat in the upstairs sitting room or sit in rocking chairs and sip lemonade on the side or front porch. They overlook this corner lot in a quiet residential neighborhood, where the trees loom taller than dormers and turrets.

▦ *2 double rooms with baths, 2 doubles share bath. Air-conditioning, fireplace in common room, canoe rental, shuttle service for bikers and canoeists. $70–$92; full breakfast, early morning coffee. MC, V. No smoking, no pets.*

Inn at Wildcat Mountain

U.S. 33 (Box 112), Ontario, WI 54651, tel. 608/337–4352

All tall white pillars, with a classic Georgian air, this inn looks like the White House of woodland Wisconsin. A Greek Revival mansion on the edge of the tiny hamlet of Ontario, it was built in 1910 with high hopes as a railroad seemed headed this way: Its builder, who had made a fortune growing ginseng and shipping it to Asian buyers in Chicago, planned to rent rooms in the house to tourists. But the proposed railroad never made it this far, and the interior of the gorgeous house was carved up into apartments.

After undergoing a monumental restoration, the building is the dream come true of innkeepers Pat and Wendall Barnes. With their children grown and gone, turning their home into a bed-and-breakfast seemed natural. "How else could I justify buying a house like this?" Pat laughs. She says she enjoyed restoring the building and likes entertaining people who appreciate the cherry, oak, and bird's-eye maple woodwork she spent years refinishing, according to her calculations.

Pat describes her former life as "collecting things," an understatement once you see the period pieces and vintage clothing hung everywhere on walls, clothes trees, and mannequins. A fan revolves on the parlor's lofty ceiling, and lace-curtained windows rise even higher than the dignified grandfather clock. The focal point of the room is a 1905 oak secretary. In the dining room, connected to the parlor by a columned entry, a silver candelabra casts a warm glow over the Philippine mahogany sideboard.

Of the four upstairs rooms, the most in demand is the Balcony Room, which has a turn-of-the-century brass bed and its own curved balcony. The back room, called Shady Rest, boasts the house's only closet, as well as a four-poster bed and a bare wooden floor.

The 5-acre woodland setting, in the lap of the forested Wildcat Mountain State Park, makes the inn especially popular with outdoor-sports enthusiasts. Guests can rent horses or canoes at nearby outfitters. Or they can just loll on Pat's wide, inviting front porch or in the spacious backyard and watch the butterflies flit by.

▦ *4 double rooms (1 sleeps 3 people) share 2 baths. Air-conditioning, ceiling fans. $50–$75; full breakfast, early morning coffee and tea, afternoon* refreshments. *MC, V. No smoking, pets in outside kennels only.*

Jones House

215 Ridge St. (Box 130), Mineral Point, WI 53565, tel. 608/987-2337

This regional showcase looks as grand as it did on the day it was built; oddly enough, it was hardly lived in. William Jones, once commissioner of the Bureau of Indian Affairs for President McKinley, erected the 16-room red-brick mansion in 1906 as a homecoming present to himself after his stint in Washington. He died soon after, and his will forbade its sale until the death of his wife and children. Boarded up intact, a housekeeper faithfully dusted it twice a week until 1986, when June and Art Openshaw purchased it.

A grand, boxy staircase winds around one of the seven unusual fireplaces. The stairs rise from the foyer to a stained-glass skylight that casts patterns on the entry carpet. The mahogany-beamed dining room is graced by forest green woodland scenes painted above the wainscoting. A green-tile fireplace warms guests during breakfast. Twin sideboards topped by graceful arches glint with beveled glass, and padded velvet window seats on either side of the fireplace overlook the broad side lawn. To complete the *après-la-chasse* feel, the hardwood floor is covered with moss green carpet.

The Persian and floral-print rugs, dark patterned wallpapers, and brass lighting fixtures, all of which came with the house, create a decidedly masculine atmosphere. The small Ladies' Parlor overlooking the front walk, however, provides respite for the frill-deprived with its garlands of roses painted on high, pale walls.

In the Master Suite, a white tile fireplace, original needlepoint chairs, and a floral covering on the daybed in the suite's sitting room also bestow a more feminine air. A screen door leads to a porch-top balcony that overlooks the town. The adjacent front bedroom, with a view of the spreading side yard as well as the avenue, boasts another white tile fireplace and a Colonial-reproduction four-poster bed with pineapple finials on the posts. The Ivy Suite, which overlooks the hills to the north of town, has a green tile fireplace and a Colonial-reproduction four-poster; the smaller back bedroom, in contrast, has a country-antique look.

There are still traces of William Jones in the house: Outside the Master Suite stand the master's antique golf clubs; his leatherbound books still line the library's shelves; and his umbrella hangs on the door of the vestibule.

▥ *1 double room with bath, 1 suite, 1 suite and 1 double share bath. Fans; 7 fireplaces. $58-$88, full breakfast. No credit cards. No smoking, no pets.*

Just-N-Trails

Rte. 1 (Box 274), Sparta, WI 54656, tel. 608/269-4522 or 800/488-4521

Ask Don and Donna Justin why they added a bed-and-breakfast to their 213-acre working farm, and they just laugh, "We'd been doing it free for 15 years anyway for all the relatives." The accommodations are "all things to all people," claim the friendly, laid-back couple, who delight in welcoming guests. Their 50 head of Holstein cattle occasionally provide visitors with a rare late-night show (no cover charge)—the birth of a calf. An athlete's nirvana, their spread has 10 miles of groomed and mapped hiking and ski trails, six nearby cycling trails (the area calls itself "the bike capital of America"), and five rivers close at hand, where guests can fish or go canoeing. And then, of course, there's always the B&B's own "traditional agrarian fitness center"—decked out with pitchfork and hay bales.

The farm is also a romantic getaway spot, with three private cabins and

Laura Ashley–decorated rooms upstairs in the farmhouse. The Granary Cottage has a front deck from which you can watch the sun sinking past the fields and wooded hills. The cabin decor includes a garden-gate queen-size bed, Amish bentwood rockers made by local craftsmen, and its own whirlpool bath. The beds are invitingly comfortable, with an abundance of pillows that make reading a pleasure.

The second log cabin, Little House on the Prairie, has a log bed, country-style furnishings, a fireplace, and a whirlpool bath in the loft under skylights. The Paul Bunyan, the two-bedroom cottage, is made of aspen logs from the farm's woodlots and is furnished with a log bed and other rustic pieces. It also boasts a double whirlpool bath, and both a rear porch and a rear balcony from which to watch deer coming out of the nearby woods. All three cottages have kitchenettes, and the Paul Bunyan is accessible to wheelchair users.

Guests in the farmstead's bedrooms—such as the Green Room, with a green, pink, and white floral scheme and double bird's-eye maple bed and matching dresser—get the same nine-pillow treatment as those in the cabins. The morning wake-up call is a wren's warble or perhaps a moo, followed by Donna's hearty, farm-style breakfast, served up in the nearby lodge. There's also a microwave guests can use when the hungries hit, as sometimes happens after a ramble on the hills up to the farm pond and down again via the Bambi Trail—so named to reassure novice skiers.

🏠 *2 double rooms with baths, 1 suite, 2 1-bedroom cabins, 1 2-bedroom cabin. Air-conditioning, fireplace and whirlpool tub in cabins, hammock, picnic tables, hiking and cross-country ski trails, ski and snowshoe rentals, snow tubes available free. $75–$250, full breakfast. AE, D, MC, V. No smoking.*

Martindale House

237 S. 10th St., La Crosse, WI 54601, tel. 608/782–4224

When Anita Philbrook opened the Martindale House in a quiet residential section of La Crosse, she was concerned that bed-and-breakfast establishments would prove to be "a fad, like the vitamin craze." But repeat guests—from as far away as England, Spain, and Scandinavia—have made her fears groundless. "I offer not just a bed, but an experience," Martindale's polished hostess maintains. Luckily, that experience includes a hearty Swedish breakfast served on the fifth-generation family china patterned in wedding-ring gold, which complements antique silver coffee spoons. This repast is served in the white, bright Scandinavian-style dining room, lined with a collection of traditional family portraits.

The imposing green-shuttered house, built in 1859, is a grand architectural mélange of Italianate cupola and Colonial clapboard, with a Victorian-style wraparound porch to boot. Combating years of disrepair, Anita restored moldings and chandeliers discovered in the basement and returned them to their proper places; she also resurrected the iron fence, hidden in the carriage house. Then she replanted the entire garden.

Inside, the parlor is a historian's delight. The room contains a stately grandfather clock, an antique chess table, antique Oriental rugs on the blond-oak floors, floor-to-ceiling windows flanked by their original shutters, and a piano that's been in her husband's family for five generations.

The white staircase in the foyer leads to four bedrooms. The Martindale Room features an 1800 cannonball bed, a warming pan, a 1740 Queen Anne highboy, and quilts from the nearby Amish community. The French Room derives its name from the carved Louis XVI bed that came from a castle in

Lyons; its other highlights are a 1640 campaign chest and an antique grandfather clock. The English Room offers a fireplace, a garden view, and a lace-canopied four-poster bed. This room has the advantage of a vast, soothing bathroom, dubbed the "rub-a-dub" by guests. The antique twin beds in the sunny Scandinavian Room came from a convent, and the Lapland dolls on display belonged to Anita's grandmother. Anita also renovated the 1860 carriage house into a two-story, three-room suite. The downstairs sitting room has a microwave, coffeemaker, and small refrigerator. The upstairs bedroom has an iron-and-brass bed and an antique Franklin stove, as well as a heart-shaped double whirlpool bath.

▦ *4 double rooms with baths, 1 suite. Air-conditioning, use of portable phones, several languages spoken. $80–$145; 4-course breakfast, evening refreshments. MC, V. No smoking, no pets.*

Westby House

200 W. State St., Westby, WI 54667, tel. 608/634–4112

Guests heading for Westby tend to book well in advance at this B&B during the merry month of May, for this is when this very Norwegian town is especially lively, thanks to the Syttendai Mai Festival. Year-round, however, the Old World Norskedalen Village, 6 miles away, attracts visitors. They arrive at a house that is archetypal Midwest American: Topped with an imposing Queen Anne witch's turret, the country manor–style abode was commissioned in the 1890s by a well-to-do Norwegian immigrant. Today, its fine oak woodwork, lighting fixtures, stained-glass accents, and imposing pillared fireplaces are still in place.

Upstairs, in an otherwise undistinguished hallway, the original dining-room buffet stands guard over a pair of spacious front bedrooms. The Tower

Room has a small bathroom and a down quilt–covered brass bed set into an alcove of bay windows. The Fireplace Room has a brass bed, tiled fireplace, and a rocking chair; a TV helps to compensate for a lackluster view of storefronts just off the town's main street. The two rooms are connected by double doors and can be rented as a suite. The Anniversary Room is almost a suite, with reproduction wing chairs and a sofa forming a conversation group in its bay window. Its brass bed merits the handmade quilt and white eyelet comforter. The Greenbriar Room's caned chairs, rag rugs, marble-top washstand, and old-fashioned white iron bed, topped with another antique quilt, have the look of Grandma's house—comfortable but not fancy.

▦ *2 double rooms with baths, 4 doubles share 1½ baths. Air-conditioning, TV in 1 room, fireplace in common rooms. $60–$80; Continental breakfast weekdays, full breakfast weekends, refreshments on arrival. MC, V.*

Other Choices

Eckhart House. 220 E. Jefferson St., Viroqua, WI 54665, tel. 608/637–3306. 3 double rooms with baths, 2 doubles share 1 bath. Air-conditioning, whirlpool bath in 1 room, TV available, refrigerator, microwave. $55–$79; full breakfast, afternoon refreshments. AE, D, MC, V. No smoking, no pets.

Geiger House. 401 Denniston St., Cassville, WI 53806, tel. 608/725–5419. 3 double rooms share 2 baths. Air-conditioning, fireplace in common room, bikes, shuttle to river ferry. $50–$60; full breakfast, morning coffee, afternoon refreshments. AE, MC, V. No smoking, no pets.

Oak Hill Manor. 401 E. Main St., Albany, WI 53502, tel. 608/862–1400. 4 double rooms with baths. Air-conditioning, TV/VCR in sitting room and parlor, fireplace in 1 room and common rooms, bikes. $60–$70; full breakfast, afternoon refreshments. MC, V. No smoking, no pets.

Parson's Inn. Rock School Rd., Glen Haven, WI 53810, tel. 608/794–2491. 3 double rooms share bath, 1 suite. Air-conditioning, TV in common room. $50–$70 ($85 for 4 in suite); full breakfast, afternoon refreshments. No credit cards. No smoking.

Sugar River Inn. 304 S. Mills St., Albany, WI 53502, tel. 608/862–1248. 2 double rooms with baths. Air-conditioning, fireplace in parlor, turndown service. $52–$62; full breakfast, wake-up coffee, afternoon refreshments. MC, V. No smoking, no pets.

Trillium. Rte. 2 E10596 Salem Ridge Rd., La Farge, WI 54639, tel. 608/625–4492. 1 1-bedroom cottage, 1 3-bedroom cottage. Fireplace and kitchen in cottages, tree house, hiking trails, picnic area with grill. $65–$70, full breakfast. No credit cards. No pets.

Victorian Garden. 1720 16th St., Monroe, WI 53566, tel. 608/328–1720. 3 double rooms with baths, single room can be rented with one of the doubles. Air-conditioning, robes. $70–$80; full breakfast, afternoon or evening refreshments. D, MC, V. No smoking, no pets.

Viroqua Heritage Inn. 220 E. Jefferson St., Viroqua, WI 54665, tel. 608/637–3306. 2 double rooms with baths, 2 doubles share 1½ baths. Phones, TVs, robes, refrigerator, and microwave available to guests. $50–$79, full breakfast. AE, D, MC, V. No smoking, no pets.

Hiawatha Valley

Arbor Inn

434 N. Court St., Prescott, WI 54021, tel. 715/262–4522

On a bluff overlooking downtown Prescott and the St. Croix River, this inn boasts two porches, both vine-covered and serene, wicker-furnished, and perfect for the watching the river below. It turns out Prescott is just upstream from the confluence of the Mississippi and St. Croix rivers and is the start of the Great River Road, which winds south along the Mississippi through Wisconsin, Minnesota, Illinois, Iowa, and Missouri. There's plenty of river traffic, but the porches are also perfect for reading or for quiet conversation—beguiling places that welcome visitors to this B&B.

In 1902 a local banker named Longworth built this Arts and Crafts home. Three owners later, innkeepers Marv and Linda Kangas took over the substantial abode and refurbished it with an eye for comfort. The living room, with exposed wood beams and original woodwork, is furnished with a mix of Linda's antiques and contemporary pieces. An overstuffed plaid sofa and matching ottoman face the large brick fireplace and are a favorite spot for guests in the winter. Linda serves her famous four-course breakfast either in the adjoining dining room, with its Victorian dining set and matching sideboards, on one of two screened porches, or in guest rooms. Linda believes in the dessert-first theory of breakfast, so she starts with her signature strawberry parfait, then moves on to fresh fruit, fresh scones or muffins, an egg dish such as quiche or an omelet, finishing up with waffles or pancakes topped with syrup made from her grandmother's recipe.

The ground-floor Silhouette Room houses Linda's distinctive collection of antique black-on-glass silhouette pictures. Linda's sister made the quilt that covers the king-size bed. An ice-cream-parlor table and chairs provide a quiet spot for breakfast. An arbor-covered private deck holds an outdoor hot tub for the use of guests who rent this room.

Upstairs, Patti's Room, decorated in shades of sage green and rose, features an antique armoire and a handmade star quilt. The huge bathroom also houses a double whirlpool bath. The Longworth Room, the inn's largest, is decorated in hunter green and burgundy, has a private deck overlooking the river and a wood-burning fireplace, and has probably the inn's most intriguing accessory—a handmade trip-around-the-world quilt, which adorns the queen-size bed.

▦ *3 double rooms with baths. Air-conditioning, TV/VCRs, fireplace in 1 room and common area, whirlpool bath in 1 room, outdoor hot tub for 1 room, bikes. $105–$145, full breakfast. MC, V. No smoking, no pets.*

Knollwood House

N. 8257 950th St., Knollwood Dr., River Falls, WI 54022, tel. 715/425–1040 or 800/435–0628

The comfortable atmosphere of the two-story Knollwood House and the warm hospitality of owners Jim and Judy Tostrud quickly transform guests into friends. Built in 1886 with red bricks from a local factory, the house, set on 85 acres in the rolling Kinnickinnic River valley, draws people into its rich history. Jim has farmed the land for many years, as his father did before him, and Judy, a horticulturalist, fills the landscape with perennials and hydroponically grown plants. Inside, you'll appreciate the Tostruds' personal touches, displayed in the plants that grace the windowsills and the family heirlooms that furnish the rooms.

Christie Ann's Room is filled with Tostrud family memorabilia. The queen-size bed with carved head- and footboards and matching dresser belonged to Jim's parents. An Amish quilt covers the bed. The suite includes an unusually spacious bathroom with tub and shower. The Country Rose Room is decorated in forest green and mauve and is furnished with an antique oak four-poster bed and an armoire of similar vintage.

The Sherlock Wales Room, a smaller room with wainscoting and an antique brass bed, overlooks a garden and small goldfish pond below the window. The aptly named Garden Room, on the first floor, allows guests access to the plant-filled solarium, which has a hot tub and to the Daybed Room, which indeed has a daybed—and a small enclosed porch. The Garden and Daybed rooms are usually rented as a suite.

The kitchen contains an antique cast-iron stove, a glazed pottery water-cooler, and a farmhouse pie cabinet with screen doors to tempt the hungry. Judy prepares a down-home breakfast featuring muffins made with the strawberries and raspberries she grows herself. The meal is served either in the solarium or on the arbor-draped deck beside the swimming pool.

There is no lack of activities at Knollwood; just about everything you could want is right outside the door. Badminton, croquet, basketball, softball, shuffleboard, boccie, a swimming pool, an in-ground trampoline, and a 180-yard par-three golf drive are found within the 3½-acre yard. The more ambitious athlete can try the 2 miles of well-maintained hiking and cross-country ski trails on land owned by the Tostruds. Ready to assist hikers are the Tostrud's two llamas, Hustler and Rivera.

▦ *2 double rooms with baths, 1 double and 1 suite share bath. Air-conditioning, fireplace in common room, ceiling fans, robes, ceiling fans and robes, hot tub, sauna, pool, hiking, cross-country ski trails. $80–$150, full breakfast. No credit cards. No smoking, no pets.*

Phipps Inn

1005 3rd St., Hudson, WI 54016, tel. 715/386–0800

This Queen Anne house has remained virtually untouched since its debut in 1884. From the octagonal tower under the witch's-cap roof to the wraparound veranda with scrolled friezes and pedimented gables, the house, which is on the National Register of Historic Places, is the showplace of the river town.

William Phipps, a prominent Hudson banker, politician, and philanthropist, moved here to serve as land commissioner for the railroad and certainly wasn't averse to living well. The interior of his former house is equipped with six fireplaces that are flamboyantly carved, guarded by Ionic columns, and set with Italian tiles. Ornate brass hardware, stained-glass windows, and parquet flooring in intricate geometric designs add to the got-it-flaunt-it look.

Innkeepers John and Cyndi Berglund bought the mansion intact but empty. This gave them the mandate of filling it with antiques from the St. Croix River valley, including an 1890s pump organ and Victorian sofas and chairs in the two parlors. In the music room, they've installed a snazzy 1920 baby grand piano; these days it's set with afternoon snacks. Guests linger over breakfast in the dining room, warmed by sun streaming through the stained-glass windows and by one of the fireplaces.

The Bridal Suite boasts a wicker canopy bed and wicker dresser, table and chairs, and a fireplace with Italian ceramic tile. The Master Suite has a canopied four-poster pine bed, another fireplace, and a large, climb-through window that leads to a private balcony. Victoria's Room, a more intimate hideaway done in a black-and-gold Victorian floral motif, is furnished with a brass bed and antique armoire; the Queen Anne's Room features hand-stenciled walls, a half-tester brass bed, and a gas fireplace that opens on both the bedroom and the adjoining whirlpool room. Guests can sit in the whirlpool bath and

look out the windows on one side and enjoy the fireplace on the other.

Above all looms the third floor's grand ballroom. Once the site of the Phipps's elegant gatherings, it has been converted into the Willow Chamber, which is furnished with willow furniture, and the Peacock Chamber, with its antique walnut half-tester bed and redwood paneling. Guests will find Jacuzzis in every bathroom.

▥ *6 double rooms with baths. Air-conditioning, fireplace in 5 rooms and in common rooms, whirlpool tubs in 6 rooms; bathrobes, picnics available with advance notice and at an extra charge. $89–$179; full breakfast, afternoon refreshments. AE, D, MC, V. No smoking, no pets.*

St. Croix River Inn

305 River St., Osceola, WI 54020, tel. 715/294-4248 or 800/645-8820

Local pharmacist C. W. Staples built this solid stone Dutch Colonial home overlooking the St. Croix River sometime after the turn of the century. Developer Robert Marshall bought it from the Staples family in 1984 and spent more than a half million dollars reconfiguring the interior and creating a luxury inn. It was money well spent. The home's original porch, along the side of the house, is now the inn's lobby area, where guests are greeted by innkeeper Bev Johnson. There's plenty of space to relax in the lobby and enjoy the eye-gratifying view of the river 100 feet below; to encourage you, Bev puts out cheese and crackers, coffee, and other drinks. Just outside the lobby is an open deck with a wooden swing—here, guests love to read or nibble on snacks as they watch the world go by.

Each of the seven guest rooms is named for a steamboat built in Osceola, and all are furnished with antique reproductions. The three lower-level rooms each open onto a private brick terrace that faces the river. These rooms have striking whitewashed stone walls—the original foundation supports of the house. The Minnie Will and Nellie Kent rooms each feature a breakfast nook that overlooks the river. In the Nellie Kent, guests can enjoy the whirlpool bath and river views simultaneously.

Upstairs, the Linn J. Room includes a bathroom with a skylight above the whirlpool bath, as well as a four-poster canopy bed and a blue velvet–upholstered chaise longue. Unfortunately, the huge arched picture window looks out on a parking lot. The G. B. Knapp Room also has a canopy bed, plus a pair of wing chairs near the fireplace. Guests in this room also have a large river-view sitting room furnished in casual wicker and a large upholstered sofa. The Jenny Hays Room, with a private balcony, is furnished with a four-poster bed from which guests, looking out the large cathedral window, can see the river.

Every morning at about 8 Bev or an assistant delivers hot coffee and a newspaper to each room. A half hour or so later a delicious breakfast of banana French toast, an omelet, or other goodies is delivered. Everything is freshly made and piping hot—even the maple syrup is warmed. Every room has a small breakfast table next to a window; no need to dress for breakfast here.

🖽 *2 double rooms with baths, 5 suites. Air-conditioning, TV in 1 room, TV/VCR in 2 rooms, fireplace in 2 rooms, stereo/cassette players, whirlpool baths, robes, grill and picnic table. $85–$200; full breakfast, afternoon refreshments. AE, MC, V. Restricted smoking, no pets.*

Other Choices

Cedar Trails Guesthouse. E4761 County Road C, Menomonie, WI 54751, tel. 715/664–8828. 2 double rooms with baths, 2 doubles share bath. Air-conditioning. $45–$65; full breakfast, afternoon refreshments. MC, V. No smoking.

Creamery. 1 Creamery Rd., Box 22, Downsville, WI 54735, tel. 715/664–8354. 3 double rooms with baths, 1 suite. Restaurant, air-conditioning, phones, TVs, whirlpool tubs; fireplaces in common rooms, bar, lounge, restaurant. $100–$130, Continental breakfast (in restaurant or in rooms). MC, V. Restricted smoking. Closed Jan.–Mar., restaurant closed Mon.

Gallery House. 215 N. Main St., Alma, WI 54610, tel. 608/685–4975. 3 double rooms with baths. Air-conditioning, ceiling fans. $70–$85, full breakfast. MC, V. No smoking, no pets.

Grapevine Inn. 702 Vine St., Hudson, WI 54016, tel. 715/386–1989. 3 double rooms with baths. Air-conditioning, fireplace in 1 room, whirlpool bath in 1 room, swimming pool. $89–$139; full breakfast, morning wake-up tray, afternoon refreshments. MC, V. No smoking, no pets.

Great River Bed & Breakfast. Rte. 35, Stockholm, WI 54769, tel. 715/442–5656 or 800/657–4756. 2-bedroom farmhouse. Woodstove in 1 room and in living room. $95 2 people, $170 4 people; full breakfast. No credit cards. No smoking, no pets.

Harrisburg Inn. W3334 Rte. 35, Maiden Rock, WI 54750, tel. 715/448–4500. 4 double rooms with baths (2 rooms can be joined to make a suite). Air-conditioning, ceiling fans. $68–$98; full breakfast, afternoon refreshments. D, MC, V. Restricted smoking, no pets. Closed Jan.–Feb.

Jefferson-Day House. 1109 3rd St., Hudson, WI 54016, tel. 715/386–7111. 3 double rooms with baths, 1 suite. Air-conditioning, fireplace in 4 rooms, double whirlpool bath in 4 rooms. $99–$169; full breakfast, afternoon refreshments. MC, V. No smoking.

Pine Creek Lodge. N447 244th St., Stockholm, WI 54769, tel. 715/448–3203. 3 double rooms with baths. Climate-controlled guest rooms, whirlpool bath in 1 room, steam room in 1 room;

TV/VCR and CD player in common room; kitchen access, masseuse on call, hiking, cross-country skiing. $85–$120, full breakfast. MC, V. No smoking.

Pleasant Lake Inn. 2238 60th Ave., Osceola, WI 54020, tel. 715/294–2545 or 800/294–2545. 3 double rooms with baths, 1 suite. Air-conditioning, fireplace in 1 room, whirlpool bath in 3 rooms, lake access, canoe and paddleboat, evening bonfires, TV/VCR in common room. $55–$125, full breakfast. MC, V. No smoking, no pets.

Rosewood. 203 S. Main St., Cochrane, WI 54622-7228, tel. 608/248–2940. 1 double room with bath, 2 doubles share bath. Air-conditioning, fireplace in common room and in 1 bedroom, TV/VCR in common room. $58–$78, Continental breakfast. No credit cards. No smoking, no pets.

Ryan House. W4375 U.S. Hwy. 10, Durand, WI 54737, tel. 715/672–8563. 1 double room with bath, 2 doubles share bath. Fireplace and TV in common room. $40–$60; full breakfast, afternoon refreshments. MC, V. No smoking, no pets. Closed Jan.–Mar.

Door County

Ephraim Inn

Rte. 42 (Box 247), Ephraim, WI 54211, tel. 414/854–4515 or 800/622–2193

In the picture of his son that inn owner Tim Christofferson carries in his wallet, another man is included—the Wal-Mart photographer who took the picture (yup, the camera timer allowed him to join the son in the photo). Tim just wanted to make sure he remembered the guy. That's the kind of good humor Tim exudes, and inn guests feel it from the time they walk in the door. A former McDonald's marketing executive, Tim had always wanted his own business; he and his wife, Nancy,

moved to Door County in 1979 when they bought Wilson's Ice Cream Parlor, overlooking the harbor in Ephraim's charming historic district. Then, in 1985, the big white house next door, where the town doctor, Dr. Sneeberger, had lived and practiced for 40 years, went up for sale. Tim and Nancy bought it and built a large addition that turned it into a sprawling horseshoe-shaped inn with a center cupola. Much to the dismay of their sons, Tim and Nancy sold Wilson's in 1987 (it's still in operation) to concentrate on the inn.

The Christoffersons live in most of the old main house; all of the 17 guest bedrooms are in the new addition, where such modern essentials as soundproofing, air-conditioning, and private baths were easy to install. Each room has its own motif, often Shaker-inspired, it shows up on the room's wooden key tags, the painted symbol on its door, and the hand-stenciled border on its ceiling. Shaker-style peg rails around the walls hold such decorative touches as dried flowers, grapevine wreaths, straw hats, and even chairs. The furniture is a mix of reproductions and antiques revealing the couple's preference for the simple, clean lines of country furniture.

The large common room with its harbor view brings guests together around a large fireplace or in a well-stocked library nook. Full breakfasts, served in three small dining areas, may include homemade granola, fresh-baked pastries, and an Ephraim Inn omelet, a quichelike dish of baked eggs, cheese, and spices.

The shorefront location, a decided asset, gives the inn wonderful water views and puts guests within walking distance not only of Ephraim's historic sights but also of an unspoiled beach just around a curve of the road. Not much farther up the road are Peninsula State Park and its fine 18-hole golf course.

🖼 *17 double rooms with baths. Air-conditioning, TVs, beach across street.*

$79–$145, full breakfast. MC, V. No smoking, no pets, 2-night minimum.

Griffin Inn

11976 Mink River Rd., Ellison Bay, WI 54210, tel. 414/854-4306

Converted from a private house to a summer hotel in 1921, the Griffin Inn is a classic country retreat, on 5 acres of rolling lawn shaded by maple trees. Long verandas with porch swings and a gazebo give guests plenty of places to sit and enjoy the breeze. Besides the main building, a Dutch reform–style house built in 1910, there are two cottages on the property, each with two guest units.

For innkeepers Paul Ennis and family, who recently purchased the Griffin from Jim and Laurie Roberts (who now own the Whistling Swan in Fish Creek; *see below*), it's a case of having come full circle. A brother and sister-in-law had managed the property in the mid-'70s. When Ennis decided to return to his northeastern Wisconsin roots from Maryland where he'd been living, his search for a business to run ended when he learned the familiar old inn was available.

Though the bedrooms are fairly small, they have been comfortably furnished with a collection of pieces reflecting the tastes of the inn's various owners throughout the years.

Common rooms include the dining room, a downstairs living room with a large fieldstone fireplace where guests gather for popcorn every night, and a small library where guests can curl up on a love seat with a good book.

The cottages, which are open from May through October, are a bit more rustic, with open-beam ceilings, rough cedar walls, and ceiling fans. Cottage guests can either pick up a breakfast basket each morning or make arrangements to join the main-house guests for the dazzling gourmet breakfast always prepared from scratch. Fresh fruit and baked goods (scones, muffins, and breads) are always on the menu, along with a changing selection of temptations such as baby Dutch pancakes topped with lemon butter and cherry sauce, stuffed blueberry French toast, and made-to-order omelets.

Only two blocks from downtown Ellison Bay, the inn is within walking distance of the waterfront. It sits on a well-traveled bike route, and the Peninsula Cross-Country Ski Trail literally runs through the backyard. Guests often play badminton or croquet on the inn grounds, a sight that conjures up images of the inn's venerable role as a summer retreat.

🏠 *8 double rooms and 2 triples share 2½ baths; 4 cottages each sleep 4 people. Air-conditioning in inn, TV in cottages. $79–$86; full breakfast for inn guests, Continental breakfast with full-breakfast option for cottage guests. No credit cards. No smoking, no pets, 2-night minimum on weekends, 3-night minimum on holidays.*

Whistling Swan

4192 Main St. (Box 193), Fish Creek, WI 54212, tel. 414/868-3442

A fixture on Fish Creek's Main Street since 1907, what is now the Whistling Swan was originally built in 1887 in Marinette—22 miles due west, more or less, across the waters of Green Bay. Dr. Herman Welcker, a legendary figure in the history of tourism in Door County, had the white-frame Victorian towed across the ice to its present location, where it became part of a resort complex that also included the current White Gull Inn (*see below*).

Now meticulously restored, the inn features such touches as floral prints, brass fixtures, and claw-foot tubs, recalling the romance of that bygone era. Guests will find fresh flowers on their nightstands, too, along with complimentary bottles of spring water. An expanded Continental breakfast is served on the sunny, glass-enclosed porch during clement seasons; come winter, full breakfast becomes the rule. Afternoon tea is served year-round.

While owners Jim and Laurie Roberts are newcomers to the Whistling Swan— they purchased the property in 1996— they're no strangers to innkeeping, after owning and operating the nearby Griffin Inn for the previous 10 years. In addition to elegant accommodations, they offer sophisticated women's fashions in their boutique on the building's main level. It's one of the many upscale specialty shops that make the neighborhood one of the peninsula's toniest.

🏠 *5 double rooms with baths, 2 suites. Air-conditioning, cable TVs, phones in some rooms. $98–$134, Continental breakfast (full breakfast in winter). AE, D, MC, V. No smoking, no pets, 2-night minimum on weekends, 3-night minimum on holidays.*

White Gull Inn

4225 Main St. (Box 160), Fish Creek, WI 54212, tel. 414/868–3517

One of the oldest lodging establishments in Door County, the White Gull Inn was founded in 1896 by a Dr. Welcker as a lodging for wealthy German immigrants who came to Fish Creek by steamer. Its current owner and manager, Andy Coulson, is a former journalist. He was traveling in Australia when a friend contacted him about joining a group of investors seeking to buy the White Gull. Andy said yes—on the condition he could run the place. The other partners happily agreed. One of Andy's first managerial decisions was to hire a new housekeeper, Jan; five years later, wedding bells happily rang.

The Coulsons have worked hard to maintain the original feel of the white-frame inn, with its inviting front porches (upstairs and down), gleaming hardwood floors covered with braided rugs, and country-style antiques. The main entry is the focus of activity; it's

here that guests watch television or gather around the large fieldstone fireplace. Besides overnight guests, crowds of people visit the inn's restaurant, famous throughout Door County for its traditional fish boils, on Wednesday, Friday, Saturday, and Sunday nights in summer (Wednesday and Saturday in winter). The restaurant serves three meals a day; breakfast may include eggs Benedict, hash browns, or buttermilk pancakes.

The inn is perfectly situated: To the left is Sunset Beach Park; to the right, the charming shops of Fish Creek and then Peninsula State Park. Accommodations are spread around a number of buildings. The main house has several guest rooms, each with a comfortable wrought-iron or carved-wood bed, and each decorated with antiques, some of them once owned by Dr. Welcker himself. Behind the inn is the Cliffhouse, whose two suites have fireplaces and lush furnishings; the inn also owns three nearby cottages, which make wonderful little family vacation homes.

🏠 *6 double rooms with baths, 3 suites, 5 cottages each sleep 2–8 people. Restaurant, air-conditioning, cable TVs, complimentary coffee, morning newspapers. $96–$185, cottages $157–$251; breakfast extra. AE, D, DC, MC, V. No pets, 2-night minimum on weekends, 3-night minimum on holidays.*

White Lace Inn

16 N. 5th Ave., Sturgeon Bay, WI 54235, tel. 414/743–1105

In 1982, a bed-and-breakfast was born when Bonnie and Dennis Statz purchased a run-down Victorian house that had been built in 1903 for a Sturgeon Bay attorney. They renovated the house inside and out, painting the exterior rose and cream and restoring the intricate wood paneling inside. Then in 1983, they bought the 1880s-vintage Garden House for the princely sum of $1 and had it moved to the grounds of their inn, right beside the flower gardens. Soon after, they bought the Washburn House, on an adjacent lot around the corner, and converted it to extra guest quarters. In 1996, the Statzes restored another nearby historic property, an 1881 Italianate known as the Hadley House. They also added an enchanting pond filled with *koi* (large Japanese-bred carp fish).

"Whimsical Victorian" is the Statzes' description of the White Lace Inn's distinctive style. Massive antique Victorian furniture—perhaps not innately whimsical—has been toned down by the use of floral fabrics, fluffy pillows, and, of course, white lace. Whether it's a framed doily, lace curtains, or pillowcases, there is at least one piece of white lace in each room. Bonnie, who holds a degree in interior design, was responsible for decorating this growing inn, and she has given each room in the four buildings its own look. All bedrooms in the Garden House and Washburn House have fireplaces; all Washburn House rooms also have whirlpool baths, as do three of the Main House rooms. The four suites in the Hadley House feature both fireplaces and whirlpool baths. Bonnie personally shops at outlet stores to find thick towels for her guests. The rooms are brightened with books of poetry and photographs, and little hand-painted rocks rest on the bed pillows, gently reminding guests to remove pillow shams before retiring.

The Main House's parlor, sitting room, and dining room serve as common areas for the entire inn complex. Guests are encouraged to mingle here; cookies and other treats are served. Walk out through the white picket fence, and you're on a quiet residential street, with tall shade trees and stately old houses, two blocks away from Sturgeon Bay's historic downtown district.

For Bonnie and Dennis, the inn is the realization of a dream shared since college days—owning a business. "We didn't know what kind of business we wanted, so we explored different things and came up with this," Bonnie said. "It's perfect because we like this kind of thing and we like people."

▦ *14 double rooms with baths, 5 suites. Air-conditioning, TV/VCR in 11 rooms, whirlpool bath in 11 rooms, stereo in 8 rooms, phones. $75–$190, Continental breakfast. AE, D, MC, V. No smoking, no pets, 2-night minimum on weekends, 3-night minimum on holidays.*

Other Choices

Barbican Guest House. 132 N. 2nd Ave., Sturgeon Bay, WI 54235, tel. 414/743–4854. 18 suites. Air-conditioning, cable TV/VCR, fireplace, whirlpool bath, stereo, and refrigerator in suites. $110–$175, Continental breakfast. MC, V. No pets, 2-night minimum on weekends, 3-night minimum on holidays.

Church Hill Inn. 425 Gateway Dr., Sister Bay, WI 54234, tel. 414/854–4885 or 800/422–4906. 32 double rooms with baths, 2 suites. Air-conditioning, cable TVs, phones, whirlpool bath in 12 rooms and 2 suites, hot tub, fitness room, pool. $124–$174, full breakfast. MC, V. No smoking, no pets.

Eagle Harbor Inn. 9914 Water St. (Box 558), Ephraim, WI 54211, tel. 414/854–2121 or 800/324–5427. 9 double rooms with bath, 16 1-bedroom suites, 16 2-bedrooms suites. Air-conditioning, cable TVs, whirlpool bath in 1 room and all suites, sauna, lap pool, fitness center. $79–$156; full breakfast for inn guests, breakfast available at additional charge for suite guests. MC, V. No smoking, no pets, 2-night minimum on weekends, 3-night minimum on holidays.

48 West Oak. 48 W. Oak St., Sturgeon Bay, WI 54235, tel. 414/743–4830. 1 double room with bath, 1 suite. Air-conditioning, cable TV/VCRs, fireplaces, whirlpool baths, phones. $95–$140. D, MC, V. No smoking, no pets, 2-night minimum on weekends, 3-night minimum on holidays.

French Country Inn of Ephraim.
3052 Spruce La. (Box 129), Ephraim,
WI 54211, tel. 414/854–4001. 2 double
rooms with baths, 5 doubles share 2
baths; 1 2-bedroom cottage. $55–$89;
cottage $485–$580 per week; Continental breakfast, evening refreshments.
No credit cards. No smoking, no pets,
2-night minimum on weekends, 3-night
minimum on holidays.

Gray Goose Bed and Breakfast. 4258
Bay Shore Dr., Sturgeon Bay, WI 54235,
tel. 414/743–9100. 4 double rooms share
2 baths. TV in guest lounge. $70–$80,
full breakfast. AE, MC, V. Restricted
smoking, no pets, 2-night minimum on
holidays.

Harbor House Inn. 12666 Rte. 42,
Gills Rock, WI 54210, tel. 414/854–
5196. 12 double rooms with baths, 2 cottages each sleep 4. Air-conditioning,
TVs, sauna, hot tub; private beach,
bicycle rentals. $49–$109, Continental
breakfast. AE, MC, V. No smoking.

Inn at Cedar Crossing. 336 Louisiana
St., Sturgeon Bay, WI 54235, tel. 414/
743–4200. 9 double rooms with baths.
Restaurant, air-conditioning, whirlpool
bath in 5 rooms. $85–$145, Continental
breakfast. D, MC, V. No smoking, no

pets, 2-night minimum on weekends, 3-night minimum on holidays.

Inn on Maple. 414 Maple Dr., Sister
Bay, WI 54234, tel. 414/854–5107. 5 double rooms with baths, 2 single rooms
with baths. Ceiling fans. $55–$75, full
breakfast. MC, V. No smoking, no pets,
2-night minimum, 3-night minimum on
holidays.

Scofield House. 908 Michigan St. (Box
761), Sturgeon Bay, WI 54235, tel. 414/
743–7727 or 888/463–0204. 6 double
rooms with baths. Air-conditioning,
cable TV/VCR in 5 rooms, whirlpool
bath in 5 rooms. $89–$190, full breakfast. No credit cards. No smoking, no
pets, 2-night minimum, 3-night minimum on holidays.

Thorp House Inn. 4135 Bluff Rd. (Box
490), Fish Creek, WI 54212, tel. 414/
868–2444. 4 double rooms with baths, 3
2-bedroom apartments, 6 2-bedroom
cottages. Air-conditioning, cable TV in
cottages, fireplace in 4 cottages and 3
apartments, ceiling fans in guest
rooms, whirlpool bath in 1 room, 3 cottages, and 2 apartments. $75–$175,
Continental breakfast. No credit cards.
No smoking in main house, no pets, 2-night minimum during high season, 3-night minimum holidays.

Wyoming

Spahn's Big Horn Mountain B&B

Jackson and Vicinity

Nowlin Creek Inn

660 E. Broadway, Box 2766, Jackson Hole, WY 83001, tel. 307/733–0882 or 800/533–0882

If you ask who lives across the street from her B&B, Susan Nowlin replies "9,000 elk" without blinking an eye. The property fronts the National Elk Refuge, which partly explains why Susan and her husband, Mark, came up with the name for their new inn: Deep within the protected park lies Nowlin Creek, named to honor Mark's great-grandfather, the refuge's first superintendent. In fact, many aspects of Jackson Hole's past supply a kind of pleasing obbligato to this inn's distinctive character.

Near the entrance sits an antique wooden model of the town's central square. Throughout the rooms, vintage photographs depict Jackson Hole "before it had trees," as Susan puts it, when it was being settled and seeded by 1880s homesteaders. Out back on a broad patio, a huge cowboy-shape sign, which once pointed the way to a trading post on the town square, has been decked out in lights to provide funky illumination for the hot tub. Susan used to be an exhibition designer at the Smithsonian Institution in Washington, DC, so it's easy to understand why this B&B has almost become a minimuseum of Jackson Hole history.

The inn—designed by Mark and Susan—is a two-story, wood house with a lodgepole railing and distinct echoes of Prairie School design. Susan has brought the outdoors into the living room by stenciling the unique rough-hewn fir floors with twining ivy borders. Windows are draped with curtains strung loosely on slender wrought-iron rods, also budding with leaves. The furnishings are sturdy and colorful: a supple teal leather sofa, end tables made by Susan and her daughters from weathered window frames, and a massive buffalo skull mounted on the wall.

Jackson Hole is the home for the nation's third-largest western art market and both Mark and Susan are active in the community as practicing artists (they also run a framing business). Throughout the rooms, Susan's drawings and handmade papers complement Audubon prints and etchings done by local artists, while Mark's sculptures adorn the grounds. They seem proudest of the trompe l'oeil wood-grained window casing Susan painted around several of the guest-room windows, which have even duped building contractors.

Above the landing, a beveled-glass window casts rainbows across the hall walls. In the pleasant dining area, breakfast may feature huevos rancheros, caramelized French toast served with sour cream and blueberries, or puffy Dutch pancakes with sautéed apples.

There are five spacious guest accommodations in the house: two downstairs and three up, each named for a regional lake. The Solitude Suite has a western motif with a lodgepole bed and shadow boxes on the walls holding an array of miscellany from poker "death hands" to a collection of arrowheads. In the Goodwin Room, a mirror-top dresser matches the antique carved-oak high-back bed. Windows face toward Snow King Mountain's ski runs. The most interesting "room," however, might be the authentic sheepherder's wagon located behind the house, which guests may choose as their sleeping quarters in warm weather. There's also a guest cabin—a historic structure with two bedrooms that can comfortably sleep five in pine pole beds. It has a full kitchen, telephone, TV/VCR, and laundry facilities, but breakfast isn't included.

▥ *4 double rooms with baths, 1 suite with whirlpool tub, one two-bedroom cabin with full kitchen and laundry, outdoor hot tub, library, reservations service for area activities. B&B rooms $105–$155, full breakfast; guest cabin with kitchen, TV/VCR, phone, washer/ dryer, $185–$210, no breakfast. AE, MC, V.*

Painted Porch

Off Teton Village Rd., Box 6955, Jackson Hole, WY 83001, tel. 307/733–1981

A stay at this cherry-color farmhouse on a large wooded lot is a retreat into an atmosphere sparked with decorative whimsy, a reflection of hostess Martha MacEachern's warm and imaginative personality. Trompe l'oeil paintings, 1950s cowboy decor, and antique knickknacks are just some of the touches she uses to bring a smile to guests' faces.

A rustic-style flagstone hallway with lemon sponge-painted walls leads to the Garden Cottage Suite—one of two cheery and imaginative guest accommodations, each of which come with their own porch and private entrance. Both bedroom and parlor positively bloom with artful combinations of Ralph Lauren fabrics in chambray, ticking stripes, and jewel-tone florals. The bedroom has a sage Berber carpet. Everywhere are clever trompe l'oeil–painted touches: a dresser whose drawers spill faux pearls, neckties, suspenders, and a delicate pocket-watch; a fool-the-eye coatrack near the door; faux flowers hanging from nails above the bed; and a painted chipmunk scurrying along the baseboard. The parlor window seat is plump with pillows beneath tab-top floral curtains on willow-branch rods—a relaxing spot from which to study the eye-filling vistas of the Grand Tetons.

Aficionados of "cow-camp" kitsch will want to stay in the Cowboy Room, with its covered-wagon lamps, bronco-shape sconces, "branded" wood furniture, and cowboy-and-Indian-pattern fabrics. Hidden within a peeled-log armoire are a TV and coffeemaker. Although the room is given a trendy spin, Gene Autry would feel right at home.

The smaller Cabin and Margaret's Room have their own charms. The Cabin has a dresser with a scene of a bear in a hammock, and special tile in the bathroom is also of bears. Margaret's Room has a blue ceiling dotted with clouds, white wicker furniture, and bright comforter and pillows.

Sharing the common areas—a tiny, square family room and a living room, with hardwood floors and a fireplace with a screen that's a silhouette of the house—Martha, her husband, Mark, and their grade-school-age son enjoy an easy rapport with guests. On any given morning, the breakfast table, positioned near a window seat filled with pillows, may be set with the MacEacherns' "bucking bronco" wedding china, with matching brown bandanna napkins. Martha's breakfasts are just as unusual, ranging from Grand Marnier French toast to her gingerbread pancakes, a fragrant recipe that once brought a moose to the kitchen window.

Guests may fish, ski at the nearby resort, enjoy the hammock, or catch some more worldly pleasures in Jackson, 8 miles distant. A word of warning: Don't head into town for a movie matinee when the cattle herds are being moved from their winter to summer pastures; there's no way you'll be on time.

🏨 *3 double rooms with baths, 1 suite. Air-conditioning, TVs, coffeemakers, turndown service, ski storage, wildlife watching. $110–$170, full breakfast. MC, V.*

Teton Tree House

Heck of a Hill Rd., Box 550, Wilson, WY 83014, tel. 307/733–3233

A little bit of childhood fancy is mixed in with a lot of adult comfort at Teton Tree House, three-fourths of a mile from Wilson. Without a doubt, a sense of quiet escape is palpable from the moment guests turn onto the steep, tree-lined road that leads to the parking area. From there, 95 steps climb gently through a forest of evergreens to the angular, multilevel wood home, with jutting balconies and wide, recessed windows.

Denny Becker and wife, Chris, designed and built this home for their family. It became a bed-and-breakfast when Denny, once a river guide, decided to try his hand at being a full-time host. When she isn't playing hostess, or being mom to their two daughters, Chris teaches at the local elementary school.

From the tree house's entry level, a spiral wood staircase curls gracefully up from the two-story Grand Room. Here, leather-covered earth-tone sofas and chairs have been gathered around an enormous stucco-and-brick fireplace fitted with a wood-burning stove. The white walls and neutral striped carpet are brightened by wood-framed windows, golden peeled-log support beams, and a collection of vivid scenic and wildlife photos. Fitted with a piano, games, and shelves full of books on varied topics, this room is an ideal place to while away part of an evening.

Guest rooms are on three of the house's four levels. Each bedroom is spacious and affords a forest or valley view through immaculate windows curtained, in some cases, only by leaves and branches. Private decks enhance the tree-house effect. However, there is plenty of luxury here: down comforters, silky cotton sheets, and bathroom baskets brimming with upscale soaps and lotions. In summer, bunches of wildflowers, such as paintbrush, arnica, and columbine, gathered from the hillside around the house, add delicate touches of color.

Denny himself made the long table where breakfast is served on glossy stoneware—handiwork of the potter down the road a ways. Cream of the West, a whole-grain, hot cereal, is always on the menu along with plenty of fresh fruit and surprises like strawberry juice, Amish friendship bread, whole-wheat pancakes, or deep-dish French toast.

Feeders hanging under the eaves guarantee birds at breakfast as well as the occasional snowshoe rabbit nibbling birdseed on the ground, and a few reckless squirrels who leap wildly from the house walls to raid the feeders.

🏨 *6 double rooms with baths. Outdoor hot tub, wildlife watching. $105–$160, full breakfast. MC, V.*

Other Choices

Inn at Buffalo Fork. Box 311, Hwy. 26/287, Moran, WY 83013, tel. 307/543–2010, fax 307/543–0935. 3 rooms with queen-size beds and baths, 1 room with two twin beds and bath, 1 king suite with bath. Snacks, outdoor hot tub, wildlife watching, cross-country skiing, snowmobiling, fly-fishing guide service, reservations service for area activities, horse boarding. $100–$165, full breakfast. MC, V.

Moose Meadows B&B. 1225 Green La., Box 371, Wilson, WY 83014, tel. 307/733–9510, fax 307/739–3053. 1 quad and 1 double with baths, 1 quad and one double share bath. TV, fireplace, and woodstove in living room; outdoor hot tub; ski packages. $65–$135; full breakfast, evening snacks. D, DC, MC, V.

Sassy Moose Inn. 3895 Miles Rd. at Tucker Ranch, H.C. 362, Jackson, WY 83001, tel. 307/733–1277 or 800/356–1277, fax 307/ 739–0793. 5 double rooms with baths. Stone fireplaces in 2 rooms, 1 room with mountain views, hot tub in 1 room. June–Sept. $85–$139; full breakfast, afternoon and evening light snacks. AE, D, MC, V.

Twin Trees, A Bed and Breakfast. 575 S. Willow St., Box 7533, Jackson, WY 83002, tel. 307/739–9737 or 800/728–7337, fax 307/734–1266. 3 double rooms with baths. Ski-slope views, ski storage, outdoor hot tub, reservations service for area activities, cat in residence. $105–$115; full breakfast, afternoon snacks. AE, MC, V. No smoking.

Wildflower Inn. Shooting Star La., Box 11000, Jackson, WY 83002, tel. 307/733–4710, fax 307/739–0914. 5 double rooms with baths. Mountain views, TVs, alarm clocks, hot tub in flower-filled sunroom, wooded 3-acre setting, creek and pond, horses, wildlife-watching. $120–$170, full breakfast. MC, V.

Window on the Winds. 10151 Hwy. 191, Box 996, Pinedale, WY 82941, tel. 307/367–2600, fax 307/367–2395. 4 double rooms share 2 baths. Fireplace in common room, hot tub in solarium with flower and herb gardens, views of the Wind River Mountains, horse boarding with advance notice. $60–$70; full breakfast, afternoon snacks, evening vegetarian meals with notice. MC, V.

Northern Wyoming

Spahn's Big Horn Mountain B&B

70 Upper Hideaway La. (off I–90), Box 579, Big Horn, WY 82833, tel. 307/674–8150

In the Rocky Mountains, 15 miles from Sheridan, Spahn's Big Horn Mountain B&B is on a pine-clustered hillside with 100-mile views spreading across a pastoral valley patterned, like a crazy quilt, with buck-rail fences.

Host Ron Spahn brings eclectic experience to his role as innkeeper. He has been a geologist, a coal miner, an attorney, and even a ranger at Yellowstone National Park. But occupation aside, it is his zest for the mountain lifestyle that makes him the consummate host in this setting. Ron, his wife, Bobbie, and their teenage son and daughter share equally in cooking and conversation.

According to Ron, an element of fantasy accompanies living in the mountains of the American West—a fantasy he intends to fulfill for his guests. Everything here—such as the solar-powered, hand-peeled-log structures built by the Spahns themselves—is part of the rustic experience.

There are two guest rooms in the main house, a log lodge with three-story living room and multilevel decks under a ruddy metal roof. The bedrooms have tongue-and-groove woodwork and peeled-log beams; ruffled curtains contrast gently with the wooden walls. Both rooms have extremely comfortable lodgepole beds.

On the hillside above the house, sheltered by evergreen trees, are two cabins. The Homestead Cabin, originally built by the Spahns as a family retreat, is compact but complete, with a tidy kitchen, wood-burning stove, living room, bedroom, and kid-size loft. The other cabin, dubbed the Eagle's Nest, is romantically furnished with white wicker, ruffled curtains, and colorful hand-stitched quilts.

Two evenings a week, Ron leads moose-photo safaris, which include a steak cookout, the promise of an unforgettable sunset, and wildlife aplenty—if not moose, then certainly deer, elk, and an abundance of birds. As for daytime activities on the mountain, the Spahns have plenty of suggestions, and may even be persuaded to come along.

Breakfast is served family-style on the deck. As often as not, binoculars for wildlife-watching are set side-by-side with an array of condiments. In cooler weather, guests eat in the dining room under a ceiling beamed in a wagon-spoke pattern. Morning meals hearken back to simplicity: pancakes, scrambled eggs and sausage with fresh fruit, and lots of good, hot fresh coffee.

🏠 *2 double rooms with baths, 2 cabins. Fireplace and piano in main house, recreation and tour packages with full meals extra. $65–$120, full breakfast. MC, V.*

Other Choices

Blue Barn. 304 Hwy. 335, Box 416, Big Horn, WY 82833, tel. and fax 307/672-2381. 3 double rooms with baths. Atrium, outdoor hot tub, horse boarding, guided hiking, fly-fishing and mountain biking packages. $75–$90, full breakfast. MC, V.

Cheyenne River Ranch. 1031 Steinle Rd., Douglas, WY 82633, tel. 307/358-2380. 2 double rooms share 1 bath, 2 bunkhouse cabins with baths. Working cattle and sheep ranch, pool, campfire meals, horseback trail riding, weeklong cattle drives in summer. $65–$75, full breakfast; weekly and family rates available; full breakfast; lunches and dinners offered. No credit cards. 3-day minimum stay.

Cloud Peak Inn. 590 N. Burritt Rd., Buffalo, WY 82834, tel. 307/684-5794 or 800/715-5794, fax 307/684-7653. 3 double rooms with baths, 2 double rooms share 1 bath. TV, fireplace in common area, whirlpool tub in sunroom, mountain-biking and photography tours available. June–Sept. $45–$75; full breakfast; lunch and dinner by arrangement (extra). AE, MC, V.

Parson's Pillow Bed and Breakfast. 1202 14th St., Cody, WY 82414, tel. 307/587-2382 or 800/377-2348. 1 double room with bath 3 queen rooms with bath. TV in living room, piano, antiques, historic building. $50–$99; full breakfast, complimentary evening snacks and beverages. MC, V.

Southern Wyoming

Ferris Mansion

607 W. Maple St., Rawlins, WY 82301, tel. 307/324-3961

This three-story, multigabled Queen Anne–style mansion with encircling porch, bay windows, and conical-roofed tower was built in 1903 by Julia Ferris, the widow of a prominent Rawlins mining magnate. She lived in it until her death in 1931. During the 1940s the elegant house was divided into apartments which, decade by decade, fell into disrepair. In 1979, when David and Janice Lubbers bought the mansion, it was a mishmash of shag carpeting, metallic wallpaper, and psychedelic-accented "crash pads." Although it seemed impossible, not to mention expensive, Janice was determined to restore and refurbish the house as a bed-and-breakfast.

By 1986, the Lubbers were renting just one bedroom. Today, the house reflects their labors of love, with four heirloom-filled guest rooms. The common areas gleam with polished woodwork and antique lamplight, and with windows framed by wide lace curtains.

The bedrooms are on the second floor, up an oak staircase that had been removed and discarded before the Lubbers pieced it together, something like a jigsaw puzzle, and had it reinstalled.

In the Lavender Room, the bed—attractively covered in a spread made of antique handkerchiefs—fills the round tower bay window, set with stained-glass panels from a church in Minnesota. A fireplace is tiled in muted green. Above it a rectangular mirror tops the carved mantel. The Blue Room has rich paisley linens, and its window overlooks the tall porch roof. The Rose Room is shaded and subdued, with an ornate bed carved with flowers. In the Gold Room, a high shelf near the ceiling is filled with intriguing bric-a-brac. Each of the guest rooms has an electric mattress pad to warm the bed. On the landing between the rooms, women's hats add splashes of color and charm to the walls.

For sing-alongs and lovers of old-time music, the downstairs foyer holds a player grand piano and a collection of more than 100 piano rolls. A gingerbread arch separates the foyer from the formal parlor, where soft teal walls are enlivened by a red-velvet sofa and a pink-tile fireplace. Pocket doors open on to a bay-windowed side parlor furnished in white wicker. The side parlor and the adjacent bird's-eye maple–paneled library alternate as the inn's breakfast site.

Breakfast itself is a sampler's dream. There are always homemade breads—anything from wheat to orange–chocolate chip—that guests can warm up in a collection of antique toasters. Jars of orange marmalade and chokecherry jelly add colorful accents on the lace-draped table. There is granola with cream, plenty of fresh fruit, and the temptation of chewy caramel buns.

🏠 *4 double rooms with baths. TVs in rooms, fireplaces in 2 rooms. $55–$65, gourmet Continental breakfast, D, MC, V.*

Other Choices

A. Drummond's Ranch B&B. 399 Happy Jack Rd., Cheyenne, WY 82007, tel. and fax 307/634–6042. 1 queen room with bath and outdoor hot tub, 1 double and 1 triple share 1 bath, 1 suite with queen and twin window seat, outdoor hot tub, fireplace, pantry kitchen, and steam sauna. Phones, terry-cloth robes, 120-acre working ranch, mountain and forest views, horse boarding. $60–$150; full breakfast, evening desserts and beverages always available. Dinner and trail lunches extra. MC,V.

Adventurers' Country B&B at Raven Cry Ranch. 3803 I–80 South Service Rd., Cheyenne, WY 82001, tel. and fax 307/632–4087. 4 double rooms with bath; 1 3-room suite with living room, atrium, king bedroom, jet tub, and walk-in shower. TV/VCR in common area, prairie and pasture views, farm animals, high mountain horseback trips, special-event and seasonal packages. $60–$125, full breakfast. Dinners and trail lunches extra. No credit cards.

Blackbird Inn. 1101 11th St., Wheatland, WY. 82201, tel. 307/322–4540. 4 double rooms share 2 baths, 1 suite. TV/VCR in common area, fireplace in library, bicycles. $45–$55; full breakfast in summer and on winter weekends, Continental breakfast on winter weekdays, afternoon snacks and beverages served on wraparound porch. No credit cards.

Porch Swing B&B. 712 E. 20th St., Cheyenne, WY 82001, tel. and fax 307/778–7182. 1 double room with bath, 2 doubles share 1 bath. TV/VCR in living room, woodstoves in dining room and enclosed porch, antiques, fishpond, lavish herb and flower gardens. $42–$66; full breakfast, afternoon and evening snacks. MC, V.

Rainsford Inn. 219 E. 18th St., Cheyenne, WY 82001, tel. 307/638–2337, fax 307/634–4506. 5 double rooms with baths with whirlpool tubs (1 bathroom is accessible with roll-in shower), 2 rooms share 1 bath. Antiques, gas fireplace in 1 room. $65–$100, full breakfast. AE, D, DC, MC, V.

Reservations Services

B&B Western Adventures (Box 20972, Billings, MT, tel. 406/259–7993). **Jackson Hole B&B Association** (Box 2766, Jackson Hole, WY 83001, tel. 800/542–2632). **WHOA–Wyoming Homestate Outdoor Adventures** (1031 Steinle Rd., Douglas, WY 82633, tel. 307/358–2380).

Notes

Fodor's Travel Publications

Available at bookstores everywhere, or call 1–800–533–6478, 24 hours a day.

Gold Guides

U.S.

Alaska

Arizona

Boston

California

Cape Cod, Martha's Vineyard, Nantucket

The Carolinas & the Georgia Coast

Chicago

Colorado

Florida

Hawai'i

Las Vegas, Reno, Tahoe

Los Angeles

Maine, Vermont, New Hampshire

Maui & Lāna'i

Miami & the Keys

New England

New Orleans

New York City

Pacific North Coast

Philadelphia & the Pennsylvania Dutch Country

The Rockies

San Diego

San Francisco

Santa Fe, Taos, Albuquerque

Seattle & Vancouver

The South

U.S. & British Virgin Islands

USA

Virginia & Maryland

Washington, D.C.

Foreign

Australia

Austria

The Bahamas

Belize & Guatemala

Bermuda

Canada

Cancún, Cozumel, Yucatán Peninsula

Caribbean

China

Costa Rica

Cuba

The Czech Republic & Slovakia

Eastern & Central Europe

Europe

Florence, Tuscany & Umbria

France

Germany

Great Britain

Greece

Hong Kong

India

Ireland

Israel

Italy

Japan

London

Madrid & Barcelona

Mexico

Montréal & Québec City

Moscow, St. Petersburg, Kiev

The Netherlands, Belgium & Luxembourg

New Zealand

Norway

Nova Scotia, New Brunswick, Prince Edward Island

Paris

Portugal

Provence & the Riviera

Scandinavia

Scotland

Singapore

South Africa

South America

Southeast Asia

Spain

Sweden

Switzerland

Thailand

Tokyo

Toronto

Turkey

Vienna & the Danube

Fodor's Special-Interest Guides

Alaska Ports of Call

Caribbean Ports of Call

The Complete Guide to America's National Parks

Family Adventures

Fodor's Gay Guide to the USA

Halliday's New England Food Explorer

Halliday's New Orleans Food Explorer

Healthy Escapes

Ballpark Vacations

Kodak Guide to Shooting Great Travel Pictures

Nights to Imagine

Rock & Roll Traveler USA

Sunday in New York

Sunday in San Francisco

Walt Disney World, Universal Studios and Orlando

Walt Disney World for Adults

Wendy Perrin's Secrets Every Smart Traveler Should Know

Where Should We Take the Kids? California

Where Should We Take the Kids? Northeast

Worldwide Cruises and Ports of Call